The Red Brush

Harvard East Asian Monographs, 231

The Red Brush

Writing Women of
Imperial China

Wilt Idema
and Beata Grant

Published by the Harvard University Asia Center
and distributed by Harvard University Press
Cambridge (Massachusetts) and London 2004

The original Chinese texts of all items translated in this book are available at:

http://digital.wustl.edu

© 2004 by The President and Fellows of Harvard College

Printed in the United States of America

The Harvard University Asia Center publishes a monograph series and, in coordination with the Fairbank Center for East Asian Research, the Korea Institute, the Reischauer Institute of Japanese Studies, and other faculties and institutes, administers research projects designed to further scholarly understanding of China, Japan, Vietnam, Korea, and other Asian countries. The Center also sponsors projects addressing multidisciplinary and regional issues in Asia.

Library of Congress Cataloging-in-Publication Data

Idema, W. L. (Wilt L.)
    The red brush : writing women of imperial China / Wilt Idema and Beata Grant.
       p. cm. -- (Harvard East Asian monographs ; 231)
    Includes bibliographical references and index.
    ISBN 0-674-01393-x (pbk. : alk. paper)
    1. Chinese literature--Women authors--History and criticism. 2. Women authors, Chinese. I. Grant, Beata, 1954- II. Title.
    PL2278.I344 2004
    895.1'099287--dc22

                                    2004018636

Index by Jake Kawatski at Twin Oaks Indexing

♾ Printed on acid-free paper

Last figure below indicates year of this printing
13 12 11 10 09 08 07

Acknowledgments

The conception, preparation, and publication of any book, but especially a book the length of this one, is dependent on the inspiration, information, ideas, and support of many people. Although it would be impossible to name all those who contributed in one way or another to this project, we would like to express our appreciation, in more-or-less chronological order, to a few of the people who were most closely involved.

First of all, we would like to thank Ellen Widmer and John Ziemer for suggesting the project to begin with. They probably envisioned a somewhat more modest result, but it is not our fault if the materials proved both more varied and captivating than we anticipated at the outset of this venture. The project might never have progressed beyond the planning stage, however, if the Radcliffe Institute for Advanced Study had not opened its doors to men, while maintaining its emphasis on issues of women, gender, and society. By awarding a fellowship to Wilt for the academic year 2001–2002, it enabled him to devote a full year exclusively to this project. Special thanks should also go to the institute's director, Judith Vichniac, for kindly inviting Beata, who was not formally a Radcliffe Fellow, not only to share in their tasty lunches and intellectual exchanges at the institute, but to also make use of their office space for several months. We are also very grateful to Edward S. Macias, executive vice-chancellor of Washington University and dean of the College of Arts and Sciences, for allowing Beata to take a year's leave from her administrative and teaching duties so that she could come to Cambridge to work on this collaborative project, as well as to her colleague Marvin Marcus for graciously agreeing to serve as interim chair of the department during her absence.

Along the way, we received all manner of collegial support, suggestions, and materials from our esteemed colleagues Ellen Widmer, Judith Zeitlin, Hua Wei, Paul Ropp, Grace Fong, and Tian Xiaofei. Eva Shi, then still an undergraduate at Harvard University, read through the entire manuscript when it was nearing completion and provided us with helpful suggestions from the student perspective. The students in the course *Writing Women in Imperial China* that Beata offered in the fall of 2003 at Washington University, especially Yang Binbin, Sookja Cho, and Rumyana Cholakova, critically read large parts of the draft as well. Wilt used the draft in his class *Writing Women in Imperial China* in the spring of 2004 at Harvard University, and he and the manuscript benefited greatly from the able assistance of his teaching fellow Jennifer Carpenter. Once submitted for review, we received very detailed and helpful suggestions from the two anonymous reviewers for which we are very grateful, even if we did not always follow their advice. And during the last stages of preparing glossaries and finding lists, we were fortunate to enlist the able assistance of Geraldine Schneider and Tian-yuan Tan, both graduate students at Harvard. Most importantly, we would like to acknowledge the indispensable editorial assistance of Cheryl Tucker, who copyedited and designed the copious pages of this volume with cheerful patience and meticulous care.

Last but by no means least, we would like to express our deep indebtedness to the many scholars and writers, women and men, past and present, from the West and from the East, whose work made our own work possible. A survey such as this one, which spans two thousand years of literary history, must rely greatly on the research of many others. We hope that this book will, in turn, inspire and encourage new generations of students and scholars to further explore this fascinating and important area of study.

Wilt Idema   Beata Grant

Contents

Chinese Dynasties and Other Useful Information   XIII

Introduction   I

Part One   Early Models for Later Ages   II

Chapter I   Women On and Behind the Throne   17
    Ban Zhao   17
    Poets, Teachers, Moralists   42
       Poets of the Inner Palace: Zuo Fen, Han Lanying,
          and Bao Linghui   43
       Teachers of Men: Fu Sheng's Daughter and Wei
          Cheng's Mother   52
       Moralists: The Song Sisters and Lady Zheng   54
    Shangguan Wan'er: Ghostwriter for Two Empresses   61

Chapter 2   Neglected Palace Ladies and Other Phantoms   73
    Slandered Virtue: Concubine Ban   77
    Fact and Fiction: Phantom Poems and Phantom Lives   82
       Reduced to a Human Pig: Lady Qi   82
       A Disputed Beauty: Empress Zhen   85

Banished Beyond the Border: Liu Xijun and
    Wang Zhaojun   91
A Lonely Suicide: Lady Hou   95
Displaced by a Rival: Concubine Plum   100
Other Phantoms   107
    The Eloping Widow: Zhuo Wenjun   108
    Abducted and Ramsomed: Cai Yan   112
    Palindromes: Su Hui   127

Chapter 3   Ladies, Nuns, and Courtesans   132
    Brilliant Daughters and Dutiful Wives   132
      The Poet of a Single Poem: Xu Shu   132
      The Poet of a Single Line: Xie Daoyun   136
      Poet and Editorial Advisor: Lady Chen   144
      Different Voices: Liu Lingxian   146
    Buddhist Nuns and Daoist Mystics   153
      Buddhist Nuns   153
        Powerful Abbesses   154
        Revealed Sutras   156
        Poems by Nuns   158
      Daoist Mystics   159
        Revealer of Texts: Wei Huacun   159
        Princess and Peasant Girl: Yuzhen
          and Wang Fajin   160
    Self-Censoring Ladies and Public Women   163
      Self-Censoring Ladies   164
        Burned Manuscripts   164
        Multiple Personalities   165
        Conversations in Dreams   167
      Public Women   174
        Poet and Traitor: Li Ye   176
        Courtesan and Collator: Xue Tao   182
        Concubine, Daoist Nun, and Murderer:
          Yu Xuanji   189

Part Two   Between New Possibilities and New Limitations   *197*

Chapter 4   Li Qingzhao   204
   Li Qingzhao's Life   204
   Li Qingzhao's Poetry   217
      The Rise of the *Ci*   217
      Lady Wei's Lyrics   221
      Li Qingzhao's Lyrics   225
      Li Qingzhao's *Ci*-Criticism 234
      Li Qingzhao and Her Critics   237
      Li Qingzhao's Poems   241

Chapter 5   Talent and Fate   244
   An Unhappy Marriage: Zhu Shuzhen   244
   Doomed Love: Zhang Yuniang   257
   A Wifely Poetics: Zheng Yunduan   269
   Guan Daosheng and Huang E   280
      Artist and Artist's Wife: Guan Daosheng   281
      An Exile's Wife: Huang E   287

Chapter 6   Empresses, Nuns, and Actresses   292
   Empresses and Palace Ladies   292
      Lady Huarui and Her Palace Songs   293
      Empress Yang and More Palace Songs   298
      Xiao Guanyin and Her Sorry Fate   300
      Empress Xu and the Bodhisattva Guanyin   304
   Nuns   319
      Chan Buddhism and Women   320
      Miaodao, Miaozong, and Other Female Disciples
        of Chan Master Dahui Zonggao   323
      Other Writing Nuns   329
   Courtesans and Actresses   333
      Courtesan, Poet, and Philosopher: Wen Wan   334
      Smartass Wang and the Romance of Su Xiaoqing   336

Part Three   The First High Tide of Women's Literature   *347*

Chapter 7   Courtesans   359
    Liang Xiaoyu and the Tale of Huang Chonggu   359
    Jing Pianpian and Ma Xiaolan   364
    Wang Wei and Yang Wan   368
    Liu Shi   374

Chapter 8   Matrons and Maidens   383
    Shen Yixiu and Her Daughters   383
        Shen Yixiu   383
        Ye Xiaoluan   390
        Ye Wanwan   406
        Huichou   410
    Gu Ruopu and Liang Mengzhao   414
        Gu Ruopu   415
        Liang Mengzhao   421

Chapter 9   Women Writers of the Conquest Period   425
    Shang Jinglan and Xu Can   426
        A Loyalist's Widow: Shang Jinglan   426
        Exiled to Manchuria: Xu Can   431
    Wang Duanshu and Huang Yuanjie   437
        Ming Loyalist: Wang Duanshu   437
        Painter, Calligrapher, and Poet: Huang Yuanjie   452
    Writing Nuns   455
        Teacher and Convent-Builder: Yikui Chaochen   457
        Pilgrimage and Poetry: Jizong Xingche   464

Chapter 10   The Banana Garden Poetry Club   471
    Gu Zhiqiong   473
    Chai Jingyi   475
    Feng Xian   477
    Qian Fenglun   478
    Lin Yining   486
    Gu Si   487

Zhu Rouze 489
Zhang Hao 492
Mao Ti 494

Interlude   Ideal and Reality 497

Chapter 11 Ideal 499
    Du Liniang and Her Female Commentators 500
    Long-Suffering Concubines 504
        Xiaoqing 504
        Skinny Mares 515
        Poems on Walls 518
    Lyrics on Flower Petals: Shuangqing 520

Chapter 12 Reality 542
    In a Script of Their Own 543
    Formalized Friendship 544
    Getting Married 547
    Autobiographical Ballads 553
    The Sorrows of Pregnancy and Motherhood 557
    How to Escape the Female Condition 562

Part Four   The Second High Tide of Women's Literature 567

Chapter 13 Poetry 578
    Poetry and Piety 578
        Tao Shan 578
        Jiang Zhu 588
    Disciples of Yuan Mei 593
        Xi Peilan 593
        Luo Qilan 612
    Poetry, Scholarship, and Vernacular Prose Fiction 620
        Wang Duan 620
        Gu Chun (Taiqing) 630

Women and Warfare   652
    Zhang Chaixin   652
    Zhang Yin   656
    Li Changxia   668

Chapter 14   Drama   677
    Cross-Dressing Heroines: Wang Yun and He Peizhu   677
    Playwright and Lyricist: Wu Zao   685
    Moral Fables and Special Effects: Liu Qingyun   702

Chapter 15   Plucking Rhymes   717
    A Rain of Heavenly Flowers   719
    Text and Performance: Zhu Suxian   729
    Karmic Bonds of Reincarnation: Chen Duansheng
        and Hou Zhi   734
    Other Plucking Rhymes   754
        More Cross-Dressing Heroines   754
        Loyalty and Patriotism   761

Epilogue   Nationalism and Feminism: Qiu Jin   *765*

Chapter 16   The Beheaded Feminist: Qiu Jin   767
    Poet and Nationalist   768
    Student and Feminist   779
    Teacher and Revolutionary   794

Reference Matter

Bibliography of Chinese Sources   811
Suggested Readings   819
Finding List   837
Glossary   872
Index   886

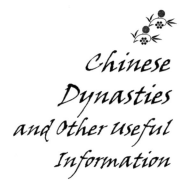

Chinese Dynasties and Other Useful Information

Xia (traditional dates 2207–1766 BCE)
Shang/Yin (traditional dates 1766–1123 BCE)
Zhou (traditional dates 1121–249 BCE)
    Period of the *Annals of Spring and Autumn* (722–479 BCE)
    Period of the Warring States (fifth–third centuries BCE)

Qin (221–208 BCE)
Han (206 BCE–220 CE)
    Western Han (206 BCE–8 CE)
    Eastern Han (25–220)
The Three Kingdoms
    Wei (221–264)
    Shu-Han (221–263)
    Wu (221–280)
Jin (265–419)

The Northern and Southern Dynasties (fourth to sixth centuries)[1]
    Southern Dynasties
        Eastern Jin (317–419)

---

1. Northern China during this period was ruled by a great number of often short-lived dynasties, whose power rarely extended beyond a few modern provinces, for example, the Later Zhao (319–352) and Early Qin (351–394).

Liu-Song (420–478)
Qi (479–501)
Liang (502–556)
Chen (557–588)

Sui (581–617)

Tang (618–906)

Five Dynasties (907–960)[2]
Liang (907–922)
Tang (923–935)
Jin (936–946)
Han (947–950)
Zhou (951–960)

Song (960–1278)
Northern Song (960–1126)
Southern Song (1127–1278)

The "Conquest Dynasties"
Liao (Khitan) (907–1120)
Jin (Jürchen) (1115–1234)
Yuan (Mongol) (1260–1368)

Ming (1368–1644)

Qing (Manchu) (1644–1911)

---

2. The power of the Five Dynasties was limited to northern China. Southern China during this time was divided into a number of smaller kingdoms. For example, the area of the modern province of Sichuan was ruled from 907 to 925 by the Former Shu dynasty, and from 934 to 965 by the Later Shu dynasty. The Southern Tang dynasty ruled from 937 to 975 over large parts of the modern provinces of Jiangsu, Jiangxi, and Anhui.

The traditional Chinese lunar year is made up of twelve months of thirty or twenty-nine days. In order to synchronize this lunar year with the solar year, five "leap months" are inserted over the course of nineteen years. The start of the Chinese year therefore can fall on different dates of the Western calendar; usually it falls sometime between January 20 and February 20. The cycle of seasons begins with spring, the first three months of the year, followed by three months of summer, autumn, and winter respectively. Thus, although the Chinese year begins roughly one month later than the Western New Year, each of the seasons begins considerably earlier.

The years are numbered continuously according to a series of sixty otherwise meaningless bisyllabic expressions (*maochen* or *kuimao*, for example) that derives from a combination of the sequence of ten "heavenly stems" and twelve "earthly branches." This same system is also used for the successive enumeration of months, days, and hours. Years are also counted according to the reign periods. At the beginning of his reign, each ruler would declare the establishment of a new reign period, the name of which often gave expression to a pious wish or marked a miraculous event. Before the Ming and Qing periods, a ruler was free to change the name of his reign period, or rather, declare the commencement of a newly named reign period, as often as he saw fit. Normally, however, each reign period lasted at least a few years. During the Ming and the Qing dynasties, it was customary for each new emperor to declare a new reign period only once, upon his ascension to the throne, the name of which would then be left unchanged for the duration of his reign. It is for this reason that emperors of these last two dynasties are often designated by the names of their reign periods. Thus, while we translate the names of the reign periods of the earlier dynasties, we leave the names of the reign periods of the Ming and the Qing dynasties untranslated.

In China, people are considered to be one year of age (in their first year) from the moment of their birth, and everyone adds another year to their age on the lunar New Year. Thus, a child born on the eve of the lunar New Year will be considered to be two years old (in the second year) on the next day. When we mention a person's age, we follow this traditional system.

When it comes to Chinese family names, the surname (usually consisting of a single syllable) comes first, followed by the personal name, which may consist of either one or two syllables. Members of the elite often have not only a personal name (which they may also use to refer to themselves) but also a "style name," which is used by others when addressing them. As a child, they may be known under a "child name," and as an adult, they may adopt any number of sobriquets. Married women are often designated by the surname of their natal family (for instance, lady Huang, lady Zhang), which at times may be also used in combination with a title (for instance, Concubine Ban, Lady Huang).

Distances are measured in *li*, roughly equivalent to one third of a mile. The basic unit for land measurement is the *mu*, roughly equivalent to one seventh of an acre. One hundred *mu* equals one *qing*.

The Red Brush

Introduction

One of the most exciting recent developments in the study of Chinese literature has been the rediscovery of an extremely long and vibrant tradition of women's writing of the imperial period (221 BCE–1911 CE). Many of these writings—poetry, prose, drama, and fiction—are of considerable literary quality. Others provide us with often moving insights—in their own words—into the lives, feelings, and thoughts of a surprisingly diverse group of women living in Confucian China, a society that perhaps more than any other is known for its patriarchal tradition.

The last few decades have witnessed a burgeoning interest, in Asia as well as the West, in the study of the women of both premodern and modern China. This has resulted in an outpouring of scholarly books and articles as well as the publication of numerous anthologies of women's writings, both in Chinese and in translation. In English, path-breaking studies such as Patricia Ebrey's *The Inner Quarters: Marriage and the Life of Women in the Sung Period* (1993); Dorothy Ko's *Teachers of the Inner Chambers: Women and Culture in Seventeenth-Century China* (1994); and Susan Mann's *Precious Records: Women in China's Long Eighteenth Century* (1997) have set the stage for more specialized studies on women writers by scholars such as Ellen Widmer, Grace Fong, Kang-i Sun Chang, and many others. Apart from these scholarly studies, there have also been some important new translations of Chinese women's poetry. For many years the only anthology available in English was Kenneth Rexroth and Ling Chung's slim volume, *Women Poets of China*, published in 1972. Now we not only have translations of individual women poets, such as Xue Tao, Yu Xuanji, and Li Qingzhao, but we also have the 900-page *Women Writers of Traditional China, An Anthology of Poetry and Criticism*, edited by Kang-i Sun Chang and Haun Saussy (1999). These works have laid the foundation for the continued study of the extremely rich tradition of writings by women in China during the more than two thousand years of imperial rule.

The challenging and stimulating scholarship of the last two decades has made possible the present anthology, which differs from previous such works in several ways. First of all, we make a special effort to provide readers with a taste of women's writings, not only in poetry, but in other genres as well, including essays and letters, drama, religious writing, and narrative fiction. This is not to say that poetry was not the major (and most acceptable) literary form engaged in by the great majority of women writers of the imperial period—as indeed, it was for the majority of men as well. Nevertheless, poetic genres, such as the poem and the lyric, created serious problems of voice for women writers. Women entering the literary arena often found themselves confronted with a ready-made feminine voice in the available writings by male authors, as traditional Chinese poetry had a long tradition of male-authored poetry written in a female voice. While these pre-existing female voices may have in certain respects facilitated women's participation in literary pursuits, it also made it more difficult for them to develop their own voices. Prose writings by women, although not as often included in anthologies, often provide us with glimpses of aspects of a woman writer's character and interests that may not be as readily apparent in poetic writings. These prose writings by women, many of which exhibit a literary sensibility comparable to that found in their poetry, range from moral tracts for women, memorials to the throne, letters to male and female relatives and friends, eulogies, funeral inscriptions, sermons and revelations, essays and prefaces, to biographical and autobiographical accounts.

In the last several centuries of the imperial period we also find women writing in new genres, such as drama and narrative fiction. The relatively low status of these literary genres in the eyes of the male literati allowed women who wrote in these genres far greater latitude when it came to indulging in fantasy or voicing subversive opinions. Unfortunately, the length of plays and narrative fiction often makes it impossible to include examples of female-authored works in these genres in their entirety even in an anthology of this size (although we have managed to include at least one complete one-act play), so we have had to limit ourselves to summaries and excerpts. Nevertheless, our hope is that the inclusion of these materials will provide a fuller picture of the diversity of women's talents as well as of their concerns. In order to make room for texts in verse, prose, drama, and fiction, we have had to be judicious in our selection of authors. Rather than trying to include as many women writers as possible, we have sought to make a representative selection of various types of women writers writing in different genres, at different periods of time, and under different social and historical conditions.

We have also decided to include a type of woman writer that appears to be particularly common in, although not necessarily unique to, the Chinese literary tradition: the woman writer who, although at least in part the creation of a male imagination, over time comes to acquire a detailed biography as well as a poetic oeuvre of her own and is eventually included in anthologies and other works on an equal footing with her more historically verifiable sisters. These women, such as the abducted widow and ransomed mother Cai Yan (ca. 200), often played an important role in the literary imaginations of both men and women, who found their own sufferings and frustrations mirrored in these women's sorrowful fates. For this reason, we cannot simply exclude writers and works of disputed authenticity; however, to deny the complexities involved would not do either. Although one might expect that such problems of misattribution and fictional authorship would be primarily characteristic of manuscript culture, it turns out that such "phantom authors" are very much a feature of later periods as well, as is shown by the popularity in the seventeenth century of the long-suffering concubine Xiaoqing and in the eighteenth century, of the trials and travails of the peasant woman poet Shuangqing.

Yet another major distinguishing characteristic of this anthology is that we have presented the selections not in isolation, but rather, to the extent that the available sources make this possible, within their respective biographical contexts. In fact, many times it is in biographical accounts and nowhere else that the works of many women writers, especially from earlier periods, are preserved. These accounts, many of which were written by the fathers, husbands, or sons of these women, usually detail the circumstances under which the particular works were written. Because traditional Chinese poetics primarily understands writing not as a strictly individual act, but rather as an immediate response to specific personal or social circumstances, these accounts help to clarify traditional Chinese ideas on the nature and function of literature as well as those on the role of the woman writer. In other words, they provide the modern reader with a clearer idea of how these poems and other writings were originally intended to be read, that is, primarily as autobiographical documents. This is why we have decided to include these biographical accounts and other materials on the lives of our women writers as far as possible in their entirety, rather than simply summarizing or paraphrasing them. Whenever available, we have given preference to the rare autobiographical writings by women writers themselves, as well as to the biographical accounts written by women about women. These biographical and autobiographical materials, whether written by men or women, often provide strikingly dramatic evidence that many of these women writers led quite interesting lives, and that their range of experiences went far beyond what one might imagine given the modern myths about the cloistered and victimized lives of traditional Chinese women.

The truth remains, however, that throughout the more than two millennia of imperial China, writing was largely regarded as man's work, since to write implied participation in the public and therefore the male domain, especially that of officialdom. Of course, this did not mean that women never wrote—the present anthology provides strong evidence that indeed they did write, and in greater numbers than until recently many have realized. The traditional equation of writing and public life, however, meant that not until the twentieth century was women's writing in China regarded as being other than marginal. In the eyes of many men, and women as well, it never ceased to be considered scandalous for a high-class woman, who was theoretically supposed to keep herself hidden within "the inner quarters," the area located in the back part of the house that was reserved for the women of the household and which was out of bounds to men unless they were close relatives. An upper-class woman was not supposed to show her face to strangers, much less bare her innermost feelings to the world at large. The very desire to see one's writings in public circulation implied a transgression of the presumably natural order of society in which women were relegated to the inner (private) sphere, while men were destined to find fulfillment in the outer (public) world. This may well have been one of the main reasons why for the first millennium, before the rise and popularization of printed texts, there are only a handful of women-authored texts preserved from what may well have been much larger collections. We know that some women authors were quite famous in their time for their literary skills and yet they have left us no trace at all of their writings. From the eleventh century onwards, once printing had been invented and come to be used for the distribution of the collected literary works of individual writers, the writings of women had a greater chance of survival, and, especially from the seventeenth century onwards, hundred of collections of women's writings were preserved.

From the beginning of imperial times up until the end of the tenth century, it was the women of the Inner Palace who appear to have played the leading roles on the female literary stage. This is easily explained by the fact that in this time of very low literacy for women (and men as well), the emperor's harem constituted by far the most significant community of literate women in China. The Inner Palace had its own complicated bureaucracy, and every woman who shared the emperor's bed might conceivably one day be called upon to rule the realm as the regent for an infant son. Because the women who filled the imperial harem were drawn from elite families, many of them had enjoyed a literary education at home. Consequently, their works constituted the bulk of women's literature of the time.

Buddhist nunneries developed in China from the third century onwards, but Buddhist nuns played a much smaller role in the tradition of women's literature than did, for example, Catholic nuns in the medieval European tradition. Daoist nunneries only developed in the wake of the Buddhist nunneries, and Daoist nuns did not enter the literary arena until the Tang dynasty (618–906). Moreover, although there were no doubt many Daoist nuns of great spiritual probity, some of the best known of the Daoist nun-poets were of a status hardly distinguishable from that of courtesans.

As the professional companions of elite men, many courtesans were trained in song and poetry, and in certain periods of Chinese history (the ninth century, for example) some of them acquired considerable reputations as writers.

The advent of printing in the ninth and tenth centuries did not immediately result in more women's writings being preserved; many of their printed works have been lost as well. Until well into the sixteenth century, it continued to be rare for a woman writer's collection to be printed and the chances of its survival remained small. Even the works of Li Qingzhao (1084–ca. 1151), probably China's most famous woman writer and the female poet best known in the West, were not preserved in their entirety. Only a little under a hundred texts from her original collection of poetry and prose remains, and these were culled from various later anthologies.

From the eleventh century onwards what did happen with the spread of printing was that the Inner Palace gradually lost its central role in the production of women's writing, as elite women outside of the court came to dominate the scene. We have snippets of information about writing nuns and writing courtesans of the period of the eleventh to the sixteenth centuries, but, as was the case for earlier periods, little of their work has been preserved.

Another change that occurred after the eleventh century is that, unlike the women before them who tended to write in a wide range of literary forms, women writers began to focus on poetry, including *shi* poems and *ci,* or song lyrics. Although originally composed mainly by male writers, *ci* lyrics were often written in the "feminine" mode, and as such offered women writers a ready-made language for the expression of "feminine" feelings.

It is really only as we move closer to the seventeenth century that we see the emergence of a more voluminous body of literature written by women. A first high tide of women's literature began to gather momentum during the last years of the sixteenth century, reached its highest point around the middle of the seventeenth century, and subsided by the end of that century. This first high tide of women's literature coincided with an unprecedented publishing boom; it is a period that in many other ways was a period of innovation and experimentation in literature and in-

tellectual life as well. This first high tide may well have been the most socially diverse period in the history of Chinese women's literature. The last
decades of the sixteenth and the first half of the seventeenth century witnessed an extraordinary flowering of the courtesan culture of the Jiangnan area, and many of the best-known courtesans established reputations
as poets. From the second half of the seventeenth century we also happen to have a few collections of writings by Chan (Zen) Buddhist nuns.
By far the greatest number of writing women of this period were women
of elite families, whose writings were published in greater numbers than
ever before. The social and political turmoil of the first few decades immediately following the collapse of the Ming (1368–1644) and the subsequent conquest of China by the Manchus appears to have allowed at least
some women a greater freedom of action in the elite cultural sphere than
they were to enjoy again for a very long time.

During the first three-quarters of the eighteenth century, there appears
to have been a lull, or perhaps simply a temporary decline in the visibility
of women's writing. Then, beginning in the last decades of the eighteenth
century, we see the rise of a second high tide of women's literature,
which reaches its highest point in the first half of the nineteenth century.
By this time both courtesans and nuns had almost totally disappeared
from the literary scene, which was now almost completely dominated by
women of the elite. These women felt increasingly freer to express their
unhappiness at the inequities and sufferings of their lives, and often
voiced both their frustrations and their aspirations by writing plays, ballads, and stories that featured heroines in male dress. While women had
written plays before this, few of these plays were preserved, but at this
point at least one play made it successfully to the stage. An even more
significant development in the tradition of women's literature is that finally more women began to write narrative fiction. Their preferred narrative genre was not the novel or the short story, however, but rather the
extremely long prosimetrical ballad known as *tanci,* or "plucking rhymes."
The story lines of these plucking rhymes often featured a female heroine,
who, dressed in male attire, outperforms men on the battlefield, in the
examination hall, and at court.

The very word "literature" presupposes a written tradition; however,
China also had a rich tradition of oral literature. The oral literature of the

imperial period has been irretrievably lost, but we may catch a glimpse of
what this oral literature might have been like from the twentieth-century
"women's script" (*nüshu*) literature of Jiangyong in southernmost Hunan.
Here, well into the final decades of the twentieth century, local peasant
women composed highly formulaic ballads, which they then recorded using a unique phonetic syllabary, thus creating a literature of their own.
This body of texts includes not only these women's renditions of local
versions of popular tales, but also many original works, including autobiographical ballads. These works form a striking contrast not only to the
writings of elite women, but also to the imagined and highly romantic
poetry ascribed to peasant women but which were most likely the works
of elite men.

It wasn't until the last two decades of the Manchu Qing dynasty
(1644–1911) that women, such as the nationalist martyr Qiu Jin (1875–
1907), began to use writing as a weapon to improve their position in society and a truly feminist literature began to take shape—the point where
this book comes to an end.

It has not been our intention to write a social history of women in imperial China, and while we have decided to present our translated selections within a narrative context, the reader should keep in mind that the
primary function of this narrative is to provide the reader with the background necessary for a better understanding of the selections. We are of
course aware that there is no such thing as a completely objective presentation of facts or selection of materials, and that the very act of choosing
particular works and writers for inclusion in an anthology of this sort
presupposes some kind of critical or theoretical stance. We have tried,
first of all, to offer a selection that does justice to the richness and variety
of women's writing in imperial China. At the same time we have made a
special effort to include writings in which women directly address the issues of the female condition in traditional society in a relatively explicit
way. In other words, we have selected texts in which women speak as
much as possible for themselves. We have supplied brief annotations and
summary historical contexts when necessary, but have avoided as far as
possible engaging in extensive interpretative commentary. There is now
an increasingly large amount of sophisticated critical work being done on
these women writers, as the bibliography of selected readings at the end

of this book amply demonstrates. While we have benefited tremendously from all of this work—indeed, we could not have compiled this book without it—we prefer to direct our readers to these articles and monographs themselves rather than attempt to incorporate all of their many critical insights and interpretations into the present anthology.

Finally, a brief word on the translations themselves: All the translations in this volume were made on the basis of the Chinese originals. Sometimes we were able to rely on fully annotated modern editions of the works concerned. In other cases, we have made use of the traditional woodblock editions of these works. When we did not have access to the complete collections of individual authors, we have relied on earlier premodern and modern anthologies. Needless to say, all errors in translation are solely our own.

In our renditions of Chinese verse, we have made no attempt to preserve the rhymes of the originals. When translating rhapsodies (*fu*) and poems (*shi*), however, we have used a line break to mark a change of rhyme in the original. In our translations of lyrics (*ci*), a line break marks a stanza break. In our translations of drama and plucking rhymes (*tanci*), indented short lines are used for extrametrical phrases, usually of three characters each, at the head of a line in the original.

Whenever possible we have provided explanations of terms and allusions in the surrounding narrative itself, although occasionally we also provide brief footnotes as well. We are well aware that many of the explanations could be expanded considerably, but we have chosen to limit ourselves to what we feel would be necessary to a first appreciation of the selected works. In many cases, we have treated certain characters and incidents in considerable detail when they are first introduced—the case of Wang Zhaojun and her marriage to a barbarian chieftain is an example—with the assumption that when they are referred to in later writings, which often they repeatedly are, the reader will be able to recognize the allusions. Readers are therefore encouraged to read this anthology from beginning to end. If they prefer not to do so, they will find the index a useful tool.

PART ONE
Early Models for Later Ages

In imperial China, the rules of behavior for (upper-class) men and women were codified in the *Rites* (*Li*). The *Rites* actually is the collective name for three independent treatises that each emphasized the importance of ritual to the social fabric and spelled out the rules of ritual ceremony, as well as everyday behavior. These three works, the *Rites and Ceremonies* (*Yili*), the *Records of the Rites* (*Liji*), and the *Rites of the Zhou* (*Zhouli*, also known as *Offices of the Zhou* [*Zhouguan*]), achieved their final form in the second and first centuries BCE. The *Rites* was designated as one of the Five Classics, the corpus of texts that were regarded as embodiments of the Way, and which served as the basis for a proper education. This education, however, was primarily a male affair, as these texts were designed to instruct a man in the correct ways of thinking, speaking, and acting, in preparation for his participation in public life, ideally as an official. The Classics and the teachings of Confucius left no doubt that it was a man's highest calling and duty to assist his ruler in establishing order in society. For a successful official career, literacy and a mastery of the art of composition were essential, since the imperial state was sustained by a large and complicated bureaucracy and every government action required extensive paperwork. While in the earliest centuries of imperial China appointment to office was primarily a matter of hereditary privilege and recommendation, eventually the examination system became institutionalized. It first made a major impact during the latter part of the Tang dynasty (618–906), and by the Song dynasty (960–1278) had become the most important avenue to high office.

Women in elite families also were taught to read and write, if only because they were expected to be able to manage their husbands' family estates after marriage and provide their sons with a primary education. There was little point in a woman studying the Classics, however, since she was excluded from participating in the public life of government. A woman might achieve great power as empress or empress dowager, but she would never actually be appointed to an official position outside the Inner Palace. The proper domain of the elite woman was the inner quarters, hidden from the public gaze. To meet the specific educational needs of women there existed a body of texts designed to provide them with instruction in their duties as daughter and daughter-in-law, mother, wife, and widow. As a rule, these texts were relatively short and written in simple prose. They consisted of, on the one hand, collections of biographical sketches of exemplary women from the past, and, on the other, guidelines for wifely behavior. The collections of biographies were largely written by men, whereas the extant guidelines for moral behavior from the first millennium and a half of imperial China were composed by women.

The earliest collection of women's biographies is Liu Xiang's (79–8 BCE) *Biographies of Exemplary Women* (*Lienü zhuan*). In the *Books of the Han* (*Han shu*), the biography of Liu Xiang tells us that this collection was compiled for the emperor (probably Emperor Cheng). Its primary purpose was to illustrate by historical example the advantages of surrounding oneself with moral and intelligent women, and the potential dangers of associating with beautiful but scheming favorites. The collection brings together a large number of short biographical sketches not only of wise mothers, chaste wives, quick-witted concubines, and filial daughters, but also of seductive favorites and malicious vixens, from ancient times up to the third century BCE. These sketches and anecdotes are classified under seven general headings: maternal rectitude, sagely intelligence, benevolent wisdom, purity and obedience, chastity and righteousness, skill in argument, and pernicious depravity. Despite its original stated purpose of providing the emperor with cautionary tales, the work soon became required reading for women, who could find in its pages both models to emulate and examples to avoid. Starting with the fifth-century *Books of the*

Later Han (*Hou Han shu*) the histories of individual dynasties usually included a chapter on "Exemplary Women," from which we will often quote in the following chapters. The dynastic histories increasingly focused on filial daughters and chaste wives and less on intelligent and quick-witted female advisors, whether they were mothers, wives, or concubines. From the Ming (1368–1644) and the Qing (1644–1911) dynasties we have a large number of quite extensive collections of lives of exemplary women.

The earliest extant woman-authored moral tract for women is Ban Zhao's (ca. 48–ca. 118) *Precepts for My Daughters* (*Nüjie*), which provides advice to young brides on how to behave toward their husband and in-laws. Other preserved examples of women-authored moral tracts include the *Classic of Filiality for Women* (*Nü Xiaojing*) and the *Analects for Women* (*Nü Lunyu*), which date from the eighth and ninth centuries. These Tang dynasty texts place primary stress on the duties of a married woman as daughter-in-law, and only secondarily describe the relationship of the bride to her husband. And, whereas Ban Zhao advocated a literary education for girls, these later texts remain silent on the subject. In short, the moral tracts written by women for women during the first millennium of imperial China appear to have placed increasingly greater emphasis on the subordination of women.

These moral texts for women, it should be noted, are prescriptive rather than descriptive and on no account can be read as actual descriptions of social reality. The extent to which examples are followed and rules adhered to will vary according to period and region, family tradition and family composition, age and personal character, and class and wealth. Examples and rules are at best ideal norms, providing a language with which to discuss and evaluate actual behavior. This universal and inescapable discrepancy between norm and reality has been a thorn in the side of moralists through the ages. Ge Hong (280–ca. 340) wrote of this very discrepancy in imperial China in a diatribe against the customs of his time. In the chapter "Hatred of Abuses," from his *The Master Who Embraces Simplicity* (*Baopuzi*), he writes with scorn of the lifestyle of the female members of the aristocracy in Jianye in the first half of the fourth century:

The *Odes* praise the ospreys, and puts great store in the segregation of the sexes.[1] According to the *Rites*, a man and a woman should not see each other before the matchmakers have reached an agreement; they should not sit next to each other; they should not ask questions of each other; and they should not wear each other's clothes. They are not allowed to hand objects to each other without an intermediary. When sisters return home after getting married, their brothers should not sit together with them on the same mat. Outside gossip should not be introduced into the inner quarters; words spoken inside the inner quarters should not be repeated outside. When seeing someone off or greeting someone, a woman should not go beyond the gate of the house; when she travels outside of the home, she must cover and hide her face. On the road, men should keep to the left and women should keep to the right. These are the clear rules established by the sages so as to ensure the separation [of men and women] and prevent the gradual [arising of scandals]. The relationship of husband and wife may indeed be called close, yet the man should not stay in the inner quarters during the day unless he is ill, and as his end approaches he should make sure not to die among women . . .

Nevertheless the women of today neglect the labor of sericulture and weaving and abandon their work on ceremonial garments. Instead of spinning their own linen, they go, hips swaying, to buy it in the marketplace! They neglect their tasks in the kitchen, and instead form friendships here, there, and everywhere, and together they go and visit each other. When they go to visit their relatives, they start out under the starry skies by the light of torches. There is no end to their outings, and accompanied by a large crowd of servants, they block the roads with their flashy displays. Their maids and servants, clerks and soldiers make up one big motley crowd that is just like a marketplace. All along the road they crack jokes— How terrible! How shameful! This time they stay for the night with a family not their own, that time they return in the darkness of night. They go on pleasure trips to Buddhist monasteries, and attend fishing parties and hunts as spectators. They climb up to high places, where they can look out over the river [to compose poetry], and they travel even beyond the borders of their home district in order to attend weddings and funerals. They open up their carriages and lift the curtains, making a public spectacle of themselves in both city and town. Cup and beaker are filled on the road, songs to strings are performed while traveling. Each in turn tries to surpass the other and bad habits become the norm. This results in relationships and affairs in which women are willing to do anything!

---

1. The first poem in the *Book of Odes* is called "The Ospreys." It is a wedding song, traditionally read as praising a queen for her lack of jealousy.

This licentiousness is the greatest sign of the moral laxity [of our times]. "If we model ourselves on the rare wife,"[2] the state will be corrected. I hope that you gentlemen will be able to restrain and put a stop to [these women]. By forbidding women to have any business outside the house, we may keep these things from occurring in the first place.

Our conflicting sources make it difficult to arrive at any but the most tentative of conclusions regarding the actual life of elite women during the centuries from the beginning of the Han to the end of the Tang. It would appear, though, that the elite women of the aristocratic society of the centuries of political disunion (fourth to sixth centuries) enjoyed a somewhat greater freedom of movement and expression than did the elite women of the unified bureaucratic empires of the Sui and the Tang. One indication of this is the number of known women writers of the earlier period, inside and outside the Inner Palace. Another is the emergence, in the wake of the introduction of Buddhism to China in the first century CE, of an independent community of Buddhist nuns, many of whom had distinguished family backgrounds.

During the Tang dynasty hardly any elite women made names for themselves through their writings, and most of the women poets of these centuries left little more than a handful of poems, if they left anything at all. One cause for this may have been the stricter demands on the educational level of the male members of the bureaucracy and the growing institutionalization of primary and advanced education outside the home, which made higher education in particular increasingly unavailable to women. Another cause may have been the enhanced status of poetry throughout society because of the examination system, which required a mastery of poetry-writing and thus turned poetry into a means of male competition. Even the unprecedented power of Empress Wu and Empress Wei during the final decades of the seventh and the first decade of the eighth centuries could not redress this tendency toward a restriction of women's access to (advanced) education and exclusion from literary life. In fact, the brazen display of power by these women may well have provoked society at large to place even greater stress on the "proper" subordinate role of women. This increased resistance to women

---

2. The quote in this sentence is derived from the *Book of Odes*.

assuming public roles may in turn have inhibited elite women from engaging in the writing of literature. As a result of these various developments, the best-known women writers of the Tang dynasty are not, as was often the case in earlier times, the sisters of well-known poets and scholars, but rather courtesans such as Li Ye, Xue Tao, and Yu Xuanji—public women for whom poetry was a professional skill.

Despite the fact that very few works of women writing in the first twelve centuries of imperial China have been preserved, many of them became models for women writers of later dynasties. One may perhaps even say that as the number and self-confidence of writing women in later dynasties increased, so did the importance of these earlier women writers as models.

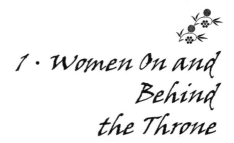

1 · Women On and Behind the Throne

Ban Zhao

A daughter in traditional China was expected to obey her father, a wife her husband, and a widow her son. If a widow was left with a son who was still a child, however, she was expected to head the household until he was old enough to relieve her of that duty. This was such a customary expectation of the widow that it also applied to the imperial family: if an heir-apparent was too young or otherwise incapable of governing, his mother, the empress dowager, would serve as the head of the household as well as the head of government. This tradition goes back to the early years of the Han dynasty (206 BCE–220 CE), when, after the death of the founding emperor, Liu Bang (256–195 BCE), his widow, the ruthless Empress Lü, became the de facto ruler of all of China. She ruled for fifteen years until her death in 180 BCE. Under almost all of the successive dynasties, women on occasion headed the imperial government as regent for an infant son, often for many years. Probably the best-known example is the infamous Empress Dowager Cixi, who ruled China from 1875 until her death in 1908.

Once a woman held the reigns of power in her capacity as regent, she often maintained her authority even after the young emperor had reached adulthood, either because the filial son deferred to his mother or because his mother simply refused to relinquish her power. Only in a single case, however, did an empress dowager ascend the throne to rule in her own name as Son of Heaven: Empress Dowager Wu Zetian took this unprecedented step in 690. Traditional historiographers, while grudgingly praising Wu Zetian for her forceful administration, have consistently condemned her for this usurpation. This was due to the traditional assumption that the actions of a widow should always serve the best interests of her son, to whom she was indebted for her position and to whom she was expected to relinquish authority as soon as he was old enough to rule.

Government in traditional China meant dealing with documents. Throughout the long history of imperial China it seems to have been assumed that empress dowagers would be sufficiently educated to handle all the demanding tasks required of the head of a large and complex bureaucracy. Except during the Ming and Qing dynasties, empresses often came from the most prestigious families of the realm and enjoyed an excellent education at home and thus were well prepared to assume their new roles. Imperial concubines and palace ladies also received a basic education, if only because they needed to handle the bookkeeping and paperwork for the female bureaucracy that was the Inner Palace. There were many opportunities for intelligent and ambitious palace ladies to acquire and use their reading and writing skills. In fact, throughout the history of imperial China the largest community of literate women was the imperial harem.

Dynastic histories, which are generally highly regarded in both traditional and modern China, are often the primary sources for the lives of these high-ranking women. The accounts in these dynastic histories must, however, be approached with caution because, although they draw on earlier sources, they are generally not compiled until centuries after the events they describe. Not only are they not always free from bias, but on occasion rumor and legend are presented as fact.

Ban Zhao was not the first woman writer in Chinese history. Compared to earlier women poets, however, including Ban Zhao's great-aunt, the imperial concubine Ban, she is the first woman to write a significant body of work in all of the genres of literature of her time. First of all, she made an important contribution to the *Books of the Han*, the dynastic history of the Western Han. This massive work was begun by her father,

Ban Biao, and then continued by her brother Ban Gu, who was unable to complete the work before he died. Ban Zhao, by then a widow, was summoned to court to finish the project. In the Inner Palace, Ban Zhao became the teacher and tutor of the young Empress Deng, who as empress dowager was the acting ruler of China from 106 to 120. Some of Ban Zhao's memorials from her days at court have been preserved. The court also greatly appreciated her talents as a poet. She is probably best known as the author of *Precepts for My Daughters*, which later came to be read as a moral tract for all women in general (and for this reason is often translated as *Precepts for Women*).

Ban Zhao came from a family that claimed a rather extraordinary pedigree. The family traced its roots to Guwutu, a bastard son of the royal family of the southern state of Chu born in 604 BCE. The story goes that the infant Guwutu had been left to die in the wilds but had survived thanks to a tigress (*wutu* in the local language) who fed him with her milk (*gu*): another word for tiger in the language of Chu was *ban* (striped). Later, his grandparents took the infant in and raised him. When the king of Qin, later known as the First Emperor, destroyed the state of Chu in 233 BCE, the descendants of Guwutu moved to the north, where they adopted Ban as their family name.

The Ban family made a fortune as cattle breeders on the grasslands north of the Great Wall. Toward the end of the second century BCE, they adopted an elite lifestyle and began to acquire a reputation for scholarship. The first member of the family to distinguish himself for his scholarship was Ban Hui. His son, Ban Kuang, moved to the capital Chang'an where he and his sons occupied a number of official posts. One of Ban Kuang's daughters entered the Inner Palace and is known to history as Concubine Ban. For a while Concubine Ban enjoyed the favors of Emperor Cheng (r. 32–7 BCE), who later, however, abandoned her for a low-class dancer. Concubine Ban expressed her anguish in a famous *fu* (rhapsody) that was included in her biography in the *Books of the Han*. Her brother, Ban You, continued the family's scholarly tradition. He collaborated with Liu Xiang, the librarian of the imperial library, in the collation of ancient texts, and the emperor let him have many of the discarded duplicates from the imperial collection. These texts greatly enriched the family's private library, which would eventually be inherited by Ban Zhao's father, Ban Biao (3 CE–54 CE), a son of one of Ban You's younger brothers.

The Western Han dynasty came to an end with the usurpation of Wang Mang, who had been a prime minister and had close ties by marriage to the reigning Liu family. He called his new dynasty the Xin and tried to institute extensive political and social reforms. His ideas were partially inspired by the *Offices of the Zhou*, which purported to describe the ideal bureaucratic system of the early Zhou dynasty. Wang Mang's efforts ended in chaos, however; rebellions broke out all across the empire, and his dynasty was toppled in 23 CE. During the ensuing civil war, Ban Biao had the foresight to ally himself with a general who in turn backed the eventual victor, Liu Xiu. Liu Xiu was a distant relative of the imperial Liu family, and because of this claimed that he was simply restoring the Han dynasty rather than establishing a new one of his own. Following his final victory, Liu moved the capital from Chang'an to the more easterly city of Luoyang, which is why his dynasty became known as the Eastern Han, as well as the Later Han.

Ban Biao held a variety of official posts under the new dynasty, but devoted most of his time to compiling a continuation of the *Records of the Historian* (*Shiji*) by Sima Qian (ca. 145 BCE–ca. 86 BCE). Sima Qian's *Records of the Historian* was a history of the (Chinese) world from earliest times (ca. 3000 BCE) up until the time of its author, who lived during the long reign of Emperor Wu (r. 141–87 BCE). Sima Qian did not present his materials as a continuous narrative, but rather divided his work into five sections: Chronicles, Tables, Treatises, Hereditary Houses, and Biographies. The "Chronicles" section provides a strictly chronological survey of the most important events at, and as seen from, the court of the kings and, later, as of 221 BCE when the king of Qin upon his unification of China declared himself to be the "First Emperor," the court of the emperors. The "Hereditary Houses" chapters offer chronological overviews of significant events at the courts of the major feudal states of the Zhou dynasty (eleventh century BCE–256 BCE). China at that time was divided into a number of states that nominally owed allegiance to the royal house of Zhou, but were in fact independent and often at war with each other. The "Tables" section synchronizes the chronologies of the "Chronicles" and the "Hereditary Houses," and also provides tables of the successive occupants of the highest offices in the bureaucracy. The "Treatises" section deals with specific aspects of administration, such as court ritual, the calendar, astronomy, taxes, and water management. The "Biographies" is the most extensive (and lively) section of the *Records of the Historian;* it includes not only biographical sketches of high officials and other famous men, but also chapters on non-Chinese peoples living on the borders of the empire. Most of the chapters in the "Biographies" are devoted to a single person, but several chapters also provide collective biographies of a specific type of person (for example, cruel officials, rich merchants, and political assassins). Whenever possible, Sima Qian based his descriptions on earlier written materials and on official archives.

Ban Biao's historiographical efforts were continued by his eldest son, Ban Gu (32–92), who was an official, poet, and scholar. Ban Gu made the important decision not to present his materials as a continuation of the *Records of the Historian,* but to present them as an independent work, limited to the period of the Western Han dynasty (including the "illegitimate" Xin dynasty). His work, now entitled *Books of the Han,* was divided into four sections: Chronicles, Tables, Treatises, and Biographies. There was no longer any need for a "Hereditary Houses" section as the Han dynasty had adopted the centralized bureaucratic administration of the Qin dynasty. The *Books of the Han,* with its fourfold division of materials, became the model for all later dynastic histories of imperial China. From the Tang dynasty onward each new dynasty would consider it its duty to chronicle the history of its predecessor in a work of the same scope and structure as Ban Gu's history of a single dynasty. Starting with the Tang dynasty (617–906) such dynastic histories were compiled by a government commission, and required the official approval of the emperor. Since the past served as a model for present and future government action, historiography was of immediate concern to the highest political authorities.

When Ban Gu lost his life in 92 because of his association with the toppled dictator Dou Xian, he had not yet completed his *Books of the Han.* Some years after his death, his widowed younger sister, Ban Zhao, was summoned to the capital in order to complete the work. We will discuss her contribution to the *Books of the Han* in more detail below. Ban Zhao's summons may have had something to do with the high position held at the time by Ban Gu's younger twin brother, Ban Chao, who, although he had also prepared himself for a civil career, later "tossed away his brush" and opted for a military career instead. In 73, Ban Chao left the capital for Central Asia, where he was instrumental in extending the power of the Han and where he eventually rose to the rank of governor-general. After almost thirty years of loyal service (and a famous memorial written on his behalf by his sister, Ban Zhao) Ban Chao obtained permission to return to his homeland. His son, Ban Yong, also served with great distinction in Central Asia and eventually attained the same rank as his illustrious father. The role of the Ban family in Chinese history would come to an inglorious end in 130 CE when Ban Yong's son, who was married to an aunt of the reigning emperor, murdered his adulterous wife in a fit of jealousy and was executed for his crime.

Little is known about Ban Zhao's youth and marriage. She must have enjoyed an extensive literary education in her parental home, which, given her milieu, was not all that unusual: both her sister-in-law and her daughter-in-law were highly literate, and her pupil, Empress Deng, had also learned to read and write at home. Ban Zhao married Cao Shishu, and later as an older widow was often referred to as Cao Dagu, or "Venerable Madam Cao." She bore her husband a son and several daughters and in 95, shortly after the death of Ban Gu, when the family's fortune may well have been at a low ebb, she accompanied her son Cao Cheng (Gu) on his journey from Luoyang to Changyuan (in the modern province of Shandong) where he had been appointed district magistrate. Ban Zhao left a record of this trip in her *Rhapsody on a Journey to the East (Dongzheng fu)*.

The "rhapsody" (*fu*), the most important genre of poetry during the Han, aimed for an exhaustive description of an object, emotion, or action and attempted to utilize all the registers of the language. The lines in a *fu* usually consisted of four or six syllables, with rhyming even lines. The length of a *fu* depended on its subject, and in a long *fu* changes in rhyme indicated a change of topic or tone. Concubine Ban, Ban Biao, and Ban Gu all wrote rhapsodies that have been preserved. Ban Gu is the author of the *Rhapsody on the Two Capitals (Liangdu fu)*, a poem of more than a thousand lines, in which a description of the old capital Chang'an is followed by a panegyric on the new capital of Luoyang. Compared to her brother's work, Ban Zhao's *Rhapsody on a Journey to the East* is only a very modest specimen of the genre. In the early sixth century, however, it was deemed worthy of inclusion in the *Selections of Refined Literature* (*Wenxuan*), a collection that quickly established itself as the most authoritative anthology of earlier poetry and prose and became prescribed reading for all writers of the Tang dynasty and after.

In the short opening stanza of the *Rhapsody on a Journey to the East,* Ban Zhao makes a point of noting that her son and she set out on their journey at an auspicious time. The second stanza begins with a description of her feelings of reluctance at having to leave the capital, the center of civilization, but concludes with an exhortation to her son to follow the straight and narrow. The following stanza is comprised of a naming of the towns and sights the travelers pass through on their eastward trip, most of which were located within the borders of the ancient state of Wei. Then in the subsequent stanza Ban Zhao calls to mind some of the famous luminaries associated with these localities: Confucius, who in Kuang was mobbed by the local population who took him for a famous bandit he resembled; Confucius' pupil Zi Lu, who was murdered when he refused to participate in the evil designs of the minister he served; and Qu Yuan (not the famous poet), who in ages past had been praised by the southern prince Ji Zha as a man of nobility. This list of exemplars of the past, famous for maintaining their virtue and integrity amid adversity, concludes with an admonition to her son to behave himself like a gentleman and to guard his integrity as he takes up his first official post. This admonition is repeated in the final section ("envoi") of the poem. The full text of the rhapsody reads as follows:

> Now, in the seventh year of Eternal Renewal
> I accompanied my son on his eastern journey.
> On an auspicious day in the first month of spring
> We chose a good time and set out on our way.
>
> I then lifted my foot and climbed into the carriage
> And that night we lodged in the town of Yanshi.
> Leaving our friends there, we headed for strangers,
> My mind was disturbed and my heart full of grief.
> By the time dawn broke, I'd still not been able to sleep,

And my lingering heart still refused to obey.
I poured myself a cup of wine to ease my thoughts,
  Suppressed my feelings, sighed and chided myself:
"We no longer dwell in nests or pry open mussels for food:[1]
  I can only exert myself and go along with my son.
So, follow tradition and take your place in the ranks,
  And accept what is assigned by Heaven and Fate.
Follow the great Way of the common road—
  If you took a shortcut, whom would you follow?"

We continued on our journey and forged ahead,
  I allowed my eyes to roam, my spirits to soar.
Passing through seven towns I gazed at the sights,
  Then we negotiated the dangers of Gong.
We watched the merging maelstrom of the He and Luo,
  Gaped at the spiraling gates of Chenggao.
Once we had escaped from those towering heights,
  We went through Yingyang and visited Yuan.
We stopped for a meal at noon in Yuanwu,
  Lodged for the night at Yangwu's Sangjian.
Passing through Fengqiu we followed the road,
  Remembering the capital I stole a sigh.
Small people tend toward love of their land,
  Ever since writing existed this has been so.
But we pressed on ahead and made some progress,
  Reaching the northern borders of Pingqiu.

Arriving in Kuang I remembered the past,
  Thought of the Master's misfortune and toil:
During those days of disaster bereft of the Way
  They mobbed and they threatened even the Sage!
Sadly I dallied and stayed there forever,
  Forgetting the time and the onset of dusk.

---

1. According to traditional Chinese historiography, early humans lived like animals until successive generations of sages brought civilization to the world. In precivilized times, people lived in holes in the ground or nests in the trees and ate raw flesh, and were ignorant of family relationships, in particular of the bonds between parents and children.

As soon as I came to the borders of Changyuan,
  I observed the people who lived in its fields,
I gazed at the hillocks and ruins of Pucheng,
  All grown over with brambles and thorns.
Startled I came to my senses and asked around
  And called to mind the might of Zi Lu.
The people of Wei laud his valor and virtue
  And even today they still sing his praises.
Qu Yuan lived to the southeast of town:
  The people still honor his grave.
Only great virtue will never decay,
  After your death your fame will endure.
The Classics and Canons teach only one thing:
  The Way and its virtue, humanity and wisdom.

Ji Zha from Wu extolled this land as "rich in gentlemen."
  His words were true, supported by the facts.
But later the state decayed, met with misfortune,
  It was despoiled and never rose again.

Know that both your nature and fate rest with Heaven,
  You must rely on your own great efforts to achieve humanity.
Maintain your lofty vision and follow after brilliance,
  Exhaust your loyalty and forgiveness on behalf of others.
If you do not waver in your love of the straight and narrow,
  Then your sincerity is bound to touch the gods.
The numinous divinities will surely shine on you,
  Protect the chaste and good and help the honest.

Envoi:

The longings of gentlemen
  Are expressed in their texts.
When speaking of their ambitions,
  They admire the men of old.
Our ancestors by their deeds
  Have set us an example.
Even though we're not their equal,
  Yet we'll take them as our norm.
High position and great riches

> May be the object of our quest,
> But we walk the Way correctly,
> 　Waiting for the proper time.
> Long or short as our life may be—
> 　Wise and fool are equal here.
> Respectfully we trust our fate,
> 　Whether fortune or disaster.
> Let us always be respectful,
> 　Full of simple modesty,
> Pure and still, without desires—
> 　May Gong Chuo your model be.

The poem ends with a reference to the *Analects* (*Lunyu*), a collection of sayings attributed to Confucius and his disciples. Once when Zi Lu asked Confucius how a real man should behave himself, Confucius is reported to have said: "Like Gong Chuo, without desires." As the final stanzas of the poem once again make clear, Ban Zhao did not write the *Rhapsody on a Journey to the East* primarily as a record of a scenic journey, but rather as a heartfelt admonition to her son as he was embarking on his public career. In this sense, it is the perfect counterpoint to her later *Precepts for My Daughters*. But whereas that later work would be written in a clear and concise prose, this grand poem is a concatenation of classical allusions. And whereas the young brides will be advised to behave obligingly, if not obsequiously, the young official is admonished by his mother to model himself on the greatest names in history and to cling to the Way and resist all temptation.

When Ban Zhao was summoned to court (it is unclear when) by Emperor He (r. 89–105), her first task was the completion of her brother's historical magnum opus. It is impossible to determine the extent of her contribution to the final version of the *Books of the Han*. She may have compiled the "Treatise on Astronomy" and she may also have compiled the "Tables" section. It is clear, however, that she did not finish the text, because later Ma Xu, an elder brother of the famous scholar Ma Rong (79–166), was ordered to complete it.

Ban Zhao was also ordered to instruct other scholars in how to read the *Books of the Han*. While there were a few punctuation marks in use at the time, texts as a rule were written out and copied without indicating the ending of sentences or the beginnings of paragraphs. For those who wanted to read (and memorize) a text, the guidance of a tutor who knew how to parse and explicate the text was absolutely essential. In the case of a traditional text, it would not be difficult to find a qualified instructor, but in the case of a new text such as the *Books of the Han,* there was not yet a scholarly tradition upon which to draw. In order to ensure the survival of the text written by the Ban father, brother, and sister, it was therefore extremely urgent that scholars be trained in how to read it, even if it had to be at the hands of a woman. One of Ban Zhao's pupils was the above-mentioned Ma Rong, the author of authoritative commentaries on the Classics. Ma Rong's subsequent praise for Ban Zhao's *Precepts for My Daughters* probably contributed greatly to its wide dissemination.

Ban Zhao not only served as historian and teacher, but also as court poet. Whenever very special tribute gifts were presented to the court, she was summoned to celebrate the event with a rhapsody. These paeans have not been preserved, with the exception of (a fragment of) her *Rhapsody on the Ostriches (Daque fu).* This *fu* must have been written before the return of her brother Ban Chao to the capital in 102, as it was he who, in his capacity as governor-general of Central Asia, had made a gift of these birds to his sovereign. The arrival at court of these "big sparrows," the likes of which had never before been seen in China, was of course interpreted as an auspicious indication of the superior virtue of the reigning emperor.

The full elder brother of the Venerable Madam, the governor-general of the western regions, the Marquis Who Subdued the Farthest Lands Ban Chao, presented a pair of ostriches to the court, and the Venerable Madam was summoned to compose a rhapsody on the subject, which reads as follows:

> How I admire the place where these "big sparrows" roost:
> They live on the numinous peaks of the Kunlun Mountains.[2]
> Although they share the small sparrow's name, they differ in size,
> And as such they are comparable to the phoenix and *luan.*
> Longing for the One with Virtue they submitted to duty,
> Winging ten thousand miles they traveled and came.
> Roosting in the royal courtyard they rest and repose,

---

2. The Kunlun Mountains are mythic mountains said to be located at the Western edge of the Chinese world, the paradisiacal abode of the Queen Mother of the West.

> Enjoying its stately harmony they feel at ease.
> High and low are unified and linked in love,
>   One hears the majestic tones of the Odes and Hymns.[3]
> From East to West, from South to North,
>   All wish to join and come and share!

Ban Zhao's memorial to the throne in support of her brother's request to be relieved of his position and allowed to return to the China heartland is considered to be one of her finest prose pieces. It has been preserved because it was included in the biography of Ban Chao in *Books of the Later Han*, the dynastic history of the Later Han, by Fan Ye (398–445):

My full elder brother, the governor-general of the western regions, the Marquis Who Subdued the Farthest Lands Chao has enjoyed the good fortune of having received great rewards beyond measure for his negligible merits. His rank has been raised to that of marquis and his position brings him two thousand *dan* of rice annually. The imperial favor has been truly exceptional, far beyond what an insignificant servant should receive.

When Chao first set out, his ambition was to sacrifice his life, and he hoped to establish some merit in order to demonstrate his efforts on behalf of Your Majesty. After the debacle of Chen Mu, all communications had been cut off.[4] But while Chao anguished all by himself out there in those inaccessible regions, he was still able to enlighten and persuade all the states in the area to submit. He relied on his troops, and whenever they attacked or gave battle, he would be the first to ascend the wall. Although he was wounded by the weapons of war, he did not shirk death. Thanks to Your Majesty's divine numinosity, he has managed to survive in the desert now for already thirty years. We may be close relatives, but having been separated in life, we would not even recognize each other. The officers and men of his age who followed him have all died. Chao is now advanced in years, he is approaching seventy. Suffering the effects of age he is beset by illnesses. Not a single black hair remains on his head; he has no feeling in either of his arms; he has lost both his hearing and his sight; and can only walk with the support of a walking-stick. Even though he would wish to do

---

3. The "Odes" (*ya*) and "Hymns" (*song*) are the names of two sections in the *Book of Odes* [*Shijing*], one of the Five Classics.

4. In 75 CE, the native population of Central Asia rose in rebellion against the Chinese governor Chen Mu, killing him and annihilating most of his troops.

his utmost to repay the emperor's favor, he has been turned by old age into a sickly dog, a decrepit steed.

It is the nature of barbarians to rebel against authority and scorn old age. But Chao may be lowered into his grave any day now and after all these years still has not been replaced. I fear that this may invite treason and incite rebellion. Yet the highest officials of the land only think of what is immediately urgent and refuse to consider future developments. If by chance Chao would suddenly die and his vital spirits no longer be able to obey his will, then all the efforts of the state over numerous generations would be lost, and all the benefits of the loyal efforts of your minister would be discarded. This would really be a shame! It is for this reason that Chao, from ten thousand miles away, addressed himself to the throne and himself explained the extreme urgency of the matter. For three years he has been anxiously waiting for a decision, but as yet his request has not been granted.

In ancient times, I have learned, one received one's weapons at fifteen and handed them in at sixty, which means there was a time of rest and recuperation and a time during which one did not serve in office. As Your Majesty rules the world with utmost filiality, You have earned the joy and gratitude of all the lands. You do not neglect even the subject of the smallest state, so how much less would you neglect someone like Chao who holds the rank of marquis! That is why I dare to risk death, implore for mercy on behalf of Chao, and beg You to permit him to spend his remaining years at home. If he may be allowed to return alive and to see the imperial palace once again, this will forever free the state from having to worry about campaigns against those faraway lands in the western regions, and from fear of disturbance and chaos. Chao may then enjoy the favor demonstrated by King Wen who buried the bones of the slain, and the generosity shown by Tian Zifang who took pity on an old warhorse. As it says in the [*Book of*] *Odes* [*Shijing*]:

> The people are worn out and weary;
> Now is the time to give them comfort.
> Bestow Your grace on the central state,
> Extend Your comfort to the border lands!

Although not yet deceased, Chao has written me a letter of final farewell; I greatly fear I will never see him again. I am truly saddened by the thought that Chao spent the prime of his life exercising his loyalty and filiality in the desert, and that now that he is exhausted and old, he is just left to die in the open field. This is truly lamentable! If Chao is not saved and rescued and later suffers a sudden reversal of military fortune, I hope that as a favor to Chao's family You will promise to exempt them from punishment as happened in the case of the mother of Zhao Kua and the concubine from Wei.[5]

I am a foolish and ignorant woman, and do not understand affairs of state, which is why I dare violate all prohibitions and taboos by writing this memorial.

Ban Zhao's eloquent memorial helped to convince the emperor to grant her brother's request to be allowed to come home. Ban Chao, by this time a septuagenarian, finally arrived back in Luoyang in 102 CE, although within a month he had passed away.

One of the few (partially) extant poems composed by Ban Zhao is called "Needle and Thread." Despite its title, this poem is not just a description of the traditional women's tasks of sewing and embroidery. As it happens, the word for needle (*zhen*) also carries the meaning of "admonition" and Ban Zhao's poem is actually written in praise of those who, with circumspection and subtlety, dare criticize, in speech or writing, the faulty actions of their superiors. In the first stanza of the poem, the "it" refers to the "needle," both as physical object and oral criticism; in the second stanza the poet describes the literary genre of the "needle" or admonition:

> Forged from the hardest essence of autumnal metal,
> Its shape, marvelously small, is straight and sharp.
> Its nature is to penetrate and then slowly advance,
> A single connection linking all manner of things.
> Truly the miracles worked by needle and thread
> Extend far and wide, although they have no source!

---

5. In premodern China, a vanquished general was often held responsible for the defeat of his troops, and upon his return might be executed together with all the members of his family. It is for this reason that, when in the third century BCE, the king of Zhao appointed Zhao Kua, the young and inexperienced son of the famous general Zhao She, as commander of the army, his mother protested. When the king insisted, she asked him to promise that should he fail in his mission, she would be spared execution. The king promised, and when Zhao Kua was defeated by the army of Qin, he kept his word. The concubine from Wei was one of the wives of Duke Huan of Qi (r. 685–643 BCE). When her husband prepared to attack her home state of Wei, she is said to have asked him what crime Wei had committed to deserve such an attack.

It rejects the corrupt, compensates for mistakes,
It is as pure as the fleece of the whitest lamb.
Buckets and baskets count for nothing at all—
But this is inscribed on stone, taken into the hall!

A bucket and a basket may be much larger than a needle (and thread), but they do not have the same efficacy. "People like bucket and basket" is a phrase that was used to characterize unenlightened officials to whom only minor tasks might be entrusted. The fourth line of the first stanza is an allusion to the well-known dictum of Confucius that the apparent multiplicity of his teaching was actually connected by a single thread or principle (that principle being, according to his disciple Zengzi, loyalty and reciprocity).

Ban Zhao's most important pupil was the woman who would eventually become the Empress Deng. Beautiful, intelligent, and highly ambitious, Deng Sui (81–121) entered the Inner Palace in 96. She had been born into one of the most prestigious families of the realm, and, according to her biography in the *Books of the Later Han*, even as a young girl had already acquired a reputation for her composure and her love of study:

The Harmonious and Illustrious Empress Deng Sui was a granddaughter of Grand Tutor [Deng] Yu. Her father [Deng] Xun was the Colonel-Protector of the Tibetans, while her mother, lady Yin, was a niece of the Brilliant and Chaste Empress.

When the empress was five years old, the wife of the Grand Tutor loved her so much that she wanted to personally cut the girl's hair. The old lady, however, was advanced in years and blind, and accidentally cut the forehead of the later empress. The little girl endured the pain without saying a word. All those present marveled at this, and when they asked her about it, she answered: "Of course it was painful! But the old lady wanted to cut my hair out of love and concern, and I did not want to hurt her feelings. So I kept my mouth shut."

By six she had mastered the *Book of Clerks*,[6] and by twelve she fully understood the *Odes* and the *Analects*. Whenever her brothers recited the Classics and Commentaries, she would pay close attention and pose hard questions. Her mind was on the canonical books, and she was not interested in household affairs. Her mother would always scold her: "You don't engage in the women's

---

6. The *Book of Clerks* (*Lishu*) was a list of often-used characters and served as a primer for reading and writing in Han dynasty China.

work of sewing clothes but only devote yourself to study. What chance is there of you being appointed a professor?" But again the empress disobeyed her mother: during the day she would tend to her women's chores, but at night she recited the Classics and canons, and everyone in the house called her "the student."

Her father Xun greatly admired her and would discuss with her in detail all matters great and small.

The biography continues with a description of the girl's extreme filiality upon the death of her father in 92 and the signs of her future greatness. After entering the Inner Palace, Deng Sui distinguished herself by her exemplary behavior, and soon became everyone's favorite. Emperor He too fell under the spell of her beauty and intelligence; in 102, immediately after deposing his main wife, Empress Yin (who had been accused of witchcraft and black magic), he elevated Deng Sui to the rank of empress. Following Emperor He's death in 106, Empress Dowager Deng dominated the court and ruled the realm as regent until her death in 120.

Empress Dowager Deng governed with a conspicuous display of frugality and austerity. She required the young princes of the imperial family to undergo a strict moral education and she herself studied the Classics with "Venerable Madam Cao." It was by appealing to the authority of the Classics that she managed to free herself from her brothers' undue influence on her actions. As a rule, when an empress dowager became regent, her father, brothers, and cousins would acquire considerable power and influence at court, often reducing the empress dowager to a mere pawn in their hands. Traditionally, such a usurpation of power by the relatives of an empress was strongly condemned. As soon as Deng Sui was raised to the rank of empress, she instructed all the local officials not to extend any special privileges to her relatives, and in the beginning at least, she also blocked the appointment of her own brothers to high positions. When their mother died in 106, Deng Sui's brothers were expected to retire from government service for the duration of the prescribed mourning period, which meant that they would have to formally request to leave the capital for at least a year. The brothers probably expected that their sister would refuse their request and ask them to stay on in their positions. Following the advice of

Ban Zhao, the empress dowager decided to grant their request, and by doing so strengthened her independence. The memorial in which Ban Zhao advises the empress dowager on this crucial matter is quoted in full in her biography in the *Books of the Later Han*. (At the end of the mourning period, Deng Sui's brother Deng Zhi returned to the capital, where he held a succession of high offices; however, following the death of Deng Sui in 121, he was forced to commit suicide.)

Another of Ban Zhao's prose texts quoted in full in her biography in the *Books of the Later Han* is her *Precepts for My Daughters*. This important text consists of a preface and seven short chapters. In the preface, Ban Zhao tells us that she wrote this text late in life to instruct her daughters who were about to be married. It would seem, however, that her daughters would already have been married by then, unless we assume that her daughters were born very late. Another possibility is that the daughters concerned were the daughters born to younger concubines of her husband.

Ban Zhao's *Precepts for My Daughters* may well be the first Chinese prose tract on wifely duties. In it, she repeatedly quotes from an otherwise unknown work entitled *Charter for Women* (*Nü xian*), which appears to have been a poem rather than a prose text. *Precepts for My Daughters* marks the beginning of a tradition of moral tracts written for women by women, in which the subordination of women to men is presented as an accepted fact of life. By the twentieth century, these tracts had come to be wholeheartedly condemned by modern Chinese intellectuals—reformists and revolutionaries, men and women—as glorifications of the oppression of women. Many a modern author has been puzzled by the seeming contradiction between Ban Zhao's elevated position and independent activities and the lessons she left to later generations of women. It may be that these contradictions are more apparent than real, however. Most likely the text was not written as a blind justification of the traditional division of labor between women and men, but rather as a practical guide for young and inexperienced girls on how to survive when they suddenly find themselves in the unfamiliar and intimidating surroundings of their husband's home. One modern scholar has even argued that *Precepts for My Daughters* was written to instruct Empress Deng in the devious ways of court politics, where flattery and dissembling were essential to success.

That may be stretching the evidence somewhat, as both the preface and the main text of *Precepts for My Daughters* address brides-to-be, rather than all women in general. In any case, one can perhaps take some cheer from the fact that *Precepts for My Daughters* was attacked during Ban Zhao's lifetime by her own sister-in-law, although what she may have taken most offense to was not Ban Zhao's moral prescriptions, but rather her description of the husband's family as a veritable pit of snakes.

The *Books of the Later Han* is the first dynastic history to include among its "Biographies" a chapter on "Exemplary Women," and it is here that we find the earliest account of Ban Zhao's life, written in the typical terse style of a traditional Chinese historian, who fills out his sparse biographical narrative by quoting some of his subject's representative writings:

The wife of Cao Shishu from Fufeng was the daughter of Ban Biao, also from Fufeng. Her personal name was Ban, and her style name was Huiban; she was also known as Ji. She was extremely erudite and highly talented. Shishu, who died young, was distinguished by his principled character and proper behavior. Ban Zhao's brother Gu wrote the *Books of the Han* but passed away before he had completed the Eight Tables and the "Treatise on Astronomy." Emperor He summoned her to the Library at the Eastern Hall so that she could continue his work and complete it. The emperor repeatedly summoned her to the Inner Palace and had the empress and consorts honor her as their teacher. She was called the "Venerable Madam." Whenever strange beasts were presented to the court in tribute, she was always sent for and requested to compose a rhapsody of praise.

When Empress Deng served as regent, Ban Zhao assisted her in the administration of the realm. Because of her diligent service both within and outside the palace, as a special mark of favor her son Cheng was enfeoffed as Marquis Within the Pass, and in his career he rose to the rank of minister to the prince of Qi.

At that time, the *Books of the Han* had just come out and there were many who could not yet understand it. Ma Rong, also from Fufeng, submitted to her tutelage and learned from her how to read the *Books of the Han*. Later, Rong's elder brother Xu would be summoned to continue Zhao's work and complete the *Books of the Han*.

In the first year of the reign period Eternal Beginning [Yongchu, 107–113], the elder brother of the empress dowager, the [later] generalissimo Deng Zhi, submitted a memorial in which he requested to be relieved of all his official duties, so that he might observe the period of mourning for his mother. The empress dowager hesitated to grant his request and asked Zhao for her advice. Zhao then submitted a memorial that reads as follows:

> Your Majesty, the empress dowager, embodies the beauty of splendid virtue and exemplifies the rulership of Yao and Shun.[7] Unlocking the gates in the four directions and opening the four kinds of sharp hearing, You consider even the blind words of madmen and take into account the proposals of grasscutters! Despite my useless ignorance, I, your servant Zhao, am allowed to shadow Your splendid brilliance. How could I dare not lay bare my innermost feelings so as to repay Your kindness, if even in a very small way.
>
> I have heard that no virtue has greater influence than modest yielding. This is why the canons and documents extol its beauty and the gods and ghosts give it their blessing. In the distant past, Bo Yi and Shu Qi left their kingdom and the entire world acknowledges their lofty purity; Taibo left Bin and Confucius praised him for his "triple yielding."[8] In this manner these men made a brilliant display of their fine virtue and left a name among later generations. The *Analects* state: "If one can rule the country with rites and yielding, what problem will there be in its governance?" As can be seen from these examples, sincerity in recommending and yielding may well bring peace to the most distant regions.
>
> Now your four brothers strictly adhere to loyalty and filiality and wish to retire from official duties. If you now refuse to grant their request on the grounds that the border regions are still not pacified, I am truly afraid that should something arise afterwards, they may never again have this opportunity to earn a name for recommending and yielding.

---

7. Yao and Shun were exemplary emperors from China's mythic past. According to legend, Yao was so impressed by the virtues of Shun, especially his filiality, that he ceded his throne to him and gave him his two daughters as wives. Shun later ceded the throne to Yu, who became the founder of the Xia dynasty.

8. Bo Yi and Shu Qi were the two eldest sons of the lord of Guzhu, but as they were convinced of the superior virtue of their younger brother, they left Guzhu so that their brother would have the opportunity to succeed to the throne. When King Wu, the founder of the Zhou dynasty, rose in rebellion against the last ruler of the Shang dynasty, the brothers urged him to desist from his campaign as it would result in regicide. When King Wu ignored their pleading, they retired to Mt. Shouyang, where they starved to death because they refused to eat "the grain of Zhou."

Taibo left the state of Bin in order to enable his younger brother Wang Ji to succeed to the throne, because he knew that Wang Ji was destined to be the father of King Wen, the father of King Wu, and the de facto founder of the Zhou dynasty.

As my insight may be defective, I am risking death by revealing my uninformed opinion. Although I am fully aware that my words are not worthy of Your attention, I wish to demonstrate my sincere loyalty.

The empress dowager followed Ban Zhao's advice and granted her brother's request, upon which they both returned to their home village.

Ban Zhao also wrote *Precepts for My Daughters* in seven chapters, which is useful in the instruction of the women of the inner quarters. Its text reads as follows:

I am simpleminded and unenlightened and not naturally intelligent. But I enjoyed the doting affection of my late father and relied on the exemplary instruction provided by my mother. When I was fourteen—now more than forty years ago—I took up dustpan and broom in the Cao family. Trembling with fear, I was always afraid of bringing divorce and dishonor upon myself, which would bring further shame on my parents and add to the burdens of my relatives. From early morning until late at night I put forth my best efforts and toiled without complaining of weariness. But from now on I know that I will be spared all of that.

By nature I am lax and lazy and have no talent for teaching. I have always been afraid that my son Gu would betray our pure court and bring dishonor upon it, but he has enjoyed the emperor's grace beyond measure, and inexplicably been honored with the gold and purple insignia. This is something we had not even dared hope for. As a man my son will be able to take care of himself, and I will no longer have to worry about him. But I am concerned about you, my daughters, who are about to be married. Because you have not been immersed in instruction and censure and know nothing of the proper behavior for women, I am afraid that you may lose face with your husbands' families and bring shame upon your ancestors.

The illness I now suffer from is serious and persistent and my life may be over any day. Whenever I think about you all, I become sad and depressed. In my leisure time I have written *Precepts for My Daughters* in seven chapters. My daughters, each of you make yourself a copy: perhaps it will be of some use and benefit to you. Do your very best once you have left home!

Chapter 1 *Lowly and Weak*

In ancient times a daughter was placed under the bed on the second day after her birth, given a tile to play with, and then her relatives fasted and announced [her birth to the ancestors]. She was placed under the bed to show her lowliness and weakness, and emphasize that she would serve others. She was given a tile to play with to show that she had to get used to hard work, and to emphasize that she would keep to her tasks. Her relatives fasted and announced her birth to the ancestors to show that she would be in charge of maintaining the ancestral sacrifices. These three things epitomize the constant way of women and are the normative teaching of the rites and norms.

To act with modesty and submission, deference and respect, to place others before oneself, to live without being praised for one's virtues and to suffer every injustice, to bear shame and hide disgrace, and to live always as if filled with fear—this is what it means to be lowly and weak and serve others.

To retire late and rise again early, and, whether at the break of day or late at night, to take care of all the household affairs without shirking either the heavy or the easy tasks, and always to complete what one has started in a proper and tidy manner—this is what it means to keep to one's tasks.

To serve one's husband and master with a proper expression and a dignified behavior, to keep oneself pure and clean, to refrain from indulging in banter and laughter, and properly prepare food and wine for the ancestral sacrifices—this is what it means to maintain the ancestral sacrifices.

I have never known anyone to worry that their good name would not be known and that they might suffer divorce and dishonor if they were perfect in these three things. But if you fail in any of these three things, there will be no good name to be spread, and divorce and dishonor will be unavoidable!

Chapter 11 *Husband and Wife*

The way of husband and wife fulfills the workings of yin and yang, and as such has the power to move the gods. It truly is the greatest duty of heaven and earth, the highest norm of human relationships. That is why the *Rites* place such value on the relationship of man and woman, and why the *Odes* expatiate on the meaning of "The Ospreys." To judge from these books, one must take the way of husband and wife most seriously.

If the husband is not wise, he will be incapable of governing his wife and if the wife is not wise, she will be unable to serve her husband. If the husband does not govern his wife, he will lose his dignity. If the wife does not serve her husband, she will be neglecting her duties. But these two tasks are one in their function. I have noticed that the gentlemen of today understand only that a wife must be governed and that one's dignity must be preserved, and for this reason they instruct their sons and test their reading ability. But they completely ignore the fact that a husband and master must be served and ritual duties must be performed. Does not instructing only the sons and not the daughters betray a total ignorance of the different norms governing the one and the other? According to the *Rites*, children should be taught to read and write when they are eight years old, and at fifteen they should be sent to school. Cannot we simply make this the general rule?

Chapter III *Respect and Circumspection*

Yin and yang each have their respective nature; men and women each have their own mode of comportment. In the case of yang, hardness is a virtue, while for yin softness is more useful; in men one prizes strength, while in women weakness is an asset. That is why the proverb says: "Even if you have a son like a wolf, you still fear he might turn out to be a wimp; even if you have a daughter like a mouse, you still fear she might turn into a tiger." And so, in cultivating one's person there is nothing greater than respect, and in the avoidance of willfulness there is nothing greater than obedience. For this reason it is said that the way of respect and obedience is the highest deportment for married women. Now, respect means nothing more than constant endurance, and obedience means nothing more than tolerant acceptance. Constant endurance results from satisfaction and contentment; tolerant acceptance results from deference and subservience. In this way the love of husband and wife will last unbroken for a lifetime.

Treating each other as equals in the home will give rise to flirtation and teasing. Once flirtation and teasing have arisen, words will go too far. Once words have gone too far, self-indulgence will arise. Once self-indulgence has arisen, you will start to lose respect for your husband. This all stems from a lack of satisfaction and contentment. Your husband's actions will sometimes be straight and sometimes crooked, his opinions will sometimes be correct and sometimes mistaken. You cannot but stand up for what is right and dispute what is wrong. But once you start fighting and arguing, there will be anger and rage. This all stems from a lack of deference and subservience. If you cannot restrain yourself in your disrespect for your husband, there will be shouting and cursing. If there is no end to anger and rage, beatings are bound to follow. Now those who are husband and wife should live in close harmony based on duty and should share an affection based on forbearance. Once the slaps and blows begin, how can duty survive? Once the shouting and cursing start, how can affection last? Where affection and duty have been abandoned, husband and wife will be torn apart.

Chapter IV *Wifely Comportment*

There are four main types of women's comportment: the first is wifely virtue; the second, wifely speech; the third, wifely appearance; and fourthly, wifely work. Wifely virtue doesn't mean you have to be exceptionally talented and bright; wifely speech doesn't mean you have to be quick-minded and eloquent; wifely appearance doesn't mean you have to look beautiful and stunning; wifely work doesn't mean you have to be more skillful than anyone else.

To be pure and chaste, to keep properly to the norms, to know shame in one's personal behavior, and to keep to the rules in whatever one does—this is wifely virtue. To choose one's words when speaking, to refrain from gossip and slander, to speak only when it is appropriate, and not to bore others— this is wifely speech. To wash away dust and dirt, to keep one's clothes fresh and clean, to bathe regularly, and not to soil one's body—this is wifely appearance. To devote oneself to spinning and weaving, not to indulge in banter and laughter, and to neatly prepare the wine and food that is to be served to the guests—that is wifely work.

These four areas of comportment constitute a woman's greatest virtue and one cannot be deficient in any of them. They are very easy to practice, all one needs is the resolve. A sage of old once said: "How could humaneness be so far away? The minute I wish for humaneness, then humaneness is there!" The same applies in this case.

Chapter V *Complete Devotion*

According to the *Rites*, the husband has the duty to marry again [upon the death of his wife], but there is nothing written about a second marriage for women [upon the death of the husband]. Therefore it is said that the husband is the sky—just as one can nowhere escape from the sky, one can never become separated from one's husband. A woman's remarriage offends the gods and ghosts and will be punished by heaven; it is a crime against the rites and against duty and your [new] husband is bound to despise you. Therefore the *Charter for Women* says: "Succeed in pleasing the one man / And you are forever settled. / Fail in pleasing the one man / And you are forever finished." Judging from this, you have to win his heart; however, you should not try to win it with "flattering charms" and "illicit intimacies." There is truly nothing more important than complete devotion and proper demeanor.

Rites and duty should govern your sitting and rising, your ears should not listen indiscriminately, and your eyes should not gaze upon evil; when you go out you should not dress seductively and at home you should not neglect your appearance; you should not assemble in crowds with your friends or peer out of the gates and doors: this is what is called complete devotion and proper demeanor. But if you are light and flippant in all your actions; are always flitting from one thing to another; leave your hair in a tangle and neglect your appearance while at home but are all charm and beauty when you go out; if you say what you should not be saying, watch what you should not be watching—this is what is called being incapable of complete devotion and proper demeanor.

Chapter VI *Compliant Docility*

"Succeed in pleasing the one man / And you are forever settled. / Fail in pleasing the one man / And you are forever finished." These words are meant to strengthen your resolve and concentrate your devotion. But how can you afford to lose the sympathy of your parents-in-law? Among living beings, some are separated by affection, and some are torn apart by duty. Now if your husband loves you, but your parents-in-law disapprove of you, he is duty-bound to divorce you.

So what should you do to win the sympathy of your parents-in-law? In this regard nothing is better than compliant docility. When your mother-in-law says that something is not the case, even if you are in the right, you had really better follow her orders. When your mother-in-law says something is the case, even if you disagree, you had still better comply with her command. On no account should you argue against her idea of right and wrong, or dispute with her as to what is crooked and straight. This is what is called compliant docility. That is why the *Charter for Women* says: "A wife like a shadow or echo / Will certainly be liked and loved."

Chapter VII *Harmony with Brothers- and Sisters-in-law*

A wife's ability to please her husband and master depends on her being loved by her parents-in-law. And the love of parents-in-law depends on her being praised by her brothers- and sisters-in-law. Your ranking and evaluation, whether of praise or blame, all depend on your brothers- and sisters-in-law, so you also cannot afford to lose the sympathy of your brothers- and sisters-in-law. All those who think they can afford to lose the sympathy of their brothers- and sisters-in-law and are incapable of living in harmony with them to save their marriage, are stupid indeed!

You yourselves are not sages, and rare are those who are without fault. That is why Master Yan praised those who could improve themselves,[9] and why Confucius admired those who did not repeat their mistakes. How much more does this apply in the case of married women! Even if you had the deportment of an intelligent woman and a bright and alert nature, how could you be perfect? Therefore, if members of the same household live in harmony, slander can be covered up, but if relatives by birth and by marriage are not united, then evil will spread far and wide. This is an unavoidable state of affairs. The *Changes* says: "When two people are united, / Their sharpness cuts through bronze. / Words that stem from unity / Are as fragrant as the orchid." This also applies to this case.[10]

Now the wives of the husband's elder brothers and his younger sister are equal in status; while there may be no bond of affection, they have become close relatives by duty. Now a pure and gentle, modest and obedient person will by adhering to duty be able to create a deep friendship and to extend affection to obtain their help. As a result, her excellence and beauty will be brilliantly displayed, her faults and defects will be concealed and hidden, her parents-in-law will cherish and commend her, her husband and master will laud and praise her, and her reputation will shine in town and village, its great glory extending to her father and mother.

But a coarse and doltish person will, when with the wives of her husband's elder brothers, rely on her family's fame to give herself airs, and when with his younger sisters, bank on his infatuation and be puffed up with arrogance. Now what kind of harmony can there be if one displays one's arrogance? And what kind of praise can one expect if affection and duty are ignored? As a result your virtues will be hidden and your faults exposed, your mother-in-law will be enraged and your husband disappointed, slander will be spread among all your relatives, and shame and dishonor will be heaped upon you. On the one hand, you will increase the shame of your father and mother, and on the other, you will add to the troubles of your noble husband!

This is the root of glory or dishonor, the basis of fame or infamy. Of course you have to be circumspect! Thus, for winning the sympathy of your brothers- and sisters-in-law there is nothing better than modesty and obedi-

---

9. Master Yan is Yan Hui, Confucius' favorite disciple.

10. The *Book of Changes* [*Yijing*] is yet another of the Five Classics. The core of the book consists of the sixty-four hexagrams (combinations of six broken and unbroken lines), and their interpretations.

ence. Modesty is the handle of virtue, obedience is a woman's mode of behavior. These two qualities should be sufficient to ensure harmony. The *Odes* says: "On that side there is no hate, / On this side there is no scheming." This applies also to such a situation.

Ma Rong praised *Precepts for My Daughters* and had his wife and daughters memorize it. The younger sister of Ban Zhao's husband, Cao Fengsheng, who was also talented and intelligent, wrote a piece critical of *Precepts for My Daughters*. This text is well worth reading.

Ban Zhao died when she was over seventy years old. The empress dowager dressed in mourning and wept before her coffin, and her emissaries supervised the funeral.

Ban Zhao's writings—her rhapsodies, odes, elegies, questions, annotations, funeral laments, letters, discussions, briefs, testaments—filled a total of sixteen scrolls. Her daughter-in-law, lady Ding, gathered them into a collection and also composed "An Encomium to the Venerable Madam."

Unfortunately, very little has been preserved of the once-voluminous writings of Ban Zhao. Her collected works were still in circulation during the Tang dynasty, but while they comprised three books in the seventh century, by the eleventh they had been reduced to only two books, and subsequently they disappeared altogether. As for Ban Zhao's poetry, only a few short fragments survive apart from the poems translated above. We also have her commentary to one of Ban Gu's rhapsodies. A seventh-century bibliography credits her with annotations to the *Biographies of Exemplary Women*, the collection of biographical anecdotes about women from ancient times up to the third century BCE that was compiled by her great-uncle's colleague Liu Xiang, but nothing of these annotations remains extant. An eleventh-century source also credits Ban Zhao with the authorship of an appendix to the *Biographies of Exemplary Women*, a collection of sixteen biographical sketches of women who lived during the Han dynasty. This appendix is included in the extant editions of the *Biographies of Exemplary Women*, but general scholarly opinion is that its author was not Ban Zhao.

Poets, Teachers, Moralists

Ban Zhao would for centuries be the role model for those writing women whose greatest ambition was to be summoned to court and serve

as tutor to the women of the Inner Palace. None of those who were selected in later times, however, displayed Ban Zhao's talent and range of
accomplishments. Zuo Fen's (second half of the third century) reputation
is based solely on her poetry; lady Song was called to court in the fourth
century to instruct male students in one of the Confucian Classics, and
the Song sisters (first half of the ninth century) are best known as the authors of a moral tract for women.

Poets of the Inner Palace: Zuo Fen, Han Lanying, and Bao Linghui

Zuo Fen was a younger sister of the poet Zuo Si (ca. 255–ca. 306), who
enjoyed a modest official career under the Jin dynasty (265–420). Like
her brother, she wrote both rhapsodies and *shi* poems. Whereas rhapsodies are often long and descriptive, *shi* poems are typically short and lyrical, and maintain the same line-length throughout. While *shi* poems with
lines of three, four, or six syllables do occur, the most common type of
shi has five or seven syllables (words) to a line. The genre developed from
popular song in the second century CE, and from then until well into the
twentieth century, *shi* poems continued to be the most widely practiced
form of Chinese poetry.

The extensive biography of Zuo Fen in the *Books of the Jin* (*Jin shu*), the
dynastic history of the Jin, provides the following brief summary of her
early life:

From her earliest years she loved books and was well-versed in literary composition; her fame was second only to that of [her elder brother Zuo] Si. Emperor
Wudi [r. 265–290] heard of her reputation and had her brought into the Inner
Palace. In the eighth year of the reign period Great Beginning [Taishi, 272] she
was appointed to be one of the nine imperial second rank concubines, with the
title Xiuyi [Lady of Cultivated Deportment].

A number of poems by Zuo Fen give expression to her longing for her
parental home. An example of this is seen in the poem entitled "Moved by
Separation," which she is said to have written in response to a long series
of poems about the sorrows of separation composed by her elder brother:

Moved by Separation

Since leaving behind my parents' loving care
Already two years have so quickly gone by.

So far so far—the distance grows and grows,
When will I be allowed to visit home?
I open and I read the scroll you sent,
Savor the words of sadness of separation.
It is as if I see your features in my mind
And I cannot restrain myself from sighing.
When will we meet together, face to face,
And feast our eyes on the *Documents* and *Odes*?
In what way can I best express my pain?
I vent my feelings through the written word.

Perhaps it was poems like the one above that elicited the imperial edict commanding Zuo Fen "to compose a text on her feelings of sorrow." The text she wrote in response to the emperor's command, *Rhapsody on Feelings of Separation*, is included in full in her biography:

Born in the lowly circumstances of a simple home,
I knew very little about texts and tallies.
I never saw the wondrous images of pictures and paintings,
And never heard the canons and counsels of former worthies.
As I am foolish and lowly and lacking in knowledge,
I am not of the sort who serve in the imperial palace.
This is no proper abode for a weed or a reed,
All the time I'm afraid and filled with fear,
Consumed by wearisome worries of loving and longing,
Beset by a myriad concerns over making it through.
Alas, my heavy cares have congealed deep within me,
They are tied up in knots—in whom to confide?
My mind is all muddied, I am deeply depressed,
My thoughts are a tangle, increasing my longing.
At night I am restless and restive and cannot sleep,
My soul hovering till dawn between waking and dreaming.

Soughing and sighing drafts arise on all sides,
Glistening and glittering frost covers the courtyard.
The sun is dark and dreary and sheds no light,
The air makes one shiver and shudder: so chillingly clear!
Filled with the many emotions of sorrow and sadness
I cannot stop my tears from coursing down.
Once long ago Han Boyu, so eager to please,

Would dress in colored clothes to cheer his parents.[11]
I am grieved by the gaping gulf of today
  That blocks me from my family forever.
It is not the distance by which we are separated
  Which may not measure more than a couple of yards!
Why are the palace restrictions so harsh and severe?
  I'd love to see their faces but it cannot be done!
Just seeing a cloud pass by makes me heave a sigh
  And my tears flow down and wet my kerchief.

When Qu Yuan was moved to laments
  He was saddened and wounded by separation.[12]
To the author of the song of the city gate
  A single day lasted longer than a month.[13]
How much more is this true for close relatives
  Who despite their yearning are ripped apart.
Forever filled with pain, I nurse my sadness,
  Looking up to blue heaven, I cry tears of blood!

Envoi:

From flesh-and-blood kin
I was turned into a stranger,
  Having left forever!
Distressed and sorrowful
My soul returns in dreams
  To see my loved ones.
Once awake I cry and moan,
My heart finds no solace

---

11. Han Boyu, who is said to have lived during the Han dynasty, was famous for his exemplary filiality. Even as an elderly man he would dress up in the brightly colored clothes of a child in order to make his senile parents believe they were still young, and he wept when the beating administered by his mother did not hurt him anymore because it meant that she was growing old and losing her strength.

12. Qu Yuan (ca. 340–ca. 278 BCE) was a minister of the king of Chu. When he had lost the king's favor because of the slander of his enemies, he was banished from court, and gave expression to his grief in a long poem entitled *Encountering Sorrow* (*Lisao*).

13. These lines refer to a poem in the *Book of Odes* in which a lover laments that a single day without his beloved feels like more than three months!

And tears drench my face.
With brush in hand I write my feelings,
Even more tears pour down my cheeks
As I voice my complaint in these verses.

We do not know whether this poem succeeded in easing the visiting rules for the Inner Palace, but probably not. After quoting this poem, Zuo Fen's biographer proceeds to describe the details of her daily life in the Inner Palace:

Later she achieved the position of one of the three imperial concubines of the first rank, with the title of Guibin. Because she was ugly, she did not enjoy the emperor's favor, but she was treated respectfully on account of her talent and virtue. She was of a delicate disposition and often ill, living in simple quarters. But whenever the emperor visited the Hualin Park, he would make it a point to visit her. When the conversation turned to literature, her answers were clear and eloquent, earning the praise of every single one of the members of his entourage.

The biography then gives us the full text of the elegy Zuo Fen composed for Empress Yang, who died in 274, as well as the entire text of an encomium she wrote in 276 for Empress Yang's successor. Zuo Fen's biography in the *Books of the Jin* concludes with the following words:

The emperor greatly admired Fen's literary talents. Whenever tribute gifts or extraordinary treasures were presented to the court, she was summoned to praise these in poetry, for which she was repeatedly showered with gifts.

Her poems and letters in response to those of her elder brother Si and some tens of rhapsodies and encomia are still in circulation.

There are no autobiographical works by Zuo Fen, but she may have left us her own self-portrait in the following poem she wrote about the woodpecker:

In Southern Hills there dwells a bird,
"Woodpecker" is the name it goes by.
When hungry it simply pecks a tree,
When night falls, it hastens to its nest.
It does not meddle in others' affairs
But instead keeps to its own desires.
Thus the pure in nature will flourish,
And the impure will be disgraced.

Of Zuo Fen's rhapsodies on a peacock, a parrot, and a white dove only a few lines remain. More fully preserved is her *Rhapsody on Pine and Cypress (Song bo fu)*. These evergreens were venerated in traditional China as exemplars of moral integrity and loyalty in adversity, and were a popular motif in poetry.

> How came about this profusion of extraordinary trees
>   Lodging on the rockiest reaches of the steepest peaks,
> Covering the winding meanders of the darkest gullies,
>   And shading the shining waves of the clearest streams?
>
> They elevate in mighty majesty their towering trunks,
>   And gather redolent fullness in their verdant needles.
> They display their mossy coats of slender sprouts,
>   And spread the flourishing growth of long tendrils.
> They arrange the clear pattern of their sparse cones—
>   Scenting their rich foliage in endless fragrance.
> Their tangled abundance spreads far and wide,
>   Their air is refreshingly clear and cool.
> They respond to the winds by shaking their boughs,
>   Which sound like the echoes of pipes and strings.
> Being endowed with nature's firmness and fortitude,
>   They will not shed their needles in coldest winter.
> Even though freezing frost assails their bark,
>   They flourish splendidly at the approach of spring.
> They are like gentlemen in their response to the times,
>   And also like hermits in maintaining their fortitude.
> Rambling below them Red Pine found the Way,
>   Eating their seeds the lover of texts extends his life.
> The *Book of Odes* sings of their glorious profusion,
>   Equal to the Southern Mountain in eternal peace!

Because of the great age that pines can attain, these trees were not only a symbol of loyalty and perseverance, but also of longevity. By abstaining from grains and eating pine nuts, humans too were believed to be able to extend their life spans. Master Red Pine (Chisongzi) is the name of a Daoist hermit who in the mythic past was said to have achieved immortality in this way. The *Book of Odes*, which is mentioned in the penultimate line of the rhapsody, contains a song in which the prayer for blessings on behalf of the reigning king ends with the wish that his good fortune and prosperity and that of his descendants may last not only as long as the sun and the moon, but also the Southern Mountains, the pine, and the cypress. By referring to this song, Zuo Fen expresses her own wish that Emperor Wudi and the Jin dynasty he founded might also enjoy everlasting good fortune.

In contrast to these paeans to immortality, Zuo Fen's *Rhapsody on a Water Bubble* (*Fu'ou fu*) laments the fleeting impermanence of all earthly existence:

> When I observe the creation of all things and beings,
>   Nothing appears as numinous as the water bubble.
> It draws on the essence of yin to display its splendor
>   And depends on a drop of rain to achieve its form.
> It is not rooted in an independent existence,
>   But rather relies on other things for its life.
> It embodies the brightness of pearly light
>   And resembles the earliest onset of frost.
> Its colors shine fresh as they glisten and glitter,
>   It looks like a heavy dewdrop about to fall.
>
> Its death is not a long dissolving,
>   Its life is not an endless stay:
> Its rise does not seek complications,
>   Its demise also takes the easy way.

❧❧❧

Shortly after the death of Zuo Fen in or around 276, the Jin dynasty in 280 completed its conquest of the entire Chinese world. In the early fourth century, however, it was again torn apart by civil wars. A number of non-Chinese ethnic groups made use of this opportunity to expand their power in Northern China, and there followed a long period of political fragmentation known as the Southern and Northern Dynasties. As of 317 the domain of the Jin was limited to southern China, which it ruled from its new capital Jianye (modern Nanjing). In the south, the Jin was eventually succeeded by the Song dynasty (420–478), which in turn was followed by the Qi dynasty (479–501). During the later decades of the

Song and most of the Qi, a certain Han Lanying was the most learned woman of the Inner Palace:

Han Lanying from Wu commandery was a woman rich in literary talents. During the reign of Emperor Xiaowu [of the Song; r. 454–464], she presented to the throne her *Rhapsody of the Restoration* [*Zhongxing fu*]. She was rewarded with gifts and brought into the Inner Palace. During the reign of Emperor Mingdi [of the Song; r. 465–472] she served in various offices in the Inner Palace. Emperor Wudi [of the Qi; r. 483–493] appointed her professor and had her teach the ladies of his harem reading and writing. Because of her age and erudition she was called "Master Han."

Zhong Rong (480–552) comments on Han Lanying in his *Ranking of Poets* (*Shipin*), the earliest extant treatise on *shi* poems. Although the fact that he mentions her work at all indicates that he acknowledges her literary talent, Zhong Rong places her poems in his third and lowest category. He discusses her poems together with those of Bao Linghui, a younger sister of the poet and official Bao Zhao (d. 466):

The songs and poems of Linghui are always original and beautiful. Although her "Imitations of Old Poems" are particularly excellent, her "Hundred Vows" is truly lascivious. Bao Zhao gave the following answer to Emperor Xiaowu [of the Song dynasty]: "My sister's talent is second only to that of Zuo Fen, while my own talent does not measure up to that of Zuo Si."

Lanying's poems are very refined, she wrote many famous works and was very good at making jokes. Emperor Wudi of the Qi once said to her: "If only the two of you had lived in earlier times, we would not have had all those rhapsodies about jade steps and songs about white silk."

The emperor's remark refers to Concubine Ban's poems, in which the poet laments her fate as an abandoned spouse (to be discussed in the next chapter). Of the many works written by Han Lanying, only a single quatrain survives. She is said to have written this poem in her old age, during the reign of the hedonistic prince of Yulin, whose short rule only lasted from the autumn of 493 to the autumn of 494. Han Lanying's quatrain is entitled "Lady Yan" and describes the sorry plight of a young woman who, after her failed marriage to a drunken lout, was taken back by her parents and placed in the Inner Palace as a serving maid:

> Strings and pipes still play before the throne,
> While sorrowful and alone she sits in a corner.
> "Discarded and rejected—everything is finished!
> Who feels sorry for this thin and wasted body?"

Han Lanying is said to have written this poem at the order of the dissolute monarch, who was so moved by it that he gave the young woman her freedom. The prince of Yulin is also said to have made use of Han Lanying in drafting the statements in support of his usurpation:

When the prince of Yulin of the Qi Dynasty first wanted to depose the [crown prince and later Emperor] Mingdi [r. 494–498], the documents were written by the Inner Palace professor Han Lanying. Han Lanying was called Master Han and she was in charge of all the affairs of the Inner Palace. She was well-versed in literary composition. When she first entered the Inner Palace she was in charge of Inner Palace protocol.

Only seven *shi* poems remain of the works of Han Lanying's contemporary, Bao Linghui. Among them are found a few "Imitations of Old Poems," but not her "Hundred Vows," so we will never know what it was about the latter poem that provoked Zhong Rong's scorn. Perhaps he felt that poems of hers such as the following were too risqué for a lady.

Postscript to a Letter; Sent to a Traveling Man

> O, ever since the day that you departed,
> I have kept to my room and never smiled.
> At night the washing stone is left unused
> And all day long the gate is closed and locked.
> Inside the curtains fireflies now are flitting,
> Before the hall the purple orchid blooms.
> The falling leaves announce the changing seasons,
> The honking geese report the freezing journey.
> Your travel money will be spent by winter's end—
> I know you will be home on New Year's Eve!

In the Old Style; Sent to a Contemporary Man

> In icy lands you do not dress in foreign style,
> But you wear felt instead of patterned silk.
> Month upon month I wait for your return—

Year after year you still cling to your seal.
 In Jing and Yang we are enjoying spring,
In You and Ji you suffer frost and sleet:[14]
Your northern cold I know but all too well,
But you don't mark my southern temperament.
 Who can report to you my bitter suffering?
I entrust my feelings to a pair of swallows.
 My body works harder than a weaving shuttle,
My beauty fades as quickly as a lightning flash.
But even when my charms are gone,
My unchanged heart will still be yours!

Sent to a Traveling Man

On the cinnamon two or three blooms,
On the orchid four or five petals—
Still you have not returned at all,
In vain the spring wind laughs at me!

The "Imitations of Old Poems" may have been more to the taste of Zhong Rong because these poems tend to be more indirect in their expression of emotion. Her "In Imitation of 'A Traveler Came from a Distant Land'" is an example of one of these:

A traveler came from a distant land
And gave to me a lacquered zither.
The pattern on the wood means "mutual love,"
Of separation sing the strings when plucked.
 But till the day I die I will not change my tune,
In coldest winter I'll maintain my love.
How I would like to play a song of spring
In which each note seeks out the other!

The above poem was inspired by a poem of the same title from the *Nineteen Old Poems* (*Gushi shijiushou*), a famous series of anonymous poems of the second century CE:

---

14. "Jing and Yang" is a general designation for the southeastern area of the Chinese world, especially the area to the south of the Yangzi River. "You and Ji" refers to the northeastern regions, especially the northern part of what is today Hebei province.

A traveler came from a distant land
And brought for me a length of pretty silk.
Separated by more than ten thousand miles:
Yet my lover's heart is still the same.
 The colored pattern: pairs of mandarin ducks—[15]
I fashioned from it a double coverlet.
That we can use when we exchange our love,
Which is a knot that cannot be untied.
 Just try to mix your lacquer and your glue:
Who in the world can separate those two?

Teachers of Men: Fu Sheng's Daughter and Wei Cheng's Mother

Ban Zhao was not the only woman in Chinese history who received an imperial command to instruct male students. In fact, she may have had a predecessor in the daughter of Fu Sheng, who in the early years of the second century BCE is said to have tutored Chao Cuo (200–154 BCE) in the *Book of Documents* (*Shujing*), a collection of speeches and essays attributed to the sage rulers of hallowed antiquity and their wise ministers. And Ban Zhao may have had a successor in lady Song, who, in fourth-century northern China at the request of the emperor instructed 120 young men in *The Offices of the Zhou*, an idealized description of the perfect bureaucracy of the early Zhou dynasty.

In 213 BCE the First Emperor of the Qin dynasty ordered the burning of all books that discussed the ideal form of government, and in the aftermath of his death, during the wars leading up to the founding of the Han dynasty, there was widespread destruction of written materials. It wasn't until the early decades of the Han that the study of the Classics made a slow recovery. One of the works that was feared lost in the turmoil was the *Book of Documents*. So when the court in Chang'an (during the reign of Emperor Wen [r. 179–157 BCE]) learned that Master Fu Sheng of Jinan still taught the *Book of Documents*, the authorities at court sent the young scholar Chao Cuo to Jinan to study the book with him. In the first century CE, the scholar Wei Hong provided in his preface to the *Book of Documents* the following account of Chao Cuo's tribulations:

---

15. Mandarin ducks are a conventional symbol for conjugal harmony and fidelity.

Fu Sheng was in his nineties, he could not speak clearly anymore and it was impossible to make sense of his words. Finally they had his daughter transmit his words to Chao Cuo so he could learn them.

Fu Sheng's daughter, therefore, was the only one who could still understand the old man and by translating her father's mumblings into understandable Chinese she may well have ensured the preservation of the tradition of the *Book of Documents*. Earlier sources concerning Chao Cuo's study with Fu Sheng, however, do not mention this essential role of Fu Sheng's daughter, so unfortunately it may have to be relegated to the realm of fable.

There is no reason for such doubt in the case of lady Song, as she has her own biography in the chapter on "Exemplary Women" in the *Books of the Jin*. While the Jin dynasty itself only ruled southern China during the fourth century, its dynastic history, which was not compiled until the seventh century under the Tang, also incorporated materials on events in northern China of that period. Lady Song taught *The Offices of the Zhou*, which is also known as *The Rites of the Zhou* (*Zhou li*). Although probably composed in the fourth or third century BCE, the work has traditionally been ascribed to the Duke of Zhou, a younger brother of the first Zhou king and later regent for his son and successor. The Duke of Zhou was credited later with the formulation of almost all of the foundational institutions of Chinese society, starting with that of marriage, and his description of the ideal bureaucracy was of urgent relevance to any regime desirous of restoring order in chaotic times. Lady Song's biography reads as follows:

It is not known from which commandery lady Song, the mother of Wei Cheng, hailed. Her family was known for generations for the study of the Classics. Lady Song lost her mother at a tender age and was raised by her father. When she was older, he taught her the pronunciation and meaning of *The Offices of the Zhou*. He told her: "Our family has studied *The Offices of the Zhou* for generations; it is a tradition that has been passed down from father to son. Moreover, this book has been composed by the Duke of Zhou himself. In it you will find a complete survey of all the offices and their documents, together with the titles of the hundred officials. I have no son to whom I can transmit this tradition, so I will now teach this text to you. Take care that this tradition is not lost!"

At that time the whole world was ravaged by war, but this did not keep lady Song from continuously reciting the text. Later great numbers of people, among them lady Song and her husband, were deported to Shandong by [the emperor of the Later Zhao dynasty] Shi Hu [319–349]. She pushed a cart and in a sack on her back carried the books her father had used to teach her. When they arrived in Jizhou, they attached themselves to a rich man from Jiaozhou, Cheng'an Shou, who offered them food and protection. At that time Wei Cheng was still a child. During the day, lady Song went out to gather firewood, while at night she taught her son, but without stopping her from spinning and weaving. Shou often sighed in admiration: "Families with a tradition of study produce gentlemen and high officials—that should apply in this case too!"

When Wei Cheng had finished his studies and made a name for himself, he served [the emperor of the Early Qin dynasty] Fu Jian [338–385] as chamberlain for imperial sacrifices. Once, when Fu Jian visited the National Academy, he inquired among the professors about the Classics and deplored the lack of knowledge of the rites and music of antiquity. Professor Lu Hu explained: "Because the tradition of study was for a long time neglected, the texts and their commentaries were scattered. After many years of collecting and editing, the Classics are now once more fairly complete, with the exception of the rites and notes of *The Offices of the Zhou*, for which we lack a teacher. I have learned, however, that lady Song, the mother of the Chamberlain for Imperial Sacrifices Wei Cheng, was born to a family that has devoted itself to study for generations. Having had the benefit of her father's teaching, she has full knowledge of the pronunciation and meaning of *The Offices of the Zhou*. She is eighty now, but her eyes and her ears are still sharp. This elderly woman is the only person who is capable of teaching this text to the younger generation."

Thereupon Fu Jian had a lecture room built in the house of lady Song and he assigned her 120 students, whom she taught from behind a red gauze curtain. Fu Jian bestowed upon her the title "Expositor of Civilization" (Xuan-wenjun) and gifted her with ten female slaves. In this way the study of *The Offices of the Zhou* was revived and everyone praised Wei's mother, lady Song.

In contrast to Ban Zhao, however, there is no record of lady Song having written any works of her own.

Moralists: The Song Sisters and Lady Zheng

The centuries of political division came to an end when the Chen (557–589), the last of the Southern Dynasties, was conquered by the founding emperor of the Sui dynasty (581–618), who earlier had unified all of Northern China. The Sui dynasty was soon replaced by the Tang dynasty (618–906), during which time the Inner Palace remained a haven for learned women such as the five daughters of Song Tingfen. Their lives and works are described as follows in the *New Books of the Tang* (*Xin Tang shu*), the eleventh-century revised version of the dynastic history of the Tang:

The intendant of the Inner Palace Song Ruozhao hailed from Qingyang in Peizhou. The Song family had been known for generations for its scholarship; her father Tingfen was skilled in literary composition. He had five daughters, all extraordinarily intelligent and skilled in writing. Ruoxin was the eldest, followed by Ruozhao, Ruolun, Ruoxian, and Ruoxun. The writings of Ruoxin and Ruozhao were the best. All of the daughters had a pure and simple character and despised cosmetics and frills. They refused to marry, preferring instead to bring fame to the family by their scholarship. As the family also was not willing to marry them off to the mediocre scions of impoverished lineages, they were allowed to devote themselves to study. Ruoxin was a stern teacher to her younger sisters. She wrote the *Analects for Women* in ten chapters, for which the basic model was the *Analects*, although for Confucius she substituted the Expositor of Civilization Wei [lady Song], and for [Confucius' disciples] Yan Hui and Ran You, she substituted the Venerable Madam Cao and others. In this work she elaborated on the duties corresponding to the wifely way. Ruozhao composed a commentary in order to provide further elucidation.

During the reign period Firm Beginning [Zhenyuan, 785–894], the military governor of Zhaoyi, Li Baozhen, described the talents [of the Song sisters] in a report to the throne, and Emperor Dezong [r. 780–804] summoned them to the Inner Palace. After examining their literary skills and questioning them about the meaning of the Classics and Histories, he praised them lavishly and retained all five of the sisters in the Inner Palace. The emperor was a fine poet, and whenever he and his courtiers gathered to compose poems, the five sisters also participated. Every time they presented their poems, they were rewarded. Moreover, the emperor greatly appreciated their lofty demeanor and did not order them around as if they were concubines or servants, but instead addressed them as "secretaries." He promoted their father to the position of Marshal of Raozhou and Palace Instructor in the Hall for the Cultivation of the Arts. He also gifted him with a house and increased the amounts of grain and silk of his salary.

When Ruoxin died in the last years of the reign period First Harmony [Yuanhe, 806–820], [Emperor Xianzong, r. 805–819] enfeoffed her [posthumously] as Lady of Henei Commandery. In the seventh year of the reign period

Firm Beginning [791], Ruoxin had been appointed to the position of Keeper of the Books in the Inner Palace. Because Ruozhao was even more capable in these matters, Emperor Muzong [r. 821–824] then appointed her to succeed Ruoxin in the position of Intendant of the Inner Palace. During the successive reigns of the three Emperors Xianzong, Muzong, and Jingzong [r. 825–826] Ruozhao was always called "Master." Empresses and concubines, princes and princesses all treated her with the respect due to a teacher. When she died in the first year of the reign period Precious Continuation [Baoli, 825–826], she was awarded the title of Lady of the Kingdom of Liang and accorded an imperial burial.

Ruoxian was then appointed to take her place as keeper of books. Emperor Wenzong (r. 827–840) had a great respect for scholarship. Because Ruoxian was skilled in literary composition and excelled in debate, he treated her with the greatest deference. During the reign period Great Harmony (Dahe, 827–835), power lay in the hands of Li Xun and Zheng Zhu. They hated the prime minister Zongmin (d. 846) and slanderously accused him of having obtained his position by getting the prince-consort Shen Yi to bribe Ruoxian with costly gifts. The emperor was enraged and had Ruoxian locked up in her private home outside the Inner Palace, where he allowed her to commit suicide. Her relatives were banished to the southern frontier. When Li Xun and Zheng Zhu were toppled [in the Sweet Dew incident of 835], the emperor realized he had been misled by slander and regretted his action. By that time Ruolun and Ruoxun had already died.

Tingfen's son, however, was too stupid to be taught and ended his life as a commoner.

We certainly would like to know more about these five remarkable sisters, but detailed information is hard to come by. There is one surviving poem attributed to each of the three eldest Song sisters. Ruozhao's poem is entitled "Written at Imperial Command, Making Use of the Same Rhyme Sound as the Poems Composed by the Hundred Officials in Response to His Majesty's Composition on the Occasion of a Festive Banquet in the Unicorn Virtue Hall." The poem is a hyperbolic and, if truth be told, rather sycophantic paean of praise to the reigning emperor, and it matters little which of the three possible Tang emperors may have been its historical addressee.

> At ease Your Majesty rules the eight directions,
> In peace the gates are open to the four sides.

This is due to Your transformation by Non-Action,
Rather than through the work of vassal and minister.
 Your culture has enticed recluses to your court,
Your might has rid the land of evil bandits,
Your virtue shines with blazing springtime brilliance,
Your virtue saturates us like a heavy dew.
 Officials in cap and gown attend the palace banquet
Where rites and music glorify the court—
"A myriad years!" they shout and raise their cups,
These thousand servants, all to the last man!

As for the *Analects for Women*, a tract with this title has come down to us, but it is a short and conventional treatise on wifely duties that does not seem to fit the description of Song Ruoxin's work in the *New Books of the Tang*; the text is divided into twelve short paragraphs and contains a preface ascribed to Ban Zhao, but lacks any reference to "the Expositor of Civilization." Whereas the *Analects* consists of brief pronouncements of Confucius and some of his disciples and their dialogues, the *Analects for Women* presents a systematically organized, continuous argument. Moreover, in the earliest known editions of this text, which are from the sixteenth century, the authorship is attributed to Song Ruohua. It is questionable, then, whether this *Analects for Women*, which some reference works flatly state has been lost, is indeed the work of Song Ruoxin and Song Ruozhao. It has been suggested that the text that in later centuries circulated under the title of *Analects for Women* may have actually been a sequel to Ban Zhao's *Precepts for My Daughters* that was written by the daughter of the statesman Wei Wen (788–845). The *Old Books of the Tang* (*Jiu Tang shu*), the dynastic history of the Tang composed in the mid-tenth century, introduces this work and its author as follows:

Wei Wen had no sons. His daughter married Xue Meng. She excelled in literary composition and wrote a sequel to the *Instructions for Women* of the Venerable Madam Cao in twelve chapters. Literati families copied it out in manuscript and it enjoyed wide circulation.

Apart from the *Analects for Women,* we have yet another moral tract for women that dates to the Tang dynasty. This work goes by the title of *Classic of Filiality for Women* and is ascribed to lady Zheng, who is said to have written it for the benefit of a niece on the eve of the young woman's marriage to the prince of Yong. This little treatise in eighteen paragraphs is written in the form of a dialogue between Ban Zhao and her daughters. The earliest references to this work date from the tenth century, and there were many illustrated versions of it in circulation during the Song dynasty.

The *Classic of Filiality for Women* first describes the various tasks of married women of different ranks (from empress to common housewife) and their filial duties toward their parents-in-law. Only when their duties as daughters-in-law have been dealt with is there any discussion of women's relationships with their husbands. Not surprisingly, the author insists that a wife's supreme duty is to support her husband. In chapter 9, however, we learn that this may sometimes entail tactfully offering advice:

The daughters asked: "We make bold to ask—is there any virtue for a married woman greater than judgment of character?" The Venerable Madam replied: "Man resembles heaven and earth, he turns his back to yin and embraces yang. His nature is bright and intelligent and can be profitably developed, especially if one applies oneself!

"Once long ago King Zhuang of Chu [r. 613–591 BCE] did not return to the Inner Palace from his morning audience until late in the evening. Concubine Fan approached him and asked: 'Why did you conclude the morning audience so late? You must be tired!' The king then replied: 'I was conversing with a wise man, which was such a pleasure that I didn't even realize that it had grown so late.' Concubine Fan asked: 'May I ask who this wise man was?' The king replied: 'It was Master Yu Qiu.' Concubine Fan covered her face with her hand to conceal her laughter. When the amazed king inquired as to the cause of her laughter, she said: 'Master Yu Qiu may be wise, but he is not necessarily loyal. It has now been eleven years since I was inducted into the Inner Palace, where I am in charge of drawing your bath, waiting on you with towel and comb, and sweeping and cleaning the floors. During these years I have introduced nine women to you. Two of them are smarter than I am, and the other seven are at least my equal. I was fully aware that these women might interfere with your love for me and that they could cause me to lose your favor, but I would not dare to harm the public good for my own profit. I wanted you to be as well informed as possible. Master Yu Qiu has now been prime minister for ten years, but the people he recommends for office are either his sons and grandsons or his nephews and great-nephews. I have never heard of him recommending intelligent people or firing incapable ones. Can he be called wise?' The king reported this to Master Yu Qiu, who didn't know what to do. He gave up his house, slept under the open sky, and had a messenger invite Sun Shu'ao to come to the court. On his recommendation the king appointed Sun Prime Minister.

"Now, because of her judgment of character displayed in this single conversation, none of the other feudal lords dared wage war against Chu. King Zhuang's eventual domination over all other states was due entirely to the efforts of Concubine Fan. In the *Book of Odes* we read:

> Find your man and you will flourish,
> Lose your man and meet disaster!

We also read there:

> Whenever words do but agree,
> The people live in harmony."

Following this discussion of a woman's relation to her husband, the *Classic of Filiality for Women* deals with the education of children. One of the chapters is entitled "Instruction in the Womb."

The Venerable Madam said: "Man receives the principle of the Five Norms. From the very beginning of life it is his nature to adapt himself to custom: the person who is stimulated by goodness becomes good himself; the person who is stimulated by evil becomes evil himself. Of course one should begin to teach the child from the very moment one begins to carry it in the womb!

"Pregnant women of antiquity did not sleep on their side, did not sit on the edge of a mat, and did not stand on one leg. They did not eat any forbidden foods and did not walk on the left side of the road. They did not eat what had not been cut properly, they did not sit on a mat that was not positioned properly. Their eyes did not look upon evil colors, their ears did not listen to debased sounds, their mouth did not utter any arrogant words, and their hands did not touch any evil things. At night they recited the Classics and during the day they discussed the rites and music. Thanks to this 'instruction in the womb' the sons who were born to them were beautiful in body and limb and excelled all others in talents and virtue. Such was their instruction in the womb."

Lady Zheng is said to have been the wife of Houmochen Mao. In an edict of 736, Emperor Xuanzong (r. 712–756) ordered his sixteenth son, Li Lin, prince of Yong, to marry a daughter of Houmochen Chao, the commander of the imperial right guard. As three-syllable surnames are extremely rare in Chinese, it seems safe to assume that the *Classic of*

Filiality for Women was written for the benefit of this consort of the prince of Yong.

The *Classic of Filiality* probably dates from the late third century BCE. Written in the form of a dialogue between Confucius and Master Zeng, the disciple best known for his conspicuous filial piety, the work emphasizes the supreme importance of filiality as a social virtue. Traditionally, it was one of the first texts memorized by schoolchildren. In fact, Emperor Xuanzong prepared an annotated edition in 722 to enhance its dissemination among his subjects and revised it later in 743. Therefore, by imitating the title and dialogue format of the *Classic of Filiality*, lady Zheng was modeling her *Classic of Filiality for Women* on one of the most widespread and prestigious texts of her time. The Song sisters went even further and modeled their tract for women on an even more famous text, the *Analects*. Proud of their family tradition, the sisters gave pride of place to the "Expositor of Civilization" lady Song, and, despite the glaring anachronism, even made Ban Zhao, the patroness of all learned women, into lady Song's pupil.

The final chapter of the *Classic of Filiality for Women* is devoted to a catalogue of evil women, which the author safely limited to ancient Chinese history. The period she chose provided her with an excuse to avoid an evaluation of both Empress Wu, who had usurped the throne of the Tang dynasty from 690 to 705, and her protégé, Shangguan Wan'er, who used her writing skills in the service of both Empress Wu and her successors.

The bibliographical chapter in the *New Books of the Tang* lists the titles of several other moral tracts for women by women of Tang times, but these have not been preserved for posterity. One text that is not listed in the bibliographies but has nevertheless been preserved is "Lady Cui's Instructions to Her Daughter" (*Cuishi furen xunnüwen*). This text, which is not a prose tract but rather a *shi* poem in twenty seven-syllable lines, must have been extremely popular—it was printed in ninth-century Chang'an and made its way as far as distant Dunhuang, where it was eagerly copied. As far as its contents are concerned, the major innovation is found in the following lines near the end of the poem:

> If your husband is drunk when he comes to your room,
> Go to him with a smile, support him, and help him to bed.

Don't scold and curse him in front of other people,
Or he will surely be angry at you when he is sober again.

Shangguan Wan'er: Ghostwriter for Two Empresses

Shangguan Wan'er would seem to be the very opposite of the exemplars of virtue discussed above. Her father was executed, her mother was confiscated by the state, and she herself was raised as a slave in the palace. Later, she only barely escaped the death penalty and was tattooed on the face as punishment. She eventually became the confidante and secretary of the omnipotent Empress Wu, the only woman in China's history to occupy the imperial throne as Son of Heaven. Shangguan Wan'er even survived the coup that brought down Empress Wu, who was replaced by her son Emperor Zhongzong (r. 705–710). Shangguan then became the ghostwriter for the emperor and his even more powerful wife, Empress Wei, as well as for the equally powerful princesses. She was eventually raised to the rank of imperial consort, despite being accused of at least two adulterous affairs. She finally lost her life when her patroness Empress Wei made a bid for power and failed.

The curious career of Shangguan Wan'er can only be understood against the background of the rise to power of Empress Wu. Wu Zhao (625–705) was born to an official family with only a modest status in the bureaucratic hierarchy. As a girl of thirteen she entered the harem of Emperor Taizong (r. 627–649), the second emperor of the Tang dynasty, who had ascended the throne after a coup d'état in which he had two of his brothers killed. He reigned ruthlessly but forcefully and went to great lengths to be remembered as an enlightened king. It is unclear whether Wu Zhao ever enjoyed the emperor's favors, but it was rumored that when Emperor Taizong was lying on his deathbed, she seduced his son and successor Gaozong (r. 650–683).

When Emperor Taizong died, Wu Zhao entered a nunnery. A few years later, Empress Wang, the wife of Emperor Gaozong, wanted to get rid of her rival Concubine Xiao, and recalling the charms of Wu Zhao, had Wu Zhao brought back to the Inner Palace. Wu Zhao soon succeeded in replacing not only Concubine Xiao but also Empress Wang herself in Emperor Gaozong's favors. Some sources hint, without being specific, that this was partly because she was willing to indulge some of the emperor's more perverted desires. Before long, Wu became pregnant and bore a daughter, who died shortly after birth. Wu Zhao accused Empress Wang of murder, and when this did not produce the hoped-for results, she accused her rivals of using black magic. This time she had more success: despite the fierce opposition of his highest official advisors, in 655 Emperor Gaozong made Wu his empress, and both Empress Wang and Concubine Xiao suffered a cruel death.

It is in the biography of Empress Wang in the *Old Books of the Tang* that we first find the statement that Empress Wu had both her rivals locked up and then strangled to death. This is followed by yet another account of their end, most likely from a different and later source:

When the former empress, now demoted to commoner status, and Concubine Xiao were locked up, they loudly cursed the Empress Wu as follows: "May that beastly Wu be reborn as a rat and we as cats, so that lifetime after lifetime, we may lunge at her throat!" Empress Wu was enraged, and from that moment on, cats were no longer kept in the palace.

Not long after both women had been locked away, Emperor Gaozong thought of them and secretly went to the place where they were held. He saw that the room had been sealed off completely, except for a single opening through which the women were supplied with food. Gaozong was deeply disturbed and called out: "Where are you, my empress and concubine?" The former empress, now demoted to commoner status, replied: "We have both committed a crime which is why we have been stripped of our ranks and demoted to palace slaves. How could we still maintain our titles and allow ourselves to be called 'empress'?" Having said this, she wept sadly. She also said: "Please, Supreme Ruler, out of consideration for our shared past, allow us to look once more on the sun and moon and stroll around in this courtyard, which afterwards we hope you will call the Courtyard of Repentance. That would be our greatest happiness!" Gaozong promised that he would look into it immediately.

But as soon as Empress Wu heard about what had happened, she had the former empress and Concubine Xiao both flogged a hundred times, their arms and legs cut off, and their truncated bodies thrown into wine vats, saying: "May the bones of these sluts drink themselves into a stupor!" Within a few days both women were dead.

It is said in the same source that, because in later years Empress Wu was continually haunted by the ghosts of her victims, she avoided the capital

Chang'an as much as possible, and spent most of her time at the secondary capital of Luoyang:

Later Empress Wang and Concubine Xiao, their hair disheveled and covered with blood as in the hour of their death, often appeared to Empress Wu. Because Empress Wu feared them, she had the ghosts exorcised by professionals and priests, and she herself also moved to the Penglai palace. But because they appeared to her there as well, she usually resided in the eastern capital.

At court, the power of the new empress grew rapidly and before long she was sitting side by side with her husband at his morning audiences, modestly shielded from the gaze of the hundred officials by a gauze curtain. In 664 a poorly organized attempt on the part of some court officials to pressure Emperor Gaozong to get rid of her ended in dismal failure. Both Shangguan Wan'er's grandfather (the celebrated poet Shangguan Yi) and her father lost their lives in this affair, and the women of the family were taken into the palace as slaves. According to one source, Shangguan Wan'er was a baby at the time; according to another, she was born later inside the palace. By the time she was fourteen years old, however, Shangguan Wan'er had already attracted the personal interest of the empress because of her intelligence:

At the age of fourteen, she was intelligent and quick of mind and the brilliance of her talent was without equal. When the empress heard about her, she made her take a written examination. Shangguan Wan'er picked up her writing brush and wrote the composition from beginning to end without hesitation as if she had prepared everything in her mind beforehand.

The power of Empress Wu continued to grow. When her husband allowed her to assume de facto control of the government of the empire, she ruled competently and efficiently, employing every possible means to strengthen her own position: she played off the members of her own Wu family against the members of the imperial Li family; she made use of informants who created a regime of terror and, after having inflicted their tortures on thousands of victims, were ultimately done away with by the empress, who did not even hesitate to have some of her own sons executed. At the same time, however, Empress Wu supported officials with proven administrative abilities, even if they were critical of her policies, and also encouraged talented men from relatively modest backgrounds. She was a highly literate woman, and left behind a voluminous body of writings. Much of her prose and poetry has since been lost, and of those texts that have been preserved, it is not clear which were written by her and which were ghosted by male secretaries and female assistants such as Shangguan Wan'er. The following quatrain, attributed to Empress Wu, is an imitation of an amorous folksong and may suggest the nature of her literary talent:

> I watched the pink turn into green—my thoughts a tangled mess,
> Racked by pain, a bag of bones, all because of love for you.
> If you do not believe how many tears I have cried of late,
> Open the chest and look at my skirt dyed red by tears of blood!!

Upon the death of Emperor Gaozong, Empress Wu's eldest surviving son, Emperor Zhongzong, ascended the throne. After two months, however, she replaced him with her youngest son, Emperor Ruizong, who implored his mother to continue to manage all the government affairs. Following a rebellion of the surviving Li princes, this compliant lad was also shoved aside, and the empress dowager occupied the throne herself. She changed the name of the dynasty from Tang to Zhou, and from then on ruled in her own name as Son of Heaven. It was probably sometime during these years that Shangguan Wan'er committed the crime (we don't know what it was) that in the estimation of the empress merited the death penalty. Although Shangguan Wan'er escaped with her life, she had to suffer the indignity of having her face branded as a criminal. She must have quickly regained imperial favor, however, since during her final years, Empress Wu increasingly left the details of administration to her:

From the reign period Community with Heaven for Myriads of Years [Wansui tongtian, 696] to the early years of Brilliant Dragon [Jinglong, 707–709] she composed all of the state documents in the name of the empress. Practically all important decisions regarding military and civil affairs as well as those concerning life and death were made by her alone.

While Empress Wu often hinted that she might turn the throne over to one of her distant nephews—Wu Sansi, for example—at the same time she recalled her banished eldest son and his wife to the capital. Eventually, a small group of high officials staged a coup d'état in 705 and restored her eldest son to the throne. The deposed and aged empress died before the end of the year and was accorded the posthumous title of "She Who Modeled Herself on Heaven" (*Zetian*). Her most lasting contribution to the enhancement of the position of women was her extension of the period of mourning for a mother from one year to twenty-seven months ("three years"), the same length as the period of mourning for a father. On the negative side, she left Chinese culture with an indelible stereotyped image of a woman's insatiable lust for sex and power.

Emperor Zhongzong turned out to be as weak-willed as his father Gaozong had been: he left the governance of the realm completely to his wife, Empress Wei, who had shared his banishment and distinguished herself at each turn by her perseverance and sharpness of mind. She and her two daughters, the princesses Changning and Anle, shamelessly abused their power. For example, they appropriated large tracts of land outside the capital for the building of pleasure estates. Emperor Zhongzong and Empress Wei relied even more than Empress Wu on the services of Shangguan Wan'er, who was the ghostwriter of their official documents and of their poems written for palace banquets and garden excursions. On these occasions, Shangguan Wan'er would not only write poems under her own name, but also judge the poems composed by the other participants in these activities. She even is said to have served as an examiner in the state examinations for officials. The following anecdote shows her as a judge in a poetry competition:

On the last day of the First Month, Emperor Zhongzong visited the Kunming Pond. When it came time to write verse, the officials composed more than a hundred poems on imperial command. A platform was set up in front of the imperial tent, and Shangguan Wan'er was ordered to select one of the poems to be the text for a melody the emperor had recently composed. The officials congregated in front of the platform. Soon the sheets of paper [of the rejected poems] fluttered down, and each person gathered up his own poem.

When everyone had returned to their places, only the poems of [the famous poets] Shen Quanqi [ca. 656–ca. 715] and Song Zhiwen [ca. 650–ca. 712] had not yet been rejected. After a while, yet another sheet of paper fluttered down. Everyone rushed to pick it up and see whose poem it was; it turned out to be

Shen's poem. Thereupon Shangguan Wan'er pronounced the following verdict: "The two poems are comparable in talent and power. But the final couplet of Shen's poem reads: 'The wood from which I have been carved is rotten, / I am ashamed to look upon the Yuzhang beams.'[16] Here he appears to lack the necessary vital force. [The final couplet of] Song Zhiwen's poem reads: 'It doesn't matter that the moon will fade, / The pearl I bring will turn the night to day!' Even here he shows his dashing boldness." Shen then conceded defeat.

Never before or after has a woman in traditional China occupied such a conspicuous and influential position in public literary life, the male domain *par excellence*. According to one early source, "It was thanks to her that outstanding talents were sought everywhere and that literary life was greatly enriched, that the State had an ample supply of gentlemen well versed in the arts so that the court was not burdened by uncultured ministers, and that for twenty years throughout the land there were no eminent persons whose talents were ignored."

Emperor Zhongzong raised Shangguan Wan'er to the rank of Consort of the Shining Countenance (Zhaorong), but this did not stop her from having an affair with Wu Sansi, the nephew of the late Empress Wu. Even after the death of his aunt, this man was one of the most powerful persons at court. He was both the lover of Empress Wei and the father-in-law of Princess Anle, the imperial couple's favorite child. Princess Anle was so confident of her parents' support and evidently considered female rule so normal that she tried to be appointed as the future successor to the throne instead of her half-brother Chongjun, the Jiemin crown prince. In reaction to her machinations, the threatened crown prince attempted a coup d'état, and had Wu Sansi killed. He also wanted to kill Shangguan Wan'er, but his attack on the palace failed and he lost his own life instead. Following the death of Wu Sansi, Shangguan Wan'er favored Cui Shi, who, in the judgment of later historians, distinguished himself more for his literary than for his administrative abilities. The same source that so greatly praises Shangguan Wan'er's twenty-year-long contribu-

---

16. Yuzhang is the name of a precious timber from southern China. In traditional Chinese poetry and prose the state and its bureaucratic apparatus are often compared to a building (a palace or temple), while the talents (*cai*) of officials and students are often compared to timber beams (*cai*).

tions to the nation's well-being cannot avoid noting as well that "[d]uring the last years of her life, she was involved in the factional struggle in the outer court and criminally abused her power; she was feared by the court."

In 710, Emperor Zhongzong suddenly died. According to our sources—which were compiled by the enemies of Empress Wei—he was poisoned by the empress because she feared the growing influence of his sister, the rich and powerful Princess Taiping. For a while, Empress Wei kept the emperor's death secret and in the interim appointed her relatives to high positions. Eventually she placed her youngest son on the throne. After two weeks, this young boy became the victim of yet another coup d'état, this one led by Li Longji, who would later become Emperor Xuanzong (r. 712–756). Li Longji was one of the younger sons of Ruizong, but the coup d'état most likely was financed by Princess Taiping. Troops led by Li Longji entered the Inner Palace and killed Empress Wei although she tried to flee, Princess Anle while she was putting on her make-up, and Shangguan Wan'er despite her readiness to serve the new powers (Tang historians preferred to describe this string of events as a failed attempt by Empress Wei to stage a coup d'état). Li Longji then placed his father Emperor Ruizong on the throne, but the latter, always obliging, abdicated in 712 in favor of his son. In 713, Princess Taiping unsuccessfully tried to unseat Li Longji, after which the young emperor graciously allowed her to commit suicide. This turned out to be the end of an unprecedented period of political power in the hands of imperial women. It also marked the beginning of a fairly long period of political stability, which lasted until the middle of the eighth century, when the aging emperor fell under the spell of his favorite concubine Yang Guifei and his empire was plunged into chaos by the rebellion of An Lushan.

Early in his long reign, Emperor Xuanzong ordered the compilation of the collected works of Shangguan Wan'er. This collection has not been preserved in its original form. If the political role of Shangguan Wan'er was indeed as great as our sources suggest, however, many of the edicts and other court documents from the period 698–710 must have been written by her. Her poems that have been preserved were mostly written on imperial command for one court occasion or another. The following poem, for example, describes a visit of the emperor and his court to the Monastery of Motherly Love (Ci'en si) on the ninth day of the Ninth Month (Double Nine). This large Buddhist monastery located in the southeastern corner of Chang'an was founded by Emperor Gaozong (r. 650–683), while still the crown prince, in memory of his deceased mother. One of the landmarks of this monastery was its large stone pagoda, which is still standing today and is known as the Big Goose Pagoda (Dayan ta). Double Nine was one of the major annual festivals of traditional China. On this day, it was the custom for the entire family to get together and climb to a high place, such as a tower or hill. Everyone would attach to their clothing a sprig of dogwood and drink wine scented by petals of chrysanthemum.

On the Ninth Day of the Ninth Month His Imperial Majesty Visited the Monastery of Motherly Compassion and Climbed the Pagoda; the Assembled Officials Wished Him Eternal Life and Drank to His Health with Chrysanthemum Wine

This land of gods, this day of Double Nine:
The emperor comes to this fragrant garden.
Warding off evil: dogwood at one's waist,
Toasting to life eternal: cups of chrysanthemum wine.
 The pagoda soars upwards, supporting the heaven,
The gate swings open, welcoming the Buddha.
Your phrases share the sky with the sun and moon,
Forever we will gaze upon their brilliant glow.

"The land of gods" is a common designation for the imperial capital, and "the fragrant garden" refers to the Buddhist monastery. In this poem, the emperor is equated with the Buddha, and his literary compositions (actually ghostwritten by Shangguan Wan'er herself) are in their brilliance compared to the stars of the Silver River (the Milky Way). Both in its excessive flattery and in its artful construction the poem is a typical example of the court poetry of the time.

The literary talents of Shangguan Wan'er went beyond a knack for writing the perfect occasional poem, however. Stephen Owen has drawn attention to her role in the development of the "estate poem," poems in

which a bureaucrat, who has temporarily retired to his country estate outside the capital, presents himself as a hermit singing, in carefully cultivated unadorned language, of the joys of a simple life in pristine nature.
The best-known representative of this type of poetry is the famous poet
Wang Wei (d. 761), who made his career at the court of Xuanzong.
Shangguan Wan'er's most important contribution to the estate poem
genre is her series of twenty-five poems written on the occasion of a visit
to the estate of Princess Changning. A sample selection of these verses is
as follows:

III

Waving gently—bamboo shadows,
Tossed by winds the sighs of pines.
There's no need for song and music,
This suffices to please one's mind.

V

Twigs and branches thick and dense:
"Harmony of form and substance."
Trees and mountain serve as friends,
Pine and cassia are neighbors.

VII

Don't tell me about peaks well-rounded,
Don't speak about islands square:[17]
None can compare to this simple lodge,
A true meeting-place of the immortals!

XVI

The springs and rocks are rich in fairy-pleasures
As peaks and gullies etch the weirdest forms.
What is there here to please your ears?
Just listen to the lilting of the streams.

---

17. "Peaks well-rounded" and "islands square" are the abodes of the immortals.

XVII

I climb steep cliffs to my heart's desire,
It clears out the eyes, delights the soul.
The wind-tossed bamboo serve as flutes,
The flowing streams as sounding zithers.

XX

A waterfall: the clear sky brings us rain,
A bamboo grove: day has turned to night.
The mountains offer much one may enjoy,
Please tell that to those pampered princes!

XXI

Sitting by a pond I wield a while my brush,
Leaning on a rock I compose a poem.
At times I strum a tune of streams and hills:
Forever let me live a hermit's life!

Shangguan Wan'er presents herself in this series as a hermit who has fled the political dangers of life at court. Stephen Owen comments:

During this period dominated by women (as opposed to the reign of Empress Wu, which was dominated by one woman), Shangguan Wan'er could unselfconsciously step into a role that previously had been reserved for men. In none of the twenty-five poems is there even a hint that the author is a woman; they do not express any of the unease women writers sometimes showed in transgressing their gender roles.

And elsewhere he writes:

If the imperial Consort of the Shining Countenance, whose face was tattooed as a criminal, could play the male hermit, then roles were not determined by one's status or by the social situation: they could be freely chosen, chosen in such a way that allowed the person to forget her other life. That element of self-fashioning in role-playing was to be one of the strongest characteristics of the period that followed, the High Tang.

If this is true, Shangguan Wan'er can claim to be the godmother of what is known as the golden age of Chinese poetry, the High Tang, famous for producing great poets such as Wang Wei, Li Bai (701–762), Du Fu (712–770), and many others.

Shangguan Wan'er has a short biography in the *Old Books of the Tang*, not in the chapter on exemplary women but rather in the chapters devoted to empresses and imperial concubines. This biography appears as an appendix to the considerably longer biography of Empress Wei, in which Shangguan Wan'er is often mentioned:

Emperor Zhongzong's concubine, the Consort of Shining Countenance, was named Shangguan Wan'er. She was a granddaughter of the Vice-Director of the Secretariat Shangguan Yi. Her father Tingzhi was executed together with Yi. Wan'er at that time was only an infant, and was consigned together with her mother to the slave quarters of the Inner Palace. When she grew up, she displayed a talent for writing and she was also well-versed in administrative affairs. During the reign of the empress Wu Zetian she was condemned to death because she had opposed the imperial will. Because the empress so valued her talents, however, she did not have her executed but only had her tattooed on the face as punishment. Starting from the reign period Holy Continuation [Shengli, 698–699] the empress often had her participate in the deliberations whenever officials submitted memorials.

Once Emperor Zhongzong had ascended the throne, he ordered Shangguan Wan'er to supervise the drafting of edicts and she enjoyed his full confidence. He then promoted her to the rank of Consort of Shining Countenance and enfeoffed her mother as Lady of Pei. After Shangguan Wan'er entered into an adulterous affair with Wu Sansi, she would, right or wrong, sing the praises of the Wu family and belittle the imperial house. The Jiemin crown prince hated her intensely. When he rebelled, he stood in front of the Suzhang Gate and demanded that Shangguan Wan'er be handed over to him. Wan'er said loudly: "His intention is, in my judgement, next to demand that Her Majesty the empress be handed over to him, and then His Majesty." The emperor and the empress were enraged and together with Wan'er they fled to the tower atop the Xuanwu Gate in order to escape the onslaught of the troops. Not long afterwards the situation was pacified.

Wan'er made the greatest effort to have learned gentlemen who excelled in literary arts widely appointed and she was an important patron of the literary officials at court. Repeatedly she was invited to banquets and excursions, where everyone would compose poems. Wan'er would on such occasions write the poems of the emperor and the empress, and of the princesses Changning and Anle. Even though she would compose several poems simultaneously, in all of them the phrasing was very beautiful, and her contemporaries all recited her works.

Later Wan'er started a relationship with the vice-minister of the department for personnel Cui Shi and she saw to it that he came to head the administration. Shi was away from the capital on a mission to open up a new road across Mt. Shang, and Emperor Zhongzong died before the project was completed. But Wan'er, who drafted the emperor's testament, greatly praised the merits of Cui Shi and showered him with honors and gifts. When the coup d'état staged by Empress Wei failed, Wan'er too was beheaded by the troops.

Emperor Xuanzong ordered her poetry and prose gathered together, which resulted in a collection in twenty books. He ordered Zhang Yue [667–731] to write a preface to this collection.

Many years earlier, when Shangguan Wan'er's mother was pregnant with her, she dreamed that someone gave her a large weighing balance. A diviner had told her: "You will give birth to a child who will ascend to the highest of positions and control the balance of power in the land." When she gave birth to a girl, he was jeered by all who heard about it, because the prediction obviously had turned out to be wrong. But when Wan'er later held all the power in the palace, the words of the diviner were substantiated after all.

But if a few women of the Inner Palace managed to rise to positions of power and display their literary talents, others were less successful. Some of these other women also left literary writings, but these, as we shall see, were quite different from those of Shangguan Wan'er in tone.

2 · Neglected Palace Ladies and Other Phantoms

Under every imperial dynasty, the heart of the capital was the Forbidden City, the large, completely walled-in complex of buildings that housed the Son of Heaven. The Forbidden City of the Ming and Qing dynasties in Beijing is still standing, although now it serves as a museum. It is made up of two completely segregated sections: the outer court and the Inner Palace. The outer court consists of a series of large courtyards, each closed off on the northern side by a terrace upon which rises a grand ceremonial hall where the emperor received his ministers and officials in audience and where the affairs of state were deliberated. The decisions prepared and executed in these halls were then passed on for implementation to the various government offices located in their own walled-in complexes outside the Forbidden City proper.

The Inner Palace in the Forbidden City (and most likely in all earlier imperial palaces as well) was made up of a maze of small courtyards and pavilions that housed the emperor and his "three thousand women," along with thousands of eunuchs whose job was to watch over these women and look after their needs. Throughout Chinese imperial history, this part of the Forbidden City was hermetically sealed off from the outside world, and no male, apart from the emperor and his infant and adolescent sons, was allowed access to it. Outsiders, including the emperor's adult sons, were only allowed to visit the Inner Palace under very exceptional circumstances. Its denizens likewise were typically not even allowed to leave the Inner Palace to visit their relatives, as we have already noted in the case of Zuo Fen. The large and complex community of women in the Inner Palace was headed by the emperor's principal wife, the empress. The empress in turn would often be assisted by three consorts of the first rank, nine concubines of the second rank, and many more ladies of lower rank and privilege. Each of these women had her own maids and eunuchs with their own well-defined tasks. There was a bureaucracy, fully staffed by women, that oversaw the everyday affairs of the Inner Palace.

It is perhaps not surprising that jealousy and envy would more readily flourish in such a hermetically sealed community characterized by luxury and hierarchy. Every palace woman's aim was to win the emperor's favor—but many died without even having seen him once. The surest way to win and keep the emperor's favor was to bear him a son, or, even better, a string of sons. The emperor's favor not only meant prestige and power within the walls of the Inner Palace, it also provided the opportunity to shower one's male relatives with honors and positions, especially if one's son was named crown prince and, even more especially, if he succeeded to the throne. But high infant mortality, endemic in any premodern society, provided the ideal backdrop for the many accusations of black magic mentioned in our sources. Empress Wu Zetian, for example, was even accused of having murdered her own infant in order to be able to blame her rivals of using black magic to bring about the baby's death. Apparently, this sort of accusation was one of the most effective means by which a new imperial favorite might dislodge her predecessors and competitors, and often the women so accused would suffer terrible fates. We have to remember, of course, that the secrecy surrounding the Inner Palace was also the perfect breeding ground for endless rumors about what went on behind its walls. While some of these rumors found their way into otherwise sober historical writings, others were transmitted in more informal records.

Women who for one reason or another no longer enjoyed the emperor's favor might be assigned to the staff of the empress dowager or locked away in the "cold palace," the sections of the Inner Palace that were never personally visited by the emperor. That those women who had enjoyed the emperor's favor were expected to feel unending passionate gratitude toward the only man in their life was a given. But those women who had never been favored by the emperor, as well as those who had briefly enjoyed his favor before being discarded, were also expected to be filled with undying love for their lord and master. It was even expected that they be willing, should the need arise, to sacrifice their lives for him.

Some of the harem ladies neglected by the emperor expressed their emotions in laments: As early as the fifth century, Emperor Xiaowu of the Song dynasty (r. 454–464) jokingly complained about the prevalence of this type of writing among palace women. In fact, this tradition of the lament of the discarded harem lady can be traced back to Ban Zhao's great-aunt, Concubine Ban, who herself apparently drew upon an even longer tradition. Some of the texts in the *Book of Odes*, the canonical collection of anonymous songs from the period 1000–600 BCE, describe in the first person the emotions of neglected, discarded, or divorced women. The earliest commentators of these texts worked on the assumption that only the direct expression of authentic emotions resulted in good poetry, and for this reason concluded that these poems written in the voice of women must have been written by women. Despite the many centuries that separated them from the time the poems of the *Book of Odes* were most likely written, these same learned commentators were convinced that they could identify not only the authors, but also the original occasion that had given rise to these poems. One example may suffice to illustrate this:

The Green Coat

Green the coat,
Green the coat, its lining yellow!
The sorrows in my heart—
Will they ever end?

Green the coat,
Green the coat, its lining yellow!
The sorrows in my heart—
How can I forget!

Green the thread—
You were the one who dyed it!

I think of men of old
So as to keep from doing wrong!

Linen, thick or thin,
Is cold when storm winds blow.
I think of men of old,
So as to win my heart's desire!

In traditional China yellow was considered a basic color and green a derived color. For this reason yellow would be used as the "upper" or outside color of a garment, while green would be considered the suitable
color for the lining. The song may therefore perhaps be read as a wife's
complaint about a concubine usurping her position. The oldest commentary to the *Book of Odes* provides the following explanation of these
verses: "'The Green Coat' is the complaint of Lady Jiang, the spouse of
Marquis Zhuang of Wei [r. 757–735 BCE]. A concubine had usurped all
the power and the Lady had lost her position. That is why she wrote this
poem." In the text of the song itself it is impossible to find any evidence
for this ascription, and a modern reader may well wonder whether in ancient times it really was a princely duty to busy oneself with such lowly
tasks as dyeing thread.

Neglected ladies who had less confidence in their literary skills might
make use of better poets to give expression to their sorrows. When, for
example, Empress Chen, the childhood sweetheart and spouse of Emperor Wu of the Han dynasty (r. 140–87 BCE) was discarded and sent
away to the Long Gate Palace, she is said to have employed Sima Xiangru (179–118 BCE), the most famous poet of his time, to write a poem for
her. Sima Xiangru's composition, *Rhapsody of the Long Gate* [*Palace*]
(*Changmenfu*), reportedly accomplished its purpose: when the emperor
read it, he changed his mind and recalled the empress to the Inner Palace.
In later centuries, the fate of the harem lady neglected by the emperor,
the wife discarded by her husband, and the courtesan abandoned by her
patron continued to be a favorite topic for male poets. In the sad fate of
these women, these men saw an analogy to their own lack of recognition
by the Son of Heaven. Many such poems were written entirely in the
voice of a woman who expresses her undying love of her man; this became a way for male poets (who were all for the most part officials or as-

piring officials) to emphasize their own total and limitless devotion to the emperor.

As long as a male poet impersonated a nameless and stereotypical woman, this rhetorical custom was too common to create confusion. When a poet assumed the voice of a specific historical woman, however, there was always the danger that later generations would interpret the text as having been actually written by the woman concerned—the more stirring the poem, the greater the danger. To this day, in cases of questionable authorship, one often encounters the argument that only a woman could have written so movingly of a woman's experiences.

Slandered Virtue: Concubine Ban

Concubine Ban was a member of the same scholarly Ban family that later would produce the poet and historian Ban Gu, as well as his learned sister Ban Zhao. Concubine Ban was one of the concubines of Emperor Cheng (r. 32–7 BCE) of the Western Han dynasty. She distinguished herself by her erudition and principled attitude. The latter aspect of her personality may have contributed to the fact that she quickly lost the favor of the fun-loving Emperor Cheng, who eventually found happiness in the arms of the former dancer Zhao Feiyan (Flying Swallow Zhao) and her sister, who were more willing to cater to the emperor's whims. Although Lady Ban survived a charge of using black magic by rebutting the accusation with exceptional clear-headedness, afterwards she opted for the safety of service to the empress dowager.

Once she was dislodged from the emperor's favor by these two women, whom texts describe as low-class upstarts, Concubine Ban gave expression to her emotions in a rhapsody, which has been included in her biography in the *Books of the Han*. Because this history was composed within a century after her death by her great-nephew and great-niece, Ban Gu and Ban Zhao, we can be confident that this rhapsody was indeed her own composition. Less unquestionable is the case of a very popular *shi* poem ascribed to Concubine Ban and entitled "Resentment." In this poem the woman neglected by her lord compares herself to a circular fan of white silk that is put away in autumn once the heat of summer has died down:

> Newly-cut white silken gauze from Qi,
> As fresh and pure as frost or snow,
> Was made into a double-pleasure fan,
> As perfectly round as the fullest moon!
> "Inside and out you take me with you,
> You wave me: I stir up a gentle breeze.
> But how I fear that when the fall arrives
> And chill winds steal away the summer heat,
> I will be discarded, stored away in a box
> And your love for me broken off midway!"

The most convincing argument against Concubine Ban's authorship of this poem is its genre. While most traditional scholars believed that fully regular *shi* poems with five syllables to a line were written as early as the second half of the second century BCE, modern scholarship prefers to date the rise of this genre of poetry to the second century CE. Such philological quibbles have not hindered the popularity of the poem in any way, and the image of the fan put away in its box continued to be used time and again for almost two millennia as a symbol for a woman abandoned by her husband, patron, or lover. The poem is representative of the many songs and poems that are believed to be the work of a famous woman but that all too often only appear centuries after her lifetime.

This is how her later descendants recount the life of the virtuous Concubine Ban in their *Books of the Han*:

Emperor Cheng's consort Concubine Ban was selected for service in the Inner Palace just at the time the emperor ascended the throne. In the beginning she was a serving girl, but very quickly, after the emperor greatly graced her [by sleeping with her], she was made a concubine and resided in the Zengcheng Quarters. Twice she went to the [birthing] lodge and gave birth to a son, but both times she lost the child after a few months.

Once, when the emperor was disporting himself in the rear garden, he wanted the concubine to share his imperial conveyance. The concubine refused to do so, saying: "When I look at the pictures and paintings of ancient times, I notice that while the wise and sagely rulers all have famous ministers at their side, the last rulers of each of the three dynasties [of ancient times] are accompanied by their favorite women. If I were to share your conveyance, would that not too closely resemble these [three last rulers]?" The emperor admired her words and desisted. When the empress dowager heard about this, she said delightedly: "In ancient times there was lady Fan but now we have Concubine Ban!"[1]

The concubine recited the *Odes* as well as pieces such as "Modest and Demure," "Image of Virtue," and "Teacher of Women." Whenever she was received in audience and submitted memorials, she based her norms on the ancient rites.

Starting from the reign period Grand Beauty [Hongjia, 20–17 BCE], the emperor increasingly showered his palace favorites with his favors. The concubine then presented her servant Li Ping to the emperor, and once Ping had been graced by the emperor, she was made a concubine. The emperor said: "Empress Wei also came from a very lowly background,"[2] and so he bestowed the surname Wei on Ping, who became known as Concubine Wei.

Zhao Feiyan and her younger sister also rose from a lowly and despised background. Violating all ritual rules they flaunted themselves ever more openly before the emperor. Concubine Ban and Empress Xu both lost the emperor's favor and from that time on were rarely received in audience. In the third year of the reign period Grand Beauty, Zhao Feiyan slanderously accused Empress Xu and Concubine Ban of employing magical charms to put a curse on herself and a spell on the emperor. Empress Xu was sentenced and reduced to commoner status. When Concubine Ban was questioned, she replied: "I have learned that 'Life and death depend on fate, riches and status rest with Heaven.' If one cannot be assured of blessings by doing what is right, what can one hope for by harboring evil desires? If the ghosts and gods are aware of our doings, they will not entertain such a disloyal request; and if they are not aware of our doings, what would I gain from making such a request? Therefore I didn't do it." The emperor found her answer admirable, took pity on her, and gifted her with a hundred ounces of yellow gold.

---

1. Lady Fan was one of the wives of King Zhuang of Chu (r. 613–591 BCE). She admonished the king against his overindulgence in hunting by refusing to eat either game or fowl. She also alerted him to the limited talents of his main advisors.

2. Empress Wei (Wei Zifu) was one of the wives of Emperor Wu of the Han dynasty (r. 140–87 BCE). She started out as a singer in the household of one of the imperial princesses, and later became one of the emperor's concubines. Empress Chen lost her position in 130 BCE, and Wei Zifu was elevated to the rank of empress in 128 BCE after she bore the emperor a son. She maintained her position for 38 years, but was then accused of using witchcraft and committed suicide when she was informed she had been deposed. Her titles were posthumously restored when later a great-grandson ascended the throne.

The Zhao sisters were arrogant and jealous, and, fearful that they would eventually find a way to trap her, the concubine requested permission to serve the empress dowager in the Palace of Eternal Trust, a request the emperor granted. Once she had retired to live in the Eastern Palace, she wrote a rhapsody lamenting her sorry fate. Its text reads:

> Having inherited the virtue of my grandfather and father,
>   How pure and numinous is my nature and fate!
> My slight frame was raised to palace and portal,
>   I occupied the lowest rank in the inner courtyards.
> I enjoyed the rich bounty of his Imperial Majesty,
>   Equal to the flourishing brightness of sun and moon!
> Praising the mighty glare of his brilliant light,
>   I basked in his doting love in the Zengcheng quarters.
>
> As I was graced beyond what I deserved,
>   I furtively aspired to these glorious moments.
> Awake and asleep I doubled my sighs,
>   And looking at my sash, was inspired by its words.[3]
> I set out pictures of great women to serve as my models,
>   Consulted their histories and questioned the *Odes*.
> Saddened by the admonition of the morning hen,
>   I lamented the crimes of the seductive Baosi;[4]
> I admired Huang and Ying, the spouses of Shun,
>   And praised Ren and Si, the mothers of Zhou.[5]

---

3. Here "its words" refers to the words of advice addressed by a mother to her daughter as she fastens the sash of her daughter's wedding gown.

4. "The morning hen" refers to a hen that, thinking she is a rooster, crows at dawn, a common analogy for a woman who meddles in state affairs. Baosi was a concubine of King You (r. 781–771 BCE) of the Zhou dynasty. Because Baosi never smiled, the king gave an order to light the alarm fires (which indicated that there was an emergency and that the king needed his vassals to come to his aid). When Baosi saw how the worried vassals hastened to the capital to assist their king only to discover that it had been a false alarm, she finally cracked a smile. But later, when barbarians actually did attack the capital and the king again had the alarm fires lit, his vassals refused to come to his aid. The capital fell and the king lost his life.

5. Huang and Ying were the virtuous daughters of the mythic sage emperor Yao, who gave them in marriage to his successor Shun. Ren was the mother of King Wen. Si was his wife and the mother of King Wu, the founder of the Zhou dynasty. Both Ren and Si are praised in the *Book of Odes* as perfect wives and mothers.

Though foolish and lowly, by no means their equal,
  How could I dare ignore these lofty exemplars?
And so all of those years I fretted and feared,
  Depressed by the wilting of flourishing flowers.
Alas that in the Yanglu Pavilion and Zheguan Hall
  My sons, when still infants, met with disaster!

What misfortune or crime of mine brought this about?
  It was due to unrelenting Fate and Heaven!
The white sun suddenly shifted its light,
  Leaving me hidden in the dark, dim and obscure.
Protected still by the rich virtue of sky and earth,
  I was not done away with for my sin and crime.

Now I serve on the staff of the Eastern Palace,
  Entrusting myself to the lowest ranks of the Eternal Trust.
I sprinkle and sweep in these curtained chambers,
  And I hope to do so until the day of my death.
May my bones be returned to the foot of His hill
  To rest in the leftover shade of cypress and pine![6]

Envoi:

Submerged in this gloomy palace, hidden yet pure:
  May the gates be closed and all the doors locked!
The dust of the painted halls settles on the steps of jade,
  The courtyards run wild as the green grasses grow.
The large rooms are somber, the curtains are darkened,
  The windows are empty, the drafts bring a chill:
Stirring both curtain and skirt, parting the red gauze,
  Rustling together—the sounds of white silk.
My mind dissolves in this place so silent,
  If You do not grace me, who is my glory?

I gaze down at the vermilion steps,
  And imagine Your embroidered shoes.
I gaze up at Your mist-covered house,
  And tears course down my cheeks.

---

6. In these lines the author expresses the wish to one day be buried by the side of the emperor's grave mound ("His hill").

I look at my servants, compose my face—
  They pour me a cup to dispel my sorrows.
All of my life since the day I was born
  Has slipped away like a floating cloud!
But I alone enjoyed Your lofty brilliance:
  For a subject there is no greater blessing.

Exert Your spirit to highest pleasure—
  I don't expect good fortune or riches.
"The Green Coat" and "The White Blossom":
  Since ancient times such has been our fate.[7]

After the death of Emperor Cheng, Concubine Ban was one of the women who took care of the sacrifices at his grave. Upon her death she was also buried in his grave garden.

Fact and Fiction: Phantom Poems and Phantom Lives

Reduced to a Human Pig: Lady Qi

The sad fate of Lady Qi shows that even a woman who bore the emperor a surviving son was not assured of a long and happy life. The development of her legend in the subsequent retellings of her story also shows how, even many years after her death, a woman could be credited with a poem regarded as a fitting expression of her deepest emotions.

Lady Qi was a concubine of Liu Bang (256–195 BCE), the founder of the (Western) Han dynasty (206 BCE–8 CE). Liu Bang came from a very ordinary background, and married Lü Qu, the daughter of the local village head. He was an ambitious man, and when upon the death of the First Emperor (r. 221–210 BCE) the empire fell into disarray, Liu Bang was one of the many who saw this as an opportunity to make a bid for power. With the assistance of wise advisors and brave generals he eventually brought down his greatest opponent, the arrogant and hitherto undefeated aristocrat Xiang Yu. The story of how Xiang Yu, on the eve of the

---

7. "The Green Coat" is a poem in the *Book of Odes* that was traditionally interpreted as a complaint of a queen who had lost her lord's favor because of a younger concubine. "The White Blossom" is another poem from the *Book of Odes*, and is said to have been written in condemnation of Baosi, the favorite concubine of the deluded King You, for usurping the position of the legitimate queen.

final battle and fully aware of the hopelessness of his situation, bids a final farewell to his trusted steed and his favorite concubine, even today continues to inspire playwrights, novelists, and film directors.

Following his final victory in 202 BCE, Liu Bang devoted himself to the pursuit of pleasure, and it fell to his wife Empress Lü to do away with those generals who might conceivably pose a threat to the throne. Together with the draconian minister Xiao He, she accomplished this task so ruthlessly that in later centuries her name became a byword for cruelty. When Liu Bang approached his end, he therefore had no illusions about the safety of his favorite concubine Lady Qi and her young son, who he had hoped would be his heir. The various precautions he took, however, were of no avail. As soon as he had died, Empress Lü, now the empress dowager, took over the reins of power, and cruelly did away with the young woman who had been foolish enough to threaten the position of the empress and her sons.

Less than a hundred years after the death of Liu Bang, the historian Sima Qian wrote in his *Records of the Historian* the following brief account of the events following the demise of the emperor:

When the Han dynasty was founded, Lü Qu became the imperial spouse of the Lofty Ancestor [Liu Bang], and her son the crown prince. But when she grew older, she lost both her beauty and her husband's affections. After that Lady Qi enjoyed his favor and occasionally moves were made to name her son Ruyi crown prince. When the Lofty Ancestor died, Empress Lü killed off all of the members of the Qi family and had the Prince of Zhao [Ruyi] executed. Only those women who had never been graced by the emperor and never had served in his proximity were safe.

In the chapter on the annals of the regency of Empress Lü in the same work, Sima Qian provides a more detailed account of the murder of Lady Qi and her young son:

Empress Lü harbored a deep hatred of Lady Qi and her son, the Prince of Zhao. She had Lady Qi incarcerated in the Long Lane Palace and summoned the Prince of Zhao [from his princedom to the capital]. Three times the messengers returned unsuccessfully, having been told by the chancellor of Zhao, the marquis of Jianping, Zhou Chang: "The Prince of Zhao was entrusted to my care by the Lofty Ancestor [before his death] and is still young. I have heard that the empress dowager hates Lady Qi and wants to summon the Prince of Zhao so as to have them both executed together. I dare not allow the prince to go. Moreover, the prince is ill and unable to obey the command."

Empress Lü was enraged and summoned the chancellor of Zhao. Once he had arrived in Chang'an, she again dispatched messengers to summon the Prince of Zhao. The prince set out but before he had arrived, Emperor Hui [the son of Empress Lü], who was of a caring and humane character and knew of the empress dowager's rage, went himself to welcome him. He met up with him at the bank of the river Ba, and took him with him to the palace. He kept him in his presence at all times and accompanied the Prince of Zhao in all his activities. In this way the empress dowager did not have the opportunity to kill him like she wanted. But in the Twelfth Month of the first year of the reign of Emperor Hui, the emperor left the palace at dawn to practice his archery. Because the Prince of Zhao was still so young, he could not get up so early. As soon as the empress dowager learned that he was alone, she had someone give him poison to drink. By the time Emperor Hui returned later that morning, the Prince of Zhao was dead . . .

The empress dowager thereupon cut off the hands and feet of Lady Qi, gouged out her eyes, seared shut her ears, gave her a medicine to drink that robbed her of her voice, and locked her up in a cesspit. She called her "the human pig." Some days later she ordered Emperor Hui to come and look at her "human pig." When Emperor Hui saw her, he asked who she was. When he found out that it was Lady Qi, he collapsed on the ground weeping loudly. He became ill and took to his bed for more than a year. He also had someone speak to the empress dowager on his behalf saying: "This is monstrous! How can I as your son rule the world?" This was the reason he drank himself into a stupor each day, indulged himself in all kinds of excess, and consequently became ill.

The horrific crime of Empress Lü did not go unavenged, however. Some years later, convinced that she had been bitten in the armpit by a blue dog, the empress dowager consulted her specialists, who informed her that the dog was none other than the ghostly apparition of the murdered prince. The wound in her armpit developed into a tumor and soon killed her.

Almost two centuries later, Ban Gu, who relied heavily on the *Records of the Historian* in compiling his own *Books of the Han*, noted the existence of the song by the imprisoned Lady Qi that supposedly provoked her ignominious death:

When the Lofty Ancestor passed away and Emperor Hui ascended the throne, Empress Lü became the empress dowager. She had Lady Qi incarcerated in Long Lane Palace where shaved, manacled, and dressed in red, she was put to work husking rice. As she husked the rice she sang a song:

> The son a prince,
> His mother a slave:
> I husk the rice from dawn till dusk.
> Here death is my constant companion.
> Three thousand miles lie between us—
> Who will let you know of my fate?

When the empress dowager heard this, she was enraged and said: "Did you think you could take advantage of your son's position?" She then summoned the Prince of Zhao in order to have him killed.

And so we see that by Ban Gu's time the legend of the rivalry between the old and unscrupulous Empress Lü and the young and defenseless Lady Qi had not only acquired a new episode, but had also transformed Lady Qi into a composer of poetry, if only of a single song. And it is as such that the voice of the luckless Lady Qi continues to be heard in many contemporary anthologies of women's writings.

A Disputed Beauty: Empress Zhen

Even if an intelligent and beautiful woman from an elite family was able to attract the attention of the emperor and bear him a son who survived to succeed his father, she was not assured of his permanent favor. This is vividly illustrated by the biography of Empress Zhen (183–221), the wife of Cao Pi (187–226). Cao Pi was the second son of Cao Cao (155–220), the warlord who, during the chaos that marked the last decades of the Han dynasty, engaged in a series of military campaigns that resulted in all of north China submitting to his power. Following the death of his father, Cao Pi accepted the abdication of the last emperor of the Han and ascended the throne as the first emperor of the Wei dynasty (221–264). In later history he was known as Emperor Wen. The domain of the Wei dynasty remained limited to north China; in southwest and southeast China, other warlords established their own dynasties. This is why this period in Chinese history is often referred to as the Three Kingdoms. More than a thousand years later, these wars leading up to the tripartite division of the empire would provide the material for China's most popular historical novel, *The Romance of the Three Kingdoms* (*Sanguo yanyi*), traditionally attributed to Luo Guanzhong (ca. 1400). In this novel, Cao Cao is depicted as a ruthless schemer, but earlier historiography depicts him as an astute politician and military genius, and his poetry has always been well received. Cao Pi also was an accomplished poet, while his younger brother Cao Zhi (192–232) is generally recognized as one of the greatest poets in the history of Chinese literature.

In Chen Shou's (d. 297) *History of the Three Kingdoms* (*Sanguo zhi*), the dynastic history of the Wei and its rivals, the early youth of Empress Zhen is described as follows:

The Cultured and Brilliant Empress Zhen was a native of Wuji in Zhongshan and was the mother of Emperor Mingdi [r. 227–239]. She was a descendant of the Great-Guardian Zhen Han, and members of her family had for generations occupied the highest positions in the bureaucracy. Her father Zhen Yi served as magistrate of Shangcai.

The empress lost her father when she was three. When later the empire was not only being ravaged by civil wars, but also undergoing severe famine, the common people all had to sell their gold and silver, pearls and jade, and other precious goods [in order to buy food]. At that time, the family of the empress had already amassed large reserves of grain, but continued to buy more in large quantities. The empress, who was just over ten years of age at the time, said to her mother: "Although the world is now at war, we continue to buy precious goods in large quantities. 'The poor man is not the one who commits a crime, it is the man who hoards his wealth who is the criminal.' Moreover, all those around us suffer from hunger and want. It would be much better to use our grain to help out our relatives and fellow townsmen and extend our favors widely." The entire family agreed to her proposal, and immediately acted on her advice.

The *History of the Three Kingdoms* is usually published together with an extensive commentary by Pei Songzhi (d. 429), who freely borrowed from many other writings on the eventful years at the end of the Han. In his commentary on the above passage, Pei Songzhi provides a rather more miraculous account of the empress's youth:

The empress was born on the day *dingyou* of the Twelfth Month of the fifth year of the reign period Brilliant Harmony [Guanghe, 178–183] of the Han dynasty. Whenever she lay asleep, the people in the house could vaguely make out some people covering her with a jade gown, and this greatly amazed everyone. When [her father] Zhen Yi died she wept beyond measure, and this earned her even more admiration, both inside and outside the family. Later, when the physiognomist Liu Lang studied her face and the faces of her brothers, he pointed to the empress and said: "The future position of this girl is incredible!"

Even as a toddler, the empress disliked childish games. When she was eight, some acrobats were putting on a performance in front of her house, and riding standing up on the backs of their galloping horses. Her sisters, together with the other people in the house, went upstairs to have a better look, and the empress was the only one to stay behind. When her surprised sisters asked her why she did not come along, she replied: "Is this something we women should be looking at?"

From the age of nine she loved to read and write. She had only to see a character once, and she knew it. Time and again she used the writing brushes and inkstones of her brothers. Her brothers told her: "You should practice sewing and embroidery. Do you think you can become a woman professor by studying all these books?" The empress replied: "All the wise women of antiquity, I have learned, studied the successes and failures of earlier generations in order to learn from them. How can I know the past without reading its books?"

The first husband of Empress Zhen was the second son of Yuan Shao, one of Cao Cao's greatest rivals. She was part of the war booty taken by Cao Cao when he crushed Yuan Shao in 206. The *History of the Three Kingdoms* describes these events as follows:

During the reign period Established Peace [Jian'an, 196–219], Yuan Shao made her the wife of his second son Xi [d. 207]. When Xi left [in 202] to take up his position as governor of Youzhou, the empress stayed behind to take care of her mother-in-law. When [in 205] Jizhou was pacified, [Cao Pi, the later] Emperor Wen took her as his wife in Ye. She enjoyed his doting affection and in time gave birth to [the later] Emperor Ming and the Princess Dongxiang.

Pei Songzhi quotes in his commentary two sources that provide a somewhat more detailed description of the first meeting between Cao Pi, who was eighteen at the time, and Xi's wife, who was then twenty-three. The first of these accounts reads as follows:

Yuan Xi had departed and was stationed at Youzhou, while the empress had remained behind to take care of her mother-in-law. When the city of Ye fell,

Yuan Shao's wife and the empress were seated in the main hall. When Cao Pi entered the house of Yuan Shao, he saw Shao's wife and the empress, who was filled with fear and had buried her face in her mother-in-law's lap, while the latter beat her breast. Cao Pi said to her: "Madam, there's no need for that! Just let the young bride lift her head!" Her mother-in-law supported the empress and got her to look up. Cao Pi approached to have a better look, and as soon as he saw her extraordinary beauty, he sighed with admiration. When Cao Cao found out about his son's love, he had her brought home as a bride for him.

The second account is slightly different:

When Cao Cao subdued the city of Ye, Cao Pi was the first to enter the mansion of Yuan Shao. Behind Shao's wife, lady Liu, stood a weeping woman with disheveled hair and begrimed face. When he asked who she was, lady Liu replied: "She is the wife of Xi." After the woman had done up her hair and wiped her face with a cloth, her beauty turned out to be without match. After Cao Pi had left, lady Liu told the empress: "You need not fear for your life!" Later Cao Pi took her as his wife and she enjoyed his loving affection.

Cao Pi's first encounter with the empress may have made a great impression on him, but it did not ensure his eternal love. The *History of the Three Kingdoms* concludes its story of Empress Zhen's life in the following manner:

In the First Month of the first year of the reign period Extended Prosperity [Yankang, 220], Cao Pi was made a prince. In the Sixth Month, he departed on a campaign against the South, while the empress remained in Ye. In the Tenth Month of the first year of the reign period Yellow Beginning [Huangchu, 220–226], Cao Pi ascended the throne. After he had ascended the throne, [the former emperor of the Han,] the Duke of Shanyang, offered both his daughters as concubines to the new emperor, and the [later] Empress Guo and the concubines Li and Yin all enjoyed his love. But Cao Pi grew increasingly displeased with the empress, who gave expression to her resentment in her words. The emperor was enraged and in the Sixth Month of the second year [of Yellow Beginning] he informed her through a messenger that he was allowing her to commit suicide. She was buried in Ye.

Empress Zhen was never formally installed as empress during her lifetime. The remainder of her biography is taken up by a long description of the efforts of her son Emperor Mingdi to clear her name and to accord her all of the honors that he felt Empress Zhen, as his mother, truly deserved.

The *New Songs from a Jade Terrace* (*Yutai xinyong*) includes the following song that Empress Zhen is said to have written just before her death:

> Look at the rushes growing in our pond:
> How their lush leaves hang tight together!
> You do your duty to the ones around you,
> No one is as acutely aware of that as am I.
> The words of many can melt the purest gold,
> They've made you separate from me in life.
>
> When I think back to when you went away,
> My lonely sorrow fills my heart with grief,
> And when I call your features to mind,
> The tangle of emotions pains my soul.
> Thinking of you I'm always filled with grief,
> Night after night I find it impossible to sleep.
>
> Do not because of present high connections,
> Discard the one you always loved before.
> Do not, because you can afford fish and meat,
> Discard the onions and the leeks.
> Do not, because you can afford hemp and silk,
> Discard the rushes and the reeds.
>
> When I go out, I feel a bitter grief,
> When I return, I feel a bitter grief.
> Sad storms blow often in the border regions,
> Just look at those trees, swaying, rustling!
> Make sure that in the army you enjoy yourself,
> May you live long and live a thousand years!

This song, however, describes not the anguished loss of imperial favor, but rather the pain of a wife of a military officer, whose husband has left her behind to serve in the army stationed on the northern borders. Other sources ascribe this poem to Empress Zhen's father-in-law Cao Cao or even to her husband, Cao Pi. All we can say is that it is a traditional song on the theme of a deserted wife, who fears that she may lose her husband's favor because of slander or because his rising fortune may cause him to look down on her.

A later legend has it that Empress Zhen had actually been in love with Cao Pi's younger brother Cao Zhi, the better poet, and that she had not been allowed to commit suicide, but rather had been murdered by her rival, the later Empress Guo. More than a year after her death, according to this version of the story, Empress Zhen's ghost appeared to Cao Zhi, and inspired him to write his grandest poem, the *Rhapsody on the Goddess of the Luo* (*Luoshen fu*). Our earliest source for this legend is a note of unknown date in the commentary to the *Selections of Refined Literature* of the early sixth century. The story is not very credible, if only because Cao Zhi was only thirteen when Cao Pi married Empress Zhen, but it became so popular in later dynasties that it must be included here:

During the final years of the Han dynasty, the Prince of Dong'a of the Wei dynasty [Cao Zhi] asked for the hand of the daughter of Zhen Yi, but did not meet with success. When Cao Cao returned [from his campaign], he gave her to the Head of Court Gentlemen for Miscellaneous Uses [Cao Pi]. Cao Zhi could not accept this, and longed for her day and night, his love robbing him of sleep and keeping him from eating.

Sometime during the reign period Yellow Beginning, he left his fief and paid a visit to the court, where the emperor showed him a headrest belonging to [the late] Empress Zhen that was adorned with jewels and encircled with gold. When he saw it, Cao Zhi could not hold back his tears—by that time she had already died because of Empress Guo's slander. The emperor also felt regret, and so he ordered the crown prince to arrange a banquet for Cao Zhi, at which he presented him with the headrest.

On the way back [to his fief], Cao Zhi passed through Xianyuan where he stopped to rest on the banks of the river Luo. All his thoughts were occupied by Empress Zhen. Suddenly he saw a woman who approached him and said: "Actually it was you to whom my heart was pledged although I was unable to consummate that love. That headrest I brought from home when I married. First I gave it to the Head of Court Gentlemen for Miscellaneous Uses, but now I give it to you. How would ordinary words have been enough to express my pleasure had I been fortunate enough to share your couch, using this headrest? But Empress Guo stuffed my mouth with chaff [suffocating me]. My hair is all disheveled and I am too ashamed to appear before you again looking like this!" When she had finished speaking, she disappeared. But she had a messenger deliver a pearl to the prince, who sent her a jade girdle-pendant in return.

Overcome by both grief and joy, he then composed his *Rhapsody on the Apparition of Empress Zhen*. But when Emperor Mingdi later read this poem, he changed the title to *Rhapsody on the Goddess of the Luo*.

Banished Beyond the Border: Liu Xijun and Wang Zhaojun

Everywhere in the world and throughout history, ruling families have traditionally cemented their political alliances with marriage ties. In East Asia too, rulers of the states bordering the Chinese empire would often seek out imperial princesses from the Central Kingdom as brides. It was thus that in the final years of the second century BCE, Liu Xijun, a daughter of Liu Jian, the Prince of Jiangdu, was dispatched by her uncle, the emperor, to the barren steppes bordering the Celestial Empire to become the consort of Kunmo, the aged king of the Wusun tribe. From a Chinese perspective it was unimaginable that a princess would find happiness in a barbarian land, and two centuries later the *Books of the Han* credits her with the following song:

> My family sent me off in marriage to the end of the world,
> Faraway to a strange country, to the king of the Wusun.
> A yurt is now my home, its walls made of felt,
> Raw meat is my food here and koumiss my drink.
> All day my heart aches with pains of home:
> Were only I a brown goose and could fly home!

While foreign rulers might insist on sisters or daughters of the reigning emperor for their brides, the emperor would usually do all he could to spare his immediate family such a sorry fate by sending a lady from the Inner Palace instead. Thus, a neglected palace lady ran the risk of being packed off to distant and barren regions, far from the Chinese heartland and the center of civilization.

In 33 BCE, Emperor Yuandi (r. 48–33 BCE) gave the palace lady Wang Zhaojun in marriage to Huhanye, the khan or leader, of the Southern Xiongnu. The Xiongnu lived on the steppe lands on the northern border and in the second century BCE constituted a constant military threat to the Han empire. In the course of the first century BCE, the Xiongnu had split into a Northern and a Southern confederation, and the Chinese court in Chang'an found it strategically useful to cultivate friendly relations with the Southern Xiongnu. The *Books of the Han* relates that Wang

Zhaojun bore her husband a son. Upon the death of Huhanye she became, according to Xiongnu custom, the wife of his son (by an earlier wife) and successor, to whom she bore two daughters. These children would subsequently play an important part in the diplomatic relations between the Han and the Xiongnu.

In later centuries, with the growth of ethnic self-consciousness in China, Chinese writers increasingly stressed the diametrical contrasts between the sedentary and civilized Chinese and the nomadic and barbarian non-Chinese. Thus, while an early source notes that Wang Zhaojun actually volunteered to be married off to the khan because she despaired of ever being noticed by the emperor, the idea of anyone voluntarily leaving the Chinese heartland would later become unthinkable. In the chapter on the Southern Xiongnu in the *Books of the Later Han* of the early fifth century, not only is Emperor Yuandi said to have regretted his selection of Wang Zhaojun, but Wang Zhaojun also begs to be allowed to return to China upon the death of her husband:

Zhaojun's style name was Qiang and she hailed from Nanjun commandery. She was the daughter of a commoner family and had been selected for induction into the Inner Palace during the reign of Emperor Yuandi. When Huhanye visited the court, the emperor ordered that he be presented with five palace ladies. Zhaojun, who after all her years in the Inner Palace had still not seen the emperor, was filled with sadness and resentment and asked the intendant of the Inner Palace to be allowed to go. At the farewell party held on the eve of Huhanye's departure, the emperor summoned the five ladies in order to show them to Huhanye. Zhaojun impressed all at court by her opulent beauty and radiant appearance. . . . When the emperor saw her, he was greatly impressed and although he would have preferred not to let her go, he could not go back on his word. So in the end he gave her to the Xiongnu to whom she bore two children.[8]

When Huhanye died, his son by his first wife ascended the throne and wanted to make Zhaojun his wife. She submitted a memorial to Emperor Chengdi requesting to be allowed to return, but he ordered her to go along with the custom of the Xiongnu and so she became the wife of the new khan.

---

8. Reflecting the influence of later legend, the *Books of the Later Han* makes a mistake here as Wang Zhaojun bore her first husband one son and her second husband two daughters.

An anecdote found in the *Various Notes on the Western Capital* (*Xijing zaji*), a collection of tales and legends concerning the Western Han dynasty compiled in the fourth or fifth century, explains why Emperor Yuandi had not noticed her until the eve of her departure, by which time it was too late:

The Inner Palace of Emperor Yuandi was well-stocked with women. Because he could not visit them all on a regular basis, he had their portraits painted and on the basis of these, would summon them to share his couch. The palace ladies paid huge bribes to the painters—sometimes as much as a hundred thousand copper coins, but no less than fifty thousand copper coins per person. Wang Zhaojun was the only one to refuse to do so, and as a result was never summoned by the emperor.

When the Xiongnu appeared at court, he requested a beauty to be his spouse. The emperor then decided, basing himself on these paintings, to have Zhaojun go. But when he received her in audience on the occasion of her departure, she turned out not only to be the most beautiful of all the palace ladies, but also quick-witted in conversation and elegant in appearance.

Later the emperor had the matter thoroughly investigated, after the painters were all executed and their fortunes—which amounted to millions!—were confiscated. Among these painters was Mao Yanshou from Duling. When he painted people, he always succeeded in capturing their likeness, whether beautiful or ugly, young or old.

In later retellings of this story, it is Mao Yanshou who deliberately makes Zhaojun look ugly in her portrait because, confident of her beauty, she refuses to pay him the bribe he demands.

As a stranger in a strange land, Wang Zhaojun had no choice but to consign her anguish and sorrow to verse. A poem ascribed to her and entitled "Resentment" is included in a work that claims to have been compiled at the end of the second century but more likely dates from the fifth century:

> How lush and lovely those autumn trees!
> Their leaves turn brown and yellow.
> And on that hill there is a bird
> That roosts in a mulberry tree.
> How she grooms her plumes and feathers,
> How brilliant are her form and features!
> She soars up high into the clouds,

And freely roams in hidden chambers.
"But housed apart I am not used:
My body is shattered and hidden away.
All my hopes have now been dashed,
Never will we fly together wing to wing!
 Even though I do not lack for food,
Yet still my heart is sad and troubled.
All alone—what shall I do?
Let me go and change my lot!"
 The swallow flitting here and there
Has come to roost with the Western Qiang.[9]
The mountains there are high and steep,
The rivers there flow wide and full.
"O my father, O my mother,
Long and distant is the road.
Alas, oh, alas, I cry, oh, alas—
Sorrow's pain so wounds my heart!"

In later centuries painters often portrayed Wang Zhaojun on horse-back as, clad in furs, she makes her way across the barren winter land-scape of the northern steppe. In her hands she holds a lute, which she plays to accompany her song. This lute originally was an attribute of Liu Xijun, but the two images were easily conflated.

Chinese emperors of the Song dynasty (960–1278) refused to grant requests from foreign rulers for Chinese brides. Playwrights of the Yuan dynasty (1260–1364) credited Wang Zhaojun with an undying love for Emperor Yuandi. They saved the emperor from the disgrace of having one of his palace ladies marry a barbarian by having her commit suicide as soon as she crossed the border and was handed over to her new master. A hill was erected on her grave, which was called the Green Hill because on this hill the grass supposedly always remained green, even at the driest times of the year.

One modern anthology of letters of famous women from China's past contains two letters from Wang Zhaojun to Emperor Yuandi. Neither of these letters seems to have been noticed until the very end of the Qing dynasty (1644–1911), and both carry all the signs of being late fakes. In

---

9. "Qiang" was in Han dynasty times a general designation for the peoples that lived to the west of China (in modern Qinghai); it was not used to refer to the Xiongnu.

one of these letters, Wang Zhaojun implores the emperor to show mercy toward the painters he is about to massacre because it would reflect badly on his reputation. About her own reputation this fictional Wang Zhaojun did not have to worry: once she is transformed from a free agent who pursues her self-interest into an innocent victim who commits suicide in order to preserve her purity, she becomes a revered exemplar of self-sacrificing loyalty.

A Lonely Suicide: Lady Hou

If Wang Zhaojun in later legend committed suicide at the far edge of the empire, other palace ladies, despairing of ever attracting the emperor's attention, committed suicide in the Inner Palace itself. One such palace lady, Lady Hou, is said to have left a group of poems describing how she felt just prior to taking her own life. But whereas there is no reason to doubt the historicity of Wang Zhaojun, there are many reasons for questioning the existence of Lady Hou.

Lady Hou supposedly committed suicide out of loyalty to Emperor Yang (r. 605–618), the second and last ruler of the Sui dynasty (580–618). Emperor Yang is one of the typical venal last rulers of Chinese history. The Sui dynasty, founded by his father Emperor Wen, had succeeded in reuniting the Chinese world after some three centuries of division. A new capital was built, again called Chang'an, and great efforts were made to integrate the empire. Within a mere generation, however, Emperor Yang would destroy everything his father had achieved by embarking on grandiose expansionist policies, undertaking megalomaniac building projects, and pursuing a life of luxury and excess. The military campaigns against the states on the Korean peninsula only resulted in a massive loss of human lives without achieving any lasting results. The construction of the Grand Canal, linking the Yellow River to the Yangzi and making it possible for the emperor to travel all the way from Chang'an to Yangzhou in barges towed by palace ladies, was carried out at a great cost of human life. In Yangzhou the emperor built a huge pleasure palace that he stocked with women with whom he could indulge his lusts. Rebellions soon broke out all over the empire, but the emperor blithely ignored the deteriorating situation. Finally the officers of his own guards took matters into their own hands and assassinated him. By using the empire solely for his own personal pleasure, the historians stress, the emperor lost both his country and his life. Future writers even went so far as to suggest that he murdered his own father in order to gain the throne.

The excesses of Emperor Yang continued to fascinate future generations and gave rise to a great number of stories and novels, each attempting to outdo the other in the invention of titillating detail. One of these tales is *The Labyrinth* (*Milou ji*), a largely legendary account of the building of the emperor's labyrinthine pleasure palace and the activities that went on inside it. It is not clear when and by whom this tale was written, but most modern scholars consider the text to be an anonymous work of the Song dynasty (960–1278), which would mean that it was written three or four centuries after the collapse of the Sui. One indication of the distance in time between the building of the actual pleasure palace and the composition of *The Labyrinth* is the fact that its anonymous author locates this maze-like palace not in Yangzhou but in Chang'an.

It is only in *The Labyrinth* that we encounter Lady Hou and her poem; earlier sources all remain silent on her life and work. In this tale, the meaningless waste of a beautiful and intelligent woman's devoted life becomes a perfect illustration of the sinful self-indulgence of Emperor Yang. When the emperor hears about her suicide and reads her poems, he is filled with admiration. Instead of being moved to allow some of his many palace women to return home and find husbands, however, he summons yet another hundred women from the Inner Palace to the Labyrinth. Lady Hou and her poems most probably derive not from fact but from the rich moral imagination of the anonymous author of *The Labyrinth*. Nevertheless, the noble death and the quality of the poems she is said to have written have ensured her a place in many traditional and modern anthologies of Chinese women's poetry.

Two of the poems attributed to Lady Hou are devoted to the plum tree, which blossoms very early in the year, even, according to the traditional Chinese calendar, before winter has yielded to spring. The white flowers open on bare branches and are very fragrant. The plum tree is a symbol of purity and chastity under most adverse circumstances, and as such often appears in Chinese poetry, especially in poetry by women, who see in its pure and fragile beauty a reflection of their own sometimes precarious lives.

In the poem "Diversion," Lady Hou compares her fate to that of Wang Zhaojun, although it is clear that hers is the more unfortunate. Zhaojun departed from the palace, according to her legend, knowing that the emperor had been smitten by her beauty, whereas Lady Hou had to die in order to make an impression on her lord and master.

Because *The Labyrinth* is too long a story to be translated here in full, we have limited ourselves to the few passages relating to the story of Lady Hou:

In the final years of his life Emperor Yang became even more unrestrained in his lust for women. One day he said to his closest servants: "As lord of men I enjoy all the riches of heaven and earth, so I want to enjoy as many pleasures as possible during my lifetime and so satisfy all my desires. Now, when the empire is prosperous and at peace and we are not being threatened from outside, is the time for me to indulge my desires. This palace hall may be grand and vast, but alas, there are no side rooms and small chambers, no dark windows or low railings. If there were, I would spend the rest of my life there!"

His eunuch Gao Chang informed him: "I have a friend, Xiang Sheng, who hails from Zhejiang and claims to be an architect who specializes in the design of palaces." The next day Sheng was summoned, and, when questioned, said: "Let me first draw up a plan." A few days later he submitted his design. When the emperor unrolled it and had a look, he was so enthusiastic that the very same day he ordered the appropriate functionaries to supply Sheng with the timber. A total of several tens of thousands of men were drafted to work on the project, and within a year the palace was completed . . .

If one happened to wander into this palace, one could pass the entire day without being able to find one's way out again. When the emperor visited the palace, he was extremely pleased, and said to his attendants: "Even if a real immortal came to enjoy himself in this palace, he too would get lost. We will call it 'The Labyrinth'" . . . He then summoned several thousands of daughters of good families from the Inner Palace and from them selected those who were to live in the Labyrinth. Whenever he visited the Labyrinth, he would stay for over a month . . .

The palace ladies were innumerable. Those women in the Inner Palace who never succeeded in sharing the emperor's couch were also very numerous. One of these women of the Inner Palace, Lady Hou, was very beautiful. One day she committed suicide by hanging herself from a roof beam. To her arm was tied a brocade sachet containing some writings. When the attendants took them to the emperor they turned out to be poems. Three of the poems, entitled "Emotions," read as follows:

I

The courtyard bears no trace of His conveyance,
The fragrant grasses are now withered weeds.
I vaguely hear a gathering's flutes and drums—
Who is the one He showers with His favors?

II

I want to cry but all my tears are gone,
Although I'm sad I force myself to sing.
The flowers in my courtyard are ablaze—
I know not how to contend with spring!

III

This spring is gloomy and it truly never ends!
What do I hope to get by pacing to and fro?
I'd rather be an idle flower or a willow
Richly blessed by rain and dew to spare.

Her two poems entitled "Looking at the Plum Tree" read as follows:

I

The snow on the steps not yet melted away—
I roll up the curtain, my brows knit in a frown.
The plum tree in the courtyard shows her sympathy:
On a single branch an early touch of spring!

II

Her fragrance pure, her wintry splendor fine:
Who else appreciates this heavenly perfection?
Once the plum sheds its jade, warm weather comes,
Passing out an easy spring to all the common flowers.

Her poem "After Completing My Toilette" reads as follows:

Self-pity fills me when my toilette is completed:
That perfect dream turned into saddest sorrow!

> I'd rather be the catkin of a poplar tree—
> Which in spring flies where it pleases!

Her poem "Diversion" reads as follows:

> The hidden room confines the fairy flower,
> The window carvings cage the one of jade:
> That Mao Yanshou deserved his punishment
> For messing with the portrait of Zhaojun!

Her poem "Lamenting My Fate" reads as follows:

> When first I came to the Chengming Palace,
> I made a deep bow in the Weiyang Hall.
> But in my seven years in Long Gate Mansion
> I've yet to see my lord and king again.
> The spring is cold and purifies my bones,
> And in my empty room alone in bed I grieve.
> Dragging my slippers, I stroll in the courtyard,
> My sad heart in pain, my sorrows in vain.
> All my life I had been loved and cherished,
> And for my future I held the highest hopes.
> Despite my beauty I've been tossed away—
> How could I have known what my fate would be!
> How truly removed I am from His favor,
> It fills my heart with distress and dismay.
> Of course I have my relatives back home,
> I left my parents aging in the hall,
> But as this body lacks plumes and wings,
> I can't escape from these high walls.
> One's life is what one values most,
> To be rejected is truly too painful to bear.
> From the red rafter hangs a length of silk,
> Inside I am seething like a cauldron!
> I crane my neck upwards, and then hesitate—
> I feel like my innards are being torn out.
> Let me be brave and die here on this spot,
> This very moment return to the land of darkness!

The emperor read her poems and was deeply moved as he recited them over and over again. When he went to have a look at her corpse, he said: "She may be dead, but she still looks as beautiful as a flowering peach or plum." He immediately summoned the eunuch Xu Tingfu and said: "We ordered you to go to the Inner Palace and select women for the Labyrinth. How is it possible that this woman was passed over?" He then had Tingfu put in jail and granted him permission to commit suicide.

The emperor recited the poems of Lady Hou every day and liked the words so much that he had his musicians sing them. He also personally selected a hundred women from the Inner Palace for service in the Labyrinth.

The Labyrinth continues with a further description of the excesses of Emperor Yang, and concludes with the Labyrinth going up in flames as the conquering founder of the new Tang dynasty (618–906) enters the capital.

Displaced by a Rival: Concubine Plum

Whereas Emperor Yang lost both his throne and his life due to his unbridled lust for countless women, more than a century later Emperor Xuanzong almost brought down the Tang dynasty because of his infatuation with a single woman, the Exalted Concubine Yang (Yang Guifei). Yang Yuhuan began her palace career as the spouse of one of Xuanzong's many sons. But when one day her elderly father-in-law became aware of the full extent of her physical attractions as she emerged from the hot springs at Huaqing Palace, he forced her to divorce her husband, enter a Buddhist nunnery (the Taizhen Convent), and then return again to lay life as his own concubine. Yang Yuhuan made a name for herself as a musician and dancer, and has left us a single quatrain in praise of a fellow-dancer:

For the Dancer Zhang Yunrong

Gauze sleeves that spread their endless fragrance:
Red lotuses that sway softly in the autumn mists—
A weightless mountain cloud caught in a sudden wind,
A drooping willow by the pond caressing its first waves.

The new favorite made sure she enjoyed the emperor's undivided attention. She also had her distant cousin Yang Guozhong appointed Prime Minister. Then, in 755, a Sogdian general in Chinese service by the name of An Lushan led a rebellion in northeast China and after a lightning campaign threatened the capital itself. Emperor Xuanzong hastily fled to the southwest with the Exalted Concubine and Yang Guozhong. When they were only one day away from the capital, however, the imperial guards who were escorting them killed Yang Guozhong, whom they blamed for the debacle, and then insisted on taking the life of the Exalted Concubine as well. The frightened emperor had no choice but to agree. One year later, after his son and successor Suzong (r.756–762), with the aid of Uighur cavalry, had expelled An Lushan and his troops from the capital, Emperor Xuanzong also returned to Chang'an. Having by this time abdicated the throne, he spent his final years reminiscing over his life with Lady Yang.

Before long, the elderly emperor's incestuous and disastrous passion for the beautiful and plump Exalted Concubine Yang became one of the most celebrated tragic love stories in all of Chinese literary history. Each detail of their relationship was elaborated on by later poets, dramatists, and novelists. One of the products of this fascination was the *Biography of Concubine Plum* (*Meifei zhuan*), which presents a perfect foil to the Exalted Concubine Yang in the person of Concubine Plum. (Both Yang ["poplar"] and Mei ["plum"] are common Chinese surnames.) While Lady Yang is depicted as a jealous woman who bewitches the emperor with her "barbarian whirling dance," Concubine Plum is regarded as the embodiment of wifely virtues: she is literate, modest, and so utterly loyal in love that, it is suggested, she preferred death to rape. And, of course, Concubine Plum expressed her enduring fidelity to her lord in appropriate verses.

One relatively late source, notorious for its unreliable ascriptions, ascribes the *Biography of Concubine Plum* to the Tang dynasty author Cao Ye (middle of the ninth century). Modern scholarship, however, is unanimous in dating this tale to the Song dynasty. Tang dynasty sources never mention Concubine Plum, and her story reads like a patchwork of themes and motifs from earlier stories and legends about abandoned concubines. Concubine Plum's fictionality has not prevented her, however, from making an appearance in later dramatic and novelistic adaptations of the romance of Emperor Xuanzong and the Exalted Concubine Yang, as well as anthologies of women's poetry.

Concubine Plum's surname was Jiang and she was a native of Putian. Her father Zhongxun had followed the family profession of physician. At the age of nine, she was able to recite the first two sections of the *Book of Odes*. She said to her father: "I may be just a girl, but I hope to model my behavior on the [examples of yielding wifehood] in these poems." Her father was filled with admiration and he called her Caipin.

During the reign period Reopened Beginning [Kaiyuan, 713–741], [the eunuch] Gao Lishi was sent to the area of Min and Yue [in search of women for the Inner Palace].[10] The concubine had by then reached marriageable age, and when Gao saw her youthful beauty, he selected her for induction into the Inner Palace. She subsequently served Emperor Xuanzong, and greatly enjoyed his loving affection. The three palaces of Chang'an [Danei, Daming, and Xingqing] and the two palaces of the Eastern Capital [Danei and Shangyang] had a total population of about forty thousand women, but from the moment the emperor acquired this concubine, he regarded the others as if they were dust and dirt. The women in these palaces also felt that they were not her equal. She was expert in literary composition and compared herself to Xie Daoyun.[11] With her light makeup and elegant gowns her appearance was brighter and more excellent than any brush could paint.

The concubine loved plum blossoms and planted plum trees all along the railings of her residence, which the emperor then named the Plum Pavilion. Whenever the blossoms of the plum trees opened, she would write appreciative poems, and she would even remain lovingly gazing up at the flowers until after midnight, unable to tear herself away. Because of this infatuation, the emperor jokingly called her Concubine Plum.

The concubine wrote the following seven rhapsodies: "The Fragrant Orchid," "The Pear Garden," "The Plum Blossoms," "The Phoenix Flute," "The Glass Cup," "The Pair of Scissors," and "The Gauze Window."

At that time the country had been at peace for many years and there was no fighting anywhere in the world. The emperor was extremely caring and loving toward his brothers; and each day treated them to a festive banquet, with the concubine always in attendance at his side. Once he ordered her to peel an orange and pass it around among the princes. When she came to the Prince of Han, he secretly placed his foot on her slipper. She immediately retired to her residence. The emperor had her summoned repeatedly, but each time she sent the messenger back, saying: "Just now the knot in the string of pearls on my slipper became undone. I will come as soon as they have been restrung." When after a long time [she had still not returned], the emperor himself went to fetch her. With trailing gown she welcomed the emperor and informed him that her whole body was aching and that she was truly unable to return to the banquet. And in the end she did not put in an

---

10. "Min and Yue" refers to China's southeasterly coastal regions. Putian is located in Fujian province.

11. Xie Daoyun (second half of the fourth century) was famous for her literary talents. She is discussed in Chapter 3.

appearance. This shows the extent to which she presumed on the emperor's doting affection.

On a later occasion, when the emperor and the concubine were engaged in a tea-tasting competition, he jokingly said to the princes: "She must be a plum sprite! When I played the jade white flute and she performed the dance of the startled goose, everyone there was overwhelmed by her brilliance. And now she beats me again in tasting tea!" Immediately she replied: "In games that have to do with grasses and plants I may happen to beat Your Majesty, but when it comes to the harmonizing of all within the four seas and preparing the offerings in the sacrificial tripods, Your Majesty has his own canonical norm—how would I be able to compete with you in those matters!" The emperor was greatly pleased [by her answer].

But when Yang Taizhen was inducted into the Inner Palace to serve the emperor, day by day she appropriated more and more of the emperor's love and affection. The emperor had no intention of abandoning Concubine Plum, but the two women were jealous of each other, and kept as much distance between each other as possible. The emperor once compared the two of them to [the two loyal wives of Shun] Nüying and Ehuang, an assessment not shared by others who knew that they were totally dissimilar and secretly laughed at the emperor [for his foolishness]. Yang Taizhen was jealous and cunning, but Concubine Plum was submissive and accommodating, and so lacked the means to beat Lady Yang at her game. Eventually, Lady Yang had her transferred to the eastern Shangyang Palace.

Once, some time later, the emperor started to think about Concubine Plum, and had a young eunuch secretly, with his lamp extinguished, bring her on one of his circus horses to the western Cuihua Pavilion. As they gave expression to their old love, they were overcome by emotion and as a result, the emperor overslept. A frightened attendant reported to him: "Lady Yang is already waiting for you outside the pavilion. What should we do?" The emperor threw on his robes, grabbed Concubine Plum in his arms and hid her between the double curtains. The moment Lady Yang entered, she asked: "Where is that plum sprite?" The emperor replied: "She is at the eastern palace." Lady Yang then said: "Please be so good as to summon her, so today we may bathe in the hot spring bath together." The emperor replied: "The woman has already been discarded. Why would you want to go [to the hot springs] with her?!" When Lady Yang became even more insistent, the emperor looked to his attendants speechlessly for help. The enraged Lady Yang said: "You have had a fine banquet here, and a woman has left her slippers by Your Majesty's bed. With whom did you engage in drunken revelry on this couch last night, such that you are not yet holding audience although the sun has risen? Your Majesty should go out and receive your ministers. I will await your return here in this pavilion." Deeply ashamed, the emperor pulled the bedcovers up, turned his face to the wall, and pretended to sleep, saying: "I am feeling ill today, I cannot hold audience." Lady Yang was furious and returned straightaway to her private quarters. When after a while the emperor looked for Concubine Plum, he found that she had already been escorted out by the young eunuch and ordered to return on foot to the eastern palace. The enraged emperor had him beheaded. He also ordered the slippers and the filigree hair ornaments she had left behind to be bundled up and returned to her. She said to the messenger: "Must the emperor go to this extreme to get rid of me?" The messenger replied: "It is not that the emperor is getting rid of you, it is just that he is really afraid of the foul temper of Lady Yang." Concubine Plum said with a smile: "If he is afraid that by loving me he will provoke the foul temper of that fat bitch, then of course he is getting rid of me."

Hoping to win back the emperor's love, Concubine Plum gave a thousand ounces of gold to Gao Lishi and asked him to locate a poet just like Sima Xiangru who would be able to write her a *Rhapsody of the Long Gate* [*Palace*]. Lishi at the time supported Lady Yang and also feared her power, so he said to her: "There is no one who can write such a rhapsody." And so Concubine Plum wrote a *Rhapsody on the East of My Residence* [*Loudong fu*] herself, which briefly reads:

> The jade mirror is covered with dust,
>   The perfume in the toilette case has evaporated.
> Too listless to artfully comb my cicada locks,
>   Or to put on gold-threaded gowns of light silk,
> Suffering a silent solitude in this fragrant palace,
>   My thoughts converge on the orchid hall.
> Truly, I am the plum blossom about to fall,
>   But hidden behind the long gate, I go unnoticed.
>
>   Moreover,
> The flower-hearts display their grief,
>   The willow-eyes exhibit their sorrow.
> The gentle breezes sough and sigh,
>   The spring birds chirp and wail.
> In my room when dusk descends,
>   I hear the phoenix-pipes and turn around;
> Under dark clouds as evening falls,
>   I intently gaze at the white moon.
> No more visits to the hot springs—
>   I recall our past pleasures in Shicui Hall;
> Forever locked away in Long Gate Palace—

I bemoan the long absence of the imperial carriage.
    I recall
The clear waves of the Taiye Pond,
  A shimmering light flitting on the water,
The music and songs of a festive banquet,
  And me at the side of His Imperial Majesty.
Musicians played marvelous tunes of dancing phoenixes,
  And we rode a fairy boat with painted rocs.[12]
Your love for me was ardent and passionate,
  You fully expressed your burning devotion,
You swore it would last forever like mountain and sea,
  Would be like the sun and moon without end!

    But alas,
That jealous beauty spared no effort,
  The blasts of envy raged uncontrolled:
She robbed me of your love and favor,
  And banished me to this gloomy abode.
Longing for past pleasures, now beyond reach,
  I relive them in stubborn dreams, all misty and vague.
I spend the flowery mornings and moonlit nights
  Too ashamed and listless to face the spring winds.
I had hoped that a Xiangru might present his rhapsody
  But nowadays there are none who possess his skill.
Before I have finished composing my sorrowful lay,
  The ringing of the distant bell resounds.
To no avail I heave a sigh, hiding my face in my sleeve,
  As I pace up and down to the east of my room.

When Lady Yang heard about this, she complained to Emperor Xuanzong: "That Concubine Jiang is too vulgar and common! Now she voices her resentment in these pathetic words! May You most graciously allow her to die!" But the emperor remained silent . . .

Once, when the emperor was at the Flower Bud Tower and was visited by some barbarian envoys, he ordered ten pecks of the pearls [they had offered in tribute] bundled up and secretly sent to Concubine Plum. She refused them, and

---

12. The roc or *peng* is a mythical bird mentioned in the opening chapter of the *Zhuangzi*, where it is described as being so large that its wings darken Heaven when it soars up into the sky.

handed the messenger a poem, ordering him to present it to His Majesty. The poem read:

> My willow-leaf brows I've long left unpainted,
> Rouge mixed with tears has dyed my silks red.
> The Long Gate Palace is not a place for dressing up:
> What need have I of precious pearls to allay my grief!

When the emperor read this poem, he felt desolate and overcome by sadness. He ordered the Music Bureau to put it to music using a new tune to which was given the title of "Ten Pecks of Pearls." This is how this tune got its name.

Later, after An Lushan occupied the capital and the emperor fled to Sichuan, Lady Yang met her death. When the emperor returned to the capital, he searched for Concubine Plum, but she was nowhere to be found. In his distress, and believing that she might have drifted off somewhere else after the fighting, the emperor issued an edict, stating that the person who located her would be rewarded with an office of the second rank and a monetary award of one million copper coins. But despite the most extensive search, her whereabouts remained a mystery. The emperor also ordered a shaman to release his spirit and, riding his vital energy, make a secret search of both heaven and earth. He too was unable to find her.

When a eunuch presented a painted portrait of Concubine Plum to the emperor, he noted that the likeness was perfect, the only difference being that it was not alive. On the portrait was inscribed the following poem:

> When long ago this concubine lived in these Purple Halls,
> She had no need for rouge and powder to enhance her looks.
> This white silk may have captured her as she was then,
> Except that her dancing eyes do not follow where you go.

Upon reading this, the emperor dissolved in tears, and he ordered the portrait copied and then carved in stone.

Later, as the emperor lay dozing on a hot summer day, he seemed to vaguely see Concubine Plum crying behind the bamboo. Holding back her tears and hiding her face in her sleeve, she resembled a flower bathed by misty dew. She said: "When not too long ago Your Majesty endured the dust of the road, I was killed by mutinous troops. Some people took pity on me and buried my bones by the side of a plum tree to the east of the pond." The startled emperor woke up in a sweat, and immediately ordered [his servants] to go to the Taiye Pond and dig her up.

They did not find her body, and the emperor grew even more disconsolate. Suddenly he remembered that by the side of the hot springs pond, there were more than ten plum trees—could that be the place? The emperor went out there himself, and ordered the body to be dug up. After digging around a few of the trees, they found the corpse. It had been wrapped in a brocade coverlet, placed in a wine vat, and then covered up with more than three feet of earth. The emperor was greatly moved, and none of his entourage could bear to look up. When they inspected her wounds, they found she had been stabbed in the side by a sword.

The emperor himself composed a dirge to lament her, and had her reburied with the full rites befitting an imperial concubine.

At this point, the *Biography of Lady Plum* embarks on an evaluation of Emperor Xuanzong, who had begun his career by ridding the court of Empress Wei, and ended it by himself falling into the snares of yet another manipulative woman. The author then draws attention to the biography itself, arguing that the most interesting texts often only become public after a considerable lapse of time, a fact that should not be used as an argument against their authenticity. Finally, the anonymous author even explains why there is no mention of Concubine Plum in any earlier works:

On those prints of recent times that depict a beauty holding a sprig of plum blossoms, she is called "Concubine Plum" and it is usually said that she was "a person of the time of Emperor Xuanzong," although her origin is unknown. Now, Lady Yang is blamed for Emperor Xuanzong's loss of his state, and that is why poets love to write about her story. But Concubine Plum was only a lesser concubine of exceptional beauty, so it is perfectly understandable why the one became famous and the other not at all.

I acquired this biography at the house of "Ten Thousand Scrolls" Zhu Zundu. It had been copied in the Seventh Month of the second year of the reign period Great Center [Dazhong, 847–859], and the calligraphy was charming and fine, although the wording was occasionally somewhat vulgar. Afraid that history might overlook her tale, I have slightly improved on the style but, fearful of distorting the facts, I have adhered closely to the original wording.

Other Phantoms

It was not only abandoned palace ladies who became the authors of a growing posthumous oeuvre, other famous women did as well. Well-known examples are Zhuo Wenjun, Cai Yan, and Su Hui. Nor was this phenomenon limited to women; some famous men were also credited with a body of work they could not possibly have written. In a discussion of the lives and works of writing women one could choose to pass over these phantom authors. In traditional China, however, these posthumous poems were generally accepted as the genuine and heartfelt compositions of these women, despite an occasional doubting voice. As such, they are integral to the tradition of women's literature as it was later constructed through anthologies and critical writings.

The Eloping Widow: Zhuo Wenjun

The moment the rich young widow Zhuo Wenjun eloped with the brilliant but poor poet Sima Xiangru, she became the heroine of one of the most popular Chinese love stories of all time. Sima Xiangru was a native of Chengdu, today the capital of the southwestern province of Sichuan. He had first tried his luck at the court of Emperor Jingdi (r. 156–141 BCE), but when he discovered that the emperor was more interested in hounds and falcons than *belles lettres*, he left the capital to join the court of the Prince of Liang at what is today Kaifeng in the province of Henan. Although the Prince of Liang loved literature and appreciated Sima Xiangru's talents, unfortunately he passed away not long after the poet's arrival. Sima Xiangru's biography in the *Records of the Historian* tells us what happened next:

When the Filial Prince of Liang died, Xiangru returned to his hometown, but was too poor to make ends meet. He had always been friends with Wang Ji, the magistrate of Linqiong. Ji said to him: "You should come and visit me now that you have traveled so much in the hopes of making a career but without success." So Xiangru went to visit him and was housed in the magistrate's office. The magistrate put on a show of treating him with great regard and esteem, going each day to pay his respects to Xiangru. In the beginning Xiangru received him, but later he would pretend to be ill and get a servant to send Ji away. This only resulted in the magistrate treating him with even greater deference.

In Linqiong there were many rich men. Zhuo Wangsun owned eight hundred slaves and Cheng Zheng also owned a few hundred. These two men said to each other: "The magistrate is entertaining an important guest. Why don't the two of us invite him over." The two of them summoned the magistrate, and by the time he arrived, the Zhuo family had laid out a feast for more than a hundred guests. At noon, they invited Sima Xiangru but he excused himself, claiming that he was ill and could not come. But since the magistrate did not dare start eating without him, he went in person to fetch him. This left Xiangru with no choice but to go along. All those present were filled with admiration [when they saw him]. When everyone was merry with drink, the magistrate of Linqiong came forward and gave a performance on the zither. Then he said to Xiangru: "I have been told that you are also fond of playing. If you don't mind, please play us a tune." Xiangru at first refused politely, but then played one or two pieces.

Now Zhuo Wangsun had a daughter, Wenjun, who had been recently widowed and who loved music. In fact it was because Xiangru wanted to seduce her with his zither performance that he and the magistrate had staged this charade. When Xiangru came to Linqiong, he was accompanied by an entourage of mounted horsemen; courteous and gracious, he was extremely sophisticated. When he joined the party at Zhuo's place and played the zither, Wenjun secretly spied on him from behind a door and fell deeply in love with him, fearing only that he would get away from her. After the gathering was over, Xiangru had someone bribe Wenjun's servant with large gifts so that she would communicate his devotion to her mistress. That very night Wenjun eloped with Xiangru, and together they hastily fled to Chengdu.

The house they lived in consisted of nothing but four bare walls. Zhuo Wangsun was enraged and said: "My daughter is really useless! I cannot bring myself to kill her but I will not give her a cent!" Whenever people would happen to mention her name to Wangsun, he would refuse to listen. After a while Wenjun started to feel unhappy and said to Xiangru: "We'd better go to Linqiong and borrow some money from my brothers so that we can get by. Why should we impose such suffering on ourselves?" Xiangru returned with her to Linqiong, where he sold all of his carriages and horses in order to buy a wine shop. They then opened for business and he had Wenjun tend the bar. He himself, wearing only his undershorts, would go together with the servants to wash the cups and dishes in the marketplace. When Zhuo Wangsun heard about this, he was so ashamed that he barred his gate and refused to go out.

Wangsun's brothers and the other gentlemen all said to him: "You have only one son and two daughters—it's not money you are short of. Now Wenjun has lost her chastity to Sima Xiangru. He, for good reason, is tired of traveling around. He may be poor, but his talent is undeniable. Yet you let them wander about. What is the purpose of dishonoring them like that?" So Zhuo Wangsun ended up giving Wenjun a hundred slaves and a million copper coins as her share of his fortune, as well as all the clothes, blankets, and other valuables from her wedding trousseau. Wenjun then returned with Xiangru to Chengdu, where they bought a house and fields and became rich.

And so the story ends happily. In the meantime, Sima Xiangru's extravagant rhapsodies had attracted the attention of Emperor Wu (r. 140–87 BCE), who summoned him to court and showered him with honors. In later centuries Zhuo Wenjun became the exemplar of the smart young woman who discerns the true potential of the brilliant but poor student, attaches herself to him despite all parental opposition, loyally supports him through all his adversities, and eventually shares in his inevitable glory.

If emperors can be fickle, so can poets. During the final years of his life Sima Xiangru served as intendant at the grave of Emperor Wen (r. 179–157 BCE). An anecdote recorded in the *Various Notes on the Western Capital*, a collection of legends and notes about the Western Han dynasty compiled in the fourth or fifth century, informs us that the old poet was at that time preparing to take a concubine, but was dissuaded from doing so by a poem written by Zhuo Wenjun entitled "White Hair Lament" (*Baitou yin*). The *Various Notes on the Western Capital* does not include the text of this poem. Although there is a poem entitled "White Hair Lament" in the "Treatise on Music" in the *Books of the Song* (*Songshu*), compiled by the statesman and poet Shen Yue (441–513), it is, however, presented as an anonymous song. Another, shorter "White Hair Lament" can be found among a group of six anonymous songs in the *New Songs from a Jade Terrace*, an anthology of poems on women and love, compiled around 540. It is this shorter version of "White Hair Lament" that has traditionally been attributed to Zhuo Wenjun:

> As brilliant as the snow on yonder mountain,
> As splendid as the moon amidst the clouds—
> I have been told that you now love another,
> And so I've come to say goodbye forever.
>
> Today we meet over a pint of wine,
> Tomorrow morning we'll meet at the Canal.
> And as we tarry by the Emperor's Canal,
> The water flows both east and west.
>
> How sad and lonely, oh, how sad and lonely!
> When one gets married, there's no need to cry:
> Just hope to find a man who'll always love you,
> And will not leave you when your hair turns white.

The fishing pole—how pliantly it bends!
The fish he's caught—how lustrous its tail!
What's precious in a man is his character,
What need is there for money and wealth?

The angler and the fish at the end of his line is an old image for the lover and the beloved. The images of the brilliant snow and splendid moon in the first two lines of this poem have given rise to a host of different interpretations. They have been regarded variously as symbols of the splendid love of former days; the pure virtue of the wife about to be deserted; the inconstancy of the husband's love; the blatancy of the husband's betrayal; and, last but not least, the white hair of the aging wife.

Even though there is nothing in this poem to link it specifically to Zhuo Wenjun, it can still be read as the lament of an abandoned wife or courtesan. The anonymous longer and earlier version in the *Books of the Song* of "White Hair Lament" may at best be interpreted as a parting song in its most general sense:

As brilliant as the snow on yonder mountain,
As splendid as the moon amidst the clouds—
I have been told that you now love another,
And so I've come to say goodbye forever.

All our lives we've lived in the same city,
But have never met over a pint of wine.
Today we meet over a pint of wine,
Tomorrow morning we'll meet at the Canal.
And as we tarry by the Emperor's Canal,
The water it flows both east and west.

East of the town there lives a woodcutter,
West of the town there lives a woodcutter.
Each one of us pushes the other forward,
We have no kith or kin—why put on airs!

How sad and lonely, oh, how sad and lonely!
When one gets married, there's no need to cry:
Just hope to find a man who'll always love you
And will not leave you when your hair turns white.

The fishing pole—how pliantly it bends!
The fish he's caught—how lustrous its tail!
A man should be an understanding friend,
What need is there for money and wealth?

Loudly chomping, all of the horses graze,
As by the river lofty men enjoy themselves.
Let us today take pleasure in each other,
I wish you all another ten thousand years!

Yet another anecdote in the *Various Notes on the Western Capital* credits Zhuo Wenjun with the composition of an elegy for her deceased husband, but no such text has been preserved. And while the *Records of the Historian* only has Sima Xiangru playing the zither and does not mention him singing any songs (Xiangru was said to have stuttered), the *New Songs from a Jade Terrace* includes the text of two songs he is said to have sung in the hopes of seducing the impressionable young widow.

Abducted and Ransomed: Cai Yan

Like Zhuo Wenjun, Cai Yan was widowed at an early age, but instead of eloping with another man, she was abducted by barbarians, ransomed twelve years later, and then married again to a husband who was subsequently condemned to death.

Cai Yan (Wenji) was the daughter of Cai Yong (132–192), a famous scholar, statesman, bibliophile, and musician. Cai Yong had quickly advanced through the ranks of the bureaucracy during the period when the military dictator Dong Zhuo dominated the court. Hoping to solidify his power, Dong Zhuo moved the emperor and his administration from Luoyang to Chang'an, but eventually lost out against a coalition of regional generals. When Dong Zhuo was killed in 192, Cai Yong also lost his life. During the civil wars that followed the fall of Dong Zhuo, Cai Yan, whose husband had died shortly after their marriage, was abducted by armies of the Southern Xiongnu. The Southern Xiongnu had originally lived in what is now Inner Mongolia, but in the course of the first century CE the emperors of the Eastern Han dynasty had relocated them to what is today the province of Shanxi, where they lived alongside Chinese communities. The abducted Cai Yan became the wife of the Second

Commander of the Southern Xiongnu, who had settled in the southern part of the province, and she bore him two sons. After twelve years, she was finally ransomed by Cao Cao (155–220), the new military dictator of Northern China and an old friend of her father's. After she returned to the capital, Cao Cao married her off to Dong Si. Already her eventful life had become the subject of works by contemporary poets.

The fact that Cai Yan did not commit suicide when she was abducted but rather remarried not once but twice would earn her much censure in later ages, when opinions on the remarriage of widows and the chastity of women had become more rigid because of the growing influence of neo-Confucianism. But she earned her place in the chapter on "Exemplary Women" of the *Books of the Later Han* for successfully defending her third husband, Dong Si, when he was condemned to death by the all-powerful Cao Cao:

The wife of Dong Si of Chenliu was a daughter of Cai Yong, also from Chenliu. Her personal name was Yan, and her style name was Wenji. She was erudite, talented, and eloquent and also had a marvelous understanding of musical matters. She married a certain Wei Hongdao from Hedong, but when her husband died before she had borne him a son, she returned to her parental home.

During the reign period Established Peace [Xingping, 194–195], the entire world was in turmoil. Cai Yan was abducted by barbarian horsemen and appropriated by the Second Commander of the Southern Xiongnu. She lived among the barbarians for twelve years and bore the Second Commander two sons. Cao Cao had been a good friend of Cai Yong's and was grieved by the fact that Cai did not have any heirs. For this reason, he had a messenger ransom Cai Yan for gold and jade and married her off once again, this time to Dong Si.

When Dong Si, while serving as commander-in-chief for the military colonies, committed a crime for which he was condemned to die, Cai Yan went to see Cao Cao and beg for his life. At that time the hall was filled with eminent ministers and famous gentlemen, together with envoys and interpreters from faraway lands. Cao Cao said to his guests: "Cai Yong's daughter is waiting outside. I will see her for your sakes." When Cai Yan entered, her hair was disheveled and she was not wearing any shoes, but when she kowtowed and begged for mercy, her words were clear and persuasive. What she had to say was extremely sad and moving, and everyone there was deeply affected. Cao Cao said: "I really pity you, but the documents [ordering Dong's execution] have already been issued, so what can I do?" Cai Yan then said: "You, Sir, have in your stables ten thousand horses, and your tiger-like troops form a forest. So why do you begrudge me a single swift courier and refuse to save a life on the brink of death?" Moved by her words, Cao Cao then revoked Dong Si's original sentence.

As it was cold at the time, Cao Cao gave Cai Yan a kerchief for her head as well as slippers and socks. He also used the occasion to ask: "Lady, I have heard that your home used to be rich in books and documents. Can you still remember them?" Cai Yan replied: "My late father left me more than four thousand scrolls, but they were all scattered during the war and now we have nothing left. What I can remember and recite are only some four hundred pieces." Cao Cao then said: "I will have ten clerks copy those out as you recite them." But Cai Yan replied: "The separation of men and women, I have learned, is so strict that, according to the *Rites*, men and women are not allowed to hand objects to each other directly. Please provide me with paper and brushes, and tell me whether the copies should be written in standard or cursive script." She then prepared clean copies of the texts, all without a single error!

Later, moved and grieving over her war experiences, she recalled her sadness and resentment in two poems. The first of these reads as follows:

> At the end of the Han, the court lost its power
> And Dong Zhuo upset the natural order.[13]
> As his ambition was to kill the emperor,
> He first did away with the wise and good.
> Asserting his force, he moved the old capital
> And controlled his lord to strengthen himself.
> All through the world loyal troops arose
> And together vowed to quell this disaster.
> When Dong Zhuo's troops descended on the east,
> Their golden armor glistened in the sun.
> The people of the plain were weak and timid,
> The troops that came were ferocious barbarians!
> They plundered the fields, surrounded the cities,
> And wherever they went, conquered and destroyed.
>
> They killed and slaughtered, spared not a soul,
> Bodies and corpses propped up one against the other.
> From the flanks of their horses they hung men's heads,

---

13. Dong Zhuo (d. 192) was one of the most powerful generals of his time. His regional power basis was Shaanxi. After his troops had plundered the capital Luoyang, he moved the court to Chang'an, where he was murdered by his underling Lü Bu. After this the emperor fled back to Luoyang.

And behind them on their horses they sat the women.
 In this way they sped through Hangu Pass,[14]
On a westward journey so perilous and far!
Looking back I only saw a distant haze,
And my innards turned to rotten pulp.
 The people they abducted were in the thousands,
But we were not allowed to stay together.
At times flesh-and-blood relatives were together,
Who would have liked to talk but did not dare.
 If you displeased them even in the slightest way,
They'd shout right out: "You dirty slaves,
We really should just kill you off,
Why should we even let you live!"

How could I still have clung to life and fate?
Their swearing and cursing was too much to bear.
At other times we were whipped and beaten,
All the bitter pains rained down on us at once.
 At dawn we set out, weeping and crying,
At night we sat down, sadly moaning.
One longed to die, but that was not allowed,
One longed to live but that too could not be.
 Blue heaven up above, what was our sin
That we should suffer this great calamity?

The border wilds are different from China,
And their people's customs lack propriety.
The places where they live are full of snow,
And the Hun winds rise in summer and spring,
 Tugging at my robes in all directions,
And filling my ears with their wailing sounds.
Moved by the seasons, I recalled my parents,
And my sad laments went on without end.
 Whenever guests would arrive from afar,
That news would always give me great joy.
But when I sought them out for tidings,

---

14. Hangu Pass dominates the narrow passage south of the Yellow River from Henan province into Shaanxi province.

They would never turn out to be from my home.
　Then out of the blue my constant wish was granted,
As relatives showed up to take me home.
So finally I was able to make my escape,
But at the cost of abandoning my sons!

A bond of nature ties them to my heart,
Once separated there could be no reunion.
In life or death: forced forever apart.
I could not bear to bid them farewell!
　My sons flung their arms around my neck,
Asking: "Mother, where are you going?
The people are saying that our mother has to leave,
And that you will never come back to us.
　O mother, you were always so kind and caring,
How come you are now so cold and cruel?
We still are children, not grown-up men,
Can it really be you do not care?"
　When I saw this, my heart broke into pieces,
And I felt as if I'd lost my mind, gone mad!
I wept and cried and stroked them with my hands,
And as I was about to depart, was filled with doubt.

The people who had been abducted with me,
Came to see me off and say goodbye.
Jealous that I alone could go home,
Their sad laments ripped me apart.
　Because of this the horses did not move,
Because of this the wheels refused to turn.
All those who watched heaved heavy sighs
And we travelers choked back our sobs.

Going and going I deadened my feelings,
The journey took us day by day further away.
And so, on and on, the full three thousand miles:
When would I ever meet with them again?
　Memories of the children born from my womb
Completely tore me to pieces inside.
Arriving home, I found I had no family,

No relatives of any kind remained!
 The city had become a mountain forest,
The courtyard was overgrown by thorns
And white bones, god knows of whom,
Lay scattered around in the open field.
 Outside the gate no sound of human voices:
Just the yelps and howls of jackals and wolves.
 Lonely I faced my solitary shadow,
As I cried out in anguish, my heart was shattered.
 I climbed to a high spot, and gazed into the distance,
And my soul and spirit seemed to fly away.
 It was as if my life was over and done,
And those around me had to comfort me.
 Because of them I forced myself to live,
But even so, on whom could I rely?
To my new husband I entrust my fate,
I do my best to make an earnest effort.
 A victim of the wars, I lost my honor,
And always fear that I will be discarded.
How many years are in a human life?
This pain will haunt me till my dying day!

The second text reads:

How poor my fate, alas, to meet such dismal times!
 My relatives were massacred and I alone survived.
I was captured and abducted to beyond the western pass,
 The journey perilous and long to that barbarian land.
Mountains and valleys stretched endlessly, the road went on and on,
 Lovingly I looked back east and heaved a heavy sigh.
At night when I should have slept, I could not find rest,
 When hungry I should have eaten, but could not swallow a thing.
Constantly awash in tears, my eyes were never dry.
 Weak in resolve, alas, I was afraid to die,
 And though I clung to life, I was dishonored and abased!

Now those regions, alas, are far from the essence of yang,
 As yin's breath congeals, snow falls even in summer.
The desert is darkened, alas, by clouds of dust,
 And its grasses and trees do not flower in spring.

The people like beasts feed on rancid flesh,
  Their speech is gibberish, their faces unsightly.
At the end of the year as the seasons pass by,
  The nights stretch endlessly behind the locked gates.
Unable to sleep in my tent, I would get up,
  Ascend the barbarian hall, look out over the wide courtyard.
Dark clouds would gather, obscuring moon and stars,
  And the piercing north wind would coldly howl.
At the sound of the barbarian reed pipe, the horses whinnied,
  And a lone goose returned, honking forlornly.
The musicians arose and plucked their zithers,
  Their notes harmonized so sadly and clear.
My heart spewed out its longings, my breast filled with rage—
  How I longed to let it all out, but I feared to give offense,
  And as I suppressed my sad sobs, my tears soaked my collar.

As my relatives had come to fetch me, I had to go home,
  But setting out on this journey meant abandoning my children.
My sons cried "Mother!" till their voices grew hoarse,
  I covered my ears as I could not bear to listen.
Running they tried to cling to me, so alone and forlorn,
  They stumbled, got up again, their faces all bleeding!
Looking back at them, I felt utterly shattered,
  My heart stunned, I fainted but did not die.

The vivid first-person accounts of the sufferings of war in these poems are extremely rare in traditional Chinese poetry. Even rarer are such narratives written from a woman's perspective. Honest descriptions of the pains suffered by a mother who is forced to leave her children behind (in traditional China, children belonged to the family of the father) are also quite unusual. But this does not mean that these poems were necessarily written by Cai Yan, or even by a woman poet. In fact, over the centuries many scholars have voiced their doubts as to the authorship of these poems. While their inclusion in Cai Yan's biography in the *Books of the Later Han* would seem to argue for their authenticity, we have to keep in mind that this dynastic history was compiled more than two centuries after the fall of the Later Han. The strongest argument against Cai Yan's authorship are the descriptions of Xiongnu life, which do not reflect the sinified lifestyle of the Southern Xiongnu during that time in southern Shanxi, but rather are stereotypical generic descriptions of barbarian life on the steppes to the north of China. It is also quite curious that none of the many literary critics from the third to the sixth century ever refer to Cai Yan as a poet. After carefully weighing the various arguments for and against the authenticity of these two poems, Hans H. Frankel concludes that the two poems could not have been written by Cai Yan, but probably were composed by two different authors, perhaps within one or two generations of her lifetime.

Frankel links the appearance of these poems and comparable works to a wider tradition of impersonation:

There was a literary development in the Han and post-Han period which was not completely understood in its own time—and even in modern times. It was a kind of impersonation or dramatic monologue. Poems and prose pieces were written in the first-person form, comparable to the first-person fiction of the Western or Japanese traditions, but distinct insofar as the Chinese stories neither told their own story nor created a fictitious personality. Rather, they took a person from history (or sometimes from among their contemporaries), identified with that person, and spoke from his or her point of view.

Frankel points out that many of the persons who speak in these letters and poems share a common fate with Cai Yan, "namely, an involuntary stay among barbarians. Contact with an alien culture is a powerful literary theme. It offers numerous possibilities, since it involves a mixture of adventurous curiosity, uneasy hostility, depressive homesickness, and a keen awareness of one's cultural and personal identity." One example of such poems, by a named male author, is the following poem by Shi Chong (249–300), in which he assumes the persona of Wang Zhaojun:

The Song of Wang Mingjun, with Preface

Wang Mingjun was originally called Wang Zhaojun, but her name was changed because it violated the taboo against using the personal name of Emperor Wen.

When the Xiongnu were at the height of their power, they requested a bride from the Han. Emperor Yuan gave them Mingjun, a girl in the Inner Palace who was from a good family. When once before a princess had been married off to the Wusun, an order was issued that lutes be played as she traveled on horseback in order to still her longings for home during the long journey. When Mingjun was sent off, much the same thing must have been the case. When the new melody was composed, it must have been replete with notes of lament and resentment. And so I record it on paper.

> Originally born to a family of the Han,
> About to depart for the Xiongnu court:
> Even before the parting words had been spoken,
> The escorts on horseback raised their banners.
> Grooms and servants dissolved into tears,
> The carriage horses whinnied sadly for me.
> Overcome by grief, my innards felt wounded,
> The tears I shed dampened the red hat-strings.
> Going on and on: every day took us further,
> Until I arrived at the town of the Xiongnu:
> They invited me inside their round yurt of felt,
> Gave me the title of *Yanzhi* as wife of the khan.
> A different race—I don't feel at home here,
> I may be a queen—but it's not what I wanted.
> Abused and raped by both father and son:
> Full of shame in their presence, and scared.
> To kill oneself is not an easy thing to do,
> So I silently suffer, and continue clinging to life.
> But what is the point of clinging to life?
> Overcome by emotion, I'm filled with disgust.
> Could I but borrow the wings of a goose,
> And leave this place here far behind!
> But the goose flies by without looking back,
> While I remain and wait, not daring to breathe.
> In former days I was a precious jade in a box,
> But now I'm a flower on a pile of dung:
> To be a morning flower is no cause for joy,
> I'd be happy to join the autumn grasses.
> I leave this message to all later generations:
> Marriage to a distant stranger is hard to bear.

The discussion on the authenticity of the two poems ascribed to Cai Yan in her biography is further complicated by the existence of a third poem, "Eighteen Stanzas for the Barbarian Reed Pipe," which is also said to have been written by Cai Yan and provides yet another first-person account of her experiences. This poem consists of eighteen stanzas of six to twelve lines, which in the tradition of Chinese lyrical poetry is exceptionally long. Although the lines within each stanza are of different length, they all rhyme (usually only the even lines carry the rhyme). The earliest appearance of this poem is in the section entitled "Songs for the Zither," in the *Collection of Music Bureau Poems* (*Yuefu shiji*) compiled in the twelfth century by Guo Maoqian in which it appears together with a poem of the same title by Liu Shang (late eighth century). According to Guo, the poem attributed to Cai Yan is the original poem, and that of Liu Shang, the imitation. Liu's poem, however, also provides a first-person narrative of Cai Yan's adventures and must have been very popular in the ninth and tenth centuries, as numerous copies of it were found among the Dunhuang manuscripts. This suggests the possibility that the poem attributed to Cai Yan translated below may actually have been the imitation, and Liu Shang's poem the original!

I

At my birth, the world was still at peace,
  After my birth, the fortunes of the Han declined.
Heaven in its heartlessness sent down disaster,
  Earth in its heartlessness made me suffer these times.
Weapons of war, day after day: all the roads unsafe,
  Everyone fled for their lives, lamenting in anguish.
Clouds of dust darkened the fields: the barbarians thrived,
  My resolve was defeated, my honor was lost!
The times brought new customs, not to my liking,
  I was brutally dishonored, but to whom could I complain?
An air on the reed pipe, a tune on the zither—
  Full of resentment about which no one knows!

II

A barbarian forced me to become his wife
And took me with him to the end of the earth.
Range upon range of misty mountains: how far the way home!
Over a thousand miles raging storms raised clouds of dust.
  The people there as fierce and cruel as snakes and vipers—
Stringing their bows and clad in armor: haughty and ruthless!

Twice I've plucked the taut strings, strings about to snap—
My resolve broken, my heart shattered: I heave a sad sigh!

III

Having crossed China's border, I entered the barbarians' land,
A refugee who had been raped: it would have been better to die!
A skirt of felt and fur: my relatives would be frightened by the sight,
Meals of rancid mutton that to me was completely revolting.
The horse drums sounded all night until dawn,
The steppe storms howled, darkening the border camps.
Pained by the present, moved by the past: my third tune is finished,
Nursing my sadness, hoarding my grief: when will I find peace?

IV

There was not a day or night when I didn't long for my homeland,
Of all beings living and breathing no one has suffered more than I!
Natural disasters and civil wars: the people left without a ruler,
But my fate was the worst of all: to be captured by barbarians!
Different customs, strange hearts: impossible to live with!
Their lust and desires unlike ours: with whom could I talk?
I recall how I endured those many hardships and dangers—
This fourth tune is finished, adding to my bitter distress.

V

When the geese flew south, I longed to entrust them with a word from
    the steppe,
When the geese flew north, I hoped to obtain from them some news
    from the Han.[15]
When the geese flew up so high that I could not make them out anymore,
To no avail my heart would break, silently filled with longing for home.
With furrowed brow I face the moon and pluck this fine zither,
This fifth tune is chilly and cold, and only deepens my despair.

---

15. Migrating geese were thought to be messengers delivering letters to loved ones far away. When Su Wu (d. 60 BCE), a Chinese emissary to the Xiongnu, was held captive by his hosts and not allowed to return home, he is said to have tied a letter to a foot of a migrating goose. When the bird was shot down in China, the emperor learned of his whereabouts, and then pressured the Xiongnu to allow Su Wu to return to China.

VI

Shivering in the ice and frost I suffered bitter cold,
Although hungry, I could not eat the offered raw meat and koumiss.[16]
At night, I heard the river Long, like sounds of choked sighs,
At dawn, I saw the Great Wall and the road, winding away.
 I think back on those days gone by and the difficult journey—
This sixth tune makes me so sad, I'd rather not play anymore!

VII

When evening fell, the winds wailed, steppe sounds rose all around,
No one knew of my sorrows, to whom could I tell them?
The vast plain lay desolate: beacon fires for thousands of miles!
The barbarians despise the old and weak, praise the young and sturdy.
 Following water and pasture, they settle down, put up their tents,
Their cattle and sheep fill the fields in droves like bees or ants.
 Then, when grass and water are gone, sheep and horses all move on—
This seventh tune runs over with disgust: how I hated to live there!

VIII

If Heaven has eyes, why didn't it see that I was alone and adrift?
If gods have power, why did they send me to live at the ends of earth and
  sky?
I never betrayed Heaven, so why did it yoke me to an unsuitable partner?
I never offended the gods, so why did they kill me in barren distant lands?
 I composed this eighth tune as if I were a common performer,
But who understands how its completion deepens my sorrow even more?

IX

The sky has no end and the earth has no border:
The sorrows in my heart are as endless as they.
Man's life lasts but a moment: a white colt passing by a crack,
But I spent the prime of my life deprived of joy.
 Filled with resentment I wanted to ask Heaven why:
But I had no connection with that blue expanse of sky.
 Raising my head and gazing upwards: clouds and mist!
This ninth tune is filled with feeling, but in whom can I confide?

---

16. Koumiss is an alcoholic beverage made of fermented mare's milk.

X

The beacon fires atop the Wall never stopped burning,
When would the fighting in those border regions ever end?
The breath of death swept again through the gates each morning,
Below the frontier moon the steppe storms howled each night.
 Cut off from my hometown without any news,
I wept until hoarse and choked on my grief.
 My whole life was hardship because of that separation—
At this tenth tune my sadness deepens and my tears turn to blood.

XI

It is not that I was greedy for life and hated to die,
There was a reason I could not leave this life behind:
I hoped to live to return to my ancestral home,
So that my bones might be buried there when I died.
 The days and months passed in my barbarian yurt,
The chieftain doted on me and I bore him two sons.
I suckled them, I nursed them: I am not ashamed,
I loved and cherished them as they grew up in that distant land.
 It was this that gave rise to this eleventh tune,
Its mournful sound lingers, piercing heart and marrow.

XII

When the east wind responded to its pitch pipe, a warm aura unfurled:[17]
I knew the Han's Son of Heaven was extending His invigorating
     harmony.
The barbarians danced about and sang their songs,
The two states made peace and put an end to the fighting.
 Suddenly an envoy of the Han claiming an official command,
Came and ransomed my body for a thousand ounces of gold.
Joyful at the thought of returning alive and meeting a sagely ruler,
Yet I sighed over the two children I had to leave and never see again.
 This twelfth tune is a mournful melody throughout:
Who can give full expression to such conflicting feelings!

---

17. Traditional Chinese cosmology aligned each season with its own musical note.

XIII

Ignoring the fact that I was being allowed to return home,
I embraced my barbarian children and tears soaked my gown.
The envoy of the Han came to fetch me, "four stallions racing,"
I wailed until my voice was gone, but who could understand?
 At that moment I had received a gift of both life and death:
Out of sorrow for my two sons, the sun lost its brightness.
Where can I find feathers and wings to take you back with me?
Each step took me farther away: my feet were unwilling to move,
My soul dissolved as their forms faded: my loved ones abandoned!
 This thirteenth tune: on anxious strings an air so sad,
A gut-wrenching experience that no one understands!

XIV

My body returned home but my sons could not follow,
My anxious thoughts are like a gnawing hunger.
The myriad beings through the four seasons all thrive and decline,
My sorrow and suffering alone do not give an inch.
 The mountains so high and the earth so wide: never will I see you again,
During the darkest watch of the night I dream that you have come.
In my dream we hold hands, filled with both joy and sorrow,
But as soon as I awake the anguish in my heart knows no end.
 This fourteenth tune: my tears stream down—
Like the waters of the River flowing east is my longing!

XV

This fifteenth tune: its rhythm so rapid—
Rage fills my breast, but who's there to know?
 I lived in a tent as the mate of a man not of my kind:
How I wished to go home—and Heaven granted my wish.
I came back here to China, enough reason for joy,
But my heart still remembers, my sorrow still grows.
 Sun and moon are impartial, yet they never shone on me:
Unbearable the memory of being separated from my sons!

We share the same sky but are as far apart as Shang and Shen,[18]
Dead or alive? No way of knowing, nowhere to inquire.

XVI

This sixteenth tune: limitless longing—
My sons and I each in a different land.
 The sun in the east still sees the moon in the west,
But we cannot be together, oh, how it breaks my heart.
I gaze at the "forget-your-pain" flower[19] but my pain is not eased,
I pluck the zither but how it wounds my heart!
 Now I left my sons and returned to my home,
An old grief has gone, but a new grief has been born.
Weeping tears of blood, I look up and lay my plaint before Heaven:
Why was I alone born to meet with such disaster?

XVII

This seventeenth tune: I can't keep from crying—
Mountains and passes, the road perilous, the journey hard!
 When I left I felt homesick but was clear in my mind,
Now I return without my children, my longing has no end—
On the border brown weeds with dried stems and withered leaves,
On the battlefields white bones scarred by swords, pierced by arrows.
 Shivering in the freezing storms of both summer and spring,
Men and horses go hungry and stumble along, all their strength gone.
Beyond my wildest dream was this return to Chang'an,
I moan and sigh and long for death, my face awash in tears.

XVIII

The barbarian reed pipe comes from the barbarian regions,
Its melody is still the same but now adapted for the zither.
 This eighteenth tune: the song may now be finished,
But its echo lingers and its mood is without end.
Thus one knows music's marvelous subtlety is the work of Creation,
Sadness and joy each follow the heart of man through all its changes.
 Barbarian and Chinese: different regions, different ways,

---

18. Shang and Shen are two constellations that never appear in the sky at the same time.

19. "Forget-your-pain" is another name for the yellow lily.

The abyss between heaven and earth: sons in the west, mother in the east.
The grief it has caused me is so vast it fills the sky:
Even the immensity of the cosmos is too small a container!

Over the last one thousand years, the ascription of the "Eighteen Stanzas for the Barbarian Reed Pipe" to Cai Yan has been passionately defended by both traditional and modern admirers, for whom quality and authenticity often seem to be synonymous. If one rejects the authenticity of the first two poems, however, there are even less grounds for accepting the authenticity of this third poem. The first scholar to express his doubts in this regard was none other than the formidable eleventh-century statesman and poet Su Shi (1037–1101).

But once the version of the "Eighteen Stanzas for the Barbarian Reed Pipe" ascribed to Cai Yan had entered into general circulation, it became extremely popular and served as inspiration to numerous poets and painters. The influential critic Yan Yu (ca. 1200) praised the poem for being "a flawless and perfect composition, without any scar or trace [of craftsmanship], as if it had flown directly from the guts of Cai Yan."

Palindromes: Su Hui

Classical Chinese is the perfect language for palindromes, since the overwhelming majority of its words consist of a single syllable, and declensions and conjugations are unknown. As it happens, China's most famous palindrome is ascribed to a woman, Su Hui, who lived in northern China during the second half of the fourth century. This particular palindrome is made up of a total of 841 characters arranged in a square with 29 characters on each side. By reading this square horizontally, vertically, diagonally, and various other ways, one can generate thousands of rhyming poems.

Su Hui has a brief biography in the chapter on "Exemplary Women" in the *Books of the Jin*. This dynastic history of the Jin (265–420) was compiled in the first half of the seventh century. While the rule of the Jin dynasty after 317 was limited to Southern China, the dynastic history also provides brief summaries of what was happening in the north during this time. As we saw earlier in the case of lady Song, the mother of Wei Cheng, the chapter on "Exemplary Women" also includes women from outside the Jin area:

Dou Tao's wife, lady Su, was a native of Shiping. Her personal name was Hui and her style name was Ruolan. At the time of Fu Jian [338–385], Dou Tao was prefect of Qinzhou, but was later banished to the "flowing sands" [of the western regions]. Filled with longing for him, lady Su wove a poem into brocade to send to him. One could read it in all directions, and the phrases were mournful and sad. It consisted of a total of 840 characters, but most of the text has been lost.

In fifth-century southern China, Su Hui had already acquired a proverbial reputation as a woman filled with yearning for her absent husband. Liu Xie, however, in his early sixth-century *The Literary Mind and the Carving of Dragons* (*Wenxin diaolong*), a systematic encyclopedia of *belles lettres*, does not mention Su Hui or her palindrome in his treatment of the genre, strongly suggesting that Su Hui's palindrome had either been lost by that time as suggested in the *Books of the Jin*, or was not known in southern China. An eighth-century encyclopedia does quote from Su Hui's palindrome, but limits itself to sixteen seven-syllable lines, which may indeed be read in both directions.

The palindrome of 841 characters that circulated under the name of Su Hui during the Ming (1368–1644) and Qing (1644–1911) dynasties was usually accompanied by a preface ascribed to Empress Wu Zetian, which provided a much more detailed account of the life of Su Hui and the circumstances under which the palindrome was composed:

Lady Su, the wife of Dou Tao from Fufeng who served as prefect of Qinzhou during the time of Fu Jian of the Former Qin dynasty, was the third daughter of Su Daozhi from Wugong, the magistrate of Chenliu. Her personal name was Hui and her style name was Ruolan. She was sharp of mind and beautiful in appearance, but behaved herself most modestly and did not seek to impress others. After she married Dou Tao, he very much respected her, but lady Su had a tendency to fly into a temper and suffered greatly from jealousy.

Tao's style name was Lianbo; he was the second son of Dou Lang, and a grandson of Generalissimo of the Right Dou Zizhen. He was a fine-looking man, who was well versed in the Classics and Histories, and who excelled in both the civil and military arts; he enjoyed a high reputation in the public opinion of the time. Fu Jian entrusted him with the most sensitive positions, and in each of the successive high offices he occupied, he established a reputation as an accomplished administrator. After he had taken up the position of prefect of Qinzhou, however, he was demoted to the garrison of Dunhuang for disobeying an imperial edict. By that time, Fu Jian had occupied the city of Xiangyang in the area of the Jin. Concerned that the city might come under attack, he relied on the talents and tactics of Dou Tao, and, appointing him with greatest honors as the Generalissimo for the Pacification of the South, stationed him at Xiangyang.

Now Dou Tao had a favorite concubine called Zhao Yangtai, whose marvelous song and dance was unsurpassed, and whom he housed in separate lodgings. When lady Su came to know of this, she requested that the girl be handed over to her after which she subjected her to the most vicious beatings and humiliations. Tao was deeply vexed by this. When Yangtai described to him in great detail all the failings of lady Su, Yangtai's slanderous calumnies made him even angrier. At the time lady Su was twenty-one. When Tao was appointed to Xiangyang, he asked her to go there with him, but lady Su was still angry at him and refused to accompany him. And so Tao took Yangtai along with him to his posting and cut off all communication with his wife.

Lady Su later regretted her actions and, filled with remorse, she wove a palindrome of brocade. The five colors contrasted vividly and their brilliance was blinding. Although the piece of brocade measured only eight inches square, it contained over two hundred poems. In total there were eight hundred odd words that, when read horizontally and vertically and backwards and forwards, always formed stanzas and sentences. Not a single dot or stroke of the characters was missing. Her marvelous talents and feelings were unmatched by anyone past or present! She called her work "The Maze Pattern." When those who read it had a hard time understanding what it said, lady Su would smile and say to them: "Turning and twisting in all directions it forms poems all by itself. But my loved one is the only one who can understand it all."

Lady Su then dispatched a servant to take it to Xiangyang. When Dou Tao carefully read the brocade characters, he was moved by their marvelous excellence. And so he packed Yangtai off to the "land within the passes" [Shaanxi], and prepared a carriage and servants with costly gifts to go and fetch lady Su. By the time she joined him in Xiangyang, their love and affection had doubled.

Lady Su composed a text of over five thousand words but it was irretrievably lost during the civil wars at the end of the Sui dynasty. But her palindrome in brocade is often seen and constantly copied. It is the original model of the boudoir complaints of recent times and serves as a normative model for all gentlemen who compose texts.

During moments of leisure between attending to government affairs, Our attention is taken up by canons and texts. As We were perusing various documents, We came across this palindrome. It is for this reason that We have provided this detailed description of Ruolan's talents. We also felt admiration for Dou Tao's ability to rectify his mistakes, which is why We wrote this text as a warning for later generations.

Composed on the first day of the Fifth Month of the first year of the reign period As-You-Wish [Ruyi, 692] by Her Imperial Majesty of the Heavenly Book and the Golden Wheel of the Great Zhou.

The learned eighteenth-century compilers of the *Basic Facts on All the Titles in the Complete Books of the Four Treasuries (Siku quanshu zongmu tiyao)*, the descriptive catalogue of the imperial collection, found it inconceivable that this palindrome could have been written by Su Hui or the preface by Wu Zetian: "No one knows the provenance of either this palindrome or the preface of Empress Wu." They considered the preface to be a hoax dating to no earlier than the twelfth century. As for the palindrome, they were willing to entertain the possibility that it might have been composed as early as the seventh century. Although the philological scholarship of the past two centuries has failed to turn up any new evidence, the belief in the authenticity of both the palindrome and the preface persists.

The story of how Su Hui was abandoned by her husband has remained popular to this very day; the most commonly performed play in the repertoire of the famous marionette theater of Quanzhou, for example, is *Dou Tao*. In this play, we find the recent top-graduate Dou Tao risking his life in defense of the empire's border against foreign invaders, while back home his wife, Su Hui, besieged by suitors, defends her chastity by blinding herself in both her eyes with her needle. But as it is only a play, the gods restore her sight when her victorious husband returns home laden with honors—or, as the Chinese phrase has it, "clad in brocade."

The continuing popularity of the story of Su Hui and her palindrome may be in part explained by the fact that it so perfectly embodies some very popular tropes. The preface pits the purely physical charms of the concubine (whose name, Yangtai, recalls the name of the place where an ancient king and a lovely goddess enjoyed the pleasures of each other's company) against the domestic and literary talents of the highborn wife. While for men, weaving was a commonly used metaphor for literary composition, for women, weaving and writing are often seen as contradictory: the drudgery of a woman's work left no time for the pursuit of literature, and we often find women writers in later ages referring to their writings as having been hastily composed in the rare free time found in between their weaving or needlework duties. Su Hui, however, seamlessly fuses her wifely duties with her literary endeavors. In the words of the contemporary scholar Ann Waltner, "her weaving, of words, combined her literary and domestic skills into one activity." Su Hui's tangible combination of the domestic and the literary is a significant accomplishment: Her embroidered characters are admired for their perfection, a reflection not only on her literacy but also on her needlework skill. Even more significant, in the eyes of traditional readers, Su Hui appears to have used her brocade palindrome to express her contrition for her insubordination and in so doing succeeded in reestablishing a proper marital relationship. In the Ming and Qing dynasties, the preface by Empress Wu Zetian, herself perhaps the greatest rebel against the norms of patriarchal society, ironically helped to establish Su Hui's palindrome as a paean to wifely duty and women's subordination to men, and as the perfect symbol of the marginal place of women's literature in late imperial society.

3 · Ladies, Nuns, and Courtesans

Brilliant Daughters and Dutiful Wives

Despite the central role of the Inner Palace in the development of women's literature during the first millennium of imperial rule in China, it was not the only place where women engaged in literary activities. After all, not all daughters of elite families entered the Inner Palace as one of the emperor's wives or concubines. In the aristocratic society of the Southern Dynasties of the centuries of disunion (fourth to sixth centuries) in particular, there appear to have been many women of elite families who, whether as wives or nuns, enjoyed a much greater freedom of action than they did during the preceding or following centuries.

The Poet of a Single Poem: Xu Shu

Some male poets are famous because of a single poem. The same holds for women poets. Xu Shu (middle of the second century CE) has only left us a single poem, but it has been enough to ensure her a modest place in the history of Chinese literature.

Xu Shu was the wife of Qin Jia. Her single extant poem is addressed to her husband, and follows in the *New Songs from a Jade Terrace* the three of his poems addressed to her. This anthology prefaces Qin Jia's poems with the following short notice:

Qin Jia's style name was Shihui and he was a native of Longxi. He served as main clerk of the commandery responsible for delivering the end-of-the-year reports to the capital. His wife Xu Shu had come down with an illness and returned to their home [in the countryside]. Since he was unable to say goodbye to her in person, he sent her the following poems.

Qin Jia's first poem would seem to indicate that he had sent a carriage to their country home with the intention of having his wife brought to the prefectural capital, but that she had sent the carriage back with a letter explaining that she was too ill. This is apparently what motivated him to write her the first of his poems after he had left for the national capital:

> A human life is like the morning dew,
> And here on earth we are beset by woes.
> Pain and sorrow are always quick to arrive,
> While joyful meetings always come so late.
> After I received my orders and departed,
> Each day took me further away from you.
> I had sent a carriage to bring you back to me,
> But empty it went and empty it returned.
> Reading your letter I am filled with sadness,
> At mealtime I find it hard to eat.
> Alone I sit here in this empty room,
> Who now will stay with me and cheer me up?
> All through the night I lie awake,
> And on my bed I toss and turn about.
> My sorrows come in one unending circle,
> But I am not a mat one may roll up![1]

Xu Shu responded with the following poem:

> Your serving-maid is alas, bereft of virtue,
> Because of an illness, I had to return home.
> Now I am stuck, alas, here in this house,
> And after all this time I'm still not well.
> I have neglected to take care of you,

---

1. The image in the last line of this poem derives from the *Book of Odes*. In one of the songs in that collection a woman protests her abiding love by stating that her heart is not a mat that can be rolled up.

In love and in respect I've fallen short.
And now, alas, you have received the order
To make the journey to the capital.
So far, so far, alas, we are apart!
I have no way to tell you of my love.
On tiptoe, I strain to see a bit further,
For a long time I stand, tarry and linger.
I yearn for you, my feelings held back,
And in my dreams I see your shining face.
But you have left and begun your journey,
Away from me—daily the distance grows.
To my regret I have no plumes and wings
To fly up high so that I may follow you—
Moaning I cannot stop from sighing,
As tears course down and soak my clothes.

In Xu Shu's original poem, each line consists of five syllables, although the third syllable is the meaningless particle *xi* (translated here as "alas"), which is used whenever a Chinese poet wants to express a particularly strong emotion. In his *Ranking of Poets*, the critic Zhong Rong, who was probably familiar only with this one poem by Xu Shu, nevertheless assigned both her and her husband's poetry to his second and middle category in his three-tiered classification of *shi* poets of the second to fifth centuries. He justified his relatively high opinion of her as follows:

As the experiences of the husband and wife were so painful, their texts are also filled with sadness and resentment. There were only a few authors of poems with five-syllable lines [in the Han dynasty], and two of them were women. Xu Shu's poem on separation is second only to the poem on the round fan [by Concubine Ban]!

Yet another reason for Zhong's high evaluation may have been his admiration for Xu Shu's moral character as a chaste widow, an indication of which is provided by the third-century scholar, Du Yu (222–284):

After Xu Shu lost her husband, she lived as a chaste widow. Her brothers wanted her to remarry, but she vowed never to do so.

In the sixteenth century, the story of Xu Shu and her husband inspired the critic Hu Yinglin to offer the following comparative evaluation of literary couples in general:

The most famous cases of couples of the Han and Wei dynasties where both husband and wife left texts are Sima Xiangru and Zhuo Wenjun, Qin Jia and Xu Shu, and Emperor Wen [of the Wei dynasty, i.e., Cao Pi] and Empress Zhen. Wenjun was a remarried widow, however, and Empress Zhen was not loyal to her first husband. Neither of these two women is worthy of emulation when it comes to the great norms of human behavior. But the historians tell us that Xu Shu did not remarry after Jia's death and even disfigured her face [to discourage potential suitors].

Later writers continued to embellish the story of Xu Shu's widowhood by adding new details. Eventually the great nineteenth-century scholar Yan Kejun produced the following summary of her life:

Qin Jia's style name was Shihui. He lived during the reign of Emperor Huan [r. 147–167] of the Eastern Han dynasty. In his official career he rose to the rank of imperial chamberlain. . . . The wife of Qin Jia from Longxi was a daughter of the Xu family, also from Longxi. Her personal name was Shu; she had literary talent and married Jia. Jia served as clerk in the capital of the commandery and Shu, because she was ill, lived in their home in one of the outlying districts of the commandery. Jia was appointed clerk for the presentation of the end-of-the-year reports in the national capital. When he was about to leave, he sent a carriage to fetch Shu so he could say goodbye to her in person. At that time he also sent her a letter, to which she replied informing him that her illness prevented her from traveling. Jia sent her yet another letter, to which she also replied with a letter. Jia then left and traveled to Luoyang, where later he was appointed chamberlain. After staying there for a number of years, he fell ill and died in Jinxiangting.

Earlier on, Shu had given birth to a daughter but had failed to bear a son. When Jia was ordered to go to the capital, she adopted a son whom she raised as her own. In this way she lived a widow's life. But as she was still beautiful and young, her brothers wanted her to remarry. She refused and, vowing to never marry again, wrote a letter to that effect to her brothers. Eventually she even disfigured her face in order not to be forced to remarry, and in so doing, won everyone's sympathy.

Upon her death, her son returned to live with his natural parents. The highest officials at court, however, changed his place of registration and decided that Shu's adopted son should continue the ancestral sacrifices of the Qin family.

Sources from the Tang dynasty and later contain the letters exchanged by Qin Jia and Xu Shu. The *Imperial Reading Matter of the Great Peace Reign Period (Taiping yulan)*, a large anthology of *belles lettres* compiled in the late tenth century, includes a letter that purports to be the text of Xu Shu's adamant refusal to remarry:

A gentleman, I have learned, leads others by means of his virtue and rectifies customs by means of the rites. That is why a brave hero is possessed of steadfast determination, and a chaste woman will not marry twice. Even though I am a mere woman, I secretly admire those who fulfill their duty by taking their own lives and put an end to everything by their death.

Disaster befell me and I lost the husband who is my heaven. But our son is still of tender age and has not yet been capped and our daughter is still young and has not yet done up her hair.[2] This is why I have forced myself to continue to live. I wish to raise these two children so they may inherit the ancestral line and continue the ancestral rituals. Once this has been accomplished, I will have no cause for shame when I meet with my husband in the land of the dead.

You, my elder and younger brothers, have proven incapable of holding to lofty norms because of the weakness of your wills, and of displaying bright virtue because of the darkness of your minds. You have promised me to someone else and pressured me to seek a partner above our status. You have even appealed to the magistrate and accused me in writing.

Now, a wise man cannot be ruined by events and a benevolent person refuses to be intimidated even by death. Even when an unsheathed knife was held to his throat, Yan Ying still refused to recant words that were proper and correct; despite the pain of disfiguring her face, the widow from Liang did not forget her duty to uphold the norms.[3] How could I not wish to emulate the brilliant behavior of such lofty exemplars?

My brothers, you are, I have concluded, incapable of guiding me according to the Way. You cannot barter me away by appealing to texts! Even though you may be called "learned," in my opinion you are not so at all.

The Poet of a Single Line: Xie Daoyun

Xu Shu's fame was based on a single poem; other poets became well known for nothing more than a single line. While we actually have a

---

2. In ancient China, the capping ceremony confirmed a young man's status as an adult. When girls reached marriageable age, their hair was done up in a bun.

3. Yan Ying (d. 500 BCE), a high minister in the state of Qi, was renowned for his probity. An otherwise unnamed virtuous widow from the kingdom of Liang, according to her entry in *Biographies of Exemplary Women*, went as far as slitting off her nose in order to dissuade the king from marrying her.

number of extant writings by Xie Daoyun, her name has remained forever associated with a single line improvised during her youth in which
she compares fluttering snowflakes to drifting willow floss:

One cold snowy day the Grand Guardian Xie [An] gathered all of his relatives
together and was discussing the principles of literature with the young men and
women when suddenly a heavy snow began to fall. Overjoyed, he said:

> To what can it be compared, this fluttering white snow?

Hu'er, a son of his elder brother, said:

> To salt being scattered in the sky it may be compared.

But the daughter of his elder brother exclaimed:

> O no! To willow floss drifting in the wind!

Xie An laughed heartily. She was the daughter of his eldest brother Wuyi, the
[later] wife of General on the Left Wang Ningzhi.

The above anecdote is found in *A New Account of Tales of the World*
(*Shishuo xinyu*), an extensive collection of bons mots attributed to, and
anecdotes concerning, eminent personalities of the second to fourth centuries, compiled by Liu Yiqing (403–444). Liu arranged his abundant materials thematically in thirty-six chapters; the anecdotes about women are
collected in chapter 19. As early as the second half of the fifth century Liu
Jun (462–521) contributed an extensive commentary to this text that includes many additional anecdotes. Text and commentary together offer a
fascinating picture of the lifestyle of the Chinese aristocratic elite of this
time. Not surprisingly, it is the century of the Eastern Jin dynasty (317–
419), the period closest to that of Liu Yiqing, which is best represented in
the collection. This period was dominated by the extraordinary figure of
Xie An (320–385), who makes his appearance in as many as one hundred
of the anecdotes.

Throughout the fourth century, northern China was dominated by a
rapid succession of dynasties. Many of these rulers and warlords belonged to non-Chinese ethnic groups. Southern China, however, was
ruled by the Jin, the Chinese dynasty that in the final decades of the third
century had ruled all of China but was later forced to move its capital to
Jianye (modern Nanjing). The leading aristocracy of southern China was
composed of great northern families who had fled the turmoil of

Northern China for the relative safety and stability of the south. The two most prominent families were the Wangs and the Xies. Although these two families engaged in incessant power struggles, they were also intimately connected by numerous marriage alliances. The most prominent member of the Xie family was Xie An. Up until the age of forty, he devoted himself to the management of his large estates in Guiji (modern Shaoxing) and kept his distance from court politics. Once he went to the capital, however, he enjoyed a dazzling career at court. In fact, by 383, when the indomitable northern warlord Fu Jian invaded the south, Xie An had become the most powerful man at court. His self-confidence is illustrated by the fact that when a messenger arrived with news of the decisive battle with Fu Jian, Xie An had him wait until he had finished his game of go. The Wangs and the Xies not only distinguished themselves by their power and wealth, but also by their many cultural pursuits. The Xie family produced a number of famous poets, the greatest of whom was perhaps the landscape poet Xie Lingyun (385–443). Wang Xizhi (309–ca. 365), who would eventually become Xie Daoyun's father-in-law, was the most famous calligrapher in all of Chinese history. Interestingly enough, Wang Xizhi studied calligraphy with Lady Wei, who traced her style of calligraphy back to Cai Yong and his daughter Cai Yan.

Xie Daoyun was a daughter of Xie An's eldest brother. Her family married her off to Wang Ningzhi, the second son of Wang Xizhi. Accustomed to the intellectually stimulating surroundings of her own family, it appears, according to an anecdote in *A New Account of Tales of the World,* that her husband was a disappointment to her:

After the wife of Wang Ningzhi, Lady Xie, married him she came to despise him greatly. When she returned on a visit to the Xie family, she expressed to them her great displeasure. The Great Guardian tried to comfort her, saying: "Not only is Young Wang the son of Wang Xishi, he himself doesn't have such a bad personality. Why must you persist in sulking?" She answered him: "Here, in just a single household, I have men like you and the general for uncles, and Feng, Hu, He, and Mo for brothers and cousins. I would never have imagined that between heaven and earth could exist such a thing as 'Young Wang'!"

The mediocre qualities of Wang Ningzhi so greatly despised by his wife apparently did not hinder him from pursuing an official career in the aristocratic society of his time:

Ningzhi's style name was Shuping and he was the second son of the General on the Right [Wang] Xizhi. He occupied successively the positions of prefect of Jiangzhou, general on the left, and governor of Guiji.

It would seem that Wang Ningzhi's younger brother, Xianzhi, was also Xie Daoyun's intellectual inferior. According to an anecdote found not in *A New Account of Tales of the World*, but rather in the biography of Xie Daoyun found in the chapter on "Exemplary Women" in the seventh-century *Books of the Jin*, Xie Daoyun once had to rescue Xianzhi from a humiliating defeat in a philosophical debate:

Once, Ningzhi's younger brother Xianzhi was engaged in a philosophical discussion with some guests. Just as he was about to concede defeat, Daoyun sent a servant girl to tell him: "Let me lift the siege for my little brother-in-law!" Then, shielding herself from their gaze behind a movable screen of green silk, she defended Xianzhi's earlier argument so skillfully that the guests were unable to defeat her.

But even her own brothers did not always live up to Xie Daoyun's high expectations:

The wife of the prefect of Jiangzhou Wang once said to Xie He: "Why is it you are no longer making any progress? Is it because your mind is so taken up by common affairs? Or is it that the gifts that Heaven has bestowed on you are so limited?"

Xie Daoyun's critical attitude toward the men around her may well have been inspired by the behavior of her aunt, Lady Liu, the wife of Xie An. One day Xie An received a visit from the official and poet Sun Chuo (314–371). No doubt expecting some scintillating conversation, Lady Liu was disappointed by what she heard:

Once Sun Chuo and his younger brother stayed the night with Xie An, but their conversation was extremely silly and trivial. Lady Liu listened in on them from behind a wall and heard every word they said. When Xie An saw her the next morning, he asked her: "What did you think of my guests last night?" Lady Liu answered him: "In the house of my late elder brother we would never have even received such guests!" Xie An was deeply ashamed.

An anecdote from the collection *On Jealousy* (*Duji*) by Yu Tongzhi (middle of the fifth century) shows that Lady Liu was very well aware of the patriarchal nature of the norms and values of traditional Chinese society. Xie An's cousins tried to persuade her to allow her husband his little pleasures by quoting songs from the *Book of Odes* that, according to the traditional commentaries, praised the queens of ancient times who were free of jealousy and allowed their royal husbands many concubines, enabling them to sire many sons. But Lady Liu had a ready reply:

Lady Liu, the wife of His Excellency Xie, did not allow her husband to keep any concubines. But His Excellency was a great lover of women, and finding it impossible to control his desires, wanted to purchase a large number of concubines and performers. His cousins, who knew only too well of his intentions, tried to persuade Lady Liu to be somewhat more accommodating. They said to her: "'The Ospreys' and 'Locusts' praise the virtue of not being jealous."[4] Lady Liu, aware of what they were up to, asked: "Who was the author of the *Odes*?" They replied: "The Duke of Zhou!" Lady Liu then said: "The Duke of Zhou was a man and wrote in defense of his own interests. If the *Odes* had been written by his wife, words such as these would not be found in the canon."

Despite Xie Daoyun's disparaging remarks about her brother, according to the following anecdote in *A New Account of Tales of the World*, Xie He continued to be her greatest admirer:

Xie He elevated his elder sister above all other women. Zhang Xuan, who always praised his own younger sister, insisted that the two women were on a par with one another. Now, there was a certain nun by the name of Ji who frequented both the Zhang and the Xie households. When people asked her for a ranking, she replied: "The spirit and feelings of Lady Wang exude an encompassing radiance, and that is why her personality impresses one as resembling that of one of the Seven Sages of the Bamboo Grove. The pure heart of Lady Gu shines like jade, so, of course, among women she is peerless!"

---

4. "The Ospreys" was traditionally interpreted as a paean to Si, the wife of King Wen, praising her for her lack of jealousy. "Locusts," another poem in the *Book of Odes*, was read as a description of the great number of sons that King Wen was able to father by his concubines, thanks to his wife's unjealous nature.

Zhang Xuan (second half of the fourth century) was a high official who belonged to the same social stratum as the Wangs and the Xies. Unfortunately, we know nothing about his younger sister apart from the fact that she was married to a member of the Gu family. Nor do we have any information on the nun who placed Zhang Xuan's sister first among women, but ranked Xie Daoyun with the "Seven Sages of the Bamboo Grove."

The Seven Sages of the Bamboo Grove were a group of seven male poets and writers of the mid-third century who ignored social conventions and distinguished themselves by their eccentric behavior, a behavior that was interpreted by later generations as indicative of their unsullied integrity. One of the Seven Sages was the poet and zither player Xi Kang (223–262), whose implied criticism of the government so outraged the authorities that eventually he was beheaded. Xie Daoyun was acquainted with the writings of the Seven Sages, and one of her two extant poems was written in imitation of a poem on a pine tree by Xi Kang:

> I look at that pine tree yonder on the hill:
> The coldest winter cannot make it wither.
> How I long to go there and rest beneath it,
> Where I can gaze forever at its branches.
> I jump up, but find I cannot soar in flight,
> Stamping my feet I wait for Wang Ziqiao.
> But time, alas, has never been on my side,
> And I am swept along by Transformation.

Wang Ziqiao was the name of a legendary Daoist immortal. According to Chinese tradition, those who wanted to take refuge from this world of ambition, hate, and slander in the realm of the blessed immortals would pray for a chance encounter with such an immortal, as only they could teach the secret techniques of longevity. These immortals were said to live on the floating islands of the Eastern Ocean and in the paradisiacal gardens on top of the lofty mountains of the far west. Xi Kang's original poem, entitled "Roaming Through the Realm of the Immortals," described in its twenty lines an ecstatic aerial journey with Wang Ziqiao to the mystical realm of the immortals, where the poet is initiated into the techniques of immortality. Xie Daoyun's much shorter poem effectively undercuts these dreams of a life eternal far from the common world, as in her poem Wang Ziqiao refuses to show up, and death is unavoidable.

Once the Chinese elite had discovered the limestone caves of Southern China, the immortals were also believed to inhabit extensive sandstone grottoes hidden deep inside the mountains. Each of these grotto-heavens constituted a cosmos unto itself, with its own sky and clouds. The second extant poem of Xie Daoyun, entitled "Mountain Climbing," describes just such a grotto-heaven:

> How they tower, those lofty eastern mountains!
> They soar straight up and pierce the azure sky.
> Within these crags are hidden empty halls,
> Their mystery deepened by a silent darkness.
> Not built either by craftsman or by artisan:
> The misty structures are produced by nature.
> What is it about these apparitions
> That propels me there again and again?
> Let me go and settle in those halls,
> And there live out my allotted years!

The first half of the fourth century was the period of the greatest popularity of "poems on roaming through the realm of the immortals" (*youxianshi*), and the subject matter of Xie Daoyun's poems may be attributed to this literary fashion. It is also quite possible, however, that it reflects the Daoist inclinations of her husband's family, who happened to be adherents of the Orthodox Unity (Zhengyi) Daoist church, another name for which was the Way of Five Pecks of Rice. Orthodox Unity Daoism had emerged in the course of the second century in the southwestern region of Sichuan, and during the third century it also found adherents in northern China. When many of the great northern aristocratic families fled south during the first decades of the fourth century, they took Orthodox Unity Daoism with them. In this form of Daoism, priests played an important intermediary role in conducting rituals, among the most important of which were those designed to cure illnesses by enlisting large armies of spirit soldiers to drive out the demons believed to cause these illnesses.

The second half of the fourth century also saw the rise of a new current within Daoism much favored by the southern elite families who had lost much of their power to the immigrants from the north. This new school of Daoism, which was called Highest Clarity (Shangqing), claimed a higher revelation and stressed mystic visions and immortality techniques. A central role in the development of Highest Clarity Daoism was played by Yang Xi (320–384), who, during the years 365–370 was said to have received a series of midnight visions, in which a great many male and female immortals revealed to him numerous new texts. Many of these texts described paradisiacal worlds populated by hitherto unknown hierarchies of male and female immortals. Xie Daoyun's poems may well reflect the influence of this new strand of Daoism.

Xie Daoyun's husband Wang Ningzhi was a firm believer in the power of the rituals of Orthodox Unity Daoism to protect him against evil. This faith cost him his life, however, when during the rebellion of Sun En in 399, he put his faith in religious countermeasures rather than taking the necessary military precautions:

The Wangs had for generations been believers of the Way of Five Pecks of Rice founded by the Zhangs, and Ningzhi was an especially ardent believer. When Sun En attacked Guiji his subordinate asked him to take precautions, but Ningzhi did not heed them. As soon as he had entered his private room and prayed, he came out and told his officers: "I have already prayed to the Great Way and have been promised spirit troops, which will be sent to our aid. The rebels will naturally be defeated." Subsequently, since he had taken no precautions, Ningzhi was killed by Sun En.

Xie Daoyun survived this debacle, as her biography in the chapter on "Exemplary Women" in the *Books of the Jin* tells us, primarily due to the courage she showed during this crisis:

During the rebellion of Sun En, Xie Daoyun remained unperturbed. But when she heard that her husband and her sons had been killed by the bandits she ordered her female servants to take her out in her sedan chair, and with drawn sword she exited the gate. When the mutinous troops came near she was captured, but only after having slain several of them with her own hand. At that time, her grandson Liu Tao [the son of one of her daughters] was just a few years old. When the bandits wanted to kill him as well, Daoyun said: "What does your quarrel with the Wang family have to do with other clans? But if you insist on killing him, I would rather be killed first." Vicious and cruel as Sun En was, he turned pale at these words, and in the end did not kill Liu Tao.

Xie Daoyun's biography in the *Books of the Jin* gives us a description of her twenty-year exemplary widowhood:

Afterwards she lived as a widow in Guiji, and the rules in her household were all extremely strict. The prefect Liu Liu had heard of her reputation and asked to be allowed to have a discussion with her. Daoyun was aware of Liu Liu's fame and so did not refuse his request. With her hair pinned up in a bun, she sat on a white cushion inside the curtains of her couch. Liu, dressed in formal attire, took his seat on a separate couch. Daoyun's demeanor was extremely lofty, and her words were pure and elegant. At first, when they touched upon the affairs of her family, she was overcome by emotion and wept copiously, but when eventually she replied to his questions, her words and reasoning were eloquent. After Liu Liu had left the room, he said admiringly: "I have truly never before met such a person as this! You have only to observe her words and her presence to want to yield to her, body and mind!" Daoyun, for her part, said: "This is the first time since the death of my relatives that I have met such a gentleman! I found listening to his questions truly illuminating!"

The *Books of the Jin* credits Xie Daoyun with "poems and rhapsodies, elegies and hymns, all of which circulate in the world." In the seventh century, an edition of her works in two scrolls was still in existence, but all that remains extant today is an "Encomium on the *Analects*" and the two poems translated above. In the end, however, the one line for which she is most famous and which has been quoted time and again through the centuries, remains the line on drifting willow floss that she improvised as a young girl.

Xie Daoyun became for women of later dynasties, especially those of the Ming and Qing, the model par excellence of a woman poet. She combined in one person all the elements that in later times would define the ideal woman poet: an exceptional talent shown at a very early age and immediately recognized by an elderly male authority figure, a life of dedication to her husband's family, and a chaste widowhood.

Poet and Editorial Advisor: Lady Chen

The biography of Xie Daoyun in the chapter on "Exemplary Women" in the *Books of the Jin* is immediately followed by a brief account of yet another woman of exceptional intelligence, Lady Chen, the wife of Liu Zhen:

The wife of Liu Zhen, Lady Chen, was also intelligent and eloquent, and skilled in the composition of texts. Once, on New Year's Day, she presented to the throne her "Hymn on the Pepper Blossom," the text of which reads:

> Heaven's dome has come full circle,
> And Triple First have their beginning.
> Now verdant yang displays its splendor,
> And the crystalline light is all ablaze.
> We picked for You, we offer You
> These numinous buds of rarest beauty.
> May your sagely countenance
> Shine on them forever and always!

Lady Chen also drew up the protocol for presentations and audiences on New Year's Day and the Winter Solstice, which were circulated in the world.

While Lady Chen never achieved the fame of Xie Daoyun, in later times she too would be referred to by women writers as a noteworthy literary ancestor.

Lady Chen's collected works consisted of seven scrolls, of which only a few fragments remain. The most interesting of these, because it shows us a woman writer coaching other women writers, may be a letter she sent to her younger sisters-in-law, offering some editorial advice regarding the elegy one of them had written for her late father:

I have read the elegy for your late father that Weifang has written. When she describes and sings of his eminent virtue, his humaneness is fully displayed, and when she voices her emotions and articulates her grief, her own filiality is thereby made manifest. Only an exceptional talent would be capable of grandly accomplishing a work like this. I recite it time and again and with every word I dissolve into tears. It evokes in me both emotion and support, sadness and comfort.

Yuanfang and Weifang, you both exhibited brilliant talents even in your early years. The style of your writings is rich and opulent, and has no equal in this world. Yet I am bold enough to express my doubts on a single matter and will express my concern in the hope that it may be of benefit to you. Your late father not only embodied and glorified humaneness and righteousness, but was also sagely and circumspect in all his actions. He attended to his parents with utmost filiality and served his lord with greatest loyalty. In his personal behavior he was respectful, and in caring for the people, he was kindly. Indeed, he may be called a man who established his virtue and his deeds, and provided a model to the people. Although the Way is long, his life was short, and during his lifetime he never met anyone who truly recognized his talents. He had not yet attained a glorious rank, and never achieved his lofty ambition; so in fact, he never distinguished himself with extraordinary achievements.

Now Laozi and Zhuangzi dismiss sageliness and reject wisdom; they look on the myriad of beings as all being equal, place high honor and low status on a par with one another, and make no distinction between sadness and joy. Such opinions are not valued by the Classics and Canons and are rejected by the Teaching of Names [Confucianism]. Why then do you insist on quoting these opinions time and again in order to make your points? I hope the two of you will carefully think about this.

Different Voices: Liu Lingxian

A number of writing women of the centuries of disunion have left more poems than Xie Daoyun, although none of them ever achieved her fame. Among these other women poets, Liu Lingxian (first half of the sixth century) may well be the most original and outspoken.

Liu Lingxian was one of the three younger sisters of Liu Xiaochuo (481–539). Liu Xiaochuo may no longer be a great name in Chinese literary history, but during his own lifetime he was highly regarded as a poet. Even as a very young man, his talents were recognized by luminaries of the preceding generation such as Shen Yue, and later, he was praised for his poetry by none other than Emperor Wu of the Liang dynasty (r. 501–549). Liu Xiaochuo was also a member of the literary salon of the Zhaoming Crown Prince, who was a great patron of the arts and the editor of the *Selections of Fine Literature*. Liu's poems not only enjoyed great popularity at the court in Jianye (Nanjing), but in north China as well:

The literary style of Xiaochuo was imitated by the younger generation. People of the time esteemed his works very highly. A piece that he had completed in the morning would by evening be found everywhere. Aficionados would recite his writings and copy them out, and they would be circulated even in the most distant regions.

Liu Xiaochuo's brothers and cousins were also known for their literary talents:

At the time, Liu Xiaochuo had seventy brothers, cousins, and nephews and they were all skilled in literary composition. Never in the recent past has such a phenomenon been seen!

Liu Xiaochuo is one of the most important representatives of what is commonly called "palace-style poetry." During the second half of the fifth century and the first half of the sixth, Chinese literary life was dominated by the salons of imperial princes, many of whom were major poets themselves. The poets in these salons wrote primarily of the scenes and objects of palace life. One of their favorite subjects was the palace lady languishing in her boudoir, and often they would adopt the voices of these neglected women in their poems. A single example from the works of Liu Xiaochuo may illustrate this:

In the Old Style

Yan and Zhao do not lack for pretty girls[5]—
The dazzling sun shows up their red rouge.
That roving man has been gone for ten years:
The sash of my gown hangs down even more.
 It is so hard to stay inside this room in spring,
But on jade steps I only cause myself pain
When I watch the swallows as they return home,
And flit about the place building their nests.
 Here and then there, they dart inside silk curtains,
High and then low, they choose a painted beam.
They still remember their old dwelling place—
How could they forget their old acquaintances?
 Longing for you I gaze open-eyed till nightfall,
And in my sleep I see your face in my dreams.
When our souls meet you are here at my side,
But turn around—and you are somewhere else.
 Startled awake I stare at my mat and pillow—
Who is the one who untied my gown and skirt?
In vain I keep the fragrant candle shining
All through the night on the ever thicker frost.

---

5. The ancient kingdom of Yan covered the northern part of the modern province of Hebei, while the ancient state of Zhao occupied most of the modern province of Shanxi. The women of these two regions were renowned for their fair skin.

Having grown up in this extraordinary literary milieu, it is no surprise that Liu Xiaochuo's sister Liu Lingxian too would try her hand at poetry and in particular, palace-style poetry. We find a few of her poems in our most important source for this kind of poetry, the *New Songs From a Jade Terrace* of ca. 531.

Liu Lingxian's poems follow the fashion of their time and in many ways are hardly distinguishable from the works of her male contemporaries. Because she was a woman, however, we may be tempted to read some of her poems as first-person confessions rather than third-person descriptions. A case in point is her "Listening to the Blackbirds":

> Above the courtyard trees the morning sky has cleared,
> I take my mirror out beyond the decorated railing.
> The breeze brings me the scent of peach tree blossoms,
> And as it passes carries the sounds of springtime birds:
> When alone they resemble a flute on southern slopes,
> But together they sound like a mouth organ on a riverbank.
> Absorbed I stand and listen as if in a trance—
> And never get around to completing my toilette!

In the original Chinese, however, this poem does not contain a single personal pronoun and there is nothing to stop us from translating the same poem as follows:

> Above the courtyard trees the morning sky has cleared,
> She takes her mirror out beyond the decorated railing.
> The breeze brings her the scent of peach tree blossoms,
> And as it passes carries the sounds of springtime birds:
> When alone they sound like a flute on southern slopes,
> But together they sound like a mouth organ on a riverbank.
> Absorbed she stands and listens, as if in a trance—
> And never gets around to completing her toilette!

Of course, even if we translate the poem in the first person, we cannot automatically identify the speaker in the poem with the historical poet. In one of Liu Lingxian's best-known works, "Poem Utilizing the Same Rhyme as the One Used in Concubine Ban's 'Resentment,'" the poet speaks in the voice of Concubine Ban after she had been supplanted in the emperor's affection by the svelte dancer Zhao Feiyan:

The sun has set, the gate is surely locked,
And sorrowful thoughts rise in a hundred ways,
The more so as the emperor's palace is so near:
The breeze carries the sounds of song and music!
I do not hate him for his change of heart,
But that false slander was simply too cruel:
I could only appeal to principle in my defense—
I am not jealous of her waist, however slim!

The modern scholar Anne Birrell has compared this text to the many poems on the same theme by male poets and praises our poet for her specifically female viewpoint and vivid emotional response. This can be seen very clearly when we compare her poem to the following poem by Liu Lingxian's brother, Liu Xiaochuo, on the same theme:

Concubine Ban's Resentment

Inside the locked gate, silence reigns—
It is not the Inner Palace anymore.
Not only that, it now is verdant spring,
And the grasses presently grow lush and green.
I may be likened to a fan in autumn,
Since You no longer deign to visit me.
Who still remembers how this humble maid
Refused to ride with You in Your conveyance?

Liu Lingxian's originality also shines through if we compare her poem to poems on similar themes by other contemporary women poets. Take, for example, the following poem on Wang Zhaojun by one of Liu Lingxian's elder sisters, the wife of Wang Shuying:

How can one settle one's life once and for all?
It is impossible to know what will befall.
The painter failed in his depiction of my form:
The mirror-case became a withered weed.
The tears I shed when I crossed China's border
Have continued to fall and are still not dry.
O envoy of the Han, when you go back south,
Please be so good as to tell this to everyone.

Not all of Liu Lingxian's poems, however, are observations or impersonations of other women. Sometimes she does seem to be speaking in her own voice, as in the following two poems written for her husband Xu Fei (d. 524), who had left her back in the capital after he had taken a provincial post:

Two Poems Written in Reply to My Husband

I

The flower courtyard in the afternoon glow:
A light breeze wafts through the orchid window.
The sun is setting as I freshen up my toilette,
Open the curtain and face the springtime trees.
The singing orioles dance among the leaves,
The playful butterflies race between the flowers.
I tune my zither, hoping for some pleasure—
But my heart is so sad, it brings me no joy.
Our joyful meeting was not long ago,
But now there cannot be a rendezvous.
If you want to know the measure of my pain,
It is as deep and dark as this boudoir in spring!

II

"Of eastern neighbors the most beautiful!"
"Of southern lands by far the brightest face!"
"Just like a goddess on a moonlit night!"
"Or like a river nymph in the morning mist!"[6]
But when I see my own face in the mirror,
I know I'm not the equal of those stunners.
Your choice of words is wonderful but nonsense,
Since your comparisons are always off the mark.
My husband, you may think me pretty—
"Earth-shattering" I wouldn't dare hope to be.

While Liu Lingxian enjoyed quite a reputation during her lifetime for her poems, her most famous work was the text she wrote for her husband's funeral ceremony. The following passage, from the *Books of the Liang (Liang shu)*, describes how this text came to be written:

---

6. These four lines all refer to proverbial examples of female beauty in early Chinese poetry.

Of Liu Xiaochuo's younger sisters, the first married Wang Shuying from Lang-ye, the second married Zhang Sheng from Wu, and the third married Xu Fei from Donghai. These sisters were all talented and learned, but the writings of Fei's wife were the most outstanding. Xu Fei was the son of Chief Administrator Xu Mian [466–535]. Xu Fei died while serving as prefect of Jin'an, and when his casket was brought back to Jianye, his wife composed for use at the funeral sacrifice a text that was extremely sad and moving. Xu Mian originally had intended to write a text of lament himself, but once he had seen her work, he laid his writing brush aside.

Xu Mian, apart from being Lingxian's father-in-law and a very high official, was also one of the most well-known writers of his time. Thus, to say that he yielded to Lingxian's superior composition is no small praise. Liu Lingxian's text has been preserved and may be rendered as follows:

In the fifth year of the reign period Great Unity [Datong, 539; NB: probably a mistake for Datong (Great Tradition), 531], I, your wife, reverently present a small offering [consisting of a goat and a pig] to your spirit, Master Xu, saying:

> Your virtue accorded with rites and wisdom,
>   Your talents combined style and elegance;
> Your learning was lofty like a mountain,
>   Your eloquence flowed like a river.
> Your insight into the Classics was exceptional,
>   You shone at court and startled the land.
> Your deportment surpassed all in Xu,
>   Your reputation outshone all in Luo;[7]
> You contained Pan Yue, outranked Lu Ji,
> Excelled Zhong Jun, outperformed Jia Yi![8]
>
> Ever since yin and yang were created,
>   Fitting partners are in the beginning apart.
> I selected sapience and relied on virtue
>   And so attached myself to you as my husband.
> You did not need me to support your governance,

---

7. Xu and Luo are place names in the modern province of Henan and refer to the "Central Plains," the core domain of the Chinese world.

8. Pan Yue (247–300) and Lu Ji (261–303) were two of the most famous poets of the third century. Zhong Jun (d. 112 BCE) and Jia Yi (200–168 BCE) both established a reputation for their talent and erudition at an early age.

My aid within the home need not be mentioned.
Luckily my weed-like nature was transformed
  By my daily contact with your orchid-like fragrance.
You taught me the harmony of zither and dulcimer
  And we exchanged writings based on the canon.

Support of humaneness is rarely rewarded,
  Spirit and feelings are easily hurt:
Hail crushes the springtime flowers,
  Frost withers the summer leaves.
With my own hands I brought the proper shroud,
  With my own eyes I saw your outstretched feet.[9]
Not even once will we see each other again,
  Not even a hundred men can buy you back![10]

Alas, alas!

We may be separated by life and death,
  But our close love is still one and the same.
I dare follow the examples of the past,
  And with my own hand mix ginger and lemon.[11]
The food on the plates dries out to no avail,
  The libation cup brims over to no purpose.
Once I raised your tray as high as my brows[12]—
How different my life has become now!

When you left me briefly to serve in the army,
  I was filled with longing in my room,

---

9. When Master Zeng was about to die, the *Analects* tells us, he called his disciples to his bedside and showed them his hands and feet to demonstrate that he was returning without blemish the body that his parents had given him at birth.

10. The image in the last line of this stanza derives from the *Book of Odes*. One of the songs in that collection praises a threesome of heroes who voluntarily follow their lord in death when he is buried, and praises their worth by stating that not a hundred men could be their equal.

11. Traditionally ginger and lemon were used to flavor food offerings for the deceased.

12. Meng Guang, the wife of Liang Hong (first century CE) showed her respect for her husband by lifting the tray on which she brought him his food as high as her eyebrows.

Even before you'd returned from that short journey,
  My hair was already a tangled mess.
But in the case of a separation like this one,
  My persistent pain will go on without end.
What is the length of a hundred years?
  Only in the grave will we be together again!

Buddhist Nuns and Daoist Mystics

The relative freedom of action enjoyed by women of elite families during the centuries of disunion is reflected in the significant role they played in the religious life of this period. Buddhism had reached China from India in the first century CE, and by the fourth century had become an established feature of Chinese life. The earliest Chinese monastics were all men, but starting from this time, many women also became nuns, and numerous convents were established. The flourishing of monastic Buddhism from the fourth and fifth centuries onward also stimulated comparable developments in Daoism, in which women played an important role as well, if initially only as teachers in the visions of male mystics. During the Tang dynasty, Buddhist convents continued to attract large numbers of nuns, but none of these women ever enjoyed the visibility and prestige of their fourth- and fifth-century predecessors. As the imperial family of the Tang claimed to descend from Laozi, the patriarch of Daoism, Tang princesses who wanted "to leave the household life" chose to become Daoist nuns, thereby enhancing the prestige of the Daoist convents.

Buddhist Nuns

We are better informed about the lives and works of the Buddhist nuns of the fourth and fifth centuries than of any other period for the next thousand years. This is primarily due to the *Biographies of Bhiksunis* (*Biqiuni zhuan*), compiled in 516 by the monk Baochang at the court of the Liang dynasty. Baochang collected sixty-five hagiographical sketches of nuns of the two preceding centuries. He was primarily interested in four types of nuns: the determined—those who persevered in their commitment and who defied their parents and in-laws in order to enter the religious life; the contemplatives—nuns who in their meditation could attain a level of trance whereby they appeared to be made of stone or wood; the preachers—nuns who lectured on the Dharma and occasionally wielded great power and influence both within the monastic community and at court; and the ascetics—nuns who in their practice of self-mortification might go so far as to immolate themselves as an offering to the Buddha.

Powerful abbesses. The majority of the nuns who have a biography in Baochang's compilation came from elite backgrounds, but not from the highest circles. In the overwhelming majority of biographies some mention is made of literacy. Usually, however, the reference is to the capacity of the nun concerned to recite one or more sutras. Only in four cases does Baochang explicitly refer to writings by the nuns, and only in one case does he actually quote from these writings, and then merely a few lines of a death poem. The most conspicuous of these writing nuns may well have been a certain Miaoyin, who lived during the final decades of the fourth century and exerted great influence at court:

It is unclear of which place Miaoyin was a native. She had set her mind on the Way when still a child. When she resided in the capital [Jianye], she studied extensively both the esoteric and exoteric writings. She was an expert in literary composition. Emperor Xiaowu [r. 373–396] of the Jin and [his brother] Daozi, the Grand Tutor and Prince of Guiji, both revered and respected her. Whenever she held discussions and composed texts together with the emperor, the grand tutor, and the scholars at court, she displayed a considerable talent, and on account of this acquired a great reputation.

   In the tenth year of the reign period Great Origin [Taiyuan, 376–396], the grand tutor established the Simple Quietude Convent [Jianjingsi] for her, of which she was made the abbess. She had more than a hundred disciples. For a while, talented and ambitious people from both within and outside the palace relied on her to promote themselves. There was no end to the gifts she received and her wealth surpassed that of everyone in the capital. High and low served her as a teacher, and every day more than a hundred carriages stopped before her gate.

Baochang continues his description of Miaoyin's life by recounting the way in which she influenced the most sensitive of political appointments at a particularly dangerous time. In the fifth century, other nuns also had access to the Inner Palace and enjoyed imperial protection, but not all of them are on record as "expert in literary composition" as was Miaoyin.

The most prolific author among the writing nuns may well have been Zhisheng (427–492), although unfortunately none of her works has been preserved. Baochang writes:

The original surname of Zhisheng was Xu. Her family came from Chang'an, but had been living in Guiji for three generations. When she was six, she went with her mother, lady Wang, on an excursion outside the capital and visited the Pottery Casket Monastery [Waguansi]. When she saw how lofty the monastery was and how beautiful its adornments, she burst into tears and begged to have her head shaved. When her mother asked her what was going on, she told her what was on her mind, but her mother, thinking that she was too young, would not give her permission [for her to become a nun].

At the end of the Song dynasty [420–478] there were many troubles, and all kinds of people lost their livelihoods. The political situation was very chaotic and this lasted for many years. Only when Zhisheng approached the age of twenty was she finally able to leave the household life. She lived in the Established Blessing Convent [Fujiansi], where her personal deportment was beyond compare and where she was inimitable in her purity. She had only to hear the *Maha paranirvana Sutra* once to be able to memorize it. Later she applied herself to the study of the *Vinaya*,[13] and her diligence was such that she never had to be taught anything twice. The fame of her comprehensive memory spread everywhere. She herself composed some several tens of scrolls of commentary. Her words were concise, but her message was far-reaching, her meaning subtle, and her reasoning marvelous.

Baochang also describes Zhisheng's connections with the court:

When the crown prince of the Qi dynasty, Wenhui [458–493], heard about her fame, he repeatedly summoned her to court, and each time she lectured on the sutras. His brother Wenxuan [460–494], the minister of works and prince of Jinling, venerated her even more. Zhisheng's determination was as firm as southern gold and her mind as brilliant as northern snow. The way in which she regulated the community of nuns truly was of the highest standards, and at the order of the crown prince, she was again made to serve as head of her convent. She was loved and revered by all, who venerated her as they would a stern parent.

In his hagiographies, Baochang often describes miracles that accompanied the lives and deaths of the nuns in evidence of their holiness. Zhisheng is no exception:

---

13. *Vinaya* refers to the extensive body of writing on the monastic rules.

Zhisheng lived in her convent for forty years but she never went out to attend vegetarian feasts or visit lay families, irrespective of rank. Pure and simple, she lived in solitude, devoting herself to meditation. That is why her reputation did not spread widely. But the crown prince Wenhui showered her with gifts, and so over time she amassed a fortune, with which she built cells and halls; the nuns of her convent lived in splendor . . .

When, in the tenth year of the reign period Eternal Light [Yongming, 483–493] she came down with an illness, she suddenly saw golden carriages and jade canopies coming to welcome her. On the fifth day of the Fourth Month, she announced to her disciples: "Now I will pass away!" While her disciples wept, she opened her robes and showed her chest. On her chest they saw a perfectly formed character *Fo* [Buddha] in cursive script. The character was radiant and white, and its color and shape were bright and rich. Zhisheng died at noon on the eighth day. At the time she was sixty-six years old, and she was buried on Bell Mountain. Crown Prince Wenhui had provided for all her medical needs, and whatever was needed for her funeral was provided for by the relevant officials.

Revealed sutras. Whereas Zhisheng only wrote commentaries to the sutras, the young girl Nizi ("Little Nun," 491–505) herself revealed twenty-one new sutras. In his comprehensive catalogue of all the Buddhist writings available in Chinese translation in the early sixth century, *Collected Notes on Texts from the Tripitaka* (*Chu Sanzang jiji*), the monk Sengyou (445–518) provides a list of the titles produced by Nizi between the ages of nine and sixteen. Sengyou also provides the following editorial note:

The sutras listed above were produced by Nizi, the virgin daughter of Jiang Bi, who during the final years of the Qi [479–501] served as an Erudite of the National Academy. Even as a toddler, Nizi would sometimes close her eyes and sit in meditation, and then begin producing these sutras by reciting them. Sometimes she would say she had ascended to Heaven, and other times she would say that a deity had taught them to her. When she pronounced the words, she spoke fluently and clearly, as if she knew them by heart. When they had someone transcribe her words, sometimes she would suddenly stop reciting, but then after one or two weeks continue again as before. In the capital, both monastics and laypeople all talked about this miracle. When the present emperor [Emperor Wu of the Liang dynasty] summoned her before him and questioned her as to how she did this, she answered each of his questions in a perfectly normal way. She firmly believed in the correct Dharma, and from an early age practiced Buddhism. When her parents wanted to marry her off, she vowed never to marry. Eventually she left the household life, took the religious name of Sengfa, and went to live in the Green Garden Convent [Qingyuansi].

After I had finished collecting the orthodox books, I began to look into miraculous rumors, and when this affair came to my knowledge, I went to her house and requested to see the sutras. Her family kept them hidden and would not show them to me, however, and I was only able to obtain the *Sutra of the Marvelous Sound of the Lion's Roar* (Miaoyin shizi hou jing). It is for this reason that I have listed her texts among the questionable sutras.

This nun died in the Third Month of the fourth year of Heavenly Supervision [Tianjian, 502–519]. When those interested in these matters obtained her texts and commentaries, it turned out that the sutras she had produced one after another added up to more than twenty scrolls. Firmly convinced that these were genuine sutras, her maternal uncle Sun Zhi commented on them and preached them, collected them and copied them. As they have been touched by brush and writing tablet, they are bound to be preserved.

Long ago, in the final years of reign period Established Peace [196–219] of the Han dynasty, the wife of a man surnamed Ding from Jining suddenly came down with what appeared to be an illness, after which she found herself able to speak in a foreign tongue. She also asked for writing brush and paper, and in her own hand wrote a book in foreign script. When later some barbarians from the western regions saw this book, they declared it to be a sutra. So if we search through antiquity, we find there have indeed been cases like this. Since Nizi's sutras were not uttered by the golden mouth [of the Buddha] nor have they been translated by a[n Indian] master, however, I was not sure whether to include or reject them, which is why I have appended them under the category of "questionable."

Nizi's sutras were not written down by Nizi herself, but rather were transcribed by someone else as she recited them. So strictly speaking, perhaps she should not be included in a history of writing women. Nevertheless, she is representative of a significant number of women in imperial China, especially of the later dynasties, who made themselves heard by the texts they revealed. As Sengyou's comments make clear, revealed texts like this were never automatically rejected as false. Buddhism, for one, provided many arguments why such texts could be regarded as authentic revelations of the Truth after all—the person who revealed them could have remembered them from a previous existence. In any case, none of Nizi's sutras remains extant today.

Poems by nuns. Whereas we have collections of biographies of eminent monks for almost every major Chinese dynasty, Baochang's *Biographies of Bhiksunis* had no sequel until early in the twentieth century. Our sources on Buddhist nuns of the Tang dynasty are mostly limited to miracle tales and epigraphical materials, this despite the relative large numbers of nuns during this period. While the *Complete Poems of the Tang Dynasty (Quan Tang shi)* contains the works of many monks and also of at least ten Daoist nuns, it includes only one poem by a Buddhist nun. This nun, Haiyin, is said to have lived in the second half of the ninth century, and her poem is entitled "At Night on a Boat":

> The color of the water merges with the color of heaven,
> The sound of the wind enhances the sound of waves.
> The traveler suffers from a longing for home,
> The fisherman is startled from his wandering dream.
> As soon as the oars are raised, the clouds arrive,
> Wherever the boat drifts, the moon follows behind.
> Now I have finished reciting the lines of my poem,
> But I still see the distant mountains stretching out.

In the thirteenth century, the polymath Luo Dagang concluded his *Jade Dew from Crane Forest (Helin yulu)*, an extensive collection of notes and essays on a wide range of subjects, with the following short entry:

The Master [Confucius] said: "The Way is not far from man." Mencius said: "The Way is near but people seek it in faraway places." There is a poem on the enlightenment of a nun, which goes:

> All day long I searched for spring but nowhere did I find it—
> On sandals of straw I trekked through the clouds atop the hills.
> When I returned, I smiled and plucked a sprig of flowering plum,
> One sniff and I found that all of spring was there on this twig!

This is also an original and enjoyable poem.

Many critics interpret the phrase "a poem on the enlightenment of a nun" as "a poem on enlightenment by a nun," and proceed to date this anonymous nun to the Tang or to the Song. The wording of the original, on the other hand, suggests that this is an anonymous poem describing a moment of enlightenment, and was not necessarily written by a nun.

Daoist Mystics

The female mystic who, through the descriptions in verse or prose of her ecstatic visions, played such an important role in the development of Western literature from medieval times onward does not really have a counterpart in imperial China. Thus most, if not all, of the extensive meditative and mystical literature compiled in both the Buddhist and the Daoist canons either is written by male authors or is anonymous. The Daoist canon admittedly contains many hymns that are ascribed to women, but in these cases we are dealing with hymns that have been revealed by female immortals to male mystics and shamans. One can accept the female authorship of these materials only if one is prepared to accept the existence of female immortals.

Revealer of texts: Wei Huacun. Of the many female immortals who revealed scriptures to their male devotees, none was more famous than Wei Huacun, who appeared regularly to the male mystic Yang Xi (330–384?). Her revelations to Yang Xi concerning the many paradises of the immortals and techniques of longevity were one of the most important sources for the rise of the new school in Daoism known as Highest Clarity. According to the biographical information provided to Yang Xi by yet another female immortal, Wei Huacun was born in 252, and was the daughter of Wei Shu (209–290), who was one of the top officials of the Jin dynasty. From her earliest youth she exhibited a love for the Way and was widely read not only in the Daoist classics but also in the writings of other schools of thought. Although from an early age she set her sights on the achievement of immortality, as soon as she was old enough, her parents married her off to a certain Liu Wen. Wei Huacun bore Liu Wen two sons, Pu and Xia, but as soon as her sons were grown, she retired from society and spent her days fasting in her room. Once, after undergoing a three-month period of austerities, she was visited by a host of immortals who revealed numerous new scriptures to her.

Wei Huacun was also said to have been a member of the Orthodox Unity church, in which she held the rank of Libationer. Together with her sons, she fled northern China during the troubles of the first decades of the fourth century and after her sons had established themselves in the world of officialdom, resumed her religious exercises with renewed energy, and finally shed her mortal form in 334. After this transformation, it is said, she continued to roam the earth for a few more years, until finally she joined the entourage of the Queen Mother of the West, the matriarch of all female immortals said to reside in the paradisiacal gardens atop Mt. Kunlun.

In Wei Huacun's biography as revealed to Yang Xi, details concerning Wei Huacun's mortal existence pale before the many descriptions of her meetings with immortals of all kinds and their discussions regarding the highest truth. While these biographical details are not implausible in themselves (Yang Xi claims to have received one of the scriptures revealed to Wei Huacun from her son, Liu Pu, in 350), the supernatural origin of the biography calls for caution. Moreover, we do not have the original biography as it was dictated to Yang Xi, but only as it was rewritten in the eighth century and included in compilations of the ninth and tenth centuries. The biography of Wei Huacun is probably best read as a description of what was considered in the second half of the fourth century the ideal life of a devout Daoist woman. For in the end, Wei Huacun is important in the history of Daoism not because of her own life, but because of the scriptures she purportedly revealed to Yang Xi.

Wei Huacun is also the only woman who is traditionally mentioned as the author of a text in the Daoist canon, although modern scholars reject this ascription. The text in question consists of a hodgepodge of writings on longevity techniques. While these writings are of a relatively early date, internal evidence dates them considerably later than the historical Wei Huacun, if she ever existed.

Princess and peasant girl: Yuzhen and Wang Fajin. As mentioned above, the development of monastic Buddhism was a major inspiration for the development of Daoist monasteries (*guan* or "observatories" for watching the stars), and eventually, Daoist convents as well. These Daoist convents enjoyed their period of greatest prosperity during the Tang dynasty, when a number of Tang emperors favored Daoist institutions with lavish gifts and elevated the status of Daoist masters. In the course of the Tang dynasty more than ten imperial princesses became Daoist nuns in ordination ceremonies that were celebrated with great pomp and circumstance.

One of these aristocratic nuns was the princess Yuzhen, a daughter of Emperor Ruizong (r. 710–712) and a sister of Emperor Xuanzong (r. 712–756). In 734 she composed the *Classic of Soaring and Flying Spirits* (*Lingfei jing*), a description of how to visualize and then summon the immortal jade maidens of the six cyclical *ding* characters for the purpose of subjugating ghosts and demons. This text is not included in the Daoist canon, but has been preserved because it was copied out by the famous contemporary calligrapher Zhong Shaojing, whose rendition was later engraved in stone.

Not all Daoist nuns of the Tang dynasty came from the most elite social circles. Wang Fajin, who also lived in the first half of the eighth century and may have been the author of a text included in the Daoist canon, was most likely born to a poor peasant family. The biography of Wang Fajin found in the *Comprehensive Records of the Reign Period Great Peace* (*Taiping guangji*) of the late tenth century clearly illustrates the wide gulf between the background and interests of noble ladies such as Wei Huacun and Princess Yuzhen on the one hand, and a simple nun like Wang Fajin:

Wang Fajin was a native of Linjin in Jianzhou. From her earliest years, she loved the Way. Her family lived close to an old Daoist temple, and even though there was no Daoist master in residence, when she played there she would never show any disrespect toward the images of the gods. When she was just over ten years old, a Daoist nun who was traveling from Jianzhou through the outlying districts stopped at their home. Wang Fajin's parents, knowing their daughter's love of the Way, placed her under the nun's protection. The nun initiated her into a minor register of the Orthodox Unity church for the extension of life, and gave her the religious name of Fajin.[14] Fajin diligently devoted herself to worship and strictly maintained the fasts and precepts. In addition, she lived on pine seeds and avoided grains, and from time to time received visions.

At that time Sichuan was beset by famine. A peck of rice became extremely expensive and five or six out of every ten people perished: people would all collect fibers from the fields and tubers from the mountains to stave off their hunger. One day three youths clad in green suddenly descended into Fajin's courtyard and said to her: "Because you have been born with the bones of an immortal, are single-minded and sincere in your belief, and have never deviated from the Way, the God on High has ordered us to escort you to the Capital on High, where you will be entrusted with a mission."

Before she knew what was happening, she had soared up into the sky, and had quickly come to the dwelling place of the God on High. He ordered that

---

14. In Orthodox Unity Daoism the priest upon initiation receives a list of gods under his or her command. Such a list of gods, including their names and detailed descriptions of their appearance, is called a "register."

she be given a jade cup of cloud brew, and then in a leisurely manner addressed her saying: "Man is the greatest of the Three Talents[15] and embodies the harmony of Heaven and Earth. It is truly fortunate to have been given a human form and to be born in China! Heaven that rotates the energies of the four seasons and Earth that provides the essences of the five elements cause the five grains and hundred fruits to grow and in this way nourish the people. But ignorant of the favor shown by Heaven and Earth in feeding and nourishing them, people carelessly discard the five grains and are so bored with silk and hemp that they throw them away! As a result the men who plow the fields and the women who spin and weave can never get enough to eat despite their diligence, nor can they protect themselves against the cold despite all their efforts. To no avail they labor and toil, but there is no one who takes pity on them. This is definitely condemned by the divine beings and will not be tolerated by Heaven and Earth! Recently this was reported by the supervisors of the earth, the holy mountains and the great rivers, in a memorial to the effect that the people of this world are so bored with the five grains that they throw them away and that they do not treat clothing and food with the proper respect. So I ordered the office of the Great Flowery Mountain[16] to lock up the gods of the five grains. What was sowed has not ripened into grain, and the people down below are suffering from famine. But the simple people do not know the origin of their transgression and therefore they do not know how to show regret and confess their sins. You are destined to become a servant girl in the palace on high, and you will serve in the mansion of Heaven. But, for the time being, I command you to return to the world below and to enlighten the people, so that they may repent of their crimes and treasure the products of husbandry and sericulture. This will be your hidden merit." He then ordered a servant girl to hand her a scroll with the ritual for thanking Heaven and Earth by means of the Pure Feast of the Numinous Treasure. He instructed her to transmit it to the world, saying: "Order the people of this world to go together to a high and quiet place on a wooded mountain and there lay out a vegetarian feast to express repentance and gratitude. If they do this twice a year, all their sins of former lives will be absolved, and Father Grain and Mother Silkworm will ensure an abundant harvest. In a dragon-and-tiger year I will summon you again." This is the current method of the Pure Feast for the Lord of Heaven for the expression of gratitude.

*In the twelfth [**NB:** probably a mistake for eleventh] year of the reign period Heavenly Treasure [Tianbao, 742–755], a renchen year, Fajin again ascended to Heaven.*

---

15. The "Three Talents" are Heaven, Earth, and Man.

16. The Great Flowery Mountain is Huashan, the sacred marchmount of the West. The god of Huashan was one of the most widely revered deities of the Tang dynasty.

There is also a slightly more elaborate version of the biography of Wang Fajin in the *Records of the Assembled Immortals of Yongcheng* (*Yongcheng jixianlu*), by the late Tang Daoist master Du Guangting (850–930). This work, which also includes a biography of Wei Huacun and has been preserved in a Daoist encyclopedia of the eleventh century, adds little of substance, however.

Of the many texts in the Daoist canon, not one bears the name of Wang Fajin as the author. The eminent modern scholar of Daoism Kristofer Schipper believes that the anonymous *Classic of the Grotto-God of the Greatest Eminence on the Extirpation of Demons and Support for the State of the Lord of Heaven* (*Taishang dongshen Taingong xiaomo huguo jing*) is the text revealed by Wang Fajin. Other scholars consider this anonymous work to be a product of the Song dynasty, at least a few centuries after Wang Fajin's lifetime. The text consists of three chapters, two of which are taken up by extended dialogues between the Old Master (Laozi) and his disciple Yin Xi. The work preaches a conventional morality and provides ritual instructions for exorcising evil demons; it also contains a number of hymns. The most important reason for linking this text to Wang Fajin is no doubt the fact that in it the Old Master himself greatly praises the efficacy of the ritual propagated by Wang Fajin.

Self-Censoring Ladies and Public Women

The female members of the elite families of the centuries of political disunion apparently felt free to engage in writing activities and were able to write, if they so wished, in any of the major literary genres of the time. This appears not to have been the case during the Tang dynasty, especially following the reign of Empress Wu. It is significant that although the volume of preserved literature from the eighth and ninth centuries is many times that of earlier centuries, women writers are notably absent. We do have a few poems for each of a handful of elite women poets, but none of these women enjoyed the reputation of their predecessors. Various sources suggest that by this time the writing of poetry had come to be seen as an unsuitable occupation for a proper lady. For instance, the female protagonist of a ninth-century miracle tale (who in the end turns out to have been a transformed tigress) says to her husband when he urges her to chant aloud the poem she appears to be silently composing:

"As a spouse one must of course know how to read and write, but if one on top of that also would compose poetry, one would look too much like a courtesan or a concubine." And indeed, the best-known women poets of the eighth and ninth centuries, Li Ye, Xuan Tao, and Yu Xuanji, were independent women, described as Daoist nuns or courtesans or both. The very visibility of these courtesan poets may well have contributed to the growing reluctance of elite women to write and publish their works.

Self-Censoring Ladies

Burned manuscripts. An elite woman of the Tang dynasty, filled perhaps with a passion for poetry but unwilling to endanger her reputation as a respectable woman, was often left with only one option: to refrain from writing altogether. She may have felt impelled to consign to flames any writings that she may have dared to secretly entrust to paper. In his *Trifling Words from the Northern Marshlands (Beimeng suoyan)*, a voluminous collection of anecdotes concerning the life of China's cultural elite in the ninth and tenth centuries, Sun Guangxian (d. 968) quotes the following three poems by a certain lady Sun:

White Wax Candle

Its light surpasses a silver lamp, its fragrance equals the orchid,
And its long jade-white purity causes one to shiver with cold.
When late on a windy spring night you find yourself in the purple palace
Drunkenly drafting an imperial edict, you'll be able to see quite clearly.[17]

Thanks for a Gift of Wine

Many thanks for sending this clear wine to this melancholy person:
Clear and transparent, sweet and fragrant—its taste is perfect!
Truly, on a night with breeze and moonlight before the green window,
A single cup whips up a heart full of spring!

---

17. The famous poet Li Bai stayed at the court of Emperor Xuanzong between 742 and 744. His finest piece of prose during this time was said to have been composed one night when the inebriated poet was summoned from a local wineshop and ordered to draft an imperial edict.

On Hearing a Zither

Jade fingers on red strings: now creaking, now clear—
The sorrows of the Xiang goddesses are too much to bear![18]
At first you think it is the fierce howling of a cold storm,
Then it sounds like the desolate dripping of evening rain.
 Close by: comparable to a gurgling spring flowing between green cliffs,
Distant: resembling a black crane swooping down from the blue sky.
At midnight after the playing has stopped, I'm overcome by grief,
As dew soaks the clustered orchids and moonlight fills the courtyard.

But what is perhaps even more interesting than these three competent but otherwise rather conventional poems is the short biographical note that introduces them:

Lady Sun of Lechang was the wife of the student Meng Changqi. She was an expert in the composition of poems, but one day she burned her collected works because she felt that poetry was not the proper work of a married woman. From that day forward, she devoted herself solely to her wifely tasks.

This may well be the earliest recorded case of a woman destroying her own writings. In later centuries many writing women would follow her example.

Multiple personalities. In other cases the tension between the desire to participate in literary life and the social pressure to refrain from writing resulted in cases of what today we might call "multiple personalities" but what was at the time identified as spirit possession. What was forbidden for a woman was permitted and even expected of the man who spoke through her mouth. For example, in his *Extensive Collection of Miracles* (*Guangyi ji*), a large collection of accounts of extraordinary events from the latter half of the eighth century, Dai Fu (ca. 730–ca. 790) recounts the story of the girl Wang Fazhi, who was possessed by the spirit of a poetically-inclined young man named Teng Chuanyin:

---

18. "The Xiang goddesses" are Huang and Ying, the wives of the mythic sage emperor Shun. When they heard of their husbands' death in the southern province of Hunan, they wept so piteously that their tears left permanent stains on the local bamboo. Then, overcome with grief, they drowned themselves in the Xiang River, after which they were revered as the goddesses of the Xiang. The goddesses of the Xiang were also credited with the invention of a zither with fifty strings.

Wang Fazhi, a girl from Tonglu, from the time she was very young venerated a deity with the appearance of a young man. Sometime during the reign period Great Continuation [Dali, 766–779], this deity was suddenly heard to speak through her mouth with the voice of an adult. Fazhi's father questioned him asking: "Are yours the words of a divinity?" The answer was: "Indeed they are! My name is Teng Chuanyin. I was a native of Wannian district in the capital, and lived in the Chongxian Ward. I have a karmic affinity with Fazhi."

If you conversed with him, he displayed a thorough understanding of principle, and the successive prefects and magistrates all regarded him very highly. The district magistrate of Tonglu, Zheng Feng, was a man of great curiosity, and repeatedly summoned Fazhi to his quarters. When he commanded her to invoke [the spirit of] Teng Chuanyin, it would be quite awhile before he arrived. His eloquent repartee was a sign of his gentlemanly style, and Feng never tired of listening to him.

Whenever Teng met with poets, he would discuss the Classics and recite poetry, happily conversing the whole day long. Once when a traveling monk stopped by Fazhi's place asking for alms, the deity engaged him in conversation and presented him with a poem that read:

> So independent, without striving: famed among the monks,
> Holding fast to your goal, you roam beyond the clouds.
> The heroes of today shake the heavens with their vigor,
> But which of them will sit for eternity on a lotus throne?

On another occasion he presented another person with the following poem:

> During my lifetime, my talents fell short,
> As for my character, I was true to my word.
> I never did give anyone cause for blame,
> So no gentleman need keep his distance.

On the night of the twenty-fifth day of the Second Month of the sixth year [of Great Continuation], I, Dai Fu, found myself at the residence of Zheng Feng, together with Xu Guang of the Military Service Section of the Left Guard; the magistrate of Longquan, Cui Xiang; the assistant magistrate of Danyang, Li Congxun; and two local men, Han Wei and Si Xiu. Then Fazhi also came, and was ordered to call down [the spirit of] Teng Chuanyin. It was a long time before he arrived. After he had exchanged a hundred or so words with Xu Guang and the others, he said: "Gentlemen, why don't each of you recite a poem!" After each of us had recited a poem, we all asked him for a poem. Without any hesitation he recited two poems, the first of which went:

When the flood rises at the mouth of the river the waters swell,
And the lotus boats rock and sway, making it hard to pick the flowers.
Your spring heart left unsatisfied, you return with nothing to show—
When the flood has subsided, you may try again to pick them!

He added: "Please, do not laugh at me!" The second poem went:

Out of the blue a single cloud drifts across the lake
And suddenly rain soaks your clothes in the boat.
You forget all about the lotus flowers you might have picked
And go home, covering your head in vain with lotus leaves!

He himself commented: "This poem is also rather lame!" Then he departed after having ordered his "younger brother" Fazhi to exchange some hundreds of words with Zheng Feng.

Because of the male spirit who spoke through her, Wang Fazhi was able to participate in male society and exchange poems with elite men, something that would have been out of the question for an elite woman who valued her reputation. Wang Fazhi's alternate personality, Teng Chuanyin, was a welcome guest at the get-togethers of the local elite of Tonglu. His popularity may have been partly due to the subtle erotic nature of some of his poems. In the poem translated above, for example, the lotus has two possible meanings. In Buddhism, it is a symbol for spiritual purity maintained even in the sinful mire of the worldly life: the lotus throne refers to the throne of the Buddha, and devout believers reborn in the Pure Land of the West of the Buddha Amitabha are each given a lotus upon which to sit. On the other hand, the Chinese word for lotus (*lian*) is also a homonym for another word that means love (*lian*). Thus, the image of young girls (often compared to lotus flowers) in their little boats, floating among a jungle of lotus flowers that rise from the water, suggests secret trysts. But then again, perhaps Teng Chuanyin's poems should be read as a daring attempt to put the assembled gentlemen in their place: they have come together to gape at a girl who composes poems like a man, but if they thought they would be able to pluck her like a lotus flower, they are in for an unpleasant surprise!

Conversations in dreams. A slightly less extreme case of literary obsession is described in the *Biography of Niu Yingzhen* (*Niu Yingzhen zhuan*). Niu Yingzhen lived around the middle of the eighth century, and during her short life became an expert in the *Commentary of Mr. Zuo* (*Zuo zhuan*, an extremely detailed narrative account of the political events in China from 721–463 BCE). She was also known for being able to discuss scholarly subjects with the greatest minds of Chinese history—although only in her dreams. Our earliest source for the *Biography of Niu Yingzhen*, the *Comprehensive Records of the Reign Period Great Peace* of 978, attributes the account to Niu Yingzhen's father, Niu Su (ca. 700–ca. 760), who once served as prefect of Yuezhou and was also the author of a large collection of miracle tales entitled *Records of Rumors* (*Jiwen*). Later sources, however, all attribute the *Biography of Niu Yingzhen* to the Inner Palace intendant Song Ruozhao, one of the five Song sisters discussed in Chapter 1. It is highly improbable that a father would include the biography of his own daughter in a collection of hearsay miracles. It may be early readers were misled by the fact that Niu Su's name appears at the beginning of the very first line of the biography. So it does not seem implausible that the *Biography of Niu Yingzhen* was indeed written by Song Ruozhao, in which case it would be her only surviving piece of prose writing.

A large part of the *Biography of Niu Yingzhen* is taken up by the text of Yingzhen's *Rhapsody on the Questioning of Shadow by Penumbra* (*Wangliang wen ying fu*).[19] As the preface to the rhapsody indicates, the motif of the dialogue between Shadow and Penumbra originally came from the *Master Zhuang* (*Zhuangzi*), a philosophical text that reflects the thinking of Zhuang Zhou (ca. 369–ca. 286 BCE) and his school, and is usually classified as a Daoist work. In the extant text of the *Master Zhuang*, one finds two slightly different versions of the dialogue between Shadow and Penumbra, one in chapter 2, and another longer version in chapter 27. The first version may be translated as follows:

Penumbra asked Shadow: "Just a moment ago you were walking and now you are standing, just a moment ago you were sitting and now you have stood up. Why are you not the master of your own behavior?" Shadow answered: "Could it be that I am acting this way because I am dependent on others? And could it be that that upon which I depend also acts the way it does because it is depen-

---

19. For a full understanding of Niu Yingzhen's rhapsody, one also should know that the Chinese word for penumbra (*wangliang*) is also used to refer to a forest imp that has the appearance of a three-year-old child, is red-black in color, and has red eyes, long ears, and beautiful hair.

dent on others? Am I dependent on the scales of a snake or the wings of a cicada? How should I know why I act or do not act the way I do?"

The *Biography of Niu Yingzhen* reads:

Niu Su's eldest daughter was called Yingzhen and she was married to Tang Tangyuan of Hongnong.

From the time she was very young she was exceptionally intelligent. She had only to hear something once, and she could immediately recite it. By the age of thirteen, she was able to recite more than three hundred scrolls of Buddhist sutras, several hundred or more scrolls of Confucian texts, and the texts of the philosophers and the historians as well. All her relatives were surprised and marveled at her abilities.

One night [when she was sleeping], before Yingzhen had studied the *Commentary of Mr. Zuo* and just as it had been decided to teach her this text, she suddenly began to recite all thirty scrolls of the *Annals of Spring and Autumn* [*Chunqiu*], beginning with [the first line], "When Lady Meng, the first wife of Duke Hui had died . . ." and ending with [the last line], "The head of the Zhi family was greedy and stubborn, which is why the Han and Wei families turned on him and destroyed him."[20] She did not leave out a single character and did not finish until the break of dawn. The entire time she was reciting, it was as if there was someone there, not only teaching her, but from time to time also engaging her in conversation. Startled and frightened, her father called out her name again and again, but she didn't respond and only woke up after she had finished her reciting. When her father asked her how this possibly could have happened, she herself had no idea. But when he ordered her to open the text, she found she already knew it by heart and could answer any questions about it.

She composed more than a hundred texts. Later, after she had achieved full mastery of the Three Teachings and her erudition had been extended to all of the arts, at night when she was sound asleep she would discuss texts with learned gentlemen, all of whom were famous men of antiquity.[21] They would pose each other questions in quick succession. They might be called Wang Bi, Zheng Xuan, Wang Yan, and Lu Ji![22] Their discussion would flare up like

---

20. The *Annals of Spring and Autumn*, which is traditionally paired with the *Commentary of Mr. Zuo*, is one of the longest of the Confucian Classics.

21. The Three Teachings are Confucianism, Daoism, and Buddhism.

22. Wang Bi (226–249) is famous for his commentaries on the *Changes* and on the *Book of the Way and its Virtue* (*Daode jing*). Zheng Xuan (127–200) was one of the greatest scholars of the second century; one of his works is a commentary on the *Book of Odes*.

torches. At other times she would discuss literary writings. Again, these learned gentlemen would rank among the most famous of antiquity. On one occasion they might discuss literary style, on another they might discuss philosophy. Often this would go on for several nights!

Yingzhen died at the age of twenty-four. I have selected her *Rhapsody on the Questioning of Shadow by Penumbra* to add to this text. Its preface reads:

In the year *gengchen* [740] I was suffering from a serious and painful illness and was bedridden for more than three months. The illness depleted my energy and emaciated my body. However much the medicines and treatments were multiplied, they brought no improvement. Moved by the meaning of the castigation of Shadow by Penumbra in the *Master Zhuang*, I borrowed the theme to write a rhapsody.

> Penumbra asked my shadow: "You are a person
> Of eminent understanding
> And brilliant intelligence,
> You have fully studied the six arts,
> And your reading encompasses the hundred schools.
> You've fed yourself on the secret words of the Daoist masters,
> And searched for the hidden meanings in the Buddhist canon.
> You've not only devoutly carried out your domestic duties,
> But have also imitated admired models from the earlier histories.
> You've committed no crime in the pursuit of fame,
> You've not slandered others to establish yourself.
> If such is the nature of your pure virtue,
> It should be enough to sustain your vital energy!
>
> So why is it then
> That your body and face are so emaciated,
> That your spirit and energy have dissipated,
> That you are beset by worries on mat and pillow,
> Just a bag of bones in gown and headscarf?
> The physical form is the only thing you can rely on—
> The physical form and you should be best friends!
> So why
> Don't you teach it to venerate virtue,

Wang Yan (256–311) was renowned for his debating talents. Lu Ji (261–303) was a famous poet and critic.

And instruct it to adhere to the norms?
You don't show the joy in the Way of Lao Laizi's spouse,
And lack the resignation to poverty of Liang Hong's wife.[23]
How could you let this chronic illness rob you of the zest for life,
Or is it because of your lowly position that you wish to neglect
your body?

Right at this moment
The seasons change and the year moves on,
The winter is finished, and spring has begun!
She spreads her bright light over suburbs and fields,
And arouses a warming energy in willow and plum.
The ice has broken on the streams that encircle your cottage,
And through your window the wind fans its pleasant breezes.
This surely can
Dispel your sorrows, relieve your ailment,
Please your spirit and nourish your longevity!
Why do you insist on
Moping in silence, doing nothing at all,
Being only yourself to blame for your troubles?"

I was then provoked to respond as follows:
"You reside in regions where there are no people,
And frolic in the land of trolls and bogeymen.
Not only has your form been depicted on the tripods of the Xia,[24]
But your name has also been recorded in the *Master Zhuang*.
So why is your insight so limited?
And why are your words so narrow?

Now,
The shadow is born because of the sun,
And adapts its shape to that of the man.
How can this be sufficiently explained by discourse?

---

23. The wives of Lao Laizi and Liang Hong both have entries in the *Biographies of Exemplary Women*. They are praised for having faithfully served their poverty-stricken husbands.

24. Yu, the mythic founder of the Xia dynasty, is said to have cast nine bronze cauldrons on which all the weird creatures of the world were depicted: by knowing their shapes and names he controlled them.

How can this be disputed by the change of season?
The shadow arises and disappears according to night and day,
 And shifts its shape according to body and bones.
The fool fears his shadow, and in so doing his rustic and stupid nature
  is revealed;
 When the wise man observes the shade, his awareness of the approach
  of the end is manifested.
My shadow's beauty or lack of it is dependent on me—
 What is its crime that it should be castigated so?

          Moreover, I have learned
That the essence of the highest Way is hidden and dark,
 That the acme of the highest Way is obscure and silent.
The man of understanding accepts the length of his life, whether long
  or short,
 The gentleman resigns himself to the turn of his fortune, for good or
  for ill:
Regret and greed cannot hinder him,
 Glory and splendor cannot seduce him;
Whatever he loses he deems not a loss,
 Whatever he gains, he deems no success.
          So why do you
Reproach me for not enjoying the fragrant spring,
 And scold me for not loving fancy adornments?
How would your wisdom be sufficient to fathom
 Why I behave this way?"

          Before I had even finished speaking, Penumbra was alarmed
    and startled, and rose with a sigh:
"I was born beyond the remotest regions,
 And grew up in far and barren lands.
Not yet understanding how a wise person behaves,
 I came to you and questioned your shadow.
Now that you have explained to me these most marvelous secrets,
 I request your permission to hide away for the rest of my life."

In the beginning, in her dreams Yingzhen would tear books apart and eat
them, and after having consumed several tens of scrolls in this way, her literary

style would always change. This occurred repeatedly, and eventually she became skillful in rhapsodies and hymns. Her writings are entitled *Lingering Fragrance*.

In the *Master Zhuang*, the dialogue between Shadow and Penumbra is a parable on the impossibility of finding a first cause. The argument made by Zhuang Zhou is that behind every action there is a cause of which the acting agency may be unaware. In her rhapsody, Niu Yingzhen keeps both Shadow and Penumbra, but introduces herself into the conversation as well. The model for her text was provided by the "hypothetical discussions" (*shewen*) of earlier centuries, in which a retired scholar, when asked why he does not take advantage of the many opportunities to make a career, answers by singing the praises of the simple life and the freedom and independence it allows. In her rhapsody, however, Niu Yingzhen's alternative is one of resignation and very little joy. A modern reader may well wonder whether Penumbra is closer to the mark than Niu Yingzhen is willing to admit when he suggests that she lacks the ability to find pleasure in the role of a self-sacrificing wife ("like a shadow or an echo"), and resents being a woman. That same modern reader may well detect a certain hollowness in the lofty language of her indignant reply, which is so much belied by the way she behaves in her dreams.

The one kind of poem a wife living in the later centuries of the Tang might be permitted to write was one in which she encouraged her husband to greater application in his preparation for the examinations. In the *Master Jade Source* (*Yuquanzi*), an anonymous collection of anecdotes compiled some time in the last decades of the ninth century, we find the following story about Du Gao (ca. 760–ca. 820) and his wife, lady Liu (or, according to another source, lady Zhao):

Du Gao's wife, lady Liu, was skilled at composing poetry. Gao had repeatedly taken the examinations but without success. He had not yet arrived back home when he received the following poem from his wife:

> My husband, you clearly have extraordinary talents,
> So why are you, year after year, always sent down?
> It has come to the point where I'm ashamed of you,
> So if you return, come under the cover of darkness!

As soon as Gao read this poem, he immediately went back [to the capital]. Later, after he had successfully passed the examinations, his wife again sent him a poem:

> Chang'an is not so very far from here,
> An auspicious air, thick and dense, hovers above.
> You, my husband, have reached your goal in the prime of your youth—
> In which bordello will you sleep off your drunken high tonight?

We may assume that lady Liu was not only concerned about her husband's alcohol consumption, but also about the company he kept. And this brings us to the subject of courtesans.

Public Women

The insistence in the *Rites* and other guidelines for women on the segregation of the sexes in elite families, even if not always strictly adhered to, greatly limited the possibilities for elite men to associate with educated women outside their own families. The need for female companionship on such occasions as festive gatherings was filled instead by professional female entertainers, trained from early youth in all the skills of music and dance, repartee, and poetry. The entertainment they provided might extend to sexual services but not necessarily. The overwhelming majority of these female entertainers lived a miserable life, but for a few women, the career of courtesan provided an opportunity to pursue an independent life outside the strict confines of the family.

The Tang dynasty is not the first period in Chinese history from which we have poems that are attributed to courtesans. From the centuries of political disunion we have a number of erotic quatrains that are ascribed to women with professional names such as Ziye (Midnight) and Taoye (Peachleaf). A few examples may suffice:

> When young, a man should not hesitate—
> Let time slip by, and quickly you'll be old.
> If you do not believe the words I say,
> Look at the grasses, now covered by frost.

> The night is long, I cannot fall asleep—
> How brightly shines the light of the full moon!
> I imagine I hear your voice calling me,
> And to no avail at all I answer: "Yes!"

How lovely the blossoms on the spring trees!
How mournful the warbling of the spring birds!
And, oh, how passionate those spring breezes
That blow open my skirt of silk.

Although attributed to named (but otherwise unknown) courtesans, these poems most likely are anonymous folksongs. Within the Chinese tradition of erotic poetry, they are remarkable for their relative sexual frankness.

The second half of the Tang dynasty provided even more favorable conditions for the rise to prominence of literate courtesans. In his *Records of the Northern Ward* (*Beilizhi*), a description of Chang'an's red-light district during its final glory years, Sun Qi (second half of the ninth century) provides us with a few brief biographies of the most prominent courtesans of the time. In these biographies, Sun occasionally also quotes one or two poems written by these women. Gao Yanxiu, another author of the second half of the ninth century, records the case of a courtesan, acquired by a certain Mr. Wei, who was not only beautiful but also an excellent musician and a perceptive textual scholar:

Her smart intelligence was really unparalleled. Once Wei had her copy out the poems of Du Fu. The text he had at his disposal was riddled with errors, but she would correct these as she plied the brush, and the literary structure [of the poems] would blaze forth with even greater brilliance! That was the reason Wei loved her so much!

This little anecdote holds out the tantalizing possibility that the transmitted text of the poetry of China's greatest poet may be as much the work of this anonymous courtesan as that of Du Fu himself!

The three best-known women poets of the Tang dynasty—Li Ye, Xue Tao, and Yu Xuanji—were both courtesans and Daoist nuns, either simultaneously or in succession. Both the nun and the courtesan lived outside the family, and both the nun and the courtesan could participate in male society by, for instance, the exchange of occasional verse. Such a free association of nuns with male patrons made the distinction between nun and courtesan at times quite hazy in the eyes of their contemporary observers.

Our knowledge of the lives of Li Ye, Xue Tao, and Yu Xuanji is very limited, since their careers did not entitle them to a biography in the dynastic histories. The information that can be culled from their poems must be combined with the scattered references to these women that we find in the works of some of their contemporaries. We also have some occasional anecdotal information, which, because it is often of a later date, is of questionable reliability.

Poet and Traitor: Li Ye. We know very little about Li Ye (style name Jilan) apart from the fact that she was a native of Wuxing, was active in the third quarter of the eighth century, mainly in southeast China, and that in 784 her life came to a brutal end. Some later sources refer to her as a Daoist nun, but among her extant eighteen poems, there is only one poem, entitled "Love for the Way; Sent to Vice-Minister Cui," that is clearly religious in character:

> Cease your useless craving for floating fame,
> Be sure to restrain your desire for high office.
> Life's hundred years are like a single day
> And what has passed all turns to emptiness.
> Your sorrowed sideburns soon turn white,
> For all your study, still no ruddy cheeks!
> The best thing you could do in India
> Would be to join the Ancient Master.

"Ancient Master" is a Daoist designation for the Buddha, so it would appear as if our Daoist nun is urging her addressee to seek refuge with Buddha.

Li Ye's other poems evince a frank sensuality that would seem at odds with a monastic vocation. This sensuality, together with her known contacts with a number of local officials, make it more likely that our poet spent most of her active life as a courtesan rather than as a nun.

Fishes Knotted of White Silk; Presented to a Friend

> A square of silk as white as snow:
> I folded it tight into a pair of carp.
> You want to know the secrets of my heart?
> Just read the letter hidden in their belly.

On Receiving a Letter from Yan Bojun

> So filled with love, before the mirror I forget to do my hair,
> The evening rain desolate, the courtyard trees autumnal.
> Don't be surprised to see tears running down in streams:
> I am heartbroken when confronted by the traces of your brush!

A Night of Full Moon; For Someone Seeing Me Off

The one departing has no words, the moon has no voice,
But the full moon has her light, and I have my feelings.
After this goodbye I will in my longing be just like the moon:
Between the clouds, above the streams, atop the highest wall!

Eight Extremes

Most near and most far: east and west,
Most deep and most shallow: limpid streams.
Most high and most bright: sun and moon,
Most close and most distant: husband and wife.

The Willow

I love most your slender form by the side of a winding stream
When the setting sun moves your shadow across the duckweed—
The east wind once again has dyed you with your annual green,
The wanderer is pained once more by a thousand miles of spring.
 Your hanging leaves can already conceal the boat at the bank,
Your highest branches surely sequester the girl on the tower.
When your dancing waist thickens, and your misty beauty ages,
Your drifting floss will scatter and flirt with the grasses below.

Love-Longing

Nothing, they say, is deeper than the ocean—
But it is not half as deep as this love of mine.
The waters of the ocean have their borders—
My love is endless and it has no bounds!
 I took my zither and climbed up the tower,
To an empty room flooded by moonlight.
There I played a melody of love and longing,
Until both strings and heart snapped in two.

Sent to Zhu Fang

I climbed the hill to gaze upon the streams:
The hill was high, the lake was oh-so-wide,
Longing for each other all the time,
Waiting for each other months and years.

The trees on the hill grow thick and lush,
The wild flowers blossom without end.
Of my boundless feelings since our parting
I will tell you as soon as we meet again.

Zhu Fang was a local magnate and minor official who lived toward the end of the eighth century. The poem suggests that the addressee has left the poet to take up an official position, perhaps at the capital. While the "trees on the hill" (or mountain) may refer to high officials, "wild flowers" may refer to the many courtesans of the capital who could well lure Zhu Fang away. Li Ye's poem may have been written as a response to the following poem by Zhu Fang, entitled "Saying Goodbye to Li Jilan":

On the old riverbank new blossoms open on a single branch,
Beside the bank and below the blossoms is where we parted.
Don't make the blossoms fall by brushing them with your sleeve,
Because that would immediately break this traveler's heart!

In China, as in many other parts of the world, "fallen flower" was a common metaphor used to refer to courtesans and prostitutes. In some poems Li Ye seems to be advertising her availability as a courtesan, especially in those poems in which she compares herself to the goddess of Shamanka Mountain (Wushan). Shamanka Mountain is one of the peaks of the mountain ranges that mark the border between the modern provinces of Hubei and Sichuan. It is through these mountain ranges that the mighty Yangzi River winds its way through the Three Gorges. Once upon a time, according to an old legend, the goddess of Shamanka Mountain appeared in a dream to the king of Chu as he lay napping on this mountain. After they had made love, she told him that she manifested herself in the early morning as drifting clouds, and in the evening as showers of rain. Since that time "clouds and rain" has been the most common Chinese euphemism for sexual intercourse, and the goddess herself became a symbol of sensuality and desire. Li Ye's identification with the goddess of Shamanka Mountain is most explicit in the following poem, which is the longest of her extant works:

I Attended Xiao Shuzi While He Was Listening to Someone Playing the Zither; The Poem Topic Assigned to Me Was "Song on the Flowing Springs Near the Three Gorges"

Originally I lived among the clouds of Shamanka Mountain,
Where I would always listen to Shamanka's flowing springs.
Imitated on the zither, they sound even more distant and pure,
And are just like those I heard in my dreams of those days!

The Three Gorges are so far away, many thousands of miles,
But all of a sudden they flow into these gloomy inner quarters.
Huge boulders and collapsing cliffs are born from the fingers,
And waterfalls and racing waves rise up from the strings!

At first their roaring rage seems to be like thunder and storm,
But then it sobs and sighs like a stream that cannot flow.
Swirling eddies and whirling maelstroms expend all their might,
To be followed again by dripping and dropping on level sand.

When long ago, I recall, Master Ruan composed this tune,
He could make Zhongrong listen to it without end.
Play the tune once again as soon as it is done,
Please make these flowing springs go on forever!

Instrumental music in the Tang dynasty was programmatic in nature, and strong contrasts in tempo and volume were greatly appreciated. Master Ruan refers to Ruan Ji (210–263), the famous poet, zither player, and untrammeled drunkard, who was later included among the Seven Sages of the Bamboo Grove. Zhongrong was his nephew Ruan Xian (234–305), who enjoyed a great reputation as a lute player.

Because Li Ye portrayed herself in her poems as the goddess of Shamanka Mountain, it should come as no surprise therefore that the earliest sources present her as a courtesan. In fact, according to an anecdote preserved in a mid-tenth-century collection, she gave indication both of her poetic talent and her lack of virtue even as a very young girl:

Li Jilan was famed for her talents despite the fact that she was a woman. When she was five or six years old, her father carried her in his arms into the courtyard, where she composed a poem on roses, the last lines of which read:

If for a moment left unsupported by a trellis,
They will tend to stray wildly in all directions.

Her father said angrily: "This girl will later be blessed with literary style, but she is bound to end up as a fallen woman." And indeed it turned out as he had said.

In his anthology of poems from the period 756–780 titled the *Restoration Collection* (*Zhongxing jianqi ji*), Gao Zhongwu (second half of the eighth century) included six poems of Li Ye's, which he prefaced with the following introduction:

For a gentleman there are the hundred rules of deportment, but for a woman only the four virtues. But not for Jilan! Since her personality is masculine, her poetry is unrestrained. Rarely since the time of Bao Zhao has her equal been seen.[25]

Once she was together with several gentlemen at the Reopened Beginning Monastery [Kaiyuansi] of Wucheng. One of them, Liu Changqing [709–780] from Hejian, was suffering from the disease of the heavy scrotum (an inguinal hernia), and so she made fun of him, saying:

The mountain's smell is finest in the evening.

Changqing retorted:

There all the birds so happily find a haven.

Everyone present roared with laughter, and the critics praised both of them equally.

Lines of hers such as "On distant streams a fairy boat is floating, / And frozen stars send off the envoy's cart" belong to the finest of five-syllable lines. While she may not be as good as Concubine Ban from the distant past, she easily surpasses Han Lanying from more recent times.

She is not worried by her advancing age; she is really an eminent dame.

One of the Chinese terms for a hernia is *shanqi*, which has the same pronunciation as *shanqi* (mountain air, mountain smell), but since one of the treatments for hernia was to wrap the scrotum tightly, the result may have been quite odorous. Li Ye addresses Liu Changqing by quoting a line from the famous poet Tao Qian (364–417), which in other circumstances would have been quite flattering (suggesting that the addressee's reputation had increased with age) as a great man is often compared to a mountain. In response Liu Changqing uses another line from the poetry

---

25. For Bao Zhao we probably should read Bao Linghui.

of Tao Qian. In its original context this line too is innocent enough, but the tree that is equally hospitable to all birds also was a common image for a courtesan who receives one guest after another, and both Liu Changqing and Li Ye were well aware that the word "bird" in more vulgar Chinese also had the meaning of "penis." The Buddhist monk and poet Jiaoran (d. 789) has left us a poem in which he more politely compares our passionate poet, who had apparently paid him a visit, to a seductive heavenly nymph:

In Reply to a Poem by Jilan

A heavenly aspara put me to the test,[26]
She wanted to dye my gown with her flowers.
But in the end my dhyana-heart was not aroused[27]
And carrying her flowers she had to return.

Li Ye was eventually inducted into the Inner Palace, probably in the early years of the reign of Emperor Dezong. But when in 783 the general Zhu Ci rose in rebellion and even occupied the capital for a while, she wrote a poem to him so flattering that the indignant Zhao Yuanyi (second half of the eighth century), the contemporary chronicler of these events, refused to include the text in his account:

At that time there was a woman of questionable morals, Li Jilan, who presented a poem to Ci. Its words are so rebellious and treasonous, that I will leave them out and not record them. When the emperor recovered the capital, he summoned her and castigated her, saying: "Why didn't you learn from Yan Juchuan's poem, which goes: 'My hands hold the ritual vases and my tears course down, / My heart thinks of the enlightened ruler but I dare not say a word'?" He then ordered her to be clubbed to death.

No further information is available on Yan Juchuan. As for Li Ye, the poetry-loving Emperor Dezong would a few years later fill her empty spot in the Inner Palace with the five talented Song sisters.

Despite her lifestyle and her ultimate disloyalty, the eighteenth-century compilers of the catalogue of the imperial library held a remarkably high

---

26. Asparas are flower-scattering heavenly nymphs in Buddhist mythology.

27. Dhyana is the Sanskrit word for meditation. A "dhyana-heart" is a mind fixed in meditation.

opinion of Li Ye's work. They regarded her poetry as comparable to that of her male contemporaries and as much better than that of the more famous Xue Tao: "We must not belittle her collection just because it includes such a limited number of poems."

Courtesan and collator: Xue Tao. Xue Tao (758–831) spent all her life in the city of Chengdu, where for many years she was the leading lady at the parties thrown by the successive governors of Sichuan. The earliest sources simply describe her as a "registered courtesan," but according to later stories, she was a native of Chang'an. Her father, who had been sent to Sichuan to take up a minor post, passed away while in Chengdu and left her mother a widow. Eventually his daughter drifted into the life of a courtesan, for which, like Li Ye, she apparently had shown an early predisposition:

One day, her father pointed to the *wutong*-tree in their courtyard, and recited:

> In front of the courtyard steps an ancient *wutong*-tree:
> Its towering trunk rises up into the clouds.

When he ordered Tao to continue the poem, she immediately responded with the following lines:

> Its branches welcome birds from north and south,
> Its leaves send off the winds that come and go.

This left her father filled with sadness for a long time.

As in the case of Li Ye, the reliability of such late, prophetic anecdotes has to be doubted.

A short biography of Xue Tao, appended to a 1609 edition of her collected poems, summarizes her life as follows:

Xue Tao's style name was Hongdu. Originally she was the daughter of a commoner family from Chang'an. Her father Yun died in Sichuan while residing there in an official capacity, and her mother, now a widow, raised her till she was of marriageable age. She became known outside the family not only for her poetry, but also for her expertise in the painting of brows and application of makeup. She was not of the same class as the gentry families, and so guests would flirt with her secretly.

At that time Secretariat Director Wei Gao [745–805] was the governor of Sichuan. He summoned her and ordered her to serve wine and compose poems [at his banquets]; this led all his subordinates and gentlemen to change their opinion of her. After one year, he proposed sending a memorial requesting an appointment for her as collator, but he was told by the military protector that this was unthinkable, and so never actually did it. Tao went in and out of the governor's offices and, beginning with Wei Gao and ending with Li Deyu, she served eleven governors in all; each of them appreciated her because of her poetry. Among those who exchanged poetry with her during those years were [famous men such as] Yuan Zhen, Bai Juyi, Niu Sengru, Linghu Chu, Pei Du, Yan Shou, Zhang Ji, Du Mu, Liu Yuxi, Wu Wuling, and Zhang Gu. The others were also famous gentlemen; in total, twenty are known by name, and with all of them she exchanged poetry.

Tao lived on the banks of the Hundred Flowers Pond, and with her own hands made small letter paper of a deep red color, which she cut to size for writing the poems she presented to these eminent personalities. People call this "Xue Tao's letter paper."

During the last years of her life, she lived in the Black Rooster Ward, where she built the Poetry-Intoning Tower, in which she would take her rest. She died at the age of seventy-five sometime during the reign period Great Harmony [Dahe, 827–835], when Duan Wenchang was serving for a second time as governor in Chengdu. Wenchang wrote a grave inscription for her.

This biography probably exaggerates the extent and the intensity of the exchanges, poetic and otherwise, between Xue Tao and the leading writers and statesmen of the early decades of the ninth century. Bai Juyi, for instance, never visited Chengdu. According to another account, it was not Wei Gao but rather Wu Yuanheng who was appointed as governor of Sichuan in 807, who initiated the unprecedented step of proposing a woman (and a courtesan no less) for an official appointment as collator, a minor post in the imperial library that often was the first appointment for students who had brilliantly passed the examinations. Yet another source tells us that Xue Tao spent her final years on the banks of the Flower-Washing Brook, clad in the garb of a Daoist nun.

The biography also neglects to mention that Xue Tao at one point offended Wei Gao so much that she was banished to the border regions, from where she sent her great patron the following contrite verses:

> I had heard about the sufferings of the border,
> But only after coming here do I know them.

Full of shame I now sing my festive songs
For our boys who serve over here in Long.

Curiously enough, Xue Tao's collection also contains the following two poems addressed to Wu Yuanheng, who apparently had also found cause to punish her by sending her to the border garrisons:

I

The fireflies above the overgrown fields, the moon in the sky:
How could such fireflies ever hope to fly and reach the moon?
May the light of sun and moon illuminate ten thousand miles—
I gaze far into the clouds, lacking any means to send a letter.

II

Atop the mountain range I halt my horse: colder than cold!
The sharp wind and fine drizzle pierce me to the bone.
If only I was lucky enough to be allowed to go home,
I would never again want to look at a landscape painting!

In later ages, Xue Tao was not only remembered for her poetry and her red letter paper, but also for her calligraphy. The rich collection of the art-loving Emperor Huizong (r. 1101–1126) of the Song dynasty contained one sample of her calligraphy, which the catalogue of the collection describes as follows:

The woman Xue Tao was a prostitute from Chengdu. In her time, she was famous for her poetry. Even though her lowly profession meant she lacked any status, she displayed the style of a recluse. And so, as soon as she produced a poem or a piece of calligraphy, people would compete to circulate it for all to enjoy. Her written characters have nothing girlish about them, and the force of her brush is strong and vigorous. The marvelousness of her running script to a large degree captures the method of Wang Xizhi.[28] If she would have studied his style even more, she would have been of the class of Lady Wei.[29] She always liked to write out the poems she had written herself.

---

28. We encountered the famous calligrapher Wang Xizhi earlier as the father-in-law of Xie Daoyun.

29. Wang Xizhi is said to have studied calligraphy with Lady Wei. Lady Wei is said to have derived her style of calligraphy from Cai Yong after having been taught by his daughter, Cai Yan.

Their phrases are artful, and the ideas behind them are extraordinary. Model calligraphy and startling lines—that is why she became famous!

As laudatory as it is, this is the earliest reference to Xue Tao's calligraphic skills, on which all our Tang sources remain silent. Since none of the calligraphy attributed to her survives, we have no choice but to take the Song experts at their word.

Xue Tao's extant collection consists of nearly ninety poems. Most of these are occasional verses; the rest are largely poems on assigned topics such as were often produced in large quantities at literary parties. The thematically rather restricted nature of her poetry was noted by critics fairly early on:

During the reign period Primal Harmony [Yuanhe, 806–820], Xue Tao, a registered courtesan from Chengdu, was skilled in literary composition and rich in eloquence. Even though her works lack the intent of indirect criticism or moral instruction, they display her talent for singing of flowers and moonlight. She truly was an extraordinary person among the garrison courtesans of the time.

Xue Tao's poems may be technically perfect, but they are also rather conventional. In fact, in her collection only a few of her poems stand out:

From: Spring Prospects, Four Songs

I

The blossoms open—but no shared enjoyment,
The blossoms wither—but no shared distress.
You ask me when it is I long for you?
When blossoms open and when blossoms fall.

IV

Unbearable! The blossoms on the branches
Turn into longing in two places.
I face the mirror and my tears course down,
But does the spring wind care?

Willow Floss

The Second Month: the willow floss, so light and ethereal,
Tossed about by the spring breeze, tugs at your gown.

But actually it is an object bereft of feeling,
Now it drifts to the south, then to the north!

Xue Tao's most popular work by far (if indeed it is hers) is a series of ten quatrains on separation:

The Dog Separated from Its Master

The most docile in this wealthy household for several years!
Fragrant fur and cleaned paws—beloved by its master.
But ever since it, without warning, bit a cherished guest,
No longer is it allowed to sleep on the red silk carpet.

The Writing Brush Separated from the Hand

Only when made of bamboo from Yue and hairs from Xuan
Can it scatter the most exquisite flowers on red letter paper.
But because through long use it has lost its sharp point,
No longer does Wang Xizhi want to hold it in his hand.

The Horse Separated from Its Stable

Snow-white ears, reddish coat, and hooves of lightest green:
Chasing the wind as far as the east and the west of the sun.
But because it startled and threw off its rich young master,
No longer is it allowed to neigh in its precious pavilion.

The Parrot Separated from Its Cage

As a solitary and lonely exile from Longxi
It could fly freely about on the brocade carpet.
But since it spoke out in an embarrassing way,
No longer is it allowed to greet people from its cage.

Swallows Separated from Their Nest

In and out of the rich man's house they'd never been chased away
Because the master often loved to listen to their twittering sounds.
But since they soiled his brocade pillow with the loam from their beaks,
No longer are they allowed to build their nest between the beams.

The Pearl Separated from the Palm of the Hand

Brilliant and pure, round and bright, and completely transparent:
Its clear light seemed to illuminate the Dragons' Crystal Palace.
But now, just because it has been tarnished by a single tiny flaw,
No longer is it allowed to spend the night in the palm of the hand.

The Fish Separated from Its Pond

It frolicked in the lotus pond for a number of years,
Flicking its red tail, it would tease the line and hook.
But for no reason at all it broke the stem of a lotus flower—
No longer is it allowed to swim in its clear waves.

The Hawk Separated from the Gauntlet

Its talons are as sharp as awls, its eyes as round as bells:
To catch a hare on the level plain is its greatest joy.
But for no reason at all it stole away beyond the clouds—
No longer is it allowed to perch on the king's wrist.

The Bamboo Separated from the Pavilion

Thick and lush, and newly planted in four or five rows,
They withstood the autumn frost with their sturdy nodes.
But because their sprouts in spring cracked the wall,
No longer are they allowed to shade the jade hall.

The Mirror Separated from Its Stand

When, forged from gold, the mirror was first uncovered,
It was a hovering full moon of the fifteenth of the month.
But because it has been covered by dust without end,
No longer is it allowed on its jade stand in the painted hall.

Xue Tao is said to have written this series of ten poems for Yuan Zhen (779–831) in the hopes of regaining his affection after she had offended him. Yuan Zhen, who is nowadays probably best known as the author of the *Tale of Yingying* (*Yingying zhuan*), arrived in Chengdu in 809 in the capacity of inspecting censor, and soon found himself embroiled in controversy as he began to document and judge numerous cases of serious official abuse of power. One may well wonder how he could have found the time to initiate a relationship with Xue Tao, break up with her, and then reconcile with her once again. Later generations, however, must have found it unimaginable that the author of one of the most romantic tales in Chinese literary history would not have enjoyed a liaison with the most famous courtesan of his time. A collection of anecdotes compiled in the final decades of the ninth century describes their relationship as follows:

As soon as Minister Yuan . . . heard that among the registered courtesans of Sichuan there was a certain Xue Tao who was competent in poetry and extremely eloquent, he continuously longed for her in his heart. When he was appointed an investigating commissioner, he asked to be posted to Sichuan, but as he was judging cases in his capacity as censor, it was impossible for him to go to visit her. When he was later [relieved of his duties and] transferred to the position of omissioner, the prefect Yan Shou, knowing of Yuan Zhen's desires, again and again sent Xue Tao over to him. When Yuan Zhen was about to depart, he did not dare take her with him. Once he had been appointed to the Hanlin Academy, he sent her the following poem:

> The rippling waves of Brocade River and the glory of Mt. Emei
> Have through the art of transformation produced Wenjun and Xue Tao,
> In speech so skillful they steal the parrot's tongue,
> In style so brilliant they earn the phoenix's plumes.
> In droves the poets all lay down their writing brushes,
> While each and every high official dreams of appointment there.
> Since our separation my longing has been blocked by misty rivers:
> The calamus flowers must be blooming—the clouds of dusk are high.

This account makes no mention of the ten poems on separation. It does provide the additional information that when more than ten years later, Yuan Zhen was appointed as governor of eastern Zhejiang and finally was about to send a messenger to Chengdu to fetch Xue Tao, he was suddenly smitten by the attractions of the actress Liu Caichun, and forgot about Xue Tao altogether. In fact, the account concludes with a poem Yuan Zhen wrote for Liu Caichun. A collection of anecdotes compiled in the early tenth century contains a story according to which the ten quatrains on separation were written by one of Yuan Zhen's secretaries, when Yuan was serving as governor of eastern Zhejiang. Apparently, this secretary, also surnamed Xue, had once become drunk and wounded his master with his chopsticks for which he was duly punished. Afterwards, it is said, he wrote this series of separation poems in the hopes of getting his job back. However, when in 900 Wei Zhuang (836–910) compiled the *Mystery upon Mystery* (*Youxuan ji*), a large anthology of Tang dynasty poetry that also included a substantial number of women poets, he credited the first poem of the series to Xue Tao. To complicate matters even further, yet another source claims that Xue Tao wrote the series in order to regain the favor of Wu Yuanheng. Most likely the series of ten poems of separation were anonymous poems that circulated orally, eagerly awaiting an opportunity to be associated with a famous name.

Concubine, Daoist nun, and murderer: Yu Xuanji. We know very little about Yu Xuanji's early years other than that she was born around the year 848 to a family of modest means. We also know that she spent most of her short life in the capital of Chang'an. At the age of fifteen she became the concubine of the censor Li Yi and accompanied him on a journey to central China. The following quatrain, "Traveling on the River," very likely dates from Yu Xuanji's days as a concubine:

> The Yangzi encircles Wuchang, which slopes down to its banks,
> Where the houses of ten thousand families stand facing Parrot Isle.
> In the painted boat our spring sleep continues past dawn:
> In our dreams we are butterflies still trying out the flowers.

Soon afterwards, though, Li Yi apparently sent her away, according to one source because he had fallen out of love with her, but according to another, because his jealous wife had forced him to do so. Yu Xuanji then became a nun at the Xianyi Convent, which at that time was the largest Daoist nunnery in Chang'an. One of her poems, "Going to Visit Refining Master Zhao but Not Finding Her at Home," describes an unsuccessful visit to a fellow Daoist (most likely a nun):

> Where has she gone with her fellow immortals,
> Leaving her servant girl alone at home?
> On her warm stove, medicines are still simmering,
> And in an adjoining courtyard tea is being brewed.
> The painted walls remain dark despite the lamp's glow,
> The poles hung with pennants throw slanting shadows.

> I leave my regards and just as I turn around:
> A few blossoming branches beyond the wall.

Yu Xuanji's life at the convent was by no means a cloistered one. In fact, she maintained warm contacts with many literary gentlemen, one of whom was the famous poet Wen Tingyun (812–870; style name Feiqing), known for his suggestive lyrical descriptions of the ennui and despair of abandoned women. Wen was also a frequent visitor in the red-light districts, and his official career suffered after he lost a few teeth in a barroom brawl. In the following poem addressed to Wen, Yu Xuanji compares him to the third-century eccentric Xi Kang:

> By the stones of the stairs, the crowded crickets chirp,
> On the trees in the courtyard, the misty dew is clear.
> Under the light of the moon, music from nearby is heard,
> As seen from my room, the distant mountains are bright.
> A chilly breeze settles on the pearly mat,
> The entrusted regret rises from the jade zither.
> If you, my Xi Kang, are too lazy to drop me a note,
> What else is there that will assuage my autumn feelings?

While Tang dynasty sources do not provide any further details on the relationship of Yu Xuanji and Wen Tingyun, Ming dynasty drama would eventually turn them into a loving couple.

The circumstances of Yu Xuanji's death are described by Huangfu Mei in his *Minor Writings from Shanshui (Shanshui xiaodu)*. Huangfu Mei wrote this collection of anecdotes in the early years of the tenth century; they represent an elderly man's reminiscences of more than a quarter of a century earlier:

The style name of Yu Xuanji, a Daoist nun in the Xianyi Convent of the Western Capital [Chang'an], was Youwei and she was the daughter of a commoner family in Chang'an. Not only was her beauty earth-shattering, but her intellectual capacities were also extraordinary. She loved to read books and compose texts, and devoted herself in particular to the writing of poetry. By the age of sixteen, her mind was focused on "the pure and empty," and in the early years of the reign period Full Communication [Xiantong, 860–873] she donned the capeline and stole [of a Daoist nun] at the Xianyi Convent. Her fine verses of appreciation and enjoyment of breeze and moonlight often circulated among the forest of gentlemen.

However, possessed as she was of the weak nature of a fragrant orchid, she was incapable of preserving her honor. She allowed herself to accept the advances of powerful bosses, and accompanied them on their excursions and elsewhere. All the men about town vied with each other to appear at their finest in the hopes of starting an affair with her. Occasionally they would come to visit her, bringing wine with them, and she would strum the zither and recite poetry, interspersing this with risqué banter. Those with insufficient learning would feel very much out of place. Her poems included lines such as the following:

> Gauze pathways: the spring outlook is distant,
> Jade zither-studs: autumnal feelings in profusion.

And:

> Filled with devotion, unable to speak,
> Red tears course down my cheeks.

And:

> Burning incense, I ascend the jade platform,
> Grasping my tablet, I bow to the golden gate.

And:

> Cloud emotions, thick and heavy—it could not be a dream:
> Fairy face, forever fragrant—far more lovely than a flower!

These several couplets were her finest.

Her servant girl, Lüqiao, was also very clever and beautiful. One day, when Xuanji had been invited by the nuns of the adjoining courtyard [in the convent], she left Lüqiao with the following instructions: "Don't go out, and if a guest should show up, just tell him that I am at such-and-such a place." Xuanji was kept longer than expected by her girlfriends and did not return to her own courtyard until evening. Lüqiao opened the gate for her, saying: "Just a moment ago such-and-such a guest showed up. When he heard that you were not in, he went away without dismounting from his horse." Now, although this guest was an old patron of hers, Xuanji suspected Lüqiao of having an affair with him.

That night she lit a lamp and, after locking the door, ordered Lüqiao to come into her bedroom so as to question her. Lüqiao said: "During all the years that I have been your servant, I have truly behaved myself properly and have never committed a transgression of the sort that would offend you. Moreover, when that guest arrived, I kept the door locked, and it was from behind the door that I informed him that you were not at home. He then went away without saying a word, spurring on his horse. You talk about love—but it has been years since I have harbored that kind of feeling in my heart! Mistress, please do not doubt me!" But Xuanji only grew more enraged. Stripping her servant naked, she lashed her hundreds of times with a cane. But Lüqiao continued to protest her innocence. She then collapsed to the ground, and requesting a cup of water, she poured it out on the ground saying: "You wish to pursue the Way of Longevity of the Three Purities,[30] but are incapable of denying yourself the pleasures of removing your skirts and sharing the couch. But because of your inveterate suspicion you falsely accuse me, who am chaste and correct! It turns out that I will be dying a cruel death under your brutal hands. If there is no Heaven, I will have nowhere to lodge my complaint. But if there is, no one will be able to thwart my stubborn soul! I swear I will not wriggle about like a worm in deepest darkness and allow you to indulge in your lasciviousness!" As soon as she had spoken these words, she passed away right there on the spot. Xuanji was filled with fear and buried her in a hole that she dug in her backyard, thinking that no one would find out. This took place in the First Month of spring in the ninth year of Full Communication [868].

Whenever someone would ask after Lüqiao, Xuanji would say: "She ran away after the spring rains cleared!" Once a guest who had been dining in Xuanji's room went out into her backyard to urinate. On the spot where Xuanji had buried Lüqiao, he noticed quite a number of green flies, which, when he chased them away, only came back again. When he looked more carefully, he noticed not only traces of what appeared to be blood, but a rancid smell as well. After the guest had left, in confidence he told his servant what he had seen. The servant, once he got home, told it in turn to his elder brother. Now this elder brother was a patrolman. He had once asked Xuanji for money, but she had ignored him, and so he harbored a grudge against her. When he heard this story, he immediately went to the convent gate to spy on her. When he overheard people speculating as to why they hadn't seen Lüqiao coming in and out, the patrolman called together some additional police officers, and with spades in their hands they rushed into Xuanji's courtyard. When they dug Lüqiao up, they found that her face looked just as it had when she was alive.

The policemen arrested Xuanji, and when she was questioned by the clerks of Chang'an prefecture, she confessed. Many of the gentlemen at court tried to intervene on her behalf but the prefecture submitted her name to the emperor

---

30. The Three Purities are the highest divinities in the Daoist pantheon.

in a memorial and when autumn came around, she was, in fact, executed. While in prison, she also wrote poems, the most beautiful couplets of which are the following:

> Easy it is to find a priceless treasure,
> Difficult it is to find a steadfast lover.

And:

> A full moon shines through the dark crack,
> A clear breeze blows open my short jacket.

Readers sympathetic to Yu Xuanji have questioned whether she was really a murderer, although they usually accept the fact that she was condemned to death and executed. Some later versions of her life, however, simply ignore the unfortunate incident of her execution altogether. For instance, Xin Wenfang, in the short notice devoted to Yu Xuanji in his influential *Biographies of Tang Poets* (*Tang caizi zhuan*) of 1304, suggests that Yu Xuanji lived a life of utmost propriety devoted to religious pursuits, and does not say a single world about her ignominious death. Readers of the Judge Dee novels by the Dutch diplomat and sinologist Robert Hans van Gulik will find that in *Poets and Murder* (1968), the last of his many novels, Yu Xuanji served as the model for the versifying nun Yulan.

Some fifty poems by Yu Xuanji have come down to us today. She may well have been a less accomplished versifier than Xue Tao, and some of her poems are simply clumsy, but these defects are compensated for by poems such as the following that are distinguished by such things as an individual voice, a felicitous image, or an expression of urgent desire:

Feelings in the Last Month of Spring; Sent to a Friend

> The chatter of orioles startles me from my dream,
> And a light makeup disguises the traces of tears.
> Above the dark bamboo, a thin new moon,
> On the quiet river, a heavy evening mist.
> With moistened beaks, the swallows carry loam,
> With perfumed beards, the bees collect their honey.
> Alone in love, my longing is without end—
> My poem intoned, the pine branches hang low.

On the Assigned Topic of Willows by the River

Their verdant color conjoins with the grassy bank,
Their misty forms enter into the distant towers.
Their shadows spread out over the river's face,
And their floss falls down upon the angler's head.
 Their old roots conceal the holes where fishes hide,
Their low branches snare the boats of merchants.
In desolate nights of sighing wind and rain
They startle me from my dreams, adding to my sorrows.

Early Autumn

Tender chrysanthemums carry new colors,
As distant mountains idle in the evening mists.
A cool breeze startles the green trees,
And pure rhymes enter the red strings:
 The longing wife: brocade on the loom,
The man on campaign: sky beyond the border.
Geese fly overhead, fish swim in the water,
But how could they ever carry any letter?

Selling Wilted Peonies

Facing the wind they evoke a sigh as their petals continue to fall,
Their fragrance fades and dissolves as yet another spring goes by.
It must be because of their high price that no one shows interest,
And because of their extreme fragrance butterflies cannot come near.
 Their red flowers are fit to be grown only inside the palace,
How could their green leaves bear to be tainted by dew and dust?
But when their roots will have been transplanted to the Imperial Park,
You, my prince, will then regret that you can no longer buy them!

One may safely assume that in "Selling Wilted Peonies," Yu Xuanji is recommending herself to an undecided patron and urging him to take action before she is snatched away into the Inner Palace as had so many other literary women before her. This poem betrays a strong self-consciousness, which we also encounter in Xuanji's quatrain entitled "During a Visit to the Southern Tower of the Veneration of Truth Monastery I Saw the New Examination Graduates Writing Their Names on the Wall." This last poem is probably the only one from this period in which a woman so nakedly voices her dissatisfaction at the limitations imposed upon her by her gender:

> Cloudy peaks fill one's eyes under a clear spring sky:
> Clearly legible "silver hooks" emerge from their fingers.[31]
> Oh how I hate this gauze gown for hiding my verses!
> To no avail I look up with envy at the names on the list.

It would not be surprising if Yu Xuanji often found herself consumed by a powerless rage. To men, literary talents brought status and riches when they passed the state exams. A woman who craved recognition for her literary talent was not only excluded from taking the examinations, but her active participation in literary exchange automatically turned her into a public woman.

---

31. "Silver hooks" refers to beautifully written Chinese characters. The simile was first used by the Tang poet Bai Juyi.

PART TWO
Between New Possibilities and New Limitations

The number of writing women was quite small during the first thousand years of imperial China. The women who did write were excluded from the government bureaucracy, of course, but this did not inhibit them from making use of all the genres current at the time and, except for the moral tracts they wrote explicitly for women, they shared in the common (male) discourse. In the second half of the Tang dynasty, however, women's writings were largely limited to poetry. And, to the extent that one might point to the emergence of a specifically feminine voice in the laments of the abandoned woman (the seminal example of which were the poems of Concubine Ban), it should be stressed once again that this voice, as we saw in Chapter 2, almost immediately became very much the preserve of male (or at least anonymous) authors.

Throughout the first millennium of imperial China, the Inner Palace represented the most important community of literate women in China. The day-to-day administration of the Inner Palace required a large number of highly educated women, and the vagaries of politics would often thrust an empress or empress dowager into a position of power as the actual head of government. Women who had established reputations as poets or scholars outside the Inner Palace were often invited to join the palace women, sometimes in the capacity of court poets and teachers. From the fourth century on, we see the development of Buddhist and Daoist female monastic communities, but these nuns appear to have left virtually no imprint on the literary tradition. Courtesans, while a permanent feature of imperial Chinese society, distinguished themselves as writers only in certain periods, such as the second half of the Tang dynasty.

The period from the ninth to the eleventh century witnessed a number of important social, cultural, and technological changes that deeply affected almost all aspects of Chinese society and culture. These changes not only influenced the way in which men read, wrote, and published, but also had a great impact on the way in which, and the extent to which, women were able to participate in the writing culture. While some developments, such as the spread of printing, increased the possibilities for women to read and write, other developments, such as the spread of the system of state examinations and the development of academies exclusively for males, almost simultaneously diminished those possibilities.

The invention of printing in the eighth (or perhaps even as early as the seventh) century, its perfection in the ninth, and its general employment from the tenth century onward, meant that more texts became available to more people at a lower price. More families now possessed the means to provide their children, including their daughters, a literary education. At the same time, the examinations became the most important and prestigious way to enter the bureaucracy. Throughout the Song dynasty, as the number of men who sat for the examinations steadily rose, the level of erudition required to pass the highest exams was also raised. As the chances of success at the highest level (and with that success, the opportunity to become a member of the national elite) became slimmer, performing well in the local examination became more crucial to maintaining local elite status. This intense focus on the examinations as defining elite status made all of society extremely education-minded and aware of the importance of a literary education. Though the social realities may have been different, most people believed that any poor student, if talented and diligent enough, might eventually pass the examinations in the nation's capital as well as the imperial palace, and as a top graduate (*zhuangyuan*) go on to a brilliant career. This Chinese version of the "rags to riches" myth was fed by novels and plays throughout the last millennium of imperial China.

To the extent that more families hired tutors to teach their children, so the opportunities for girls to acquire a basic literacy also increased. Elite families in eleventh-century China, such as the household of the famous statesman and poet Wang Anshi (1021–1086), were well known for the high level of literary accomplishments of their female members (later legend would also provide the well-known poet Su Shi [1037–1101] with an erudite and quick-witted sister). At the same time, girls were now almost totally excluded from all forms of higher education because this was increasingly provided outside the home in government schools and private academies (*shuyuan*). The only way for a girl to penetrate these male bastions would have been to disguise herself in male attire (one such tale, that of Liang Shanbo and Zhu Yingtai, did develop in the course of the Song dynasty; see Chapter 9). Confined to their homes, women writers of the Song dynasty and later, like those of the last century or so of the Tang dynasty, devoted their literary energies primarily to poetry.

The same period that had witnessed the invention and proliferation of printing had also seen the birth of a new poetic genre, the *ci* or lyric. While rhapsodies continued to be written, the most important form of poetry from the very beginning of the Tang dynasty, if not before, was the *shi*; it would retain this status well into the twentieth century. In a *shi* poem, the poet was expected to articulate an unmediated reaction to a situation in the world around him (or her) and to testify to the feelings called forth by his (or her) experiences. While both men and women writers wrote *shi*, readers would assume that the "I" in the poem was male, unless there were explicit indications to the contrary. *Ci*, or lyrics, on the other hand, originated as the songs of courtesans, each melody setting its own specific pattern. Not surprisingly, the most important subjects of *ci* were love, longing, and loneliness, usually as seen from the perspective of a (discarded) woman. For the first two centuries of the genre's existence, however, the known authors of *ci* were male; among the most famous early practitioners of the genre was the bon vivant Wen Tingyun (whom we have already encountered as an acquaintance of Yu Xuanji). These early male poets often wrote their lyrics for performance by women in the entertainment quarters, and in so doing developed a "feminine" poetic style supposedly expressive of typical female experiences, emotions, and concerns. By the time the genre had become respectable enough to be practiced by elite women in the second half of the eleventh century, it had already developed a language with which to describe "feminine" experiences. What this meant is that once women themselves began to write lyrics, they had, whether they liked it or not, a ready-made emotional vocabulary to draw upon. Sentiments and situations that had been read as fictional (and therefore of lesser value) when expressed by men such as Wen Tingyun, were now regarded as truthful and authentic when used by women in their poetry.

Chinese society from the second to the eighth century had been strongly aristocratic in character, and status was primarily determined on the basis of heredity. As the examinations gained in importance, social status was no longer a given, but rather had to be achieved. Apart from a short hiatus during the first several decades of the Yuan dynasty (1260–1368), the examinations dominated the life and thought of Chinese elite men throughout the last thousand years of imperial China. While largely literary in character, these examinations were not primarily intended to test the candidates' literary talents as such, but rather their mastery of the Confucian canon: status and power were achieved by a competitive display of orthodoxy in writing and in daily life. This social development was closely tied to the emergence of neo-Confucianism (or "Learning of the Way"), a reinterpretation of the tradition that was greatly spurred on by the wider availability of books and facilitated by the spread of schools and academies. Whereas earlier versions of Confucianism had placed relatively more stress on Confucian learning as the command of statesmanship, ritual forms, historical scholarship, and literary genres, neo-Confucianism placed more emphasis on the adherence to proper ritual forms in one's daily life and a deeply felt personal commitment to the Way of the Sages. With some exaggeration, one might even call neo-Confucianism a Protestant, even a puritanical, variant of Confucianism. The various schools of neo-Confucianism were largely synthesized in the course of the twelfth century by Zhu Xi (1130–1200), and when the Yuan dynasty reinstituted the examinations in 1313, Zhu Xi's interpretations of the Classics became the only ones that were acceptable, making neo-Confucianism the de facto state ideology. It would maintain that position until the abolition of the state examinations in 1905.

Neo-Confucianism, with its emphasis on the conspicuous display of orthodoxy and proper ritual behavior, meant the imposition of increasingly strict rules on women. For instance, the patriarchs of neo-Confucianism were adamant in their condemnation of the remarriage of widows, and placed a particularly high value on women's chastity. This stricter interpretation of the traditional norms and values was often internalized by the women themselves. This internalization of strict and constrictive norms had its physical counterpart in the female custom of footbinding, which had begun to be widespread by the end of the Song dynasty. Anxious to ensure the marriageability of their daughters, mothers would tightly bind the feet of their little girls, stunting the growth of the feet, and occasionally even breaking the bones. Women with bound feet had great difficulty walking and this severely restricted their mobility. The origin of the custom is still not completely clear, but it seems to have gained popularity among elite women in some parts of China during the Song dynasty. In later centuries its popularity would spread beyond the elite to ever larger segments of society; women took great pride in their tiny feet, the tinier the better.

It is worth noting that the two best-known women poets of this period, Li Qingzhao and Zhu Shuzhen, were active in the first half of the twelfth century, when printing had increased the availability of books and the lyric had become a respectable literary genre, but before neo-Confucianism had become dominant in elite circles. The best-known Buddhist nuns of the Song dynasty, many of whom came from elite families, also lived in this period. However, as early as the eleventh century, the famous statesman and historian Sima Guang (1019–1086), in his *Family Rituals* (*Shuyi*), had criticized the widespread practice of instructing girls in the writing of poetry:

From the age of five girls should be taught simple embroidery. From the age of six they should learn the *Classic of Filiality* and the *Analects* by heart. When they turn eight years of age, the *Classic of Filiality* and the *Analects* should be explained to them, together with the *Biographies of Exemplary Women* and *Precepts for My Daughters*, and they should understand at least the main points.

Wise women of the past all read historical works so as to find models for themselves. Women such as the Venerable Madam Cao [Ban Zhao] were well-versed in the Classics, and their writings were clear and proper. Nowadays it happens that people teach their daughters poetry and popular music—but that is not the way it should be at all!

Also in the late twelfth century, the famous poet Lu You (1125–1210), in a grave inscription he wrote for a distant relative, lady Sun (1141–1193), praised her for having in her youth rejected instruction in the writing of poetry offered by none other than Li Qingzhao:

From her earliest youth lady Sun displayed a pure disposition. Lady Li, the spouse of Zhao Mingcheng, the late prefect of Jiankang, was famous for her literary writings and wished to transmit her learning to lady Sun. At the time lady Sun was only eleven or twelve, but she regarded her offer as improper and refused it, saying: "Talent and rhetoric are not a woman's business."

In the fourteenth century, the poet Yang Weizhen (1296–1370) was even more dismissive in discussing the works of Li Qingzhao and Zhu Shuzhen:

When it comes to women who recite books and compose texts, the histories praise the Venerable Madam Cao [Ban Zhao] of the Eastern Han dynasty. In recent times, women like Li Qingzhao and Zhu Shuzhen have achieved fame because of their writings. Each of their poems or songs, it seems, is capable of moving people. But their works issue from limited learning and restricted wisdom; confined by the vulgar character of their energy and habits, they fall short of the proper norm for feelings and human nature. The Venerable Madam was able to serve as teacher and model to the women of the Inner Palace. Li and Zhu and their ilk may temporarily dazzle their fathers and elder brothers with their compositions, but they [and Ban Zhao] cannot be mentioned in the same breath!

To place these remarks in context, one has to point out that they appear in the preface of a (lost) collection of poems by a contemporary woman poet, presumably one who, avoiding the vulgarity of Li Qingzhao and Zhu Shuzhen, was considered to be of the same moral stature as Ban Zhao.

Some of the family rules of these centuries even explicitly prescribe that daughters and daughters-in-law be educated to read the moral tracts for women and collections of biographies of exemplary women, but prohibited from reading the Classics and poetry—and under no circumstances should they be allowed to engage in writing themselves.

This situation continued until the end of the sixteenth century, when an expanding economy facilitated a boom in publishing, and when philosophers and critics started to valorize "feelings" (*qing*) as the basis of authenticity. These developments would lay the groundwork for an explosion in the number of writing women, particularly from the elite class, in the seventeenth century and beyond.

4 · Li Qingzhao

Li Qingzhao's Life

Li Qingzhao was a native of Shandong province. Shortly after her birth, however, her father Li Gefei was appointed Erudite at the National Academy in the capital and the family moved to Kaifeng. Li Gefei was a very learned man; one of his works was an extensive commentary on the *Notes on the Rites* (*Liji*). He also befriended such eminent poets and statesmen as Su Shi (1037–1101) and Zhang Lei (1052–1112). Li Qingzhao's mother, the granddaughter of a chancellor, was also highly educated.

Li Gefei's later official career suffered from the factional struggles within the bureaucracy during the last decades of the eleventh century. But by 1101, when his daughter married Zhao Mingcheng (style name Defu; 1081–1129), he had attained the rank of vice-director in the Ministry of Rites. Li Qingzhao's father-in-law, Zhao Tingzhi, was also a native of Shandong, and belonged to the bureaucratic faction that was in power in the early years of the twelfth century. In 1101, he was vice-minister in the Ministry of Personnel. In 1105 he was appointed chancellor alongside Cai Jing (1046–1126), although in the following year Cai was cashiered, leaving Zhao the sole occupant of this office. In 1107, it was Zhao Tingzhi's turn to be dismissed, while Cai Jing was reinstated in the position of chancellor. Zhao Tingzhi died soon after this event. Zhao Mingcheng had received his first official appointment in 1105, but following the death of his father he retired with his wife to the ancestral estate in Qingzhou for the prescribed period of mourning.

After the requisite three-year mourning period, Zhao Mingcheng and Li Qingzhao continued to live in Qingzhou for another ten years. Zhao did not go back into active service until 1121, when he was appointed prefect of Laizhou (or Donglai, in Shandong). One of the few preserved *shi* poems written by Li Qingzhao, entitled "Emotions," describes the couple's life shortly after their arrival in their new home:

On the tenth day of the Eighth Month of the *xinchou* year of the reign period Proclaiming Harmony [Xuanhe, 1101–1125], we arrived in Laizhou. We sat all by ourselves in a single room, without any of the objects that we had been used to seeing around us all our lives. There was nothing on the table but a copy of the *Ministry of Rites' Rhyming Dictionary*. So I opened it at random with the agreement that we would each write a poem using the rhyme of the page to which the book opened. The character *zi* fell to me, and so I used words from that rhyming category in the rhyming positions of my poem, which is a poem of emotions.

> A cold window and a broken table without any books,
> How sad that in your career you had to end up here,
> Where all day long Clerk Alcohol and Bully Money
> Delight in stirring up a motley crew of troubles.
> I kick them out and lock the gate so I can write my poem,
> Inside this "palace," a frozen fragrance elicits fine thoughts.
> The silence allows me to seek out my trusted friends,
> Master Mere Imagination and Sir Fantasy.

In 1124, Zhao Mingcheng was appointed prefect of Zizhou (also in Shandong). During these years in Qingzhou, Laizhou, and Zizhou, Zhao Mingcheng could devote all his time to his greatest passions, archaeology and epigraphy, which at that time in China were young and exciting branches of scholarship. Li Qingzhao shared her husband's intellectual interests, and over time the couple built up an impressive collection of books, paintings, rubbings, and antiquities.

This idyllic existence was brutally shattered when in 1126 the armies of the Jürchen thoroughly defeated the troops of the Song before going on to conquer northern China. The Jürchen had proclaimed their own Jin dynasty in what is today Manchuria in 1115. The Song dynasty then allied

itself with this new power in northeast Asia to fight their common enemy, the Liao dynasty. The Liao dynasty had been founded by the Khitan; throughout the tenth and eleventh centuries it was a major power in
southern Manchuria and northern Hebei. All of the earlier Song dynasty
attempts to dislodge the Liao dynasty had ended in failure and, ultimately,
in the payment by the Song court of a humiliating annual tribute to the
Liao to maintain the peace. When the Song and the Jin combined forces
against the Liao, the Jin quickly destroyed the Liao and then turned on
the Song and invaded northern China. They met with very little resistance, and in the spring of 1126 their troops showed up at the gates of the
capital Kaifeng, but left after having been promised a large tribute. The
art-loving Emperor Huizong (r. 1101–1126) then retired in favor of his
son, Emperor Qinzong (r. 1126). But in the autumn of the same year, the
armies of the Jin again showed up right outside Kaifeng. This time they
took the two emperors captive and embarked on a systematic conquest
of the Song empire.

The years that followed were chaotic ones. Northern China was
quickly subjugated by the Jin, but in southern China one of the younger
sons of Emperor Huizong was placed on the throne by Song loyalists.
Initially the chances of this regime's survival seemed slim, as Emperor
Gaozong and his court were chased by Jin troops all over southern China
and at times had to flee to the high seas for safety. Gradually, however,
the resistance against the Jin gathered strength, and eventually the river
Huai came to mark the borderline between the two competing empires.
Despite the stiff opposition of the refugees from the north, who continued to hope for the reconquest of their home districts, the Southern
Song in 1141 concluded a peace with the Jin, and agreed both to recognize
the Jin emperor as the "elder brother" of the Song emperor and to pay a
large yearly tribute.

By that time, Zhao Mingcheng had been deceased for many years. In
1127 he had traveled to Jiankang (Nanjing) because his mother had passed
away there. Soon afterwards, Li Qingzhao followed him with part of their
possessions—the books alone filled fifteen carts. Before the end of the
prescribed period of mourning, Zhao Mingcheng reentered government
service. After having served as prefect of Jiankang, he was appointed prefect of Huzhou, but on his way to his new post he fell ill and died. For

his widow, there followed a period of trekking back and forth across southern China, in constant flight from enemy raids and local rebellions. Over the years, her riches melted away like snow in the sun as a result of plundering, theft, and false accusations. Only in 1132, when she followed the court to Hangzhou, would her life settle down a little, although by then she was living in very reduced circumstances. She had hoped to be invited into the Inner Palace as a teacher, but this never happened, although once in a while she was invited to supply songs and couplets for court festivities.

Our most important source for the life of Li Qingzhao from her marriage in 1101 to Zhao Mingcheng to the mid-thirties of the twelfth century is the postface she composed for her husband's *Inscriptions on Bronze and Stone* (*Jinshi lu*). This work originally consisted of the texts of two thousand inscriptions ranging in date from the second millennium BCE to the tenth century CE, together with 520 appended notices (only the table of contents and the appended notices survive). Li Qingzhao's postface is a description of how she and her husband had built up this collection, as well as how it was later scattered and lost. But the preface's many details about their married life and her travels through southeastern China make it a major autobiographical document. To a modern Western reader it may be surprising to find Li Qingzhao's account of her eventful life in the interstices of a description of her husband's library and other collections. One should keep in mind, however, that China at this time did not have much of a tradition of autobiographical writing. Our most important autobiographical statements in prose from the preceding centuries are postfaces to books, in which the authors explain how and why they felt moved or compelled to write the work concerned. By writing this postface in which she reveals her husband to have been a slave of passions that ultimately ended up as fruitless and futile, and by inserting herself into the narrative, Li Qingzhao may well have demonstrated even more originality than she did in writing her lyrics.

What is this *Inscriptions on Bronze and Stone* in thirty scrolls? It is the work of his lordship Zhao Defu [Mingcheng]. It brings together two thousand rubbings of inscriptions on bells, tripods, steamers, pots, plates, basins, beakers and vessels, as well as of the records of the deeds of eminent personalities and obscure gentlemen carved on large steles and tall columns—whatever may be found inscribed on bronze or stone—from the period beginning with the Three Dynasties and ending with the Five Dynasties.[1] For each of these texts mistakes have been corrected, and everything has been included that, following a critical selection, sufficiently accords with the Way of the Sages or might serve to remedy the omissions of the historiographers—it is truly voluminous!

Alas, ever since the disasters that befell Wang Ya and Yuan Zai, manuscripts and paintings have shared the same fate as pepper.[2] And what is the difference between Changyu's obsession with money and Yuankai's obsession with the *Commentary of Mr. Zuo*?[3] The labels may have been different, but both were equally addictions!

I married Zhao Mingcheng in the *xinsi* year of the reign period Established Mean [Jianzhong, 1101]. At that time my late father was a vice-director in the Ministry of Rites, while the chancellor [my father-in-law] was vice-minister in the Ministry of Personnel. His lordship was twenty-one, and was a student of the National Academy. Both the Zhaos and the Lis were families of modest origins, poor and frugal people. On the first and fifteenth of every month his lordship was allowed to visit his family, at which time he would pawn his gown, take the five hundred copper coins, and walk over to the Assisting-the-State Monastery [Xiangguosi] to buy rubbings and fruit. When he returned home, together we would pore over the rubbings and nibble on the fruit, certain that we were as [carefree as the] subjects of the [ancient emperor] Hetian.[4] Two years later, when he first served in a provincial post, he would, as soon as we had supplied ourselves with the minimum daily necessities, roam though the farthest and remotest regions, collecting records of ancient writing and unusual characters from all over the world. As time went by, his collection gradually grew and expanded. When the chancellor held the post of prime minister, our friends and

---

1. The Three Dynasties are the Xia (traditional dates 2207–1766 BCE), the Shang (also known as Yin; traditional dates 1765–1122 BCE), and Zhou (traditional dates 1121–249 BCE). The Five Dynasties refer to the sequence of five dynasties that ruled Northern China from 907 to 960.

2. When the house of the murdered chancellor Wang Ya (d. 835) was plundered, all the objects of gold and silver were taken away, but the books and paintings were simply tossed out on the street. When the corrupt chancellor Yuan Zai in 777 was allowed to commit suicide and his possessions were confiscated, the authorities found no less than eight hundred large sacks of pepper in his house.

3. He Qiao (style name Changyu; d. 292) was known as a miser, while Du Yu (style name Yuankai; 222–284) devoted all his life to the study of the *Commentary of Mr. Zuo*.

4. Hetian is said to have ruled in an ancient time when people, living simply, were happy.

relatives often served in the government archives and libraries. They would repeatedly bring us lost odes and neglected histories and all sorts of texts not to be found among the books recovered from the wall [of Confucius' home] in Lu or from the [royal] tomb in Ji.[5] His lordship would then copy them as fast as he could, and eventually he came to find such pleasure in this kind of work that he could not make himself stop.

Later as well, whenever his lordship would happen to see a piece of calligraphy, a painting by a famous master past or present, or an extraordinary vessel from some early dynasty, he would take off his gown and hand it over in payment. I remember that once during the years of the reign period Exalted Peace [Chongning, 1102–1106] someone brought us a painting of peonies by Xu Xi, for which he asked two hundred thousand copper coins.[6] But in those days even the scions of noble houses would have found it difficult to come up with two hundred thousand copper coins! So we kept the painting for two nights but in the end had to return it as we had no way to come up with that amount of money. For several days the two of us, husband and wife, were filled with regret and disappointment.

Later, during the ten years we lived in retirement in the countryside, we had to scramble to make ends meet, but at least we were well supplied with food and clothing. When his lordship then served as prefect of two prefectures in succession, he spent all of his income on the collation of books. Whenever he would acquire a text, the two of us would immediately compare it to other editions, incorporate it in our collection, and provide it with a title slip. And whenever we obtained a piece of calligraphy, a painting, a vessel, or a tripod, we would hold it in our hands in appreciation or unroll it if it was a scroll, and point out any flaw or defect. It was our rule that we could go on at night until a single candle had burned down to the nub. When it came to the quality of the paper [of our books] and the complete accuracy of their characters, we were able to surpass every other book collector.

Now I happen to have a good memory, and each time when we would sit in the Hall of Returning Home after dinner, we would point to the pile of books and histories and say which event was found in which book, in which chapter,

---

5. When the house of Confucius was torn down to make way for an extension of the palace of the prince of Lu in the second century BCE, a number of manuscripts were found in one of the walls. It was believed these manuscripts had been hidden there after "the burning of the books" by the First Emperor in 213 BCE. In 281 CE, a number of hitherto unknown texts were discovered in Ji when the tomb of one of the kings of the pre-imperial state of Wei was opened.

6. Xu Xi is one of the most famous painters of the tenth century.

on which page, and in which column of text—the person who made no mistakes would win and was allowed to drink his or her tea first. Whenever I hit the mark, I would raise my cup and laugh out loud, at times even spilling my tea on my clothes, and would stand up without even having had the opportunity to drink a drop! I would have been happy to be allowed to grow old in this realm! And so our resolve was not affected even though we were living in a time of sorrow and hardship.

When our collection of books was complete, we built a book vault in the Hall of Returning Home. The big chests were recorded in a register and we prepared a list of the books. When we wanted to teach or read a book, we had to ask for the key and have our name recorded in the register, after which the relevant scrolls were located and brought out. If there was some slight damage or soiling, we were always required to have the book cleaned or repaired, and the ease and informality of earlier times was gone. So, while our desire was to seek enjoyment, we actually created trouble and worries for ourselves. I could not bear this, and so I started to deliberately omit the second meat from my meals; I also stopped wearing clothes of more than one color; in my hair I no longer wore any ornaments of bright pearls and kingfisher feathers, and in my rooms I kept no utensils that were painted in gold or decorated with embroidery. Whenever I came across one of the Classics or Histories or one of the Hundred Philosophers, as long as the characters were not defective and the edition was without mistakes, I would immediately purchase the book to keep as a second copy. In our family there was a tradition of studying the *Book of Changes* [*Yijing*] and the *Commentary of Mr. Zuo*, and so the texts relating to these two Classics were the most complete. As a result the books lay arranged in rows on tables and desks and were strewn in disorder on mat and pillow. They satisfied our minds, our hearts, our eyes, and our spirits, and the pleasure was beyond any provided by music or sex, hounds or horses.

In the *bingwu* year of the reign period Quiet Force [Jingkang, 1126], his lordship served as prefect of Zichuan. When he heard that the Jin bandits had invaded the capital, he looked all around him in desolation. The stuffed cases and overflowing chests filled him with longing and with desperation, as he realized that most certainly they would soon be his possessions no longer. The following spring, in the Third Month of the *dingwei* year of the reign period Established Upsurge [Jianyan, 1127], he had to hasten to the south because of the demise of my mother-in-law. As we were unable to transport all our luxury goods, we first put aside all the big and heavy books as well as those that were printed editions; next, we put aside the paintings on many sheets of paper, and finally we put aside all the ancient vessels without inscriptions. In addition, we later put aside those books that were directorate editions, run-of-the-mill paintings, and the large and heavy vessels. After all these various sortings, we still had fifteen cart-loads of books. When we came to Donghai, we crossed the Huai with a string of boats. We then again crossed the Yangzi and arrived in Jiankang. In our old home in Qingzhou we had left behind under lock and key more than ten rooms of books and sundry objects, and we had intended to transport them by boat [to the south] as well in the spring of the following year, but in the Twelfth Month the troops of the Jin conquered Qingzhou and the "more than ten rooms" were reduced to ashes.

That autumn, the Ninth Month of the *wushen* year of the reign period Established Upsurge [1128], his lordship reentered active service and served again as prefect, this time of Jiankang prefecture. The following spring, the Third Month of the *jiyou* year [1129], he was cashiered. We went up to Wuhu by boat, and then entered Gushu where we planned to settle down on the bank of the river Zhang. That summer, in the Fifth Month, we arrived at Chiyang. There his lordship received his appointment as prefect of Huzhou, with the order to proceed to the palace for an audience with the emperor. We temporarily made our home [on the river] in Chiyang, since he would be going by himself to the imperial court. But it was not until the thirteenth of the Sixth Month that he shouldered his luggage and left our boat. As he sat on the bank in his ramie gown with his cap pushed back, he exuded a tiger-like spirit, and his eyes flashed. Gazing into the boat he bid me goodbye. I felt extremely uneasy, and called to him: "What should I do in case I hear of some disturbance in the city?" With his hands on his hips he answered me from a distance: "Just follow the crowd! If worse comes to worst, first throw away the household goods, then the clothes and bedding, then the books and paintings, and then the ancient vessels. But the vessels for the ancestral sacrifices you must carry with you and guard with your life. Don't forget!" Then he galloped away.

Hurrying along the road, he exposed himself to extreme heat and fell ill. By the time he arrived at the Temporary Residence, his illness had taken a turn for the worse, and toward the end of the Seventh Month, I received a letter informing me that he was bedridden. I was alarmed and distressed, because I knew that his lordship had always been of an impatient nature—so what to do? If his illness was a serious one, he might run a fever, and in that case he would have to take cold medicines, which would make his illness even more worrisome. So I unmoored our boat and traveled downstream, covering three hundred *li* in a single day and night. When I arrived, I found he was indeed taking large quantities of medicines such as *chaibu* and *huangjin*; he suffered from bouts of fever and diarrhea, and his illness was so critical that he was on the brink of death.

Shedding tears of sorrow and filled with panic I could not bring myself to inquire about what he thought should be done after his death. On the eighteenth day of the Eighth Month, he was no longer able to get out of bed. He grabbed a brush and wrote a poem. He died immediately after having finished it, without leaving any instructions as to what to do upon his death.

After his burial, I had nowhere to go. The imperial court had disbanded the Inner Palace and sent its palace women away; it was also rumored that it was forbidden to cross the Yangzi.[7] At that time I still had twenty thousand scrolls of books and two thousand rubbings of bronze and stone inscriptions, and sufficient cups and plates, carpets, and cushions to entertain a hundred guests—as well as comparable quantities of other luxury items. Now it was my turn to fall seriously ill and I survived by only a single breath. As the political situation became ever more pressing, I remembered that his lordship had a brother-in-law who held the position of vice-minister in the Ministry of War and was serving in the imperial guard in Hongzhou.[8] I therefore dispatched two trusted clerks to go on ahead with my luggage as I intended to take refuge with him. But that winter, in the Twelfth Month, the Jin bandits conquered Hongzhou, and so all my goods were lost. The books that had once crossed the Yangzi "in a string of boats," were now once again all scattered like clouds and mist. The only things that still remained were a few small and lightweight paintings and calligraphy pieces, manuscript editions of the collections of Li Taibai, Du Fu, Han Yu, and Liu Zongyuan, a *Tales of the World* and a *Discourses on Salt and Iron*, some twenty or thirty copies of rubbings of bronze and stone inscriptions from the Han to the Tang, twelve or thirteen large and small tripods from the Three Dynasties, and some baskets filled with manuscripts from the Southern Tang, things I had amused myself with when I was ill and had been storing in my bedroom—this was all that survived of all that wealth.

It was now impossible to travel upstream on the Yangzi [to Hongzhou], while the might of the renegades was beyond calculation. My younger brother Hang was serving as an editor in the office of imperial edicts, so I joined him. When we arrived in Taizhou, the prefect of that city had already fled. When we arrived in Shan, we traveled overland . . .[9] We then threw away all our clothes and bedding and fled to Huanyan, where we hired a boat, and taking to sea we fled with the Traveling Court. At that time His Majesty had made a stop in Zhang'an. Following the imperial fleet, we traveled over the open sea to

---

7. Li Qingzhao had probably hoped for an appointment in the Inner Palace; she also found it impossible to return to Qingzhou.

8. Hongzhou refers to modern-day Nanchang in Jiangxi province.

9. Here there appears to be a gap in the text.

Wenzhou, and then went to Yuezhou. In the Twelfth Month of the year *gengxu* [1130] the court dismissed all of its officials, and so we went to Quzhou. That spring, in the Third Month of the *xinhai* year of the reign period Shaoxing [1131], we went again to Yuezhou. In the *renzi* year [1132] we went again to Hangzhou.

Earlier, when his lordship had been critically ill, he was visited by Secretary Zhang Feiqing who brought along a jade vase. After he had seen his lordship, he left taking the vase with him. Actually the vase was made of nephrite. This became the subject of gossip, and later it was even falsely rumored that he had offered it to the Jin, and I was also told that a censor had submitted a secret memorial of accusation. I was overcome with fear and did not dare to speak out, and so I collected all the bronze vessels and other objects in our house in order to present them to the court as soon as I arrived. But when I arrived in Yuezhou, the court had already moved to Siming. I did not dare keep these objects at home, so I sent them with a letter to Shan. Later, when government troops subjugated some mutinous soldiers, they took all of these things with them, and I have heard that they all ended up in the home of the late general Li. Of "all that survived of all that wealth," now some fifty to sixty percent had disappeared.

I now had only about five or seven baskets of calligraphy pieces and paintings, inkstones and inksticks. I could no longer bear to store them elsewhere, and so I kept them always under my own bed, and I always unlocked and locked the bedroom myself. While in Guiji, I lodged with a local family surnamed Zhong. But one night someone made a hole in the wall and carried off five baskets. I was inconsolable and offered a large reward for their recovery. Two days later a neighbor, Zhong Fuhao, appeared with eighteen scrolls demanding the reward. In this way I knew that the thieves had been local people. Despite all my efforts to recover my possessions, the other things were never returned. I now know that they were all purchased for a very low price by Transportation Commissioner Wu Yue. So now of "all that survived of all that wealth," seventy or eighty percent had disappeared. But yet I love and cherish the few scattered and incomplete books and quite ordinary pieces of calligraphy in my possession as I do my life—what foolishness, is it not?

When today I happened to read through this book, it was as if I saw the departed one before me. And I thought back how his lordship in the Hall of Tranquil Governance in Donglai, when the scrolls had first been mounted, provided them with a title strip and binding string, and wrapped every ten scrolls together in a single cover. Each day, after the end of the evening watch, he would collate two scrolls and write a postface to one. Of the two thousand scrolls in this collection, five hundred and twenty have such a postface. Now the work of his hands is still fresh, but the trees on his grave have already grown tall. How sad!

Long ago, Xiao Yi upon the collapse of Jiangling paid no heed to the collapse of the dynasty and destroyed all of his books and paintings, and Yang Guang, after the collapse of Jiangdu, did not grieve over his death, although he did come back to reclaim his paintings and books.[10] Can it be that even in death one cannot forget the objects to which one is attached by nature? Is it perhaps the case that Heaven deems us unworthy of enjoying such extraordinary things because of our insignificance? Or could it be that the dead retain their mental powers and, still devotedly loving and cherishing these things, are unwilling to leave them behind in the world of men? How is it possible for them to be scattered so easily when they had been acquired with such difficulty?

Alas! From the age of eighteen, two years younger than Lu Ji when he wrote his *Rhapsody [on Literature]*, to the age of fifty-two, two years older than Qu Yuan when he acknowledged his mistakes, during all these thirty-four years, I have been endlessly worried about gain and loss.[11] But where there is possession, its opposite must follow, and where there is collection, dispersal must follow: this is the cosmic law. If one man loses his bow, another man will find it—no need to waste words on it. The only reason why I have recorded the course of events in such detail is in the hope that it may serve as a warning for all those in later ages who love antiques and strive for erudition.

Written in the Studio of Simple Peace, on the first day of the Eighth Month of the second year, a ren *year, of the reign period Continued Restoration* [Shaoxing, 1132].

There is an important incident in the life of Li Qingzhao that is not mentioned in her postface to *Inscriptions on Bronze and Stone*. In the early summer of 1132, shortly after the end of the prescribed mourning period for her first husband, Li Qingzhao, then forty-nine years old, married a

---

10. Xiao Yi reigned from 552 to 554 as Emperor Yuan of the Liang dynasty in Jianling (in Hubei province); following the collapse of the dynasty, he set fire to his extensive library. Yang Guang was the last ruler of the Sui dynasty (581–617); following a life of debauchery he was killed in Jiangdu (Yangzhou). When the new authorities tried to transport part of his collection back to the capital, the boat sank: the ghost of Yang Guang had reclaimed his books.

11. The famous Tang dynasty poet Du Fu states in one of his poems that Lu Ji (261–303) wrote his magisterial *Rhapsody on Literature* at the precocious age of twenty. Qu Yuan (not the famous poet but the noble officer of Wei also mentioned by Ban Zhao) is said to have realized at the age of fifty all the mistakes of his preceding forty-nine years.

low-ranking official named Zhang Ruzhou. This second marriage was a total disaster: within a hundred days she had not only filed for divorce, but also formally accused her husband of corruption. For a woman to apply for divorce represented an act of insubordination, and it landed Li Qingzhao briefly in jail. In a letter to the high official Qi Chongli, a distant relative by marriage who had helped her out in this affair, she wrote that she had been misled by the glib talk of Zhang Ruzhou, who turned out to be a corrupt official interested only in her money. Moreover, she claimed, he had physically abused her when he found out that most of her wealth had disappeared.

Li Qingzhao's letter to Qi is riddled with allusions, so we limit ourselves here to a translation of one section of it:

Since youth I have been versed in the norms of righteousness and have had a rough understanding of the *Odes* and *Rites*. Not long ago, because of a serious illness, I was hovering at the brink of death, unable to even distinguish between buffaloes and ants, and my casket had already been prepared. Even though I still had my weak younger brother to taste my medicine for me, we had only one old soldier to guard the gate. In my panic, I acted too rashly; I believed Zhang's stories which were as glib as a bamboo reed, and was misled by his words which were as beautiful as brocade. As my younger brother was easily deceived, he took the man at his word as soon as he showed him his letters of appointment. As I myself was about to die, I had not the slightest suspicion that Zhang would not be "a jade mirror stand." He brought unspeakable pressure to bear on us and we found ourselves in an insoluble quandary. Even before I had recovered from my illness, he had taken me by force to his home.

As soon as I could again see and hear clearly, I realized it would be impossible for me to live with him. How could I, in the twilight of my life, bear to be married to such a greedy scoundrel? While I myself had earned public contempt for my disgusting behavior, he was determined not only to carry off the prize but also to kill me. And so he gave free rein to his brutal violence, and each day I suffered his beatings. You will understand that the arms of [a peaceful person such as] Liu Ling were no defense against the fists of [a barbarian rebel such as] Shi Le![12] I complained to Heaven and Earth, but how could I dare imitate

---

12. Liu Ling (mid-third century) is best known for his love of wine, but one anecdote has him refusing to fight a challenger with the words: "How could my chicken breast be a worthy match for your noble fists!" Shi Le (274–333), one of the fourth-century war-

Tanniang and complain to all and sundry![13] Yet I was also unwilling to resign myself to my terrible fate and take my misery for happiness. As outside help was nowhere to be found, there was no harm in lodging a complaint myself. But how could I have predicted that such a trifling affair would come to the notice of the emperor! A decision was taken in the Palace that this case was to be assigned to the highest court. Shackled hand and foot I gave my deposition, and was forced to make my case together with the worst criminals. I felt deeply ashamed, just as did the young scholar Jia Yi when he had to stand in the same row as [old army men such as] the Marquis of Jiang and Guan Ying, or the Old Master [Laozi] because he shares the same chapter [in the *Records of the Historian*] with [the legalist] Han Fei.[14] I only prayed for escape from death, I did not hope for a restitution of my money.

It was not Heaven's punishment that I was forced to live with this cruel and violent man for a hundred days; it was not the doing of someone else that I had to spend nine days in prison. If one tries to chase away a sparrow by throwing gold at him, what profit will come of it? If one smashes a disk of jade with one's head, one is bound to suffer a loss. I have only myself to blame for this stupid mistake and it was my lot that I should come to know the inside of a jail . . .

Li Qingzhao's second marriage was common knowledge among her contemporaries, but from the Ming dynasty (1368–1644) to the present, critics have tried to prove time and again that the letter to Qi Chongli was a fake and that the second marriage never actually took place. The stridency of their arguments can be attributed to the increasingly tight grip of a neo-Confucian morality that condemned the remarriage of widows. In traditional China, poetry was read as a reflection of the author's character, which meant, by extension, that only a high-minded person could produce fine poetry. To these critics, then, it was inconceivable

lords of northern China, in his youth had been a local thug who would beat up his neighbors in fights over fields.

13. Tanniang is one of the main characters in a popular Tang dynasty skit about a drunkard and his wife: when he comes home drunk and beats her up, she runs off to the neighbors to complain.

14. The Marquis of Jiang (Zhou Po) and Guan Ying were old soldiers who had assisted Liu Bang in founding the Han dynasty, whereas Jia Yi was a brilliant young scholar. When Jia Yi's proposals of reform threatened their position, they engineered his banishment to Chang'an. Laozi is considered the founder of Daoism, while Han Fei is one of the representatives of Legalism, a political theory that through most of Chinese history has been condemned as amoral.

that a great poet like Li Qingzhao could have remarried after the death of her husband; that she could have initiated a divorce was completely beyond their imagination. During the Song dynasty, when ideas on the remarriage of widows were still somewhat more liberal than they would become later, it was not Li Qingzhao's remarriage as such, but rather her quick divorce that was considered scandalous.

Little is known about the final years of Li Qingzhao. Following a stay in Jinhua, in 1138 she returned to Hangzhou. The last date in her life that can be ascertained is 1149, and she probably died soon thereafter, since she is referred to as deceased by 1151. She left a voluminous collection of writings, most of which has been lost. All that remain are a few prose texts, a handful of *shi* poems, and some fifty lyrics, collected from a wide array of anthologies and other sources. It is especially these song lyrics that have earned her the title of China's greatest woman poet.

Li Qingzhao's Poetry

The Rise of the Ci

The latter half of the Tang dynasty saw the rise of a new genre of poetry, originally called *quzi ci* (lyrics for songs), but later simply known as *ci* (lyrics). The Tang dynasty was characterized by its cosmopolitanism. One area of the culture of this period that was especially open to foreign influence was music. Orchestras and individual performers from Central Asia acquainted China with a wide variety of new musical instruments and melodies, which interacted in numerous ways with China's indigenous musical traditions, resulting in a host of new and popular tunes to which lyrics might be written. As in premodern Europe, it was quite common for songwriters to write new lyrics to existing melodies. Each of these melodies would have its own title, often taken from the words of the song that first made it popular.

Needless to say, given their origin in popular song, these lyrics made abundant use of formulaic motifs and images, and they used a register of language that is quite distinct from the one usually employed in *shi* poems.

Each individual melody imposed its own requirements on the songwriter. Whereas the older *shi* poems were made up of lines of equal length, with a requisite rhyme at the end of the even lines, *ci* lyrics could have any number, even or uneven, of lines, and the length of each line could be different, all depending on the melody to which the song was written. The melody also determined the prescribed word tones within each line as well as the placement of the rhymes. While in the earliest *ci* lyrics it is sometimes still possible to discern a link between the name of the individual melody and the content of the *ci* lyrics that were written to that tune, later this link was often lost.

Although originally the number of lyric melodies was rather limited, new melodies continued to appear throughout the tenth and eleventh centuries. Because the original melodies have almost all been lost, what we have now are the metrical patterns that still carry the names of the original tunes. Later handbooks that codify these metrical patterns list more than a thousand different tunes; if we also count the variations, they include more than sixteen hundred different patterns.

The earliest lyrics are relatively short, and consist of only a single stanza. An example of such a single stanza melody is "Dreaming of South of the River" (*Meng Jiangnan*). Each lyric written to this melody consists of only five lines: an opening line of three syllables, followed by one line of five syllables, two lines of seven syllables each, and a concluding line of five syllables; the rhyme is carried by the final syllables of the second, fourth, and fifth lines An example of a song to this melody is the following lyric by Yu Xuanji's one-time friend, Wen Tingyun, who in his works often adopts a feminine persona:

To the Melody of "Dreaming of South of the River" (*Meng Jiangnan*)

> After completing my toilette
> All alone I lean from the riverside tower:
> A thousand sails pass by but still no sign of the right one!
> The setting sun slowly sets and the river flows on and on,
> Breaking my heart at White Rushes Bank.

Another example of a single-stanza melody is "As in a Dream" (*Rumengling*). In this case, the lyric required seven lines: two of six syllables each, one of five syllables, one again of six syllables, two of two syllables each, and a final line of six syllables. All of the lines except the third line rhyme. Li Qingzhao wrote several lyrics to this melody, one of which reads:

To the Melody of "As in a Dream" (*Rumengling*)

I often recall that night in the pavilion by the brook:
We were so drunk that we forgot how to get home.
The mood over, we returned by boat in the dark,
And got lost by mistake in a jungle of lotus flowers.
We struggled to cross,
And struggling to cross
We stirred from their sleep a bank full of herons and gulls.

Before long, however, it became common to repeat the melody and to have lyrics consisting of two stanzas, between which one can usually discern some kind of contrast. One of the most popular two-stanza melodies from the earliest years of the genre was "Bodhisattva Barbarian" (*Pusaman*). In this melody, both stanzas consist of four lines, but whereas the first stanza consists of two lines of seven syllables followed by two lines of five syllables, the second stanza consists of four lines of five syllables; the rhyme scheme is aa bb//cc dd. An early example of a lyric to this melody is provided by Wen Tingyun:

To the Melody of "Bodhisattva Barbarian" (*Pusaman*)

Once darkness falls, the bright-white moon climbs to its zenith,
Silence reigns behind closed gates and no human voice is heard.
In the hidden room the musk-incense lingers,
I lie down without removing rouge and powder.

Oh, how I still cherish those years gone by—
Unbearable those memories of the past!
The dew on flowers and the fading moon:
The brocade coverlet knows the chill of dawn.

One of Li Qingzhao's lyrics to this melody may be translated as follows:

To the Melody of "Bodhisattva Barbarian" (*Pusaman*)

A tender breeze, the sun still weak as spring has just begun,
It feels so good to be able to again wear only a lined jacket.

When I wake up, I feel a slight chill;
The plum blossom in my hair has wilted.

My old home—where is it to be found?
The only way to forget is by drinking.
The aloeswood was burning while I slept,
Its fragrance is gone—I still feel the wine.

The most important performers of these new songs were professional female entertainers, the courtesans. While it is not inconceivable that some of the anonymous lyrics of the ninth and tenth centuries may have been composed by these women, all the known authors of the ninth to eleventh centuries are male. Though the earliest preserved anonymous lyrics were quite direct in their expressions of rage and despair, male literati songwriters preferred a highly suggestive and indirect language when dealing with the same themes. During the tenth century the genre enjoyed a growing popularity at the courts of the southern kingdoms: the earliest anthology was compiled at the court of the Early Shu in Chengdu, and the most famous *ci* poet of this period, Li Yu (937–978), was the (last) emperor of the Southern Tang in Nanjing. In the eleventh century, many of the leading literati wrote lyrics, but given the still relatively low status of the genre, few cared to include them in their collected works. If an author's lyrics were collected, they would circulate as a separate collection. Even though the genre had become more respectable by the second half of the eleventh century when even women of elite families wrote *ci* lyrics, authors and readers alike were still very much aware of the close link between the genre and musical entertainment, if not with the entertainment quarters.

Given the origins of the lyric, it is no surprise that love has been one of its most important themes. In some of the earliest examples of the genre one may find lyrics in which the implied speaker is a man, but the overwhelming majority of lyrics, intended to be sung by a woman, adopt a female voice and comment on love from a supposedly female perspective. All aspects of love are dealt with, from the very first exchange of glances to the implied consummation of passion, but the genre manifests a distinct predilection for the description, directly or indirectly, of the despair and ennui of the abandoned woman. Often her loneliness is contrasted with the luxury of her surroundings: a boudoir filled with painted screens and golden animal-shaped incense burners, looking out into a small, enclosed courtyard. Or the abandoned woman has climbed to the highest floor of a tower or pavilion from where she looks out over the fields and gazes into the distance, following with her eyes the river or road along which her husband or lover may one day return. Only occasionally is the unremitting gloom relieved by a memory of happier days together.

Lady Wei's Lyrics

Fairly representative examples of the genre are provided by the ten or so surviving lyrics of Wei Wan (better known as Lady Wei). Wei Wan was the wife of Zeng Bu (1036–1107), a younger brother of the famous prose writer and one-time prime minister Zeng Gong. No less an authority than Zhu Xi pronounced: "Lady Wei and Li Qingzhao are the only two women of the present dynasty who can write." Later critics, however, agreed that "while she [Lady Wei] was no match for Li Qingzhao, she did demonstrate a rare talent." A brief look at some of Lady Wei's lyrics will give us some idea of her talent; it will also allow us to appreciate Li Qingzhao's far greater originality.

To the Melody of "Master Ruan Returns" (*Ruanlanggui*)

Beyond the tower at dusk fallen blossoms drift,
The azure of the clear sky drapes down on all four sides.
The departing sail in the blink of an eye reaches heaven's edge—
A single plume of smoke spirals up into the empyrean's blue.

A traveler atop this tower—
My hair has turned gray.
No date has been set for your return.
Feeling lost I dare not descend the steep stairs—
In the shade of the *wutong* the moon's shadow shifts.[15]

---

15. The name of the *wutong* tree is homophonous with the expression *wutong* (we together).

To the Melody of "Bodhisattva Barbarian" (*Pusaman*)

The hills in the river appear, then disappear in the light of the setting sun,
When the mirrored image of the tower moves, the mandarin ducks are
    startled.
On the opposite bank a handful of houses,
Above their walls red apricot blossoms.

The road below the dike of green willows
Goes all day long by the bank of the river.
Three times I've seen the willow floss drift,
But the one who left has still not returned.

To the Melody of "Bodhisattva Barbarian" (*Pusaman*)

The east wind has already colored green the grasses on the immortals' isle,
In the painted tower the screens are rolled up on this clear frosty morning.
Purer even than the flowering plums of West Lake,
The blossoms open but as yet don't fill the branches.

An endless sky—no news or letter has arrived.
Again I see the geese making their way south.
Where does one most feel separation's sorrow?
In the capital, on a full moon night, atop a tower.

To the Melody of "Bodhisattva Barbarian" (*Pusaman*)

The red tower slanting and leaning by the bend of the river,
The river's water in front of the tower was frozen cold jade.
Punting our boat of magnolia wood,
We in that boat were still so young.

The lotus flowers charmingly made as if to speak,
As smiling we entered the mandarin ducks' channel.
Over the waves a dark mist descended—
Singing a song by moonlight we returned.

To the Melody of "Magnolia Flower Abbreviated"
(*Jianzi mulanhua*)

A full moon above the western tower:
The pear blossoms appear, then disappear: a thousand trees of snow.

To the top of the tower I return,
And filled with sorrow listen to the lone goose above the orphaned city.

Where could he be, that man of jade?
Again I see the spring coming to an end here, south of the River.
News from you is nowhere to be had—
Since you left, peach blossoms have blanketed the flowing stream.

To the Melody of "Tying Up My Skirt" (*Xiqunyao*)

The light of the lamp flickers weakly as the hours drag on and on.
Since you left me,
The nights are cool.
The western wind moans desolately as I wake from my dream:
Who thinks of me,
Alone in my bed,
With knitted brows?

The brocade screen and the embroidered drapes conspire with autumn:
My heart is about to break,
Tears furtively trickle down.
Again the full moon appears to the west of my small window.
Oh, how I hate you,
Oh, how I love you,
But what do you care?

To the Melody of "Dotting Red Lips" (*Dianjiangchen*)

Over the waves a clear breeze:
A painted boat, the full moon, after he has returned.
Slowly the after-effects of the wine fade away,
And all alone I lean for a long while against the balustrade.

Union and separation all happen so fast,
This pain I carry with me year after year.
Again I look back:
A light mist and sparse willows,
And the indistinct calls of the watchman on the wall.

To the Melody of "Little Town on the River" (*Jiangchengzi*)

How easy it was to say goodbye, how difficult to meet with him again!
And so, whatever one may say,
I have no desire to look into the mirror.
My figure has wasted away
And suddenly I notice my clothes fall too loosely.
Outside the gate the red plum is about to wither—
Who would have thought
I never even saw it bloom?

My morning toilette done, from the tower I gaze toward the capital city,
But fearing the light chill,
Do not lean on the balustrade.
How I hate you, eastern wind,
For blowing resentment onto my brows!
Go and tell him that he should hurry and come home,
So he won't waste my
One spring of leisure!

To the Melody of "Springtime in Wuling" (*Wulingchun*)

The little courtyard: no one around, the screen half rolled up—
All alone I lean on the balustrade.
Too loose by far my goldthread gown of spring!
Wasted away—but no one knows!

Lately letters from the man of jade have been few,
It must be they are delayed because of my resentment.
When will he return from Chang'an in my dreams?
With tear-filled eyes I watch the setting sun.

The lyrics of Lady Wei are almost perfect illustrations of the generic characteristics of the lyric. While one of the lyrics is devoted to the evocation of a happy memory, the majority of them focus on the stock situation of the abandoned woman longing (in vain) for the return of her husband or patron. Lady Wei restricts herself to a limited number of melodies and develops her theme by relying on a small set of stock images. In fact, her lyrics are so conventional that few critics would be tempted to confuse the persona in her lyrics with the historical author. Li

Qingzhao, however, shows a much greater individuality even when she treats the same themes as Lady Wei. Moreover, she uses a greater variety of melodies, shows a more creative use of language, and on occasion inserts what appear to be personal details. This latter characteristic of her work invites critics to read not only some, but all of her lyrics as direct expressions of her personal and deeply felt emotions.

Li Qingzhao's Lyrics

Though Li Qingzhao's style is unique, her lyrics generally adhere closely to the thematic conventions of the genre, so well exemplified by the preceding lyrics of Lady Wei. In the following lyrics, for instance, Li Qingzhao makes use of two very common motifs: the scene inside the boudoir and the vista from the tower.

To the Melody of "Dotting Red Lips" (*Dianjiangchen*)

The silent and lonely inner chamber:
Each inch of my tender innards a thousand threads of sorrow!
I cherish spring but spring departs,
As drops of rain hasten the blossoms' fall.

I lean against the balustrade
And am filled by feelings of listlessness.
Where is he?
Fragrant grasses up to the horizon:
I gaze at the road along which he'll come home.

To the Melody of "Remembering the Flute-Player on Phoenix Terrace" (*Fenghuangtai shang yi chuixiao*)

The incense chilled in golden lions,
The coverlet rumpled like red waves:
I get up but am too lazy to comb my hair.
Let the precious mirror be covered with dust,
And the sun climb as high as the curtain hook,
I'm so frightened of the bitter loneliness of separation!
There are so many things like this
That I would like to say but don't.
The reason I have grown so skinny lately

Is not because of too much wine,
Nor is it due to autumn sadness.

Over! It's all over!
When you left this last time,
Not even a thousand, ten thousand "Yang Pass" songs
Could keep you here.[16]
Remembering my Wuling fisherman now so far away,
Mist locks in the tower.[17]
None but the flowing stream in front of the tower
Seems to remember me
As all day it fixes me with its gaze.
And fixing me with its gaze,
As of now it adds
Yet a new sorrow.

A theme that is quite common in song lyrics is the complaint about the passing of time and the brevity of human existence. Such feelings are easily aroused by autumn, when all of nature seems to be dying. One of Li Qingzhao's best-known works is the following autumn lament:

To the Melody of "Reduplications, Extended" (*Shengshengman*)

Seeking, seeking, searching, searching:
Chilly, chilly, cheerless, cheerless,
Dreary, dreary, dismal, dismal, wretched, wretched—

---

16. "Yang Pass" songs are songs of parting. The term originally referred to a poem by the Tang dynasty poet Wang Wei entitled "Sending Mr. Yuan on his Way on a Mission to Anxi," the last two lines of which read: "I urge you to finish one more cup of wine: / Once you travel westward beyond Yang Pass you'll be without friends." This poem was widely sung as a parting song.

17. Tao Qian (365–427), in his *An Account of Peach Blossom Spring*, tells the story of a fisherman from Wuling who, passing by a grove of blossoming peach trees and entering into a cave, discovers a paradisiacal community—but once he returns to his own village, he is unable to find the Peach Blossom Spring again. In later tellings this story was conflated with another legend of woodcutters who deep in the mountains accidentally come across a community of immortals. The woodcutters spend some time with a few lovely female immortals, who are left desolate when their lovers return to the world of men.

The weather suddenly warm, then cold again
Makes it hard to regain strength.
How could two or three cups of weak wine
Be a match against
The gusting winds as darkness falls?
Migrating geese fly by—
What pains me now:
Once long ago they were my friends.

Chrysanthemums cover the ground in heaps:
Wilted, withered, damaged.
But who today takes pleasure in them and will pick them?
Sitting by the window
All by myself, I wish it would turn dark!
The *wutong* tree, and then that drizzling rain,
That—into dusk—
Drip-drops, drip-drops!
How can all of this
Be disposed of by
The one word "sorrow"?

Chrysanthemums, which flower in autumn, are often used in Chinese poetry as a symbol of loyalty in adversity, so perhaps this lyric also invites a political reading. In yet another autumn lament the sadness of autumn is linked to the pain of parting:

To the Melody of "One Cut-Out Plum" (*Yijianmei*)

The red lotus has lost its fragrance, the jade mat feels autumnal—
I slightly loosen my gauze skirt,
Alone I board the orchid boat.
Who will send me from the clouds a letter of brocade?
As the V-shaped formations of geese return,
The moon fills the western tower.

Blossoms tossed and scattered, the river flowing on—
One and the same: the longing,
In two places: the idle sorrow.
This feeling—I simply don't know how to make it go away:

Barely has it descended from my brows,
Then it ascends again into my heart!

Spring as well as fall evoked deep feelings of sadness, either because the new blossoms of spring made the observer aware of the contrast between the cyclical renewal of nature and the irreversible fading of youth, vigor, and beauty, or because the fading or falling blossoms remind the observer of the ephemeral nature of existence. Li Qingzhao's most famous spring lyric is probably the following one-stanza song:

To the Melody of "As in a Dream" (*Rumengling*)

Last night the rain was scattered, the winds blustery,
Even a deep sleep has not cleared my head of wine.
I ask the girl who is rolling up the blinds,
She answers: "The crab apple is the same as it was before."
Doesn't she know?
Doesn't she know?
She should've said: "The green is fatter, the red skinnier"!

The following spring song by Li Qingzhao is said to date from her stay, late in life, in Jinhua in 1135:

To the Melody of "Springtime in Wuling" (*Wulingchun*)

The breeze has dispelled the dust, all the fragrant blossoms are gone:
The day's half passed but I'm too lazy to comb my hair.
The time is right but he's not here, nothing's worth doing—
Before I can speak, the tears flow down.

I've been told that spring on Couple Brook is still fine,
I too would like to boat there in a scull.
But I'm afraid that such a tiny boat on Couple Brook
Wouldn't be able to move
             with all my sorrows.

Of course, despair caused by the absence of a loved one and frustration over the irreversibility of time often go together. These feelings are experienced even more intensely on seasonal festival days such as Double

Three and Double Nine. Double Three was celebrated on the third day of the Third Month, the last month of spring according to the traditional Chinese calendar. Tall swings sometimes would be erected in the garden, allowing girls to catch a glimpse of life outside the garden walls—or to be seen by passers-by. Double Three was also associated with the ancient Cold Food Festival, during which no fires were to be lit for three days, and which was celebrated one hundred and five days after the shortest day of the year:

To the Melody of "Niannu's Charms" (*Niannujiao*)

The courtyard desolate,
Again that slanting wind and drizzling rain—
The double gates securely locked.
Pampered willows, charming blossoms: Cold Food draws near
With many kinds of annoying weather!
The rhymes were hard but the poem is done,
Propping up my head, clearing it of wine:
This moment holds a special flavor!
The migrating geese have all passed by,
Impossible now to send you the thousand, ten thousand secrets of my
    heart.

Atop the tower, spring these few days has been cold,
The blinds hang down on all four sides,
And I'm too listless to lean on the jade balustrade.
The coverlet is chilly, no incense burns as I wake up from my latest
    dream,
And although filled with sorrow I still must get up.
Clear dewdrops form at dawn,
The new *wutong* has started to grow,
Giving rise to thoughts of spring excursions.
When the sun rises higher and the mist disperses,
Let's see whether we will have a clear day today!

The following lyric by Li Qingzhao does not so much describe the feelings occasioned by the day of Double Three itself, as those evoked by the evening following it:

To the Melody of "Resentment against My Prince" (*Yuanwangsun*)

In the Capital spring draws to a close—
A deep courtyard behind double gates:
Grasses have turned green around the steps,
Under the evening sky the geese are gone.
Atop this tower—who'll bring a letter from far away?
My pain lingers on and on.

Passionate as I am, I just bring it all on myself!
I simply cannot give him up!
Once again it is the Cold Food Festival:
The swings deserted, the streets empty, no one about,
The pure-white moon about to set
Drenches the pear tree blossoms.

While the preceding Double Three lyric may well date from sometime before 1126, the following Double Three song was most likely written during Li Qingzhao's later years:

To the Melody of "The Butterfly Loves Flowers" (*Dielianhua*) On Double Three I Invited My Relatives to a Banquet

The endless night stretches on and on, my pleasures are few.
To no avail I dream of Chang'an,
And recognize Chang'an's streets.[18]
People tell me this year the spring colors are fine—
Flowers' luster and moon's shadow surely shine on each other.

Even though the makeshift cups and plates are nothing special,
The wine is good, the food is fine,
Just the thing to delight the heart.
But don't stick flowers in your hair when tipsy, and flowers do not laugh:
While spring may be the same again, people grow old.

Double Nine was celebrated on the ninth day of the Ninth Month, the last month of autumn in the traditional Chinese calendar. Friends and fam-

---

18. Chang'an was the name of the capital of the Western Han and the Tang dynasties. In Song times, the term was often used to refer to the new capital of Kaifeng.

ily would gather to ascend to a high place together to enjoy the moon and drink wine scented with the petals of chrysanthemum flowers. The following lyric by Li Qingzhao, however, reflects a more solitary and melancholic experience of this particular holiday.

To the Melody of "Tipsy in the Shade of Flowers" (*Zuihuayin*)

Light mist and heavy clouds: depressed all through the day,
As ambergris dissolves in golden beasts.[19]
A festival: again it's Double Nine—
A jade headrest, gauze curtains,
Penetrated only after midnight by the chill.

By the eastern hedge I poured the wine even after dusk,
And the chrysanthemums' dark fragrance still fills my sleeves.
Don't say that this will not dissolve your soul:
The curtain lifted by the autumn wind,
And I more skinny than those yellow flowers!

This lyric would later give rise to an extremely popular, if most likely apocryphal, anecdote about an exchange of poems between Li Qingzhao and her husband, probably when he was away from home studying at the National Academy:

Yi'an [Li Qingzhao] sent her lyric on Double Nine written to the melody of "Tipsy in the Shade of Flowers" in an envelope to Mingcheng. Mingcheng sighed in admiration. He felt ashamed that he was not her equal and wanted desperately to surpass her. For three full days and nights he refused to see any visitors and forgot to eat or sleep. After he had written fifty lyrics [on the same subject and to the same melody], he inserted Yi'an's lyric in with them as well, and showed them all to his friend Lu Defu. After the latter had read them carefully a number of times, he said: "There are only three lines that are of exceptional beauty." When Mingcheng pressed him to tell him which three, he said: "Don't say that this will not dissolve your soul: / The curtain lifted by the autumn wind / And I more skinny than those yellow flowers." These were the lines from Yi'an's lyric!

---

19. "Golden beasts" are animal-shaped incense burners made of bronze or sometimes even more precious metals.

One of the other major yearly festivals was First Night, which was celebrated on the fifteenth (also called "Three Times Five") of the First Month, the first full moon night of the year. The festival marked the end of the many activities surrounding New Year. In Song dynasty times, the festival of First Night was celebrated with elaborate displays of lanterns and men and women would stroll along the streets and admire them. Li Qingzhao describes this festival in a lyric that must have been written sometime during the latter part of her life, after she had fled the north and settled in Hangzhou:

To the Melody of "Eternal Pleasure" (*Yongyule*)
First Night

The setting sun melts into gold,
The evening clouds merge into a disk of jade,
But where on earth is he?
The mist that dyes the willows is so heavy,
The flute that plays "The Plum Tree" sounds resentful—
God knows how many, many thoughts of spring!
The festival of the First Night,
A weather that is nice and pleasant—
But later there is bound to be some wind and rain.
People come to fetch me—
Fragrant carts and finest horses—
But I decline the invitations of those companions of poetry and wine.

In those glory days of Kaifeng
Leisure reigned in the inner quarters
And I remember how we relished the Three Times Five:
Kingfisher-feather little chaplets,
Snow-willow hairpins rolled of gold,
As each tried to outdo the other with her headdress!
But now I am a bag of bones,
My hair disheveled and turning gray—
You'd be afraid to see me out at night.
Far better I should from
Behind a lowered blind
Just listen to other people's laughter.

The onset of spring was marked by the beautiful sight of the bare branches of the plum tree suddenly dotted with white blossoms, occasionally even before New Year. Li Qingzhao shows a special affinity to plum blossoms in a number of her lyrics.

To the Melody of "Pride of the Fisherman" (*Yujia'ao*)

Despite the snow I know that news of spring has arrived:
Blossoms of winter plum adorning branches sleek with ice.
The fragrant cheeks half-opened, seductive in their charms,
Across the courtyard:
A jade-white beauty who has just emerged from her bath.

Creation has no doubt purposely on her behalf
Ordered the full moon to illuminate her with its soft light.
So together let's savor the "green ants" in golden cups
And drink till we are tipsy:[20]
These blossoms are quite different from ordinary flowers!

To the Melody of "Venting My Innermost Feelings" (*Suzhongqing*)

Last night I was too tipsy to remove my headdress,
In my hair I still wear a branch of blossoming plum.
When I wake, its fragrance shatters my spring dream,
Leaving my soul stranded far away.

Everyone's still asleep,
The moon still lingers,
The screens hang down.
Once again I rub the plum's remaining petals,
Once again I press out its leftover fragrance,
Once again I enjoy it for one moment more.

To the Melody of "Orphaned Goose" (*Guyan'er*)

Whenever people of the present generation try to write lyrics on the plum blossom, as soon as they put brush to paper their works turn out to be

---

20. The "green ants" refer to the froth on the wine.

vulgar. As I have also tried my hand at writing such lyrics, I have come to realize that the above words are true.

Rattan bench and paper curtains, I wake at dawn,
Unable to express all my unhappy thoughts.
The aloeswood incense sputters, the jade burner has grown cold,
And the feelings that won't leave me are like water.
After three tunes of the flute the plum-heart is startled
By these countless spring feelings.

A slight breeze, a light rain's desolate drizzle
Again impel me to shed a thousand tears.
The one who played the flute is gone, the jade tower is empty,
My heart is broken—with whom to climb it?
I have plucked a branch,
But on earth below and in heaven above
There is no one to whom I can send it.

Li Qingzhao's Ci–*Criticism*

One of Li Qingzhao's preserved prose writings is entitled *On Lyrics* (*Cilun*) and is a short essay on the art of the song lyric. In it, Li Qingzhao stresses the musical requirements of the genre. She also briefly discusses two developments in the genre that took place during the course of the eleventh century. The first of these was the growing popularity of longer and longer melodies, occasionally in three stanzas, requiring longer texts. This development is often attributed to the songwriter Liu Yong (987?–1053?), whose sensitivity to the genre's musical requirements is highly praised by Li Qingzhao. At the same time, she condemns the vulgarity of his language (a criticism later Song dynasty critics would also level against Li Qingzhao herself). In her own lyrics, Li Qingzhao continued to prefer the shorter melodies.

The second development was the tendency of many poets of the second half of the twelfth century (most famously Su Shi, 1031–1101) to use lyrics to treat subjects that had been traditionally restricted to *shi* poetry. Li Qingzhao protested strongly against this tendency, which she felt would reduce the lyric to a genre that differed from *shi* solely in terms of form. She argued that the lyric constituted a separate genre because of both its subject matter and its formal requirements, and criticized some of the leading poets of her age for departing from the genre's conventions. In later centuries, some of the greatest names in the history of Chinese literary criticism held this against her, even though her remarks were no more outspoken than those of some of her male contemporaries. Li Qingzhao's (conservative) insistence on the "feminine" characteristics of the genre, however, should perhaps be interpreted as an attempt to protect the lyric from being subverted by the male-dominated *shi* genre and to ensure that women had "a genre of their own."

Li Qingzhao opens her brief essay with a story illustrating the power of song:

Ballads and song-poems emerged simultaneously and flourished especially during the Tang dynasty. During the reign periods Reopened Beginning [Kaiyuan; 713–741] and Heavenly Treasure [Tianbao; 742–755] there lived a certain Eighth Master Li, whose singing was the best in the whole world. Once, on the occasion of a celebration banquet for the newly passed graduates at Serpentine Pond, a famous gentleman on the list summoned Li ahead of time and ordered him to change into different clothes and not to reveal his name. Li put on an old, shabby gown and cap that made him look very pitiful. The gentleman took him along to the banquet, and said: "Please let my cousin sit at the far end," after which no one paid attention to him. When the wine had been passed and the music had begun, the singers entered, among whom were Cao Yuanqian and Niannu, the most famous singers of the day. After they had sung their songs, all present sighed in admiration and voiced their praise. Then the gentleman pointed to Li and said: "Please let my cousin sing a song!" Everybody smiled in derision and some even got angry. But then Li cleared his throat and started to sing, and after only one song they were all in tears; gathering around him, they bowed and said: "You must be Eighth Master Li!"

Ever since that time the tunes of Zheng and Wei have become more popular daily and the changes in ornamentation daily more elaborate.[21] At the time there already existed lyrics for tunes such as *Pusaman* [Bodhisattva Barbarian], *Chunguanghao* [How Fine is Spring], *Suojizi* [Sedge-Chicken], *Genglouzi* [The Watches of the Night], *Huanxisha* [The Sands of Washing Brook], *Meng Jiangnan* [Dreaming of South of the River], and *Yufu* [The Fisherman]—too many to list in their

---

21. "The tunes of Zheng and Wei" is a general designation for popular songs on erotic themes.

entirety. The Five Dynasties [907–960] was a period of warfare, during which the world was cut up like a melon and divided like beans, and the Way of "This Culture of Ours" was in shambles. Only the rulers of the Li family and their ministers south of the Yangzi venerated literary elegance, and so they produced lyrics with lines such as "On the small tower one blows forth the cold of the jade flute," and "This blows all the water of the spring pond into crackle patterns."[22] Such lines may be extremely unusual, but they partake of the "mournful sadness of the sounds of a decaying state."

Once the present dynasty was founded, rites and music, culture and might were grandly established. But it would take another one hundred years of nurturing to produce a Liu Yong, who changed the old tunes and turned them into new ones. He authored *A Collection of Texts for Music* [*Yuezhang ji*], and in his time was greatly renowned for his tunes. But although he adheres to the notes and scales, his words and phrases are vulgar and common. After him appeared men like Zhang Xian, Song Qi and his brother Song Xiang, Shen Tang, Yuan Jiang, and Chao Duanli, but even though they may from time to time have produced marvelous lines, such lines are too incidental to earn these poets the appellation of "famous masters." As for Yan Shu, Ouyang Xiu, and Su Shi, their learning encompassed both Heaven and Man, so when they composed a short song lyric, it was just as if they had poured out a ladleful of water from their great ocean. Their lyrics, however, are all nothing more than *shi* poems but with lines of unequal length. They also often fail to adhere to the tones and scales. Why is this? Now *shi* and prose only distinguish between level and oblique (in word tones), but song lyrics distinguish among the five notes, among the five tones, among the six scales, and between high and low, light and heavy. Moreover, recent tunes such as *Shengsheng man* [Reduplications, Extended], *Yuzhonghua* [Flowers in the Rain], and *Xiqianying* [Joy at the Moving Oriole] not only have rhymes in the level tone but also in the entering tone. *Yulouchun* [Jade Tower Spring] not only has rhymes in the level tone, but also has rhymes in the ascending and leaving tones, and also in the entering tone. Originally it had rhymes in the oblique tone, but it only fits if one uses rhymes in the ascending tone—it is impossible to sing the tune if one uses entering tones.

The prose of Wang Anshi and Zeng Gong reads like that of the Western Han, so whenever they wrote short song lyrics, everyone would fall over laugh-

---

22. The court of the Southern Tang dynasty (936–975) in modern-day Nanjing was renowned for its elegance. The last ruler of that dynasty, Li Yu (937–978), is one of the most famous authors of lyrics.

ing because they were impossible to read out loud. From this we know that the lyric is a genre unto itself and that there are few who really understand it.

Later, only Yan Jidao, He Zhu, Qin Guan, and Huang Tingjian were capable of understanding the genre. Even so, Yan Jidao suffers from a lack of developed exposition, and He Zhu is deficient in classical decorum. Qin Guan focuses on the delineation of feeling but does not employ enough allusions. His works may be compared to a beautiful woman of a poor family: she may be exceedingly voluptuous and dazzling, but in the end she does not have the bearing of one born to wealth and status. Huang Tingjian loves allusions, but his works contain many faults and failings; they may be compared to a beautiful jade, the crack in which diminishes its value by half.

In her own lyrics, and in keeping with her own argument, Li Qingzhao largely limits herself to the conventional themes of the genre, lamenting her loneliness and the brevity of youth. On occasion she also expresses the desire to leave this world behind forever:

To the Melody of "Pride of the Fisherman" (*Yujia'ao*)

Cloudy waves to the horizon merge with the morning mist,
The River of Stars about to turn, a thousand sails dancing.
It is as if in a dream my soul had returned to God's abode,
I heard the words of Heaven,
Which kindly inquired where it was I intended to go.

And I replied: "The way was long, alas, the evening draws nigh.
I practiced poetry but few of my lines were startlingly new.
A wind of over ninety thousand miles that lifts the giant roc:
Please, let that wind cease not
But blow my little boat straight to the Isles of the Immortals!"

Li Qingzhao and her Critics

If the lyrics of Li Qingzhao are so self-consciously conventional both in form and subject, why then are they so highly regarded by both traditional and modern Chinese critics? First of all, these critics praise the authenticity and depth of the emotions she expresses. As we have stated before, the lyric as a genre originally was very fictional in character, written largely by male authors who gave expression to the supposedly typical feelings of women in a supposedly typically "feminine" language. The writers of song lyrics did not even pretend to describe their own feelings; like songwriters all over the world they were providing performers with the words to voice typical feelings in typical situations. However, the Chinese reader of poetry of imperial times assumed that the poet and the "I" in his (or her) poems were one and the same; any perceived discrepancy between the historical author and the "I" in the poem was regarded as a sign of frivolity and bad faith that detracted from the value of the poem. This is why in imperial China, literary critics usually reserved their highest praise for those authors whose compositions, whether *shi* poems or *ci* lyrics, could be read as autobiographical statements. Traditional critics have, for example, insisted on reading the lyrics of Li Yu, the last ruler of the Southern Tang, as just such autobiographical statements, even though his works hardly depart from the thematic conventions of his time. But for the majority of male-authored lyrics such a reading was very difficult (an important Qing dynasty school of criticism insisted on reading such lyrics allegorically in order to safeguard them for literature). In contrast, it was generally considered that lyrics written by women could be more easily read as being spontaneous and authentic, direct and unmediated, and expressive of deep feeling.

Traditional Chinese critics, therefore, read Li Qingzhao's lyrics as truthful expressions of her rich emotions. Some of Li Qingzhao's lyrics invite such a reading as they often carry a short preface specifying the occasion for which the lyric was written or contain explicit references to her own life. However, many of her other extant lyrics are highly generic and do not provide such autobiographical information. Yet this does not stop critics from attempting to determine which works date from which period in her life—although they by no means agree on the dating of each individual work. Another problem these critics encounter is that the original collection of Li Qingzhao's lyrics compiled shortly after her death has been lost, and that the collection we have today has been reconstructed on the basis of much later anthologies, which do not always agree in the ascription of authorship. Some of the lyrics that were traditionally ascribed to Li Qingzhao may well have been the work of earlier, male poets. Among these contested pieces are some of Li Qingzhao's best-known works, such as the following:

To the Melody of "Dotting Red Lips" (*Dianjiangchen*)

After exerting herself on the swing,
She gets off, too tired to redo her toilette—
Such delicate hands.
Heavy dew on a skinny flower:
Her light gown damp with beads of sweat.

The moment she sees the guest enter,
She, in her stockings, gold hairpins slipping,
Feels embarrassed and runs off.
But leaning on the gate she glances back,
And takes a whiff of the green plum in her hand.

In some cases the willingness of critics to reject the authenticity of a lyric is motivated primarily by their conviction that a great poet such as Li Qingzhao could not possibly have written such light and frivolous, even flirtatious, songs as the above or the following:

To the Melody of "Magnolia Flower Abbreviated" (*Jianzi Mulanhua*)

Out of the basket of the flower-seller
I bought one single branch that was about to bloom:
Lightly and evenly dyed by tears,
Still bearing the traces of rosy dawn and morning dew.

Afraid that he might wonder
If my face is perhaps not as lovely as that of this flower
I'll stick it in my cloudy locks,
And have him compare the two of us whenever he looks!

The modern Chinese literary historian Su Zhecong, a specialist in Chinese women's poetry and the author of a monograph on women's literature of the Song dynasty, praises Li Qingzhao above all for her ability to make abstract concepts such as sorrow almost tactile by her use of concrete images. As an example, she quotes Li Qingzhao's lyric to the melody of "Springtime in Wuling," in which the weight of sorrow is described as being such that it can sink a boat. She also praises Li Qingzhao's ability to fuse the description of scene and emotion, and her skill in delineating complex emotions. Other aspects of Li Qingzhao's that elicit this particular scholar's praise are her original comparisons ("And I more skinny than those yellow flowers!"), her subtle use of personification, her deft handling of parallelisms, and her spectacular (and later often imitated) use of reduplicated words (as in the lyric to the melody of "Reduplications, Extended"). And finally, she notes Li Qingzhao's capacity to surprise her readers by inserting into a rather bland style such startling lines such as "Pampered willows, charming blossoms," and "The green is fatter, the red is skinnier."

Critics also praise Li Qingzhao for her daring inventiveness in incorporating colloquial words into the conventional idiom of the lyric. However, this willingness to make use of "vulgar" language was criticized by certain contemporary writers who wanted to elevate the status of the genre. For example, in 1149 Wang Zhuo wrote the following in his survey of contemporary lyric writing:

Yi'an jushi [Li Qingzhao] is the daughter of the late judicial intendant for the eastern circuit of the capital, Li Gefei [style name Wenshu], and the wife of the late prefect of Jiankang, Zhao Mingcheng [style name Defu]. From her youth she has been famous for her *shi* poetry; her talent and forcefulness are rich and ample, and she is a close match to earlier generations. Even among gentlemen and high officials such qualities are rarely to be found. Among women of the present dynasty her literary brilliance has to be ranked as number one. After Zhao died, she remarried, but obtained a divorce from her second husband after a court case. Now in the evening of her life she drifts about without a home.

In writing song lyrics, she is able to analyze the human mind in minute detail. Her works are light and artful, sharp and fresh, and can assume a hundred different postures. She makes use of the wild and lascivious words of alleys and lanes with abandon. Since ancient times, never among the literate women of gentry families has there ever been anyone who showed such disregard for propriety.

Reading such a comment one can understand why Li Qingzhao failed in her attempts to find a safe haven in the Inner Palace, but it is difficult, apart perhaps from the frequent references to wine and drinking, to discern in her extant lyrics any trace of the unrestrained licentiousness referred to by Wang Zhuo.

Li Qingzhao's Poems

In her own lifetime, as Wang Zhuo's appreciation makes clear, Li Qingzhao was known primarily for her *shi* poems. Only a handful of these poems, however, has been preserved, among them the following quatrain entitled "The End of Spring":

> Why do I suffer from homesickness as spring draws to a close?
> Feeling ill, I comb my hair and my despair could not be greater.
> That pair of swallows on the rafters chatter all through the day,
> The faint breeze from yonder roses fills the door with fragrance.

This poem elicited from a later critic the following dismissive note:

The *shi* poems of Qingzhao are not very beautiful, but she excels in lyrics, which are outstandingly elegant and merit recitation. A line such as "The faint breeze from yonder roses fills the door with fragrance" from her quatrain, "The End of Spring," may be well crafted but really belongs in a lyric.

Modern Chinese anthologies rarely fail to include the following poem as an example of Li Qingzhao's staunch patriotism:

> In life one should be a hero amongst men,
> Then in death a stalwart amongst ghosts.
> To this day everyone remembers Xiang Yu,
> Who refused to cross to south of the Yangzi.

Xiang Yu (232–202 BCE) was born to a noble family in the ancient southern state of Chu. Following the death of the First Emperor of Qin in 210 BCE and the subsequent collapse of his empire, he recruited three thousand young men in the area south of the Yangzi and fought other contenders for the spoils. Initially he achieved great success, but ultimately he lost out to the low-born Liu Bang, who eventually emerged victorious because of superior planning (whereas Liu Bang surrounded himself with capable advisors, Xiang Yu failed to make use of the talents of the strategist Fan Zeng). When in the end, Xiang Yu was left without any troops, a boatman offered to ferry him back to south of the Yangzi River so he could recruit fresh soldiers. Xiang Yu, however, could not bear the thought of having to face the parents of the young men he had led into battle. Instead, he turned back and fought his foes one more time, until, surrounded by enemy commanders, he finally took his own life. It is clear that Li Qingzhao's poem was meant to be read as a reproach to those in the Southern Song government who preferred to enjoy the "stolen peace" in southern China rather than fight to the death for the recovery of the north.

Yet another of Li Qingzhao's poems, "Dawn Dream," can also probably be read as a satire of these peace-loving gentlemen:

> My dawn dream follows the sounds of bells,
> And airily I tread the colored clouds.
> By chance I meet there Master Anqi,
> And also happen to run into Elühua.[23]
> Just now the autumn wind is naughty,
> And blows away the Jade Well flowers.
> Together we see lotuses as large as boats,
> And we eat dates that are as big as melons.
> Dashingly elegant: the guests in attendance
> Are marvelous of mind and fine of speech.
> With jesting words they debate and dispute,
> Over the fire they brew the freshest tea.
> This may not be of any use to one's Lord,
> But still the pleasures are without limit.
> If one can live out one's human life like this,
> What need is there to return to one's old home?
> But I stand up, straighten my gown, sit down,
> Cover my ears, disgusted by their clamor.
> I realize I will not see my home again,
> But every memory still makes me sigh.

In the People's Republic of China the works of Li Qingzhao have engendered considerable discussion. In the decades when literary criticism was dominated by Marxism her writings were often condemned as reactionary; critics found it difficult to ideologically justify the sentimental laments of a wealthy upper-class gentry woman. But since the early eighties of the twentieth century the verdict has been that "the songs from the

---

23. Master Anqi is a famous immortal who has a short entry in *Biographies of Immortals* (*Liexian zhuan*), the earliest collection of hagiographical sketches of immortals. Elühua is a female immortal who in the middle of the fourth century appeared to Yang Quan.

earlier period show a warm love for life, while their basic attitude is healthy, and the songs from her later period manifest a patriotic thought that is deeply moving," which then leads to the conclusion that there exists an affinity between Li Qingzhao and the laboring masses. This opened the way for the construction of a beautiful museum in her memory in Ji'nan, and an unending stream of annotated editions and other publications.

5 · Talent and Fate

Li Qingzhao and Wei Wan were both prolific authors. The collections of their writings that were made after their deaths have not been preserved in their entirety, however; all we have now are the fragments preserved in much later anthologies. The same applies to practically all the other writing women of the Song, Yuan, and early Ming periods, despite what fame they may have enjoyed during their lifetimes. A few writing women—Zhu Shuzhen, Zhang Yuniang, and Zheng Yunduan—were more fortunate and for one reason or another their complete collections are still extant today. These women were not necessarily the best-known female authors of their time: while the works of Zhu Shuzhen enjoyed a wide popularity in the thirteenth century and later, Zhang Yuniang and Zheng Yunduan at best only had a local reputation.

An Unhappy Marriage: Zhu Shuzhen

Zhu Shuzhen is known as the author of a collection of *shi* poems entitled *A Broken Heart* (*Duanchang ji*). Modern editions of this collection consist of a first section in ten chapters (*juan*), a second section in eight chapters, and two chapters made up of later additions, and ends with fifty song lyrics that have been assembled from various later anthologies. *A Broken Heart* is arranged not by genre or date as is common in the poetry collections of male writers, but rather according to season and topic. The ten chapters of the first section include three chapters of spring poems, one of summer poems, two of autumn poems, and one again of winter poems; this is followed by three chapters of poems on miscellaneous subjects, including a chapter of "inner quarter laments" (*guiyuan*). The eight chapters of the second section are made up of one chapter each devoted to spring, summer, fall, and winter, followed by one chapter devoted to plants, another to historical subjects, and finally two chapters on miscellaneous subjects. This sort of arrangement primarily by season is quite rare in the Chinese tradition.

Our major source for information on the life of Zhu Shuzhen is the following preface to *A Broken Heart* written in 1182 by Wei Duanli (style name Zhonggong):

Combining phrases and linking sentences, I have learned, is decidedly not the proper business of women. Occasionally, however, their heavenly style manifests itself brilliantly, their nature and spirit combine in intelligence, and the words and phrases they produce and utter may even outclass those of the most extraordinary of men. Even if one would want to conceal their fame, it would be impossible. Among them, Lady Huarui of the state of Shu[1] and, in recent times, Li Yi'an [Qingzhao] are by far the most famous examples. Their palace songs and lyrics circulate in this world, but if you ask about their genuinely popular poems, there are only one or two—how could they all be beautiful?

When I went to Hangzhou, I noticed that the aficionados staying at my inn were always reciting the lyrics of Zhu Shuzhen. I secretly listened to their recitations, and these works in each case were original and elegant and filled with longing and passion, and were able to give expression to the things on one's mind; they were beyond the level a shallow mind might attain: each time "one song was followed by three sighs."

When Zhu Shuzhen was young, unfortunately her parents lacked the discernment to select a fitting match for her. Instead, they married her off to a common family of the marketplace. All her life she felt frustrated at being unable to fulfill her ambitions, which is why her poems are full of words of sorrow and regret. Whenever, touched by the breeze or in the presence of the moon, her heart was wounded by the sights before her eyes, she would lodge her feelings in poetry in order to give expression to her lifelong feeling of having been treated unfairly. But she never did find a true friend and she died depressed and

---

1. Lady Huarui and her "palace songs" are discussed in the next chapter.

full of frustration. Although since ancient times beautiful women have often had short lives, this is not simply a case of "if one's face is like a flower, one's life will be like a leaf!" If one carefully reads her poems, one can form a mental image of the person—truly, it was because she was mismatched to such a vulgar fellow that her life was ruined! When she died, he was not even capable of burying her bones in the earth so that she might be [properly] mourned [like Wang Zhaojun] at the Green Mound. Her father and mother cremated her and her poems together on a single pyre. The poems that have been handed down to the present make up only one percent of her works—a second misfortune! Alas, how she has been wronged!

As I felt that my sighs were insufficient, I took up my brush to write this down. I hope in this way to bring some comfort to her fragrant soul on the inhospitable banks of the Nine Springs[2] and ensure that she will not go unrecognized. As for a full description of the facts, there is her biography by Wang Tangzuo of Lin'an, so I have only noted the highlights as an introduction to her life. I have entitled her collection of poems *A Broken Heart*. Gentlemen-aficionados of later times should not think that there is no basis for my words.

Written by Wei Zhonggong (Duanli) of Wanling, Layman of Drunken . . . , on the day of the full moon of the Second Month of the year renyin *of the reign period Pure Prosperity* [Chunxi, 1182].

This is a strange preface indeed. The author ends it by defending his own reliability, and appeals for authority to a full-length biography of Zhu Shuzhen by an otherwise unknown author that he does not include in his edition, and which no one has ever seen. Wei Duanli was apparently himself responsible for the compilation of *A Broken Heart* since he was the one who gave the collection its title; the collection was definitely not compiled by Zhu Shuzhen's husband or her parents. For those of his contemporaries who insisted on some physical proof of the historical existence of Zhu Shuzhen, Wei Duanli had a ready answer: the reason there is no grave is that the body was cremated. The absence of biographical information on Zhu Shuzhen, apart from what may perhaps be inferred from her poems, allows Wei Duanli to offer his own version of her life, which presents her as the perfect embodiment of the widespread belief that women of great beauty or extraordinary talent must inevitably suffer an unhappy fate. Wei Duanli's Zhu Shuzhen is the brilliant daughter of a gentry family who is married off to a merchant's son, and as her husband

---

2. "Nine Springs" is the conventional designation for the underworld of the dead.

is a vulgar lout, she dies of sorrow after a lifetime of frustration. More-over, only a few of her poems are saved from destruction by fire.

A clue to the motivation behind Wei Duanli's version of the life of Zhu Shuzhen can be found in Wei's reference to the Green Mound, the place where Wang Zhaojun was buried by the Xiongnu following her death on the barren steppe. Just as Zhaojun, a Chinese princess, was married off to a barbarian chieftain, so Zhu Shuzhen, a high-born lady of talent, was married off to a merchant's son. But while Zhaojun was at least accorded a traditional burial, Zhu Shuzhen's body was cremated—a Buddhist, and therefore a "barbarian," way of disposing of the dead. Just as Wang Zhaojun is an exemplar of loyalty despite unrecognized beauty, Zhu Shuzhen is an exemplar of loyalty despite unrecognized talent. The appeal of such an image for Southern Song literati is obvious: the expansion of the examination system during this time meant a dramatic increase in the number of participants and an equally dramatic decrease in the number of successful graduates. By identifying with Zhaojun and Zhu Shuzhen, the (primarily male) readers of *A Broken Heart* could imagine themselves to be loyal but unappreciated servants of the throne, with all the talents needed for service at court or on the border.

While Wei Duanli may be quite specific as to how he wants his male readership to read Zhu Shuzhen's poems, he is very vague when it comes to the facts of her life and even the period in which she lived. Wei's preface, which is dated 1182, suggests that she was not his contemporary. However, it is unclear whether she lived under the Northern Song, and thus prior to 1126, or after the Jürchen conquest of Northern China. Modern scholars have argued for both possibilities, but the poems and lyrics contain no incontrovertible indications regarding this point (scholars that favor one period over the other usually have been better at disproving the claims of their opponents than in establishing their own).

The debate over Zhu Shuzhen's dates points to a general characteristic of *A Broken Heart*: the presence of factual inconsistencies within the collection itself. Scholars who have attempted to reconstruct her life on the basis of the clues provided by the poems and lyrics have reached radically different conclusions. Some argue that she was married to an official who was often away from home in the course of his duties, whereas others postulate that she was married to a narrow-minded clerk. Others claim that she was unhappy in her marriage and returned to her parental home, while others maintain that she obtained a divorce. Some even argue that she had a lover before, and even after, her marriage, and that she eventually committed suicide. It has even been argued that Wang Tangzuo, the purported author of the biography quoted by Wei Duanli, was actually her second husband. And it has also been put forth that Zhu Shuzhen was the only daughter of the high official Zhu Xiyan (1133–1200), and the wife of another high official Wang Gang (d. after 1237), and that she ended her life in a nunnery.

Each of the fanciful scenarios outlined above blatantly contradicts the information provided by Wei Duanli in his preface. However, this same preface also provides us with a hint as to how such internal contradictions might have arisen in the first place. The poems and lyrics of Zhu Shuzhen, Wei Duanli stresses, were highly popular among the literati of the capital, by whom they were often recited. In fact, Wei Duanli mentions only having heard the poems, and never refers to a written text, whether in manuscript or in print. If (the extant) *A Broken Heart* was based, wholly or in part, on an oral tradition, many poems other than those composed by Zhu Shuzhen could easily have found their way into what were commonly referred to as the "Zhu Shuzhen poems."

While the size of the collection and its unity of tone would seem to argue in favor of the historicity of Zhu Shuzhen, one might go even further and question the actual historical existence of a specific single person of that name—after all, her name is homophonous with an expression one might translate as "all pure maidens." Perhaps it is safer to read the poems in *A Broken Heart* not so much as the compositions of one specific woman, but rather as a reflection of what twelfth-century men considered to be typical poetic expressions from the inner quarters. In other words, it is not at all inconceivable that at least a sizable portion of the Zhu Shuzhen poems might be the work of anonymous male authors impersonating a female voice.

Whether or not they were actually written by a woman writer, the poems attributed to Zhu Shuzhen enjoyed much popularity in later centuries. Following the arrangement of *A Broken Heart* we first present a seasonal selection of Zhu Shuzhen's *shi* poems beginning with spring:

Getting Up, Two Poems

I

I get up but take no pleasure in applying rouge and powder,
I have to force myself to look in the mirror at my sickly face:
My skinny waist, a sign of how I am plagued by idle sorrows,
My copious tears, caused by my deep sadness at being parted.

II

Too listless to face the mirror and pencil my black brows,
Who cares if the locks framing my face hang like mist!
But the servant girl hasn't the slightest idea how I feel,
And insists on sticking a branch of plum blossom in my hair.

Feelings on a Spring Day

On official business to east and west, never his own master,
Father and mother a thousand miles away, always in tears.
Not only is there no goose to deliver a letter to my home,
But the call of the cuckoo stirs up the traveler's sorrow.[3]
The sun warm, the birds singing—this lovely scene for naught,
The flowers' gleam, the willows' shade fill my eyes in vain.
Atop the tower dispirited and despairing I lean on the balustrade,
And my heart follows the white clouds floating to the south.

End of Spring Feelings

Weary of facing the drifting blossoms that fill the path,
In the stillness I hear the croaking frogs in the spring stream.
Where is my friend now? The grass turns rich green for naught,
Except to throw my heart into turmoil here at one end of the sky.

In Front of My Study Window, (One of) Two Poems

The blossoms fall but spring says not a word,
As spring takes its leave, the birds still sing.
Most passionate of all the butterflies and bees,
Flying off to the west over the whitewashed wall.

---

3. The call of the cuckoo was said to sound like *burugui* (Better go home!).

Sleeping Alone during the Hottest Month

Dozing under the gauze netting—the days now so long!
Removing the red skirt—the fine mat feels cool.
Smoke from an incense burner cages in the noon pillow,
Icy skin beaded with perspiration: white lotus fragrance.

Written on a Summer Night

The steamy heat of the summer night is truly unbearable!
I move my bed outside to sleep by the light of the moon.
Late at night I feel the chill of clothes now wet with dew,
And from a dream of Yang Terrace am rudely awakened.[4]

Shamed by Swallows

Laying down my needle, wordlessly tears fill my eyes—
I'm not only wounded by spring, but saddened by summer.
From beyond the flowers a pair of swallows come flying:
For each time they swoop by, I feel a pang of shame!

Autumn Nights, (One of) Two Poems

Outside the window crickets chirp, announcing autumn,
The endless clear night brings to mind outings gone by.
The moon, resplendent, drifts over the western tower,
Adding yet another sorrow to the one left behind.

Hearing a Flute at Mid-Autumn

Whose flute could that be playing so light and clear,
Stirring up the pillow-feelings of the one left behind?
It's because my heart is broken that I can't bear to listen—
It's not that the tune being played breaks my heart.

Describing My Feelings on an Autumn Day

Although women's eyes may not be strong,
It doesn't mean they're always weeping.

---

4. The goddess of Shamanka Mountain was said to have shared the couch of the king of Chu on Yang Terrace.

It is all because my circumstances are so bad
That I have wiped away five lakes of autumn floods.

Impending Snow

Freezing sparrows silently huddle along the bamboo fence,
Icy clouds hang down all around as the snow threatens to fall.
The north wind disregards the feelings of human beings,
And keeps the plum blossom from opening on its branch.

New Year's Eve

Stop lamenting the passing of time,
In the blink of an eye spring will return.
Pepper trays surround the red candles,
Cypress wine spills over the gold cups.
 The final watch of the Last Month is over,
Horns at dawn announce the New Year.
In the race to be first who will win?
It can only be the back garden plum!

As the above selection shows, nearly all of the *shi* poems in *A Broken Heart* are short pieces, either quatrains (*jueju*) or so-called "regulated verse" (*lüshi*) in eight lines, and most deal with personal emotions and experiences. There are, however, a few longer *shi* poems that deal with social issues. For example, anthologies of women's poetry from the People's Republic of China rarely fail to include the following poem as evidence of Zhu Shuzhen's social consciousness:

Moved by What I Heard the Farmers Say during a Heat Wave

The sun-wheel pushes its fiery way, scorching the sky:
These are the three hottest weeks of the Sixth Month.
Layer upon layer of drought's red clouds bring no rain—
The earth cracked, rivers dry, the dust raised by the wind.

The farmers fear that in their fields the grain will die,
And tread the waterwheel without pause, hoping to save them.
All day long they hunger and thirst, their throats parched,
Sweating blood they labor and toil, but who speaks for them?

They sowed and planted, plowed and weeded, left nothing undone,
But still they worry that at autumn's end they will have no harvest.
If no rainbow appears in the clouds, their labor will have been in vain—
How can they not lift their heads and cry out to Heaven?

"Inquire on our behalf of those carefree rich young playboys:
What is the good of your silken caps and feathered fans?
In the fields the green rice plants are withered and brown—
Sitting comfortably in your high hall, what could you know?"

This poem has a counterpart in a long poem entitled "Delighting in the Rain," which is seldom included in these same modern anthologies, perhaps because of its fulsome praise of the reigning emperor:

Delighting in the Rain

The fiery red sun had scorched the earth to the eight extremities,
In the absence of rain, the young rice plants in the fields were turning
     brown.
But the agency of Heaven did not allow the old dragon to grow lazy:
Flashing lightning and rumbling thunder, clouds gather all around![5]
 Millions of barrels of precious pearls poured down from the sky,
Ponds, tanks, lakes, and marshes filled to the brim with water.
The high fields, the low fields, all soaked through and through:
The farmers delighted that their grain would not wither and die.

The sagely virtue of Our Emperor extends over the cosmos:
So, in the Sixth Month a clear sky sent down this sweet rain!
All within the four seas enjoy the grace of this great downpour,
Each of the Nine Provinces is released from the fear of drought.
 By the time the torrential rains end, not a speck of dust remains,
The sleeves of our gowns now feel cool—we can put away our fans!
The several peaks above the river now appear clearly on the horizon,
Our vista has been opened up, our hearts filled with pleasure.

The fiery heat has been washed away, leaving not a trace,
Suddenly I feel a cool breeze arising from under my arms.

---

5. Dragons were believed to be the dispensers of rain.

The gauze nettings and bamboo mat have a new freshness,
As submerged plums and sliced melons float in icy water.
 Beside the pond is where this autumnal feel is best captured,
Strands of leftover pearls of water adorn the round lotus.
Above the tower the moon ascends, the clouds have all gone—
Distant rivers join the sky, the sky merges with the waves.

Since the lyrics attributed to Zhu Shuzhen have not been preserved in a Song dynasty edition but have been culled from later anthologies, we do not know how they were originally presented. Like the *shi* poems, however, the Zhu Shuzhen lyrics readily fall into seasonal categories. Here is a sampling of these lyrics, arranged by season:

To the Melody of "Magnolia Flower, Abbreviated" (*Jianzi Mulanhua*)

Alone I walk, alone I sit,
Alone I sing, alone I drink, and still alone I go to bed.
I stand and wait with wounded heart:
Defenseless against the annoying springtime chill.

These feelings—who's there to notice?
Tears have washed away more than half of my rouge.
Sorrow and sickness follow in succession,
I've trimmed the cold wick to the nub—but dreams don't come.

To the Melody of "Clear and Level" (*Qingpingle*)

How quickly the season hurries by:
The Third Month, and suddenly the thirtieth day!
I'd like to make spring stay, but my schemes are all too late—
On the green fields the mist grieves, the dew sheds tears.

Who can I ask to deliver my message this spring night?
On top of the city wall painted drums lightly sound the watch.
Please tell the departing spring of my loving attachment,
And come early next year on the branch of the plum!

To the Melody of "The Butterfly Loves Flowers" (*Dielianhua*)
Seeing Off Spring

Outside the tower millions of threads of weeping willow:
I wish I could tie up the verdant spring,
But even if it stayed for a while, in the end spring would go.
Willow floss keeps drifting along on the breeze,
Following spring in the hope of seeing where it goes.

Green fills mountain and stream, I hear the cuckoo's call—
Even if one had no feelings,
How could one not be grieved by one's pain?
When I pour wine to see spring off, spring says not a word,
But when dusk falls, sends down a desolate drizzle of rain.

To the Melody of "Clear and Level" (*Qingpingle*)
A Visit to the Lake on a Summer Day

Annoyed by the mist, provoked by the dew,
You urged me to stay a little bit longer.
Holding hands along the road by the lake of lotus flowers,
A single moment of fine summer rain!

Pampered and foolish, not caring what people might think,
I went along and for a time left my sorrows behind.
The hardest part was when I let go of your hand—
Back home, too listless to sit down before the mirror.

To the Melody of "Immortals at the Bridge of Magpies" (*Queqiaoxian*)
The Night of Double Seven[6]

Ingenious clouds adorn the evening,
A western wind dispels the heat,

---

6. On the Night of Double Seven (the night of the seventh day of the Seventh Month), the Cowherd and the Weaving Maiden, two stars on opposite sides of the Heavenly River (the Milky Way), are allowed to cross over a bridge of magpies for a yearly reunion. The Cowherd and the Weaving Maiden were believed to be grandchildren of the Jade Emperor who were so in love with each other that they neglected their duties, and so were placed on opposite sides of the Heavenly River and allowed to see each other only once a year.

A light rain cleans out the sky, the moon sets.
Cowherd and Weaving Maiden have been through so many autumns,
But still how many
Feelings of separation, tears of despair.

A light chill enters my sleeves,
A secret pleasure fills the stars:
Satisfaction both in Heaven and down here below.
How much better were it every evening, every morning,
And do away with this
"One meeting once a year."

To the Melody of "Bodhisattva Barbarian" (*Pusaman*)

A mountain pavilion, a water kiosk—the midpoint of autumn:
The phoenix-curtains forlorn and silent—no one around.
My sorrow and melancholy are all new,
But my brows are furrowed as before.

Rising I stand by the embroidered door,
Occasionally a lonely firefly flits by.
Thank you, moon, for taking pity on me:
Even you do not want to be full tonight.

To the Melody of "Dotting Red Lips" (*Dianjiangchen*)
Winter

The wind so fierce, the clouds so thick:
Defenseless against the evening chill that seeps through the gauze nettings.
My chignon is done up in a slanting fashion,
I blow on my hands so I can make my toilette.

A bit of drinking, pure pleasures:
Time and again sparks flew from the silver candle.
Such desolation!
But I've noticed the handiwork of spring
That has pried open the fragrant bud of the plum.

The overwhelming majority of poems in *A Broken Heart*, whether *shi* poems or song lyrics, are written very much in the "feminine" mode. Although the collection includes a chapter of poems on historical themes, in them we find no sign of the outspoken patriotism that was so characteristic of Li Qingzhao. An example is the following poem on the tragic hero Xiang Yu:

> The virility to dominate the world, the strength to rip out mountains:
> How could *he* have realized that Heaven intended Liu Bang to rule?
> Fan Zeng was a man to be trusted but Xiang Yu was unable to trust[7]
> And in vain he lamented that in the blink of an eye his life was over.

Very few of the Zhu Shuzhen poems stand out for their originality of theme or expression. The eighteenth-century editors of the catalogue of the imperial collection even went so far as to dismiss her work in the following words: "[Zhu Shuzhen's] poems are shallow and weak and do not go beyond the [poetic] conventions of the inner chambers. It was because the world pitied her sorry fate that her work was passed down to later times." It may therefore come as somewhat of a surprise to find in *A Broken Heart* two poems that express a strongly voiced complaint against the limitations imposed by gender on a literate woman with writing ambitions:

Self-Reproach, Two Poems

I

A woman who dabbles in writing truly deserves condemnation,
Especially if she composes lines on the moonlight and breeze.
To grind a hole through an iron inkstone is not our business,
We should take pride in plying our gold needles till they break.

II

Feeling low I thought to cheer myself up by reading poetry,
But discovered that poetry speaks of nothing but separation.
This just adds to my sorrow, increases my desolation—
Now I know one should not be clever, better to be dull!

---

7. Fan Zeng was the loyal, but unheeded, advisor of Xiang Yu.

Doomed Love: Zhang Yuniang

Zhang Yuniang is the author of a small collection of poetry entitled *Orchid and Snow* (*Lanxue ji*), which was not printed until the second half of the seventeenth century. When we look at what is known about her life, we find many of the same issues we encountered in our discussion of Wei Duanli's preface to *A Broken Heart*—a lack of reliable information on the life of the poet, doubts about the authenticity of her works, and the desire to turn her life into a model of female chastity and, by extension, a symbol of male loyalty to the ruler.

We do know that Zhang Yuniang lived in the Songyang district of southeastern Zhejiang province, although the precise dates of her life are unclear; some modern reference works date her to the Song dynasty, others to the Yuan. In any case, she must have been alive after the fall of the Song dynasty, since one of her poems, the only one quoted in the local gazetteer for Songyang, is on the subject of the tomb of General Wang, a local hero from Songyang who died resisting the Mongols. Originally he fought under the famous Song loyalist Wen Tianxiang, but when Wen was taken captive by the Mongols, Wang returned to his native place, where he raised his own troops and continued the fight. Eventually he perished in battle below Wangsong Ridge, and that is also where he was buried. Zhang Yuniang's poem, which is not particularly representative of her collection, reads as follows:

The Tomb of General Wang

On the ridge the pines like banners,
Lush and sturdy, like iron and stone.
Beneath them rests the soul of a hero,
On them grow the creeping vines.
 The hero's virtue will never change,
The green of the pines will grow richer.
If you want to know the heart of that hero,
Just look at the branches of these trees!

Assuming that this poem is indeed by Zhang Yuniang, it probably could not have been written before the last decades of the thirteenth century, which would suggest ca. 1260 to ca. 1285 as likely dates for our poet.

The poems and lyrics in *Orchid and Snow* otherwise provide little biographical information about Zhang Yuniang, although there is one quatrain about a student named Shen, whom later writers describe as her fiancé:

Weeping over Student Shen

In mid-journey we had to part forever,
Never again will we be able to meet.
If only I could take the thoughts of today,
And change them into Yang Terrace clouds![8]

At the end of the collection we find yet another poem with the same title, together with a poem by student Shen addressed to Zhang Yuniang, but its placement suggests that we may well be dealing here with a later addition to the collection, inspired by the legend that developed around the couple. This legend would stress Zhang Yuniang's loyalty to her fiancé, the female counterpart of an official's loyalty to his lord.

The Songyang district gazetteer includes a short biographical note on Zhang Yuniang. We have consulted the 1875 edition of this gazetteer, which is based on a much earlier edition of 1654. Given the habit of compilers of gazetteers to copy biographical materials wholesale from earlier editions, however, it is not implausible that the redaction of this notice may date back to the early Ming—or even the late Yuan. This optimism is inspired by the fact that the redaction of this account is much shorter than, and apparently unrelated to, a much longer account of her life composed around 1500 by Wang Zhao. Still, this gazetteer notice must date from a period at a considerable remove in time from Zhang Yuniang's life, as it seems to reflect a well-developed legend associated with a local monument:

Zhang Yuniang's style name was Ruoqiong. When her father instructed her in the *Classic of Filial Piety* and the *Instructions for Women* (*Nüxun*), she had no sooner looked them over than she was able to recite them. Now, the Zhangs were an

---

8. Yang Terrace is the place at which, according to a rhapsody by Song Yu (3rd century BCE), a king of the southern state of Chu had a dream tryst with the goddess of Mt. Wu (Shamanka Mountain); upon her departure the goddess informed the king that she manifested herself as clouds and rain.

official family who collected books and passed down the arts. Yuniang secretly read her father's books, which only deepened [her love of literature]. When it came to her literary compositions, they were not inferior to those of Concubine Ban of the Han dynasty. Subsequently she adopted the sobriquet of Layperson of Total Chastity [Yizhen jüshi].

Her parents selected as her fiancé a descendant of the top graduate Shen Hui [1084–1149]. However, before they were married, student Shen fell ill while on a journey with his father to his official post and passed away soon afterwards. Yuniang was twenty-four at the time. She swore to remain loyal to him, and at his funeral was overcome by grief, her greatest regret being that she could not have died with him.

One night she dreamt that student Shen came to fetch her driving a carriage. She immediately put on her clothes and sat up, saying to her servant girls: "Everything has been settled." She stopped eating and before the month was out, she passed away. Her parents grieved for her and buried her together with the student in a grove of maple trees next to the city wall. The talking parrot that was Yuniang's pet, and her servant girls Qinghong and Cuihong all died, crying out with grief. They were all buried together with their mistress, and the grave was called the Parrot's Grave. The manuscript collection left behind by Yuniang, entitled *Orchid and Snow*, was taken by someone to the capital. When the Imperial Secretaries Yu Bosheng [Ji] and Ouyang Xuan, reading her poems, came to the lines:

> Over the highest mountains
> The moon appears so small.
> Small as the moon may be,
> It still shimmers and shines!
> There is a man that I love
> Out there on a distant road
> Each day that I see him not,
> My heart is troubled and sad!

they pounded the table with their fists and sighed: "This may be compared to the 'Grass-Insects' in 'Airs of the States.' How could a mere girl have attained such a level!"

Yu Ji (1272–1348) and Ouyang Xuan (1288–1357) were two of the leading scholar-officials of the Yuan dynasty. Whether or not they actually read Zhang Yuniang's poems and praised them in this way is difficult to ascertain at this remove in time. "Grass-Insects" is a poem in the *Book of Odes*.

According to this classic's earliest commentary, which dates from the Han dynasty, the text of this poem "shows how the wife of a great officer safeguarded propriety." The editor of the above account may well have inserted these favorable comments by Yu Ji and Ouyang Xuan not only to highlight Zhang's literary talent, but also to defend her reputation against possible allegations of immoral conduct, specifically a premarital affair with her fiancé, student Shen.

During the early Ming dynasty, around the second half of the fourteenth century, the poem quoted in the local gazetteer enjoyed a considerable reputation, at least locally. This is evident from a derogatory remark by Ye Ziqi in his *Master Grass and Tree* (*Caomuzi*) of 1378, which is the earliest dated external reference to the poetry of Zhang Yuniang. It was Ye Ziqi who states that Zhang's fiancé was actually her cousin; he is also the one who first suggests that she overstepped the bounds of their relationship:

In recent years there was a woman surnamed Zhang—I don't know whose daughter she was—who was good at literary composition. Once she sent her cousin a poem that read:

> Over the highest mountains
> The moon appears so small.
> Small as the moon may be,
> It still shimmers and shines!
> There is a man that I love
> Out there on a distant road.
> Each day that I see him not,
> My heart is troubled and sad!
>
> I gather bitter herbs
> On the south side of the mountain.
> O the sorrows of my troubled heart—
> How can I bear them!

And another of her poems reads:

> Your heart is firm like metal and stone,
> My deportment is pure like ice and frost.
> We had exchanged a hundred-year vow,
> But suddenly one morning we were parted.

> Morning clouds and evening rains: our hearts come and go,
> A thousand miles of love-longing share the full moon.

These two poems may be beautiful, but to me they sound too much like "Between the mulberries, on the bank of the Pu"!

The phrase "Between the mulberries, on the bank of the Pu" (*Sangjian Pushang*) was traditionally used to refer to so-called lascivious songs and music associated with love affairs and secret rendezvous, and moral degeneracy in the public and private realm in general. It is as strong a term of opprobrium as can be found in the traditional discourse on poetry and on poets. Ye Ziqi hailed from Longquan district, which bordered on Songyang district and belonged to the same prefecture. He was a major Confucian scholar of his time, who in his youth was closely associated with the leading literati of the early Ming. It is therefore quite possible that his contempt was directed not only at our female poet, but also at the great literary luminaries of the Yuan dynasty who had praised her poetry so highly.

Sometime in the middle of the Ming dynasty, Wang Zhao wrote a more detailed biography of Zhang Yuniang. Wang Zhao was a student from Songyang who enjoyed a local reputation both for his poetry and for his filial behavior. His biography in the local gazetteer reads as follows:

Wang Zhao's sobriquet was Longxi [Dragon Brook] and he was a student in the local school. During the period of mourning for his parents, with his own hands, he hauled the earth required to build their tomb [a filial act], which resulted in the appearance of white sparrows and gray doves. In his studies he was very argumentative. Whenever he read about the virtuous behavior of people of the past, he would immediately take up his brush and note down the circumstances.

Once, while visiting the Zhiping monastery, he heard a rustling sound coming from the top of the sutra [-hall]. When he climbed up a ladder to have a look, he discovered a manuscript that described the deeds of the gentlemen who had followed their king during the Pacification of the South [i.e., those officials who remained loyal to the Jianwen emperor during the Yongle usurpation]. Many of the characters had become so damaged that they were illegible, and he was only able to reconstruct a few words from the eulogies of Liang,

Guo, and about ten other people. [This manuscript] was entitled the *Remarkable and Secret Record of Loyal Statesmen* [*Zhongxian qimi lu*] . . .

Although Wang Zhao's discovery of this damaged manuscript is an important clue to the dates of his life, all one can say for sure is that he must have lived considerably later than the reign period Yongle (1403–1424). The placement of his biography in the local gazetteer strongly suggests that he lived sometime during the second half of the fifteenth century.

Whereas the much earlier Ye Ziqi professed not to know even the name of Zhang Yuniang's father, Wang Zhao is able to reconstruct the family genealogy in considerable detail. He also claims to know the name of her fiancé, whom he identifies as Shen Quan, who took second place at the palace examinations of 1270. Wang Zhao does not compare his heroine with Concubine Ban but with the even more famous Ban Zhao; he also provides her servant girls with different names. And interestingly enough, he is able to come up with a great many details regarding the love affair between the two cousins:

Zhang Yuniang's style name was Ruoqiong. She was a native of Songyang and was the daughter of a scholarly family of the Song dynasty. Her father's name was Mao, his style name was Keweng, and he sported the sobriquet of Rustic Fellow of Dragon Rock. He was once commended for his filial behavior and in his official career attained the rank of Supervisor. Her mother, lady Liu, was a wise and good person, who assisted her husband by managing the household. [As head of the family, Zhang Mao] behaved most strictly. Although he was already nearly fifty years old, Yuniang was his only child. From the time she was born she displayed an extraordinary beauty and her quick intelligence was exceptional. This only increased her parents' love for her.

Her grandfather was called Jiye; his style name was Guangda. As the Head of the List in the prefectural examinations he attained the rank of Court Gentleman for Promoted Service. Her great-grandfather was called Zaixing; his style name was Shunchen. He became a presented scholar in the eighth year of the reign period Pure Prosperity [Chunxi, 1174–1189], and he attained the rank of Left Gentleman for Meritorious Achievement in the Court of Scrutiny. Her great-great-grandfather Ruchi's style name was Jinggu, who thanks to a gracious edict had been named a Gentleman for Rendering Service.

Zhang Mao made his home wherever his official duties took him. Yuniang benefited from the inherited tradition and "peeked" at the family studies. In this way she greatly deepened [her erudition] day by day. As soon as she was old enough, she assisted her mother in overseeing the ancestral sacrifices and she purified herself in order to take part in the reception of guests and the preparation of food. She applied herself to her needlework and mastered numerous skills. In her search for [embroidery] patterns, again and again she came up with new models. Her prose writings were rich in content, comparable to those by men who ranked highly in the literary examinations, but her poetry compositions resembled the style of the great masters even more. Her contemporaries compared her to Ban Zhao. She herself adopted the sobriquet of Layperson of Total Chastity. She had two servant girls, Ci'e and Shuang'e, both of whom were talented, beautiful, and good at writing. The parrot she kept could talk and was also very intelligent, and was able to grasp people's intentions. She referred to [her two servant girls and her parrot] as "The Three Purities of the Inner Chambers."

When Yuniang reached marriageable age, she was engaged to the student Shen Quan, who was a descendant of Shen Hui, the top graduate in a Palace Examination held during the reign period Proclaimed Harmony [Xuanhe, 1119–1125] of the Song. Quan and Yuniang were cousins. But shortly afterwards, Zhang Mao [her father] went back on his word [and broke off the engagement]. Quan and Yuniang secretly became even more devoted to one another, as she could not bear to abandon him. Shen Quan was quite an exceptional scholar. Once when his father traveled on official business to the capital, Shen went with him. There, at the age of twenty-two, he suffered two bouts of pneumonia. The exorcist [called in to cure him] said: "He is beyond cure, his illness is too serious." The servant girls who conveyed Yuniang's messages to him would sometimes whisper in her ears that his illness was the result of his unquenchable longing for her. She was even more saddened because of this and secretly sent him a note in which she vowed to be loyal to him until death: "If I cannot be your wife, I wish to die so that I may share your grave!" When he read this, he said: "Ruoqiong, will you be able to follow me?" Sighing deeply, he wept copiously, and then closed his eyes forever.

Yuniang was overcome by grief and fell into a depression. When her parents noticed this, they secretly arranged to find another man for her to marry in order to settle her future. When Yuniang found out about this, she became even more anxious and said: "The only reason I haven't died yet is because you two are still alive!" It happened to be First Night and her parents were going out to look at the lanterns. They whispered instructions to her female companions to try to get her to go out as well, but she refused, feigning illness. She was leaning on a little table, when all of a sudden student Shen appeared in the flickering shadows of the candle and spoke to her saying: "Ruoqiong, take good care of yourself. What I most wish is that you will not forget your former vow!" Yuniang was both startled and happy. She rushed forward to grab hold of his gown but he eluded her. Watching the shadows of the lamp, she clutched her chignon with her hands and, with tears of grief streaming down her face, she said: "Whatever I keep from you will melt away like this candle!" Having spoken these words, she woke up, and when she found that he was no longer there, she fainted with grief. Eventually she revived, and exclaimed: "Have you abandoned me?" After this she fell ill and died. She was only twenty-eight years old.

Her parents were moved by her determination and obtained permission from the Shen family to have them buried together in a maple grove next to the city wall. Both of her servant girls mourned her greatly, and a little over a month later Shuang'e died of grief. Ci'e said: "How can I bear being the only one to remain alive? I am duty-bound to follow my mistress in death." She then hung herself and so joined them in death. The next morning the parrot let out a mournful cry and died as well. The entire household marveled at this and buried them all with Yuniang. At that time the tomb was called the Zhang tomb; it is the same place now known as the Parrot's Grave.

This biography of Zhang Yuniang concludes with a final evaluation by Master Mushuo, most likely a pseudonym of Wang Zhao:

Lady Zhang was an outstandingly fine girl living in troubled times. A certain someone has condemned her for breaching the rites and secretly maintaining contact [with her fiancé] during his illness. This was in fact the case. But in the past, Zhongli [Chun] discussed affairs at length in the court of Qi, and Meng Guang independently chose Liang [Hong to be her husband]. Yet they were not condemned by their contemporaries and gentlemen praised and lauded them. The one could not avoid presenting herself [in court] and the other disobeyed her parents' orders. They were not women who strictly adhered to the letter of the ritual classics!

From his biographical notice in the local gazetteer we know that Wang Zhao was a local antiquarian and a devoted Confucianist who practiced what he preached and was very much concerned with questions of loyalty. In the case of Zhang Yuniang, the fact that her marriage never actually took place, and that it was her own father who broke the engagement, not only adds greater poignancy to her determination to be faithful to the man she loved, but also illustrates the conflict she faced between the demands of filiality and loyalty. Zhang Yuniang opts for loyalty, since traditionally, once two families agreed on an engagement, the couple were considered to be virtually man and wife, whatever their parents might decide later on. The loyalty she showed in death canceled out any seeming improprieties that may have occurred earlier. Thus, our Master Mushuo does not hesitate to compare our beautiful heroine with two proverbial exemplars of womanly virtue, both of whose biographies were included in Liu Xiang's *Biographies of Exemplary Women*, and both of whom combined physical unattractiveness with independence of action in seeking a husband. It is obvious that Master Mushuo here refutes, without ever mentioning him by name, the disparaging remarks of Ye Ziqi. Zhang Yuniang's loyalty to her husband is further reinforced by that of the servant girls and the pet parrot to their mistress. In Wang Zhao's insistence on the virtue of loyalty unto death, his glorification of Zhang Yuniang fits in neatly with the growing emphasis on female chastity in Ming dynasty China.

Wang Zhao's treatment of the life of Zhang Yuniang also shows the influence of the romantic tale in the classical language. One of the most popular classical tales during the Yuan and the early Ming was *Wang Jiaoniang and Feihong* (*Jiao Hong zhuan*) by Song Yuan (second half of the thirteenth century). This tale, which was repeatedly adapted for the stage, recounts the tragic love affair between the talented and beautiful Wang Jiaoniang and her cousin Shen Chun. It is remarkable for its length and for its inclusion of many poems and lyrics said to be secretly exchanged between the lovers. While the plot of this tale is much more complicated than Wang Zhao's biography of Zhang Yuniang, contemporary readers may well have been struck by the similarity and have assumed that his biography, including the poems it accompanied, were fictional as well.

Until the very end of the Ming dynasty, Zhang Yuniang was only a local celebrity and it would appear that her writings had until then only circulated in manuscript form. The first known printed edition of her collection was produced in the early years of the Qing dynasty by Meng Chengshun (1599–1684), a native of Shaoxing. During the last decades of the Ming dynasty, Meng Chengshun had made a name for himself as an author and printer of plays. During the reign period Shunzhi (1644–1661), Meng Chengshun served for a brief while as an assistant instructor in the district school in Songyang. He relinquished his post in 1656, following an incident in which he supported a student protest against the new Manchu government. While in Songyang, Meng Chengshun not only expended great efforts in restoring the district school, but also devoted himself to reviving the memory of Zhang Yuniang. He led the students in offering sacrifice at her grave and took the initiative in erecting a shrine to her memory. It is clear that Meng Chengshun and his contemporaries perceived Zhang Yuniang as a symbol of loyalty and an inspiration to those who mourned the demise of the Ming dynasty. (The restored grave would survive as a local landmark until the latter half of the twentieth century, when this "remnant of the feudal past" was leveled during the Cultural Revolution.)

Following his return home, Meng Chengshun not only saw to the printing of Zhang Yuniang's collected writings, but also wrote a long play based on her life and death, which he had printed with the financial help of friends in Shaoxing and Nanjing. In his preface to the play, Meng argues for the authenticity of Zhang's collection, pointing out that it would have been impossible to find a literate ghostwriter in such a backward place as Songyang:

From ancient times there have been women who have excelled in literary composition—but have there ever been women whose poetry was as skillful as that of Yuniang? From ancient times there have been women who remained chastely loyal to their fiancés—but have there ever been women who combined literary talent and chaste loyalty and whose talent and deportment were as perfect as that of Yuniang? Yuniang's talent was the most remarkable talent in the whole world and her deportment was the most remarkable deportment in the whole world. Now, some may have their doubts because the writings of women are often false attributions. [However,] ancient Bailong corresponds to present-day Songyang. Songyang is located between mountain torrents and steep ravines. It has had its share of talented poets but if you were to look for someone of the quality of Yuniang, you would never be able to find anyone. So who was there who could have been her ghostwriter?

Now, it is quite common for a woman to follow her husband-to-be in death even though the marriage has not yet formally taken place. But it is quite uncommon to find someone like Yuniang, who by her own death moved Ci'e, Shuang'e, and her parrot to follow her to the grave. One might say therefore that the rare occurrence was not so much her death but the fact that these others followed her to the grave. . . . If they had not been moved by Yuniang's sincere passion, Ci'e, Shuang'e, and the parrot definitely would not have followed her to the grave. So the rarity does not apply to the ones who followed but rather to the one who led. This is why I say that Yuniang's talent was the most remarkable talent in the whole world and that Yuniang's deportment was the most remarkable behavior in the whole world.

This fulsome praise of the personality and the poetry of Zhang Yuniang found no echo in the eighteenth-century catalogue of the imperial collection, whose editors summarily dismissed her works as follows: "Her poetical style is shallow and weak and does not go beyond the affectations of the inner chamber." That this judgment may have been too harsh is shown by the following translations:

Sitting Idly; An Impromptu Song

Alone I sit, a flower without a branch,
Without a word, my tears course down.
The silly maid just doesn't understand
And asks me who it is I'm angry with.

The Autumn Night Is Long

The autumn wind makes for a chilly night,
The chilly wind prolongs the autumn night.
But I so love to watch that harvest moon—
Let the clear dew soak my skirt and gown!

The End of Spring

Outside the door, a myriad dots of drifting petals,
And on a branch the single tune of a singing bird.
It calls me back from sleep and dreams of spring—
I lean on the railing, lost in feeling the entire day.

From: Six Inscriptions on Paintings
The Fisherman's Boat

The autumn stream and autumn sky are equally clear:
The willow's shade does not tie up the small light skiff.
I do not dream of halls of jade and horses with gold saddles,
But of moonlight, reeds, getting drunk, and waking up together.

To the Melody of "As in a Dream" (*Rumengling*)
Written in jest, following the rhymes of Li Qingzhao

Outside the gate horses and carriages busily rush by,
In my embroidery room I am still rapt by spring wine.
I wake up with a start, and the green duvet feels cold,
Although that fellow is still at my side as before.
But does he know,
But does he know
Why all the chrysanthemums will become so skinny?

To the Melody of "Jade Butterflies" (*Yuhudie*)
Feelings of Separation

Gazing at the distant trees on the horizon,
My brows knit in a frown,
As I lean on the balustrade.
The green bamboos, closely massed, swish and rustle,
While my bracelets and pendants jingle and jangle.
The fragrance of my snow-white skin:
Translucent as the jade of Jingshan Mountain!
My cricket-locks a tangled mess,
As on Mount Wu the clouds grow cold.[9]
I wipe away the traces of my tears,
But, too ashamed to face my own reflection,
I turn my back on the bronze mirror.

Oh, when will we again, beneath the moon and stars,
In the clear chill of night
Comfort each other?
In Ji and Yan autumn is at its height[10]
But my man of jade, I'm sure, is not yet ready to come home.
I count the new geese,
And would like to entrust them with a letter,
But I lay down my brush,
Unable to give expression to my sadness.
By the time dusk falls,

---

9. Mount Wu is Shamanka Mountain.
10. "Ji and Yan" refers to the regions of northernmost China.

The withered lotus and the scattered rain
Will have repeatedly melted away my soul.

A Wifely Poetics: Zheng Yunduan

Some women poets chose not to limit themselves to noting the change of seasons outside the window of their boudoir. Zheng Yunduan (1327–1356) in her brief preface to her collection of poems titled *Reverential Harmony* (*Suyong ji*) explicitly distances herself from the conventional themes of the "feminine" tradition as represented by Li Qingzhao and Zhu Shuzhen:

I, lady Zheng, was born to a noble family that for generations has revered Confucian studies. My father and elder brothers instructed students in the Classics and so made a name for themselves throughout Wu [Suzhou]. Because from my earliest years I was taught by my father, I was able to read and recognize characters. Later, my mind became set on study and by pilfering and stealing the various leftover [texts of my father's] I acquired a rough understanding of duty and principle.

When I came of age, I married Shi Boren from our same prefecture. Boren also came from an old family with a tradition of scholarship. He was a man of Confucian culture and our interests were very much alike. In the leisure allowed by my wifely duties, I had even greater opportunity to play and sport with writing brush and ink and to chant and express my feelings and my inner nature.

When women and girls of the present age write poetry, to my constant consternation, I find their work lacks the intent of "giving expression to one's feeling in response to external stimuli" and "creating in order to chastise." Ordinarily, they do nothing but lightheartedly chant about breeze and moonlight and give vent to their feelings and longings; delicate and voluptuous, dispirited and decadent, they dwell on the passing of time. For this reason [in my own writings], I have done away with all these old habits and rejected the popular trends of the day.

Whenever I would write songs and poems, I would lock them away in chests and baskets, waiting for a master wordsmith to correct them, and only later would I show them to other people. However, now I have been ill for many years and I may die at any time. Afraid that these poems might be lost without leaving a trace, I have copied them out once again and put them in proper order. I will place them in the family school so they may be shown to later generations. Long ago, there was a Tang dynasty hermit who had a poetry-gourd inscribed with the words: "Only the one who finds this will understand my bitter heart."[11] I could say the same.

Written by Zheng Yunduan of Yingyang on the day of Clear and Bright of the bingshen *year of the reign period Utmost Orthodoxy* [Zhizheng, 1356].

This preface not only sheds light on Zheng Yunduan's views on women's poetry, it also serves as our major source on her life. Zheng Yunduan's grandfather, whose own grandfather had been a prime minister during the Song dynasty, had established himself in Suzhou after having served there as assistant prefect. The Zheng family was immensely wealthy (they were said to own "half of the prefecture"), and we may assume that Zheng Yunduan's husband's family enjoyed a comparable status. However, in 1356, during the chaotic final decades of the Yuan dynasty, Suzhou was occupied by the warlord Zhang Shicheng and his troops. Zheng Yunduan's home was burned to the ground, and she herself died shortly afterwards.

Zheng Yunduan's preface raises a serious question: what were the options for serious women poets who rejected what their contemporaries considered to be the "feminine" mode? Despite the protestations she makes to the contrary in her preface, Zheng Yunduan did not manage to completely free herself from this "feminine" mode: there are many poems in her collection with titles such as "Moved by Spring" and "Drifting Petals." But even when she does take up a "feminine" subject such as "Calls of the Flower-Seller," she tries to infuse it with a moral message:

> The beauty removes the embroidered screen in her courtyard;
> The calls of the flower-seller drift across the jade balustrade.
> Ordinary folks may crowd and squabble over peach and plum,
> But is there anyone who asks the east wind about the peony?

The collection also contains a number of poems inspired by events within the family. Some of these poems reflect the chaotic conditions of the time, an instance of which is the following "Thinking of My Younger Sister":

> My younger sister followed her husband,
> When he took up his post near Mount Lu.

---

11. Hollowed-out gourds were commonly used as containers. This hermit apparently kept his poems in a gourd.

That was already more than a year ago,
We have yet to receive a letter with news.

Recently we learned of the rise of bandits
Throughout the Jiangxi province.
Wherever they go, they plunder the cities:
The blood of the butchered fills the ditches.

I do not know whether she is still alive,
Or has died in the midst of these troubles.
Oh, the emotions of "wagtails on the plain"—
Alone, I sit filled with boundless sorrow.

The final couplet of this poem contains an allusion to a poem from the *Book of Odes*, which reads: "Wagtails are on the plain, / My brothers are in great distress." The traditional commentators explain that the wagtail is a waterbird, and that its presence on the high plain is a sure sign that the world is out of balance.

One of the most conspicuous features of Zheng Yunduan's collection is the large number of poems (at least thirty) on paintings. While it is true that poems on paintings were quite popular with poets of the time, the large number of such poems in Zheng's collection is particularly significant. Even for a rich young woman with a sympathetic husband, the world outside the home was only indirectly accessible. The opening poem in Zheng Yunduan's collection is entitled "Song of a Landscape Painting on a Folding Screen." In this poem, a description of the painting is followed by the speaker's complaint that the restrictions imposed on her by her gender (symbolized by tiny bound feet) make it impossible for her to visit the actual scene depicted on the screen. The fact that Zheng Yunduan chose this poem to open her collection suggests that it had programmatic value for her:

I am the owner of a roll of fine white silk from the east,
Upon which are painted the many mountains of Jiangnan:
The brushwork is by no means inferior to that of Li Qingqiu, [12]
While the composition far surpasses that of Yang Qidan.

---

12. Li Yingqiu is the Five Dynasties painter Li Cheng, who hailed from Yingqiu in Shandong province. Yang Qidan (Khitan Yang) was a famous painter of the Sui dynasty (581–617).

Fine craftsmen and skilled artisans are not easily found,
But this painting has been most impressively laid out:
Rows of mountains and layered cliffs converge then open,
Strange-shaped rocks and majestic pines rise face to face.

A wooden bridge and thatched cottage at the forest's edge,
Waterfalls and cascades crash and peal like thunder:
It is as if I were sitting at the foot of Mount Lu,
Suddenly I feel completely cleansed of worldly dust.

This body of mine has already grown old in the inner quarters,
I resent not having the chance to go out in search of the hidden.
Stockings of linen and black shoes have ruined my life—
Facing this painting I'm filled with a helpless frustration!

The landscape depicted in this scene was specifically that of Mount Lu in Jiangxi province, one of the most scenic spots in the region known as Jiangnan (south of the Yangzi). Mount Lu was famous for its many Buddhist and Daoist monasteries and temples, and over the centuries attracted a great number of famous monks and poets, including the Tang dynasty poet Bai Juyi (772–846).

In her many poems on paintings, Zheng Yunduan only rarely refers to the name of the painter. One of these exceptions is "Apricot Flowers by Xu Xi." Xu Xi was a famous tenth-century painter, who had also captured the fancy of Li Qingzhao and her husband. Zheng's poem reads as follows:

I really love Xu Xi's lifelike paintings of plants and flowers,
As I hold the scroll and savor his work, my eyes are dazzled.
I remember how once after a heavy spring downpour,
A single sprig protruded at a slant beyond the plastered wall.

As a rule, Zheng Yunduan seems to have been more interested in a particular painting's narrative content and moral message than in its artistic merits, as we can see from her poem entitled "A Scroll-Painting of Qiu Hu Trying to Seduce His Own Wife." According to the traditional story, Qiu Hu of the ancient state of Lu left his wife of less than a week home with his mother and went off to pursue an official career at court. When some years later he returned as a high official to his home village, he noticed a pretty young woman picking mulberry leaves. Not realizing that the woman was actually his own wife, he tried to seduce her with a gift of gold. Not recognizing her husband, she indignantly refused his offer. When she returned home that evening and discovered that her would-be seducer was none other than her own husband, she was so ashamed that she committed suicide by drowning herself. The chaste virtue of Qiu Hu's wife was celebrated as early as the Han dynasty in Liu Xiang's *Biographies of Exemplary Women*, and her story remained popular through the ages. Zheng Yunduan's poem reads as follows:

> How lovely was that Lady Jiang of Lu!
> She went out to pick mulberry leaves.
> Then a traveler arrived from far away,
> And by the roadside dismounted from his steed.
> With yellow gold he conveyed his glib words—
> A stripling youth, but also a noble lord!
> Still she, a wife, maintained her pure resolve,
> Her guts were made of iron and of stone.
> How could she be swayed by material things?
> Waves were stirred up in the ancient well.
> "Please convey my regrets to the one on the road,
> And ask him to chant the stanza 'Walk on Dew.'"

"Walk on Dew" is a song from the *Book of Odes*, which, according to the traditional commentaries, was written in condemnation of sexual assault and rape.

Apart from these poems on exemplars of virtue depicted in paintings, Zheng Yunduan also wrote poems on more unconventional subjects, an example of which is her poem entitled "On a Picture of Liu Ling and the Man with a Spade on His Shoulder." The subject of the painting concerned must have been provided by the following anecdote in *A New Account of Tales of the World*:

Liu Ling's style name was Bolun; he was a native of Peijun. He had an unbridled and eccentric character, and he found the whole cosmos too limited. He rode about in a carriage drawn by deer, with a jug of wine under his arm, and followed by a man carrying a spade, who, should Liu Ling die, could dig a hole and bury him on the spot. He regarded his body as nothing more than earth and wood, and all his life just followed his whims.

Zheng Yunduan's poem reads as follows:

> A hundred years flashes by in no more than a blink of an eye:
> How often in this single life can one enjoy oneself to the full?
> As long as there's wine in the jug, I'll drink myself into a stupor!
> The fellow with the spade following behind can bury me if I die.

Zheng Yunduan's collection also contains a number of poems inspired by her reading. Among the works she mentions by title are dynastic histories, philosophical treatises, and the collected writings of Song loyalists. She also read the writings of Ban Zhao, as we can see from the following poem entitled "On Reading the Seven Chapters of the *Precepts for My Daughters* by the Venerable Madam Cao":

> The Ban family for generations cultivated scholarship,
> And so brought forth this sagely "Venerable Madam."
> Her fragrant name has been famous through the ages,
> Because her literary writings are beautiful and elegant.
> The chapters for her daughters lay out instructions,
> The Way of the Wife here truly finds its model.
> With reverent attention I read them again and again,
> These norms I admire I would never dare transgress!

Zheng Yunduan is far more complex, however, than these moralistic poems would suggest. For one thing, she was convinced that as a woman poet she was destined to die young. As we saw earlier in our discussion of Zhu Shuzhen, there existed in late imperial Chinese society a widely shared belief that women of unusual beauty and/or talent were destined to suffer a "poor fate," and more often than not die young. By the same token, Zheng Yunduan's chronic illness may have strengthened her confidence in her own mission as a poet.

A Passing Mood

> Heaven granted me talent and fame but not longevity,
> How will I ever be able to enjoy them both in this life?
> Now that I am thirty, I am afraid that in two or three more years
> I won't be around to see my sons married and my daughters wed.

Untitled

The blossoms of the flowering peach and apricot fill the branches,
This is precisely the time when the splendor of spring is at its best.
I laugh at myself: since my illness my talents and ideas are less—
The spring nearly half over, and I haven't written a single poem!

Autumn Window, Describing My Emotions

The bones of a poet have never accumulated any fat,
Ill and wasted, I can't sustain the weight of my clothes.
When this morning I tried to put on my gauze skirt,
I found I was skinnier by half than I was this spring.

Throughout her many illnesses Zheng Yunduan found comfort in the notion that in a former existence she had been a heavenly immortal on the Three Isles (floating mountains) of the Immortals in the Eastern Ocean, and that she had been an attendant of the Queen Mother of the West, the ruler of all female immortals. She was also visited in her dreams by other heavenly immortals such as Hemp Maiden (Magu), with her famously long nails, who urged her not to postpone her return to her original home.

Expressing My Emotions

I used to be an immortal on the ocean,
Until suddenly I was ensnared by earthly thoughts
And fell down into the web of the world:
Since that time twenty years have passed.
Recently I received a letter from Hemp Maiden,
Asking me when I was planning to return.
To no purpose do I hesitate here in the wind,
Lifting my head toward those holy mountains.

Record of a Dream

Hemp Maiden, that immortal of ancient times,
Unexpectedly appeared in one of my dreams.
At first glance, I did not recognize her at all,
Looking as she did like an unmarried girl:
Her age was perhaps seventeen or eighteen,

But with fingernails more than a foot long;
A gown of blue and rose, her hair coiled high,
With some strands hanging down in tresses.
 She told me that she had come to fetch me,
 Now that three times the fields had turned to seas;
 And she'd just gone by the Isles of the Immortals,
Where the Weak Waters had become a clear stream.[13]
She beckoned me to journey to my western home,
Where at Jasper Pond I would meet Amah.[14]
 I simply smiled and without saying a word,
Lightly floated upwards borne by the winds,
Gazing all the while up at the misty clouds—
Waking from my dream, I let out a long sigh!

While waiting for her final return to the world of the immortals, Zheng Yunduan tried to write serious women's poetry. It is clear that she wanted to write poems on issues of particular concern to women that were infused with the same degree of moral seriousness that characterized the best poetry in the Chinese tradition. This may be one of the reasons why her collection consists of only *shi* poems and why she eschews the song lyric. But whereas the rich social experience available to male authors afforded them with varied occasions to write poems of high moral seriousness, women lacked the wider exposure to social reality that was, in the Chinese view of things, a prerequisite to the writing of this kind of poetry. One of Zheng Yunduan's few poems of social criticism that is not based on a painting, her reading, or some small incident in her daily life, is her "Ballad on the Way in Which the People of Wu Marry off Their Daughters." This ballad is preceded by a short preface:

I have observed that commoner families often marry their daughters off to high officials and men of high status. Even though these girls may for a time dazzle others with their status, in the end they never succeed in growing old together with their husbands. And so I wrote this poem as an admonition to them.
 Written in the bingshen *year of the reign period Utmost Orthodoxy* [Zhizheng, 1356].

When planting flowers, don't plant them by the side of the official road,

---

13. The Weak Waters, which are unable to support even a feather, encircle the earth and separate the world of mortals from that of the immortals.
14. Amah here refers to the Queen Mother of the West.

When marrying off a daughter, don't marry her off to a lord or a prince.
If you plant flowers by the side of the road, others will steal them away,
If you marry your daughter off to a prince or a lord, she won't last long.
 As flowers fall and beauty fades so feelings of love are bound to change,
Separated phoenixes, halves of a broken mirror: they will be torn apart.
It is far better to marry your daughter off to a local farmer boy
Who will take care of her into old age and never send her away.

Zheng Yunduan also drew on traditional legends and stories for her poems. Even if the titles do not always specify this, we may assume that many of these poems were inspired by painted illustrations of these legends. An example is her poem entitled "The Husband-Watching Rock," inspired by a legend told in many parts of China about a loyal wife who, after waiting for her absent husband's return for many years, is finally transformed into a rock so she can keep watch for her husband for all eternity:

Her husband went off on a distant campaign,
And stayed away at the other end of the world.
He promised to be back in three years' time:
How many autumns have gone by since then?
 She climbed the mountain to its highest peak,
And craning her neck, watched for his homing boat.
But his homing boat she never did get to see,
She tarried and lingered and fretted in vain.
 Turned into a rock there on the mountain top,
Towering high, she leans against the blue sky.
To this very day her heart remains unchanged,
As night and day she gazes into the distance.
 Stone is strong but still one day it will erode;
Seas will run dry and turn into mulberry fields.
When stone erodes and the seas run dry,
Then surely the traveler will come home!

In yet other cases Zheng Yunduan derived her moral messages from events and objects in her daily life, as can be seen in her poem "Trying Out My Walking Staff after Recovering from an Illness":

At fifty, one may use a staff at home—
But I am only thirty years of age!
Bedridden with an illness for a year,

I could sit up, but barely walk or stand.
 This morning I tried to go for a stroll,
But still at each step I almost stumbled.
Supported by my staff I walk very slowly,
And my limbs have regained their ease.
 How lovely that I can go where I please!
Only now do I appreciate my sturdy staff!
A skinny pole that barely fills my hand,
But taller than me, exactly seven feet high.
 It's not a bamboo from the heart of the Yangzi,
In fact, it is made of pear wood from the hills.
The nodes have turned into gnarled warts,
The grain of the wood is fine and dense.
 Capable of supporting a sickly body,
It can also assist a weakened frame.
When you are in a precarious position,
It's bound to be of even greater use!

For a full understanding of the import of this poem one needs to know that the word denoting "nodes," which is often used in describing bamboo, also has the derived meaning of "norms," and has come to refer in particular to a woman's chastity.

At other moments, however, apparently neither the hope of an eventual return to the Isles of the Immortals nor the reiteration of eternal values seems to offer Zheng Yunduan any comfort. The following poems lament the ephemerality of human existence.

My Mirror

Bright and shiny this mirror in its case
Has kept me company for many years.
To what might one compare its clarity?
To the full moon hanging up in the sky.
 Long ago, when I was just about sixteen,
My complexion was as fresh as any flower.
Performing my morning toilette in front of it,
I tried to outdo my own reflection in charm.
 But lately the years have begun to add up,
And I have been plagued by poverty and illness.
Gradually I have become so old and ugly

That I no longer make use of powder and rouge.
 This morning the mirror too has grown dim,
Dusty and dirty and eaten away by rust.
We look at each and sink into darkness:
How can one distinguish between ugly and fair?
 In human life there's splendor and decay,
Both things and feelings undergo change.
For everything in the world this holds true,
What is the point then in sighing any further?

A Dirge for Myself

Where there is birth, there must be death:
As constant a principle as day and night.
Some make it to old age, some die young,
What's the use of comparing spans of life?
 While still in the prime of my life,
I came down with an illness without a cure.
For over a year I was bound to my bed,
And my life dangled by no more than a thread.
 Then one morning I bid goodbye to the world,
My soul and spirit wafted away in the air.
My shriveled body, like a withered tree,
I shed and left behind in the empty hall.
 My good husband caressed me and wept,
And my darling children cried at my side.
I was laid in a coffin of unplaned wood,
And was wrapped in a padded linen skirt.
 They sent me off and took me out of town,
Where I was buried in the southern hills.
This dark hall is hidden deep in the earth,
Where even the fiercest sunlight never enters!
 Friends and relatives have done their weeping,
Set out the goblets and arranged the wine.
To no avail they pour libations on the grave,
And hang paper coins from white poplars.
 There is no shaman who can summon back my soul,
And the bereaved all mourn in vain:
After a thousand years, ten thousand offerings,
We will have dissolved into nothing at all.

My only regret is that while in the world,
I did not make a name for myself by doing good.
If one has a reputation to be handed down,
It will grow more fragrant with passing time.
I myself wrote the words of this dirge,
Words that are filled with sadness and grief.
But there are no mourners to sing this dirge,
So having these words doesn't mean a thing.

This last line may perhaps be regarded as a premonition on the part of Zheng Yunduan, for although her poems have been preserved, they have not brought her enduring fame. The eighteenth-century compilers of the catalogue of the imperial collection refer to her poems as "shallow and weak"—a common way of dismissing women's poetry—and claim she committed "many mistakes of meter and rhyme." However, these learned gentlemen may well have misjudged her originality. It would appear that the conspicuous simplicity of her diction was deliberate: Zheng Yunduan wanted to write as a woman about women for women. To what extent she was unique in doing so or was part of a more general development in women's poetry at the time is difficult to determine, but Yang Weizhen's preface to the lost collection of lady Cao would seem to indicate that more women than we will ever know about reacted to the growing ideological pressure of neo-Confucianism by trying to break away from the "feminine mode" and strike out in new directions.

To the extent that the name of Zheng Yunduan was known in later times, it is ironic that she was, like Zhu Shuzhen, viewed as a young woman condemned by her great talent to an unhappy existence. Thus, an early seventeenth-century source is able to reduce her life to the following short paragraph:

Zheng Yunduan was the wife of Shi Boren of Suzhou. From her earliest years she was extremely intelligent and skilled in literary composition. But because her husband was of a boorish and evil character, her marriage was unhappy, and she wrote her poems to give vent to her feelings.

This contradicts both Zheng Yunduan's own testimony about her companionate marriage and her literary aspirations. But apparently later readers were only able to discern possibilities for poetry in feminine suffering.

Guan Daosheng and Huang E

Apart from the few female poets from elite families whose collections have been preserved, there were many other women authors of comparable status from this period who were less fortunate and for whom only a handful of poems are extant. Some of these women poets, such as Guan Daosheng and Huang E, enjoyed considerable reputations during their lifetimes. Guan Daosheng was the wife of the famous painter, calligrapher, and poet Zhao Mengfu (1254–1322), and a major painter, calligrapher, and poet in her own right. Huang E was the wife of the well-known polymath Yang Shen (1488–1559).

Artist and Artist's Wife: Guan Daosheng

Guan Daosheng's husband Zhao Mengfu was a native of Wuxing, located about halfway between Suzhou and Hangzhou. He was a member of the imperial family of the Song dynasty, established a reputation as the finest painter of his age, and early on held an official post under that dynasty. Following the final conquest of southern China in 1276–1278 by the Mongols, he retired to the hills. Because of his fame, he was repeatedly pressured to come to the capital, Dadu (present-day Beijing), and finally, in 1287, he made his first trip north to take up a post under the Yuan dynasty (1260–1368). He soon returned to the south, but in 1289 he again traveled north, this time accompanied by his young wife. Throughout his life Zhao Mengfu would feel torn between his loyalty to the preceding dynasty and the attractions of honor and wealth, an ambivalence which he often expressed in his poetry, but which did not stop him from pursuing a successful career.

Our most important source for the life of Guan Daosheng is a grave inscription written by her husband. It was customary for such a text, engraved in stone, to be buried with the coffin of the deceased—but of course it was usually also preserved in the collected writings of the author.

A Grave Inscription for Lady Guan, Lady of the State of Wei

The personal name of the Lady was Daosheng, her surname was Guan, her style name was Zhangji, and she was a native of Wuxing. Her ancestors were scions of Guan Zhong, who had fled the troubles in the state of Qi by coming to Wuxing.[15] Because people considered them to be sages, the village where they settled is still called Xixian [Sages' Roost]. Her father's personal name was Shen and his style name was Zhifu; her mother was surnamed Zhou. Sir Guan had an eccentric character, and was renowned throughout the village for his chivalry. He had an extremely high opinion of his daughter who had shown herself to be of extraordinary intelligence from the moment of her birth, and he was determined to find her a suitable match. I was living in the same neighborhood, and her father also held a high opinion of me. He was convinced that I would rise to a high position, and so the Lady married me.

In the twenty-fourth year of the reign period Ultimate Prime [Zhiyuan, 1271–1294], Emperor Shizu [Khubilai Khan] summoned me to court. From being a common citizen I was appointed Grand Master for Admonishment and Director in the Ministry of War. When in the twenty-sixth year I returned on official business to Hangzhou, the Lady accompanied me back to the capital. Later I was appointed Secretary Serving in the Hall of Assembled Sages Concurrently Serving as Prefect of Jinan. When Emperor Chengzong summoned me to serve in the Bureau of Historiography, the Lady again accompanied me. When I resigned my appointment because of illness, she returned with me to Wuxing. At the end of my term as Inspector-General of Confucian Schools in Jiangnan and Zhejiang, I was appointed prefect of Taizhou. When the present emperor was still the crown prince, he dispatched an envoy to summon me, whereupon I was appointed Reader in the Hanlin Academy. Again the Lady accompanied me to the capital. This was in the winter of the third year of the reign period Ultimate Greatness [Zhida, 1308–1311]. In the following year, the emperor ascended the throne, and as a special mark of favor I was appointed Secretary in the Hall of Assembled Sages and Grand Master for Palace Attendance, while the Lady was enfeoffed as Lady of the Commandery of Wuxing.

During the first year of the reign period Imperial Blessing [Huangqing, 1312–1313], I requested leave to return home where I erected a stele on behalf of my ancestors. Now the Lady had wanted to name an heir to the Guan family as there was no surviving adult son, but, unable to find a suitable person, she turned the old family home into the Guan Family Household Daoist Shrine of Filial Remembrance and assigned a Daoist priest to take care of the ancestral

---

15. Guan Zhong (d. 645 BCE) was the most important minister of Duke Huan of Qi (r. 684–643 BCE) and greatly contributed to the growing power of Qi during this period. Soon upon Duke Huan's death, however, Qi was devastated by civil war as various princes disputed over who would succeed to the throne.

sacrifices for her father and mother, as I have described in my "Record of the Daoist Shrine."

During the next year, envoys arrived one after the other, and the Lady once again followed me to the capital. In the fourth year of the reign period Extended Happiness [Yanyou, 1314–1320] I was appointed as [one of the six] Chancellors of the Hanlin Academy, while the Lady was enfeoffed with the higher rank of Lady of the State of Wei. In the winter of the fifth year she again fell ill with her old disease beriberi, and the emperor dispatched a succession of imperial physicians to take her pulse. In the sixth year, when the illness had grown even more severe, I requested and obtained permission from the emperor to return home. On the twenty-fifth day of the Fourth Month we departed from Dadu. On the tenth day of the Fifth Month, after our boat had reached Linqing, the Lady, who was fifty-eight years old, succumbed to her illness.

Together with our son Yong I escorted her casket back to Wuxing. On the . . . day of the . . . Month of that year we buried her on the plain at the foot of Mount Dongheng in Deqing district, all in accordance with the rites.[16] She had given birth to three sons: Liang [who died in infancy], Yong, and Yi, and six daughters. The Lady had by nature a cheerful disposition. She was impeccable in each of the four wifely virtues of deportment, speech, features, and work. Although she had no formal training she was accomplished in calligraphy and literary composition. When it came to regulating household affairs she treated relatives and outsiders fairly. She would personally take care of both the yearly and the seasonal sacrifices to the ancestors, unless prevented from doing so by her illness. This she would do in the most proper manner, [herself preparing] a full array of dishes, while dressed in formal attire. If any member of the clan would happen to become enslaved, she would in each case buy their freedom. When she encountered someone in need, she would provide for them without any stinginess. In her treatment of guests and when dealing with problems, she would always do so in an appropriate manner according to the rites.

The Lady was deeply devoted to Buddhism, and she personally wrote out tens of copies of the *Diamond Sutra* for distribution to famous monasteries and famous monks.

The Son of Heaven ordered the Lady to write out the *Thousand Character Text*, and then had jade carvers polish jade knobs for the scroll, which he had sent to the Imperial Library so her calligraphy could be mounted and included in the

---

16. Funerary inscriptions often were prepared a long time before the actual burial. In the draft of the document, which often served as the basis for the text at the time of the compilation of an author's collected works, the exact date of burial would be left blank.

collection. Then he also ordered me to write out this same text in six different styles; Yong also wrote it out once. The emperor said: "In this way later generations will know that during our reign there lived a lady who was accomplished in calligraphy. It is also unusual that all the members of a single family should be accomplished in calligraphy." In addition, the Lady painted both monochrome and colored paintings of bamboo for presentation to the throne, which also met with the emperor's approbation, and for which she received a gift of a jug of wine of the highest quality from the imperial store. When once the Lady was received in audience by the empress dowager in the Xingsheng Palace, she was allowed to sit down and was honored with a meal—she was showered with favors. To be thus acknowledged by both the emperor and the empress dowager was truly to bask in glory!

When the Lady died, her relatives on both sides of the family were all deeply moved, and all those who had once enjoyed her company shed tears: from this one can appreciate the extent of her virtue.

It was perhaps to avoid the charge that his wife was a bluestocking that Zhao Mengfu stressed her natural, rather than acquired, talents for painting, calligraphy, and poetry. A fair number of paintings attributed to Guan Daosheng have been preserved, but in many cases their authenticity is disputed. The few of her poems that are extant today have almost without exception been preserved because they were inscribed on her paintings.

Sent to My Husband: Painted Bamboo

The day you left, my lord and master, the bamboo had just been planted,
Now the bamboo has grown into a grove, but you have not yet returned.
Once my jade-white face has lost its beauty, it will be gone forever,
Unlike flowers that fall, only later to blossom yet again and again.

Painted Plum Trees

After the snow, white branches are fragile,
Covered with frost, jade pistils are cold.
Yonder village is no place for them:
Move them to the moon for viewing!

Guan Daosheng's best-known poems are probably the four song lyrics she wrote to the tune of "Fisherman's Song" (*Yufuci*). These lyrics were originally written as an inscription on one of her own paintings, said to have been executed sometime between 1310 and 1312 when she was in Dadu (Yan). In this set of lyrics, she contrasts the harried life of a court official, burdened with obligations, with the carefree existence of a fisherman in her home district of Wuxing:

I

From afar, I think of my mountain cottage with its several plum trees:
Despite the icy cold, jade blossoms open on their southern branches.
The mountain moon shines,
The morning wind blows—
It is all because of their pure fragrance that I so long to return home!

II

Gazing south toward Wuxing, four thousand miles of road—
When will I be able to return to the banks of the river Zha?
Fame and profit
I'll leave to Heaven,
Smiling, I'll fetch my angling rod and board my fishing boat.

III

My body is here in the Yan mountains near the imperial residence,
But with homesick heart I think of Wuxing by night and by day.
Pouring fine wine,
Mincing fresh fish:
I know of nothing to compare with that life of pure leisure!

IV

The highest honor in human life is the rank of prince or duke,
But for fleeting fame and passing profit one gives up freedom.
How could that compare
With a single boat—
So let's go home, enjoy the moonlight, and chant in the breeze!

It is not surprising to find in a grave inscription a catalogue of the virtues and honors of the deceased, rather than an impassioned declaration of love. However, by so strongly emphasizing the fact that Guan Daosheng accompanied him on all his travels, Zhao Mengfu suggests that the two of them must have been very close. Quite often an official's wife would stay behind in his home village in order to take care of her parents-in-law, look after the family estate, and raise the children, while her husband, with or without the comfort of a concubine, trekked from place to place and from post to post. Yet, according to one very popular, if rather late, legend (first written down around 1600), Zhao Mengfu is said to have once suggested to his wife that his status (and his wife's age) called for the acquisition of a few concubines:

Once, when Zhao Mengfu wanted to buy some concubines, he wrote the following short lyric in order to sound out Lady Guan's feelings on the matter:

> I am a Secretary,
> You are a Lady.
>   You must have heard that
> Secretary Tao had his Peach Leaf and Peach Root,
> Secretary Su had his Morning Cloud and Evening Cloud.[17]
>   Now if I could obtain a few
> Maidens of Wu and beauties of Yue, it would befit my position.
> You are already over forty years of age,
> Yet in this jade hall you still want to monopolize spring!

Lady Guan replied as follows:

> You and I
> Share an ardent passion.
> When passion is ardent,
> It burns like fire.
> Take one lump of clay
> Knead one you,
> Sculpt one me.
> Smash them both into pieces,
> Mix them with water,
> Knead another you,
> Sculpt another me:
> In my clay there is you,

---

17. Secretary Tao is Tao Gu (903–970), a high official of the Song dynasty. On a mission to the "decadent" court of the Southern Tang, although he seemed to be a pillar of morality, it turned out he was susceptible to female charms after all, as he was easily seduced by a wily courtesan. Peach Leaf (Taoye) and Peach Root (Taogen) were actually the names of two of the favorite concubines of Wang Xianzhi (344–388). Secretary Su is the famous Song dynasty poet Su Shi (1036–1101).

In your clay there is me.
In life you and I share a single coverlet,
In death a single grave!

When her husband received this song, he laughed heartily and did not pursue his intention any further.

An Exile's Wife: Huang E

Huang E was the second daughter of the famous scholar Huang Ke (1449–1522) and the second wife of the well-known exile Yang Shen (1488–1559). Yang Shen was a native of Xindu district in Sichuan province. His father had been a high court official and he himself passed the metropolitan examinations in 1511 at the top of the list. He appeared to be destined for a brilliant career, but in 1524 he provoked the ire of the young Jiajing emperor (r. 1522–1566) and was banished as a common soldier to Yongchang in westernmost Yunnan. Despite the pleas of Yang's former colleagues, the Jiajing emperor repeatedly refused to pardon him, and Yang spent the rest of his life in faraway Yunnan, where he found the time to write on every conceivable topic and in every known literary genre. His wife Huang E is said to have been "well read in the Classics and Histories, and a fine prose writer."

Huang E had initially accompanied her husband to his place of exile, but after the death of her father-in-law in 1529 she returned to Xindu, where she managed the family estate. She and her husband continued to exchange poems. According to her biographical sketch in the *Collected Poems of the Successive Reigns* (*Liechao shiji*) by Qian Qianyi (1582–1664) and his wife, Liu Shi, "she rarely wrote *shi* poems, and did not leave a collection: not even the younger members of the family ever saw her poems. However, the song lyrics and short songs she sent to Yang Shen were handed down and recited by the literary crowd." And so not long after her death, collections of "her" works started to appear. Early in the seventeenth century, for instance, a Suzhou publisher printed a collection of arias (*qu*) under her name. The *qu* is a more vernacular genre of song lyric that had become popular in the thirteenth century and later. The arias in this Suzhou collection are unusual in their uninhibited description of the pleasures of love. When one compares the contents of this collection with those of Yang Shen, though, it is clear that the overwhelming majority of the arias are indeed his compositions, or those of other anonymous male authors (the literary crowd that recited "her" works). The same sorts of questions surround the other publications that bear Huang E's name. Modern editors who have tried to reconstruct a collection of her authentic compositions have inevitably found that they must append cautionary notes to almost all the titles they include.

The best known of Huang E's *shi* poems addressed to her husband is the following:

> Even the geese on their return south never fly past Hengyang,
> How then am I to send my brocade characters to Yongchang?
> The Third Month's blossoms and willows: such is my poor fate,
> The winds and miasmas of the Six Commands: your heart is broken.
> Rumor after rumor of homecoming—I grieve throughout the year,
> Prayer after prayer for rain—we resent the bright scorching sun.
> To no avail we pity each other, and cling to the promise of return,
> But when will the Golden Cock descend to the land of Yelang?

This poem is filled with allusions, some of which may need some clarification. Traditionally, migrating geese were believed to fly no further south than Hengyang in Hunan province. Geographically speaking, Yongchang is not that much farther south than Hengyang, but during this time it was considered to be the back of beyond. In fact, Yunnan province was only incorporated into the empire during the Ming. Before that, it was at different times the home of various non-Chinese states, such as the Six Commands (Liuzhao) during the Tang dynasty. Located as it was in the deep south, Yongchang was considered to be a hot and humid place, where pestilential miasmas spelled disease and early death. Lines five and six of Huang E's poem both open with references to two poems in the *Book of Odes*, one in which the rumors of a speedy return (of soldiers on campaign) always turn out to be false, and the other in which hopes for relief from a terrible drought are repeatedly dashed. If the emperor himself is often compared to the sun, his mercy is many times compared to a reviving rain. Yelang was in Tang dynasty times the designation of a vassal kingdom in present-day Guizhou province; the poet Li Bai (701–762) was banished late in his life to this tropical area, but, unlike Yang Shen, was pardoned before he reached his destination. Finally, the Golden Cock, the name of a star, is the symbol of amnesty, as ancient

Chinese believed that an oscillation of this star foretold a general amnesty.

The following quatrain, entitled "Sent to My Husband," in contrast to the one above, is quite straightforward:

> Too listless to send this letter to "the side of the sun":
> Since you left one year has passed and then another!
> You are the one who makes no plan to come home,
> Where on the verdant hills does the cuckoo not call?

In the call of the cuckoo the traditional Chinese heard the words *burugui* ("Better go home!"). According to an old legend, an ancient king of the state of Shu (modern-day Sichuan) turned into a cuckoo out of shame after raping the wife of his prime minister. The bird is believed to weep tears of blood, which give the flowers of the azalea their red color. It may be, then, that the last line hints at a bit of jealous suspicion on the part of Huang E.

There is some disagreement about the likely date of the composition of this poem. The expression "the side of the sun" usually refers to the capital, close to the emperor. This might lead one to think that this poem was written before 1524 (and Yang Shen's exile), but as far as we know, during these years the newlyweds were never separated for more than a short time, much less for "one year" and then another. If one insists on reading "one year" literally, this would mean that "to the side of the sun" must refer to Yang Shen's place of exile in the deep south, not close to the emperor, but to the scorching sun. But then the complaint over the unwillingness of the absent husband to return home becomes unfair: Yang Shen was only too willing to return home, but was not allowed to do so. If one wishes to read the poem as the composition of a young bride, then the line "one year has passed and then another" may be read simply as a playful hyperbole. If, on the other hand, one wishes to read the poem as the composition of the wife of an exile, one might read the third line as an expression of grief over the husband's absence that is so intense its cause is projected onto the husband. And then again, the poem may not have been written by Huang E at all!

We reencounter the cuckoo in the final couplet of the following untitled poem by Huang E:

My pearly tears fall in profusion into the inkstone's well:
A broken heart finds it hard to write "broken-heart poems."
Ever since that hour when we held hands and said farewell,
Up to this very day I feel too listless to paint on my brows.
 No medicine can cure the sadness that fills my nights;
No amount of money can buy back the years of our youth.
I'll do anything to persuade that bird of the spring hills
To tell the traveler south of the Yangzi to come home!

Not all of Huang E's *shi* poems are obsessed with the theme of her husband's return, as the following quatrain entitled "A Spring Day" shows:

With my golden needle I poked a hole in the paper window
So as to let in a whiff of the plum blossom's fragrance.
Even the ants lose no time in becoming enamored of spring,
As moving backwards they haul a petal up the eastern wall.

Most of the arias attributed to Huang E are of a highly generic character, and it is extremely difficult to find anything in them that would help us link them more directly to our author. Many traditional and modern anthologies include a series of four arias to the tune of "Yellow Oriole" as representative of her work in this genre. The first aria in this series reads as follows:

The ceaseless rain brews up a light chill,
Look how the abundant blossoms
Wither on each and every tree.
Nothing but muddy roads—I'm tired of climbing high and gazing afar!
Rivers flow—how many bends?
Cloudy hills—how many turns?
I strain my eyes toward the horizon, but it only breaks my heart.
Impossible to send a letter:
Those heartless migrating geese
Will not fly as far as Yunnan!

One of the more playful arias attributed to Huang E is the following suite of songs entitled "A Painting of Palace Ladies":

To the Tune of "Cursing the Lover" (*Ma yulang*), followed
by "Grateful for the Emperor's Favor" (*Gan huang'en*) and
"Tea-Picking Song" (*Caicha ge*)

One is picking a rose—entangled in thorns a golden hairpin falls,
One is gathering up kingfisher feathers,
One is holding up her mermaid-silk scarf.
One is leaning by a painted screen.
One is concealed by the bamboo's shadow,
One is hidden behind the willow's colors,
One is veiled by the scholartree's shade.
One—in green—is sketching a banana tree,
One—in red—is picking cherries.
One stands with her back to pond and hill,
One looks into basin and pool,
One walks to the pavilion terrace.
One blows the pipe of the phoenix-flute,
One plucks strings joined with *luan*-bird glue.[18]
One leans on the balustrade and looks down,
One ascends the tower to gaze afar.
One peeps through the cracks of the blinds.
One shows a brow furrowed by sorrow,
One shows a face flushed with wine.
One looks into the water as she evenly applies her rouge,
One stands near the flowers as she arranges her kingfisher hairpins.
One holds a green plum as she clambers up the low wall,
One kicks the swing and makes it soar higher than the trees,
And one pulls back a sleeve and waves it like a fan.

---

18. The *luan* is a mythic bird very much like the phoenix. "*Luan*-bird glue" is glue said
to be made of the bones of the *luan*-bird.

6 · Empresses, Nuns, and Actresses

Empresses and Palace Ladies

As mentioned before, up until the end of the Tang dynasty the women of the Inner Palace played a central role in the tradition of women's literature. Following the spread of literacy and the increased availability of books from the Song dynasty onwards, though, the Inner Palace lost its privileged position. While the palace ladies remained as literate as before, few of them made a name for themselves in literary history. There was, however, still one genre of poetry in which empresses and palace ladies were at an advantage: the "palace songs" (*gongci*). The genre was invented by the mid-Tang poet Wang Jian (766–ca. 835), who composed a series of a hundred quatrains on the topic of life in the Inner Palace. These poems were very much appreciated, but suffered in the eyes of traditional Chinese critics from one major weakness: Wang Jian had no personal access to the Inner Palace and had derived his information secondhand from palace eunuchs. As poems should be based on personal experience, only a resident of the Inner Palace was truly qualified to write authentic palace songs. In due time, emperors, empresses, and palace ladies obliged. The art-loving Emperor Huizong (r. 1101–1126) is credited with a series of no less than three hundred palace songs (of which many may actually have been written by his courtiers). The popularity of the genre at Huizong's court may have been spurred on by the discovery in the archives a few decades earlier of a set of palace songs attributed to Lady Huarui. Empress Yang of the Southern Song dynasty was also credited with a series of palace songs, although this attribution was not made until much later, during the Ming dynasty. The number of palace songs ascribed to Lady Huarui and Empress Yang tended to increase over time. Empresses and palace ladies did not limit themselves to the genre of palace songs, however; in the early Ming dynasty, Empress Xu, the formidable principal wife of the Yongle emperor, made a name for herself with the composition of a moral handbook for women and the publication of a Buddhist sutra that had been revealed to her.

Lady Huarui and Her Palace Songs

Following the collapse of the Tang dynasty, the Chinese world was divided into a number of opposing states. Whereas most of northern China remained unified under one central authority (although five different dynasties followed one another in quick succession), southern China was divided among both large and small, more or less long-lived, kingdoms constantly at war with each other and with whichever northern dynasty was in power at the time. The area of what is today the province of Sichuan remained independent for most of this period. It was first ruled by the Former Shu dynasty (907–926) founded by Wang Jian, and subsequently by the Later Shu dynasty (930–965) of Meng Zhixiang (r. 930–934) and Meng Chang (r. 935–965). The courts of both these local dynasties were centers of culture, especially known for their patronage of scholarship, painting, and the art of song.

When in 965 the territory of the Later Shu dynasty was conquered by the troops of the newly established Song dynasty, they hauled all the treasure of the vanquished dynasty (including books and palace ladies) off to the Song capital at Kaifeng. When, more than a century later, Wang Anguo (ca. 1028–ca. 1076), a younger brother of the famous statesman Wang Anshi (1021–1086), went through the remnants of the palace collection of the Later Shu dynasty, he discovered two manuscripts containing palace songs ascribed to Lady Huarui. Originally the manuscripts had included "some eighty or ninety quatrains but only thirty-two were preserved." A few examples from this series may suffice to provide a sense of the themes and style of this genre of poetry:

I

Inside the phoenix walls, towers and pavilions like five-colored clouds;
The trees and flowers always fresh, the days and months passed in idleness.
The thirty-six palace courtyards are all connected to the Inner Garden:
The Son of Heaven of Great Peace makes his home on Mount Kunlun![1]

III

The nine bends of the Dragon Pond from afar are interlinked,
The threads of the willows tugged by the wind on the banks.
Here it always resembles the fine scenery of South of the Yangzi:
Where painted boats ply in all directions on the emerald waves.

VII

The kitchen-boat brings food: an assortment of delicacies!
Those who take part in the banquet are all His closest aides.
At noon His Majesty expresses a desire for a raw fish filet—
Behind the flowers the fishermen are urged to make it quick.

XV

The emperor's favorite concubine lives near Dragon Pond;
The floor has been swept and incense is burning by noon.
While waiting for the arrival of His Majesty at her courtyard,
She watches her parrot being taught to recite a palace song.

XVIII

My morning toilette done, a spring breeze caresses my face,
As I stealthily break off a flowering branch on the riverbank.
When I am spotted from a distance by one of the eunuchs,
I pretend to be trying to hit the yellow orioles with red beans.

XXIII

In front of the hall, the palace ladies with waists so slender,
Learn to ride for the first time—frightened, but so charming.

---

1. The mythical Mount Kunlun (elsewhere also translated as the Kunlun Mountains) was said to be located far to the west of China and believed to be inhabited by immortals.

As soon as the horses they have mounted make ready to gallop,
They drop the reins and cling for dear life to the saddle-bridge!

XXVI

Clustered in groups the palace ladies are out picking lotuses,
Startling the gulls that fly up from the banks on both sides.
Raising the magnolia oars they beat the water in unison,
Racing their boats, their gauze blouses are soaked through.

XXXII

On the first of the month they receive their flower-buying money:
Within the palace there must be more than a few thousand ladies.
When their name is called out, many of them do not say a word,
As they walk by the Imperial Couch with a blush on their faces.

During the Ming dynasty, Huarui's palace lyric collection appeared in several editions, each more extensive than the next (the lyrics that were added were often plagiarizations of palace lyrics by Wang Jian), until one hundred quatrains had been included. In the early eighteenth century, the *Complete Poems of the Tang Dynasty* further expanded the number of poems in the collection to one hundred and sixty-seven.

Since the original thirty-two palace lyrics had been found among the manuscripts of the palace collection of the Later Shu, Wang Anguo and his contemporaries concluded that Lady Huarui must have lived during that dynasty. Soon there appeared anecdotes that referred to Lady Huarui as the favorite concubine of Meng Chang and stressed her noble character. We find, for example, the following notice in a collection of critical comments on poetry from around 1100:

Lady Fei was a native of Qingcheng in Shu. Because of her talent and beauty she was inducted into the Inner Palace. The Last Lord [Meng Chang] fell in love with her and enfeoffed her as Lady Huarui. In imitation of Wang Jian, she wrote one hundred palace lyrics. When the state of Shu was destroyed, she was inducted into the Inner Palace [in Kaifeng]. When Emperor Taizu [the founder of the Song dynasty, r. 960–975] heard about her, he summoned her and had her show him her poems. She then recited a poem about the fall of Shu, which reads:

> From the wall, my lord and king raised the banner of surrender—
> As a woman, hidden deep inside the palace, how could I know?
> A hundred and forty thousand troops laid down their weapons,
> Among them not a single one worthy of being called a man.

When Emperor Taizu heard this he was very pleased because the troops of the Song had only numbered a few tens of thousands whereas the troops of the Shu had numbered one hundred and forty thousand men.

Many traditional readers will probably have read this poem by Lady Huarui as an expression of her loyalty: by chiding Meng Chang's soldiers for their lack of valor, she implies that if she were a man and had been in their position, she would have put up a much more valiant defense. Lady Huairui's reputation for loyalty is also reflected in the following anecdote recorded a generation later by Cai Tao in which Lady Huairui is said to have attempted, out of loyalty to her former master and despite the fact that she was a woman, to assassinate Emperor Taizu herself.

When Our Dynasty had subjugated the western state of Shu, Lady Huarui followed Meng Chang to the capital, Kaifeng. About ten days after her arrival, she was summoned to the Palace, and [not long afterwards] Meng Chang died. Later, Emperor Taizu grew besotted with her beauty. She repeatedly tried to poison him but was ultimately unsuccessful, even though he repeatedly suffered from her attempts.

When [the younger brother of Emperor Taizu and eventually his successor] Emperor Taizong was still the Prince of Jin, he warned his brother time and again [of Lady Huarui's intentions], but the latter could not bear to banish her from his side. One day, Taizong accompanied the emperor while he was shooting animals in the Palace Park with Lady Huarui at his side. Taizong took an arrow, drew the bow, and pretending to be aiming at a fleeing animal, instead suddenly turned around and shot at the Lady. She died immediately.

While these Song dynasty authors were unanimous in their praise of the virtue of Lady Huarui, they were not quite as certain about her identity, and by the mid-twelfth century, we find that her surname has been changed from Fei to Xu. By this time, she had also become credited with a poem in which she predicts Taizu's infatuation with her:

Meng Chang, the illegitimate ruler of Shu, took the daughter of Xu Kuangzhang as a wife, and enfeoffed her as Lady Huarui. . . . When the state of Shu was destroyed, Emperor Taizu ordered her to be taken to Kaifeng. On the road she wrote the following lyric to exonerate herself:

> Leaving the province of Shu, my heart feels shattered,
> The pain of parting lingers on and on.
> Each spring day seems to last a year,
> On horseback, again and again I hear the cuckoo's call.

> The three thousand women of the Inner Palace are all like flowers,
> But none is as alluring as I.
> Now I go to see the emperor,
> I fear only that my lord and king will love and favor me alone.

Some say that her surname was Fei, but that is wrong.

The anecdotes about Lady Huarui's activities at the court of Taizu are interesting as legend but hardly reliable as history. The poem on the fall of the Later Shu attributed to Lady Huarui, for example, is actually based on a poem found in a mid-tenth-century source, where it refers to the fall of the Former Shu. And we know so little about the life of Lady Huarui at the court of Meng Chang that it is doubtful there was ever such a lady at his court. It has also been suggested that the palace lyrics attributed to her were the work of one of the wives of Wang Jian, the founder of the Former Shu dynasty. The existence of this lady, the younger sister of Wang Jian's empress, is well attested to in historical sources. She was also surnamed Xu, was also enfeoffed as Lady Huarui, and was also known to have written poetry. However, these same historical sources describe this Lady Huarui as being a rapacious shrew who during the reign of Wang Jian's son, Wang Yan, monopolized power together with her sister. Following the conquest of the Former Shu by the Later Tang dynasty in 925, Wang Yan, his mother, and Lady Huarui were all executed. This Lady Huarui is a more likely, if less likable, candidate for the authorship of the set of poems discovered by Wang Anguo (although, of course, if any male author wanted to pass off his own palace lyrics as the authentic works of a palace lady, no story would be more convincing than that of claiming to have discovered them in a pile of discarded manuscripts in the palace library itself).

Empress Yang and More Palace Songs

In the second half of the fifteenth century, Lang Ying published a set of thirty palace songs that he claimed had been written by Empress Yang (1162–1232) of the Southern Song dynasty. Among them we find the following quatrains on springtime in the palace:

III

Willow branches snatch from the rain freshest green,
Peach buds show in the breeze a first hint of red.
It is here in Heaven that spring's glow first appears
Amidst the many-hued clouds of towering palaces.

IV

The spring breeze even and mild, the river expansive and wide—
Holding hands we cross the small bridge in search of fragrance.
But there is sadness when the eyes wander over field and ponds:
The countless mandarin-ducks only come in couples and pairs!

VI

The window at dawn turns white, the oriole already singing!
The palace trees in bloom—on which branch does it sing?
Smoke no longer rises from the censer but the scent still lingers,
As I return from my dream of hidden chambers and red doors.

VII

The spring wind of the Second Month cuts out the shape of leaves,
The floating and drifting strands of willow now even more lovely.
Silently I lean on the carved balustrade with nothing at all to do,
Except count the shadows of swallows flitting through the flowers.

VIII

The screen filled with drizzling rain, I dread the chill of spring,
Hidden deep here inside the Inner Palace, idle the entire day.
Fallen blossoms cover the ground, their red not swept away,
Still the oriole on its branch continues to warble on and on.

XI

How secluded the scene of these deep, hidden rear courtyards!
Rare flowers and famous bamboo sway tenderly in the spring.
His Majesty's presence has not graced this place for over a year,
And many of the pavilions and terraces are in need of repair.

Lang Ying based his edition of these palace lyrics on "a manuscript in his private collection," and claimed that the series had originally numbered fifty quatrains. In the early seventeenth century an edition was published that indeed consisted of fifty quatrains, but at least three of the added poems were copied from Wang Jian and three others from Lady Huarui. The following two quatrains are at least not such blatant plagiarizations as the others.

XXXVII

All of a sudden our lord and king is in a happy mood:
The tall swings are set up amidst the hundred flowers.
The one who shows the most skill in turning and soaring
Will become the champion of this battalion of women.

XLIII

Last night the Inner Garden reported: "The flowers have opened!"
Both within and without, the arrival of His Majesty is announced.
From a distance I watch how the tumultuous crowd of young girls
All compete with each other to be the first to offer a cup of wine.

Empress Yang grew up inside the Inner Palace; her original surname is unknown and she only adopted the surname Yang later on. She is said to have been "widely read in the books and histories and well-acquainted with the affairs of past and present." Her "crafty and suspicious character" served her well in the course of her long and fierce struggle to achieve pre-eminence. She was a powerful woman who served as regent for her husband, the mentally impaired Emperor Ningzong (r. 1195–1224). She is known to have written poems (some, inscribed on paintings, have recently been identified), but neither her long biography in the *History of the Song* (*Songshi*) nor any contemporary source makes mention of her palace songs.

The silence of her contemporaries and the interval of more than two centuries between her demise and the appearance of the palace songs attributed to Empress Yang, call into question the authenticity of the first set of thirty palace lyrics published under her name by Lang Ying. Some critics have also pointed out the discrepancy between the actual position of the empress and the recurrent persona of the neglected palace lady that is the subject of most of the palace lyrics attributed to her.

Xiao Guanyin and Her Sorry Fate

The ladies of the Inner Palace at the courts of the so-called "conquest dynasties"—the Liao, the Jin, and the Yuan—also engaged in literary activities, including the composition of Chinese verse. One of the empresses of the Liao dynasty who is said to have been "skilled at poetry" was Xiao Guanyin. Her biography in the *History of the Liao* (*Liaoshi*), compiled in the early years of the Yuan dynasty, reads as follows:

Lady Xiao, the Xuanyi Empress, wife of Emperor Daozong [r. 1055–1100], was called Guanyin as a child; she was a daughter of the Military Affairs Commissioner [Xiao] Hui, a younger brother of the Qin'ai Empress. Not only was her appearance exceptional, but she was also an accomplished poet and an excellent debater. She composed her own songs and lyrics and excelled especially on the lute. During the reign period Doubled Prosperity [Chongxi, 1032–1054], when the emperor was Prince of both Yan and Zhao, he took her as his concubine, and in the first year of the reign period Pure Peace [Qingning, 1055], he gave her the name of Yide Empress.

The wife of the imperial grand-uncle Zhongyuan prided herself on her voluptuous beauty. When the empress saw her, she castigated her, saying: "A woman of a noble family should not find it necessary to go to such extremes!"

The empress was the mother of the crown prince Jun and she enjoyed the emperor's undivided favor. She loved music, and the musician Zhao Weiyi was in constant attendance at her side. In the first year of the reign period Great Force [Dakang, 1075] the palace maid Shan Deng and the entertainer Zhu Dinghe falsely accused the empress of having a relationship with Zhao Weiyi. The Military Affairs Commissioner Yelü Yixin brought the matter to the attention of the emperor, who summoned Yixin and Zhang Xiaojie in order to look into the accusation. When they had produced sufficient evidence, Weiyi and all his relatives were executed. The empress was allowed to hang herself, and her body was returned to her family [for burial].

In the first year of the reign period Strong Control [Qiantong, 1101], when her son ascended the throne, the empress was awarded the posthumous title of Xianyi Empress, and was buried together with her husband in the Qingling Tomb.

The Liao dynastic history elsewhere specifies that the empress died in 1075, but does not quote any of her writings. For that we have to wait for a much-embroidered account of the affair entitled *Burnt Pepper* (*Fenjiao lu*), said to have been written by the academician Wang Ding (d. 1106) in 1089, although it does not make its appearance until much later. Though from as early as the seventeenth century the authenticity of this account has been questioned, the eighteenth-century compilers of the catalogue of the imperial collections accepted the work at face value. According to this account, the emperor and empress grew apart after she submitted a memorial remonstrating against the emperor's hunting expeditions. After having fallen out of favor with the emperor, we are told, she tried to rekindle his love by writing the following series of ten songs:

I

I sweep the hidden hall,
Closed for so long, its gold paint darkened:
Floating threads of cobwebs and heaping piles of dust,
Rubbish and verdant moss thickly covering the steps.
I sweep the hidden hall,
Waiting for my lord's feast.

II

I clean the ivory couch,
Only in my dreams can I get to Gaotang.[2]
One half of the couch is battered and worn: that's where I sleep;
The half of the couch that's meant for You is bereft of its luster.
I clean the ivory couch,
Waiting for my lord and king.

III

I change the fragrant pillow,
One half has lost its many-hued brocade.

---

2. Gaotang is one of the names of the place where the goddess of Shamanka (Wu) Mountain shared the king of Chu's couch.

Ever since autumn arrived, I've been restlessly tossing and turning,
In addition, it has been soaked through by the tears from my eyes.
I change the fragrant pillow,
Waiting for my lord to lie down.

IV

I spread the kingfisher cover,
Ashamed by the sight of mandarin ducks in pairs.
I still remember the time when it was called "double-pleasure"
But now it covers only this lonely huddle of love-longing.
I spread the kingfisher cover,
Waiting for my lord to sleep.

V

I arrange the embroidered netting
But do not yet dare put up the golden hooks.
I take down the night-illuminating pearls at the four corners,
So they will not shine on my grief-stricken appearance.
I arrange the embroidered netting,
Waiting for my lord's gift.

VI

I fold the brocade beddings,
Layer upon layer, spread out in vain.
My only wish is that I could be the body white as jade,
I have no wish to be the one who suffers a "poor fate."
I fold the brocade beddings,
Waiting for my lord's arrival.

VII

I unroll the jeweled mat,
The flowers laugh amidst the emeralds of Han.
They laugh at me for having newly made this bed of jade,
Since ancient times a wife's joy has never outlasted the night.
I unroll the jeweled mat,
Waiting for my lord to rest.

VIII

I trim the silver lamp,
I have to make sure it shines as clearly as before!
Only when my lord comes does it glow with resplendent light,
When facing me, it burns with but a bluish flickering flame.
I trim the silver lamp,
Waiting for my lord to come.

IX

I light the incense burner
That can rescue me from my lonely despair.
Others may say that my body is completely tainted and soiled,
But its skin has been saturated by the emperor's fragrance.
I light the incense burner,
Waiting for my lord's pleasure.

X

I string the sonorous zither,
Its charming voice like that of an oriole.
Ever since I have played on its strings the melodies of the bedchamber,
They've always harmonized with the wind and rain outside the window.
I string the sonorous zither,
Waiting for my lord to listen.

Wang Ding also credits Xiao Guanyin with the following lament, which she is said to have composed just before committing suicide:

Despite a meager fortune I was greatly blessed,
  By being married into the imperial family.
I enjoyed the covering protection of august Heaven,
  And close to the sun and moon I shared in their splendor.

Entrusting myself to the smaller planets, I fixed my position,
  But suddenly I shone with the radiance of a major star.
And even though I encumbered the imperial couch,
  I committed no crime against the ancestral temple.

I only wished to be presented to the throne as one of many,
  But carried aloft by His manly virtue, I rose up to Heaven.

How could this disaster stem from my disrespect toward Him?
I was subjected to villainous slander from inside the palace.

I will lay bare my heart to show my innocence,
  Hoping for the returning light of the bright sun.
How could I, like a common woman filled with shame,
  Bring down the flying frost and strike the land?[3]

Gazing at my children, I am overcome with pity,
  Facing my companions, I feel even greater pain.
Together with the western light that is about to set,
  I will now leave these pepper-scented chambers.

Calling upon Heaven and Earth I am overcome by grief,
  Who in all eternity ever came to such an end?
But I know that once we are born, we are bound to die,
  Why then should I still cling to this one moment?

Empress Xu and the Bodhisattva Guanyin

The written works of Empress Xu (1361–1407) consist primarily of works of a moral and religiously didactic nature, including a twenty-chapter treatise entitled *Household Instructions* (*Neixun*), a twenty-chapter moral booklet entitled *Exhortations* (*Quanshan shu*), and a Buddhist sutra, which she claimed was revealed to her by none other than Guanyin, the Bodhisattva of Compassion (in Mahayana Buddhism a bodhisattva is a being who has devoted him or herself to the liberation of all sentient beings). She also sponsored the compilation of yet another instruction book for women entitled *Biographical Sketches of Women of Chastity from Ancient Times to the Present* (*Gujin lienüzhuan*), for which her husband wrote a preface (in fact, all of her three sons wrote commentaries and postscripts for her various writings). As we shall see, Empress Xu's composition, compilation, and

---

3. When Dou E was beheaded for a crime she had not committed, she prayed that her blood might stream upwards, that frost might fall in midsummer, and that the district in which she lived might be devastated by a three-year drought. The story was very popular with Yuan dynasty dramatists. Of the various known adaptations, the most famous is Guan Hanqing's *Injustice to Dou E* (*Dou E yuan*).

publication of these works, even the sutra, were to a large extent motivated by political as well as aesthetic and religious concerns.

Empress Xu was the wife of the Yongle emperor, who ascended the throne in 1402 after having disposed of his eldest brother's son, who occupied the throne in 1398 after the death of the Ming dynasty founder, and who is known to history as the Jianwen emperor. This was widely seen as an act of usurpation, which is why it is not surprising that much of the Yongle emperor's considerable administrative, military, and intellectual energies were subsequently devoted to ensuring that no one questioned the moral legitimacy of his rule. One way he did this was by claiming that his father, the Hongwu emperor, had actually intended him, rather than his nephew, to inherit the throne. His wife, Empress Xu, helped him in this quest for legitimacy by means of her writings in which she claimed a special relationship to the Hongwu emperor's Empress Ma, as is also made clear in her biography in the *Ming History* (*Mingshi*):

The Humane and Filial [Renxiao] Empress of the Yongle Emperor, Lady Xu, was the eldest daughter of the Prince of Zhongshan [Xu] Da. From her earliest years, she was chaste and quiet and because she was fond of reading, she was called the "Girl Student." When the Hongwu emperor [r. 1368–1398] heard of her sagacity and modesty, he summoned [her father] Da and said to him: "You and I have a friendship that goes back many years. In ancient times, when there was a mutual affinity between lord and subject, it was often sealed by a marriage alliance. You have a fine daughter so why don't we arrange a match for her with my son, Di [Zhu Di, the future Yongle emperor]?" Da kowtowed in gratitude.

In the ninth year of the reign period Hongwu [1376] Lady Xu became the principal wife of the Prince of Yan [the Yongle emperor before he ascended the throne]. The Empress Ma [the wife of the Hongwu emperor] loved her deeply. Lady Xu [even] followed the prince when he went to his border fiefdom. During the three-year mourning period following the death of the Filial and Compassionate Empress Ma, she ate only vegetarian food exactly as prescribed by the rites. She had committed to memory each and every one of the words of wisdom left by the Empress Ma, and never forgot any of them.

The Prince [in 1399] had raised his troops to quell the disturbances and had left the capital in order to carry out a surprise attack on Daning. Li Jinglong then availed himself of this opportunity to advance upon and surround Beiping [Beijing]. At the time, the Renzong emperor [the heir-apparent who would take over the throne in 1425] as eldest son was left in charge of the defense of Beijing, but in all matters regarding defensive preparations, he sought the advice of [his mother] the empress. Jinglong vigorously attacked the city. Because there were too few soldiers inside the city, the empress roused the wives of officers, gentry, and common people, who after having been provided with armor, climbed the ramparts in order to defend the city. In the end, the city was not taken.

When the Prince [in 1402] ascended the imperial throne [in Nanjing], Lady Xu was named empress. She said: "Every year there has been fighting and warfare in both the north and the south; both the soldiers and the common people are weary and worn. It would be fitting for them to be allowed to rest." She also said: "The wise and talented of this generation were all bequeathed by the Hongwu Emperor so it is not appropriate for you to make distinctions between the new and the old." She also said: "In the bestowal of His grace, Emperor Yao began with those closest to Him."[4] In each case, the emperor valued her suggestions and adopted them.

In the beginning, the empress's younger brother Zengshou often relayed information regarding state affairs to the Prince of Yan and for this was executed by the Jianwen emperor. When the Yongle emperor ascended the throne he wanted to confer upon him a hereditary rank, but the empress argued strongly against it. The emperor did not listen to her, and in the end awarded him the title of State-Stabilizing Duke and ordered that [Zengshou's] son Jingchang should inherit that title. When he then told the empress about this, she said: "This was not something that I wanted," and never thanked him for it. On another occasion, she said that [her two sons] the Prince of Han and the Prince of Zhao were unruly characters, and that the government would do well to choose someone from the ranks of the officials to take charge of the affairs of their princedoms.

One day, she asked [her husband]: "With whom does Your Highness decide matters of administration?" The emperor replied: "The Six Ministers manage administrative affairs and the Hanlin Academy [scholars] takes care of strategy and planning." The empress then requested that all the wives of the officials be summoned to court and gifted with items of clothing as well as money. She then instructed them saying: "How could it be that the service of a wife to her husband is limited to ensuring that he is provided with food and clothing? There should also be other ways in which she assists him. As regards the words of a friend, there are those that he follows and those that he rejects; when it comes to the words exchanged between husband and wife, they are pleasant and accommodating and easily accepted. From morning until night I wait on His

---

4. Emperor Yao is a sage emperor of hoary antiquity.

Highness, and my only concern is for the well being of the people. This is what all of you should diligently devote yourselves to as well." Basing herself on selections from the *Charter for Women* and [Ban Zhao's] *Precepts for My Daughters*, she wrote her *Household Instructions* in twenty chapters. She also arranged in classified order the notable words and worthy actions of the ancients, which she made into a book entitled *Exhortations*. All of these books were promulgated throughout the empire.

In the Seventh Month of the fifth year of the Yongle reign period, the empress fell gravely ill. Still her sole concern was to urge the emperor to love and cherish his subjects, to seek far and wide for wise and talented [officials], to treat the members of the Imperial House with gracious propriety, and not to be arrogant toward members of other families. In addition, she spoke to the heir apparent and said: "In the past, the wives of the officers of Beiping took up arms and defended the city walls on our behalf. I regret that I have not been able to accompany the emperor on one of his northern tours and reward them for their efforts." That month, on the day *yimao*, the empress passed away at the age of forty-six.

The emperor was filled with grief, and ordered great [vegetarian] feasts prepared on her behalf at the Linggu and Tianxi Monasteries. He permitted the officials to present offerings, and the Court of Imperial Entertainments supplied the sacrificial paraphernalia. On the *jiawu* day of the Tenth Month, Empress Xu was posthumously awarded with the title of Empress Humane and Filial. In the seventh year of the Yongle reign period [1409], construction began on a tomb on Mount Tianshou in Changping, and when four years later the tomb was completed the empress's body was placed inside it. This is none other than the Changling or Eternal Tomb. The emperor did not install another empress after her death. When [her son, the emperor] Renzong ascended the throne, he conferred upon her the posthumous title of Cultured Empress Humane and Filial, Compassionate and Virtuous, Sincere and Bright, Sedate and Devoted, Match for Heaven and Equal to the Sages [Renxiao Ci'i Chengming Zhuangxian Peitian Qisheng Wen Huanghou] and [ordered that] she be worshipped in the great ancestral hall.

As we can see from this biography, Empress Xu felt strongly that despite women being relegated to the inner quarters or the Inner Palace, their duties to their husbands and family members were by no means limited to making sure that their families were fed and clothed: rather, they also had important roles to play as moral advisors. In her preface to *Household Instructions*, the empress makes it clear that morality and proper behavior did not come naturally to women, but that they had to be learned. In true Chinese style, the best way to learn the proper norms of behavior was to study and, even more importantly, emulate female moral exemplars of the past. She makes a point of setting up her mother-in-law, Empress Ma, as just such an exemplar.

From my earliest years, I received instruction from my father and mother. I recited the *Book of Odes* and the *Book of Documents* and carefully attended to the duties of a daughter. Thanks to the accumulated goodness and ample blessings of my ancestors, I was fortunate to be chosen to become a member of the royal family. I served the Filial and Compassionate Empress Ma and attended her from dawn until dusk. Empress Ma taught all the wives of her sons, and was always meticulously observant of the rites and regulations. Reverently I absorbed her exemplars and norms and daily listened to her words of instruction, which I both respected and accepted and dared not in any way transgress. I have now served the present emperor [the Yongle emperor] for over thirty years, and in my management [of the royal household] have always obediently adhered to the ideals of the late empress.

I feel that, as regards my position in the Inner Palace, I must be ashamed that my virtue has been insufficient, and deplore that in my supervision of those below me, I have had nothing to contribute to the quality of the present emperor's regulation of his household, and have been unable to add in any way to the instructions of the Empress Ma.

I have often perused the historical biographies in search of wise women and chaste maidens from times past, and [have noticed] that although these women had a reputation for possessing virtuous characters, there was not a single one of them who did not become that way due to having been taught. However, in ancient times, teaching always required exemplars. When boys were eight years old, they entered the elementary school; when girls were ten years old, they listened to their mothers' instruction. The texts used in the elementary school were not handed down; only after Master Zhu [Xi, 1130–1200] of Hui'an had edited and compiled a text, did there come to be a proper text for beginning students. There is still, however, no comprehensive text designed solely for the education of girls. For generations [people] would simply use Venerable Madam Cao's *Precepts for My Daughters* from Fan Ye's *Books of the Later Han*, which has always been faulted for its brevity. There were also the so-called *Charter for Women* and *Regulations for Women* [*Nü ze*] for all of which we have only the titles. In more recent generations, an increasing number of educational books for women have begun to circulate that are made up of selections of the most important passages from the "Detailed Rites" and the "Household Rules" [sections of the *Book of Rites*], the small prefaces to the "Southern Zhou" and "Southern Shao" [sections of the] *Book of Odes*, together with various biographies.

The words of instructions provided by our Empress Ma alone surpass those of past times, and are worthy of being handed down as exemplars to the myriad of generations to come. Because I heard them often, I stored them away in my heart, and so in the winter of the second year of Yongle, I set down in writing Empress Ma's instructions, and in the course of expounding them, composed the twenty chapters of the *Household Instructions* in order to instruct the women of the Inner Palace.

Now, when it comes to attaining a state of sageliness, there is nothing more absolutely essential than nourishing one's virtuous nature in order to cultivate the self; therefore [the chapter] "Virtuous Nature" comes first, followed by "Cultivating the Self." In cultivating the self, there is nothing more urgent than being attentive to one's speech and actions; therefore, the next [chapters] are "Mindful Speech" and "Careful Action." Extending this even further, we come to the next [chapter], "Unremitting Effort" and "Constant Attentiveness." When it comes to the acquisition of long-lasting good fortune, there is nothing that surpasses the accumulation of goodness. To be able to refrain from committing any transgressions, there is nothing more important than to move toward goodness. Therefore, the next [chapters] are "Accumulating Goodness" and "Moving toward Goodness." As to all the things that are essential to the self, and from which one may take as models, one must adhere to our empress's instructions, therefore this is followed by [the chapter] "Venerating Sagely Instruction." We are selecting exemplars from the distant past, therefore the next [chapter] is "Displaying Wise Models." Regarding one's relations to one's superiors, we then have the chapters "Serving One's Parents," "Serving One's Husband," "Serving One's In-laws," and "Maintaining the Ancestral Sacrifices." And then we continue on to "Maternal Duties," "Familial Harmony," "Care for the Young," "Treatment of Servants," and finally "Treatment of Natal Relatives." Unfortunately, my words and phrases are shallow and vulgar and incapable of giving full expression to these profound principles, and its particulars are rather crude and simplistic. Readers should not get bogged down in the words, however, but should rather simply extract their meaning. In this way, these words may be of some small aid in the regulation of the inner quarters.

This preface was written on the day of the full moon of the First Month of the third year of the reign period Yongle [1405].

We see that the empress arranged the twenty chapters of the *Household Instructions* in order of importance, beginning with the basic "cultivation of a virtuous nature." She then proceeds to address the various responsibilities of a woman of the inner quarters, paramount of which were the care of one's parents and, after marriage, the care of one's husband's parents. Then follows all of the other various duties, again in order of importance. The very last chapter, after the chapter on how to deal with one's servants, is devoted to how one should treat one's own relatives, as opposed to those of one's husband. As we saw from the story in Empress Xu's biography from the *History of the Ming* of how she opposed the enfeoffment of her younger brother, the empress apparently made a point of avoiding the slightest appearance of favoritism. This is not surprising, of course, since it was precisely this sort of favoritism on the part of empresses and concubines that was traditionally said to be the cancer that ultimately brought about the fall of a dynasty. And, of course, Empress Xu's abiding concern was to help her husband validate his rule, not to undermine it. In later centuries, the *Household Instructions* was often printed together with the *Precepts for My Daughters*, the *Classic of Filiality for Women*, and the *Analects for Women* as the *Four Books for Women* (*Nü sishu*), which enjoyed wide popularity as a primer for women.

The emperor, as we see from Empress Xu's biography, was grief-stricken after her death and as part of the funeral ceremonies, "ordered great [vegetarian] feasts prepared on her behalf at the Linggu and Tianxi Monasteries." This is the only reference to Empress Xu's avid, if not purely religious, interest in Buddhism. It is curious that there is no reference in the biography to the Buddhist sutra with which she is associated, the full title of which is *The Rarest Sutra of Great Merit Spoken by the Buddha and Received by the Empress Humane and Filial of the Great Ming in a Dream* (*Da Ming Renxiao huanghou menggan Foshuo diyi xiyou dagongde jing*). Empress Xu was not the first woman, nor was she the last, to receive such texts through revelation. As we saw earlier, in the late fifth century, the young girl named Nizi or "Little Nun" was said to have revealed not one but twenty-one new sutras and later in the Ming Dynasty, the Empress Dowager Li, the mother of the Wanli emperor (r. 1573–1619), also had a sutra revealed to her in a dream. However, Empress Xu's case is unusual in that the sutra she claimed was revealed to her was, like her other didactic materials, put to the service of the moral legitimization of her husband's rule.

Before discussing this sutra, we need to take a brief look at its central figure: Guanyin, or Guanshiyin. Guanyin's original Sanskrit name is Avalokiteshvara, and her original form, inasmuch as Buddhist deities have form, was that of a male. In fact, it is as a handsome prince that Avalokiteshvara was first introduced into China. One of the characteristics of this particular bodhisattva is the ability to assume as many as thirty-three guises, including several female guises, in order to access and convey the Buddhist teachings to different sorts of people in different walks of life and stages of religious development. Although this ability was never lost, from approximately the eleventh century onward in China, there was a growing tendency to imagine and to depict this deity in female form. And, because in the Chinese tradition, everyone, even gods and divinities, should have a proper historical, biographical and, most importantly, familial context, before long there emerged a full-fledged story about the female Guanyin. This story about her life on earth as the Princess Miaoshan not only gave her parents and sisters, but also provided an explanation for the odd form in which Avalokiteshvara (and many other deities of Indian provenance) was sometimes depicted in paintings and sculpture; that is, with a thousand arms and an eye on each palm of the hands. The symbolism of this depiction is clear: as a bodhisattva of compassion dedicated to the succor of sentient beings, the more hands with which to proffer assistance, and the more eyes with which to perceive people's needs, the better.

The legend of Princess Miaoshan proved to be immensely popular and is still widely known in the Chinese world today. Like all legends, it went through modifications over the years, and can be found in many different versions, although the basic elements of the story are relatively consistent. Guanyin was popular with both men and women, but perhaps it is not surprising that women found her particularly accessible. An early version of the legend of Miaoshan, and the earliest to include her visit to hell, *The Biography of the Mahasattva Guanyin* (*Guanyin dashi zhuan*), is known to us as the work of Guan Daosheng, though it is unclear whether she actually composed the text or only wrote it out as a calligraphic exercise.

Guanyin was born in the western regions.[5] Her personal name was Miaoshan and she was the youngest daughter of King Miaozhuang. From childhood on, she abstained from meat and strong spices and adhered to the [Buddhist] precepts. She found joy in the simple and bland and was extremely intelligent. When it was time to be married, the king sought out for his three daughters sons-in-law who would come to live in the palace. His eldest daughter Miaoyin and his second daughter Miaoyuan went along with their father's wishes, but Guanyin opposed the king and as a consequence was stripped of her [royal] rank. The king supplied her with only the bare minimum of food and clothing and ordered the palace ladies to persuade her to change her mind, but she remained adamant.

In his rage the king sent her away to White Sparrow Convent, where he ordered the abbess to pressure his daughter into obedience. He threatened the abbess saying: "If you do not report back in seven days [that you have succeeded in changing her mind], all the nuns in the convent will be burned to death!" The frightened nuns put Guanyin to work as a slave, but she only became even more determined in her resolve. She worked the well and the mill all by herself and it was as if she was assisted in her labors by supernatural beings. When the frightened abbess told the king about this, he did not believe her and had the convent surrounded and set ablaze. The five hundred nuns were all burned to cinders, and no one survived except for Guanyin, who sat on her lotus seat reciting sutras, untouched by the flames.

The king then recalled her to the capital, hoping to change her mind by explaining to her [the laws of] fortune and disaster; profit and loss. But Guanyin replied saying: "Those who have grown old will never again become young, and those who have died will not come back to life again. The unceasing cycle of birth and death means unending and bitter suffering. The only reason why I, your daughter, refuse glory and riches is because I desire life eternal."

When the king heard these words, he became even angrier and ordered her to the execution ground to be decapitated. However, as soon as the sword touched [her neck] the sword spontaneously shattered into pieces. A tiger then appeared on the execution ground and, with a roar, bore her away. The king assumed that she had been devoured by the tiger.

The tiger carried Guanyin on its back to a forest located over a thousand miles away. Guanyin did not regain consciousness immediately but rather dreamed that two youths dressed in black took her on a tour of the underworld. There she was most respectfully welcomed by the divinity known as King

---

5. "The western regions" also includes the area of India.

Yama. She also witnessed the bitter sufferings of the sinners who were being sliced, burnt to ashes, or pulverized by pestle or mill, and was able to liberate them by reciting the sutras.

When she regained consciousness [back in the forest], the poisonous dragons and evil beasts of the forest vied to bite her and chase her about. Guanyin did not feel at all comfortable there, and as she was building herself a hut [for protection], an old man appeared, gave her a peach to eat, and led her to Incense Mountain. The scenery at Incense Mountain was tranquil and peaceful and untainted by even a single speck of dust. It was here that Guanyin undertook religious austerities for a number of years. People believe that this is the place where she attained insight into the Way and achieved Buddhahood.

One day, when Guanyin was meditating in her cell, she saw from a distance that the king was suffering from sores and about to die; he had issued a proclamation offering a reward of gold hoping to attract a physician [who would be able to cure him] but no one had responded to the proclamation. And so Guanyin, assuming the illusory guise of an old monk, said to the king: "Only the arms and eyes of one of your closest relatives can heal you." Assuming that his two daughters were [what was meant by] his closest relatives, he had them summoned, but neither of them was willing to put her life in jeopardy [by sacrificing their flesh].

When the king asked the monk what he should do next, the monk told him that on Incense Mountain there lived an immortal who was able to assist all sentient beings—the king would only have to say the word and he would be given what he desired [that is, the immortal's arms and eyes]. The king sent an official messenger to the immortal with his request, to which the immortal immediately acquiesced by cutting off both arms and gouging out both eyes and giving them to the envoy. The envoy took them to the monk who added them to the medicinal [broth]. As soon as the king drank it, he was healed.

The king wanted to make the monk a high official and to bestow upon him many precious gifts, but the monk refused, saying only: "The immortal has done you a great service. Tomorrow morning you must go in person and offer your thanks." The king agreed, and when his carriage was readied, he hastened there at great speed. He then saw that the immortal was covered with blood and indeed was missing both arms and both eyes.

Although overcome with grief, the king could not help but notice the striking resemblance of the immortal to Guanyin—she could be no other than his third daughter, Miaoshan! Prostrating to heaven and earth, he begged them to make her whole again and instantly, the immortal sported a thousand arms and eyes! Guanyin then stepped down and kneeling down before the king, gave expression to the [proper] feelings between father and child. Overjoyed, she urged her father to cultivate virtue. Following her advice, the king cleansed his heart and changed his ways. Guanyin then died and flew up to heaven together with the king.

Guanyin ascended to the Western Paradise where she became part of the Buddha assembly. Constantly she opens the gate [of the Buddhist teaching] to save beings from suffering; widely she points out the way to those with karmic affinity. Everywhere she perceives the sounds of the world both past and present; universally, she distinguishes the good and evil of the human realm. That is why she is called Guanshiyin [Perceiver of the Sounds of the World].

The legend of Miaoshan is primarily concerned with Guanyin's life on earth before she assumed her divine form and ascended to Heaven. Empress Xu, on the other hand, is taken in a dream for a visit to Guanyin's home territory, the Western Paradise. Central to Mahayana Buddhism, which is the form of Buddhism that ultimately took hold in East Asia, is the notion that through many lifetimes of selfless and compassionate activity, bodhisattvas can, by virtue of their accumulated merit, once they have become a full-fledged Buddha, create a "pure land," in which especially devout believers may be reborn after death and from which, it is believed, it is much easier to attain final enlightenment. These pure lands, in some ways comparable to the heavens of Christianity and Islam, are said to be of nearly inconceivable beauty: trees of gold hung with the seven precious gems—gold, silver, lapis lazuli, crystal, agate, rubies (or red pearls), and cornelian; ponds of divine nectar filled with magnificent and sweetly scented lotus blossoms, and lovely birds of all sizes and colors sweetly singing the music of the Buddha. In Mahayana Buddhism, there are many such Buddhas and many such pure lands, although in China, the Western Pure Land of the Amitabha Buddha is the one that became the most popular and the most vivid in the religious imagination of devotees. The Bodhisattva Guanyin is traditionally associated with the Amitabha Buddha and his Western Pure Land. It is to such a pure land that Empress Xu is transported in a dream and which she attempts to describe in the first part of her preface to the sutra she claims to have received during this visit. The last half of the preface relates how the empress was immediately able to use the beneficial powers of the sutra (as it happens, she "received" the sutra just before her husband embarked on his war against his nephew and the legitimate Jianwen emperor). According to the empress, Guanyin had asked her to take back the sutra with her and also assured her that others could benefit from the sutra as well if she were to have it printed and circulated widely.

In the spring of the thirty-first year of the Hongwu reign period [1398], on the first day of the First Month, I lit some incense and sat quietly inside my chambers. I was perusing some ancient sutras and classics, my mind and spirit focused and settled, when suddenly a purplish-gold radiance completely filled every corner of my room. Indistinctly, as if I were asleep and dreaming, I saw the Bodhisattva Guanyin appear from within the radiance in the form of the Great Compassionate One. Standing on her thousand-petaled jeweled lotus, she held in her hand a rosary made of the seven precious gems. She moved in front of me, and before I knew it, I was riding a kingfisher-blue cloud-vehicle, above which there opened a five-colored jeweled canopy, an array of pearly banners and precious flags inviting us to come forward. Flapping and fluttering, they waved over the distance without seeming to be rooted anywhere at all.

After a little while, we came to a towering magnificent gate the likes of which are not to be seen in the human world. Its golden placard was inscribed with the words "The Realm of Vulture Peak." On the other side of the gate were encircling clusters of deep kingfisher-green and dark purple-blue mountains, with steep and precipitous verdant cliffs and red escarpment and jagged, uneven high crags and ridges and a winding stream that encircled the mountains at their base. I followed the twists and turns of this for several tens of *li* or so. The stream's flow was so deep and pure, and its green so clear that one could see every strand of hair [in its reflection]. [There were] beautiful flowers and lovely grasses, iris and epidendrum, fully-opened lotus flowers, various kinds of peonies, tuberoses and redbuds: all as beautiful as springtime, full of sap and gleaming brightly.

The road gradually came to an end at a bridge, which I crossed over. Its steps were made of blue and gold crystal, agate and white jade, and covering the bridge was a building with several tens of columns in front: the pillars made of aloeswood; the beams of sandalwood and the variegated colors with which the walls were painted added even more to its beauty. Above hung a sign with the words "The Bridge of Wisdom" written in large gold letters. This bridge was several tens of *zhang*[6] in length and about the same in height. Crossing the bridge, I wound my way for several tens of *li*. From a distance I saw three splendidly lovely peaks, their grand and imposing shapes soaring upwards to touch the clouds and mist. Its forests of trees were dense and luxurious, their

---

6. One *zhang* is equivalent to approximately six feet.

mists and vapors dimming the sun's glare, and hidden away towers and pavilions could be glimpsed through the treetops. After traveling another several *li*, I again saw a gate, above which was inscribed in golden letters the following words: "The Principle Bodhimandala of Vulture Peak." Passing through the gate, [I found] the road completely covered with crystals, gold, coral, cornelian, and all kinds of precious jewels. There were groves of bamboo and dense trees, their leaves and branches rich and flourishing, graceful and elegant, lush and luxuriantly spreading their ample shade. There were unusual flowers and extraordinary blossoms that were dense and rich with a pungently sweet fragrance. Auspicious and lovely fruits, shining dark red and blue-purple, hung from the branches.

Peacocks, parrots, *yuan-* and *luan*-birds, and wild swans flew and danced, their calls like the tinkling of bells. In addition there were unusual birds who sang in Sanskrit, their pure rhymes sounding out in mutual harmony. By the side of the road there was a wide pond from which sprung out five-colored, seven-petaled lotus flowers. They were as large as cart wheels and from them rose the most fragrant of vapors. On the pond, there were widgeons and gulls, swans and geese, mandarin ducks, egrets and cranes, and other sorts of waterbirds, mallards, and ducks swimming about and flapping their wings.

Eventually, I came to a place halfway up the mountain where there were groups of young maidens dressed in gowns of many colors and divided into two rows. The ones in the front row held up flags and banners, while those in the back row played on pipes and drums and welcomed me with the harmonious and measured sound of Buddhist music. Blue lions and white elephants vigorously led the dance, as young boys went back and forth with offerings in golden trays and colorful baskets.

I ascended the mountain and arrived at the summit where I followed Guanshiyin up to the seven-jeweled lotus platform. Atop this platform were majestic and splendid palaces and halls with deep and hidden corridors and passageways, as well as ten thousand buildings and a thousand gates of multistoried towers and pavilions. Their golds and jade-greens gleamed brightly and their ornate colors were fresh and beautiful, as were their carved roof-tiles, embroidered doors, pearl archways, and carved pillars. Their jewel-like windows softly glowed, their precious nettings were clear and transparent, and the railings of the balconies and the foundations of the pillars were all covered with masses of gems. [There were] lovely adornments fashioned from all kinds of jeweled flowers, flags and banners with fancy tassels, jades and pearls in dazzling disarray; masses of delicate heavenly flowers would suddenly fall, and then just as suddenly flutter about, their extraordinary scent refined and subtle, their fragrant vapors spreading and brimming over. The jeweled radiance became concentrated, and its brilliance transmuted into a million different hues. Over the distance, a vast expanse of sky stretched out without boundaries, while below, one could see an array of lovely mountain landscapes.

Gazing at these wondrous marvels, I sighed that there had never before been anything like it and then thought to myself: "My virtue has always been meager and paltry: what sort of positive karmic conditions could I have possibly accumulated that would have enabled me to come to this place?" Guanshiyin smiled and said: "This is the bodhimandala where the Buddha has preached throughout as many kalpas as there are sands in the River Ganges. None can come up to this place unless they have a karmic affinity with the Way of the Buddha. Your Highness, with the virtuous disposition, perfected goodness, and wisdom gained in a previous lifetime, has marvelously achieved the true realization. Because you are about to meet up with great difficulties, I have especially brought you here in order to liberate you from your worldly troubles. *The Rarest Sutra of Great Merit Spoken by the Buddha* is the crown of all of the sutras, and has the power to put an end to the miseries suffered by sentient beings. If one assiduously recites it for a full year, single-mindedly and diligently, one will be able to attain the fruit of 'stream-enterer'; if for two years, one will obtain the fruit of a 'once-returner'; if for three years, one will obtain the fruit of 'non-returner'; if for four years, one will obtain the fruit of 'arhatship'; if for five years, one will attain the fruit of the Bodhisattva path; and if for six years, one will attain the fruit of Buddhahood.[7] Because the religious merit of the people of the world has been so paltry, many kalpas have passed without them having heard of this sutra. Your Highness will in the future be the mother of all under Heaven, a deep and capacious vessel of merit, with a perfected and completed enlightened nature. Thus you are marvelously worthy of being entrusted [with this sutra] with which all living beings may be raised up and rescued."

Then, Guanshiyin lifted up her pure vase filled with the dew of compassion and sprinkled the dew over my head. All I knew is that my mind and body felt cleansed and purified, and my ten thousand cares had all disappeared and I was able to remember and completely understand everything without forgetting. She then produced a scroll of scripture, which she ordered me to repeat after her.

---

7. A "stream-enterer" has entered the stream of enlightenment and is assured eventual enlightenment. A "once-returner" is someone who will be reborn only one more time, after which he or she is assured of achieving enlightenment. A "non-returner" is someone who will achieve enlightenment in this life. An arhat is a person who has attained enlightenment, although unlike the bodhisattva, he or she does not take the vow to return to the world and aid all sentient beings to achieve liberation.

This was none other than the *The Rarest Sutra of Great Merit*. The first time I recited it, I roughly understood its overall meaning; the second time, I fully comprehended it and became enlightened; and by the third time I recited it, I had flawlessly committed it to memory. Guanshiyin said: "We will meet again ten years from now." She seemed about to say something more to me but when I leaned forward to listen, I suddenly heard the sounds of the palace women and was startled awake.

I felt both overjoyed and filled with wonder. Trembling, I sighed and said: "This was indeed a divine dream!" Quickly I fetched brush and paper and wrote down the sutra and the *dharanis* that I had received, without omitting a single word. I was aware only of an unusual flavor in my mouth and fragrant vapors and mists that lingered in my chambers for seven days without dispersing. The heavens rained down flowers for three days and then stopped, and from that moment onwards, I assiduously recited this sutra day and night without ceasing.

In the autumn of the thirty-second year [1399] the dynasty was indeed endangered, and His Imperial Majesty raised his troops and left on a defensive campaign. In the city itself we were also repeatedly threatened by dangers and difficulties. I steadfastly recited this sutra, which buoyed our energy and freed us from fear. The emperor, assisted by Heaven and Earth, and with the help of the gods and spirits, under the protective cover of the flourishing virtue and great blessings of the late founding emperor, and the late Filial and Compassionate Empress, in the thirty-fifth year [1402] pacified and quelled the disastrous calamities, brought peace to the ancestral temples, and inherited the imperial succession. I accordingly became empress of the realm.

With my meager virtue and limited capabilities, I clearly would not be able to be of any great assistance. However, each and every word and line of *The Rarest Sutra of Great Merit Spoken by the Buddha* revealed to me in my dream was one of true principle, unimaginable subtlety, and marvelous significance. For so many kalpas people had not yet had the chance to hear it. The Buddha saves and liberates out of compassionate benevolence: for the manifestation of the hidden karmic causes one must await the appropriate time. Among the mysterious words of the three treasures and the twelve sections [of the Buddhist canon] there are none that cannot dispel the many delusions and spread the true teaching.

Now I do not dare keep [this sutra] secretly to myself and so I am having it carved, printed, and distributed widely so that it may serve as a ford or bridge by which people may be freed of suffering, a shortcut to the road to enlightenment. It will serve as a wide-reaching and greatly skillful means of benefit to the world. Now, the Way does not distance itself from people, it is people who distance themselves from the Way. If those who aspire to study Buddhism are sincere, they will be able to find in this sutra the ultimate marvelous principle: they will then fully understand the myriad dharmas and become enlightened as to the true vehicle. In an instant, they will achieve the supreme wisdom, in the snap of a finger they will achieve Nirvana, and liberating themselves from the mundane world, they will attain true enlightenment. I am now writing this preface so as to assist and support its dissemination, and cause it to be spread, so that the marvelous Way may continue forever.

Written on the eighth day of the First Month of the first year of the reign period Yongle [1403].

The sutra itself is in two chapters. The first chapter talks about central Mahayana Buddhist notions such as the idea that the mind, or nature, of the Buddha is in essence no different from that of you and me, it is simply that we do not realize this identity and as a result undergo untold sufferings. The empress's formulation of these ideas is by no means original, and makes ready use of language and imagery found in other, rather more legitimate Buddhist sutras that were popular among monks and literati of the period. The second chapter is twice as long as the first, and consists primarily of numerous *dharanis*, powerful chants which, if recited with faith and persistence, will save one from all manner of dangers— including death by fire or water, poisons, and wild beasts. Such recitations were also said to bring such blessings as a male heir, deliverance from hell, and in general, countless blessings and virtues. It is this second part that was clearly the most important part of the sutra, since it offered its readers not just ideas, but rather something tangible that could be done to ease the inevitable sufferings of life. As Empress Xu tells us in her preface, she herself found the recitation of her sutra to be most invaluable during the dangerous times when her husband was making a bid for the throne. Reciting the sutra, she claimed, helped them not only to endure but, ultimately, to triumph.

Nuns

Our first introduction to Buddhist nuns in China was through the *Biographies of Bhiksunis*, compiled in 516 by the monk Baochang at the court of the Liang dynasty. Baochang's sixty-five hagiographical sketches of nuns of the fourth and fifth centuries provide an interesting glimpse into the lives of women who entered the religious life, often in defiance of their parents. We also saw that, although some of these nuns gained fame as preachers, and most, given their elite backgrounds, were fairly literate, Baochang makes very little reference to their writings. This neglect of the writings of nuns appears to have been common through the following dynasties as well: it is not really until the seventeenth century that we see significant extant collections of writing by Buddhist nuns. It is difficult to say, however, whether this was because these nuns were not writing or because their writings were simply not being preserved. In any case, we do know that there were nuns during the Song dynasty who were well known for their religious as well as their literary achievements.

Chan Buddhism and Women

Many of these Song nuns belonged to the school of Chinese Buddhism known as Chan, which in the West is more commonly known by its Japanese pronunciation, Zen. The word Chan is actually the Chinese pronunciation of the Sanskrit word *dhyana*, which means "meditation," and the school is known for its emphasis on the experience of meditation—the meditation by means of which the Buddha was said to have found enlightenment under the Bodhi tree. This experience was considered to be ultimately beyond language and words altogether. Thus, the Chan tradition traces its beginnings to a story about the Buddha who one day as he was preaching to the multitudes, suddenly fell silent and then wordlessly held up a white flower. All of the audience were puzzled by this and did not know what to think—except for one of the Buddha's senior disciples, Mahakashyapa, who, when he saw the flower, broke into a smile, indicating that he had understood the Buddha's "mind-to-mind transmission."

The Tang dynasty is generally considered to be the golden age of Chan Buddhism, and it is during this period that we find the names of many of the great iconoclastic Zen masters such as Nanchuan Puyuan [745–835], who held the monastery cat in his arms and threatened to cut it in half if his students did not respond quickly to his spiritually probing questions, and his famous disciple Zhaozhou [778–897], who in response to a question posed to him by a student, simply placed his sandals on his head and walked out of the room. The point of these seemingly mad, and often quite violent, actions was to shake the complacent spiritual seeker out of his or her conventional, rational, and inevitably, dualistic, ways of thinking and thus break into a higher, intuitive realization of the Buddhist truth of non-duality.

The Tang masters used a variety of techniques to "wake up" their students [the word "Buddha" actually means the "Awakened One"], including shouts, hand motions, and beatings with a stick. They also used language, often very paradoxical language, designed to put students into a mental bind from which they could emerge only by trying to make sense of the words in a way that was neither nonsense nor commonsense, but something beyond both. Poetry also served as a means by which masters could convey their sometimes ineffable teachings, and students used it to demonstrate their understanding. Much of this poetry made use of traditional Chinese imagery, especially nature imagery, although it was given a Buddhist metaphysical twist, often imperceptible to the untrained, or rather unenlightened eye.

Part of the Chan Buddhist problem with language is that it tended to keep people rooted in duality—existence and non-existence, good and bad, right and wrong—and it is this duality that Chan Buddhists regarded as the root of all human suffering. Perhaps one of the most important of such dualities is, of course, that between male and female, and here too, the Chan Buddhists employed what Miriam Levering has called a "rhetoric of equality," which affirmed that the ultimate truth was to be found beyond all dualities, including that of gender. Thus there exists a number of well-known Chan stories that illustrate this. One of the most famous of these is from the *Lotus Sutra*, an Indian Buddhist scripture, which (in Chinese translation) became one of the most popular of all Buddhist scriptures in China. This is the story of the daughter of the dragon king who, when she hears the Bodhisattva Manjusri preach the *Lotus Sutra*, attains immediate, and supreme, enlightenment. Later, another of the Buddha's eminent disciples, Sariputra, questions how it could be that a person could attain enlightenment so quickly when it took the Buddha many lifetimes, and more importantly, how could this person be a woman, since women were supposedly subject to the five hindrances, the last of which specifically stated that a woman could not become a Buddha. The dragon king's daughter replies not in words, but in action: she quickly turns herself into a man, thus demonstrating that her spiritual insight has endowed her with the ability to determine her own gender, since she has transcended both.

One would think that there would be a great number of accounts of historical women who, taking inspiration from this story, devoted themselves to the search for enlightenment. In fact, even though there were many Buddhist nuns during the Tang dynasty, only a very few of them belonged to the Chan school, and even fewer were known as Chan masters. It is not until the thirteenth century when we finally start to see significant mention of women practicing and teaching Chan. This change came about only because of one very enlightened male Chan master who openly acknowledged his female disciples' achievements.

There are, however, a few references to women embedded in the many stories of the Tang masters: women such as Liu Tiemo, or Iron-Grinder Liu, whose nickname gives some indication of her powerful charisma, and Moshan Liaoran, who became famous for the "dharma battle" in which she bested the arrogant monk Guanqi Zhixian who, in admiration of her insight, became a gardener at her convent for three years. In this dialogue Moshan tries to get Guanqi Zhixian to understand that there is no essential, unchanging essence that one can call "man" or "woman."

For the first time [Zhixian] bowed and said, "What is Moshan [Summit Mountain] like?"
    She replied: "It does not expose its peak."
    He asked: "What is the owner of Summit Mountain like?"
    She replied: "It does not have male or female appearance."
    He then gave a shout and asked, "Why doesn't it transform itself?"
    She replied: "It is not a god and it is not a ghost: What should it transform itself into?"
    With this he admitted defeat and worked as a gardener [in her temple] for three years.

Moshan Liaoran is the only nun who has a record of her own in the *The Jingde Period Record of the Transmission of the Lamp* (*Jingde chuandeng lu*), a collection of biographical accounts of monks of the Chan Buddhist lineage compiled in 1004.

From the Song dynasty onwards, Chan Buddhism, although it prided itself on being a form of Buddhism that "did not rely on words," in fact, produced an immense amount of religious literature. This literature included collections of *gong'an* (in Western literature more commonly referred to by its Japanese pronunciation, *koan*; the recorded exchanges between the great Chan masters and their interlocutors), Chan lineage histories, and hagiographical accounts of the lives of the masters. Of the latter, the first of these, entitled the *Collection from the Halls of the Founders* (*Zutang ji*), was compiled in 952, and the second, the *The Jingde Period Record of the Transmission of the Lamp*, appeared in 1004. These were followed by many other compilations of the same kind.

We know from various sources that there was a significant number of Buddhist nuns during the Song period: in 1021, for example, there were nearly 61,240 nuns, or about 13 percent of the entire monastic population at that time. One would expect then, that the numerous compendia of biographies and recorded sayings would reflect somewhat the role played by these nuns in the religious and literary life of their times. The male compilers of these collections were quite slow, however, to include female monastics: it is in a compendium titled *Outline of Linked Lamps* (*Liandeng huiyao*) compiled in 1183 that we first find several bona fide biographical entries for female Chan masters. *The Jiadai Universal Record of the Lamps* (*Jiadai pudenglu*), compiled in 1204, contains fifteen such biographical accounts, out of a total of more than one thousand. But despite the small numbers, these entries do show that male Chan masters were beginning to fully acknowledge the ability of women not only to engage in spiritual practice and to be considered exemplars of morality and piety, but also to serve as teachers—women who would ascend the platform in the dharma halls to deliver sermons, would take disciples, and would pass on the dharma lineage, whether orally or in writing.

Miaodao, Miaozong, and Other Female Disciples of Chan Master Dahui Zonggao

The male Chan master credited with legitimizing women's participation in the "public" sphere of Chan religious life was the famous Linji Chan Master Dahui Zonggao (1089–1163), and his female disciples Miaodao and Miaozong are considered to be the most outstanding women of the time. Both of these women came from upper-class scholarly families.

Miaodao was a native of Yanping, located in present-day Fujian province. She was the daughter of Huang Shang (1044–1130), who was the top graduate of the metropolitan exams of 1082 and subsequently held a number of high official posts, including that of head of the Ministry of Rites. Her biography in the *Jiadai Universal Record* tells us that from childhood onwards, she showed such a strong and determined predilection for the religious life that when she reached the age of twenty, her father allowed her to enter the monastic life. After becoming a nun, she studied with several eminent Chan teachers, and in 1134, met with the man who was to become her principle teacher, Dahui Zonggao. Dahui, who himself was just coming into his own as one of the most effective and forceful teachers of this period, took Miaodao under his wing and provided her with the guidance and instruction she needed to achieve the spiritual breakthrough she longed for. Later Dahui would often recount the story of Miaodao's struggles and her subsequent enlightenment to his other students. In one of these accounts he describes Miaodao's first enlightenment experience, which took place during an intensive retreat in the summer of 1134.

At that time it was as hot as a furnace. There were only seventy or so monks and they came to my quarters [for private interviews] twice a day. I instructed Miaodao to investigate [the phrase]: "It is neither the mind, nor the Buddha, nor a thing."

On one occasion, the monastery librarian Kuang came into my quarters. Miaodao was outside and [when she] overheard [our conversation] she experienced a flash of joy. Then one day she suddenly said to me: "Not long ago when I heard you speak with Monastery Librarian Kuang about [the phrase]: 'It is neither the mind, nor the Buddha, nor a thing; I realized I already understood [what you meant]." Then I asked her: "'It is neither the mind, nor Buddha, nor a thing.' In what way do you understand [what this means]?" She answered: "This is just the way I understand it." Before she had finished speaking, I gave a shout and then said: "That is one too many 'This is just the way I understand it.'" Then, for the first time, she caught a glimpse [of the truth].

After her enlightenment experience had been verified by Master Dahui, Miaodao began teaching herself. There is little information about this period of her life, although we do know that she was the abbess of several nunneries, the first in her hometown of Yanping, and the next two, the Zisheng Nunnery and the Jingju Nunnery, in Zhejiang province. Her accomplishments as a teacher are reflected in the name by which she was known during her lifetime and afterwards: Dingguang dashi, Great Teacher Radiance of Concentrated Meditation. She appears to have had a great many students, although the official Chan genealogical histories do not provide any names of dharma heirs. However, her biographical accounts in these same histories do provide a few examples of her sermons and dialogues, which are, as one scholar puts it, "elegant, polished, and literary." Here is one of these sermons:

"Chan is not a matter of concepts and thoughts. To set up concepts is to deviate from the teaching. As for speaking of great merit: to establish merit is to miss the point. Listen to the phrases beyond the pure sounds and do not seek [to apprehend the truth] in concept. Turn the receiving and responding power of the teacher around and get it into your own hands, grab the cudgel and tongs away from the Buddhas and patriarchs and control them yourselves. Where there is Buddha, host and guest are interchangeable. Where there is no Buddha, the winds sough and sigh. The sort of person whose mind and thoughts are at peace, whose echoes and sounds are in harmony—tell me, where would this person settle down?" After a while, Miaodao added: "Throwing on my raincoat, my rainhat askew, beyond a thousand peaks, I draw water and sprinkle the vegetables in front of the Five Stars."

Miaozong (1095–1170) was the granddaughter of the prime minister Su Song (1020–1101), and before becoming a nun had been married to a scholar-official by the name of Xu Shouyuan. Coming as she did from an upper-class family, Miaozong was highly educated and appears to have had an impressive command of Buddhist literature as well as the Confucian classics and Daoist texts. She was particularly well known for the latter. Although unfortunately no longer extant, there appears to have been a *yulu* or "discourse record" for Miaozong, which may well have been printed and circulated during her own lifetime. Such discourse records included accounts of a master's exchanges with his or her own disciples, sermons, hymns, letters, and poetry, both religious and secular.

Miaozong's best-known poems were in the form of poetic responses to well-known *gong'an*, a literary tradition made famous by the Chan Master Xuedou Chongxian (998–1052), who compiled a collection of a hundred *gong'an* to each of which he appended a commentary in verse, designed to further challenge rather than elucidate. In the twelfth century, the students of another Chan monk, Yuanwu Keqin (1063–1135)—who was the teacher of Dahui Zonggao—took Xuedou's *gong'an* and verses, added their own teacher's commentaries, and thus produced the famous book known today as the *Blue Cliff Record* (*Biyan lu*). Miaozong continued this tradition by writing her own quatrains on selected *gong'an*. A Yuan dynasty collection, stored in a library in Japan, contains forty-three of these quatrains, and these same forty-three verses can also be found in a collection of poetic commentaries to *gong'an* by two seventeenth-century Chan Buddhist abbesses, Baochi Jizong and Zukui Jifu, proving the continued popularity of Miaozong's verses in the milieu of Chan nuns. The latter collection, entitled *The Harmonious Echoes Collection of Poems about Ancient [Cases]* (*Songgu hexiang ji*), presents forty-three relatively famous *gong'an*, some of them quite extensive, others only a sentence or two in length. Each story is followed by a quatrain by Miaozong, Baochi Jizong, and Zukui Jifu.

Perhaps the most well-known example of these poetic commentaries composed by Miaozong is her poetic response to the following story involving the Tang dynasty Chan Master Yantou Quanhuo (828–887). The story is as follows:

When Yantou was in Shatai, he was a ferryman at Ezhu Lake. On each side of the lake he hung a board. When someone wanted to cross, he or she would knock on the board and Yantou would call out, "Who is it?" or "To which side do you want to cross over?" Then he would ply his oars and go to meet them. One day, it so happened that an old woman appeared carrying a child in her arms and said: "Ply your oars and make them dance. And since you don't ask, then tell me where this child I have in my arms came from?" Yantou then struck her. The old woman said: "I have given birth to seven children: six of them did not get the tune; and this one I have no need for either." She then threw it into the water.

This rather cryptic, and somewhat horrifying, story is clearly meant to be read metaphorically and understood intuitively. It may help to keep in mind that in Buddhist thought, the sufferings of life and death, or samsara, are often compared to a river, and the Buddhist teachings to a raft with which to cross this river. The ferryman, therefore, would be someone who helps others cross the river of suffering and attain enlightenment. In Chan literature, old women are often actually quite wise, and serve to test those who call themselves Chan masters. In this story, the children may possibly refers to the illusions created by the six sense perceptions, which Chinese Buddhism often refer to as the six thieves; Confucianism talks about the seven emotions. In both cases, they refer to attachments that keep people in a state of delusion. Thus Yantou's response to her question, which is not a verbal one, seems to both answer the old woman's query and also allow her to get rid of her last illusion and attain enlightenment.

Miaozong's poetic response to this story, not surprisingly given her interest in Daoism, makes use of the famous story in the *Zhuangzi*, which gathers the teachings of the Daoist philosopher Zhuang Zhou (369–286 BCE), in which the master, upon waking from a dream of a butterfly, wonders if he was a man dreaming he was a butterfly or whether he is now a butterfly dreaming that he is a man. The central hypothesis, that maybe the self as we mentally conceive of it may not be what we think it is, is the same as the point of the *gong'an* quoted above. Miaozong's quatrain on this *gong'an* reads:

> A leaf of a boat drifts across a vast stretch of water;
> His oars plying and dancing, he distinguishes between "do" and "re."
> Clouds over the mountains, moon in the sea: all tossed away,
> And by so doing, Zhuang Zhou's butterfly dream goes on and on.

The enigmatic quality of this type of verse, unfortunately, does not invite translation, and so we limit ourselves to this single example.

Another sign of the appreciation by Miaozong's teacher, Master Dahui, of women's religious activities is the admiration he expressed for the writings of a nun by the name of Daoren Mingshi (also known as Benming). He found her poetry quite exemplary and brought it to the attention of his students. In 1140, Daoren Mingshi wrote a series of verses, which so impressed an eminent male Chan teacher that, after her death, he published them together with a laudatory colophon of his own. Mingshi's verses read:

> Don't you know that afflictions are nothing more than wisdom,
> But to cling to your afflictions is nothing more than foolishness?
> As they rise and then melt away again, you must remember this:
> The sparrow hawk flies through Silla without anyone noticing! [8]

---

8. Silla is the name of an early kingdom in what is today Korea (57 BCE–935 CE). The kingdom reached its cultural apogee in the ninth century, also a time when Buddhism

Don't you know that afflictions are nothing more than wisdom,
And that the purest of blossoms emerge from the mire?[9]
If someone were to come ask me what it is I do:
After eating my gruel and rice, I wash my bowl.[10]

Don't worry about a thing!
Don't worry about a thing!
You may play all day like a silly child in the sand by the sea: [11]
But you must always realize the truth of your original face![12]
If you suffer the blows delivered by the patriarchs' staff—
If you can't say anything, you will perish by the staff!
If you can say something, you will perish by the staff!
In the end, what will you do
If you are forbidden to travel by night but must arrive by dawn?[13]

Dahui also expressed his admiration for the poetry of the nun Zhenru. As a young girl she had been inducted into the Inner Palace because of her considerable talents and abilities, and there she became an attendant to a certain Concubine Qiao. Concubine Qiao was herself a Buddhist devotee, and so did not put up any resistance when Zhenru expressed a desire to leave the palace and study with Dahui Zonggao, who at the time

---

flourished there. The image of a sparrow hawk flying through Silla is used in Chan Buddhist texts to refer to the swift and sudden manner in which an opportunity for enlightenment may present itself and, if the disciple is not sufficiently alert, be lost.

9. The reference here is to the lotus flower.

10. This refers to a famous exchange found in the discourses of Zhaozhou. A monk comes to the master for an interview and asks the question: "What is my self?" Zhaozhou replies with a more down-to-earth question: "Have you had your breakfast yet?" When the monk replies in the affirmative, Zhaozhou says simply, "Then go wash out your bowl."

11. In the famous chapter of the *Lotus Sutra* entitled "Expedient [or Skillful] Means," we find the following lines: "Even if little boys at play / Should collect sand to make a Buddha tower, / Then persons such as these / Have all attained the Buddha way."

12. One true original face is one of the many Zen metaphors for one's original Buddha-nature. To know one's original face is to experience enlightenment.

13. During the Song dynasty, it was forbidden to travel by night. The paradox of not traveling by night and yet still arriving at dawn is one that is often found in Chan Buddhist texts. The last lines of these poems describe the psychic and spiritual double-bind confronted by a student struggling with seeming paradoxes of this kind.

was living and teaching in exile in the south. One of her poems is the following:

> Suddenly I find myself upside-down on level ground:
> When I pick myself up, there's nothing I can say!
> If someone should ask me what this is all about,
> Smiling, I'd point to the pure breeze and bright moon.

Other Writing Nuns

Miaozong's sister-in-law also became a nun and became renowned for her spiritual accomplishments. Known as Woman of Dao Kongshi (Empty Room) and later as Chan Master Zhitong Weijiu, she was the daughter of Fan Xun, an archivist in the imperial Dragon Diagram Hall, and was briefly married to Prime Minister Su Song's grandson, Su Ti. Shortly after her marriage she became weary of worldly ways, and returned home to ask for permission to become a nun. When her father objected, she stayed home and engaged in religious practice on her own. After her parents passed away, she accompanied her brother, Fan Zhuan, to his official post in Jiangxi province where she met the eminent Chan Master Sixin (Deadened Mind) Wuxin (1044–1115), one of the four great Chan masters of the Song dynasty. The following is a record of the dharma dialogue they are said to have exchanged. It is an exchange filled with paradox, allusions, and symbolism, and is meant to be expressive of the notion of a non-dual "emptiness" that cannot be understood with the limited rational mind, which must be "deadened" or transcended in order to achieve a more authentic intuitive realization of truth (*prajna*).

Master Sixin, knowing of Kongshi's accomplishments, asked her: "The Sadprarudhita Bodhisattva[14] sold off his heart and liver—who could have taught him this intuitive wisdom [*prajna*]?"

---

14. One of the twenty-seven bodhisattvas named in the *Great Prajnaparamita Sutra*. It is said that his name, which means "always weeping" (*changdi*), derives from the fact that he weeps at the sight of the sufferings of sentient beings. Another story says that for the benefit of sentient beings, he once wept for seven days and seven nights without stopping. Yet another story says that when he was young, he was always crying, which is why he got this name. He was known for his determined cultivation of Buddhist wisdom and dreamt that in the east there was a practitioner of the Prajnaparamita. He trav-

"If you are of no-mind [*wuxin*] then I, too, will stop," Kongshi replied.

Master Sixin then asked: "Although moistened by a single rain,[15] the root and the shoot are different: on a piece of land where there is neither sun nor shade, what can be grown?"

"A single flower with five petals,"[16] Kongshi replied.

Master Sixin then asked: "Where do you settle yourself during the twenty-four hours of the day?"[17]

"The Master is good at borrowing [other people's] eyebrows!"

Master Sixin hit her and said: "This woman is making a mess of the sequence of things."

She respectfully bowed. Since Kongshi had derived some insight from his words, she sought to express her appreciation by means of the following *gatha*.

> Fine and flourishing, his deadened mind,
> The numinous source is very deep!
> In his ears, he sees the colors,
> In his eyes, he hears the sounds.
> The commoner is illumined, the sages ignorant,
> The one behind is rich, the one in front poor.
> Benefiting beings and liberating creatures,
> Taking a drop of mud and turning it into gold.
> Reds and blues cannot duplicate his image,
> Which is neither of the past nor the present.

Master Sixin probed her understanding with the following:

> The deadened mind is not the true [form],
> So what is it you are praising?
> If you praised the deadened mind,
> The deadened mind has no form.
> If you praised the empty void,

---

eled east undergoing many hardships along the way, including having to sell off his body parts.

15. A reference to the rain of the Buddhist teaching that falls on all alike, although each person benefits from it differently according to their individual karmic propensities.

16. A reference to the five schools of Chan or Zen Buddhism that developed after the Sixth Patriarch, Huineng.

17. Literally, the twelve hours: the Chinese divide the day into twelve sections of two hours each.

The empty void leaves no traces.
Without form and without traces,
What words can you find for them?
If you can find the words,
Then you will have seen the deadened mind for yourself!

She responded saying:

The deadened mind is not the true [form];
The true form is not the deadened mind.
The empty void has no form,
The Marvelous has no shape.
After it is over, then it is born again,
And you will see the deadened mind for yourself.

Master Sixin nodded his head in approval and he wrote the following *gatha* to present to her:

Empty, empty, room, room: emptiness is not empty:
The empty place that is not empty realizes the true emptiness.
Mixing it up with the dusty world that is not the dusty world,
It is only within the dusty world that is not the same as the dust.

When Zhitong Weijiu was still a layperson and living in Jinling (present-day Nanjing), she had a bathhouse built at the Baoning Monastery and wrote a poem that was inscribed on a placard over the entrance. In this poem she plays on the Mahayana Buddhist notions of non-duality (which declares that the distinction between purity and defilement is relative rather than absolute), on the belief that there is an intrinsic Buddha-nature in all sentient beings that has been pure from the beginning and has never been stained, and finally, on the belief that despite the absolute distinctions, one must still keep oneself clean through religious practice and good actions in everyday life.

Since there is nothing that exists,
What are you bathing?

If there is even a speck of dust,
From where does it arise?

If you produce a single profound phrase,
Then everyone can come in and bathe.

The most the ancient holy ones can do is scrub your back:
When has a bodhisattva ever illuminated anyone's mind?
If you want to realize the stage beyond impurity,[18]
You should sweat from every last pore of your body.
 It is said that water is able to wash away impurities;
But how do you know that the water is not also dirty?
Even if you erase the distinction between water and dirt,
When you come in here, you must still be sure to bathe![19]

Zhitong Weijiu is also known to have composed a work, no longer extant, entitled *Record of Mind Illumination* (*Mingxin lu*), which was published along with a preface and several verses by several eminent male Chan Buddhist masters of the time.

Zhitong Weijiu was not the only Song dynasty nun whose writings were printed during her lifetime or shortly after her death. We know, for example, of the existence of a collection of discourse records for the nun Huiguang (Jingzhi dashi) from Chengdu, whose uncle was the writer Fan Zuyu (1041–1098), a Confucian scholar-official known for his book *The Mirror of the Tang* (*Tang jian*), a concise history of the Tang dynasty. Huiguang was known for her erudition and eloquence, and in 1121 was appointed abbess of the Miraculous Wisdom (Miaohui) Convent in the capital Bianjing (Kaifeng) by the Emperor Huizong, who greatly admired her learning. The famous Song poet Lu You, who wrote a piece in her honor, mentions having visited the nun's burial site on West Mountain in Yuzhang in 1165, and then, several years later in 1172, coming across a collection of her writings in Chengdu—writings he found to be truly extraordinary. In fact, he goes so far as to compare their overall tone and spirit to the poetry of the great Song writer, Fan Zhen (1008–1088). Unfortunately, none of her writings remains extant today.

In the case of many other nuns, all that remains is a handful of poems. One such example is lady Ye, a granddaughter of the high official Guo Sanyi (active ca. 1100). After she became a widow at a young age, she en-

---

18. Literally, the second of the ten bodhisattva stages or bhumis, characterized by a transcendence of all passion and impurity.

19. The story of the bathing bodhisattvas originally comes from the *Surangama Sutra*. Later it was used as a koan and can be found in collections of koan such as *The Blue Cliff Record*.

tered a convent that had been built for her by her family, the Dharma Cloud Cloister in Songjiang prefecture (present-day Shanghai), and adopted the religious name of Zhengjue. Although almost none of it survives, she was quite famous for her poetry, of which the following quatrain is an example:

> A spring morning on the lake: wind and rain—
> Worldly matters like flowers fall and blossom again.
> Retire to meditate behind closed doors: a place of true joy.
> The leisurely clouds come and then go the whole day long.

Courtesans and Actresses

Courtesans were a very visible presence in urban China throughout the Song, Yuan, and Ming dynasties, but few of them distinguished themselves by their writings. We have to wait until the final decades of the Ming (and a later chapter) before we see these courtesans once again playing a major role in the development of women's literature. During the period from the tenth to sixteenth centuries, courtesans were primarily noted as performers, rather than writers, of lyrics, and later of arias, and if a courtesan is occasionally listed as an author, it is usually only of a single poem, lyric, or letter. For example, an unnamed Song dynasty courtesan from Sichuan is credited with the following song lyric, addressed to a patron who had made her promises that he was not keeping:

To the Melody of "Magpie Bridge Immortals" (*Queqiaoxian*)

> You swore an oath, proclaimed a vow,
> Spoke of your love, declared your affection:
> Time and again, spring sorrow filled your letters.
> You must have learned to recite the *Sutra of Deceit*—
> Which Master could have taught you that?
>
> I don't drink any tea, I don't eat any rice,
> I don't open my mouth, don't say a word
> And because of all this, I've wasted away.
> I've never learned to be an expert in love longing—
> I haven't got the time to curse you out!

Courtesan, Poet, and Philosopher: Wen Wan

The most egregious exception to the general rule that few Song courtesans were active as writers is the case of Wen Wan of the second half of the eleventh century. She is not only credited with an extensive collection of five hundred poems (now lost), but also, interestingly enough, with a commentary on the *Mencius*, entitled *The Meaning of Mencius Explained* (*Mengzi jieyi*; also lost). The story of Wen Wan's life is told in *Anecdotes from Gantang* (*Gantang yishi*) by an author writing under the pseudonym of "Master of Pure Vacuity," and thirty poems said to be hers are quoted in a sequel to that tale entitled *Postface to Anecdotes from Gantang* (*Gantang yishi houxu*) by the otherwise unknown Cai Zichun. The modern compilers of the *Complete Poems of the Song Dynasty* (*Quan Song shi*) have not included Wen Wan and her works, undoubtedly because they considered both her and her work to be fictional creations. Nevertheless, Su Zhecong, an eminent authority in the field of Chinese women's literature, has written extensively on Wen Wan and her poetry. Nor is she alone among contemporary scholars in believing that *Anecdotes of Gantang* deals with a "real person and real facts."

Wen Wan's mother is described in our sources as an official's wife who, following the death of her husband, becomes a prostitute in Shaanzhou. Wen Wan is raised by her mother's younger sister and her husband in Fengxiang. Dressed as a boy she attends school and soon impresses all around her by her precocious talents. When she is about to be married, however, her mother reclaims her and takes her back to Shaanzhou, where Wen Wan eventually also becomes a courtesan. She soon becomes the local prefect's favorite hostess at the parties he throws for visiting officials, and he writes a poem for her that ends with the lines: "If women were allowed to take part in the examinations, / You would be Shaanzhou's first woman 'top graduate.'" Wen Wan even impresses the stern moralist and historian Sima Guang with her proper behavior:

Around this time the prime minister Sima Guang [style name Junshi] had requested leave to return to his hometown in order to offer sacrifices to his ancestors. He arrived in Shaanzhou after having been away for a long time. As soon as he arrived, the local officials treated him to a dinner and Wan was ordered to wait on him. As Sima Guang hailed from Shaanzhou, he had long heard about Wan but he had never met her, so he asked those present: "Shaanzhou is my hometown. I have heard that you have here a registered courtesan who is an expert on the *Mencius*. Who might that be?" The host answered by pointing out Wan. Sima Guang thereupon questioned her on the meaning of the *Mencius*, but modestly she refused to answer. When he persisted in his request, she replied: "Master Meng is almost equal to the Sage [Confucius], so who am I to dare comment on his writings?" And then, when Sima Guang persisted further, she said: "I am only a woman. If I were to discuss the *Mencius* in front of eminent scholars like you, I would be like someone trying to leap across the northern seas with Mt. Tai under her arms, someone who does not know the limits of her strength and is oblivious of her station." A pleased Sima Guang said to his host: "You gentlemen should appreciate such modesty and capability in a mere woman." The prefect was even more taken with her, and treated her even better than before.

Wen Wan pins her hopes of leaving the "fiery pit" of a courtesan's life on a military officer who promises to marry her, but unfortunately, he loses his life while in service in the border regions. Disgusted with her life as a courtesan, Wen Wan dons male clothing and tries to run away to her aunt in Fengxiang. She is caught, however, and brought back to Shaanzhou. Later she persuades her mother to give up her way of life, and together they move to Kaifeng, where they live a quiet and completely secluded life. The Master of Pure Vacuity notes that Wen Wan's writings included not only poems and the commentary on the *Mencius*, but also commentaries on "the Nine Classics, the twelve histories, and the hundred philosophers, as well as literary and discursive writings from the Western and Eastern Han dynasties onwards: astronomy, strategy, numerology, and Buddhism and Daoism."

The following are just a few of the thirty poems of Wen Wan's recorded by Cai Zichun:

Sent to Someone Far Away

As in the silent little flower courtyard the east wind rises,
Pairs of swallows and orioles brush against peach and plum.
Leaning against the red wall I ask the fate of one far away—
Beyond the tower thousands of miles of spring mountains.

Describing My Emotions

Those who by nature are rich in feeling suffer from feeling:
Hidden by a dark window I'm fed up with the courtesan's life.

Don't ridicule me for spending my time on "chapter and verse":
I don't see why Xie Daoyun should claim all the fame for poetry!

Written by Moonlight

Everyone loves the white moon drifting across the sky
And the moonlight that impartially shines down on all.
If Chang'e were not filled with the slightest spring feeling,
Why would she want to follow after someone—to no avail?

Unfortunately, nowhere in his extensive writings has Sima Guang (or, for that matter, any of Wen Wan's other supposed contemporaries) left us even a hint of the historical existence of this truly extraordinary woman poet and philosopher.

Smartass Wang and the Romance of Su Xiaoqing

In the course of the thirteenth century the song lyric had become an increasingly elite literary form, practiced by high-class connoisseurs and aficionados. Eventually, however, the popularity of the song lyric was superseded by that of the aria (*qu*), which developed in ways that were quite different from the traditional song lyric. This was particularly true in northern China where the spoken language had by this time developed into what was essentially an early form of modern Mandarin Chinese, in which polysyllabic words predominated. In addition, the music used for these arias was such that it was possible to combine several tunes in the same mode into a longer suite, all the while maintaining a single rhyme from beginning to end. Suites of arias might be included in a form of prosimetrical storytelling called *zhugongdiao* ("all keys and modes"), which flourished in the twelfth and thirteenth centuries, and in the form of drama that arose in northern China from the thirteenth century onwards and goes by the name of *zaju* ("variety play" or comedy). Individual arias and aria suites could also be performed independently, in which case they were referred to as *sanqu* ("scattered arias").

Drama went through a period of rapid development in the thirteenth century, and by the end of that century had emerged as the major form of entertainment in the big cities of the Mongol Yuan dynasty (1260–1366), such as Dadu (present-day Beijing), Kaifeng, Pingyang (in Shanxi province), Dongping (in Shandong province), and, later, Hangzhou.

As drama gained in popularity, it provided a new area of activity for courtesans who could now perform on stage as actresses. In the final days of the Yuan dynasty, Xia Tingzhi (ca. 1316–ca. 1370) compiled a small book entitled *Houses of Pleasure* (*Qinglou ji*), which was composed of brief biographical notes on the most famous actresses of the preceding century.

As was the case with the song lyric, arias were usually written by men. Not until the final decades of the Ming dynasty do we see, for the first time, the names of any female dramatists. In the *Complete Arias of the Yuan Dynasty* (*Quan Yuan sanqu*), though, we do find two suites of arias written by women. One of these, entitled "The Rendezvous," is ascribed to "the courtesan, lady Zhang." This suite of songs is written entirely from the perspective of a male patron eagerly anticipating his tryst with a young girl who, despite her youth, is an accomplished professional and makes him wait.

The second suite is ascribed to "lady Wang, a Dadu actress," and is entitled "Sent to My Loved One." Although the title of this suite might lead one to expect a romantic love letter in verse, the suite in fact turns out to be a long and extremely angry dramatic monologue written in the voice of Su Xiaoqing (Su Qing), the female protagonist of a love story that was extremely popular from the twelfth to the fifteenth century. The story was repeatedly adapted as a *zhugongdiao* as well as a drama, although nothing but scattered fragments of these versions remain extant today. Su Xiaoqing is said to have been an eleventh-century courtesan who plied her trade in the city of Luzhou. She fell in love with the young, brilliant, and handsome student Shuang Jian, who loved her greatly and stayed for some time at her establishment before leaving for the capital to take part in the exams. He promised her that he would return as soon as possible and marry her upon his return. While he is gone, however, Su Xiaoqing's stepmother, the madam, sells her off as a concubine to a tea merchant from Jiangxi named Feng Kui. Tea was a government monopoly, and tea merchants were often depicted in drama as being immensely wealthy, but also old, ugly, and completely uncultured. Su Xiaoqing protests vehemently, of course, but eventually gives way after being handed a letter of divorce, which she is led to believe comes from Shuang Jian, but has been actually substituted by the madam for a letter in which he informs her of his success in the examinations and promises to come back to her soon.

Feng Kui takes Su Xiaoqing with him back to his home in Jiangxi, traveling south by boat on the Grand Canal. At the spot where the Grand Canal crosses the Yangzi River, the couple stop to visit Jinshan (Gold Mountain), a small island in the river close to Zhenjiang and famous for its great Buddhist monastery. Before continuing their journey up the river, Su Xiaoqing, who by now has found out about the madam's trickery and knows that Shuang Jian has actually been faithful to her after all, leaves a poem on one of the walls of the monastery, in which she informs Shuang Jian of Feng Kui's destination. Not long afterwards, Shuang Jian also stops at Jinshan on his way to Jiangxi where, as it happens, he has been appointed magistrate of Yuzhang following his success in the examinations. He sees the poem and immediately sets off in pursuit. That same night he catches up with the heavy junk of the tea-merchant, abducts his beloved Su Xiaoqing, and quickly proceeds to his official post. When Feng Kui arrives home, he angrily appeals to the authorities for the restitution of his "stolen property," but the case is ultimately decided in favor of Shuang Jian who is allowed to keep Xiaoqing. And thus the story ends happily. Lady Wang's suite of arias below describes the heroine's state of mind as she and Feng Kui arrive at Jinshan—before Su Xiaoqing can even guess at the happy denouement her story will enjoy.

Sent to My Loved One
In the Zhonglü mode: To the Tune of "Powdered Butterflies" (*Fendie'er*)

The river scene is desolate and bare,
On top of that, the Chu skies, the autumn dusk!
Shivering in the west wind, the willow yields, the lotus withers.
Standing in the slanting sun,
Freezing with cold, I wait in vain.
In this river land, at the ancient ford,
The waters touch the corners of the sky.
Tears spill over: the evening hills, the misty trees.

To the Tune of "Drunken Spring Breezes" (*Zui chunfeng*)

Alone and lonely: when the days grow long,
Those who are separated suffer the most.

She turned a proper family letter into a false writ of divorce.
And before I knew it, Feng Kui came to take me away in marriage,
Marriage!
How could I have known that *he* had leapt the Dragon Gate,
That he had headed the tiger list:[20]
I wonder where my old lover can be!

To the Tune of "Red Embroidered Slippers" (*Hongxiuxie*)

Once, we'd nestle together under our hibiscus quilt in winter,
And we'd roll out rattan mats and curtains of gauze in summer.
Whenever I went out I changed into a set of fine new clothes,
Never giving a thought to that Mister Tea Merchant Feng Kui,
Mister Tea Merchant, Uncle Cash!
I assumed my handsome Master Shuang would be my companion.

To the Tune of "Greeting the Immortal Guest" (*Ying xianke*)

I see an ancient temple,
Which is built in a very rustic way.
I see a monk reciting sutras, counting the beads of his rosary.
I thought at first it was a little novice,
But it turns out to be the old abbot himself.
I am a lay follower and donor:
I'll ask the reverend what I should do.

To the Tune of "Pomegranate Flower" (*Shiliuhua*)

I looked at the pleasing river landscape painted there on the wall:
They expended quite some effort on its adornment.
And then I noted the river sky, the evening snow and the cold scholar,
Gazing out over the flat sands for a place to spend the night.
The geese alight but without bringing any news.
In vain I followed the homeward-bound sails as far as the distant isles.

---

20. The Dragon Gate is the name of the rapids in the Yellow River. Carp swimming upstream that managed to cross these rapids were believed to turn into dragons. "To pass the Dragon Gate" therefore means to pass the examination. The list of the successful candidates was called the "(dragon and) tiger list."

The misty temple, the evening bells, the slanting lights of dusk—
The autumn moon over Dongting shines on me here all alone.

To the Tune of "Fighting Quails" (*Dou anchun*)

My sorrow is as great as the shiny mists over a mountain market,
My tears are as many as the night rain over the Xiao and Xiang.
I am missing the one talented young man in my heart,
Instead I have one too many husbands under my feet.
Every day it's tea and only tea, rice and only rice, and a hundred kinds of
    mistakes:
Who is there I can complain to!
The highest pain of separation reaches to heaven;
The deepest longings of love reach down into hell.

To the Tune of "The Joy of the World" (*Putianle*)

The anguish in my gut,
The lines in this poem—
Don't ask about missing the title and dropping the rhyme,
Or whether I'm "riding a donkey" or "straddling a mule."
I think of that time when I felt fulfilled,
When I felt satisfaction:
The tip of the writing brush has but to touch on the broken heart
And helplessly I let out short sighs and long moans.
I order you, monk, to note this all down.
Was I, Su Qing, the one who left him behind?
I had no clue what had happened to Shuang Jian!

To the Tune of "Ascending the Small Tower" (*Shang xiaolou*)

Of course I'll disclose my innermost feelings:
They've all been entrusted to this poem.
Here I am pacing and remembering, pacing and yearning,
Pacing and writing, pacing and reading,
My tears raining down like pearls.
All of this is something I can't express in words,
Can't express in writing:
Melancholy sadness, thoughts of sorrow,
In the end I cannot stifle the sound of sobs and tears.

To the Same Tune

How can he know that I have been married off to another?
I know that he has passed the examinations.
But now: submerged like a fish, vanished like a goose,
The vase shattered, the hair clasp broken,
The letters have stopped, no news has come.
In the blink of an eye more than six months have passed,
But I've yet to receive a single word.
Master Shuang, where are you?
I am being forced to follow *him* onto his tea ship.

To the Tune of "The Twelfth Month" (*Shi'eryue*)

I've not had the fortune to remain united with friend and companion,
But my lot has been to suffer an unshared pillow and extra mat.
When I think about it, my longing turns most bitter,
In vain I try to dream of you, but can't summon even one that is good.
Slapped away are the limpid songs and marvelous dances,
Now I suffer this loneliness and desolation.

To the Tune of "Song of People of Yao" (*Yaomin ge*)

Fleeing from me, above the phoenix terrace the solitary moon,
Taking advantage of the force of the wind, he bears down on eastern Wu.
Now I can raise the mast, lift the oars, and float on the rivers and lakes,
But I'd rather get drunk between gauze nettings until I keel over.
Hovering,
Hovering.
At Heaven's edge the goose wanders,
In vain it has mistaken the auspicious date.

To the Tune of "The Doll" (*Shuahai'er*)

This boor knows nothing of past and present, only buying and selling,
Always trading and bartering—how depressing this life on the road!
Nursing this melancholy depression: how can I make it go away?
Truly he is an ox, a horse, decked out with collar and sleeves;
Vessels made of only straw: of what use are they?
Walls made of dung and dirt cannot be whitewashed.

I think of my money-grabbing madam's deceptive tricks:
She doesn't distinguish between the good and the weak,
She makes no distinction between wise and foolish.

To the Tune of "The Third Precoda"

Ay, madam, how cruel you are, how cruel you are,
So very hateful and vicious, so very hateful and vicious,
With not even the slightest maternal feelings in your innards.
May your house be burned down in three thousand places, may you
    suffer Heaven's wrath,
May you break out in boils, and abscesses grow on ten thousand places
    on your back.
How can you not provoke feelings of rage in my heart?
You enjoy yourself in piles of money,
And so toss me away into the water to meet with banishment.

To the Tune of "Second"

Boarding his boat is like mounting the scaffold,
Going down into the hold is like descending into hell.
Leaning against the mast pole is like leaning against an execution pole,
This is a floating prison that follows the wind as the rudder is turned,
And carried by the stream, borne on the waves, I ride the prisoners' cart.
As I accompany this despicable creature,
He pesters me as if he were a wronged ghost
And pursues me like a shadow.

To the Tune of "First"

This is truly a case of: "As soon as Feng Kui is in his cups,
Su Qing's sorrows abound"!
Leaving the boat, I walk to a place where there are no people.
I am like the daughters of Emperor Yao whose weeping for Shun added
    markings to the bamboo,
I am like the lovely maiden Cao who wept by the river—but without a
    suit of mourning clothes.[21]

---

21. Emperor Yao, impressed by the virtues of Shun, gave him his two daughters as
wives. After Shun's death in Hunan, the two widows' tears of grief permanently stained
the local bamboo. The maiden Cao (Cao E) is said to have lived during the Eastern Han

But I am afraid that he will see through to my inner feelings.
So pretending to have something in my eyes, I secretly wipe away my
    bitter tears;
Making as if to yawn, I let out a few long sighs.

To the Tune of "Coda"

These pearls of tears, what sun can dry them?
These grieving brows, when will they unknit?
If I were to gather together all of the anxieties in the world,
They would still not equal a half-day of Su Qing's sorrows!

It would be interesting to know more about lady Wang, the author of this suite. But according to the Venetian traveler Marco Polo who visited China in the last decades of the thirteenth century, there were more than twenty thousand "public women" living in the suburbs of Dadu alone. Moreover, Wang is an extremely common Chinese surname: in his *Houses of Pleasure*, Xia Tingzhi includes brief biographical accounts of five different actresses surnamed Wang. One of these actresses, who went under the stage name of Heavenly Splendor, was married to a man surnamed Hou, excelled in bandit plays, and made a forceful impression on audiences with martial acrobatics executed on the tiniest of feet. Xia also praises the acting skill of another actress named Wang, "The One Who Eloped," who, he tells us, happened to be a hunchback and for that reason the man who bought her as a concubine was ridiculed by his friends. Yet another woman, Wang Yumei, was a fine actress but was even better known as a singer.

Xia provides a somewhat more extended account of the remaining two of these five actresses surnamed Wang. The first of these was named "Ten-Percent":

She was surnamed Wang and was a renowned courtesan of the capital. In singing and dancing she had no equal, and her intelligence was without compare. One day, Commander Ding gathered together with the poets Liu Shichang and Cheng Jishan for a small drinking party in the River Village Garden, and Wang was also there to assist with the drinks. At the gathering, a young courtesan sang

---

dynasty. When she was unable to find the corpse of her father, who had drowned in the Cao E River, she wept for days on the banks of the river before jumping in and drowning herself as well.

"Chrysanthemum Party," a song in the Nanlü mode, which went: "Red leaves are dropping flames: dragons shed their scales, / The verdant pines are dry and weird: pythons bare their fangs." Ding interrupted her saying: "These are the opening lines of the tune 'Drunk on the East Wind.' Let's ask lady Wang to finish the song." Lady Wang immediately came up with:

> Red leaves are dropping flames: dragons shed their scales,
> The verdant pines are dry and weird: pythons bare their fangs.
> A good theme for a poem,
> A fine subject for a painting.
> Let's enjoy the cups and tallies
> Now we're gathered at this feast.
> *Wein, Wein, Wein,*
> I pour out again and again.
> *Trinke nur, Brüderlein, trink!*
> Don't help me onto my horse until I am drunk!

Everybody sighed with admiration and from that day, both her fame and her price doubled.

The impromptu composition of Ten-Percent Wang is not too impressive as poetry, and certainly not in translation (the lines in German represent a feeble attempt to reproduce something of the effect of the lines in transliterated Mongol in the original). But it may be enough to qualify "Ten-Percent" as a possible candidate for the authorship of "Sent to My Lover."

There is, however, one more possible candidate provided for us by Xia Tingzhi: the fifth of his lady Wangs, Smartass Wang:

She enjoyed quite a reputation in the capital for her singing and dancing and for her good looks. Chen Yunqiao became intimate with her, and she wanted to marry him. Her madam secretly told her fellow actresses to get her to change her mind by warning her: "The wife of Master Chen is a daughter of Chancellor Tie, and is extremely jealous and cruel. If you should end up in his house, you'd be bound to suffer her abuse." But Wang said: "I am only a common whore. If Master Chen is so kind as to allow me to serve him as a concubine, I will have no regrets even if it means my death."

When the madam realized that Wang was not going to change her mind, she secretly moved her brothel to a hidden place that Chen did not know. After a week, Wang secretly sent someone to let Chen know: "My madam tried to trick you and is keeping me captive at such and such a place. She has arranged for a rich merchant to come on such and such a day. Please do what must be done. If not, I'm afraid you'll be too late!"

On the specified date, the merchant did indeed show up. Wang excused herself pleading illness, and pitifully wept with grief. The merchant drank until midnight and then wanted to sleep with her. Wang pinched him all over his body until he was black and blue, and so escaped being raped. In the fifth watch of the night, Chen, in accordance with a plan he had carefully thought out, suddenly burst through the door, tied up the merchant, and pretended to be about to take him to the Ministry of Punishment for sleeping with his wife. The merchant was scared shitless and pleading with him, said: "I really didn't know! Please let this matter rest! I will be happy to contribute two hundred strings of copper coins toward the wedding expenses!" But Chen said: "That won't be necessary!" and after paying Wang's madam handsomely, he took Wang with him to the area south of the Yangzi.

When Chen died, Wang together with Chen's main wife Tie managed and maintained the family estate as widows, and both were widely praised.

Chen Yunqiao is better known as Chen Bo. In his youth Chen occupied a number of metropolitan posts and acquired the reputation of a bon vivant; later he served as district magistrate, and in 1339, he died in Hangzhou at the age of sixty. So perhaps it was Smartass Wang who needed a week to write her impassioned suite of songs that she then sent to Master Chen as a plea to save her from the clutches of the madam and the embrace of the merchant just as Shuang Jian had once saved the hapless Su Xiaoqing.

PART THREE
The First High Tide of Women's Literature

As our previous chapters have shown, there have always been writing women in imperial China. For a great many centuries, however, only rarely were complete collections of their works preserved, and even the most well-known women authors have left us no more than a handful of poems and other writings. This situation changes drastically from the seventeenth century onwards. Not only does the number of known women writers dramatically increase, but there is also a significantly greater number of extant collections of writings by women. The standard bibliography of women's writings lists the names of four hundred women writers for the Ming dynasty and more than three thousand for the Qing dynasty, and for the latter dynasty, we find the titles of more than two thousand extant collections. Even taking into consideration the far greater numbers of male writers during this period and the greater survival rate of women's writings as we move closer to modern times, the sudden explosion of women writers in the final decades of the Ming dynasty and their conspicuous presence throughout the Qing dynasty is nothing short of extraordinary. The phenomenon becomes even more striking when we realize that it was very much a regional development: the overwhelming majority of writing women of this period came from the Jiangnan region, and within this region from the greater Suzhou-Hangzhou area.

One factor behind the sudden emergence of so many women writers was the economic development of the Jiangnan area in southeastern China. China had suffered a period of economic stagnation in the fifteenth century, but in the course of the sixteenth century the economy revived, and by the end of the sixteenth century the country was enjoying what might be called an economic boom. No area profited more from this development than the Jiangnan area, which was one of China's richest agricultural regions, and which was also located at the crossroads of China's main internal thoroughfares: the Yangzi River and the Grand Canal. As agriculture, handicraft industries, and trade continued to develop, huge private fortunes were amassed, which in turn stimulated the development of luxury industries and scholarship. While advanced education in government schools and academies remained inaccessible to women, a significant number of elite families were both able and willing to allow their daughters and wives the opportunity to acquire a basic literacy, and, even more importantly, to read widely and to engage in literary activities themselves. One indication of the growing literacy among women (at least in elite families) is the appearance in print during the last century of the Ming of numerous newly composed and often lavishly illustrated moral tracts on wifely virtues (by this time mostly written by men) and collections of biographies of exemplary women, both of which were designed primarily for women readers.

Educated women were also more than happy to read other sorts of materials as well, including the many works of poetry, fiction, and drama that proliferated during this period. One extremely important aspect of this burgeoning economy was the growth and development of the printing industry. The last quarter of the sixteenth century saw the onset of a publishing boom that lasted for almost a hundred years. Meeting the demands of a larger and more demanding readership, publishers of all kinds rushed to print all kinds of books, and once the stock of existing texts had been exhausted, they eagerly sought out new materials, including fiction and drama. For the first time in Chinese history, an extensive range of leisure reading materials became available to the reading public. While much of this leisure reading was directed at a primarily male audience, we know from various sources that there were also many women to be found among the enthusiastic readers of romantic tales, and that moralists voiced their fear that this might put dangerous thoughts into women's heads.

More significant for the history of women's writing is the fact that, in their search for new subject matter, publishers began to take into account the possibilities offered by women's writings. The seventeenth century saw the appearance of a rapidly increasing number of individual collections by women as well as large anthologies of women's writings. These anthologies enhanced the visibility of women's writings and in turn probably inspired more women to write.

On an ideological level, the growth of women's literature was helped along by what is known as the "the cult of *qing*," which was immensely popular during this period. The word *qing* has a wide range of meanings, but most are associated with emotion and feeling, including love and passion. Intellectuals of the second half of the Ming dynasty grew increasingly critical of the neo-Confucian orthodoxy enshrined in the prescribed texts for study for the state examinations. This selection of texts was largely based on the synthesis of neo-Confucianism (or "Learning of the Way") as formulated by the great Song dynasty philosopher Zhu Xi (1130–1200). Zhu Xi had not only prescribed a strict moral code, but also had advocated an understanding of the Way through the study of principle, in particular the moral principle operative in history. In contrast to this rather bookish approach, the Ming dynasty statesman and philosopher Wang Yangming (1472–1529) proposed a more intuitive approach to the highest truth. He taught that all human beings were born with an innate "knowledge of the good" that would enable one to understand the Way directly by trusting one's authentic or "genuine" feelings. Wang Yangming's students and later followers further radicalized his teaching by placing an even greater emphasis on its egalitarian aspects, thus transforming it into, among other things, a critique of societal hypocrisy. The cult of *qing* would find its literary embodiment in *Peony Pavilion* (*Mudanting*), a play by the late Ming playwright Tang Xianzu (1550–1616). This play is about a teenage girl who falls in love in a dream, and whose passion is so strong that she both dies of it and then because of it returns from the grave. This play enjoyed an enormous popularity on stage and in print, and among both male and female audiences.

The cult of *qing* had a direct impact on literary criticism. Whereas most of the fifteenth and sixteenth centuries were dominated by "archaist" (*fugu*) critics who stressed the importance of studying the models of the great masters of the past, the late sixteenth century and early seventeenth century saw the emergence of critics who emphasized instead the unmediated and spontaneous expression of *qing*. According to these critics, those engaged in the search for wealth and power were inevitably alienated from their innate "knowledge of the good" by rote book learning and slavish imitation. For this reason, the only place where one could find expressions of pure feeling was outside the public sphere of officialdom and the examinations; in short, among peasants, children, and women. In terms of the literary world, this resulted in a reevaluation of drama, fiction, popular song and, even more significant for us, women's poetry.

The clearest expression of this new appreciation of women's poetry is found in the preface to the *Selections of Poems by Famous Ladies* (*Mingyuan shigui*) of ca. 1620, one of the first major anthologies of women's poetry to be published during the seventeenth century. The compiler of this anthology, and the author of this preface, is traditionally considered to be the famous critic Zhong Xing (1574–1624), but his link to the work is often questioned. The preface reads as follows:

Poems are sounds that arise naturally. One cannot become skillful at writing them by following norms and rules or by imitating models. The three hundred songs of the *Book of Odes* were all inspired by climbing mountains, traveling afar, and singing out one's love for someone [which is why] their words lend themselves to be sung and recited. Their most essential qualities are tenderness and gentleness: where do you find in them any "norms and rules"?

Nowadays, those who devote themselves to poetry all start by talking about "norms and rules" before they even come near their writing paper. All their talk is about such-and-such a person imitating such-and-such a style, and such-and-such a poem belonging to such-and-such a school. This is why the poets and gentlemen of today begin by harboring in their breast [the examples of] Cao Zhi [192–232], Liu Zhen [d. 217], Wen Tingyun [ca. 812–870], and Li Shangyin [ca. 813–858] [rather than the bamboo or any other object] and then writing their poems in imitation [of these poets]. In contrast, the famous women poets of past and present use their feelings as a point of departure and base themselves on their nature. They never write in imitation and they know nothing about schools. They make no distinction between Nanpi and Xikun schools, but just let their sadness and elegance flow.[1]

Now a woman starts out as a girl who cannot distinguish artful from primitive, has no idea of dark sorrow, and keeps her head covered with a dark red scarf to shield herself from impropriety. But once her hairpins begin to dangle in profusion, dew moistens her light frame, and [the willow's] yellow has turned green, she finds herself caught up in all sorts of matters. One moment she is filled with a joy that would turn ice into flowers; the next moment she is depressed, and heavy clouds turn into snow. She feels either as pure as bathing emerald or as desperate as dreaming red. All of a sudden she finds herself alone and forlorn, and a single thread strings together a hundred emotions. This is the origin of the profuse loftiness and charming graciousness [of women's poetry]. All those who in later days [are regarded as] skilled in poetry were writers who in their own time did not know what it meant to be skillful!

Having stressed the spontaneous character of women's poetry, the author of this preface then goes on to praise women's poetry primarily for its purity, and it becomes very clear that to him this "purity" derives from women's seclusion, protected as they are in the inner quarters from the sordid hustle and bustle of the wider world outside.

The Way of Poetry may have many beginnings, but no matter what the circumstances, I will always opt for purity. Once . . . I wrote: "Poetry is born of purity. . . . When it comes to conception, it loves ease, when it comes to surroundings, it prefers cleanliness. When it comes to subject matter it prefers serenity; commotion will not do." But even if a man can combine all these elements in his person, he will still be unable to do better than a girl. This is because girls never have to deal with carters and porters, grooms and sedan-chair bearers. Delicate mosses and fragrant trees nourish and surround them with their fragrant scents and lend them their sweet elegance.

A man still has to rely on travels through the four directions in order to know the four directions. Just think of Yu Shiji [d. 618] and his *Description of the*

---

1. The Xikun school of poetry of the eleventh century was renowned for its ornate and allusive language, very much in the manner of Li Shangyin. "Nanpi" is not commonly used as a name of a school of poetry, but because it is mentioned by Cao Zhi in one of his poems as a place where he and his friends had met for literary activities, the term here probably refers to poetry in the simple and unadorned style of Cao Zhi and his contemporaries.

Ten Commanderies [*Shijun zhi*]: he had to catalogue all of the mountains and rivers before he was able to paint the mountains and rivers; he had to catalogue all the prefectures and districts before he was able to paint these prefectures and districts; he had to catalogue all the walls and moats before he was able to paint the official buildings. But women are different. Lying in their beds they can see villages and districts, and in their dreams they can visit the border passes. This is all because of their purity.

If one is pure, one becomes ingenious. At the age of fourteen, Lu Meiniang could embroider the complete *Classic of Numinous Treasure* [*Lingbao jing*] on a single square foot of silk. Although the characters were as tiny as grains of rice, each line and dot was clearly distinguishable. She also made with a single thread a golden parasol [decorated] with depictions of the Ten Continents and the Three Isles [of the immortals] with all their terraces and palaces, phoenixes and unicorns.

The cult of *qing* provided the arguments to defend hitherto marginal forms of literature such as drama and fiction, folksongs and women's literature. Not all male readers, however, were convinced of the superior quality of the women's poetry printed in such large quantities at the time, as becomes clear from the somewhat sarcastic remarks of Xu Shipu, quoted by Zhou Lianggong (1612–1672) in his *Shadows of Books* (*Shuying*):

In the transmission of prose and poetry much depends on luck. If a text is fortunate enough to have been written by a child, it has a ninety percent chance of survival. If they are texts that are fortunate enough to have been written by a woman or a girl, they are transmitted to the world as soon as they drop from their lips. There are only a few women nowadays who are expert in poetry, but because they are women, nobody dares demand perfection from them, nobody has high expectations of them, and as a result even their worst poems are printed.

Xu Shipu continues his remarks by noting the recent fashion of publishing poetry written by proper, married women, which he contrasts with the women's writings of the past produced primarily by courtesans and palace ladies. In fact, it is quite true that in selecting women's poetry for publication, some (male) editors applied different standards from those applied in the selection of poetry by men. In his preface to a collection of biographies of less-known women writers published in 1659, *Female Poets* (*Nü caizi shu*), the editor frankly admits that:

One will not find in this book any famous women of past or present who have a biography in the histories, even though their writings may be excellent. This collection consists only of the orderly presentation of forgotten events and hidden facts. Despite the fact that the poems of these women poets are occasionally extremely shallow and poor, we could not bear to omit any of them. When one discusses the poetry of women, one cannot compare their work with that of literati. Even if the quality of their works ranks only a ten out of a hundred, one still should praise it as if it were a hundred out of a hundred. The reader should not conclude that the editor is completely lacking in any critical discernment and for that reason condemn him.

Despite the cult of *qing*, writing by women in elite families was at best tolerated as an avocation, a leisure activity, but not as a primary occupation. For Chinese men, in the words of Charlotte Furth, "writing . . . was an ontological central and civilization-defining activity. It was also a public social practice which legitimized careers and through which men competed for status." While men were expected to dedicate their lives to the study of literature and prove their mastery in extremely competitive examinations, the poetry of women was praised for the direct expression of emotion, free from convention and artifice. Often poetry written by young adolescent girls was fulsomely praised by admiring male relatives, not for its craft but for its naïveté. In fact, what might be decried in the writings of men as conventional or cliché, might sometimes be praised in women's poetry as honest and authentic.

If women of seventeenth-century Jiangnan elite society were living in surroundings that allowed them greater opportunity to engage in writing and see their works in print, they still had to be very circumspect. To again quote Charlotte Furth, "For a woman's writings to be seen or known was for her to be perceived sexually by outsiders. The Chinese woman who was published and read by an impersonal public of readers unknown to her occupied a space more like that of a Muslim woman who walks the city streets without a veil." Other historians of Chinese women's culture in the seventeenth century have stressed the extent to which the writing of poetry by elite women took place in a sphere of their own. Although the writing of poetry was as much of a social activity for women as it was for men, women exchanged poetry primarily with other women, either within the family circle or within a larger local or regional network of women friends. Moreover, as a rule, in their writings they limited themselves to a rather narrow range of subjects and emotions—aware, no doubt, of the social and conventional boundaries that defined their activities. The preface to the *Selections of Poems by Famous Ladies* provided not so much a charter of freedom for women's poetry as a strict program. Women's direct expression of emotion was praised because all proper women were supposed to be "pure" in their feelings; they were therefore expected to express only proper sentiments in proper language (a program that in many places all over the world was traditionally imposed by apparently well-intentioned male critics of women's writing). Despite the popular rhetoric praising their spontaneous expression of untrammeled emotion, women poets themselves were very much aware of the restricted conditions under which they were allowed to write, as is shown by the following passage from a letter by the late Ming woman poet Liang Mengzhao to her younger brother:

It is more difficult for those of us in the inner chambers to write poems than it is for sophisticated gentlemen and pen-pushers. A [male] poet can indulge himself in mountains and streams, and once he has a broad experience of the world, he feels no inhibitions when chanting his words and discussing the affairs [of the world]. For this reason the songs he voices often are filled with an extraordinary and wide-ranging energy. The situation is different for those of us in the inner chambers. Our feet do not cross our thresholds, and our experience does not extend beyond our home villages. Even if we are inspired, we still have to show decorum. When our texts are unbridled, we offend against elegance. If even a writer like Zhu Shuzhen was criticized on this account, how much more so those who are not her equal! Even when singing of our nature and feelings, we are not allowed to give free rein to our thoughts and speak our minds, but must express ourselves in a soft and suggestive way. This sort of style, however, easily slips into weakness. Poets esteem Li Bai and Du Fu as the greatest writers who ever lived. But how would it be considered fitting for those of us in the inner quarters to write with Li Bai's reckless abandon or with Du Fu's strange density and tragic heroism?

Even if a woman writer were to write a poem that might in any way reflect poorly on her virtue, it would have most likely been edited out of her collection, either by the poet herself or by her male relatives. For women were almost totally dependent upon the good offices of their male kin if they wanted to see any of their works in print, and there was little chance that a filial son or grandson would publish anything that might detract from the positive image of his mother or grandmother. This process of self-censorship and censorship can be sensed behind the statement, found in the prefaces to numerous poetry collections by women, that the author would actually have preferred to burn her poems and that the poems in the collection represent those that have been saved from destruction by fate and filial piety.

Another contributing factor to the self-restraint of elite women in literary activities was the need to distinguish their own writing activities from those of courtesans. The same large private fortunes and liberal attitudes that allowed for the development of leisure reading and women's literature also provided the basis for the last great flowering of Jiangnan courtesan culture. Courtesans constituted a highly visible aspect of the major urban centers, and the *grandeur et misère* of their life provided subject matter for many contemporary plays and novellas. The leading courtesans of the final decades of the Ming dynasty distinguished themselves by their artistic accomplishments, including calligraphy, painting, and poetry. Some of them pursued widely publicized affairs with leading literati, others are reported to have written sexually explicit poetry. None of them enjoyed a more spectacular career than Liu Shi (Rushi), who first had a relationship with the dashing young poet Chen Zilong (1608–1647) and later became the wife of the elder statesman and poet Qian Qianyi (1582–1664). She helped the latter in the compilation of a large anthology of Ming dynasty poets, *Collected Poems of the Successive Reigns*, and was apparently responsible for the section devoted to women's poetry, contributing to both the selection of poems and the writing of the authors' biographies. Nevertheless, the marginal status of the courtesan in elite society, a status that she could not shed even by becoming the wife of a high-ranking official, is highlighted by the fact that after Qian Qianyi's death, Liu Shi was pressured into committing suicide by his rapacious relatives.

Many elite women were forced by the political developments of the mid-seventeenth century to pursue a far more public career than they would have otherwise. The collapse of the Ming dynasty in 1644 was followed by an extended period of warfare and social dislocation as the Manchus pursued the conquest of the whole of China, a unification that would not be fully achieved until 1683 with the incorporation of Taiwan into the empire. Throughout this period of nearly four decades, many elite women were forced to make their own living when their husbands were killed or the family fortune was lost, and some of them did so by becoming teachers, selling their brushwork, or, in exceptional cases, engaging in editorial activities. The chaotic circumstances of the conquest years, together with the lack of a clear center of political and moral authority, allowed women a greater latitude of action in society than would have been imaginable in earlier times—and which would be quickly curtailed again once things had settled down by the last quarter of the seventeenth century.

This increase in the possibilities open to women in mid-seventeenth-century China may also be observed in the sphere of Buddhism. Late Ming China had seen the beginnings of a revitalization of both lay and monastic Buddhism in which nuns played a small but significant role. In addition, many women from gentry families, like their male counterparts, took refuge from the chaos of the times in monastic establishments. Some of these women became quite eminent abbesses and religious leaders. Many of the nuns in the Chan school now followed the tradition of male Chan teachers who would have their various sermons, poems, letters, and other writings gathered together into collections known as "discourse records" or *yulu*. Given the greater interest in women's writings of this time, many of these collections were published, printed, and circulated—usually with support of men, both monastic and lay, who admired women's teachings and writings and felt that they should be known widely, if only because they might serve as models of exemplary female behavior. For the first and only time in imperial China, a number of these collections of writings by nuns were included in a privately published edition of the Buddhist Tripitaka, thus preserving some of them and allowing us a more detailed view of their thoughts and activities as wives and widows, nuns and abbesses, teachers and writers.

This first high tide of women's literature during the late imperial period gradually came to a close during the last quarter of the seventeenth century. As Chinese (male) intellectuals pondered the causes of the downfall of the Ming, they increasingly came to view the liberalism and loose morals of the latter half of that dynasty as the primary cause of the debacle. As a result they advocated a return to the full tenets of the Learning of the Way, stressing the need to adhere strictly to all the traditional ritual prescriptions. In general, a turn toward orthodoxy on the part of men usually manifests itself most strongly in the increased restrictions they impose on women. An example of this particular mindset can be seen in the following passage from *Instructions for My Sons* (*Tingxun*), written by the high official Jin Fu (1632–1692):

Of course it is a good thing for women to be literate and thus able to understand the highest principles, but it doesn't usually turn out this way. As a rule they prefer to read plays and novels, which inspire in them all kinds of improper thoughts. In the worst cases, misconstruing the meaning of what they have read, they commit the most heinous crimes. Given that this is the result [of female literacy] it would be better that they didn't learn how to read and simply resigned themselves to their ignorant fate. Chen Jiru [1558–1639] once said: "In women a lack of talent makes for virtue." How very true!

The phrase "in women a lack of talent makes for virtue," which may or may not have been coined by Chen Jiru (1558–1630), continued to be quoted often in later centuries, and in modern times has been often decried as epitomizing Confucian prejudice against women.

The reversion to neo-Confucian orthodoxy on the part of the Chinese intellectuals fitted in well with the authoritarian bent of the Manchu emperors, who presented themselves as champions of orthodoxy. Moreover, in the chaos of the last days of the Ming, many of the large fortunes of the Jiangnan region had been destroyed, and changes in the tax structure made it more difficult to amass the kinds of fortune that had maintained the elite lifestyle of the late Ming. This may also partly explain the fact that from the last two decades of the seventeenth century onwards, publishers no longer rushed to produce new titles for upper-class leisure reading. The last major anthology of women's literature of the seventeenth century was published in 1690, and we must wait for over three quarters of a century for the next major anthology to appear in 1773. This growing reluctance of publishers to engage in new projects and their tendency to favor reprinting new editions of old, well-established texts may also have been because of the growing control of the new authorities over printed materials and the extreme sensitivity of the Manchus to any real or perceived slights to themselves or their forebears.

It is impossible to say whether or not the actual number of writing women diminished from the last quarter of the seventeenth century onwards. What is true is that although writing women appear prominently in the major works of fiction written during the first half of the eighteenth century, actual writing women appear to be much less visible in the written records of this period than they were either before or after. And, by the time a second high tide of women's writing begins to gather momentum in the last quarter of the eighteenth century the cultural milieu has greatly changed. For one thing, writing courtesans and nuns have for all intents and purposes disappeared from the literary scene, leaving the stage almost exclusively to elite women. Many of these gentry women enjoyed the patronage and tutelage of some of the leading poets of the time, and their newly acquired visibility provoked an ongoing public debate over "women's learning." In addition, whereas women of the seventeenth century limited themselves largely to the composition of poems, song lyrics, and letters, women writers of the second half of the eighteenth century and beyond branched out into a wider variety of genres, including narrative and drama, which often provided them with greater freedom to speak their minds.

7 · Courtesans

Liang Xiaoyu and the Tale of Huang Chonggu

No late Ming courtesan writer was more prolific than Liang Xiaoyu. Her biographical notice, written by Liu Shi, in the *Collected Poems of the Successive Reigns* reads as follows:

Liang Xiaoyu was a native of Hangzhou. At the age of seven she composed, following prescribed rhymes, a poem on a fallen flower, and at the age of eight she copied out the *Daling tie*.[1] As an adult she perused books of all kinds. She wrote a *Rhapsody on the Two Capitals* [*Liangdu fu*], which took her half a year to complete. Her collection of poetry in two chapters was entitled the *Langhuan Collection* [*Langhuan ji*].[2]

Her poem entitled "On Myself" makes use of the two rhyme words "cold" [*leng*] and "fragrant" [*xiang*] throughout. The following couplets are from this poem:

> The setting moon, imitating the orchid burner, has already grown cold,
> The drifting flowers, enticing the wine cup, still remain fragrant.

> The brook ripples through the boulders' weeds: my cloudy chignon feels
> cold,

---

1. Examples of the calligraphy of Wang Xianzhi (344–388).
2. Langhuan is the name of the library of the Heavenly Emperor.

The rain washes away the traces of moss: my kingfisher sleeves are
    fragrant.

Peach blossoms float on the stream, their dark red rouge grown cold,
The willow trees sway in the wind, their kingfisher-green so fragrant.

"Fighting for grasses" in the spring wind, the inscribed sash grows cold,[3]
Gathering caltrops from autumn streams: even the mirrored flower is
    fragrant.

Rain coats the pear blossoms: spring dreams are cold,
Wind blows through the lotus leaves: evening toilette's fragrance!

On the isle with its rushes, the rhymes of the wind are cold,
Below the bean arbor, the traces of the rain smell fragrant.

When the rising vapor is without smoke, the gods all feel cold,
When bones are wrapped in colored vapors, even the marrow is fragrant.

All these lines may be called beautiful. But her other poems often are rough and
forthright and do not avoid being vulgar. She even goes so far as to discuss her
amorous feelings and talk at length about "secret games." The flowing cinnabar
is fully expressed:[4] she goes to the extreme in ornate lasciviousness. It can be
said of her what Gao Zhongwu said [of Li Ye]: "Female and yet unrestrained."

Liang Xiaoyu once evaluated the famous courtesans from past and present,
placing Xue Tao at the head of them all [on her home altar], with [the famous
courtesans] Su Xiaoxiao and Guan Panpan sharing in the offerings.[5] She hung a
plaque over the entrance [of the room] that read: "Temple of the Three Queens
of the Flowery Altar." On the first day of each quarter of the year she would
honor them with a libation. She designated herself as the main priestess of this

---

3. "Fighting for grasses" is the name of a variety of games: one involves finding as
many different kinds of flowers as possible, another involves coming up with as many
different names of flowering plants as possible.

4. "Flowing cinnabar" most likely refers to the red ink used for writing an oath of
love. Here it probably refers to the more physical aspects of love.

5. Su Xiaoxiao is said to have been a Hangzhou courtesan of the Six Dynasties period; she is credited with the authorship of one poem. Guan Panpan, who lived around
800, was a courtesan who later became the concubine of a high official and starved herself to death after he died. Four quatrains by Guan Panpan have been preserved.

cult. But I fear that "the woman of the Swallow Tower" [i.e., the loyal courtesan Guan Panpan] would not have accepted this incense. It would actually have been a more appropriate ritual, however, if she had replaced [the loyal courtesans Su Xiaoxiao and Guan Panpan] with Li Ye and Yu Xuanji!

Apart from the titles mentioned in the above biographical notice, Liang Xiaoyu is credited with eight additional titles. As these works, many of which appear to have been of considerable length, have been lost, there is little point in listing all of them, although some of their titles do arouse one's curiosity, such as her *Description of All the Countries in the Classic of Mountains and Seas* (*Shanghai qunguo zhi*). One of these titles, *A History of Women Past and Present* (*Gujin nüshi*), testifies further to her interest in women's history.

One of Liang Xiaoyu's extant poems, inspired by the ruins of the Guanwa Palace outside Suzhou, deals with the posthumous reputation of the famous beauty Xi Shi. The Guanwa Palace had been built in the early fifth century BCE by King Fuchai of the ancient state of Wu as a residence for Xi Shi, a beautiful girl from the neighboring state of Yue. When the state of Yue was defeated by Wu, Yue sought revenge by selecting the most beautiful girl in the land and training her in the arts of seduction in the hope that she would be able to captivate King Fuchai of Wu and cause him to neglect the affairs of state. Despite the protestation of the loyal minister Wu Zixu (who was subsequently ordered to commit suicide, after which his body was sewn into a rhinoceros-hide sack and thrown into a river), King Fuchai accepted Xi Shi, was charmed by her beauty, and lost his kingdom:

> Once the leather sack sank into the river, the hegemonic aura was lost,
> Yet from the ruins that remain one can still imagine the heroic style.
> The story is not true that Xi Shi was capable of bringing down the state:
> Nobody realizes that it was Wu itself that brought about its own collapse.
>
> The song and dance have been transformed into two orchestras of frogs,
> The silk and gauze have changed into a thousand clusters of climbing fig.
> Where once she received His Majesty's favors, her soul still resides,
> And her pure blood, year after year, continues to dye the azaleas red.

The poem may be read not only as a vindication of Xi Shi, but also as a general defense of the courtesan: if a man allows himself to be seduced by the charms of a courtesan, he has only himself to blame. The courtesan, on the other hand, is only doing what she is trained to do.

As might be expected, the anthologies of women's poetry shy away from including Liang Xiaoyu's poems on the "secret games" of sexual intercourse, and prefer innocuous quatrains such as the following:

> The rustling pine trees play their purest tunes,
> The gurgling spring rinses away the earthly dust.
> The white clouds make a fitting present for a guest:
> The full moon knows how to make a person linger.

"Secret games" poems can be found in various albums of erotic woodblock prints, but although the authors always hide their identity behind fancy pseudonyms, we may assume that they were usually male. While it is possible that some of these poems might have been written by Liang Xiaoyu, we have no way to identify them. Some of Liang Xiaoyu's poetry must have been pretty outrageous, however, judging from Liu Shi's disdainful comment at the end of Xiaoyu's biography that in view of her lifestyle she would have done better to venerate the "criminals" Li Ye and Yu Xuanji than such exemplary courtesans as Su Xiaoxiao and Guan Panpan, who remained faithful to their lovers to the very end. Other critics share Liu Shi's low opinion of Liang Xiaoyu's poetry. One of them, after praising her prose, even exclaims: "How is it possible that one cannot find a single outstanding phrase in all her hundreds of poems?"

Liang Xiaoyu is also known for being one of the first female playwrights in Chinese literary history. Her lost play *United Primes* (*Heyuan ji*) was based on the tale of Huang Chonggu. This story has been preserved in the *Comprehensive Records of the Reign Period Great Peace*, a comprehensive collection of anecdotes and tales from the first to the tenth centuries, and reads as follows:

Once when Zhou Xiang, the so-called prime minister of the "Shu dynasty" of Wang Jian and his son, was serving on the staff of the governor of Qiongnan, he was put in charge of the administration of the prefecture.[6] At that time the district of Linqiong sent him for judgment Huang Chonggu, who had been ac-

---

6. Wang Jian's Former Shu dynasty ruled Sichuan province from 907 to 925.

cused of criminal negligence that had resulted in a fire. As soon as Huang had been put in jail, he presented Zhou with the following poem:

> It was by chance I left my hidden hermitage to live in Linqiong,
> My deportment is as firm and true as the pine tree in the valley.
> Why would you, whose justice is as pure as water and mirror,
> Want to shackle a crane from the wilds and lock it in a cage?

After reading this poem Zhou summoned Huang [to his office]. Huang claimed to be a provincial graduate of about thirty years of age. His answers [to Zhou's questions] were detailed and intelligent, and so Zhou immediately ordered him to be released. A few days later, Huang presented him with a song that Zhou admired greatly and so Zhou sent him to study with the other students in the academy. Huang was good at the game of go and was also a fine zither player; he excelled at calligraphy and painting as well. The next day, Zhou recommended his name for appointment as acting prefectural administrator for fiscal affairs. [Once he had taken up this position] Huang enjoyed an excellent reputation: clerks and runners submitted to him in awe, and his documents and briefs were well written and clear.

Zhou not only appreciated his extraordinary intelligence, but also admired his elegance and sophistication. After Huang had served for over a year in this position, Zhou wanted to give him his daughter's hand in marriage. Huang tucked the offer of marriage in his sleeve and excusing himself, offered the following poem:

> Since I stopped gathering kingfisher feathers along the emerald river,
> I have kept to my poor and humble abode, just chanting my poems.
> Since donning the blue gown of office and living the life of a clerk,
> I have forever foresworn the phoenix-mirror and the painting of brows.
> My deportment is extraordinary, displaying the virtue of the green pine,
> My ambition is out of the ordinary, manifesting the beauty of white jade.
> But if you, Governor, deign to accept me as your "bare-bellied guy,"[7]
> We'll have to first beg Heaven to quickly turn me into a man!

Zhou was completely flabbergasted when he read this poem and summoned Huang for questioning: As it turns out, "he" was the daughter of prefect Huang!

---

7. When one of Wang Kuang's colleagues sent one of his students to check out Wang Kuang's sons to see which would be most appropriate as a son-in-law, the spy was most impressed by the insouciance of the one son who had lain around bare-bellied. This turned out to be Wang Xizhi (309–ca. 365), the famous calligrapher. Since then the term "bare-bellied guy" has been used to refer to a son-in-law.

At a tender age she had lost her parents after which she lived together with her old wet nurse. She had never been married. When Zhou [heard about this] he was filled with even greater admiration for her chastity and purity and everyone in the prefecture was astounded by this amazing story.

Subsequently, Huang requested that she be dismissed and returned to her former secluded hermitage in Linqiong. No one knows whether she is still alive or not.

This tale was first adapted for the stage as a five-act *zaju* by the maverick sixteenth-century playwright Xu Wei (1521–1593). Xu has his Huang Chonggu participate in the metropolitan examinations administered by Zhou Xiang. After Huang passes the exams at the head of the list and subsequently excels in all his duties, Zhou wants "him" to marry his daughter. This twist of events forces Huang to disclose her true sex, whereupon Zhou contrives a happy ending by having her instead marry his son, who has just passed the military examinations with highest honors. Later, the tale was repeatedly dramatized by female playwrights, including Liang Xiaoyu, but unfortunately none of these versions has been preserved. To judge from the title of her play, Liang followed Xu Wei in having Huang Chonggu marry Zhou Xiang's son.

Jing Pianpian and Ma Xianglan

The courtesan who has the most poems in the *Collected Poems of the Successive Reigns* is Jing Pianpian. Whereas other courtesans as a rule are represented by only a handful of poems, the editors saw fit to include fifty-three of her works. Her introductory biographical notice in the anthology reads as follows:

Jing Pianpian, who had the style name Sanwei, was a girl of the "green towers" from Jianchang [in Jiangxi province].[8] On the strength of her romantic spirit, she made a vow to remain loyal to the student Mei Ziyu who, although he had promised to marry her, did not follow up on his promise. Eventually she died in dire poverty. Her collection was called *Flower-Scattering Chants* [*Sanhua yin*].

Wang Bogu once wrote a poem dedicated to her that goes:

> In Fujian lives a girl who is skilled at writing poems:
> She sent me her collection, *Flower-Scattering Chants*.

---

8. "Green tower" is a euphemism for a courtesan's house.

I've yet to gaze upon this heavenly maiden's face,
But her words are as good as the taste of lichees.

Although Pianpian had her home in Xujiang, she often visited Jian'an, which is why Bogu thought she was a Fujian girl.

Like Liang Xiaoyu, Jing Pianpian apparently modeled her life on the courtesans of the second half of the Tang dynasty. The title of her collection, for example, is a clear reference to the poetic exchange between Li Ye and the monk Jiaoran. Other sources not only praise her qualities as a poet ("Of all the famous courtesans of the Ming dynasty amusement quarters renowned for their poetry, Sanwei must be considered the most excellent"), but also as a singer. As to the end of her life, some sources indicate that she was eventually bought as a concubine by the merchant Ding Changfa, but hanged herself when her husband was thrown in jail on a false accusation.

Most of Jing Pianpian's extant poems are in the form of quatrains. The following, written in the tradition of Music Bureau songs (*yuefu*), are among the ones most often singled out for praise:

Songs of Resentment

I

How can you say the road is long?
It is your mind that makes you stay.
My heart is like a wagon wheel:
Each day it goes ten thousand miles!

II

I am the water in the brook:
That flows, but never leaves the rocks.
Your heart, my lord, is willow floss
Floating on the wind, leaving no trace.

Rain on the First Day of the Fourth Month

The ninety days of springtime splendor have silently passed by:
What is the message of the flowers by the painted balustrade?
It is that you should know the rain's intention, sorrow's promise:
As soon as the rain comes to your couch, sorrow too abounds.

It should be noted, however, that modern anthologies of women's writings rarely accord Jing Pianpian the same prominence as does the *Collected Poems of the Successive Reigns*.

Wang Bogu was the style name of Wang Zhiheng (1535–1612), a prolific writer who played a leading role in Suzhou literary life for over three decades. While his contacts with Jing Pianpian seem to have been limited to a single poem, his relationship with the famous Nanjing courtesan Ma Xianglan (1548–1604) was widely known. Ma Xianglan's biography in the *Collected Poems of the Successive Reigns* reads as follows:

The personal name of courtesan Ma was Shouzhen; her childhood name was Xuan'er, and her style name was Yuejia, but because she was skilled in the painting of orchids, she was best known by the name of Xianglan ["Xiao River Orchid"]. Her figure and face were quite ordinary, but she was always high-spirited and as carefree as the early oriole in the spring willow; spouting her phrases and casting her glances, she was able to cleverly gauge each person's mood, and none who saw her could avoid being captivated by her charms.

Her establishment was located at the finest spot on the Qinhuai River. Its ponds and halls were clear and sparse, its flowers and rocks were elegant and pure; with its winding corridors and secret chambers it was a labyrinth from which one could not escape. She had her girl apprentices instructed in the theatrical arts and each day they would provide entertainment to the banqueting guests: the sounds of drum and lute would mingle with those of gold strings and red ivory clappers.

By nature she was given to acts of light-hearted largesse. Time and again she would shower money on young men. Although richly ornamented hairpins that happened to fall to the floor would often end up at the pawnbroker's, she did not care.

Once when she was threatened by Mo Cilang,[9] Mister Wang Bogu saved her from disaster. She then wanted to become his concubine, but he refused her request. In the autumn of the *jiachen* year of the reign period Wanli [1604], Bogu turned seventy and Xianglan came to Suzhou from Nanjing to arrange a banquet for him in celebration of his birthday. The eating and drinking went on for several months and the singing and dancing lasted each day until dawn. It was the most elaborate celebration Suzhou had seen in decades. Shortly after her return [to Nanjing] Xianglan fell ill. She lit a lamp, paid homage to the Buddha, after

---

9. Perhaps *mocilang* should rather be translated as "criminal" (a fellow whose body has been tattooed).

which she bathed and changed into a fresh set of clothes. Then, at the age of fifty-seven, she passed away seated in the lotus position. She left a collection of poetry in two chapters.

Although in his preface to her collection Wang Bogu compliments Ma Xianglan profusely, other critics have been more sparing in their praise. And indeed, she may not have been a particularly accomplished poet, even if some of her poems are not without a certain simple charm, such as the following poem on a parrot:

> All through the day I watch the parrot,
> As it passes its life in this gilded cage:
> Green wings adept at brushing feathers,
> A red beak skilled in imitating sounds.
> Its heart must be longing for its Long trees,
> Yet it has been taught to mimic Wu speech.
> My Snowdress, I love you if no one else does:
> Always your partner in inner quarter feelings.

The native Chinese parrots of the Long mountains of the border regions between the modern provinces of Shaanxi and Gansu, known for their vivid green coloring, had by the fourteenth century been hunted into extinction but lived on in poetic cliché. White parrots, often called "Snowdress" after a famous white parrot owned by Yang Guifei, were an imported species from the Moluccas. Perhaps it is just a lapse on the part of our poet to draw our attention first to the parrot's green feathers and then to address the pet as "Snowdress." Or is it possible that she wanted to draw attention to the emptiness of the coy and charming pet names often given to courtesans despite the fact that their lives were often ones of great misery?

Ma Xianglan is also known to have written a play, *A Tale of Three Lives: The Story of the Jade Hairpins* (*Sansheng zhuan yucanji*). This play was an adaptation of the tale of Wang Kui, whose callous lack of gratitude had provided a subject for playwrights from as early as the thirteenth century. Wang Kui, so the story goes, is a poor student whose courtesan-lover provides him with the means to travel to the capital and sit for the examinations. Before he leaves, he vows eternal loyalty to her in the temple of the god of the sea, but once he passes the examinations, he marries a high official's daughter instead. Not only that, he also refuses to have anything to do with his heartbroken former lover, who in the end commits suicide, leaving it to her avenging ghost to drive Wang Kui to madness and ultimately suicide. It is not difficult to see why such a story might appeal to a courtesan-playwright. Two scenes of this play have been preserved in a contemporary anthology. Unfortunately, however, only a few lackluster arias are included, without the stage directions and the intervening dialogue.

Wang Wei and Yang Wan

In their *Collected Poems of the Successive Reigns*, Qian Qianyi and Liu Shi provide the following biographical notice for Wang Wei (d. 1647), whom they include not with the courtesans but with the "wives and daughters":

Wei's style name was Xiuwei and she was a native of Yangzhou. At the age of seven she lost her father and eventually she ended up in a bordello. When she grew up, her talent and feeling were extraordinary. She would travel up and down between Suzhou and Shaoxing in a small skiff, accompanied by her books. The people she associated with were all famous gentlemen of a superior category.

Later she experienced sudden enlightenment and converted to the joys of Chan. With a linen pack and a bamboo staff, she traveled throughout the Yangzi region. She climbed Dabieshan, visited the famous sights of Yellow Crane Tower and Parrot Isle, went on pilgrimage to Wudangshan, and climbed Heaven's Pillar Peak. Traveling up the Yangzi, she ascended Mount Lu and visited the straw-thatched cottage of Bai Juyi [772–846], and at Wuru she sought instruction from the great master Hanshan Deqing [1546–1623]. Upon her return, she had her future grave built in Hangzhou,[10] and calling herself the Person of the Way of the Straw Cape, she was prepared to live out her life in this manner [as a recluse].

Once when she was visiting Suzhou, however, she was raped by a vulgar lout. Afterwards she became the concubine of Xu Yuqing from Huating. Xu served as a censor, and at a time when the administration was in disorder and the dynasty was about to fall, he often spoke his mind. During this period of heroic self-sacrifice and later following his retirement as well, he received a great deal of assistance from Xiuwei. Upon the collapse [of the Ming dynasty], they

---

10. The building of this tomb was financed by Wang Ruqian, a wealthy patron of courtesans based in Hangzhou, who later also played a major role in introducing Liu Shi to her future husband, Qian Qianyi.

stuck with each other throughout the period of warfare [that followed]. In the course of their peregrinations, they swore to follow each other in death.

Three years later Wang Wei died and Xu mourned her deeply. A gentleman might say: "Xiuwei was like a blue lotus rising high above the mud from which it has extracted itself, or like a white piece of jade from Kunlun Mountains, indestructible even by the fires that come at the end of a kalpa. This may be called 'returning to one's true home.'" How fortunate!

For her poetry collection *Poems of Foliage Hall* [*Yueguan shi*] she wrote her own preface, which reads:

> If one is not actually born a man, one cannot cleanse the world of evil. Yet, while serving my husband, and in the time left over from my meditation and recitation, [I wrote] these single words and single chants. Sometimes I sought distraction from my mood with flowers and rain, at other times I noted my longing for streams and mountains. The poems had their origin in profound emotions, and were completed as soon as I had lodged my intention in them. Wrongly it is said that in this world spring depends on its flowers and autumn depends on its leaves, and that everything becomes a poem if you embellish it with these. Can one even speak of poetry under such circumstances? Or would it not be better to refrain from speaking of poetry?

She loved famous mountains and streams and compiled a collection of descriptions of famous mountains in a few hundred chapters, for which she wrote a preface so that it might be published.

The famous critic Chen Jiru (1558–1639) is said to have expressed his appreciation for her poems as follows: "Her *shi* poems are like those of Xue Tao and her song lyrics resemble those of Li Qingzhao, but she doesn't bear even the slightest resemblance to those powdered and painted little girls, and even men with beards and whiskers should be filled with awe [when reading her work]." However, only 130 of her songs and poems have been preserved in various contemporary anthologies.

After Returning at Night I Remember the Girl on the Neighboring Boat

Sharing spring, we talked and talked, forgot to sleep:
By the bank of the river I gathered up an idle sorrow.
Yet it seemed as if I had seen you once in a dream:
A single branch of spring glowing in the cold mist.

Checking on the Plum

When my friend said goodbye to me and left,
He promised: "When the plum tree blossoms!"
Last night when those words came back to mind,
I rose to look at the branches of the courtyard tree.

Resentment against the Plum

The courtyard tree looks as it did yesterday,
When is it then that my friend will return?
All the other flowers have opened before you,
Why do you alone take so long to blossom?

Yang Wan was a sworn sister of Wang Wei. In their biographical sketch of Yang Wan in the *Collected Poems of the Successive Reigns*, Qian Qianyi and Liu Shi explicitly contrast the different life trajectories of these two courtesans:

Yang Wan's style name was Wanshu and she was a famous courtesan from Nanjing. She excelled in poetry, and her works contain many fine lines; she was also good at cursive calligraphy.

She became the concubine of Mao Zhisheng from Tiaoshan who admired her talents and treated her with exceptional favor. Wan was repelled by Zhisheng, however, and for this reason had many outside relationships. Zhisheng prided himself on being a magnanimous hero, and did not interfere in her affairs even though he knew about them.

After Zhisheng's death, it happened that Tian Hongyu, a relative of the dynastic family by marriage, was ordered by the emperor to make a pilgrimage to Putuoshan. On his return to the capital, he passed through White Gate [Nanjing]. His idea was to marry Wan in order to get his hands on her riches, while Wan wanted to leave the Mao family in order to marry someone else. Thinking that Tian would help her to accomplish this, she eloped with him, bringing along all her possessions. But Tian treated her like an old serving woman and put her to work teaching his young daughter.

After Tian's death, she was preparing to elope again, this time with Liu Dongping, but just as they were about to set out, the city [of Beijing] fell. She then disguised herself as a beggar woman, but when she attempted to return to Nanjing by country roads, she was killed by bandits out in the fields.

Wan was a sworn sister of the Person of the Way of the Straw Cape [Wang

Wei], who repeatedly strongly admonished her [for her behavior], even though Wan was unable to follow her advice. Wang Wei was as shining and pure as the flower of the blue lotus that rises high above the dust, but Wan finally sunk into the mud and dirt and became a laughing stock. How sad!

Mao Zhisheng was the style name of Mao Yuanyi (1594–ca. 1641), a good friend of Qian Qianyi's. He was a native of Gui'an, but lived for most of his life in Nanjing. Mao Yuanyi's grandfather, the famous prose writer Mao Kun (1512–1601), had made a name for himself in military campaigns against the native tribes of Guangxi, and Mao Yuanyi's father had also held quite important official positions. Mao Yuanyi himself was best known as the compiler of the *Treatise on Military Preparedness* (*Wubeizhi*) of 1628, a huge and extremely comprehensive encyclopedia on military technology and strategy. He participated in campaigns against the Manchus in the twenties and thirties, but his official career never got off the ground, and later in life he began to drink heavily. In the preface he wrote for Yang Wan's collected poems, Mao Yuanyi describes her artistic development:

When Wan married me, she was barely sixteen. She could read and her calligraphy in the small regular style was accomplished. When I noticed that her forehead was always stained with the ink from her brush, I taught her the *Pictures of the Battle Formations of the Brush* [*Bizhen tu*],[11] and immediately her calligraphy improved greatly. When I taught her poetry, I began with the three hundred pieces [of the *Book of Odes*], and only when that subject had been fully mastered did I follow the historical development [of poetry] until we came to the literary writing of today.

When it came to calligraphy, Wan would sink her brush in the inkwell and in the process ruin her clothes. When it came to poetry, however, she would play around and read in a desultory fashion without really concentrating. But after three years she suddenly started to compose quatrains. They were excellent and profound . . . and comparable in quality to that of her calligraphy. Although I was pleased I also had my doubts.

Whenever she wrote poetry, as soon as she had completed [even] a single stanza or single line, she would immediately fall ill. This eventually became a debilitating disease and although she was repeatedly warned by the physician [to

---

11. *Bizhen tu* is a short treatise on the basics of calligraphy, which is variously ascribed to Wang Xizhi and Lady Wei.

refrain from writing], she never reformed her behavior. Only then did I realize that she had stored within her heart all the plunder of her readings.

One of Yang Wan's most interesting works is a series of five poems entitled "Watching Beauties Flying Kites." For a full understanding of the series one should keep in mind that the Chinese word for "string" or "thread" (*si*) is homophonous with the word for "thought" or "longing" (*si*). Chinese kites, which are made of bamboo and paper, can be extremely beautiful. Flying kites was a competitive sport, however, and people would often try to cut the strings of each other's kites, causing them to drift off.

I

Together we watch the jade-white arms holding the fragile strings,
As carried aloft by the wind the kites unhesitatingly rise and soar.
Then, in the blink of an eye, I see them far away at heaven's edge,
As they pass the clouds and brush the trees in order to rendezvous.

II

I'd like to let soar my sorrow, but to no avail,
I've cut the string, but have not cut the sorrow.
If this kite were as heavy as is my sorrow,
It too would find it hard to soar up in the sky.

III

How they cross the clear sky for ten thousand miles!
Alas, I may be lightweight but I'm not as light as they.
If at heaven's end you meet with that wandering man,
Would you kindly give him my letter of just a few lines?

IV

Feelings paper-thin, as heartless as the bamboo;
You have on purpose broken off every string.
Once you'd flown away, you became unstoppable—
Where at heaven's edge will I find news of you?

V

The time came when you disappeared like floating clouds,
You drift about as free as can be, taking nothing seriously.
This is the way of passionate lovers who don't keep faith—
The beauty wrongly blames it all on the east winds of spring.

The talent and sensibility so highly praised by Mao Yuanyi can also be seen in the following poems:

Autumn Feelings

Solitary, I rest my chin on my hand, overcome by sorrow,
I'd like to tell of my passion, but am then filled with shame.
Since ancient times, life has been like this for the "poorly-fated,"
How dare I seek to be like mandarin ducks, growing old together?

Geese

Flying on and on for ten thousand miles they cross the blue sky,
What could the moon possibly mean by sending me their shadows?
I know full well they must have flown over where my lover lives,
But passionate lovers, I know all too well, only rarely send letters.

To the Melody of "Partridge Sky" (*Zhegutian*)
About the Weaving Maid One Day after Double Seven[12]

The long-expected rendezvous so quickly finished again!
There is no way the magpies' bridge can be kept in place.
The wind has blown this couple of mandarin ducks apart,
In the moonlight she longs in vain for her phoenix-companion.

Ever since they were parted,
Both have been filled with sorrow—

---

12. The reader may remember that the Cowherd and the Weaving Maiden are two stars on opposite sides of the Milky Way (in Chinese, the Heavenly, or Silver, River). Because they had neglected their duties when they fell in love with each other, the Jade Emperor turned them into stars and allowed them to meet only once a year, on the night of the seventh day of the Seventh Month, when magpies form a bridge for them across the Milky Way.

But whom can she ask to deliver a sealed letter of brocade writing?
Too listless to throw the golden shuttle—it only increases sorrow.
Along with the Silver River, her tears stream down without end.

Liu Shi

No courtesan's life is known in more detail than that of Liu Shi (1618–1664). This is to a large extent due to the labors of the modern scholar Chen Yinke, who devoted a massive, three-volume monograph to her life and work, and in so doing provided us with one of the greatest monuments of twentieth-century Chinese philology.

Little is known about the early years of Liu Shi, though it has been surmised that she may have been born in a literate family and only later sold to a courtesan's establishment in the town of Shengze in Wujiang district. At the age of fourteen she was sold to the household of the former minister Zhou Dengdao. Although she started out there as a servant of the minister's mother, it was not long before she became a concubine of the minister himself: "She was his most favored concubine. Although still extremely young, she was extraordinarily bright and intelligent, and her master would often place her upon his knee in order to teach her the literary arts. It is for this reason that she came to be hated by all the other concubines." The following year, Zhou sold her back to her original establishment.

Liu Shi then embarked on the next stage of her career. Using her madam's establishment as a home base, she cruised the area between Suzhou and Shaoxing in a lavish houseboat. As the former concubine of a minister she now belonged to the highest rank of courtesans, and in the Eleventh Month of 1632 she participated, together with many other famous courtesans such as Wang Wei, in the celebration of the seventy-fifth birthday of Chen Jiru. It was at this time that she also met the young poet Chen Zilong for the first time. Following a relationship with one of the most promising students of Songjiang, Song Zhengyu (Song's mother had the magistrate ban Liu Shi from Songjiang as "a danger to public morals"), Liu Shi in the spring of 1633 fell in love with his friend Chen Zilong. Chen Zilong was one of the leading intellectuals of his time, and also played a major role in the revival of the song lyric as a major genre of poetry. After Chen Zilong's return from the metropolitan examinations in 1633, in spring 1635 the couple moved into the Southern Garden in Songjiang. Throughout these seemingly idyllic two years, the couple exchanged numerous poems and song lyrics. In the early summer of 1636, however, Chen Zilong's main wife, with the support of his grandmother and stepmother, forced Chen Zilong to send Liu Shi home. The couple nevertheless continued to exchange poetry in later years.

In the following years, Liu Shi had intimate relationships with a number of patrons. One of the most notable of these was the rich merchant Wang Ruqian, at whose Hangzhou house she stayed in 1638. It was Wang who introduced her to the famous poet Qian Qianyi (1582–1664) from Changshu. Qian Qianyi had passed the metropolitan examinations in 1610 as the "third on the list" and had occupied several important bureaucratic posts in the twenties and thirties. Liu Shi admired Qian's poetry and Qian had expressed his admiration for one of her lines. In 1639, Liu Shi joined Qian Qianyi for a boating trip on Hangzhou's famous West Lake. In the Eleventh Month of 1640, Liu Shi, dressed as a man, went to Changshu to call on Qian, who immediately built a studio for her on his estate. After having spent New Year's Eve there together, the couple left for a pleasure trip by boat of many months. On board their boat, Qian Qianyi formally married Liu Shi on the seventh of the Sixth Month according to the full ritual for marrying a wife. Marrying a courtesan not as a concubine but as a wife was improper enough in itself, but Qian's main wife, lady Chen (d. 1658), was still very much alive, and Qian's actions caused a great scandal:

In the Sixth Month of the *xinsi* year, Yushan [Qian Qianyi] married Liu Shi on their boat at Rongcheng. He was dressed in cap and gown [i.e., formal court dress], and the wedding ritual was complete with joined cups and flowery candles. Qian recited altogether eight poems on "Hastening the Toilette." The gentry of Yunjian [Songjiang] was in an uproar and attacked him for soiling the famous vessels of the dynasty and damaging the honor of the literati, and it almost came to fistfights. The boat sailed off under a barrage of tiles and bricks, but Yushan was the happiest man on earth!

After Qian Qianyi and Liu Shi had returned to Changshu, he built a new library for Liu Shi, even though he had to sell his prized Song dynasty editions of the *Books of the Han* and the *Books of the Later Han*. Here the couple collaborated in the collating and editing of texts.

After the fall of Beijing in 1644, when Ming officials in southern China tried to organize resistance against the invading Manchus and establish a government in Nanjing, Qian Qianyi joined the so-called Southern Ming court with the rank of President of the Ministry of Rites. Liu Shi had followed him to Nanjing and when the city was about to fall to the troops of the Manchu Qing dynasty the following year, she is said to have urged Qian to commit suicide out of loyalty to the Ming. Qian Qianyi declared himself unable to take his own life, and in fact headed the delegation of Nanjing officials who welcomed the Manchu troops into the city. As a reward, Qian was summoned to Beijing for appointment. In the summer of the next year (1646), however, he retired from his new post, pleading illness, and returned to Changshu with Liu Shi. In 1647 (some argue in 1648) Qian was arrested for participating in anti-Manchu activities and taken to Nanjing, but after a few months of detention he was released, partly thanks to the efforts of Liu Shi on his behalf. A daughter was born to the couple in 1648.

Following their return to Changshu, Qian Qianyi completed the compilation of his *Collected Poems of the Successive Reigns*, which was printed in 1649. Liu Shi had collaborated on this project by editing the section on women poets. Most of Qian Qianyi and Liu Shi's remaining years were taken up by various undercover activities on behalf of the anti-Manchu struggle in the lower Yangzi region, but none of these activities was successful. The couple also increasingly turned to Buddhism for solace. Two years after her daughter was married in 1661, Liu Shi even shaved her head in the style of a Buddhist nun. When Qian Qianyi died the next year, powerful relatives immediately descended on the estate to (re)claim huge amounts of money. Unable to withstand their constant extortions, Liu Shi committed suicide by hanging herself a month after her husband's death. Following her death, Qian Qianyi's son had her buried with his father as his main wife in second marriage. Liu Shi's ghost continued to haunt the room in which she had hanged herself, until it was turned into a temple in her memory in 1808.

The poetry of Liu Shi does not make for easy reading as it is laden with obscure allusions and topical references that often continue to baffle even the most erudite Chinese scholars. This also severely restricts the number of poems that lend themselves to translation. Most of the pre-

served works of Liu Shi date from before her association with Qian
Qianyi. The period during which she was involved with Chen Zilong was
particularly productive, as the couple exchanged many songs and lyrics.

Sitting Alone, Two Poems

I

The time of spring completes my lonely sitting,
Pure harmony destroys my fragrant years.
On the emerald bank: cold the mist-wrapped chignon;
By the dark brook: returned from a jade-like dream.
 The numinous wind endless as in the past,
But I take no pleasure in the stream.
To what purpose this reddening of the grass?
Yet the love of swallow and oriole persists.

II

Last night my sorrowful thoughts were many,
Now my grief is about to be doubled.
Gods and immortals may loftily live in bliss,
Flowers and birds are free to drift and soar.
 The jade mirror is filled with spring charms,
The golden hook chilly throughout the night:
I do not know whether this evening's moon
Truly regrets having lit up this empty room.

The above poems may well have been written when Chen Zilong was
temporarily away to take part in the metropolitan examinations. The following song lyric is assumed to date from the period they lived together:

To the Melody of "Sound Reduplications" (*Shengshengling*) On Flying Kites

Willow floss returned from dreams:
Who is in charge of spring's splendor?
Under the bright sky they seek out a place to go wild.
Crossing clouds and grasping rain—
At other times
Flying close to Heaven

Afraid of only
Being unable to catch the other.

The string is long, the wind is light
In front of the painted tower
In the glorious sunlight.
Even at the edge of the sky they can be made out side by side,
Deeply attached one to another,
Unable to part.
Truly tied up:
From time to time in sorrow above indistinct trees.

The following song lyric is said to have been written after the couple had been forced to split up:

To the Melody of "Walking through the Sedge-Grass" (*Tasuoxing*)
Sending a Letter

Flower-patterned, moon-shaped:
"Sorrow" it opens, "Grief" it ends—
When I started out writing I already had no tears left.
Now that I've done writing a sneaky wind blows,
A sneaky wind that blows my devotion to pieces.

Half of the screen the lamp's flame,
Once again as in a dream:
My soul dissolves as you appear in the light.
When I open my eyes I have to think very hard—
My dream so small, he is nowhere to be found.

In 1638, the year Liu Shi spent in Hangzhou, she wrote many poems and lyrics on the city's famous West Lake and its scenic surroundings dotted with numerous monasteries, temples, and cloisters. The Dragon Well on the Phoenix Range to the southwest of West Lake was renowned for the purity of its water, from which an excellent tea could be brewed:

Visiting the New Cloister at Dragon Well

Hidden birds multiply their songs at dusk,
The beautiful one extends her evening sorrow.

In the mountain hall lofty words are chanted,
By the clear pond a dark crane cries out.
 Endlessly the valley streams rush down,
Gazing into the distance one is filled with thought.
I play a zither among the flat boulders—
What is the need for rock-osmanthus branches?
 The moon arises from the pond of flowing gold,
The clear songs are the same as those of my prime.
Creepers grow on the northern mountain,
Mist settles on the painted eaves.
 We returned and soared to this fine feast—
When can we look forward to another gathering?
I crane my neck and heave a deep sigh,
And all around me are also moved to lament.

On the banks of West Lake could also be found (and can still be found) two of China's most famous patriotic shrines, one dedicated to the memory of the Song dynasty general Yue Fei (1103–1141) and one to the fifteenth-century minister of war Yu Qian (1398–1457). Yue Fei, it was widely believed, had been on the verge of reconquering all of northern China when he was called back to the capital due to the calculated machinations of the prime minister of the Southern Song, Qin Kui, who was secretly in the pay of the Jürchen Jin dynasty and preferred a life of luxury and leisure to the exertions and sacrifice of war. At the urging of his wife, Qin Kui later had Yue Fei killed in prison. Yu Qian served as the minister of war in 1449, when the reigning emperor of the Ming allowed himself to be persuaded by his eunuchs to personally lead a campaign against the marauding Mongols, who by this time had been unified under a leader named Esen. The Ming campaign ended in total disaster: at the battle of Tumu, the Chinese troops were decimated and the emperor himself was captured. Yu Qian saved the dynasty by taking charge of the defense of Beijing, installing the emperor's younger brother as his successor, and refusing to negotiate with Esen. The latter did not have the military means to press his advantage, and one year later allowed his captive to return to Beijing. In 1457 a coup d'état returned the former emperor to his throne and Yu Qian was executed. Both Yue Fei and Yu Qian were posthumously restored with all the honors due to them, and subsequently became widely venerated exemplars of loyalty. Liu Shi's later loyalty to the beleaguered Ming dynasty is foreshadowed in the poems she wrote after visiting these two shrines:

The Shrine of the Martial and Revered Prince Yue

Qiantang was once upon a time the capital and home of the Emperor,[13]
The Martial and Reverend Prince's grave is still to be found on this hill.
The banners and flags that roved by moonlight killed the panther's tail,
The wind and rain that loved the lake blocked his standard's advance.
 The palace buildings of yesterday linked up with the barbarian horsemen,
The endless sky of tonight stretches out to the border's watchtowers.
This very day the world is filled with the news of battles:
In front of Tian Heng's grave one is moved to even greater sorrow.[14]

The poem on "The Shrine of the Loyal and Dignified Prince Yu" reads as follows:

The Junior Guardian was a hero without equal,
The fame of his merit fills the farthest regions.
How decisive was he in attack and defense
Whenever he was commanding the troops!
 His energy swallowed the dragon-wastes,
His achievements surpass cloud-pavilions.
Sitting still he witnessed the emperor return,
And the death of the caitiffs' chief in the desert.
 Only when Heaven's Mandate had shifted,
Could a plot be hatched against this Rangju.[15]
Over the Western Market white clouds arose,[16]
As his storm and thunder reverted to silence.

---

13. Hangzhou (Qiantang) was the capital of the Southern Song dynasty (1127–1278).

14. Tian Heng was a scion of the royal family of the ancient state of Qi. When the Qin dynasty collapsed, he raised troops and set himself up as king of Qi, but later was defeated by one of Liu Bang's generals. He then fled with five hundred followers to a little island off the coast. When he was summoned by Liu Bang, he committed suicide rather than submit. Five hundred of his retainers followed him in death.

15. Sima Rangju was a general of the ancient state of Qi, who later also served as the country's prime minister. In the end he was executed without cause, which makes him a fitting counterpart for Yu Qian.

16. The Western Market was where executions were traditionally carried out. In Chinese cosmological thinking, the western direction was associated with autumn and death.

How could he not have known their treacherous plot?
But His Lordship had studied the numbers of fate.
How moving his gratitude for exceptional favor—
This is why he suffered the blade of the sword.
 Although all this happened two hundred years ago,
His spirit is present still in hills and ravines.
 When I visit the banks of the West Lake,
His temple, however, is in disrepair.
In the rampant grass the crickets chirp,
The sky is crisscrossed by osprey and hawk.
 Cypress and pine darken the hills and heights,
Sparrows chatter on withered mulberry trees.
Useless are the tears I shed in the setting sun—
On what may his heroic manner now rely?
 How many have matched his excellence
Since his departure from this world?
This is the reason why this solitary wanderer
Sheds tears for his hegemonic strategies.

Liu Shi's concern for the safety of the dynasty as peasant rebel armies laid waste to central and western China and the Manchus built up their power along the empire's northeastern border and from time to time conducted raids deep into China also informs her poem "Swordsmanship" of a slightly earlier date:

Why is it that foxes and birds roam freely over the western hills,
And on overgrown slopes squirrels and weasels screech in broad daylight?
By chance I met a man whose courageous vitality was boundless,
His beard and brows were chillingly cold, as solid as thickest ice.
 Although in his hands he did not hold wind or clouds, he was fast and
    fierce,
He took me away and on two horses we traveled to the southwest.

Before on horseback I'd heard the words "Dragon-like Soaring,"
I'd already seen the bows and lances hanging before the gate.
Arranging my clothes, I wanted to flee the coral turning dark,
But of the vast world he did not speak, only of swordsmanship.

In a moment thunder and lightning rose from the branch tips,
Black gibbons and red panthers invaded the empty empyrean:

The inverted shadows of the freezing blade were unknowable—
On the dark cliffs the wind rustled sadly through the bare trees.

Alas, such transformations can only be the work of a hero,
In times of danger his swords sliced through rocks and bones.
"To no avail does my energy fill the entire world,
White-haired in Yangzhou my heart is overcome by sorrow.
Gazing at this straw-thatched cottage—what can I accomplish?
Heroic talent and great strategy are now but sorrow and grief.
 However, just see how the stars and planets move as I lift my sleeves,
And ocean-lads and river maidens are forced to come out.
Dashing like a giant serpent shooting through the thick underbrush,
Forceful like a striking eagle swooping down from the cloudy sky,
 Crowded like myriads of gods gazing down into a ravine,
Flashing like a length of silk following a striped badger.
I see nothing in front of me but demon-birds and orphaned owls—
In vain then are the actions of an old crane in the dark clouds.
 A real man with a tiger's gait who studies the Way
May one day perhaps yet follow the numinous gods.
Filled with noble outrage I myself still nourish this intention,
Confronted with such towering threats, how can I just let go?"

This poem inspired an early critic to the following remarks: "In her early years Liu Shi was besotted with the strange, and she often fell into the trap of disorganized rambling. . . Even her finest works such as 'Swordsmanship' . . . lack careful pruning, and so are not easy to recite. But time and again one comes across startling lines, and again and again she surprises you with the crashing and flashing of thunder and lightning, and the thrusting and beating of swords and lances, showing an extraordinary style among women writers."

In later years, however, Liu Shi also produced poems such as the following quatrain on the bamboo, which are far more pared down and concise:

It refuses to show off with flowers since it does not aim for glamour,
Its independent stance is reflected upside down in the inkstone's well.
Every single branch and every single leaf deserves our respect:
Once it grew on a famous mountain and spurned the Seven Sages. [17]

---

17. The Seven Sages is a group of eccentric scholars of the middle of the third century, including Xi Kang and Liu Ling, who spurned the common run of corrupt officials. The bamboo in its purity spurns even the Seven Sages!

8 · Matrons and Maidens

Given that writing courtesans were such a highly visible presence in late Ming society, it is understandable that elite women with literary aspirations would want to avoid the public domain and make use of their own all-female networks for the exchange of poems and letters. Often, these informal networks were composed of family members, as in the case of the group constituted by Shen Yixiu (1590–1635), her daughters Ye Wanwan (1610–1632), Ye Xiaowan (1613–1657), and Ye Xiaoluan (1616–1632), and various other female relatives. In other cases, these groups would be extended to include members from outside the family and would take the shape of a more formal literary society. The best-known example of this phenomenon is the Banana Garden Poetry Club of Hangzhou, which will be discussed in Chapter 10.

Shen Yixiu and Her Daughters

Shen Yixiu

Shen Yixiu was the daughter of a high official named Shen Chong (1562–1622), who after a long official career rose to the position of vice-commissioner of Shandong province, and one of her uncles was the famous Suzhou dramatist Shen Jing (1553–1610). At the age of sixteen, Shen Yixiu was married to Ye Shaoyuan (1589–1648), a descendant of a rich landed family of Wujiang who in his youth was renowned for his good

looks: their marriage was widely considered in Suzhou circles to be a perfect match. Although the couple did indeed share an interest in painting,
Buddhism, and poetry (they actively collected women's poetry together),
they did not see much of each other during the early years of their marriage because Ye Shaoyuan spent much of his time at the home of his
adoptive father, Yuan Huang, preparing for the examinations. Despite
this, Shen Yixiu managed to bear her husband eight sons and five daughters. Ye Shaoyuan eventually passed the metropolitan examinations in
1625, but after a short and frustrating career retired from the bureaucracy
in 1631 and devoted the remainder of his life to literary pursuits and philological studies, while his wife and daughters devoted themselves to
poetry.

Shen Yixiu was an accomplished poet, and for many years was also the
central figure of a large group of women poets comprised mostly of
members of the Shen family and relatives by marriage. Nevertheless, giving birth to so many children one after the other occupied much of her
time and energy, and in the end, she never recovered from the death in
quick succession of one of her sons and two of her daughters. Basing
their account on the copious biographical materials provided by Ye
Shaoyuan, Qian Qianyi and Liu Shi compiled the following summary of
the life of Shen Yixiu:

Shen Yixiu's style name was Wanjun and she hailed from Wujiang. She was the
daughter of the vice-commissioner of Shandong province, Shen Chong, and the
wife of the bureau director of the Ministry of Works, Ye Shaoyuan [style name
Zhongshao]. In his youth, Zhongshao was known for his good looks, which
were compared to those of [the paragons of male beauty] Wei Jie [ca. 300] and
Pan Yue [247–300]. At the age of sixteen Wanjun came to him in marriage, and
like a carnelian branch and a jade tree they brilliantly illuminated one another
and were extravagantly praised by all the people of Suzhou.

Shen Yixiu gave birth to three daughters: the eldest was named Wanwan, the
second Huichou [Xiaowan], and the youngest Xiaoluan [Qiongzhang]. With
their orchid-like hearts and figures, they were all heavenly beings. After Zhongshao met with misfortune in his official career, he plunged himself into philological studies, while Wanjun and her three daughters wrote about the blossoming trees and flowers, and sang of the moon and clouds. Their inner quarter
verses were the equal of those of the Xie household [Xie Daoyun], while the
writings of the cherished daughters at times surpassed those of lady Zuo [Zuo

Fen]. All of their female relatives, whether old or young, related by blood or by marriage, would lay aside their scissors and rulers to devote themselves to poetic composition, and abandon their spinning and weaving to perfect their writing skills. Atop Songling Ridge and alongside Fen Lake, literary talents emerged one after the other from the women's apartments, and "gifts of red brushes" were all the rage.[1]

At seventeen, Xiaoluan was engaged to a son of the Zhang family of Kunshan, but on the eve of her marriage she died. Shortly afterwards, Wanwan, who had returned to her maternal home to lament her sister's death, also died. Wanjun's spirit was wounded and her heart had perished: wracked by sorrow, she wasted away, and after three years, she too passed away. Zhongshao subsequently gathered all of Wanjun's poems under the title *Oriole Pipings* [*Lichui*], all of Wanwan's poems under the title *Words of Sorrow* [*Chouyan*], and all of Xiaoluan's poems under the title *Fragrance of a Returned Life* [*Fansheng xiang*], and together with many funerary and commemorative texts, he published them as a single collection.

Although Shen Yixiu's collection of poetry is much more extensive than those of her daughters, it must be said that few of her poems match the intensity, detail, and narrative power of the biography she wrote for her daughter, Qiongzhang (Xiaoluan), which appears later in this chapter. The majority of her preserved poems appear to have been written after the death of her daughters, as many of them are written in their memory. Of these poems, the most moving are those in which she records her dreams of absent or deceased family members:

Dreaming of Junyong[2]

Sad and distressed, and again, sad and distressed,
There is no limit to the pain of separation.
Since you left us, seven autumns have passed:
I can vent my sorrows only through my sighs.
 Of late you have often entered my dreams—
But how could such a dreamscape even exist?

---

1. "Red brushes" refer to women's writing brushes, which often had a red-colored handle.

2. Junyong was one of Shen Yixiu's younger brothers. He spent many years in northern China before his death.

Whenever you dream of your old hometown,
You couldn't possibly still remember the place.
 And although I dream of Heaven's farthest reaches,
I could not know my way on the roads there.
In other words, both of us are completely lost:
And the long night is a darkness without end.
 Unending is the way it wounds my heart:
The moon is setting by the green wood's edge.
Then I look up and see the wagtails flying by—
When can I too lift my feathered wings and fly?

Dreaming of My Deceased Daughter, Qiongzhang

The eastern breeze tonight has just returned,
But at the silk window the cold is still fierce.
Pacing up and down I am unable to fall asleep,
As the bronze water clock hurries on.
 When I doze off, I meet you in a dream,
Your flower-face brighter still than snow.
Overcome by joy, flooded by thoughts—
Unable to express the sadness of parting.
 Conscious only of the joy of seeing you,
I forget that we are separated by death.
I ask about your elder sister's whereabouts,
And why it is you did not bring her along.
 You point to the east side of a little room
Where quietly she sits reading her books.
As I grasp her hands, my feelings surging,
A sudden sob wakes me from my dream.
 Awake and yet I still clutch at the gown,
As the dying lamp sputters and then fades.
Lying on my pillow I swallow my cries,
But my innards are torn into smithereens.

On a Sleepless Summer Night Thinking of My Deceased Son

The endless night drags on and on, accompanied by a hundred sorrows,
I trim the lamp, rise then sit down again, then let out a heavy sigh.
The empty courtyard silent except for the frogs croaking in the grass,
The tall bamboo a shield against the rain pouring through the railings.

My heart has completely turned to ashes, unvisited now by grief.
I cried my eyes out, yet to no avail I brush aside my tears.
The Ninth Heaven far away turns a deaf ear to my questions—
Now that the orchids have been destroyed the jade trees are cold.

Shen Yixiu's collection also includes a large number of lyrics. This reflects both the general revival of this genre during the final decades of the Ming dynasty (and into the following Qing dynasty) and the special affinity many women writers appeared to have felt with this genre. One of Shen Yixiu's best-known lyrics supposedly came to her in a dream:

To the Melody of "Remembering the Prince" (*Yi wangsun*)

To heaven's farthest reaches I follow my dream over green, green grasses.
The color of willows hides the ten- and five-mile pavilions along the road;
The yellow orioles in their branches resent the blossoms for falling down.
Mountains stretch into the distance,
Below them drifting clouds pass by endlessly without a worry in the
    world.

Some of Shen Yixiu's lyrics were, like many of her *shi* poems, written in memory of her deceased daughters:

To the Melody of "Remembering the Beauty of Qin" (*Yi Qin'e*)
On a Cold and Sleepless Night, Remembering My Deceased Daughter

The west wind is piercing,
The bamboo battered by rain, the grieving cold intense.
The grieving cold intense:
My heart has been broken a hundred times,
My innards are twisted into a thousand knots.

The jasper flowers lured away our whitest pear blossoms too soon:
Now the Sparse Fragrance One has gone, my sorrow is unspeakable![3]
My sorrow unspeakable:

---

3. Sparse Fragrance was the name of Ye Xiaoluan's study.

The joys and laughter of times gone by
Today have turned into tears of blood.

To the Melody of "Walking through the Sedge-Grass" (*Tasuoxing*)
Weeping for My Daughters

The plum bud startled by the storm,
The pear blossom wasted by the rain:
Only traces of their sparse fragrance are still as of old.
Orioles and swallows chirp and chatter all over again,
But peach and plum remain mute from dawn till dusk.

Of the three parts of spring
Two parts are already gone,
But when I sum up my sorrows, they cannot be counted.
To no avail did my broken heart urge all my tears to flow—
Their fragrant souls have disappeared to who knows where.

Shen Yixiu was a follower of Great Master Lezi, a medium from Suzhou who claimed to have the ability to transmit messages from a female divinity by the name of Fangtai Lezi. Because this medium was so completely identified with this divinity, he himself came to be referred to as the Great Master Lezi.

Offered to the Great Master Lezi

Busily we float up and sink down without a moment of respite,
Looking back on my life, nothing has turned out as it should.
My parents' efforts not yet repaid—in vain my heart breaks;
Children tugging at my sleeves—secretly I wipe my tears away.
 I know it is not easy to free oneself from the realm of illusion,
Until one has put a stop to "empty flowers" one will only hesitate.
Lost in delusion, I hope that you will deign to take pity on me,
And lead me to the raft of compassion—oh please, hear my prayer!

The Great Master Lezi informed Ye Shaoyuan that he had received messages from the divinity indicating that not only his daughters, but also his wife had passed on to a higher stage of consciousness upon their death. Ye Shaoyuan has left extended descriptions of the messages he received through the intermediary of Lezi, the contents of which Qian Qianyi and Liu Shi summarize as follows:

In Suzhou there was a deity who manifested herself through the planchette. She called herself Fangtai Lezi and claimed to have been a senior disciple of the Great Master Zhizhe [Zhiyi 538–597, known as the founder of Tiantai Buddhism], who had in a subsequent lifetime taken on a female body but had fallen into the path of demons and spirits; she made use of the planchette to manifest herself and teach the Dharma. According to this planchette, women of exceptional intelligence who upon their death were destined to achieve deliverance in a female body were taken to the Leafless Hall where they would be instructed in the practice of the four rules and esoteric truths and marked for rebirth in the Western Paradise. The name Leafless Hall refers to the realization of the essentials [literally, the trunk rather than the leaves] of the Buddhist sutras and the pure and authentic truth. Wanjun and Zhaoqi [Wanwan] both entered Leafless Hall. Wanjun took the religious name of Zhiding and the style name of Xiyan; Zhaoqi took the religious name of Zhizhuan and the style name of Zhulun. Xiaoluan had once served as a library attendant in the Moon Mansion and originally her name was Hanhuang, but now she was again given the name of Ye Xiaoluan.

[The spirit of] Qiongzhang was summoned, and sometime later, she arrived and composed some poems. She replied in great detail to the questions of the members of her family. When Lezi explained the workings of ignorance, and the causes and conditions of the sufferings of birth, illness, and old age, Qiongzhang said: "I would like to receive the teachings from you, Great Master, instead of returning to the mansions of the immortals." When the Master questioned her on the Buddhist precepts, Qiongzhang replied without any hesitation, and entirely in the elegant language of Six Dynasties parallel prose! Greatly amazed, the Master said: "I would never dare to regard you as [a mere] divine immortal! You can be said to have gone far, far beyond them." She then gave her the religious name of Zhiduan and the style name of Jueji. The adherents of this cult now address Qiongzhang by the name of Juezi or Chan Master Jue. From that time on, Master Lezi and Xiyan, mother and daughters, descended countless times through the planchette, composing poetry in which they urged people to engage in religious practice.

Shen Yixiu's daughters, Wanwan, Xiaowan, and Xiaoluan, distinguished themselves at an early age by their precocious intelligence. When she was only three years old, Wanwan reportedly could recite Bai Juyi's lengthy *Song of Lasting Regret* (*Changhen ge*) and already at the age of thirteen could write poetry of her own. Xiaoluan, the youngest daughter, who was raised by an uncle and aunt who had no children of their own, is said to have been able to recite poetry by the age of four, to be able to write poems by the age of twelve, to have become an accomplished go player by the age of fourteen, and to have mastered the zither by the age of sixteen. Ye Shaoyuan, who firmly believed that his youngest daughter had become an immortal after her death, lost no time in publishing the collected poems of his wife and two deceased daughters. He attached to these poems many of his own extensive critical notes as well as copious biographical materials, and also appended to the collection an anthology of women's poetry compiled by his wife as well as some of his own writings. (A later edition of this collection, compiled by his son Ye Xie [1627–1703], also included a four-act *zaju* play written by Ye Xiaowan in memory of her two sisters.) Ye Shaoyuan's compilation, entitled the *Noon Dream Hall Collection* (*Wumengtang ji*), enjoyed a wide circulation at the time, in large part because it appealed to contemporary sensibilities regarding the purity and sincerity of the literary expressions of young women who had suffered much and died young. Ye Shaoyuan was not unique in publishing the writings of his prematurely deceased daughters. At a somewhat earlier date the official and dramatist Tu Long (1542–1605) had seen to the printing of the poems of both his daughter and his daughter-in-law, who had died at the ages of twenty-seven and twenty-one, respectively.

Ye Xiaoluan

Ye Shaoyuan's *Noon Dream Hall Collection* was inspired primarily by the sudden death of his cherished third daughter, Ye Xiaoluan. Xiaoluan had been raised by her uncle, Shen Yixiu's younger brother, Shen Junyong, and his wife Zhang Qianqian, who happened to be Shen Yixiu's cousin as well as best friend. After Zhang Qianqian's untimely death at the age of thirty-four, Shen Yixiu wrote an extended biographical account of her life, later summarized by Qian Qianyi and Liu Shi as follows:

Qianqian was the wife of Shen Zizheng [style name Junyong] from Wujiang and was the daughter of Shen Yixiu's aunt. Shen Yixiu herself had been raised in her youth by her aunt [Qianqian's mother], and Qianqian was four years her junior. With shining eyes and sparkling teeth, they would discuss the *Rites* and try their hand at poetry: they were truly girls of the highest caliber.

When Qianqian married Junyong, none of the sons and daughters she bore survived, and so she raised Shen Yixiu's youngest daughter, Qiongzhang [Xiaoluan], as if she were her own. Qiongzhang was extremely intelligent and already as a small child could recite the *Book of Odes* and the *Songs of the South* (*Chuci*), which Qianqian had taught her. As a young man, Junyong loved to dress in furs and ride a fine horse and would often squander a thousand ounces of silver [on a single occasion]; he would boast that he was talented enough to rule the world with his eloquence, and he loved to roam about both in the Capital and in the regions beyond the northern border. Beautiful and intelligent, Qianqian endured solitude and poverty until, unable to bear her sadness, at the age of thirty-four she fell ill and died.

Qianqian was skilled at writing poems and lyrics, but whenever she wrote anything, she would immediately toss it out. Qiongzhang, however, [managed to] commit some of her poems to memory. When Qiongzhang died, Shen Yixiu not only grieved for her daughter, but also felt a need to memorialize Qianqian so she wrote a biography of Qianqian to which she appended the poems [by Qianqian] that Qiongzhang had memorized.

Following the death of her aunt, Xiaoluan returned to her natal family. In later years she would continue to remember fondly her adoptive parents and the love and care they lavished on her. This affection is very apparent in the following quatrain by Xiaoluan:

Spring of the Year *yisi* (1629): Weeping at the Grave of My Aunt, the Wife of Shen Liu

I have no way to repay the ten years of your loving care,
You can't hear my weeping deep down below the earth.
But every year the color of the grass in spring
Will break my heart here at this lonely grave.

When we read the comments that Ye Shaoyuan appended to the following quatrain Xiaoluan composed in 1627 at the age of twelve, it becomes obvious that he was convinced of the extraordinary literary abilities of his daughter from early on:

Morning Toilette on a Spring Day

I hold up my mirror in the clear morning breeze:
These moth-like brows are not a work of artifice!

Just as I finish inserting the flowers in my hair,
I hear the songs of orioles beyond the willow trees.

> *[Ye Shaoyuan:] At the age of twelve, when she had just learned [to write poetry], [already she was able to] come up with lines like these. They are truly the result of an innate intelligence! Why should she be ranked lower than the Four Stalwarts of the Effortless Rule period* [Chuigong, 685–688]![4]

Her father lavished this high praise not only on Xiaoluan's *shi* poetry, but also on her prose. In the collection of Xiaoluan's writings in the *Noon Dream Hall Collection*, Ye Shaoyuan includes two of his daughter's short prose essays, the first of which, entitled "Record of a Night at the Banana Window," according to the note appended to the title, she wrote "in jest, in the year *xinwei* [1631]." In this little piece, Xiaoluan assumes for herself the sobriquet Master of the Cooking Dream, an obvious allusion to the Tang dynasty tale of the "yellow millet dream." This famous tale recounts how a young and ambitious scholar stops at a roadside inn and, weary from his journey, falls asleep while waiting for his meal of millet porridge to finish cooking. In his dream he experiences an entire lifetime, including a long and distinguished career and its inevitable end. The student wakes up and, finding that his meal is still not ready, realizes the vanity of all worldly ambition.

The Master of the Cooking Dream hides herself away in a single room, devotes herself solely to poems and wine, and is not the slightest bit concerned with the affairs of this world.

Once on the night of the sixteenth of the Ninth Month, a white moon illuminated the sky and a long breeze entered her door. The leaves that had fallen from the branches danced in the wind, and the grasses, which had been depleted of their colors, knew that they were doomed. The Master of the Cooking Dream had brought along a goblet and a jug of wine and was drinking by herself in the courtyard. After a long while the moonlight moved to the west and the shadows of the trees turned to the east. Once her goblet was empty and her

---

4. The "Four Stalwarts" are Wang Bo (649–676), Yang Jiong (650–ca. 694), Lu Zhaolin (ca. 634–ca. 684), and Lo Binwang (before 640–684), usually designated as the "Four Stalwarts of the Early Tang." They are often credited with reviving the moral élan of Chinese poetry following the vogue for "palace-style poetry."

jug had run dry, in her elation she became filled with a yearning for the [company of the] immortals, and in her frustration wrote the following poems:

I

Penglai lies so far away across the Weak Waters;[5]
I find it hard to keep my sad sorrows at bay.
If the moon's pale beauty has any feeling at all,
She will shine down especially upon this room.

II

The whistling fades and the bright moon descends,
The singing finished, the bright clouds drift away.
I wish I could go to the Queen Mother of the West,
And borrow from her a goblet of crystalline brew!

[After writing these poems] she went into her room. Raising the wick of the dying lamp, she opened a book, but after a while, leaning on her armrest she dozed off. Outside her window she heard a shuffling sound, like the sound of footsteps. Peering through a crack in the window, the Master of the Cooking Dream saw two girls clad in green. They both had hair in locks like the wind and chignons like rain; they were graceful and elegant and had many charms. They sat down on the stone table in the front side of the courtyard. Laughing and jesting, they began by admiring the beauties of breeze and moon, but after a while, as they started to tell of the secrets in their hearts, sorrow furrowed their brows and tears streaked their cheeks. They spoke of far more than she could remember and in fact, she could only really remember the gist of their songs, such as when the older of the two girls raised her sleeves in the wind and sang:

> Below the bright moon, oh, how I long for my loved one,
>   The clear dew rolls down, oh, so many sorrows fill my breast.
> Wandering along lakes and hills, oh, I idly sing my sad song,
>   My fragrant heart will not be moved, oh, though overwhelmed by feeling.

The youngest one then chimed in with the following song:

---

5. Penglai is one of the floating islands of immortals in the Eastern Ocean. Weak Waters, a body of water that cannot support even a feather, separates the world of mortals from that of the immortals.

From the folds of my emerald sleeves, oh, a pure fragrance wafts,
And I long for my loved one, oh, at the other end of the sky!
I gaze up at the geese heading south, oh, my longing heart hurts—
That I might borrow their wings, oh, and fly together with them!

Even after their songs were finished, their lingering echoes and the girls' fine fragrance continued to assail her, but by the time she opened the window to ask them who they were, they had already shaken out their sleeves and hidden themselves among the banana trees.

The Master of the Cooking Dream comments: "Alas, could they possibly have been the numinous spirits of the banana trees?"

Here, Ye Shaoyuan limits himself to the following remarks: "It is indeed unusual that a gentle and graceful beauty from the women's quarters should adopt the name of Master of the Cooking Dream! The significance of the two words 'Cooking Dream' is even more novel. How could they signify nothing more than that her dream had already transported her, even before the yellow millet had finished cooking, to the realm of Huaxu?[6] These manifestations of the immortals are too many to all be described in full—and even if you did, people would probably not believe you."

If Ye Shaoyuan was somewhat circumspect with his comments on his daughter's first essay, he unhesitatingly compares her second prose piece, titled "A Record of the Lake Fen Stones," to no less than the works of the greatest Tang dynasty masters of old-style prose, Han Yu (768–824) and Liu Zongyuan (773–819): "One doesn't have to be a great master such as Liu Zongyuan or Han Yu! She had barely begun to learn how to write ancient-style prose essays, and already she could write like this. This is proof of a truly divine preternatural intelligence. If Heaven had allowed her some more years, she would have surpassed Ban Zhao and Cai Yan!" Although this fatherly praise may be a bit fulsome, nevertheless Xiaoluan's essay is certainly good enough to be included in any anthology of informal essays (*xiaopin*) from the late Ming dynasty:

The Lake Fen Stones are so called because they were found in Lake Fen. Once, the water level had fallen leaving the banks high and dry: [in fact] the flow had

---

6. The realm of Huaxu is a mythic domain where people live happily in an eternal dream.

dried up leaving the steep sides exposed. The people [living there] informed us "On the shore of the lake you can find stones, lots of them, in piles!" And so we ordered them to bring the stones to our place by boat. Large and small, round and misshapen, wide and long—they were all different. Their colors were dark and their shapes were marvelous and they were all beautiful! When we asked the people who lived by the side of the lake who it was who might have left them there, they said they didn't know.

Could it be that in the past this had been a place of wealth and luxury that over many centuries had disappeared without any record? Or had these stones been born in this lake at the beginning of time? If they had been born in this lake, then they have only now had the good fortune of being discovered! But if they had once belonged to a place of wealth and luxury that had disappeared without leaving a trace, they were indeed much to be pitied! When the people [of this place] installed these stones, I imagine there must have been flowers and trees that both shaded and illuminated them and ponds and terraces that surrounded and supported them: There, singing lads and dancing girls must have roamed and dallied, and scholars must have whistled and chanted along with poets. Woods and valleys would have vied in beauty, and colored mists would have had their owner. Would not these stones also have participated in the pleasures of wandering and gazing?

But now into what have they been transformed? Not even a single trace remains of a crumbled wall or abandoned well, an overgrown path or an ancient trail: nothing there that one can research. There are only these stones, which, for who knows how many centuries, have lain dejected along the banks of the lake. Now that they have been discovered, isn't it enough just to feel sad for them? Still, when the rushing waves crashed into them and bore them away, when fish and shrimp swam around them and hollowed them out, then the autumn wind blew mournfully over the flowering rushes and the cold nights resounded with the honking of migrating geese. Reeds covered with white dew stretched out endlessly into the dark mists. Anglers' skiffs and fishermen's sails bobbed up and down while transverse flutes were played; hairpins of cress and sashes of water mallow enveloped and surrounded these stones as they did the black conches. Did it then seem as though the existence of these stones between heaven and earth would forever share the destiny of the lake's waters in their forgotten corner?

Now that they have been placed in our courtyard, they have again been piled up like mountains. Shaded by flourishing trees and covered with dark mosses, they are interspersed with the most resplendent red blossoms and intermingled with the most fragrant white petals. Here the fine grasses are green in spring, and the full moon shines brightly in autumn. Kingfishers circle above their peaks, drifting petals adorn their crags. Between the railings they ascend high terraces and send off returning clouds, next to the windows they brighten distant scenes and give rise to clear breezes. Should they reminisce about their [former] pleasures of whistling and chanting, dallying about, roaming and gazing, are they not enjoying themselves once again here and now? If so, the stones may be pitied for having been buried in the water, but it also should be a cause for joy that they have now had the fortune to be discovered. If the water level had not dropped, if the lake had not dried up, they would [still] be buried under the deep waves. Stones too certainly have their moment!

Lake Fen was located on the southeastern border of Wujiang district, which in turn was bordered on the west by Lake Tai, one of China's largest inland lakes and long famous as the source of the so-called Lake Tai rocks: strangely-shaped pieces of sandstone that have long been popular as ornamental features in traditional Chinese garden design. Xiaoluan's essay was prompted by the chance discovery of comparable rocks in Lake Fen.

Ye Xiaoluan also wrote lyrics and arias. Only one of her arias has been preserved and we translate it here, if only to show that for Xiaoluan and her sisters, poetry could sometimes also be the vehicle for mischievous, if not slightly malicious, fun:

To the Tune of "Yellow Oriole" (*Huang ying'er*)

There was a girl who although already quite old was still not married, so we all made fun of her and I wrote this song in jest:

Leaning on the jade balustrade from beginning to end,
She counts her spring sorrows—
When will they cease?
Her fragrant skin a bag of bones, and still her heart is broken.
Her silk gown is now speckled with tears,
The orioles and flowers are now all gone.
Her rosy cheeks have grown so old, to no avail she sighs.
Behind closed doors
The jade flute sings her grief:
When will she ever drive paired phoenixes?

It is the song lyric, however, that Ye Xiaoluan found to be particularly suited to her poetic talents. She wrote at least ninety lyrics to thirty-six different melodies, something even her father was surprised to discover: "I only knew that she was accomplished in writing lyrics, but I didn't know she had written this many!" Many of these lyrics are devoted to the description of trees and flowering shrubs. Others describe visits to the realm of the immortals, which, although a common enough theme in *ci* poetry, were regarded by her parents after Xiaoluan's death as proof that their daughter was a banished immortal destined to die young and return to her home in the celestial realms.

To the Melody of "Sands of Washing Brook" (*Huanxisha*) Expressing My Emotions

Whenever I try to call out to Heaven, Heaven just seems farther away.
I realize that in this life I will never reach the mountains and streams:
But why have I by nature always felt a kinship with mists and clouds?

Counting the years on my fingers, I'm startled by their number:
Time emptily floats away and I have no desire for worldly glory:
When can I ride astride a crane to the home of the immortals?

> [*Ye Shaoyuan:*] *This was also one of her later pieces. How could she have possibly been detained for long in this dusty realm, given that she possessed the air of an immortal as well as bones that predestined her to the Way? It is useless for me to be saddened by grief.*

To the Melody of "Partridge Sky" (*Zhegutian*) On a Spring Night in the Year *renshen* (1632), I Wrote the Following Five Lyrics in a Dream

I

One scroll of the *Lankavatara Sutra*, one stick of incense:[7]
The prayer mat my companion, now I've forgotten the world.
The green rivers of the Three Isles to my soul are not so far[8]—
A clear breeze on half of my pillow and my dream lingers on.

---

7. The *Lankavatara Sutra* is a central text in the tradition of Chan Buddhism.

8. The Three Isles are the three floating islands of the immortals said to be located in the Eastern Ocean.

As I trace the bending paths,
Follow the winding corridors,
The bamboo hedges and thatched cottages provide a splendid view.
In vain do I pity the swallows returning and then setting off again—
Why must they spend their days so busily building their nests?

II

After the rain the mountains turn a kingfisher-green:
And the overgrown gate opens toward the setting sun.
In the morning I depart with my companion in search of mushrooms,[9]
In the evening, we return home, having bought ourselves a jug of wine!

My body supported by a rock,
My hand holding up a cup:
Who cares if this jade mountain collapses in a stupor—
We cannot know today what will happen tomorrow,
If I stay sober, I will be allowing Time to push me in vain!

III

The paths through the spring fields are overgrown with grasses,
As beneath the green clouds at daybreak the riotous orioles sing.
The tune of the purple reed-organ can be heard even on top of Mt. Hou:
The melody of the crystal-clear chime breaks the silence on
    Vulture Peak.[10]

Dazzlingly red,
Lushly green:
Peach blossoms and swaying willows share the mountain creek.
In the distance, I see a swathe of mists and clouds,
 Spring sails are lowered in the rain as the sun prepares to set.

---

9. The "mushrooms" here refer to the *lingzhi*, the magical mushrooms that bestow eternal life.

10. Mt. Hou (in Henan province) is mentioned in the *Biographies of Immortals* (*Liexian zhuan*) as being an abode of immortals. Vulture Peak is renowned as the place where the Buddha preached the *Lotus Sutra*.

IV

After the rain the dark mountain's colors are even lovelier:
Leaping streams and waterfalls threaten to invade the stairs.
Who can tell these many medicinal plants one from the other?
The mountain flowers have purposely waited for my arrival to bloom.

Just for fun I climb the heights,
Make no special arrangements:
Whistling, reciting, singing, and chanting I leave my cares behind.
I long to float along lightly, to ride off astride the wind,
To go to live on the White Jade Terrace of Jasper Pond.[11]

V

I traveled West on a visit to the Queen Mother's pond,
Where the Qiongsu wine floated in cups of nine colors,
All of the stars of Heaven were mine for the picking,
And my body felt as if it were clothed in clouds and mist.

Riding astride white tigers,
Driving along green dragons,
The assembled immortals sang lyrics to the tune of "Pacing the Void,"
And when I was leaving, Shuangcheng gave me a gift, [12]
A gift of a mushroom of five colors with a golden stem.

> [*Ye Shaoyuan:*] *Ever since the year of her enlightenment* [renshen, or 1632], *she longed to leave this world behind. These lyrics are the more extraordinary as she completed them in a dream. I have often suspected that in a former life she must have been a Daoist recluse who cultivated herself in the mountains, but why was she then born a beautiful girl in this life? If you say it was because she had not yet freed herself completely from her attachment to this dusty world, then why did she die on the eve of her marriage and before she had resolved her emotional entanglements? It remains an insoluble mystery.*

---

11. The Jasper Pond is one of the features of the abode of the Queen Mother of the West located in the mythical Kunlun Mountains.

12. Shuangcheng is a well-known female companion of the Queen Mother of the West.

As early as 1631, Ye Xiaoluan had written a gatha (Buddhist verse), in which she describes her moment of enlightenment in Buddhist terms, although the "Great Teacher" she refers to in her poem most likely refers to the Suzhou medium Master Lezi. As mentioned before, following the death first of Xiaoluan, then of Wanwan, and finally of Shen Yixiu, this spirit transmitted messages to Ye Shaoyuan from his departed wife and daughters and in so doing continued to fuel Ye Shaoyuan's ardent belief in the medium's efficacy. The gatha written by Ye Xiaoluan can be translated as follows:

Rising Early One Morning, I Heard the Sound of Sutras Being Recited and Had an Experience of Enlightenment

Several notes of clear chimes, the prolonged sound of chanting
Startle the frost of the Ninth Month in the cold forest.
The Great Teacher makes no distinction between "self" and "other,"
Although in this floating life we busy ourselves with only profit and fame.
Having experienced enlightenment, my heart is now cold as ice,
In my delusion, how could I have known the fragrance of musk?
How it grieves me to see the suffering of this world of Jambudvipa,[13]
When will we all be ferried across on the raft of compassion?

> [*Ye Shaoyuan:*] *What insight is shown by a girl of sixteen in writing a gatha like this! There was not even half a strand of the dusty web in her bosom!*

Shortly following Xiaoluan's death, her mother Shen Yixiu commemorated her talented daughter with the following long and moving biography:

A Biography of My Youngest Daughter Qiongzhang

My daughter's name was Xiaoluan and her style name was Qiongzhang; another of her style names was Yaoqi. She was my third daughter.

At the age of just six months, she was sent to be raised by the family of my brother Junyong. In the spring of the following year my father retired from office and returned home from Eastern Lu, so I went to visit my natal family. At that time my child was only a year old and exceedingly beautiful. Her aunt

---

13. In Buddhist cosmology, Jambudvipa is the name given to the continent on which the Buddha Sakyamuni preached the Dharma, and by extension, the world in which human beings such as us reside.

was my sister-in-law lady Zhang, a woman of classic beauty and clear wisdom. Time and again she would say to me: "This child shows evidence of a preternatural intelligence, in time she will surely be the equal of Ban Zhao and Cai Yan. Her features also are out of the ordinary!" At the age of four, my child was able to recite "Encountering Sorrow," which she completely understood after having only repeated it a few times. She was also taught to read and write, and if later one would deliberately try to fool her with the wrong character, she would say: "This is not correct. Mother, did you make a mistake?" Her uncle and aunt loved her very dearly.

At the age of ten, she returned to live with our family. Around that time, it had just started to turn cold, and we were sitting together by the clear light of a lamp. Beyond the railing the bamboo mournfully rustled in the wind, and in front of the screen the glow of the moonlight was as bright as day. I then said: "The osmanthus so cold, soaked by the clear dew," and my child immediately responded with the line: "The maple feels the chill when its red leaves fall." At that time I was delighted by her quick-witted intelligence, which reminded me of "the willow floss in the wind." Alas, could this line have been after all a portent of her premature death? Unfortunately later her aunt died, after which her uncle stayed on in Beijing. Whenever their names were mentioned, she would recall their love and care and was always moved to sighs and tears.

My child's build was tall and lovely. At the age of twelve, her hair already covered her brow and she was as graceful as a creature of jade. Her father took her with him to Nanjing, where she visited [famous local spots such as] Changgan and Taoye. Her father also taught her how to chant, and she soon became accomplished in poetry. But now, although I have searched her chests, I have been unable to locate a single poem from those days, probably because she herself threw them away thinking them to be unskillful childhood dabblings. By the age of fourteen, she had become an accomplished player of the game of go. When she turned sixteen, an aunt who was a good zither player gave her some lessons, and immediately she was able to play some tunes. Clear and limpid, they were lovely to listen to, and fit Xi Kang's descriptive lines: "The fine notes rise and disperse— how colorful, how splendid!" She was also skilled at copying the scrolls of painting that we kept in our home. This last summer, when my younger brother Junmu sent me a fan, my child made a very precise copy of it. She would also observe the falling petals and drifting butterflies [drawn] on *teng* paper, which were extremely elegant, but since she did not have a teacher to instruct her and had not studied painting for a long time, she still lacked the necessary skill.

By nature she was lofty and untrammeled and disdained riches and luxury. She loved the mists and clouds and was well-versed in the principles of Chan

Buddhism. Confident in her excellent features, she once said: "I want to surpass all in past and present!" This was the reason her father doted on her, although among her sisters she would never take advantage of being her father's favorite. Whenever he would give her something she would share it with them—even though these presents from a poor scholar were limited to paper and brushes, books and incense. She didn't like new clothes. In the spring and summer of this last year, I made her some new gauze shirts and skirts to replace her old ones, but I never saw her wearing them, and when I looked for them after she had passed away, I found that they had never even been unfolded. This shows how frugal she was. Because the day of her marriage was drawing near and we were too poor to provide her with a proper dowry, her father did all he could to scrape some money together. This did not please her at all, however, and she said: "Father, thorn hairpins and linen skirts are the usual dress for a poor scholar's [daughter], why do you make so much trouble for yourself?" But neither was she a stingy miser: she looked upon gold and money as if they were dirt. Indifferent to the world, she had few needs and took pleasure in simple elegance.

My child had jet-black hair and a white forehead, long brows and alabaster cheeks, red lips and sparkling teeth, a straight nose and charming dimples, bright eyes and artful glances: her beauty was such that you just wanted to eat her up! She would never assume seductive or extravagant poses and cared nothing for rouge and powder. If you tried to compare her to a plum blossom, you would find yourself blaming the plum blossom for being too thin, and if you tried to compare her to a crab apple, you would blame the crab apple for being deficient in purity. And so, if you were to call her an opulent beauty, you would find that in fact she exuded a transcendent elegance, and should you think that women of such charm could not but be frivolous, you would find that she was serious and impeccable. In short, she combined in her person the style of the forest recluse Xie Daoyun, and the beauty of the inner quarter wife of Mr. Gu. When her father once said to her jokingly: "You are extraordinarily beautiful," my child was very distressed and replied saying: "Father, what is there to be prized in a girl's city-toppling charms? Why must you insinuate that I have them?" In the year *jisi* [1629], when she was fourteen years old, I took her along to my parents' home, and as we were leaving, her uncle Junhui presented her with a poem that contained the following lines:

> In southern lands without compare: you should cherish yourself,
> Unequaled in the northern regions: to none should you give way!

If you'd fly to the Wide Cold, you'd be the very image of its goddess,
In comparison to Jade Pavilion your face is much sweeter.[14]

My child didn't like these lines at all. One day, rising very early she came and
stood by the side of my bed. Even though she had not yet washed the cream off
of her face nor combed her tousled hair, her looks and her charms were so
completely unequaled, that I jokingly said to her: "You are always angry when
people praise you for your beauty, but now, even when not properly dressed
and with such a wild head of hair you still look as lovely as this. This is truly an
example of 'every smile generates fragrance, every step moves with grace.' Even
I fall in love with you when I see you, so who can predict what 'the man who
will paint your eyebrows'[15] will think of you!" Alas! Who could have imagined
that I would never again see my child standing beside my bed, and that bride
and groom would never see each other face to face?

When writing poetry she did not like to write suggestive lines, and if such
lines are by chance found in her collection, they are due to the convention
of describing objects [in *New Songs of a Jade Terrace*] or to the genre of the song
lyric [in which she was writing], and may be compared to those of Qin Shaoyou
[Guan; 1049–1100] and Yan Xiaoshan [Jidao; eleventh century], writing in the
voice of women of the inner quarters. But the lyrics to the tune of "Partridge
Sky," which she composed in a dream, express her own aspirations. Every day
she would copy out either Wang Zijing's [Xianzhi; 344–388] version of
the "Rhapsody of the Goddess of the Luo" [*Luoshen fu*] or examples of the cursive script of Huaisu [ca. 725–ca. 785]. In both winter and summer she would
practice quiet sitting by her northern window, with nothing but a single incense
burner for company throughout the day. She would only emerge when I called
her to come out into the courtyard. Otherwise she would enjoy herself quietly
with her zither and her books. She surpassed all others in her love of clear
serenity and peaceful tranquility. But she also greatly disliked being restrained or
controlled in any way. She could hold her liquor and was good at jesting and
joking. She demonstrated her carefree spirit in many ways: lofty and untrammeled, she left behind the cares and worries of society. By nature she was
mild and loving, magnanimous and sincere, and never once did she scold her
maid Hongyu. The mirror of her intellect was bright and perspicacious, and she

---

14. Wide Cold is the name of the palace of Chang'e, the goddess of the moon. The
Queen Mother of the West met with King Mu of Zhou in a "jade pavilion," and so Jade
Pavilion here most likely is used as a designation for this stern female deity.

15. "The man who will paint your eyebrows" refers to her future (loving) husband.

grasped completely the affairs of both present and past as soon as they
were raised. Whenever we engaged in a discussion, she always came out ahead
of me, and I would say to her "You are not my daughter, you are my younger
friend."

After breakfast on the fifteenth of the Ninth Month, as usual she taught her
fifth younger brother Sheguan and her youngest sister Xiaofan to recite the
Songs of the South. On that same day, the family of the groom delivered the gifts
that would make it possible for the bride to complete her toilette, but that very
night my child fell ill and on the eve of her departure from home for the wedding, she took to bed with a fatal illness. On the tenth day of the Tenth Month
her father felt obliged to allow the groom to come and fetch the bride [on the
sixteenth]. As soon as her father came into her room, he said to her: "I have
given them this date. You must make the effort to pull yourself together so that
you won't miss your wedding!" My child remained silent, but as soon as her father had left, she called Hongyu over to her and asked: "What day is it today?"
"The tenth of the Tenth," Hongyu replied, at which my child sighed and said:
"How can I possibly be ready by such an early date!" But nothing was to
be done because, despite the fact that she had not yet shown any improvement,
the family of the groom was putting a terrible pressure on us. Who would have
known that at dawn on the following day this horrendous calamity would befall us?

When a sick person's body becomes heavy, I've been told, it means her situation is critical. But even when my child had no strength left, her body was light
and when we had to lift her, she was easy to move. Her spirit remained clear
and alert and to the very end she showed not a trace of despair or delusion.
There was a moment when she wanted to sit in an upright position. Because I
was afraid that she would lack the strength after her long illness and would not
be up to the exertion, I supported her in my arms. Moments later, her eyes shining brightly, and reciting the name of the Buddha in a voice that was loud and
clear, she passed away. I called out her name again and again, but she could no
longer hear me.

When I first realized that my child had died, I was so alarmed and distraught
that I didn't know what to do: my innards felt as if they had been ripped apart
and I wept tears of blood until my eyes ran dry. When later I pondered the matter at length, I came to the conclusion that she could not have been a mere
mortal. If she wasn't a jade maiden from the Jasper Isles,[16] she must have been

---

16. The Jasper Isles are the abode of Daoist immortals.

an attendant at Vulture Peak. Most likely she was a divine creature who had returned to this world for one last time, so how could she have remained for long in this world of dust?

After her death we continued to hope that she would come back to life, and so we waited until the seventh day before we placed her in the coffin. Even though her fragrant body was extremely emaciated, her face still shone like snow and her lips were as red as always. With tear-filled eyes I wrote the two characters Qiongzhang on her arm, which was still soft and white and adorable. Only her bones jutted out and were oh-so-cold. Such grief!

Some years ago, when my boys went to school outside of the home, they all took with them a sheet of paper that they would fill up with their writing. I made them a tablet of wood to use instead, which would not so easily be damaged. In the early days of the Ninth Month, my child [Xiaoluan] asked me to make her this kind of tablet as well, and on it she wrote in her own hand the line "On the stone path the spring breeze engenders the green moss." When I asked her why she'd written this line, she said: "I love these words so much!" Although I did not realize it at the time, now I remember that this is a line from a poem by Liu Shang [second half of the eighth century], and that the preceding line reads: "Although the immortals come and go they leave no trace in passing." Could it not have been an omen? There can really be no doubt that my child left to become an immortal!

On the night of the second of the Eleventh Month, our fifth son Shidan dreamed that he saw my child in a thatched hermitage between deep pines and flourishing cypress trees. She was leaning on a table reading a book, her hair was covered by a scarf and her gown was of a light color, and her expression was cheerful. By her side stood someone brewing tea. She did not allow our fifth son to enter her room, but spoke with him through the window, after which he left. Our fifth son is still very young, and so he could only remember the landscape in the dream but had no memory of what she had said. Our fifth son said: "I seem to vaguely remember the name of the monastery, but by the time I woke up I had forgotten it." A few days later, our eldest son Shiquan dreamed that his sister gave him some cups of pine seeds. I remembered the lines from a poem by Chen Zi'ang [661–702]: "And then again I met Master Red Pine / Sitting by the heavenly road, he invited me along."[17] From the time she was born, my child was extraordinarily intelligent—she must indeed have been invited to go to the city of the immortals. Some people will say that it is all nonsense, and

---

17. Master Red Pine is one of the immortals mentioned in the *Biographies of Immortals*.

that this is only an imitation of the *Song of Lasting Regret*.[18] Alas! Ever since my darling daughter died, the pain in my heart has not subsided and I think of her with tears in my eyes. I am recording only the facts, how could I imitate those writers of talent who compose fictional tales to deceive the world?

My daughter was born during the *mao* hour of the eighth day of the Third Month of the year *bingchen* [1616], and she died at the age of seventeen during the *mao* hour of the eleventh day of the Tenth Month of the year *renshen* [1632] of the reign period Chongzhen. She was betrothed to Zhang Liping from Kunshan, who was one year older than my child and already renowned for his literary accomplishments. The wedding date was set for the sixteenth of that month, but five days before that date she died, and bride and groom never met face to face. The horror that I have yet to experience is, I fear, something such as has not yet existed in this world. Such grief! Such pain! My innards feel torn to shreds and so I have briefly noted down one or two details: I am incapable of providing a full description.

Ye Wanwan

The death of Ye Xiaoluan was quickly followed by that of her elder sister, Wanwan. At the time of her death, Wanwan had been unhappily married for seven years to a son of her father's adoptive brother. Qian Qianyi and Liu Shi summarize the facts of her life as follows:

Wanwan's style name was Zhaoqi. Her appearance was beautiful and alluring, brilliant like gold and sleek like jade. At the age of three, she could recite the *Song of Lasting Regret*, and by the age of thirteen she was able to compose poems. Her calligraphy was strong and forceful and of the Jin dynasty style. She was unhappy throughout the entire seven years of her marriage to a son of the Yuan family of Zhaotian.

In the autumn of the year *renshen* [1632], when her youngest sister was about to get married and she had just finished writing a wedding song for her, the news of her sister's death arrived. She returned to her maternal home where, overcome with grief and mourning over her sister's death, she fell ill and died. Earlier Zhaoqi had taken refuge in Buddhism: she recited Buddhist sutras every

---

18. Bai Juyi's *Song of Lasting Regret* describes the disastrous passion of Emperor Xuanzong and Lady Yang. The final section of the poem is a description of the lingering passion of the aging emperor for Lady Yang following her enforced suicide and of a meeting between a shaman and the soul of Lady Yang in her heavenly abode.

day and maintained a strict discipline in her devotions. When her illness became critical, she forced herself to sit upright, and seated thus she passed away, reciting the name of the Buddha. She was twenty-three years old at the time. After her death, there were signs concerning her "passage through the world of darkness," as is described in the biography of Xiaoluan.

Ye Shaoyuan includes Wanwan's poems in the section of his *Noon Dream Hall Collection* entitled *Words of Sorrow*, and in his preface describes the nature of its contents as follows:

Alas, how can one bear to speak of poems marked by sorrow! Cao Zhi [192–232] once said: "What a shape-shifter is this thing called 'sorrow'! When you summon it, it doesn't come, but when you push it away, it won't leave. If you powder and paint it, it will not increase in luster, if you feed it delicacies, it will not gain weight; moxabustion and [acupuncture] needles cannot dissolve it, gods and offerings cannot diminish it. No artful smile can please it and music and songs only deepen its sadness. Sorrow's persistency is truly inexorable, isn't it?" For the entire seven years since my daughter tied the marriage knot at seventeen until her premature death this year at twenty-three, she made her home in the city of sorrow. . . . She observed the drifting petals falling from the trees and watched the fragrant grasses forming a tapestry; she heard the single leaf that is the harbinger of autumn, and bathed in the moonlight shining on half a bed; she sighed when the spring wind entered her door and felt depressed when the night rain pounded on her lantern; she was saddened by the letters to the south brought by the border geese and was distressed by dreams of the north in frosty autumn; she wept for the tears of dew dropping from the lotus flowers and her grief was awakened by the singing oriole in the willow tree; the evening warmth of the golden incense burner filled her with despondency, and the morning verses woven into brocade made her weep: the single emotion of sorrow was elicited by all of the ten thousand phenomena. . . . Here I will not discuss in detail my daughter's virtuous behavior and admirable demeanor, her filial respect and scrupulous conscience. If I have discussed her *Words of Sorrow* at such length, it is in the hope that her readers may commiserate with her feelings, and by inscribing them on bronze and stone, ensure her immortality in death.

The tone of the collection is set by the poem with which it opens:

Feelings While Looking at Flowers on a Spring Day

How many people grieve when spring takes its leave!
And when spring comes, they're happy and pleased.

Its coming and going doesn't matter the slightest to me,
Whose heart is bound up by futile feelings of sorrow.
A sorrowing heart does not ask about the flowers,
In front of the steps, I find myself choked by grief.
Let the Lord of the East make them explode in color![19]
That Lord of the East is far too hot.
None but this woman gazing at the flowers,
Has cold thoughts that are like snow and ice.

This poem elicited the following comment from Wanwan's father: "In this one poem each word is a tear, and in it can already be discerned the general nature [of her poetry]. There is no need to expound further on her boundless sorrow! . . ." *Words of Sorrow* also includes the text of the long poem Wanwan wrote with the intention of presenting it to Xiaoluan on her wedding day. This poem contains a detailed description of the happy childhood shared by the two sisters:

Sending Off My Younger Sister Qiongzhang upon Her Departure from Home to be Married

The shadows of red candles in the painted hall sway the light,
The loud sounds of pipes and drums envelop mat and roofbeam!
From behind the screen you are pressured to finish your toilette,
As we gaze at each other in silence, each of us brokenhearted.
The precious mirror on its phoenix stand reflects the face of parting,
The mandarin duck sash and gauze gown begrudge the long separation.
Behind the chamber screen the thick incense settles on your bright fan,
Inside the curtain hangings the light breeze caresses your new toilette.

For your new toilette you will have no need of face powder:
Plum and snow have always felt ashamed when comparing colors.
"A toppler of states, a toppler of cities," you are most extraordinary,
But, surprisingly, the immortals Feiqiong and Biyu are your friends.[20]

We gaze at one another full of feeling: I secretly brush away a tear,
What a pity it is!—you have yet to know the pain of separation.

---

19. The Lord of the East is the divinity in charge of spring.

20. These two lines may be paraphrased as follows: despite your truly extraordinary beauty, which would turn every man's head, you are more interested in spiritual matters.

On this night, you will be far, far away from your fragrant pavilion,
I can't bear to watch your cortege moving farther and farther away.

I wanted to write a long song to send you off once and for all,
But before even taking up the brush, tears came pouring down.
Remembering how we used to play together in times gone by,
I am overcome by grief because we are now so very far apart.

In times gone by we played, we laughed, and we talked together,
Inseparable from morning till night, we knew no sorrow or pain.
In the spring pavilion we practiced calligraphy on tables side by side,
On our autumn bed we listened to wind and rain under a shared duvet.

I remember too that at that time, though you were still very young,
Already your beauty displayed an immortal's bewitching charms.
The verses on snow that you composed were out of the ordinary,
And very few were those who could match your lyrics' rhymes.

Those days of yore are lost and gone, empty memories for me,
And now never again can they be relived—sadness without end!
Let's not speak of those days gone by that will never come again,
I only hope you will not miss the date we've set to meet once more.
 Once you've left we'll be parted a long while and only rarely meet,
Geese who fly in flocks have a better life than do we human beings!
My boundless feelings of loneliness will follow your departing boat,
As an unending regret over parting impels me to grab at your gown!

Regretting your leaving and grasping at your gown won't detain you,
The sail is raised, the music played and then the stream carries you off.
How sad that this departure should be an occasion for joy and laughter,
But don't let your longing to return home fill you with idle sorrow!

[Ye Shaoyuan:] Not long after Wanwan had written this poem, her younger sister died, and shortly afterwards Wanwan herself passed away. Who would have thought that this one poem urging the bride to finish her toilette would end up as a conversation between two ghosts? How could such sad and strange things be possible between heaven and earth!

Huichou

Ye Xiaowan (style name Huichou), the second daughter of Ye Shaoyuan and Shen Yixiu, was married to a cousin by the name of Shen Yongzhen. Shortly before her death in 1653, she entrusted her writings, along with the following quatrain, to her married daughter, Sujia:

During the Time When I Was Ill, I Put My Scattered Drafts in Order, After Which I Entrusted Them to My Daughter Sujia

Wounded by partings, weeping for the dead, poor and ill,
I vented my sadness and desolation for over twenty years.
I entrust them to you, so take them home and shed a tear:
Be sure not to leave a name as a woman writer of talent!

Upon her death, Ye Xiaowan's younger brother, Ye Xie, collected her surviving poems and lyrics and added them to his edition of his father's *Noon Dream Hall Collection*.

Of these works, the best known are those written in memory of Huichou's elder and younger sister, such as the following two poems accompanied by a preface:

In the Second Month of spring of the year *yihai* [1635] I returned home to visit my father and mother. All the trees and shrubs in the courtyard were in full bloom with the exception of the old plum tree in front of the Pavilion of Sparse Fragrance [where Xiaoluan used to live] whose trunk was covered by moss and on whose branches there was not a single petal! My younger brothers told me: "This tree has not blossomed for the three years since Eldest Sister and Third Sister passed away." Alas! Plants and trees have no feelings, so how could this be? Plucking a branch, I could not keep my tears from flowing down like rain.

I

The light chill, cutting out leaves and petals, locks in the flower terrace,
In front of the mirror, overwhelmed by emotions, I am filled with grief.
When I sit by myself in their empty chamber I feel abandoned and alone,
As I idly stroll along the winding path, my shadow paces back and forth.
The garden is filled with grasses of jade green that sway with the mist,
And on the trees, red clusters of flowers blossom in the rain.

There is none but the soul of the plum that knows the sorrow of parting,
Which is why it does not bring the colors of spring here to this window.

II

The fragrant flowers stab the eyes under bright and sunny skies,
My sisters gone, now just the Sparse Fragrance filled with gloom.
This lovely scenery offers me nothing but sorrow for company,
This floating life of mine tends to entangle itself in grief.
 Only by seeing the Second Month do I know of the First Month,
And it is out of pity for this year, that I speak of years gone by.
Fallen leaves, departed kin, all become but a dream—
The tears that stain my windblown sleeves are fresh.

Xiaowan's greatest claim to literary fame, however, is not her poetry, but a play she wrote entitled *Mandarin Ducks' Dream* (*Yuanyang meng*). As we saw earlier, there had been some plays written by courtesans but the plays they wrote were of the kind known as *chuanqi*. There also existed an earlier type of drama, known as *zaju*, which had become popular during the Yuan dynasty, but was only occasionally performed during the late Ming, by which time it had become primarily a literary rather than performative genre. Xiaowan's uncle, Shen Zizheng (Xiaoluan's adoptive father), claimed that his niece was the first woman author to have composed a full-length four-act *zaju*. The play enjoyed a moderate success in its own time and was included in later editions of the *Noon Dream Hall Collection*.

Xiaowan's play recounts the story of three immortal maidens who swear loyalty to one another at the Feast of the Peaches of Immortality held in honor of the Queen Mother of the West. Because their partiality for one another went against the emotional detachment required of immortals (though it was not considered to be as offensive as that between golden boys and jade maidens), they are banished to earth in order to purify themselves of their worldly feelings. They are reborn as three male students, Hui Baifang, Zhao Qicheng, and Qiong Longdiao (clearly meant, despite their gender, to represent the three Ye sisters). The "wedge" or introductory act of the play is taken up by a description of the students' first meeting, during which the three express their mutual

admiration of each other's unconventional characters, swear brotherhood, and then make plans to meet again the following day. The first full
act of the play describes their pleasant comradely excursion together to
Phoenix Terrace near Nanjing, an excursion over which Hui Baifang
reminisces in the second act of the play. In the third act, Hui Baifang,
adverted by a dream, hastens to the home of Zhao Qicheng only to find
him at death's door. At this time, he also learns of the death of the third
member of the brotherhood, Qiong Longdao. After both of his friends
have died, leaving behind them forever the "sea of suffering," Hui
Baifang vows to seek enlightenment. Finally, in the last act of the play, after much travel and many travails, he meets the immortal Lü Dongbin.
Lü Dongbin is a member of the famous group of the Eight Immortals;
he was a widely revered deity in Ming-Qing China, believed to roam
the earth working his miracles and searching for people ready to be
enlightened. Usually in plays that treat the topic of deliverance from the
world, the teacher has a hard time weaning his unwilling disciple away
from his or her attachments to the world and may even have to resort to
drastic measures to do so. In this play, however, the grieving Hui Baifang
is only too eager to listen to Lü Dongbin's liberating words, and immediately undergoes conversion. He is then reunited with his sworn brothers,
and together the three of them return to their home in the realm of the
immortals.

A modern reader may well be disappointed by the relative lack of action in this play, but the traditional reader would have appreciated the
ways in which different moods (elation, nostalgia, grief, deliverance)
found expression in the sets of arias assigned to Hui Baifang in each of
the successive acts. The following translation of the opening songs of the
final act may provide the reader with a sense of the expressive qualities of
these arias:

[*The male lead enters*] I am Hui Baifang. After Zhao Qicheng and Qiong Longdiao
passed away, I came to realize the impermanence of samsara. Ever since that
time I have been roaming unhindered among the clouds and along the streams
looking for the Way and searching for the Truth. I have heard that on Mt.
Zhongnan there lives a Man of the Way who knows past and future, and so I
will go there to pay him a visit. [*sings*]

Zhonglü Mode: To the Tune of "Powdered Butterfly" (*Fendie'er*)

Ever since I left my home village,
I have traveled to famous mountains one after the other:
In the blink of an eye, gray has streaked my locks.
How can I free myself from the red dust,
And escape from the temptations of Mara?[21]
Endless the cycle of rise and fall that runs through past and present,
In a moment's time, the seas have turned into fields and back again,
In vain we follow the endless coming and going of the busy crow and
       hare.[22]

To the Tune of "Drunk on the Spring Breeze" (*Zui chunfeng*)

In the mournful wind my coat of feathers feels cold,
The road rocky and hard, the ancient path overgrown.
Creepers and vines, brambles and thorns
Take pleasure in snaring my sandals:
They're really out to resist me,
Resist me!
Just look at those steep cliffs, bizarre peaks,
Those tall pines and verdant cypress trees,
That spring brew of green streams!

To the Tune of "Welcoming the Immortal Guest" (*Ying xianke*)

The echoes of the waterfall's thundering roar lingers on,
Soaring to dizzy heights, the mountains block like screens:
I'll emit a drawn-out whistle to fill the expanse of heaven and earth!
I have only just rid myself of the red dust,
But surprisingly, I have no need of fantasy!

---

21. Mara is the Buddhist equivalent of the Tempter, who tries to distract religious aspirants away from their goal.

22. In Chinese mythology, the sun is said to be inhabited by a three-legged crow and the moon by a hare.

This dazzling landscape made of rivers and streams
Is far better than pretty enclosures and silken screens!

To the Tune of "Red Embroidered Shoes" (*Hongxiuxie*)

Look at those pines like interlocking stakes and contorted pythons,
And those rocks ringed all about by climbing fig and rampant weeds:
My linen coat is always suffused with the fragrance of wild flowers.
To my sorrow, our three lives are as unsubstantial as a dream,
But to my joy I've worn immortal's garb for half of my years.
Look here:
Now that I've made my way around this mountain crag,
There is the vast expanse of Heaven!

These four songs describing Hui Baifang's trek through the mountains culminating in a splendid view of Heaven's limitless expanse may be read as symbolic of his long struggle to attain enlightenment, which will be crowned with success when he finally meets with the immortal Lü Dongbin. It is then that he undergoes the enlightenment that will allow him to return home with his two soulmates to the immortal paradise of the Queen Mother of the West. In this way, Ye Xiaowan gives her play the happy ending that was denied her and her two sisters.

Gu Ruopu and Liang Mengzhao

During the final decades of the Ming dynasty and for the last three centuries of imperial China, the southeastern city of Hangzhou was one of the main centers of Chinese women's literature. Hangzhou's women poets for the most part belonged to the elite, as their fathers, brothers, husbands, and sons often achieved success in the examination system and went on to pursue official careers. There are a great number of noteworthy women poets from Hangzhou, but for reasons of expediency we will limit ourselves here to a discussion of the writings of Gu Ruopu (1592–ca. 1681) and her late Ming contemporary Liang Mengzhao. In a later chapter, we will also look at the women poets of the Banana Garden Poetry Club, which was active in Hangzhou in the early decades of the Qing dynasty.

Gu Ruopu

Gu Ruopu was born into an eminent literati family, and later married Huang Maowu (style name Dongsheng), the son of Huang Ruheng (Yuyong; 1558–1626), who was a high official and a friend of the famous dramatist Tang Xianzu. In 1619, after thirteen years of marriage, Gu Ruopu was widowed and left to raise her sons alone. Gu Ruopu's collection of poetry, entitled *Drafts from the Reclining in the Moonlight Studio* (*Woyuexuan gao*), was published by her sons in a gesture of filial piety on the occasion of her sixtieth birthday (which would be 1652); however, the preface to this collection, written by Gu Ruopu herself, is dated 1626. The collection includes the following "Short Biography" by a certain Bao Hongtai:

Gu Ruopu had the style name Hezhi and hailed from Qiantang [Hangzhou]. She was the daughter of the vice-director of the Office of Imperial Parks, Gu Youbai, and the wife of the student Huang Dongsheng, the eldest son of the Provincial Education Commissioner Huang Yuyong. From the time she was born, she demonstrated an innate intelligence and already in her early youth was well-versed in the *Odes* and *Documents*. Dongsheng was also a master of ancient prose and lyrics, but unfortunately was of a sickly disposition, and eventually succumbed to illness. The two sons and daughters he left fatherless were refined and courteous and wrote well, thanks to Ruopu's instruction. Reading her preface to *Drafts from the Reclining in the Moonlight Studio*, one can also get a general impression of her character.

Huang Yuyong was one of the arbiters of literature of his day, and only rarely approved [of contemporary writings], and yet Ruopu's poems were all edited by him. In his epitaph for Dongsheng he wrote: "His wife is intelligent and wise; she understands the principles of literature and has the requisite qualities of a mother." This, I believe, is a factual record. Moreover, the Gus, from Cangjiang to Xiyan, Yue'an, and Youbai, all were famous for their literary compositions. So Ruopu's excellence in poetry was probably due to this family tradition as well.

In the preface to her poetry collection, alluded to in the above biography, Gu Ruopu provides a more modest account of her path toward poetry, and presents her accomplishments very much as a by-product of the education of her children:

When I read the *Odes*, I learned that the tasks of women are limited to the care of wine and food, so how could I dare toy with brush and ink in order to compete with literary gentlemen? Still, from ancient times it has been true that "creatures cry out when they suffer injustice." In the past, such pure exemplars of womanhood as Ban [Zhao] and Zuo [Fen] composed many texts to amuse themselves, thus demonstrating that "red reeds" [used in making women's writing brushes] and "needle reeds" can be displayed side by side. So perhaps [writing] is not completely foreign to our lot [as women].

Lacking in talent, I could not as a child live up to my mother's instructions, and when after my marriage I became responsible for running the household of a well-known family, I was constantly fearful of bringing even greater shame to my father and mother. I busied myself with the [sacrificial] wines and brews, seal-cords and sashes without once complaining about the work, and in this way, several decades have passed as if a single day. The year I married Dongsheng, my father-in-law had just resigned from his post as magistrate of Zhongling and was awaiting his next appointment in the Capital. My father and mother loved me dearly and did not want me to go so far away. My husband took a niece as a concubine, which made it possible for me to stay home and take care of my parents.

I quickly lost the support of my husband. His body became so emaciated and weak that it could not even hold up his clothes! My father-in-law was an incorruptible official. As he did not concern himself with the economic activities of the household, there was nothing in the house but a few books. So I pawned my hairpins and earrings to provide [my husband] with a meal of chicken as he studied by the window. Later on, he repeatedly failed in the provincial examinations, and feeling frustrated and depressed, started to cough up blood. Gradually, his condition became increasingly serious. Before my husband was able to repay the boundless favors [of the emperor and his parents], he contracted a life-threatening illness, which increased his despondency even more. Although night and day he applied himself even more to his studies, he had less and less vitality. Alas, I served my husband for thirteen years but for more than half of them, I kept company with the stove for boiling medicinal brews. Later, as our sons and daughters grew older, the money needed to buy food increased, and I rarely had the leisure to tend exclusively to the garden of literature. If by chance I would recite some verses, they were never written down in their entirety. Most of the poetic compositions made during these idle moments were written as I sat with Dongsheng, worrying and suffering.

Then suddenly his bones crumbled, his soul dissolved, and he passed away. For a long time I wept over the coffin wishing I were dead. How would I be able to live on in this human world ? How would I ever again create compositions that "delineate feelings in ornate detail"? It is only out of concern that the interest of our children would be neglected that I eschewed loyal suicide, which would have been the simpler way, and instead chose the hard struggle of a widow's existence. I had no choice but to follow the example of those women of old who raised their children to adulthood [even if it meant] concocting pills out of bear gall for their sons and teaching them by writing characters in the sand with a reed. At that time, my father-in-law was the educational commissioner for Jiangxi province and my parents and brothers were living even farther away. The Classics and Histories were the last thing on my mind: rather I was concerned with how to teach my children and see them to maturity. Each day I was anxious and afraid, fearing that in the end I might betray my original resolve and not succeed in following my husband into the grave. And so, when there was time to be spared from my household duties, I would take out the books that were in the house, starting with the *Four Books* and the Five Classics, and continuing on to the *Mirror of Ancient History* [*Gushi jian*], the *Continuous Chronicle of the August Ming* [*Huang Ming tongji*], and the *Record of Great Administration* [*Dazheng ji*]. I would read them night and day, fearful of not being able to keep up with my two sons. Whenever an outside teacher would come to the house, I would have him light a lamp, and sitting in a corner, explain [these texts] on my behalf. In this way, my own understanding would grow along with that of [my children]. Oh, I would go on until midnight and, in the joy of repeating my lessons, would not realize how tired I really was!

As time went by, my knowledge grew. The Classics and the traditions of the Saints and Sages nourished my virtue and cleansed my heart. I also extended my readings to include the *Songs of the South* and the rhapsodies. I roamed through them and rested in them, hoping to be able [in this way] to express my own mournful feelings and relieve my frustration and depression. Fortunately, I did not sink into the illness of intense brooding, but [as] the birds of spring and the insects of autumn are moved by the season to send forth their calls, so I too would regularly take up the brush [to write poems], storing them away afterwards in chests and baskets. Nevertheless, these poems cannot be put into the category of "crying out because of injustice," and how would I dare have them compared to the writings of ancient exemplars of pure womanhood such as Ban and Zuo, thereby earning myself the criticism of trying to "imitate the Handan strut"? 23

---

23. To "imitate the Handan strut" means to engage in something that one will never be able to master.

When a year later my father-in-law returned to a life of retirement in Hangzhou, he had his grandsons bring him these writings [of mine] and he was so kind as to edit them. Despite my deficient intelligence, I only hope that they may someday be found to contain a single word at least that conforms to the Way. The title he gave to the collection was *Drafts from the Reclining in the Moonlight Studio*. The Reclining in the Moonlight Studio was the name of the place where my husband used to rest and recollect himself.

Written by the Hangzhou widow Huang Gu Ruopu in the last month of spring of the year bingyin [1626] *of the Tianqi reign period*.

Gu Ruopu not only saw to the education of her sons, but also hired a teacher for her daughters as well. Despite the increasing literacy of many elite women at the time (we even hear about the existence of schools for girls), providing one's daughters with a literary education was still not something of which everyone approved. Clearly Gu's decision to hire a teacher for her daughters was still capable of provoking criticism from an older generation of women, as we can see from the following text in her collection:

Purposely Written as a "Rebuttal of Ridicule"[24] After Having Been Criticized for Hiring a Teacher to Instruct My Daughters

As soon as yin and yang were separated,
  Social norms were created and laid out:
The husband should establish righteousness,
  And the wife and daughter should be chaste.
But without studying the *Odes* and *Documents*,
  One cannot fulfill one's nature and one's life.
Now some old crone has lambasted me:
  "You've fallen short of the Wifely Way!
You have hired a teacher for your daughters,
  As if she were going to sit for the exams.
She'll pay no attention to her needlework,

---

24. *Rebuttal of Ridicule* is the title of a text by Yang Xiong (53 BCE–18 CE), written very much in the style of a rhapsody, in which he defends his contentment with his lowly position against the criticisms of those who argue that his scholarship should be able to secure him a much higher position.

And will focus instead on reading books!"
When I heard these words, [I said:]
   "You fail to understand my intention!
In life, men and women are segregated.
   But wifely virtue is not so easily achieved!
How can we, just because we're women,
   Refuse to take the ancients as our teachers?
The wives of both King Wen and King Wu
   Are praised among the 'Ten Administrators';[25]
The Venerable Madam left us her instructions,
   The 'Inner Quarters' Rules' must be understood.
I am ashamed of my own ignorance,
   And find I cannot minimize my faults,
And yet, I feel pity for those of today
   Who worry about their looks and pretty clothes.
If I did not instruct them in their youth,
   The reputation of our family would suffer.
It is through study that children are molded,
   Questions and discussions sharpen and refine.
The 'Four Virtues' and 'Three Obediences':
   Those ways of the ancients remain the norm.
But by chiseling and by adorning,
   One can make one's person pure and good.
How could I be thinking of luster and glory?
   I wish only to admonish against error and wrong!
If you can't accept these simple words of mine,
   Then you should put your question to the wise!"

We do not know who "the old crone" mentioned in this text refers to, but we do know that it cannot have been Gu Ruopu's mother-in-law, as she died within a month of Gu Ruopu's marriage. Gu Ruopu speaks of her mother-in-law's death in a letter written in 1632 to her two married sons on the occasion of the division of the family property. In this letter, Gu Ruopu emerges as a forceful character, very much aware that the

---

25. The "Ten Administrators" are the ten sage ministers who assisted King Wen and King Wu in the founding of the Zhou dynasty.

continued prosperity of the Huang family has in large part been the result of her own efforts.

Even if a literary education for women was defended primarily on moral grounds by many, including Gu Ruopu, it included as a matter of course the study and composition of poetry. The most striking of Gu Ruopu's own poems are some of the quatrains she wrote in remembrance of her husband:

Remembering My Husband

At the end of spring, days are long and grasses lush,
Fragrance rises from the orchids outside as dusk falls.
Inexpressible the thousand knots of parting's sorrow:
Resting my chin on my hand I idly recall those years.

Untitled

Quietly I turn the sutra pages late at night inside the tower,
But, alas, ten thousand gallons of sorrow drench my heart.
Now spring has come, I fear stepping on the grass outside:
For the entire day the embroidered screen is left hanging down.

Rising Early, an Impromptu Poem

In my dream I was idly reciting my late husband's poems,
When the maid suddenly said: "There is snow on the steps."
I got up but, lacking the strength to sweep the courtyard,
I sat down in front of the mirror to count my gray hairs.

Gu Ruopu wrote other sorts of poems as well. The allusion to Wang Zhaojun in the following poem may well have been an indirect reference to the growing menace that the Manchus posed on the northeastern border of the Ming empire in as early as the first two decades of the seventeenth century:

What has become of all the border victories of Li and Wei?[26]
In the end, it is a tender girl who must cross the desert river.

---

26. "Li and Wei" refers to Li Guang (d. 119 BCE) and Wei Qing (d. 106 BCE), two of the most successful generals in the various campaigns of Emperor Wu of the Han against the Xiongnu in the second half of the second century BCE.

Beyond Black Dragon border, spring is about to burgeon,
But on the Red Phoenix Tower, regrets already multiply.[27]
 The guardsman's gong, smothered by frost, startles the huddled geese;
She plays the lute in the falling snow, her brows knitted in a frown.
Hardly any of her companions from the palace are still around—
Go tell our generals to rest their heads on their halberds at night!

Liang Mengzhao

Gu Ruopu by no means was the only prominent woman poet of Hangzhou during the final decades of the Ming dynasty. One of her female contemporaries was the defiant poet Liang Mengzhao, whom we have already encountered in the introduction to this section. The preface to her collection praises her talents in the following rather hyperbolic terms:

She is naturally gifted with intelligence and beauty. As regards her *shi* poetry, she writes in the style of the Han, Wei, and Tang dynasties and when it comes to painting, she works in the style of the Jin, Song, and Yuan dynasties. She is a consummate master of every genre, and in all of them she reaches the summit. This is surely a "gift of Heaven," for does it not surpass [mere] human endeavor?

A slightly later critic was less convinced of the qualities of her poetry: "In her *shi* poems she strives for startling strangeness, but ends up with nothing but messy prolixity. Even if one finds one or two fresh and original pieces, it is like looking for hidden orchids in a tangle of thorns." This critic far prefers Liang Mengzhao's letters.

Liang Mengzhao wrote poetry and prose, but also authored a play entitled "The Inkstones of Mutual Love" (*Xiangsi yan chuanqi*), which unfortunately was lost. It was based on a story of two inkstones, one inscribed with the character for "mutual," the other with the character for "love." The former ends up in the possession of a reincarnation of the Herdboy and the latter in that of a Weaving Maid, and, needless to say, the inkstones and their owners are happily reunited in the end.

Liang Mengzhao was married to a great-grandson of the famous prose writer Mao Kun. She once accompanied her husband on a boat trip from

---

27. The Black Dragon River is said to mark the border between the realm of the Han dynasty and that of the Xiongnu. The Red Phoenix Tower refers to the imperial palace.

Hangzhou to Nanjing, where the couple spent a number of years. The following poems were probably written during that journey:

Scenes from a Journey by Boat, Two Poems

I

From afar, the boatman calls for the fisherman to come over,
When buying the fresh catch, they don't haggle about the price.
The taste of the wine from the village is like human nature:
Whether it is bland or fragrant depends on the patron's will.

II

Not many people pass by along the two reed-covered banks
And all you can hear is the screeching of the boatman's oar.
Every direction obscured by heavy rain and sodden clouds,
The road as yet untraveled, the days all going by in a blur.

Filled with Emotions

In my yearning for nature's scenes, I set out on this journey;
On the boundless misty river, we moor the boat for the night.
The new moon only knows it's grand to be beyond the clouds,
She doesn't mean to move us to sorrow by waxing and waning.

Following a visit to Suzhou, Liang Mengzhao's journey took her along the Grand Canal to the Yangzi River, and from there on to the southern capital, Nanjing:

Setting Sail at Dawn on the Yangzi

I

The boundless expanse of the Long River: a myriad shining miles,
As the glow of the sun first pierces through the light mists of dawn.
The flat billows, wave upon wave, roll along with the clouds,
The low willows, tree after tree, grow along both sides of the stream.
The shadows of the hills come from afar and sink with the banks,
Suddenly we hear the sound of the storm startling us like the tide.
My heart feels as if it has stretched out a million acres wide:
These beautiful thoughts I'll entrust to my brush to express.

V

As we gradually near the southern capital, the river's force subsides,
The greenish clouds at day's end make the scenery especially serene.
How could I have known that these flowers and plants were the finest in
    the world?
I had no idea that these winds and waves would cause the greatest sorrow
    on earth!
 The distant waves come pressing on urging the nearby waves forward,
Then as they are blown back against the current, they turn into whirlpools.
Few are those who realize the beauty in all of this,
Compared to our West Lake, it is superior by far!

In one of her poems Liang Mengzhao describes the scene of Nanjing's
Qinhuai River at night. The Qinhuai River ran through the heart of Nanjing's entertainment district, and at night courtesans and patrons would
ply the river in boats lit up by lanterns.

Evening Entertainments on the Qinhuai River

One would think that the mermaids had come out,
Defying the current and playing with their pearls.
The golden glow spreads a net across the water;
And the pale moon delicately ripples on the lake.
 I am reminded of a painting of the Hill of Cinnabar,
Think I am seeing a picture of "Emerging from the Water."[28]
Even the divine immortals, should they come here,
Would sell their jewels in order to buy ambrosia.

The many attractions of Nanjing did not, however, stop Liang Mengzhao
from feeling nostalgic for her hometown of Hangzhou:

On the Sixteenth of the Fifth Month

I stand alone in the little courtyard, the moon right above me,
Still and silent, not a sound—I am overwhelmed by sorrow.

---

28. The Hill of Cinnabar is one of the abodes of the immortals. "Emerging from the
Water" is very likely a reference to a painting on the topic of Cao Zhi's famous *Rhapsody
on the Goddess of the Luo River.*

I would like to get Chang'e to deliver a letter,[29]
Conveying my somber feelings to Hangzhou.

Like Gu Ruopu, Liang Mengzhao also left us a poem about Wang Zhaojun:

From all sides the sounds of the border, hemmed in by shadows,
She sits up all night until lonely dawn, her sadness ever growing.
Since ancient times, Sons of Heaven have made fickle lovers:
Married to a commoner, this would never have been her fate!

In later sources, the names of Gu Ruopu and Liang Mengzhao are sometimes coupled with that of Zhang Qiongru, yet another Hangzhou woman poet of the final decades of the Ming dynasty. The following is one of the few poems by Zhang that has survived.

Dragon Well

Dimly discernible hangings and banners, the green trees low:
The sloping road to the convent's gate as the evening sun sets.
The steep steps of the ancient altar: a thousand-layered cliff,
The narrow stream feeds far away into the nine-bend brook.
 Sounds from the pine valley harmonize with the clear chimes,
The cloudy mists amid the bamboo hide the small pavilion.
The meditation-mind is already cut off from dusty karma,
And is not disturbed by the lonely gibbon's midnight cry.

---

29. Chang'e is the name of the goddess said to inhabit the moon.

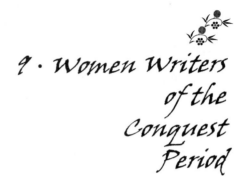

9 · Women Writers of the Conquest Period

The collapse of the Ming dynasty and the conquest of the Chinese world by the Manchus was a particularly momentous time for many women. For several years, the most prosperous parts of China were ravaged by warfare, and occasionally women even went so far as to actively participate in battle. The officials of the former Ming dynasty had to choose between loyalty to the Ming or serving the new Qing dynasty. If they chose to remain loyal to the Ming, they faced the possibility of being executed or forced to commit suicide. If they went over to the Qing, they would earn the hatred of the loyalists and the distrust of their new masters. Many Ming loyalists avoided this dilemma by going into hiding or assuming the identity of a monk. Whatever the eventual choice of fathers and husbands, it greatly affected their daughters and wives, as we can see from the lives of Shang Jinglan and Xu Can.

The conquest period, and in particular the first twenty years of the Qing dynasty, however, also opened up new possibilities for women writers. The dislocations caused by warfare and the absence of a clear center of moral authority created a society that was in many ways more fluid than it had ever been before or would ever be afterwards. Some women writers during this period traveled widely and maintained extensive contacts not only with other women writers but also with leading male thinkers and writers. The most remarkable woman writer in this respect is Wang Duanshu. Other elite women were forced by circumstance to make a living from their literary and artistic talents, serving as tutors and selling their paintings, as was the case of the woman poet Huang Yuanjie.

Shang Jinglan and Xu Can

A Loyalist's Widow: Shang Jinglan

Shang Jinglan (1602–1676) and her husband Qi Biaojia (1602–1645) were both natives of Shaoxing. Qi Biaojia held a number of different offices under the Ming and played an active role in the anti-Manchu resistance put up by the Southern Ming court at Nanjing. After the debacle of the Southern Ming, he returned to his estate in Shaoxing (Yu Garden), where he committed suicide by drowning himself in a pond. While it was not at all uncommon for loyalists who committed suicide to be voluntarily followed in death by their wives and children, Shang Jinglan chose to stay alive expressly for the purpose of caring for her sons and daughter, as we read in one of her two poems entitled "Mourning My Husband":

> You have achieved the reputation of a thousand ages,
> While I still cling to this one single life.
> Lord and minister: indeed the great norm,
> Sons and daughters: human feeling too.
> You "broke the railing" when you were alive,
> The stele you have left is your posthumous fame.[1]
> Although life and death are different roads,
> In purest chastity we complete one another.

Most of Shang Jinglan's preserved poems would appear to date from the late forties and early fifties, when she lived in Shaoxing with her two sons, two of her daughters, and her two daughters-in-law. Together with her daughters and daughters-in-law she engaged in many different kinds of literary activities, and for a while had as her guest the well-known woman poet and teacher Huang Yuanjie. In Shang Jinglan's poems, as

---

1. When a Han dynasty official angered the emperor with his remonstrations and was dragged off by two members of the guard, he clung to the railing, persisting in offering his sincere advice until the railing broke. The Tang dynasty poet Bai Juyi makes the point in one of his poems that a reputation established among the people is ultimately a more enduring monument to one's memory than any inscribed stone stele.

might be expected, an acute awareness of the absence of her departed husband is a recurrent theme:

On a Spring Day in Yu Garden Gazing at the Plum Blossoms

The plum and willow compete in springness: the entire garden quiet.
The shrubs and trees here in his absence stir up sorrows over the past.
It is only the spring wind that still has the same inexhaustible drive,
And, as it did before, completely infuses the branches with fragrance.

Yu Garden

The old garden has now grown wild:
On returning, my feelings are multiplied.
All through the garden, plums blossom white,
Along both banks willows unfurl their green.
 Fragrant grasses burgeon in profusion,
And the sound of waterfalls is everywhere.
Evening crows urge the sun to set,
But I keep walking in the moonlight.

Sweeping the Graves on a Spring Day

A boat passing through mist, trees hidden in darkness,
Rain blown by the hard wind obscures the river village.
The silence of the overgrown wilds causes me to weep,
The desolation of the old graves nearly breaks my heart.
 In the long dike's dense willows roosting birds are startled,
People passing along both banks hear the cry of the gibbon.
A single square of linen sail but nowhere a road leading home;
As evening falls, the gates of people's houses are shut tight.

My Feelings on My Fiftieth Birthday

Music is played, a fine banquet arranged:
The sound of songs renews my old grief.
The orphaned *luan* is in the end left alone,
And the colored phoenix will never return.
 I clutch my hair, locked in clouds of sorrow,
I unfurrow my brow revealing a moon of pain.

The tears from the feelings of these ten years
Today fill the mirror-stand in my private room.

Self-Description at Fifty

The Tenth Month of the year *jiawu*:[2]
The year that I turn fifty years old.
Although I'm still unable to "know my fate,"
It is a perfect day to acknowledge my faults.[3]
 In the hall the big drum is beaten,
And flutes and pipes line up against the walls.
My eldest son offers me a rhinoceros-horn cup,
And my youngest son lays out the jasper mats.
 Their wives have powdered their faces white,
My grandsons stand like the trees in a forest;
Their bowings and kowtows beyond counting,
Their colorful clothes as dazzling as brocade.
 Each and everyone wishes me a very long life,
The filled cups number almost a hundred,
The nine-*wei* lamps brighter than the moon,
And everyone present is an honored guest.
 Words of praise produce the rarest of flowers,
And pearls, round and baroque, drape me like a cloak.
Of all the festive gatherings in this life of mine,
There has been no festive gathering as perfect as this.
 Yet I am grieved at heart and in it can find no joy,
I feel like crying but cannot find the tears.
A wounding wind that stabs at my eyes:
Today only doubles my painful memories.
 Both of my sons kneel down and ask:
"Mother, what is the cause of your distress?
Is it because we did something wrong?
Or is our filial piety not up to par?"
 I bow my head but cannot speak,
As I weigh the deep feelings in my heart:

---

2. The year *jiawu* here corresponds to 1654.

3. In the *Analects*, Confucius claims to have known his fate at fifty. Qu Yuan, as we saw before, realized at the age of fifty all the mistakes he had made in the preceding forty-nine years.

The phoenix pair was unable to stay together,
The solitary *luan* has long since lost her colors.
  The branches, intertwined, have been divided:
No wings to place together on the limpid pond.
I did not see the sun and moon collapse,
But stream and mountain are all changed.
  I am like a torn-off remnant of silk
That will never be woven to completion.
I fight against my tears and tell my sons:
"There's been no negligence on your part.
  It may be the proper time to celebrate,
But trouble can be avoided by restraint.
We are a filial and a loyal family,
Our actions define the norm for the entire age.
  Our deeds should set the standard of purity,
Luxurious display to us is quite unknown.
In all matters, the ancestors are our models,
We rule our body as we rule our house.
  Through study you'll become great scholars,
There is no need for me to urge you on:
I have the nature of the cypress and pine,
And willingly withstand the coldest frost.
  Achieve your fame and bring glory to your parents:
That kind of longevity endures like bronze and stone."

Soon after Shang Jinglan's fiftieth birthday, disaster struck once again. Her two sons became involved in a loyalist conspiracy and were arrested by the Qing authorities. Lisun, the eldest son, was eventually released after the family paid a hefty bribe, but the youngest son, Bansun, was banished to Liaodong (although in 1667, he escaped and lived incognito as a monk in Suzhou, where he died in 1673). Shang Jinglan describes both the relatively carefree days of her early widowhood and the crisis involving her sons in a preface she wrote late in life for the poetry collection of Zhang Chayun (Hao), a woman poet from Hangzhou, who was one of the members of the Banana Garden Poetry Club.

Preface to the *Remaining Drafts of Zither Tower*

I am a seventy-two-year-old widow who has again and again found herself on the brink of death. When my husband, the vice censor-in-chief, died in the year *yiyou* [1645], I did not dare follow him in death because our sons and daughters were still in their infancy. In the year *xinchou* [1661] my second son met with disaster [at the hands of those envious] of his talents; his family fell into ruin and [eventually] he lost his life. The reason I did not commit suicide immediately was that I was afraid this would bring him a reputation for unfiliality. It has been my bad fortune to live on as a widow until now, when old age will soon be upon me.

I do not know how to write, so how could I assume to write about others? Still, all my life I have been fond of the soft brush. The wife of my eldest son, Zhang Dehui, the wife of my second son, Zhu Derong, and my daughters, Xiuyan and Xiangjun, all know how to read. Whenever we could take time from our needlework, we would select topics and assign rhymes and earnestly strive for elegance. Sometimes we would delve into history, at other times we would discuss current affairs. Whenever we met with talented ladies or pure maidens, we would force them to stay and would not let them depart. Our passion even surpassed Qu Dao's addiction to the water caltrop[4] and Xi Kang's love for working metal. But it has now been almost thirty years since I threw out my ink and burned my brushes.

By chance, I noticed on my son's desk this *Remaining Drafts of Zither Tower* [*Qinlou yigao*], written by Zhang Chayun from Wulin [Hangzhou]. Chayun was both a talented wife and a filial daughter, and her poems are therefore honest and mild; they express her nature and feelings, and embody the meanings of the *Book of Songs* as they have been handed down. Finding myself unable to put the book down, I said to my daughters and daughters-in-law: "I know that you are capable of Chayun's talent, and I know that you are capable of Chayun's filiality, so I hope that you will make an effort to emulate the beauty of her talent and the purity of her filiality." My daughters and daughters-in-law asked: "Given her talent and filiality, why didn't Heaven grant Chayun more years in which to enrich her learning and adjust her virtue?" Smiling, I said: "This is something you do not understand. In general, when a gentleman is reduced to poverty, he is not reduced to it by Heaven, but rather by his addiction to poetry, and when a girl dies prematurely, it is not because of Heaven that she dies prematurely, but rather because of her abundance of talents. These are cases where people exert themselves when they shouldn't. But if Chayun had enjoyed honors and riches and lived to a ripe old age, she would not have been praised by later times and

---

4. Qu Dao was a dignitary of the ancient kingdom of Chu. His love for the water caltrop was so strong that he instructed his children to make offerings of this plant at the ancestral sacrifices they made for him after his death.

would have lacked that which makes her Chayun." My daughters and daughters-in-law were all overcome by sadness.

I now note down these simple words exchanged at home as a record of the love, respect, and deep emotion that we felt at that time. Chayun's unique qualities will ensure her undying fame. How would I dare consider my writing to be good enough to [adequately] praise Chayun?

Exiled to Manchuria: Xu Can

Xu Can was the second wife of Chen Zilin (d. 1666), who was from Haining in Zhejiang province. Her husband had served the Ming court, but when the dynasty fell, he switched his allegiance to the Qing and quickly rose to the highest ranks of the Qing court. He became the owner of one of Suzhou's most famous gardens, the "Inept Administrator's Garden" (*Zhuozhengyuan*), and in 1650 published a collection of song lyrics by his wife entitled *Song Lyrics of the Inept Administrator's Garden, First Collection* (*Zhuozhengyuan shiyu chukan*). In 1656 Chen was accused of conspiracy and banished to Shenyang in what is today Manchuria. Later he was recalled and reinstated in his official position, but then was banished again in 1658, accused this time of bribery and collusion with a corrupt eunuch. Xu Can and the couple's two sons joined Chen Zilin at Shangyang Fort where, eight years later, both Chen and the two sons died. As soon as her husband passed away, Xu Can stopped writing poetry. She had to wait until 1671 before she was allowed by the Kangxi Emperor (r. 1662–1722) to take her husband's remains home for burial and, once there, she adopted a Buddhist lifestyle.

Xu Can's biography, written by her nephew Chen Yuanlong and included in the Chen clan genealogy, summarizes Xu Can's life as follows:

The lady's personal name was Can and her style name was Xiangping. Her family had lived in Suzhou for generations. She was the second wife of the Junior Guardian Su'an [Chen Zilin].

From her earliest years her ladyship displayed great intelligence. She understood the books and histories and grasped their major significance. She was doted upon by her father, the vice-minister of the Court of Imperial Entertainments, Xu Zimao. Su'an's first wife, lady Shen, had died prematurely and by the time he asked for her ladyship as his second wife, he had been a graduate of the provincial examinations for three years. Now the Xu family had two daughters, and her ladyship was the younger of the two. But because the rank of the man who had come to ask for her hand was so high, the family agreed to the requested marriage. After she was married, she served her father-in-law the vice censor-in-chief and her mother-in-law lady Wu with greatest filiality. She was very young to have risen to such a lofty status, but she was graceful and modest and did not display any pride or arrogance. And when she was together with her sisters-in-law, she was oblivious to the fact that she was a bejeweled and titled lady.

Later in life she suffered many hardships. She followed Su'an when he was banished to the regions beyond the border. Twelve years [after their banishment] she was finally able to move Heaven by her laments and was allowed to bring his coffin back for burial. Relatives of other people who had been banished in those times were never allowed to do this and even if they petitioned the palace, they were never given [this kind of] permission. The only one to receive this permission was her ladyship. When her ladyship came home, the clan members met her at the border and asked her how she had managed to accomplish this. Her ladyship replied: "The grace of our lord and father is as high as the sky and as thick as the earth. The roaring thunder and the fertile rain are both due to his grace. All of the others insisted on their innocence but I was the only one to admit to my guilt. That is why the emperor was so kind as to take pity on me." This shows the extent to which both her humility and her cleverness surpassed that of others.

From her early years she loved to hum and chant [poetry] and she took a special pleasure in lyrics. Su'an personally compiled a collection of her lyrics, which he entitled the *Song Lyrics of the Inept Administrator's Garden, First Collection* and which he had printed and circulated widely. As soon as she was left a widow beyond the border, she stopped writing poetry and not a single character [of her later writing] is to be found in this world.

Because she had to follow her husband to his official posting and so was unable to personally serve the finest of dishes to [her mother-in-law] lady Wu, she once made a great vow to paint 5,048 images of the Mahasattva [Guanyin] so that her mother-in-law would enjoy a long life. Later in life she became an even more devout Buddhist. She adopted the religious name of Zidan, and subsequently painted almost ten thousand such scrolls, which people treasured greatly. She continuously nurtured her inner spiritual radiance through meditation, and when she died, a rare fragrance filled the room. Even though it was the hottest part of summer, [her body] did not appear any different from when she was alive.

Alas! Her ladyship suffered hardships and faced dangers, but she never slackened and she never tired. Even a real hero could not have surpassed her. When it came to her final actions, she was as confident as if she were returning home, and did not swerve from the road to enlightenment. She was surely a "once-returner!"[5]

An anecdote from a later date adds to the above account with a story about how the marriage of Chen and Xu Can came about:

Before the Junior Guardian, his Excellency Su'an, had passed the metropolitan examinations, he went to Suzhou because his wife had died. Surprised by a sudden downpour, he took shelter in the Xu Family Garden. Leaning on the balustrade gazing at the fish, after a while he fell asleep. The owner of the garden, old Master Xu, had dreamt that night of a dragon sleeping on the balustrade, and when he saw [Chen Zilin leaning with his eyes closed on the balustrade,] was startled by how similar it was to his dream. When he found out that the young man was a son of the vice censor-in-chief and had already passed the provincial exams, he gave him his daughter in marriage. She was lady Xiangping [Xu Can].

Xu Can is best known for her song lyrics, a great many of which have been translated into English. Here we limit ourselves to a single example, a lyric composed to "Full River Red," a melody often used for the expression of patriotic sentiments. Although Xu Can's husband served the Manchus, many of Xu Can's own lyrics lament the collapse of the Ming dynasty:

To the Melody of "Full River Red" (*Manjiang hong*)
Moved by Events

Gone in a flash the splendors of spring,
As the chill and dreariness return again
In this time and season of cool autumn.
I hear all around me
The quickening sounds of clothes being fulled,
And the mournful cries of migrating geese.
The recent past a source of grief: we heard the Jade Tree tune;[6]
The lotus-picking songs are gone: the weeping cuckoo bleeds.

---

5. A "once-returner" is a person so perfected in Buddhist virtues that he or she only needs to be reborn one more time as a human being in order to achieve final enlightenment.

6. "Jade Trees in the Back Courtyard" is the name of a musical tune associated with the last ruler of the Chen dynasty (557–588), the last of the Southern Dynasties, which had its capital at Nanjing.

The glories and riches of days past,
Alas, have been carried eastward by the river's flow,
The golden goblet lies in pieces.[7]

When will there be an end
To the rains and the storms?
I crane my neck and gaze
Toward the moon over my home,
And see the world still filled with spears of bronze,
And the myriad mountains swathed in clouds.
By the side of cauldron and axe, the lingering pain remains,
Those tall warships crossing the sea were swallowed by waves.
To this very day
Shattered hearts have tried in vain to erect a stele
In memory of the heroic deed.

Although best known for her lyrics, Xu Can was also a prolific writer of *shi*. Her surviving poems date mostly from the years when her husband was at the height of his career. Among them, we find a number of poems on "border subjects" written before she followed her banished husband to Manchuria:

Zhaojun's Resentment

To grow old hidden deep inside the palace,
Or to stand before the emperor in her youth:
Whether she goes or stays, she's poorly fated,
Who really cares whether she lives or dies?
The freezing moon looks in the autumn mirror,
The steppe storm breaks off the night strings:
Her jade features are completely wasted away,
Now she thinks that the portrait was charming!

Moon on Border Mountains

The single moon above the inner quarters
Also hovers far away over Jade Pass.[8]
The old hometown ten thousand miles away—

---

7. The golden goblet is an often-used symbol for the integrity of the empire.
8. Jade Pass marks the westernmost end of the Great Wall.

The traveler in the last month of autumn.
 Filled with resentment, it rises over the Liao;
Wracked by sorrow, it sets on Mt. Long.[9]
Night after night the beacons warn of battle:
The moon always curved like the horn bow.

There are also a few of Xu Can's poems that date from her years living in Manchuria:

Gazing on Shenyang

From far away I gaze on the high walls in the setting sun,
We lived here "on a single branch" in times gone by.
When I left, I had watched the plum trees blossom three times,
When I returned, I was surprised to see the willows fatter by half.
 Don't in these distant lands be depressed by your sudden fall,
Freed for a while from the dusty web, enjoy the lack of guile.
When the bright sun rises to the middle of the autumn sky
Is when the migrating geese and the exile will return together.

New Year's Eve of the Year *Yihai* (1659)

The entire family has taken refuge in the Dharma and prays to the
    Buddha:
But we can't yet free ourselves from the pain of exile and the dreams
    of kin.
With my icy brush I have swept away all my idle sorrows,
As the revolving Jade Dipper melts away this long night.[10]
 I have come to rejoice in the whirling snow over the border grasses,
And can tell from afar that plum and willow are stirring by the Yangzi.
May the mild yang soon return, bringing us a warm easterly wind,
That will send the carved carriage on its way to the Phoenix Gate.

Seeing Off Lady Fang on Her Return to the West

Since our times in the Capital we have been old acquaintances,
For three years we suffered together the dust of the border lands.

---

9. During the Tang dynasty, the Liao River marked the easternmost limit of China's northeast expansion. Mt. Long (or the Long Mountains) marked the border between the provinces of Shaanxi and Gansu.

10. Jade Dipper is the Chinese designation for the constellation Ursa Minor.

Suddenly you've donned your jade pendants: spring has arrived,
The orchid lamp shines brightly again: the flowers blossom anew.
 Our friendship has been strengthened by our many shared hardships,
After the pardon, you soar to the clouds, our shared karma over.
But I know that whenever you in your carriage turn to look back,
I'll still be standing here in the desert, the one who still can't return.

The most ambitious work Xu Can wrote during her years in Manchuria was a series of eight poems entitled "Autumn Feelings" (*Qiugan*), an obvious allusion to a very well-known series of poems by the great Tang poet Du Fu entitled "Autumn Emotions, Eight Poems" (*Qiuxing bashou*). Du Fu's poems were written toward the end of his life when he was far from home, and in them he reflects on both the personal failures of his own life and the chaotic years of the An Lushan rebellion. The first two poems of Xu Can's series begin by describing the situation of the poet and her husband in their place of exile.

I

I had heard played on strings songs about leaving for the border regions,
But who would have thought that in this life I too would travel that road?
The frost invades the shadows of the blinds, bringing on an early chill,
The wind carries the notes of the reed pipe, often entering my dreams.
 Even a bird has to become an immortal to return to its hometown,
There are no fish, so what stranger will angle in the murky stream?
What can the bright moon over our house and hills look like today?
Night after night it hovers over the banks of the emerald brook.

II

In autumn a hundred feelings arise in the heart of the exile,
All alone below Yellow Dragon Pass tears dampen my gown.
The wind that blows over the open field is even fiercer at night,
The sky in the last month of autumn is often gray during the day.
 How can embroidered curtains protect against the northern clime?
The jasper zither is still tuned to the sounds of the south.
Those who then took to the sea together with their kith and kin
Are nowhere to be found in the immensity of water and clouds.

Xu Can's series continues with poems on her husband's service under the Ming, on the collapse of that dynasty, and on the historical dynasties whose rule was limited to southern China. These are then followed by poems in which she describes her sojourns in Nanjing and Hangzhou. She concludes the series with the following poem:

VIII

The loom for weaving brocade grows cold as the white season begins,
The insistent sounds of the washing blocks quicken my evening sorrow.
As I gaze toward the hills of Wu, clouds descend from high above,
On the banks of the Liao, three times I saw the geese coming and going.
 Who was the one playing the lute in sympathy over our leaving?
Often we heard the fife on the ruined terrace express resentment.
Greased cart wheels accommodate our books, the rest are empty bags,
In which to carry back with us the lovely colors of the many hills.

Wang Duanshu and Huang Yuanjie

Ming Loyalist: Wang Duanshu

Wang Duanshu (1621–before 1685) was without a doubt one of the most unusual and extraordinary women writers of the seventeenth century. She was born in Shaoxing, the second eldest daughter of a family of eight boys and three girls, the youngest of whom later became a nun. Her father was a high official named Wang Siren (1575–1646) and her mother, lady Yao, was his concubine.

Wang's precociousness became evident from a very early age, so much so that her father was moved to declare that "I have eight sons, but none of them measures up to this one daughter!" A biographical account by Wang Xianding describes her childhood as follows:

She was lovely in face and figure from the moment she was born, and naturally intelligent and wise. . . . At the age of four, she saw a play about Sudhana after which she would imitate him by bowing endlessly to her mother as if she were Guanyin.[11]

At the age of six, she would listen to her father tell all sorts of stories about loyal, filial, and wise women of the ages, and she would remember them all and never forget them. For fun she would dress up as a boy, and cutting out banners of paper, she would put on a performance, with her mother as the strategist, the

---

11. Sudhana (Shancai), one of Guanyin's acolytes, is often depicted as a little boy bowing in front of her.

maids lined up like soldiers and officers, and herself leading the troops with flag
upraised. When her father saw her, he laughed and said: "Why don't you [plan
on becoming] a woman scholar?" . . . She then followed along with her elder
and younger brothers when they went out for tutoring, and was taught the *Four
Books* and the *Book of Odes*, which she was able to recite after having looked
them over once. She herself wrote that she regarded Confucius as her master, and
every time before sitting down to eat she would insist on paying homage to him.

Wang Duanshu's childhood appears to have been a happy one, but
adolescence brought many difficulties and sorrows, including the illness
and death of her beloved mother, during which time she distinguished
herself by her filial behavior. When she was sixteen she was married to
Ding Shengzhao, to whom she had been betrothed as a child, and two
years later went with him to Beijing where he had family connections.
Here too she was called upon to show her filiality in the service of her
husband's family.

In 1643, the year before the fall of the Ming dynasty, Wang Duanshu
returned to Shaoxing with her husband. The subsequent years were
marked by great poverty and difficulty, and in 1646, Wang Duanshu was
devastated to learn of the death of her father, who had died a loyal martyr to the fallen Ming. It is not surprising that by this time Wang had become a fervent and outspoken loyalist herself. Indeed, it is this loyalism
that becomes the central organizing principle of her writings. Later, the
newly established Qing court, apparently willing to overlook her loyalist
sentiments and impressed by her reputation as a writer and scholar, invited her to Beijing to become a tutor in the Inner Palace, an invitation
she adamantly refused.

Throughout all of this political unrest Wang Duanshu and her husband continued to maintain their intellectual and literary interests. In
Shaoxing and later in Hangzhou, they often met together with other
Ming loyalists, a group which included many famous writers, dramatists,
and painters of the day, including Zhang Dai (1597–1684?). Wang
Duanshu also had very good relationships with other well-known loyalist
women poets, such as Liu Shi. In fact, despite the political and social turmoil whirling around them, and their own straitened circumstances, Wang
Duanshu and her husband appear to have led a rich and varied life that included poetry gatherings with plenty of wine to aid the inspiration, boat
trips on West Lake, and other convivial pleasures. She was known for her

beauty and wit and was in considerable demand not only among the loyalist crowd, but also among less politically minded artists and writers such as the famous playwright and wit Li Yu (1611–1680) (she contributed a preface to one of his plays). And during all this time, she kept up her work of writing and editing.

Wang Duanshu was a talented and prolific writer in an exceptionally wide range of literary genres, as well as a noted anthologist, critic, painter, and calligrapher. She wrote, compiled, and edited an impressive number of works, including an anthology of prose writings by women, a study of imperial princes and concubines through the ages, and various collections of her own prose and poetry. Unfortunately, most of these works have been lost, leaving only their titles behind. Still preserved, however, is Wang Duanshu's first collection of poetry and prose, published between 1651 and 1655. This work in thirty chapters is entitled the *Chantings of Red Collection (Yinhong ji)* and was published by her husband and other male members of their poetry group. Although by this time collections of women's writings were by no means unusual, the *Chantings of Red Collection* was unique both because of its range of writing forms and styles (including a substantial amount of prose) and because its topics went far beyond the traditional "feminine" subjects of love and longing. Also still extant is Wang Duanshu's anthology of women's poetry, *Classic Poetry of Famous Women (Mingyuan shiwei)*, which she began in 1639 and completed in 1664. This collection, finally published in 1667, again with the help of her husband and friends, features about fifteen hundred poems by over a thousand women of the Ming dynasty. Each entry in this anthology is preceded by a short biographical sketch and critical appreciation of the poet concerned. Like the *Chantings of Red Collection*, the work was enthusiastically received when it was published and sold so well that copies quickly became difficult to obtain.

It is clear that writing was the main activity in Wang Duanshu's life. She was very close to her husband Ding Shengzhao, who appears to have regarded her more as an intellectual and artistic companion than just a housewife or helpmate. She was apparently not interested in the traditional womanly occupations of needlework, housekeeping, or childrearing—in fact, she used her own money to purchase a concubine for her husband and later adopted the daughter born to this same concubine.

Loyalty to the fallen Ming dynasty is a central theme in the writings of Wang Duanshu, and she expresses her fervent loyalist sympathies in both poetry and prose. Wang Duanshu apparently never tried her hand at writing fiction, but she was undoubtedly an avid reader of popular stories, novels, and drama. She did write commentaries on drama, however, and many of her prose pieces are strongly marked by a well-developed narrative, a dramatic sensibility, and a talent for characterization. This is particularly true of her biographical sketches of loyalists, of which she wrote quite a few. Six of these biographies were of well-known male loyalist martyrs, and were included in a collection compiled by Wang Duanshu and her husband's friend, the famous literatus and writer Zhang Dai. In a postface to these biographies, Wang Duanshu explains the circumstances under which she wrote them:

I wrote the six biographies, from that of Guan Wenzhong to that of the Beggar of Jinling, during the years *mao*[*zi*] [1648] and *ji*[*chou*] [1649]. This was after the ruin and confusion [of the dynasty's collapse], and our family finances were in bad shape. We were living at the time at Plum Mountain, but I had no interest in women's work and so once in a while, I would take up my brush and ink in order to relieve my low spirits. I am ashamed that these [biographies] are not yet polished, and as to the language, I am afraid I will inevitably be criticized for wielding an axe in front of Lu Ban.[12] But these six biographies are based on what I have actually heard and seen and I daresay that not a single word is exaggerated in either its praise or censure. Nevertheless, they are roughly written and cover only the main facts. As to the worthiness of the lives [of these men], they all have their own epitaphs, biographies, and family records, and there is no need for me to add to them. My husband's poetry society friend, Zhang Tao'an [Zhang Dai], was going to put together a book called *Stone Chest Writings* [*Shigui shu*] and wanted to include these six biographies.[13] He came and asked for them many times but, worried that they were not up to par, I did not dare let them out of my hands and stubbornly refused. But the more I put him off, the more insistent he became. And so I copied them out and handed them over to him. Now they can be found in his *Stone Chest Writings*. In the end not a single word was changed or deleted! How could Tao'an's self-effacement go so far as this! And so I here respectfully note for the record that they were casually written.

---

12. Lu Ban is the god of carpenters. "To wield an axe in front of Lu Ban" means to make a fool of oneself by a conspicuous display of one's limited skill or talent.

13. Zhang Dai enjoyed a life of luxury during the final decades of the Ming but lost most of his fortune following the collapse. He is now best known for his nostalgic memoirs of the days of his youth.

The following is one of these biographies. It is a sketch of the life of a famous loyalist martyr by the name of Huang Duanbo (?–1645), who was known for his upstanding integrity as an official as well as his piety and devotion as a Buddhist layman.

Biography of the Loyal and Virtuous Master Huang Duanbo

Huang Duanbo had the style name of Yuangong as well as the sobriquet of Haiping and he was a native of Xincheng in Jiangxi province. He passed the metropolitan examinations in the year *maochen* of the reign period Chongzhen [1628], after which he was awarded the post of judge in Ningbo prefecture. In the year *gengwu* [1630] he was assigned to the southern capital [to supervise the examinations]. People he selected, like Yang Tingshu and Wen Deyi, were all outstanding famous scholars. He requested leave because of illness, and in the year *jiamao* [1635] was appointed to a post in Hangzhou. He loved the people as he would his own children, and was sparing in his punishments when settling cases. The common people all praised him and called him "Huang the Buddha."

Before long, he had to leave because of the difficulties of the *jiashen* [1644] transition. Magnanimous and brave, he was selected for the position of secretary of the Bureau of Ceremonies of the Ministry of Rites [at the Southern Ming court in Nanjing]. In the Fifth Month of the year *yiqiu* [1645], after the fall of Jinling [Nanjing], most of the civil and military officials capitulated and were recommended for posts in the new government. But the honest Huang Duanbo vowed that he would rather die than give in, and for more than ten days he refused to send in his statement of official rank. The [Qing] commander pressured him again and again, but he simply lay prostrate on the ground and refused to move. The commander then sent a horse and rider to seize him. Duanbo, dressed in a cornered turban and a wide-sleeved robe, came in and stood erect facing south. The attendants said: "What sort of official are you that you do not follow the protocol for an official audience?" Duanbo said: "The Chongzhen emperor has already passed away, and the Hongguang emperor has 'left the capital on a hunting trip.' So who is there to have an audience with?" The attendant said: "Prince Yu of the Great Qing!" Duanbo said: "He is your family's Prince Yu, what does he have to do with the subjects of our Ming court?" When the commander heard the interpreter's report, he said: "Mister Huang, you insist on being stubborn and unyielding. What I have witnessed so far, I must report to the emperor. Will the gentleman please tell me which official post he would like—I myself can give you whatever you want." Duanbo only shook his head and did not reply. The interpreter went back and forth more than ten times, but like before, Duanbo did not say a word. When this was reported to the commander, he said: "If you do not submit to the new dynasty, the punishment will be extremely severe. Aren't you scared?" Duanbo craned his neck and shook his head.

The commander, in great anger, ordered him taken out and beheaded, and moreover, secretly said to the executioner: "Start slowly with the punishment. If Mister Huang is willing to change his mind, I would still like to make use of him. We will see what Mister Huang says when he finds he is about to be executed." Then he sent the officials who had recently surrendered together with some of Duanbo's friends over to urge him repeatedly to submit. Duanbo came striding out and taking off his clothes, faced the sun, and bowed to the ground, shouting: "Taizu Emperor Gao! Virtuous Emperor Yizong!"[14] Then without saying another word, he stretched his neck out for the executioner. When all of the officials who had surrendered saw that his resolve could not be shaken, they reported this back to the commander. The commander said: "Since he is not willing [to submit], then let us give him the fame he craves."

Duanbo was sixty-one years old when he met his fate in this way. In eastern Zhejiang, the regent of the resistance regime bestowed upon him the special posthumous title of Loyal and Virtuous Chief Minister of the Court of Imperial Sacrifices, and also in his honor gave one of his sons a special exemption from the extra qualification examinations for an official post. He was then buried with praise for his loyalty.

Duanbo's nature was simple and straightforward. He was extremely fond of the Chan Buddhist school, and after the age of thirty would neither eat meat nor drink wine, nor get involved with women and sex. He was truly an honest and straightforward gentleman. Duanbo belonged to the circle of the first son of my departed father-in-law, which is why I know that [what I have written] is reliable: I would not dare to be overly fulsome in my praise.

In another section of her collection, Wang Duanshu includes a fair number of biographical sketches of women loyalists. In the following account of the undaunted lady Jin who is wiser and braver even than her husband, who is a general, and ultimately gets her posthumous revenge, we can get a feeling for Wang Duanshu's strong loyalist patriotism as well as her flair for graphic, and sometimes rather gory, dramatic detail.

---

14. These are the ritual designations of the founder of the Ming dynasty Zhu Yuanzhang, the Hongwu emperor, and of the last ruler of the Ming, the Chongzhen emperor.

The Upright and Loyal Lady Jin (and Her Husband Zhang Qinchen)

Lady Jin was a native of Guiji [Shaoxing] and the wife of the loyalist Ming general Zhang Qinchen. Born and raised in a well-known family, she was proper and serious, chaste and quiet; and her appearance was very lovely. After her marriage to Qinchen, she earned a reputation for serving her in-laws capably and filially.

In the year of *maozi* [1648], the countryside of Yue was covered with military encampments, and so the lady removed her hairpins and earrings [and sold them in order to raise money]. She pressured Qinchen to raise some troops, which he then stationed in the area of Mt. You, where he battled the Qing troops. After five or six months of fighting, over half of his troops had either been killed or wounded. Looking around for grain to feed them, he raided the fields of the countryside, which made life very difficult for the people of Yue. Lady Jin wept and cried and bitterly remonstrated with him saying: "If you don't have the common people on your side, how will you succeed in your great task? I can only foresee your failure." Qinchen did not listen to her and confiscated the grain with even more urgency. As a result, he was betrayed by his own men, and he and his wife were both arrested and sent to the capital of the prefecture.

Qinchen was actually willing to comply with [the enemy] and weeping, he made excuses for himself and pleaded for his life. His wife glared at Qinchen and said: "You are a general. Since you have not been able to succeed, you should have surrendered your life a long time ago. And now you still want to beg your captors to let you live? Aren't you shamed to death?!" Greatly angered, the [Manchu] commander took a knife and pointed it at her throat, but lady Jin cursed him with even more deafening vehemence. In the end, Qinchen was condemned to death by slicing, and his wife was ordered to be handed over to the troops as a reward. At this, lady Jin gave out a great scream and said: "If my husband dies, then how could I even think of remaining alive? I also want to die right away." The commander said: "Since you want to die, I will order you to be cut in half at the waist." But lady Jin [protested] saying: "Since my husband has been condemned to death by slicing, why should I be [simply] cut in half? I should also be condemned to death by slicing." So the commander agreed to her request.

As soon as the executioner raised his knife, lady Jin cursed him loudly, and when his knife reached her lower body, she pressed her two legs tightly together and died. A soldier by the name of Ma poked her lower body with his sword and scornfully said: "You dirty slut! Playing the fool! You were ordered to marry some fellow but you refused. And now today it has come to this!"

The next day this same Ma saw the lady, wearing a gold headdress and ceremonial robes, and accompanied by several tens of attendants. She pointed at Ma
and loudly cursed him saying: "The execution by slicing was justifiable, but why
did you have to defile my body?" She then ordered her attendants to beat him up.
This Ma fellow began to spit blood through mouth and nose; his body became
covered with dark bumps and he died a gruesome death on the spot. When the
commander heard about this, he said: "Of the officials and common people of
Yue city, as many as they are, none was the match of this one woman."

Therefore I have written a poem that goes: "The more people thought it
gruesome, the more she rejoiced, / The flesh flew off sliver by sliver, like petals
of fragrant flowers." This poem can be [regarded] as an evaluation of lady Jin's
reputation, which was certainly not an empty one.

Wang Duanshu must have been quite taken with the story of lady Jin,
since she also wrote a poem about her. In the latter version, though, lady
Jin's husband comes off looking a lot better than he does in the text
translated above. In the poem, Wang Duanshu portrays both of them as
a perfect loyalist couple, comrades both in resistance and in death.

Weeping for the Death of the Loyalist Wife Jin and Her Husband

The peaks of Yue, the hills of You all cherish this woman hero;
Her snow-pure essence was bathed in the waters of Mirror Lake.
Her virtuous visage, full of beauty and grace, worthy of an immortal—
Husband and wife, a fortunate match, took an oath to die together.
 Given the times, they clearly realized that there was no recourse,
Assisting her husband she bared her arms, took up bow and arrow.
The husband marveled that he had a wife of the same disposition,
The wife urged the husband: we must finish what we've begun.
 Together they cried out and vowed that they would not stop,
Displaying their loyalty they allowed themselves to be sliced.
Their determination was that of leaders, fearless until the end,
Fearless and united till the end, their eyes never left each other.
 People said that the worse it got, the more joyful they were:
The pain they suffered was shared by both to the same degree.
The flesh flew off sliver by sliver, like petals of fragrant flowers,
The bones as pure as frost, and even more fragrant than the iris.
 I don't wish that their graveyard be covered with lush green,
I don't wish them the fame of loyal martyrs that have suffered death:

I don't wish them the offerings of five sacrificial vessels in their honor,
I don't wish them records of a thousand autumns on bamboo and silk—
  I only wish that their heroic spirits will remain together without parting,
So they may come again, sweep over the land, and avenge this shame.

Many of Wang Duanshu's political poems are striking for their graphic imagery, as we can see in the following poem about a battlefield:

Lament at the Qiantang Battlefield

Lush and overgrown the riverbank grasses, the rain desolate and dreary;
The fighters dead: their lances cold but their hatred not yet dissolved.
On the battlefield, the glow of fireflies darkens in the moon's shadows;
In their dark rooms, ghosts weeping and wailing in the autumn night.
  As the last bell sounds from the distant peaks and all falls still,
The bark of a dog pierces the deserted village, the cry of a goose.
Then silently, silently, the startled spirits follow the defeated boats,
And lushly, lushly, the old millet mourns over the unstringed bows.
  At the roots of the wild flowers there's only rancid blood,
Passing strangers at dawn sing of demons blackened by ink.
The valorous ambition now turned cold with the mist and moon—
Fragrant names: where are the paper banners summoning their spirits
    home?
  In the depths of the inner chambers there is a woman by a solitary lamp:
Don't listen for the sound of the river, or wait for the evening tide.

In Chinese poetry, contemporary events are often described in terms of well-known historical incidents. For a woman poet like Wang Duanshu, the figure of Cai Yan offered a ready analogy to her own experiences as well as those of many other women during the wars of the conquest period:

Ballad of Resentment

Cold and dilapidated the house of Han, gone the caps and robes:
The fields of grain nothing but deserted mounds: people's efforts lost.
Invading soldiers, encroaching bandits all praise their khan,
The stalwart men of the nine provinces have died in their saddle.
  The beautiful woman followed the horses—a tale to make one grieve,
"Shields and spears bring turmoil and trouble, traveling is hard.
I make my residence in this remote place and do not seek comfort—

The sound of the leaves fluttering down, the water overflows."
  The moon urges the cold shadows over to the balustrade,
Long I chant the *History of the Han,* reading deep into the night.
Thinking of how it flourished then fell, I flick away my cold tears,
The cry of the cuckoo pierces through the third watch.
  Why is it that the men are lacking the nerve, the guts?
Fortune and fame all dangle temptingly from a fishing pole.
There was one who attacked the First Emperor, but he was all alone:
His scheme failed, but his heart had revenged the kingdom of Han.[15]
May Heaven's wind blow and air out the rank-smelling blood,
And summon sages from hidden valleys to display their worth.

Wang Duanshu also wrote many poems in which she viewed the disturbing events of the times through the lens not only of her own predicament, but also those of her intelligent and creative husband and friends whose opportunities for fully developing their talents were derailed, if not completely destroyed, by the fall of the dynasty. A straightforward description of her family's difficult circumstances can be found in the following poems:

Lunar New Year's Eve (1649)

Who says that New Year's Eve is full of activity?
I feel dull and cold, but happy there's no trouble.
Midnight marks the start of the year of *gengyin,*
When we can laugh at the worries of the year *jichou.*
  How wise—the words of Confucius:
The Way is not abandoned when poor!
How stupid—the writings of Han Yu:
In vain he wrote "Sending off Poverty."[16]
  Arms around my knees I face the cold lamp:
Firecrackers—where are they being set off?

---

15. After the First Emperor of Qin had conquered the kingdom of Han, Zhang Liang, a scion of a long line of ministers, tried to take revenge. The man he had hired to kill the First Emperor, however, mistakenly struck the wrong carriage with his huge hammer. Zhang Liang later became one of the most important advisors of Liu Bang, the founder of the Han dynasty.

16. The Tang dynasty writer Han Yu (768–824) wrote a piece in which he addresses Poverty, urging him to leave, whereupon Poverty lists the benefits (largely moral) that he has brought to him.

When My Woman Friend Dong Da Surou Came for a Visit, There Was No Cooked Food

In the desolate and dusty bare wastes, a cold thatched hut:
A sudden gust of autumn wind brings a slight chilly shiver.
The first dawn light in the bamboo windows vague and misty,
Dew sealed the path's grasses after my good husband left.
 Whenever my husband goes out, he returns late at night,
Now a woman friend comes to visit, there's no rice in the kitchen:
It's true enough that poems and books cannot stave off hunger,
But if I threw away my poems and books, I wouldn't have a life.
 My little boy doesn't understand and keeps whining away,
Seeing my girls adds to my sorrow: they all sob and whimper.
Gently I admonish my son that he must not cry so much:
Mother will pawn her gowns of gauze for rice and firewood.
 The sons of the rich and wealthy who know not how to read:
With fox-skin robes and fine steeds they live in great mansions,
And accompanied by pipes and drums feast on sweet flavors—
Their bumper harvest of grain piled up with plenty to spare.
 If people are a bit intelligent, Heaven becomes jealous:
I swear that I should burn my books and bury my brushes.
Ashamed to listen, the wealthy bar their door against my song,
As I chant about not having cooked food and so mark this day.

Telling My Story

So unexpectedly the prime of my life has passed,
As white hairs appear on the sides of my temples.
The flowing water goes its way, never to return:
And blue hills stand blocking my way forward.
 I look out over heaven and earth's expanse,
Within which I cannot call a single speck my own.
This world lacks people with a discerning eye,
Who can tell the foolish from the wise?
 They delight in the crooked, don't love the straight:
Comparable to the curved bow and the taut string.[17]

---

17. According to a folk song of the Han dynasty, those who are as straight as the taut string of a bow are doomed to endure a life of poverty, while those who are as crooked as a bow will make a successful career.

The lotus flower springs from the tip of my tongue,
But purse and chest are ashamed of the single coin.
I myself know that one must mind one's time,
Once the party is over, one's ashamed over its vanity!
At dawn one plans to travel to Qin and Jin;
At dusk one thinks of going to Qi and Yan.[18]
I sigh that I lack the ambition that soars;
Tired and weary, I can only struggle on.
I always feel as stupid as the cuckoo bird,
Ashamed of trying to fill the sea with pebbles.
The azure heaven cannot be questioned;
Who says that the wise will come first?

It would be wrong to assume that all of Wang Duanshu's writings were of such a serious and rather somber nature. In fact, she appears to have managed to enjoy herself tremendously. She derived a great deal of pleasure from exchanging poems and letters with fellow women poets, and a great number of poems are written to her women friends or recount her memories of happy outings:

My Woman Friend Zheng Er Mingzhan Stopped to See Me on Her Way to Her Maternal Home for the First Time (Since She Was Married)

The leaves were falling, autumn halfway through,
When a guest came to visit me at my humble home.
Waist-pendants trailing she dallied among the flowers,
Hairpins tinkling she set the quiet birds chattering.
I envy your being able to return to our old home,
I pity myself having to stay in this lonely village.
Together we write about these feelings of ours—
Then the boat leaves and the sun slowly darkens.

Feelings on the Double Ninth

Climbing to a high place to drink and carouse without a care,
Strolling at leisure in scarf and skirt and light raw-silk shoes.

---

18. "Qin and Jin" stands for northwestern China; "Qi and Yan" for northeastern China.

At dawn we played among the lotus flowers in a little boat,
At dusk we lodged in a fancy tower near the flower market.
 Unpainted screen leaning aslant, kingfisher sleeves rolled up:
Flourishing the brush, laughingly recording lovely girls' names.
The clouds brightly thronged around the moon as the night falls,
And the sounds of harps and sandalwood clappers began to rise.
 Don't you know about all the withered trees on the bare hills?
Human affairs are always changing, the garden pavilion is gone.
This year I try to find the flowers and continue the old excursion,
But the sound of girdle-pendants has faded, the girls have passed away.
 We raise our cups halfheartedly—close friends are few:
Nothing left but bits of cloud floating over the autumn waters.

When Wang Duanshu was compiling her comprehensive anthology of
women poets, which took her twenty-five years to complete, she made a
point of asking poets she knew as well as readers of her works to submit
either their own poems or other poems that they might have in their possession. That she was very appreciative of other women poets can be
seen in the following brief preface she wrote for *Together with Autumn Poetry Collection (Tongqiu shixuan)*, the collected poems of a woman poet by
the name of Xuan Huazi:

Preface to the *Together with Autumn Poetry Collection* of Xuan Huazi

Between heaven and earth, lucid and pure talent is not reserved just for men:
one half of it is also the work of women. When Confucius edited [the *Book of
Odes*], he made sure that [women-authored songs such as] "How the Creepers
Spread" and "The Mouse-Ear" were praised on a par with the Six Classics.

When I first opened up [this book], and read the various chantings of Xuan
Huazi, I found their conception to be chilly and solitary, and their structure
forceful and elegant; they were as graceful as rolling pearls and linked jade, and
as lofty as the moon over the mountain peaks where the clouds gather. They
were like the [poems] of the Han and Wei and yet they were not [the poems]
from the Han and the Wei; they were like the [poems] of the Three Periods [of
the Tang] and yet they were not poems from the Tang. They nonetheless captured the spirit and style of all of these.

Alas! Xuan Huazi truly is worthy of sharing the platform with these writers
of old. Now all of these chantings have been gathered together, the world will
forgive my verbosity if it has enlightened eyes. I recite these chantings and in-
tone them over and over again, and cannot bear to let them out of my hands.

Respectfully, I write this rough preface, so that [others may] know that this woman scholar of ours from Yue [Shaoxing] still far surpasses most of woman-kind. Alas! How should I be worthy of writing this preface for [the works of] Xuan Huazi?! I offer it as tribute to Xuan Huazi that [her works] may never perish.

Wang Duanshu herself experimented with a wide variety of poetic styles, including both ancient and modern five- and seven-syllable verse, quatrains, song lyrics, *yuefu* or ballads, rhapsodies, and even a few reli-gious hymns or gathas. She also had fun writing palindromes, a literary pastime that appears to have been particularly popular during this time. In the case of Wang Duanshu's palindromes translated below, each sec-ond line is the inverse of the preceding line:

To the Melody of "Bodhisattva Barbarian" (*Pusaman*)
Spring Lament (In Imitation of the Style of Zhu Huiweng)

The water loves the flowers' reflection, and imitates new makeup,
Imitating new makeup, the fresh reflections of the flowers love the water.
This lyric is chanted because I am thinking of you,
I am thinking of you because of chanting this lyric.

Returning to Beijing, accompanied by melancholy close by,
Close by is the melancholy that accompanies Beijing's return.
The door closes on the willow in the golden dusk,
Dusk turns golden as the willow closes the gate.

To the Same Melody
Summer Lament

Tunes and songs line the path, flowers scorching the green,
The green-scorched flowery path lined by songs and tunes.
The lotus dream resents the startled cicada,
The cicada startles the resentful dream of the lotus.

Bits of clouds and mist blown at random,
At random are blown the mist and cloud bits.
The zither is lovely as the night's watch grows deep.
In the deep watch of the night a lovely zither.

To the Same Melody
Autumn Lament

The butterflies coldly chase smiles and, suppressing feelings, are timid.
Timidly, feelings suppressed, smilingly we chase the cold butterflies.
The autumn shine of the moonlight floats,
The floating light of the moon shines on autumn.

Desolate geese cry out long and sad,
Sad and long cry out the geese in desolation.
A foolish illness I know is difficult to cure,
To cure it is difficult, I know this illness is foolish.

To the Same Melody
Winter Lament

Slapping the face the bitter cold wind soughs and sighs,
Sighing and soughing, the wind coldly and bitterly slaps the face.
Stretching out frozen hands I turn the pages of my book,
The book's pages I turn as my hand freezingly stretches out.

I pity the branch of plum as skinny as a stone,
Stone-skinny the plum branch is pitiful.
The blinding snow presses the clouds low,
The low clouds press the snow blindingly.

If Wang Duanshu excelled at the writing of long ballads as well as more extended works of prose, she also appears to have had a special fondness for the shorter, more lyrical, quatrain form. There are several such quatrains in her collected works. The following represents just a sampling:

Impromptu Verses

I

Wine I love to drink when melancholy,
Poetry I only chant when I am ill.
Blinding frost and solitary moon are cold,
As the first geese pass over at night.

II

Cold birds at dawn arrive in their colors,
Their winging cries not the usual tune.
"Ding, ding" the hidden valley echoes,
Who's chopping the South Mountain trees?

III

A lecherous man is fond of face and figure;
A lettered man values talent and thought.
The Han palaces were filled with lovely women,
But history has always praised Concubine Ban.

Painter, Calligrapher, and Poet: Huang Yuanjie

In her own day Huang Yuanjie enjoyed a reputation that easily equaled that of Wang Duanshu, not only as a poet, but also as a painter and calligrapher. She had contacts with many of the leading women poets of mid-seventeenth-century Jiangnan, and was also highly regarded by well-known poets such as Qian Qianyi and Wu Weiye. But little of her work has survived, which makes it difficult at this distance in time to fully appreciate why she was so highly regarded.

Huang Yuanjie hailed from Xiushui in Zhejiang province. Her exceptional talents became evident from an early age and later she married a local student. Legend has it that even before her marriage her fame was so widespread that the famous literatus Zhang Pu (1602–1641) asked for her hand, but that she refused his offer of marriage. Following the destruction of the Manchu invasion, Huang Yuanjie and her husband left their hometown and embarked upon a peripatetic life in Jiangsu and Zhejiang. Huang Yuanjie provided the primary income by serving as a family tutor for girls and by selling her paintings and calligraphy (it was probably because of her fame as a professional woman painter that she was invited to contribute a preface to a play by Li Yu about a professional woman painter who ends up, after having married first a natural eunuch and then a woman in male disguise, as a concubine of the famous painter Dong Qichang). One of the many families Huang Yuanjie stayed with was that of the widowed Shang Jinglan in Shaoxing. Wang Duanshu includes in her anthology a number of poems that Huang Yuanjie wrote during this stay:

Composing Poems to the Same Rhyme in Yu Garden Together with Lady Qi (Shang Jinglan), Qi Xiuyan, Qi Xiangjun, Zhang Chuhuai, and Zhu Zhaobi

We stir the flowers on winding paths and cut through the morning fog,
The landscape's murky haziness doubles all the woods and springs.
The wide-spaced railing shows off even more the size of the grounds,
The dense trees obscure the roundness of the setting sun.
 Close to a stream, the floating mist enters doors and windows,
Brushing the clouds, the high pavilion houses divine immortals.
In this season of frost, there still are flowers blooming and falling,
Sprinkled and doused, the red of their petals is doubly fresh.

On the First Prime[19] of the Year *yiwei* (1655) Lady Wu Zixia Invited the Club-Sisters Wang Yuyin, Wang Yuying, Zhao Tongwei, and Tao Gusheng for a Gathering at Floating Emerald Pavilion. We Waited for Qi Xiuyan and Zhang Wanyan but They Didn't Come. I Was Assigned the Rhyme Word "*Yuan*" (Prime)

Clutching fly whisks like immortal companions,
We're treated to a banquet on this First Prime:
These flowering talents develop female learning,
Elegant sophistication gathers in Liang Garden![20]
 The green of the bamboo is split up by the distant paths,
The fragrance of nearby flowers surrounds the pavilion.
The plates seem to be filled with dishes made of jade,
Sitting here, it is like being at Peach Blossom Spring,
 As decorated candles are further illuminated by torches,
And again and again we float our cups of ambrosia.
The moon, fully round, looks like a precious mirror,
And the sparkling lamps spin a wheel made of pearls.
 Who will be the first one to find a perfect line?
Together we yearn to discuss our deep longings.
Gazing at each other, with words still left unsaid,

---

19. The First Prime refers to the fifteenth of the First Month.
20. Liang Garden was the abode of the poets patronized by the prince of Liang in the second century BCE.

As we say goodbye, our thoughts continue to linger.
The returning boats set off to the north and the south,
Each and every one of them startling the traveler's soul!

When Huang Yuanjie left Shaoxing, Shang Jinglan and all of her daughters and daughters-in-law wrote parting poems full of praise for Huang Yuanjie's superior talents. Huang Yuanjie also stayed for a while with Liu Shi. Later, when she was invited to Beijing to teach, she lost her son in a boating accident in Tianjin, and within a year her daughter also died, after which she returned to the south.

A hundred or so of Huang Yuanjie's poems are preserved in various seventeenth-century anthologies. Wang Duanshu includes sixteen of her poems in her *Classic Poems of Famous Ladies*, and in her introduction quotes a critic to the effect that Huang Yuanjie's paintings were better than her calligraphy, and that her calligraphy was better than her poetry. Some of her poems, however, do have a certain charm and are worthy of translation.

On the Road through Nine Pines

The stream can print the moon and display it in each location,
The mountains, not leaving the mist, are everywhere green.
For nine miles the sounds of the pines lightly brush my ears,
As the evening cool, rustling and rustling, ascends the reeds.

Springtime Window

Inside the house one feels the north wind's chill,
Outside the window the birds all sing at one time:
I've yet to see the colors of flowers and willows,
But I hear they're filling the brook down the road.

Watching the Clouds on a Summer Day

Each and every one—there's too much to see!
Their miraculous transformation has no cause.
Rising like mountains, they threaten each other,
Meeting each other, they do not utter a word.
Why is it that you keep shifting your shapes?
I want to find out—I'll get to the bottom of it!

In the Mountains

Entering the mountains I don't see any stones:
The stones have become the walls of my house.
Entering the forest, I don't see any trees:
The trees have become the beams of the roof.
 So I say to all of you living in the mountains:
What need to raise those pavilions of yours!

Suffering from the Rain

Who, traveling far from home, can bear the rain and the wind?
My bitter longing for home communicates with the drifting cloud.
All alone I ascend the dilapidated tower and fancy myself in Heaven,
 I laugh at myself for being afraid of seeing my sorrowful face in the mirror.
The branches are cold, the blossoms freezing, the orioles want to fly away,
My bags empty, the tip of my brush worn to a nub—it's hard to write well.
But what I most hate is that although spring has long gone, I am still
    around,
In a corner of the room insects chirp, blaming me for being so damned
    poor!

Writing Nuns

The late Ming and early Qing dynasties were a time of great religious fervor at all levels of society—from emperors and empresses (for instance, the mother of the Wanli Emperor) to elite officials and their families (as we have seen in the case of the Ye family) to ordinary men and women too humble to have left any records of their lives. This religious fervor took many shapes and forms, from the worship of local deities and spirits, to the invocation of shamans and mediums, the pursuit of Daoist immortality through adherence to various types of practices and dietary programs, and the simple piety of offering incense to the Buddha and invoking his blessings. Women were involved in all these religious activities to some extent.

The Buddhist convent represented yet another religious alternative for women. As was true in premodern Europe, the convent often offered refuge to women who had no other place to go—women whose husbands had died or abandoned them, or who had no families upon whom they could depend. And, indeed, it probably was the case that many Buddhist nuns were in the convent not out of choice, but as a place of last resort. It is also likely that a great number of these women, although they might learn to recite a sutra or two, were illiterate. Yet there were Buddhist nuns who came from elite families and who had received a classical education even before entering the convent. Their motivations were varied—some indeed were widowed at an early age, others appear to have felt a strong pull toward a religious life even as young children. For these women, the convent was not simply a place to hide away; rather, it was a place where they could exercise many of their talents—religious, administrative, educational, and literary—to an extent that may have been impossible in the inner quarters. This was not a new phenomenon, of course. As we saw earlier, during the Six Dynasties period and later during the Song dynasty there were many famous and influential Buddhist nuns. Some of these, such as the Chan Buddhist master Miaozong of the Song dynasty, were known for their literary skills. Although only a handful of their writings survive today, these writing nuns may have had much larger collections of works that circulated widely. In the centuries that followed, names of such nuns continue to appear in the sources, and during the seventeenth century in particular, their poems and other writings often appear in the anthologies of women's writing that were popular during the time. Collections of their writings were also published and circulated independently; for the seventeenth century, we have the titles of over thirty such collections. Not everybody, and in particular, not every elite male, was happy about this phenomenon, as we can see from the following diatribe by none other than Qian Qianyi:

In these degenerate days of the Dharma, the Chan school has lost its way. Witchlike nuns and their demonic kin ascend the [dharma] hall, preach to the congregation, and circulate their discourse records. This is all due to a generation of heterodox teachers and blind Chan followers who indiscriminately bestow the seal of transmission. Oiled heads and rouged cheeks wrangle over who will grasp the fly whisk; untouchable slave girls are elevated to the status of lineage masters.

Even Qian Qianyi, however, was able to name a few Buddhist nuns whom he knew personally and who were, in his eyes, quite worthy of admiration.

Teacher and Convent-Builder: Yikui Chaochen

Fortunately, several of these collections of writings by Chan Buddhist nuns of the third quarter of the seventeenth century were preserved in an edition of the Buddhist canon known as the *Jiaxing Extended Tripitika* (*Jiaxing Xuzang jing*). The collections contain sermons, letters, and poems as well as prefaces and autobiographical and biographical accounts of these women's lives. Since many of these nuns lived at approximately the same time (around the middle of the seventeenth century) and in approximately the same part of China (the lower Yangzi area known as Jiangnan), they knew each other, either as teachers, disciples, friends, or simply as spiritual mentors and models. One such nun is Chan master Qiyuan Xinggang (1597–1654), abbess of the Crouching Lion Chan Cloister (the lion lying in ambush was often used as a metaphor for the way in which an enlightened Chan master would make use of unconventional methods to "surprise" a student into a higher realm of understanding). Qiyuan Xinggang had seven official dharma heirs, two of whose collections of writings, together with those of their teacher, are preserved in the *Extended Tripitika*. One of these dharma heirs was Chan master Yikui Chaochen (1625–1679). In her collection, we find both a short autobiographical piece and a considerably longer biographical account written by one of her disciples. These two texts complement each other both in terms of purpose and emphasis and together they provide a rare glimpse into the world of an educated Buddhist nun of the seventeenth century.

Let us begin with the short autobiographical piece that Yikui Chaochen wrote, as she tells us, "for the edification of my disciples." In this piece, Yikui emphasizes her role as abbess, which included training and watching over a community of disciples, as well as taking part in fundraising and construction activities. She also describes her devotion to her teacher, especially after her teacher's death.

My secular surname was Sun, and [my family] had lived for generations in Lüli [southwest of Suzhou in Jiangsu province]. When I was twenty-six, I left the household life and took the tonsure with Qiyuan Xinggang of the Crouching Lion [Chan Cloister] in Meixi, which was in the same county. The master was a dharma granddaughter of the Venerable Miyun Yuanwu [1566–1642] from Tian-tong; Miyun was a thirtieth-generation descendant in the lineage of Linji [Jpn. Rinzai, d. 866].

In the *renchen* year [1652] of the Shunzhi reign period [1644–1661], when I was twenty-eight, I took the precepts. In the Sixth Month of my thirtieth year, my mother died, and in the Ninth Month, my master also passed away. At that time, my elder dharma sister Yigong assumed the leadership of the Crouching Lion, while I mourned our teacher's death. After the [prescribed mourning] period was over, I wanted to build a thatched hermitage for myself but lacked the financial wherewithal to do so. Fortunately, my second eldest brother Zilin shared my aspirations; he had made a headstart in his investigation of Chan and fully understood the [truth that] the Three Teachings all return to a single source. And so he built a hermitage to which he gave the name of Cantong [The Unity of the Three], and asked Master Hongjue [Muchen Daomin, 1596–1674] to write [the characters for Cantong] on a plaque [to be hung at the entrance to the convent]. This is how the Cantong Cloister got its name.

It consisted of secluded rooms with cassia windows and the abbess's quarters with its winding corridors, and beyond the kiosks by the ponds and the waterside pavilions there were flowering plants and slender bamboo. In the year *bingshen* [1656] the buildings were finished and everything was ready, and in the Second Month of the winter, I was invited to take up residence there. At that time, there were only six or seven people living in the hermitage, and I was able to fully enjoy the pleasure of the forest. The white clouds sealed the gates and it was quiet and tranquil with no one around. Six years passed like a single day. Then, unexpectedly, in the spring of the year *xinchou* [1661], my elder dharma sister Yigong suddenly came down with a serious illness. She called me to her bedside and entrusted me to take care of things after her death, [especially] the printing of our late master's discourse records. She herself had already built [the master's] stupa, appointed a convent manager, and issued instructions to the community of nuns, but given that she and I belonged to the same dharma family, she wanted me to complete our late master's unfinished business. The lay donors also came to Cantong especially in order to request that I do so. I was concerned, though, about my aging father, and so, [writing] a gatha, I firmly refused. Who would have expected that the following winter my honorable father would also pass away, and that the convent manager would become critically ill.

At the insistent pleading of the lay donor from Xunxi, Madame Dong, in the First Month of the year *renyin* [1662], I reluctantly agreed to her request. When I returned, I saw that our late master's stupa garden was located on a road out in the wilds where it was difficult for people to care for it. Greatly perturbed in body and mind by this, I returned to live at the Crouching Lion Chan Convent.

For six years my sole concern was to deal with the matter of the stupa, and I did not become involved in worldly affairs. By the Twelfth Month of the year *bingwu* [1666], I had begun the work of moving the stupa to a location left of the Cantong Cloister. I also built a completely new reliquary for the ashes of my elder dharma sister Yigong right next to our master's stupa. By the time of the Clear and Bright Festival in the year *dinghui* [1668], the work of stupa construction was completed, and in the Eighth Month I retired from the Crouching Lion Chan Convent [and returned to Cantong Cloister].

That winter, we put up three buildings, and in the spring of the year *wushen* [1668] we began to build a six-*jian* gate. In the year *jiyu* [1669] we built a three-*jian* bathhouse on the eastern side, and in the year *gengxu* [1670] on the Buddha's birthday, we [began] construction of the Great Hall. When I left the household life, I had given away every bit of the marriage dowry [which had been given to me by my own] Sun family, as well as my share of the goods from [my husband's] Sheng family: this is something everyone, whether monastic or lay, knows well. I have spent twenty-six years toiling for this dharma family, ten years of which have been devoted to the task of building, as gradually this cloister has come into being. All of this has come from the trusting hearts of donors from all ten directions. It is for this reason that night and day I exhort and admonish you, my disciples: if we do not disregard our bodily [desires] and make our minds as if dead [to the world], how will we be able to ensure that [this cloister] will continue for a long time without falling into decay? If you want to repay your dharma ancestors, you must respectfully adhere to the pure regulations, and sincerely fulfill your vows. In this way, the simple and austere "family style" will last forever. Only by following these words will we be able to live together as a community and ensure that it be sustained for generation after generation. You must not betray that which has been the primary aspiration of my entire life!

Our admiration for Yikui Chaochen's entrepreneurial abilities as displayed by her fundraising and building projects is only increased when we realize that she carried out these activities during one of the most unsettled periods of Chinese history.

After Yikui Chaochen's death, her disciples gathered all of their master's sermons, poems, and other writings together, added a long biographical account, and then found a couple of famous officials to write prefaces for it and have it published and circulated. These prefaces often remark on the master's gift for language, both as a preacher and teacher and as a poet and writer. Although, as usual, much is lost in translation, the following is an example of a sermon or dharma talk that

Yikui Chaochen delivered to her disciples on New Year's Eve. In traditional China, the eve of the lunar New Year was celebrated with a festive meal for the whole family. The "white ox of the open field" mentioned in the first sentence of this sermon is a common metaphor for the enlightened mind.

The master said: "The ancients would cook 'a white ox of the open field' to share with the community for the New Year. I thought it over, [and have come to the conclusion that] there is no need, no need! 'A white ox of the open field' is something the elder and younger sisters of this community naturally have— what need to add more wine when you are already drunk? But since this year at Cantong we have built a new refectory, I cannot avoid raising the word 'new' in my talk to you. But what new thing shall I talk to you about? Every household and every family is raising a noisy hullabaloo, pasting new pairs of couplets on their doorways, and changing into new sets of caps and gowns. In this regard, one can say that, from the outside, they are all spanking new; however, one doesn't see the ignorance within: everything that is bad and pungent, stale and bitter, remains unchanged and no one pays attention to them. But in the households of those of us who are people of the Way, we must clearly and meticulously continue on as usual: we have no new clothes or new hats, nor do we exchange our old adornments for new ones. All we do is take the three hundred and sixty days of the year and reckon them up from beginning to end. Are there any smelly and dirty jars that have not been washed clean? Are there any debts accumulated in the course of the year that have not yet been repaid? Are there any karmic habits brought with us into our mother's womb [from another life] that have not yet been eliminated? Are there any karmic roots that have been there since beginningless time that have not yet been uprooted? Each and every grain of dust or negligence must be gone over, then when the thirtieth day of the Twelfth Month arrives, finally you must closely inspect each and every thing [you have done], without leaving even the slightest stain of dirt on your mind-field; everything must be completely turned over, and you must renew and replace your determined daring and keen understanding, and raise the *huatou* that you are investigating. Renew yourself day after day and then again daily. If you concern yourself solely with this sort of progress—that is what is meant by the phrase 'brand new'! So this is how we should deal with this festival.

> In the Cantong Cloister, buildings and terraces have gone up,
> Like blue lotuses that have been planted atop the stones.

Among fireworks' noise, what remains of the old year departs,
Within the plum blossom fragrance, springtime is escorted in.

Take good care of yourselves. You may now go back to your rooms."

Yikui's collected writings also contain a large number of poems. Many of these are actually religious instruction in verse. But others contain more explicit expression of her personal feelings. In the following poems, for example, she expresses her sorrow over the loss of Master Zhiyuan Xinggang, whom she regarded very much as a second mother.

Lamenting My Teacher, the Venerable Nun Zhiyuan

I

She who spent years humbling, shaping, and polishing us,
Is now gone like a broken noon dream and I am still in tears.
Alas, it was far too soon for me to have been parted from her—
Her personal things are now in ashes and know not sorrow.

II

Since when have spring and fall passed without me serving her?
The cries of the nightjars fill the branches left bare of blossoms.
Broken-hearted, I sorrowfully listen to their repeated calls,
Then just shut the brushwood gate against the wind and rain.

Many of Yikui Chaochen's poems are addressed to her various dharma sisters, that is, the nuns with whom she received her religious training at the Crouching Lion Cloister. One of her closest companions was Chan Master Yigong Chaoke (1620–1667), who Yikui Chaochen mentions in her autobiographical piece excerpted above. After the death of Master Zhiyuan Xinggang in 1654, Yigong Chaoke, together with yet another of Yikui's dharma sisters, Yichuan Chaolang, had taken over the administration of the Crouching Lion Cloister. Yichuan, however, passed away only two years after her own teacher's death, leaving Yigong with complete responsibility for the convent, as Yikui Chaochen notes in her piece. In the following poem that Yikui Chaochen wrote to her during this time, she praises Yigong for the conscientious way in which she undertook her responsibilities:

Sent to My Elder Dharma Sister Yigong

I

The ancestral hall is tall and lofty, and as pure as autumn.
"The myriad shapes so majestic," this phrase says it all.
Spring arrives and naturally the flowers produce brocades—
When sound and fragrance fill the world, who can grieve?

II

You have kept the lamp glowing as it did with our master,
The Chan community flourishes and puts out new shoots.
The gates and halls are in order all thanks to your efforts:
It is truly the time to throw out the bait and cast the line.

All of this work took its toll on Yigong Chaoke's health, and before she had a chance to "throw out the bait and cast the line," and retire to a life of quiet contemplation, she fell gravely ill and died shortly afterwards. Her death meant the loss of yet another person who had become a family member to Yikui Chaochen, as we can see in this short poem:

Lamenting My Elder Dharma Sister Yigong

Waking from my dream, full of sorrow I listen to the morning bell:
No point in strumming "Tears of Blood Dye the Red Maples."
I think back on how together we sang the songs of the Unborn:
How could I have known the wind would blow in a different tune?

Still other of Yikui Chaochen's poems deal with her inner spiritual life, and in particular the practice of meditation—both its difficulties and its joys.

Sleepless Due to a Cold

My whole body burns with fever, I cannot keep from coughing;
Rising I sit, my robes pulled about me: my breath slowly clears.
When I emerge from meditative realization, the night is done,
And I hear nothing but the neighbor dogs barking in the village.

Written to the Rhymes of "Sitting in Meditation Gathas": Five Poems

I

Once the layered gates are smashed open, wherever you are is peaceful,
Once the mind is not attached to things, then you will be fully satisfied.
Whenever I have some time, back straight, I sit in the shade of the pines,
And watch as the toad in the moon slowly rises to hover in the east.

II

When one freely speaks of the Dharma, the heavenly flowers fall;
When one deliberates and debates, one only becomes confused.
With the right opportunity and good luck, nothing is impossible:
Tapping Emptiness, extracting the marrow become a way of life.

III

How wonderfully sublime to discuss mysteries layered like clouds:
It is truly rare to meet someone who can be called a kindred soul.
The red-hot stove blazes forth with an aspiration to transcendence!
Because of our karma we have the chance to turn the Dharma Wheel.

IV

In this toiling life, disordered and confused, greed and anger reign,
But when the mind-flower suddenly opens, the world becomes Spring.
Melting snow to boil water for tea, I while away the entire day:
Inside, I feel as vast and expansive as the ice-cold disk of moon.

V

A tiny boat in the moonlight stirs up foam-flowers on the water,
Blossoming water-lilies send across their fragrances in the dark.
Hearing, seeing, knowledge, and consciousness—all one Dharma:
Now this bald nun can be lazy and let her hair hang down.

One last example of the poetry of Master Yikui Chaochen is the follow-ing two poems written to another Buddhist nun with whom she clearly felt a close bond, not only of friendship but also of spiritual affinity. It is worth noting that although we so far have used the words dharma sister and dharma daughter in our translations, Buddhist nuns referred to their teachers, fellow students, and disciples, by male kinship terms—grandfathers, brothers, sons, and grandsons—even when they were in fact female.

On Chan Master Dongyun's Fiftieth Birthday

I

You've forgotten the dusty world and realized your own inner ease,
In middle age, your longing for the Way is as it was in the beginning.
Examining errors, rectifying mistakes you've awakened from the dream,
And in the fragrance of the lotus, you have realized the complete truth.

II

Of a hundred years half have disappeared into the distant past,
Now you have put the convent in order, everything goes well.
Our grandfathers' fields have been tilled and are ready to harvest:
Sons and grandsons will forever find their way to the source.

To My Chan Companion Dongyun

The ancient hall stands tall and proud, completely renewed:
Locked inside the cloud-shrouded cave is a kindred soul.
Burning incense, sitting silently, we attune to one another—
The words of a tongueless person are the most intimate of all.

Pilgrimage and Poetry: Jizong Xingche

Chan Master Jizong Xingche (b. 1606) was born and received her initial training in Hunan province, and it was only later that she came to the Jiangnan area to study with various Linji Chan teachers. Jizong Xingche provides us with a brief autobiographical account, which opens as follows:

I come from Hengzhou prefecture in Huguang [present-day Hunan province]. My family name is Liu, my father's given name was Shanchang and my mother's family name was Song. One night, my father dreamed that an old monk came and asked if he might have a room for the night and my father said yes. Not long afterwards, my mother became pregnant and a year later gave birth to me. On the night I was born, the eighth day of the Eighth Month of the *bingjia* year of the Wanli reign period [1606], the birds sang out repeatedly and a white light that was brighter even than the moon filled the room. Everyone present remarked on this amazing occurrence.

Even at a young age, I disliked eating non-vegetarian food: just one taste of meat and I would spit it out! When I became a little older, I took pleasure in reading Confucian texts and Buddhist sutras. I felt revulsion for the dust and confusion of the world and I thought deeply about the matters of life and death. I begged my father to let me sacrifice myself and enter the religious life, but he refused. Later, I was engaged to marry a man named Chen, but after only a few years, he perished on his way to take up a government post.

I then built a cloister in which I installed a [Buddha] image and began to engage in the cultivation of my merit field. At dawn and dusk, I would take time from my other duties to sit in quiet meditation; I took such delight in adhering to the precepts and [religious] discipline that I became determined to leave the householder's life. In the days that followed, I began to seek interviews with teachers of knowledge and wisdom.

As it happened, one day when I was visiting Master Haitian, I noticed on his desk a copy of the *Nanyue Chan* [*Lineage Transmission of the Lamp*], which had been printed and circulated by the monk Shanci. When I read it, I realized that it contained nothing less than the essential principles of the lineage by the worthies of the past. When I asked Haitian where Master Shanci had hidden himself away, he informed me he had built himself a modest hermitage on Yanxia Peak [located on nearby Mount Heng] and so I went to pay him a visit . . .

Thus began Jizong Xingche's life as a Chan Buddhist practitioner: the remainder of her autobiographical account relates the various dharma dialogues (completely mystifying to those of us who are not involved in Chan Buddhist practice) with which she engaged her teacher and which ultimately resulted in her first experience of awakening. She studied for many years with Master Shanci Tongji who, unfortunately, died prematurely in 1645 after mistakenly eating some poisonous wild greens. After her master's death, she took up her walking staff and set out to visit some of the eminent Linji Chan masters living in the Jiangnan region. She clearly thought that this would be a pilgrimage, and planned to return to her beloved Mt. Heng afterwards. Her travels lasted longer than expected, however, as we learn from a letter she wrote to her brothers many years later:

The several decades since I left home have sped by more quickly than the blink of an eye. You can imagine all of the changes the world has undergone since then! Gazing far away in the direction of home, I really can't imagine what it might be like anymore. Carrying with me only a tattered robe and wooden walking stick, I made do wherever I landed and in this way I completely traversed the rivers of Chu and the mountains of Wu. This is what Fashi meant when he said "I share the same root with Heaven and Earth, I share the same substance with the myriad things."[21] My feet have carried me every which way, completely ignoring this body of mine covered with mud and my ragged robe dragging along the ground.

Jizong's travels were, of course, an integral part of the traditional Chan training, which required visiting a number of different teachers to deepen one's understanding. Accordingly, Jizong made a point of visiting some of the most important Linji Chan monks in the area. One of these, Chan Master Wanru Tongwei (1594–1657), was so impressed with her that he made her his formal dharma heir. He also insisted that she remain in the Jiangnan area to teach. And so began several decades of teaching, primarily as abbess of the Huideng Cloister in Suzhou, although it appears that she also lived for a while in the Protection of Goodness Cloister that was associated with Yikui Chaochen's dharma sisters, Chan masters Yiyin Chaojian and Yigong Chaoke.

In the course of her years in the Jiangnan area, Jizong Xingche appears to have acquired a significant following, both among monastics and elite laymen and women. The following letter written to Mrs. Xiang, the wife of a Hanlin scholar, gives an example of her teaching:

The masters of old said: "In practicing Chan one must look for enlightenment; if there is no enlightenment, there will be no way by which one may escape the great sea of birth and death. Nowadays [so-called] followers of the Way mistakenly swindle by means of mouth and ear the denizens of the inner chambers when they tell them that they do not need to be enlightened in order to be liberated from life and death; glib and loquacious, they vilify the great wisdom of insight, and even go so far as to completely obscure its sacredness. This demonstrates a lack of gratitude toward the sages of the past. How can it not be lamented! Since you have taken refuge with me, I hope you will seek the Great Way and urgently strive to distinguish between the different paths of clarity and blindness. All you need to do is to focus on a *huatou* and then proceed straight

---

21. Fashi (ca. 382) was one of the four students of Kumarajiva, the famous Buddhist missionary and translator.

ahead without indulging in distractions. . . . If you practice, you should practice the real practice, enlightenment should be the real enlightenment. When you have become very clear about this, then you can be resolute and firm, then you can be considered dharma material!"

Jizong was most famous for her poetry, in particular her poems describing the beauties of Mount Heng, to which she finally returned to live out the last years of her life.

Mount Heng, although not one of the four famous Buddhist mountains (Emeishan, Wutaishan, Jiuhuashan, and Putuoshan) and often associated with Daoism, has played a major role in Chinese Buddhist history and imagination since the fifth century. The history of Mount Heng's sacred geography actually goes back even further to the Han dynasty, when it began to be regarded as one of the Five Peaks (*wuyue*), which were thought of as part of the official cosmological system. Within this cosmology, Mount Heng corresponded to the South, thus its formal name of Nanyue, or Southern Peak. In fact, Mount Heng is not a single mountain, but rather a range of mountains running parallel to the Xiang River that consists of seventy-two peaks, five of which are considered to be major.

For centuries, Mount Heng's peaks and valleys, pagodas, abbeys, and temples have stirred the poetic imagination of both clergy and laypeople. All of the local gazeteers of this area contain several chapters devoted to poems and other writings (arranged by dynasty) written in praise of its beauties. Of particular note are the many poems by great Tang poets such as Du Fu and Li Bai, as well as writings by famous Tang and Song dynasty monk-poets such as Jiaoran and Foyin Yuanliao. The mountain continued to be a popular subject of poetry during the Yuan, Ming, and Qing periods as well. It is clear that Jizong Xingche's poems on Mount Heng were considered to rank among the best of these: hers are the only ones written by a nun—or by a woman, for that matter—that are included in these compilations.

The following poems are selected from a series of twenty-five poems entitled "Living in Seclusion on Southern Peak," which was most likely written after Jizong Xingche had left Jiangnan and returned to live in the mountains.

I

From the mountain torrent the wind gusts fiercely,
When the heart is empty, all things are mysterious.
Here there is no sound of clattering carts and horses:
Far from neighbors and from dusty worldly cares.
 When the leaves fall, you know autumn is ending;
When the trees are bare, they reveal the waterfall.
I've abandoned all plans: now seagull and egret
Are as close to me as the most intimate of friends.

II

The gate borrows stray clouds to guard it,
And a pure solitude borders my quarters.
Forest gibbons go in search of ripe fruit,
Roosting birds fly deep into the forest.
 I've thrown off the net of floating fame,
And aimed higher: a mind that delights in the Way.
The emptiness of emptiness, beyond the four phrases:[22]
A fulfillment as rare as finding a needle in a haystack.[23]

III

Peacefully I watch the lovely lights of autumn,
As the maple-reds fill my ears with their rustling.
The pine winds link together the crying of the cranes,
The valley echoes reply to the chirping of the cicadas.
 The travelling guest's robes and cap are old-fashioned,
The crazy monk's manner and bearing are pure-hearted.
Raising their heads, they gaze toward the far horizon:
In the marshes of Chu, there are still heroes to be found.

V

I sit by the window and face toward the west:
Jade peaks line up in rows of kingfisher green.

---

22. This is a reference to famous tetralemma of Mahayana Buddhism, which speaks of that which exists; that which does not exist; that which neither exists nor does not exist; and that which both exists and does not exist.

23. In the original Chinese, this idea of very slim odds is expressed by the metaphor of a mustard seed tossed from a great distance landing on the point of a needle.

White clouds skim past the tips of the peaks,
Fresh breezes encircle the low bamboo hedge.
The mountain hut is replete with clear dreams,
The creek pines are wrapped with jade moss.
These deserted woods have an undifferentiated flavor:
When the fruit ripens, the birds will come for them.[24]

VII

A jumble of boulders amidst thousands of mountaintops,
A thatched hut leaning precariously against jade peaks:
Yellow orioles sing in the kingfisher-green willows,
White egrets punctuate the sweet-smelling woodlands.
The winding path cuts narrowly through the clouds,
The bramblewood gate is deep among the fallen leaves.
Moving from one vantage point to another and another,
Until all the mountain scenes have been captured in verse.

VIII

On worldly roads, in wind and dust I've grown old—
Time to return home: wild greens to eat aplenty.
If you are frugal, even in poverty you will have enough;
If you are detached, even disasters in the end are light.
Learning comes from not despising the beginnings,
Wisdom relies on the purity of being free of affairs.
Let the bookish scholars and holders of high positions
Exert themselves to exhaustion for the rest of their lives.

IX

Secluded birds hover around their hibernation place,
Cloud-like flowers shine brightly from the cliff face.
The trees are so deep one can just glimpse the deer,
The temple is so distant one cannot hear its bell.
The bamboo forcefully parts the blue-grey clouds,
The spring leaps up then dangles from the jade peak.
There is no one else who knows where this place is:
Alone I face the ten-thousand-year-old pine trees.

---

24. The allusion here is to the fruition of karmic actions.

XI

To dwell in noble solitude has been the dream of a lifetime,
So from now on I will live my life here on this mountain.
I have seen through the illusions of this dusty world,
And am no longer embroiled in this floating existence.
 The stalactites—stone nipples—can be sucked when needed,
The wisteria flowers can be pulled down as the mood dictates.
Heaven and Earth: an emptiness that is so great and so vast—
Who understands the leisure to be found in all of this?

XII

The forest ravine locked in by fair-weather clouds,
Several plum trees standing there tall and solitary.
Sipping spring water, humming and singing I set out;
Gathering herbs, wrapped in fragrance I return home.
 On the leaves, the gathas of Hanshan,[25]
In the clouds, the terraces of Wisdom.
I follow my bramblewood staff where it goes:
To a stone table covered with verdigris moss.

XX

The azure sky in the window gleams pure and clear;
I open the door to let in the blue-green of the hills.
From out of the rosy mists, the lone crane returns,
Circling the rocks, then aimlessly soaring the clouds.
 A low bed of moss can be used as a meditation mat,
The scattered leaves on the eaves can serve as a robe.
The setting sun has disappeared far into the west—
The weary birds instinctively know their way home.

---

25. Hanshan (Cold Mountain), a famous monk-poet said to have lived in the seventh century, is credited with a collection of three hundred poems on Buddhist subjects.

10 · The Banana Garden Poetry Club

By the last quarter of the seventeenth century order had been restored. As both the Manchu state and the Chinese intellectuals embraced an orthodox neo-Confucianism as the leading ideology, the limits on women's freedom of movement and freedom of expression became strict once again, and women poets very much retreated to a sphere of their own. As one representative example of this development we discuss the Banana Garden Poetry Club of Hangzhou.

Some sources credit the Banana Garden Poetry Club with having five members, others with seven, but actually the membership seems to have been very fluid. Some sources claim that Gu Ruopu's niece, Gu Zhiqiong (Yurui), took the initiative to organize this club, but others suggest that the credit should go to either Chai Jingyi (Jixian; d. 1680) or Feng Xian (Youling). In any case, many of the members of the club were the sisters, daughters, or daughters-in-law of these three women. Qian Fenglun (Yunyi; 1644–1703) was a daughter of Gu Zhiqiong, and Lin Yining (Yaqing; 1655–1730) a daughter-in-law. Gu Si (Qiji) was also related to Gu Zhiqiong. Zhu Rouze was a daughter-in-law of Chai Jingyi. Other members of the club were Zhang Hao (Chayun) and Mao Ti (Anfang). (The Suzhou woman poet Xu Can [ca. 1610–after 1677] in later years was often listed as one of the members of the Banana Garden Poetry Club, although actually she never took part in its activities.) Many of these women were poets but also painters and calligraphers. The Banana

Garden Poetry Club seems to have been most active in the decade 1665–1675, when life had returned more or less to normal. In a well-known contemporary anthology (1688) of lyrics by women, the activities of Chai Jingyi and her fellow women poets are described as follows:

At that time, talented poets of the inner chambers such as Qian Yunyi [Fenglun], Lin Yaqing [Yining], Gu Zhongmei, and Feng Youling [Xian] would travel in a string of carriages and take turns hosting parties where, wielding brush and ink, they would write poems in which they matched each other's rhymes. People remarked that not since the days of lady Zhang Qiongru, lady Gu Ruopu, and lady Liang Mengzhao, had such an impressive gathering of elegant ladies been seen.

Another observer pointed out the marked contrast between the elegant pastimes of these women poets and their less sophisticated sisters' gaudy displays of jewelry:

At that time, the fashions in Wulin [Hangzhou] were lavish and extravagant. On mild spring days when the scenery was bright, the painted boats and embroidered tents by the [West] Lake would compete with each other for brilliance. [The women] with their bright earrings and kingfisher-feather headdresses, pearly locks, and "cricket" gauzes, would vie to blind each other with their blazing splendor. The only exception would be Jixian [Chai Jingyi], who would be accompanied in her small boat by such eminent ladies as Feng Youling, Qian Yunyi, Lin Yaqing, and Gu Qiji [Si]. Dressed in white skirts and with their hair done up simply, they would take up their brushes and divide up sheets of paper [for writing poems on the occasion]. As soon as the partying women on the neighboring boats would catch sight of them, they would lower their heads and hesitate, deeply ashamed that they did not measure up to them.

The most detailed description of the poetic activities of the Banana Garden Poetry Club is provided by Lin Yining in her postface to the poetry collection of Feng Xian. Having described her first meeting with Feng Xian, she continues:

Each month we would meet a number of times, and at each meeting we would randomly choose a rhyme and assign a topic, and [in this way we would] chant our verses till the end of the day. Moreover, each of us would recommend [for membership in the club] female relatives such as Chai Jixian [Jingyi], Li Duanming, Qian Yunyi, and Gu Qiji. We became as friendly "as gold and orchid," and each of us was rich "in snow and floss." The collection of our linked verses grew bigger every day!

Many of the poems and lyrics of the women poets of the Banana Garden Poetry Club were inspired by the collective activities of the club as well as other sorts of exchanges among the members. We also find many poems dedicated to famous women of the past, as well as poems and other works written either to encourage brothers, husbands, and sons to persevere in their studies or to console them when they failed in their exams.

Gu Zhiqiong

It was Gu Ruopu's niece, Gu Zhiqiong, also from Hangzhou, who, according to at least one source, founded the Banana Garden Poetry Club. Although she is not formally listed as one of its members, Gu Zhiqiong would certainly have had the status to take such an initiative, as her husband Qian Sheng served in the Hanlin Academy, the emperor's "think tank." As the following poems suggest, Gu Zhiqiong did not accompany her husband to his posting in the capital.

To the Melody of "Jiangnan Spring" (*Jiangnan chun*) Remembering an Absent Husband

The stars glow and glimmer,
My thoughts linger on and on.
Obscure dreams wind over passes and mountains,
As my soul darkly flies through the storm and rain.
The Jiangnan spring is glorious and carefree!
So why does that traveling man
Tarry and not come home?

To the Melody of "Hard to Forget" (*Yinanwang*) Sent to My Husband

Willow floss drifts about on the wind,
Which audaciously blows through my gown and strokes my face—
What outrageous behavior!
I find it impossible to stop these spring feelings,

And can't keep my noon dreams from lingering!
The white fan so pure,
The stone screen so cool,
So what's to stop me from getting drunk?
But in a moment the relentless breeze blows away
The fragrance coming from the embroidered duvet.

Waking up, my gauntness arouses a dread of the gauze skirt.
I tie a "shared-hearts knot" and send it to my loved one,
Praying that in life after life we'll fly together,
That in every one of our days we will be a pair.
Spring leaves quickly,
Butterflies busy themselves in vain,
And fragrant flowers blaze in the setting sun.
I fear that yet again his search for fame may not succeed,
Leaving my beauty neglected.

To the Melody of "Poorly-Fated Girl" (*Baomingnü*)

The late night so still—
The servant girl urges me to get some sleep,
But I find it too early yet,
Unable to find any distraction.

Pray tell me the source of these springtime sorrows:
I remember how long ago, when still young and lovely,
Embroidering mandarin ducks, I would be filled with longing:
Startled at daybreak by the sound of the bell.

To the Melody of "Sands of Washing Brook" (*Huanxisha*)
Spring Outing

My body, skinny and wasted, cannot bear even the weight of gauze,
And, alas, with the arrival of spring my illnesses have only increased.
Filled with feelings, without a word, my reflection in the clear waves.

The drooping arms with golden bracelets, slim fingers so fine—
The jade hairpins sagging down, the face flushed with wine.
By the small bridge, from the returning boat a fisherman's song!

Chai Jingyi

Chai Jingyi (d. 1680) was one of the five original members of the Banana Garden Poetry Club. She and her sister, Chai Zhenyi, were daughters of Chai Shiyao, a literatus who had passed the provincial examinations. Her elder sister married the student Huang Jiemei and was known for both her poetry and painting, while Jingyi married Shen Hanjia, who attained the rank of district school instructor. Later critics such as the eighteenth-century poet and anthologist Shen Deqian praised Chai Jingyi for avoiding in her writings some of the more stereotypical "feminine" topics and moods: "[Her poems] are rooted in the chastity of her nature and feelings, and develop from the orthodoxy of her study and reading; her harmonious words regularly entail remonstration and exhortation, something not to be found in [poems on] breeze and clouds, moonlight and dew." The following poem may be an example of what Shen had in mind:

Huangtiandang: On Lady Liang

From jade-white face and cloud-like hairdo she wipes the dust of battle,
With her little band of lotus flowers she assembles by the river bank.
Her job is not drawing water or winnowing rice, but beating the drum—
Who would believe that this stalwart hero is in fact a beautiful woman?

During the battle of Huangtiandang of 1129, the Song dynasty general Han Shizhong inflicted a decisive defeat on the troops of the Jürchen Jin dynasty after they had crossed over into the area to the south of the Yangzi River. His victory was in large part credited to his wife Liang Hongyu, a former courtesan, who tirelessly beat the drum, stirring the Song army to greater efforts. In the third quarter of the seventeenth century, following the Manchu conquest of southern China, Liang Hongyu's name often appeared in poetry as an exemplar of patriotic loyalty.

An example of Chai Jingyi's "remonstration and exhortation" is provided by the following poem:

Written to Comfort My Eldest Son Yongji upon His Return from the Capital

Don't you see:
In the houses of the nobles, banquets are laid out night after night,

But who spares a man of talent a cup of wine or a morsel of bread?
Three times you went up to the capital but without meeting success,
Returning home once again with disheveled hair and sunburnt face.
 Alas, the affairs of the world change a thousand times every day,
People only compete in driving fine carriages and dining on meats.
Do find your pleasure in studying books and strumming the zither:
Since ancient times, wise men have endured poor and humble lives.

Whether studying with famous teachers, seeking patronage, serving on the private staff of high officials, taking part in the examinations, or traveling to and from official posts, the men in these elite families spent a large part of their lives on the road. Many of Chai Jingyi's poems are addressed to absent relatives, such as the following poems addressed to her son:

Thinking of My Son in Jiangxi Province

The storm-tossed waves of Lake Pengli roar without respite,
Where will you moor your traveling boat when the sun sets?
Tomorrow morning you'll surely shed some tears for your mother,
And the stream will carry them down to the old ford of Qiantang.

To the Melody of "Wind Entering Pines" (*Fengrusong*) In Imitation of "Border Lyrics"

Why do young men want to follow the army on distant campaigns?
Ahead of the horses, the sun starts to set.
The passes and mountains cut off the road to village and home—
When one looks back,
All one sees are brown clouds.
By the light of the moon a single line of sobbing geese,
And, blown by the wind, a myriad miles of flying dust.

The interminable grass of the steppes has no knowledge of spring—
No one can bear to listen to the painted horn.
It is impossible to send a letter home to the comfortable inner quarters,
So what is the use
Of returning in dreams, time and again?
With a few songs sung to the lute, wine is poured out:
Here in the desert we have our own red skirts!

While as a rule women stayed behind to manage the family estate, take care of their parents-in-law, and see to the education of the children, occasionally one of them would accompany her husband on his official journeys. Many of Chai Jingyi's poems as well as other writings by members of the Banana Garden Poetry Club mention the departure of one of their members, Gu Qiji, for Beijing:

Seeing Off Gu Qiji on Her Northern Journey

The wide expanse of the peach blossom stream,
Clear and abundant, sends off your traveling boat:
Now spring has arrived with a myriad willows,
Whose every leaf speaks of parting's sorrow.
  When I, worn down by misfortune as I am,
Met you, we found we shared the same ideas.
Mists and rainbows—we would ply our brushes,
Breeze and moon—often we ascended the tower.
  We should be sitting in the perfume of incense—
Who can bear this journey, the beating of oars?
When once in Beijing you will look back
At the clouds hanging white over Hangzhou.

Feng Xian

Feng Xian was also from Hangzhou. She was the daughter of the district magistrate Feng Zhongyu, and later became the wife of the student Qian Tingmei. The following poem appears to have been written after her husband had returned home after failing once again in the higher examinations:

Following the Rhymes of My Husband's "Expressing My Emotions"

Li Guang was also not yet enfeoffed as a marquis at your age,[1]
Why should a student always have to suffer from "sad autumn"?
As long as you have your tongue, you'll one day get power,
As your ambition is high, you've come home a library prisoner.
  The colored clouds that fill our eyes are only an illusion,

---

1. Li Guang (d. 119 BCE) was one of the most successful generals of Emperor Wu's campaigns against the Xiongnu.

The pine and bamboo in the courtyard must be given their due.
When we two while away our time by writing and painting,
I feel as if we were already living in a hundred-foot tower!

Qian Fenglun

Qian Fenglun was a daughter of Gu Zhiqiong; her brother, Qian Zhaoxiu (1652–1711), attained the high rank of censor. At the age of sixteen, she married the "tribute student" Huang Shixu, a grandson of the formidable female poet Gu Ruopu. Qian Fenglun's writings were printed in 1702 under the title of *Ancient Fragrance Tower Collection* (*Guxianglou ji*), and included a preface written in 1680 by Gu Ruopu at the age of eighty-nine. This preface contains the following biographical sketch:

My grandson's wife Qian Fenglun is the second daughter of lady Yurui. Since her early childhood she has written about flowers and birds, and even then she was already said to exhibit the characteristics of Xie Daoyun. Her parents loved her dearly. At the age of sixteen she married my second grandson. At that time our family found itself in straitened circumstances. In the time she had free from needlework, she did not shirk physical labor; but when she had a few free moments after setting out the food, she would continue to apply herself to her literary endeavors. From time to time she asked for instruction from me. When I looked over her poems, [I found] her to be like a fine bird warbling in spring, like a fresh flower in the bright sun. Even though her scholarship was as yet lacking, her outstanding beauty and lofty thoughts at times far surpassed others—isn't it true that "whatever it is that one finds in one's own nature is great"?

Later, my second grandson participated several times in the provincial examinations. Each time he received news of his rejection, he would become depressed and heave deep sighs . . . but then she would light a lamp and sit with him as he studied deep into the night.

Some of Qian Fenglun's poems are inspired by famous heroines from Chinese history, and often she takes on their voices. In the following poem, for example, she speaks in the voice of Pang E, a woman from the Later Han dynasty whose father was killed by Li Shou. When Pang E's three elder brothers all died in an epidemic, Li Shou rejoiced, thinking that there was no way that a mere girl would be able to avenge her father's death. Needless to say, he was sadly mistaken: Pang E tracked him down and stabbed him to death.

Weeping for My Elder Brothers

When many years ago High Heaven was knocked down,
There was no hope for the survival of the hatching eggs.
So you, my brothers, did not directly follow him in death,
Even though your desire for vengeance was fully justified.
　How you caressed and stroked your pairs of daggers,
Each night you got up twice, and then got up again!
Ten thousand catties were as light as a single hair,
Fearing only that Heaven would not come to your aid.
　The years and months slowly crept by,
A hidden suffering entered your marrows.
But you were all carried away by sudden illness
Before you could pierce the great villain's chest.
　Stretched out on the bier you refused to close your eyes:
"If I don't carry on, I'm not my father's child!
As long as I, Pang E, am still alive,
You, Li Shou, should not rejoice!"

In the following lyric, Qian Fenglun takes on the voice of lady Yu, the lover of the doomed hero Xiang Yu. When Xiang Yu found himself surrounded by the troops of Liu Bang near Crow River and deserted by even the most loyal of his men, he begged his beloved concubine to flee to safety. Our earliest sources are silent on what she ultimately decided to do, but later tradition holds that she committed suicide out of loyalty to Xiang Yu. The "Land Within the Pass" mentioned in the poem is a reference to the Wei river valley in modern Shaanxi province, where Xiang Yu's rival, Liu Bang, had established his capital.

To the Melody of "Lady Yu" (*Yu meiren*)
On the Original Topic

All around one hears songs of Chu played on decorated horns:
They blow the moon down from above the border fortress.
The eight thousand young stalwarts long followed the dragon,
But in a single night the carved saddles and gilded breastplates
　　　　scattered beneath the endless sky!

I'd rather my jade be shattered by my lord's side,
Let my blood dye your battle dress crimson red!
My chaste soul refuses to enter the Land Within the Pass—
Year after year, as the waves rise on the Crow River,
        my weeping will turn the spring red.

Most of Qian Fenglun's poems and lyrics, however, are devoted to spring outings and other communal activities of the fellow women poets:

To the Melody of "A Phoenix Roosting on the Acacia" (*Feng xi wu*)
A Spring Outing

They've heard the crab apple tree is about to shed its blossoms,
So as the sun ascends the agate tower,
They quickly finish combing their cloud-like chignons,
And lightly apply their cosmetics with slender fingers—
Their spring dresses oh-so-delicate
Are scented with orchid and musk.

Swallows and orioles flit across the green fields,
And playful girls frolic about,
"Fighting with flowers," they want to have fun.
When they have stolen a handful of tender branches,
They hit each other with them,
Reducing the petals to dust!

Lotus Gathering Songs

I

The lotus flowers are ablaze and vie in red apparel,
The two oars on the stream muddle the evening sun.
Repeatedly I tell the servant girls: Don't laugh so loudly,
I fear you may disturb the ducks sleeping there in pairs!

II

All day long the painted boat floats in the light breeze,
In the waves emerald sleeves sway and reflections dance.

What made us forget the road home here among the flowers?
We so love to gaze at the lake's double-budded lotuses.

To the Melody of "Azure-Tipped Brows" (*Meifeng bi*)
Playing a Game of Go with Yaqing

A secluded courtyard, a spring day of leisure:
Curling incense smoke spat out by gilded beast.
A single cup of clearest tea, a single game of go,
In the season of apricot rains and drifting petals.

How fluent the parrot's new words!
Startled, I suddenly turn around.
Carelessly I have lost a jade hairpin,
Leaning against a screen, I smile and sniff a blossoming branch.

To the Melody of "The Water Dragon's Chant"
(*Shuilongyin*)
Thinking Fondly of My Sister-in-Law Chai Jixian, I
Also Thank Her for Her Painting of Plum Blossoms

Idly we leaned on the red railings and curved balustrades,
As pine and bamboo intermittently shaded the deep hidden courtyard.
The red maple had been completely dyed,
The yellow chrysanthemum had just bloomed,
Its color so deep, its fragrance light.
Linked verses on jade tablets,
Shared rhymes on brocade billets:
Pearls and gems, gleaming and fresh,
But without any purpose at all.
Then the herdboy's flute sounded again and again,
Urging the sun to set,
The square pond to darken.

Since we parted, the reed-lined waterway stretches out so far.
Just as I returned to my empty room from a hazy pear-blossom dream,
A gust from heaven blew down to earth
This painting in reds and blacks

Of spring in bloom on Mt. Luofu.[2]
Sparse shadows in a crosshatched jumble,
A subtle fragrance lightly stirring:
Painted with a brush and yet as if real.
The painted screen will be left hanging
For fear that otherwise in the morning the kingfishers
Will fly away in pairs.

To the Melody of "Phoenixes Exchanging Their Nest" (*Huanchao luanfeng*)
Seeing Off Gu Qiji (and Her Husband) on Her Journey to Beijing

The sun is warm and the spring is glorious:
I envy the pair of colored phoenixes on the wing,
Freely roaming toward the capital city.
In a golden cup we pour the wine of parting,
On jade tablets we write of our new sorrow,
Even before the "Black Colt" song is sung, the tears pour down.[3]
How can we bear to say: "All aboard the light skiff!"
Once you have left,
Will you remember
Those with whom you discussed poetry
            in your embroidery pavilion?

Hand in hand—
When will we again trim the lamp,
And by the window, whisper together as evening falls?
Above the Wu hills, the clouds will tarry,
Over Beijing's gate, the moon will set:
In both places, we know, brows will be knit.
A beautiful tale that for a thousand years
Will be spoken of everywhere:
That Wenjun found yet another friend with high ambitions!
In a fine carriage, on a proud horse,

---

2. Mt. Luofu in Guangdong province was famous for its plum blossoms.
3. The "Black Colt" song is a parting song.

You two will see all the blossoms and willows
of the Imperial Park.

A Letter to Lin Yaqing

One of the five people who first met in the Banana Garden, Qiji, has recently left on a boat journey to the North. The [remaining] four of us live only a few steps away from each other, but, occupied by all kinds of sundry affairs, we have not seen each other for over a year. All to no avail, this has deepened my yearning for the clouds above the mountain ranges and the moon above the rafters, a pleasure that eludes me whenever I spread out a sheet of paper below the blossoms or trim the candle by the window. Recently, seeking to capture that spirit, I myself painted a picture of our elegant gathering in the Banana Garden. I placed the five of us among towering pines, thick bamboo, clear springs, and white rocks, so that the essential spirit of the five of us might forever remain united and this marvelous occasion might be passed on through eternity. Of course I would not dare to compare our cultural achievements to those of the Seven Sages and the Six Hermits, but our profound enjoyment can stand by itself!

Some of Qian Fenglun's works are written in memory of her sister-in-law Yao Lingze (Roujia):

To the Melody of "Southern Song" (*Nangezi*)
Early Summer: Visiting the River Isle Again and
Remembering Roujia

The path is blocked as green mountains converge,
The gate is hidden by the slanting green willows.
Village girls in clusters pick the new tea,
And together, as the sun sets on the stream,
      board the small fishing rafts.

Emerald bamboo caged the slender moon,
Evening crows clamored in a solitary pine.
On the stone bridge the two of us once grew tipsy on evening colors,
Lovely leaning against the spring breeze, you asked me with a smile
      to pluck a branch of peach blossom.

To the Melody of "Sorrowfully Leaning on the Balustrade" (*Chou yilan ling*)
Weeping for My Sister Roujia

Leaning on the balustrade, I always look for your fragrant traces,
Yearnings and memories without end.
I remember how your jade hooks tread so lightly,
Leaving an imprint on the fallen red.

In the small garden the flowers are drunk at the height of spring,
Their fragrance wafts about,
Enticing the spring scene.
Now I regret that before, when we would hold our gatherings,
We were always in such a hurry.

Still other of Qian Fenglun's lyrics and letters are addressed to her younger brother, Qian Youkun, and to her son:

To the Melody of "The Candle Shadows Swaying Red" (*Zhuying yaohong*)
Seeing Off My Younger Brother Youkun on His Journey to Beijing

Tossed about by the waves for years on end:
Each and every experience rends the heart.
Without any reason you suddenly sing the "Black Colt" song again,
As brother and sister are split up between north and south.
A traveler on the long road at the year's end—
You ready your luggage: a single pack of books.
A thousand mountains blocked by snow,
Ten thousand valleys covered by clouds,
And on the great river a lonely boat.

The wonderful sights you will inscribe
With a brush of brocade like that of Jiang Yan.[4]
Under that distant sky geese will often fly south,
So entrust your writings to their paired wings.

---

4. After Jiang Yan (444–505) in his youth had in a dream been presented with a writing brush of brocade, the quality of his writings greatly improved.

When will you, weary of wandering through Beijing,
Compose your own "Let's Go Home" and choose the hermit's life?
Amidst the songs of the yellow oriole, in the shade of the green willows,
A straw cape and bamboo hat in mist and rain.

A Letter to My Younger Brother, Youkun

Where in the world does one find talented people who enjoy riches and glory in peace? For to have talent and enjoy riches and glory in peace, it is necessary that one's talent not be rejected by the Creator. But the Creator always has been a naughty boy who will go to great lengths to put down the greatest heroes and intellects. How could you be the only one to be filled with indignation?

My talent does not measure up to yours and for half my life I have been trailed by misfortune, turning my black hair to gray. Within the four walls of my empty room, I spend all my days in sorrow. Although I do not have [even] two *qing* of fields outside the city, I do have the responsibility for eight hungry mouths that cry out for food. Lately, all one sees are shields and spears, as the migrating geese honk sadly, and we are kept forever preoccupied with worries about our country and our people.

But soon I will hide my traces on a secluded isle. There, I'll ride a deer-drawn carriage and prepare my angling rod and line. I'll build my cottage on a rock and channel a spring to irrigate my rice field. I'll harvest caltrop from a pond, and where there is sufficient water, I will grow mulberry and hemp. I will call the rooster down from the tree and hug the calf high up on the mountain. And when I have time to spare, I will immerse myself in *The Old Master* and *Master Zhuang* and feed myself by ingesting the mystic breath. One moment I will play Wang Ziqiao's mouth organ, at another moment, I will copy out Lady Wei's calligraphy models.[5] In this way, I will live out my years in utter contentment and nourish my natural harmony.

When on one of your free days, you rent a boat and come to visit, I will treat you to dark-essence rice and purple-sprouts tea, and we will discuss the waxing and waning of heaven and earth, and the rise and fall through past and present. Together we will walk through the woods and over the fields, taking in the views of the rising moon and the setting sun, the emerging clouds and the thickening mists. The rustling bamboo and strummed zither, the whooping cranes and crying gibbons will all be more than enough to wash away your worries and cares and release you from your worldly bonds.

Please, cherish your talent and just don't be too depressed.

---

5. Wang Ziqiao is one of the ancient immortals; Lady Wei is said to have been the calligraphy teacher of Wang Xizhi.

To My Son Zhao

A hundred years last but a moment, the succession of seasons passes by in a flash. If one does not exert oneself while young and strong, one will suffer in vain in old age.

Now, if one uses the past as a mirror, it can serve as a teacher of future events. I hope you will cultivate and embody the Way and virtue, savor and digest the *Odes* and the *Documents*, deport yourself in a proper manner, and respond positively toward others. Your elbows may show through your patched gown, but poverty is not a disease; when you use your bent arms as a pillow, pleasure may be found therein. Because lately we have lacked the means to allow you to travel in search of scholarship, you have had to be taught by your mother, [whose limited knowledge is such that she] measures the ocean with a ladle and gauges the sky through a tube, so it is my fault that your studies are not yet deep and your mind not yet broad.

As principle is subtle and the Way is great, at this point you really must make an effort. Whenever you come across enlightened teachers and good friends you should rely on them to your own benefit, you must modestly ask them for their instruction, and then choose the best to follow. Don't be a slacker, don't be a superficial person!

In a moment of leisure I have noted down these few words for you, so please copy them out and hang them up by the side of your seat.

Lin Yining

Another Hangzhou woman poet was Lin Yining. Her father Lin Lunnü had passed the metropolitan examinations, and her husband Qian Zhaoxiu, a brother of Qian Fenglun, attained the rank of censor. Her collected writings were printed in 1697, together with appreciative comments by Chai Jingyi and Qian Fenglun.

Crossing the Confluence of the Yi and the Luo

Crossing the most perilous mountains and rivers,
One comes to realize the hardships of travel.
A cold storm roars in the wide valley,
Strange rocks block the eddying stream.
 At every fork in the road I am filled with fear,
And at journey's end my eyes are still not dry.

The glistening waves must be laughing at me,
As all alone I ascend the bank of the river.

On Receiving a Letter from My Husband

A full year filled by the feelings of parting,
The letter I got barely a square foot in size.
Your love makes it endlessly meaningful:
Raising the lamp I read it a hundred times.

Falling Petals

In eerie silence, the spring wood shields the emerald pond,
The cuckoo cries till the moon gives way to the early dawn.
Since she has no one at Long Gate to deliver her many tears,
They change into the red that drifts into the Weiyang Palace.

Voicing My Ambition

A lifetime's failure and success are all an idle dream,
But the value of one's writing is a different matter.
I have the ambition to ferret out literature's secrets,
And emerge from the inner chambers a great scholar.

Gu Si

Gu Si was the daughter of the vice-supervisor of the Household of the
Heir Apparent Gu Ceyun, and married the student E Ceng. Her husband
is said to have loved to travel, and Gu Si accompanied him at least once
on a trip to Beijing, as we already learned from the parting poems her
fellow members of the Banana Garden Poetry Club addressed to her.

Inscription on a Painting by Lin Yaqing

Plum blossoms and bamboo leaves intermingle together,
The moist ink vivid and forceful, straight lines and curves.
I now remember how last night by the light of the moon
Their scattered shadows fell across the silk of my window.

To the Melody of "Sands of Washing Brook Expanded" (*Tanpo Huanxisha*)
Moonlight Shadows

Passing over the red towers, piercing through the green window silk,
Covering half of the misty willows, covering half of the blossoms:
The poorly-fated Chang'e understands how I feel—[6]
I'm so grateful!

Feeling lost on my pillow in recurring dark dreams,
Home a thousand miles away at the edge of the sky.
The night watches have an end, but not my road,
So don't set in the west!

To the Melody of "Full River Red" (*Manjiang hong*)
Comforting My Husband on Our Boat Tied Down for the Night on the Huai

A slender boat, no bigger than a leaf:
The lightweight sail is lowered,
As we rest for the night by this ancient bank.
Beyond the light of the lamp
A few branches of scattered trees,
Village houses just barely visible.
The Washerwoman's Shrine overgrown with weeds,
Above Han Xin's Terrace cut off by the cold clouds.
Alas, this place has always repressed heroes,
Although the streams and mountains remain.

The flavor of poverty's sorrow
You have tasted to the full,
And you no longer sigh
At the evil of human nature.
We'll get some wine from the village ahead,
I'll pay for it with my hairpins of gold.
I won't refuse to lift the tray: tonight we'll get drunk,
The ambition inscribed on the bridge you'll fulfill some other year.

---

6. Chang'e, the goddess of the moon, leads a life of eternal chilly loneliness.

Listen, at midnight the raging waves rise on the river,
As the fish turn into dragons!

The above lyric appears to have been written on the couple's journey from Beijing back to Hangzhou after her husband's unsuccessful trip to the capital. Gu Si first compares her husband to the famous general Han Xin (d. 196 BCE), who in his youth was so destitute that he only survived thanks to the kindness of a poor washerwoman. In the second stanza she also makes a reference to the legend that when the young poet Sima Xiangru left his hometown Chengdu to make a career at court, he wrote an inscription on the bridge outside town declaring that he would not return unless he was driving a carriage drawn by five horses.

Zhu Rouze

Zhu Rouze (style name Shuncheng; Daozhu) was the daughter-in-law of Chai Jingyi. Her husband was Shen Yongji, a well-known poet at the time, who spent most of his adult life traveling throughout the empire. He lived for many years in Beijing, where he enjoyed the patronage of one of the Manchu princes.

Songs Sent to an Absent Husband

I

Living at home you didn't have a worry,
Husband and wife enjoyed a carefree life.
Time and again we would link rhyming verses,
And often we would play a game of go.
 A serving girl would pour out wine and sing,
Your darling son would play the *sheng* for fun.[7]
So who forced you to leave and go traveling?
So far away—I hate that pain of parting!

II

Endless banks of flowering watercress:
Interminable sorrow over separation.
Letters you send arrive from the Capital,

---

7. The *sheng* is the traditional Chinese mouth organ.

But you I have to look for in my dreams.
 Even the longest day comes to an end at dawn,
But fragrant cheeks will soon turn to autumn.
In the old nest there are still swallows
Peeping into the room where you studied.

III

Oh how I hate not having had the weeping willow
To tie down your jade saddle with the greatest of care!
The evening was warm on the backs of the crows,
But in the spring snow the horse's hoofs were cold.
 Trying your luck, you're no good at fawning and flattering;
Relying on others, you find it hard both to leave and to stay.
Your infant son cries in my arms:
Last night I dreamt of Chang'an.

IV

The howling wind is growing wilder,
The endless rain has not yet ceased.
Filled with pity for our son because his blanket is so thin,
I remembered that your traveler's clothes are not padded.
 The swallow struggles to raise the chicks in its nest,
The migrating goose is freezing without its mate.
For me here at home and you on the road
The hardship and pain is one and the same.

V

I have heard that on the streets of Beijing
The struggle for life for many is hard.
To one's shame one bothers a patron for food,
Who wants to beg for a teacher's meager pay?
 To stay there for long is not the best choice,
Back home at least there are fields that need plowing.
Your kind mother's coffin still stands above ground,
You must quickly decide on the spot for her grave.

Zhu Rouze sent her husband the above poems along with one of her own paintings, which she entitled "Hometown Landscape." When Shen Yongji's patron saw the painting, he inscribed on it the following verses:

"She must have known her husband still had no plans to return, / So she painted the hills of home and sent them to the one so far away." He then gave Shen Yongji some money and sent him home to his wife and family.

One of the most famous sights of Hangzhou was the bore on the Qiantang River. Slightly to the north of the city the river passed between two mountains, a spot that was called Sea Gate or Heavenly Gate, after which it opened up into a broad V-shaped mouth as it met the sea. This natural configuration made for a spectacular bore, which attracted the attention of poets since the second century BCE. The bore was at its most spectacular on the fifteenth (the night of full moon) of the Eighth Month. There was a popular legend that the threatening white-capped waves were the vengeful spirit army of the great sixth-century BCE hero Wu Zixu, who died an unjust death. Another legend told of how Qian Mu, the tenth-century ruler of the Hangzhou area, tried (unsuccessfully) to subdue the bore by having three thousand soldiers shoot into it all the arrows from their crossbows. Any poem on the Hangzhou Bore that was more than several lines long would most certainly contain allusions to these legends.

A Song of Watching the Bore on Hangzhou's Qiantang River

Outside the city, masses of people look out for the bore,
After the noon hour, a wild wind starts blowing fiercely.
Making three curves, the river flows on in huge waves,
As ferocious billows crash into the Heavenly Gate.

The Heavenly Gate offers a dismal picture below stormy clouds,
The distant mountains, range upon range, are impossible to see.
At first you'd think that some clouds are drifting in from the sea,
Then you are startled by the expanse of white silk across the river.

The silver sea pours out all the snows of the Himalayas,
Crashing like pounding drums, swirling below the blue sky.
Towering masts and big junks rock to and fro without respite—
Who dares to shoot the strongest bow, the stiffest crossbow?

As the sun sets and mists rise, we descend from the tower,
But still the waves are unruly and continue to roll in.
Where have the white horses and chariots returned to?
A single bend of dark blue river, a myriad miles of fall.

Another poem by Zhu Rouze is addressed to her husband's concubine Gu Chunshan:

Making an Appointment with Gu Chunshan for Enjoying the Plum Blossoms on the Isle in the River

Let's meet to view the spring sights on the river isle,
On a single boat against the wind the trip will not be far.
Around the tower there are three thousand plum trees:
Until you show up, my beauty, they will not flower!

A later source contains the following anecdote concerning this poem:

[Zhu Rouze's husband] Fangzhou had a concubine named Gu Chunshan. Daozhu [Zhu Rouze] set a date with her to go and enjoy the plum blossoms. This poem contained the line: "Until you show up, my beauty, they will not flower!" The readers concluded from this that Daozhu was compassionate and harbored no feelings of jealousy; it also increased Chunshan's fame and price by tenfold.

Zhang Hao

Zhang Hao was a daughter of the provincial graduate Zhang Buqing and married Hu Daying. She died prematurely at the age of twenty-five. A short biographical notice devoted to her in Deng Hanyi's *Summary of the Poems of the Most Famous Masters of the Whole World (Tianxia mingjia shiguan)* reads:

Hao's style name was Chayun. She hailed from Qiantang [Hangzhou] in Zhejiang province. She was the eldest daughter of the provincial graduate Zhang Buqing [Tanzhi]. Her father was extremely poor and made a living by teaching in different places. Although her mother lady Chen did not teach her anything other than needlework, Hao loved to read books. No sooner had she glanced at the texts of the canons than she had grasped their literary principles. The poems, lyrics, and fictional narratives she wrote were all skilled compositions. When her elder cousin Zuwang by chance came across one of Hao's poems containing the line "The remnant wind and remnant snow at Broken Bridge," he was filled with grief and said with a sigh: "My younger cousin will become famous for her poetry, but she will be poorly fated."

In the year *kuimao* [1663], when she was nineteen, she married the student Hu Daying [style name Wenyi]. Their marriage was extremely harmonious. In the year *dingwei* [1667], her father traveled to the capital in order to take part in the metropolitan examinations, and there died. When she received news of her father's demise, Zheng Hao was so overcome by grief that she wanted to die, and wrote the lines: "Orphan Hill, how can you be so cruel / As to turn into my father's grave?"[8] All those who read this took pity on her.

Only after a year did she rise from her bed. Once, while she was discussing poetry with her husband, they came to speak of the quatrains of Guan Panpan, and she said: "How can one not become famous if one's poems are of this quality!" Later, after she had finished her morning toilette, she dressed in formal attire and sat by the window. Then, after a while, she stared at the clouds and suddenly said: "My heart is broken!" By the time a servant came to help her to bed, she had already closed her eyes forever.

Earlier she had dreamt that a white crane had spread its wings in her courtyard and in a human voice said to her: "Why don't you climb on my back to return? The predestined seven years of your marriage are over." She then climbed on his back and rose into the air as if she were a god or immortal! It is only after she had died that people realized that this had been an omen!

Zhang Hao left a collection entitled *Chants of Rushing through the Courtyard* (*Quting yong*), which was carefully edited by her elder cousin Zuwang and printed by her husband Wenji so that she might become famous.

While Zhang Hao's poetry enjoyed a wide circulation (as we saw from Shang Jinglan's preface), none of her fictional narratives (*baiguan xiaoshuo*) appears to have been preserved, at least not under her own name. As an example of her poems, we include the following work, yet another description of the Hangzhou Bore:

Watching the Bore

The wind is fierce, the autumn river darkens,
The bore resounds as the sunlight grows dim.
From far away it is as if a thousand lengths of silk
Were draping down like a single tall white mountain.
How filial was that Cao E in her determination!

---

8. Orphan Hill is the name of a little island situated in Hangzhou's West Lake.

How loyal was that Wu Zixu, how wise a minister!
After a thousand years their rage still lingers on:
They make it known by means of the angry waves!

Cao E was a woman of the Later Han dynasty, who, when her father had drowned in the river, jumped into the waves after him. Several days later, her floating body was found with her father's body on her back.

Mao Ti

Mao Ti was a daughter of the famous poet Mao Xianshu (1620–1688). She married Xu Ye (style name Huazheng), and died at the age of forty. Her work includes both lyrics and poems.

To the Melody of "Full River Red" (*Manjiang hong*)
Rising at Dawn

Rising at dawn I comb my hair:
Dust covers the bright mirror on its jade stand.
When I push open the window,
The east wind, when compared,
Is even fiercer than the west wind.
I love to hear the chatter of the yellow orioles in the mass of trees,
But am too listless to stroll along the small garden's fragrant paths.
Most pitiful are
Those blossoms half-lovely, half-wilted:
Spring like an illness.

Coldness and warmth
Share the administration,
And wasp and butterfly
Must be in competition,
But that green, green prince of spring
Just sits majestically on his throne.
The fragrant grasses are perfectly capable of welcoming the balmy air,
The clustered orchids perfect their hidden nature all by themselves.
The small corridor
With its winding balustrades
On which one may lean.

For a full appreciation of the following poem one should keep in mind that it was considered an elegant pastime when it snowed to have a servant gather some of the fresh snow and brew tea with it.

Snow

In the mountains, hungry crows clamor on a thousand trees,
I myself brush the icy flakes together, I myself brew the tea.
I don't care that the freezing cold causes me to shiver all over:
I worry only that the snow may crush the old plum blossoms.

After Mao Ti's death her father prefaced her collection of poetry as follows:

I love poetry. When Ti was just over ten, she wanted to learn poetry from me, but I brushed her aside and said: "This is not something for you." She went away but then secretly took out the *Old Poems* and read them. After she was married, she returned to her parental home for a visit and again [asked for instruction by] showing me her poems. These poems showed considerable thought and principle. Now [her husband] Huazheng was always traveling throughout the empire, so her feelings and emotions upon climbing up to high places and looking out all resulted in sad songs filled with intense grief.

Ti once said: "I am almost forty and still have not borne any sons. These poems are a product of the divine luminosity in me, they are my sons!" She also once asked me whether she could have them printed. I said: "Yes, you can, but you should wait until your later years when you will have collected more. It won't be too late to have them printed then . . ."

In the Sixth Month of this year Ti fell ill and died. When I recalled what she had said earlier about her poems being her sons, I felt even more saddened. Moreover, Huazheng was afraid that if we postponed [the printing of her works], they would end up scattered and lost, so he had them printed. How painful!

INTERLUDE
Ideal and Reality

11 · Ideal

According to the historian Dorothy Ko, Chinese literati of the seventeenth century displayed "a morbid fascination with the death of teenage [girl] poets." While seventeenth-century women poets such as Ye Xiaoluan might have lived up to the ideal of the beautiful, talented, and suffering young heroine, the overwhelming majority of women poets of the late Ming and early Qing dynasties were mature women who had active lives as mothers and estate managers, teachers and editors, brazen courtesans and feisty abbesses. This social reality in no way diminished the hold over the Chinese imagination during this time and later of the image of a young woman's virtuous suffering and passion, the most striking embodiment of which was probably Lin Daiyu, one of the central characters in the famous eighteenth-century novel *Dream of the Red Chamber* (*Honglou meng*) by Cao Xueqin (1715–1763). Ever since the first printing of this novel in 1791, the overwhelming majority of Chinese readers, both male and female, have appeared to prefer the moody and overly sensitive Lin Daiyu over her rival, the cheerful and accommodating Xue Baochai. Lin Daiyu's lonely death in her room on the night the love of her life, Jia Baoyu, reluctantly marries Xue Baochai was and continues, for most readers, to be the most poignant scene in the 120-chapter novel. Significantly, just before her death, Lin Daiyu consigns all of her poems to flames.

A century earlier, readers would have found the perfect embodiment of the suffering young woman poet who dies an early death in Xiaoqing, who was believed to have been the beautiful and talented concubine of a spineless Hangzhou man with a jealous wife. Her grave later became a pilgrimage site and the story of her unhappy life was repeatedly adapted for the stage. In the eighteenth century, yet another despondent young woman poet enters the scene, this time a simple peasant girl by the name of Shuangqing, who, despite her exquisite beauty and talent, is forced to endure the verbal and physical abuse of a nagging mother-in-law and a brutish husband. There is a great deal of biographical information about these two humble girls' lives of patient suffering—more even than we have about many of our elite women poets who lived longer. Even if one is willing to accept the historicity of Xiaoqing and Shuangqing—as we will see, there is good reason to assume that they are as fictional as *Dream of the Red Chamber*'s Lin Daiyu—one will find it hard to deny that the descriptions of their unhappy fates presented in such loving detail by their largely male biographers seem to be more informed by cultural stereotypes than by historical fact. Nevertheless, these two heroines took on a life of their own under the writing brushes of their biographers, and the poetry and prose attributed to them was read by male and female readers alike.

Du Liniang and Her Female Commentators

The characterizations of both Xiaoqing and Shuangqing are indebted to that of Du Liniang in Tang Xianzu's play *Peony Pavilion* of 1598. In this play of fifty-five acts, Du Liniang is the young and sensitive daughter of a stern and self-righteous Confucian official. In one of the first scenes, the young girl's deep and spontaneous capacity for passion is contrasted to the rigid and pedantic moralism of her male tutor. When he teaches her the first ode of the *Book of Songs*, "The Ospreys," she immediately reads it as a love song, while he insists on the established scholastic interpretation: a poem written in praise of a king's wife for her lack of jealousy.

Soon after her session with the tutor, Du Liniang wanders into an abandoned flower garden behind her father's office, which she finds in full bloom. When she returns to her room, she falls asleep, and in a dream revisits the garden where she now meets a handsome young man who makes love to her by the garden's Peony Pavilion. She wakes up from her dream, but finds that she cannot get the young man out of her thoughts. Passionately in love with her dream lover and in despair of ever meeting him in real life, she wastes away and before long is at the brink of death. Before she dies, however, she paints a portrait of herself that is placed in the Red Plum Chapel located in the garden. Her grief-stricken parents bury her in the flower garden as she has requested, after which they leave for another posting.

Not long afterwards, Liu Mengmei, who turns out to be none other than the handsome young man Du Liniang had met in her dream, passes through town on his way to the capital to sit for the metropolitan examinations. He decides to stay in the town to prepare for the exams, and rents a study in the very garden where Du Liniang is buried. He then comes across her self-portrait hanging in the Red Plum Chapel, and immediately falls in love with her, after which her spirit appears to him in his dreams. Finally, Du Liniang is restored to life, Liu Mengmei succeeds in the examinations, Du Liniang is reunited with her grieving parents, and the young couple lives happily ever after.

From the time this play first appeared in print, the first half of the play, with its detailed description of the sensitive Du Liniang's lingering death, is what most attracted readers. Some women readers are said to have been so affected by the reading of *Peony Pavilion* that, like the play's heroine, they fell ill and died. As we shall see, Xiaoqing too is depicted as just such a reader of this play. In addition, many women poets, including Ye Xiaoluan, wrote poems about the play and its heroine. In 1694, the Hangzhou author Wu Ren even published an edition of the play to which he appended a commentary written, he claimed, by his three "wives": Chen Tong (1650–1665), who had been engaged to Wu Ren but died before the wedding could take place, supposedly wrote the commentary to the first part of the play; Tan Ze (d. 1674), who was married to Wu Ren but died shortly afterwards, wrote the commentary to the second part; and finally Qian Yi, his second wife, edited and completed the manuscripts left by her two predecessors. This edition of *Peony Pavilion*, which also included prefaces by a number of well-known women writers of the day, immediately became very popular. From the beginning there were those, however, who questioned the authorship of the commentaries attributed to Wu Ren's "three wives." One of the main reasons for this was that Wu Ren had first circulated the commentaries under his own name (in order, as he would explain later, to protect the reputation of his wives), and later was never able to produce any of the original manuscripts. Unfortunately, he said, they had all been lost in a series of fires.

The spirit in which we should read the "three wives' commentaries" as well as the writings about and attributed to Xiaoqing and Shuangqing is perhaps best suggested by the following short story, ascribed to Wu Ren's second wife Qian Yi, which introduces Wu Ren's edition of the play:

In the last month of the winter of the year *jiaxu* [1694] the carving of the printing blocks of *Peony Pavilion: The Return of the Soul* was completed. Our son checked the text for mistaken characters, a task that he completed by the end of the year. On the First Night when the moon came out, I set up a clean table in the courtyard and on it I placed a carefully bound copy [of the play]. I then set up a soul tablet inscribed with Du Liniang's name, plucked a branch of red plum blossoms, which I placed in a "gall-bladder" vase, lit some candles, and laid out offerings of fruit and wine.

My husband laughed loudly and said: "Don't you think you are really being too foolish? Tang Xianzu himself has said that Du Liniang is a made-up name and that such a person has never existed. So why do you make offerings to her?" I answered: "That may be so, but the breath [*qi*] of the Great Clod is infused with intelligence. Even a stone may serve as the habitation of some creature, and even a tree may serve as the dwelling of a god. When Qu Yuan first sang of the Goddess of the Xiang and when Song Yu wrote his rhapsody on the Goddess of Shamanka Mountain,[1] these [women] originally may well have been allegorical, but later many temples [were established in their honor]. So how can you and I be absolutely sure whether or not Du Liniang really existed?" My husband said: "You are right and I was wrong."

---

1. The Goddess of the Xiang is the subject of the third of the "Nine Songs," a collection of hymns included in *Songs of the South* and traditionally ascribed to Qu Yuan (traditional dates 340–278 BCE). According to legend, the Goddess (some traditions speak of more than one) of the Xiang was the daughter of Yao, who had married Yao's successor Shun, and when her husband died sometime later, she drowned herself in the river. The poet Song Yu, said to have been a pupil of Qu Yuan's, wrote the *Rhapsody of the Divine Woman (Shennü fu)*, which describes the Goddess of Shamanka Mountain (Wushan) and her dream rendezvous with a king of the state of Chu.

At midnight we went to sleep, but shortly afterwards, awakened by the sound of my sighs, my husband got up and got dressed. Nudging me with his elbow, he said: "Wake up! Just a moment ago I had a dream that you and I went together to a garden that seemed to be the one with the 'Red Plum Chapel.' In front of the pavilion, peonies of all different varieties were in full bloom, their five different colors intermingled. Suddenly a beautiful woman appeared from behind the pavilion. Her dazzling beauty was so blinding that it robbed all the flowers of their colors, and secretly I wondered whether this might not be Du Liniang herself. But when you asked her for her name and dwelling place, instead of answering, she just turned around and plucked a little green plum, which she rolled between her fingers. And when you asked her: 'Are you Du Liniang?' she only smiled and did not reply. A moment later, a blustery storm rose and blew all the peony flowers off into the sky, leaving none behind. Then, when I became aware of you heaving endless deep sighs, I woke up."

The dream he described corresponded with my own dream, and we both were astounded by this amazing coincidence. My husband said: "Long ago, when Ruan Zhan [early third century] argued that ghosts didn't exist, a ghost appeared to him. Could it be that Du Liniang really does exist? This proves what you said!" We heard the fifth watch of the night being announced at the city gate, and since the lamp we had placed on the wall was still burning, I got up as well, and called the servant girl to get the fire going and brew us some tea. After I had finished combing my hair and sweeping up, I immediately asked for a writing brush and paper so that I could record this event. At that moment the light of the lamp had turned a pale red and the first light of morning was already shining through the window.

My husband said: "It cannot have been by accident that you and I had the same dream. If there was a reason why Du Liniang should appear to us, it probably was so that an image of her likeness might be transmitted to the world. You have been a [painting] student of Li Xiaogu's, and you have devoted yourself in particular to line drawings. Why don't you recreate her [appearance] in your mind and paint her portrait?" I protested that I was afraid that I might not be able to capture her spirit, but my husband urged me to take up the brush. When the portrait was finished, I felt I had captured her inner harmony. To the painting I then appended a poem, which reads:

> That I could glimpse your beauty for a moment cannot have been by chance:
> I saturated my brush and sketched your portrait so as to preserve your beauty.
> From now on everyone will recognize your spring breeze face,
> Heart-broken for your lover after a dream at dawn.

When I showed the portrait to my husband, he said: "This captures her like-ness!" Then he also wrote a poem, making use of the same rhyme that I had used:

> You pictured her true form in black and white quite naturally:
> One longs to ask from where this immortal beauty floated in.
> Idly she toys with a green plum but without saying a word—
> How vexing this unfinished dream among tattered flowers!

We now invite those who share our interests to also write matching poems.

Skeptical readers may note the extent to which Qian Yi appears to serve as her husband's puppet, but the moral of this story, which would be taken up with such gusto in the next century by Cao Xueqin, is clear: fiction becomes truth through the willing suspension of disbelief. Not all contemporary readers, however, were as willing to suspend their disbelief. Gu Si, one of the women poets of the Banana Garden Poetry Club in Hangzhou, is on record as having commented: "Du Liniang's appear-ance in a dream must have been the projection of the author."

The "three wives" edition of *Peony Pavilion* enjoyed great popularity in the eighteenth and nineteenth centuries, and may well have inspired the publication of yet another annotated edition of the play, entitled *The Tal-ented Scholar's Peony Pavilion (Caizi Mudanting)*. This latter edition, which was printed in 1762 and is now very rare, includes extensive commentar-ies by Wu Zhensheng (1695–1769) and his wife Cheng Qiong, which pas-sionately condemn hypocritical morality and equally passionately stress the complete naturalness of physical love. One of the most remarkable features of these commentaries is the way in which almost every line of Tang Xianzu's play is interpreted in sexual terms. This highly idiosyncratic feature probably also goes a long way to explain the oblivion this edition has suffered from until quite recently.

Long-Suffering Concubines

Xiaoqing

The earliest preserved biography of Xiaoqing was written by an unknown author who concealed himself behind the pseudonym of Master Narrow-Minded. He may have composed his biography of Xiaoqing as early as 1612, and by 1624 it had appeared in print. Some scholars have suggested that Master Narrow-Minded is yet another of the many pseudonyms of Feng Menglong (1574–1624), an extremely prolific author and editor of plays, novels, vernacular stories, and popular songs, as well as classical tales and many other types of writings. Feng Menglong included Master Narrow-Minded's biography of Xiaoqing in his *History of Passion* (*Qingshi*), an extensive, thematically classified collection of eight hundred classical tales on love.

Xiaoqing was the concubine of a gentleman from Hangzhou, but she herself was a native of Yangzhou. As she and that gentleman shared the same surname, I will avoid using her surname and refer to her simply by her style name, Xiao-qing.

Xiaoqing's predestined fate was extraordinary. When she was ten, she met an old nun who taught her the *Heart Sutra,* which she understood completely after having gone over it only once or twice. Then she repeated it without omitting a single character.[2] The nun said: "This child is precociously intelligent, but her luck is poor. I hope you will allow her to become my disciple, but if you won't do that, [at least] don't teach her to read, because if you do she may not live past the age of thirty." Xiaoqing's relatives, thinking the nun was a fraud, ridiculed her.

Xiaoqing's mother was a teacher in a school for girls, and Xiaoqing later learned to read and write from her. Her mother's friends were all famous ladies, and from them she acquired a refined understanding of all the arts and a marvelous grasp of poetic prosody. Now, Yangzhou is a scenic spot, and from time to time the most brilliant of the ladies would gather like clouds; selecting teas and playing go, they would form a lively crowd. Xiaoqing would have a response ready for any situation, and in each case she would surprise everyone, so much so that everyone's greatest fear was that she would not be in attendance [at their gatherings]. Even though she always behaved most properly, her appearance was exceptionally dazzling. Graceful and elegant, such was her nature.

At the age of sixteen she married the aforementioned gentleman. He was a rich young wastrel, a loud-mouthed fool lacking in sophistication. Moreover, his [main] wife was extremely jealous. Xiaoqing made every effort to placate her but never succeeded in mitigating her animosity. One day Xiaoqing accompanied her on a visit to the Tianzhu Monastery and the main wife asked her: "The Buddha of the Western Paradise, I have been told, is Amitabha, so why do all

---

2. The *Heart Sutra* is a very popular short Buddhist text that teaches the ultimate equivalence of emptiness and form.

the people in the world honor and revere the Mahasattva [Guanyin]?" Xiaoqing answered: "Because of her compassion." The main wife realized that this was meant as a criticism of her, so she said with a smile: "I will show you my compassion!" She then had Xiaoqing moved to the family's villa on Orphan Hill [a little island in West Lake], and warned her: "If my husband arrives without my express permission, don't let him in! Even if a letter from him arrives without my express permission, don't you dare accept it!" Well aware that since the wife had banished her to such an out-of-the-way place, she was bound to secretly keep an eye on all of her doings and would make use of any plausible pretext to do away with her, Xiaoqing behaved herself in a most circumspect way.

Occasionally, the main wife would order Xiaoqing to share her boat when she went out to a party. Whenever the other women with them would catch sight of the rich young playboys on the banks racing their horses or shooting pellets, they would point them out and make jokes, running from one side of the boat to the other. Xiaoqing, however, would remain seated and completely ignore them. Now one of the relatives of the main wife was a lady who was both talented and wise. She had once taken go lessons with Xiaoqing, and loved and pitied her very much. And so she repeatedly fetched huge beakers of wine for the main wife, and once the wife had become completely intoxicated, whispered to Xiaoqing: "This boat has an upper deck, let's go upstairs, you and me!" When they had climbed to the upper deck, they gazed for a long while into the distance. The lady patted Xiaoqing on the back and said: "It is too bad that this scenery is so beautiful! Even the Willow of Zhangtai was able to lean out from her red tower to catch a glimpse of Master Han speeding by on his horse.[3] Do you want to be a prayer mat and watch in vain?" Xiaoqing replied: "But I fear the sharp blade of Chancellor Jia!"[4] The lady said with a smile: "You are wrong, the chancellor's blade is dull, it is the female chancellor who is to be feared!"

After a while, once the lady had made sure that they were all alone with no others around them, she chided Xiaoqing at greater length: "Your talent and grace, beauty and artistry are unequaled, and you do not deserve having ended up in this land of *rakshas*![5] Even though I am not a female knight-errant, I still

---

3. The "Willow of Zhangtai" was a Chang'an courtesan. According to a well-known Tang dynasty tale, she was the paramour of Captain Li. When he noticed how much she admired the poor poet-student Han Yi (Junping; ca. 730–ca. 800), he generously allowed them to become a couple.

4. Chancellor Jia is Jia Sidao (1213–1275), who, from 1259 until his death, dominated the court of the Southern Song dynasty at Hangzhou. Suspecting his favorite concubine Li Huiniang of having an affair with a poor student, he had her beheaded.

5. *Rakshas* are evil demons from Buddhist mythology.

have the strength to save you from this pit of fire! You must have understood what I meant when I mentioned the Willow of Zhangtai a moment ago. How could there be a lack of men like Han Junping in this world? Moreover, when she sees that you are gone, she will be freed from a thorn in her eye. And even if she were to accept you, do you want to be the serving girl bringing lamb and wine to the bedside of General Dang?"[6] Xiaoqing excused herself saying: "Please stop this! As a little child I dreamt that I plucked a branch of flowers, but then each and every petal was blown by the wind into the water. This is just my fate. How could I hope for someone else as long as my old karma has not yet been expiated? The register of marriages in the bureaucracy of the netherworld is not my wish-granting pearl: I would only make myself a laughingstock." The lady sighed and said: "You are right. I will not pressure you. But take good care of yourself. You will have to be even more cautious when she starts to wine and dine you with friendly words. If there is anything you need at short notice, you must let me know." They gazed at one another, and their copious tears dampened their clothes. But then, fearful that one of the slave girls might overhear them, they carefully wiped their tears away and returned to their seats. After they had parted ways, the lady would often speak of this conversation to her relatives, and all those who heard about it were saddened.

From this time on, Xiaoqing entrusted all her dark frustration and piercing resentment to poems and short lyrics. But when later the lady [who had comforted her] followed her husband to a distant official posting, and Xiaoqing had no one with whom to share her songs, her despondency turned into illness, which after a year or so became increasingly critical. The main wife sent for a physician, and later sent a servant over with some medicine. Xiaoqing feigned gratitude, but as soon as the servant had left, she flung the medicine onto the bed, and laughing loudly said: "It is true I have no desire to live, but I wish to take refuge [with the Buddha] with a pure body so I can [rise to Heaven like] Liu An's chickens and dogs.[7] How would one cup of your poison be enough to kill me?"

---

6. General Dang, often used as an example of a boorish character, is said to have lived in the tenth century. On snowy days, he would simply drink himself into a stupor inside his cozy bed curtains, in contrast to the elegant Tao Gu, who would collect the snow and melt it to brew tea.

7. Liu An (d. 122 BCE) was the prince of Huainan; he rebelled against imperial authority and was executed. During his lifetime he was the patron of a group of scholars who composed the *Huainanzi*, a philosophical work with a strong Daoist coloring. Later legend turned Liu An into a magician who, after successfully preparing an elixir of immor-

Her illness worsened, and she no longer ate or drank anything apart from a single cup of pear juice every day. She would nevertheless continue to prop herself up in bed with cushions, fully dressed in her most dazzling gown and beautifully made up. Occasionally, to while away the time, she would summon a blind woman to sing narrative ballads to her to the accompaniment of the lute. Even when she was suffering frequent fainting spells, she would never lie down with disheveled hair. One day she told her old maid: "Go and tell that husband of mine to whom I am tied by bad karma to find me a good painter." When the painter came, she ordered him to paint her portrait. When he was finished, she took a mirror and after looking carefully at herself, said: "He has caught my formal likeness, but has not yet [captured] my spirit." She then laid the painting aside. When he had done yet another painting, she said: "The spirit is right, but my posture is too stiff. My eyes would seem to be expressionless and my hands heavy when he looks at me. It must be because I am posing too much." So she laid this painting aside as well, and told the painter to remain by her side with his brush [and observe her] as she ordered the maid about and talked to her, fanned the tea stove, sealed a letter, personally straightened the folds in her clothes, or mixed all the different kinds of colors for him [hoping in this way] to inspire his imagination. When sometime later the [third] painting was finished, it truly captured all of her charms, and with a smile she said: "That's it!" After the painter had left, she placed the painting on an altar table in front of her bed, lit some incense, and preparing a libation of pear wine, said: "Xiaoqing, is this to be your karma?" She stroked the table, her tears pouring down like rain, and overcome by emotion, she passed away. She was only eighteen years old when she died.

It was almost dusk before her husband came sauntering over. But when he opened the bed curtains and saw the radiance of her face and the beauty of her figure, just as it was when she was still alive and before she had fallen ill, he started to weep and stamp his feet, and coughed up over a pint of blood. Carefully looking around, he discovered a scroll of poetry and a painting, as well as a sealed letter addressed to the lady [who had been her friend]. When he opened the letter, he found that it contained a description of her grief and pain, followed by a quatrain. In distress he cried out: "I have betrayed you!" When the main wife heard about this, she was enraged and, rushing over, demanded to have the portrait. But he had hidden the third portrait, and gave her only the first painting, which she immediately burned. She also demanded the poems, and as soon as they were in her possession, she burned them as well. He later

---

tality, ascended to Heaven with his entire household, including those chickens and dogs who happened to have also swallowed some of the elixir.

searched for the drafts [of the poems], but by then they had all been scattered and lost.

But just before her death, Xiaoqing had given some filigree hairpins and other things to her maid's daughter. She had wrapped these objects in two sheets of paper, upon which, it turned out, she had written the drafts of some of her poems! In this way, nine quatrains, an old-style poem, and a lyric were recovered. Together with the letter sent to the lady, this makes for twelve texts.

The author of this biography of Xiaoqing proceeds to quote all twelve of these texts in full. These texts—*shi* poems in various forms, lyrics, and letters—represent the range of literary genres an educated woman in seventeenth-century China would have been expected to master. The old-style *shi* poem attributed to Xiaoqing describes snow falling on a cold winter day:

> The threat of snow stops the clouds from going on their way,
> The old clouds weigh heavily upon the clouds that are new.
> The mad splashes of Mad Mi drip in front of the window[8]—
> The finest spot of the pine tree ridge just across from my room.
> If I pull down the screen I'm afraid I'll miss out on the fine scene,
> But if I roll up the screen, I'm afraid the wind will whirl about.
> The screen pulled down, the screen rolled up—which is the hardest?
> Bereft of feeling, bereft of emotion, who is there to understand?
> The burner's smoke grows slimmer, the sound of trimming weaker,
> And then to top it off, the distant honking of an orphaned goose.

In the first of the nine untitled quatrains attributed to Xiaoqing, the poet addresses the bodhisattva Guanyin and expresses the hope that in her next life she will be reborn not in Heaven, but rather in this world as a happy and requited lover. Two lotus flowers growing from a single stem were often used as a symbol of a happy couple.

> I bow my head and pray to the Mahasattva up on her cloud of compassion:
> May I not be reborn in the Western Paradise, may I not be reborn in
>   Heaven,
> But may I become a drop of water dripping from your willow branch,
> That sprinkled on the earth becomes a double-blossomed lotus flower.

---

8. Mad Mi refers to the famous, and somewhat eccentric, painter Mi Fei (1057–1107).

In the second quatrain, the poet claims that she has shed enough tears of blood to dye deep red every one of the white blossoms on the plum trees at the West Lake home of the recluse Lin Bu (967–1028):

> My spring blouse: tears of blood spot the light gauze—
> Blow them away to the house of the recluse Lin Bu,
> And the three hundred blossoming plums on the ridge
> Will immediately be turned into flowers of azalea-red!

In some of her quatrains, Xiaoqing compares herself to famous unhappy beauties from Chinese history such as Wang Zhaojun:

> If I, newly made-up, would've been compared with paintings,
> Who knows what number I would rank in Zhaoyang Palace?
> I gaze at the reflection of my gaunt face in the spring stream:
> You must surely feel pity for me just as I feel sorry for you.

In one of her quatrains, Xiaoqing describes herself as reading the *Peony Pavilion* and recognizing her own unhappy fate in that of Du Liniang:

> Cold rain outside the dark window—such a mournful sound!
> I trim the lamp and leisurely read the *Peony Pavilion*.
> In this world there are people even more foolish than I:
> Xiaoqing is clearly not the only one with a broken heart.

In yet another quatrain, Xiaoqing compares her own fate to that of beautiful birds buffeted by autumn storms:

> A couple of birds, from who knows where, roost on the balustrade:
> With all their reds and greens they look like a pair of phoenix-birds.
> But now how many are there who pity them for their vivid colors?
> For they too will have to struggle against the storms of autumn.

Xiaoqing's lyric to the melody of "Heavenly Immortal" [*Tianxianzi*] reads as follows:

> Cai Yan became a bride far away on Zhaojun's steppes,
> Now again it is Xiaoqing who pays the dues of passion.
> How I wish a single black tornado would swoop down,
> Like a wheel of fire,
> And carry me off,
> All by myself, away from everyone, to a world clear and cool!

I do not want to be one of those lovesick mandarin ducks.
Don't think that I am nothing but longing and yearning.
All alone I think, all alone I ponder, and all alone I muse.
My heart is still here,
My soul is still here—
I change my blouse and play with the double sash of my skirt.

The long letter Xiaoqing is said to have written to her lady friend concludes with the following few lines:

When at some future date you moor your boat by the bank, come look for me on Plum Hill, open the gate of my western pavilion, and take a seat on my couch in the green shade. Then it will all be as if I were still alive. When you see a silent whirlwind inside the empty curtains, will you believe that I still exist or not? Alas, light and darkness follow different roads, and I now take my leave for all eternity. When I think that my jade white arms and rosy cheeks will soon be buried in the earth, there is no point in feeling moved so deeply.

The quatrain appended to the letter reads:

Twisted innards in a hundred knots, tears streaking my face:
When you return, you will find nothing but the old red gate.
The shadow of peach blossom in the endless evening glow
Is bound to be, as you must know, the lovely Qiannü's soul.[9]

Master Narrow-Minded ends his biographical narrative with the following words: "One of the gentleman's relatives collected these writings and had them printed under the title *Saved from Burning* [*Fenyu*]." (This title would be echoed in the titles of many collections of women's poetry in the centuries to come.) He then appends the following commentary of his own:

When I read the compositions of Xiaoqing, I find that although they may be sad and mournful, they do not lack in energy and structure. What a pity that her complete collection has not been preserved! In short, [this collection is as

---

9. Qiannü is a character from a well-known Tang dynasty tale. In this story, she is promised in marriage to a cousin, but later her parents go back on their word. When her cousin leaves, her soul follows him, while her body remains behind in a coma. After [the soul] of Qiannü had lived with her cousin as his wife and borne him two children, the couple returns to her parents' home, where her body and soul are finally reunited.

small as a] fragment of a coral tree one inch in diameter, but that makes it only more admirable!

When I heard that the second painting was kept by her maid, I spared no efforts in purchasing it from her. Charming and proper, Xiaoqing resembles the blossom of the autumn crab apple. Her gown is lined with pearls on the inside and covered with kingfisher feathers on the outside, and her superlative beauty has the grace of a cultivated gentleman. But this is still only a copy, the one of which Xiaoqing said: "The spirit is right, but my posture is too stiff."

Her maid once told me: "The young lady loved to read. When she lacked a book, she would obtain it from her husband, and what she could not get from him, she would borrow it from that particular lady. From time to time, she would execute a small painting. She [also] painted a fan, which she loved so dearly that she wouldn't give it to her husband even after he heard about it and insistently asked for it." The maid also said: "The young lady loved to talk to her reflection in the mirror. And in the late afternoon sun by the flowers, when the mists had disappeared and the water was clear, she would gaze at her reflection in the pond, and whisper as if she were conversing with her reflection. But after the slave girls once caught her doing this, she refrained from ever doing it again, although on her brow one could see a hint of distress, as if she were about to weep." When I read the third quatrain in her collection, I realized that this story was true.

Alas! It is impossible to count all those in this world who, like Xiaoqing, end up hapless despite their talents and must tarry in the dust with only their reflections to pity them, before disappearing without a trace!

The last lines of this commentary suggest that literati such as the anonymous Master Narrow-Minded may have been moved to record the sad life of Xiaoqing not merely for its inherent interest, but also because her experiences seemed to mirror those of many men who felt frustrated and betrayed when it came to their own career.

This allegorical reading of the story of Xiaoqing probably explains in large part its extraordinary popularity throughout the seventeenth century. Her biography was rewritten again and again, and in many of these rewritings, poems attributed to her were inserted into the narrative at appropriate spots. Yet other versions of the story contain embellishments; for instance, one emphasizes that it was the reading of the *Peony Pavilion* that precipitated her death, and in another we are told that Xiaoqing and her husband both had the surname of Feng. While the original biography was written in classical Chinese, the tale of her life was also rewritten as a vernacular story, and for the seventeenth century alone, one finds titles of fifteen independent dramatic adaptations, some of which became quite famous. The nature of the drama, however, required that these stage adaptations have a happy ending, if not in this life then certainly in the one following. And finally, many women poets in the seventeenth century and later would write their own poems about the sorry fate of Xiaoqing. One of these women poets was Wang Duanshu, who entitled her poem simply "Xiaoqing":

> There was a girl from Yangzhou, her name was Xiaoqing,
> Born and raised deep in the women's quarters till sixteen.
> Soft and delicate, sweet and graceful, lovely and modest,
> Her talents worth praising, far surpassing those of Miss Xie.
> Her parents she lost early, she was left all alone,
> And weak and vulnerable, she became a concubine.
> She married a scoundrel from far away, a leaf in the wind.
> He already had a jealous wife with a thunderous temper.
> Smashing gold, shattering jade, she burned the Five Classics,
> In a hidden house the wife shut her away as if she were a prisoner.
> The lonely wind and desolate moon pierced the window sills,
> She longed to walk on the fallen leaves, leave the painted screens.
> Let that parrot stop repeating things over and over again!
> Raising high the lamp she idly reads the *Peony Pavilion*.
> The rain drips on the empty steps, but she cannot bear to listen,
> Then a female knight tried to help her escape the layered doors.
> But the wife took her to Orphan Hill, a most lonely spot:
> A branch of winter pear shades the shattered vase.
> The hour is still, the mourning goose weeps on the sandy isle.
> She forces herself to comb and bathe, timid and graceful.
> She softly orders the painter to capture her sickly form,
> And herself holding the spotted brush, she writes "fragrant tea."
> Respectfully I read your writings and pour out a libation of wine,
> To my regret I cannot follow you into the Underworld.

Even at the height of the "Xiaoqing craze" in the seventeenth century, there were those who expressed their skepticism about her historic existence. Qian Qianyi and Liu Shi, for example, do not include any poems by Xiaoqing in the section of women poets in the *Collected Poems of the Successive Reigns*, nor do they provide her with a biographical account of her own. She is, however, briefly mentioned in an appendix to the biography of another writing concubine, Yu Sulan, a flamboyant personality who ended up the victim of a gruesome unsolved murder:

Sulan's [White Orchid] personal name was Ru and her style name was Jinghe; her place of origin is unclear, but some say she hailed from Suzhou. She was born to an eminent family, but was married off to a "toad."[10] She was romantic and unbridled, and eventually was murdered. . . . She was a competent calligrapher and excelled in the painting of orchids. She had orchids and cattails growing on the small table of fragrant wood in front of the light-filled window where she recited her books and chanted her poems. This is why she adopted the pseudonym of Sulan [White Orchid]. When the full moon was in the sky, when everyone had all gone home and the streets were empty, she would have her servant girls dress up as barbarian grooms and she would wander about astride a fine horse until midnight. On beautiful spring and autumn days, she would take off in a small boat, and she visited almost all the mountains and streams of Wu and Yue.[11] During the third watch of a night in the Ninth Month of the seventh year of the Tianqi reign period [1627], she was hacked to death by an unknown person. Despite a full judicial inquiry, the name of the perpetrator was never discovered. Following her marriage, Sulan had felt frustrated and wrote sixteen poems on the subject of the water bubble to give expression to her understanding [of life]. She left two scrolls of poetry, which were prefaced and printed by some busybody.

Then there is the case of the so-called Xiaoqing. This person never existed; it was our fellow townsman, the student Tan, who invented both her biography and her poems. Jokingly, he said to his friends: "The name Xiaoqing [small green] was created by separating the heart radical, which resembles the character *xiao* [small], from the phonetic element in the character *qing*. Some say her family name was Zhong, and by putting these two characters together, one gets Zhong Qing [concentrated passion]." Neither the biography nor the poems are very good, but they are more widely circulated by the day, and her story has even been turned into plays. It has reached the point that there are even people who, visiting the "grave of Xiaoqing" on Orphan Hill, write poems as inscriptions! It is just a vulgar and baseless tale that has gone so far as to be depicted in

---

10. The word "toad" could refer to a hunchback, an old lecher, an impotent husband, or an actor.

11. Wu refers to Suzhou and surroundings, while Yue refers to the eastern part of the modern province of Zhejiang.

paintings—it makes one want to vomit! As she [was supposed to have] lived in Yushan [Changshu], we append her story here.

Ellen Widmer has suggested that the student Tan mentioned by Qian Qianyi and Liu Shi may refer to Tan Yuanchun (1585–1637), a man who counted many publishers of the time among his friends. The names of at least five other male authors have also been put forward, however, as being the ones responsible for the creation of Xiaoqing.

Skinny Mares

Xiaoqing was said to hail from Yangzhou. Throughout the seventeenth and eighteenth centuries Yangzhou was renowned for its ample supply of high-quality "skinny mares," that is to say, girls who had been raised and groomed for the concubine market. The Yangzhou trade in "skinny mares" attracted customers from all over China. Though Xiaoqing is not explicitly identified as a "skinny mare," the description of her unhappy life certainly suggests that she belonged to this category. One of these many unfortunate girls, He Guizhi (possibly late Ming) described her state of mind on the eve of her "marriage" in the following words:

Despair

On the night of the sixth of the Sixth Month the rain pours down,
And this girl cannot fall asleep, overcome by emotions of despair.
She cocks her ear to the east—but everyone is still loudly snoring,
She leans on her bed with lowered head—her handkerchief soaked.

I do not know how to express my grief,
To whom can I tell what I have to say?
Here I sit at midnight facing the rain,
Moved to sighs by my unhappy fate.

Originally I am a girl from the provincial capital of Guangxi,
My father and mother here in this place are not my real parents.
When I call to mind the events of some eight or nine years ago,
My little heart beats furiously as alone, I am overcome by grief.

When I was six or seven, I remember,
My father and mother abandoned me.

I was entrusted to the care of poor relatives,
Poor relatives who harbored evil intentions.

Someone on the staff of the commanding officer of Xunwu
Made use of his connections to suddenly flaunt his power.
He gave them some money—I have no idea how much—
And they were happy to sell me to him as a female slave.

At that time I was still a child so I could only go along—
Poorly fated, dependent on others, and completely helpless.
That same year he took me with him to the city of Yangzhou,
A journey of ten thousand miles over mountains and rivers!
 Once I had entered the house of my boss here in Yangzhou,
No one took pity on me as the years went by one after the other.
At dawn I brought them rice and tea, at night their hot water:
When cold I had no clothes to wear, when hungry I got no food.

When the boss would once in a while show a hint of pity,
His wife would whip and beat me—what unbearable pain!

But about a year ago all of a sudden their attitude changed:
They started to treat me as if I were their own daughter!
They allowed me to address them as "father" and "mother,"
And expended great efforts to fix my hair and bind my feet.
 How could I have known that theirs was a fiendish trap,
That their many favors were not really deeper than the sea!

After I had mastered playing the flute and plucking the lute,
I was also taught to master the games of cards and backgammon.
As soon as lady Li had been called in to teach me singing,
I also had to study embroidery with Missus Zhang.

Every detail had to be perfect: the supervision was strict—
Who would have guessed their planning and scheming?
Spring came, autumn went, and quickly the time passed by,
They said that I had grown up into a beautiful girl,
And that I would marry a rich man, a noble prince,
And that I would live a life of luxury without end!

Yesterday a guest arrived in the wide open hall,
And I was told to go to the hall to welcome him.
He was some good-for-nothing—I'd no idea who—
But he looked me over carefully from head to toe.
I noticed that my parents were very pleased indeed,
But I felt so ashamed that I fled back to my room!

I could only guess, I didn't dare ask,
But I knew it could only spell trouble.
When I listened in on their discussion,
The words I heard filled me with gloom:
 Only then did I learn that this guest
Was a man who hailed from Hangzhou.
 A Ministry of Works supervising censor, he occupied a high post,
Sixty years old but without a son, he was buying a new concubine!
There was not going to be a nice and proper marriage ceremony:
The only thing I heard them really discuss was the matter of money.
 Oh, how I hated my parents for their total lack of feeling—
A thousand *liang*, a hundred *liang*: no end to the haggling!
Since even I did not know the day and the hour of my birth,
They simply made up a date and time to tell the other party.
 The engagement was set for the fifth, the wedding for the seventh:
Because he had a deadline to meet, they said, they needed to be quick.
Alas, to no avail is my face as beautiful as a flower,
Alas, in truth my fate is like a leaf in the wind!
 Today these people still insist on calling me child,
But tomorrow another family will call me concubine.
This is why my heart is broken and I sigh with sorrow,
Late at night I wipe my tears as my innards are crushed.
 Had I known that my powdered face would be sold for gold,
I should long ago have plunged into the moonlit Yangzi River.

It is finished and done: what point is there in weeping?
Don't you see that it has long been the custom in Yangzhou
To marry one's own children off to the edge of the sky?
To the edge of the sky and to the ends of the earth!
Toward their own flesh and blood they act like wolves!
So why then should I still be dissolved by tears?

> Dissolved by tears and still my grief has not stopped,
> But the Yangzi's floods will never flow back to the west.
> The ancients already deplored this stubborn custom!
> This is my advice to all the unmarried girls with rosy cheeks
>   and dark hair:
> Make sure to never in a future life be reborn in Yangzhou!

According to one account, He Guizhi's husband died within a year, after which his main wife took pity on Guizhi and allowed her to remain with her. Together the two women dedicated the rest of their lives to Buddhist devotions.

There were other "skinny mares" who wrote poetry as well. The famous eighteenth-century poet Yuan Mei (1716–1798) records the following anecdote in his *Notes on Poetry from the Sui Garden* (*Suiyuan shihua*):

Zhao Juntai from Hangzhou went to Suzhou to buy a concubine. He found a girl with the surname of Li. She had a beautiful face but because her feet had not been properly bound, Zhao remarked: "Too bad that despite all her fine features she is so 'firmly planted on the ground.'" "Firmly planted on the ground" is a Hangzhou expression for having big feet. The old matchmaker then responded: "But this girl can write verse: please put her to the test here and now." Thinking he would ridicule her, Zhao assigned her the topic of "curved shoes." Right there on the spot the girl wrote:

> In ancient times these three-inch-long curved shoes did not yet exist:
> When seated, the Mahasattva Guanyin reveals two bare natural feet.
> Nobody knows when the custom of footbinding really originated,
> But it must have originated with the meanest men of this world!

Flustered, Zhao left.

Poems on Walls

As we have seen, the seventeenth century witnessed the remarkable popularity of the tale of Xiaoqing, but the literati of the time appeared to also be obsessed with "poems written on walls" by damsels in distress. While Chinese literati have always left poems on various surfaces, they developed a knack for discovering poems left by women only during the final decades of the Ming dynasty. One of the earliest and most famous cases was the anonymous "girl from Guiji," who was said to have left her poems on a wall in Xinjia. The account provided in *History of Passion* reads as follows:

It is unknown from where she hailed, but her poems and preface were found on the wall of the government inn in Xinjia. The prose preface reads:

I was born and raised in Guiji, and from my earliest years I devoted myself to the Classics and Histories. As soon as I reached marriageable age, I was wed to a merchant from Yan. Despite my elegant features I had to serve a "general" who turned out to be completely unfaithful: each day I suffered repeated scoldings by his ferocious and jealous wife. When one morning I dared to complain to him, I became the target of her rage. I was whipped and beaten and treated worse than a common slave. Filled with indignation I could hardly rise!

Alas, I am like a bird in a cage and my life has no value for me anymore. But I was afraid that if I hid myself amid the bushes, I would die without leaving a trace. I therefore temporarily postponed my death, and when the others had all finally fallen fast asleep, I stole to this back courtyard, and using my tears to mix the ink, I wrote three poems on the wall. If a sympathetic friend should read these, and be saddened by my unlucky fate, my death will not have been in vain.

The poems read:

I

My silvery-red singlet is partly covered by dust,
Only a single dying lamp to keep me company.
I am just like the pear blossom after a rain storm:
Strewn all about and never making it to spring.

II

All day long I lived in a den of tigers and panthers—
Filled with emotion, silently brooding: limitless grief!
Old Heaven arranged for my birth with no other purpose
Than to provide romantics with a topic of conversation.

III

To whom could I complain of my myriad sorrows?
In the presence of others I smiled, but alone I wept.

> Do not look upon this poem as just an ordinary poem:
> Each line of verse is made up of thousands of tears.

As soon as these poems became known, literati competed in writing poems to match them.

Many seventeenth-century readers were indeed deeply moved by these poems and their preface. The same applied to the many other "poems written on walls" that became known in the subsequent decades. A particularly large number of verses of this kind were produced during the troubled decades of the middle of the century, although there were those who questioned the authenticity of at least some of these poems. As a result, the authors of "poems on walls" on occasion felt a need to stress their own authenticity. For example, in 1654 Deng Hanyi (1617–1689), an anthologist of contemporary poetry, discovered written on the wall of an inn in Shandong the poems of a "girl from Xiangyang." The preface on the wall expresses the hope that these poems will be included in a later anthology of women's writings. Even more significantly, the reputed author also feels impelled to protest her own reality: "I do not entrust myself to the fictional imagination of a Xiaoqing, but I am humbled by the expressions of grief by the girl of Guiji."

Lyrics on Flower Petals: Shuangqing

All of our information about Shuangqing as well as all of her written works ultimately derive from a single source, Shi Zhenlin's (1693–1781) *Scattered Records of Xi and Qing* (*Xiqing sanji*). Shi Zhenlin, who hailed from Guazhu in Jiangsu province, passed the metropolitan examinations in 1736, after which he stayed on in Beijing for another two years before returning south to care for his ailing mother. During his lifetime he was a well-known writer, and also enjoyed a considerable reputation as a poet, calligrapher, and painter.

Shi Zhenlin published his *Scattered Records of Xi and Qing* in 1738. The book consists of essays, records, and musings from the years before he passed the highest exams, and are all written in a very personal and lively style. The work was quite popular in his time, a success that may have been due largely to the descriptions of his and his friends' meetings with Shuangqing. In a later work, Shi Zhenlin would characterize these passages as "dreams," a word that could refer both to the lost pleasures of his youth and to the fictional character of his descriptions. It is, of course, not unthinkable that Shi Zhenlin was inspired by a real flesh-and-blood woman, and to this day many readers, both male and female, remain convinced of Shuangqing's historical existence. Nevertheless, there is no doubt that one of Shi Zhenlin's goals was to portray what he considered to be the embodiment of a cultural ideal: the long-suffering woman of extraordinary talent. His Shuangqing is both more talented and more patient than Xiaoqing, her background is more humble, and her devotion to her despicable husband even greater. In a succession of descriptive passages, Shi Zhenlin attempts, at times at the cost of internal contradiction, to perfect this characterization of his heroine.

Shuangqing has already inspired two English-language monographs, both of which include practically all the passages dealing with her in Shi Zhenlin's *Scattered Records of Xi and Qing*. In these various passages, Shi Zhenlin is as much concerned with his and his friends' infatuation with Shuangqing as he is with Shuangqing herself. Here we limit ourselves to a translation of those passages in which Shuangqing is the main protagonist:

Shuangqing was a girl from Xiaoshan whose family had been farmers for generations. From birth she exhibited an innate intelligence and whenever she heard the sound of books [being read], she would happily smile. When she turned ten, she started to practice needlework, in which she became exceedingly skilled. Her uncle on her mother's side was a schoolteacher who taught in a school located next door. When she heard him [recite the texts he was teaching], she would secretly memorize [them all], and in this way she started to practice composing poems and lyrics instead of doing her needlework. She also learned the Little Seal style of calligraphy; her dots and strokes were correct and charming, and she was able to write out the entire *Heart Sutra* on a single osmanthus leaf. When one of the neighbor girls married a student, she made fun of Shuangqing because, having been born in a peasant family, she could never hope to even look upon the face of a student!

When Shuangqing turned eighteen, there was no one there in the hills who appreciated her talents, although they all vied in praising her dazzling beauty. And so in the fall of that year, she was married to the son of a peasant family surnamed Zhou. Her mother-in-law was a wet nurse. The couple rented a hut from Mengzhan and worked his fields as tenants.[12] Whenever they saw their landlord, they would address him as "Mr. Official." Shuangqing's husband was more than ten years older than she was, and when he looked at the almanac, he had to make a great effort to recognize the characters for "big" and "small" used to distinguish the months.

That summer, in the Fourth Month, I escaped the heat by going to live in the Hall of Paired Plowing in Xiaoshan. [My friend,] the Lover of Flowers, Duan Yuhan, also showed up there. When I accompanied him to have a look at the evening hills, Shuangqing happened to appear outside her door with a spade in her hand. She was also carrying a bamboo basket, and [was preparing to] plant melons and gourds on the river bank to the west of the bridge. Her expression was cheerful, but not without a trace of sadness.

The next day we found one of her lyrics to the melody of "Sands of Washing Brook" [*Huanxisha*], which she had written with powder on the leaf of an herbaceous peony. It read:

> The warm rain, which has no feelings, comes down in threads,
> The herdboy has stuck a tender flowering branch aslant in his hair:
> This is when the new wheat is brought in from the small fields.
>
> Planting melons and drawing water, I am blamed for being too early,
> Boiling the millet despite the morning mist, then they call me lazy!
> While all through the long, long day my tender back aches in pain.

She had also written a lyric to the melody of "Gazing to Jiangnan" [*Wang Jiangnan*] with powder on a tuberose leaf:

> Spring has disappeared,
> Searching for it, you came to the west of the bridge.
> The pale red that entices dreams fools the powdered butterflies,
> The dark green that locks up sorrow deceives the yellow oriole:
> Don't speak again of this hidden pain!
>
> All the people are gone—
> Is a meeting such as this good or is it wrong?
> Praying to the moon, the incense teases my sleeves in vain,
> Pitying the flowers, my tears are gone but my gown is soaked,
> As the evening sun sets behind the distant hills.

---

12. Mengzhan is the name of one of Shi Zhenlin's friends.

She composed this lyric to poke fun at the Lover of Flowers, who became infuriated. When Shuangqing heard about this, she said: "Having been born and raised in a peasant family, I had resigned myself to the fact that I would never meet a student. So now that I have had the good fortune of making the acquaintance of all these poets in *Scattered Records,* every night I burn incense and bow to Heaven [in gratitude]. I am like a caged bird that aspires to be a soaring phoenix!" But then she turned aside and sighing, said: "Although my peasant husband may be a vulgar lout, still he is capable of taking good care of me. How could I bring myself to despise him? In this life I don't want to make the acquaintance of any students!" Then she wrote a lyric to the melody of "Soaked Gauze Gown" [*Shi luoyi*]:

> Most difficult to express in this world are one's deepest feelings,
> I swallow all my tears, but then they gather again.
> Between my fingers, I press a wilting flower,
> And silently lean against a screen.
>
> I gaze at myself in the mirror,
> And am startled by how skinny I've become.
> A spring portrait—oh no!
> An autumn portrait—oh no!
> But it is me, Shuangqing!

The Lover of Flowers wrote several tens of song lyrics, but when he asked her to match them, she did not respond. By chance he saw Shuangqing at the gate. Her expression was extremely distressed, quite different from before. The Lover of Flowers bowed to her from a distance and when he left, asked Mengzhan to hire a skilled painter to paint her portrait. He also wrote a parting lyric and repeatedly asked her to match it. She then rolled a small note into a ball and sealed it very tightly, ordering the Lover of Flowers not to open and read it until he was somewhere on the road where there was no one else around. Delighted, he put it in his sleeve and left, without me or Mengzhan knowing anything about it. When the next day we sent a maid to ask her about it, Shuangqing only smiled, and recited a poem she had written on white silk, which read:

> There actually exists a naïve and passion-filled immortal like me,
> Who has now managed to leave this student guessing for a while!

An old man from Xiaoshan told me: "Shuangqing has a carefree nature and a friendly disposition. Lightly floating, she has the air of soaring beyond the clouds, with none of the trivial and niggling mannerisms of women. She considers her talents a bane, and those who visit her home never see a trace of her brush and ink. She is married to a peasant whose poverty is extreme, and on top of that, her mother-in-law works her very hard and shows her no compassion. Yet Shuangqing serves her well, and even though she doesn't love her husband, she always puts on a happy expression when she sees him. Even though she may be burdened and emaciated by starvation and toil, she still continues to laugh and joke."

We later learn that in the secret letter she had given the Lover of Flowers, Shuangqing had included a portrait of herself together with some lyrics in which she poked fun at him. We also learn that Mengzhan does indeed hire a painter, who eventually succeeds in painting two portraits of Shuangqing. When Mengzhan shows the paintings to Shuangqing and asks her to write inscriptions for them, she promises to do so, but then reneges on her promise and refuses to return the paintings. It is only after Mengzhan has written her a long letter that she relents. The song lyric she supposedly writes on the paintings is composed to the melody of "Jade Metropolis Autumn" (*Yujingqiu*):

> Brows half in a frown,
> The springtime red already fully faded,
> The old sorrow still not paid off:
> The skinny image in this painting—
> I'm so ashamed I want to run away!
> Not yet fully recovered from my recent illness,
> Some simple make-up
> Lightly applied but all in vain.
> Coolness gives rise to a night moon, bright as if just washed—
> A white beauty without blemish!
>
> The traces of tears on emerald sleeves are proof
> That by the side of the crab apple
> I've wept tens of thousands of them.
> But more recently, alas,
> I pay no attention to my appearance,
> And care nothing for salty or sour.
> Perspiration congeals my fragrance,
> And soaked in darkest green water

My gauze handkerchief time and again wipes my icy mat.
Who is there to care
That I'm a flower goddess, temporarily banished?

The second stanza of this lyric alludes for the first time to Shuangqing's suffering from malarial fever, a theme that will be developed in many of the subsequent passages. These passages are remarkable in Chinese literature for their detailed descriptions of the hardships of peasant life. It must be said, though, that they also can be seen as indications of the intense aesthetic pleasure Qing dynasty literati apparently derived from the minute observation of female suffering:

At the beginning of the Ninth Month, Shuangqing's malaria still had not subsided. At that time people were harvesting the rice, so she forced herself to go out and start working again. In the fields, she bundled the cut stalks, bending down low then lifting them up high, then drying them, then stacking them. Whenever she grew dizzy with exhaustion, she would sit down on a pile of straw, but as soon as she had recovered she would get up again. When one of her women neighbors urged her to stop, she tearfully said: "My husband leaves the house early with his sickle in his belt, walking on the frost with his bare feet and cutting his toes and ankles, in order to slave in the fields. How could I allow myself to sit at ease and watch him! My mother-in-law is old and still takes part in the work! Moreover, how could such a poorly-fated person as myself dare compare herself to those rich and noble girls who fear both wind and sun and avoid dust and grime?" The women neighbors all sadly sympathized with her.

Shuangqing was wearing an old blue gown. She had rolled up her white sleeves, and [her arms] were as fresh and pure as snow. When she was sweeping the threshing floor, her sleeves opened up and a little piece of paper fell out. When Tong Zilin picked it up, he found on it written the line: "The lamplight shadow is hardly discernible, as befits my illness," which was an expression of her unending desperation.

Whenever she went out, she would keep her head bowed and her eyes cast down and would not look at anything. Once when she was gathering firewood to the west of the bridge, she put down her basket below a willow, and tying two branches into a knot, she said: "This is my tree of compassion."

❧❧❧

By the end of the Ninth Month, the weather was clear and mild and the farmers were busy harvesting the rice. On the dikes surrounding the paddies and in the gardens, the bundles of stalks rose up like walls. All the women left their homes to labor in the fields. Shuangqing was suffering from a severe bout of malaria, but although the alternation of cold shivers and high fever made her dizzy and her face looked lifeless and sallow, her mother-in-law became only more demanding, and whenever Shuangqing would pause for a moment, would loudly curse her. By afternoon, she was freezing and shivering all over, but still she forced herself to rise and put on a lined and padded garment. When she held a bundle of grain in her hands, each stalk and ear would be quivering. When she had an attack of fever, she would put on an unlined shirt but her face would be red and she would gasp for breath. Since there was no boiled water to be had, when she was thirsty she had no choice but to go down from the field to the river and scoop up some water to drink. Although her mother-in-law would look at her from the corner of her eyes and criticize her with sarcastic remarks, Shuangqing would only smile, and did not dare say a word. She obeyed her mother-in-law in everything and was quick to supply her needs: she would vie to be the first to do the heaviest work, which she dared not leave to her mother-in-law. Each time she and her mother-in-law brought their bundles to the threshing floor, Shuangqing brought a few hundred bundles for every few tens of her mother-in-law's.

Whether leaning over or looking up, whether quick or slow, there was always grace in her movements. Her thin eyebrows looked as if they had been painted on and her earrings shimmered in the sun like stars. Whenever she used her lapel to wipe away her perspiration, her face became even more radiant. Her mother-in-law was extremely suspicious and would not let any man come near her and speak with her. But Shuangqing was by nature very circumspect; even if you spoke to her, she would not respond . . .

♦♦♦

Shuangqing was working one night on the threshing floor. Her mother-in-law and husband had called it a day and had gone off to take a bath. The moon had darkened and a wind had started to blow and in the distance could be heard the barking of dogs. She was sitting all by herself on the ground bundling straw, and then, when she was finished bundling, stacking it up in piles. Tong Zilin stealthily approached her from behind and suddenly called out her name; this startled Shuangqing and caused her malaria to become even worse. Sometime earlier Anshu [Tong Zilin], convinced that she was a witch, had written a poem of exorcism, and as a joke had tried to subdue her by writing out an exorcistic charm. Now whenever Shuangqing saw Tong Zilin she would smile and say: "Have you come to exorcise me again?"

Shuangqing loved chrysanthemums. She grew wild chrysanthemums in a broken pot so she could look at them while engaged in her activities, whether pounding rice or preparing food. She also wrote the following lyric on the blooming chrysanthemum to the melody of "The God Erlang" [*Erlangshen*]:

The tender branches of willow
Still continue to sway, cutting through the light mist.
In the setting sun,
In the shade of the autumn hills
These flowers to my joy have not yet grown skinny.
They have managed to survive Double Nine with its dreary rains,
And have been able to endure up until this Indian summer.
Who knows if tonight
They'll be covered by frost,
And, abandoned by the butterflies, droop their heads?

What cruel suffering—
The new cold pierces my bones,
As my illness acts up again.
But would I, Shuangqing, be so fickle in my affections
As to discard you after dusk has fallen?
Under the cold moon, I lean sleepless on the balustrade.
It's been several nights
Since I've untied my gown.
It is to no avail
That you flower in this poor household:
To my sorrow I have no wine to offer you in libation.

One day she had cooked some millet [as a meal to take to her husband in the fields]. When she was late [in getting it to him], he became enraged and tried to hit her with his hoe. When Shuangqing returned home, she wrote the following lyric to the melody of "Lonely Phoenix" [*Guluan*]:

The noontime shivers right on schedule:
As soon as I feel the attack coming on,
I put on an extra green blouse.
Too listless to comb yesterday's chignon,
I hastily wrap my head in a gauze scarf.
I've been too busy to wash my white skirt,
And along the seams

Broken threads unravel on either side.
These days my jade-white arms are as coarse as silkworm cocoons,
But my fragrant cheeks still feel soft.

I am ready to endure a lifetime of misery,
And even to be turned into dust and ash.
Be careful before you get married:
That brocade-like longing, that flower-like passion,
Will all be blackened by the smoke of the stove.
In the eastern field he blames me for bringing his meal too late—
A cold tide returns,
No one cares if it was hot when it went out.
Back home I air out the cotton in the sun,
And soon it's time to cook the evening meal.

One evening she was coming home from the threshing field with a broom in one hand and a spade in the other, when she saw a lonely goose that, calling out sadly, landed in a paddy for the night. She stopped and facing west, gazed at it. When her mother-in-law came up to her from behind and scolded her for this, the spade fell to the ground. Shuangqing had never been very brave and was easily startled, and because of her long illness she was even more nervous. Every time she heard an unexpected sound, she would be seized with terror, which is why her mother-in-law tortured her like this. Shuangqing then wrote the following lyric on the lonely goose, to the melody of "Cherishing the Chrysanthemums, Long Version" [*Xi huanghua manci*]:

The distant sky a pure azure,
Evening colors scattering their gauzes:
Torn and cut bits of brightest red.
When you hear her, her sorrow is close by,
When you see her, you fear she is too far.
The lonely goose, a solitary bird,
To whom does she yearn to go?
The white frost has already frozen over the reed-clad banks,
So don't hope for
The sympathy of gull and crane,
Silently you sleep all alone.
Even though to be a phoenix may be fine,
It is far better to be married.

Sad and forlorn—I beg you to be silent,
Find a small beach and half a stream,
Where you can live out your fleeting years.
The rice and corn have just been brought in,
And net and cage are oh-so-cruel.
The dreaming soul is easily startled
By the cold mist in different places.
Your broken heart resembles the emotions of this charmer:
How many entanglements
Can be contained in such a tiny heart?
Not even at night do you feel at ease
Flying on, tired as you are, you mistakenly rest in the open field.

♣♣♣

On the twentieth day of the Tenth Month of the year *kuichou* [1733], I returned from Menghe. Shuangqing was still suffering from malaria, and the physician said: "... Make sure she has no cause to worry." Shuangqing had a weak constitution and a meek disposition, but because she had an accommodating character, she always put on a happy expression even when she was depressed. When she saw a woman neighbor fight and curse her husband, she urged her to desist, whereupon the neighbor started cursing her: "Are you such a dead frog that you have no pride at all?"

One day, when Shuangqing was pounding rice, she was out of breath and she rested with the pestle in her arms. Her husband thought she was being lazy and gave her a push. When she collapsed by the side of the mortar, the pestle [fell on her] and crushed her back. She cried out, but despite her pain, got up and resumed her pounding. While her husband angrily glared at her, she apologized with a smile: "This rice really deserves a beating!"

Once she had an attack of malaria before the gruel had finished cooking. As the fire flared up, the gruel boiled over. When Shuangqing in her panic doused it with water, her mother-in-law started cursing her, grabbed her by her earring, and cried: "Get out!" Her earring had been ripped out and the blood streamed down onto her shoulders. She wept as she tried to hide the wound with her hands, but then her mother-in-law threatened to hit her with a ladle, shouting: "Weep, if you dare!" Shuangqing then cleaned the mortar. When the cooking was done, her husband did not allow her to share the noontime meal because she had let the gruel boil over. Shuangqing had no choice but to remain there next to them pounding the rice with a smile on her face. When that same woman neighbor asked her: "Are you hungry?" she replied in the negative, whereupon the neighbor teased her saying: "Does our frog have some pride after all? How could you have eaten your fill?"

Shuangqing then cleaned out the mortar, and as she leaned over, she said with a sigh: "Heaven, allow me, Shuangqing, to suffer this endless suffering on behalf of all the exceptional beauties of the world, so that beauties may never in all eternity be forced to live as I am living!"

She then asked Tong Zilin to make a copy of the *Scattered Records*, which she wanted to be buried with her when she died, along with the nine quatrains on her handkerchief of white gauze. These she had written on the gauze using rouge. Mengzhan wanted to see them, but she would not allow him to do so until he swore the following oath: "May I in my next life become as poorly fated a beauty as Shuangqing if I do not return this handkerchief!" In this way he obtained the poems and copied them, after which he immediately returned the handkerchief to her. There were stains on the handkerchief, which were most likely the traces of tears. The poems were as follows:

I

I've not yet been allowed to cultivate myself in a secluded little cloister,
My even and untroubled heart of ice resembles a transparent pool.
Don't blame the hungry swallow for being late with loam for the nest,
Who will pity the sickly silkworm for spinning such a thin cocoon?

II

This year no fattening rain fell from the autumn clouds,
So I again pawned my skirt in order to pay the new rent.
As long as there is protective warm padding for my man,
My heart is as sweet as honey—would I dare hate you?

III

I closely stitch his hemp sandals—how often I double the thread!
Tomorrow morning he will climb the western peaks to cut firewood.
Suddenly it began to freeze and last night the wind became fierce—
Don't blow on my husband, direct all your wrath toward me!

IV

The cold kitchen, a low and separate shed, is filled with chilly smoke,
I have to apologize to the phoenix-pair for burning up the *wutong*-wood.

I myself fetch the vegetables from the fields, wash them in freezing
water—
Even though the chrysanthemum suffers pain, she can still endure the frost.

V

My fate like the wing of a cricket is thinner than the lightest silk,
But once upon a time I was as pretty as the neighbors' daughter.
Would my own mother still recognize her child if she saw her?
My face is gaunt with suffering and the joyous bloom is gone.

VI

My little speck of a heart is soaked through with springtime grief,
The occasional dreams I had when I was ill have quickly faded away.
My mirror and hairpins I've sold to pay for the medicine prescribed,
Looking at myself in the stream, I stick willow branches in my hair.

VII

The distant shade of Four Screen Mountain looks like a terrace,
My husband descends it again and again with loads of firewood.
When he returns home I tell him to sleep late in the morning,
And when the sun is high, secretly keep others from waking him.

VIII

The hen and rooster, resting together, poke fun at the phoenix,
Roosting side by side, wing to wing, purple combs touching.
When the lamp gives out and starts to sputter with a greenish glare,
I'd rather lean against the stove than lonely on some balustrade.

IX

I live in a humble cottage, but next to a painted tower;
Fragrant night breezes waft down the inner chamber sorrows.
From open sleeves drop down the lines on autumn leaves
About wilting grasses, setting sun, dreams of distant journeys.

♦♦♦

A neighbor woman said to Shuangqing: "What is the purpose of living if one is
as poorly fated as you?" Shuangqing replied: "This is all a result of my karma
from a former life. If I do not repay [my karmic debts in this life], I will not es-

cape [the same fate] in the next life. Now the men in this village are so incoherent and stupid that they hardly even resemble human beings. Compared to those creatures without feeling, my husband is not so bad. My mother-in-law may be strict, but she adheres to the Wifely Way, and if I serve her diligently, I will have nothing to fear. Why would I dare to be filled with resentment? The only reason people call me poorly fated is because of my good looks and my talents. All those without looks and talents without exception also long for fine husbands—I, Shuangqing, am not the only one! Talent and beauty are the means by which Heaven kills Shuangqing. Now would it not be really foolish to kill myself just to please Heaven!"

The neighbor continued: "Even the wives of gentlemen are allowed to have an occasional affair. So why do you insist on remaining completely loyal to that country hick?" Shuangqing replied: "Even when the poor are forced to live on bran and chaff, they will be ashamed to steal corn and meat. Now even if the distance in taste were as far apart as that between bran and chaff and corn and meat, I still would not care, let alone if the taste were exactly the same. My person would be greatly dishonored and I would be committing a crime deserving of execution. If my person becomes soiled, two families will be dishonored; the mistake of one moment will result in a lifetime of shame; and that one sin will cause everything to come to naught. Although I, Shuangqing, may be foolish, I could never bring myself to do that!"

The neighbor then asked: "But why then do you allow your poems and lyrics to be seen by people outside of your family?" Awash in tears, Shuangqing replied: "This is a case of which it may be said: 'The lotus nature may be present in embryonic form, but the threads [longings] of the lotus root are difficult to kill off.'[13] Brilliant thoughts and beautiful phrases come to me in profusion as soon as my feelings are aroused. I also hope that all the poorly-fated beauties of the world will feel consoled by my example, and that they will understand the *Odes* and practice the rites in order to guard their purity and bring honor to their parents, husband, children, and grandchildren. I too am filled with remorse over this."

✦✦✦

On the twenty-sixth day of the Tenth Month, Shuangqing cut a three-inch-long leaf from a reed, and using powder, on it wrote the following letter to her uncle:

---

13. The lotus is often associated with the Buddha, and the lotus nature therefore refers to the Buddha nature that is in principle present in all living beings. At the same time, the word for lotus (*lian*) has the same pronunciation as one of the words for love (*lian*), with the result that "lotus" is used as a pun for "love."

Although everyone thinks of me as poorly fated, my fate is not so poor. In this world there are quite a few pure maidens in red towers and graceful women by green windows who are lost without a trace in the deep inner quarters. Remembering their joyless nights, in spring they cannot weep. It is the red peach blossom that dies prematurely, while the poor green bamboo endures forever. Of course, they hope that others will sing of them and cry for them, but as their life is surrounded by taboos and prohibitions, they are rarely lauded and praised, and brilliant as their bright pearls may be, they are locked away in the sunless depths of the sea.

Now, when a resentful bird calls out its notes and a desiccated tumble weed displays its colors, they find themselves on the eloquent tongues of great poets, and are engraved on the jade tablets of banished immortals. How much more should this apply to someone [like me], who by nature is as noble as pepper and orchid, but who has been brought as low as dirt and dust!

Those who recite my lyrics on the chrysanthemum and on the lonely goose all claim that I, Shuangqing, am filled with resentment. As I am lacking in virtue, I cannot but feel resentment. But even though I feel resentment, I will never go so far as to hate my husband. Of that I am confident. Long ago, Xiaoqing wanted to not be reborn in Heaven, but instead to be reborn as a double lotus. I want in my next life to be reborn in the body of a man, in order that I may practice the Chan of a broken heart and recite gathas that dissolve the soul. That would be enough for me.

Whenever Shuangqing would write a poem or lyric, she would write it not on paper but on a leaf, using powder rather than ink. The leaves would quickly decay, and because it was not mixed with glue, the powder would easily fall off. She did this because she did not want to leave behind any trace of her writing.

❦❦❦

Once when Shuangqing admonished her husband for his gambling, he became infuriated and locked her up in the cooking shed. Leaning against the firewood, she sat weeping with only a fading lamp for a companion. She then wrote a lyric on the fading lamp:

> Although she's already fading, I forget to blow,
> Who'll trim her when she wants to brighten?
> She shows no flame, looks just like a firefly.
> I hear the cold rain on the earthen steps,
> Dripping, dripping, on into the third watch.
> Completely alone I am restless and sad,

Unable to free myself
From all these many feelings.
The fragrant oil is used up,
But her pure heart is not yet cold,
And she accompanies me, Shuangqing!

Like a tiny star,
Slowly waning, it doesn't move:
Still I hope you will continue to burn,
And perhaps give off some sparks.
You are much better than that wildly swaying
Fisherman's lamp tossed by the winds.
Alas, since the autumn moths have flown away,
My illness has returned—
When will it ever recede?
For a long time we gaze at each other,
Until I finally doze off,
Doze off, only to be startled awake.

❦❦❦

I left Xiaoshan on the eighth day of the Twelfth Month of the eleventh year of the reign period Yongzheng, a *kuichou* year [1733]. I had packed my luggage and was about to head home, since the following year I would travel north [to sit for the metropolitan examinations]. I comforted Shuangqing, saying: "Take good care of yourself! Don't let worry, pain, toil, and suffering worsen your illness and shorten your years! This journey will make the name of Shuangqing famous throughout the world!"

There was a neighbor girl, Han Xi, who was recently married and had come back for a visit to her parental home. She was by nature very intelligent, and whenever she saw Shuangqing drawing water or pounding rice all by herself, she would assist her. And when an attack of malaria would force Shuangqing to sit down on a bench, she would weep on her behalf. She did not know how to read, but she loved Shuangqing's calligraphy, and asked her not only to copy out the *Heart Sutra* for her, but also to teach her how to recite it. When she was about to return to her husband's family, her parents threw her a farewell dinner to which they also invited Shuangqing. When Shuangqing was unable to attend because of an attack of malaria, Han Xi refused to eat anything either and, taking half of her own portion, she wrapped it up, and took it to Shuangqing.

Shuangqing shed tears and wrote the following lyric to the melody of "Groping for Fish" [*Moyu'er*]:

> To our joy the sky has cleared,
> And evening colors appear in the west,
> While the cold hills beyond the mist are a light green.
> The dry spots on the patterned moss support your fragrant shoes,
> Which leave pointed imprints on the purple loam that is still soft.
> Hearing the clamor of voices,
> I quickly come to the unpainted door:
> To no avail I have betrayed your deepest, deepest wish!
> The single thread of mutual love—
> By the light of the new moon I roll a sharp tip,
> And threading together sorrows and regrets,
> I turn all my tears into a string of pearls.
>
> Once darkness has settled in,
> Who will pity me as I lay panting after a bout of fever?
> The wind pierces the small window like an arrow,
> The spring flowers and autumn dew are oh-so-dazzling,
> But a flower like me is never chosen.
> It'll be a while before I see you again,
> As I am told
> That you have already, to my grief, held your farewell party.
> The setting sun stabs my eyes,
> So let me gaze no longer at the horizon,
> A horizon that shows nothing more
> Than a few shreds of cold clouds.

She wrote this in tiny characters using light-colored ink on a red leaf. She also wrote the following lyric to the melody of "Remembering the Flute Player on the Phoenix Terrace" [*Fenghuangtai shang yi chuixiao*]:

> Inch after inch of the palest of clouds,
> Thread upon thread of fading sunlight,
> Now here, now there, now bright, now dull, still not dissolved.
> This breaks the heart—a broken heart,
> Glittering, glowing, swaying, and waning.
> I gaze and gaze at hills and hills and streams and streams,
> As you go on and on,
> Disappearing, disappearing, farther and farther away.

From this day on
This painful pain and grievous grief
Will always remain as it is this night.

Spring has gone away—
I ask Heaven about it but Heaven is deaf.
Look at this frail, oh-so-frail Shuangqing,
Tossed about by the winds, without support:
Who will I see, who will be seen,
Who will be wounded by tender flowers?
Who hopes for happy joy or joyous happiness?
Using white powder I secretly
Write and scribble, draw and paint.
Who cares about
Life after life, age after age,
Night after night, day after day?

❦❦❦

I had planned to return to Guazhu on Tao Lake on the tenth, but did not leave because of heavy rain. On the night of the eleventh, I was discussing my *Scattered Records* with Yuhan. Stroking the manuscript, I said: "How moving are these many affairs in heaven and on earth! But those that love its style may doubt its veracity, and those who adhere to Principle may well find fault with my words. But since I had no particular purpose in writing this, I would feel no remorse even if I burned it." Yuhan chimed in saying: "Shuangqing is an exceptional creature; I have never seen or read about such a woman whether from the past or present. You should simply be a little more reserved." I replied: "Earlier, when I was in Yangzhou, I burned ten scrolls of old drafts at the house of Xu Shufeng. Why don't I also burn the *Scattered Records of Xi and Qing*! Man's life passes like a flash, even our spiritual intelligence will not be preserved and will eventually disappear. So why should words and writings be worth caring for?"

When Shuangqing heard about this, she wrote me the following letter:

When I was fifteen, my uncle once said: "The Zhounan and Shaonan [sections of the *Book of Odes*] contain many romantic works, while the Zheng and Wei [sections] are filled with erotic poems. When Confucius did not throw them out, none of his seventy disciples protested. If only I had been a pupil of Confucius' [I would have corrected the Master]!"[14] I then said [to my uncle]: "You would only have been [good enough to be] a student of Zai Yu, and study with him how to sleep during the daytime!"[15]

He also said: "The story of the man [in the *Mencius*] who begged at the graves [but bragged to his wife and concubine about his high connections] is much too painful a case, and the fable of the man stealing a chicken [also in the *Mencius*] is a tale of fantasy. If I had been Mencius' pupil, I would have demanded that he throw them out." I then said: "Even if you'd been the pupil of Chen Zhongzi, I'm afraid you would've been unable to even learn to crawl![16] And you would like to have been a fellow student of [Mencius' best-known disciples] Wan Zhang and Gongsun Chou?!"

The Great Way has no directions and the great teaching knows no limits. When this kind of village schoolteacher expounds the *True Mean* [*Zhongyong*], he does nothing but shower the page with his spittle, the foam from his mouth soaking his beard. He considers himself to be Zi Si's most meritorious servant and Zhu Xi's most authoritative friend, but the eyes of his eight or nine ignorant pupils just glaze over and they fall asleep.[17] Whenever I would see this, I would feel scorn for how he deceived the deaf and dazzled the blind.

The Immortal Lad Who Enjoys the Moon [Yuhan] would purportedly see ghosts in broad daylight. It is not my way of acting to be pure in words but sinful in behavior, to be negligent in my language and like a windlass in my actions. If this book would be better consigned to flames, then I, Shuangqing, should never have opened my mouth. A butterfly does not speak and yet desires the flowers, a maggot does not speak and yet is addicted to dung. Those who in this world deceive others by not speaking are

---

14. The *Book of Odes* was traditionally believed to have been edited by Confucius, who made a selection of three hundred poems from the three thousand at his disposal. Shuangqing ridicules her uncle for being a typical narrow-minded neo-Confucian scholar who even wants to correct Confucius himself!

15. Zai Yu was one of Confucius' students; he once was found napping during the daytime.

16. Chen Zhongzi lived in the ancient state of Qi. When the king of Chu, learning of his wisdom, invited him to his court, Chen Zhongzi followed the advice of his wife and fled. Later he made a living as a gardener.

17. The *True Mean*, attributed to Zi Si, formed together with the *Analects*, the *Mencius*, and the *Great Learning* (*Daxue*) the Four Books. The Four Books had been popularized by the great synthesizer of neo-Confucianism Zhu Xi (1130–1200) as the summation of wisdom, and formed the core of the educational curriculum in Ming and Qing times.

butterflies when they encounter fragrance but turn to maggots as soon as they encounter dung. Whenever I, Shuangqing, see these [kinds of] people, my malaria flares up!

Now Shuangqing was like a dream. What one encounters in a dream is all topsy-turvy and confused. But when one wakes up and thinks about it, there is no need to feel any remorse. Whether people know me for my true worth or condemn me does not entirely hinge on this.

Reading the above passage one cannot escape the impression that Shi Zhenlin had originally intended to end his description of Shuangqing here. He characterizes her as a dream apparition and considers the option of destroying his writings about her, but takes heart after reading Shuangqing's letter, which represents an undisguised attack on the narrow-minded learning of the Way and the heavy-handed ritualism of his day. But apparently the image of Shuangqing Shi Zhenlin had created was so attractive that he could not resist returning to her a few more times before bringing his *Scattered Records of Xi and Qing* to a close:

I left Xiaoshan in the year *kuichou* [1733]. In the summer of the year *jiayin* [1734] I visited Menghe, and in the spring of the year *yimao* [1735] I stayed in Lanling, where I acquired even more detailed information regarding Shuangqing.

The neighbors praised her filiality. Although her husband became increasingly violent, she would adroitly accommodate herself to his moods and never dared to go against him. She engaged in physical labor all year long. She had locked away her tattered books and old brushes in a broken basket, and didn't dare even take a peek at them—although she didn't have any leisure time to do so anyway. Once during First Night [of the New Year] she had the *Surangama Sutra* [*Lengyan Sutra*] in her hands and was reciting it by the light of the stove lamp. When her mother-in-law returned home from viewing the lanterns, she grabbed the book and cursed her, saying: "Half a book of rotten paper! Paste it on the face of a student and he'll die of poverty! Blockhead, are you thinking of taking the examination for women?!" And once when she was rinsing off her inkstone, her husband spotted her and angrily said: "As soon as you can steal away, you play around with that lump of clay! The soot from the cooking pot can at least be used for fertilizer!"

Although Shuangqing's calligraphy was noble and elegant, she did not use it for anything except keeping the daily accounts of her husband's tofu and wine on scrap paper. Although her husband couldn't read, he would stand next to her and arrogantly scold her: "This character is upside down," he would say, to which she would reply with a smile: "No, it isn't."

She wrote the following lyric on the plum blossoms:

> I smile at my own listlessness—
> After spending so much time on springtime chores,
> I go and inspect the tips of the branches:
> The wasted jade-white faces—
> On whose account have they been multiplied?
> Ever since I fell ill, my fate is to despise blossoms.
> In the First Month and the Last clothes have to be washed,
> But spring's waves are so cold—
> I dread them splashing my white arms!
> In the hard easterly breeze
> These blossoms spread their cold fragrance to no avail—
> The new moon but a narrow sickle.
>
> Overcome by passion, the whole sky filled with falling powder:
> Only another burden for me, Shuangqing,
> As in my dream, I pluck them in vain.
> I recall the souls of dead butterflies,
> Wipe away the tears of orioles,
> And late at night secretly recite the *Surangama*.
> I write the finest lines of springtime grief,
> Its pain and suffering—
> Life and death equally sweet.
> I pray for a year of flowers,
> Bow my head before Guanyin,
> And pull out every one of the divination slips.

She also wrote the following lyric, using the word "spring" in almost every line, on taking food to her husband plowing the fields:

> Springtime sun on purple paths—
> A springtime scarf around my head,
> As I take food to the springtime plowman.
> The small plum trees are springtime skinny,
> The fine grasses are springtime brilliant,
> As spring bursts out at every step on the springtime fields.
> I remember that year when the fine spring taught springtime passion

> To the springtime swallows,
> But now this year
> Springtime letters and springtime tears
> Have all turned into springtime ice.
>
> I love spring, I hate spring, all these many springs!
> The endless expanse of springtime mist
> Has locked in the springtime oriole.
> What was given to springtime me
> I now pass on to springtime you,
> So is it me or is it you, that radiance of spring?
> I count the heads of spring, the tails of spring,
> But cannot count the springtime dreams and springtime awakenings.
> Because of some spring demon
> I suffer springtime illness all through spring:
> Spring's ruining me, Shuangqing!

These two lyrics both were written to the melody of "Spring Descends from Heaven" [*Chun cong tianchang lai*].

In the first month of summer, the wild roses were blooming on the banks. You had only to touch their light reds or pale whites with your hand, and the rich fragrance would last all day. Shuangqing was out harvesting wheat and, afraid that the [rose petals] might fall, gathered up an apronful of them. Back home, she sat down by the earthen window and cut characters out of the petals, which she then scattered on her pillow and mat, and, surrounded by flowers, dozed off. When she swept, she put some petals in the water she used to sprinkle the floor, and in front of the bed, she brushed her shoes and then tread slowly on the flowers. Surrounded by flowers, she simultaneously laughed and cried. Her husband angrily said: "People who destroy flowers will be ugly in their next life. Why do you persist in destroying flowers since you are already so ugly?"

Shuangqing loved cleanliness. Even though she lived between dust and dirt, she kept her chignon spotlessly pure. But her husband was such a filthy swine that his stench made you want to throw up. His neck was covered with so much grime you could roll it into balls. Whenever Shuangqing urged him to take a bath, he would fly into a rage, and so she did not dare say another word.

Shuangqing asked Zhang Shilin to paint her an image of the White-Robed Mahasattva [Guanyin]. She made her offerings of pure water and at night silently worshipped her. Her husband would curse her saying: "Why do you need to pray for good fortune? Isn't it happiness enough that you were able to marry me?" Even though Shuangqing had recovered from her malaria, she patiently let him rant and rave. But her energy grew less by the day and she was reduced to a bag of bones. To her neighbor Han Xi she once said: "Everything tastes bitter to me. And when I eat something sweet, it is even worse. Why?"

And with this plaintive "Why?" Shuangqing disappears from the pages of Shi Zhenlin's *Scattered Records of Xi and Qing*. Later admirers provided Shuangqing with the surname He and collected all the poems, lyrics, and letters of Shuangqing contained in the *Scattered Records of Xi and Qing* and published them as a separate collection, as if she were not a fictional creation but a real woman of flesh and blood. As time went by, Shuangqing's reputation continued to grow, and in the nineteenth century we find a male critic praising her as follows:

The lyrics of Shuangqing resemble the whispering chatter of little girls as they discuss the everyday details of their life. In meticulous detail and noting down every fact, she describes both the things she has seen or heard, as well as those that have come up in her mind. Although the author herself does not presume that her works are lyrics, and her readers also forget that they are lyrics, the feelings [they express] are true and their words are apt—direct successors to the *Book of Odes*. Hers is a heavenly sound, an extraordinary talent! The poverty she experienced is without precedent among the talented lady poets of the past. Whenever I recite one of her lyrics, before I know it, I find myself awash in tears.

Yet another male critic of the final decades of the Qing dynasty goes so far as to state:

Her lyrics represent the acme of both purity and serenity. They are like olives and betel nuts: the more slowly they are savored, the more distinctive their taste becomes . . .

12 · Reality

In his *Scattered Records of Xi and Qing*, Shi Zhenlin himself admits that his picture of Shuangqing is not very realistic: "Those who doubt the existence of Shuangqing all say she could not exist: although she is a peasant woman, she not only knows how to read but also how to write, and not only does she know how to write, but she is also skilled in each genre." The truth is that the overwhelming majority of peasant women in eighteenth-century China were illiterate. This does not automatically imply that these women had no literary life at all. Women were an important audience of the rich tradition of oral and performative literature of imperial China, and some of them also played even more active roles as performers and composers. But authentic oral literature is an evanescent genre: once the performance is over, nothing is left behind. For this reason, it is almost impossible at this remove in time to paint a clear picture of women's participation in oral and performative traditions during the premodern period.

Although the great social and cultural changes of the twentieth century do not allow us to project information gleaned from the last few decades onto the society of the nineteenth century and earlier, we do know that in certain parts of China there existed oral traditions, often in the form of wedding and funeral laments, that were exclusively practiced by women. We have descriptions of such traditions for places as far apart as the New Territories in Hong Kong and Nanhui outside Shanghai. In these areas the traditions survived into the second half of the twentieth century, but have since disappeared as living traditions. Wedding laments appear to have been an especially important genre, as they allowed a bride to voice—in a ritually recognized way—her affection for her family members on the eve of her departure from home, as well as her ambivalent feelings about her unpredictable future and her resentment against all those who had conspired to make her leave her native village. In so doing, a bride was not expected to mince her words, and she would even be allowed to heap curses on the matchmaker, the groom and his family, and even on her own parents for "selling" her into a certain "death." In the words of the Australian sinologist Anne McLaren, "no other group in China besides peasant women appears to have been given a generic license, as it were, for this uninhibited outpouring of anger, anxiety, and grief."

In a Script of Their Own

There is one exceptional case that can provide us a more immediate glimpse into a specifically female literary tradition from the countryside. Until quite recently, there were, in a few villages of Jiangyong district in southernmost Hunan province, peasant women who made use of their own script, called "women's script" (*nüshu*), to record their ballads and songs. Some of these ballads and songs were their own compositions, while others (especially the longer narrative texts) were transcriptions of more well-known narratives. But even in the latter case, it is interesting to consider which of these narratives the women of Jiangyong chose to record in women's script and what changes they introduced into the stories when they did so.

Women's script is, in essence, a syllabic transcription of the local Jiangyong dialect. Scholars have hotly debated the origins of this women's script, and some have even tried to trace it back to characters inscribed on oracle bones of the late second millennium BCE, or even earlier. It is more likely, however, that women's script evolved from the regular Chinese script by means of a process of progressive simplification, until a single symbol remained for each of the syllables in the local dialect. Women's script may not even have evolved until as late as the eighteenth century, and was apparently used only in a few villages in Jiangyong district, where it was passed on from one generation of women to the next. It began to disappear in the twentieth century when girls started to attend school like their brothers and learned to read and write traditional Chinese characters.

There are various local legends on the origin of women's script. One such legend credits its invention to a local girl who was taken into the imperial harem, and wishing to inform her family of her loneliness and despair without being found out by her keepers, penned her complaints in a script that only made sense when pronounced in the local dialect. Another legend ascribes its invention to a local girl of exceptional qualities who simply wanted to have a reliable means of getting in touch with her women friends. Local stories also link women's script to a temple in Jiangyong dedicated to two goddesses where women would deposit their written prayers and laments.

Women's script was never a secret script, however. While some of the texts written in women's script, such as letters exchanged between adolescent girls, were not meant to be shown to men, the majority of texts were actually recited in public at weddings and other sorts of festivals. Despite the fact that women's script ballads were performed in public, in the early 1950s efforts were made to ban women's script because it was suspected of being a secret code, and in the following decade because it was regarded as a shameful reminder of China's feudal past. As a result, by the early 1980s there were only a few elderly women still around who were able to read and write women's script. Many of the texts in women's script available today were copied out from memory by these few women—in particular, by two women named Gao Yinxian and Yi Nianhua. Irrespective of topic and purpose, practically all the texts written in women's script are composed in rhyming lines of seven syllables each, and the language of the texts is often quite formulaic.

Formalized Friendship

Some of the local customs of Jiangyong are reflected in the writings in women's script. One such custom, found in other areas of traditional China as well, was the formalized and intense friendship between unmarried girls who became "sworn sisters."

A Sworn Sisters Song of the Twelve Months of the Year
(Sung by Wu Longyu from Heyuan and edited by Zhou
Shuoyi on the basis of a tape recording)[1]

New Year's Day of the First Month is a fine festival,
But if the two of us are not together, I can feel no joy.
When the Second Month arrives, the trees all blossom,
When the trees all turn green, their blossoms are fragrant.
 In the Third Month, the color of the plums begins to change,
As they continue to change, you show up and we are together!
The Fourth Month is spring's busiest time with lots of work to do,
Please come for the End of Spring so we can do something together.
 In the Fifth Month the weather is hot, hotter than flames,
As you sit on the upper floor embroidering colors.
The long days of the Sixth Month are a time to have fun—
Should not a pair of mandarin ducks be brought together?
 In the Seventh Month all of us stop doing needlework,
So I cannot be together with you to do my stitching.
In the Eighth Month we receive a guest in the main hall,
Seeing you upstairs, my eyes become flooded with tears.
 In the Ninth Month we all together start spinning thread,
When I think of my situation, I can't bear to mention it.
In the Tenth Month storm and frost strip the trees bare,
How pitiful the two of us, who cannot share our joy!
 In the Eleventh Month all the geese are at heaven's end,
But I have no idea where you, my girl, could possibly be.
In the Twelfth Month we have to clean up at year's end,
And then there's next year for which we have to prepare.

Our Mutual Love Will Not Be Broken
(Written down by Gao Yinxian)

I went to the garden to pick spring vegetables,
Beyond the wall they've begun harvesting the rice.
The two of us fought off the sadness of returning,
As all around on the street people watched us.
 Our mutual love will not be broken!

---

1. Zhou Shuoyi is a local cultural worker in Jiangyong district who has been very
important in preserving "women's script" documents.

The two of us were sitting on the upper floor,
Threading our needles and embroidering colors.
Not caring for what other people were saying,
We embroidered flowers and chatted together.

We embroidered a pair of golden roosters roosting on a tower,
We embroidered pairs of birds of all kinds soaring up to heaven.
We embroidered a pair of yellow dragons leaving their caves,
Yellow dragons leaving their caves and crossing the oceans.
 We embroidered a pair of carps living in the depths of the sea,
Couples of them, pair upon pair, each of them inseparable!
Our mutual love will never be wrenched apart,
It will last forever, and will never come to an end.

I write you a letter, record it on paper,
And in my words speak my mind freely.
The two of us enjoyed a wonderful time,
Like immortals playing a game of go.
 The two of us were sitting on the upper floor,
Threading our needles, facing one another.
Your father and mother were really pleased
That the two of us got along so well.
 Whatever the opinions of passers-by may be,
The birds soar up high into the clouds!
You are in all respects an honorable girl,
Even though at times you are misjudged.
 In good friendship we were sitting upstairs,
Everything proper, each and every thing!
In all respects, there was nothing amiss,
Your good name will be spread all around.
 You did your hair and I held up your mirror,
Which mirrored you, a pair against a pair.
The two of us would never sit apart,
The room upstairs was open on all sides.
 Let people have their ignorant opinions,
We are a couple and, like eyebrows, a pair!

This period of intense adolescent friendship was often regarded as the happiest time in a girl's life. Marriage, however, often spelled the end of this happiness.

The Dog Barked Out Front: A Guest Had Arrived (Written down by Yi Nianhua)

We had finished our meal, / and I had cleared the table,
When the dog barked out front: a guest had arrived.
When I went to the gate to have a look for myself,
I saw that it was my sister who had come to see us.
 With my left hand, I took my sister's umbrella from her,
With my right hand, I took my sister's basket from her.
In the main room there was a red-lacquered bench;
I bade my sister sit down as I poured her a cup of tea.
 Even after drinking one cup, she didn't open her mouth,
Even after drinking two cups, she still said not a word.
"Is it because my mother has done you some wrong,
Or is there some misunderstanding between us two?"
 "It is not because your mother has done me wrong,
It is not because of a misunderstanding between us two.
It is because *his* family has no decency at all,
And on the fifteenth of the Eighth Month will fetch me as bride.
 His family is much too hasty in fetching me to be his bride,
Because they tear apart this couple of fine mandarin ducks!"
 "This is of no importance! / Don't get upset!
We'll buy paper money and candles and go to the temple,
Where we'll pray to the gods till our wish is granted:
That every single one in his family be doomed to die!
 When old and young, high and low have all died,
Then the two of us can be together forever more!"

Getting Married

Despite the possibility suggested in the above song, in reality the girls of Jiangyong probably expected that they would all end up getting married, which would mean leaving the village where they had grown up and starting a completely new life in another village. Among the writings in women's script one finds many poems meant to be sung or recited by the bride when the time came to say goodbye to all of her relatives, as well as to all of the familiar objects in her old home. The bride would then be escorted to her husband's home where the wedding ceremony would be performed. On the second day after the wedding ceremony (referred to as "the Third Day" below), the bride would receive so-called "Third Day Letters" from her friends and relatives. In these letters, friends would complain bitterly about their forced separation, while relatives would urge the bride to serve her parents-in-law well and to do whatever necessary to lessen their displeasure over her meager dowry. But in the end, in these letters friends and relatives alike concur that the best thing the bride can do is resign herself to her new situation, not only because that is the way things have been since ancient times, but also because the institution of marriage was established by no less an authority than the emperor or, in some cases, even the Jade Emperor himself.

With a Brush Made of Goat's Hair, I Write a Letter to You in Your Noble Mansion
(Written down by Yi Nianhua)

I take in my hand a brush made out of goat's hair,
And write a letter to you in your noble mansion.
I see, my girl, that the Third Day has arrived,
So with this letter, I inform you that we should meet.
 When the day before yesterday we hurriedly saw you off,
Being separated from you was a knife through my heart.
I turned around and went home, and I wept for grief—
Never again to be together and comb each other's hair!
 At night I lit a lamp and went to the upstairs room:
I sat in the upstairs room, my eyes flooded with tears.
I resented your parents for all the pressure they applied,
For forcing us mandarin ducks to go our separate ways.
 The others in their upstairs rooms are all in couples,
But here in my upstairs room, I am alone and lonely.
And I did not feel like filling up the lamp with oil,
And as my eyes closed, the lamp gave out too.
 So I sat till the fifth watch, in the still of the night,
When I heard a pair of geese calling out several times.
I imagined that one of the geese had lost her mate,
And that her situation was very much like mine.
 As I sat alone in my empty room, my heart would not be still,

It is hard to accept that you have gone your separate way.
During all twelve hours of the day you are on my mind,
I could not sleep the entire night, tears flooded my eyes.
 Since you abandoned this cold room I'm like a lonely bird,
And as I sit here in this room, I feel alone and empty:
My only hope, my friend, is that you still remember me,
And that you think of your soulmate, wrenched apart.
 I hope that when you come home, we will sit together,
Just as of old, just as before, the two of us together.
When we were little we became friends, over ten years ago,
And never has a cross word been exchanged between us.
 United by deepest friendship we were truly inseparable,
And I always revealed to you all the secrets in my heart.
So I ask you, my girl, do you feel the same sorrow,
And do you find it impossible, like me, to bare your heart?
 After being friends for three years, we are truly like sisters,
We may be compared to children born of the same mother.
From childhood we have been friends and will be to the end—
Like the river that flows forever, like the deep sea!
 Today I would also like to offer you my congratulations,
Please convey my best wishes to your parents-in-law.
Mandarin ducks share the same room, a match made in Heaven,
A dragon is paired to a phoenix, for a full sixty springtimes!
 Please take good care of yourself in your noble mansion,
Rise higher with every step, do better than all the others!
I hope your parents-in-law will soon give you a leave,
As I hope that my friend will soon come back home!

With a Writing Brush I Write These Words on a Paper Fan, Congratulating Your In-laws Whose Entire House Is [Decked in] Red
(Collected and edited by Zhou Shuoyi)

With a writing brush I write these words on a paper fan:
Congratulations to your in-laws whose entire house is red.
I am your eldest brother's wife and now write you this letter,
Since I see that the Third Day of the bride has arrived.
 The day before yesterday, when we saw you off, your heart was in
    turmoil,

And your eyes were flooded with tears as you gazed back toward home.
You must truly have found it difficult to leave all of that behind,
From the day you were born, you were the apple of your parents' eyes.
 In your dealings with the wives of your brothers you were always kind,
And toward your father and mother you were filled with filial piety.
Your hands would always find some useful work to do,
You can read and write and know the rites: you are the finest.
 You and I have been together now for almost five years,
And never once has a cross word been exchanged between us.
But now is the time for you to shine as brightly as the red sun,
And, alas, it is also the time when your girlhood days must end.
 Don't say that this separation is causing you grief,
Since ancient times girls have left their villages, that's how it is.
Fortunately, your parents-in-law are excellent people,
And as a couple, you are like the golden rooster and phoenix.
 Once you arrive there, you must be quiet and docile,
And serve your parents-in-law according to the rites.
Your brother and sister-in-law still remain here at home,
So do not worry that your mother will be lonely.
 And explain once again to your parents-in-law
That if the dowry your parents have provided is small,
It is because the family has fallen on hard times,
So the ritual gifts may not be as fine as those of others.
 You have arrived at their noble mansion at a young age,
And there are still many things we have to teach you.
Once the wedding guests at your noble mansion have departed,
They'll soon allow you to come home for a day or two.

A Third Day Letter to Her Daughter by the Wife of Wang Xianzhi in Baishui, Who Had Been Married Off by Her Husband to a Second Man
(Written down by Yi Nianhua)

I take up my brush and write a letter to your noble mansion,
And send it to the parents-in-law of your fine family there.
In a noble mansion, people understand rites and righteousness,
So I hope that all of you will listen to what I have to say.
 When I was nine years of age, my marriage was settled,
And it was decided that I would marry Wang Xianzhi.

After the engagement, ten years quickly passed by:
"Red as a flower, green as a willow," I entered his home as a bride.
 After I had been there for three years, going on four,
I gave birth to a daughter, so I was worth my money.
The entire family came together and was filled with joy,
Like immortals celebrating a festival in their grotto-heaven.
 I was like a red plum tree, its heavy branches hanging down,
Each and every branch in bloom, filling the house with red,
But the branches were broken by a witchlike storm:
We were wrenched apart by a witchlike monster.
 I've learned the truth of that witchlike monster Gui'e:[2]
There are many people who call each other "sister,"
But that witchlike monster Gui'e commits crime after crime,
She killed her father with a knife and married me off!
 Now that my own daughter has grown up to be an adult,
She does not remember how I bore her and cared for her.
In a single day she would drink three pints of my milk,
In three days' time she would drink nine pints of my milk.
 A mother's milk is not endless like the waters of the Yangzi,
It is better to compare my milk to the sap of a tree.
Who would have guessed my daughter would be so unkind,
And not recognize her mother once she had grown up?
 My daughter has left the village and gone to another mansion,
While I live in the house of another, my heart not at peace.
I wanted to return home for my daughter's wedding,
But that witchlike monster Gui'e played the bride's mother.
 I, your own mother, saw you off at the back of the crowd,
I wept till my heart was pained and my tears poured down.
I wept for my beautiful daughter—as if cut by a knife:
She discards her own mother and chooses someone else.
 I wept for my darling daughter till my heart broke,
But we were wrenched apart by that enemy of mine.
I nurtured my daughter as if she were a precious pearl,
And at every moment I worried about her in my heart.
 But, my girl, your father has a nature that is evil,
He wed that witchlike monster and married me off to another.
I did not want to give up my darling daughter and wept my heart out,

---

2. Gui'e apparently is the name of the second wife.

But they pressured me so much I had to leave my darling daughter!
It was he who married me off and made me go away,
He wouldn't let me take you along to that other village.
It is not that your mother left you behind, my daughter,
So that once grown, you would forget what I did for you.

Jiangyong is one of several places in southern China where the practice of "delayed-transferral" marriage was common. Following the wedding, the young bride would often return for long stretches of time to her mother's home (where her husband could visit her), only to take up permanent residence at her husband's place after she had become pregnant with her first child.

Going to My Mother's Place in the Burning Heat of the Sixth Month
(Written down by Yi Nianhua)

In the Sixth Month it's burning hot, burning like flames,
I take a fan in my hands and place it over my heart.
But how can that fan dissolve the flames in my heart?
Living here in this strange family I do not feel at peace.
 In an entire month he came to me not even seven times,
And I would never dare just go to him for nothing at all.
My mother accompanied me, Jintuo, for a mile or two,
And I still remember how long that journey was.
 I plucked a sprig of thorn brush, a sprig of pomegranate,
A sprig of thorn brush on my journey back home.
Before, at my mother's place, we had so much fun,
But now my mother is all alone in her empty room.
 In the first watch, I light a lamp and kneel in prayer:
Now I am serving the parents of another household!
In the second watch, I am thinking of my loneliness,
To have mistakenly been born a woman pains my heart!
 I sleep till the third watch, when everyone is still asleep,
It really pains my heart to think of my mother.
Just as I am about to fall asleep in the fourth watch,
I see the parents who gave me life there before me.
 When I wake up with a start, it turns out to be a dream—
My mother is in the east, and I am in the west.
I sleep till the fifth watch when the clear dawn breaks,

There is nothing to be done but get up out of bed.
When I have gotten up and finished my chores,
I formally ask my mother-in-law for permission to go back.
Father and son, neither of the two will consent,
But I insist on going back to see how my mother fares.
My mother raised me, her daughter, as a widow,
Now she has married me off, she's bound to grieve.
In my left hand I take my cool black parasol,
In my right hand I take it—and so I go home.
When I get halfway there, I'm overcome by emotion,
Weeping as I walk, I rush toward my mother.
My mother cries out: "My darling daughter Jintuo,
It must be that over there, you are worried and grieved:
When you left, your cheeks were the color of peach blossom petals,
Now that you return, they are as yellow as chrysanthemum flowers.
Your parents-in-law over there must really hate you,
In truth, there may be a Heaven but it is missing a sun!"
My mother comforts me and says to me: "Jintuo,
A woman can only acquire a family with patience.
Let's hope that High Heaven will protect you,
And soon send a darling son to your noble house!"

Autobiographical Ballads

One of the most intriguing types of women's script literature are the
autobiographical ballads. These ballads as a rule dwell almost exclusively
on the sufferings of the author; if there is any mention at all of moments
of happiness, it only serves to further emphasize the suffering that immediately follows. The prevalence of this type of text may well have
something to do with the practice of leaving a written list of one's heart-
aches and woes in the local temple of the two goddesses. One can also
imagine that the recitation of these texts may have been intended to publicly shame derelict relatives. In quite a number of these texts, a mother
chastises her son for neglecting her in favor of his wife.

Her Own Story by He Huanshu from Baishui
(Written down by Yi Nianhua)

I write this letter myself on a paper fan,
The misery of mother and daughter is found on this fan.

Alas, when my father departed from this world,
He left us, mother and daughter behind, such a sorry fate!
 The two of us, mother and daughter, have had no luck,
Our fate worse than that of others, it makes one's heart break:
Whereas others sit at ease in their embroidery rooms,
We must suffer a thousand kinds of hardship and cold.
 We rise at the crack of dawn and are busy till dark,
Washing clothes and starching skirts with no one to help.
We also have to go into the hills to cut our firewood,
And there is work in the fields that also has to be done.
 During the famine of the Sixth Month, we usually go hungry,[3]
During the freezing days of frost and snow, we sleep on straw.
We don't have the money to make ourselves padded clothes,
And we don't make any money from raising pigs or chickens.
 I am my mother's only child, I have no brothers at all,
So on whom can she rely when she grows old?
All the people around feel pity for us,
They pity us for being unable to help ourselves.
 If others can't help themselves, they have one problem,
But when we can't help ourselves, we have a hundred headaches.
I don't know what we may have done in some former life,
That the two of us should now have to suffer like this.
 Sitting here in my upstairs room, I let out a heavy sigh,
Hoping that Heaven will pity us and send away the black clouds.
I hope that the black clouds will all be blown away
And the sun will come out in the east showing its light.
 Who could have known I would sit before the gate till dark,
I don't see my mother—where could she be?
I only see the hundred birds roosting in the trees,
But still I cannot see any sign of my mother.
 From the day my mother, alas, gave birth to me,
I have not experienced a single moment of joy.
I pray to High Heaven to send down a terrible rain,
And drown us both, mother and daughter, in its floods!

---

3. By the Sixth Month the new crops will not yet have been harvested but the old harvest will have been depleted.

I Have Been a Widow Since the Age of Twenty-Eight and My Daughter-in-Law is Unfilial
(Written down by Yi Nianhua)

As I sit here in my empty room, I am thinking
That I will narrate my misery and make it known to all.
When I had been married for three years, going on four,
I gave birth to a daughter and we were greatly pleased.
 My husband and I had a good understanding,
Even though life was bitter, the water tasted sweet.
After I had been there for five years, going on six,
I gave birth to a darling boy, and my heart was pleased.
 Husband and wife lived together for a full eight years,
Not even a single cross word was exchanged between us.
We had one son and one daughter, so we were pleased,
And this family of ours was untroubled by cares.
 Who'd have known that Heaven would withdraw its love,
And that my husband would come down with an illness?
We were just poor folks without any money at hand,
And each day his condition grew worse and worse.
 After falling ill he was bedridden for several months,
His illness worsened and he left this world for the shades.
He left behind a son and a daughter, both of them still small,
I too was still very young when I became a widow.
 But my father and mother cruelly refused to take me back in,
The three of us in that empty house—on whom to rely?
The man who'd fathered them wasn't there to raise them,
How long would I, a widow, be able to raise them?
 I got up at the break of dawn and wept until dark,
I could not sleep the entire night, but nobody knew.
I wrote a letter to be taken to the prefecture,
Imploring my younger brother to take pity on me.
 But the road was too long and it didn't work out,
And my brother had no idea of my thousand miseries.
 One bowl and two chopsticks—no deathbed instructions,
We could not stay on in the house where we lived.
 There was no one to take care of the work in the fields,
I passed every moment of the time weeping for sorrow—
If it weren't for the fact that he lived much too far away,

My brother would have looked after us and tilled the fields.
 When our daughter reached the age of twelve,
She too passed away and departed this world.
Given that I had no way at all to vent my frustration,
I was so frustrated that in that moment I almost died.
 I also considered the possibility of finding a husband,
But then my darling son, alas, would have no one to rely on.
When I went to bed at night, straw served as my blanket,
When I got up in the morning, there was no rice for breakfast.
 I borrowed a few ounces of rice that I would nibble at a little.
And pretending to be happy, I would pass the days in this way.
But I pulled my darling son through and we scraped by:
He grew up to be a man who can fend for himself!
 Whether above or below, I had no one to rely on,
And neither did I have any full brothers.
Considering my choices, I had no other way out
But to hire myself out to hull grain for others.
 They also paid me for doing needlework,
And despite all the hardship I managed to raise my boy.
Every day I would get up to slave for others once more,
It was under black clouds like these that I passed my years.
 With nothing to rely on but High Heaven's compassion—
No protective star kept the three of us from suffering.
When my husband died my son was only two,
Since the age of twenty-eight, I have lived a widow's life.
 After my husband's death, when my son was twelve,
He earned a living by herding the water buffalo of others;
On freezing cold and snowy days, it was really hard to survive,
Suffering to the limit that freezing cold, he slept in the snow.
 He had no clothes to cover himself with—like freezing water,
On his bed he had no blanket, the suffering was too much to bear!
Suffering starvation and cold I raised my son,
But was worried that my boy would not find a wife.
 So when my son was eighteen years of age,
I wanted my boy to have a marriage partner.
I searched far and wide for a sensible girl,
Who would marry and be the wife of my son.
 Aunts and uncles and relatives all helped out,
Willing to assist me to arrange the engagement.

One year after the engagement, going on two,
"Red as a flower, green as a willow," she became a bride!
 Everyone told me that now my bad times were over,
That I deserved credit as a widow for getting him a wife.
So I was happy when he had married that bride,
And I reckoned that she and I would be always together.
 For the first two years, everything was fine,
But then some busybody set her up against me,
Set her up against me, and so she turned me out,
Turned me out of the house to live on my own.
 At no feast or festival is there a share for me,
 I just lift up my head and I peek inside:
They have dishes of meat, but nothing for me,
And my boy doesn't dare come look for his mother.
 Each day they eat white rice at all three meals,
While I have to go to others to beg for some soup.
Those who take pity on me will give me a little,
But others will say: "You have your own darling son!"
 When at night I go to bed, I weep through the night,
When will I weep myself to death, this old, old body?
At the end of this year, I'll be sixty-six years old,
I'll make seventy if I put off dying another four years.

Unfortunately the length of these autobiographical ballads, some of which go into considerable detail about the author's adventures and misadventures, makes it impossible to include more examples of these extremely interesting texts here.

The Sorrows of Pregnancy and Motherhood

Yet another type of women's script texts are those that have been transcribed from sources originally written in traditional Chinese characters, and that very clearly reflect the concerns of their female audience. First of all, there is a group of texts that are designed to mentally prepare the young bride for her future life as a wife and mother. They go to great lengths to warn the young woman that her life will be one of hardship and that, even if she is fortunate enough to successfully bear her husband a son, her life will still be filled with anxiety and worry.

The Ten Months of Pregnancy[4]
(Collected and edited by Zhou Shuoyi)

Let me say to you a few simple words:
As human beings we must repay our parents' care.
If we do not repay the care of our parents,
We will have lived this human life in vain.
 In this book I will not discuss but one thing:
I'll speak only of the sufferings of pregnancy.

Pregnant in the First Month, on the first of the First:
It has no form, it has no shape, it makes not a sound,
It is exactly like the watercress drifting on the river—
Will it eventually put out roots and settle down?
 Pregnant in the Second Month, under a sunny sky:
Now the embryo has truly installed itself inside you,
Your wobbly legs have no desire to walk long stretches,
Your listless hands have no desire to do any needlework.
 Pregnant in the Third Month, on the third of the Third:
Of the three meals of the day you only eat two.
You don't want any tea, don't long for any rice—
All you crave are astringent plums and sour soup.
 Pregnant in the Fourth Month: slowly it grows,
Your body wracked by pain, you can hardly walk.
To be with child when young may still be all right,
But as one gets older, it is like a debilitating disease.
 Pregnant in the Fifth Month, at Double Fifth—
It's really a burden to be heavy with child!
Had I known that being pregnant would be so painful,
I would have shaved my head and entered a convent!
 Pregnant in the Sixth Month, the dog days of summer:
I burn incense and paper money and pray to the gods,
Praying to the gods that they will take pity on me,
And protect me from harm when it's time to deliver.
 Pregnant in the Seventh Month, at harvest time:
Everyone in the household is busy with work.

---

4. In China a pregnancy is said to last ten months, as the pregnancy is counted from
the month in which the mother becomes pregnant to the month in which the baby is
born.

Cutting firewood for heating water, I ascend the ridge in sorrow,
Carrying water for washing clothes, I descend the slope in pain.
 Pregnant in the Eighth Month, in the chill autumn wind:
My husband is oh-so-busy delivering grain.
Don't go away on a distant trading trip,
Make the trip short and come home soon!
 Pregnant in the Ninth Month, a belly like a balloon:
There are all sorts of things you can't do anymore.
I would love to go back to my mother's home,
But I'm afraid my son might be born on the road!
 Pregnant in the Tenth Month: it's about to be born!
The child in my belly has grown oh-so-heavy.
I've no strength in my arms and my legs are swollen,
I never feel comfortable no matter what I do!
 And then as soon as the period of labor begins,
I find myself a paper-thin distance from dying.

The pain of one contraction is enough to make you faint,
The pain of two contractions can cause your soul to flee!
Clenching your teeth, you bite through a nail,
And your hands and feet feel as icy as snow.
 Even if the child is delivered without a hitch,
The fate of the mother still hangs in the balance.
When the child is born and lets out a first cry,
The parents-in-law in their room sigh with relief.
 When the child is born and lets out a second cry,
The mother in her room opens up her eyes wide.
When the child is born and lets out a third cry,
People inspect it to see whether it's a boy or a girl.
 A tub is filled with water to wash the child's body,
And then the child is swaddled in a silken skirt.
Someone takes the good news to the mother's mother,
And a rooster is killed in gratitude to the gods.
 When the mother's mother hears the news, she is pleased:
"Now my daughter has given birth to a grandson!"
She too grabs a chicken and some eggs as well,
In her old clothes, not taking the time to change.
 A lucky date is selected for the Third Day:
Gifts in baskets, in sacks, all jumbled together!

Pleased and filled with joy they make their way over,
Until talking and laughing they arrive at the gate.
 When the parents-in-law see them, they are pleased,
And welcome the mother's mother into the house.
They ask the mother's mother to take the best seat,
And the Third Day is celebrated in good cheer.

Let's forget the Third Day and speak of it no more,
Instead let me talk about the relationship of mother and son.
For one year, for two years, he drinks his mother's milk,
For three years, for four years, he never leaves her side.
 At five years and six years he learns how to talk,
At seven years and eight years he learns how to read.
Paper and ink, brushes and inkstone are bought as is proper,
And she expends all her efforts in teaching him to read.
 Once a boy has learned to read, then he will go to school,
While his mother stays home, waiting for him to return.
After he leaves in the early morning, she waits till noon,
And from noon she then waits till late in the day.
 She worries that her son might catch a cold,
She worries that her son might still be too young,
She worries that her son might climb up a tree,
She worries that her son might go too near the river;
 She worries that her son might catch an illness,
She worries that her son might suffer a fright,
She worries that her son might catch smallpox,
She worries that her son might not grow up;
 She worries that her son might have no talent,
She worries that her son might not find a wife—
Each day she looks forward to her son growing up,
To grow up into a man who will take a wife!
 She brings up her son and when he is eighteen or nineteen,
She finds him a wife and then her duty is done!
When he marries a decent and a sensible wife,
His parents can at last put their minds at ease.

They hope that their son and wife will show filial piety,
That flowers will again bloom and the moon be again round.
 If you respect your parents for four ounces,

Your children and grandchildren will do for half a pound.
 Those who are filial will have filial children,
Rebellious children will have evil offspring.
If you don't believe me, just look at the water on the roof:
Each drop falls to the ground on the very same spot!
 If you yourself are not filial, it is still a small matter,
But if your son is not filial, you'll be sorely grieved.
If you bring up a boy, he'll never appreciate his mother's sufferings,
If you bring up a girl, she'll repay all of her parents' cares!

This section we'll leave aside and not discuss any further,
Let me go back now and speak of the mother's concerns.
 If a child wets the bed on the left, she moves him to the right:
She lets him sleep on the dry part, and takes the wet part herself.
And if both sides are soaked through and through,
She'll cradle the baby in her arms all night until dawn.
 In just one day he drinks three bellyfuls of milk,
 In three days he drinks nine bellyfuls of milk,
But a mother's milk is not like the waters of the Yangzi,
Nor is it like the roots of the ferns in the mountains.
 Every drop that he drinks is the blood of his mother,
But he keeps on drinking till her body turns all yellow.
I won't even speak of a father's many sufferings—
A mother, in raising her son, gives it all she's got!
 I cannot relate all the sufferings of pregnancy,
May sons and daughters never forget their parents' care!
Each one of us will one day become a father or mother,
So teach your children to keep that in mind!

Still other women's script texts paint the nightmare of the unfilial son in even more graphic detail. There is also a text that presents the negative model of a lazy housewife: a glutton who cannot keep her own house in order and is subjected to everyone's ridicule.

A great number of transcribed texts deal with stories of loyal wives. In the story of Third Daughter Wang, the heroine is urged—by her own mother—to leave her poor husband and find, as her sister has done, a rich man to marry. Third Daughter Wang decides to stick by her destitute husband, however, and by sheer perseverance (and the timely intervention of the gods) the couple eventually becomes rich. In the meantime, the heroine's mother and sisters have fallen onto hard times and the mother is reduced to begging at the gate of the daughter she once despised. In the story of Meng Jiangnü, one of China's most popular folktales, shortly after she is married, her husband is hauled off to serve as a laborer on the construction of the Great Wall. When winter approaches, Meng Jiangnü travels north to take him his winter clothes, only to discover that he has died and been buried inside the Great Wall itself. She then vows to stay at the spot where her husband's bones have been buried and shed tears until the Great Wall crumbles down. In still other stories, the heroines resist all sorts of pressures to remarry despite the absence of their husbands for three years or even eighteen years. Each of these stories features women who are determined in the pursuit of their ideals and who do not hesitate to confront authority to achieve their goals. The same may be said of many stories in which the female protagonists are innocent victims of crime and determinedly seek redress. When compared to the other versions of these very popular stories, many of which are not specifically directed to a primarily female audience, it becomes clear that the women's script versions place far greater emphasis on the initiative and agency of their heroines.

How to Escape the Female Condition

Finally, there are two stories that deal with the way in which a woman can escape her female condition with all its attendant hardships, and join the world of men. The first of these is the tale of Liang Shanbo and Zhu Yingtai, one of the most popular Chinese love stories of all time. An early summary of the story reads as follows:

Yingtai was the daughter of the Zhu family in Shangyu. Dressed as a man, she left her home village to pursue her studies. She devoted herself to her books together with Liang Shanbo from Guiji, whose style name was Churen. Zhu Yingtai was the first to return home. The next year Liang Shanbo came to pay her a visit, and only then, to his great surprise, did he discover that she was a girl. He got his parents to ask for her hand, but her parents already had promised her to a son of the Ma family.

Shanbo later served as magistrate of Yinxian district. He fell ill and died, and was buried to the west of the district capital of Maoxin district. Zhu Yingtai was on her way to the home of the Ma family for her wedding, and as her boat passed by his grave, stormy waves made it impossible to go any further. When she learned that the grave of Liang Shanbo was nearby, she went to visit it. As she bitterly wept, suddenly the earth opened up and she fell into the grave and so was buried there together with Shanbo.

The Jin dynasty chancellor Xie An reported this incident in a memorial to the throne, after which the grave was called the Grave of the Loyal Wife.

While this summary set the story in the fourth century (we encountered Xie An as the uncle of Xie Daoyun), it is more likely that it originated in the Song dynasty, when literacy among elite women had increased, but when the advanced education provided by the many new government schools and private academies of the time was not accessible to them.

The version of the story of Liang Shanbo and Zhu Yingtai in women's script may be summarized as follows. The first reaction of Zhu Yingtai's parents when she expresses a desire to study at an academy is bafflement and refusal. Eventually, when even her father is fooled by her male disguise, they relent and allow her to go. At an academy in Hangzhou, she shares a room with Liang Shanbo. Liang Shanbo has his suspicions, but Zhu Yingtai convincingly answers his questions: she never undresses completely because of a vow she has taken, her large nipples are a sign of good fortune, and she pees in a squatting position to show her respect for the gods. But as she has fallen in love with her roommate, she urges him to visit her parents' home and ask for the hand of her "sister."

When the date set for the communal student summer bath approaches, Zhu Yingtai realizes she will not be able to maintain her cover any longer if she stays, and so she makes her excuses, saying she has received a letter telling her to come home. As Liang Shanbo sees her off, Zhu Yingtai hints in various ways that she is in love with him, but he is now so convinced of her male identity that he doesn't pick up on any of her hints. It is only when he visits her sometime later at her parental home that he realizes she was a girl after all. When he asks Zhu Yingtai's parents for her hand in marriage, he is told that she is already engaged to be married to someone else. Grief-stricken, Liang Shanbo falls ill and dies. On the day of her wedding, Zhu Yingtai asks her sedan-chair bearers to take her by Liang Shanbo's grave. As soon as she arrives at the grave, it opens up and she leaps into it. Ever since that day, this version of the story tells us, the grave of the two lovers has been frequented by a pair of mandarin ducks (in most versions, the souls of the lovers turn into butterflies).

In the twentieth century, the tale of Liang Shanbo and Zhu Yingtai has been read primarily as an expression of the rebellion of the young against arranged marriages, and of women's desire for an advanced education. In traditional society, however, the tale may also have been read by women as a cautionary tale against the dangers of falling in love, as well as the perils of attempting to participate fully in the world of men. It may be deceptively easy, the story shows, for a woman to fool most men most of the time, but eventually her body will tell on her, and any attempt to cross the line between the sexes is fraught with danger. The only realistic expectation a woman had of transcending the limitations imposed by her physical condition was to live a life of religious piety in this life and hope for rebirth as a man in the next life, as the women of Jiangyong and elsewhere in China learned from stories such as that of Fifth Daughter Wang.

Like the tale of Liang Shanbo and Zhu Yingtai, the story of Fifth Daughter Wang (in many other places better known as lady Huang) was widely known all over China in the late imperial period. The basic outline of the story as told in the women's script version is as follows. Fifth Daughter Wang has from earliest childhood been extremely pious, maintaining a strictly vegetarian diet and assiduously reciting the *Diamond Sutra*. Despite her desire to become a nun, her parents marry her off to a butcher, to whom she bears a son and a daughter. When she reproves her husband for his sinful trade and urges him to look for another occupation, he refuses, saying that he does not believe in karmic retribution, and besides that, he and his forefathers have been making good money as butchers for many generations. Moreover, he tells her, she is actually much more sinful than he is himself, since she pollutes the gods of the rivers and earth each time she menstruates and every time she gives birth. His wife is so upset by this final argument that, from that moment on, she insists on living apart from her husband and refraining from all sexual activity.

Because of her superior command of the *Diamond Sutra*, Fifth Daughter Wang is one day summoned to the Underworld. On her way to her interview with King Yama, she passes through the ten courts of Hell, witnessing the impartial sentencing of deceased sinners and their punishments. King Yama is extremely impressed by her mastery of the *Diamond Sutra*, and as a reward orders that she be reborn as a man. Fifth Daughter Wang is pleased, of course, and requests only that she be reborn in China (so she won't have to learn a foreign language) and as a sedan-chair carrier (so she won't have to commit any sin in order to earn a living), but King Yama decides she will be reborn as the son of the very rich and pious Zhang family.

Sure enough, Fifth Daughter Wang is reborn as a boy named Zhang Shifang. A brilliant student, he passes the examinations with highest honors, and asks the emperor to be appointed as prefect of his/her former hometown. There Zhang Shifang discloses his/her identity to his/her former husband and children, who this time around are quickly convinced of the wisdom of changing their ways. Zhang Shifang gives up his/her official post, and together the reunited family devotes the rest of their life to religious cultivation.

While the story of Liang Shanbo and Zhu Yingtai and the tale of Fifth Daughter Wang both show a keen awareness of the disadvantaged position of women, they also teach that "body is destiny." Even if one is as talented as Zhu Yingtai, the attempt to escape the limitations imposed by one's body is eventually doomed, and the only hope to improve one's lot is to resign oneself to the segregation of the sexes, and to hope for a better rebirth. For the overwhelming majority of Chinese women in traditional society, realistically speaking, there hardly may have been any alternative.

It is interesting to see which stories appealed enough to the women of Jiangyong for them to want to transcribe them into women's script; it is also of interest to consider which stories were ignored. In the women's script repertoire we find none of the many extremely popular stories of male heroes subduing traitors at court, rebels in the provinces, and foreign enemies all around China. We also do not find any of the stories of brilliant young students seducing and satisfying high-born ladies and courtesans alike. All of these stories are, of course, endlessly recycled narrative constructions of the ideals of Chinese masculinity, and so it should perhaps not surprise us that these stories held little appeal for the women of Jiangyong. More surprising perhaps is the absence of tales of women warriors. While the heroines of such tales have been hailed in recent years as early exemplars of female empowerment, it perhaps makes better sense to see these figures primarily as reflections of male fears of the devouring woman. In vernacular fiction of the last two dynasties, the most famous women warriors, such as Mu Guiying and Fan Lihua, are barbarian princesses who inflict heavy losses on Chinese armies until they are subdued with great effort by a Chinese hero. Even those elite women who in their long prosimetrical ballads dwell at great length on the adventures of a girl in male disguise (as we will see in a later chapter) show a preference for female victories in the examination hall and at court over female victories on the battlefield. Especially following the fall of the Ming dynasty, elite women poets did often celebrate military heroines, but the daring and determination of these heroines usually function as a foil for the hypocrisy and spinelessness of the men who, unwilling to fight to the end, were only too eager to serve the new dynasty.

It should also be pointed out that the same period that witnessed the remarkable flourishing of the morbid male fascination with the figure of the suffering young female also saw the equally remarkable popularity of the theme of the virago, or the jealous wife, who subjects her husband to endless scorn and humiliations. If Xiaoqing became the model of the innocently suffering young woman, the main wife of her husband became a model for the virago. The specter of the virago haunted the male imagination throughout the seventeenth century, and the male authors of plays and novels would go to great lengths to portray the virago in all her fearful ferocity.

PART FOUR

The Second High Tide of Women's Literature

If the first half of the eighteenth century continues to be a low tide in the development of women's literature in China, it does so only in relative terms. The resurgence of neo-Confucian thought, with its emphasis on the proper adherence to ritual, and the growing strength of the Qing state, which stifled publishers with its censorship, may have contributed to the diminished public visibility of women's literature from the last decades of the seventeenth century onwards. There is no indication, however, that the literacy rate of elite women was negatively affected by these circumstances, and women probably continued to write very much as they had done before. Certainly the prominence of writing women in the great novels of the eighteenth century, Cao Xueqin's *Dream of the Red Chamber* (published in 1791/92) and Wu Jingzi's (1701–1754) *The Scholars* (*Rulin waishi*; published in 1806), indicate that writing women were very much a feature of the elite society of the time.

Cao Xueqin was the grandson (or great-grandson) of Cao Yin, a bond-servant of the Manchu imperial family, a trusted confidant of the Kangxi emperor, and eventually the director of the imperial weaving establishments in Nanjing and Suzhou. Although the latter position made him one of the richest men of the empire, once the Kangxi emperor was succeeded by the Yongzheng emperor, the family fortunes plummeted, and Cao Xueqin himself spent most of his life in poverty in Beijing. His novel describes in great detail the life of the wealthy Jia family, and may be read both as a mythologizing memoir of the lost grandeur and opulence of the author's own family, and a scathing inquiry into the moral causes of their fall from grace. While Cao Xueqin carefully avoids mentioning the name of the dynasty under which his story unfolds, it is clear that his descriptions were inspired primarily by the contemporary scene.

The main character of the *Dream of the Red Chamber* is Jia Baoyu, a rather unusual adolescent boy who prefers the company of girls to that of his male companions. Thanks to the intercession of his elder sister, an imperial concubine, he is allowed to spend his days with twelve half-sisters and female cousins in the pavilions and gazebos of the beautiful garden in the heart of the Jia family compound. It goes without saying that the women of the Jia family and the families they are related to through blood or marriage are, because of their elite status, taught how to read and write, and also how to compose poetry. When in chapter 48 of the novel one of the servant girls expresses an interest in learning to write poetry, the young ladies are only too happy to act as her teachers. So it comes as no surprise that at one point one of the girls organizes a poetry club. Cao Xueqin tells us in considerable detail about all of the energy that goes into the formal organization of the club, which includes choosing fitting pseudonyms for each of its members and deciding on the menus of the many meals that will be served at each gathering. Finally, in chapters 37 and 38 the young women (and Jia Baoyu) finally get down to the business of writing poems on assigned topics and using assigned rhyme words that are then collectively judged and ranked. In Cao Xueqin's hands, these poems become one of the many devices he uses to delineate the distinctive characters of his novel's numerous female protagonists (yet another poetry contest takes place in chapter 50 of the novel).

Cao Xueqin's tongue-in-cheek descriptions of the activities of the poetry club make clear that for many of the club's members the composition of poetry was little more than one pastime among many. But for one of them at least, poetry is the primary means she has of expressing her deeply felt emotions. This is our Lin Daiyu, the silently suffering, introverted, and tubercular cousin of Jia Baoyu. Lin Daiyu and Jia Baoyu are secretly in love with each other, but each time they are on the brink of declaring their love for one another, they are hindered from doing so by some incident or misunderstanding, and Lin Daiyu is left to pour out her anguish in poetry. One of the other major female characters in the novel, the well-adjusted and robust Xue Baochai, often warns Lin Daiyu of the potentially harmful consequences of her addiction to poetry. More specifically, she warns her against the dangers of obsessively reading romantic plays such as *Peony Pavilion*. Xue Baochai is also worried that Lin Daiyu's poems may find their way outside the inner quarters:

"Because it really would be terrible if they were passed around. The proverb says: 'In women lack of talent makes for virtue.' For us the most important qualities are chastity and modesty, followed by a talent for needlework. All the rest, including poetry, are nothing more than hobbies to while away the time in the women's quarters—it is of no importance how good you are at it. Girls from families like ours do not need a reputation for literary talent!"

Eventually the family decides that Jia Baoyu must marry Xue Baochai, although they can only get him to actually do so by tricking him into believing that he is marrying Lin Daiyu. On the night of the marriage ceremony, Lin Daiyu, coughing blood, dies alone in an agony of betrayal and sorrow, but only after she has carefully burned all her poems.

While Cao Xueqin seems to have been heavily influenced by the popular figures of suffering young women such as Xiaoqing and Shuangqing in creating the character of Lin Daiyu, his contemporary, Wu Jingzi, chose another approach to satirize women's infatuation with literature. His novel *The Scholars* is a panoramic survey of the foibles and failings of the literati of his time. In one of his chapters, he narrates in detail the unhappy life of Mademoiselle Lu, the only child of a scholarly father, who was a former compiler in the prestigious Hanlin Academy. Her father raises her as if she were a boy, teaches her to write examination essays, emphasizing at each step that a mastery of the structure of the examination essay serves as the basis for all compositional skills:

Whenever they were sitting together without anything to do, he would repeatedly remind his daughter: "If you can write a good examination essay, then you will be able to handle any genre, whether of prose or poetry: with the first lash of your whip you will draw a welt, and with the second you will inflict a wound. But if the structure of your examination essay is defective, everything you write will be either utter nonsense or heretical ravings."

The girl took in all of her father's words, and on both her cosmetic table and her embroidery table lay piles of essay collections, which she studied every day with the greatest of care, annotating them in detail. She never even glanced at the poems and lyrics, the ballads and rhapsodies that were sent to her. Of course there were some popular anthologies of poems and stories about the poet Su Shi and his talented younger sister,[1] but those she gave to her serving girls, Caipin and Shuanghong, to read. When she really had nothing else to do, she would teach the two of them how to knock together a poem, but that was only for fun.

Mademoiselle Lu's father goes to great lengths to find her an equally talented husband, but the man she marries turns out to be interested only in poetry: he detests examination essays, which he considers to be utterly vulgar and, in fact, hasn't the slightest interest in studying for the examinations at all.

Before we dismiss Wu Jingzi's portrayal of Mademoiselle Lu as nothing more than a misogynist satire, it should be pointed out that many women did indeed study examination essays. The short biographical notices in the comprehensive *Correct Beginnings: Women's Poetry of Our August Dynasty* (*Guochao guixiu zhengshi ji*), compiled in 1833 by the woman anthologist Wanyan Yun Zhu (1771–1833), often mention with pride that this or that woman poet excelled in the composition of examination essays. There is also the example of Wen Pu, whose father dressed her up as a boy and taught her to write examination essays:

Wen Pu's style name was Chuheng and she hailed from Shimen in Jiangsu province. She was the daughter of Provincial Treasurer Wen Yuyan, and the author of *Collection of Poems from the Tower of the Drunken Crane*.

Because her father had no son, he had her dress as a boy and tutored in the Classics. By the time she was fourteen, she had become skilled in the composition of examination essays. Her father wanted her to sit for the exams, but someone advised him against it, saying: "Wouldn't it be better for her to become a Ban Zhao rather than a Huang Chonggu?" And so her father abandoned the idea.

---

1. Later legend provided the famous Song dynasty statesman and poet Su Shi (1037–1101) with an erudite and brilliant younger sister. A vernacular story of the early seventeenth century recounts how, on their wedding night, she subjected her husband, the well-known poet Qin Guan (1049–1100), to a grueling set of literary tests before she would agree to consummate the marriage.

From that time on, Wen Pu no longer received guests, although she continued to dress as a man. She looked after her parents and never married.

Cao Xueqin and Wu Jingzi would have been quite surprised by the proliferation of women's literature in the second half of the eighteenth century and beyond. By the middle of the eighteenth century, Chinese intellectual life had become increasingly dominated by "evidential scholarship," which not only valued philology over philosophy, but also, because of its interest in collecting and editing texts of all kinds, contributed to a growing awareness of the richness and diversity of the Chinese past. At the same time, the Manchu rulers gradually became less suspicious of conspiracy and slander, and over time, began to relax their fierce censorial grip. Some of the leading poets of the day, such as Yuan Mei (1715–1797), once again felt free to stress the direct expression of authentic emotion as the hallmark of true poetry. During the final years of Yuan Mei's life, when he was living in retirement in Nanjing, the elderly poet not only went so far as to accept female disciples, but also to publish an anthology of their verses. Other male poets surrounded themselves by a coterie of female disciples as well. Somewhat earlier, the Suzhou literatus Ren Zhaolin was at the center of a group of ten female poets, whose works he anthologized in 1789, and, at a slightly later date, Chen Wenshu (1771–1843) served as mentor for a group of women poets in Hangzhou. As these place names make clear, the central area of this resurgence of women's literature was, as before, the Jiangnan region.

The enhanced visibility of writing women in the public sphere had, by the end of the eighteenth century, provoked an ongoing debate over what women should be learning. The debate centered very much on Yuan Mei's role as a champion of women's literature, and was in part also fueled by his reputation as a libertarian bon vivant. One of his most outspoken critics was the historian Zhang Xuecheng (1738–1801), who hailed from eastern Zhejiang province, a region in which women's literature was less valued, even in elite families, than it was in Hangzhou and Suzhou. Zhang Xuecheng did not mince words when describing Yuan Mei's activities:

Nowadays there is a shameless fool who takes pride in his *savoir vivre* and uses it to mislead and poison [the minds of] young ladies of eminent families. He misleads them with [stories of] "talented poets and beautiful ladies" such as actors stage in their performances. In Jiangnan, many women of good families and noble houses have been seduced by him: he has collected their poems and printed them, and so has made their names known all over the place. He shows no respect for the [proper] segregation of the sexes and ignores the fact that they are [proper] women. These kinds of girls from eminent families cannot be said to be engaging in "women's learning": they are victims of a corrupt mind.

The publication in the final years of the eighteenth century of Yuan Mei's anthology of poems composed by his female disciples inspired Zhang Xuecheng to write his *Women's Learning* (*Fuxue*), a tract in which he provides a survey of women's literature since earliest times, and advocates a return to the norms of antiquity. Zhang Xuecheng insisted that the public domain was the preserve of men, and strongly disapproved of the entry of women into this domain through the publication of their writings. In his view, the sole purpose of women's poetry was to give expression to the "wifely way." This is not to say that Zhang Xuecheng believed that men and women had different kinds of intelligence, or that men were necessarily more intelligent than women. If a woman really had talent, he wrote, she should develop it to the full, as long as she adhered to her womanly duties and remained within her proper sphere of activity. He was concerned, however, that less talented women might publicly make fools of themselves. In his opinion, it was much better for a woman to remain illiterate than to risk making a show of her ignorance. Apparently Zhang Xuecheng did not think much of the published poetry of contemporary women poets.

This debate concerning the place of women in society, the proper education of women, and the proper evaluation of women's literature (and scholarship) is reflected in one of the most original novels of the nineteenth century, Li Ruzhen's (1763–1830) *Flowers in the Mirror* (*Jinghua yuan*), a paean in prose to the multifaceted intelligence of women. We know little about Li Ruzhen apart from the fact that he was an excellent phonologist. The action of his novel is set during the Zhou dynasty (690–705) of the female "Son of Heaven," Empress Wu Zetian. One New Year's Eve, the empress issues a command in the form of a poem to all of the flowers in her Imperial Park, ordering them to start blossoming that very night, regardless of the fact that spring has not yet arrived:

Tomorrow morning We will visit the Park,
So, quick as fire, inform the Spring of this:
Every flower must start blooming this night,
And should not wait for the breezes of dawn.

This unnatural command of Empress Wu is obeyed by a hundred flower-fairies who, as a punishment, find themselves banished to earth by the Queen Mother of the West, where they are reborn as young maidens. We next meet the literatus Tang Ao who travels to the capital to take part in the examinations, but is rejected because of his outspoken criticism of Empress Wu's regime. When he returns home, he and his daughter Tang Guichen accompany his brother-in-law Lin Zhiyang on an extended ocean journey. Along the way, they visit many island states, the local culture of each representing in one or more aspects the inverse of that of China. In one of these countries, for example, merchants vie to lower the price of their wares, while customers do their best to drive the prices up. In another country, they find that even the youngest elementary school girl student knows more, regardless of the subject, than the learned Tang Ao. One of the best-known episodes from the novel is the visit by the travelers to the Country of Women, where women rule and take male concubines, and where men are subjected to the tortures of having their ears pierced and their feet bound (it is here that Lin Zhiyang catches the fancy of the local queen and is taken into her harem, only barely escaping at the last minute). At each island they visit, they are joined by another one or two of the banished flower-fairies, and in this way, all of the hundred flower-fairies are eventually reunited. But when the travelers eventually return to China, Tang Ao decides to stay behind on an island called Little Penglai.

In the second part of the novel, Tang Guichen makes yet another short ocean trip. Upon her return, the hundred girls travel on to the capital in order to participate in, and of course, pass with flying colors, a literary examination for girls that has been convened by Empress Wu. On their journey to the capital, as well as at the many parties celebrating their success after taking the exams, the hundred girls indulge in all sorts of intellectual and literary pastimes, the description of which makes the novel an extremely witty "encyclopedia of literati leisure culture." The novel ends with the husband and brothers of the hundred girls defeating the nephews of Empress Wu in allegorical battles, whereupon she cedes the throne to the rightful heir, and the Tang dynasty is restored.

It will come as no surprise that in the twentieth century *The Flowers in the Mirror* was often hailed for its feminist stance. More recent years have brought a more nuanced evaluation, however; scholars point out that although Li Ruzhen describes a number of alternative societies and in so doing illustrates the cultural arbitrariness of all social norms, including those of gender, he never goes so far as to advocate full political and social equality for women. He is still unable to imagine an unsegregated world in which men and women's spheres of activity are not carefully distinguished. Thus, while in his novel women can sit for examinations, these are examinations held especially for women. Nor is success in the examinations followed, as it would be for men, by an appointment to an official post, whether at court or in the provinces. The public domain of officialdom remains the prerogative of men, and it is men who, at the conclusion of the novel, are called upon to restore political order.

The Flowers in the Mirror was not the first novel to describe literary examinations for women. *The Plum in the Golden Vase* (*Jinpingmei*), *A Sequel* (*Xu Jinpingmei*) and *Examination for Women* (*Nü kaike zhuan*), both published in the seventeenth century, contain descriptions of literary examinations for courtesans. The first of these novels, by Ding Yaokang (1599–1669), is set in the years immediately following the collapse of the Northern Song dynasty. In it we find a description of an examination organized in Yangzhou by the Jürchen conquerors for the purpose of evaluating and selecting talented courtesans for induction into the Inner Palace. The second, an anonymous novel of ca. 1700, is set in the Ming dynasty and describes how three students organize a literary examination for the gifted courtesans of Suzhou and end up marrying the three women with the highest marks. This happy denouement, however, is reached only after many complications, including the students being accused of high treason for privately conducting what was normally a state activity. It seems clear that in both of these novels, the idea of examinations for courtesans was designed to titillate, if not scandalize, male readers rather than offer a serious social alternative to the established patriarchal order.

In contrast, Li Ruzhen does indeed seem to be questioning the established order when he describes how elite women, not courtesans, dressed in female attire rather than disguised as men, take part in examinations for women (even if these examinations were especially convened for them, and even if they were sponsored by Empress Wu Zetian, the *bête noire* of Chinese historiography). Despite its limitations—especially as viewed from a contemporary feminist perspective—*Flowers in the Mirror* must have been regarded as quite daring in its day. In the context of the imperial Chinese political system, claiming the right for women to sit for the examinations was equivalent to suggesting that women had the right to vote. The women of imperial China lived in a society in which an individual could make his voice heard in the halls of power not by voting, of course, but by taking part in the examinations and joining the administration. Even during times when the likelihood of succeeding in the examinations was greatly diminished, as increasingly more men were competing, the primary rationale for education continued to be that it was the prerequisite for acquiring an official post. Thus, the most devastating critique that could be made of female literacy was that it was completely useless—since it did not, and could not, lead to participation in the examinations for a post. *Flowers in the Mirror* marked the first time in Chinese literature that someone ventured to imagine what such examinations for women might be like, and under what circumstances they would be feasible.

Li Ruzhen's suggestion that such things as women's examinations could only exist during anomalous times (as exemplified by the reign of a female "Son of Heaven") may well have been prophetic: in fact, the only time an officially sponsored "national" examination for women was ever held in China was in 1853 in Nanjing, which was then the capital of the Heavenly Kingdom of Great Peace (*Taiping tianguo*). This regime had been founded by a man named Hong Xiuquan, who regarded himself as "the younger brother of Jesus." In the early years of his rebellion he advocated the absolute equality of men and women. As his movement grew in power, however, he gradually reverted to more traditional views on sex and gender. The destruction wreaked by Hong Xiuquan's campaigns of conquest and the subsequent efforts of the imperial government to defeat and subdue them was without precedent in Chinese history. The area that suffered most from the many years of fighting was the Jiangnan area, and cities that had been the centers of women's literature up to the mid-nineteenth century (Nanjing, Suzhou, Hangzhou) would only recover very slowly. It is for this reason that during the last decades of the Qing, Beijing and Shanghai would become the major centers of cultural activity in China.

Chinese women's literature of the second half of the eighteenth century and the first half of the nineteenth century differs in many ways from that of the seventeenth century. During this second high tide of women's literature, the stage was clearly dominated by elite women: the Jiangnan culture of literary courtesans was one of the many victims of the societal and cultural changes that accompanied the Manchu conquest. The absence of courtesans on the literary scene may well have made it easier for elite women to associate with the leading poets of the time. Whereas in the seventeenth century Qian Qianyi scandalized many by marrying the most famous courtesan of his time, by the eighteenth century, poets like Yuan Mei served as mentors for elite women, many of whom were married. And while there is no slackening in piety among elite women, only very few nuns have left us with collections of their writings, perhaps because of the decreased popularity of the more intellectual Chan Buddhism of the seventeenth century, and the ascendance of more devotional and "domestic" forms of religious piety.

But while the social basis for women's literature may have been somewhat more uniform during this period, the genres in which women wrote and the range of subjects they wrote about was much more varied than it had been during the preceding period. Admittedly, the most important genre for women writers continued to be poetry, both *shi* and *ci*. The high status of these genres ensured that the topics women could deal with and the style in which they could do so would remain subject to strict limitations. But women during this period did not only write poems and lyrics, they were also busy compiling anthologies. Most of these were of women's poetry but in one case at least, of men's poetry as well. They also wrote works of criticism and some women tried their hands at various forms of scholarship. Even more significantly, a number of women writers were active as playwrights, and fortunately a relatively large number of their works have been preserved. The publication of the *Dream of the Red Chamber* in the last years of the eighteenth century, with its detailed descriptions of life in the inner quarters and its stories of doomed love, turned women into even more avid readers of fiction. Although it would be many years before women would write vernacular prose fiction themselves, they did discover the narrative possibilities of the "plucking rhymes" (*tanci*), a very popular form of prosimetrical ballad. It is in many of these *tanci* texts written by women for women that we find women authors indulging in fantasies of dressing up in male disguise and outperforming men on the battlefield, in the examination halls, and at court.

13 · Poetry

Poetry and Piety

Tao Shan

By the eighteenth century neo-Confucianism had reasserted itself as the primary official philosophy of the gentry class, but Buddhism continued to play an extremely important role in their lives, especially in the lives of gentry women. In fact, characteristic of this period was a form of lay Buddhism that was extremely eclectic, combining elements from Pure Land and Chan Buddhism, as well as from Daoism and Confucianism. We can see these religious influences with particular clarity in the poetry of an eighteenth-century woman poet by the name of Tao Shan (1756–1780).

Tao Shan, whose style name was Qingyu, was born in Changzhou in Jiangsu province. According to her biographers, even as a very young girl she demonstrated deep religious devotion and considerable spiritual insight. She appears to have imbibed some of this piety from her mother, who was a Buddhist devotee. By the age of nine, she had already made the decision to become a vegetarian.

Tao Shan was artistically inclined as well. When she was nine years old, her parents, noting her precocious intelligence, engaged a tutor for her and her younger sister, Ren. Together, the two sisters read and memorized the classics of poetry and history and began to learn the technical niceties of poetic composition. The first poem in Tao Shan's collection is on the theme of the pine tree, a traditional symbol of high-minded integrity, a rather surprising choice of topic for a young girl of thirteen.

Pine Tree

A cold wind whistles through the myriad ravines,
A new moon hovers over the eastern mountains.
Stern and majestic, its trunk supports the heavens;
Lush and gleaming, its form rises from the earth.
Not priding itself on its integrity of the superior man,
Yet it willingly accepted the title of "grandee."[1]
It is because of the scraggly trees all around it
That the green of its gnarled branches seems deeper.

In many of Tao Shan's earliest poems, we see a pronounced inclination toward the life of cultivated seclusion represented by such famous figures as the fourth-century poet Tao Qian, who in disgust at the corruptions of the bureaucratic life, quit his official post and returned to live in the countryside.

A Spring Day: Living in Seclusion

The small courtyard is filled with a perfect stillness:
I lean on the railing where fragrant grasses cluster.
In the spring breeze, a few homing swallows;
In the setting sun, a lone crowing rooster.
Bamboo colors north of the bamboo window;
Flower fragrances west of the flowerbeds.
Who is there who lives as leisurely as do I?
The fisherman angling in the creek beyond.

Late Autumn Afternoon

On Su terrace frost is cold as the geese head south,
Yellow chrysanthemums turn into evening fragrances.
Late afternoon rain: idly listening to the flute in the jade tower;
Autumn breezes: lazily cutting out cloth with golden scissors.

---

1. An early emperor once formally appointed a pine tree to the rank of grandee to express gratitude for it sheltering him during a thunderstorm.

Courtyard scholartrees of drooping green sough and sigh,
Butterfly wings extending their yellow flit gaily about.
This is the purest and freshest time of the entire year:
Rivers full, mountains bare, white clouds here and there.

As the years went by, Tao Shan continued to write poems in which the emphasis is on purity and stillness and emotional detachment, all of which are often associated with Buddhist thought. In the following poem, this association is made quite explicit:

Winter Day: An Impromptu Verse

It is early winter: I lay aside my needlework,
And huddle by the stove idly intoning verses.
Pine seeds fall onto my cold inkstone,
Plum blossoms cover up my old zither.
 As dirt and dust dissolve worldly affairs,
So by ice and snow my heart is purified.
I ask those who would plunge into Chan:
Where is the true Chan to be found?

Tao Shan's early poems are by no means limited to descriptions of the quiet and secluded life within the inner quarters. In fact, it would appear that at least twice a year her family would spend a fortnight at a home they had in Suzhou. Many of Tao Shan's poems are joyous celebrations of walks in the hills, accompanied—or so she would have us believe—only by her own thoughts and perhaps a book of poems.

Reading

On the empty mountain the fallen leaves lie deep,
The returning afternoon light enters through the pines.
You may ask why I am brushing off this boulder?
That I may sit to read and amuse myself a while.
 There is a special feeling to this place,
Every day splendid in a different way.
Turning to look, I freeze in my tracks,
As the mountain peak spits out a new moon.

But Tao Shan was not always alone. She was extremely attached to her younger sister, and as they grew up, they were practically inseparable.

They often exchanged poems with one another, and although none of Ren's poems survive, we do have this one by Tao Shan:

Pillow Talk with Younger Sister in the Quiet Mountains

Deep in seclusion we share the spring chill,
As I trim the lamp so as to speak with you.
During our life between heaven and earth
How does one distinguish between foolish and cunning?
 The foolish are always peaceful and contented,
While the cunning are caught up in their worries.
But the Great Way is impartial from the start,
And the white clouds are carefree by nature.
 Lost in silence, we've both "forgotten words,"[2]
The human realm is different from the pure.
A solitary dog barks in the middle of the night—
Bramble gate shut against the wind and the snow.

Not too long after this poem was written, Ren had become engaged to a young man from a prominent family from nearby Wuxi. When the young man died before the wedding, the family began to look for a second husband for her. It is not clear exactly how Ren felt about this, but it would appear that she felt a sense of loyalty to her original fiancé, and was not eager to marry someone else. It may have been due to this stress that she fell into a deep depression and before long fell critically ill and passed away.

Tao Shan herself had been engaged at the age of sixteen to a young man by the name of Peng Xiluo, a nephew of Peng Shaosheng (1740–1796), one of the most important lay Buddhist figures of the time, and author of a collection of biographies of pious laywomen from the fifth century to his own day. This collection, entitled *Biographies of Pious Women* (*Shannü zhuan*), was eventually printed in 1781 and included a biography of Tao Shan, who had died just the year before. Peng Shaosheng was especially known for his devotion to Pure Land Buddhist practices, which, unlike Chan Buddhism, consisted not of meditation or *koan* investigation,

---

2. According to a famous passage in *Master Zhuang*, the primary function of language is to convey a message or meaning, and once one has caught the meaning, one can forget the words; just as having caught the hare, one can do away with the trap.

but rather devotion to the Buddha Amitabha and the invocation of this Buddha's name and presence.

Tao Shan did not go to her husband's home until eight years after her engagement, perhaps because her parents agreed to give her some time to recover from her younger sister's death, which had not only come as a great shock to her, but had also opened her eyes to the evanescence of human life and turned her mind even more toward Buddhism. It would appear, in fact, that she spent most of the time between her engagement and her marriage studying Buddhist sutras and practicing Buddhist devotions. Toward the end of this protracted period of study and meditation, as she was preparing to leave her parent's home and become a member of the Peng household, she wrote a series of quatrains, entitled *Chants of Shame and Remorse (Cankui yin)*, which may be regarded as a poetic confession. Confession in Buddhism, as in many religions, is regarded as an important first step for those desiring to commit themselves more fully to the religious path. Tao Shan's preface to this series of poems gives us an indication of how she felt about her religious life, not only as a woman, but also as a poet:

During the long summers of leisure, I often thought about my life experience, and in particular, I looked deep in my heart and asked myself: "What kind of person do you wish to become?" Now it happens that, being a woman and lacking the wherewithal to rescue body and mind, I find myself still floating along in the [cycle] of birth and death and have no way of knowing where my future lies. A truly perilous position to be in! Fortunately, however, I still have enough [awareness] left of my True Mind to know something of the [sense] of shame. Whenever I find my thoughts inspired by some situation, I express my feelings in verse, and so I have written a number of seven-syllable quatrains. The Buddhist sutras say that those who know no remorse are indistinguishable from birds and beasts; the Daoist texts say that one should always keep this [sense of] shame in mind; and Confucius says that "only he who, in his conduct of himself, maintains a sense of shame [is worthy of being called a superior man]." This is exactly what I mean when I speak of "shame." All these sages of the Three Teachings, in liberating both themselves and others, based themselves exclusively on this sense of shame. Common people neglect it, but superior people retain it: in fact, this is what distinguishes the two. Writing has its limits, but shame has none. It is for this reason that I have entitled this series [of quatrains] *Chants of Shame and Remorse.*

Many of these verses contain complex religious and philosophical allusions that lend resonance to the poems but do not always survive the process of translation. The first of these poems shows that Tao Shan was acutely aware that in Buddhism, birth as a woman was considered to be unfortunate and the result of unwholesome deeds committed in a past life. There was also the belief that women were hindered by an inherent inability to attain the five supreme spiritual states, including that of a Buddha. Some Buddhist traditions, especially Pure Land, even went so far as to claim that the best thing a woman could do was create sufficient merit to ensure her rebirth either in the Pure Land where there was no gender, or in this world as a man:

> I am ashamed for not having cultivated virtue in my last life,
> Which is why I was given this body with its five obstacles.
> Still, I was fortunate to have been given a human body at all,
> So why should I complain that it is only a female one?

In the last poem of this series, Tao Shan seems to find encouragement in the fact that the stepmother of the Buddha himself, Mahaprajapati Gotami, was able to attain enlightenment despite being a woman, as was Lingzhao, the daughter of the famous Tang dynasty poet and lay Buddhist Pang Yun. Tao Shan, however, is still ashamed of not being up to their standards:

> Mahaprajapati Gotami made a vast and limitless vow
> To save every last woman in this world of Jambudvipa.[3]
> I am ashamed that the karmic obstacles from lives past
> Have deprived me of Lingzhao's knack for enlightenment.

In the preface to this series translated above, Tao Shan notes that "writing has its limits." This is a theme that we find reiterated a number of times in her verses:

Early Spring: An Impromptu Description of the Secluded Life

> Last year, my poetic inspiration evaporated,
> And I did not write more than ten poems.
> This year, why is it that yet again

---

3. Jambudvipa in Buddhist cosmology is the continent on which the Buddha preached.

I've not penned even a single verse?
It may be that these days my mind
Sees nothing special about writing:
No, not that writing is nothing special,
But that I fear the mockery of the wise,
The wise ones who remain still and silent,
As joyfully the mind comes to know itself.

In 1778, at the age of twenty-three, Tao Shan finally moved into the home of her husband, Peng Xiluo. It is quite likely that she would have preferred not to marry; in his biography of her, Peng Shaosheng tells us that for the first few weeks after she had moved in, she not only spoke constantly to her new family of the truth of impermanence, but also apparently expressed her desire to remain a virgin, a notion that elicited only ridicule. In time, Tao Shan resigned herself to cultivating the wifely way (*fudao*) and, according to Peng Shaosheng, quickly won the affection of her mother-in-law and of her relatives. She efficiently carried out her household duties, and provided her young husband with the support he needed as he prepared for the examinations. She continued to pursue her religious practice, however, rising early every morning to study the sutras and recite the name of Amitabha Buddha. Nor did she give up writing poetry. Many of the poems written during this period express the notion that the Pure Land, ordinarily thought of as being very far away from this defiled world, is to be found in the here and now.

How do these trees differ from the jeweled ones of the Pure Land?
On their branches can also be heard the songs of heavenly birds.
Spontaneously they explicate the Dharma in the easterly breeze,
Preaching with a hundred thousand subtle and marvelous sounds.

Once you've penetrated the layered gates, Truth is everywhere,
Never again will I lose my way, as I have in days gone by.
The six realms of samsara without a beginning or an end:
Flowing water, drifting clouds, it is always spring.

Originally there was neither form nor emptiness:
Speaking of Daoism, talking of Chan, both superfluous.
A single "Amitabha," the emptiness of one's nature:
Who is this I? Who is that Other?

A little over a year after her marriage, Tao Shan gave birth to a son. Soon afterwards, she fell seriously ill and died, although not before trying to comfort her husband by telling him that their karmic connection had been fulfilled and that he was not to grieve unnecessarily over her death. Only twenty-five years old when she died, Tao Shan was commemorated by her husband in the following biographical sketch:

Madame Tao's given name was Shan, and her style name was Qingyu. She was the eldest daughter of Master Jixuan, a "tribute student" from Suzhou prefecture. When she was young she was precociously intelligent and fond of reading. At the age of fourteen she wrote a poem entitled "The Hundred Flowers" that was like the work of a mature scholar. Her nature was such that she made a great effort to remember; she had read widely in the Classics and Histories, and was able to recite a wide variety of texts from memory. Within the women's quarters, she kept to her purpose cheerfully, and in all respects maintained propriety and virtue.

When she was sixteen years old, her father betrothed her to [me], Xiluo, but it was not until eight years later that we were finally married. At the time she was twenty-three years old, two years older than me. She served my mother, who delighted greatly in her; and she got along with her sisters-in-law, and did not engage in idle chatter. In ordering the maids and servants, she was generous but firm and reasonable. She was particularly thrifty and simple as regards her personal expenditures. My mother would say to everyone in the family: "Because my daughter-in-law's nature is somewhat like my own, I find I need not worry quite so much anymore [about family affairs]."

My own nature had always been rigid and stubborn and I found it hard to accommodate myself to others, but after my marriage to my wife, I was able to be a little more forgiving and encouraging [toward others]. I was able to control myself to a considerable extent, and my temperament gradually became more peaceful.

Last autumn, before the examinations, she encouraged me to study diligently, and took over the management of all the household affairs so that I would be able to devote myself single-mindedly to my studies. Then, after I took the examinations but was unsuccessful, my wife consoled me by explaining to me my duty and fate.

It was around this time that my wife first became pregnant. Whether active or quiescent, eating or resting, she in all respects adhered to the rules for "teaching in the womb" laid out by the ancients. In the beginning of the Twelfth Month, [our son] Yunhui was born, and for the first months all went well. My wife said to me: "Before this, Mother-in-law had not yet had a grandson, so having this one will bring her much comfort." Who would have known that half a month later, suddenly things would take a turn for the worse. With the help of strong medicines she was able to prolong her life until the New Year, but in the end she lost the battle. What sadness!

When my wife was nine years old, she had already begun to take pleasure in vegetarian fasts and when she was a little older, she would go with her parents to listen to the Dharma of leaving the world. When she read Buddhist texts, her faith deepened and she was able to understand them completely. With her own hand she copied out the *Repaying Compassion* [*Bao'en*], the *Diamond* [*Jingang*], and the *Amitabha* [*Mituo*] sutras in a firm and ordered calligraphic style. [Later,] when she read works written by my paternal uncle [Peng Shaosheng], such as his *Treatise on the Sutra of Unlimited Life* [*Wuliang shou jing lun*] and his *Biographies of Buddhist Laymen* [*Jushi zhuan*], she then began to aspire to [rebirth] in the Pure Land. Every day she would carry out regular devotions: at dawn she would rise and after washing and getting dressed, she would recite the name of the Buddha along with a number of *dharanis* and sutras. She felt pity for the extravagant butchering [of animals for meat] on the part of the ordinary folk of Wu, and so made a donation so that a thousand copies of the *Precious Mirror of the Compassionate Heart* [*Cixin baojian*] compiled by Mr. Shen of Wujiang [could be printed and circulated].

When she composed the sixty poems of the *Chants of Shame and Remorse*, my uncle evaluated them as follows: "Her [spiritual] roots are superlatively planted, and her faith and aspiration are also great. If she diligently cultivates herself, she certainly will be able to preach the Dharma even as she manifests the body of a Ban Zhao." In this way, my uncle expressed his approval of her conduct.

One month before she passed away, she said to me: "You and I have only the karmic connection of a single lifetime, so after I die, you must not grieve. I regret that I will not be able to continue to serve my mother-in-law, so if you wish to remember me, you will kindly comfort my mother-in-law and not forget my own mother and father. These are my wishes." When her illness became critical, one of her maternal uncles personally came to give her a medical examination, but could only tell her white lies in order to comfort her. Just before her death, she recited the name of the Buddha several times and then the *dharani* of rebirth [in the Pure Land]. Saying "The Great Monk has come from the West, I am leaving now," she then passed away.

Alas! Her personal effects are still like new, but the lady herself has suddenly become hidden away. When I look back at the dusty world of the past, it is truly like a dream. Because my wife had wise karmic roots from a previous lifetime, she experienced not a single obstacle in the interval between her coming and going. When I lost my father when I was just a boy, I was lonely and felt sorry for myself. And now, again I experience the sorrow of losing my partner, and the responsibility for my mother greatly adds to my grief and anxiety. How can I ever carry out my wife's lofty instructions and forget the lingering sorrow of my solitary dawns? So I briefly note the story of her life and append it to the family records as a testimony for those who come after. My wife was born on the twenty-second day of the twenty-first year of the Qianlong reign [1756] and died on the twenty-third day of the First Month of the forty-fifth year of the Qianlong reign [1780]. She was twenty-five years old and had one son, Yunhui. Written with endless mourning by Peng Xiluo.

Following Tao Shan's death, her uncle Peng Shaosheng edited her poems and provided the resulting collection with the following preface:

In the year *gengzi* [1780], a few days before the middle of the Second Month, I returned south after a trip on official business, and visited with all of the sons of my eldest brother. When I asked after the health of lady Tao Qionglou, I was told that she had passed away twenty days earlier. I then placed a sprig of plum blossoms in a vase of clear water and wrote a text as an offering to her. Afterwards, when I was gathering together all of the scrolls she had left behind, I found the ten poems she had written to the rhymes of my own "Solitary Retreat" poems. I read them and sighed, saying: "How extraordinary! They resonate in their melancholy elegance with the sounds of the *kalavinka* birds from the Buddha Land of the western regions singing in the seven-jeweled trees, and give voice to thoughts of the Buddha, the Dharma, and the Sangha. It is all here!" And so I printed all of the poems that she had written during her lifetime, which came to several scrolls, which, after editing, left more than ninety poems. I retained the old title of *Draft Chants of the Lovely Tower* [*Qionglou yingao*].

When Qionglou first began to write poetry, she entrusted her thoughts to breezes and flowers, and assuaged her feelings in mountains and streams. She came up with [verses] that were limpid and far-reaching, unstained by any dust or dirt. When she was a little older and had read the texts of the sages and saints and the Buddhist patriarchs, she gradually learned how to pare away flowery phrases, and force herself to approach the heart of things. Was it not her aspiration to emulate those of the past who studied for their own enlightenment? In those ten poems [written in imitation of my work] she penetrated and mastered the Dharma source, and purifying all of her feelings of doubt, gave rise to the energy of her karmic roots, and also displayed her literary talent. This was not something those of limited knowledge and shallow roots would be able to fathom.

Reading the poems of Qionglou, one would take some of them to be those of a poet of genius, others to be those of a lofty recluse, and still others to be those of a man of the Way. This Qionglou is like a flower in the void, like the moon in the water: neither identical nor dissimilar, neither Self nor Other. If one looks at [her poems] in this way, it can be said that Qionglou continues to exist to this very day.

The story of Tao Shan, indeed, does not end here. Nearly five years after her death, in the spring of 1784, a group of Pure Land devotees gathered together for the first of a series of eleven spirit-writing sessions in Suzhou. Peng Shaosheng attended some of these sessions, and at one of them he thought to inquire as to the fate of his nephew's departed wife, Tao Shan. He tells us that at first Tao Shan herself communicated to him by means of poems and sermons, but that when later he tried to get in touch with her again, he was informed that she had assumed the body of a man and been reborn in the Pure Land. The poem that Tao Shan's spirit delivered to Peng Shaosheng was as follows:

> In the interval between rains the fragrant grasses multiply,
> And the events of five years have slipped by like a weaver's shuttle.
> Hidden deep inside the cave amidst traces of mist and clouds:
> A gust of fragrant breeze sends the guest on his way.

Jiang Zhu

Jiang Zhu (1764–1804) was a contemporary and an acquaintance of Tao Shan's. Like Tao Shan, her poetry reveals a strong and abiding interest in Buddhist ideas—as we can see from her sobriquet, which was Little Vimalakirti (Xiao Weimo). Weimo was also the sobriquet adopted by the famous Tang dynasty poet Wang Wei, and Jiang Zhu certainly may have had him in mind when she chose it for herself. On the other hand, both of them may have been thinking of the original Vimalakirti, known in Buddhist literature as the famous layman who, although he lived in the secular world, had such a profound understanding of the highest truth of non-duality that not even the most highly advanced buddhas and bodhisattvas dared engage him in dialogue and debate for fear of being bested.

Jiang Zhu was an extremely active member of the Clear Brook Poetry Club of Suzhou, a group of ten women poets who wrote and studied under the aegis of a Suzhou man of letters by the name of Ren Zhaolin (active 1776–1823). Like his more famous contemporary, Yuan Mei (1716–1798), Ren Zhaolin took it upon himself to instruct his women disciples in the art of poetry, and also to help publish and publicize their poetic works. Thus the appearance in 1789 of an anthology of the writings of these ten women, published by Ren Zhaolin and edited by his wife, Zhang Yunzi (b. 1756), whose sobriquet Clear Brook (Qingxi) was used to name the poetry club. Of these ten women, Jiang Zhu was noted primarily for her erudition. In fact, she clearly saw herself as a lady scholar—when a male poet hinted that her works might be plagiarized from the work of her brother (the distinguished scholar Jiang Fan), she protested with great indignation in one of her poems: "Although I admit my talents are shallow and unpolished, / I venture to say that I am not second to my brother." This bravado is reflected as well in one of the many other skills for which Jiang Zhu was known—sword fighting.

Jiang Zhu was very eager to exchange poetry and conversation with her women friends. As we can see from the following song lyric, even before the Clear Brook Poetry Club was established, she was encouraging Zhang Yunzi to think about the possibility of forming just such a literary society.

To the Melody of "Flowers Fill the Garden" (*Manyuan hua*)

After I read the poetry drafts of Madame Clear Brook, I wrote this in jest, and sent it as well to all of our younger and elder fellow women students.

These fine lines are difficult to stop chanting,
As mysteriously my soul feels about to be transformed!
Pray tell when can we form our ladies' association?
My obsessive longings have worn me out!
Permit me to tell you about my thatched hut,
Which I just happen to have built on a cloud-covered cliff,
Where the bamboo and boulders are elegant but wild,
And inside are zithers and books to uplift the soul.

There the spring waters are like wine,
And the spring hills are like paintings.
If you wait until the peonies bloom,
It should provide a place for a peaceful holiday.
Couldn't you get a painted boat to come,
And raise your wine cup amidst the flowers?
We'd talk about things that ease the feelings,

And when I'd acknowledge that you had won,
I'd be willing to bow in defeat.

In another song lyric she nostalgically recalls their animated discussions:

To the Melody of "The Candle Shadows Swaying Red" (*Zhuying yaoyong*)
Feelings on a Rainy Night

The night rain sad and sorrowful,
What's left of the candle melts in drops, its light the size of a pea.
These writings—where is it we wept over the westerly wind?
I truly cannot bear to look back.
But I remember the moonlit nights, the flowery dawns,
As ink-soaked, I scribbled away, staining the hem of my sleeves.
Tipsy with wine, we talked about swords,
Excitedly we discussed the world,
Turning dreams into realities.

These things are gone, are gone.
 My wild spirit has been ground to dust,
And is nothing like it was before.
No need to compose regrets or write about sorrow:
It's your fate, don't you know that yet?
Unfurrow the wrinkled lines between your brows,
Liberate yourself from your worldly karma,
And attend to sitting on your meditation mat.
A thousand invocations to the ancient Buddha,
A single stick of pure incense
Make it possible to endure.

Yet other lyrics and poems give expression to a desire to escape the burden of intelligence and sensitivity:

To the Melody of "Tossing over Fragrance" (*Fanxiang ling*)
A Late Spring Impromptu Verse

The green fat, the red skinny: indolent butterflies and bees—
Grabbing the blossoms, lingering by the willow floss: hating to hurry.
Let me have a curtain of fragrant rain,
And a few curls of steam from the tea
To keep out the easterly wind.

Because of my feelings I'm like a pathetic little insect—
I wish I could dissolve this wisdom and be stupid and deaf.
So I can get drunk on wine and fill my belly,
And then foolishly flying high,
Return home in the dark sweetness.

We saw in our discussion of Tao Shan that after her death Peng Shaosheng attended a spirit-writing session and apparently was able to contact the spirit of Tao Shan. Jiang Zhu also once attended a spirit-writing session of this sort with her elder brother. The spirit who manifested itself on this occasion was none other than the playwright Tang Xianzu, the author of *Peony Pavilion*, which, as we have seen, had always been extremely popular with women readers. Jiang Zhu herself had read and delighted in the play and Tang Xianzu was one of her literary heroes. Although the play celebrates the power of love over death, the spirit that spoke to Jiang Zhu by means of the planchette did not encourage Jiang Zhu in her expression of her feelings and literary talent. Rather, it informed her that it was because of her inordinate fondness for poetry in a previous life that she had been born into an (inferior) female body in the present one. The spirit then urged her to repent of her addiction to poetry if she wanted to be reborn as a male in her next life. After the session, Jiang Zhu wrote three poems about this experience:

Poems Written in Response to the Spirit of the Planchette

On the first day of the Fourth Month, Master Tang Linquan [Tang Xianzu] descended by means of the planchette and presented [my brother] Zhengtang and me with several tens of poems. He also told me that I had a karma of words and explained to me some things about my three lives [past, present, and future]. The gist of what he said was that it was [because of my] fondness for embroidered words that I fell into the body of a woman and that I should diligently cultivate pure karma in order to atone for my previous transgressions. Ay! Were the master's words true or were they not? With this in mind, I wrote three quatrains.

I

Breeze and flowers, moon and water—vast and vague.
Dare I believe my writing is the karma of an earlier life?

I will make a record of our meeting in a painting
To testify to your words before both men and gods.

> *In a poem presented [by Tang Xianzu were the lines]: "With a fine steed you can return home to the fragrant seas, / When we meet we should commemorate it with a painting."*

II

The path full of brambles and thorns is hard to travel,
The distant fragrant seas can only be returned to in dreams.
Embroidered words no longer need remorse and shame:
My madness is done with, leaving only my foolishness.

III

A single dream can truly cause one to mess up an entire life.
The grieving cricket once in a while cries out in frustration.
Sitting on the meditation mat, I slowly become a Buddha:
Sweeping clean the troubled mind, waiting for the moon to shine.

In other poems, Jiang Zhu also makes reference to her addiction to words, even as she makes deft use of them, often in a spirit of playfulness, as a way to endure illness and generally get through life's trials and troubles.

I Had Recovered from My (Previous) Illness, but This Fall, I Again Came Down with a Strange Illness: I Could Not Sleep Either in the Day or at Night, and Whenever I Ate Any Rice, I Would Throw It Up and Could Not Eat It. I Did Not Eat or Sleep for Over a Hundred Days, and Yet Was Able To Walk and Sit Normally As If I Were Not Sick At All and Was Just Play-Acting. So in Fun I Wrote a Poem in Order To Amuse Myself for a While

> With the medicine found in a book bag, I get by year after year;
> That seems to be my way of life—something truly to be pitied!
> Following my whims I go through poems as if chanting *gathas*;
> With wild phrases, I pretend to be a ghost discussing Chan!
> If you compare the body to fallen leaves you understand illusion;
> The silver fish that dines on words can truly become immortal.

Appearing to be ill, I just roam and play in the rain and flowers:
The altar of the mind is just there in front of the lantern.

Drinking in Come-Again Pavilion

The wine flows, the flowers gleam white;
The breeze comes, the bamboo path hidden.
Discussing poetry in itself presents no obstacles,
Asking about the Dharma dissolves worries.
The realm of Chan is clearer than water;
The empty hall is as peaceful as autumn.
I am ashamed of dragging my feet in the dust;
Bound and tied, I've yet to turn myself around.

Enjoying the Moon at South Tower

With a cup of wine in my hand I climb the south tower:
A few calls of returning geese heading into the sandy isle.
A jade platter suddenly emerges from the depths of the sea,
As the Western Hills tip over into the chilly river's flow.
I can distinguish clearly that it is water and not the moon,
A stretch of vast expanse floating along the extended void.
Lush and luxuriant the jasper groves are five hundred feet tall,
A single branch blows in the autumn in the human world.
I sing and I dance and I offer my poems to the immortals.
I grab its icy shadows, cling tight to its flowing fountains.
Climbing up on the ladder of clouds, I call out to Chang E:
Why shouldn't I be able to turn into the toad in the moon?[4]

Disciples of Yuan Mei

Xi Peilan

Of the many female disciples of Yuan Mei, Xi Peilan (1762–ca. 1820) is
the best known. She has the largest number of poems included in Yuan
Mei's anthology of his female pupils' works, and later critics have confirmed Yuan's judgment concerning the quality of her poetry. Her qua-

---

4. While most legends about the moon-goddess Chang E describe her as a beautiful
woman, some identify her with the toad that inhabits the moon and causes the regular
waning and waxing of the moon by eating and regurgitating the moon.

trains show a remarkable wit, and the longer poems written when she was young provide us with revealing glimpses into the ups and down of her married life.

We do not know very much about Xi Peilan's youth, apart from the fact that she was born in Changshu and when she was fifteen was married to Sun Yuanxiang (1760–1829), also from Changshu. One of Xi Peilan's earliest poems is the following:

Longing for My Mother

At fifteen I had never been separated from you for a single day,
So how could I bear to be apart from you for weeks on end?
Last night in bed, filled with longing for my mother, I cried,
And in my dreams clutched her skirts as I had at our tearful parting.

Xi Peilan bore her husband two sons in quick succession before he left in 1779 to join his father in Shenyang. A few months later her own father died, and she returned home to assist her ailing mother, who had been left with the care of her four younger siblings, two brothers and two sisters (one of Xi Peilan's younger brothers would grow up to become one of her husband's best friends). On the eve of her return to her husband's family, she wrote the following poems:

Admonishing My Younger Brothers

In the courtyard the lamps are aglow,
In the hall, the wine has been set out.
 My younger brother has just begun to grow a queue,
My baby brother can barely pull himself up by the bed.
In their white caps they beat the floor with their heads,
As they weep for their father, your heart is saddened.
 My younger brother, knowing how his father cared,
Has a full understanding of his instruction and nurture.
Now he has become an orphan at the age of fifteen,
All day long he grieves without limit, without bounds.
 My baby brother, unable to find his father,
Imitates my mother in everything she does.
When Mother weeps, he too starts weeping,
His emotions stem from his natural goodness.
 At the sight even passers-by are filled with sorrow,

How much more then does it break my heart!
 Younger brother of mine, come over here:
Father may have died, but mother is still here.
You'll have to support her from morning till night,
If she falls ill, you will have to take charge.
 Set an example of filiality for your baby brother
And make an effort to uphold the norms.
If you don't show your brother proper friendship,
Mother will be at a loss what to do.
 My baby brother, just come over here:
You must stay by mother's side the entire day!
When mother weeps, you must wipe away her tears,
When mother walks, you must hold on to her gown.
 If you serve your elder brother with brotherly devotion,
Then your brother will not have to discipline you.
But if you show your elder brother no respect,
Mother will be disappointed in her hopes.
 Mother fell ill because of father's illness,
She was determined to die if father died.
If rather than dying she has recovered from her illness,
It is only because she was thinking of you, my brothers!
 If you, my brothers, live in happy harmony,
It may perhaps relieve her sadness at his death.
It is to my regret that I was not born a man,
And so cannot be the head of this household.
 The truth of my words speaks for itself,
So I hope you will keep in mind what I say:
Do your best to live up to your father's virtue,
And do not diminish the luster of this house!

An Exhortation for My Younger Sisters on My Departure

Lonely and quiet has become our mother's life,
So from dawn to dusk ask her often how she feels.
Always be there to wipe away her tears,
And make sure too that she eats her food.
 I am very sorry that this visit is so brief,
And that I cannot fulfill life's greatest duty.
Later you will understand how I suffered
For not having brought her joy as a child.

The prolonged absence of her husband inspired Xi Peilan to a number of witty variations on old themes:

In the Old Style

My love is like the moon over the inner courtyard,
And his handmaid is like the moon over the border.
Each of our hearts so brightly illuminates the other's
That one can even see the bones of our mutual love.

A Song of Sending Winter Clothes

I want to sew a winter gown for you, but cannot cut the cloth,
And again and again my frozen tears sprinkle the frost-like silk.
I can no longer assume you are the same size as when you left:
In my dreams I look for you so I can take your measurements!

Song of a Merchant's Wife

Since you left: months and years as deep as the Yangzi;
That solitary sail on the Yangzi: your handmaid's heart.
No amount of money can buy the beauties of spring,
So what is the use of leaving home in search of gold?

When Xi Peilan's husband eventually returned, it was to take her and his mother to Lu'an (Shangdang) in northern Shanxi, where his father had been posted as prefect.

Rejoicing That My Husband Has Finally Returned

I am suddenly startled from somber dreams at my dawn window
By the bright morning and magpies chattering more than usual:
I was counting on my fingers how long before you returned,
When I heard in my ears the sound of you entering the gate.
 Even though wind and dust may have emaciated your face,
I see that your heart is still as pure as the moon in the river.
Go quickly to your mother's place and ask how she fares,
Only then I'll dare tell you how much I missed you, my darling!

Since We Are Going to Leave for Shangdang, I Return to My Maternal Home to Say Goodbye to My Mother

I remember how long ago when I was just married,
I would weep night and day, longing for my mother.
I would go home for ten days out of every month,
And filled with devotion, sleep by my mother's side.
 I had only to be separated from you by a single foot,
And my dream-soul would hover around your house.
The year before last my father passed away,
Leaving you, my mother, lonely and alone.
 I would often come home to comfort your sorrow,
And in your room I would ask you what you desired.
Together we would cut and stitch gowns and skirts,
And I would prepare you delicacies of fish and meat.
 Still fearing that my mother would not be happy,
I would often admonish my brothers and sisters.
So now how can I bear to make this distant journey
Of a thousand miles, chased by the autumn wind?
 First a long way by boat, then a long way on horseback,
River after river followed by mountain after mountain!
But however high the Taihang Mountains may be,
They'll never be able to block my gaze in your direction.
 The longing for you will only deepen in your daughter,
Although it won't be able to hasten your daughter's return.
And your daughter will never know how you long for her—
Who will be there to comfort my mother's heart?
 Now the moment of my departure approaches,
My tears fill bushel-baskets with their pearls.
But there is no way of avoiding this journey,
Custom forbids I disobey my husband's command.
 Furthermore I must accompany my mother-in-law:
I cannot be equally filial to the both of you.
And so, bowing twice, I take leave of my mother,
And beseech her not to worry about her child.
 My younger brothers will serve you from dawn till dusk,
My younger sisters will look after your comfort.
Since the family is poor, there is not much to do,
Do not be distressed by thoughts of the past.

My little heart remembers your spring-like warmth,
I would never dare forget your nurturing love.
I will wait for the cold season of the year
To send a letter home tied to the leg of a goose.

The long trip from Changshu to Lu'an, first by boat on the Grand Canal, and then in horse-drawn carts, resulted in poems such as the following:

Crossing the Yangzi

All of a sudden this boat feels like a leaf,
Tossed about on myriad acres of billows.
The turgid waste stretches high and low,
The empty expanse knows neither east nor west.
 Our ferry launch is submerged by palest clouds,
As the heart of the waves bathes the reddest sun.
In the inner quarters I never saw anything like this,
Now as I take in the sights, my spirit grows manly!

Traveling at Dawn and Watching the Sunrise

At dawn we travel through the dense mountains,
In the pitch-black darkness we can't see the road.
Silently I sit behind the cart's lowered curtains,
But I can still feel the freezing cold nip my face.
 When the hooves of the horses lose their grip on the ice,
My courage disappears and my heart flutters with fear.
In front, I'm aghast at the ravine's precipitous decline,
Behind me, I'm frightened by the steep cliff like a wall.
 I shut my eyes and do not dare open them,
But even when I open them, I can't see a thing!
Then suddenly, through all the clouds and mists,
A single thread of dazzling red pierces through!
 First it stretches out like Sichuan brocade,
And then slowly takes shape like Suzhou silk.
Suddenly it breaks, as if split by Juling's ax,
Then again it looks like Nüwa's melted stones.[5]

---

5. With a single stroke of his axe, Juling (Giant Spirit) is said to have separated the Taihang Mountains from Mt. Hua, thereby providing the Yellow River with an outlet to

Palaces of silk are constructed in an instant,
Phantasmal towers soar aloft then change again.
The five colors are like the five flavors,
Which are all mixed together into a whole.
Like a sword—but its gleam more hidden,
Like a pearl—but its essence more subdued:
There where its essential light concentrates,
A golden mirror appears in its midst.
Shattering the sky as if with a blast,
Exploding outwards as if in a flash.
A wheel of fire spins through a vermillion palace,
Pillars of gold are laid across the courts of heaven.
Then suddenly the gloomy vapors all melt away,
And everything in the world is brilliantly displayed.

In 1783, while in Lu'an, Xi Peilan gave birth to yet another son. The child, however, contracted a debilitating disease, from which he only recovered after Xi Peilan and her husband returned to Changshu the following year:

Our Youngest Son A'an Suffered from a Strange Disease. When We Returned from Shanxi to the South, He Finally Recovered, and Filled with Joy, I Composed the Following Poem

In the First Month of last year our son was born,
And already at two months, he was able to smile!
My parents-in-law in their room were overjoyed,
But when happiness is at its peak, disaster strikes.
His face that was so lovely suddenly became swollen,
Oozing pus gave way to blood, as if pierced by needles.
It happened just when my husband was away on a journey,
With tear-filled eyes I hugged my baby and spoke to him softly.
My husband was kept away for over half a year,
And in my empty room, I worried day and night.
He came back but then again had to go to Bingzhou,
And only in the First Month of this year did he return.

---

the sea. The goddess Nüwa is said to have repaired the dome of Heaven with five-colored stones after one of the pillars separating heaven from earth was knocked down.

I recalled that it had been a full year since our son's birth,
And still the pus and blood were pouring out like water.
We willingly spent a thousand to buy the best medicines,
And we also burned incense and made our vows to the gods.
But the gods stayed in their heavens and couldn't be bothered,
And the medicine was no better than stones—it did no good.
His skin turned a scarlet red, his eyes turned white,
And his breath had the rancid smell of fish or shrimp.
His stomach filled with air and expanded like a balloon,
His spirit gone, his breath stopped, wordlessly he cried.
By that time it was the fifteenth of the Fourth Month,
As beneath the dim lamp in the black moonless night,
I cradled my son in both my arms, my son as stiff as wood—
With my whole body I hugged my son, my son as cold as ice.
A single thread of breath was all that there was left,
I yearned to put off his dying, but dared not hope for his life.
My own heart grown cold, my tears run dry, I had already died,
And Earth was as if completely cut off from a heartless Heaven!
At midnight the ghosts began to wail like falling rain,
As my son stopped breathing and no longer responded to our call.
I could no longer hold him, but could not bear to put him down,
At this moment I, too, was not my own self.
There seemed to be gods there before me and behind me—
Could it be that my son's body had been possessed by a god?
Then, after his lengthy silence, he suddenly started to wail!
It had been three long months since I had heard that sound.
So when I first heard it, I thought it was some other child!
When I realized it was him, my arms felt limp with shock.
The son in my arms, I believed, had come back to life,
And when I stroked his limbs, they felt slightly warm.
A storm wind had carried off all the ghostly vapors,
And the lamp flared brightly like a single blue lotus.
My son's fate had suddenly saved him from calamity,
Heaven made this weak body travel through the windy dust.
My son had met with calamity but was destined to live:
We traveled by cart through mountains as if on level plains.
And our solitary sail heading southwards filled us with joy:
His skin turned as white as snow, and his eyes turned black.
The excess air left his body, and his belly returned to size,

His hands clutched fish and meat and he wolfed them down.
And just as when he first was born, he started to smile again,
Only then seeming to recognize his father and mother again!
 When we arrived home, our kith and kin wouldn't believe us,
And they thought he was a baby no more than five months old.
When I think back on the past, I relive again the sadness and joy,
The scene of hanging out bow and arrows by the door is still vivid.[6]
 Because of my son's illness, my own illness worsened,
Even if hungry, whether early or late I would forget to eat.
At night I would go to sleep without taking off my clothes,
And my fingers were always busy scratching the baby's head.
 At times I was so tired I wanted to lie down for a moment,
But was afraid that his crying might startle me from a dream.
Alas, my bitter suffering did not last just a single day:
It lasted from the spring of *kuimao* to the fall of *jiachen*.[7]
 Now the feeding and caring is still hard work,
But compared to the toils of the past, it is nothing!
My son! My son!
How hard and difficult it has been to take care of you!
 Now your thread-like fate has been replaced by a sturdy cord,
Later, when you grow up, you'll bring our family greatness:
But then with whom will you discuss what happened today?
Alas! The limitless nurture bestowed by our parents!

As is clear from the above poem, for most of her stay in Lu'an, Xi Peilan's husband was away in Beijing sitting for the provincial examinations. He ultimately failed to pass the examinations, however, and he returned home to Lu'an feeling discouraged and downcast. Xi Peilan consoled him with the following poem, in which she compares him to the famous Tang dynasty poets Li Bai and Du Fu:

A Poem to Comfort My Husband upon His Return Home after Failing the Examinations

 Don't you see:
The rustic graybeard from Duling excelled in poetry,

---

6. According to ancient custom, the birth of a son was announced to the community by hanging a bow and arrows from the front gate.

7. That is, from 1783 to 1784.

The Banished Immortal poet had a lofty reputation.[8]
Recognized for their abilities as the greatest masters ever in the realm of
    poetry,
They failed in their own lifetimes to make a name for themselves in the
    exams.
You, my husband, have studied the poetry of both Du Fu and Li Bai,
If you don't defeat them then you surpass them—you are free of frills.
Your lofty chants time and again shatter Heaven's clouds,
And your deep feelings are as limitless as spring's rivers.
 When sometimes you toss aside your brush in frustration,
Who would not believe the ghost of Du Fu guides your hand?
When you show off your excellence and your ambitions soar,
It is obvious that Li Bai remains still very much alive today!
 Principle requires that wealth in one means poverty in the other:
Perhaps you should not have had such a store of natural talents!
This last spring you made ready your luggage and left for Beijing,
Confident you would pluck the purple as you would a mustard seed.
 But now as the winds of autumn have started to blow,
You return home in a student's blue gown as before.
Your sacks are stuffed with the brocades of your writings,
When you call for a lamp and read them to me by the gauze window,
 The mountains and rivers of Yan and Jin materialize before my eyes,[9]
The breeze of spring and moon of autumn are hidden in your verse.
The world's examiners do not even dare accept you as their disciple,
They cede you to Li Bai and Du Fu so you can become their pupil!
 Although poetry was prized in the Tang, still they were not chosen;
Even less would've they been now that there's no poetry in the exams.
If you write your poems and persevere in your studies,
That is enough to be remembered for a talent like yours.
 Even though as a woman my insight may not be great,
I know well that to beg for mercy is cause for shame.
Merit and fame are best earned by studying without cease.
If in one's lifetime, then that is wonderful, if you die, that's it!
      Don't you see:

---

8. The "graybeard from Duling" is Du Fu; the "Banished Immortal" is Li Bai.

9. The ancient state of Yan occupied the northern part of what is today the province of Hebei, while the ancient state of Jin covered the area of the modern province of Shanxi.

Since ancient times sages and worthies have emerged from the poor and
lowly!

Sometime in 1788, Xi Peilan bore another son, Lu'er, but that same
year, both he and A'an died, as did Xi Peilan's own youngest brother:

Songs of a Broken Heart

I

I still recall that the day my son was born his grandfather was promoted,
And it was he who bestowed on him the auspicious name of Lu'an.
To far beyond tropical mists and miasmic rains we must today
Send the one-line letter to inform the white-haired old man.

> *My son was born in the official quarters of Shangdang prefecture. The prefect loved
> him dearly. This spring we received a letter that he was taking part in the campaign
> against Nepal.*

II

When in his swaddling clothes, on the Third Day, he was first bathed,
Everyone came to see him, filled with admiration, in the prefect's hall.
The guest offered auspicious gifts of jade seals and rhinoceros coins—
Who could have known that these would end up as his burial gifts?

III

On the fifteenth of the Fourth Month, the moon was cold and chill:
My son died, then revived, and I both laughed and cried.
Had I known then that today he would again leave, this time forever,
My one spasm of grief would have turned into two spells of crying.

> *After his birth my son suffered from a wasting disease for a full year and was
> repeatedly on the verge of death. Alas! Wouldn't it have been better for him to die as
> an infant before he could even laugh or talk rather than die after he had grown up
> and had shown himself to be so bright?*

IV

For six years I held you as if you were an Udumbara flower,[10]
When happy you smiled, when angry you did not strike out.

---

10. The Udumbara flower is said to blossom only once every three thousand years,
and is thus used as a metaphor for that which is rare and precious.

In the end, lying there in bed and on the very brink of death,
One time you cried out "Mother," another time "Father!"

V

Your father said that you were extremely intelligent:
By the age of six already you could recite the *Odes*.
How painful it is when the first morning bell sounds—
And I seem to hear you reciting poems in your bed.

> *My son was particularly fond of the poems of Li Bai and Du Fu and he knew them
> by heart. Each day he would recite some pieces from memory in his bed. It was such
> pleasure to listen to him.*

VI

Verses by Green Lotus and lyrics by Washing Flowers:[11]
Your skilled parallel couplets clearly were a bad omen.
In a moment the blossoms fell and the clouds dispersed,
And Zhang Qian and his raft were nowhere to be found.[12]

> *My son was skilled at composing parallel couplets such as: "If one has feeling, one
> loves Song Yu, / But nowhere can one find Zhang Qian"; and "Rivers are like green
> jade, mountains are like obsidian, / Clouds recall her gown, flowers recall her face."
> When you would assign him a difficult sentence, he would immediately come up [with a
> matching line . . .]*

VII

With brush stand and the inkstone case you had a karmic bond,
All day you carried them about, protecting them with your life!
You'd cut yourself bits of paper as big as the palm of your hand,
And then your extraordinary thoughts would soar to the blue sky.

> *As soon as my son started to study books, he loved to make poems, but his words
> were often inappropriate. His "Sunrise at Dawn" reads: "Who drives the wheels of*

---

11. Green Lotus was one of the sobriquets of Li Bai; Washing Flowers (Brook) was a
sobriquet of Wei Zhuang (ca. 836–910), one of the first, and most well-known, writers
of lyrics, or *ci*.

12. Zhang Qian (d. 114 BCE) was dispatched by Emperor Wu as an envoy to the non-
Han tribe from Central Asia known as the Yuezhi and returned only after many years.
Later legend had him sail up the Yellow River on a raft and return by way of the Heav-
enly River (the Milky Way).

flaming fire | And scatters the blue of Highest Heaven?" These ten words truly defy interpretation.

VIII

On the Day of Flowers he fell ill and quickly wasted away,[13]
With frail hands he ground the ink but too lightly to blacken.
On a corner of his box he copied out a line of tiny characters:
"Sealed the thirteenth day of the Second Month of the year *maoshen.*"

> *During his illness my son himself put away all his writing implements and toys. The seal he wrote is still there now, but where is he?*

IX

A servant losing a silver bowl, a maid overturning the gruel:
For all of them he'd take the blame, and bear his father's ire.
But now all of them are scolded for each of their own misdeeds,
And as a result everyone in the household weeps themselves raw.

> *My son was doted upon by his father. Whenever the servants and maids made a mistake and feared being scolded by their master, they would always blame my son for their misdeeds, and he was happy to bear the blame on behalf of others. After his death, all of them wept copiously.*

X

A single bowl of gypsum became the cause of his death:
Who handed the hilt of the sword to that terrible quack?
At the Yellow Springs don't blame the quack for his fault,[14]
It is your parents that you must blame for that fatal error.

> *On the eighteenth day, my son felt a little better and ate some rice-gruel. But that terrible quack, Zhang Bingkui, prescribed gypsum, and the next night my son suddenly died. Alas! Why did he do this?*

XI

Amidst plum blossom fragrance you closed your eyes,
Under the endless blue vault you stared stiffly ahead.

---

13. The Day of Flowers fell on the twelfth or fifteenth of the Second Month.
14. The Yellow Springs is another name for the underground abode of the dead.

As you have chosen to die on the birthday of Guanyin,
You'll either become a Buddha or be reborn in Heaven.

> *Buddhists celebrate the birthday of Guanyin on the nineteenth of the Second Month.*

XII

Your pair of eyes cut from water are now frozen and still,
Your snow-white body is still wrapped in your red blanket.
Even if a painter had the skill to capture your spirit,
He'd find it hard to paint the intelligence of your heart.

XIII

The words of the soul banner that I wrote on icy silk:
"My six-year-old darling son who was known as A'an."
You had grown into a little lad of exceptional talent,
How could you be "an infant death not worth mourning"?

> *According to the* Rites, *children of less than seven years old are "infant deaths not worth mourning, for whom one weeps [only] a day." The startling intelligence of my son surpassed [that of] adults. Would it not have been wrong to bury him according to the ritual for deceased infants even if I had wanted to?*

XIV

Two dying birds with a common fate: uncle and nephew—
At the grave we are overcome by our feelings of loss.
But how can I bear, my eyes now as dry as wells,
To hear the widowed mother weeping for her son?

> *On the day following the death of my son, my youngest child, Lu'er, also died. After another three days, my younger brother, Xingchun, also died. In the space of five days, I wept for three boys who died when still children.*

XV

The younger later, the elder first—even greater the grief:
A pair of pearls dropped down onto the Terrace of the Springs.[15]
Crying like a baby he hopes that you will take care of him well,
It has only been ten days since he was weaned from the breast.

> *At that time Lu'er was just three.*

---

15. The Terrace of the (Yellow) Springs is another name for the realm of the dead.

XVI

I offer a cup of chilly brew as libation in front of the coffin,
Sprinkling the Yellow Spring's Terrace, broken-hearted I weep.
How much of it is wine and how much of it is tears?
You will know when you get a taste of its bitterness.

The year 1788 is the same year Xi Peilan met Yuan Mei for the first time (she would only meet the grand old man three or four times in all). In an entry in his *Addenda to the Sui Garden Poetry Talks* (*Suiyuan shihua buyi*), Yuan Mei describes Xi Peilan as "very intelligent looking," with "a beautiful, rather frail face." Nevertheless, at first Yuan Mei suspected that her poems were actually written by her husband, Sun Yuanxiang, whom he may well have met during Sun's regular visits to Nanjing to sit for the triennial provincial examinations. It did not take long, however, for Yuan Mei to become convinced of Xi Peilan's authorship and her considerable talent. He later contributed the following short preface to her poetry collection:

Each and every word issues from her natural intelligence. Without collecting the purple passages of the ancients, she is capable of the marvelous purity of a heavenly loom, and her tones and rhythms resound like jade. Such a poetic talent only rarely finds its match in the women's quarters! The excellence of her poems lies in the fact that she always begins with an idea she wants to express and only then does she write a poem. She puts to shame many of those who are now famed as poets.

A letter from Chancellor He Xizhai [Lin] written while on campaign reads: "Whenever I obtain a scrap of paper or a single word from you, I recite it from morning till night as religiously as if it were a Buddhist sutra." Whenever I obtain some verses from Xi Peilan, I do much the same thing!

Unfortunately, many of the poems Xi Peilan wrote after becoming Yuan Mei's pupil are much more formal in style, and lack the charm and spontaneity of her earlier work. Among the exceptions are the following poems:

Song of the Old Tree Felled by the Storm
on the Night of Double Seven

When one dragon raises its head, all the dragons dance:
The old tree, withstanding the storm, roared like a tiger.
But suddenly branches as thick as tubs were broken off,

And soared up into the clouds as weightless as feathers!
 Had it been struck by the hand of Juling who split Mt. Hua?
Had it been hurt by the ax of Wu Gang who lives on the Moon?[16]
Had it been borrowed by Zhang Qian to build himself a raft?
Had it been taken home by the Weaving Maid for a spool?
 At this moment, the palace of Heaven itself is shaken,
White billows like mountains surge on the silvery channel.
The Two Stars amuse themselves driving clouds and wind,[17]
Their laughter turning into storm, their tears into rain.
 But here below it frightens the wits out of young lovers,
Late at night there is no one who dares even whisper.
Tomorrow morning its green shade will no longer be whole,
And the scorching heat of the blazing sun will strike at noon.

The Ancient Mirror

A full moon from the time of the Qin,
Its pure brilliance eternally fresh:
When I face you I only find myself:
How many others have you tested?
 It is impossible to stop the years,
And now I hate my actual appearance.
 But if I were to cover you carefully,
Then not a speck of dust would show!

Sun Yuanxiang persevered in his studies and, after repeated failures, finally passed the Jiangsu provincial examinations in 1795:

Summer Night, for My Husband

The night is late, your clothes are thin, and drops of dew congeal,
Often I longed to call you to bed, but feared you wouldn't respond.
But now a wind from Heaven, lucky me, knows what's on my mind,
And in front of the window blows out the lamp by which you study.

---

16. Wu Gang is one of the inhabitants of the moon; a Chinese Sisyphus, he is believed to be engaged in the endless task of cutting down the cassia tree on the moon.

17. The Two Stars are the Cowherd and the Weaving Maid. They are lovers who are only allowed to meet once a year on the night of the seventh day of the Seventh Month, when magpies form a bridge for them to cross the Heavenly River (the Milky Way). When there are clouds and rain on that night, it is said to be their lovemaking.

Congratulating My Husband on the Report of His Success in the Provincial Examinations

From outside the gate comes the raucous sound of clanging gongs,
Inside my room, even before my spinning wheel has come to a stop,
A servant with disheveled hair comes in with a smile on his face,
And in his hands an announcement on paper embossed with gold.
 Over the years I have grown accustomed to the word "almost,"
So this time I hesitate and fear that the message may not be true.
I sneak a look at the list to see whether the name is indeed correct,
Or whether it could be someone around here with a similar name.
 I don't even know over half of the well-wishers coming in crowds,
The neighbors' kids climb on the wall, point him out to each other.
Having no other way to provide for wine at such short notice,
I undo my chignon and happily remove my hairpins and earrings.
 I still remember how you came home in the winter of *kuimao*
From the capital, filled with shame at your failure in the exams.
At that time both of your honorable parents were still alive;
They treated you, disconsolate man that you were, to a banquet.
 And I too offered some words and comforted you with a joke:
You're a poet and have to wait for a poet-examiner to succeed!

> *In the* kuimao *year I comforted my husband with the lines: "The world's examiners do not even dare accept you as their disciple / They cede you to Li Bai and Du Fu so you can become their pupil!"*

Who'd have known this joke would be a happy omen,
But that for it to be realized you'd have to wait a dozen years!
 Qian and Liu are, like Li Bai and Du Fu, both equally famous,

> *The main examiners were the Chief Minister of the Court of Imperial Sacrifices Liu Yunfang and Hanlin Compiler Qian Yunyan.*

And you were truly lucky to be among their "peaches and plums."[18]
Although I dissolve in tears and my face becomes filled with joy,
You weep copious tears and in your sadness you begin to cry:
 "Even though this single success brings luster to this simple home,
Both my parents have already entered the world of the Yellow Springs.

---

18. "Peaches and plums" here refers to disciples. All the students who passed an examination would automatically become the disciples of the men who had examined them.

In vain I announce my ranking at my parents' grave with tears and wine,
I am not in the mood for yet another celebratory festive banquet!"
My husband, allow me once again to just say a few words:
This is only the start of your career, the glorification of your parents.
Next year, when you enjoy the flowers of the Imperial Park,[19]
Please remember the one in the inner quarters who waits for the news!

The following poem by Xi Peilan dates from the early spring of the
following year, and was probably written for her husband as he was preparing to set out for Beijing to sit for the metropolitan exams. In it, she
warns him against the temptations of the capital (keep in mind that the
word for "thread" [*si*] is homophonous with the word for "love" and
"longing" [*si*], and that flowers are a common metaphor for courtesans).
After all, Sun Yuanxiang's father had had at least one concubine and no
doubt Xi Peilan was eager to avoid the sorts of complications that this
had brought upon the family.

An Admonition on Love, Written for My Husband

Don't say that love is like the clouds,
One moment thick, one moment thin.
Don't say that love is like the flowers,
That easily bloom and as easily wilt.
 True love is strong like bronze and stone,
The same today as it was yesterday:
That flower's fragrance wafts forever,
Those clouds are always plump and full.
 The only worry is a false intention,
Or tears and smiles that are not true.
Those clouds will soak your dreamtime clothes,
Those flowers dazzle you with their mirrored buds.
Their postures show off their extraordinary beauty,
But still one cannot trust them with one's heart.
 If an empty beaker is thrown into a great marsh,
The water will have dried up before it is retrieved.
If you pull up the sprouts to help them grow,
You can't expect to have a harvest in the fall.
When a flying insect lands in a spider's web,

---

19. Passing the examination is often described as "plucking the flower."

He will find himself entangled, to his dismay:
It is far better to turn around in a timely way,
And happily escape from the shackles and fetters.
 A chronic illness can still be cured,
If you aren't afraid of the bitterness of the pill.
There is no taste to those dishes of meat,
They are nothing but the butcher's dregs.
 A flower displayed in a painting,
A cloud reflected in the waves,
Belong to empty insubstantiality,
An idle love that's easily discarded.
 The threads in the roots of the lotus
         may be tens of feet long or more,
But all that is needed to cut through them
         is a single blow from a keen sword.

Again it took Sun Yuanxiang several tries before he finally passed the metropolitan examinations in 1805. He was then appointed to the prestigious Hanlin Academy, but returned home after having only served for a few years. As we have seen from some of the above poems, Xi Peilan often praised her husband's poetic talent, and it is probably thanks to her encouragement that he ultimately devoted himself to the writing of the poetry for which he still enjoys a reputation today.

Xi Peilan's most widely anthologized poem is probably the following:

Spring Night Moon

At midnight the little serving girl opened the window to have a look,
And then came to tell me that the entire courtyard lay deep in snow.
When I got up this morning, not even the tiniest little patch remained—
Only then did I realize how very brightly last night's moon had shone.

The opening line of the quatrain above was inspired by one of Li Qingzhao's most famous lyrics, while the last line recalls this extremely popular poem by Li Bai:

Quiet Night Thoughts

The light of the moon before my couch:
I thought the floor was covered by frost.

Raising my head, I gazed at the moon,
Bowing my head, I thought of home.

Xi Peilan lived to be a great-grandmother. Her sizable collection of poetry was later published as an appendix to her husband's even more extensive collection.

Luo Qilan

Luo Qilan (1755–1813) vividly exemplifies the many difficulties confronting a woman who wanted to make a name for herself as a poet in a man's world. In 1795, the collected poems of Luo Qilan, who was by then widowed, were printed by her husband's family, the Gongs of Nanjing, with prefaces by Yuan Mei, the painter Zeng Yu (1759–1830), and the poet-calligrapher Wang Wenzhi (1730–1802). In 1797, Luo Qilan herself added to this six-*juan* collection of her poems a *juan* of poems by her friends. Her preface to this latter section reads as follows:

For a woman it is harder to become skilled in poetry than it is for a man, and it is harder for a woman poet to establish her fame than it is for a gentleman of talent. This is because she lives in the women's quarters and her experience is extremely limited. Not only does she not have friends with whom she can, through discussion and study, purify her nature and intelligence, she also lacks the opportunity to climb mountains and gaze upon rivers in order to display her talent and style. If she does not have a worthy father or elder brother, who on her behalf can trace the stream to its source and distinguish between correct and false, she will not be able to complete her studies. Then, once she has married, she must toil at drawing water, pounding rice, and serving her parents-in-law, and given all her many household responsibilities, usually she will not have the leisure to pursue her studies.

Gentlemen of talent obtain the purple [robes] and succeed in the examinations, they compete in the examination halls, and their network of contacts grows wider by the day. Furthermore, their names are praised by the most famous lords and the highest ministers, and their reputation becomes even more glorious and dazzling. Now, if a woman poet has the good fortune to be matched to a man of sophisticated culture and to enjoy a companionate marriage, he of course will cherish her and make sure that she is known and that her name does not simply vanish. But if the man she is destined to marry turns out to be scarcely human and lacks all understanding of "chanting and reciting," her poetry manuscripts will end up as the covers of pickle jars. Is it not difficult for women poets to make a name for themselves?

Moreover, the hardships are of many kinds. Since my earliest years I studied poetry with my late father, and even before [I had reached adolescence and] my hair had been done up, I had already mastered the tonal rules. When I grew up and married into the Gong family, their family fortunes were on the wane, and so my husband and I had to interrupt our "humming and singing" in order to make a living. Still later, I became a widow and had to assume the responsibility for the family. From Yangzhou I moved to a place west of the district capital of Dantu. In a cramped old house I provided lessons to girls by the light of an autumn lamp, and brush and ink took the place of spinning and weaving. This is after all the common lot of those who endure a life of poverty.

Later on, every day, more and more people would ask me for a poem or painting. And yet some who read my poems doubted their authenticity, and claimed that the poems in *Manuscripts from the Listening to Autumn Study* [*Tingqiuxuan*] had all been written by others at my request. I am unpolished and forthright by nature, so if they would have said that I was incapable of achieving skillfulness in my poems, I would in all sincerity and humility have felt ashamed. But when they claimed that I could not write poems [at all], this I indignantly refused to accept. When I had the leisure to travel, I would visit the most famous men and greatest scholars north and south of the Yangzi, and face-to-face with them [write poems on] assigned rhymes. In this way I thought to clear my name and shut the mouths of those liars who falsely accused me of hiring others to do my writing. I became a disciple of the three gentlemen Yuan Mei, Zeng Yu, and Wang Wenzhi. I showed them my old manuscripts and although I asked them to point out my mistakes, I was greatly praised by these three gentlemen. Those who in this world take hearsay for direct experience may have the nerve not to believe me, but they wouldn't have the nerve not to believe Yuan Mei, Zeng Yu, and Wang Wenzhi!

But even as the voices of doubt died down, the voices of criticism arose. Now they said that it was not fitting for a woman to write poetry, and that it was even more outrageous that I should maintain regular contact with these three gentlemen. But I would like to point out that more than half of the three hundred songs [in the *Book of Odes*] were written by women. "Spreading-Out Dolichos" and "The Mouse-Ear" were composed by a queen and a royal consort; "Gathering Southernwood" and "Gathering Duckweed" were composed by the wife of an official and a titled lady; and "The Cock's Crowing" and "Grey Dawn" were written by the wives of gentlemen. If the Great Sage [Confucius] had actually adhered strictly to the dictum that "words from the inside should not go out," he would have removed or omitted them a long time ago. So why are these poems still included in the Classic?

Now, Yuan Mei, Zeng Yu, and Wang Wenzhi are all white-haired old men. They enjoy the highest status and reputation, and are on a par with the members of the Luoyang Association.[20] All those gentlemen in the world who write poetry venerate them as if they were Mt. Tai or the Big Dipper.[21] After a hundred generations there will still be those who know their names and love their purity. I consider it the greatest fortune of my life to have been able to visit them personally in their homes and have been permitted to receive their instruction. To say that it is not fitting to associate with these three gentlemen is to say that it is forbidden for women to gaze upon Mt. Tai or to look up at the Big Dipper. Those who voice such opinions should keep their mouths shut and laugh at themselves! Now, not to know of a person's talent and for this reason to doubt her is to be small-minded. And to be well aware of a person's talent and yet to criticize her is to be cruel. Small-mindedness and cruelty are not the attitudes of a sincere gentleman.

I am now forty-two years old. Recently I have been reading the esoteric canons and have taken to meditation on emptiness. I intend to seek refuge in the Way in order to admonish myself. I am now unconcerned with blame and praise, and I deeply regret that in the past I loved fame so dearly that I made myself into an object of scandal. But I have not yet been able to free myself from my old habits. Whenever the cool moon penetrates the blinds and I burn incense and sit in meditation, some of the poems that women poets from both far and near once gave to me or sent to me still come to mind. Unable to forget them, I recite them once again, and as I experience the deep feeling and sincere intention that lies beyond the tones and rhymes, it is as if I am sitting next to their authors. It is for this reason that I have gathered these poems together and put them in order in readiness for delivery to the printers. In this way the critics will know that the problem is not that there are so few talented poets among women, but only that it is much harder for them to make a name for themselves. Is it not true of those who are quick to judge people that the less they know, the more they condemn?

As I put together this collection, I lamented the fact that my fortune and my fate have not been as great as that of others. But it is glory enough for me to be able to add my name to those of these lady poets.

---

20. During the latter part of his life in Luoyang, the famous Tang dynasty poet Bai Juyi commissioned a painting of himself seated together with a number of friends and colleagues who were much older than him; he also celebrated the occasion in verse.

21. The Big Dipper is the Chinese name for the constellation Ursa Major.

Written in the autumn of the year dingsi [1797] *of the reign period Jiaqing by the woman scholar of Juqu, Luo Qilan* [style name Peixiang].

This preface provides us with an outline of Luo Qilan's life, but it also shows us that famous male authors did not always seek out women poets to offer them patronage; rather, sometimes women poets would take the initiative and seek the patronage, and the vindication, of male poets they admired.

Luo Qilan's birthplace, Juqu, was located at the foot of Maoshan, one of the holiest places of Daoism. Here, legend had it, immortals centuries earlier had revealed their heavenly secrets to the three Mao brothers. In Luo Qilan's time, Maoshan was still an important religious site, and in one of her later poems Luo Qilan describes a pilgrimage she herself made to the mountain:

Climbing the Highest Peak of Maoshan

I had heard that the three peaks of Maoshan
Rise dimly discernible beyond the clouds,
And that the middle peak soars even higher,
And reaches straight to the blue empyrean.
 Having been born in Juqu, day and night
I would gaze up at their luxurious woods.
Alas! Hampered as I was by my woman's scarf,
It was impossible to tread that holy ground.
 But this spring my women friends and I
Lit incense, abstained from eating meat,
And set a date to make the pilgrimage:
Finally my wish was to be fulfilled!
 The first leg of the journey was a winding road,
But reaching the summit, the view was vast and wide.
Looking up, you could touch the stars and planets,
Looking down, you could see only a hazy mist.
 The distant trees as level as a field of grass,
The passing clouds hanging down like parasols.
Before, I was a bird locked up in its cage,
But now I was a boat leaving the Gorges!
 People are all enmeshed in worldly matters,
Wherever they go, they meet with obstacles.
The worthy and the wise are equally fettered,

Not to mention we who are women in skirts.
 I have a karmic bond with the immortals,
Who wait for me on their famous mountains.
Eventually I'll bid farewell to this world,
And live on ambrosia until the end of time!

Both Luo Qilan's wanderlust and her resentment against the limitations imposed on her by her gender are encountered in numerous poems written at different times in her life:

Resting at White Cloud Cloister after Climbing Mt. Tianping

When you are in the clouds, you can no longer see the clouds:
At the start of the climb, you forget how scorching is the sun.
When you turn to look at the road by which you have come,
You hear nothing but the sound of the spring behind the trees.

Mocking Myself

When I was young, by nature I loved the rough and honest,
So much so that people would call me a man among women.
If I just donned a helmet, they said, and served on the border,
A portrait of me would be painted for the gallery of heroes!

Records of Dreams, Eight Poems, with a Preface

When I was very young, I often had strange dreams, although when I woke up I would remember only half of them. The ancients said: "Dreams may indicate either omens or desires." My dreams mostly concerned things that I could not even begin to wish for—to call them omens would be even more ridiculous. Once, on a day of leisure I turned those dreams I could still remember into poems in order to record them. I am a foolish person recounting my dreams and can only smile at myself.

III

In my dream, I was a student dressed in blue,
The talented were summoned: I took the exams!
After a long journey in a speeding state carriage,
I showed off my brilliance in the literary battles.

In the palace offices I changed my gown to green,
At Heaven's gate my name was displayed in gold.
Riding on horseback, I inspected all the flowers,
A score of miles darkened by fragrance and dust!

VII

In my dream I headed the imperial troops,
Gripping our lances we cleared the dust.
The troops seemed to descend like a flash,
The formation was one of birds and snakes.
 At the border I displayed my heroic tactics,
On the dome of the sky I wrote my ambitions.
Until suddenly I awoke at the sound of a bell,
To find myself still wearing three-inch shoes.[22]

Other poems by Luo Qilan offer us little vignettes of her life:

Enjoying the Cool on a Summer Night

The windows open all around, the small courtyard empty:
The round fan lightly stirs up the wind under the bamboo.
But I am very much afraid tomorrow it will be even hotter:
This is the first time the moon has shone like a wheel of fire!

An Inscription for My Painting of "Teaching Girls by the Autumn Lamp"

South of the Yangzi trees shed their leaves, geese prepare to leave,
And the hazy light of the moon shines through the window gauze.
In the old house, one half of the room is lit up by the single lamp,
As deep into the night, I teach the girls how to read their books.

My Servant Girl Wenqin Married a Certain Man. When a Year Later, I Heard That the First Wife Kept Her Imprisoned and Treated Her Most Cruelly, I Used My Money to Buy Her Back. I Then Wrote the Following Two Poems to Show Her

---

22. The ideal length of bound feet was said to be three inches.

I

For over twelve years, you mixed my powder and scented my clothes,
So when all of a sudden you had to leave me, I was deeply grieved.
Who'd have known that you would be like a swallow in the eaves,
And that after a year you would return back to your mistress of old?

II

Your old clothes still perfectly fit your tiny figure,
At dawn you again wait on me as I make my toilette.
From now on you should put aside any thought of dusty bonds,
And spend your days in this boudoir embroidering Buddhas.

Passing By My Old House in Yangzhou, Two Poems

I

I moor the boat and return again to the city of green willows,
The gate and lane so desolate, changed in the blink of an eye!
Then I meet an old neighbor who should still recognize me:
Over the wall she'd have heard us reading our books out loud.

II

Here I once turned my boudoir into a poetry salon,
Each day we would recite linked couplets till dawn.
Since we wrote these lines on the wall—twelve years!
I wipe away the dust mixed with tears to have a look.

Like Xi Peilan, Luo Qilan also addressed many poems to her poetic
mentor, Yuan Mei.

Visiting Master Yuan Mei in His Sui Garden, (One of) Two Poems

II

In the women's quarters I had heard his name for twenty years,
But only today was I allowed to personally make his acquaintance.
He was quick to ask my style name in front of his study window,
But I had only new poems to offer in lieu of a disciple's gifts.

"Song of the Large Mirror"; Written at Master Jianzhai's (Yuan Mei) Command

The mirror is eight feet long and just as wide.[23] Provincial Administration Commissioner Zhang Songyuan had bought it in Canton and when the Master of Sui Garden [Yuan Mei] visited Hangzhou and saw it, he immediately fell in love with it. The Commissioner then gifted it to the Master, who was overjoyed. He brought it back with him to Sui Garden [in Nanjing] where, after putting it on display in his Xiaocang Mountain Study, he ordered all his disciples to write a poem about it.

Commissioner Songyuan possessed a large mirror,
Measuring eight feet square and as pellucid as snow.
When the Master of Sui Garden visited Hangzhou,
He developed a pure interest in it as soon as he saw it.

The Commissioner prized friendship above objects,
And so very generously gave it to him to take home.
The largest of junks was needed to transport this "cold soul,"[24]
Dragons were startled by the lustrously rippling ocean waves.

On his return he displayed it in his spacious courtyard,
As in the Six Month the rustling autumn winds arose:
Luminous and clear as if cleansed by the waters of the Yangzi,
Its resplendent light causes one to forget the bronzes of the Qin.

The wooded valley of the Sui Garden is serene and secluded,
But, invited into the mirror, the landscape entered the house—
Fine flowers, now hidden, now visible: a myriad layers of spring,
Distant peaks, just barely discernible: a thousand points of green.

In addition, he lit up hundreds upon hundreds of lamps of glass;
Their transparent glow shone everywhere, raising high the spirits.
The Milky Way soundlessly dropped down all of its stars,
And the people below felt as if they'd gone up to the moon.

---

23. Chinese mirrors were traditionally made of bronze and were small in size. Large glass mirrors were an imported rarity in eighteenth-century China.

24. Here the mirror is being compared to a luminous, but chilly, "soul" or spirit, i.e. the moon.

The mirror of the Master's mind illuminates eternity,
The radiance of its precious flames there for all to see.
The Master's disciples all have exceptional talents,
When brushes are in hand, multicolored silks emerge.[25]

The river's water reflects the sky and the moon fills the tower,
The icy vase is bright and clear and marks the start of autumn.[26]
Now take the images of every mountain and river in the world,
And gather them all in this one mirror of perfect intelligence!

Poetry, Scholarship, and Vernacular Prose Fiction

Wang Duan

Wang Duan (1793–1839) may well have been both the most learned author and the most productive poet of the first half of the nineteenth century, but—and we will see why this is—the combination of these two qualities has not endeared her to nineteenth- or twentieth-century anthologists.

Wang Duan hailed from Hangzhou. As a child prodigy she was able to write verse even at an early age and could also, we are told, memorize the most taxing rhapsodies at a glance. After the early death of her mother, she was raised by her aunt, Liang Desheng, an important woman writer in her own right. In 1810, Wang Duan married Chen Peizhi, the son of the indefatigable Hangzhou champion of women's poetry, Chen Wenshu (1771–1843). Although Chen Wenshu never passed more than the provincial examinations, he enjoyed the patronage of the high official Ruan Yuan, and eventually served a number of times as district magistrate. Whereas the nationally known Yuan Mei did not become active as a patron of women poets until the last years of his life, Chen Wenshu, whose fame was much more local, was active in the promotion of women from the very beginning of his literary career. One of his many projects was the restoration of monuments associated with famous women of the past, including the reputed grave of Xiaoqing. This latter project was commemorated in verse by many poets, both male and female. Chen

---

25. Fine writing is often compared to beautiful brocade.
26. "Icy vase" refers to the moon.

Wenshu also wrote commemorative poems and short biographies for five hundred famous women from past and present who were said to have had a connection (at times rather tenuous) to Hangzhou's West Lake. This collection was eventually published under the title *West Lake Collection of Poems about Women* (*Xiling guiyong ji*). Chen Wenshu was assisted in the final editing of this collection by his female poetry disciples, including, among others, his daughter-in-law Wang Duan, and the woman dramatist Wu Zao (1799–1863).

Wang Duan had a great interest in history: she was said to have been able to correctly answer any question on the subject that her father-in-law might pose. She was especially interested in the period of the Yuan-Ming transition, and expressed a great sympathy for Zhang Shicheng, who ruled Suzhou and the surrounding area virtually independently from 1353 to 1367 until he was defeated by Zhu Yuanzhang, the founder of the Ming dynasty. Wang Duan had lived in Suzhou for a number of years during the second decade of the nineteenth century, when her father-in-law was teaching there. This was a time of revived local self-consciousness among Suzhou literati, which may well have contributed to Wang Duan's own interest in the history of the Zhang Shicheng regime. She praised Zhang's moral qualities highly, contrasting them favorably with Zhu's cruelty, and in so doing set herself up against the traditional view that the victor in a struggle for the control of the throne must necessarily be the most virtuous. This distaste for Zhu Yuanzhang also explains the high evaluation she gives in her *Selections of Thirty Poets of the Ming* (*Ming sanshijia shi xuan*) to the poet Gao Qi (1336–1374), a Suzhou native who was executed in 1374, a victim of Zhu Yuanzhang's suspicious paranoia.

Wang Duan's aunt Liang Desheng contributed to this anthology the following preface in which she stresses the interrelation of poetry and history in her niece's work:

Thirty Poets of the Ming was compiled by my niece, Wang Yunzhuang. Yunzhuang is the youngest daughter of my elder sister Yingjuan. Her grandfather, Wang Ganbo, passed the metropolitan examinations at an early age, after which he was awarded the position of observer in the Ministry of Justice. At the age of twenty-four, he applied for leave and returned home without ever again resuming his official career. His library was the most comprehensive in Hangzhou. Her father, Tianqian, was an erudite scholar who was also skilled in the writing of poetry. He lived at home and did not seek office. His sons and daughters all excelled in study, but Yunzhuang was the most intelligent. At the age of seven, she dashed off in just one minute a poem on spring snow. After reading the *Rhapsody on the Ocean* [*Haifu*] of Mu Hua [second half of the third century CE] only twice, she could recite it from memory without omitting a single word. She had only to skim through a book and it would be imprinted on her memory forever—all because of her extraordinary talent.

She married Chen Mengkai [Peizhi] from the same district, the son of magistrate Yunbo [Chen Wenshu]. The magistrate was renowned throughout the world for his poetry and prose, and having been instructed by his father, Mengkai had established a reputation when he was very young. My late uncle, Secretary Shanzhou, and my husband, Master Zhousheng, both encouraged him and appreciated his talents. The couple was considered a match of golden lad and jade maiden.

This work claims to be an anthology of poetry but is really a treatise on history. The preceding Ming dynasty, which lasted for three hundred years, was founded by Zhu Yuanzhang, who conquered the empire on horseback and treated literary scholars like dirt. The Yongle emperor expelled his own nephew and mowed down the loyal and good, and in those centuries there was no end to people who toadied to the power of the eunuchs. Moreover, although the state selected its officials on the basis of examination essays, it had no true understanding of, or brilliant insight into, fine writing or ancient prose. Even though the Former and Later Seven Masters dominated the literary scene [with their classicist poetry], they only competed in outward appearance. The Way of Literature had become the way of the marketplace.

Qian Qianyi's *Collected Poems of Successive Reigns* is rich but also contains much that is worthless and, on top of that, is not systematically arranged. Zhu Yizun's [1629–1709] *Compendium of Ming Poetry* [*Ming shi zong*] is well organized, but is too inclusive and not very discriminating. Shen Deqian's [1673–1796] *New Selection of Ming Poetry* [*Mingshi biecai*] is nothing but an abbreviated version of the *Compendium of Ming Poetry*. These works all reiterate the old views of earlier authorities and are not worthy of study. Yunzhuang in her selection takes sublime purity and classical elegance as her criterion and does away completely with the likes of the Former and Later Seven Masters. In her introductions to writers [of the earliest years of the Ming] such as Wencheng [Liu Ji, 1311–1375], Qingqiu [Gao Qi], Qingjiang [Pei Qiong, d. 1379], and Mengzai [Yang Ji, ca. 1334–ca. 1383], she pays special attention to the causes of right and wrong, success and failure—and she pays even greater attention to reasons for rise and decline, order and chaos. Upon reading this book, not only does the full development of poetry during these three hundred years become as clear as if they were standing right there in front of your eyes, but the right and wrong, success and failure of those three hundred years become as obvious as if they were lying right there in the palm of your hand. An anthology such as this really deserves a wide distribution.

On reading this book, I am saddened by the thought that my elder sister died so young and did not live to see the fine results of her daughter's scholarship. But I also deem it a blessing that my niece, despite my elder sister's demise, achieved such fine results in her scholarship. Now that I have read the book, I return it to her and write this at the beginning so it may serve as a preface.

Liang Desheng's preface is not included in the woodblock edition of *Selections of Thirty Poets of the Ming* found at Harvard University's Harvard-Yenching Library. The Harvard edition opens rather with a description of the "guidelines" or editorial principles behind the compilation of the anthology, and following the table of contents is Wang Duan's own "Record of a Dream." This latter text, which we include here as an example of Wang Duan's narrative and argumentative skills, was intended as an explanation of why the anthology includes no poems by Song Lian (1310–1381) but includes a sizeable selection of the poems of Liu Ji (1311–1375). Song Lian and Liu Ji had both started out as trusted Confucian advisors of Zhu Yuanzhang. A few years after the Ming dynasty was officially established in 1368, however, both men retired from active government service and Liu Ji died seven years later in 1375. In 1380 Zhu Yuanzhang grew suspicious of his prime minister, Hu Weiyong, suspecting him of designs on the throne. Among other crimes of which Zhu Yuanzhang accused Hu was that of having poisoned Liu Ji. Thousands of other officials, including Song Lian, were accused of complicity in Hu Weiyong's nefarious plots. Thanks to the intervention of Empress Ma and the heir apparent, Song Lian's life was spared, but he was banished to the western border and died en route. Song Lian's reputation as a representative of neo-Confucian moralism was greatly enhanced when his favorite disciple Fang Xiaoru was condemned to a horrific death by the Yongle emperor after Fang criticized him to his face for having usurped the throne. Song Lian's name would not be completely cleared until 1541, when he was posthumously awarded the title of Cultured and Exemplary Duke. Wang Duan's text reads as follows:

After I had finished compiling my *Thirty Poets of the Ming*, one night I dreamt that I came to an old monastery. In the main hall there was a shrine, within which there was a [statue on a] lotus pedestal. The standing image of over three feet high was dressed in a gauze cap and a scarlet gown, and its impressive-looking face sported a white beard. Next to the statue stood an elderly woman in a brown dress who smiled at me and said: "Do you know who this is? It is the Chan monk, Fenggan.[27] During the Ming dynasty he was reborn as Song Lian, and now he has become a Buddha. Why don't you pay your respects to him?" "So this is the Cultured and Exemplary Duke!" I said, "I have revered him all of my life!" I immediately bowed to him, and then said to the woman: "If the Cultured and Exemplary Duke is here, there should also be images of the other gentlemen such as Liu Ji and Gao Qi. I would like to pay obeisance to all of them." The woman pointed to another room and said: "They are all in there. You will be able to recognize them yourself." When I walked into the room, I saw some tens of sculpted images: some in official gown and cap, some in the garb of a Confucian student, some dressed in full armor, and some in straw capes and bamboo hats. Before each image rested a pear-wood tablet inscribed with a name, but when I tried to look at the tablets more closely, I found the characters had been smudged by the incense smoke that wafted up from the burners and so I was unable to read them. I then woke up with a start.

I then had the following thoughts: "Liu Ji and Song Lian were equally famous for their contribution to the foundation of the Ming dynasty. Liu Ji became well known for his military planning, while Song Lian was famous for his literary prose. Now although Liu Ji's poems are gloriously represented in the first chapter of my anthology, Song Lian's poems have not been included at all. This must be the first cause of his unhappiness. Moreover, in my anthology I discuss at length the authors and their times. The selections of poems by Gao Qi and the others are all preceded by an evaluation, and the cases of slander and praise, failure and right of the several centuries of the Ming, I have completely corrected and revised. Yet I do not devote a single word to the Cultured and Exemplary Duke. That must be the second cause of his unhappiness.

Furthermore, the Cultured and Exemplary Duke served the founder of the Ming for tens of years and was the acknowledged leader of the Confucian scholars. Even though it is doubtful he committed any crime, [the emperor] did not relent in the least even after he had executed [Song Lian's] sons and grandsons but rather availed himself of the opportunity to drown both him and his descendants. Even when Empress Ma and the heir-apparent came to his rescue, the Cultured and Exemplary Duke still could not avoid being banished to the

---

27. Fenggan is best known as a companion of Hanshan, the semi-legendary poet-monk of the Tang dynasty.

southern wilds, and upon his death, his family was not permitted to take his corpse back to his hometown for burial. This is truly lamentable! Moreover, he is listed among the officials of the Yuan dynasty by Wang Shizhen [1526–1590] in his *Miscellaneous Writings* [*Zabian*], and Wang Ao [1450–1521] states in his *Brush Records* [*Biji*] that he had been a compiler in Yuan dynasty times. Now, Liu Ji twice served the Yuan dynasty, but that is never regarded as a blemish on his achievements in supporting the Mandate. So what is wrong with the Cultured and Exemplary Duke having served the Yuan? If one checks the facts in his biography in the *History of the Ming* [*Ming shi*], one finds that he was recommended to serve as compiler in the Hanlin Academy sometime during the Zhizheng reign period [1342–1367], but that he declined the appointment because of his parents' old age and never took it up—he retired to the Longmen Mountains and devoted himself to writing. In Liu Ji's collection, one can find the text of a poem written to see Song Lian off upon entering the Way. Both the *Collected Poems of the Successive Reigns* and the *Compendium of Ming Poems* mention the fact that Song Lian declined the appointment and retired from the world. It should therefore be an incontrovertible fact that he never actually served the Yuan. Wang Shizhen and his ilk heap abuse on their betters and besmirch both their careers and their characters. What kind of attitude is that?

In his *Nanjing Collection* (*Moling ji*), my father-in-law has completely cleared the names of all the civil and military officials of the early Ming who were unjustly condemned. . . . I believe that I too have spared no effort to reach a fair judgment on the gentlemen of the Ming. The reason that I appear to be in default with respect to the Cultured and Exemplary Duke is that even though his poetic talent and force may have been wide and expansive, his poems are not as refined and pure as his prose writings. Now, in my anthology I include people on the basis of their poetry, which is not the same as selecting poetry on the basis of the person. If I were to include his poems in the main selection, I would have to lower my standards, but if I were to include him in an appendix, I am afraid I would be belittling him. For that reason I did not include him in my anthology. This is a guideline that applies to the book as a whole. Because I did not include his poetry, I also did not discuss the facts of his life—that is based on another guideline. This means that the injustice the Cultured and Exemplary Duke suffered has not been made manifest to later generations in this book. Could this be the reason that he appeared to me in a dream?

The Cultured and Exemplary Duke's character was most correct, his scholarship was most solid, he served the emperor longer than anyone else and offered him more counsel than anyone else. As he was also fully conversant with Buddhist scholarship, it is indeed quite fitting that he, having been a reincarnation of

Fenggan, should be reborn in heaven as a buddha. It was my good fortune that in my dream I could pay my respects to him with a little incense. Even though I did not include his poems, I cannot help but discuss his personality. I therefore have appended this account in order to record my mistake. It may also serve as a warning to all those later generations in the whole world who are too severe in their judgment of earlier men and besmirch the reputation of the famous and worthy.

It is said that when Gu Sili [1655–1722] completed his selection of Yuan dynasty poetry, several hundred people in ancient-style caps and gowns appeared to him [in a dream] to express their gratitude. In my dream, I also saw some tens of statues that were the recipients of smoke offerings upon which their souls could rely. But how could I dare accept the suggestion that this has been due to my efforts to open up and display that which has been obscured and hidden."

Written by Wang Duan on the tenth day of the first month of winter of the kengchen *year of the Jiajing reign period* [1820].

Wang Duan's *Selections of Thirty Poets of the Ming* was unusual in that it was the first published anthology of male poets compiled by a woman. For at least two centuries prior to Wang Duan there had been women critics and anthologists of women's poetry, and contemporary and later women anthologists continued to devote their efforts to the writings of women writers. In the introduction to this section, we quoted from the *Correct Beginnings: Women's Poetry of Our August Dynasty*, which aimed to include representative poems and short biographies of as many Qing dynasty women poets as possible. This anthology was compiled by Wanyan Yun Zhu, who assembled 1,700 poems by 933 poets; later, her granddaughter would compile a sequel of more than nine hundred poems by yet another 459 women authors. Another work, *Comments on Poems by Famous Ladies (Mingyuan shihua)*, edited by Wang Duan's friend Shen Shanbao (style name Xiangpei; 1807–1862), represented the first work of poetry criticism (rather than an anthology of poems with critical commentary) written by an author of either sex, exclusively devoted to women. A woman named Yan Heng (1826–1854) collected almost eighty anecdotes about literary and artistic women of the Qing dynasty. She entitled the book *Tales of the World about Women (Nü shishuo)*, indicating that she saw it as belonging to the long tradition of collected anecdotes about notable personages. When women writers of the first half of the nineteenth century engaged in philological scholarship, they also placed a particular emphasis on works and subjects of special concern to women. For instance, Wang Zhaoyuan (1763–1851), from Fushan in Shandong province, is best known for her 1812 annotated edition of Liu Xiang's *Biographies of Exemplary Women*, although she also wrote a short treatise on dreams, and is said to have assisted her husband, the scholar Hao Yixing (1757–1825), with his annotations to the *Books of the Jin* and *Books of the Song* and his commentaries to the *Book of Odes*. For a woman scholar to pass critical judgment on male literary achievements (and moral attainments), however, as Wang Duan did in her anthology of Ming poetry, was without precedent.

Wang Duan's interest in the period of the Yuan-Ming transition resulted in a long novel in eighty chapters as well, entitled *Anecdotal History of the Yuan and Ming* (*Yuan Ming yishi*). In contrast to the writing women of tenth-century Japan or seventeenth-century Western Europe and later, Chinese women writers have always shown a remarkable reluctance to engage in prose fiction, especially vernacular fiction. While it has been suggested that some of the relatively short "novels of poets and beauties" (*caizi jiaren xiaoshuo*) on the (mostly chaste) love affairs of brilliant young students and sophisticated young ladies of the seventeenth and eighteenth centuries may have been written by women, there is no positive evidence to support this claim. The only woman writer of the seventeenth century who is on record as having written "fictional narratives" is Zhang Hao, one of the members of the Banana Garden Poetry Club, but unfortunately none of these tales has been preserved. Factors that may have contributed to the reluctance of women writers to try their hand at vernacular fiction are the low status of the genre and its often satiric and bawdy discussion of social abuses. The fact that most vernacular novels have an explicit narrator who is clearly identified as male, and usually relatively low class, may also have been a contributing factor. It is clear that by the early nineteenth century, in large part due to the immense popularity of the *Dream of the Red Chamber* and *Flowers in the Mirror*, women had become avid readers of fiction, and it is therefore not surprising that the earliest known women authors (Wang Duan and Gu Taiqing) of vernacular fiction both lived in the nineteenth century.

Wang Duan's marriage to Chen Peizhi appears to have been a happy one. She bore her husband two sons, the youngest of which died in infancy. Chen Peizhi died in 1828 in Hankou while on his way to take up an official post in Yunnan. When the couple's surviving son, by then a teenager, developed severe mental problems because of the death of his father, Wang Duan turned to religion for solace, and partly under the influence of her father-in-law, devoted the remaining years of her life to religious devotions. Unfortunately, convinced of the need to make a complete break with the vanities of the secular world, she destroyed the manuscript of her as-yet-unpublished novel.

A large portion of Wang Duan's more than one thousand surviving poems consists of "poems on historical subjects" (*yongshishi*). These scholarly poems are as a rule heavily laden with allusions, and even though Wang Duan herself supplies them with extensive annotations, one example may suffice to show that they do not lend themselves easily to translation. The subject of the following quatrain is Li Si, the infamous prime minister of the equally infamous First Emperor. Li Si was a native not of Qin, but of one of its neighboring states. As a young man he had come to Qin, which was then rapidly expanding its territory, to pursue a career. When at one point the state of Qin wanted to expel all foreigners, Li Si submitted a famous memorial in which he argued for the usefulness to the Qin state of foreign materials, artifacts, entertainments, and people, and succeeded in having the xenophobic decree rescinded. As prime minister of the Qin empire, however, Li Si tried to stamp out dissension by not only "burning the books" but also burying alive overly opinionated scholars. Following the death of the First Emperor, Li Si lost out in the ensuing power struggle to the chief eunuch Zhao Gao, who had him executed. When Li Si and his son were taken to the execution grounds of the Qin capital of Xianyang, Li Si was said to have expressed regret only for the fact that he would never again be able to go out hunting with his dogs.

> Cruel and vindictive, Li Si assisted the First Emperor of Qin,
> By the time the Classics' ashes had scattered, the state too had collapsed.
> If he had much earlier allowed himself to be expelled as a foreigner,
> He wouldn't be sighing now in Xianyang over his brown hunting dogs.

A related genre of poetry that is well represented in Wang Duan's work is that of "lamenting the past" (*huaigu*), poems written on the occasion of a visit to a famous place in Chinese history where, often from a high position overlooking the ruins, the poet becomes aware of the ephemeral nature of glory and the insignificance of a mere human being in space and time. An example of a *huaigu* poem by Wang Duan is "Xuanwu Lake." Xuanwu Lake was located in Nanjing, behind Cock-crow Hill. The state archives of the Ming dynasty had once been housed in a library on the shores of this lake, and the desolation of this location, which had been abandoned following the Manchu conquest, had earlier inspired the famous seventeenth-century poet Wu Weiye (1609–1672) to write one of his best-known works. Wang Duan's poem, as the first line suggests, was not inspired by an actual visit, but rather by a painting of this site:

> The painting of Cockcrow Hill's scenery unfolds:
> On the waves of Xuanwu Lake green algae drift.
> The former dynasty's archives lost in wind and rain,
> The new era's towers filled with orioles and flowers.
> In the cool mist, the waterfowl disappear into the clouds,
> In the setting sun, fishing boats arrive singing of the night.
> All that remains of the past is the new song by Wu Weiye:
> The willows at the water's edge are overcome by grief.

The majority of the remaining works in Wang Duan's collection are occasional and social poems. The following poem, describing a visit to Tai Lake outside Suzhou, is one of her very few nature poems:

> The heavens' blue here looks like mist and rain,
> The mountain peaks are reflected here in a mirror.
> And thirty thousand acres of cool clouds
> All of a sudden surround this Tai Lake.
> On the banks between fields idle petals fall;
> A distant flute mourns in a fishing village.
> I climb on high, express my autumn sorrow:
> Where is there a Zither Terrace in this world?

The final line turns what might have been a simple nature poem into a work of social criticism: the Zither Terrace was built by the population of Danfu district to commemorate Confucius' disciple Mizi Jian's virtu-ous administration of their locality. Thus to say that there is no Zither Terrace is to say that in this day and age there are no administrators of virtue.

Gu Chun (Taiqing)

Gu Chun, better known by her style name Gu Taiqing, is generally regarded as the greatest female Manchu poet of the Qing dynasty. She was born in 1799 to a family that had come down in the world because of a disgraced grandfather—a Manchu prince who, several decades earlier, found himself on the losing side of a bitter factional dispute and was executed. Much speculation has gone into explaining why Gu Taiqing, a Manchu, has the Han Chinese surname of Gu. One of the theories is that when she married, in an effort to escape the shadow cast by her grandfather, she adopted the surname Gu. Another is that she was raised by a Chinese bondservant family by that name. In any case, little is known for certain about her early life, although from her poems it would appear that it was quite an unsettled one and may have involved a considerable amount of moving around.

When Gu Taiqing was twenty-six, she became the concubine of a Manchu prince by the name of Yihui (style name Zizhang). Yihui, who, like Gu Taiqing, was born in 1799, was a grandson of the fifth son of the Qianlong emperor and was actually related to Gu Taiqing's family as well. He was a very talented young man, known for his love of poetry and extensive scholarship in a wide range of subjects, including music, philosophy, Buddhism, mathematics, and architecture. A good Manchu aristocrat, he was also extremely proficient at hunting and riding. Because of their family connections, Gu Taiqing met and fell in love with Yihui long before they were married. Again because of her shameful antecedents, however, his relations put up considerable resistance to accepting Gu Taiqing into the family, and it was only after overcoming many obstacles that she finally became his concubine. Yihui had married his first wife, Miaohua, when he was fifteen. Gu Taiqing appears to have gotten along quite well with her, and wrote a number of poems describing excursions they took together. In 1828, Miaohua died prematurely at the age of thirty-one. Because Yihui and Gu Taiqing had such a compatible marriage, he did not remarry. The years the couple had together between 1828 and Yihui's premature death in 1838 at the age of forty, were ones of great happiness for Gu Taiqing.

To a large extent, it was from Yihui that Gu Taiqing learned the art first of writing *shi* poems and then song lyrics, and they wrote a great number of poems to and in reply to each other. The earliest poems written to her husband (or to the rhymes of a poem written by her husband) are in the *shi* form and, true to generic convention, they often deal less with emotion and more with historical and philosophical themes. They make generous use of allusions to historical, literary, and philosophical texts (including Daoist and Buddhist ones) that she no doubt read and studied together with her husband. Gu Taiqing also wrote many poems on the occasion of excursions taken with her husband, as in the following two poems, the first in *shi* form, the second a song lyric:

Ascending to the Heavenly Wandering Pavilion with My Husband on Summer's Longest Day

On summer's longest day we climb the tower with our worries:
Year after year of unbearable drought—what is there to be done?
In the sky filled with a red-hot sun, the cicadas buzz urgently;
Over the five-sided red balustrade, the orioles' shadow lingers.
Atop the western peaks, the drifting dust could hardly mean rain;
In the eastern suburbs, the old trees have half-withered branches.
And although these halls and pavilion are free of that blazing heat,
How much more we long for copious rains to pour down soon.

To the Melody of "High Hills and Flowing Rivers" (*Gaoshan liushui*)
Written to the Rhymes of a (Lyric) Composed by My Husband at the Clear Breeze Pavilion

The many mountains with their myriad ravines draw out the long winds
Which penetrate the woodland marshes.
The dawn's light is splendid;
Beyond the tower the green shadows are deep,
Leaning on the railing, we point especially toward the east.
The waters of the Yongding River,
Like the arc of a rainbow,
Cool and fresh as can be.
The valleys filled with the chattering of hidden birds:
Green mist and drizzling rain.
Let the sea and the heavens be boundless and vast,
We will fly and leap amidst being and non-being!

The cloud's shape
Looks like a Guanyin but also a shaggy old dog!
To those of No-Mind
Such transformations are all Emptiness.
The slender grasses cover the craggy cliffs,
The cliff flowers so fine turn red in the sun.
The Clear Breeze Pavilion
Reaches up to the Milky Way,
The peaks lined up like children.
Which year will we be able to return.
And laughing and teasing, see who's champion?

Yihui fathered nine children; Miaohua bore him four children—two girls and two boys, and Gu Taiqing gave birth to five children—two girls and three boys. The last of these, however, was still an infant when he died in 1834. Gu Taiqing wrote the following short poem to express her grief and sorrow:

On the Twenty-second Day of the Twelfth Month, Weeping for Ninth Son, Zaitong

My son Tong had not yet lived a full year,
When early one morning he left us and died.
Who says that after a time one will forget?
The tears keep on falling without any end.

Gu Taiqing's grief was even greater when, just four years later, Yihui suddenly passed away. Gu Taiqing was heartbroken and from the many poems she wrote in subsequent years, often on the occasion of his birthday, one can see that this grief took a very long time to subside:

On His Birthday in the Year *Gengzi* (1840), Mourning My Departed Husband

Forty-two years have gone by like a dream—
Easterly breezes, warm sun: another spring.
Half a life of wearisome toil: to whom can I trust to speak of it?
To two words "fleeting" and "cease" I entrust this self of mine.
 Contemplating change, I can for a bit forget these vulgar trials;
With my books for food, perhaps I can relieve this pure poverty.

I send word to the Nine Springs below that he must wait for me:[28]
Alone I sit and raise the wick, my kerchief soaked with tears.

Barely three months after Yihui's death, Gu Taiqing was forced to take her four surviving children and leave the family home. It is not clear why; some scholars speculate that Yihui's eldest son, Miaohua's child, kicked them out when he inherited his father's title, others that Yihui's relatives, who never approved of her marriage in the first place, suspected Gu Taiqing of carrying on an affair with the noted poet Gong Zichen (1792–1841), something she vehemently denied. The following poem describes what happened:

On the Seventh Day of the Seventh Month, My Husband Departed This World and on the Twenty-eighth Day of the Tenth Month, I was Ordered to Take My Two Sons, Jian and Chu, and My Two Daughters, Shuwen and Shuyi, Leave the House and Move Out of the Neighborhood. Since We Had Nowhere to Go, I Sold Off My Gold Phoenix Hairpins, and by So Doing Was Able to Get a Place to Live. I Wrote This Poem as a Record of This

The immortal has already become a crane among the clouds—
Is there a year he will come back once again to his old home?
Who will on my behalf clear my name of that false accusation?
Uproot the vines and repair the rooms is what I must do alone.
I have already seen the phoenix wings soar away in the wind,
But there are still the flowers whose gleam shines on the eyes.
Sitting motionless I cannot bear to think of how it was before:
Anxious sorrow rends my guts, my heart is filled with grief.

Once the immediate problem of where to live had been settled, Gu Taiqing turned back to memories of her departed husband. She greatly missed his support as husband and father, and also the times they spent writing and enjoying poetry and other aesthetic pursuits together:

---

28. The Nine Springs is another name for the Yellow Springs (the abode of the dead below the earth).

I Had Not Written Any Poems Since the Death and Burial of My Late Husband. That Winter I Gathered Together the Drafts of Poetry He Had Left Behind, Which Contained Many Poems We Had Written Together; When I Saw Them I Was Deeply Moved and Since Old Habits Are Hard To Forget, I Penned a Few Words; I Dared Not Complain, So I Briefly Noted Some of the Misfortunes I Have Suffered in This Life To Show to My Two Sons, Jian and Chu

> Dark and overcast, the sky threatens snow,
> Huddled by the brazier, I sit in the south light.
> Unrolling the scroll I read the poems left behind,
> My pain so great that I cannot utter a word.
> And then, this gaunt and sickly body,
> The tears so many my eyes are dim—
> The immortal has joined the other immortals;
> He has drifted back to the Jade Capital.[29]
> I have sons whose nature is foolish and stubborn,
> I have daughters who are still just little babes.
> A peck of grain and a length of cloth—
> A home to which we can no longer go.
> In a narrow lane, a small little house,
> That feels just like a deserted valley.
> My sons and daughters cry and wail,
> My grieving heart flutters like a flag.
> I feel like being buried underground,
> But I dare not treat this body lightly.
> I should not be thinking of myself:
> For you, I must see my children grown.

To the Melody of "Treasuring the Autumn Flowers" (*Xichouhua*)
On the Twenty-first of the Seventh Month of the Year *ren-geng* (1842), I Was Very Moved When I Saw Once Again the Heavenly Wandering Pavilion Where We Used to Stay

---

29. The Jade Capital is one of the celestial abodes of the immortals.

The Heavenly Wandering from my old dreams,
Leaning against the pellucid sky, is still
The tower pavilion of those years.
But over the elegant doorway and latticed windows
Spider webs secretly draw a screen.
Wild grasses grow every which way around the steps,
And on the secluded paths
Only mallow-weeds and wild oatgrass.
Lonely and desolate . . .
Cawing in the slant of afternoon sun
Black magpies are still busily building their nests.

I can just make out a corner of the balustrade,
And in a spot covered with a jungle of weeds,
I glimpse the red heart of a crab apple tree.
The scenery is as always:
The people have changed.
But to whom can I speak of this?
So awful to relive these four years:
Thinking of the disappointments
The wounded feelings, the repulsed heart.
Unstoppable:
Facing the west wind,
My tears come gushing down.

The years that followed were ones of relative poverty and hardship, but Gu Taiqing managed to raise all of her children successfully, and see them all married off and settled. When her eldest son attained an official post, she was finally able to live in relative comfort once again. She also continued to write, and by the time of her death, sometime around 1876, she had produced an impressive body of poetry: over eight hundred *shi* poems and over three hundred song lyrics. It is these lyrics for which she has become most famous.

Many of Gu Taiqing's song lyrics are conventional in terms of their themes of love and longing, but demonstrate a very subtle sensibility, reminiscent at times of the song lyrics of Li Qingzhao. A contemporary critic said of her song lyrics:

The beauty of Taiqing's song lyrics resides in their overall atmosphere rather than in [specific] words and phrases. If one looks for it in the total form or general organization, one finds it impossible to put one's finger on any one or two things, or on the artistry and craft of this sound or that word.

Like many women poets before her, Gu Taiqing showed a special fascination for the plum tree, the flowers of which blossom on bare branches in the earliest days of spring, and sometimes even during the last days of winter according to the traditional Chinese calendar. In the first stanza of the following lyric, Gu Taiqing compares the purity of the plum blossoms to immortal maidens who have descended to earth after having performed the dance of "Rainbow Skirt" at the heavenly court of the Queen Mother of the West at Jasper Pond. (Legend had it that in a dream, Emperor Xuanzong of the Tang had been taken to the heavenly realms to enjoy a performance of this dance.) The second stanza then shifts to a characterization of the author herself as a plum blossom, and of the inner apartments of the princely mansion as a grotto heaven.

To the Melody of "Entering the Pass" (*Rusai*)
Potted Plum Trees

Beautiful flowers,
Pure and fragrant,
Just about to blossom:
Like immortals who having finished a performance
Of "Rainbow Skirts" descended from Jasper Pond—
Red suits them well,
White suits them too.

The night is cool in the little tower as the moon's shadows shift,
Behind the low screen
The blanket is cold, dreams stay away.
Hidden from view in a grotto heaven, she guards her icy form,
Unbeknownst to the humming bees,
Unbeknownst to the butterflies.

As Gu Taiqing spent most of her adult life in Beijing and surroundings, the spring scenes she describes in her poems were often different from those of the women poets of the Jiangnan region. For one thing, snow was a far more frequent occurrence in the northern capital Beijing.

To the Melody of "Shouting Fire" (*Hehuoling*)
One Day after the Beginning of "Waking of Insects" of the Year *Yihai* (1839) I Went to Visit Yunlin While Snow Was Falling. When I Returned, the Snow on the Road Had Become Deep. Thereupon I Composed This Short Lyric by the Light of the Lamp

Long separated: our feelings even more ablaze,
Deepest friendship: no end to our discussions.
My good friend had me stay and poured a fragrant cup,
Until the hour when the crows fly off to roost,
And window-shadows turn to evening twilight.

The east wind blowing in my face is cold,
The spring snow falls down across the sky.
Returning tipsily I do not fear the city gate will close.
The entire road as if made of alabaster,
The entire road empty of cart tracks,
The entire road of distant hills and nearby trees
All decked out to make a jade-white universe!

To the Melody of "Beautiful Weather" (*Fengguanghao*)
Admiring the Blossoms at Heavenly Peace Monastery (Tianning si), I Saw from Afar the Massed Snow on the Western Hills

What a fine easterly wind—
And what balmy weather!
The azaleas in the flower plots dazzle the eyes with their red,
And intoxicate the roving bees.

A stretch of green mist: the willows of the nearby village—
As if embroidered by spring!
Myriads of layers of massed snow on the Western Hills:
Like lotus flowers of whitest jade.

Spring might come later in the north, but one of its first harbingers is the tender yellow of weeping willows:

To the Melody of "Beautiful Weather" (*Fengguanghao*)
Spring Day

How beautiful the weather
Now the days grow longer!
It is the First Month, so the roving bees leave their hives,
And busy themselves for us.

The finest place to look for spring is by the river's bank
Where misty threads are swaying.
Who was able to dye these supple branches such a tender yellow?
They make a great composition!

    The departure of spring was marked both by falling flowers and drifting willow floss, in the north as well as the south:

To the Melody of "Little Town on the River" (*Jiangchengzi*)
Falling Flowers

Flowers bloom and flowers fall all through the year,
Yet I do pity the tattered reds,
And blame the easterly winds.
Greatly annoyed by the unruly crowds,
Like snowflakes blown against the curtain.
I sit and watch the drifting flowers, their season past,
As spring once again
Departs in far too great a hurry.

Who on earth shares my grief, my pity for the flowers?
Too listless even to make my morning toilette:
That's how much I am overcome by sorrow!
When the swallows arrive,
A red rain falls to the east of the tower.
They cannot bear away this springtime sorrow of mine:
Those utterly bumbling
Bees that buzz about!

To the Melody of "A Courtyard Filled with Fragrance" (*Mantingfang*)
Following the Original Rhyme Words of "On Willow Floss" by Yunlin Zhuren

Tired of embroidery I put down my needle,
Laying out my books I lie down for a while:
This is the moment the flitting orioles are at their most diligent.
As the east wind stirs the curtains,
Again spring sees off the souls of the flowers.
It is truly impossible to tie down the splendor of spring—
Lost in infinitude,
It comes and goes without a trace.
And without a cause:
That weak willow floss also knows
How to tumble about in the wind.

Reckless and foolish it flits here and there,
Stirring people's emotions and thoughts,
Secretly it goes on from early till late.
Riling the red ropes of the swaying swings,
And the brushwood gates beneath the moon.
In wild profusion it sinks into the grass and mud,
And without rhyme or reason
Activates the roots of sorrow.
At the edge of the world
Thousands of snowflakes in a cloudless sky
Drift and dance into the garden next door.

To the Melody of "As in a Dream" (*Rumengling*)
Sending Off Spring

Yesterday I sent spring back home:
On the branches the red becomes less and less.
Beyond the curtains the green shadows increase,
The ground is strewn with fallen petals—who will sweep them up?
Don't sweep them up!
Don't sweep them up,
Just let the easterly winds blow them into old age!

The oppressive heat of the summer apparently rarely inspired poems or lyrics, but the inspiration to write was always bound to return with the coming of autumn.

To the Melody of "Phoenix on Her Hairpin" (*Chaitou huang*) Autumn Crab Apple

Clear, clear dew—
Pure, pure it forms.
Tender red delicate dots spit out from the flower's heart.
Flowers like tears,
Leaves like kingfishers' feathers—
Flower after flower, leaf after leaf,
All with the same sour taste.
Take note!
Take note!
Take note!

The insects sound scolding,
The westerly wind is jealous.
Once autumn comes, who then will they order about?
Idle sorrows accumulate,
No one can get to sleep.
A tattered half of a full moon,
A chill rises in the embroidered quilt.
Doze off!
Doze off!
Doze off!

To the Melody of "One Cut-out Plum" (*Yijianmei*) On a Moonlit Night Drinking Alone

Lonely in the empty courtyard, the moon up in one corner—
Inside the window, the light of the lamp;
Beyond the curtains, the light of the sky.
Alone I fill the cup to the brim to fend off the slight chill:
Poetry exhausts the withered heart,
Wine fills up the melancholy heart.

Crossed branches of flower shadows will not line up straight—
No sooner do they descend the hall,

Than they climb up the eastern wall.
The third watch has already sounded, the night is so long!
I straighten up the square bed,
Put some incense in the burner.

To the Melody of "Song of Meeting of Metal Wind and Jade Dew" (*Jinfeng yulu xiangfeng qu*)
On the Day Following the Mid-Autumn Festival, When Visiting, Together with Yunlin, Xiangpei, and My Relative Xiaxian, Eight-Treasure Hill (Babaoshan) in the Rain, the Sky Cleared at the End of the Day; Following the Rhymes of Xiangpei [30]

A cold mist envelops the trees,
A chill wind whips our faces,
Pointed peaks beyond the clouds lined up like a screen:
We do not break the date we had set, and meet in the rain,
Just as once, a long time ago,
Dai Kui braved the snow in Shanyin.[31]

Look out the window toward the east,
Look out the window toward the west:
Everywhere autumn's splendor is utterly pure.
Pouring wine I ponder a poem as the evening sky starts to clear,
And the light of the setting sun falls
On shattered steles and broken columns.

To the Melody of "Celebrating the Fresh Coolness" (*He xinliang*)
In the Rain We Departed Early from Nangu; Using the Rhymes of Jiang Zhushan

Here and there the cocks have started to crow,
And I hear the desolate

---

30. Xiangpei is the style name of Gu Taiqing's woman friend Shen Shanbao.

31. One of the best-known anecdotes in *A New Account of Tales of the World* recounts how once Dai Kui was struck with a sudden desire to visit his friend one evening during a snowstorm. He departed immediately but by the time he arrived at his friend's door early the next morning, the urge had passed and so he went home without even seeing him.

Rustling rain that never ends,
As the sky is slowly lit up by the dawn.
We pack the luggage and insist on an early departure:
It will be a mostly rocky mountain road—
Because of the autumn floods
Even fewer people are traveling.
On either side of the road, the mountain flowers are like a tapestry:
All our carts and chests are too small
To transport this autumn splendor.
Cinnabar nuts
Combine with wild jujubes.

The endless sky refuses to wipe away the somber clouds,
Weeping willows everywhere
Shake their misty threads.
As chilly crickets chirp their aging,
Barley and millet far and wide on the high plain—
All blown to the ground by a night of westerly wind.
Rapidly rising rivers
Completely encircle lonely villages.
As we round the cloudy ridge I once again look back,
And vaguely make out
The lofty mountain range at the edge of the sky,
As the clouds again rise
On the hills all around.

Traditionally, neither winter nor summer was the preferred season for poetry. The following unusual lyric not only describes a winter scene, but also testifies to Gu Taiqing and her husband's shared interest in Buddhism.

To the Melody of "Partridge Sky" (*Zhegutian*) On a Winter Night I Was Listening to My Husband Expounding the Way, When Suddenly the Water-Clock Announced the Third Watch. The Fading Blossoms of the Potted Plum Trees Gave Out a Fragrance, I Experienced a Moment of Enlightenment, and Composed the Following

Staying up late, discussing the sutras—the clock announced midnight:
The wondrous expediencies of life are in the end not miraculous at all.

We people of the world should not long for the flower's fragrance:
For when the fragrance is most intense, the flower is about to fade.

The bees produce their honey,
The silkworms spit out thread:
How can their labors go unrecognized once they are done?
The sands of the Ganges can be counted but kalpas never can—
The great myriad of phenomena serves as our greatest teacher.

Some of Gu Taiqing's lyrics were occasioned by social activities in and around Beijing and document her interactions with her network of women friends. Other lyrics delineate the emotions on receiving letters from women friends living in the Jiangnan region.

To the Melody of "River Town Plum Blossom Intro" (*Jiangcheng meihua yin*)
On A Rainy Day Receiving a Letter from Yingjiang

My friend has sent me a letter from a thousand *li* away:
Hurry up and open it!
Open it up slowly!
Who knows if what's in the letter is happy or not—I cannot guess!
Since we parted heat and cold have changed according to season.
You to the south of the Yangzi, I to the north:
Moved by the grief of separation,
I cannot help but pace to and fro.

Pacing to and fro,
Pacing to and fro,
My feelings extend forever!
The sky on one end,
The water on one end,
I dream and I dream,
But in my dream cannot see
The gown and hairpin of those days.
Who'd know the westerly wind would lift its head and reduce my heart to ashes.
Next year when you return home and see me again,
I won't be the same

As how, when we parted,
I used to look.

As is clear from the above lyric, dreams played a major part in Gu
Taiqing's life and often inspired her to poetry.

To the Melody of "Settling Stormy Waves" (*Dingfengbo*)
A Bad Dream

Each and every affair on careful consideration has its cause,
For half a life I've suffered every sort of bitter misfortune.
Faraway I see migrating geese who have nowhere to land:
As evening falls,
The "wagtails on the plain" move me to tears.[32]

Wanting to express my sorrows, I drown my heart in wine—
A bag of bones
Completely befuddled, quite unlike the self of my youth.
I wake up from a bad dream, heart even more anxious,
As through the window
Drifting flowers and falling leaves join forces to scare me.

To the Melody of "Little Town on the River" (*Jiangchengzi*)
Record of a Dream

Mist locks in the cold stream, moonlight locks in the sand,
As riding a magical raft
I visit the immortal realms—
All the way along the clear brook
                    the two oars slice right through the mist.
As soon as I pass a small bridge, the landscape changes:
By the light of the moon
I see plum trees in bloom.

Myriads of blossoming plum trees, their shadows in wild profusion,
By the edge of the hills,
By the edge of the stream—

---

32. "Wagtails on the plain" is an allusion to a song in the *Book of Odes* said to express
the speaker's anxious concern about close relatives.

Reflected in the rippling lake
> their springtime splendor is beyond praise.
But just as I am about to wander at will through this sea of fragrant snow
I am startled awake from my dream—
Oh, how I hate those cawing crows!

Gu Taiqing did not limit herself to the conventional subject matter of the lyric, such as spring sights, autumn melancholy, and dream visits to celestial realms. She also wrote song lyrics on somewhat less usual topics, such as marionettes, children at play, and pets (especially her little puppy, Double-Topknot).

To the Melody of "Partridge Sky" (*Zhegutian*)
Marionettes

When the marionettes take the stage they act with abandon:
Their tall tales and ancient legends entrance little children.
Their stories of the kings of the Tang and the Song are all baseless,
Their wonderful skill lies in bringing demons and devils to life.

Riding crimson leopards,
Followed by striped vixen,
With their flashy caps and gowns they put on heroic airs.
But what use are they once brought down from the stage and hung up
> high?
Carved wood and pulled strings: just a moment of time.

To the Melody of "Regret over the Parted Hairclasp" (*Xifenchai*)
Watching Children Play with a Noisemaker

Spring is almost here,
Fair weather days:
Idly I sit a while and watch the children play.
Using heaven's winds
It drums along inside;
Braided colors for a cord,
Whittled bamboo for a pole:
Boom! Boom!

In this world of men
One sees both fools and sages.
The construction of this toy is deeply symbolic:
Principle will never be exhausted,
Affairs will never come to an end.
The solid can make a sound,
The hollow can take it in:
Rattle! Rattle!

To the Melody of "Sands of Washing Brook" (*Huanxisha*) Describing My Puppy, Double-Topknot

I

Warmly resting on my chest, hiding in my sleeves,
The fluffy down of his two ears tied up with gold rings,
The nickname Double-Topknot is just exactly right!

Bamboo leaves above the window: startled at the moon shadows,
Flowering branches reflected on the walls: barking at the lantern's light.
Then as the night grows deep, he lightly sleeps next to my pillow.

II

The words "soft" and "silly" describe his nature,
So very sweet and gentle and especially clever:
That he should win people's affection is natural!

When he sleeps, his curled-up paws are worth painting,
When he plays, cleverly he raises his small little feet.
He makes yapping noises but is still learning to bark.

Her collection also includes lyrics in which she expresses her support and admiration for the literary efforts of other women writers. The following lyrics provide an example of this:

To the Melody of "Ballad of Golden Threads" (*Jinlüqu*) Inscription for Lady Scholar Yu Caizhuang's *Wisdom and Happiness Tower Poetry Collection*

Happiness and wisdom cultivated at the same time!
I ask her age:

Sixteen years
And already so intelligent!
She took out her book of new poems to show me:
Their loveliness comparable to jade, their purity to gold.
I would truly not be ashamed
With her as a literary disciple.
In her book, I single out the lines on reading the histories:
Not at all the usual "playing with moon and chanting of the breeze,"
"Flowers in the hair" style,
"Silver hook of the moon" words.

The immortals of the Jasper Pond must surely be like this!
I love her grace and elegance,
Her attitude so warm and soft,
And her face grave and proper.
If there were an immortal youth they'd make a fine match,
Like a pair of jade figures, both of them lovely,
Worthy of being praised
For both beauty and talent.
People would also speak of her understanding of the way of filiality:
Attending to her widowed mother-in-law she will bring her much joy.
"Happiness and wisdom,"
Who would fit it better?

> *I was especially fond of the two lines from "Reading the Annals of Xiang Yu":*
> *"To no avail his hundred battles for the empire of the Qin, / The Nine Provinces*
> *in the end became the hills and streams of the Han."*

Gu Taiqing has long been recognized for her poetry, but it has been recently ascertained that she was also the author of a sequel to the famous novel *Dream of the Red Chamber,* which she entitled *Shadow Dream of the Red Chamber (Hongloumeng ying)*. It was published in Beijing in 1877, shortly after her death. Written under a pseudonym, it was not until some lost poems by Gu Taiqing bearing the same pseudonym were discovered in Japan in 1989 that Gu Taiqing was first credited with this novel.

Although Gu Taiqing's decision to write a novel was quite daring, the style of the novel itself is not. As a result, for over a hundred years nobody suspected that this novel had been written by a woman, let alone Gu Taiqing. However, as soon as one knows the novel was written by her, one is struck by a number of telling details, such as references to

Manchu customs and objects, a detailed description of childbirth, and a very sympathetic portrayal of a widow much like Gu Taiqing herself (who, at a poetry party with like-minded women, produces a set of poems that were in fact Gu's own).

Gu Taiqing's twenty-four-chapter novel is nowhere near as long as the original *Dream of the Red Chamber*; it is, however, still much too long to include in its entirety in an anthology such as this. We have limited ourselves to the following passage from the novel in which the author describes the birth of the son of Jia Lian, a cousin of Jia Baoyu. In Cao Xueqin's novel, Jia Lian's first wife had been Wang Xifeng [Sister Feng]; Sister You had committed suicide when he did not marry her after he had seduced her. In Gu Taiqing's novel, Jia Lian has taken Ping'er, the maid of his deceased wife, as his concubine.

[Jia Lian] had no sooner fallen asleep when he saw Elder Sister Feng come in laughing and giggling with Second Elder Sister You. Sitting on the edge of the *kang*,[33] she said: "We've come to tell you the good news!"

"What good news?" Jia Lian asked.

Elder Sister Feng smiled and said: "We now have a son!"

Jia Lian laughed and said: "Ping'er is pregnant, but she has not yet delivered. How can you know whether it is a son or a daughter?"

"What is that then?" said Elder Sister Feng pointing at Second Sister You. Looking over at her, he saw that sure enough Second Sister You was holding a baby in her arms. Second Sister You, her eyes filled with tears, gazed at Jia Lian and nodded her head. Jia Lian, forgetting that both Feng and You had long since died, then asked Second Sister Feng, "Who is raising this child?"

Elder Sister Feng sighed and said, "The elder madam told me that you and I were finished and that we could not have any heirs. Because in the past Ping'er has always been compassionate and helpful to the aged and the poor, accumulated good merit wherever she goes, and is always proper in her speech, in the future she will be honored with a title. It is for this reason that I have come to warn you to control yourself a little when it comes to alcohol, sex, and money. Alcohol is the thing that can wreak the most havoc on your character: as soon as you start feeling high, you end up tossing propriety, rites, and the established norms of morality out the window. And as for 'sex,' that is even more critical: for the sake of a moment's pleasure, you not only ruin someone else's reputa-

---

33. In northern China people often sleep on a *kang*, a raised brick platform that is warmed from underneath by the smoke of the stove.

tion, you also ruin your own personal conduct. And then there are those good deeds you can do with your mouth, the most important of which is that you never should spread rumors about murky affairs in the inner apartments of other families. Now, as soon as you see someone else rise in the official ranks, you feel envious; as soon as you see that someone else has money, then you feel jealous, and inevitably you get angry. You are already over thirty years old, your parents are getting older, and yet how many friends do you have? You should follow my advice and make an honest woman of Ping'er: it will be advantageous for you, and it will also reflect well on the child. Although now she takes care of everything, when it comes down to it, if the servants do not submit to her, there is bound to be some pushing and shoving. You all keep well. I will come back to see you!"

Then turning around, she said to Second Sister You, "Let us go deliver it to her." As she spoke, she stood up and they left together. At this point, Jia Lian seemed to recall that they were both dead, and he woke up weeping from his dream to see the dwindling light and [the maid] Feng'er still sleeping soundly with the blankets over her head. Jia Lian sighed and then fell into a vague sleep.

In the meantime, Ping'er woke up, got down off the [*kang*] and, opening up the lamp, turned it up. After going to the bathroom, she washed her hands in cold water, and climbed back up onto the *kang*. She lay down and as soon as she had closed her eyes, she saw Elder Sister Feng come in with Second Elder Sister You, who was holding a child next to her breast. Ping'er greeted them saying:

"Mistress, you have returned! What a happy coincidence that you should come together!"

Elder Sister You said: "Because you are so worried about the child to come, I have come to thank you."

Ping'er said: "What do you mean by that, Mistress?" She then felt her heart beating wildly and waking up, she felt a huge heavy sodden weight in her lower body, and frightened, she cried out: "Grannie Zhao! Hurry! Get up! Things are not good!"

Mama Zhao, startled awake from her dreams, heard a child's cry, but her lamp had gone out, and she could not find her shoes. So she got down off her *kang* in her bare feet and went looking for some touch-paper to light the lamp with, muttering: "My young lady, why didn't you say something earlier!"

Ping'er said: "I didn't know myself!"

Jia Lian had not yet gone to sleep, so when he heard a child bawling and crying, and the two of them talking, he went and got Feng'er up, then, holding up his lamp, he looked at the clock: it was exactly midnight. He threw on some clothes and came over, and seeing Grannie Zhao there still looking for some touch paper, he grabbed the lamp saying "Miss Feng, you take her and pull her up, so that I can get a hold of the child."

When Feng'er leaped onto the *kang* and pulled at Ping'er, Ping'er said "Just take it easy! I can't sit up yet!" Not until Mama Zhao had pulled the covers to one side to have a look did she hurriedly pull Ping'er's undergarments down, and seeing the infant lying there next to her belly, she reached out and took it up in her arms.

When Jia Lian saw the baby's red feet, all covered with blood, he was anxious, but funnily enough said: "Mama, put some socks on him so he doesn't catch cold!" Then he ordered Feng'er to help Ping'er sit up. He went to the window of the room and called for Elder Sister Qiao's Mama Li to come. Mama Li got up on the *kang*, and washed off both P'ing'er and her baby. Just at this moment, the old ladies all got up as well, and they boiled up a hot calming broth. Mama Li cut the umbilical cord, and taking up the child, gave it to Ping'er to hold. She then cleaned up all traces of blood from the *kang*.

When Jia Lian saw that it was a boy, he suddenly remembered the dream he had had just a while earlier. He wanted to tell Ping'er about it, but was afraid that it might make her feel hurt and afraid. But after Ping'er had drunk her calming broth, she slowly began to describe her own dream to Jia Lian.

Jia Lian then said: "Was your mistress wearing that snow-white dress that she used to wear all the time?"

"How did you know that?" Ping'er asked.

Jia Lian then described the dream he had had that night, and everyone marveled at the coincidence.

One of the most important bits of evidence of Gu Taiqing's authorship of this sequel to the *Dream of the Red Chamber* was a poem she had written in mourning for the death of one of her closest woman friends (her sworn sister, in fact) Shen Shanbao (style name Xiangpei), who, it has now been discovered, in 1861, the year before she passed away, had written a preface to Gu Taiqing's *Shadow Dream of the Red Chamber*. Shen Shanbao was not only a critic of women's poetry but also a poet in her own right: in one of her most famous poems she expresses her profound admiration for the great heroes of the past and laments, in no uncertain terms, the fact that even women of great talent have rarely had the opportunity to show their mettle either in offices of state or on the battlefield. It is this heroic spirit to which Gu Taiqing refers in the opening lines of the following verse. In the last lines, she makes reference to the disturbances caused by the Taiping rebellion that had disrupted life in Hangzhou, Shen Shanbao's hometown.

Weeping for Third Younger Sworn Sister Xiangpei

After a friendship of thirty years, we were as close as foot and hand;
I demand a reason from Heaven for having taken this person away!
All her life she exhibited the mind and character of a valiant knight:
Demonstrating a masculine talent although in the body of a woman.

The illusory world of the Red Chamber is not based in fact:
Once in a while, I take up my brush and add a few chapters.
Her lengthy preface brought it far more praise than was due:
Repeatedly she sent me letters asking me for all of the book.

> *I have been working off and on on a sequel to* Dream of the Red Chamber *in several chapters called* Shadow Dream of the Red Chamber. *Xiangpei wrote a preface for it, and could not wait for me to let her see it. She often scolded me for my laziness and she would tease me saying "You will soon be seventy years old. If you don't hurry up and finish this book, I am afraid that it will never get done."*

Lost in deep talk, we hated being separated by layered walls;
Holding hands we would cling to each other, loathe to go separate ways.
With this single sentence in the end I make you a promise on this day:
That you and I will, forever and for always, be sworn sisters.

> *Younger Sister passed away on the eleventh day of the Sixth Month of the first year of the Tongzhi reign period* [1862]. *When I went to visit her on the twenty-ninth of the Fifth Month, she suddenly asked: "How can I repay the affection of Elder Sister?" I replied saying: "Why even speak of repayment between elder and younger sisters? I hope that in the next lifetime the two of us will be as we have been in this lifetime." Younger Sister said: "Why stop at just the next lifetime: we will be sworn sisters for eternity." I said: "That is a promise." Ten days after we said goodbye to each other, she passed away: how could I not be pained!*

Every time she spoke of the hills of home, her eyes filled with tears,
Which caused cloudy shadows to dim the shining waves [of her eyes].
I am deeply worried and all my thoughts are of grief about her grave:
If only she could get a team of phoenix-like birds to take her home.

Because of the disturbances in Hangzhou,[34] *I have been unable to get through and inquire whether or not the location of the gravesite has been determined or not, or whether her relatives are still alive: it is for this reason [my grief and weeping] that I have lost the sight in my right eye.*

In years past, when we had time we would always visit one another,
But nowadays, I think of you but there is no date set for our meeting.
I can still see your smiling face and your voice here before my eyes:
I take up my brush to write, I fear, the poem of a broken heart.

Women and Warfare

Warfare is a subject that only rarely makes its appearance in the poetry of women poets of the eighteenth century. China at this time enjoyed many years of internal peace while the Qing emperors expanded the power of the Manchu dynasty deep into Central Asia. This does not mean that the topic is absent, however. Women poets would sometimes recount the martial deeds of famous heroines from China's history in their verse. By the middle of the nineteenth century, however, the long period of internal peace came to an end as internal rebellions and foreign wars threatened the very survival of the dynasty and laid China's most prosperous regions to waste. These troubles directly affected the lives of several of the women authors of this period, as we have seen in our discussion of Gu Taiqing and her friend Shen Shanbao. Some women poets would react to these troubled times by invoking the names of male and female heroes from China's past, or by describing in detail the horrors of war, and the ways it affected their own lives as well as those of their friends and family.

Zhang Chaixin

Zhang Chaixin hailed from Hanshan in Anhui province. Her husband, Qing Xilun, passed the metropolitan examination in 1852 and subsequently served in a succession of military posts in northern China, even as their home province was being ravaged by the Taiping rebellion. Following the death of her husband, Zhang Chaixin escorted his coffin from

---

34. In 1860 Hangzhou was conquered by the Taiping rebels after a long and destructive siege. Later, the city was retaken by Qing troops.

the north back home to Anhui. In her collection we find a number of poems commemorating heroes from China's history. In the following poem, the heroic patriotism of Yue Fei, who was widely celebrated throughout the Qing dynasty, is contrasted with the treacherous villainy of Qin Gui, the chancellor of the Southern Song, who was willing to cede one half of all of China's territory in order to buy peace with the enemy.

Mourning at the Tomb of Prince Yue

He let those bandits devour one half of our mountains and streams,
But he never would allow the General to turn the world around:
That noble hero had the sword to smite those barbarian invaders,
But the chancellor had no intention of repaying his country's favors.
Twelve imperial orders written in gold were sent to his camp,
Three thousand ironclad warriors wept and tried to block his way.
Now all that remains here today is this solitary grave mound,
Its pine and cypress somber and dark as the bright sun sinks.

According to the legend, when Yue Fei finally decided, under insistent imperial pressure, to discontinue his heroic campaign to reconquer northern China and return to Hangzhou, his men tried to dissuade him by weeping before his gate, but to no avail.

One of Zhang Chaixin's best-known poems celebrates the late Ming female hero, Shen Yunying. Shen Yunying's father, Shen Zhixu, was the commander of Daozhou in modern Hunan province. In 1643, Daozhou was overrun by the armies of the "peasant rebel" Zhang Xianzhong, and Shen Zhixu died valiantly defending the city. After his death, his daughter Yunying then assumed command, retrieved her father's body, and succeeded in defending the city against the rebels. The court, which at this time had also been relying on the support of non-Chinese troops from Sichuan under command of the female chieftain Qin Liangyu (d. 1648), formally appointed Shen Yunying to be her father's successor—a very unusual occurrence. Not long afterwards, however, her husband Jia Jian died in the defense of Jingzhou, and Shen Yunying relinquished her post to return home. In the eighteenth century, the story of the two female military heroines, Shen Yunying and Qin Liangyu, became the subject of a popular sixty-act play.

In Zhang Chaixin's verse treatment of the life of Shen Yunying, she is not only a formidable warrior and a filial daughter, but also an erudite writer, although no works of Shen Yunying have been preserved. In this respect, Zhang's characterization of Shen Yunying may have been influenced by the character of Liu Shuying, a female author of the midseventeenth century who is known to have personally participated in the armed struggle against the Manchus.

The Ballad of General Shen

Lord Shen had a daughter, the finest flower of the inner chambers,
And he instructed her in the Six Classics from her earliest years:
At night she would read to her heart's content in books of history,
During the day she would indulge in embroidery with colored silks.

When the father joined the army, the daughter went with him:
Heaven-startling bronze drums surrounded the towering walls.
A storm arose: the sun darkened by the fluttering of banners,
Clouds gathered: a crashing tide of troops astride their steeds!

True to his oath the commander was willing to die for his country,
And he personally led his small army to meet the rebels in the field.
His imposing figure, bristling with rage, filled the bandits with fear,
But even so, alas, the decision of Heaven could not be reversed.

Lightning flashed, thunder roared, the rain poured down:
In the heat of the battle he did not make a timely retreat.
His horse slipped in the mud and the commander fell,
No longer able to display his might with bow or sword.

The General, when young, had the style name of Yunying,
Pounding the earth, crying to Heaven—life had no value!
She herself led a small group of ten or twelve stalwarts
And ventured on to the battlefield on horseback, alone!

The armies of rebels fled in all directions, like mice, like sparrows,
They spun around and showed their backs, scared out of their wits!
Their horses spat peach-colored foam, dyed red by the blood,
Their armor filled with holes like coins, slivered by the sword.

In a moment's time she had cut off more than thirty heads,
And great masses of men had returned to the unborn state.

After her return, she opened the gate, ready to fight again,
But the bandit swarms in their panic had already moved their camp.
From then on the orphaned city, unassailable, remained untroubled,
And all the neighborhoods sang praises of her meritorious service.

When the Imperial Court was informed, it rewarded her most lavishly,
By a special act of grace she was allowed to succeed to her father's post.
Restoring order among the remaining troops, storing fodder and food:
Intending to revenge her father's death, she prepared for swift action.

But, alas, Jingzhou was overrun by bandits, and her husband
Jia Jian vowed to risk his life defending the gates of the city.
Hit by an arrow he departed forever from this mortal world—
Her marching orders arrived together with the news of his death.

Awash in tears she declined to obey the Emperor's summons:
"My heart a tangled mess, I am unfit now to fulfill my duties.
I implore you to allow me to return home while still alive,
And I ask that our heirs be exempted from taxes and duties.
My father gave his life in your service, my husband also died:
Their hearts were loyal, they wanted only to repay Your favor.

Who will take care of their abandoned coffins on my behalf?
I wish to bury their bones next to the graves of their ancestors.
I'm resigned to growing old in poverty, dressed in a linen skirt,
Since I can't rid the world of dust and smoke and bring it peace."

While traveling home rumors reached her of the Emperor's death,
And right away she wanted to plunge into the river and drown.
But her mother beseeched her and implored her: "My child,
Our clan's survival is not yet secure while I'm old and weak.
 Would it not now be better to stay alive for a little bit longer,
And, for my sake, to remain in this world a few days more?"
In the end the daughter gave in to her mother's entreaties,
Overcome by emotions both of them were awash in tears.
 She locked the gate: her only wish was now to serve her mother—
Without firewood by daytime, without rice for the evening meal.
Managing to scrape by in poverty for more than ten years—
Until one day she died of an illness and was laid in her grave.

The General combined literary talent with military arts,
Her filial piety and loyal chastity will be known forever.
She bound up her hair, joined the troops—just like Mulan;[35]
Taught the Classics behind a red screen—like lady Song;
Composed a poem out in the desert—another Cao Zhi;[36]
Stabbed bandits and rebels in battle—a new Xie Daoyun!

Gods and hosts still stand in fear of her majestic merit,
She spent the last years of her life writing books.
The trees atop the clouds on the mountain slope of Mt. Kan
Still seem to rattle like the spears and swords of those days!

Zhang Yin

Zhang Yin (1832–1872) was a native of Tongguan in Shaanxi province. Her father at one point served as the governor of Shandong province, and her husband Lin Shoutu, from Minhou in Fujian province, rose to the rank of provincial administration commissioner for Shaanxi province. Zhang Yin's adult life coincided with a period of considerable social and political chaos caused by the Taiping rebellion, as well as other rebellions and bandit movements with which the country was plagued at this time.

In his *Compendium of Qing Poetry* (*Qingshihui*), Xu Shichang provides the following brief sketch of Zhang Yin's life and works:

In her youth, Zhang Yin attended school together with her elder brother, Shuyan, and learned to read. She was extraordinarily intelligent and her parents loved her dearly. She took pleasure in the arts, and excelled in the painting of flowers and birds. Whenever she would copy a famous piece of calligraphy, it looked strikingly like the original. She also was good at embroidery and was praised as a "goddess of the needle." Her mother, lady Wu, also instructed her in sewing and cooking. She loved physical work and did not put on any of the airs of a high-born young lady.

---

35. Mulan is the heroine of the *Song of Mulan* of the sixth (?) century. When Mulan's elderly father is summoned for military service, Mulan dresses up as a man and takes his place among the troops. After twelve years of military campaigns she returns home, without her comrades-at-arms ever having discovered her true sex.

36. The reference to Cao Zhi in this context is a bit odd, and may, given the mention of the desert, well be a mistake for a reference to Cai Yan.

After she had married Lin Shoutu, she served her mother-in-law with great filiality, and she showed even greater concern for his daughter by his deceased first wife than she did for her own children. Her husband was an expert in poetry. Zhang Yin certainly was a person capable of writing poetry, and if something struck her fancy she would show even greater skill, but unfortunately she was often distracted by her household duties. Her husband remarked: "Sometimes, after not having written a single line for a whole year, she would write tens of lines in a single evening. She did not care for ornamentation and tonal rules, for her the most important thing was to give expression to her nature and feelings. If she hadn't had to take care of the children, she would have improved day by day. Now there is no way of knowing whether her work will be handed down or not."

More than twenty years after Zhang Yin's death, her son discovered a bag of manuscripts inside a double wall of the old home, more than half of which had already been devoured by insects. Later he printed her works in Fujian . . .

In the following poem, Zhang Yin provides us with a glimpse of her youth. She also offers us yet another example of a father who was even more supportive of the literary education of his daughter than her mother was:

Thoughts upon Reading the "Biography of Ban Zhao"

When long ago I applied myself to brush and inkstone,
The opened books would lie around me in profusion.
Once in a while my mother would order me to stop,
And snatch them away: "Your father'll be angry!"
 But each time my father would say to my mother:
"You must have heard of the Venerable Madam Ban!
Her 'Treatises' surpassed the history by Sima Qian,
Her careful choice of words followed the Annals.
 The ladies of the Palace took her as their teacher,
No less a scholar than Ma Rong became her pupil.
And thanks to the high position of his mother
Her son then rose to the rank of marquis!"
 When I heard this, I would be filled with joy,
My ambition would soar higher than the clouds.
Now that I am able to read the book she wrote,
I feel depressed and am overcome with sorrow.
 Her history has all the three qualities,

It is not just the beauty of her style!
The Concubine provided her a norm,
No Zuo or Xie could hope to be her equal!
 My talents are lesser by far than theirs—
The people of ancient times provide us with models,
Especially for those of us here in the inner quarters—
Closing the book, my spirit roams together with them!

Zhang Yin gives us a detailed description of her married life in the following poem, which she wrote on the eve of her stepdaughter's wedding:

For My Daughter Quan

The ancient sages left us with a saying:
"Within the seas all men are brothers."
And besides that, your mother and I
Were just as close as E and Ying.[37]
 Moreover, you were raised by me:
Of course I love you like my own!
But now today you are grown up,
The wedding ceremony draws near.
 More then ten years we've been together:
The thought of this makes my heart break.
When I came here, I still recall, as a bride,
You were then no more than a toddler:
Your stiff hair covered your shoulders,
And you could hardly reach the tabletop!
 But you were all that your grandma had,
She regarded you as the apple of her eye.
The dialect is different in north and south:
We had trouble understanding one another.
 So as soon as I tried to come near you,
You would immediately shy away;
As soon as I would beckon to you
You would look around anxiously.
 I often would be trembling inwardly,
Desperate to communicate my love.
But fortunately, as you grew older,

---

37. The sisters E and Ying were the daughters of the mythic sage emperor Yao. They were both married to Yao's assistant and successor, Shun.

You came to see me as a part of your life.
 At dawn, you came and I combed your hair,
At night, you came and you slept in my bed,
When hungry, you would come to me for food,
When cold, you would come to me for clothes.
 One time, when I went to the kitchen,
Before I knew how to cook southern style,
You came to me and secretly informed me:
"Minced fish is used for making stew!"
 And then again at certain annual holidays,
Before I knew the hairstyles of Fujian,
You came to me and secretly informed me:
"Wrap red thread around the 'bridge' of your chignon!"
 When later I gave birth to little sister,
And could not look after your needs myself,
Your grandma called you, but by then
You only wanted to remain with me.
 When sister cried, you took her in your arms,
When sister was hungry, you prepared her food.
You would not leave my side for a single moment,
Who could have known that you were not my own!
 Both your grandma's family and my own
Are descended from the Nanxuan Zhangs,
But are as far apart as Fujian and Shaanxi,
It's hard to be precise about the family line.
 Yet grandma favored me right from the start:
"Don't think of me as your mother-in-law—
Since I never had a daughter of my own,
It would be best if you called me 'Mother.'"
 The reason grandma loved me so sincerely,
Was in part because you did so well!
 From time to time my natal family
Would come and fetch me for a visit.
I would take you and your sister with me,
And when together we would enter the house,
 My mother would always then say to me:
"This girl is very beautiful indeed!"
My elder brother also was very fond of you.
And every time he would emphatically say:

"Make sure you take good care of her,
Because she is very much my niece!"
Your face was truly pure and handsome,
Your nature truly proper and correct!
 When uncle taught you how to write,
Your brushstrokes were so bright and clear,
And when he taught you how to read,
Each word of yours resounded like a bell.
 Some time ago, your father remained in Shaanxi,
And left the whole family behind in the capital.
 At that time I was suffering from an illness:
By the tea-stove there always hung a medicine bag,
But you anticipated all of my wishes,
And made sure that I was never disturbed.
 Last year your father sent us a letter,
Ordering us to start out on the journey.
Grandma was already elderly and weak,
And I was just a dried-up bag of bones.
 Along the road we relied entirely on you,
To help us forget the distance we had to go.
 Your father once said to me:
"In selecting a son-in-law we should be careful.
If we can find someone who will ride the dragon,
Why should we stick to our own hometown?"
 I was a woman who'd married far from home,
And so the thought of this filled me with worry:
How could I impose what I had hated so myself
On my daughter and make her suffer as well?
 Your father has told me that your betrothed
Is well established in Suzhou and Hangzhou.
His grandfather is a censor-in-chief,
His father is a metropolitan official.
 Your groom is just twenty years old,
But his talents are most exceptional.
He's a student in the School for Sons of State,
And soon will succeed in passing the exams.
 All my wishes have been fulfilled,
So why is it I am still awash in tears?
I have just heard that a letter has arrived:

The wedding gifts will be delivered this fall.
 There is no way we can stay together forever,
And so when you go, you must swallow your cries.
 That may well be so, but I have heard it said
That both your husband's parents are still alive:
 Present them at the proper times with the finest dishes,
Prepare with your own hands their stews and teas.
The offerings to the ancestors are the duty of a wife,
So steam and taste the foods in autumn and in spring.
 There are also in his household two elder sisters,
Renowned citywide for their chastity and brilliance.
And there is also an infant younger brother,
In storm and rain he'll stand beside your bed.
 Remember well the virtue of Qu Yuan,
Don't let it be by thorn trees overgrown.
If your marital harmony is based on deep respect,
Then you'll find that his love will last forever.
 Whether in riches or in want, exert yourself,
Do not let your pleasures get in the way of your study.
 If by chance he should disappoint your hopes,
You'll have to serve him with even firmer purpose.
And if from time to time there is some disagreement,
You'll have to be the one who surrenders her place.
 The Way of Man values modesty and restraint,
The Way of Heaven resents flourishing wealth.
Do not pride yourself on your father's status,
And do not show off your hairpins and jewels.
 Exert yourself! The Venerable Madam's
Instructions for My Daughters lays out the rules.
Very soon now you'll become somebody's wife,
After which you'll have to leave your natal home.
 Do not act in a pampered and foolish way,
Nor should you be sad or grieved of heart.
Your grandma is already quite advanced in age,
Your mother has been gone now for many years.
 That leaves no one but your father and myself,
And we are no longer in the prime of our lives!
 I still regret that you have had to exert yourself,
But I must be meticulous in my instructions.

So sharp and clear, the scent of the autumn chrysanthemum,
So rich and sweet, the fragrance of the vermillion osmanthus!
　Out of my simple heart I write these words,
I'll put them in the chest with your scarves and things.
Each single character may be counted as a tear,
That, drop by drop, takes on the luster of pearls.

　In the poetry of most elite women, there is little evidence of any interest in gardening, apart from plucking the occasional flower or two.
Zhang Yin, however, appears to have taken a more active interest: in fact,
during the time her husband held office in Shaanxi, she even grew her
own vegetables.

Planting Vegetables

By nature I love working in the garden,
Besides, here there's plenty of empty land.
The spring breeze blows invigoratingly,
But people are still slow and lethargic!
　The kitchen maid in her bare feet,
Her cooking done, falls into a snoring sleep.
When I try to teach her how to read,
Her eyes don't recognize the *Books of Odes*.
　But when I send her for the spade and hoe,
She is happy to come along with me as I go.
Thorns and brushes cleared the very same day,
The broken earth also leveled in one day.
　So here we put in the pods of beans,
And there we sow the cluster mallows!
The autumn cabbage and the springtime garlic
Each get, dry or moist, a spot that suits them best.
　Along the straight lines all properly laid out:
I am secretly proud of what I have achieved!
Whenever my household duties leave me free,
I come here in order to lift and please my spirits.
　If, by good fortune, a light rain has just fallen,
The moisture will have sped up their growth:
Then jade sprouts emerge, breaking the earth apart,
And in the breezes their green leaves unfurl.
　Amazed at this, I cannot keep from smiling:
Like the poorest peasant become newly rich!

It would appear that the same kitchen maid who helped Zhang Yin lay out her vegetable garden also provided her with the materials for a long poem on the abuses of government troops when they were taking part in campaigns far from home:

Ballad of a Soldier's Life

I'd always heard a soldier's life is bitter,
But now I see that a soldier's life is fun.
How could a soldier's life really be fun?
Is it not one that is both brutal and cruel?
 We have here in the house a kitchen maid,
Whose family lives close to Luoyang.
Cooking done, hands tucked in her sleeves,
She recounted to me this story of her life:
 "The troops that were just now at Tongguan
Have lately been making their way to Hubei.
 Whenever they come across a wine shop,
They guzzle great quantities, like cattle!
And when they leave—without paying—
The owner still scrapes and bows to the ground.
 Once they are drunk, they visit the brothels,
At their command pipes and flutes are played.
If you are favored with their loving affection,
Then they snatch your jewels as they depart.
 When one night there was news of approaching rebels,
People everywhere were as frightened as wind-tossed cranes.
 But the troops on the other hand, rejoiced at the news,
And they leapt and hopped about like sparrows!
 All the village shops they passed along the road
Were ordered to provide them with sandals of straw.
The soldiers showed no sign of the Creator's love and care,
And were as demanding as the most destitute bandits.
 As soon as anyone caused them any displeasure,
A thousand cruel swords would hack him down!
When the people complained to the authorities,
The magistrate was frightened and taken aback.
 He went and asked to meet with the commander,
But the commander kept himself aloof:
'Our bodies and our very lives,' he said,

'We have entrusted to these boys, have we not?
 The small and trifling matters of which you speak,
Are like a single hair, my man, of nine buffaloes!'
Bowing his head, the magistrate said not a word,
As all the blame had now been put on him!
 The next day as the troops prepared to move on,
They plundered each house where they had stayed.
There was no horse that we weren't forced to feed,
And for each ten, they stole as if for a hundred.
 The soldiers did not shoulder their own luggage,
But had carts ahead that were linked to carts behind.
And whenever they would meet a merchant,
They would search and empty all his bags.
 They whipped the men just as if they were dogs,
And shot the people just as they would shoot birds.
And if anything would rile them even just a bit,
A chopped-off head would drop to the ground!
 Each chopped-off head was worth two dimes:
They'd get their bounty from the quartermaster![38]
 That pretty girl—who are her parents?
It doesn't matter whether she is married!
That little boy—who are his parents?
He has a golden chain around his neck!
 The girls they took with them on their horses,
The boys they tied to the harness of their steeds.
The husbands follow in the tracks of the army,
The parents stumble in the clouds of dust.
 Eventually, after more than ten miles,
The sun sets behind the western hills.
When dawn breaks they see a pile of corpses
That have been roughly thrown into a ditch.
 The relatives are deeply moved and weep,
They beat their breasts and tear their skin.
The village head pleads their case at the army camp,
The army camp where the soldiers party:
 Prostitutes lined up in front of the painted screens,

---

38. Since soldiers were rewarded for each enemy they killed, some would take advantage of this situation to murder innocent citizens in the hopes of collecting a reward.

Jewels and pearls piled up in mountains and hills.
Before the man has even opened his mouth,
He finds himself shackled in fetters.
 They tie him to the flagpole of the camp,
He figures he's surely going to lose his head.
When suddenly he sees some men with a rooster
He knows because of its distinctive colors:
 'Today you will be devoured by this crowd
When just yesterday you ate my grain and corn!'
 In a while the soldiers were all completely drunk,
And shouting loudly they then began to gamble.
'The black one wins,' they cried without restraint,
And threw around their money without a thought,
 Believing as they did that the source was endless—
There were all those things illegally acquired.
 He grabbed the opportunity and made his escape,
Back home, he hopes the commander will consider
Why men, three hundred miles away from home,
After having marched only a few days,
Start to behave in such unlawful ways,
Only too happy to be a soldier!"
 Alas, all of you soldiers over there,
How can you commit such flagrant crimes?
Not only are you like a guest who abuses his host,
You're also like a strongman who bullies the weak.
 I have heard that now in Hunan province
You have acquired a bad reputation as well.
Didn't you also leave a son behind at home?
Don't you have a daughter who is married?
 But as soon as the army goes on campaign,
There's no way for you to avoid the slaughter.
The Way of Heaven is truly hard to fathom,
In composing this song, I plead for a reply!

Recovery efforts by the government officials in the wake of destruction by warfare and widespread depopulation are the subject of yet another of Zhang Yin's poems:

Because of the Long Rains I Was Concerned about the Peasants, and So I Wrote This Poem as a Prayer on Their Behalf

Even though the bandits had fled far away,
There were no people left to plow the fields.
My husband, having served here for a while,
Was deeply worried as he looked all around.
 And so he donated both oxen and seeds,
So that each family could support themselves.
Those who had run away eventually returned,
And rice seedlings were planted everywhere,
 Once again there was hope for rich harvests,
And the happy peasants sang the song of peace.
Then, alas, from Heaven fell rains without end,
The sky refusing to clear once they had begun!
 What is the sin these peasants have committed
That this year too their labors come to naught?
My family will have enough to eat—
But thinking of the others, my tears flow down.
 I write this poem and pray to God on High
That He may look into this earnest plea.

The cruelty of the mother-in-law toward her son's wife is a recurrent motif in modern accounts of traditional Chinese marriages. Zhang Yin, however, appears to have had a close and loving relationship with her mother-in-law. We saw a hint of this in the poem she wrote for her stepdaughter, and we see it again in the moving poems she wrote after her mother-in-law passed away:

Leaving through the Passes[39]

That year so long ago when I came to Xi'an,
I shared the carriage with my white-haired mother-in-law.
But this year as I am about to depart Xi'an,
I see nothing apart from the carriage crushing the snow.
 The black crows that swoop in the snow

---

39. The Passes refers to the Hangu Pass on the border of Shaanxi province and Henan province.

Cause me to feel overcome by sorrow,
As I consider that my mother-in-law and I
From now on will be separated forever.
 Why does your soul-flag delay and tarry?
Why does your hearse refuse to move?
As on my journey I approach the Passes,
I linger for a while not daring to depart,
 Hoping as I am that your soul will return,
So we may go through the Passes together.
I will take you with me back to the South,
Where you'll be buried with the ancestors.
 In your coffin you are separated from me by only a plank,
But your soul has gone straight away to the Yellow Springs.
Your voice and your face grow daily more distant,
And I throb with a pain that my voice can't express.
 In the deep mountains the foxes are many,
And in the still of the night, the cuckoo cries:
Who will bring you clothes when you are cold?
Who will prepare your food when you're hungry?
 You'd be far better off on this long journey:
At dawn and dusk you'd receive our libations.

Record of a Dream

In last night's dream I saw my mother-in-law,
Who looked just as she did when she was alive.
Talking incessantly she had no special instructions,
But seemed concerned that I looked so gaunt.
 "Make sure not to let your son remain ignorant,
He has to work hard at his *Documents* and *Odes*.
When a girl grows up, it's right she should marry,
How can her instruction be a trifling matter!
 Your husband is a naïve Confucian scholar,
With no idea of how to manage a household,
For thirty years he has served as an official,
Yet he still doesn't own even a single beam.
 He very much relies on you for his daily care!"
Hearing these words, I was beset by worries,
And was deeply moved, even more than I knew:
When I woke up, I cried until my eyes ran dry.

And I could still hear her voice in my ears:
Why are the candle's shadows so blurry?
My filial care regretfully was not enough:
And at this thought I sigh, but all in vain.

Sitting in Meditation during the Daytime

When long ago my mother-in-law was still alive,
I would rise early and see to breakfast preparations.
The neighbor's rooster had barely crowed at dawn,
And already I had quickly finished with my toilette,
 I would then hasten to go to the kitchen
To supervise the cooking of the dishes.
From the time the sun rose until it set,
I would be as busy as a frightened bird.
 But now when I am tired, I sleep late,
Often 'til the sun is already high in the sky.
I find it very hard, despite everything I do,
To pass the long five, six hours of the day.
 Heaven revolves now slowly and now fast,
The mind of man is now sad, now happy.
The more so on this endless summer day,
When a hundred thoughts spin all about.
 Those still living—a thousand miles apart,
Those already gone—all at the Yellow Springs.
When sadness comes, it cannot be dissolved,
It is like sitting atop a bed of nails.
 A single day is like an entire year,
The driver of the sun is missing his whip!
Thinking all these anxious thoughts,
My hair has suddenly turned gray.

Li Changxia

Another woman poet of the mid-nineteenth century whose work testifies
to the horrors of war is Li Changxia (ca. 1830–ca. 1880). Her father, Li
Tu, served as an official, and her husband was the student Ke Heng from
Jiaozhou in Shandong province. We know little about her life beyond
the data that may be gleaned from her poems, but the family must have
been a scholarly one: her eldest son, Shaojing, passed the metropolitan

examinations in 1889; another son, Ke Shaomin (1850–1933), was the author of the *New History of the Yuan* (*Xin Yuanshi*); and her daughter, Ke Shaohui, left a collection of poetry.

In her poems, Li Changxia describes the dislocations and misery caused by the Nian rebellion as it affected Shandong province in the 1860s. In her description of the sufferings caused by warfare Li Changxia often modeled herself on the great Tang dynasty poet Du Fu, known particularly for his poems on the havoc wrought by the An Lushan rebellion.

On the Road between Jiaozhou and Laizhou

My carriage stops by the ancient road,
The dense trees cold in the setting sun:
The falling leaves almost hide our way,
The distant bells are largely in the clouds.
 The brook's waters are swollen after the rain,
The mountain's colors are split up by the mist.
Gazing back at my hometown not far away,
My heart is filled with a tangle of sorrows.

Stopping for the Night at a Mountain Inn and Listening to the Rain

We are going to stop for the night at this mountain inn,
For in the rocky ravines the evening mist has thickened.
The out-of-the-way path leads through fragrant grasses,
The unused gate is blocked off by masses of pine trees.
 A weak lamp: the rain at midnight,
In bed: the bell from beyond the brook.
When tomorrow we come down the mountain,
The peaks will be hidden by clouds all around.

On the Night of the Fifteenth of the Eighth Month, I Think of My Father (Who Is Serving in the Metropolitan Area)

As the dew settles I await the crickets' cry,
Pacing up and down along the empty steps.
Shiny stars appear through the clouds,
And a chilly moon rises by the door.

Dreams wander to the far Sanggan River,
And over Jinan, the autumn sky is high.
As we gaze at each other, I pity my little brother:
He too must still be able to remember the Capital.

On a Spring Day Longing for Home

On the empty steps grow all shades of green,
The unmoving grasses entice the bright sun.
Butterflies appear chasing falling petals,
Swallows flit by with bits of willow floss.
 My many sorrows doubled by dreams:
Long separated I envy those who return.
I gaze into the distance toward Beijing:
My desire for the source thwarted so long.

Poems in the Ancient Style from the Year *gengshen* (1860), Four Poems

IV

A guest arrived from a faraway place,
He said he was a peasant from Hubei:
"There is misfortune all through the South,
And not a single family has been spared.
 The great generals celebrate daily,
Sending in their reports of victory.
But, alas, their exhausted troops
Melt away like floating clouds.
 Everywhere places are being plundered and looted,
There is no distinction between rebels and soldiers.
It is not that the nature of Heaven is to love warfare:
The hordes of bandits are all starving peasants."

Written in a Besieged City

Bereft of assistance: the orphaned city so small—
And no geese fly over it under the autumn sky.
Now the common people are in such straits,
What will be the outcome of the defense?
 The drums of alarm are close by at midnight,

And so many fires of distress flare up at dusk.
Those in authority have laid the best of plans:
When will they bring this cruel war to a close?

Journeying to Weiyang

Yesterday we departed from the banks of the Jiao
To make the long and distant journey to Qianzhou.
In the villages we saw hardly any signs of life,
As under the cold sky the road stretched out.
 Rough wooden doors closed in the daytime,
Ashes and charred ruins still scattered about.
A number of old widowed women
Told me their story, faces covered with tears:
 "Last spring when we sowed the summer wheat,
Bandits came to the southern part of the district.
The wheat fields became their battleground,
The wheat sprouts became their horses' fodder.
 Without the wheat we might still have survived,
Were it not that in autumn there appeared Pious Liu:[40]
The young and strong became the bandits' coolies,
The old and feeble died by the side of the road.
 Their souls remain but cannot yet be summoned,
For there are no bones one can go and gather.
 He who dies as an official earns great glory,
His good name remembered for a thousand years.
He who dies as a soldier earns a rich reward,
How bountiful are the Emperor's good graces!
 But when we peasants die we simply vanish,
Just like water bubbles floating on the stream!
They leave behind them a tender infant son,
They leave behind their white-haired mothers,
Their farms are lost and cannot be recovered,
And still the taxes of the state must be paid.
 Those who have died are gone away forever,
Those still living are constantly beset by cares."

---

40. Pious Liu was the name of a local bandit leader.

The Inn at Nanliu

Oh fierce, so fierce, the northern wind is bitter cold,
Dipping and swaying, the light of the lamp's candle.
I cannot sleep because of the journey's sorrow,
Troubled and worried, the cold night drags on.
 My youngest daughter in her threadbare clothes,
Lies at my side, tossing and turning about,
 "Where are we going this time," she asks,
"Trudging and tramping, where will we end?"
 Hearing these words, I am deeply moved,
My tears pour down, dampening my clothes.
Long ago, whenever I thought of my parents,
I regretted not living in the same district as they.
 But now that we are getting closer to them,
I feel myself becoming even more distressed.
When one has a home, one is attached to the soil,
If one hasn't a home, why should one feel pain?
 I get up and gaze at the moon in the window,
Then looking around, I see the moon on the bed.
The pines and cypresses more distant every day,
How can I console them with annual sacrifices?

Fleeing from the Bandits by Taking to the Sea

The endless expanse of blue ocean opens itself to my gaze,
The mountain forms of the two Laos tower high in the dusk.[41]
A terrible wrath rising to heaven shakes the stars and planets,
A fierce storm whips up a flood that overturns rocks and isles.
 Around the beaches, the evil miasma becomes even worse at dusk,
In the orphaned city, the painted horn sounds more mournful at night.
How can we endure this raging rampage of mounted troops!
Surely the government soldiers will come to our rescue!

Returning to Our Old House in West Village

For three years this was our house in West Village:
Upon returning once again, my thoughts are stirred.
Arriving at the gate, I think I see my mother,

---

41. The Lao Mountains are located on the southern coast of Shandong province, to the east of the city of Qingdao.

As in a dream, I remember when I first arrived.
The snow is gone and moss covers the roof,
The spring is cold, no willows turning gold.
But there in the courtyard the old crows
Still fly up to roost on rooftop and branch.

In most of her poems, Li Changxia limits herself to a straightforward description of the travails of her family and the miseries she observes around her. In some of her poems, however, a more philosophical mood prevails:

Traveling, Three Poems

I

The sporadic willows hide the lonely village,
And the sinking light sets on the misty ranges.
Huts have been built up against the rocks,
And hibiscus planted along the clear stream.
In distant gardens scattered yellow flowers,
And new rushes upraise their purple plumes.
The last rays illuminate the level fields:
High and low the shadow of "grain and millet."[42]
The sight makes one yearn for a hidden retreat,
What is the point of wishing for a fancy mansion?

II

I drive my carriage along the foot of Ox Mountain;[43]
Dried-up tumbleweeds roll through the yellow dust.
On the cold mountain the spring grasses are short,
And in the fierce storm the hoary pine trees moan.
Among them lies the grave of a king of Qi,
Overgrown and ruined by tares and weeds.
On top of the grave, hungry crows caw,
While all around it, mice dig their holes.
But the white bones know nothing anymore

---

42. One of the poems in the *Book of Odes* describes how the ruins of a former capital have become overgrown with grains and millet.

43. Ox Mountain is located outside Jinan, now the capital of Shandong province, and was once the capital of the ancient state of Qi.

Of all the desires he cherished when alive.
So let me go on and on, and never look back—
For if I look back again, my heart will shatter.

III

Yesterday I left from the city of towers,
Today I pass by the village of Fu Sheng.
The overgrown mound is not plowed in spring,
The damaged stele, though broken, still juts out.
Hungry rabbits run off hipping and hopping,
Startled squirrels scamper up medlars and pines.
I recall how in the days of the First Emperor
Fu Sheng served as an Erudite Scholar.
Knowing early on that books would be burned,
He hid his traces and returned to his hometown.
Asking for only sweet-grass to eat, he relied
On his daughter to help him pass on the Classics.[44]
As he was old and weary, nothing could be done,
To transgress the norms is a cause for shame.
How despicable was that Master Shusun,
Who with his court rituals flattered the ruler.[45]

As we have seen, many of Li Changxia's poems focus on the disruptions of war, but in some poems we also get a glimpse of how life can go on even under these difficult circumstances.

Memories after the Destruction of Our Library

The shelves with five thousand books
Completely destroyed by a single torch.
Everyone suffered the same cataclysm,

---

44. Fu Sheng was one of the few scholars who, following the "burning of the books" by the First Emperor of the Qin (and the destructions wrought by the civil wars following the collapse of the Qin dynasty), was still able to recite from memory the *Book of Documents*. By the time the scattered texts of the Classics began to be reassembled in the early Han dynasty, however, Fu Sheng was so old that no one but his daughter could make sense of the old man's mumblings. See Chapter 1.

45. Shusun Tong was the Confucian scholar who devised the ritual protocol for use at the new court of the Han dynasty: his glorification of the emperor at the expense of his officials greatly pleased the founder of the Han dynasty, the low-born Liu Bang.

So how dare I even speak of this grief?
 With our library gone, the boys can be lazy,
By the idle window the long day bores them.
Reciting poems, I feel sorry for my young daughter,
As on an empty stomach I explain the "Three Tangs."[46]

Sent to Younger Lady Yao

To Fujian's mountains it is seven thousand miles,
For twelve years now there've been alarms of war.
There is no way of knowing if in the bright mirror
Your head as well has become covered with snow.

Living in a Village

A rainfall has dispelled the lingering summer heat,
Longing for home, autumn has again come around.
The first frost can be seen mostly on the bamboo,
And even short dreams only give rise to sorrow.
 The ancient leaves are enveloped by cobwebs,
And on the bright moss, snails leave their trail.
We've been in this village for about three years,
And we still don't know when we can go home.

While the poetry of Du Fu was the most important model for Li Changxia in writing her own works, the following poem was clearly written in imitation of Du Fu's elder contemporary, Li Bai:

Fighting South of the City

Fighting to the south of the city,
The south of the city in the wilds:
Brave soldiers pursue the defeated,
Not even stopping when night falls.

How long will the horsemen fight the remaining bandits?
For there is a rumor that today their commander has died.

---

46. The "Three Tangs" refers to the three major periods in the development of Tang poetry: Early, High, and Late.

Green fireflies illuminate the field where skeletons converse,
It must be they were companions-in-arms a long time ago.
The general has died in battle, his bones not yet recovered:
Who in the camp will beat the big drum at the feast?

In her later years, Li Changxia spent some time in central China. The
following poem was written after she learned that her younger brother
had died.

How Mournful

I had a younger brother staying in Hebei,
Still young, but with nowhere to settle down.
Last year returning from the examinations,
On the way home, he died in Zhengzhou.
 Nothing in this human life is constant,
Disaster and fortune befall as by chance.
When last we parted it was for ten years;
But with this parting we'll never meet again.
 Last night you appeared in my dream,
Your pale face just as when you were alive.
Looking distressed, you were about to speak,
But before you spoke, I woke up with a start.
 Along the Yangzi the autumn rains are heavy,
And in the morning storms, no one can cross.
Where is there a place for your spirit to rest?
Oh how desolate are those green maple trees.

14 · Drama

Several women writers of the seventeenth century tried their hand at drama, but, unfortunately, only one of these plays has been preserved. Women playwrights of the second half of the eighteenth century and beyond, however, while not necessarily more numerous than before, had a better chance of having their works preserved. Moreover, some of these later women playwrights did not limit themselves to composing a single play, but wrote a number of dramatic works. To what extent their works were actually performed is difficult to ascertain; only in the case of Wu Zao's *The Fake Image* (*Qiaoying*) do we have evidence of a successful staging. For the time being, we have to conclude that women playwrights wrote primarily not for the stage, but for the study, and that they may have preferred drama to prose fiction because of the higher status of drama (*zaju* and *chuanqi*) in the eyes of literati.

Cross-Dressing Heroines: Wang Yun and He Peizhu

The Chinese scholar Hua Wei has noted that many plays by women playwrights deal with cross-dressing and gender-switching. Earlier we discussed Liang Xiaoyu's lost play about Huang Chonggu—a woman who presents herself as a man so convincingly that not only is she assigned an official post but also is asked to marry the prime minister's daughter; when her true identity is revealed, her talents are still admired.

Huang Chonggu was also the protagonist of a lost play by Zhang Lingyi, a daughter of the Grand Secretary Zhang Ying. The preface Zhang Lingyi wrote for her play in 1717 does survive, fortunately. In it, she writes:

Intelligent and talented as Huang Chonggu was, in the end she did not achieve her ambition and eventually had to revert to her original [female] dress. But could she just return to making herself up with rouge and powder, serving her husband with towel and comb, and begging others for pity? It is for this reason that I, basing myself on the images of the divine immortals, have made her into a lofty bird [soaring] amidst leisurely clouds free from the fetters of *qian* and *kun* [yin and yang; the whole cosmos]. In so doing, I have created a play for the enjoyment of both the educated and the uneducated, and which may also add luster to us women!

As we saw, Ye Xiaowan also wrote a play. Although it did not have any female characters in male disguise, the play did feature three male protagonists who were clearly meant to be the alter egos of herself and her sisters.

In order to fully understand the implications of cross-dressing on stage, we have to be aware of the extent to which dress and hairstyle marked class, status, and gender in premodern China. It was one thing for socially despised professional actors to cross-dress on stage (that is, for women to play male roles and men to play female roles), but quite another thing for ordinary folks to transgress the dress code for men and women in daily life, and then for actors to portray these sorts of transgressions on stage. As an example of this strongly negative attitude toward cross-dressing, we have the following brief anecdote found in the *History of the South* (*Nanshi*) about Lou Cheng, a woman who, dressed as man, managed to engage in an official career during the Southern Qi dynasty (479–501):

Lou Cheng, a woman from Dongyang, cross-dressed and presented herself as a man. She was quite skilled at playing go and was widely read. She served in the entourages of all the high ministers of the land and attained the official post of officer in the consultation section of the office of the governor of Yangzhou. When her [true sexual identity] was discovered, Emperor Ming [r. 484–498] threw her out of the bureaucracy and ordered her to return to Dongyang. Putting on her women's clothes again, she sighed and said: "Isn't it a shame that despite all of my talents, I have been turned into an old crone!?"

The historian who recorded this story clearly regarded Lou Cheng as an anomaly that signaled the imminent fall of the dynasty: "She was a freakish monster [*renyao*]. Although she was yin, she wanted to be yang, but such cannot be, and so she was exposed. This augured the [subsequent] rebellions of Jingze, Yaoguang, Xianda, and Huijing."

The only circumstances under which traditional morality allowed for a woman to assume male dress was if she was in immediate danger of losing her life or her virtue. A woman could also be forgiven for donning male dress if her action was motivated by filiality. The most famous case of this is found in the story of Mulan, the central protagonist of the "Song of Mulan," a narrative ballad that may date from fifth- or sixth-century northern China. This ballad tells of how, when Mulan's elderly father is called to serve in the army (her one brother is still a child), she dresses as a soldier and fights valiantly for twelve years without her fellow soldiers discovering her true sex. At the end of the war, the ruler wants to reward her for her service, but her only wish is to be allowed to return home as quickly as possible. As soon as she arrives back home, she sheds her armor and happily puts on her own women's clothes once again. This ending is essential to the narrative, as it provides the evidence that throughout all those years during which she pretended to be a man, Mulan was inspired solely by filial piety, rather than by any unnatural and dangerous desire to be a man. This central filial motivation is always maintained, even in later, and sometimes rather different, versions of the story. In some versions, for example, Mulan is portrayed as a Turkish maiden fighting the Chinese, but in others as a Chinese maiden fighting the Turks. Only in the final years of the Qing is Mulan turned into a Han dynasty Chinese maiden patriotically fighting the northern Xiongnu, which is the version most well known today.

In other stories about filial cross-dressing women, a daughter who was the only child of her parents might even be miraculously and permanently transformed into a proper male. There were usually terrible consequences to willful cross-dressing, however, as we have seen in the sad story of Liang Shanbo and Zhu Yingtai.

The emotional value of proper dress was also demonstrated in the middle of the seventeenth century when the Manchus imposed their dress code on all officials serving the Qing dynasty. They even went so far as to force all Chinese males to shave their foreheads and grow a long braided queue. Many Chinese literati committed suicide or became monks (if one shaved one's entire head, one would not have to wear a queue) in order to avoid the indignity of submitting to what they considered to be barbarian customs. The Manchus also tried to ban the Chinese custom of footbinding for girls, but here Chinese opposition was so tenacious that the Qing authorities allowed Chinese women (but not Manchu women) to continue binding their feet.

Picking up on the tradition of plays portraying Huang Chonggu, the eighteenth-century playwright Wang Yun in the twenty-five acts of her *Dream of Splendor* (*Fanhuameng*) portrays a female heroine who, in male guise, sits successfully for the exams—and goes on to marry one or more wives. Wang Yun (1749–1819) was from Chang'an (Xi'an) in the northwestern province of Shaanxi. Her father, Wang Yuanchang, had passed the metropolitan examinations in 1748, and served in various places as district magistrate; her son, Wang Bailing, would pass the metropolitan examinations in 1802. When Wang Yun completed *Dream of Splendor* in 1768, her father showed the play to the official Zhang Fengsun, who sent it on to his younger sister, Zhang Zhao, the mother of the famous scholar and high official Bi Yuan. It was Zhang Zhao who put up the money to have the play published, whereupon it appeared in print in 1778, with prefaces by Wang Yun's father and son, and a poem by Zhang Zhao.

Wang Yuanchang explained his daughter's reasons for writing this play as follows: "My daughter Yun from her earliest years showed signs of an extraordinary disposition. She understood histories and other books after a single glance and always resented being born a woman. So she wrote *Dream of Splendor* in order to give expression to the pent-up feelings in her breast." This statement is echoed and expanded in the preface by Wang Yun's son: "The lady, my mother, has an extraordinary disposition. She understood the histories and other books and she always regretted that she could not achieve success in the examinations and attain high office. So she wrote this piece in order to give expression to her pent-up feelings."

The name of the central female protagonist in Wang Yun's play is Wang Menglin, whose name means "dream of the unicorn." Following the traditional introductory scene, she makes her entrance in the second act (which in *chuanqi* plays is customarily reserved for the introduction of the male lead), and immediately reveals her character by declaiming the following lyric to the melody of "Partridge Sky" (*Zhegutian*):

> Submerged and buried in the women's quarters for over ten years,
> I cannot achieve a high position, I cannot become an immortal.
> When reading books, I always envy Ban Chao's ambition,[1]
> When pouring wine, I constantly recite the poems of Li Bai.
>
> My heart's manly energy
> Yearns to soar to heaven,
> But I am not predestined for the deeds of a Mulan or a Huang Chonggu.
> It's not my lot in this life to join the ranks at Jade Gate and Golden
>   Horse,[2]
> I can do nothing, then, but entrust my deepest feelings to a dream.

But Wang Menglin does not just want to pursue a man's career at court and in the provinces, she also wants to find herself a beautiful wife. After she has hung up on her wall "a painting of a beautiful woman brought from Suzhou," she continues:

If I were a man, I would definitely find myself a beauty like this for a wife. Let me pray to her—who knows, she may step down from the painting. [*Acts out burning incense and bowing in front of the painting, and sings*]

To the Same Tune

> Devout in heart, devout in mind,
> I bow and beseech you to appear!

[*Looks at the painting*]

> Her spirit is floating, her figure is floating,
> Her "autumn waters" seem to make a pass at me.[3]

---

1. When Ban Zhao's brother Ban Chao was a young man, he grew so bored by the drudgery of clerking that one day "he threw away his writing brush" and took up a military career instead.

2. Jade Gate and Golden Horse Gate are the names of gates located in the imperial palace.

3. "Autumn waters" is a common metaphor for clear and beautiful eyes.

[*Calls out*] Beauty! My beauty!

> Once I shout loudly,
> Once I call softly,
> Why does she show me no pity at all?
> If I want to engage her in conversation,
> I can only hope to vaguely see her in a dream.

I remember how last year in Handan, I got together with mademoiselle Huang from Suzhou and mademoiselle Hu from Hangzhou, who were truly extraordinary beauties. But after meeting just once, we were soon parted, and there is little possibility of ever seeing them again. "Lost in the distance, hidden by cloudy mountains: / My love-longing can only be transmitted by dreams." Alas, even though my father is now an official and enjoys fame and glory, I am in the end only a girl, so how can I pursue a career? [*Weeps*]

> Thinking of body and world multiplies my sad sighs,

[*Yawns*]

> All of a sudden I feel drowsy and tired!

Wang Menglin falls asleep and, as Act Three opens, she is transformed in her dream into a man through the good offices of Shancai, Guanyin's young acolyte. Shancai is played by a *xiaosheng*, while Wang Menglin is played by a *sheng*.[4]

[*While melodic music is played offstage, the* xiaosheng *takes out a mirror, and then wakes up the* sheng. *He fetches a gown and cap, which the* sheng *puts on, and then after waving a brush over the body and face of the* sheng, *leads the* sheng *back to the place where the* sheng *had been sleeping*]

When Wang Menglin discovers that she has been transformed into a man, "he" leaves for the Jiangnan area in search of the two beauties he had once met in Handan. He looks everywhere, including the courtesan houses. When he finally finds them, he promptly marries them, although only after he has first dutifully married the wife chosen for him by his parents. He also passes the examinations with flying colors, coming out at the top of the list.

---

4. *Xiaosheng* and *sheng* are the names of male role types, usually handsome young men, in Chinese drama.

Wang Menglin then wakes up from her dream, only to find herself still inhabiting a woman's body. Deeply disappointed, she falls asleep again, and in a second dream, meets the Daoist female divinity Hemp Lady (Magu), who enlightens her as to the insubstantiality of all phenomena ("a dream, an apparition, a bubble, a shadow"). The final aria of the play is as follows:

To the Tune of "Clear River Intro" (*Qingjiangyin*)

All of a sudden I wake up, my spring dream vanished,
In vain I rushed about in my dream.
Throughout three lifetimes my feelings have been foolish,
Today I laugh: what was the point?
Only now do I understand that both women and men
        should reform their ways and convert!

And so the play ends, rather reluctantly, on a note of resignation: a woman's dream of living a man's life has turned out to be no more than just that, and the only way to transcend the frustration of being a woman is to realize the dream-like quality of all existence, a realization that transcends gender distinctions altogether.

As we saw, Wang Yun's Wang Menglin wanted to sit for the examinations but also to be reunited with her female companions. One may speculate on the extent to which her *Dream of Splendor* was an expression not just of social ambition but also of homoerotic desire. If Wang Yun indeed harbored such desires, the only way she could envision their realization was by turning her heroine into a man, and only in a dream as well. In He Peizhu's *Pear Blossom Dream* (*Lihuameng*), a five-act play from the first half of the nineteenth century, these homoerotic desires do not dissimulate their true nature behind the mask of a dream: the heroine of this play, a cross-dressing young bride, would seem to be longing above all to be reunited with her beloved female companions.

He Peizhu was from Shexian in Anhui province and her husband was from Yangzhou. She spent a considerable amount of time together with him in Tianjin, where he served in an official post. The modern scholar Hua Wei says of He Peizhu's play, which was probably written around 1840: "It gives expression to the bafflement and bewilderment about marriage on the part of a newly-wed young wife leaving her home village far behind, as well as to her passionate feelings of attachment to her female friends from before; the plot is extremely monotonous."

As the play's main character, Du Lanxian, is traveling north by boat with her new husband, she finds herself overcome with longing for her female friends of days gone by. She dozes off, and in her dream meets a beautiful female immortal who asks her to write a poem on the sprig of pear blossoms the immortal is holding in her hand. Du Lanxian then wakes up, but finds herself consumed with longing for the woman in her dream. She even paints a portrait of the lovely immortal in an attempt to assuage her desire. As spring turns into summer and summer into autumn, Du Lanxian, still yearning desperately for the lovely vision of her dreams, falls gravely ill. Hovering on the brink of death, she has a second dream, in which she visits the realm of the immortals. In this dream she meets with the Pear Blossom Immortal and the Lotus Flower Immortal. The three of them spend a wonderful and enjoyable time together, but then the two immortal friends explain to Du Lanxian that delightful encounters such as they have enjoyed are rare, and are bound to be followed immediately by separation. At this point, Du Lanxian is awakened from her dream by the sound of a bell.

In the first act of the play, Du Lanxian introduces herself as follows:

I am Du Lanxian. From the day I was born, I have had a manly appearance and the talents of Ban Zhao, as well as the air of the immortals and the bones of the Way. Whenever I step with swaying hips, willows appear at Linghe Palace; whenever I let out a breath, lilies open on the Li River. At the age of ten I excelled in embroidery, and in [the time it takes to take] seven steps I was able to complete a poem. But what bothers me is that I have a partner on Phoenix Ridge who is skilled at applying my kingfisher-green eyebrows.[5] I will not leave my name on Goose Pagoda,[6] and to the end will be ashamed of having been nothing but rouge and powder. I now accompany my husband on his northward journey. The entire way I have suffered greatly, with the dew forming on the curtains and the wind blowing through the blinds. I remember how in Yangzhou I vied to identify the grasses and evaluate the flowers, cultivated

---

5. Phoenixes are a symbol of a happily married couple; it is the loving husband who is supposed to paint on his wife's eyebrows.

6. In Tang dynasty Chang'an the students who successfully passed the metropolitan examinations would, during one of the subsequent celebrations, write their names on the walls of the Great Goose Pagoda—a structure that still stands today.

the clouds and there beneath the moon, got tipsy with my girlfriends, among whom was one who wished that I was a man so that she could refill my incense and carry my inkstone. Today the spring colors are splendid and I am consumed with longing. And so to amuse myself, I sit here alone, dressed up as a man . . .

A modern reader could not be blamed for wanting to read passages such as the one above as an expression of lesbianism, but it is questionable whether the author would have understood her work in this way. This is not because lesbianism did not exist in premodern China, but rather because homoerotic relationships were not necessarily regarded as exclusive, nor were they considered to be the primary basis for the formation and definition of one's identity. In fact, He Peizhu's play could just as easily be read as an expression of the difficulties of leaving behind the passionate girlish attachments of youth and assuming one's role as a married woman. The heroine may dress up as a man, but she knows it is only in jest, done "to amuse myself."

Playwright and Lyricist: Wu Zao

The only woman writer whose play became a stage hit was Wu Zao (1799–1862), the author of the one-act play *The Fake Image* (*Qiaoying*).

Wu Zao was a native of Hangzhou. Her literati contemporaries often pointed out that she did not come from a literati family, and that both her father and husband were merchants who "never even glanced at a book." Wu Zao never mentions her husband in her work, and it has been suggested that she was estranged from him, although for most of her life she appears to have been financially comfortable. And it is clear that even though they were raised in merchant families, Wu Zao and her sisters enjoyed a literary education that was not much different from that of other women writers of her time. Moreover, Wu Zao maintained regular contacts with writing women in the area once her reputation was established. From a very early age, she showed a special affinity for music, and while she also wrote *shi* poems, most of her extant poetry consists of lyrics and arias. She was probably in her early twenties when she wrote her one play, *The Fake Image*, which after circulating in manuscript form for some time, was staged to great acclaim in Shanghai by the male Suzhou actor

Gu Lanzhou. According to the colophon to the first edition written by Wu Zaigong, the play was first printed in 1825:

In the autumn of the year *yiyou* [1825], when I was staying in Shanghai, a friend showed me this text. As I read it, I had the feeling that Qu Yuan's longing for "fragrant grasses" was still with us. That it should be found in the women's quarters makes this text the most unusual work of all time! At the time, the Suzhou actor Gu Lanzhou, an excellent performer of extended high-pitched melodies, was [staying in Shanghai] and I taught him this play. When he performed it in public, he drew out the long notes and, whether singing or crying, completely exhausted the emotions and postures [of the heroine]. Those who saw his performance tapped to the beat, and those who heard about it vied to make copies of the text—the price of paper suddenly soared![7] For this reason, I turned the play over to the block carvers for printing, so that it might be distributed in theatrical circles and thus obviate the need for copying it out by hand.

The play consists of a single extended monologue in a combination of prose and arias, which are sung and spoken by a character called Xie Xucai. Xucai's name ("Floss-Talent") recalls the figure of Xie Daoyun. Echoing some of the most popular scenes from *Peony Pavilion*, Xie Xucai paints a portrait of herself dressed in male attire. She then sits down to contemplate her self-portrait as she drinks her wine and reads "Encountering Sorrow" (*Lisao*). In the Chinese poetic tradition, solitary drinking has always signified the occasion for somber musings on the sad fact that one's talents have failed to be recognized by the world. In her play, Wu Zao quotes an extremely well-known poem on the topic of solitary drinking by the Tang dynasty poet Li Bai. As an example of unrecognized talent and loyalty, Li Bai is surpassed only by Qu Yuan, who is supposed to have lived around 300 BCE. After the king of Chu ignored Qu Yuan's loyal warnings against the kingdom of Qin (which eventually would conquer Chu and annex its territory), Qu Yuan fell victim to slander and was banished from court. He then wandered along the rivers of south China, venting his despair and frustration in his long allegorical poem, "Encountering Sorrow." This poem is now the centerpiece of the *Songs of the South*,

---

7. To say that "the price of paper goes up" means that a certain book is a bestseller: it sells so well that it causes a shortage of paper, which in turn results in a rise in the price of paper.

the collection of poems ascribed to Qu Yuan and his disciples. Some of the other poems in this collection alluded to by Wu Zao in her play include "Questions to Heaven" (*Tianwen*), which is basically a long list of unanswered queries about the mysteries of ancient Chinese mythology, and the "Great Summons" (*Dazhao*) and the "Small Summons" (*Xiaozhao*), both said to have been written by Qu Yuan's disciple Song Yu after Qu Yuan had committed suicide by drowning. Throughout the centuries, Qu Yuan remained the exemplar of the brilliant but misunderstood and slandered official, the figure with which all disappointed intellectuals could identify: one of the best-known plays of the early Qing dynasty was You Tong's *Reading "Encountering Sorrow."*

While it is true that Xie Xucai can be seen as the thinly disguised alter ego of the author (Wu Zao is also known to have painted a portrait of herself in male dress), we should nevertheless not overlook the additional freedom the author has created for herself by voicing her concerns through the mouth of a fictional character. What must remain unspoken, or at least muted, in songs and lyrics believed to be the actual voice of the woman poet, could be expressed much more forcefully in the voice of an obviously fictional (male) character. In Wu Zao's play, the role of Xie Xucai is played by a "young male" (*xiaosheng*), a role type that specialized in playing brilliant young students. Both actors and actresses specialized in this role type, adding yet another layer to the blurring of gender roles in the play.

The songs in the play alternate between "northern" and "southern" tunes. The "northern" tunes, which are typically associated with a certain manly heroism, refer to those Kunqu tunes that originally derived from the northern-style music of *zaju*. Generally speaking, however, most Kunqu tunes are southern in origin and are traditionally considered to be better suited to the expression of feminine languor.

The Fake Image

[*The* xiaosheng *enters in a long gown, hair in a scarf*]

Northern: To the Tune of "New Water Tune" (*Xinshuiling*)

A single tree with scattered flowers protects my cozy study,
To guard the place, I've arranged brush-stand and tea-stove.

I always carry with me a goblet of jade,
I've changed into a well-fitting blue robe.
My skirts and shoes are splendid,
But I'm embarrassed to paint on curved brows!

[*Sits down*]

Steel, a hundred times melted, yet pliable enough to bend:
The noble ambitions of a man, the sorrows of a woman.
Today all of this has been made into a heartrending song
That will wipe away the shame of the world's women!

I am Xie Xucai. Although I was born and raised in the inner quarters, I am by nature addicted to books and histories. I am ashamed of my female dress and I despise powder and rouge! I dare not boast of texts engraved on purple crystal that will earn me an [official position], but I love to discuss the swordsmanship of the knight-errant. If I were allowed to give free rein to my innermost desires, they would be no different from those of the flying roc that soars beyond the clouds. But unfortunately my body is not in harmony with the world, and in the end what I most resemble is a sick crane locked behind bars. Alas, this is because I am fettered by my physical form, and I can only sigh all alone over my sadness. If one considers the matter carefully though, while miraculous transformations depend on Heaven, the initiative rests with oneself. That is why a few days ago I painted a small portrait of myself dressed in male attire, which I have titled "Drinking Wine and Reading 'Encountering Sorrow.'" I dare not call myself an extraordinary beauty, but I secretly congratulate myself for being a sophisticated gentleman. Today I've changed my female dress. Now that I am here in my study, let me lift my spirits by enjoying this painting for a while.
[*Stands up and walks around the corners of the stage*]

Southern: To the Tune of "Each Step Lovely" (*Bubujiao*)

The actor's cap and gown can be exchanged at will:
This conception is quite original.
Filled with sorrow I offer a libation of wine,
Who in the world understands
My noble and heroic feelings?

[*Takes a book from her sleeve*]

In my sleeve I carry the "Encountering Sorrow,"
In the courtyard, petal clusters of red and blue swirl about.

[*On the stage a painting has already been hung up. Set up table and chairs, and place a wine cup on the table. The* xiaosheng *looks at the painting*]

Just look: a jade tree in the wind, a bright pearl at the side, extended eyebrows and long nails, a black cap and a blue gown—painted quite exceptionally!

Northern: To the Tune of "Snapping Off a Sprig of Cassia" (*Zheguiling*)

You say that a female student like this is truly unheard of,
That it is just an illusory image, an empty flower,
That it is, after all, the fate I must suffer.
This new painting of you looking like a wild-hearted fellow,
Truly means your fate is as thin as paper,
Don't tell me anymore about your heart being as lofty as Heaven!
But to be like this unfettered body,
A cap donned sidewise on bundled hair,
Is much better than a listless toilette, limbs bound by light silk.
Why do I have to be crushed powder, vexed fragrance,
Beset by illness, overcome by sorrow?
I only fear that the single cup of red mist there in the painting,
Will be no match for the red tides early and late in the mirror.

[*Drinks wine*] Long ago, Li Bai said in one of his poems: "Amidst the flowers, a single jug of wine: / I drink alone, without a companion. / I raise the cup, invite the bright moon, / Together with my shadow, that makes three." If you look at it this way, the person in the painting must be Xie Xucai's closest friend! [*Walks over to the right side to look*]

Southern: To the Tune of "River's Water" (*Jiangershui*)

I carefully study that carefree air:
Grown up to be quite handsome!
Your dashingly romantic face may be finer even than the lotus flower,
But I fear such a somber person will be laughed at by the blossoming
    peach,
So how can your unfortunate fate not be more meager than a pear
    blossom petal?

Xucai, Xucai!

Again I foolishly call out to the painting:

When someone is as brilliant as you,
Who, apart from me, will share your tune?

Bah! Since my eyes find the present world wanting, my ambitions soar beyond this dusty realm. My lofty feelings don't run after pear blossom petals, and my extraordinary energy can swallow the marshes of Yunmeng[8]—so why should I be talking to this picture and acting in this foolish manner? Let me describe once and for all the greatest desires of my life! [*Takes a position center stage*]

Northern: To the Tune of "The Goose Falls" (*Yanerluo*), Followed by "Victory Tune" (*Deshengling*)

I want to avail myself of the misty waves to sail my painted craft,
I want to drive the winds of heaven and visit the isles of the immortals;
I want to pluck a bronze lute and on the Yangzi sing a song,
I want to take hold of a precious sword and whistle by lamplight.
Oh,
I want to use the rainbow as line and lower it into the sea to hook the
    golden turtle,
I want to drink like a whale and pawn my gold and sable to buy some
    wine,
I want to tune the red strings and play the tune of "Hidden Orchid,"
I want to don a palace gown and scoop up the moon from the river.
I want to play the flute,
To be just like Wang Ziqiao, but only much younger,[9]
I want to use the word "cake" [in my poems],
And laugh at Liu Yuxi, who in vain took himself to be a hero, [10]
And laugh at Liu Yuxi, who in vain took himself to be a hero!

Alas! It is all fantastic nonsense, I really am an idiot recounting his dreams! Those who know me may yet sympathize with me for my pure and unconventional character, but those who do not know me will only say that my way of life is scandalous. How could they know that these feelings of depression and frustration have been with me since birth? [*Weeps*]

---

8. The marshes of Yunmeng, located at the confluence of the Yangzi and the Han, were the extensive hunting preserves of the kings of the ancient state of Chu.

9. Wang Ziqiao was an immortal of ancient times.

10. The Tang dynasty poet Liu Yuxi (772–842) once wanted to use the word "cake" in a poem, but in the end decided against doing so because the word did not occur in the Classics, and so using it would run the risk of being considered too vulgar.

Southern: To the Tune of "Oh So Cute" (*Jiaojiaoling*)

All my life I've prided myself on my arrogant bones,
In an earlier existence were planted the sprouts of sorrow.
Don't blame me for writing my failure in the air like Yin Hao,[11]
It's nothing but an attempt to defend myself against detractors,
It's nothing but an attempt to defend myself against detractors.

To open a jug and read a book like this can indeed dispel one's sorrow. Now how can I get myself some dancers and singers with skirts like breezes and fans like the moon? Isn't that the elegant pastime of the literati?

Northern: To the Tune of "The Conquest of the South" (*Shou Jiangnan*)

Ah,
All I lack is a red-sleeved companion, refilling the incense, to sit opposite me on a spring night,
Of course I will, despite the cold, equally reject all the half-sleeve jackets,[11a]
And I'm bound to forget my jet and kohl—the ten pecks I mixed [in the past].
Carefully tracing out the black lines,
Slowly beating the red-ivory clappers—
Only that will display beauty and scholar dissolving your soul!

[*Laughs loudly*] What fun! I impose on you the penalty of drinking one large beaker! [*Acts out drinking wine and reading the book*] In my opinion, Qu Yuan is the greatest human being there ever was: in later generations there has never been anyone to equal him. But at this moment, there's not that much difference between him and me, Xie Xucai, when it comes to haggard wanderings by river and pond, and traveling and chanting along the banks of the marsh.

---

11. Yin Hao (306–356) in 350 was a commander-in-chief who led a Jin attempt to re-conquer the north. He was soundly defeated by northern troops, however, and subsequently dismissed. Afterwards, he spent his days tracing the character *zhuozhuo* ("alas, alas") in the air with his hand.

11a. Once when the high official Song Qi (917–996) was partying with his many concubines, it suddenly became chilly and he asked that a jacket be fetched. All his courtesans offered him their own jackets, but he refused them all, fearing that by accepting one of them, he would be showing preference to the owner.

Southern: To the Tune of "Fine Gardens" (*Yuanlin hao*)

I make a lotus gown, its fragrance wafting, its powder wafting,
I gaze toward the river Xiang, its mountains far, its waters so far,
And recite "Encountering Sorrow" to the end.
I scratch my head and ask,
But the azure heaven is far away.
I scratch my head and ask,
But the azure heaven is far away.

[*Weeps bitterly*] Come to think of it, Qu Yuan's spirit may have returned to Heaven, but his fame has remained in this world. What is more, he had a disciple who summoned his soul, and who scattered his tears throughout the South. So his situation after death was still not too bad. But I, Xie Xucai, will disappear without a trace, and since this minuscule soul of mine will disappear into the endless void, what will become of me?

Northern: To the Tune of "Buying Fine Wine" (*Gumeijiu*) followed by "Great Peace Tune" (*Taipingling*)

Somberly I ponder: who'll summon my soul?
Somberly I ponder: who'll summon my soul?
Once the spirit is ready to leave,
Dream's labor will be lost.

In ancient times there were people who offered sacrifices to people still alive and there also were people who wrote their own funerary texts. As for me today,

On this paper, spring breeze has come to its end,
I'll sing a dirge of Chu,
And pour some pine-brew:
How many evening suns and fragrant grasses can I experience?
How many waning moons and breezy dawns can I endure?
There is no end to manuscripts of brokenhearted songs,
On top of that, there is this portrait that wounds my mind.
Oh,
Let me do away with these golden hairpins, these kingfisher hairpins,
I'll ready a gourd for my poems, a gourd for my wine.
Oh,
In front of the flowers I repeatedly grieve over her image. [*rolls up scroll*]

To the Tune of "Clear River Intro" (*Qingjiangyin*)

Brown rooster and white sun propel us on to old age,
When will we wake up from this butterfly dream?[12]
Forever I'll follow the one in the scroll,
And from now on be a *kalavinka* bird.
Indistinguishable: image and body have fused into one!

Xie Xucai's desire to be entertained by female performers and to find herself a companionate wife has earned her creator, Wu Zao, the reputation of being "a lesbian merchant wench." And it must be said that in her song lyrics as well, one can find works that betray what would appear to be strong homoerotic feelings. An example is the following lyric written to the melody of "Song of the Cave Immortals" (*Dongxiange*) addressed to the Suzhou entertainer Qinglin:

With your jingling and jangling interconnected bones[13]
You're like an immortal companion of the Emerald Palace.
As soon as I saw your smile, I was completely at a loss for words.
Holding a flower in your hands,
You lean against the bamboo as a cool rises from the green.
In this empty valley
I imagine that I can see my own deepest thoughts.

The orchid candle dims its light and shade,
As we drink wine and discuss poetry,
And then sing those heartbreaking lines of "Remembering the South."
Both of us are talented poets with painted brows,
But I in my wild-heartedness
Would like to enjoy,
Jade-like one, your devotion.
At this moment vast and boundless—
The misty waves of the Five Lakes in spring:
Let me buy a red boat
And take you along with me, away!

---

12. The philosopher Zhuang Zhou once dreamt he was a butterfly. When he woke up he wondered whether he might not be a butterfly dreaming to be Zhuang Zhou.

13. Bodhisattvas are said to have interconnected bones. In one legend, a beautiful prostitute is identified as actually being a reincarnation of Guanyin when her grave is opened up and her bones are discovered to be interconnected.

The final aria of *The Fake Image* makes clear, as did Wang Yun in her *Dream of Splendor*, that for many women the contradiction between a woman's gender and her ambition could find resolution only in a realization of the insubstantiality of all phenomena, a realization that renders irrelevant all dualities, including that of male and female. The *kalavinka* is a bird said to have a particularly melodious voice and is often used in Buddhist scriptures as a metaphor for the beautiful sounds of the Buddhist teachings. This line suggests, then, that Buddhist practice may offer a way out of her dilemma. Later in her life, Wu Zao did in fact take up Buddhist practice.

Her play attracted the attention of Chen Wenshu, the male patron of women poets in the Hangzhou area, whom she met in 1826 on a visit to Suzhou. She became Chen Wenshu's literary disciple, and celebrated his restoration of the grave of Xiaoqing with a long set of songs, which would be widely performed. Chen Wenshu later characterized Wu Zao (whose sobriquet can be translated as The Master of the Flower Screen) in a poem that was inspired as much by the portrait of her in male dress and her play, as by Wu Zao herself:

> Her jade feelings and jasper resentment have no equal,
> Her peerless charm and grace are of the highest class.
> Jewels and powder cannot dispel the air of a man of talent,
> Lakes and hills easily move this beautiful person to sorrow.
> Over a cup of wine the scanty rain's chill evokes a dream,
> The unmoving clouds in the painting have the cold look of fall.
> Disconsolate are the words from the strings of the black zither,
> The Flower Screen's shadow is thin in the Water Bright Tower.

In Suzhou, Wu Zao met a number of Chen Wenshu's other disciples, including Wang Duan, who, after returning to Hangzhou in her later years, would share in Wu Zao's Buddhist devotions. Wu Zao also met Zhang Xiang, a general's daughter who could ride and shoot. This visit to Suzhou remained one of the high points in Wu Zao's life, and later she would recall her time there in a series of eight lyrics written to the melody of "Remembering the South" (*Yi Jiangnan*). The fifth lyric in this series is dedicated to Zhang Xiang and reads as follows:

> When I think back on the South,
> The first thing I recall is that dark green shade:

In the eastern pavilion, downing our cups, we examined our swords,
In the western garden, we rode our dappled colts side by side,
We women are heroes too!

Wu Zao's early lyrics were collected in the *Flower Screen Lyrics* (*Hualianci*) of 1829. The preface for this collection, written by Zhao Qingxi, suggests that the predominant tone of the poems was one of unmitigated "sorrow":

There is no year that lacks falling blossoms, there is no place that lacks fragrant grasses, and there is no day that lacks a setting sun and a radiant moon. But how many people in past and present have been able to speak of falling blossoms and fragrant grasses? And how many in past and present have been able to speak of setting sun and radiant moon? This shows how extremely difficult it is to describe objects and to describe sorrow. But the Master of the Flower Screen is skilled in sorrow, and her lyrics excel in describing sorrow. . . . Her lyrics are about the falling blossoms, the fragrant grasses, the setting sun, and the radiant moon. These objects do not necessarily evoke sorrow. But if one feels sorrow when there is no necessity for sorrow, then one will perceive the entire world as being filled with objects that are conducive to sorrow, and filled with scenes that are conducive to sorrow. This is the reason why the Master of the Flower Screen excels in sorrow, and this is also the reason why she excels in the writing of lyrics.

While writing this preface, Zhao Qingxi may have had in mind the following lyrics by Wu Zao:

To the Melody of "Incense Offering" (*Xingxiangzi*)

The long night drags on,
The falling leaves rustle,
As the wind continues to pound on the paper window.
The tea is tepid, the mist is cold,
The burner dark, the incense finished.
At this moment the little courtyard is empty,
The two doors are shut,
The one lamp trimmed.

I can't rid myself of sorrow,
I can't find myself a dream,
And under my cold duvet even sleep brings no comfort.

This desolate situation
Is the same every night:
There's the slow dripping of the water-clock,
The bitter sound of the bell,
The high call of the geese.

To the Melody of "Shouting Fire" (*Hehuoling*)

The bamboo mat is chilly as if it had just been washed,
Behind the screen no dream has yet been summoned.
I want to sleep, but rise again to arrange the icy silk,[14]
And by the green-gauze window
Silently select some incense to burn.

My sorrow I am afraid to tell to Heaven,
My poems are mostly wrought while ill.
This night as of old resembles the night before:
The same red candle,
The same distant clock,
And when I wake up from my wine-induced slumber,
That same setting moon above the branches in bloom.

To the Melody of "Romantic Lover" (*Fengliuzi*)

The covered walkway, twelve times curving:
Again I look around—
How can I bear to pour the golden goblet?
Depressed by last night's scattered rains,
Today's blustery winds,
The fallen petals on narrow pathways,
The drifting floss on level ponds.
At the gathering to send spring on its way
The two or three stanzas of parting songs
Are augmented by melancholy lyrics.
If fragrant flowers have feelings,
Their green is bound to deepen like this;
If the setting sun does not take care,
Their red cannot last long.

---

14. The "icy silk" refers to the strings of the zither.

Where does this springtime splendor go?
The weeping willows cannot tie it down,
Still swinging their misty threads.
Instantly both in the world of men and in Heaven,
The incense cools, the clouds drizzle.
In the courtyard as twilight draws near,
The bamboo curtain is half rolled up.
I stand for a while on the jade steps
Counting all the dots of crimson—
The few brokenhearted songbirds
Perch on the empty branches.

In a number of lyrics this expression of sorrow is combined with references to "Encountering Sorrow" and other texts from *Songs of the South*, texts to which Wu Zao referred to in her play as well.

To the Melody of "Ballad of Golden Threads" (*Jinlüqu*)

Depressed I demand a statement from Heaven,
And pose this question to the sky above:
You brought us forth into this world,
How can you bear to ruin and destroy us?
Since ancient times the vigor of brave men has been indestructible—
But even they can only helplessly inscribe their frustrations in the air.
At this moment I read
These verses of a broken heart,
And when I come to the most moving passage,
　　　　　I suddenly start to laugh,
To laugh because it is clear
That sorrow is my private fortune:
All of it is concentrated
On the tip of my brush.

Great heroes and passionate lovers, it all makes no difference—
After a thousand years, alas,
Their final gesture is just the same,
As all their tears turn into blood.
I want to lightly put away these spineless feelings,
Avoid the breeze and moonlight near the willows.

So let me make ready
A bronze lute and an iron plectrum.
After reciting "Encountering Sorrow" I'll pour out my wine
Into the great river that streams eastward and sing a few stanzas:
My voice will soon come to a halt,
And the dark clouds split open!

To the Melody of "Sands of Washing Brook" (*Huanxisha*)

On one side "Encountering Sorrow," on the other a sutra:
My innermost feelings of ten years, my lamp of ten years.
How many drops of autumn on the banana leaves?

I'd like to weep but when I can't, I force myself to smile,
I outlaw sorrow, but when that fails, I study oblivion.
The one thing that still ruins my life is my intelligence.

To the Melody of "Pallid Moon behind the Curtain" (*Sulian danyue*)

In the darkening dusk, drowsy with drink—
And what is more, gusts of westerly winds
Have torn the paper window to shreds.
Yesterday and again tonight
It is the same damp chill.
Hairpins aslant, chignon sagging, behind the gauze curtain:
Sleep will not come,
So forget about dreams!
Flowers in vases—their fragrance so weak,
Flowers from brushes—brilliant but cold,
Flowers from candles—red yet wilting.[15]

What is the need in the end
To confess one's regrets before the Lotus Altar?
I only regret the root of sorrow is not yet cut,
Don't utter the words "intelligent" or "smart."
Each and every sheet of writing paper
Is completely awash in rivers of tears.

---

15. The "flower of a candle" refers to the charred tip of a candlewick.

The autumn orchid always serves as my girdle pendant,
And with each and every word
I chant the song of the "Mountain Goddess."[16]
Ill as I am, how can I bear,
To grow ever more haggard and gaunt,
As the splendors of the year depart.

In yet other sorrow-filled lyrics, Wu Zao compares herself by allusion to the Song poet Zhu Shuzhen, who, like her, hailed from Hangzhou and had been married to a merchant. The following is a Qing dynasty anecdote about Zhu Shuzhen:

From the time Zhu Shuzhen of Qiantang married an incompatible husband, her lyrics became filled with dark resentment. Each time spring arrived, she would sit in meditation behind lowered bed curtains. When people asked her the reason for this, she would answer: "I cannot bear to witness the glories of spring!"

Wu Zao alludes to this anecdote in the following poem:

To the Melody of "Intertwined Branches" (*Lianlizhi*)

I do not fear the blossoming branches' anger,
I do not fear the blossoming branches' scorn—
But I do blame the spring breezes
For bringing these days every year
And again such sorrow to this place.
When I sit in meditation behind my lowered curtains,
The bees and the butterflies all raise a fuss.

Will heaven ever age and then grow old?
And can the moon be perfect at all times?
Below my eyes, above my brows,
There is no love, yet there is grief,
But when I ask, nobody can reply.
I've never since I was born, betrayed my lofty talent—
Could it be that my intelligence is my undoing?

---

16. "Mountain Goddess" is the title of one of the songs in the "Nine Songs" section of *Songs of the South*. Like the other texts in the "Nine Songs," it evokes the image of a beautiful but ever elusive goddess.

Wu Zao's lyrics in this first collection, however, are somewhat more lighthearted than the above compositions would suggest. Many of the lyrics not only testify to her remarkable mastery of the lyric form, but also to her wit and humor, as the following examples will show.

To the Melody of "River Town Plum Blossoms Intro" (*Jiangcheng Meihuayin*)

Last night a gentle rain fell endlessly on my study—
I feared spring had arrived,
Indeed spring had arrived!
So now that spring has finally arrived,
A hundred things must be put in order.
My makeup lightly applied, my brows not yet painted,
Without saying a word
I quietly lifted the curtains,
And stepped out on the emerald moss.

Emerald moss, emerald moss: I tread on empty steps,
Then rested my embroidered shoes,
And leaned against the jade terrace.
I counted and counted again but was unable to count them all:
The flowers falling, the flowers blooming.
Instead I just asked the willow branches:
"To whom are you lifting your green eyes?"
The swallows and orioles all suddenly fell silent
As if, their backs to the easterly winds,
They wanted to hazard a guess,
And answer the question themselves.

To the Melody of "As in a Dream" (*Rumengling*)

The swallows have not yet left with the springtime,
They hide themselves inside the embroidered blinds.
Twittering softly they talk to me for a long while,
It must be that they want to remain here with me.
I hesitate,
I hesitate,
Then answer with a smile: "It's not allowed."

To the Melody of "Zhu Yingtai" (*Zhu Yingtai jin*) On My Shadow

The low balustrade
In the secluded courtyard—
At the end of the day too tired to comb my hair.
Into the endless sea of regret
I feel I have already plunged.
What is more, that busybody of a lamp,
As soon as dusk has fallen,
Provides me with
A single lonely shadow!

And what is most annoying:
Even though I make an effort to pity you,
You are unable to pity me!
So why, there by the window, do you
Persist in following me whether I walk or sit?
Impossible, I know, to chase you away,
But I have a trick for avoiding you:
Pull the bed curtains shut,
And pretend to be asleep!

In 1837 Wu Zao moved to a house to the south of West Lake. Her time was increasingly taken up by religious devotions, often in the company of Wang Duan. Her later lyrics were gathered together in a collection entitled *Lyrics from South of Incense Mountain and North of Snowy Mountains* (*Xiangnan Xuebei ci*) and published in 1844. Many of the lyrics in this collection reflect her growing acceptance (or perhaps resignation) to the ultimate evanescence of all phenomena:

To the Melody of "Sands of Washing Brook" (*Huanxisha*)

A heart and mind of snow and ice: my lines seek transcendence,
It is right for this body to age and grow old by the side of the lake:
The room by the stream is dark in spring when the plum petals fall.

I find a hairpin: how many people have lost their precious baubles?
I refill the incense and, all alone, I tune the strings of the zither:
I'm feeling fine, more and more different from the years gone by.

The quiet life of Wu Zao in later years, however, did not mean that she abstained from all social contacts. She edited the collected lyrics of Shen Shanbao, a friend of both hers and Wang Duan's, before Shen Shanbao left with her husband for Beijing; she also instructed Huang Xieqing, the major male playwright of the mid-nineteenth century, in musical matters.

Moral Fables and Special Effects: Liu Qingyun

By far the most prolific woman playwright of the nineteenth century was Liu Qingyun (1842–1915) from Haizhou. Her father was a high official and her husband, Qian Meipo (1841–1909), rose to the rank of vice-prefect. The couple lived a life of luxury and ease until they were reduced to poverty when Hongze Lake flooded over and destroyed their house. Liu Qingyun wrote poems and song lyrics, but she also wrote over twenty plays, ten of which were printed in 1900 with a preface by the famous philological scholar, Yu Yue (1821–1907):

In the spring of the year *dingyou* [1897], when I was staying at West Lake, Magistrate Zhang Xiju showed me the poems and lyrics of the woman scholar Liu Qingyun, who was from his hometown Haizhou. I wrote a preface and then returned the collection to him. When I learned that she had also written twenty-four plays and I asked to see them, he came up with ten of them.

When I inquired about the remaining plays, he told me that Liu Qingyun had them at home. Liu Qingyun was from Haizhou, and her husband Qian Meipo from Shuyang, quite a distance from where we were in Hangzhou, which meant it would not be easy to go and get them. In the autumn of that year it rained incessantly and Hongze Lake flooded over. Liu Qingyun's house was destroyed by the flood, and the manuscripts of her plays were submerged and soaked by the mud and dirt, and bricks and stones, and were lost. Thus all that remains of her work are these ten plays.

Judging her work on the basis of these ten plays, we find that even when she makes use of well-known materials, she often comes up with new ideas, and the plot and the rhythm of her plays are always extremely lively. In her arias, she puts less effort into phraseology, but instead seeks a natural style of beauty, often achieving the *samadhi* of the playwrights of the Yuan dynasty. If one compares her to Li Yu and his ten plays,[17] she may lack his talent and energy, but she would seem to surpass him in elegance and purity. As the remaining four-

---

17. Li Yu (1611–1679) is the author of a collection of ten witty *chuanqi* plays that enjoyed a great popularity throughout the Qing dynasty.

teen plays are no longer to be found, should one not circulate widely on her behalf the ten plays that have fortunately survived?

Mister Wu Jiying of Hangzhou is a man of culture and initiative. Having recently acquired a press for lithographic printing, he offered to print the plays so as to ensure that they would be widely distributed, and Magistrate Yang Guyun from Louxian volunteered to do the proofreading. At that time, Yang Guyun was temporarily serving as magistrate of Longyou, but despite the huge pile of official documents [on his desk], he did not let it get in the way of the work of correcting the proofs, which shows the superior ease with which he carries out his business. Unfortunately, Zhang Xiju has already passed away and did not live to see the completion of this book.

I would feel blessed and it is my hope, as it is that of both Mr. Wu and Mr. Yang, that if Liu Qingyun retains the pearl of memory in her breast, she will once again be able to write out clean copies of the fourteen plays that were lost, so that we can make complete this edition [of her works].

While the fourteen lost plays were never recovered, recent research has unearthed two additional manuscripts of plays that Liu Qingyun wrote after 1900.

Liu Qingyun's plays are all relatively short, the longest ones comprising no more than twelve scenes. As Yu Yue noted in his preface, her work is notable for its simple style, especially when it comes to the language of the arias. Liu Qingyun does not share her predecessors' fascination with cross-dressing; most of her plays are moral fables, featuring exemplars of traditional virtues. Three of her plays are dramatic adaptations of stories from Pu Songling's (1640–1715) famous collection of ghost stories, *Stories of the Strange from Make-do Studio* (*Liaozhai zhiyi*). Her play *Kept Promises* (*Danqingfu*) is an adaptation of Pu Songling's story "Tian Qilang." The story describes the friendship of the wealthy magnate Wu Chengxiu and the fierce hunter Tian Qilang, to whose rescue Wu once came after Tian had killed someone in a brawl, and the way in which Tian Qilang repays Wu for his help when Wu himself gets in trouble with the law because of the machinations of his local rival Wu Lai. In Liu Qingyun's play, when Wu Lai and a corrupt magistrate are discussing their plans to do away with Wu Chengxiu, they are surprised by Tian Qilang, who kills off Wu Lai, and then slashes his own throat. But when the magistrate, who had escaped the hunter's wrath by jumping into a cesspit, returns to inspect the corpse, Tian Qilang suddenly comes back to life, cuts off the magistrate's head and carries it out into the street, after which he once again collapses and dies. Subsequently, Tian Qilang reappears transformed into a god, and the play ends with an encounter between an elderly Wu Chengxiu and Tian Qilang's son, now a high military official, at Tian Qilang's old home, which has since been converted into a temple. The most memorable female character in this play is Tian Qilang's mother, who tries in vain to discipline her son and warns him against associating with Wu Chengxiu, who, as she can clearly see just by "reading" his face, spells disaster.

The violence and didacticism of the play is relieved by a few lighter touches of social satire, especially in the descriptions of the venal magistrate, as well as of Wu Changxiu's obsequious and self-serving secretary and his spiteful catamite. This last character plays center stage in the beginning of scene seven, which in many ways can be read as a parody of the famous garden scene from *Peony Pavilion*:

[*The* chou[18] *enters, gaudily dressed and drunk*] . . . I am Master Wu's favorite boy Lin'er. The Master loves me in a hundred ways and is forgiving of my thousand faults. Whatever I wish, I obtain; whatever I ask for, I get. I have more influence than anyone in this entire mansion. It goes without saying that the other boys don't even dare breathe on me—even the secretaries and other household officers are always currying my favors. But I won't talk about that. I've heard that the Eldest Son has married himself a new bride who is quite pretty, but I've never seen her. Now I've just heard from the studyroom boy that she is out in the garden all by herself looking at the flowers, so I'll have to go to the study and wait for the opportunity to play my little trick. And then let's see what happens! [*Nods, smiles, and exits. The* dan[19] *enters with a tired expression, accompanied by her servant girl*] . . . I am He Wanqing. I was born and raised in an illustrious family, and when I came of age, I married into this noble family. I am pampered by my parents-in-law and dearly loved by my husband. At this moment the inner quarters are silent, the secluded courtyard is quiet, so let me play a tune on the zither to while away the long hours of daylight. Servant girl, bring me my zither! [*Notices the flowers in the vase*] Where do these come from? [*Servant girl speaks*] Oh, madam, you should know that on the east side there is a flower garden built by the Old Master with his own hands. Originally it didn't look like much, but later, after the Old Master had built pavilions and terraces, and planted shrubs

---

18. The name of a role type, usually a low-class male.
19. The name of a role type, usually a young woman.

and trees, it was so transformed that it came to look like a heavenly palace. Madam, why don't you go there with me to have a look? [Dan *ponders*] I am afraid that won't do; sure there are people out there coming and going. [*Servant girl speaks*] Today the Master is receiving guests in the main hall, so there is not even a shadow of a man to be seen in the garden. Let's go for a stroll. What are you afraid of? [Dan *speaks*] Are you sure? [*Servant girl speaks*] Yes, I am sure! [Dan *gets up*] Let's go then, but we will come back immediately! [*They go there together.* Dan *speaks*] This is really a wonderful flower garden! [*Stops suddenly*] I forgot my handkerchief on my toilette table, go and get it for me! [*Servant girl exits.* Dan *sings as she strolls about*]

To the Tune of "Spring in the Imperial Park" (*Shanglin chun*)

My slow steps stir up a fragrance, the imprint of my lotus-shoes is small,
Following dark paths and curving corridors I stroll about.

[*Offstage a parrot speaks*] A guest has come! [Dan *looks around*]

All of a sudden I hear a call from behind the blinds,
It's that white cockatoo that's just trying to annoy!

Just look what a quiet and secluded spot this is, next to the hill and close to the stream, connected to the house, at the back of the hall! [*Looks up*] "Like an Orchid Study": this must be my father-in-law's meditation room. If the outside is so elegant, the inside must be even more special, so let me go inside and have a look. [*Prepares to enter. The* chou *rushes on stage and greets her*] I did not know, madam, that you were going to visit this place, so forgive me for not coming out to welcome you! [*The* dan *acts out being surprised and steps back. Calls out to her maid*] Servant girl, there's someone here, let's go back! [*The* chou *smiles but blocks her way*] Madam, now that you have done me the honor of visiting me, please be so kind as to sit down, so I may offer you some tea. [*The* dan *becomes angry*] Who are you that you dare act with such disrespect? [*The* chou *speaks*] Madam, don't be angry. The proverb says it well: "Where one arrives, there one settles." How could you go back empty-handed? [*Attempts to pull the* dan *over to him. The* dan *is frightened and eludes him. The servant girl enters*] I looked for you everywhere and couldn't find you, but it turns out you were here! [*Hands the* dan *the handkerchief. The* dan *speaks*] Let's go back! [*Tries to leave. The* chou *blocks her way*] Where are you going? Why don't you be nice and stay with me for a little tête-à-tête! [*Servant girl speaks*] Lin'er, you're in big trouble! Who do you think this is that you behave in such an outrageous manner? [*Turns to the* dan] Madam, don't be upset, let me go and tell the Master to have him killed! [*The* chou *speaks*] Bah, you cheap slut! Be careful or I'll beat you up! [*He grabs her and hits her. The servant girl cries for help. The* sheng *enters, strolling leisurely*] Hey, who is that there making such a fuss? [*Stops and listens, then gets angry*] Servants! [*Two bit parts enter*] Master, what is your command? [*The* sheng *speaks*] Go into the study and grab that Lin'er. I'll be waiting for you in the hall. [*Exits. The* chou *becomes frightened, releases the* dan *and exits running. The* dan *and the servant girl exit*]

This excerpt not only illustrates the prevalence of dialogue in Liu Qing-yun's plays, but also the naturalness of her language. While we have no references to any performances of her plays, the detailed stage directions show that she carefully envisioned the action on stage.

Another of Liu Qingyun's adaptations of Pu Songling's *Stories of the Strange from Make-do Studio* is a play entitled *Sword of Vengeance* (*Fei-hongxiao*), which is based on the story "Gengniang." The action of this play is set in the last decades of the Ming dynasty, when central Henan province was suffering the depredations of roving bandits. You Geng-niang is the young wife of Jin Dayong from Kaifeng. When bandits approach the city, the couple flees south, together with Jin Dayong's parents. They are soon separated from their servants, and eventually join up with Wang Shiba and his wife, after which they continue their journey by boat. Wang is in league with the boatmen, however, and that very night he kills off the elderly couple and throws both his own wife and Jin Dayong overboard as he has set his sights on Gengniang. Both Jin Dayong and Wang's wife are later rescued by a man who takes them to his house and insists that the two marry each other. In the meantime, Gengniang has preserved her chastity by promising Wang that she will marry him when they get to his home in Nanjing. On the night of their wedding, however, she kills off Wang Shiba, and his mother and younger brother as well, before committing suicide by jumping into the river. This tale of wifely fortitude in a time of warfare and danger may well have held a special appeal for Liu Qingyun—after all, she had lived through one of the most unsettled and dramatic periods of Chinese history.

But the story of Gengniang does not end here, as we learn from scene seven, "Opening the Grave":

[*The bit player enters, dressed as a woodcutter with his ax and a jug of wine*] As soon as I've sold a bundle of firewood, / I'll buy myself three pints of brew. I am Zhang

Three. [*The* jing[20] *enters dressed as a fisherman, punting his boat*] As soon as the fish is cooked in the wok, / We'll have a good chat over our drinks. I am Li Four. [*Waves. The bit player boards the boat and takes a seat opposite him. The* jing *speaks*] Zhang Three, the two of us have suffered bitterly for most of our lives, and we've not even saved a single copper or half a dime. Now, when we've become resigned to the fact that we were just born to be poor—who'd have thought that old Heaven would take pity on us! Last night I had a dream in which a spirit instructed me to open the grave of the female martyr Liu and promised that we would make quite a lot of money. Now tell me, do you think that we can really pull that off? [*The bit player speaks*] If that old guy is telling us to do it, of course we can pull it off! Let's first finish this wine, and then discuss it. [*They play drinking games and drink heartily. The* jing *becomes drunk, gazes at the sky, and turns to the bit player*] It's getting dark, so let's go! As soon as we get there, we'll get to work. [*The bit player speaks*] Whatever you say! [*Exit, together rowing the boat. The* tie[21] *enters, dressed as before and, holding a flag, leads the* dan. *They circle the stage and exit. The* jing, *carrying a spade, and the bit player, holding the ax, enter together. They walk around the stage*]

To the Tune of "Consulting the Oracle" (*Fanbusuan*)

Once the layers of mist are cleared from the field,
The shining stars begin to glow in full brilliance.
Distant paths and nearby lanes all interconnected:
We walk on until the soles of our shoes wear out.

[*The* jing *speaks*] Here we are, let's get started! [*He digs. The* tie *enters, leading the* dan. *She pushes the* dan *to the ground and speaks*] Gengniang, listen carefully! The earthly life of you and Jin Dayong is not over yet and husband and wife will be reunited. So wait patiently, and don't forget. [*Exits. The bit player speaks*] No need to dig any deeper, we've reached the coffin. [*The* jing *speaks*] To reach the court always spells trouble![22] [*The bit player speaks*] Stop making jokes! [*Takes his ax and splits open the coffin. The* dan *sighs. The bit player throws aside his ax and shivers all over. The* jing *picks up the ax and curses him*] You useless bastard! Bugger off! Just watch me do it! [*Lifts up the coffin's lid. The* dan *heaves a deep sigh. The* jing *collapses in fright*

---

20. The name of a role type, usually a villain.

21. The name of a role type, usually a female character of secondary importance.

22. In Chinese the words for "coffin" (*guan*) and "official" (*guan*) have the same pronunciation. We here have translated "official" as "court," a word that at least begins with the same sound as "coffin."

and screams] It's not my fault! It's all Zhang Three's idea! I beseech you, Your Excellency, just arrest him and spare me! [*The* dan *sings softly*]

To the Tune of "The Cold Carved Window" (*Suochuanghan*)

Lost and bewildered—for how many years?
It feels as though I'd just woken from sleep.
When I turn around and relive my dream,
The dangers and hardships were a million.
I tried to bury myself with him in the white-capped waves,
So how can the red string of marriage be tied once again?
But if it is not to be,
Why then should I so clearly appear once more in this world of form?
What a pitiful fate:
I was peacefully resting below a clod of brown earth,
So why must I be forced to look upon the blue sky again?

[*Stands up very, very slowly and then sits down. The bit player comes forward, kneels down, and kowtows*] I, Zhang Three, originally didn't dare to come. It is all the doing of that Li Four! [*Kowtows repeatedly*] Please let me go! [*Points to the* jing] He is the one you should arrest! [*The* dan *speaks*] Don't be afraid, I don't blame you for anything! [*Removes her hair ornaments and stands up*]

To the Same Tune

Thank you for saving me and bringing me back to life!

I have nothing else with which to express my thanks. [*Hands them her hair ornaments*]

I give you these jade ornaments and golden hairpins to buy yourself a drink.

[*The bit player and* jing *kneel down and refuse the gift, not daring to accept it*] Madam, we really cannot accept this wonderful gift. Just tell us where you live, so that we can escort you home! [*The* dan *sings*]

All I want is to seek refuge in a cloister,
Burning my incense before the Buddha,
From morning bell until evening drum
Confessing and repenting my many sins.

[*Hides her tears*]

I no longer have any attachments to the endless cycles of samsara.

An empty memory:
In this boundless expanse of Heaven and Earth—
How do I know at whose side my husband lives?

If you are willing to do this good deed, there may be some money in it for you. [*The* jing *and the bit player speak*] We've never committed any evil or crime, we only did this dastardly deed because we were instructed to do so in our dreams by a spirit. Madam, you have no family to which you can return, but in Zhenjiang there lives a lady Geng, a widow without children, who is immensely rich. If you seek refuge with her, she will certainly take you in. Isn't that better than becoming a nun? [*The* dan *speaks*] So let's go there first. [*The* jing *speaks*] Zhang Three, quickly get your boat, so we may take her there this very night! [*The bit player exits, then re-enters rowing his boat*] Li Four, help the lady! [*The* dan *speaks*] There is no need to help me, I can board by myself. [*Boards the boat. The bit player and the* jing *together act out punting the boat. The* dan *speaks*] I love this day because of the return of the pearl, / But in what year will the swords be reunited? [*Exit together*]

This scene derives much of its originality from its portrayal of the woodcutter and the fisherman, usually depicted as exemplars of the contented simple life, as greedy but ineffective grave robbers. As it turns out, the wealthy and pious lady Geng is indeed only too eager to take Gengniang in as an adoptive daughter. Eventually Gengniang is reunited with her husband, who, as so often happens in stories of this type, ends up with two wives.

Liu Qingyun's third adaptation of one of the *Stories of the Strange from Make-do Studio*, entitled *Guided by Heaven's Storm* (*Tianfeng yin*), is a rewriting of "The Rakshas and the Seamarket" (*Luocha haishi*). The main character of the well-known tale is Ma Longmei, a handsome young man who, at the urging of his parents, has abandoned a scholarly career in order to become a merchant. When his ship is wrecked in a typhoon, he is the only survivor. On the island of the rakshas (demons from Buddhist lore), where he is stranded, people are assigned to official positions on the basis of their ugliness, and Ma Longmei discovers that his beauty only frightens everyone away. It is only by painting his face that he is able to obtain a position at court, but as soon as his opponents realize that his ugliness is only a painted mask, he is slandered and maligned. Friends help Ma Longmei to leave the raksha island for the seamarket, where all the peoples of the ocean meet to barter their jewels and precious stones. Here Ma Longmei attracts the interest of one of the dragon princes, who takes him to his father in the dragon palace at the bottom of the sea. Ma's poetic compositions impress the latter so much that he gives Ma his daughter's hand in marriage. Pu Songling's tale ends with Ma Longmei's eventual return to China and his reunion with his parents; although without his dragon wife, who cannot live in the human world. After his departure, she gives birth to twins, whom she sends to live with their father.

In the play there is a scene entitled "A Mother's Offering" (*Ciji*) in which Ma Longmei's mother expresses her regret over having urged her son to become a merchant and makes sacrifices to him, thinking he has died at sea:

[*The* laodan[23] *enters, sick and leaning on a staff*] I am lady Wu. When I was very young, I became a bride of the Ma family. They have been merchants for generations. I have only one son who from the time he was a boy was pressured by his father from morning till night to go out into the world to make money. In fact, he did end up making some profits. [*Chokes*] But I don't know what miserable scoundrel talked him into making an ocean journey. People have told us that he ran into a storm and that the boat and the entire crew went down. When his father and I first heard this news, we fainted from the shock. Now it has been over a year, and given that we've not received any further news, most likely there's no hope left. Today at the crack of dawn, his father went again to the pier to see if there was any news. My son, all day long, your mother

To the Tune of "Finer Than Flowers" (*Shengruhua*)

Remembers you when walking,
Can't forget you while sitting,
Thinks of you, longs for you, and is filled with sad remorse.
Had I known at the start that you would lose your life in the ocean's
    waves,
I would never have let my darling son become a merchant and make
    distant journeys!
On whom can I now rely in my twilight years?
In the evening
I sit by the dark candle that flickers mournfully in the dismal darkness,
In the morning
The pale light of a joyless dawn pokes through the window railings.
When I doze off,

---

23. The name of a role type, usually an old woman.

I seem to hear my son's clear voice as he recites his books.

[*Weeps*]

> But it only is the honking of the migrating geese,
> So sorrowful it tears my heart to pieces,
> So sorrowful it tears my heart to pieces.

My son, when you were a child and we had predictions made for you, we were always told that you were predestined to become very wealthy and to rise high in the ranks. Moreover, on the day I gave birth to you, I dreamt that a divinity descended from the sky carrying in its arms an infant as white as powder and jade, which it then handed over to me, instructing me to take good care of the child, whose father and mother it was taking with him to paradise. Then I suddenly woke up and gave birth to you. I always thought that even if you could not rise to high rank, you would have no problem becoming a millionaire. But who could have thought that it would have ended up like this? My son, my grief over you is killing me! [*Hides her tears*] Enough of this! Today is your birthday; you, who died before your time. I remembered it last night, and so this morning I prepared soup and rice; how could I ever have forgotten it? [*Wipes away her tears*] Let me get everything together and make an offering to you, wherever you may be. My son, this suffering over you will be my death! [*Weeps and exits, enters carrying incense sticks and paper money. She lights the incense sticks and pours out the wine, and sits down on the ground weeping and shouts loudly*] My boy, you were so smart and intelligent! My boy, it was too cruel of you to die before your time! Do you realize that your mother is here sacrificing to you? [*Gets up to burn the paper money*]

To the Same Tune

> I burn the paper ingots,
> Pour out the cold wine;
> Come quickly and accept these offerings!

[*There is a sudden gust of wind*][24]

> As you wind yourself around me, whirling and swirling,

My son,

> Why don't you quickly take your mother with you?
> How can you bear to leave your mother behind alone?

---

24. A sudden gust of wind or a whirlwind was believed to signify the arrival of a ghost or spirit.

If I could only leave this land of sorrow, this land of pain,
I'd be freed from the pain in my heart, the pain in my mind.
Instead of living here in misery,
I'd rather go to the Yellow Springs,
Where we would be all reunited in greatest joy.

My son, you were so smart and intelligent! My son, it was too cruel of you to die before your time! Why don't you even answer me, even just once?

> Before the offering table my tears course down,
> Before the offering table my tears course down.

[*The* mo[25] *enters in great haste, with a smile on his face and a letter in his hand*] A letter from across the sea from my son / I hastily bring to my bedridden wife. My wife, soon you won't have to weep any longer! [*The* laodan *does not react. The* mo *speaks*] Here's a letter from your son! [*The* laodan *speaks*] Is he back? Where is he? [*The* mo *speaks*] He has not come, but I have here a letter in his own hand. [*The* laodan *speaks*] What does he say in the letter? Where is he now? [*The* mo *speaks*] Take those candles away, and then we will go inside and I will read the letter to you. Our son is now a prince-consort in the dragon palace, and soon he will send for us, to share in his good fortune. [*The* laodan *speaks*] Can it be true? [*The* mo *speaks*] Of course it is true! [*The* laodan *smiles happily and presses the palms of her hands together*] Thank Heaven, thank Earth! Hail, Amitabha Buddha! [*Exit together*]

The final scene of the play is devoted to the reunion of Ma Longmei and his parents in the dragon palace: the childhood predictions turn out to have been true after all.

One remarkable aspect of *Guided by Heaven's Storm* is the ample use Liu Qingyun makes of masks, elaborate costumes, and special effects. A good illustration of this is the following scene of the play in which Ma Long-mei, after marrying the daughter of the dragon king, is taken on a tour of the sights of the ocean world, including the seamarket.

[*The* xiaosheng *enters, his hair tied up in a scarf, (wearing) a ghost mask, riding a seahorse, and holding a flag*] Listen, you mermen! The king's command is this: today the prince-consort will visit the seamarket, so, to avoid being censored for transgression or negligence, you must make a great display of your treasures, lay out all your rarest goods, and put up phantasmal oyster-towers as well.[26] [*From back-*

---

25. The name of a role type, usually an elderly male.
26. "Phantasmal oyster-towers" are mirages seen on the sea.

stage voices are heard shouting "Understood!" The xiaosheng *exits. The* chou, *dressed as the chief of the mermen, enters at the head of the mermen who are pushing their carts filled with treasures. One of the mermen speaks*] Brother, this seamarket of ours is held once a year, just as it has been since ancient times. All the people of the nine continents and the ten thousand countries and all the dragon kings of the five lakes and four seas are free to come and go as they please and no one has ever interfered. So why is it that today we have been ordered to set up earlier than usual? It must be because they want to tax us! [*The* chou *speaks*] No, that is not what it is. When I went into town yesterday to see some friends, the prince-consort was just then returning from a banquet in the southern ocean. I can't describe to you all the zithers that were strummed on horseback and all the chimes that were played in the carriages, all that pomp and glory! When I sneaked closer to have a look, it turned out to be that beggar the Third Prince picked up here a few days ago. I secretly asked people there: "How come they didn't give that fine girl who is like a leaf of jade, a sprig of gold, to one of the many dragon-sons or dragon-grandsons, but instead married her off to *him*? Isn't that an injustice?" But everyone expressed their surprise at my question and said: "You shouldn't regard this prince-consort too lightly! Not only does our king respect him greatly for having written the *Rhapsody on the Seamarket*, but he is also respected by the dragon-lords of the four seas. In a mere three days' time, the fame of his great talent has spread through all of the four seas. The king even wants to hold a special seamarket just for his entertainment!" [*All speak*] If that is the case, we will put our treasures on display! [*The* chou *speaks*] Not so fast! Brother Oyster, come over here! [*The* jing *enters dressed as an oyster spirit, speaks*] From time to time I spit out clouds and fog, / Which in a blink turn into terraces and towers. Brother Merman, I have no rare jewels or extraordinary treasures, all I have are these illusory vapors. What do you want them for? Are you going to tell me there are people interested in buying vapors? [*The* chou *speaks*] This is not the time for jokes. His Majesty has ordered you to use your skill to create a big city that will enclose our seamarket. This city must have six main streets and three bazaars, ten thousand doors and a thousand gates, and everything must be perfect. No error or mistake will be tolerated! [*The* jing *counts on his fingers*] One, two, three, four, five, six, seven: the seamarket is only held for one single day! Bah, let me have a look at that royal command!! It's clear you are trying to have fun at my expense! [*Makes as if to walk away. The* chou *grabs him*] Nobody is having you on! This is really His Majesty's command: he orders you to come up with your finest ornamentation, so that the prince-consort can come and visit us. [*The* jing *speaks*] Friends, my fake vapors can only deceive momentarily; how will he think that they are real? [*The* chou *speaks*] You are right—what should we do? [*The* jing *speaks*] You all just put your treasures on display, and then I will exhale some fog to cover them up. When the prince-consort approaches, just go back to your business as usual. This will be both miraculous and original. [*All clap their hands and laugh wildly*] That's a brilliant idea! What fun indeed! Brothers, let's get to work! [*At the back of the stage, a tall three-tiered scaffolding has been erected. All arrange their treasures on the scaffolding. The* jing *emits smoke and produces a black sheet to cover the scaffolding. The* chou *looks on from a distance*] Wonderful! Let's go and have a rest now. [*Exits, leading all the others*]

The scene continues with Ma Longmei being taken on a tour of all the great underwater sights. One of these sights is a mountain of pebbles, which, it is explained to him, has been created by the Jingwei bird in her futile attempts to fill up the sea with little stones. Another sight is, oddly enough, the Lute Pavilion, in which Wang Zhaojun's original lute is said to be preserved:

[*The* sheng *(i.e. Ma Longmei) speaks.*] As the original lute of Wang Zhaojun is still preserved, let me have a closer look. [*Dismounting from his horse, he takes the lute in his hands, and hides his tears*] Zhaojun, even though during your lifetime you were forced to travel to barbarian lands, this is yet another case of the truth that

To the Same Tune

> Beauties are poorly fated, in the past as well as now.
> Don't blame the painter for the portrait he painted—
> If you'd been the emperor's favorite concubine,
> Would your Green Hill grave enjoy everlasting honor?

Oh lute, even though you are an object venerated because of the person, it was you who on behalf of Wang Zhaojun, suffering on horseback such unspeakable sadness and grief,

> Piercingly gave expression to her innermost feelings!

[*Paces to and fro, overcome by tears*] Zhaojun refused to bribe Mao Yanshou and was banished from the Han palace because of her misleading portrait. When I was swept off course by the typhoon, I was barred from the country of ghosts because of my actual appearance. Even though the circumstances are different, the sadness is the same.

Eventually Ma Longmei and his party arrive at the location of the sea-market, which is invisible to them until suddenly revealed:

[They halt their horses, uncertain of what to do. The jing *takes up a position at the stage entrance, then enters emitting smoke; he takes the sheet down and exits. The* chou *leads the other mermen in kneeling down in front of Ma's horse]*

While modern accounts of traditional Chinese drama often suggest that the stage was normally kept bare except for a small table and two chairs, there were some highly popular forms of drama that, like the plays of Liu Qingyun, relied for their appeal on elaborate costumes and scenery as well as special effects. Such forms of theater were classified under the general designation of "lamp-and-props shows" (*dengcaixi*). How elaborate such performances could be is illustrated by a rare description in chapter 5 of Gu Taiqing's novel *Shadow Dream of the Red Chamber*. The occasion of the performance is a First Night (the fifteenth of the First Month), which happens to coincide with the celebration of the first full month since the birth of Jia Baoyu and Xue Baochai's first child. The performance has been staged as a gift from relatives and it is held in one of the mansion's courtyards at night after dinner for the entertainment of the women of the Jia household (when Jia Baoyu's father, the dour Confucian Jia Zheng, finds out how much the performance has cost, he mutters: "What's so wonderful about it? They just scrape the fat off ordinary people in order to impress their relatives and acquaintances!")

Four large Heavenly Kings leaped out onto the stage, with brightly burning wax candles fastened both to the magical weapons in their hands and the hair ornaments on their heads.[27] There were also eight cloud-lads who held in their hands five-colored cloud lamps made of silk. In the center [of the stage] the Jasper Pond had been laid out, with peach trees visible on either side.[28] Strings of peaches of immortality hung down from their branches, and to each of them a little red lamp had been attached. After the cloud-lads had danced for a while with their lamp clouds, the Queen Mother of the West entered, riding a carriage drawn by two phoenixes. The tassels that hung down from the four corners of her carriage were all in the shape of authentic-looking fruits made of glass, in each of which burned a small white wax candle. Four immortal maidens surrounded her, each of them carrying a flower basket symbolizing eternal honor and riches, in which red candles were burning. After the Queen Mother of the

---

27. The Four Heavenly Kings are fierce protective deities of Buddhist monasteries.

28. Jasper Pond is one of the features of the palace of the Queen Mother of the West atop Mt. Kunlun.

West had sung a song to the tune of "Dotting on Vermillion" [*Dianjianghong*], the Eight Immortals, the Three Star Gods of Fortune, Wealth, and Longevity, and the Five Graybeards appeared carrying all kinds of colorful lamps, and were singing a song to the tune of "River-Disturbing Dragon" [*Hunjianglong*]. Then everyone heard the sound of flutes playing, and the Mahasattva Guanyin appeared on stage, her feet resting on a thousand-petaled lotus-lamp, and [her acolytes] Shancai and Dragon-Girl standing on lotus petals on either side. Then, singing a song to the tune of "Oil Calabash" [*Youhulu*], they circled the stage as Guanyin's white parrot circled overhead by means of some invisible contraption. Aunt Xue said: "I have seen many lamp shows, but nothing comparable to this!" The widow Li Wan said: "How marvelous! How can that lotus flower move so easily?" And lady Wang said: "But that is not so amusing as that parrot flying about!" As they were talking, the gongs were sounded and the Hemp Maiden entered carrying the raft of the immortals, upon which had been arranged the gourds of a hundred sons and a thousand grandsons and in each of which had been lit a small wax candle.[29] After all the immortals had paid homage to the Queen Mother of the West, a white gibbon suddenly entered with a somersault, and holding a large peach of immortality in his paw, he jumped down from the stage and knelt down in the middle of the courtyard. Then, with the help of some sort of fuse, from the peach poured out an endless number of firecrackers. All the guests were full of praise: it was a good thing they had this courtyard, because if it had been even just a little bit smaller, there would not have been enough room for the monkey to perform his tricks! After everybody had had a good laugh, they all handed tips to the performers.

It must be admitted that Liu Qingyun's special effects, as imaginative as they were, pale in comparison to those described in Gu Taiqing's novel!

---

29. Spreading vines hung with gourds have from earliest times been a symbol of large numbers of progeny.

15 · Plucking Rhymes

Women writers up to the end of the imperial period only very rarely tried their hand at prose fiction, whether long or short. Starting from the second half of the eighteenth century, however, an increasing number of women wrote prosimetrical narratives and often of an astounding length. The prosimetrical narratives by women are an important but late chapter in the development of prosimetrical literature in China, which has a history of written texts going back at least as far as the eighth century CE. In prosimetrical texts, passages in verse (normally composed of lines of seven syllables) alternate with passages in prose. As the passages written in prose were intended to be narrated in performance, while the passages in verse were meant to be chanted or sung, in Chinese the many varieties of prosimetrical literature are subsumed under the term *shuochang wenxue* (literature for narrating and singing); for this reason, some sinologists use the term *chantefable* (borrowed from medieval French literature) to refer to these types of texts.

Women have always been enthusiastic audiences of prosimetrical narratives, whether performed by blind performers who knew their texts by heart or read aloud from printed texts by a literate member of the household. We have already seen how the lonely Xiaoqing tried to lift her spirits by inviting performers to recite prosimetrical narratives for her, and in the anonymous sixteenth-century novel *Plum in the Golden Vase* (*Jinpingmei*), which chronicles the profligate life of the merchant Ximen Qing and contains detailed descriptions of the daily lives of his six wives in the inner chambers, we find many descriptions of nuns entertaining the ladies of the house with their recitation of "precious scrolls" (*baojuan*). Precious scrolls originated as prosimetrical narratives on Buddhist themes. A very early example of the genre is the *Precious Scroll of Incense Mountain* (*Xiangshan baojuan*), an anonymous text that claims to have been composed in the early twelfth century and is mentioned in one source that dates from 1509, even though the earliest preserved printing dates only from 1773. This precious scroll recounts the trials and travails of the royal princess Miaoshan who, by the end of the story, is revealed to be none other than the Bodhisattva Guanyin. Another highly popular precious scroll, mentioned in *Plum in the Golden Vase*, was the *Precious Scroll on Lady Huang* (*Huangshi baojuan*), which recounts the popular Buddhist legend of a pious wife who is reborn as a man. As time went by, the subject matter of narrative precious scrolls expanded and by the nineteenth century the genre could include any moralistic tale, irrespective of religious affiliation. From the sixteenth century onward, however, the format of the precious scroll was also used by many sectarian groups to spread their teachings.

While many precious scrolls appear to have been composed with a female audience in mind, female authorship seems to have been quite rare. The only known female author of precious scrolls, a nun by the name of Guiyuan who lived in the Baoming convent outside of Beijing during the second half of the sixteenth century, wrote no less than five precious scrolls, all of which were sectarian works propagating the cult of the Eternal Mother (*wusheng laomu*). According to the teachings of various sixteenth- and seventeenth-century sects, all human beings are the wayward children of the Eternal Mother, who from up in her heavenly paradise longs for their return. In many of these texts, the bodhisattva Guanyin is only one of the many earthly manifestations of the Eternal Mother who attempt to pry these lost children away from their attachment to the world and lead them back to a paradise of endless happiness.

When elite women in the second half of the eighteenth century and later took up the writing of prosimetrical narratives, however, they wrote not precious scrolls but rather "plucking rhymes" (*tanci*), an extremely sophisticated genre of prosimetrical narrative characteristic of the Jiangnan region. This genre derived its name from the fact that in performance the verse sections were sung to the (plucked) accompaniment of the lute (in contrast to the "drum rhymes" [*guci*] of northern China). As a genre of performative literature, plucking rhymes were often performed by women, and their subject matter more often than not consisted of complicated love stories. These factors may well have facilitated the adoption of the genre by elite women, who quickly developed a female narrative voice once they had taken it up. In many plucking rhymes texts written by women the narrator presents herself as a filial daughter who only writes in order to entertain her mother. While in recent years great strides have been made in the study of plucking rhymes written by women, there is still much that remains to be done. One reason this field has been neglected until only very recently is the very low status of prosimetrical literature in the eyes of both traditional literati and most modern intellectuals. Another reason is the enormous length of many of the plucking rhymes authored by women—their convoluted plots easily put most modern-day soap operas and television serials to shame. The most extreme example in this respect is the *Pomegranate Blossom Dream* (*Liuhuameng*), the 360-chapter lifework of Li Guiyu (d. 1841). This work is almost five million characters in length; in its first printed edition it ran to ten volumes of more than six hundred pages each, each page consisting of one hundred lines of verse! Some of the plucking rhymes written by women enjoyed a considerable popularity, and inspired adaptations as prose novels and plays. While the women writers of plucking rhymes refrained from explicitly questioning the status quo, their works often featured heroines who in male guise show themselves to be the equal of, if not superior to, any man.

A Rain of Heavenly Flowers

The earliest plucking rhymes text written by a woman author is often said to be *A Rain of Heavenly Flowers* (*Tianyuhua*), composed by Tao Zhenhuai from Liangxi (Wuxi), dated 1651. In her preface to this work, Tao Zhenhuai introduces herself as follows:

I was born in a time of warfare and destruction and lived through an era of suffering and hardship. Whenever I read the biographies of noble heroes, I am deeply moved by their deeds of loyalty and filiality. Again and again I am stirred to sighs by the fact that the Han dynasty was destroyed by the power of the eunuchs, that the House of Tang was plunged into chaos by an emperor's infatuation with a favorite, and that during the Tianqi reign period [1621–1627], [the Ming dynasty] suffered because of both of these failings. Although this dynasty was supposed to last for countless generations, it ended up slaughtering the loyal and good with even greater ferocity than had any of the previous dynasties. Thus, the fact that it was eventually replaced by another dynasty, was a disaster it brought down upon itself!

Alas! When it came to knowing people, my father had the clarity of water or a mirror, and he was fond of cultivating the Way of the recluse in a secluded valley. Pitying me for my bound feet, he was willing to discuss his most intimate aspirations with me. When he told me that I possessed both the capabilities of Mulan and the determination of Cao E, I felt truly ashamed.[1] I am also grateful to him for the rich treasury of stories that he transmitted to me through his oral teaching. But now the trees [on his grave] are always swaying restlessly. He fathered me, he understood me, he raised me, he instructed me—how can my feelings [of gratitude] ever be adequate!

In the letters I send to [my husband who may be compared to] Qin Jia[2] and who serves as an adjutant far away from here, I lament the premature death of my infant son and atop the high tower, I am filled with memories of my child. So I gathered together the various fragments and old drafts and compiled them into a complete book.

Both the identity of the author and the date of this preface are problematical. No further information is available on Tao Zhenhuai apart from what may be gleaned from her own work. As her name may be read as "Pleasing Chaste Feelings," it has been suggested that the name actually is a pseudonym; a nineteenth-century source asserts that this plucking rhymes text was in fact composed by a man named Xu Zhihe to amuse his mother. But, while it is quite possible that the name "Tao Zhenhuai" is a pseudonym, many contemporary critics have noted the central role that the father-daughter relationship plays in this work, and it is now generally accepted that it was, in fact, written by a woman. Some modern

---

1. Cao E is said to have lived during the Eastern Han dynasty. When her father was drowned in a river, she was overcome by grief, and when she could not find his corpse, she drowned herself in the same river, which later was named after her.

2. Qin Jia was the husband of Xu Shu, one of the earliest known women writers of *shi* poetry.

scholars have suggested that Tao Zhenhuai may be a pseudonym for Liu Shuying, a woman author of the mid-seventeenth century, who personally raised troops and fought the Manchus, but this remains pure speculation.

If *A Rain of Heavenly Flowers* was indeed completed in 1651, it would mean that the work was written within a period of just a few years, given that it discusses in considerable detail the causes of the fall of the Ming dynasty. The composition of a work of such length in so short a time span would in itself be quite remarkable, but it would also have been quite premature, as the Manchu conquest of southern China was far from over in 1651, and for some time there would continue to be incidents of Ming loyalist resistance. The central character of the story is a man by the name of Zuo Weiming ("Support of the Ming"). He is not meant to be a historical figure, but represents rather the perfect embodiment of perfect loyalty (along with a host of other manly virtues). Such a portrayal would fit in much better with the intellectual climate of the mid-eighteenth century, which witnessed the growth of a cult of pure loyalty that was so pervasive that former Ming officials who had gone over to the Manchu regime were now reclassified in the official historical records as "renegades" (*erchen*), while those who had chosen suicide over surrender were praised by the Manchu court for their integrity. This intellectual climate also produced prose novels such as *A Rustic Greybeard's Idle Words* (*Yesou puyan*), which features a hero that is the embodiment of all the manly virtues, and creatively rewrites the political history of the Ming dynasty. This work also shares *A Rain of Heavenly Flowers'* condemnation of all forms of "superstition." It is thus quite possible that *A Rain of Heavenly Flowers* was a product of the mid-eighteenth century. This would explain why we have to wait until the early nineteenth century for the earliest external reference to this work. It is quite conceivable that the original author purposely provided her preface with a much earlier date, either to give her work a spurious aura of antiquity, or to avoid possible trouble from the censors.

The modern scholars Tan Zhengbi and his daughter Tan Xun provide the following summary of the contents of *A Rain of Heavenly Flowers*:

During the reign of the Wanli Emperor [r. 1573–1619] of the Ming dynasty, Zuo Yi (style name Shoulun) from Xiangyang in Hubei province is serving as

Supreme Commander. Campaigning against the northern barbarians, he is defeated and dies a martyr's death. His eldest son, Weiming (style name Juyuan), has from his earliest years shown himself to be extraordinarily intelligent; excelling in both literary and military skills, and ready to act whenever duty calls. Zuo Yi's second son, Weizheng, is the adopted son of his maternal uncle, Su Pei. When the provincial administration commissioner's son, Sun Guoying, oppresses his tenants and forcibly abducts the wife of [the peasant] Tao An, Weiming comes to her rescue, and when in the process he also causes Guoying to suffer at the hands of a shoemaker's daughter and his own vindictive wife, everyone is overjoyed.

After Weiming has passed the provincial examinations at the head of the list, he marries Heng Yingzheng's sister, Qinggui. He then goes to the capital to take part in the metropolitan examinations, where he passes at the top of the list in both the departmental and the palace examinations, and is appointed senior compiler. Weiming's good friends, Wang Zhengfang (the son of the minister of war); the prefect's son, Zhao Shengzhi; the son of the commissioner of the Office of Transmission, Du Hongren; and his brother-in-law, Heng Yingzheng (a son of the chief minister of the Court of Imperial Entertainments), all pass the examination at the same time with high honors.

When Weiming is nineteen, he becomes left vice censor-in-chief in the Surveillance Court. That year, lady Heng gives birth to a son, Yongzheng, and in the next year to a girl, Yizhen. When the northern barbarians cross the borders, Weiming volunteers to campaign against them so as to take revenge for his father. The barbarian king is defeated in battle and surrenders, after which Weiming is promoted to left censor-in-chief and president of the Ministry of Justice, and later becomes governor of Zhejiang province. While in this latter office, he repeatedly resolves difficult cases, establishing the innocence of those who have been wrongly accused, and delivering the people from scourges. At the end of his term, he resigns from active service and returns to his hometown in order to take care of his mother. Later, lady Heng gives birth to two more daughters, Dezhen and Wanzhen.

Weiming is adamantly opposed to the taking of concubines. His mother has a servant girl named Guixiang, who harbors the ridiculous hope of becoming Weiming's second wife. She gets his mother to take her side, but even though his mother puts pressure on him to marry her as a concubine, Weiming is not willing to do so. Once, when Weiming is drunk, Guixiang pretends to be lady Heng and shares his bed, but after Weiming has sobered up again, he continues to refuse to have anything to do with her.

After five years, Weiming's mother falls ill and dies. At the end of the mourning period, Weiming returns to the capital and resumes his career. At that moment, the elder brother of the Honored Consort, Zheng Guotai, and the prime minister, Fang Congzhe, are scheming to appropriate the imperial throne for themselves. Because Weiming is upright and straightforward, they want to secretly do away with him. When later Zheng Guotai and his son plot to kill the crown prince, Weiming makes use of a clever scheme to discover and arrest them, after which they are stripped of their ranks and reduced to the status of commoners. Moreover, when Fang Congzhe and his son plot to do away with Weiming, they are also exposed by Weiming and punished. Despite the many attempts that Zheng Guotai and his son make on Weiming's life, they are never successful.

Yongzheng is now already engaged to Zhao Shengzhi's daughter, Shun'e, while Yizhen is engaged to the son of Heng Yingzheng, Heng Yu, and Dezhen is engaged to the son of Wang Zhengfang, Wang Liqian. Du Hongren's son, Shunqing, falls in love with his maternal cousin, Huang Jingying. Jingying's father dotes on his concubine and has no love for his daughter. When he sees her coming home with a poem by Shunqing tucked in her sleeve, he falsely accuses her of improper behavior and forces her to jump into a river, but she is saved by Zuo Weiming. Later, Weiming makes it so that Jinying's father himself acts as the matchmaker and promises his daughter to Shunqing, and in this way, brings about the couple's marriage. One after the other, all the other young men, once they have passed the examinations, also marry their respective brides.

Following the demise of the Wanli Emperor, the Taichang Emperor [r. 1620] succeeds to the throne. His favorite concubine, Chosen Attendant Li, wants to become empress, and plots to that end together with Fang Congzhe and Zheng Guotai. Fang and Zheng have by this time been restored to their former posts and, availing themselves of Weiming's [absence from court because he is leading his] second northern campaign, poison the Taichang Emperor with a red pill they give him, and also rob the crown prince of his title. After Zheng Guotai ascends the imperial throne, he abducts Weiming's daughter Yizhen with the idea of making her his empress. When Yizhen makes use of a ruse in order to kill Guotai, his son Youquan takes the opportunity to steal the throne, and locks Yizhen up in the "cold palace" [the part of the palace reserved for disgraced concubines]. As soon as Zuo Weiming hears about this, he hastens back to the capital, and once he has succeeded in entering the city, he executes Youquan and enthrones the crown prince, who will reign as the Tianqi Emperor [r. 1621–1627]. Zuo Weiming is then given the title of Loyal and Brave Marquis, and is appointed prime minister.

Later, the palace eunuch Wei Zhongxian usurps all the power, and even though he is still alive, in every locality a temple in his honor is established as a way of currying his favor. Weiming is greatly opposed to this, and Wei Zhongxian tries every possible means to have him killed, but whether he employs hired assassins or uses black magic, he never succeeds in his purpose. The Tianqi Emperor's wet nurse, lady Ke, has an affair with Wei Zhongxian. Wishing to select husbands for her three daughters, Meijiao, Taojiao, and Hejiao, she opens her private garden to the public and invites people to come and visit it. When Yongzheng, Heng Yu, and Shunqing mistakenly wander in, they are forcibly detained, and when they resist, are nearly killed. When Zuo Weiming is informed of this, he comes to their rescue with his private guards. Later Weiming resigns from his office. When Wei Zhongxian tries, with the help of some beautiful women, to trap his son and sons-in-law, his plot is not only foiled by Weiming but also results in the death of Wei Zhongxian's own nephews. As the enmity between the two parties deepens, Yongzheng and the others come to the realization that they cannot stay on any longer in their official posts, and they all hand in their resignations and return to their hometowns.

When in the fifteenth year of the Chongzhen reign period [1644] the "roving king" Li Zicheng captures the capital, the Chongzhen Emperor hangs himself on Coal Hill and the Ming dynasty comes to an end. In consultation with the Heng, Wang, Zhao, and Du families, Zuo Weiming decides to die for the dynasty. All the male members of these families who have once served the dynasty, and all the women who have received titles, board a ship together. Once the ship reaches the middle of the river, they sink it and die out of loyalty.

This summary, focusing on the political career of Zuo Weiming as a stalwart supporter of the Ming dynasty, fits well with the purpose of *A Rain of Heavenly Flowers* as formulated by Tao Zhenhuai in the opening of her preface:

Why was *A Rain of Heavenly Flowers* written? Saddened by the utter confusion of rules and norms, I imagined a person capable of upholding the rules and establishing the norms, so that even the most stubborn stone might nod its head in agreement. And why did I develop my story using the plucking rhymes [form]? Because I wanted to incite people to moral effort. Now, those who cannot be regulated by means of the rites, may yet be moved by music; for those who cannot be moved by music, one writes plays; and those who may not even be reached by plays, may yet be roused by plucking rhymes.

While the hero Zuo Weiming and his exploits are purely fictional, the main villains in *A Rain of Heavenly Flowers* (Concubine Zheng and Zheng Guotai, Fang Congzhe, Wei Zhongxian, and lady Ke) are all historical characters. *A Rain of Heavenly Flowers* is above all an inquiry into the causes of the collapse of the Ming. As was common in the early part of the Qing (and the Manchus would not have had it otherwise), these causes were to be found primarily in the moral decay of the Ming court and bureaucracy itself.

A summary such as the one provided by Tan Zhengbi and Tan Xun does not do full justice to the importance of the father-daughter relationship in *A Rain of Heavenly Flowers*. Zuo Weiming is obsessed by the moral behavior of the women in his family, and at the slightest suspicion of impropriety (such as a visit to a flower garden), he inflicts upon them draconian punishments, all in the name of virtue. Most interesting is the relationship between Zuo Weiming and his eldest daughter, Yizhen. Her relationship to her father is one of both devotion and rebellion. Scholars have, of course, speculated as to the extent to which this fictional relationship may be a reflection of the special connection the author tells us in her preface that she had with her own father.

In *A Rain of Heavenly Flowers*, when Yizhen turns seven, Zuo Weiming decides to take her away from her mother and raise her himself, together with his son Yongzheng, because, in his opinion, she is far too smart for her mother to handle:

> "Now when it comes to our daughter Yizhen,
> She is by nature extraordinarily talented.
> She is nimble and smart and quite quick-witted,
> Her character is stubborn, her energy heroic.
> She is quick of tongue, and strong-willed,
> Heaven truly gifted this girl with intelligence.

But intelligent people may turn out to be good or evil. When I observe this girl, [I can tell that] you are not the person to teach her. On the one hand, I'm afraid you will only spoil her; on the other, she is too talented to submit to your authority. From now on you should treat her as if she were a son and hand her over to me. I too will not treat her as a daughter but rather look upon her as a son. All I ask is that you not interfere and try to protect her. Just devote all your attention to [our daughter] Dezhen. I will be the one to instruct this one son and one daughter." His wife said: "Yongzheng and Yizhen are just like you, devious and mean! Once today's decision is made, I'll let you and the two children join together in evil!

> But if later some problem arises with Dezhen,
> I will expect you not to interfere with me."

When Weiming heard this, he said with a smile:

> "A daughter should obey her mother's instructions,
> How could I as a father meddle in that?

As far as Yizhen is concerned, I will only teach her some writing and ritual. I will not concern myself with her women's work at all!"

In this way, Yizhen is educated as if she were a boy, and develops a fascination for her father's swords, which are called "coiling-dragon swords," because they can expand and contract at will. At the earliest opportunity she asks her father to give them to her, but at first he refuses to do so. When later he does give them to her, she uses them first to kill an evil spirit in the flower garden that she and her sisters visit against her father's strict orders, and then to kill the evil usurper, Zheng Guotai. Her desire for her father's swords can be said to symbolize Yizhen's desire to take over her father's position and indeed, to be a man herself—a desire that is, of course, ultimately doomed to failure.

While Yizhen consistently tries to model herself on her father, her relationship with him is also riddled with conflict. Once, for example, her father locks up her mother for visiting the flower garden, and Yizhen has the temerity to let her mother out. When her father demands an explanation, she defends her insubordination with the following words:

"I cannot deny responsibility for my action today. If you, my father, had locked up anyone else, I definitely would not have dared to act so brazenly. But, alas, the one who locked the door was you, my father, and the one who was locked up was my mother. If I had sat by while my mother suffered, how would I have been able to explain my actions should my mother have berated me? Today I am berated by you because I disobeyed you, and I will not deny that. But I hope that you will be able to explain to me more clearly the right and wrong of this case, so that I may benefit from your instruction. If you say that this is a case of a senior disciplining an inferior and that "might makes right," it means that you, my father, are strong and my mother is weak. But if, just hypothetically, mother had been the stronger party and you had been the one locked up in the garden, would it then have been right for me as your child to open the gate, or should I have left it locked? My father, please be so kind as to instruct me in this, so that I may know what my mistake has been."

Toward the end of *A Rain of Heavenly Flowers*, Yizhen's father orders her unruly third sister, Wanzhen, who has tried to kill her mother-in-law by laying a curse on her, to commit suicide by jumping into the garden pond. Moreover, he summons Yizhen to come and watch her sister die, with the idea that it will be a good lesson in morality for her.

> When Yizhen returned to the Zuo mansion,
> Sister Shun'e came out of the hall to greet her.
> She asked how she was, then they went inside,
> And in the hall, took their seats as guest and host.
> Yizhen then asked her sister-in-law:
> "My father is of course in his study?"
> Her answer was: "He is now in the garden,
> So please go there if you want to see him."
> When Yizhen heard this, she said with a smile:
> "It is the middle of winter and the weather is freezing,
> There are no flowers, no willows, he'll shiver with cold,
> So what is my father doing out there in the garden?"
> . . .
> After they had chatted for a while, she stood up,
> Took leave of her sister-in-law, and went outside.
> The servant girls Caihong and Biyun accompanied her,
> As she went to the flower garden, past the corner pavilion.
> She ordered one of the servant girls to go ahead and see
> Where in the garden her father might actually be.
> After she had gone to look, the servant girl reported:
> "The Master is sitting inside the riverside pavilion!"
> When Yizhen heard this, she was even more amazed,
> And she hurried over to the place where he was.
> Her servant girls at her side, she entered the pavilion,
> She went up to him, and greeting him said, "Father!"
> She was about to bow, but as soon as she said "Father!"
> He made her sit down, although without saying a word.
> When Yizhen raised her head to look at him,
> She was terrified by the murderous expression on his face!

He did not betray even the slightest hint of pleasure,
And she secretly wondered what the reason might be.
 She then opened the conversation by asking her father:
"My father, why is it you are sitting out here today,
On a day when the wind blows as cold as ice?
What's more, you are sitting in the river pavilion!
This westerly window has no bars or shutters,
You have to be careful in this freezing wind!"

Zuo Weiming said: "I have come here today to end a life, I didn't come here for my amusement! I asked you to come here simply because, little wench, you are not someone who is resigned to her fate. And so I want you to watch this as a warning. Yizhen, listen carefully, and don't be alarmed." Right away she asked him: "Father, whose life do you want to end?" Before her father could answer, Caihong called out from below the pavilion: "Third Miss is here!"

Despite Wanzhen's pleas and Yizhen's entreaties, Zuo Weiming persists in his demand that his youngest daughter take her own life by jumping into the garden pond, and eventually Wanzhen accepts her fate:

"Ah, father, I will carry no grudge,

My only regret is that I will never again see my mother,
And that I could not say a final goodbye to my husband.
Never will I be reunited with my brother and two sisters."
When she had finished speaking, she was overcome by grief.
 When Zuo Weiming had heard all these many words, he said:
"Only now am I seeing true and sincere repentance!
When a man is at his wit's end, his true heart speaks,
Make sure that in your next life you are a good person."
                    At that they watched
As she lifted the hem of her gown to cover her head,
And in a single leap, jumped down from the pavilion.
Her windblown sleeves danced in the air:
Crushed jade, vanished fragrance—sinking further and further!
 All they heard was the splash in the pond,
And that was the end of a beauty of eighteen.
The water closed over her as she sank to the bottom,
No trace remained of her white complexion and fragrant skin.
 A trampled flower, a hidden moon, a bright pearl crushed:
At this moment Old Zuo's heart felt gouged out by a knife!

> He saw the waves that had been stirred up on the pond,
> A bright pearl had slipped from his cupped hands:
> "It is not that your father here is excessively cruel,
> There really was no other way out for me.

That's it! She must have expired as soon as she leaped into the pond. I'll have the servants buy a coffin, and tomorrow they can dredge up the corpse."

> At this moment he let go of Yizhen's hands,
> And as fast as he could he left the pavilion.
> As soon as he had left in such a great hurry,
> A weeping Yizhen collapsed on the floor.

She quickly got up again, and went out to have a look at the pond below the pavilion.

Yizhen then discovers that her sister has in fact not drowned and quickly takes action to save her life. When she returns with her rescued sister to face their father, he declares that Wanzhen's survival had all been part of his plan and that he only wanted to frighten her into mending her ways.

While *A Rain of Heavenly Flowers* sets out to present a perfect embodiment of moral values in the person of Zuo Weiming, it may also be compared to other fictional works of the eighteenth century (such as Wu Jingzi's *The Scholars*) that indirectly question traditional morals by showing how barbaric the behavior of those who are fanatically committed to those same morals can be. If this is a correct reading, if even perfect fathers are shown to be ineffective in society and can only control their daughters by killing them, then this particular plucking rhymes text can be regarded not only as a lament for a fallen dynasty, but for a doomed culture as well.

Text and Performance: Zhu Suxian

The plucking rhymes written by elite women of the second half of the eighteenth century and later were as a rule intended to be read. There is one case, however, in which the author of a plucking rhymes text, a woman by the name of Zhu Suxian, taught her composition line by line to a blind female performer by the name of Xiang Jin. This collaborative effort is described in the following 1805 preface to Zhu Suxian's *Linked Rings of Jade* (*Yulianhuan*):

Lady Zhu from Yunjian [Songjiang] was born to a poor family and was widowed when still young. She had a virtuous character and was addicted to study; extremely erudite, she annotated the *Changes* and excelled in the writing of poems and rhapsodies.

In her later years, she became very fond of the plucking rhymes of blind performers [*mangci*], and would regularly invite sister Xiang Jin from Taicang to strum and sing all kinds of tales. She would say to people: "When you listen to their notes, their lovely sounds are enough to stop the floating of the clouds, but when you consider their words, they are not sufficient to correct and rectify lascivious evil. These tales can only amuse the ears of worldly folks, they are incapable of pleasing those with more perceptive vision!"

She then composed *Linked Rings of Jade*, which is also titled *A Tale of Concentrated Passion* [*Zhongqing zhuan*], and taught Xiang to sing it. At first listening, it makes a bland impression; but the second time around, it is stirring; and eventually, it endlessly pleases and amuses both one's feelings and nature.

Some years later, lady Zhu and Xiang Jian died one after the other, and the sounds and rhymes of *Linked Rings of Jade* disappeared together with them. Alas! Why did *Linked Rings of Jade* have to suffer such a fate?

Linked Rings of Jade was eventually printed in 1823. As is clear from the above preface, Zhu Suxian thought of her work as a moral alternative to the conventional fare. In fact, she even lists for her readers sixteen reprehensible or "defective" plot elements that the audience will *not* find in *Linked Rings of Jade*: 1) men dressing up as women; 2) secret vows of marriage; 3) premarital sex; 4) elopements of adulterous women; 5) widows losing their chastity; 6) robbery and murder; 7) imprisonment; 8) murder for political motives; 9) secret conspiracy with foreign countries; 10) obsequious flattery of the powerful; 11) instruction in the methods of the immortals; 12) evil depravity of ghosts and monsters; 13) plots hatched by monks and priests; 14) prognostic dreams; 15) burglary and theft; 16) abduction and forced marriage. As it turns out, however, even our well-intentioned author has not been able to completely avoid all of these plot elements, as we can see from the following summary by Tan Zhengbi and Tan Xun of *Linked Rings of Jade*:

A certain Liang Qi (style name Ziyu), who has lost his father at an early age, is living with his mother, lady Wang, and his sister, Hongzhi. On his way to Nanjing to take the provincial examinations, he pays a visit to his old teacher Xie

Daoqing, whom he finds to be ailing. His teacher entrusts his young daughter Huixin to his care, and she and Liang Qi become sworn siblings.

The next-door neighbors of the Liangs are Censor Sun Chun and his family. Sun Chun's son, Sun Hao (style name Lingyun), asks for Hongzhi's hand in marriage, but because Sun Hao is a good-for-nothing, Liang Qi's mother refuses his request. Sun Hao then goes to his maternal aunt in Piling to ask for the hand of his cousin Wang Wencai in marriage. Wencai's style name is Xianxia; her father, Wang Tingzuo, who occupies the post of magistrate of Jiangyin, is temporarily away as he has been appointed as examination officer in the provincial capital. Later, fleeing a mutiny, Sun Hao escorts his aunt to Suzhou, but along the way, they become separated from Wencai, who disappears without a trace.

When Liang Qi passes the provincial examination at the head of the list, his examiner, Wang Tingzuo, promises him his daughter Xianxia in marriage, and Liang Qi in turn presents Wang Tingzuo with [a set of] linked rings of jade as an engagement gift. On his way back home, Liang Qi again passes by the home of Xie Daoqing, but his old teacher has already passed away, and Huixin has been abducted by bandits. Liang Qi goes to their camp and rescues her. While they are resting in an abandoned temple, he meets with Wang Wencai who is dressed as a man. Liang Qi and Wang Wencai become sworn brothers, and Liang Qi promises to give Huixin to Wencai as a bride, after which they all go back to Suzhou together. When Wencai arrives at Liang Qi's place, she immediately goes to the home of Sun Chun, where she is reunited with her mother and puts on her women's clothes again. Liang Qi goes there to visit her, and when he sees her dressed in women's clothes, he falls in love with her. He asks his mother to request Wencai's hand in marriage, but Sun Chun demands that she first agree to the marriage of Hongzhi to Sun Hao. Left without any choice, Liang Qi's mother agrees, and takes Sun Hao into her house as a live-in son-in-law.

When Liang Qi learns that Wang Wencai's mother has moved to a house she has rented, he goes there to see Wencai and learns that Wencai is none other than his own fiancée, Wang Xianxia. When Wencai meets with Huixin, she urges her to join her in marrying Liang Qi.

When Liang Qi successfully passes the metropolitan examinations at the head of the list, he is ordered to subdue the pirates. After accomplishing this with great merit, he is appointed Grand Secretary of the Central Pivot Hall and Pacifying the Oceans General, after which he marries both Wencai and Huixin. Later the two of them also purchase a concubine named Zhang Pingping for him. When Sun Hao sees how beautiful Pingping is, he tries to seduce her, whereupon she jumps into a river. In his anger, Liang Qi wants to kill Sun

Hao, but he is dissuaded from doing so by Wencai. But Sun Hao still does not mend his ways, and once his parents have died, abandons himself even more to uncontrolled whoring and gambling. When Hongzhi's remonstrations have no effect, she follows the advice of her sister-in-law, and buys him a beautiful concubine, Zhao Yuege. By this time, Sun Hao has already spent all his money and is forced to sell his house and lands. Hongzhi instructs Yuege to dress as a man, take on the name of Xuzhai, and purchase Sun Hao's fields. After a short time, Sun Hao's money is exhausted once again, and he considers selling his wife. The enraged Hongzhi pretends to marry Xuzhai. But Sun Hao soon exhausts the money he gets in exchange for her, and there is no longer anyone willing to lend him money. He is retained as a servant by Zhao Xuzhai, who gives him the sobriquet of Huichu (Regret for the Past). When, a few days after being hired, Sun Hao again wants to go out and gamble, Xuzhai gives him a sound beating. From that moment on, Sun Hao gradually changes his ways and devotes himself to his studies. When he takes third place in the prefectural examinations, Xuzhai becomes his sworn brother. When Sun Hao falls ill out of longing for his wife, Hongzhi—since he has repented and reformed his behavior—tells him the truth and husband and wife are reunited. Furthermore, Sun Hao formally marries Yuege as a wife.

Liang Qi has a younger cousin, Liang Jun (style name Ziwen), who is in love with Shuxiu, the daughter of the prefect of Suzhou, Xiahou Bangyan. With the help of her mother, the couple take advantage of Bangyan's absence to secretly marry. But when he returns, he angrily has Liang Jun flogged and takes Shuxiu back home. When Bangyan is promoted to another post and leaves some time later, Shuxiu cannot accompany him because of a serious illness, and goes to live in a nunnery. Liang Jun, who has been severely wounded because of the flogging, is revived by Yumei, a daughter of one of the prefect's private secretaries, Zhuang Wenqing. With the help of Zhuang, Liang Jun escapes and later he passes the provincial examinations. Then, thinking that Shuxiu is dead, he makes Yumei his wife. Shortly afterwards, he happens to encounter Shuxiu in the nunnery, resulting in the reunion of husband and wife.

Liang Qi attains the rank of chancellor in his official career and fathers five sons. He also invites his sister to come to the capital. Carrying thorns on his back [as a sign of repentance], Sun Hao apologizes to Liang Qi for his crimes. Eventually both Liang Jun and Sun Hao pass the metropolitan examinations. Liang Jun is appointed a vice-minister, and Sun Hao joins the Censorate. From then on, the three families all enjoy wealth and glory.

While Zhu Suxian made an attempt to improve the moral quality of the plucking rhymes that were performed, other women authors of plucking rhymes rather stressed the difference between their own fictions and those that either served as the basis for performances by professionals or were derived from them and thus designated as "performance texts of plucking rhymes" (*tanci changben*). One of the reasons why an author might insist that her text differed from performance texts was to emphasize the literary qualities of her own work. We see an example of this in the following advertisement of *The Painted Portrait* (*Huizhen ji*), a plucking rhymes text by an anonymous woman writer, published in 1812:

This book is not a performance text. It is designed purely to amuse and please the feelings and nature of literary scholars and beautiful ladies as, incense wafting from the burner, they enjoy their tea after their studies or their embroidery.

In *A Rain of Heavenly Flowers*, Wanzhen's personal ownership of numerous performance texts of plucking rhymes is yet another piece of supporting evidence that convinces her father, Zuo Weiming, of his daughter's complete depravity:

Lord Zuo said with a scornful smile: "You neither busy yourself with needlework nor read books of history. Since that is the case, how do you spend your time each day at home?" At that question, Wanzhen fell silent and did not say a word. But just as Zuo Weiming spoke these words, two servant women brought in a chest. When her mother asked them where the chest came from, they replied that it was Wanzhen's chest of books. When Zuo Weiming asked what kind of books she had, Wanzhen replied: "Only some plucking rhymes texts, novels, and plays." Zuo Weiming then ordered the chest opened so that he could take a look. The servant women opened up the chest and then stacked the books up one by one on the table. After Zuo Weiming had inspected the titles and read each one of the books, he discovered that the performance texts of plucking rhymes dealt with nothing but illicit trysts by the light of the moon and secret vows to elope and that most of the novels and plays were about nothing more than talented students and beautiful maidens in love with each other's beauty and talent.

There is no question that Zhu Suxian's own *Linked Rings of Jade* presents a gallery of model students and resourceful women, but one cannot help but notice that it does not avoid various kinds of reversals of gender roles and authority relations: women dress as men and husbands (temporarily) become the servants of their concubines. As we shall see, this reversal of normative patterns can be found to an even greater extent in other plucking rhymes by women writers.

Karmic Bonds of Reincarnation: Chen Duansheng and Hou Zhi

The most famous plucking rhymes text written by a woman author is Chen Duansheng's *Karmic Bonds of Reincarnation* (*Zaishengyuan*). This work presents itself as a sequel to yet another plucking rhymes text, *The Jade Bracelet* (*Yuchuanyuan*). This latter work may date from the second half of the seventeenth century, and there are some indications that it may have been written by a mother-and-daughter team. The only preserved edition of this work is one heavily revised by Hou Zhi (1764–1829). Hou Zhi was a daughter of the Nanjing poet and official Hou Xueshi; her husband was the well-known literatus Mei Chong, and her son, Mei Zengliang, was a pupil of Yao Nai [1732–1815], one of the most respected prose writers of his time. Hou Zhi belonged to a large network of women poets, and actually began her literary career primarily by writing poetry. From 1810 onwards, however, she devoted all her energy to the revision and composition of plucking rhymes (for commercial publishers) in the hopes that this would offer her a greater chance of establishing her reputation than would the highly competitive field of poetry. Apart from her extensively revised version of *The Jade Bracelet*, Hou Zhi also produced an edited version of Chen Duansheng's *Karmic Bonds of Reincarnation*, and was herself the author of a sequel to this work, *Recreated Heaven* (*Zaizaotian*), as well as another plucking rhymes text entitled *Flowers on Brocade* (*Jinshanghua*).

A near-contemporary of Hou Zhi, Zheng Danruo (d. 1860) was another woman writer who turned to plucking rhymes because the genre was not (yet) dominated by men. In her plucking rhymes text entitled *Dream Affinities* (*Mengyingyuan*), Zheng Danruo says as much in the following lines in the opening chapter of her work:

> Plays for the most part are written by famous male writers,
> It is impossible to compete with them and become the best.
> Novels too are written by men of talent during days of leisure,
> How could I take up my brush and try to equal their talent?

> A chicken's bill or a buffalo's tail:[3] this takes some thought,
> But in the end I'd better
> Sweep clean the field of plucking rhymes if I want to express myself!

The plot of *The Jade Bracelet* has been characterized as "relatively simple." If that characterization applies, it does so only in the context of the genre itself, as will be immediately clear from the following summary of the story by Tan Zhengbi and Tan Xun:

> During the reign of Emperor Ningzong [r. 1195–1224] of the Song dynasty, Minister Xie Min from Luoyang in Henan province and his wife, lady Yao, have a son, Yuhui (style name Yunqing), and a daughter, Yujuan (style name Xiang'e), whom people call the "two treasures of the Xie family." Yuhui is studying at the cloister of his aunt, the widow Yang. One day Meiying, the second daughter of the Hanlin scholar Xue Zheng, comes to the cloister to burn incense, and Yuhui falls in love with her the minute he sets eyes on her. At his request, his mother sends a matchmaker to the Xue family and Xue Zheng and his wife are just about to happily agree to the proposal. It so happens, however, that the brother of Xue Zheng's wife, Cheng Duanlin, is staying with them. Because in the past, while serving as district magistrate, he had been indicted by Xie Min, and because earlier he himself had unsuccessfully asked for Meiying as a bride for his own son, he falsely accuses lady Yao, the prospective mother-in-law, of being a violent shrew, and as a result the negotiations are broken off.
>
> Then, when the emperor suddenly issues a call far and wide for lovely maidens for his harem, Cheng Duanlin submits the names of Meiying and Xiang'e to the authorities. Yuhui is grieved at the thought that Meiying should suffer such a dire fate, and unable to bear being separated forever from his sister, he and Xiang'e exchange clothes, and he goes to the capital in her stead. Before his departure, he instructs Xiang'e to come to the capital in male dress and take part in the examinations under his name. Yuhui then leaves together with Meiying, Zheng Ruzhao, and Cao Yanniang, and the four of them become close friends. Once they have entered the palace, they become palace ladies.
>
> At this point, the two concubines Zhu and Liu compete in the palace for the emperor's favor. Concubine Zhu Yuexian has Concubine Liu Suxia killed, and she orders Cao Yanniang to strangle Concubine Liu's baby son, the crown prince Zhenxiang. By this time Yuhui has already disclosed the true state of af-

---

3. In other words, is it better to be a "chicken's bill," a prominent figure in a small enclosure (i.e., a famous author writing in the marginal genre of plucking rhymes) than "a buffalo's tail," a small figure in an important field (i.e., a minor author of verse).

fairs to Meiying and, promising to marry her, has given her a gold-plated jade bracelet as an engagement gift. When Meiying hears from Yanniang what she has been ordered to do, she confers with Yuhui, after which Yuhui reports this state of affairs to Empress He. Empress He, aware that Yuhui is a man in female dress, orders him to take the infant crown prince to the palace of the emperor's uncle, the prince of Rong; she also instructs the prince of Rong not to condemn Yuhui for his deception. The eldest son of the prince of Rong, Tingyu, admires Yuhui's talents and keeps him in the palace as his study companion.

Xiang'e in fact does come to the capital under Yuhui's name and passes the examinations at the head of the list. The prime minister, Wang Fu, has a daughter called Liying (style name Shuxian), and makes Xiang'e his son-in-law. When Yuhui goes and visits Xiang'e, brother and sister are reunited.

Meiying, still in the palace, dreams that the bodhisattva Guanyin presents her with a miraculous medicine, which she in turn presents to the emperor. Cured from his disease, the grateful emperor adopts her as a daughter, bestowing upon her the title of Princess Yong'an.

After Concubine Long is accidentally poisoned by Concubine Zhu, she appears in a dream to the emperor and discloses to him all the crimes of Concubine Zhu. In this way, the emperor learns that the crown prince is still alive, and he condemns Concubine Zhu to strangulation. Because of his merits, Yuhui is not only cleared of all crimes, but is also honored at court for heading the list in the literary and military examinations. Meiying, Yanniang, and Ruzhao are all allowed to leave the palace and Xiang'e is given the title of Female Scholar. The consort of the prince of Rong takes a liking to her and Empress He acts as the matchmaker, giving Xiang'e an engagement present of a ring of intertwined dragons, upon which Xiang'e becomes the wife of the prince's eldest son Tingyu. Wang Shuxian, who has been given the title of Princess Yongping, also marries Yuhui and, what is more, Yuhui also marries Hua Chuyun.

After Concubine Zhu has been executed for her crimes, her brother Zhu Liang not only rebels in the provinces, but also joins forces with the troops of the Jin dynasty, which invade the Song. Yuhui is at his own request appointed commander in the campaign against the rebels, and Wang Zhaohua serves as his vanguard commander. The outcome of the first battle is very positive. The commander-in-chief of the Jin troops, Princess Minghua, however, is skilled in the use of black magic and her vanguard commander Li Zhenqing is very brave. Yuhui is defeated by them, and although he is almost captured, fortunately he is saved by [one of the Eight Immortals,] Imperial Relative Cao, and taken to the magic mountain island Penglai where he is taught the techniques of the immortals. When Wang Zhaohua cannot find Yuhui, he immediately tells the emperor, who then enters into the field of combat himself. When, after another major defeat, the emperor is surrounded on all sides by the Jin troops, Imperial Relative Cao dispatches Yuhui to rescue him. Yuhui saves the emperor and inflicts a heavy defeat on the Jin troops. The defeated Jin dynasty sues for peace, and both Princess Minghua and Li Zhenqing also become Yuhui's wives.

The victorious generals escort the emperor back to the capital where he generously rewards all his meritorious officers and troops. Yuhui is enfeoffed as Prince of Expansive Peace, and his entire family is raised to glory.

Although all of the main characters of *The Jade Bracelet* ascend to Heaven upon their deaths, some of them make a reappearance on earth in *Karmic Bonds of Reincarnation*. In this plucking rhymes text, Xie Yuhui becomes Huangfu Shaohua; Zheng Ruozhao, a concubine of Xie Yuhui, is reborn as Meng Lijun; Chen Fansu becomes Su Yingxue; and Cao Yanniang is punished for her jealousy by being reborn as Liu Yanyu, the sister of Huangfu Shaohua's arch-enemy Liu Kuibi. The time has moved on to the early years of the fourteenth century, and the Song dynasty setting has been replaced by that of the Mongol Yuan dynasty. The plot of *Karmic Bonds of Reincarnation* has been summarized as follows by Tan Zhengbi and Tan Xun:

During the reign of Emperor Chengzong [r. 1295–1307] of the Yuan dynasty, Minister Meng Shiyuan returns to his hometown of Kunming to carry out the prescribed period of mourning for a deceased parent. Shiyuan has a daughter called Lijun, who is both beautiful and talented. She spends her time in the inner chambers together with Su Yingxue, the daughter of her wet nurse lady Su, and the two are very close. Shaohua, the son of Commander-in-Chief Huangfu Jing, and Liu Kuibi, the son of the emperor's father-in-law, Liu Jie, on the very same day send a matchmaker to ask for Meng Lijun's hand in marriage. When Meng Shiyuan orders a shooting match and Liu Kuibi loses, Shiyuan promises Lijun to Shaohua. Filled with resentment, Kuibi tricks Shaohua into staying at his house and plies him with wine until he is drunk. He tries to burn him to death, but his sister Liu Yanyu, who has fallen in love with Shaohua, rescues him: after Shaohua secretly promises to marry her—she is willing to become a concubine—she helps him escape from the compound.

Around this time, the marshal of Liaodong invades Dengzhou and the border officials request help from the court. Liu Jie uses this opportunity to recommend that Huangfu Jing be appointed commander of this campaign. When Huangfu Jing and his vanguard commander Wei Huan have been captured by means of black magic, Liu Jie falsely accuses them of having surrendered to the enemy. The enraged Yuan emperor orders Huangfu's entire household confiscated and Shaohua just barely manages to escape in disguise. While traveling he meets up with Xiong Hao, and the two of them go into the mountains to study the Way. Shaohua's sister, Changhua, and his mother, lady Yin, are arrested by the imperial commissioner and sent off to the capital, but along the way, their party runs into some robbers. The leader of these robbers is Wei Huan's daughter, Yong'e, who has disguised herself as a man. She abducts mother and daughter to her mountain camp, where she honors lady Yin as her mother and Changhua as her elder sister.

Now that the Huangfu family has been destroyed, Liu Kuibi asks for an edict proclaiming Lijun to be his wife. Kuibi's elder sister is the main wife of the Yuan emperor, and when she speaks to him on behalf of her brother, the emperor approves Liu Kuibi's request. Unable to openly defy the emperor's order, the unwilling Lijun pleads with Su Yingxue to assume her name and take her place, and, dressed as a man, she flees together with a servant girl. Su Yingxue is not willing to marry Kuibi either, so she secretly hides a sharp knife in her bosom and vows to revenge the Huangfu family. On the night of the wedding, she ends up stabbing Kuibi on his forehead. After this, she tries to commit suicide by jumping into Kunming Lake, but is saved by the wife of Prime Minister Liang Jian, who adopts her as her daughter, gives her the name of Suhua, and takes her along to the capital.

Once Meng Lijun has escaped, she changes her name to Li Junyu (style name Mingtang). While traveling she meets the rich merchant Kang Xinren, who adopts her as his son. When later she goes to the capital to take part in the examinations, she passes the departmental exams at the head of the list. The chief examiner Liang Jian chooses her as a live-in son-in-law. Yingxue at first is unwilling, and only agrees to the wedding after she has been informed by a spirit in a dream that the top graduate is none other than Lijun. After Lijun also has passed the palace examinations at the head of the list, she [quickly] attains the highest rank in the bureaucracy [because of her superior medical skills] and is ordered to supervise the military examinations. Shaohua and Xiong Hao take part in these examinations under false names, and Shaohua passes at the head of the list. At the same time, Kuibi, who had been leading a campaign against Wei Yong'e, is captured by Wei, while Liu Yanyu, rejecting her arranged marriage with Cui Panfeng, escapes to a nunnery. In this way the Liu family gradually loses its power.

Shaohua requests permission to subdue Yong'e and together with her fight Wu Bikai in order to bring peace to the realm. The emperor agrees to his request, and appoints Shaohua as Grand Marshal, and Xiong Hao as general. The two go on campaign across the ocean. Later, when the enemy sues for peace, Shaohua obtains letters exchanged between Liu Jie and the enemy. Upon his return to court he recounts how he himself changed his name and how his family was exterminated, together with the facts of Liu Jie's conspiracy with the enemy. The Yuan emperor is enraged. Empress Liu has already died, and so he has all members of the Liu family thrown into jail. He bestows upon Shaohua the noble title of Loyal and Filial Prince, and on his father Jing that of Martial and Exemplary Prince. All of the rest are rewarded as well according to their merits.

When Yanyu in her nunnery hears that her father has been condemned, she comes to the capital to save him. The Loyal and Filial Prince recalls the favor she had shown him earlier by saving his life, and also remembers that he has promised to marry her, and so requests the emperor to release all the members of the Liu family except for Kuibi. After Shaohua has married Yanyu, he treats her as a second wife, and vows that he will not consummate his marriage with her until he has found Lijun, whose whereabouts he does not know. Li Junyu [Lijun] harbors a resentment against Shaohua, however, because of his impetuous assistance to the Liu family and his marriage to Yanyu, and she refuses to disclose the true state of affairs. Eventually, the Yuan emperor finally realizes that she is a woman in male disguise and, wishing to make her his consort, assiduously courts her. By this time, Changhua has already succeeded Lady Liu as empress, and she does her best to plot on behalf of Shaohua. Only when Lijun's mother, lady Han, has fallen ill out of longing for her daughter and Meng Shiyuan invites Junyu to treat her, does Lijun secretly disclose her identity to her mother. When Changhua hears this rumor, she immediately informs the empress dowager. They trick Junyu into drinking wine until he/she is drunk, and then discover the truth by taking off her/his shoes [Junyu is discovered to have bound feet].

Once this fact has been disclosed, the Yuan emperor again pressures Lijun to become his consort and will not allow her to reveal her true identity as Meng Lijun. Fortunately, the empress dowager issues an edict pardoning Lijun [for the crime of deceiving the court by taking on a false identity], and adopts her as a daughter, bestowing upon her the title of Baohe Princess. Eventually Shaohua is married to Lijun, as well as to Yingxue.

Karmic Bonds of Reincarnation is not a feminist work in the modern sense of the word. While Wei Yong'e as a general and Meng Lijun as prime minister easily outperform their male counterparts, they do not advocate a fundamental change of system. If Chen Duansheng's work subverts the system, it does so, as in the case of *Linked Rings of Jade*, in a more subtle way: reveling in a reversal of sexual and social identities, *Karmic Bonds of Reincarnation* reduces all such identities to roles that may be played equally by men and women. Meng Lijun/Li Junyu takes her/his role playing so far that she/he accepts the offer of her/his examiner and teacher to become his son-in-law. She has no idea that her bride-to-be, Liang Suhua, actually is her former servant girl Su Yingxue. Su Yingxue/Liang Suhua may have been informed in a dream of the true sex of her groom-to-be, but such information is of course not always reliable. As the bride wears a heavy red veil throughout the marriage ceremony, the newlyweds (Meng Lijun/Li Junyu and Su Yingxue/Liang Suhua) only see each other face-to-face at the end of the day in their bedroom:

Our story goes that, after Li Mingtang had securely locked the bedroom door, he took a red candle from in front of the window and stepped inside the embroidered bed curtains.

> There he saw the precious young lady Liang Suhua,
> Sitting on the bed with lowered head, her face like a flower:
> A light tinge of emerald green spreads across the jet of her brows,
> An almost invisible red blush covers her cheeks with its hue.
> Bashful and diffident, she is demure and does not say a word,
> Leaning against the silken curtains her bridal skirt hung aslant.
> Her fragrant face is gorgeous: she is truly lovely,
> Her alluring posture is charming: surely deserving of praise!
> As soon as Junyu caught sight of her, he was very surprised,
> And holding the candle he stood there dumbfounded, and thought:

"How strange! She looks so familiar! I'd say she is the spitting image of Su Yingxue!

> How strange! The daughter of Minister Liang
> Looks exactly the same as Su Yingxue.
> For as long as heaven and earth we'll be husband and wife,
>   But this really makes me
> Call to mind Su Yingxue, and pain fills my breast.
> How pitiable was the bitter death of that lovely girl,
> Buried deep in the cold springs, her grief must be mounting.
> Now when I suddenly see this fragrant face here today,
> My heart suddenly shatters into smithereens!

Come to think of it, Teacher Liang also hails from Yunnan. Could it be that he rescued Yingxue after she jumped into the lake?

> Even if that were the case, it can't be mentioned!
> Now she is the daughter of Minister Liang.
> If she really was Su Yingxue,
> How could she marry again after jumping into the lake?
> At present there is no way to resolve my doubts,
> > And I find myself in a bind
> That the truth of my disguise might also be revealed!"
> Once Junyu had recovered from his pleasant surprise,
> He placed the shining candle close to his bride.
> Lifting the sleeve of his gown, he took her lovely hand,
> And uttering the words slowly, softly said: "Darling!"
> The bride turned away, not knowing how to answer,
> Her heart in turmoil, she was flustered and afraid.
> Fearful that her groom might be a man after all—
> Even if she did not lose her virginity, she might lose her honor.
> As she could no longer suppress all the doubts in her belly,
> She quickly opened her beautiful lips and said in lovely tones:

"My dear Head of the List! To me you do not sound like someone from Huguang province, your accent rather seems to be from Yunnan. Please tell me the truth of your innermost feelings!

> Your Yunnanese accent is not the strangest thing about you,
> Your marvelous beauty is rare in this world.
> > The way I see it,
> You are not a man, you are a woman!
> You have something to hide and your words are a lie.
> Quickly tell me in detail from the very beginning
> The most secret and deepest feelings in your heart.
> But if you, my Head of the List, continue to prevaricate,
> I'll inform my parents and have them resolve my doubts."
> When she had finished speaking, she observed his expression:
> > Head of the List Li
> Had become flustered and panic-struck, fearful of scandal.
> The white face had turned red, the eyes expressed fear,
> The heart was in turmoil, the mind at a loss.
> "I should have known that my features were too fine,
> > I cannot deceive

The sharp eyes of such an intelligent girl.
Let me try to fool her with my words—
If she fails to believe me, I'll beg for her mercy!"
　The Head of the List, secretly filled with fear,
　Regained his composure and tugged at her gown:

"My Lady, why do you say such things?

This lowly official has only insignificant talents,
But yet had the fortune to be passed by your father.
I succeeded in each examination at the head of the list,
And now I serve in a position at court.
　If I really were a girl in skirt and hairpins,
　　　　　How would I dare
Enter the minister's mansion as a son-in-law?
Where do you, my Lady, come up with such ideas,
And take your bridegroom for a girl in skirts?"
　When the Head of the List had finished speaking, he smiled.
　　　　　Little Miss Liang
Blushing even behind her ears, was completely dumbfounded.
But when she lifted her eyes and looked him over once more,
He clearly was a girl—no need to guess about that!
　Once she had reached this decision, she stood up,
　And opening her ruby-red lips, spoke to him as follows:

"My Head of the List, why don't you tell me the truth? Let me tell it to you on
your behalf! Head of the List Li, now listen to me!

Because the emperor's edict ordered you to marry Liu Kuibi,
You preserved your honor, fled disaster, and traveled afar.
When you met Mister Kang, he adopted you as his son, and
　　　　　Thanks to your talents
You thrice succeeded at the head of the list and entered the Hanlin.
　Let me disclose to you your true name and surname:
　　　　　You are originally
That sophisticated young lady from Yunnan, Meng Lijun!"
Before the bride had even finished speaking, she had
　　　　　Frightened out of his wits
That multitalented, most erudite, Hanlin scholar Li:
　The two peach-petal-like cheeks had turned to white,
　The pair of willow-leaf-like eyebrows was knit in a frown.

Overcome by fright her heart pounded wildly:
"This surely must be Su Yingxue who has come back to life!"

Although both works subtly subvert accepted gender norms, *Karmic Bonds of Reincarnation* goes far beyond *Linked Rings of Jade* in its long extended elaboration of Meng Lijun's refusal to resume her female identity. Meng Lijun refuses to acknowledge her identity not only when confronted by Huangfu Shaohua (arguing that as his examiner and teacher it would not be proper for her to become his wife and subordinate), but also when confronted by her parents, to whom she even presents another young woman in the hopes that they will be fooled into believing she is their daughter. Moreover, she retains her false identity when directly questioned by a suspicious (and amorous) emperor. It is only when she, now the prime minister and the favorite of the emperor because of her/his medical skills, is called on to treat her mother's illness and her mother pretends to faint, that Meng Lijun/Li Junyu's determination is shaken:

> Just as the prime minister was about to feel the lady's pulse,
>   He suddenly heard
> A wild shouting inside the gauze bed curtains:

"Oh, how suffocating! Away with these bed curtains!"

> She shouted and screamed and she tugged away at the curtains,
> And the red gauze curtains surrounding the bed all then opened.
> He saw the lady sitting there underneath her quilts,
> Her face was wasted away by sickness and she was wildly panting.
> A piece of silk covered her chignon, a duvet surrounded her waist,
> And both her cheeks were burning red as if with a fever.
> With stretched-out hands she pulled at the curtains, showing herself to
>   the physician,
>   Looking all around—
> With wide-open eyes she peered in all directions!

As soon as Prime Minister Li saw lady Meng pull down the curtains and stare wildly about, he hastily got to his feet.

> Not only was he taken by surprise, he was also flustered,
> He retreated a few steps, walking toward the window.
> Secretary Meng quickly grabbed him to keep him from leaving
>   And said:

"No need to stand on propriety now that she is so ill!"
Minister Li could do nothing but again go to her bedside,
But still he could not help
His face from showing, however slightly, his panic.
At the side of the bed, he sat down outside the curtains,
And with his jade-white fingers lightly took her pulse.
 Now that the curtains had been removed, lady Meng,
Opening her eyes, observed Mingtang carefully:
She noticed
That he had the imposing mien of a first rank official,
Clad in his python-gown, with gold and sable on his head.
 But the face like a lotus flower betrayed a touch of fear,
And the brows like willow-leaves were partly knit in a frown.
With knees close together he was sitting on the folding chair,
And his dashing and elegant face was without peer.
 "Truly amazing, oh what a joy,
This person is the daughter I bore, my Meng Lijun!"
When lady Meng had reached this conclusion,
She was filled with sadness, filled with joy, filled with pain.
 Before she had spoken a word, her tears coursed down,
And she threw herself upon him without further delay.
Tightly clutching the purple gown, she would not let go,
And cried with a voice filled with sadness: "My child!

Oh, my child! You are my daughter! How can you be so cruel as to refuse to recognize your mother!"

As she loudly wailed and clutched at his skirt,
She frightened that fake Minister Li out of his wits!
He was dumbfounded, he was flummoxed and confused,
His face changed color and he was in a panic.
 He got to his feet and started to move backwards,
Tearing the sleeves of his gown out of his mother's hands.
Lady Meng did not have the strength to keep him with her,
And overcome by grief
She loudly vented her grief as she dissolved into tears:

"Oh, this is killing me!"

After she had let out this shout, she closed her eyes,
Collapsed on the edge of the bed and lost consciousness.

Her two legs were spread out, her body did not move,
Her teeth were clenched tightly, her life was about to end!
  Even though Secretary Meng knew she was pretending to faint,
            On purpose he
Rushed over with long strides and threw himself on her quilt:

"Oh, my wife, don't die! What do you want that unfilial daughter for?

  She's now been gone for many years, most likely will never return,
Despite her parents' longing and all their sorrow and care.
            You
Carry her memory in your heart like a jewel or treasure,
            But she
Has forgotten all about you as if you were dirt.
  Why do you have to torment yourself like this on her behalf?
How would Lijun be willing to show any love for her parents?
Even if her eyes were to witness her own mother's illness,
She would still look upon her as if she were a stranger!

Oh my wife, please don't die! Don't destroy your body on account of that heartless daughter!"

. . .

Our story goes that Mingtang, when lady Meng grabbed at her, panicked and
could do nothing but step backwards. When she not only witnessed her
mother's fainting spell, but also heard the angry words of her father and
brother, it was as if a thousand keen swords were stabbing her innards, a million
steel daggers piercing her heart!

  Dressed in formal robes she was sitting there dumbfounded,
She said not a word and hadn't the slightest idea what to do.
Her brows were furrowed like spring hills, sorrow had arisen,
Her eyes overflowing with autumn floods, on the verge of tears.
            Overcome by sadness,
  She felt as if she had been showered with freezing water,
            Terrified,
The slightest trace of red had bleached from her cheeks
With bowed head she pondered, her heart about to break,
Her mind turned in a thousand ways—unbearable pain.
            Neither could she
  Walk over to the bedside and summon her back to life,
            Neither could she

Walk out of the room and simply avoid getting involved.
   . . .
As soon as she saw this, Mingtang was greatly terrified,
        All of a sudden
She felt bereft of her soul, did not know what to do:
"If today I still refuse to disclose the state of affairs,
        I will have murdered
The mother who bore me, a crime beyond words!

Oh, this is too painful! Let me forget about the fact that a teacher cannot take a student as a spouse! I'll first acknowledge my mother, and then figure out what to do!"

As this scene only takes place in chapter 44, and we still have many chapters to go before the story reaches its denouement, naturally Meng Lijun does not find it difficult to persuade her parents that she has no choice but to maintain her male disguise:

"My parents, just think about your child's situation! If Prime Minister Liang reports this state of affairs to the emperor, he would have to tell him that I have deceived the Son of Heaven, fooled the great ministers, upset the relationship of yin and yang, and although a woman, married a bride. Each one of these accusations would be enough to condemn me to death by slicing! Father and mother, now let me know your opinion: should I disclose this state of affairs or would it be better if I did not?

And even if Minister Liang did not report to our ruler,
How would I deal with his darling daughter?
She is the only child of the all-powerful prime minister,
        Why should she be willing
To become a little concubine of the Loyal and Filial Prince?
Now she is married to your child and enjoys great status,
Acknowledged as the proper wife of an official of the first rank.
If you now would ask her to become a lowly concubine,
Wouldn't she feel ashamed, and wouldn't she be enraged?
        Moreover,
Just when I was down and out, nothing going right,
I became the adopted son of the Kang family.
Now that I am enjoying riches and honor, fame and glory,
        I have brought
My adoptive parents to live with me in the capital.

If I, despite my position, were to be condemned to death,
　　　　　　Most likely
They too will suffer in my misfortune and lose their status.
All these many problems and questions are not easily resolved,
So how could your child go ahead and disclose the truth?

My dear parents, the way I see it, the best solution is that I acknowledge you as my parents in secret but not in public.

Even though by doing this you, my parents, lose a daughter,
You still have my sister-in-law and my elder brother.
They can keep you company from daybreak to dusk,
And at family reunions you will not have to feel lonely.
　Even if you wanted me to return to the bosom of the family,
　　　　　　You would have to
Marry me off to another family to serve my parents-in-law.
Seen from that angle, I'd be of no use to my parents at all,
　　　　So it would be much better
To allow your child to continue to act the husband.
　Better still, we will all be living together here in the capital,
Not at all far from each other by horse and by carriage.
As soon as you, father or mother, want to see me,
You only have to send a messenger to come get me.
　There is no problem in us seeing each other often,
　　　　· So why insist
On my taking back my surname and marrying Huangfu Shaohua?

My parents, people all say that it is the Way of a wife to share in her husband's glory and shame. But if I had not fled defilement and saved my honor by taking to the road, I most likely would have suffered the same misfortune as the members of the Huangfu family. Now he indeed has made a brilliant career, but your child does not care to share his glory.

I may be a girl in skirts, her hair fastened down with pins,
But at this moment I stand before the steps of the throne!
This boundless favor binds me for a myriad generations,
My rank none other than one of the three prime ministers.
　Why should it be so urgent that I marry a husband?
　　　　　　Why should I care
For the title and rank of a prince's main wife, a royal consort?
　　　　　　What is more,

> The official salary of a prime minister is as high as the sky,
> I am fully capable of taking care of myself!

My dear parents, there is still another point. When I was appointed as the president of the Ministry of War, Shaohua's whereabouts were unknown and he had not yet made a name for himself. So, in response to my proposal to the emperor, a military examination was decreed.

> Only then could Shaohua spread his wings like an eagle,
> Under the name of Wang Hua, he came to the capital.
> The emperor had appointed me as chief examiner:
> I gathered heroes to safeguard the national borders.
> At that time I, Lijun, became his teacher and master:
> I selected him as head of the list at the exercise grounds.
> All the people of the prefecture know about this situation:
> And all the "eagles" of the day gathered inside of my home.

Now father and mother, dear sister-in-law and elder brother, just try to remember whether from ancient times to the present there ever has been

> A teacher who ended up married to one of his students?
> I am quite sure that such a thing has never yet been seen.
>   Why should I be willing
> To become the all-time laughing-stock of the whole wide world?"

Meng Lijun clearly relishes her masquerade as Li Junyu and the tangled web of social contradictions that result from it. Women audiences loved the story of Meng Lijun/Li Junyu, and it enjoyed great popularity in late imperial times, not only as a plucking rhymes text but also as a novel and as a play.

Karmic Bonds of Reincarnation's author, Chen Duansheng (1751–1796), was a granddaughter of Chen Zhaolun (1701–1771), a scholar-official who, in the course of his long career, held several of the highest metropolitan offices. He also appears to have held relatively enlightened views on the education of women. Chen Duansheng's younger sister, Changsheng, was a poet and one of Yuan Mei's literary disciples. Changsheng's husband, Ye Shaokui (d. 1821), was a son of the well-known woman poet Li Hanzhang, and enjoyed a long and distinguished career, attaining the rank of governor of Guangxi province in 1817. Chen Duansheng herself was far less fortunate in life. Her husband, Fan Tan (Qiutang), was implicated in a case of examination corruption in 1780, and was subsequently banished to Xinjiang as a common soldier. By the time he had been pardoned and allowed to return home, Chen Duansheng had already passed away.

Even though Chen Duansheng wrote the first sixty-four chapters of *Karmic Bonds of Reincarnation* before her marriage, later readers saw a clear link between the circumstances of her life and the contents of her work:

People say that Mrs. Duansheng, the granddaughter of Chamberlain for the Imperial Stud Chen Goushan [Zhaolun] from Qiantang, married a man from the Fan family, and that when her husband was implicated in an examination case, she put away all of her cosmetics, and [devoted herself to the] composition of a plucking rhymes text entitled *Karmic Bonds of Reincarnation*. She herself appears in that work in the guise of a girl of the Yuan dynasty called Meng Lijun, who, dressed as a man, takes part in the examinations, changing her name to Li Junyu. After passing the examinations, she becomes prime minister, and although she and her husband serve in the same court, they are never reunited. In this way, Chen Duansheng expressed her regret over her separation from her husband: she would say: "This book will not be completed until my husband comes home!" Later Fan was pardoned and returned home, but by that time she had passed away.

The work was completed by Xu Zongyan and his wife, Liang Desheng, who turned it into a complete jewel. All the women of the land who could recognize at least a few characters would have read this book.

Only the first sixty-eight chapters of *Karmic Bonds of Reincarnation* were written by Chen Duansheng herself. In a long autobiographical introduction to chapter 65, she describes how she wrote the first sixty-four chapters in the course of just a few years while still at her parental home and with the enthusiastic encouragement of her mother. At the urging of her female friends, who wanted to see the fictional lovers reunited, she resumed her work in 1784 (the forty-ninth year of the Qianlong reign period) after an interval of twelve years:

> I scratch my head and call out to Heaven, wishing to ask Heaven,
> Ask Heaven whether the Way of Heaven can be turned around!
> Having tasted to the full all the bitter sufferings of this world,
> I recall the days of my earliest youth in the inner chambers:
> We sisters shared a couch as we listened to the night rain,
> And our parents assigned us rhymes and taught us poetry.
> From across the wall, red apricot petals drifted over the clean snow,

And shading our benches, the tall scholar-trees were wrapped in mist.
Tired from our embroidery, at noon we continued to lay out the threads,
And when we had tasted the springtime tea, we added some more water.
We lived quite close to the Eastern Ocean, always threatened by floods,
Living on Penglai's fairy isle, we believed we'd turn into immortals!
Thousands upon thousands of towers and terraces took form in the sky,
And beyond the island, two or three sails and masts were hung up aloft.
I accompanied my father to his official post and there I grew up,
My parents lavished their love on me, they loved me far too much!
My talents couldn't compete with "willow floss tossed by the wind,"
And I could not live up to "In a Bowl," or "Pepper Blossom."[4]
Still, in my ignorance I dared take a peep at the affairs of the past:
With brush in hand, I wrote *Karmic Bonds of Reincarnation* for fun.
I knew too well that the cloud had no intention to leave the peak,
But still I gazed at the beautiful moon in front of the window.
                    I wrote some chapters
  On separation and reunion, sadness and joy, and miraculous meetings,
                    I wrote some chapters
On loyalty and treason by high and low in the midst of great danger,
On noble men and chaste wives, wishing to repay the favors shown,
On determination only strengthened by separation in death or in life.
My dear mother was amused and often offered her suggestions,
As her silly child continued to spin out her fantasies further and further.
But once my mother started to waste away,
I had to put aside my scented books and shining brush.
At that point Li Mingtang's shoes had been taken off and her feet
    inspected,
But the marriage settled by the shooting match had not yet been
    consummated.
When I lost my mother in the thirty-fifth year, it was the first month of
    autumn;
When we returned to the south in the thirty-sixth year, it was the early
    summer.
On the boat home I wondered whether I should revise the text,
Then in the leisure of the inner chamber I prepared to rewrite it.

---

4. "In a Bowl" refers to a poetical composition by the wife of Su Boyu, and originally was written in the form of a spiral designed to be read from the center outwards. The text of "In a Bowl" is included in *New Songs of a Jade Terrace*. "Pepper Blossom" refers to the "Hymn on the Pepper Blossom" by Lady Chen.

But soon I came to the realization of the emptiness of existence,
And once home, alas, I found myself taken up by worldly duties.
Fortunately my parents-in-law took pity on my weak person,
And to my joy, my husband was a champion amongst scholars.
By the light of the lamp we studied together and boiled water for tea,
Making a mark on the candle we wrote poems and laughter abounded.
With the joyous harmony of a brocade zither, our hearts were united,
And soon a bright pearl dangled from my palm [a daughter was born].
Enjoying our good fortune, our comfort and joy was extraordinary,
But then he was caught in the fetters of profit, the snares of fame.
Once a string on a zither has snapped, it is broken forever;
The half of a broken mirror can never be made round again:
A migrating goose, far from the flock, in the setting sun,
A man of sorrow, far from home, stuck beyond the border.
From that moment on, my heart was hurt, my soul was lost,
And for all these years, my torn innards have been seething.
My desire to repay my husband's favors remains unfulfilled,
My determination to care for our children grows only stronger.
I sit inside a wall of sorrow, frozen are my tears of blood,
When my spirit travels the thousand miles, it is blocked by storms.
Ever since this marriage was determined as if by a shooting match,
These past few years all its pleasures have been crushed to pieces.
Could it possibly have been an omen of our fate today
That long ago I called this work *Karmic Bonds of Reincarnation?*
During the day, my face in the mirror always provides the proof,
"Following daybreak, an orphaned star" truly does apply to me.
As it happens, my book has enjoyed a reputation for a time,
And has found its way throughout the province of Zhejiang.
As ridiculous as this light diversion from my youth may be,
   It still far surpasses
My serious writings of adversity that are not worth a cent.
My friends of the inner chambers have often voiced their admiration,
My elders in their screened halls have all let themselves be amused.
They've buzzed about my ears, urging me to complete the book,
   As they all longed to see
The star-crossed lovers, that perfect couple, brought together at last:
"Huangfu Shaohua must be matched with his beautiful bride,
Minister Li Mingtang must finally consummate her marriage!
As you have played the role of matchmaker on their behalf,

You should not play the Son of Heaven and keep them apart!"
The Creator should not blame me for this state of affairs,
   I am only
A woman with a broken heart grieving over her lonely life.
I've revised my old drafts and added some new ones,
And after revising the longer work, I've written a short sequel.
 It is now the second month of spring of the forty-ninth year,
And by my window I again work on *Karmic Bonds of Reincarnation*.
All the endless affairs of the last twelve years
Have passed in a tipsy dream of Li Mingtang!

It took Chen Duansheng almost a year to finish chapters 65 through 68, by the end of which the lovers were still not reunited. Some critics have suggested that as an author, Chen Duansheng saw no way to extricate Meng Lijun/Li Junyu from the quandary she had landed her/him in. Her Meng Lijun remains guilt-ridden because of her unfilial behavior toward her father and mother, but apparently content to maintain her male disguise and to continue to enjoy all of the benefits it allowed her. As mentioned above, it was left to the well-known Hangzhou woman poet Liang Desheng and her husband, Xu Zongyan (1768–1819), to bring the work to a conventional conclusion. Xu Zongyan was one of the greatest scholars of his day, and Liang Desheng, whose name we have encountered earlier in our discussion of Wang Duan, was a sister of the equally learned Hangzhou scholar, Liang Yusheng (1745–1819). Modern critics have dealt harshly with Liang Desheng, accusing her of subverting the "feminist" thrust of Chen Duansheng's work by arranging for the final marriage of Huangfu Shaohua and Meng Lijun. It is clear from the long autobiographical passage translated above, however, that if that was not the ending that Chen Duansheng intended, it was, at least, the ending she knew that her readers expected.

 In *Recreated Heaven*, Hou Zhi's own sequel to *Karmic Bonds of Reincarnation*, the central character is Meng Lijun's daughter, Feilong (Flying Dragon), who is said to be a reincarnation of Wu Bikai. Feilong's admired model is Empress Wu Zetian, as is clear from a poem she writes in praise of the empress in the first chapter of *Recreated Heaven*:

As a female ruler she occupied the throne,
And her fame spread throughout the world:

The khan of the Huns came suing for peace,
And the king of Korea laid down his arms.
 People all blame her for her use of vixen-like charms,
But what ruler has measured up to her imperial fortitude?
In the Southern Court she punished her favorite eunuch,
In the Phoenix Pavilion she dressed down her virile lover.
 Her law made no allowance for personal favors,
For her ministers she selected the finest men.
She recognized quality, and rewarded it well;
She even admired a rebel for his fine writing.
 For what lack of virtue should she feel ashamed?
There was no one talented enough to put her down.
She was a golden goblet, with no defect or failing,
The most divine of monarchs in a thousand years!

Such an attitude, of course, can only lead to disaster. As soon as Feilong becomes Yingzong's secondary empress, she supplants all the other women around the emperor, and collaborates with traitors and eunuchs. Eventually, her machinations backfire, and in the end, she is condemned to death by being allowed to commit suicide, whereupon peace and order are restored to both court and country.

Feilong is described as being a rambunctious tomboy practically from the moment of her birth. In *Recreated Heaven,* she encounters her match in the person of her maternal aunt and mother-in-law, the empress dowager Huangfu Changhua, who is depicted as an embodiment of female virtue. Feilong can only exert her influence at court after the empress dowager is laid up with an illness. As soon as Huangfu Changhua recovers, however, she takes decisive action to restore order, though always careful to do so unobtrusively and without publicly taking credit for her contributions to the stability of the state and the dynasty. If Hou Zhi in *Recreated Heaven* seems to condemn the public display of female talent as a danger to the family and the nation, her work also displays, in the words of Ellen Widmer, "a latent respect for the woman who can handle the administration of a household, perhaps even a state, if duty called. This latent respect is Hou's compromise with the far bolder celebration of feminine talent and ambition in *Zaisheng yuan.* [*Karmic Bonds of Reincarnation*]"

Other Plucking Rhymes

More Cross-Dressing Heroines

Women dressed as men who passed the examinations, achieved the highest government positions, and collected a bevy of brides along the way, continued to be a popular subject with the women writers of plucking rhymes. One of the several women authors who tried to outdo Chen Duansheng in her characterization of Meng Lijun was Qiu Xinru, the author of *Flowers from a Brush (Bishenghua)*.

Qiu Xinru, who was married to a man surnamed Zhang, lived in the first half of the nineteenth century. Following the death of her husband, her son, and her parents-in-law, and the marriage of her daughter, she returned to her parental home twenty years after having left it, and subsequently made her living as a schoolteacher. Most of the meager information on her life derives from the sometimes quite extensive autobiographical introductions to the chapters of her plucking rhymes text. Her *Flowers from a Brush* is comprised of only thirty-two chapters, but each of these chapters is as long as a short novel. Qiu Xinru is said to have written the first five chapters before her marriage, the following fourteen chapters after her marriage, and the remaining chapters after her husband had died and she had returned to her parental home.

The heroine of Qiu Xinru's life's work is called Jiang Dehua, although once she assumes male dress, she uses the name of Jiang Junbi. At various points in her long and successful career she finds herself forced to marry a wife. While her original fiancé early on suspects the true sex of "Jiang Junbi," readers have to wait until the very end of the tale before Jiang Dehua reverts to female dress. The character of Jiang Dehua was clearly designed to outdo Meng Lijun in virtue: whereas Meng Lijun is conspicuous for her lack of filiality, Jiang Dehua can never be accused of such a sin. At the beginning of her first chapter, Qiu Xinru explicitly articulates her goal of improving on her predecessor's work by elevating the moral character of her heroine:

> *Karmic Bonds of Reincarnation*, just recently published,
> Is today eagerly circulated by aficionados of the genre.
> Its literary style, graceful and restrained, is not at all vulgar,
> The sophistication of its artistic composition is quite admirable.

In the ranking of "plucking rhymes," it deserves the first place,
But still it suffers in its conception from some minor failings:
> Liu Yanyu
Promised herself to Huangfu Shaohua without parental permission,
> So how could she have been enfeoffed
As a Chaste and Filial Lady and be so highly praised?
> The "Rules for Women" says:
"If one is remiss in even one virtue, all one's virtues suffer."
> How much more does this apply
To marrying without a matchmaker's help, a scandalous act!
> Li Junyu
Was completely perfect in talent, looks, and in deportment,
And she excelled in both public administration and literary writings.
But if one must point out her faults, she was extremely unfilial,
> She even
Completely suppressed the natural feelings of gratitude.
When she threatened to resign in the golden hall of the palace,
She shamed her father and fooled her lord—this goes too far!
Despite her many qualities, this truly must be deemed a defect,
> As it is always said
That of the hundred virtues of humanity, filiality comes first.

But Qiu Xinru's Jiang Dehua is as reluctant as Chen Duansheng's Meng Lijun/Li Junyu to give up her life as a man with all its attendant privileges. Thus, when her identity is finally revealed, she drafts her resignation with a certain reluctance:

> She wanted to draft the memorial but felt no inspiration,
> She smoothed the yellow paper but didn't lift her brush.
> Abruptly she pushed her inkstone aside, rose from her desk,
> And collapsed inside the bed curtains in her embroidered gown.
> Her heart was in turmoil, her mind in a whirl,
> Recalling the past, imagining the future, overcome by grief!

"Ah, this is really too vexing!

> Since my old father caused me to be born with many talents,
> > Why, oh why
> Was I not born a boy? Why did I have to be born a girl?
> > In the last few years,
> Thanks to all my hard work, I've made a success of my career.

> How could I know
> I'd have to see riches and honor return to ashes and dust as before.
> To no purpose
> Has my talent been as high as the Dipper—what use is it now?
> To no purpose
> Have I been ranked among ministers—now I am dismissed."

If Meng Lijun, Jiang Dehua, and the many other cross-dressing hero-ines of plucking rhymes by women authors all eventually revert, however reluctantly, to female dress and take up again their roles as dutiful daugh-ters, there is at least one case of a fictional heroine who maintains her male identity and dies rather than reverting to female dress, and one case of a heroine who maintains her male identity and lives happily with her bride for the rest of her life. This latter story is found in *The Golden Fish Affinity* (*Jinyuyuan*), written between 1863 and 1868 by Sun Deying. The plot of this plucking rhymes text, set during the reign of Emperor Lizong (r. 1253–1264) of the Song dynasty, is too complex to summarize here in full, so we will limit ourselves to a brief outline of the adventures of just one of the female heroines. Qian Shurong is the daughter of a loyal min-ister of the throne who is forced to battle the evil machinations of a trai-torous minister and a depraved eunuch. When the family is imprisoned on trumped-up charges, Shurong runs away, only to be abducted by a lo-cal bully who wants to make her his concubine. She escapes his clutches with the help of his wife. On the run yet again, this time in male disguise, she is adopted as a son by the former governor of Guangxi, and assumes the name of Zhu Fengrui (style name Yunping). After she has passed the provincial examinations, she marries Yu'e, the daughter of a censor. Yu'e discovers her husband's true sexual identity, but the two of them swear that they will remain together forever as man and wife. Shurong then passes the metropolitan examinations and embarks on a brilliant career. She succeeds in bringing about the downfall of the treacherous minister, which leads to further promotions. When later on there are some who suspect that Zhu Fengrui actually may be Shurong, the empress tests her by presenting her with a few palace ladies. When Shurong accepts the gift, the emperor refuses to listen to any further questioning of Shurong's identity. Eventually, Shurong does reveal her true identity to her close relatives, but she continues to maintain her male identity in public. Later she retires from the bureaucracy and lives together with Yu'e on the banks of Hangzhou's West Lake.

The Golden Fish Affinity includes two prefaces. The first of these argues that women may be capable of the same heroic exploits as men. The second, written by Sun Deying's sister-in-law, Niu Ruyuan, contains a detailed biography of the author, which clearly suggests that the career of Shurong reflected, at least partially, the aspirations of the author herself:

Since ancient times, authors have been remembered because of their texts, and texts have become famous because of their authors. And so, if the author is extraordinary, the text will be even more extraordinary.

Every period has its men who stand out for their writings, but one rarely hears of women who take hold of the writing brush and set forth their opinions. Of those famous ladies and pure maidens, there are none who do not nourish the numinous beauties of hills and streams and cherish the immortal talents of exceptional insight. But rare indeed are those who do not follow the established conventions of rouge and powder. The only one who has been able to link together past and present, to understand [how things] rise and fall, to turn her back on the hustle and bustle of worldly affairs, to look upon honor and riches as floating clouds, and to make zither and books the only lasting pleasures of her life, is my younger sister-in-law.

My sister-in-law's style name is Deying, and she sports the sobriquet of Immortal Fairy Rising Beyond the Clouds. Our Sun family was originally registered in Eastern Zhejiang and is an established lineage of Gui'an [Wuxing]. Since my father-in-law was employed as a private secretary in Jiangxi and was married in Jiujiang, the family has now been living here for over thirty years. When I married my husband, my sister-in-law did not yet wear her hair tied up in a bun, but even then she did not indulge in sports and games, but loved only study and meditation. By nature she was bright and intelligent, far above the run of the mill. Every moment she could spare from her needlework, she would take up a book: she was widely read and had memorized not only the Classics and Histories and the Philosophers, but also the heterodox teachings and miscellaneous chronicles. Behind closed doors, she would tell stories of both near and far without omitting any details, and her listeners were never the slightest bit bored. I secretly admired her for this.

When she [reached marriageable age and] had her hair tied up in a bun, she exhibited an even greater earnestness and elegance. Even though she had never received any formal instruction in her youth, she excelled in poetry. The verses she wrote were clear and pure, natural and unrestrained, very much in the style of a recluse. Even though she never explicitly expressed her desire to care for her parents in their old age instead of getting married, I early on guessed from her writings and discussions that this is what she wanted. Her parents, however, did not know of her desire, and my sister-in-law became despondent and unhappy whenever there was talk of an engagement. Shortly afterwards, her mother suffered a stroke, and having become paralyzed on the right side of her body, she required the help of a nurse not only to eat and drink but also to sit up and lie down. My sister-in-law's resolve to take care of her parents was only strengthened by this, and so she told her parents straight out [that she did not want to marry]. Her parents and the clan elders, however, were concerned that this might eventually create problems, so they admonished and reprimanded her, and in a hundred ways tried to make her change her mind. But none of this made any difference and so they had no choice but to yield to her resolve.

Not long after this, the people from Guandong-Guangxi [the Taiping rebels] were threatening to invade our prefecture, so we rented a boat and fled the fighting. The unsettled situation caused the illness of her mother to suddenly worsen: she coughed up mucous, became delirious, and was unconscious of what was happening around her, and medicines were of no avail. Within an hour, she had departed from this world, leaving us behind! My sister-in-law wailed sorrowfully and cried tears of blood, and was so grieved that she lost her desire to live. Only when my husband and I comforted her was her grief somewhat assuaged. From this time onwards, she lived alone in her tiny room and refused all contact with the outside world, spending her time either reciting the *Diamond Sutra* and practicing meditation, or writing about events of the past and composing books. She would not take even half a step out of her cell unless it was to pay her respects to her father or to take part in the worship of the ancestors. All members of our clan who heard of this were filled with admiration.

She began her *The Golden Fish Affinity* in the year *kuihai* [1863] and finished it in the year *mouchen* [1868], having completed the work in six years. When my husband and I read it, we praised it greatly—how could she have written it so quickly and so well! Even though this work is a prosimetrical text, it well merits reading. It truly may be compared to the Classics and Histories inasmuch as it deals with the major issues of morality and the basic causes of order and chaos, and it is of even greater value as regards the moral transformation of the inner quarters. It should be printed and widely circulated so that her feelings of compassion will not have been wasted. My sister-in-law said: "I wrote this simply as a diversion to while away the time, so why cut down pear trees and date trees for printing blocks?" But I said: "Authors are remembered because of their texts, and texts become famous because of their authors. How could we bear to keep hidden such an extraordinary author and such an extraordinary text?" So we turned the manuscript over to the printer so that it might find a wide readership, in the hope that from this single spot one might deduce the entire leopard.

Respectfully written in the Study for Enjoying the Moon in the last decade of the Fourth Month, in the summer of the year xinwei, *the tenth year of the reign period Tongzhi* [1871], *by your sister-in-law Niu Ruyuan.*

If in *Karmic Bonds of Reincarnation* Meng Lijun in male and female dress had to fend off the amorous advances of the emperor, this sexual problematique undergoes a new twist in Cheng Huiying's *Phoenixes Flying Together (Feng shuang fei)*. Cheng Huiying was a female schoolteacher of the second half of the nineteenth century. The main characters in this very long work are handsome young men who are pursued by male lovers who, when they fail to achieve their objectives, don't hesitate to accuse others of homosexual practices. One wonders to what extent the author chose this unusual subject matter in order to bring the issue of unwanted intimacies closer to home for a male readership. It may also have been that the author thought handsome young men more realistic alter egos for her own aspirations than girls in male dress, especially since it allowed for a more detailed description of society. In fact, the subject matter may have been less remarkable at this time in Chinese history than one might imagine: Victorianism only reached China in the twentieth century, and one of the most popular novels of the second half of the nineteenth century was Chen Sen's *Precious Mirror of Ranked Flowers (Pinhua baojian)*, which describes the love affairs between members of Beijing's high society and the young men who performed as female impersonators in the Peking Opera.

Despite the conspicuous presence of male homosexuality in the extremely complicated story of *Phoenixes Flying Together*, which defies any attempt at a brief summation, female characters also abound in this lengthy work, and one of them explains a woman's lot to her husband as follows:

> She said: "Master, do not say anything like that!
> How can someone like you who can read be so deluded?

Please, don't blame me for quoting the following phrases:
'In general it's misfortunate people who have daughters.'
They spend their money and waste their efforts,
Raising her till she's grown, as beautiful as a flower,
         But just when
She could help her mother by taking over her tasks,
         They insist on
Marrying her off to other people as a bride.
         If she happens to have
Parents-in-law familiar with the rites, and a good husband,
         She can be assured of
A quiet and peaceful existence for the rest of her life:
Without a worry she will enjoy a thousand pleasures,
And never complain that her parents have discarded her.

This shows the uselessness of having daughters.

         But if she encounters
A family that eats dung for dinner and is ignorant of the Way,
         They are bound
To criticize her every move, and be concerned only about her dowry.
Her parents-in-law will curse her, her husband will abuse her,
And whenever they open their mouth, they'll malign her parents.
When she cannot stand the stress and abuse any longer,
         She will
Return to her parental home to complain, weeping and crying,
         With the result
That her father is pained by pity, her mother all in a fix,
         And they will
Go back with her to her place and raise a terrible stink.
         But in the end,
'Once the cloth falls in a vat of blue dye, it'll never be white again,'
And their precious pearl has already fallen into the mud and mire.

Their daughter never can come home. This is the damage caused by having daughters.

         And so it is said:
'When she enters the bridal sedan, she enters the grave.'"

Cheng Huiying was also the author of a collection of poetry, *Songs of Lament by the Northern Window* (*Beichuang yingao*), as we learn from the following brief notice:

Cheng Huiying [style name Chenchou] from Yanghu is the author of *Songs of Lament by the Northern Window*. She was poor and made a living as a lady school-teacher. She also wrote the plucking rhymes text *Phoenixes Flying Together*. Her talent was so overflowing that at the time the price of paper went up.

The poems she wrote are pure in the expression of her life's experiences, and could never have been written by ordinary literary ladies. It is truly a memorable thing that the world of fiction has produced such a woman. Her poem entitled "Written at the End of *Phoenixes Flying Together*, for Yang Xiangwan," reads:

> To whom can I tell my heart's secrets of half a life?
> Let me use this frosty brush to reveal them to you.
> There is no need for tears and laughter to always fit the beat,
> Dare but speak your wrath and curses and you'll have a text!
> Deeds that will frighten even Heaven—dreams of autumn months,
> Sadness and joy that move the Earth—it's only clouds.
> I want this book to be opened only by a true friend,
> I would rather it be unknown by the common crowd.

Loyalty and Patriotism

One of the other plucking rhymes texts of the second half of the nine-teenth century that enjoyed an enduring popularity was Zhou Ying-fang's *Utter Loyalty* (*Jingzhong zhuan*). Zhou Yingfang (d. 1895) hailed from Hangzhou. Her mother Zheng Danruo, herself the author of a plucking rhymes text entitled *Dream Affinities* (*Mengying zhuan*), had died in 1860, when Hangzhou was overrun by the armies of the Taiping. Zhou Yingfang's husband, Yan Jin, attained the rank of prefect and died in 1865 in Guizhou province while fighting a local rebellion. She escorted her husband's coffin back home for burial, after which she de-voted the rest of her life to the writing of her plucking rhymes text on the life and death of Yue Fei (1103–1141), the famous general of the Southern Song dynasty. After many years of war against the Jürchen Jin dynasty, which in 1126 had conquered northern China and abducted Emperors Huizong and Qinzong, the Southern Song wanted to make peace with the Jürchen. Yue Fei, it was said, had been on the verge of reconquering the north and freeing the captive emperors, when he was summoned back to court. It was only his utter loyalty to the throne that persuaded him to obey the insistent summonses to return, even though he knew they were misguided. As soon as he returned to the capital, he was thrown in jail and subsequently murdered. In her *Utter Loyalty,* Zhou Yingfang describes the cosmic reverberations that accompanied Yue Fei's death:

> The colored clouds scattered, the moon sank in the west,
> The wild storms shook the earth and bellowed with rage.
> Rolling boulders and flying dust darkened heaven and earth,
> And the darkened candles filled everyone with terror.
> The Great Wall, the whole world, bereft of its ruler,
> Mt. Tai, that holy mountain, collapsed, the earth's power lost.
> His soul was carried aloft by cranes, "never, alas, to return!"
> His heroic energy melted away like the ice of spring.
> From then on rivers and mountains had to lose their color,
> With this rare man gone, the world was left without heroes.
> > Was it because
> Of Heaven's envy of his perfect talent and wisdom?
> > As it turns out
> This was the end of his merits that topped even Heaven.
> > Alas,
> His desire to free the emperors thwarted by traitors,
> > Alas,
> This jade pillar, this Great Wall, this night has been slain!

Yue Fei was buried on the banks of Hangzhou's West Lake. His heroic life and tragic death soon became the subject of plays and novels and in later centuries he was venerated as a patron saint of loyalty, and, as such, his cult received the full support of the Manchu Qing court. In the perception of many of the Manchus' Chinese subjects, Yue Fei was also, or even primarily, a patriotic hero, whose brave struggle against foreign enemies was thwarted by traitors at court and a spineless emperor who placed his own comfort above national honor. With the resurgence of both anti-Manchu and anti-imperialist feelings in the final years of the nineteenth century and the first decades of the twentieth,

Yue Fei re-emerged as an icon of this new Chinese nationalism. While Zhou Yingfang may have written her *Utter Loyalty* to drum up support for the tottering Manchu Qing dynasty for which her husband had given his life, in fact, her work was published and read as an expression of Chinese patriotism.

EPILOGUE
Nationalism and Feminism: Qiu Jin

16 · The Beheaded Feminist: Qiu Jin

Whereas many women writers of the eighteenth and nineteenth centuries wrote about women who disguised themselves as men in order to perform great deeds, Qiu Jin (1875–1907) not only actually dressed as a man but was also an active participant in the revolutionary movements of early twentieth-century China. The political realities of the final decade of the Manchu Qing dynasty, however, turned out to be far less accommodating than the fictional world of drama and plucking rhymes. When Qiu Jin, together with her revolutionary comrades, attempted to stage an armed uprising, she was arrested by the authorities and on July 15, 1907, she was executed by beheading.

Qiu Jin's life and works exemplify the end of the tradition of Chinese women's literature of the imperial period. She started out by writing in the traditional "feminine" mode, but in the course of her revolutionary activities, came to reject, at least theoretically, both traditional social conventions and traditional modes of women's writing. Nevertheless, while she did her best to acquire a more modern and more practical education during a stay in Japan, and while she plunged into various kinds of educational, editorial, and revolutionary activities upon her return to China, she often found herself making use of traditional forms of women's writing to spread the new message of nationalism and feminism among her female friends and women in general. It was not until the appearance of a new generation of feminists and women writers, soon after the establishment of the Republic of China in 1912, that these traditional forms would be finally abandoned.

Poet and Nationalist

Qiu Jin was born to a Shaoxing family with a long tradition of official service. Her great-grandfather served in several localities as magistrate, and eventually attained the rank of prefect. Her grandfather, also a prefect, was in charge of the coastal defense of Xiamen (Amoy) in southern Fujian, one of China's first treaty ports. Xiamen was also the place where Qiu Jin was born. Her father passed the provincial examinations and made a living by serving as private secretary for a number of high officials. His work took him and his family to places as distant from one another as Changsha and Taiwan. Despite the family's somewhat peripatetic existence, Qiu Jin enjoyed a good education, which included horse riding and fencing.

In the mid-1890s, Qiu Jin's father served in a secretarial post in the central province of Hunan, which at the time was one of China's most progressive regions. Here he married his daughter off to Wang Tingjun, the youngest son of the rich merchant Wang Fuchen, who was related through marriage to the well-known reformer, Zeng Guofan (1811–1872). Zeng had risen to become one of the most powerful officials in the empire, largely thanks to the part he played in the suppression of the Taiping Tianguo rebellion, which swept through central China in the years 1849–1863. Zeng's locally-raised troops had succeeded in quelling the rebels where the regular armies of the Qing dynasty had failed. Afterwards, Zeng Guofan held high positions in the government and took an active role in the military modernization of China. His relatives and friends continued to occupy important positions in China's political and economic life well into the twentieth century.

The Taiping rebellion, led by a leader who claimed to be the younger brother of Jesus Christ, was only one example of how the destabilizing influence of imperialism made itself felt in China. Following the Opium War (1839–1842), in which China had been defeated by Great Britain, China had been forced to open five cities to foreign trade. These so-called treaty ports included Canton, Xiamen, and Shanghai. The resulting shifts in trade routes led to large-scale unemployment in the Canton hinterland, which together with an economy that was suffering from the effects of rapid population growth and soil exhaustion, created the breeding ground for the Taiping rebellion. This rebellion was one of many in the middle decades of the nineteenth century that nearly brought about the fall of the Qing dynasty. Weakened internally, the Qing dynasty had to give in to the growing demands of the Western imperialist powers (soon joined by Japan) for ever greater freedom and flexibility with regard to trade, exploration, and missionary activity. Confronted with the superior technology of the West, a small but growing number of Chinese intellectuals began to devote themselves to "Western studies" in order to better understand the sources of Western power. Initially these studies focused on military technology, but soon they expanded to include all of the sciences as well as foreign languages. The discomfort over the relative discrepancy between East and West in terms of technological development turned into a deepening conviction of critical backwardness, however, when the "Great Qing Empire" was soundly defeated by its eastern neighbor, the traditionally despised "Japanese dwarfs," in the Sino-Japanese War of 1894–1895, a military engagement that resulted in China having to cede Taiwan to the Japanese.

After this, the ruling Manchus began to be blamed by ever-widening segments of the Chinese population for China's international weakness and internal stagnation. It was feared that soon China would be cut up like a melon and divided amongst the imperialist powers, an anxiety that was fed by the social Darwinism popular with both reformers and revolutionaries of the time. Social Darwinism interpreted the process of world history as a struggle of race against race, in which only the fittest race would survive. The Chinese intellectuals of the early years of the twentieth century took the fate of American Indians and African Negroes as a dire warning: unless the Chinese race renewed itself, it would be either annihilated by the white race or reduced to slavery or colonial serfdom. An important component of the resulting yearning for cultural and political renewal entailed questioning the traditional position of women in society, and reformist male intellectuals such as Kang Youwei (1858–1927) and Liang Qichao (1873–1929) began to take the lead in this effort. Kang Youwei and his supporters were given a chance to implement some of their ideas when in 1898 the Guangxu emperor (r. 1875–1907) came of age and took over the reigns of power from the and empress dowager Cixi, who had dominated court politics for decades, stepped down. Kang Youwei's reforms, however, so angered some of the more conservative elements of the court, that after only a hundred days, the empress dowager staged a coup d'état and imprisoned the young emperor.

Following this debacle, Kang Youwei and Liang Qichao were forced to flee China. From his base in Japan, Liang Qichao in particular became an extremely influential publicist, and lashed out against the illiteracy of Chinese women and the custom of footbinding. His argument was that ignorant and deformed mothers would never be able to bear and raise healthy and intelligent soldiers for the nation, and that their ignorance and immobility condemned them to a parasitical existence that was of no benefit whatsoever to society as a whole. While Liang Qichao did admit that at least some Chinese elite women were not only literate but also active as poets and scholars, he totally denied, as early as 1897, the social relevance of this traditional form of female literacy, which he contrasted unfavorably with the more tangible social utility of, for example, the medical education undertaken by Kang Aide (Kang Cheng, Ida Kahn, 1873–1930), one of China's first American-trained female physicians. In the view of men such as Liang Qichao, the emancipation of Chinese women came to be seen as a necessary condition for the regeneration of the Chinese race and the Chinese nation. But, by the same token, since women's emancipation and nationalism were so completely interconnected, a complete emancipation of Chinese women would have to wait for the reassertion of Chinese nationhood.

It is not quite clear when Qiu Jin first came in contact with this feminist and nationalist discourse, although after she had left her husband, she would write to her brother that from the very start she had experienced marriage as a kind of double slavery: all Chinese were the slaves of the Manchus, and as a wife she was the slave of her husband. Qiu Jin's earliest preserved poetry, however, shows little sign of such precocious awareness, and her poems on flowers and trees and spring days and autumn rains for the most part reflect the traditional styles and moods of the women's poetry of the time. One of her earliest preserved lyrics reads as follows and may have been written while she was living in her hometown of Shaoxing:

To the Melody of "Midnight Song" (*Ziyege*)
Cold Food Festival

The Day of Flowers has now passed, again it's Cold Food:[1]
Nothing is more wearisome than the season of Spring!
Outside the window, the grass is like mist,
Inside my room, I'm too lazy to roll up the screens.

Crimson peach-blossoms blaze along the river,
Verdant bamboo smile against the wind.
Oriole and swallow who know not sorrow,
Together swoop and fly around the little tower.

One of Qiu Jin's earliest preserved poems dates from her first stay in Hunan province:

Written on the Occasion of My Departure from Changde: Traveling by Boat, I Am Filled with Emotion

Since leaving the river city, I've been filled with a hundred emotions!
When it comes to friendship, who is there to compare to Wang Lun?[2]
And even he lacks the depth of feeling of the willows along the dike:
They cannot keep themselves from seeing me off even from afar!

The following poems were written while Qiu Jin was living in Xiangtan and date from the earliest years of her marriage:

A Record of a Visit to a Garden in Bloom, Four Poems

I

A woman neighbor sent me a letter inviting me on a garden outing,
Tomorrow, she said, we'll have clear skies, no doubt about that!
So last night I laid out ahead of time everything I would wear:
Tiny shoes with phoenix heads, a blouse of embroidered gauze.

---

1. The Day of Flowers was celebrated on the twelfth (or fifteenth) of the Second Month; the festival of Cold Food fell on the one hundred and fifth day after the shortest day of the year.

2. Wang Lun is referred to in one of Li Bai's best-known poems as a man whose friendship is more than a thousand feet deep.

II

On winding paths our pendants tinkle, the fragrant grass so thick!
Hand in hand we cross together to the east side of the bridge.
This particular stretch of flowing water lacks any feeling at all:
Instead of carrying off our sorrows, it carries off the fallen reds!

III

In the deepest shade of the willows a yellow oriole chants,
The fragrant grasses grow lushly, their green fills the dike.
Pointing and smiling: "Whose house has the finest pavilions?"
"A screen of pearls rolled up aslant, a crab apple branch."

IV

The western neighbor also comes to visit the garden in bloom,
As hand in hand we walk amidst flowers, she says with a smile:
"Yesterday you visited the Shrine of the Royal Tutor Jia Yi,
And today I ascend the Terrace of Prince Ding of Changsha."[3]

Visiting Again a Spot I Had Visited Before, I Mused on the Speed with Which Time Passes, an Impromptu Poem

Last year I came here once to visit the garden in bloom,
Hand in hand we trod on the verdant moss by the dike.
Chatting together we admired the variety of flowers,
A communion soon replaced by the pain of parting.
 I wrote my sorrows on the wall: the poem is still there,
We set a date, but she's yet to return from the inner quarters.

---

3. The Shrine of the Royal Tutor Jia Yi and the Terrace of Prince Ding are both famous landmarks and tourist spots in Changsha. Jia Yi (201–169 BCE) quickly rose to prominence at court during the early decades of the Han dynasty, but his farsighted proposals for reform angered the authorities. He was banished to Changsha, in those days a southern outpost of the empire, where he served as a tutor to the local prince. Unaccustomed to the tropical climate, Jia Yi soon fell ill and died, but not before he had written a number of poems in which he tried to express, and thereby transcend, his deep frustration over his fate. Prince Ding was a Han dynasty prince who, when he took up residence at his fief in Changsha, was so filled with longing for his mother that he had a terrace built from which he could gaze toward the capital where she lived.

All alone I am lost in thought, how I long for a friend.
In this garden, I regret that I lack the talents of Zuo Fen.

While poems like these do not show much evidence of a nascent feminism, they do testify to an urgent desire for female friendship. The following quatrain about Xie Daoyun may perhaps be read as a commentary on Qiu Jin's own unhappy marriage:

> Singing of willow floss, her words so quick-witted:
> All that is vulgar swept away by her pure talent!
> What a pity that Xie Daoyun
> Did not marry Adjutant Bao![4]

Qiu Jin bore her husband a son and a daughter (who would grow up to become China's first female aviator) and in no later than 1903 followed him to Beijing, where he had acquired an official post. The Beijing of the early twentieth century still showed the scars of the combined destruction wrought first by the Boxers, and then by the allied armies of eight imperialist powers led by Germany. The Boxers originated in northern China and formed a movement that combined religious teachings with the practice of martial arts; later, convinced of their invulnerability, they turned against Western missionaries together with their churches and their converts. The Manchu court, dominated once again by the formidable empress dowager Cixi, first tried to suppress the Boxers, but then, in 1900, turned around and enlisted their help in order to attack the foreign legations, which resulted in a siege that lasted for fifty-five days. When the foreign powers retaliated, the empress dowager and the Guangxu emperor fled to Xi'an, and Beijing was looted by the allied troops. Eventually, the empress dowager and the emperor were allowed to return to Beijing, but only after they had agreed to pay huge indemnities to the foreign powers, and to allow them to station their troops in Beijing in order to protect the foreign legations.

While in Beijing, Qiu Jin avidly read the impassioned nationalist publications put out in Japan by Liang Qichao and other exiled reformists, and soon her own poetry began to reflect this nationalistic spirit as well. An example of this is her "Song of the Precious Sword."

---

4. Adjutant Bao here refers to the famous poet Bao Zhao (d. 466), the brother of the woman poet Bao Linghui.

The palaces of the house of Han in the light of the setting sun:
After more than five thousand years the old nation has died—
For over hundreds of years it has been sunk in a deep sleep,
No one aware of our shameful state of slavery!

Long ago, I recall, our very first ancestor Xianyuan
Rose to power from his base in the Kunlun Mountains.
He opened up the lands of the Yellow and Yangzi Rivers,
And his flashing great sword pacified the Central Plain.

My bitter weeping over Plum Hill is completely useless:
The imperial city overgrown, the bronze camels buried.[5]
Whenever I am moved to turn and gaze upon the capital,
The sad song of a defeated nation fills my eyes with tears.

When the allied troops of the eight powers marched north,
We again handed our mountains and rivers over to others.
Those white devils coming from the West served as a bell,
That woke us Chinese up from our slaves' dream!

You, my lord, gave me this gold-speckled sword,
Today as I receive it, my mind is virile and brave.
These are the days when red-hot iron rules,
And a million heads are not worth a feather.

Bathed by the sun and moon, shinier than jewels:
Risking my life, I am suddenly filled with elation.
I swear I'll find a way to lead us from death to life:
World peace now depends on military armament.

Don't you recall Jing Ke's visit to the court of Qin?
When the map was unrolled, the dagger appeared!
Although he failed to stab him there in his palace,
He still managed to rob that evil tyrant of his soul!

---

5. In the late third century Suo Jing predicted the destruction of the capital Luoyang by pointing at the bronze camels in front of the imperial palace and sighing: "I will see you overgrown by weeds."

I personally long to save the land of my ancestors,
But a race of slaves has overrun the land of Yu.
What can one do about those whose hearts have died?
With brush in hand, I write the "Song of the Precious Sword."
 May this "Song of the Precious Sword" strengthen their courage,
And bring back many souls from the land of the dead.!
A precious sword, heroic bones: who is our equal?
All my life I've known who are my enemies and friends.
Don't despise this foot-long iron for not being brave:
The rare merit of saving the nation is yours to garner!
 Could I but use heaven and earth as my oven, and yin and yang as my
  coal, and gathering all the iron of the six continents,
Produce thousands, ten thousands of precious swords to purify this
  sacred land,
And continuing the glorious power and fame of our first ancestor, the
  Yellow Emperor,
Cleanse once and for all what, in its thousand-, its hundred-year-long
  history, has been its vilest shame!

This poem, one of the many works that reflect her lifelong obsession with swords, can be read as Qiu Jin's personal nationalist credo. China's long history and its glorious past under the rule of the mythic founders of the Chinese polity (Xianyuan, the Yellow Emperor, and Yu) is contrasted to the present situation in which the Chinese are the willing slaves of the Manchus, who in their turn bow and scrape before the foreign powers. The Chinese people, writes the poet, are as if asleep, unaware of their humiliating condition, and must be woken up before they are completely annihilated. Plum Hill (or Coal Hill, Meishan) behind the Forbidden City in Beijing marks the spot where in 1644 the Chongzhen emperor, the last emperor of the Chinese Ming dynasty, hanged himself when the capital was overrun by peasant rebels (who were later ousted by the Manchus). Jing Ke was a famous assassin who, in 227 BCE, made an attempt on the life of Ying Zheng (259–210 BCE), the cruel king of the state of Qin. Jing Ke, acting on behalf of the crown prince of the threatened state of Yan, was unsuccessful in his attempt to kill the king, who later became the First Emperor of Qin, and lost his life. Jing Ke thereafter became the symbol of someone willing to lay down his life for a higher cause, and as such, had a special significance for the revolutionaries of the early twentieth century.

In Beijing, the strained relationship between Qiu Jin and her husband quickly deteriorated (he wanted to buy a concubine; she attended meetings outside the house in Western-style men's clothing), and Qiu Jin found her female condition increasingly irksome, as can be seen in the following lyric, which she wrote to the melody of "Full River Red" (*Man-jianghong*):

> Recently I've come to the capital,
> And already it is again the fine Festival of Mid-Autumn.
> The chrysanthemums are in full bloom below the hedge,
> The countenance of autumn is as clean as if just dusted.
> With songs being sung all around them, Chu finally met defeat,
> My experiences of these eight years all a hopeless yearning for Zhejiang.
> Alas, they sent me off by force to be mere "rouge and powder,"
> The last thing I wanted!
>
> My body will not allow me
> To mingle with the men,
> But my heart is far braver
> Than that of a man.
> All my life, has not my liver and gall
> Burned for others?
> But how could they with their vulgar minds understand me?
> In adversity the hero must suffer troubles and woes.
> Where in this world of red dust can I find a true friend?
> My blue gown is soaked with tears.

The line "With songs being sung all around them, Chu finally met defeat" is an allusion to one of the most famous incidents in early Chinese history. Following the collapse of the Qin dynasty, the two main contenders for the imperial throne were the aristocratic southern general Xiang Yu, the hegemonic ruler of Western Chu, who had yet to be defeated in battle, and the sly peasant Liu Bang, who would eventually become the founder of the Han dynasty. On the eve of the final battle between these two men, Zhang Liang, one of Liu Bang's many capable advisors, suggested that the troops of the Han should encircle Xiang Yu's encampment and sing southern songs. When Xiang Yu's troops heard these songs, they assumed that they were being sung by men from the south whose home districts had been conquered by Liu Bang. Believing that this meant that their homes in the south had been vanquished, they then defected en masse, forcing Xiang Yu to concede defeat and commit suicide. Qiu Jin may have used this allusion to refer to the defeat of China in the Sino-Japanese War, but given the following line, in which the author expresses her longing for her maternal home, it is more likely that she is saying that, like Xiang Yu, she has been tricked into defeat—in her case, the defeat of marriage to someone she regarded as her social and intellectual inferior.

One advantage of the large foreign presence in Beijing was that it enabled Qiu Jin to come into contact with Japanese women, from whom she learned about the women's movement that had been gathering momentum in Japan since the last years of the nineteenth century. The following lyric was written by Qiu Jin for one of her Japanese women friends:

To the Melody of "Walking through the Sedge-Grass" (*Tasuoxing*)

Facing the mirror I mumble and murmur,
Sighing and sobbing, I write in the air.[6]
It is not a headache of wine or woes of parting:
A prison of sorrow has been raised in my heart,
There is none to whom I can explain this feeling.

My ambition is manly,
My life is too narrow,
To no avail is my mind filled with heroic daring!
Let me question High Heaven about my bad fate:
Although a mere woman, I suffer like the poet Qu Yuan!

Qiu Jin's relationship with her husband ("That unreliable, immoral, whoring and gambling liar and cheat, who will harm others to profit himself and abuses his relatives, that conceited and arrogant no-good playboy reeking of money," as she described him in one of the letters she later

---

6. After the fourth-century general Yin Hao was defeated in battle, he is said to have spent the rest of his life tracing the character *kong* ("emptiness," "in vain") in the air.

wrote to her brother) finally reached a breaking point and she decided to go and study in Tokyo. She tried to get some money together by selling what jewelry had not been stolen by her husband, and also made a short fundraising trip to Shaoxing and Shanghai. She was, however, greatly disappointed by the political apathy that she encountered in the mercantile metropolis of Shanghai:

An Inscription on a Wall in Shanghai

By boat I crossed the sea and returned once again to the South,
After staying a while in Shanghai, my hopes have been dashed:
Amidst the dust of horse-drawn carriages true friends are rare,
The music of rapid strings and shrill pipes lacks proper notes.
 Do they ever shed tears, impassioned by the political situation?
They only compete in luxury, flaunting their evening dresses!
The vulgarity that fills one's eyes gives rise to unending sorrow:
Like the daily downward flow of a river, society is on the decline.

Completely disillusioned, Qiu Jin left Shanghai and traveled by steamboat to Tianjin. She left us a record of what for her was clearly an exhilarating experience in the following two poems:

A Trip by Steamboat, Two Poems

I

Looking around me, not a shore to be seen:
The wide open sea truly a feast for the eyes.
The ship crosses it faster than a flying bird,
The mountains coil round like fierce dragons.
 The myriads of crashing billows resound,
A thousand peaks gather below the clouds.
Amidst the endless expanse of water and mist,
Thoughts of home cause my furrowed brow.

II

Water and sky share the same color,
Like a tower, a single peak soars high.
Gazing afar, the mind grows elated,
Through the porthole, an expansive view.
 Silvery billows rise up like cliffs,

> The dark sea makes one shiver with cold.
> But soon the imperial province grows near,
> So do not sing *The Road is Hard to Travel*!

After settling her affairs in Beijing, Qiu Jin then sailed from Tianjin in late June of 1904, arriving in Tokyo on the third of July.

Student and Feminist

While in the last decade of the nineteenth century and the first decade of the twentieth century there were a few Chinese students who traveled to Europe or America to study, a far larger number went to Japan. Japan's successful modernization in the Meiji years (1868–1912) demonstrated that an Asian nation could beat the Western powers at their own game, and so Chinese students flocked to Japan to learn from her experience. Although the overwhelming majority of Chinese students were men, there were a few women as well. Many of the women were quite involved in various student activities, including the numerous student publications that circulated during this period. These women wanted to be more than just good mothers of citizens in the modern nation-state to come; they wanted to be full-fledged citizens themselves. They took their inspiration from Mulan, who in publications of the first decade of the twentieth century was transformed from a filial daughter into a patriotic fighter defending her Chinese motherland against foreign encroachment. But they also modeled themselves on non-Chinese women such as Sofia Perovskaya (1853–1881) and Madame Rolland (Jeanne Manon Philipon, 1754–1793). Sofia Perovskaya, who had been condemned to death and executed for her part in the murder of Czar Alexander II, had become the subject of an (unfinished) Chinese novel as early as 1902. Madame Rolland had played, together with her husband, a major role in the early years of the French Revolution and died under the guillotine in 1793, only to be revived in China in 1904 as the heroine of a short plucking rhymes text entitled *The Female Hero from France* (*Faguo nü yingxiong tanci*). Encouraged in part by the public outcry that had followed the execution of these Western revolutionary heroines, some of the modern Chinese female students did not hesitate to make use of the old and proven means of public suicide to dramatize their objections against both Manchu rule and the traditional order.

Upon her arrival in Tokyo, Qiu Jin first enrolled in a Japanese language school, and then later entered a teacher's college. A large part of her time in Japan, however, was taken up by her revolutionary activities. The American sinologist Mary Backus Rankin summarizes her life in this period as follows: "She dressed in men's clothing, carried a short sword, practiced bomb-making and marksmanship." Qiu Jin also became acquainted with some of the leaders of the revolutionary movement residing in Japan, and joined several revolutionary organizations.

During her years in Tokyo, Qiu Jin showed a particular interest in the "new" art of public speaking as a means of reaching larger groups of (largely illiterate) women. Her lecture, *An Address to My Two Hundred Million Women Compatriots in China*, published in October 1904, may well represent the most systematic exposition of her feminist views:

Alas, the most unfair treatment in the entire world is suffered by us, my two hundred million women compatriots. And this is true from the moment we are born: if you have a good father, things may still be all right, but if your father is a muddleheaded, unreasonable type, he will only keep shouting: "What bad luck! Yet another useless one!" And he will want to snatch you and crush you to death! With the thought constantly in mind of the saying "Later she will belong to another family," they will treat you harshly and with disdain. As soon as you are a few years old, they will, completely ignoring the consequences, take your snow-white and so very tender natural feet and bind them tightly with white linen—even when you are asleep, you will not be allowed to loosen them even the tiniest bit! Eventually all the flesh will rot away and the bones will be broken, just so that relatives, friends, and neighbors may say: "Such-and-such little girl has such tiny feet!"

And that is not the worst of it! When it comes to selecting a marriage partner, they will completely rely on the words of two shameless matchmakers. As long as the family of the groom has money and power, they don't care whether or not he is from a respectable family, and without knowing whether the groom's character is good or bad or whether his scholarship is wide-ranging, they will agree to the match. When it comes to the day of the wedding, they will force you to sit inside a gaudy red and green sedan chair, and you will hardly be able to breathe. When you arrive [at the home of the groom] if you have good fortune from a former life you will be allowed to enjoy it in this life if the fellow is a decent sort, even if he is nothing special. But if you've been married off to a good-for-nothing, all they'll have to say is: "That is your bad karma from a former life," if not: "That's just your bad luck." If you utter even a few words of complaint or say a few words of reproof to your husband, they'll change their tune, and you'll be beaten and cursed. When outsiders hear about it, they'll just say: "She's stupid and does not understand the Wifely Way." Dear listeners, is this not a case of suffering an injustice and having nowhere to lodge a complaint?

There is also still another unfair matter. When a man dies, a woman is forced to dress in mourning for three years, and she is not allowed to marry again. But when a woman dies, the man may braid a few blue threads into his queue, but some men find this to be very unattractive and will not even do that. Before their wife has been dead for three days, they will go out and visit prostitutes, and before the "sevens" are over,[7] a new wife will have already entered the gate.

When High Heaven originally gave birth to humankind, there was no discrimination between men and women. Let me ask you, if there were no women in this world, who would give birth to man? So why this injustice? Those men who day in and day out yammer on about: "The mind is fair, we should treat people fairly," why do they treat women as if they were Negroes from Africa?[8] And how is it that things have become so unfair?

Dear listeners, you have to realize that in this world it does not do to be dependent on others, you must rely on yourselves! When long ago those rotten Confucians started to spout such nonsense as "Man is lofty, woman lowly," "In women a lack of talent makes for virtue," and "The husband is the yardstick to his wife," we women should have had the guts to mobilize our comrades and oppose them. And when the Last Ruler of the Chen dynasty began the practice of footbinding,[9] we should have been shamed into raising an army and routing out that villain! But nothing like that happened—how is it that we bind our own feet whenever someone else wants to shackle our legs?

Men are afraid that if we acquire understanding and knowledge, we will climb up over their heads, and so they do not allow us to study. Why is it that we obey them and do not oppose them? It is all because we women have ourselves abdicated our responsibilities. Whatever it was, as soon as we saw that the men were there to take care of it, we ourselves were content to be lazy and take it easy. If men say we are of no use, then we are of no use. If men say we are no good,

---

7. In Buddhist funerary practice, sutra readings for the benefit of the soul of the deceased were held on every seventh day after death, up until the forty-ninth day.

8. The Chinese translation of Harriet Beecher Stowe's *Uncle Tom's Cabin* had a huge impact on Chinese intellectuals in the first decade of the twentieth century.

9. Chen Shubao, known as the Last Ruler of the Chen dynasty (r. 582–589), is well known for his indulgence in women and song, but the beginnings of the custom of footbinding are more commonly traced back to Li Yu, known as the Last Ruler of the Southern Tang dynasty.

then we are happy to be their slaves and ask no questions as long as our present comfort is assured. And as we increasingly "enjoy emoluments without meriting them," we become afraid that they may not last forever. So as soon as we learn that men are fond of tiny feet, we rush like crazy to bind them, so that men will be pleased when they see them, and in this way, we hope we can continue to be fed without having to work. If they don't want us to learn to read and write, that is an even greater blessing—of course we are all in favor of it!

Dear listeners, just think it over: is there anyone in the entire world who is entitled to enjoy ready-made happiness? Of course it is the men who have studied, who are learned, who work as hard as they can, and who have all the power, and so we have become their slaves. And since we are their slaves, of course we suffer oppression! But since we ourselves are to blame, how can we carry a grudge against others? I myself also feel bad just talking about these things. But you must have all experienced the same thing, so there is no need for me to elaborate.

But I hope that from now on we sisters will do away with the state of affairs from the past and exert ourselves to create new circumstances. It is as if we had died and been reborn as human beings. Those of you who are advanced in years should not say: "I am old and of no use." If you have a good husband who wants to establish a modern school, you should not stop him, and if you have a worthy son who wants to study overseas, you should not stop him. Those of you in your twenties and thirties who are wives should not be a millstone around your husbands' necks, placing all sorts of obstructions in their way and making it hard for them to succeed in their work or achieve fame. If you have a son, you should send him to a modern school, and you should do the same with your daughters—and on no account should you bind your daughters' feet! As for you young girls, it would be best if you would enroll in a school, but if you cannot go to a modern school, you should incessantly read books and practice writing at home. You wives of men who are rich or who hold official posts should urge your husbands to establish modern schools and factories and to take initiatives that will benefit the common people. You who are married to men without money should support your husbands in their labors and not spend your days in idleness, dining on unearned food. This is my hope.

Dear listeners, do you realize that our nation is about to perish? Men cannot be sure of their own survival, so how can we continue to rely on them? If we do not lift ourselves up now, it will truly be too late once the nation has perished. Dear listeners, do not let me down!

Qiu Jin, more than many other women writers of the time, stressed the need for women to acquire marketable skills and achieve economic independence, not only so that they would no longer be a burden on society, but also, and primarily, so that they might achieve true independence for themselves.

The themes that are touched upon in the "Song of the Precious Sword" and in the above lecture recur in many of the writings that Qiu Jin produced while in Japan. Her view was that China was like a sinking ship, and it was the duty of all of China's citizens to willingly sacrifice their lives in order to save the nation. Above all, she felt that women could play a major role in this work of liberation only if they freed themselves from old ways of thinking and old customs (such as footbinding) and allowed themselves to be inspired by examples of female military commanders from the past such as Qin Liangyu (d. 1648) and Shen Yunying (1624–1661). Qiu Jin's poetry makes frequent use of modern neologisms, which shows the influence of the "poetry revolution" of the last decade of the Qing dynasty, when many reformist and revolutionary writers tried to revitalize the conventional literary forms by writing on subjects "never before attempted in rhyme."

Filled with Emotion (Written during My Stay in Japan)

Sun and moon have grown dim, heaven and earth have grown dark.
But who is there to save the deeply submerged world of women?
I have pawned my hairpins and my rings to travel over the ocean,
Taking leave of my own flesh and blood, I left China behind.
 Unbinding my feet, I washed away a thousand years of poison,
Filled with hot blood, I summon the souls of the hundred flowers.
Alas, my scarf woven of mermaid-silk
Is half-soaked by blood and half by tears.

Song of a Red-Haired Barbarian's Sword[10]

A single expanse of autumn water flashing pure and slender:
Seen from afar it's hard to tell it is the gleam of a sword.
I'm amazed at this jade-white dragon hidden in its sheath:
Once it rides on wind and thunder, it soars beyond the clouds![11]

---

10. "Red-haired barbarian" was an epithet initially used to refer specifically to the Dutch "barbarians," but which came to be used as a general designation for all Westerners.

11. Swords are often said to be the transformations of dragons.

This sharp blade, I'm told, comes from the Red-Haired Barbarians,
Damascus and Japan to their shame have failed to produce its equal.
When it is dipped in blood it causes joints and bones to come apart,
Severing heads even before weapons have come into contact.
 When this sword is drawn from its sheath, then heaven shakes,
And sun and moon, stars and planets quickly obscure their light.
The ocean's waters are roused by the sound of it hitting the earth,
And the dark winds howl when an inch of its blade is exposed.
 How many have come face-to-face with this sword?
Their skulls form a mountain, their blood rises in billows.
The million souls of the slain weep at the tip of this sword,
With this sword in hand you can rob and kill the whole world.
 If you take it out, hang it on the wall, and for a time leave it unused,
It will wail and sob night after night making the cries of an owl:
Its heroic spirit thirsts to drink the blood of battle,
Just as a restless heart needs a libation of wine.
 Red-Haired Barbarians, don't be so proud and arrogant!
Your weapon may indeed be sharp, but I will toss it away:
Self-strengthening depends on people and not on weapons,
What is there to boast about a single puny little sword?

To the Melody of "Full River Red" (*Manjianghong*)

In this ugly and dirty world
How many men, I ask you, are heroic and wise?
Only from the ranks of those with painted eyebrows
From time to time do stalwarts emerge!
The memory of Qin Liangyu's fame soaks my gown with tears,
At the thought of Shen Yunying's deeds my heart starts to pound.
Tipsy, I stroke my long sword, which cries like a dragon,
Its voice stifled by sadness.

The incense of liberty
Is what I want to burn.
When can I wash away
The shame of the nation?
I urge those of you present here
To exert yourself to the utmost.
Be fired by the desire to ensure the future of your race,

Prosperity does not depend on showing off your jewels.
These bow-like shoes, three inches long, condemn us to inaction:
This must change!

To the Melody of "Watching the Tide" (*Wang haichao*) Seeing Off the Two Sisters Chen Yan'an and Sun Duokun on Their Return to China

Beset with emotion at our parting,
Moved to tears by the age we live in:
Internal weakness and foreign aggression together wreak havoc.
The political situation is alarming,
The stranded ship fills me with fear,
But why do our countrymen remain so befuddled and foolish?
At this thought my heart flutters.
I envy you for having left before me,
Cutting through the waves and riding the wind.
Just half a month we lived together,
As we now hurriedly take our leave I heave a sigh.

At this moment we each go our different ways—
Now that you are returning home, I am sure,
You will revive the old and sick.
The thirst for knowledge is awakened,
Our rights have not yet been recovered.
You will, I hope, apply yourself to changing outdated customs,
And ensure that the study of how to reform the rotten may flourish!
Thanks to your marvelous eloquence
You'll enlighten the blind and shake up the deaf.
And call out to the millions of our sisters
To pay heed to the bell that announces the last watch!

To the Melody of "Rivers and Mountains Like This" (*Ruci jiangshan*)

In her lonely study Xie Daoyun recites the *Rhapsody of Sorrow.*
How desolate, as the incessant rain drips down from the roof!
A true friend is hard to find,
Time flies by in an instant,

And the hair at my temples has started to gray.
I dare not complain of my sorrows:
At the end of the road as evening falls, I fear
I'll be alone in my sufferings.
This world, so sad and chill,
Alas, gave birth to me, a woman sad and chill!

If you tell me: "Go home!"
Where on earth is my home?
When I turn around and look,
My ancestral land is still snoring away as before:
Invaded by foreign aggression,
And corrupt and rotten within,
Without a manly hero to take the lead.
Heaven, you're so blind:
Can you bear to see these rivers and mountains
In the possession of foreign barbarians?
Divided up like beans, cut up like a melon—
It is all our land of old!

While in Japan, Qiu Jin also started work on a twenty-chapter plucking rhymes text, entitled *Stones of the Jingwei Bird* [*Jingwei shi*]. In early Chinese mythology, the *jingwei* bird was said to be the transformation of a princess who drowned in the sea, after which the bird angrily tries to fill the sea by dropping pebbles into the water. Qiu Jin only completed five chapters of this work, which was never published during her lifetime. The first chapter opens with a long indictment of the sorry state of affairs in the realm of Huaxu, with its snoozing emperor, its muddleheaded and myopic officials, and its domineering men:

> To my regret
> My country has now long had a reputation for its darkness,
> A heroic woman myself, I have the ambition but not the strength.
> There is nothing to be done, I can only bide my time,
> And grasp my brush and write the song of the Jingwei:
> Something to read for sisters who are of like mind,
> To be discussed after tea by the light of the lamp.

The story goes that in the East there was the realm of Huaxu,[12] which had been there now for no one knows how many years. All that is known about it is that the kings of this country were all surnamed Huang [Yellow], that they were honored as emperors of China, and that the throne had been passed down in a single unbroken line of succession. The earliest emperors of China had all been very heroic and enlightened men, but who would have guessed that later on, their sons and grandsons would by nature have a proclivity to sleep, a situation that would become worse with every succeeding generation. In the end there were emperors who were asleep all of the time and because they did not even know how to wake themselves up, occasionally they would remain in this state and end up sleeping their lives away until the day they died. The dragon throne would often be stolen and occupied by foreigners without the people of that country knowing about it. How could that be? This was because the officials inside and outside the court all suffered not only from muddleheadedness, but from extreme myopia. So, even when foreigners occupied the throne, they would day in and day out knock their heads against the floor, praising the emperor for being so heroic and enlightened, divine and martial, and so deeply humane and greatly beneficent that he nourished his subjects with the produce of the land and with a virtue as lofty as heaven and as rich as earth! Wagging their tails they would fawn and flatter him, without realizing that the court had been taken over by people of an alien race, who day in and day out oppressed the common people and ordinary folks of our own race by extracting provisions and increasing taxes, and who plotted for the privilege of autocracy, so they might live off the common people and order the officials about. But because the officials were thinking only about their own benefit and wanted to be able to hand down their official positions to their descendants, they would not hesitate to kill their own compatriots to please this alien race. If farsighted people who were not muddleheaded would accuse them [for having allowed the] foreigners to steal and occupy their land, these officials would pee in their pants in fear. And claiming that the accusers were committing a crime against nature, a crime of lèse-majesté, they would arrest them and have them executed. Anyone among the officials who was not muddleheaded and not nearsighted would find it impossible to keep his position. And strange to tell, it was evidently the case that as soon as a perfectly normal person took up an official career, he would for one reason or another begin to suffer from muddleheadedness and myopia. People who discussed this phenomenon concluded that the reason they had

---

12. "The realm of Huaxu," a mythic domain where all the people live a life of undisturbed happiness because they are always asleep, is an obvious reference to China.

begun to suffer from these diseases was that the desire for profit had obscured their minds and the stench of corruption dimmed their eyes. When the foreigners saw that these officials were all so muddleheaded, they all coveted their land, and this one cut off a piece here for himself, and that one took a piece there for himself. The lord and his ministers were completely unconcerned about this, and simply continued to enact their daily play and enjoy the charade of peace and prosperity. They did nothing but hunt down the patriots who were not muddleheaded and not nearsighted and have them killed. This, until recently, was the state of affairs in the Flowery Kingdom.

They had also upheld for many thousands of years the most inequitable, most unliberated and evil tradition of honoring men and denigrating women. All these men were able to do was come up with some primitive books [justifying this state of affairs] and practice their primitive oppression in order to keep women in fetters and ensure that they remained stupid. They contrived the saying: "In women, lack of talent makes for virtue," so that women would not read books and would lack any knowledge, as a result of which men could remain on top and be the boss. They even went so far as to look upon women as the slaves and cattle of men. They could not even conceive that by birth, men and women are equal as to their limbs and senses, their talent and understanding, and their intelligence and valor, and that they also have the same natural rights. But because the women never read books and never left the house to travel or to work, all they knew how to do was bury themselves in the inner chambers where they would grow old and die sitting there by their windows. They completely ignored their own abilities and allowed the men to occupy their superior positions and come up with ever more ways to suppress women. Tell me: isn't this disgusting?

> With their theories and tricks men deceive us,
> > Since they claim
> That Heaven established men's superiority over women.
> How can a woman speak about affairs outside the home?
> > Inside the home
> It is the rule that husbands should lead and wives follow.
> A woman is only admirable if she never leaves her room,
> Universal criticism will greet her words if they leave the house.
> In women a lack of talent is bound to ensure that she is virtuous,
> So it is not fitting that she should become literate and read books.
> A woman's place is in the kitchen preparing food and drink,
> Twisting hemp, weaving cloth, and sewing clothes.
> The Three Obediences have been her norm since ancient times,

The Four Virtues have always been her unchanging rule.
 A widowed woman should remain loyal to her husband,
But for a man there's no harm in having many wives.
There are also those who hate their wives for being principled,
And send them away, quoting the "seven reasons for divorce."[13]
 They cook up an obvious lie meant to deceive even Heaven,
　　　　　But all they want
Is that women have no recourse but to serve them meekly.
　　　　　And being afraid
That women might secretly come and overhear their schemes,
　　　　　They stipulate
That when descending the hall her girdle pendants should tinkle!
 A chaperone should always be at her side, so that she'll stay within
　　bounds;
And if she has to be on the streets by night, she should take with her a
　　lantern.
 And then there was that stupid Last Ruler of the Southern Tang,
Who acted in a reckless manner, and lacking all propriety.
　　　　　Once upon a time
Just for fun, he tightly bound up the feet of a consort,
Bound them into crescent moons: each step a lotus!
 As soon as this story entered the ears of those fools,
It delighted those people who love to torture women.
They claimed that bound feet were particularly lovely,
And that they alone lent women an elegant grace.
 Once this rumor got around, everyone adopted the custom:
When choosing a wife, they wanted one with small feet!
 And as women already had acquired the attitude of slaves,
And relied on their lord for a life of shame or glory,
When they learned of the fashion, they all bound their feet
With thin strips of linen, daily vying to be the most novel.
　　　　　Even though
A mother might look upon her child as her treasure,
　　　　　When it came to footbinding,
She simply ignored the pain of her darling daughter:
　　　　　With tear-filled eyes,

---

13. Chinese custom recognized seven valid reasons for a man to divorce his wife, one
of which was garrulousness!

When the girl would in vain implore her mother for mercy,
Her mother would treat her as if she were an arch-enemy!
 Wounding and maiming her own flesh and blood—how cruel!
She was like an executioner inflicting the punishment of amputation.
                    Alas! These girls—
Why did they have to suffer this mutilation at such a tender age?
A bloody mess of broken bones—they could hardly walk!

What a painful thought that these girls, once their feet had been bound, could do nothing but spend the day sitting in their rooms! They were unable to move about, and the things they were able to do before, they could no longer do because they could not use their feet to walk. They were truly like half-dead people: their faces became jaundiced and their flesh atrophied, while their joints and bones diminished in size. All day they sat like a dried-out tree trunk, and because their blood did not circulate through their veins, they easily contracted consumption. And even if they did not contract consumption, they lacked any strength in their limbs and all the joints in their body ached. If you look at those who suffer from "breath-pain disease,"[14] they are all women—you never hear of a man suffering from breath-pain disease. Women consider difficulties in childbirth, when their life can hang by a thread, to be dangerous. This too is all because of the damage caused by footbinding: because of it, the blood cannot flow and the frame of the body is stiff and not mobile. If you have natural feet, you can be constantly active, you will be free and independent, and you can manage your own affairs, and I assure you that you will not suffer from these sorts of diseases! I have never heard that in any other country, whether East or West, that there are so many women who die in childbirth. Nor have I ever heard of any foreign country in which they have the disease of breath-pain. This disease is found in only one country: China. This goes to show the endless damage caused by footbinding.

Why are our women willing to risk their lives and endure all that suffering for a pair of feet, to put up with every kind of pain, even to the point of having their bones broken? Often the diseases of women multiply by the hundreds and cannot be cured! But is it true that they cannot be cured? It is their own fault for considering themselves as totally worthless. They do not try to acquire a craft or knowledge of use to their own lives, they know only how to rely on men and devote their entire lives to serving them. They flatter men and try in a hundred ways to win their approval. As soon as they hear that men like small feet, they neglect their own lives, and begin to tightly bind their feet. After they have

---

14. "Breath-pain disease" is a specific condition in traditional Chinese medicine.

bound them with a two-meter-long strip of footbinding cloth, they wrap them with a piece of cloth. On top of that go the oh-so-tight pointed socks and oh-so-narrow shoes. As a result they have to seek support from a wall, each step requires three attempts, and even then, they cannot even move half an inch: they can do nothing but sit alone all day in their rooms like a lame invalid or ceramic doll. Even if you can make your husband love you after you have plastered your face with rouge and powder and dressed yourself in silk and gauze, he will regard you merely as a plaything and treat you as if you were a bird in a cage—you never will have the right to autonomy! Moreover, there is no guarantee that your husband really will love you forever just because you have small feet and know how to dress up. If after a time, he gets fed up with you, he can immediately marry someone else and neglect you, his wife, and completely ignore you. Then you will be as if condemned to the cold palace and locked up in Long Gate, and you'll sob and wail with grief, and each day will feel as long as a year. If you dare to complain, your husband can beat and curse you, and there will be no one to say he does not have the right to do so. If you complain to others, they will tell you to your face that you are a jealous woman who will not allow her husband his little pleasures and you will become a laughing-stock. And they will lock you up securely, as if you were a prisoner on death row, and then you will not be able to vent your suffering to anyone. Even if you die from rage or are subjected to violence, there will be no one around anywhere to lend a word of sympathy!

If, in addition to all of this, you have an evil mother-in-law, she will feel as though with every daughter-in-law another inmate has been added to her prison; or she will act as though she were from the American South and had acquired one more black slave: she will abuse you in all sorts of ways and make sure that you have no human life at all! If her son should commit a crime, she will always blame her daughter-in-law, and if something goes missing, she will claim that it has been stolen by her daughter-in-law who has taken it to her own mother's place. If her son has always been a never-do-well and good-for-nothing, she will claim that her son has always been a fine boy but that he began to be led astray as soon as her daughter-in-law showed up. If the family loses money in business or if someone dies—whenever something bad happens—it will be because the daughter-in-law is fated to bring misfortune. To her, you will be like a nail in the eye and a thorn in the flesh, and she will not rest until she has caused your death. She will urge her son to abuse his wife and torture her to death. After all, you are not her own flesh and blood, so she has no feelings for you. As soon as you have been lowered into your grave, the matchmaker will be invited, and within just a brief time a new bride will enter the room to replace the one who died. These men always regard women as playthings, as cattle, and for them it is quite normal to discard an old wife upon finding a new one. If they act this way while you are alive, it goes without saying how they will act upon your death. If today they still lament your passing, tomorrow they will have a new bride like jade. When will they ever show the slightest sympathy or marital love? They even have the saying: "There's no worse luck than a wife who doesn't die within three years." There is no need here even to speak of the fate of child brides who suffer all sorts of horrible beatings: no one knows how many of them die as victims of abuse.

This then is the cruel world of women. This is all because women do not make arrangements for a field of study or a craft that will allow them to make a living for themselves. It is because they specialize in binding their feet and dressing themselves up to please men, know only how to be dependent on men, and are incapable of independence. That's why they suffer these gruesome tortures. Now, there are also women who are loved by their husbands and never have had to suffer these tortures. So they enjoy their riches and high status, which they consider to be an incomparable joy. They have no idea that their fellow women suffer these gruesome tortures, and even if someone informs them about it, they are of the opinion that the sufferings of others are of no concern to them and that they should not have to pay for others' mistakes. They completely fail to realize that the women who day in and day out burn incense and pray to the Bodhisattva [Guanyin], do so because [they believe] the Bodhisattva can save them from suffering and disasters. Ladies and gentlewomen, as you are not willing to show compassion and save others from sufferings and disasters, you go completely against the intention of the Bodhisattva, so what kind of luck can you expect for yourselves? If you ladies with good fortune and with money were to be filled with compassion, and either with your money or your influence were to assist either in the establishment of factories or of modern schools for women, in order that all women might learn a craft and acquire a profession so they could support themselves and never again have to suffer these cruel tortures, then this merit would be a thousand times, many tens of thousands of times, greater than that of burning incense, reciting sutras, and bowing before the Bodhisattva! In my opinion, all those women who will have been saved in this way from the sea of suffering will be filled with gratitude, and will venerate these ladies and gentlewomen even more than they venerate the Bodhisattva. This truly will establish your reputation for thousands of years and bring you immeasurable merit, so why are none of you willing to act in this way?

My sisters, my compatriots! Those who cannot be independent should be determined to become independent. Those who can be independent should nourish the desire to save all their sisters in the world from the sea of suffering, they can put it off no longer! We women suffer a myriad kinds of oppression that are truly unbearable! Allow me to explain to you once more what the cruel laws of the oppression of women are like!

> Layer after layer of nets and snares in earth and heaven,
> Alas, lock women up deep inside the inner quarters.
> Unable to bear the abuse, they try to end their lives
> By taking poison, hanging themselves, or drowning.
>   Deepest darkness:
> The souls of the wronged wail in the hell of suicides,
>   Blackness of night:
> Many are the prisoners of the inner quarters praying to Heaven.
> This is the real hell, worse than the court of King Yama:[15]
>   Why do we women
> Have to suffer all these tribulations, what is our crime?

And what is even more hateful, even more lamentable, even more painful, and even more ridiculous is that

> Parents rely entirely on the words of the matchmakers,
> And hurriedly their daughter's marriage is concluded.
>   All they care about is
> Equality of status, fine clothes, and good food to hand,
>   Without wondering whether
> This match of a lifetime may be the wrong combination.
> Uselessly, they regard their daughter as a rare treasure,
> They're not looking for a suitable groom, they only go for money.
> But once you have entered his gate and become his wife,
> You will have to entrust your future fate to Heaven.
> A phoenix cannot spread her wings when she follows a crow,
> The prisoner locked up in jail will never be pardoned.
> The cries of injustice rise up to Heaven and fill the world,
>   Causing even
> The Queen Mother of the West at Jasper Pool to tremble!

The Queen Mother of the West then selects from her entourage a number of golden lads and jade maidens to be reborn on earth, where they will rescue the Flowery Kingdom from its torpor and backwardness. The

---

15. King Yama is the head of the bureaucratic court of the Underworld.

remaining completed chapters describe how a group of educated Chinese girls, fully conscious now of the discrimination from which they are suffering, set sail to Japan to pursue their studies. The preserved titles of the subsequent unwritten chapters indicate that Qiu Jin planned to have her male and female revolutionary heroes return to China and establish schools and factories. In the end, they would stage a successful military uprising, drive out the barbarians, and establish a new republic.

Teacher and Revolutionary

Soon after Qiu Jin left Beijing for Tokyo, Japan declared war on Russia. The Russo-Japanese War of 1904–1905, however, was mostly fought on Chinese soil, since Japan was contesting the Russian sphere of influence in northeast China. The Chinese government could do little but watch from the sidelines. The increasingly radical protests of Chinese students in Japan against the cowardly attitude of the Qing government resulted in the Qing government asking the Japanese government to limit these student activities. The Japanese government was only too eager to oblige, and in protest, many Chinese students, including Qiu Jin, left Japan and returned to China. Qiu Jin wrote the following poem on her way home from Japan:

Aboard a Ship on the Yellow Sea, Someone from Japan Requested Some Lines from Me, and Showed Me a Map of the (Developments in the) Russo-Japanese War

Riding the wind for a myriad miles: I left and now I return,
All alone on the eastern sea I bring along the thunder of spring.[16]
How can I bear to look at this map—my face is drained of color,
I refuse to let our rivers and mountains be reduced to ashes.
 There is no wine that can dissolve my sorrow for the nation—
The current crisis demands persons of extraordinary talents.
Even if it takes the blood of hundreds of thousands of people,
We will have to turn the whole world around by our efforts.

---

16. The "thunder of spring" here refers to the revolutionary message Qiu Jin is bringing to China.

Upon her arrival in Shanghai, Qiu Jin first went to Shaoxing, where her mother and brother were living at the time. Here she had herself photographed in male dress:

An Inscription for a Portrait of Myself (in Male Dress)

Who could this person be, looking so sternly ahead?
A previous life of heroism, alas, entrusted to this body!
The physical form that I now inhabit is but a phantom,
But in a subsequent life I trust that it will be more fitting.
 To my regret I met you late—feelings overwhelm me,
As I look up and sigh over our times, my energy is stirred.
If at some later date you see my friends of former days,
Tell them on my behalf that I have swept aside convention!

Qiu Jin then returned to Shanghai where, during the spring term, she taught at a girls' school in Nanxun. She was offered the directorship of a Chinese girls' school in Java, but in the end declined the offer. While in Shanghai, she treated her women friends and fellow activists Xu Zihua (1873–1935) and Wu Zhiying (1867–1936) to her performance of a sword dance. One of the best-known photographs of Qiu Jin shows her dressed as a Japanese lady but holding a short sword. This may well be the sword she brought back with her from Japan. Both Xu Zihua and Wu Zhiying have left us descriptions of Qiu Jin's sword dance. That of Xu Zihua reads:

The lady scholar had a great capacity for alcohol; she showed no sign of drunkenness even after downing ten or twenty large cups and when in her cups, her discourse would become even more unrestrained. Although I do not enjoy drinking, she always forced me to join her and I would get drunk. One day after we had been drinking, and I was leaning out of the window with a book in my hands, she grabbed my book and said: "Stop reading, lady scholar, and just watch me doing a sword dance!" "Great!" I replied, and she immediately got out the Japanese sword she had recently acquired and, whirling around, she began to dance. The glint of the sword lit up the entire room, and she herself displayed the force of a hero flushed with wine, drawing his sword and hacking the ground. Then she handed the sword to me and said: "You try it!"

Wu Zhiying's account reads:

Later, when she returned from Tokyo, she passed through Shanghai and told me all about her difficult struggles during her study abroad. Then she showed me the Japanese sword she had recently acquired, and said: "As a weak woman I have repeatedly traveled thousands of miles all by myself. When traveling by boat I always took a third-class cabin, which I shared with low-class laborers. During the long trip I was overcome by the heat and became so sick that I almost died. The only thing I could rely on to protect myself was this sword! That is why it accompanies me like my shadow." I said jokingly to her: "In this dark age, there is quite a groundswell to study abroad, it is a tide that cannot be stopped. Didn't the customs officials take you for a female revolutionary when they checked you?" She answered with a smile: "Revolutionaries and revolution are two different things. You know I am not a new-style youth revolutionary!" Then wine was served. After she had drunk, she pulled out her sword, got up and danced, singing some couplets of a Japanese song and ordering my daughter to accompany her on the harmonium.

After Qiu Jin had turned down the offer to go to Java, she tried to launch a popular journal for women, *China Women's Journal* (*Zhongguo nübao*), but her attempts to raise the necessary capital failed, as is clear from the lead article she wrote for the first issue, which eventually appeared on January 14, 1907:

To My Sisters

My dearly beloved elders and younger sisters! Even though I may be a person who lacks great learning, I am someone who most fervently loves the nation and my compatriots. Isn't it said that in China now we have four hundred million compatriots? Of those, two hundred million men have already begun to enter the world of civilization, their knowledge has increased, their experience has been broadened, their learning has accumulated, and personally they make daily progress, all thanks to the effectiveness of journals [published] in the past. Now that today they have reached this point, tell me, aren't they to be envied? That is why people say that journals are the easiest means by which to expand people's knowledge.

Alas, while these two hundred million men have entered the new world of civilization, my two hundred million women compatriots remain submerged in the deepest darkness of the eighteenth level of hell, and lack the desire to even clamber up a single level! They bind their little feet oh-so-tightly, and they comb their little heads until their hair is bright and shiny. In their hair they stick little flowers and little sprigs, tied together or encased in gold; they wrap their bodies in satins and silks, embroidered or patterned, and make themselves up with the whitest powder and the reddest rouge. All they know is how to be dependent on men all of their lives: for their food and clothing they rely entirely on men. They softly and pliantly please his body, and they suffer his moods in silence. They are incessantly shedding tears, and they spend their lives in anguish. They are prisoners for their entire lives, and cattle for half. Let me ask you, my sisters: Have you ever in your life enjoyed the happiness of freedom?

Then there are those women compatriots who are rich and glorious and whose families have many possessions. They have a hundred slaves and maids at their beck and call. When they leave the house they are both preceded and followed by a throng of servants: their glory is truly incomparable! When they stay at home, every one of their whims is obeyed: their power is truly tremendous! They themselves are of the opinion that they are fortunate and that it is because of what they have earned in a former life that they can now rely on a good husband and lead a life of enjoyment. Outsiders will also sigh with admiration and envy: "That lady is lucky!" "That lady enjoys good fortune!" And they will praise her, exclaiming "What glory!" "What honor!" But what they do not know is that at home she is always the victim of his rage and always must undergo sufferings. Those little flowers and little sprigs are best compared to shackles of jade and fetters of gold, and the satins and silks to ropes of brocade and embroidered sashes that bind one oh-so-tightly! Those slaves and maids are jailers and wardens that keep one behind bars. And that husband, it goes without saying, is one's prosecutor and one's judge. No matter what his command, one must obey him and him alone. Let me ask those rich and noble ladies and gentlewomen: although you enjoy a life of luxury, do you have even the slightest right to independence? In each and every case, men occupy the position of authority and women occupy the position of slaves. Because they want to depend on others, they themselves do not have the slightest desire for independence. These prisoners locked up in their inner apartments do not have even the slightest inkling of their own suffering!

Alas, my sisters, in the myriad countries of the whole globe there is not a single person who would be willingly called a slave, so why are we sisters so happy to be called such without feeling any shame? You sisters will say: "We women are not capable of earning our own money, nor have we acquired any skills, so all our life we are dependent on our husband for either our glory or our shame. Even if we have to suffer all sorts of troubles, there is nothing to be done about it, and we must accept it as our fate." This talk is truly bereft of courage. In each and every human being, what is to be feared most is a lack of courage. If you have the courage, you can always find the basis for independence or the training you need in order to earn your livelihood. At present there are many modern schools for women, and there are also jobs for women. As long as you have learned a science or a skill, you can become a teacher or start a factory. Of course you can earn your own livelihood! In this way you will not be a parasite who is a burden on her father, brothers, or husband. In the first place you can contribute to the household income, and in the second place, you will earn the respect of men. Once you have rid yourself of the curse of uselessness, you will reap the happiness of freedom. At home you will be welcomed by your relatives, and outside the home you will benefit from the counsel of friends. Husband and wife will walk hand in hand, and elder and younger sisters will chat side by side. Quarrels and fights will be a thing of the past. Those whose ambitions are higher and whose minds are finer may even enjoy a lofty reputation or perform great deeds, such that they will be praised in China and abroad and revered throughout the land. Tell me, wouldn't this beautiful world of civilization be great?

It can't be true that you, my sisters, are truly happy living the life of cattle and slaves and that you do not long to free yourselves! If it is, it is only because living in the seclusion of the inner chambers you are unable to learn about outside affairs, and you do not have any journals that can expand your knowledge and thought. Now, there was a *Journal of Women's Studies* [*Nüxuebao*], but for some reason it stopped publication after only a few issues. Nowadays we do have the *Women's World* [*Nüzi shijie*], but its style is far too abstruse. Since eight or nine out of every ten sisters are illiterate, if a journal is written in a simple style, it can still be read out to them as vernacular speech, but if the style is too abstruse, they simply can't understand it. In editing this *China Women's Journal*, I have taken this into consideration and the articles in the journal will be written in both the classical and the vernacular languages to facilitate its perusal by my sisters. May this be appreciated as an effort on behalf of my compatriots.

When it comes to publishing a journal, it is of course a much easier job if you have sufficient capital. If you don't have the money, you're bound to encounter all kinds of problems. That is why I wanted to start by raising ten thousand *taël* of capital by selling shares [at twenty dollars a share], so that I could rent a building, install the [necessary] equipment, print the journal and edit books, and hire writers, editors, and other staff, and in this way be able to publish the journal on a regular basis and far into the future. The *China Women's Journal* would truly add luster to my two hundred million women compatriots. It would also mean that we would not fall behind, that we would be able to establish a basis for ourselves, and in the future everything would be so much easier. For this reason I published the statutes [for the journal] in the *China and the World Daily Newspaper* [*Zhongwai ribao*]. I also printed them separately and mailed them to every modern school for women, so I am quite sure that you, my sisters, must have seen them. But quite a few days have passed, and apart from a few people who have purchased a few shares, no one has even made any inquiries. From this, one can also imagine the situation of our women's world! It really pains my heart to think of this!

In speaking of this, tears come to my eyes, pain grips my heart, and the brush falls from my hand. Under these circumstances, wouldn't it be better not to publish the *China Women's Journal*? But, then again, I cannot bear to see my beloved sisters forever buried in this hell, which is why I could not but scrape together a little money, and with my blood and tears produce this lithographic paper for my sisters to read. Even though today the first issue has appeared, and I will do my best to produce the next one, the expenses are really a problem. As with all things under heaven, what a single person finds difficult to accomplish is easily brought to completion by a collective effort. If there are enthusiastic sisters who are willing to join with me in this venture, that would be the best thing that could happen to the *China Women's Journal*!

A second issue of *China Women's Journal* appeared on March 4, 1907. One of Qiu Jin's own contributions to this issue was a song, published with musical notation:

A Fighting Song for Women's Rights

We women love our freedom,
So let's raise our glasses to freedom!
The equality of men and women is bestowed by Nature,
So how can we accept discrimination?
 Let us exert ourselves and free ourselves,
And cleanse ourselves once and for all of our shameful past.
Joan of Arc will fight on our side,
As we restore these rivers and mountains with our bare hands!

The old traditions are extremely shameful:
Women treated as if they were no different from cattle!
The light of dawn now brings the tide of civilization,
We'll take the lead in independence.
 Let's eradicate our slavery,
Become proficient in knowledge and learning.
We'll shoulder that responsibility,
We women heroes of our nation will never betray its trust!

Qiu Jin did put together a third issue of *China Women's Journal*, but because her life was about to take a dramatic turn, that particular issue was never published.

Early in 1907, Qiu Jin had become the principal of the newly established Datong School for girls, just outside Shaoxing. An important component of the education offered in this school was military-style physical exercise. The tone of the education in this school may also be gauged from some of the songs that were published by the authorities upon Qiu Jin's arrest as proof of her guilt:

Song of China Expelling Its Demons

Our neighbors encircle us and we wish to expel them,
But still we continue forfeiting rights and ceding territories.
These sort of people are really too muddleheaded,
They seem to be dreaming, to be drunk, to be half dead!
 Alas!
The energy of our country has gradually been exhausted,
How is it possible that we have still not raised ourselves up?
A lack of heart, a lack of courage, a lack of brains:
These must be reckoned the greatest of China's demons!

Lament for China

Alas, our country cannot compete with those of the West!
Alas, the glory of ancient times has now all fallen into ruin!
Can it be that High Heaven no longer deigns to watch over us,
And intentionally fills the skies with a poisonous miasma?
 The inherited nature of our compatriots is perfect and fine,
So why do we find it impossible to surpass those white men?
It is because we are locked in a prison of darkness,
Which silences the successors to the divine sages!

We Envy the Peoples of Europe and America

They have liberty, they enjoy peace and prosperity,
In ample ease and greatest joy they pass each year.
The life of their nations lasts for thousands of years,
And their people's energy is sustained by their rights.
 Their trade, their armies, and their industries improve daily,

Their politics and their scholarship become ever more perfect.
Their armies are strong, their economies prosper, their territories expand,
Each year more, each month better, each day renewed!

Isn't this the image we have of those grand and imposing civilized countries?
Alas, our Chinese compatriots suffer oppression and suffer vexation. Our country is poor, its people are ill—such sorrow!

Qiu Jin clearly used the Datong school as a basis for the coordinated military uprising that she and others were planning to carry out in both Anhui and Zhejiang province on the tenth day of the Sixth Month (July 19). In Zhejiang, the plans called for an uprising in Jinhua, the idea being that once the imperial troops from the provincial capital Hangzhou were dispatched to quell it, the rebel troops from Shaoxing would then march on the undefended city. The plans leaked out, however, and when the authorities began to arrest revolutionaries in Jinhua, Xu Xilin (1873–1907), who was the person responsible for the activities in Anhui, decided he could not wait any longer and on July 6 tried to instigate an uprising by shooting the governor of Anhui at the ceremony being held for the first graduating class of Anhui's modern police academy. The shooting failed to provoke an uprising and Xu Xilin was executed that same day. Moreover, the authorities, by now thoroughly alarmed, moved swiftly against the other known participants in the plot. Qiu Jin refused to flee and was arrested by the Shaoxing local authorities on July 11. Several days later, on July 15, she was executed by beheading.

As part of the various materials assembled as evidence of Qiu Jin's revolutionary thought, the authorities later published the following lyric that was found among her papers and which probably dates from her stay in Japan:

To the Melody of "Partridge Sky" (*Zhegutian*)

Overcome with emotion at the nation's decay,
I traveled overseas in order to find myself true friends.
Since the golden beaker is chipped, it must be restored,
For the sake of the nation I'll happily sacrifice my body.

Alas for the dangers,
Tossed by the winds:

The many miles of hills and passes I traveled like a man.
Don't say that there are no heroes among us women:
Night after night on the wall my Dragon Spring cries out![17]

One of Qiu Jin's colleagues at the Datong school, writing under the name of Fonu, has left us a detailed description of Qiu Jin's final days and execution, which was published later in 1907 in Shanghai in the *Divine Land Women's Magazine* (*Shenzhou nübao*):

Alas! As I wrote the account of this case, my heart broke, my innards felt shredded, and my tears welled up like a tide! How could I bear to write this record! But a bunch of despicable villains, people like Guifu and Zhang Zengyang, Yuan Di, and Hu Daonan,[18] either made secret accusations thus precipitating this disaster, or contrived false confessions in order to justify her sentence. Bereft of human feeling, completely insane, and lacking any regard for human life, they deceived themselves so as to deceive others and flaunted public opinion, all in the hopes that this wrongful case would remain forever hidden at the bottom of the deep sea. That is why, despite the pain, I could not but write this account, so that my sisters might have an inkling of the real facts of this case.

At about eight o'clock in the morning of the fourth day of the Sixth Month, Mr. ———, the music teacher, arrived from the Middle School [the Shaoxing Prefectural School], and reported that Guifu had gone to Hangzhou to mobilize two detachments of troops, which had reached Shaoxing that very morning. Guifu was then planning to go to Dongpu to search the house of the Xu family [the house of Xu Xilin], after which he would immediately come and search the [Datong] School.

Sometime after eleven o'clock, the cook returned from town and said to the lady scholar: "A little while ago, I heard people in the teahouse say that prefect Guifu is going to arrest you, so please leave quickly." She replied saying: "This has nothing to do with me! It is nothing but nonsense! Even though this school may have been founded by Xu Xilin, he is only one of the old teachers, so why should the teachers of the school be implicated in this case? I am a pure and

---

17. "Dragon Spring" is a conventional name for an exceptionally fine sword.

18. Guifu was the Manchu prefect of Shaoxing in 1907. Zhang Zengyang was the governor of Zhejiang province. Hu Daonan was a member of the local gentry and head of the Shanyin Bureau for the Promotion of Education (Shanyin was one of the districts making up Shaoxing prefecture). It is not certain who Yuan Di was, but one can assume that he also was a local official of some kind.

spotless woman and haven't committed the slightest crime, so why should I run away and provide people with an excuse to accuse me of fleeing like a coward!"

I happened to be there as well, and so I urged her saying: "You are doubtlessly right, but these rapacious officials are bound to abuse the law in order to further their careers. I'm afraid that it may not be in your best interest to refuse to flee." The lady scholar said: "Is there no justice in this world then?" I replied: "It is a mistake to try to talk justice with barbarian officials who do not have the requisite understanding of what justice means." She then said: "They may be barbarians, but they won't be that barbaric. Since I have not committed any crime, why should I run away? But if you are afraid, you should feel free to flee." When I saw that her mind was made up, I let it rest at that.

A moment later the clock sounded and together we went to the dining hall for lunch. As soon as we had finished eating, her brother arrived together with a lady. He told Qiu Jin that according to the unanimous opinion of the people in the streets, the troops were coming to search the school for rifles and that they also intended to make arrests, and that it would be best if the teachers and the students fled as quickly as possible. The lady scholar replied saying: "The rifles in this school were procured with the permission of ex-prefect Xiong, and prefect Guifu has seen them many times, so what need is there for a search? If they are worried about these rifles, we will happily return them if so requested. What is the point of making arrests?" When her brother heard these words, he agreed with her, and immediately left with the lady. By that time it was already two o'clock in the afternoon.

After an hour or so, the lady scholar began to play the zither and I went on an errand outside the school. On my way back I ran into Mr. Sun, who said to me: "Guifu surrounded the Datong School with more than four hundred troops, and when students tried to escape, many were killed by gunfire. When the lady scholar Qiu, Cheng Yi, and others came outside to see what was happening, they were all arrested and taken away. The soldiers beat them repeatedly along the way. When they came to a certain spot, a soldier flung two pistols to the side of the road, saying that they had fallen out of the trousers of the lady scholar. By now they have been taken to the prison of the prefecture, and all the Datong School's funds, more than five hundred silver dollars, as well as all of its moveable goods have been plundered and looted."

When I heard these words, I was filled with both fear and rage. I immediately asked Mr. Shen to send someone to the prefectural office to make a full inquiry. Mr. Shen said to me: "You are one of the teachers of the Datong School. It is very unwise for you to be out here on the street." So I went with him to his house, and he sent the younger brother of a judicial clerk to make full inquiries.

The next morning [the fifth day] the younger brother of the judicial clerk came to Mr. Shen's house and gave us a full report. He reported that the lady scholar Qiu had been taken to the Shanyin district office to be interrogated.[19] Although questioned repeatedly, she refused to say a word, and even when placed on the rack, remained silent despite the pain. When they forced her to sign her name to a confession, at first she wrote only the character for "autumn," [*qiu*][20] but under [continued] pressure she completed the line as follows: "Autumn rains and autumn storms kill me with their sorrow." The other six people were also interrogated separately, beginning with Cheng Yi, but even under torture refused to confess.

At twelve o'clock that night the brother of the judicial clerk returned to Mr. Shen's house again, and told us that Qiu had been condemned to death, that the confirmation of the verdict by the provincial government had already arrived, and that she would be executed the following day at the break of dawn. Was it not cruel that a tender maiden should be condemned to death merely because of the line "Autumn rains and autumn storms kill me with their sorrow"!

At three o'clock on the morning of the sixth day, Mr. Shen, because of the alarming news of the previous night, went to the Shanyin district office to see what was happening. It was still dark when he got there and saw that Li Jiasheng, the district magistrate of Guiji, was the one presiding over the court and overseeing the preparations for the execution. This was because Li Zhongyue, the district magistrate of Shanyin, knew that the lady scholar had been condemned unjustly. His most vehement protests had gone unheeded, and so, unable to bear being a party to this injustice, he had pleaded illness and had been replaced by the magistrate of Guiji.

During all of this, the lady scholar Qiu lost none of her customary composure, and made four requests of magistrate Li [Jiasheng]: 1) that she be allowed to write a letter to her family; 2) that she not be stripped of her clothing [like a common criminal]; 3) that her head not be publicly displayed [after being removed from her body]; and 4) that the more than five hundred dollars that had been stolen from the school by the soldiers be retrieved and deposited in the Ever-Level Granary Bureau so as to benefit the poor. Magistrate Li, however,

---

19. The city of Shaoxing, the capital of Shaoxing prefecture, belonged partly to Shanyin district and partly to Guiji district.

20. The same Chinese character is used to write the Chinese word for autumn (*qiu*) and the rare family name Qiu. The authorities are pressuring Qiu Jin to sign the prepared confession of her participation in the plot because, according to traditional law, a case could only be settled if the criminal confessed and accepted the punishment as fitting the crime.

did not agree to any of her requests. The lady scholar let out a deep sigh, and remained silent. She was then fettered and shackled according to the rules and escorted by a platoon of soldiers to Xuanting Crossing. . . . After she had been beheaded, her body was tossed away. Because none of her relatives dared to come forward to claim the corpse, it was prepared for burial and placed in a coffin by a charitable society. Because the coffin had not been firmly nailed shut, after a while the coffin lid was blown off by the wind. Scorched by the sun and drenched by the rain she suffered the extra punishment of having her corpse exposed to the elements. Not only do I find writing this detailed record of the circumstances of her beheading and the exposure of her corpse unbearable, but I trust that readers must also find it impossible to endure having to read about these events.

After the lady scholar had been executed, Guifu tried to pressure Cheng Yi and the others into making a false confession in order to justify the sentence of the lady scholar. Although he interrogated them under such tortures as having to kneel down on red-hot irons, Cheng Yi and the others in the end did not confess and chose to suffer the pain rather than make a false accusation. Guifu had no choice but to sentence Cheng Yi to prison; the others all received different sentences. And because Li Zhongyue had disagreed with him, he relieved him of his position. Although Li Zhongyue had not supervised the execution, he had interrogated the lady scholar under torture and, for this reason, felt that he had betrayed both Guifu and Qiu Jin. Overcome by remorse and regret, he eventually hanged himself.

Alas! For over a year now we have been hearing declarations about the Preparation of a Constitutional Government.[21] Of course everyone knows that our rulers are only deceiving themselves in order to deceive others. But that they should go so far in their disregard for a human life really exposes their true nature! Guifu may be stupid, but he would not hasten the annihilation of the Manchus just for his own personal reasons. Even after pondering this matter a hundred times, I still could not explain it. So I again asked Mr. Shen to request the younger brother of the judicial clerk to make an investigation. Only then did I learn that the wrongful death of the lady scholar was due to a secret accusation made by those animals Yuan and Hu! When the case of their friend [Yuan and others had been friends of Xu Xilin] was exposed, they were afraid of being implicated, and that is why they made use of this extremely evil and dastardly method of betraying a weak woman to save their own skin. There could be

---

21. In 1905 the imperial government had announced that it would gradually transform itself into a constitutional government.

nothing more vicious than this! Alas! How can one exert oneself on behalf of the national cause when such rotten elements are to be found in the circles of education?

When later I went to Shanghai, I read the newspapers' accounts of Qiu Jin's crimes, which included her confession. As this was completely at variance with the facts as I knew them, I sent a telegram to the younger brother of the judicial clerk asking him to make inquiries. After seven days I received his reply and learned that the publicized confession had been concocted by Chen Mofang [a judicial investigator of Shaoxing prefecture] together with Guifu and others. Alas! Although fully aware of the power of public opinion, they still came up with this false and unfounded "confession" as if they could cover all the eyes of the world with a single hand!

Qiu Jin's speedy execution by the authorities turned her into a martyr for the revolution and a national celebrity. From the moment of her death her life immediately became the subject of an endless stream of plays and novels, by male and female writers. Her friend Wu Zhiying, famed for her prose and calligraphy, composed the following formal biography in the year of her death:

The lady scholar Qiu Jin, whose style name was Xuanqing, hailed from Shanyin in Zhejiang. From her earliest youth she was educated at home, and already by the time she had reached the age of marriage, was well-versed in the Classics and Histories. She loved to write songs and poems, most of which were filled with laments for the times. At the age of nineteen, she married such-and-such official of such-and-such a rank from such-and-such a district and bore him one son and one daughter.

As she had lived for a number of years in the capital, the events of the year *gengzi* [1900] filled her with pain and rage, and she took upon herself the responsibility of promoting schools for women. She devoured every single one of the new books and journals and, as result of this, she not only acquired a deep understanding of the affairs of China and the outside world but also became more and more stimulated and affected by the high tide of foreign ideas.

One day, she removed her hairpins and earrings and sold them to defray the costs of tuition, took leave of her husband, sent her son and her daughter to her mother's home to be raised, and traveled by herself to Japan to study. Upon her departure, all her sisters and friends in the capital organized a banquet in the Taoran Kiosk to the south of the city to see her off and wish her a smooth journey. When she arrived in Tokyo and saw all the different sorts of corruption and decadence among the students abroad, she immediately went into a rage. By nature she was forthright and outspoken, and whenever she would run into someone who did not understand the needs of the time, she would mercilessly berate him to his face and contradict him in public, which caused many people to resent her. She would be pleased when, on occasion, people compared her to Sophia or Madame Rolland, and she adopted the sobriquet of Female Knight-Errant of Mirror Lake.

Later, when she was subjected to restrictions on her activities, she left Tokyo and returned to China and in Shanghai, edited the *China Women's Journal.* Receiving news of her mother's death, she hastily returned to her native village where she was invited to be a teacher at the Mingtang School for Girls, although she did not accept the position. On the twenty-sixth day of the Fifth Month of the present year, Xu Xilin was arrested in Anhui. Qiu Jin was accused by high officials in Zhejiang of being one of Xu's accomplices and was executed.

[*The author comments:*][22] Although this lady scholar was always fond of acting impulsively, she did not die because she was a criminal. The officials may have been violent and rapacious, but they would not have gone to such cruel lengths: it must be that there was someone who held a private grudge against her and plotted her downfall by availing himself of this case against some revolutionaries in order to ingratiate himself with his superiors. So it is not just the officials who are to be blamed. Alas! And this is called the period of "Preparation for Constitutional Government!"

As the Manchu Qing dynasty was still the government in power, Wu Zhiying wisely refrained from stressing Qiu Jin's links to the revolutionary movement in the public testament she wrote to her friend's character.

Qiu Jin was initially buried in Shaoxing, but in 1908, her friends Wu Zhiying and Xu Zihua had her reburied on the banks of Hangzhou's West Lake, close to the grave of Yue Fei. When the Manchu authorities became aware of this, they forced Qiu Jin's family to move her grave yet again and have her reburied in Hunan alongside her deceased husband. But as soon as the Manchu Qing dynasty collapsed in 1911, Qiu Jin was once again buried on the banks of West Lake. Now she could be celebrated as a martyr of the new Republic and there was no longer any need to keep silent about her revolutionary activities.

❧❧❧

---

22. In a formal biographical account such as this one a factual survey of the deceased's life is followed by a more personal evaluation by the author.

Qiu Jin was far from being the only writing woman feminist of the last decade of imperial China. The first woman writer to argue for a modern education for women, for example, was Kang Tongwei (1858–1927), a daughter of the well-known reformer Kang Youwei. Women students in Japan and small groups of educated women in Shanghai and elsewhere spearheaded a vociferous feminist movement, which turned into a suffragette movement when the long-awaited Chinese Republic denied women the vote. Many of the members of this movement would eventually go on to long and distinguished careers in education and other fields. After the examination system was abolished (the last metropolitan examinations were held in 1905), China embarked on the modernization of its educational system, a project that was pursued even more vigorously after the establishment of the Republic. Growing numbers of girls began to attend the new, modern-style public and private schools at all levels, and all the professions were, in principle at least, opened to women.

A second wave of feminism, led by a new generation of students, began with the May Fourth Movement of 1919. The feminists of the final years of the Qing dynasty had enjoyed a traditional education, and they still struggled to express their new ideals in the classical language and in established genres. The feminists of the Republican period, on the other hand, often had the benefit of a modern education and not only rejected traditional values and conventions, but also the language and genres in which these values and conventions had been expressed. They followed the lead of their late-Qing predecessors in stressing the oppression women had suffered (and were still suffering) in the traditional society, as exemplified by illiteracy, footbinding, and arranged marriages. Despite the appearance in the twenties and thirties of a few monographs devoted to the rich tradition of women's literature in imperial times, no place was found for it in the educational curriculum of high schools and universities—apart, of course, from the occasional obligatory nod in the direction of such luminaries as Ban Zhao and Li Qingzhao.

REFERENCE MATTER

Bibliography
of Chinese
Sources

Bao Zhenpei 鮑震培, *Qingdai nüzuojia tanci xiaoshuo lungao* 清代女作家彈詞小說論稿. Tianjin: Tianjin Shehui kexueyuan chubanshe, 2002.

Baochang 寶唱, *Biqiuni zhuan* 比丘尼傳. Nanjing: Jinling kejing chu, 1885.

Cai Tao 蔡絛, *Tieweishan congtan* 鐵圍山叢談. Beijing: Zhonghua shuju, 1983.

Cantong Yikui 參同一揆, *Cantong Yikui chanshi yulu* 參同一揆禪師語錄, in *Mingban Jiaxing Dazangjing* 明版嘉興大藏經, reprint. Taibei: Xinwenfeng, 1987, vol. 39.

Cao Xueqin 曹雪芹 and Gao E 高鶚, *Honglou meng* 紅樓夢. Beijing: Renmin wenxue chubanshe, 1964.

Chen Dongyuan 陳東原, *Zhongguo funü shenghuo shi* 中國婦女生活史, reprint. Shanghai: Shanghai shudian, 1984.

Chen Duansheng 陳端生, *Zaishengyuan* 再生緣, ed. by Du Zhijun 杜志君. Beijing: Huaxia chubanshe, 2000.

Chen Gaohua 陳高華, comp., *Yuandai huajia shiliao* 元代畫家史料. Shanghai: Shanghai renmin meishu chubanshe, 1980.

Chen Wenhua 陳文華, ed., *Tang nüshiren ji sanzhong* 唐女詩人集三種. Shanghai: Shanghai guji chubanshe, 1984.

Chen Wenshu 陳文述, *Xiling guiyong* 西泠閨詠, woodblock ed. N.p.: Jiahuitang dingshi, 1883.

Chen Xiang 陳香, comp., *Qingdai nüshiren xuanji* 清代女詩人選集. Taibei: Taiwan Shangwu yinshuguan, 1977.

Chen Yan 陳衍, comp., *Yuanshi jishi* 元詩紀事. Shanghai: Shanghai guji chubanshe, 1987.

Da Ming renxiao huanghou menggan Foshuo diyi xiyou da gongde jing 大明仁孝皇后夢感佛說第一稀有大功德經, in *Xuzangjing*. Hong Kong: Longman shudian, 1967 (reprinted from the *Dainihon zokuzokyō*. Kyoto: Zokyo Shoin,1905–1912), vol. 1.

Daoyuan 道源, *Jingde chuandeng lu* 景德傳燈錄, in Takakasu Junjirō et. al., eds., *Taishō shinshū daizōkyō*. Tokyo: Taishō Issaikyō Kankōkai and Daizō Shuppan, 1924–1932, vol. 51.

Deng Hanyi 鄧漢儀, *Tianxia mingjia shiguan* 天下名家詩觀, woodblock ed. N.p.: Nanyang Dengshi Shenmotang, 1672.

Du Deqiao 杜德橋 (Glen Dudbridge), *Miaoshan chuanshuo: Guanyin pusa yuanqi kao* 妙山傳說：觀音菩薩緣起考. Taibei: Julin tushu gongsi, 1990.

Du Fangqin 杜方琴, ed., *He Shuangqing ji* 賀雙卿集. Zhengzhou: Zhongzhou guji chubanshe, 1993.

Du Xun 杜珣, ed., *Zhongguo lidai funü wenxue zuopin jingxuan* 中國歷代婦女文學作品精選. Beijing: Zhongguo heping chubanshe, 2000.

Ge Hong 葛洪, *Baopuzi* 抱朴子, in *Zhuzi jicheng* 諸子集成. Beijing: Zhonghua shuju, 1954, vol. 8.

Gu Huizhi 谷輝之, comp., *Liu Rushi shiwen ji* 柳如是詩文集. Beijing: Zhonghua quanguo tushuguan wenxian suwei fuzhi zhongxin, 1996.

Gu Ruopu 顧若璞, *Woyuexuan gao* 臥月軒稿, in *Wulin wangzhe yizhu qianbian* 武林往哲遺著前編. Hangzhou?: Jiahui dingshi, between 1875 and 1900.

Gu Taiqing 顧太清 and Yihui 奕繪, *Gu Taiqing Yihui shici heji* 顧太清奕繪詩詞合集. Shanghai: Shanghai guji chubanshe, 1998.

Guan Dedong 關德棟 and Che Xilun 車錫倫, eds., *Liaozhai zhiyi xiqu ji* 聊齋誌異戲曲集. Shanghai: Shanghai guji chubanshe, 1983.

Guang Tiefu 光鐵夫, comp., *Anhui mingyuan shici zhenglüe* 安徽名媛詩詞徵略. Hefei: Huangshan shushe, 1986.

Guo Maoqian 郭茂倩, comp., *Yuefu shiji* 樂府詩集. Beijing: Zhonghua shuju, 1979.

Guo Yanli 郭延禮, ed., *Qiu Jin yanjiu ziliao* 秋瑾研究資料. Jinan: Shandong jiaoyu chubanshe, 1987.

Han shu 漢書. Beijing: Zhonghua shuju, 1962.

Hou Han shu 後漢書. Beijing: Zhonghua shuju, 1965.

Hu Wenkai 胡文楷, *Zhongguo lidai funü zhuzuo kao* 中國歷代婦女著作考, rev. ed. Shanghai: Shanghai guji chubanshe, 1985.

Hu Yinglin 胡應麟, *Shisou* 詩藪. Shanghai: Shanghai guji chubanshe, 1958.

Hua Wei 華瑋, *Ming Qing funü zhi xiqu chuangzuo yu piping* 明清婦女之戲曲創作與批評. Taibei: Zhongyang yanjiuyuan Zhongguo wenzhe yanjiusuo, 2003.

Hua Wei, ed., *Ming Qing funü xiqu ji* 明清婦女戲曲集. Taibei: Zhongyang yanjiuyuan Zhongguo wenzhe yanjiusuo, 2003.

Huang E 黃娥, *Yang furen shiji* 楊夫人詩集, in *Yang Shen ciqu ji* 楊慎詞曲集. Chengdu: Sichuan renmin chubanshe, 1984.

Huang Yuanjie 黃媛介, *Huang Jieling shi* 黃皆令詩, in *Shiyuan ba mingjia ji* 詩媛八名家集, woodblock ed. N.p., 1655.

Ji Yougong 計有功, ed., *Tangshi jishi* 唐詩紀事. Beijing: Zhonghua shuju, 1965.

Ji Yun 紀昀, ed., *Siku quanshu zongmu* 四庫全書總目, reprint. Taibei: Yiwen yinshuguan, n.d.

Jiang Yikui 蔣一葵, comp., *Yaoshantang waiji* 堯山堂外紀, in *Xuxiu Siku quanshu* 續修四庫全書. Shanghai: Shanghai guji chubanshe, 1995–1999, vols. 1194–1195.

Jin Fu 靳輔, *Tingxun* 庭訓, in Xu Zi 徐梓, ed., *Jiaxun* 家訓. Beijing: Zhongyang minzu daxue chubanshe, 1996.

Jin shu 晉書. Beijing: Zhonghua shuju, 1974.

Jiu Tang shu 舊唐書. Beijing: Zhonghua shuju, 1975.

Jizong Che chanshi yulu 季總徹禪師語錄, in *Mingban Jiaxing dazangjing*, vol. 28.

Legge, James, trans., *The Chinese Classics*, Vol. 4, *The She King*, rev. ed., reprint. Taibei: Wenshizhe chubanshe, 1971.

Li Fang 李昉, comp., *Taiping yulan* 太平禦覽. Beijing: Zhonghua shuju, 1960.

———. *Taiping guangji* 太平廣記. Beijing: Zhonghua shuju, 1961.

Li Ruzhen 李汝珍, *Jinghua yuan* 鏡花緣. Hong Kong: Zhonghua shuju, 1965.

Li Shiren 李時人, comp., *Quan Tang Wudai xiaoshuo* 全唐五代小説. Xi'an: Shaanxi renmin chubanshe, 1998.

Liang Desheng 梁德繩, *Guchunxuan wenchao* 古春軒文鈔, woodblock ed. N.p., 1849.

Liang shu 梁書. Beijing: Zhonghua shuju, 1973.

Liaoshi 遼史. Beijing: Zhonghua shuju, 1974.

Liu Fu 劉斧, comp., *Qingsuo gaoyi* 青瑣高議. Shanghai: Shanghai guji chubanshe, 1983.

Liu Xin 劉歆, *Xijing zaji jiao zhu* 西京雜記校註, ed. by Xiang Xinyang 向新陽 and Liu Keren 劉可任. Shanghai: Shanghai guji chubanshe, 1991.

Liu Yanyuan 劉燕遠, ed., *Liu Rushi shici pingzhu* 柳如是詩詞評註. Beijing: Beijing guji chubanshe, 2000.

Liu Yiqing 劉義慶, comp., Liu Xiaobiao 劉孝標, ann., Zhu Zhuyu 朱鑄禹, ed., *Shishuo xinyu huijiao jizhu* 世說新語彙校集注. Shanghai: Shanghai guji chubanshe, 2002.

Liu Yulai 劉玉來, ed., *Qiu Jin shici zhushi* 秋瑾詩詞註釋. Yinchuan: Ningxia renmin chubanshe, 1983.

Lu Qinli 逯欽立, comp., *Xian Qin Han Wei Nanbeichao shi* 先秦漢魏南北朝詩. Beijing: Zhonghua shuju, 1983.

Lu Xun 魯迅, comp., *Gu xiaoshuo gouchen* 古小說鈎沉. Hong Kong: Xinyi chubanshe, 1967.

———. *Tang Song chuanqi ji* 唐宋傳奇集. Hong Kong: Xinyi chubanshe, 1967.

Lu You 陸游, *Lu You ji* 陸游集. Beijing: Zhonghua shuju, 1976.

Luo Dajing 羅大經, *Helin yulu* 鶴林玉露. Beijing: Zhonghua shuju, 1983.

Luo Qilan 駱綺蘭, *Tingqiuxuan shiji* 聽秋軒詩集, woodblock ed. Nanjing: Gong shi, 1795.

———. "Guizhong tongren jishi xu" 閨中同人集詩序, reproduced in Robyn Hamilton, "The Pursuit of Fame: Luo Qilan (1755–1813?) and the Debates about Women and Talent in Eighteenth-century Jiangnan," *Late Imperial China* 18 (1997), pp. 39–171.

Ma Rong 馬蓉, ed., *Nü caizi shu* 女才子書. Shengyang: Chunfeng wenyi chubanshe, 1983.

Meng Chengshun 孟稱舜, *Zhang Yuniang guifang sanqing yingwumu Zhenwen ji* 張玉娘閨房三清鸚鵡墓貞文記, in *Guben xiqu congkan erji* 古本戲曲叢刊二集. Shanghai: Shangwu yinshuguan, 1955.

Miao Lianbao 妙蓮保, ed., *Guochao zhengshi xuji* 國朝正始續集, woodblock ed. N.p., 1863.

Milou ji 迷樓記, in *Tang Song chuanqi ji*.

Mingshi 明史. Beijing: Zhonghua shuju, 1974.

Nan Qi shu 南齊書. Beijing: Zhonghua shuju, 1984.

Nanshi 南史. Beijing: Zhonghua shuju, 1975.

Nianchang 念常, *Fozu lidai tongzai* 佛祖歷代通載, in *Taishō shinshū daizōkyō*, vol. 49.

Peng Jiqing 彭際清, *Xifang gongju* 西方公據, in *Xuzangjing*, vol. 109.

Pu Ji 普濟, *Wudeng huiyuan* 五燈會元, in *Xuzangjing*, vol. 138.

Pu Jiangqing 浦江清, *Pu Jiangqing wenlu* 浦江清文錄. Beijing: Renmin wenxue chubanshe, 1958.

Qian Qianyi 錢謙益, *Liechao shiji xiaozhuan* 列朝詩集小傳. Shanghai: Gudian wenxue chubanshe, 1957.

———. *Muzhai youxueji* 牧齋有學集, in *Xuxiu Siku quanshu*, vol. 1391.

Qiu Jin 秋瑾, *Qiu Jin ji* 秋瑾集. Shanghai: Shanghai guji chubanshe, 1979.

Qu Wanli 屈萬里, ed., *Shijing quanshi* 詩經詮釋. Taibei: Lianjing chubanshe, 1983.

Quan Han fu 全漢賦. Beijing: Beijing daxue chubanshe, 1993.

Quan Tang shi 全唐詩. Beijing: Zhonghua shuju, 1960.

Quan Tang wen 全唐文. Taibei: Huiwen shuju, 1961.

Sanguo zhi 三國志. Beijing: Zhonghua shuju, 1959.

Sengyou 僧祐, *Chu sanzang jiji* 出三藏記集. Beijing: Zhonghua shuju, 1995.

Shang Jinglan 商景蘭, "Shang Furen Jinnang ji" 商夫人錦囊集, in *Qi Biaojia ji* 祁彪佳集. Beijing: Zhonghua shuju, 1960.

Shen Lidong 沈立東, comp., *Lidai houfei shici jizhu* 歷代后妃詩詞集注. Beijing: Zhongguo funü chubanshe, 1990.

Shi Shuyi 施淑儀, comp., *Qingdai guige shiren zhenglüe* 清代閨閣詩人徵略, reprint. Taipei: Dingwen shuju, 1971.

Shi Zhenlin 史震林, *Xiqing sanji* 西青散記, in *Zhongguo wenxue zhenben congshu* 中國文學珍本叢書. Shanghai: Shanghai zazhi gongsi, 1935, vol. 9.

Sima Guang 司馬光, *Sima shi shuyi* 司馬氏書儀, in *Congshu jicheng chubian*. Shanghai: Shangwu yinshuguan, 1936, vol. 1040.

Sima Qian 司馬遷, *Shiji* 史記. Beijing: Zhonghua shuju, 1959.

Songyang xianzhi 嵩陽縣志, in *Zhonghua fangzhi congshu, Huazhong difang*. Taibei: Chengwen, n.d.

Su Zhecong 蘇者聰, *Zhongguo lidai funü zuopin xuan* 中國歷代婦女作品選. Shanghai: Shanghai guji chubanshe, 1987.

Sui Shusen 隋樹森, comp., *Quan Yuan sanqu* 全元散曲. Beijing: Zhonghua shuju, 1964.

Tan Zhengbi 譚正璧, *Zhongguo nüxing wenxue shihua* 中國女性文學史話, reprint. Tianjin: Baihua wenyi chubanshe, 1984.

Tan Zhengbi and Tan Xun 譚尋, comps., *Tanci xulu* 彈詞敘錄. Shanghai: Shanghai guji chubanshe, 1981.

———. *Pingtan tongkao* 評彈通考. Beijing: Zhongguo quyi chubanshe, 1985.

Tang Guizhang 唐圭璋, comp., *Quan Song ci* 全宋詞. Beijing: Zhonghua shuju, 1965.

Tao Shan 陶善, *Qionglou yingao* 瓊樓吟稿, in *Xuzangjing*, vol. 138.

Tao Zhenhuai 陶貞懷, *Tianyuhua* 天雨花, ed. by Li Ping 李平. Zhengzhou: Zhongzhou guji chubanshe, 1984.

Wang Ding 王鼎, *Fenjiao lu* 焚椒錄, in *Zhongguo guyan xipin congkan* 中國古艷稀品叢刊. Taibei: n.p., n.d., vol. I, *Ruyijun zhuan deng shizhong* 如意君傳等十.

Wang Duan 汪端, *Ming sanshijia shixuan* 明三十家詩選, woodblock ed. Hangzhou?: Yunlan yinguan, 1873.

Wang Duanshu 王端淑, *Yinhong ji* 吟紅集, woodblock ed. N.p., ca. 1670.

Wang Duanshu, comp., *Mingyuan shiwei chubian* 名媛詩緯初編, woodblock ed. Hangzhou?: Qingyintang, 1667.

Wang Qi 王琦, ann., *Li Taibai ji* 李太白集. Beijing: Zhonghua shuju, 1977.

Wang Renjun 王仁俊, comp., *Yuhan shanfang jiyishu xubian sanzhong* 玉函山房輯佚書續編三種. Shanghai: Shanghai guji chubanshe, 1989.

Wang Wencai 王文才, ed., *Yang Shen ciqu ji* 楊慎詞曲集. Chengdu: Sichuan renmin chubanshe, 1984.

Wang Xuechu 王學初, ed., *Li Qingzhao ji jiaozhu* 李清照集校註. Beijing: Renmin wenxue chubanshe, 1979.

Wang Yongkuan 王永寬 et. al., eds., *Qingdai zaju xuan* 清代雜劇選. Zhengzhou: Zhongzhou guji chubanshe, 1991.

Wang Zhuo 王灼, *Biji manzhi* 碧雞漫志, in *Zhongguo gudian xiqu lunzhu jicheng* 中國古典戲曲論著集成. Beijing: Zhongguo xiju chubanshe, 1959, vol. I.

Wanyan Yun Zhu 完顏惲珠, *Guochao guixiu zhengshi ji* 國朝閨秀正始集, woodblock edition. N.p.: Hongxiang guan, 1831–1836.

Wu Jingzi 吳敬梓, *Rulin waishi huijiao huiping ben* 儒林外史會校會評本, ed. by Li Hanqiu 李漢秋. Shanghai: Shanghai guji chubanshe, 1984.

Wu Zao 吳藻, *Hualianci* 花簾詞, in Xu Naichang 徐乃昌, ed., *Xiaotanluanshi huike guixiuci* 小檀欒室彙刻閨秀詞, woodblock ed. N.p.: Xiaotanluanshi, 1896.

———. *Xiangnan xuebei ci* 香南雪北詞, in *Xiaotanluanshi huike guixiuci*.

———. *Qiaoying* 喬影, in Zheng Zhenduo 鄭振鐸, comp., *Qingren zaju erji* 情人雜劇二集. N.p., 1934 (reprinted in Zheng Zhenduo, *Qingren zaju chu er ji hedingben* 清人雜劇初二集合訂本. Hong Kong: Longmen shudian, 1969).

Wu Zeng 吳曾, *Nenggaizhai manlu* 能改齋漫錄. Beijing: Zhonghua shuju, 1960.

Xi Peilan 席佩蘭, *Changzhenge ji* 長真閣集, woodblock ed. N.p.: Qiangshi Nangao caolu, 1891.

Xia Tingzhi 夏庭芝, *Qinglou ji* 青樓集, in *Zhongguo gudian xiqu lunzhu jicheng*, vol. 2.

Xiao Tong 蕭統, comp., *Wen xuan* 文選. Beijing: Zhonghua shuju, 1977.

Xiao Yi 蕭繹 (Liang Yuandi 梁元帝), *Jinlouzi* 金樓子, in *Zhongguo zixue mingzhu jicheng* 中國子學名著集成. Taibei(?): Zhongguo zixue mingzhu bianyin weiyuanhui, 1978 (?), vol. 90.

Xin Tang shu 新唐書. Beijing: Zhonghua shuju, 1975.

Xu Can 徐燦, *Zhuozhengyuan shi yu* 拙政園詩集, in *Xiaotanluanshi huike guixiuci*. N.p., 1896.

———. *Zhuozhengyuan shi ji* 拙政園詩集, in *Baijinglou congshu* 拜經樓叢書. Shanghai: Boguzhai, 1922.

Xu Ling 徐陵, comp., Wu Zhaoyi 吳兆宜, ann., Cheng Yan 程琰, ed., *Yutai xinyong jianzhu* 玉臺新詠箋注. Beijing: Zhonghua shuju, 1985.

Xu Shichang 徐世昌, comp., *Qingshihui* 清詩匯. Beijing: Beijing chubanshe, 1995.

Xu Shiwen 徐式文, ann., *Huarui gongci jianzhu* 花蕊宮詞箋注. Chengdu: Ba Shu shushe, 1992.

Xu Shumin 徐樹敏, *Zhongxiangci* 眾香詞. Shanghai: Dadong shuju, 1933.

Xu Zhenbang 徐振邦, ed., *Gudai nüzi aiqing shixuan* 古代女子愛情詩選. Beijing: Dazhong wenyi chubanshe, 1998.

Yan Kejun 嚴可均, *Quan Shanggu Sandai Qin Han Sanguo Liuchao wen* 全上古三代秦漢三國六朝文. Beijing: Zhonghua shuju, 1965.

Yan Yu 嚴羽, *Canglang shihua jiaoshi* 滄浪詩話校釋, ann. by Guo Shaoyu 郭紹虞. Beijing: Renmin wenxue chubanshe, 1983.

Ye Shaoyuan 葉紹袁, comp., *Wumengtang ji* 午夢堂集. Beijing: Zhonghua shuju, 1998.

Ye Ziqi 葉子奇, *Caomuzi* 草木子. Beijing: Zhonghua shuju, 1959.

Yuan Mei 袁枚, *Suiyuan shihua* 隨園詩話. Nanjing: Jiangsu guji chubanshe, 2000.

Yuncha waishi 雲槎外史, *Hongloumeng ying* 紅樓夢影. Beijing: Beijing daxue chubanshe, 1988.

Zeng Yongyi 曾永義, *Shuo suwenxue* 說俗文學. Taibei: Lianjing chuban shiye gongsi, 1980.

Zhang Chao 張潮, comp., *Yuchu xinzhi* 虞初新志, in *Yuchu zhi heji* 虞初志合集. Shanghai: Kaiming shudian, 1935 (reprint Shanghai: Shanghai shudian, 1986).

Zhang Fuqing 張福清, comp., *Nü jie* 女誡. Beijing: Zhongyang minzu daxue chubanshe, 1996.

Zhang Xuecheng 章學誠, *Zhang Xuecheng yishu* 章學誠遺書. Beijing: Wenwu chubanshe, 1985.

Zhang Yuniang 張玉孃, *Lanxue ji* 蘭雪集, in *Tuobachan congke* 託跋廛叢刻. Yanghu: Taoshi Sheyuan, 1925.

Zhang Yunzi 張允滋, comp., Ren Zhaolin 任兆麟, ed., *Wuzhong nüshi shichao* 吳中女士詩鈔, woodblock ed. N.p., 1789.

Zhang Zhang 張璋 and Huang Yu 黃畬, eds., *Quan Tang wudai ci* 全唐五代詞. Shanghai: Shanghai guji chubanshe, 1986.

———. *Zhu Shuzhen ji* 朱淑真集. Shanghai: Shanghai guji chubanshe, 1986.

Zhanzhan waishi 詹詹外史, comp., *Qingshi* 情史. Shenyang: Chunfeng wenyi chubanshe, 1986.

Zhao Liming 趙麗明, ed., *Zhongguo nüshu jicheng* 中國女書集成. Beijing: Qinghua daxue chubanshe, 1992.

Zheng Acai 鄭阿財, "Dunhuang xieben 'Cuishi furen xunnü wen' yanjiu," 敦煌寫本《崔氏夫人訓女文》研究, in his *Dunhuang wenxian yu wenxue* 敦煌文獻與文學. Taipei: Xinwenfeng chubanshe, 1993, pp. 277–301.

Zheng Yunduan 鄭允端, *Suyong ji* 蕭雝集, in *Hanfenlou miji san* 涵芬樓秘笈三. Taibei: Taiwan shangwu yinshuguan, 1967.

Zhengshou 正受, *Jiadai pudeng lu* 嘉泰普燈錄, in *Xuzangjing*, vol. 137.

Zhenhua 震華, *Xu biqiuni zhuan* 續比丘尼傳, in *Biqiuni zhuan quanji*. Taibei: Fojiao shuju, 1988.

Zhong Huiling 鐘慧玲, *Qingdai nüshiren yanjiu* 清代女詩人研究. Taibei: Liren shuju, 2000.

———. *Qingdai nüzuojia zhuanti: Wu Zao ji qi xiangguan wenxue huodong yanjiu* 清代女作家專題：吳藻及其相關文學活動研究. Taibei: Lexue shuju, 2001.

Zhong Rong 鍾嶸, *Shipin zhu* 詩品注, ann. by Chen Yanjie 陳延傑. Beijing: Renmin wenxue chubanshe, 1980.

Zhong Xing 鍾惺, *Mingyuan shigui* 名媛詩歸, in *Siku quanshu cunmu congshu* 四庫全書存目叢書. Jinan: Qilu shushe, 1997, vol. 339.

Zhou Lianggong 周亮工, *Shu ying* 書影. Shanghai: Gudian wenxue chubanshe, 1957.

Zhou Shutian 周書田, ed., *Liu Rushi ji* 柳如是集. Shenyang: Liaodong jiaoyu chubanshe, 2001.

Zhou Xunchu 周勛初, comp., *Tangren yishi huibian* 唐人軼事彙編. Shanghai: Shanghai guji chubanshe, 1995.

Zhuangzi jishi 莊子集釋. Beijing: Zhonghua shuju, 1961.

Suggested
Readings

Introductions to Chinese Literature and Poetics

Wilt Idema and Lloyd Haft, *A Guide to Chinese Literature*. Ann Arbor: Center for Chinese Studies, University of Michigan, 1997.

Victor Mair, ed., *The Columbia History of Chinese Literature*. New York: Columbia University Press, 2002.

William Nienhauser, Jr., ed., *The Indiana Companion to Traditional Chinese Literature*. Bloomington: Indiana University Press, 1986.

———. *The Indiana Companion to Traditional Chinese Literature*, Vol. II. Bloomington: Indiana University Press, 1998.

Stephen Owen, *Traditional Chinese Poetry and Poetics, Omens of the World*. Madison: The University of Wisconsin Press, 1985.

———. *Readings in Chinese Literary Thought*. Cambridge, Mass.: Harvard University Press, 1992.

General Anthologies of Chinese Literature

Cyril Birch, ed., *Anthology of Chinese Literature: From Early Times to the Fourteenth Century*. New York: Grove, 1965.

———. *Anthology of Chinese Literature*, Vol. II: *From the 14th Century to the Present Day*. New York: Grove, 1972.

Victor Mair, ed., *The Columbia Anthology of Traditional Chinese Literature*. New York: Columbia University Press, 1994.

Stephen Owen, ed. and trans., *An Anthology of Chinese Literature, Beginnings to 1911*. New York: Norton, 1996.

Anthologies of Chinese Women's Poetry

Kang-i Sun Chang and Haun Saussy, eds., *Women Writers of Traditional China: An Anthology of Poetry and Criticism*. Stanford: Stanford University Press, 1999.

Beata Grant, trans., *Daughters of Emptiness: Poems of Chinese Buddhist Nuns*. Boston: Wisdom Publications, 2003.

Kenneth Rexroth and Ling Chung, trans., *Women Poets of China*. New York: New Directions, 1972.

General Reviews of Studies on Women in Imperial China

Jennifer Holmgren, "Myth, Fantasy, and Scholarship: Images of the Status of Women in Traditional China," *Australian Journal of Chinese Affairs* 6 (1981): 147–170.

Paul S. Ropp, "Women in Late Imperial China: A Review of Recent English-language Scholarship," *Women's History Review* 3 (1994): 347–383.

Jinhua Emma Teng, "The Construction of the 'Traditional Chinese Woman' in the Western Academy: A Critical Review," *Signs* 22 (1996): 115–151.

Ellen Widmer, "The Rhetoric of Retrospection: May Fourth Literary History and the Ming-Qing Woman Writer," in Milena Doleželová-Velingerová and Oldřich Král, eds., *The Appropriation of Cultural Capital: China's May Fourth Project*. Cambridge, Mass.: Harvard University Asia Center, 2001, pp. 193–225.

Part One: *Early Models for Later Ages*

Chapter 1: *Women On and Behind the Throne*

Robert Joe Cutter and William Gordon Crowell, trans., *Empresses and Consorts: Selections from Chen Shou's* Records of the Three States *with Pei Songzhi's Commentary*. Honolulu: University of Hawaii Press, 1999.

Bret Hinsch, *Women in Early Imperial China*. Lanham: Rowman and Littlefield, 2002.

Rowen R. Tung, *Fables for the Patriarchs: Gender Politics in Tang Discourse*. Lanham: Rowman and Littlefield, 2000.

Ban Zhao

Yu-shih Chen, "The Historical Template of Pan Chao's *Nü-chieh*," *T'oung Pao* 82 (1996): 229–257.

Lily Xiao Hong Lee, "Ban Zhao (c. 48–c. 120): Her Role in the Formulation of Controls Imposed Upon Women in Traditional China," in her *The Virtue of Yin: Studies on Chinese Women*. Broadway NSW: Wild Peony, 1994, pp. 11–24.

Nancy Lee Swann, "Biography of Empress Teng," *Journal of the American Oriental Society* 51 (1931): 138–159.

————. *Pan Chao, Foremost Woman Scholar of China, First Century A.D.: Background, Ancestry, Life and Writings of the Most Celebrated Chinese Woman of Letters.* New York: The Century Co., 1932 (rep., with a new introduction by Susan Mann, 2001).

Tienchi Martin-Liao, "Traditional Handbooks of Women's Education," in Anna Gerstlacker et al., eds., *Women and Literature in China.* Bochum: Brockmeyer, 1985, pp. 165–189.

John E. Wills, "Ban Zhao," in his *Mountain of Fame: Portraits in Chinese History.* Princeton: Princeton University Press, 1994, pp. 90–99.

Xiao Tong, *Wen Xuan or Selections of Refined Literature*, Vol. 11, trans. by David Knechtges. Princeton: Princeton University Press, 1987, pp. 173–179, "Rhapsody on an Eastward Journey."

Zhang Mingqi, "The Four Books for Women: Ancient Chinese Texts for the Education of Women," trans. by Gary Arbuckle and Rosemary Haddon, *British Columbia Asian Review* 2 (1988): 174–184.

Poets, Teachers, Moralists

Patricia Buckley Ebrey, trans., "The *Book of Filial Piety for Women* Attributed to a Woman Née Zheng (ca. 730)," in Susan Mann and Yu-yin Cheng, eds., *Under Confucian Eyes: Writings on Gender in Chinese History.* Stanford: Stanford University Press, 2001, pp. 47–70.

Julia Murray, "The *Ladies' Classic of Filial Piety* and Sung Textual Illustration: Problems of Reconstruction and Artistic Context," *Ars Orientalis* 18 (1988): 95–129.

————. "Didactic Art for Women: The *Ladies' Classic of Filial Piety*," in Marsha Weidner, ed., *Flowering in the Shadows: Women in the History of Chinese and Japanese Painting.* Honolulu: University of Hawaii Press, 1990, pp. 27–53.

Beatrice Spade, "The Education of Women in China During the Southern Dynasties," *Journal of Asian History* 13 (1979): 15–41.

Shangguan Wan'er: Ghostwriter for Two Empresses

Stephen R. Bokenkamp, "A Medieval Feminist Critique of the Chinese World Order: The Case of Wu Zhao (r. 690–705)," *Religions* 28 (1998): 383–392.

Chen Jo-shui, "Empress Wu and Proto-Feminist Sentiments in T'ang China," in Frederick Brandauer and Chun-chieh Huang, eds., *Imperial Rulership and Cultural Change in Traditional China.* Seattle: University of Washington Press, 1994, pp. 77–116.

Stephen Owen, "The Formation of the Tang Estate Poem," *Harvard Journal of Asiatic Studies* 55 (1995): 39–59.

John E. Wills, "Empress Wu," in his *Mountain of Fame*, pp. 127–148.

Chapter 2: *Neglected Palace Ladies and Other Phantoms*

Priscilla Ching Chung, *Palace Ladies of the Northern Sung, 960–1126*. Leiden: E.J. Brill, 1981.

Slandered Virtue: Concubine Ban

David Knechtges, "The Poetry of an Imperial Concubine: The Favorite Beauty Ban," *Oriens Extremus* 36 (1993): 127–144.

Burton Watson, trans., *Courtier and Commoner in Ancient China: Selections from the History of the Former Han by Pan Ku*. New York: Columbia University Press, 1974, pp. 247–278, "Accounts of the Families Related to the Emperors by Marriage (Excerpts)."

Fact and Fiction: Phantom Poems and Phantom Lives

Paul Rouzer, *Articulated Ladies: Gender and the Male Community in Early Chinese Texts*. Cambridge, Mass.: Harvard University Asia Center, 2001.

A Disputed Beauty: Empress Zhen

Robert J. Cutter, "The Death of Empress Zhen: Fiction and Historiography in Early Medieval China," *Journal of the American Oriental Society* 112 (1992): 567–582.

Banished Beyond the Border: Liu Xijun and Wang Zhaojun

Cao Yu, *The Consort of Peace*, trans. by Monica Lai. Hong Kong: Kelly and Walsh, 1980.

Eugene Eoyang, "The Wang Chao-chün Legend: Configurations of the Classic," *Chinese Literature: Essays, Articles, Reviews* 4 (1982): 3–22.

Ma Chih-yüan, "Autumn in the Palace of Han," trans. by Donald Keene, in Cyril Birch, ed., *Anthology of Chinese Literature, from Early Times to the Fourteenth Century*, pp. 422–448.

Ning Chia, "Women in China's Frontier Politics: *Heqin*," in Sherry J. Mou, ed., *Presence and Presentation: Women in the Chinese Literati Tradition*. New York: St. Martin's Press, 1999, pp. 39–76.

Other Phantoms

The Eloping Widow: Zhuo Wenjun

W. L. Idema, "The Story of Ssu-ma Hsiang-ju and Cho Wen-chün in Vernacular Literature of the Yüan and Early Ming Dynasties," *T'oung Pao* 70 (1984): 60–109.

Burton Watson, trans., *Records of the Grand Historian of China, Translated from the Shih-chi of Ssu-ma Ch'ien*, Vol. II. New York: Columbia University Press, 1961, pp. 297–342.

Abducted and Ransomed: Cai Yan

Rewi Alley, *The Eighteen Laments of Ts'ai Wen-chi: Later Han Dynasty*. Peking: New World Press, 1963.

Hans H. Frankel, "Cai Yan and the Poems Attributed to Her," *Chinese Literature: Essays, Articles, Reviews* 5 (1984): 133–156.

Itakura Masaaki, "Representations of Politicalness and Regionality in Wen-chi's Return to China," *Acta Asiatica* 84 (2003): 20–41.

Dore J. Levy, *Chinese Narrative Poetry: The Late Han through T'ang Dynasties*. Durham: Duke University Press, 1988.

———. "Transforming Archetypes in Chinese Poetry and Painting," *Asia Major* Third Series 6 (1993): 147–168.

Robert A. Rorex and Wen Fong, *Eighteen Songs of a Nomad Flute: The Story of Lady Wen-chi*. New York: Metropolitan Museum of Art, 1974.

Chapter 3: *Ladies, Nuns, and Courtesans*

Lienü zhuan and Other Collections of Women's Biographies

Sherry J. Mou, "Writing Virtues with Their Bodies: Rereading the Two Tang Histories' Biographies of Women," in Sherry J. Mou, ed., *Presence and Presentation: Women in the Chinese Literati Tradition*. New York: St. Martin's Press, 1999, pp. 109–148.

———. *Gentlemen's Prescriptions for Women's Lives: A Thousand Years of Biographies of Chinese Women*. Armonk, N.Y.: M.E. Sharpe, 2004.

Albert Richard O'Hara, *The Position of Woman in Early China, According to the Lieh Nü Chuan, "The Biographies of Eminent Chinese Women."* Washington D.C.: The Catholic University of America Press, 1945.

Lisa Raphals, *Sharing the Light: Representations of Women and Virtue in Early China*. Albany: State University of New York Press, 1998.

Marina H. Sung, "The Chinese Lieh-nü Tradition," in Richard E. Guisso and Stanley Johannesen, eds., *Women in China: Current Directions in Historical Scholarship*. Youngstown, N.Y.: Philo Press, 1981, pp. 63–74.

Brilliant Daughters and Dutiful Wives

The Poet of a Single Line: Xie Daoyun

Lily Xiao Hong Lee, "Xie Daoyun: The Style of a Woman Mingshi," in her *The Virtue of Yin: Studies on Chinese Women*. Broadway NSW: Wild Peony, 1994, pp. 25–46.

Richard Mather, trans., *Shih-shuo Hsin-yü: A New Account of Tales of the World*, by *Liu I-ch'ing, with commentary by Liu Chün*. Minneapolis: University of Minnesota Press, 1976.

Beatrice Spade, "The Education of Women in China during the Southern Dynasties," *Journal of Asian History* 13 (1979): 15–41.

Different Voices: Liu Lingxian

Anne Birrell, "In the Voice of Women: Chinese Love Poetry in the Early Middle Ages," in Lesley Smith and Jane H. M. Taylor, eds., *Women, the Book and the Worldly*. Cambridge: D.S. Brewer, 1995, pp. 49–59.

———, trans., *New Songs from a Jade Terrace: An Anthology of Early Chinese Love Poetry*. London: George Allen and Unwin, 1982 (rep. as Penguin Classic).

Maureen Robertson, "Voicing the Feminine: Constructions of the Gendered Subject in Lyric Poetry by Women of Medieval and Late Imperial China," *Late Imperial China* 13 (1992): 63–110.

Buddhist Nuns and Daoist Mystics

Buddhist Nuns

Ann Heirman, "Chinese Nuns and their Ordination in Fifth Century China," *Journal of the International Association of Buddhist Studies* 24:2 (2001): 275–304.

Li Jung-hsi, trans., *Biographies of Buddhist Nuns: Pao-ch'ang's Pi-chiu-ni-chuan*. Osaka: Tohokai, 1981.

Kathryn Ann Tsai, trans., *Lives of the Nuns: Biographies of Chinese Buddhist Nuns from the Fourth to the Sixth Centuries: A Translation of the Pi-ch'iu-ni chuan, compiled by Shih Pao-ch'ang*. Honolulu: University of Hawaii Press, 1994.

Daoist Mystics

Charles Benn, *The Cavern Mystery Transmission: A Taoist Ordination Rite of A.D. 711*. Honolulu: University of Hawaii Press, 1991.

Suzanne Cahill, "Performers and Female Taoist Adepts: Hsi Wang Mu as the Patron Deity of Women in Medieval China," *Journal of the American Oriental Society* 106:1 (1986): 155–168.

———. *Transcendence and Divine Passion: The Queen Mother of the West in Medieval China*. Stanford: Stanford University Press, 1993.

———. "Smell Good and Get a Job: How Daoist Women Saints Were Verified and Legitimated during the Tang Dynasty (618–907)," in Sherry J. Mou, ed., *Presence and Presentation: Women in the Chinese Literati Tradition*. New York: St. Martin's Press, 1999, pp. 171–186.

———. "Discipline and Transformation: Body and Practice in the Lives of Daoist Holy Women of Tang China," in Dorothy Ko, Jahyun Kim Haboush, and Joan Piggott, eds., *Women and Confucian Cultures in Premodern China, Korea, and Japan.* Berkeley: University of California Press, 2003, pp. 251–278.

Thomas Cleary, ed. and trans., *Immortal Sisters: Secrets of Taoist Women.* Boston: Shambhala, 1989.

Catherine Despeux, "Women in Daoism," in Livia Kohn, ed., *Daoism Handbook.* Leiden: E.J. Brill, 2000, pp. 384–412.

Livia Kohn and Catherine Despeux, *Women in Daoism.* Boston: Three Pines Press, 2003.

Self-Censoring Ladies and Public Women

Self-Censoring Ladies

Glen Dudbridge, *Religious Experience and Lay Society in T'ang China: A Reading of Tai Fu's Kuang-i chi.* Cambridge: Cambridge University Press, 1995.

Josephine Chiu Duke, "The Role of Confucian Revivalists in the Confucianization of Tang Women," *Asia Major* Third Series (1995): 51–94.

Public Women

Victor Xiong, "*Ji*-Entertainers in Tang Chang'an," in Sherry J. Mou, ed., *Presence and Presentation: Women in the Chinese Literati Tradition,* pp. 149–170.

Courtesan and Collator: Xue Tao

Jeanne Larsen, trans., *Brocade River Poems: Selected Works of the Tang Dynasty Courtesan Xue Tao.* Princeton: Princeton University Press, 1987.

Genevieve B. Wimsatt, *A Well of Fragrant Water: A Sketch of the Life and Writings of Hung Tu.* Boston: John B. Luce, 1954.

Concubine, Daoist Nun, and Murderer: Yu Xuanji

Suzanne Cahill, "Material Culture and the Dao: Textiles, Boats, and Zithers in the Poetry of Yu Xuanji (844–868)," in Livia Kohn and Harold D. Roth, eds., *Daoist Identity: History, Lineage and Ritual.* Honolulu: University of Hawaii Press, 2002, pp. 102–126.

Genevieve B. Wimsatt, *Selling Wilted Peonies: Biography and Songs of Yü Hsüan-chi.* New York: Columbia University Press, 1936.

David Young and Jiann I. Lin, trans., *The Clouds Float North: The Complete Poems of Yu Xuanji.* Hanover: Wesleyan University Press, 1998.

Part Two: *Between New Possibilities and New Limitations*
Chapter 4: *Li Qingzhao*

General Studies on Lyrics

Kang-i Sun Chang, *The Evolution of Chinese Tz'u Poetry: From the Late T'ang to the Northern Song*. Princeton: Princeton University Press, 1980.

Grace S. Fong, "Engendering the Lyric: Her Image and Voice in Song," in Pauline Yu, ed., *Voices of the Song Lyric in China*. Berkeley: University of California Press, 1994, pp. 107–144.

James J. Y. Liu, *Major Lyricists of the Northern Sung AD 960–1126*. Princeton: Princeton University Press, 1974.

Marsha L. Wagner, *The Lotus Boat: The Origins of Tz'u Poetry in T'ang Popular Culture*. New York: Columbia University Press, 1984.

Studies on Women in Song Society

Bettine Birge, "Chu Hsi and Women's Education," in Wm. Theodore de Bary and John W. Chaffee, eds., *Neo-Confucian Education: The Formative Stage*. Berkeley: University of California Press, 1989, pp. 325–367.

Beverly Bossler, "Women's Literacy in Song Dynasty China: Preliminary Inquiries," in Tian Yuqing et. al., eds., *Qingzhu Deng Guangming jiaoshou jiushi huadan lunwenji*. Shijiazhuang, 1997, pp. 322–352.

Patricia Buckley Ebrey, *The Inner Quarters: Marriage and the Life of Women in the Sung Period*. Berkeley: University of California Press, 1993.

Jian Zang, "Women and the Transmission of Confucian Culture in Song China," in Dorothy Ko, Jahyun Kim Haboush, and Joan Piggott, eds., *Women and Confucian Cultures in Premodern China, Korea, and Japan*, pp. 123–141.

Studies and Translations of Li Qingzhao

Siu-Pang E. Almberg, "Li Qingzhao: Letter to the Academician Qi Chongli," *Renditions* 41/42 (1994): 79–84.

Patricia Buckley Ebrey, *Women and the Family in Chinese History*. London: Routledge, 2003.

James Cryer, trans., *Plum Blossom: Poems of Li Ch'ing-chao*. Chapel Hill: Carolina Wren Press, 1984.

Sam Hamill, trans., *The Lotus Lovers: Tzu-yeh and Li Ch'ing-chao*. St. Paul: Coffee House Press, 1985.

Lucy Chao Ho, *'More Gracile than Yellow Flowers': The Life and Works of Li Ch'ing-Chao*. Hong Kong: Mayfair Press, 1968.

Hu Pin-ching, *Li Ch'ing-chao*. New York: Twayne, 1965.

Stephen Owen, "The Snares of Memory," in his *Remembrances: The Experience of the Past in Classical Chinese Literature*. Cambridge, Mass.: Harvard University Press, 1986, pp. 80–98.

Kenneth Rexroth and Ling Chung, trans., *Li Ch'ing-chao: Complete Poems*. New York: New Directions, 1979.

Jiaosheng Wang, trans., *The Complete Ci-poems of Li Qingzhao: A New Translation*, *Sino-Platonic Papers* 13 (1989).

Timothy Wixted, "The Poetry of Li Ch'ing-chao: A Woman Author and Woman's Authorship," in Pauline Yu, ed., *Voices of the Song Lyric in China*, pp. 145–168.

Chapter 5: *Talent and Fate*

An Unhappy Marriage: Zhu Shuzhen

Wilt L. Idema, "Male Fantasies and Female Realities: Chu Shu-chen and Chang Yü-niang and their Biographers," in Harriet Zurndorfer, ed., *Chinese Women in the Imperial Past: New Perspectives*. Leiden: E.J. Brill, 1999, pp. 19–52.

Doomed Love: Zhang Yuniang

Wilt L. Idema, "Male Fantasies and Female Realities: Chu Shu-chen and Chang Yü-niang and their Biographers," in Harriet Zurndorfer, ed., *Chinese Women in the Imperial Past: New Perspectives*, pp. 19–52.

Guan Daosheng and Huang E

Ch'en Hsiao-lan and F. W. Mote, "Yang Shen and Huang O: Husband and Wife as Lovers, Poets, and Historical Figures," in Marie Chan et. al., eds., *Excursions in Chinese Culture: Festschrift in Honor of William R. Schultz*. Hong Kong: The Chinese University of Hong Kong, 2002, pp. 1–32.

Morris Rossabi, "Kuan Tao-sheng: Woman Artist in Yuan China," *Bulletin of Sung-Yuan Studies* 21 (1989): 67–84.

Chapter 6: *Empresses, Nuns, and Actresses*

Empresses and Palace Ladies

Empress Yang and More Palace Songs

Genevieve Wimsatt, *Apricot Cheeks and Almond Eyes*. New York: Columbia University Press, 1939.

Xiao Guanyin and Her Sorry Fate

Aidong Zhang and Wayne Schlepp, "Xiao Guanyin: Her Tragic Life and Melancholy Poems," *Journal of Sung-Yuan Studies* 28 (1998): 213–221.

Empress Xu and the Bodhisattva Guanyin

Glenn Dudbridge, *The Legend of Miao-shan*. London: Ithaca Press, 1978 (rev. ed. Oxford University Press, 2004).

Chün-fang Yü, *Kuan-yin: The Chinese Transformation of Avalokitesvara*. New York: Columbia University Press, 2000.

Nuns

Ding-hwa E. Hsieh, "Images of Women in Ch'an Buddhist Literature of the Sung Period," in Peter N. Gregory and Daniel A. Getz, Jr., eds., *Buddhism in the Sung*. Honolulu: University of Hawaii Press, 1999, pp. 148–187.

———. "Buddhist Nuns in Sung China (960–1279)," *Journal of Sung-Yuan Studies* 30 (2000): 63–96.

Miriam L. Levering, "The Dragon Girl and the Abbess of Mo-shan: Gender and Status in the Ch'an Buddhist Tradition," *Journal of the International Association of Buddhist Studies* 5:1 (1982): 19–35.

———. "Stories of Enlightened Women in Ch'an and the Chinese Buddhist Female Bodhisattva / Goddess Tradition," in Karen L. King, ed., *Women and Goddess Traditions in Antiquity and Today*. Minneapolis: Fortress Press, 1997, pp. 137–176.

———. "Miao-tao and her Teacher Ta-hui," in Peter N. Gregory and Daniel A. Getz, Jr., eds., *Buddhism in the Sung*, pp. 188–219.

———. "Women Ch'an Masters: The Teacher Miao-tsung as Saint," in Arvind Sharma, ed., *Women Saints in World Religions*. Albany: State University of New York Press, 2000.

Courtesans and Actresses

J. I. Crump, *Songs from Xanadu*. Ann Arbor: Center of Chinese Studies, University of Michigan, 1983, pp. 171–192, "The Lost Love Story."

Wilt Idema and Stephen H. West, *Chinese Theater 1100–1450: A Source Book*. Wiesbaden: Franz Steiner Verlag, 1982, pp. 142–171, "Some Views of the Social Position of Actors and Actresses."

Part Three: *The First High Tide of Women's Literature*

Kang-i Sun Chang, "A Guide to Ming-Ch'ing Anthologies of Female Poetry and Their Selection Strategies," *The Gest Library Journal* 5 (1992): 119–160 (also in Ellen Widmer and Kang-i Sun Chang, eds., *Writing Women in Late Imperial China*. Stanford: Stanford University Press, 1997, pp. 147–170).

———. "Ming-Qing Women Poets and the Notions of 'Talent' and 'Morality,'" in Theodore Huters, R. Bin Wong, and Pauline Yu, eds., *Culture and State in Chi-*

nese History: Conventions, Accommodations and Critiques. Stanford: Stanford University Press, 1997, pp. 236–258.

————. "Gender and Canonicity: Ming-Qing Women Poets in the Eyes of the Male Literati," *Hsiang Lectures on Chinese Poetry* 1 (2001): 1–18.

Clara Wing-chung Ho, "The Cultivation of Female Talent: Views on Women's Education During the Early and Late Qing Periods," *Journal of the Economic and Social History of the Orient* 38 (1995): 191–223.

Dorothy Ko, *Teachers of the Inner Chambers: Women and Culture in Seventeenth-Century China*. Stanford: Stanford University Press, 1994.

Maureen Robertson, "Changing the Subject: Gender and Self-Inscription in Authors' Prefaces and *Shi* Poetry," in Ellen Widmer and Kang-i Sun Chang, eds., *Writing Women in Late Imperial China*, pp. 171–217.

Marsha Weidner, ed., *Views from Jade Terrace: Chinese Women Artists 1300–1912*. Indianapolis: Indianapolis Museum of Art, 1988.

Chapter 7: *Courtesans*

Victoria Cass, *Dangerous Women: Warriors, Grannies, and Geishas of the Ming*. Lanham: Rowman and Littlefield, 1999.

Dorothy Ko, "The Written Word and the Bound Foot: A History of the Courtesan's Aura," in Ellen Widmer and Kang-i Sun Chang, eds., *Writing Women in Late Imperial China*, 1997, pp. 74–100.

Wai-yee Li, "The Late-Ming Courtesan: Invention of a Cultural Ideal," in Ellen Widmer and Kang-i Sun Chang, eds., *Writing Women in Late Imperial China*, pp. 46–73.

Paul S. Ropp, "Ambiguous Images of Courtesan Culture in Late Imperial China," in Ellen Widmer and Kang-i Sun Chang, eds., *Writing Women in Late Imperial China*, pp. 17–45.

Liu Shi

James Cahill, "The Paintings of Liu Yin," in Marsha Weidner, ed., *Flowering in the Shadows: Women in the History of Chinese and Japanese Painting*, pp. 103–121.

Kang-i Sun Chang, *The Late-Ming Poet Ch'en Tzu-lung: Crises of Love and Loyalism*. New Haven: Yale University Press, 1991.

————. "Liu Shih and Hsü Ts'an: Feminine or Feminist?" in Pauline Yu, ed., *Voices of the Song Lyric in China*, pp. 169–187.

Chapter 8: *Matrons and Maidens*
Shen Yixiu and Her Daughters

Dorothy Ko, *Teachers of the Inner Chambers: Women and Culture in Seventeenth-Century China*, pp. 179–218, "Domestic Communities: Male and Female Domains."

Ann Waltner and Pi-ching Hsu, "Lingering Fragrance: The Poetry of Tu Yaose and Shen Tiansun," *Journal of Women's History* 8/4 (1997): 28–53.

Gu Ruopu and Liang Mengzhao

Dorothy Ko, *Teachers of the Inner Chambers: Women and Culture in Seventeenth-Century China*, pp. 219–250, "Social and Public Communities."

———, trans., "'Letter to my Sons' by Gu Ruopu (1592–ca. 1681)," in Susan Mann and Yu-yin Cheng, eds., *Under Confucian Eyes: Writings on Gender in Chinese History*. Stanford: Stanford University Press, 2001, pp. 149–154.

Chapter 9: *Women Writers of the Conquest Period*

Dorothy Ko, *Teachers of the Inner Chambers: Women and Culture in Seventeenth-Century China*, pp. 115–142, "Margins of Domesticity: Enlarging Woman's Sphere."

Ellen Widmer, "The Epistolary World of Female Talent in Seventeenth-Century China," *Late Imperial China* 10 (1989): 1–43.

———, trans., "Selected Short Works by Wang Duanshu," in Susan Mann and Yu-yin Cheng, eds., *Under Confucian Eyes: Writings on Gender in Chinese History*, pp. 179–196.

Writing Nuns

Beata Grant, "Female Holders of the Lineage: Linji Chan Master Zhiyuan Xinggang (1597–1654)," *Late Imperial China* 17 (1996): 51–76.

———. "Severing the Red Cord: Buddhist Nuns in Eighteenth-Century China," in Karma Lekshe Tsomo, ed., *Buddhist Women Across Cultures: Realizations*. Albany, N.Y.: SUNY Press, 1999.

———. "Through the Empty Gate: The Poetry of Buddhist Nuns in Late Imperial China," in Marsha Weidner, ed., *Cultural Intersections in Late Chinese Buddhism*. Honolulu: University of Hawaii Press, 2001, pp. 87–113.

Chapter 10: *The Banana Garden Poetry Club*

Dorothy Ko, *Teachers of the Inner Chambers: Women and Culture in Seventeenth-Century China*, pp. 219–250, "Social and Public Communities."

Interlude: *Ideal and Reality*

Dorothy Ko, *Teachers of the Inner Chambers: Women and Culture in Seventeenth-Century China*, pp. 68–112, "The Enchantment of Love in *The Peony Pavilion*."

Judith T. Zeitlin, "Shared Dreams: The Story of the Three Wives' Commentary on *The Peony Pavilion*," *Harvard Journal of Asiatic Studies* 54 (1994): 127–179.

Chapter 11: *Ideal*

Xiaoqing

Ellen Widmer, "Xiaoqing's Literary Legacy and the Place of the Woman Writer in Late Imperial China," *Late Imperial China* 13 (1992): 111–155.

Poems on Walls

Grace S. Fong, "Signifying Bodies: The Cultural Significance of Suicide Writings by Women in Ming–Qing China," *Nan Nü* 3 (2001): 105–142.

Judith T. Zeitlin, "Disappearing Verses: Writings on Walls and Anxieties of Loss," in Judith T. Zeitlin and Lydia H. Liu, eds., *Writing and Materiality in China: Essays in Honor of Patrick Hanan.* Cambridge, Mass.: Harvard University Asia Center, 2003, pp. 73–132.

Lyrics on Flower Petals: Shuangqing

Elsie Choi, *Leaves of Prayer: The Life and Poetry of He Shuangqing, a Farmwife in Eighteenth-century China: Selected Translations from Shi Zhenlin's West Green Random Notes.* Hong Kong: The Chinese University Press, 1993.

Grace S. Fong, "De/Constructing a Feminine Ideal in the Eighteenth Century: *Random Records of West-Green* and the Story of Shuangqing," in Ellen Widmer and Kang-i Sun Chang, eds., *Writing Women in Late Imperial China,* pp. 264–281.

Paul S. Ropp, *Banished Immortal: Searching for Shuangqing, China's Peasant Woman Poet.* Ann Arbor: University of Michigan Press, 2001.

On Women's Traditions of Oral Literature

Fred Blake, "Death and Abuse in Marriage Laments: The Curse of Chinese Brides," *Asian Folklore Studies* 37 (1978): 13–33.

Anne McLaren, "The Oral and Ritual Culture of Chinese Women: Bridal Lamentations of Nanhui," *Asian Folklore Studies* 59 (2000): 205–238.

Rubie S. Watson, "Chinese Bridal Laments: The Claims of a Dutiful Daughter," in Bell Yung et. al., eds., *Harmony and Counterpoint: Ritual Music in Chinese Context.* Stanford: Stanford University Press, 1996, pp. 107–129.

On Women's Script Literature

William W. Chiang, *'We Two Know the Script; We Have Become Good Friends': Linguistic and Social Aspects of the Women's Script Literacy in Southern Hunan, China.* Lanham: University Press of America, 1995.

Wilt L. Idema, "*Changben* Texts in the *Nüshu* Repertoire of Southern Hunan," in Vibeke Bordhal, ed., *The Eternal Storyteller: Oral Literature in Modern China.* Richmond: Curzon, 1999, pp. 95–114.

Pei-wen Liu, "The Confrontation Between Fidelity and Fertility: *Nüshu, Nüge*, and Peasant Women's Conceptions of Widowhood in Jiangyong County, Hunan Province, China," *Journal of Asian Studies* 60 (2001): 1051–1084.

Liu Shouhua and Hu Xiaoshen, "Folk Narrative Literature in Chinese *Nüshu*: An Amazing New Discovery," *Asian Folklore Studies* 53 (1994): 307–318.

Anne McLaren, "Women's Voices and Textuality: Chastity and Abduction in Chinese *Nüshu* Writing," *Modern China* 22 (1996): 382–416.

———. "On Researching Invisible Women: Abduction and Violation in Chinese Women's Script Writing," in Antonia Finnane and Anne McLaren, eds., *Dress, Sex, and Text in Chinese Culture*. Clayton: Monash Asia Institute, 1999, pp. 164–179.

Cathy Silber, "From Daughter to Daughter-in-law in the Women's Script of Southern Hunan," in Christina Gilmartin et. al., eds., *Engendering China: Women, Culture and the State*. Cambridge, Mass.: Harvard University Press, 1994, pp. 47–68.

Chapter 12: *Reality*

How to Escape the Female Condition

Beata Grant, "The Spiritual Saga of Woman Huang: From Pollution to Purification," in David Johnson, ed., *Ritual Opera, Operatic Ritual*. Berkeley: IEAS Publications, 1989, pp. 224–311.

Yang Hsien-yi and Gladys Yang, trans., *Love under the Willows: Liang Shan-po and Chu Ying-tai (A Szechuan Opera)*. Peking: Foreign Languages Press, 1956.

Part Four: *The Second High Tide of Women's Literature*

Clara Wing-chung Ho, "Conventionality versus Dissent: Designations of the Titles of Women's Collected Works in Qing China," *Ming Qing yanjiu* 3 (1994): 47–90.

———. "The Cultivation of Female Talent: Views on Women's Education during the Early and High Qing Periods," *Journal of the Economic and Social History of the Orient* 38 (1995): 191–223.

———. "Encouragement from the Opposite Gender: Male Scholars and Women's Publications in Ch'ing China," in Harriet Zurndorfer, ed., *Chinese Women in the Imperial Past: New Perspectives*, pp. 308–353.

Susan Mann, "'Fuxue' (Women's Learning) by Zhang Xuecheng (1738–1801): China's First History of Women's Culture," *Late Imperial China* 13 (1992): 40–62.

———. "Talented Women in Local Gazetteers of the Lingnan Region during the Eighteenth and Nineteenth Centuries," *Jindai Zhongguo funüshi yanjiu* 3 (1995): 123–141.

————. "Women in the Life and Thought of Zhang Xuecheng," in Philip J. Ivanhoe, ed., *Chinese Language, Thought, and Culture: Nivison and His Critics*. Chicago: Open Court, 1997, pp. 94–120.

————. *Precious Records: Women in China's Long Eighteenth Century*. Stanford: Stanford University Press, 1997.

Paul S. Ropp, "Love, Literacy, and Laments: Themes of Women Writers in Late Imperial China," *Women's History Review* 2 (1993): 107–142.

William T. Rowe, "Women and the Family in Mid-Qing Social Thought: The Case of Chen Hongmou," *Late Imperial China* 13 (1992): 1–41.

Haun Saussy, "Women's Writing Before and Within the *Hong lou meng*," in Ellen Widmer and Kang-i Sun Chang, eds., *Writing Women in Late Imperial China*, pp. 285–305.

Ellen Widmer, "Considering a Coincidence: The 'Female Reading Public' Circa 1828," in Judith T. Zeitlin and Lydia H. Liu, eds., *Writing and Materiality in China: Essays in Honor of Patrick Hanan*, pp. 273–314.

Chapter 13: *Poetry*
Poetry and Piety

Beata Grant, "Who is this I? Who is that Other? The Poetry of an Eighteenth Century Buddhist Laywoman," *Late Imperial China* 15 (1994): 47–86.

————. "Little Vimalakirti: Buddhism and Poetry in the Writings of Chiang Chu (1764–1804)," in Harriet Zurndorfer, ed., *Chinese Women in the Imperial Past: New Perspectives*, pp. 286–307.

Dorothy Ko, "Lady Scholars at the Door: The Practice of Gender Relations in Eighteenth-Century Suzhou," in John Hay, ed., *Boundaries in China*. London: Reaktion Books, 1994, pp. 198–216.

Disciples of Yuan Mei

Robyn Hamilton, "The Pursuit of Fame: Luo Qilan (1755–1813?) and the Debates about Women and Talent in Eighteenth-Century Jiangnan," *Late Imperial China* 18 (1997): 39–71.

David Hawkes, "Hsi P'ei-lan," *Asia Major* Second Series 8 (1959): 113–121.

Poetry, Scholarship, and Vernacular Prose Fiction

Grace S. Fong, "Writing Self and Writing Lives: Shen Shanbao's (1808–1862) Gendered Auto/Biographical Practices," *Nan Nü* 3 (2000): 259–303.

Nanxiu Qian, "Milk and Scent: Works about Women in the *Shih-shuo hsin-yü* Genre," *Nan Nü* 1 (1999): 187–236.

————. *Spirit and Self in Medieval China: The* Shih-shuo hsin-yü *and Its*

Legacy. Honolulu: University of Hawaii Press, 2001, pp. 283–318, "Milk and Scent: Women *Shih-shuo*."

Ellen Widmer, "Ming Loyalism and the Woman's Voice in Fiction after *Hong lou meng*," in Ellen Widmer and Kang-i Sun Chang, eds., *Writing Women in Late Imperial China*, pp. 366–396.

Harriet T. Zurndorfer, "The 'Constant World' of Wang Chao-yüan: Women, Education, and Orthodoxy in 18th Century China—A Preliminary Investigation," in *Family Process and Political Process in Modern Chinese History*. Taipei: Institute of Modern History, Academia Sinica, 1992, pp. 579–619.

————. "How to Be a Good Wife and a Good Scholar at the Same Time: 18th Century Prescriptions on Chinese Female Behavior—A Preliminary Investigation," in Léon Vandermeersch, ed., *La société civile face à l'état dans les traditions chinoise, japonaise, coréenne et vietnamienne*. Paris: École Française de l'Extrême Orient, 1994, pp. 249–270.

Chapter 14: *Drama*

Wei Hua, "The Lament of Frustrated Talents: An Analysis of Three Women's Plays in Late Imperial China," *Ming Studies* 32 (1994): 28–42.

Paul S. Ropp, "'Now Cease Painting Eyebrows, Don a Scholar's Cap and Pin': The Frustrated Ambition of Wang Yun, Gentry Woman Poet and Dramatist," *Ming Studies* 40 (1999): 86–110.

Chapter 15: *Plucking Rhymes*

Mark Bender, *Plum and Bamboo: China's Suzhou Chantefable Tradition*. Urbana: University of Illinois Press, 2002.

Thomas Shiyu Li and Susan Naquin, "The Baoming Temple: Religion and the Throne in Ming and Qing China," *Harvard Journal of Asiatic Studies* 48 (1988): 131–188.

Tze-lan D. Sang, *The Emerging Lesbian: Female Same-Sex Desire in Modern China*. Chicago: University of Chicago Press, 2003.

Marina Sung, *The Narrative Art of Tsai-sheng-yuan: A Feminist Vision in Traditional Chinese Society*. Taipei: Chinese Materials Center, 1994.

Ellen Widmer, "The Trouble with Talent: Hou Zhi (1764–1829) and her *Tanci Zaizaotian* of 1828," *Chinese Literature: Essays, Articles, Reviews* 21 (1999): 131–150.

Epilogue: *Nationalism and Feminism: Qiu Jin*

Chapter 16: *The Beheaded Feminist: Qiu Jin*

Studies on Late Qing Feminism

Charlotte Beahan, "Feminism and Nationalism in the Chinese Women's Press, 1902–1911," *Modern China* 1 (1975): 379–416.

Louise Edwards, "Chin Sung-ts'en's *A Tocsin for Women*: The Dexterous Merger of Radicalism and Conservatism in Feminism of the Early Twentieth Century," *Jindai Zhongguo funüshi yanjiu* 2 (1994): 117–140.

Grace S. Fong, "Alternative Modernities, Or a Classical Woman of Modern China: The Challenging Trajectory of Lu Bicheng's (1883–1943) Life and Song Lyrics," *Nan Nü* 6 (2004): 12–59.

Paula Harrel, *Sowing the Seeds of Change: Chinese Students, Japanese Teachers, 1895–1905*. Stanford: Stanford University Press, 192.

Hu Ying, "Reconfiguring Nei/Wai: Writing the Woman Traveler in the Late Qing," *Late Imperial China* 18 (1997): 72–99.

———. *Tales of Translation: Composing the New Woman in China: 1899–1918*. Stanford: Stanford University Press, 2000.

———. "Naming the First 'New Woman,'" in Rebecca E. Karl and Peter Zarrow, eds., *Rethinking the 1898 Reform Period: Political and Cultural Change in Late Qing China*. Cambridge, Mass.: Harvard University Asia Center, 2002, pp. 180–211.

Joan Judge, "Talent, Virtue, and the Nation: Chinese Nationalisms and Female Subjectivities in the Early Twentieth Century," *The American Historical Review* 106 (2001): 765–803.

———. "Reforming the Feminine: Female Literacy and the Legacy of 1898," in Rebecca E. Karl and Peter Zarrow, eds., *Rethinking the 1898 Reform Period: Political and Cultural Change in Late Qing China*, pp. 158–179.

———. "The Ideology of 'Good Wives and Wise Mothers': Meiji Japan and Feminine Modernity in Late-Qing China," in Joshua A. Fogel, ed., *Sagacious Monks and Bloodthirsty Warriors: Chinese Views of Japan in the Ming-Qing Period*. Norwalk: Eastbridge, 2002, pp. 218–248.

Rebecca E. Karl, "'Slavery,' Citizenship, and Gender in Late Qing China's Global Context," in Rebecca E. Karl and Peter Zarrow, eds., *Rethinking the 1898 Reform Period: Political and Cultural Change in Late Qing China*, pp. 212–244.

Thomas L. Kennedy, trans., *Testimony of a Confucian Woman: The Autobiography of Mrs. Nie Zeng Jifen, 1852–1942*. Athens: The University of Georgia Press, 1993.

Ono Kazuko, *Chinese Women in a Century of Revolution*. Stanford: Stanford University Press, 1989.

Peter Zarrow, "He Zhen and Anarcho-Feminism in China," *Journal of Asian Studies* 47 (1988): 796–813.

Studies on Qiu Jin

Amy D. Dooling and Kristina M. Torgeson, eds., *Writing Women in Modern China: An Anthology of Women's Literature from the Early Twentieth Century*. New York: Columbia University Press, 1998.

Lionel Giles, *Ch'iu Chin: A Chinese Heroine*. London: East and West, 1917 (rep. in *Nine Dragon Screen, Being Reprints of Nine Addresses and Papers Presented to the China Society, 1909–1945*. London: The China Society, 1965, pp. 1–21).

C. Y. Hsu, "Ch'iu Chin, Revolutionary Martyr," *Asian Culture Quarterly* 22 (1994): 75–94.

Gong-way Lee, "Critiques of Ch'iu Chin: A Radical Feminist and National Revolutionary," *Chinese Culture* 32 (1991): 57–66.

Mary Backus Rankin, "The Emergence of Women at the End of the Ch'ing: The Case of Ch'iu Chin," in Margery Wolf and Roxanne Witke, eds., *Women in Chinese Society*. Stanford: Stanford University Press, 1975, pp. 39–66.

Tao Cheng-chang, *The Life of Chiu Chin*, trans. by Lionel Giles. Leiden: E.J. Brill, 1913.

Finding List

Translated passages and quotations are identified below by the first few words of the first line of text, rather than by their titles.

Part One: *Early Models for Later Ages*

"The *Odes* praise" (p. 14): Ge Hong, *Baopuzi*, in *Zhuzi jicheng*. Beijing: Zhonghua shuju, 1954, vol. 8, p. 148.

Chapter 1: *Women On and Behind the Throne*

"Now, in the seventh year" (p. 23): *Quan Han fu*. Beijing: Beijing daxue chubanshe, 1993, pp. 366–367; *Wen xuan*. Beijing: Zhonghua shuju, 1977, pp. 144–146; Su Zhecong, *Zhongguo lidai funü zuopin xuan* (hereafter "Su"). Shanghai: Shanghai guji chubanshe, 1987, pp. 40–43.

"The full elder brother" (p. 27): *Quan Han fu*, p. 370.

"My full elder brother, the governor-general of the western regions," (p. 28): *Hou Han shu*. Beijing: Zhonghua shuju, 1965, pp. 1584–1586; Su, pp. 44–46.

"Forged from the hardest" (p. 30): *Quan Han fu*, p. 369.

"The Harmonious and Illustrious," (p. 31): *Hou Han shu*, p. 418.

"The wife of Cao Shishu" (p. 34): ibid., pp. 2784–2792.

Poets, Teachers, Moralists

Poets of the Inner Palace: Zuo Fen, Han Lanying, and Bao Linghui

"From her earliest years she loved books" (p. 43): *Jin shu*. Beijing: Zhonghua shuju, 1974, p. 957.

"Since leaving behind my parents' loving care" (p. 43): Lu Qinli, comp., *Xian Qin Han Wei Nanbeichao shi* (hereafter "Lu Qinli"). Beijing: Zhonghua shuju, 1983, p. 730; Su, p. 56.

"Born in the lowly circumstances of a simple home" (p. 44): *Jin shu*, pp. 957–958; Su, pp. 57–58.

"Later she achieved the position" (p. 46): *Jin shu*, p. 958.

"The emperor greatly admired" (p. 46): ibid., p. 962.

"In Southern Hills" (p. 47): Lu Qinli, p. 730.

"How came about this profusion" (p. 47): Yan Kejun, comp., *Quan Jin wen*, p. 1533 (13: 2a), in his *Quan shanggu sandai Qin Han sanguo liuchao wen*. Shanghai: Shanghai guji chubanshe, 1990; Su, pp. 58–59.

"When I observe" (p. 48): *Quan Jin wen* 13:2a–b.

"Han Lanying from Wu commandery" (p. 49): *Nan Qi shu*. Beijing: Zhonghua shuju, 1984, p. 392.

"The songs and poems of Linghui" (p. 49): Zhong Rong, ann. by Chen Yanjie, *Shipin zhu*. Beijing: Renmin wenxue chubanshe, 1980, pp. 69–70.

"Strings and pipes still play" (p. 50): Lu Qinli, p. 1479.

"When the prince of Yulin" (p. 50): Xiao Jian (Liang Yuandi), *Jinlouzi*, in *Zhongguo zhexue mingzhu jicheng*. Taibei (?): Zhongguo zhexue mingzhu bianyin weiyuanhui, 1978 (?), vol. 90, p. 326 (1: 26b).

"O, ever since the day" (p. 50): Lu Qinli, p. 1314.

"In icy lands you do not dress" (p. 51): Lu Qinli, p. 1315; Su, pp. 70–71.

"On the cinnamon" (p. 51): Lu Qinli, pp. 1314–1315; Su, p. 71.

"A traveler came from a distant land" (p. 51): Lu Qinli, pp. 1313–1314; Su, p. 70.

"A traveler came from a distant land" (p. 52): Lu Qinli, p. 333.

Teachers of Men: Fu Sheng's Daughter and Wei Cheng's Mother

"Fu Sheng was in his nineties" (p. 53): Wang Renjun, comp., *Yuhan shanfang jiyishu xubian sanzhong*. Shanghai: Shanghai guji chubanshe, 1989, p. 25.

"It is not known from which commandery" (p. 53): *Jin shu*, pp. 2521–2522.

Moralists: The Song Sisters and Lady Zheng

"The intendant of the Inner Palace Song Ruozhao" (p. 55): *Xin Tang shu*. Beijing: Zhonghua shuju, 1975, pp. 3508–3509.

"At ease Your Majesty rules" (p. 57): *Quan Tang shi* (hereafter "*QTS*"). Beijing: Zhonghua shuju, 1960, p. 68.

"Wei Wen had no sons" (p. 58): *Jiu Tang shu*. Beijing: Zhonghua shuju, 1975, p. 4380.

"The daughters asked" (p. 58): Zheng shi, *Nü xiaojing*, in Zhang Fuqing, comp., *Nüjie*. Beijing: Zhongyang minzu daxue chubanshe, 1996, p. 9.

"The Venerable Madam said" (p. 59): ibid., p. 11.

"If your husband is drunk" (p. 61): "Cuishi furen xunnüwen," in Zheng Acai, "Dunhuang xieben 'Cuishi furen xunnü wen' yanjiu," in his *Dunhuang wenxian yu wenxue.* Taipei: Xinwenfeng chubanshe, 1993, p. 285.

Shangguan Wan'er: Ghostwriter for Two Empresses

"When the former empress, now demoted" (p. 62): *Jiu Tang shu*, p. 2170.

"Later Empress Wang and Concubine Xiao" (p. 63): ibid.

"At the age of fourteen, she was intelligent" (p. 63): *Jinglong wenguan ji*, in Li Fang, comp., *Taiping guangji.* Beijing: Zhonghua shuju, 1961, pp. 2132–2133.

"I watched the pink turn into green" (p. 64): *QTS*, pp. 58–59; Su, p. 98.

"From the reign period Community with Heaven" (p. 65): *Jinglong wenguan ji*, p. 2133.

"On the last day of the First Month" (p. 65): Ji Yougong, ed., *Tangshi jishi.* Beijing: Zhonghua shuju, 1965, p. 28.

"It was thanks to her" (p. 66): *Jinglong wenguan ji*, p. 2133.

"[d]uring the last years of her life" (p. 67): ibid.

"This land of gods" (p. 68): *QTS*, pp. 60–61.

"Waving gently—bamboo shadows" (p. 69): ibid., pp. 62–63.

"During this period dominated by women" (p. 70): Stephen Owen, "The Formation of the Tang Estate Poem," *Harvard Journal of Asiatic Studies* 55 (1995): 53.

"If the Imperial Consort" (p. 71): ibid., p. 52.

"Emperor Zhongzong's concubine" (p. 71): *Jiu Tang shu*, pp. 2175–2176.

Chapter 2: *Neglected Palace Ladies and Other Phantoms*

"Green the coat" (p. 75): Qu Wanli, ed., *Shijing quanshi.* Taibei: Lianjing chuban shiye gongsi, 1983, pp. 46–47.

"'The Green Coat' is the complaint of Lady Jiang" (p. 76): James Legge, trans., *The Chinese Classics*, vol. 4, *The She King*, rev. ed., reprint. Taibei: Wenshizhe chubanshe, 1971, p. 41.

Slandered Virtue: Concubine Ban

"Newly-cut white silken gauze from Qi" (p. 78): Lu Qinli, pp. 116–117; Su, pp. 24–25.

"Emperor Cheng's consort Concubine Ban" (p. 78): *Han shu.* Beijing: Zhonghua shuju, 1962, pp. 3983–3988.

Fact and Fiction: Phantom Poems and Phantom Lives

Reduced to a Human Pig: Lady Qi

"When the Han dynasty was founded" (p. 83): Sima Qian, *Shiji.* Beijing: Zhonghua shuju, 1959, p. 1969.

"Empress Lü harbored" (p. 83): *Shiji*, p. 397.

"When the Lofty Ancestor passed away" (p. 85): *Han shu*, pp. 3937–3938.

A Disputed Beauty: Empress Zhen

"The Cultured and Brilliant Empress Zhen" (p. 86): *Sanguo zhi*. Beijing: Zhonghua shuju, 1959, p. 159.

"The empress was born," (p. 87): ibid., p. 159, note 1.

"During the reign period Established Peace" (p. 87): ibid., p. 160.

"Yuan Xi had departed" (p. 88): ibid., p. 160, note 1.

"When Cao Cao subdued" (p. 88): ibid.

"In the First Month" (p. 88): ibid., p. 160.

"Look at the rushes growing in our pond" (p. 89): Xu Ling, comp., Wu Zhaoyi and Cheng Yanshan, ann., *Yutai xinyong jianzhu*. Beijing: Zhonghua shuju, 1985, pp. 56–57; Su, pp. 48–49.

"During the final years of the Han" (p. 90): *Wen Xuan*, pp. 269–270.

Banished Beyond the Border: Liu Xijun and Wang Zhaojun

"My family sent me off" (p. 91): *Han shu*, p. 3903; Su, pp. 19–20.

"Zhaojun's style name was Qiang and she hailed from Nanjun commandery" (p. 92): *Hou Han shu*, p. 2941.

"The Inner Palace" (p. 93): Liu Xin, *Xijing zaji jiao zhu*. Shanghai: Shanghai guji chubanshe, 1991, p. 67.

"How lush and lovely" (p. 93): Lu Qinli, pp. 315–316; Su, p. 22.

A Lonely Suicide: Lady Hou

"In the final years" (p. 97): Anon., *Milou ji*, in Lu Xun, comp. *Tang Song chuanqi ji*. Hong Kong: Xinyi chubanshe, 1967, pp. 209–213; Su, pp. 93–96.

Displaced by a Rival: Concubine Plum

"Gauze sleeves that spread their endless fragrance" (p. 100): *QTS*, p. 64.

"Concubine Plum's surname was Jiang" (p. 102): *Tang Song chuanqi ji*, pp. 282–286.

"Now on those prints of recent times" (p. 107): ibid., p. 286.

Other Phantoms

The Eloping Widow: Zhuo Wenjun

"When the Filial Prince" (p. 108): *Shiji*, pp. 3000–3001.

"As brilliant as the snow" (p. 110): *Yutai xinyong jianzhu*, pp. 14–15; Su, pp. 20–21.

"As brilliant as the snow" (p. 111): Lu Qinli, pp. 274–275.

Abducted and Ransomed: Cai Yan

"The wife of Dong Si of Chenliu was a daughter of Cai Yong" (p. 113): *Hou Han shu*, pp. 2800–2803.

"There was a literary development" (p. 119): Hans H. Frankel, "Cai Yan and the Poems Attributed to Her," *Chinese Literature: Essays, Articles, Reviews* 5 (1983): 153.

"Wang Mingjun was originally called Wang Zhaojun" (p. 120): Lu Qinli, pp. 642–643.

"At my birth, the world was still at peace" (p. 121): Guo Maoqian, comp., *Yuefu shiji*. Beijing: Zhonghua shuju, 1979, pp. 860–865; Su, pp. 34–39.

Palindromes: Su Hui

"a flawless and perfect composition" (p. 127): Yan Yu, *Canglang shihua jiaoshi*, ed. by Guo Shaoyu. Beijing: Renmin wenxue chubanshe, 1983, p. 189.

"Dou Tao's wife, lady Su, was a native of Shiping" (p. 128): *Jin shu*, p. 2523.

"Lady Su, the wife of Dou Tao from Fufeng" (p. 128): *Quan Tang wen*. Taibei: Huiwen shuju, 1961, pp. 1257–1258 (97: 14b–15b).

"No one knows the provenance of" (p. 130): Ji Yun, ed., *Siku quanshu zongmu*, 148: 33b, reprint. Taibei: Yiwen yinshuguan, n.d.

"her weaving, of words, combined her" (p. 131): Ann Waltner and Pi-ching Hsu, "Lingering Fragrance: The Poetry of Tu Yaose and Shen Tiansun," *Journal of Women's History* 8–4 (1997): 34.

Chapter 3: *Ladies, Nuns, and Courtesans*
Brilliant Daughters and Dutiful Wives

The Poet of a Single Poem: Xu Shu

"Qin Jia's style name was Shihui" (p. 133): *Yutai xinyong jianzhu*, p. 30.

"A human life is like the morning dew" (p. 133): ibid.

"Your serving-maid is, alas" (p. 133): ibid., p. 32.

"As the experiences of husband and wife" (p. 134): *Shipin zhu*, p. 31.

"After Xu Shu lost her husband" (p. 134): Du You, *Niiji*, quoted in Li Fang, comp., *Taiping yulan*. Beijing: Zhonghua shuju, 1960, p. 2031.

"The most famous cases of couples" (p. 135): Hu Yinglin, *Shisou*. Shanghai: Shanghai guji chubanshe, 1958, p. 133.

"Qin Jia's style name was Shihui" (p. 135): Yan Kejun, *Tieqiao mangao*, quoted in Hu Wenkai, *Zhongguo lidai funü zhuzuo kao*, rev. ed. Shanghai: Shanghai guji chubanshe, 1985, p. 2.

"A gentleman, I have learned, leads others by means of his virtue" (p. 136): Yan Kejun, *Quan Hou Han wen*, p. 991 (96: 9b–10a), in his *Quan shanggu sandai Qin Han sanguo liuchao wen*.

The Poet of a Single Line: Xie Daoyun

"One cold snowy day" (p. 137): Liu Yiqing, comp., *Shishuo xinyu huijiao jizhu*. Shanghai: Shanghai guji chubanshe, 2002, p. 119.

"After the wife of Wang Ningzhi" (p. 138): *Shishuo xinyu huijiao jizhu*, p. 587.

"Ningzhi's style name was Shuping" (p. 139): *Jin shu*, pp. 2102–2103.

"Once, Ningzhi's younger brother" (p. 139): *Jin shu*, p. 2516.

"The wife of the prefect of Jiangzhou" (p. 139): *Shishuo xinyu huijiao jizhu*, pp. 588–589.

"Once Sun Chuo and his younger brother" (p. 139): ibid., p. 695.

"Lady Liu, the wife of His Excellency Xie" (p. 140): Yu Tongzhi, *Duji*, in Lu Xun, comp., *Gu xiaoshuo gouchen*. Hong Kong: Xinyi chubanshe, 1967, p. 362.

"Xie He elevated his elder sister" (p. 140): *Shishuo xinyu huijiao jizhu*, p. 589.

"I look at that pine tree" (p. 141): Lu Qinli, p. 912.

"How they tower, those lofty eastern mountains" (p. 142): ibid.

"Ningzhi was an adherent" (p. 143): *Shishuo xinyu huijiao jizhu*, p. 119.

"During the rebellion of Sun En" (p. 143): *Jin shu*, p. 2516.

"Afterwards she lived as a widow in Guiji" (p. 144): ibid., pp. 2516–2517.

Poet and Editorial Advisor: Lady Chen

"The wife of Liu Zhen, Lady Chen" (p. 145): *Jin shu*, p. 2517.

"I have read the elegy" (p. 145): *Quan Jin wen*, p. 2291 (144: 9b).

Different Voices: Liu Lingxian

"The literary style of Xiaochuo" (p. 146): *Liang shu*, Beijing: Zhonghua shuju, 1973, pp. 483–484.

"At the time, Liu Xiaochuo had seventy brothers" (p. 147): *Liang shu*, p. 484.

"Yan and Zhao do not lack" (p. 147): Lu Qinli, p. 1837.

"Above the courtyard trees" (p. 148): *Yutai xinyong jianzhu*, pp. 261–262.

"Above the courtyard trees" (p. 148): ibid.

"The sun has set" (p. 149): Lu Qinli, p. 2130; Su, pp. 78–79.

"Inside the locked gate" (p. 149): Lu Qinli, p. 1824.

"How can one settle" (p. 149): Lu Qinli, pp. 2129–2130; Su, p. 75.

"The flower courtyard" (p. 150): Lu Qinli, p. 2131; *Yutai xinyong jianzhu*, pp. 255–256; Su, pp. 77–78.

"Of Liu Xiaochuo's younger sisters" (p. 151): *Liang shu*, p. 484.

"In the fifth year of the reign period Great Unity" (p. 151): Su, pp. 79–81.

Buddhist Nuns and Daoist Mystics

Buddhist Nuns

Powerful Abbesses

"It is unclear of which place Miaoyin" (p. 154): Baochang, *Biqiuni zhuan*.
Nanjing: Jinling kejing chu, 1885, 1: 10b–11a.
"The original surname of Zhisheng" (p. 155): ibid., 3: 5a–5b.
"When the crown prince" (p. 155): ibid., 3: 5b–6a.
"Zhisheng lived in her convent" (p. 156): ibid., 3: 6a–6b.

Revealed Sutras

"The sutras listed above" (p. 156): Sengyou, *Chu Sanzang jiji*. Beijing: Zhonghua
shuju, 1995, pp. 230–231.

Poems by Nuns

"The color of the water" (p. 158): *QTS*, p. 9061.
"The Master [Confucius] said" (p. 158): Luo Dagang, *Helin yulu*. Beijing:
Zhonghua shuju, 1983, p. 346.

Daoist Mystics

Princess and Peasant Girl: Yuzhen and Wang Fajin

"Wang Fajin was a native," p. 161
"Wang Fajin," *Xianzhuan shiyi*, in *Taiping guangji*, p. 327.

Self-Censoring Ladies and Public Women

Self-Censoring Ladies

Burned Manuscripts

"As a spouse one must of course" (p. 164): Xue Yusi, "Shentu Cheng," *Hedong
ji*, in *Taiping guangji*, p. 3487.
"Its light surpasses a silver lamp" (p. 164): "Sun shi," *Beimeng suoyan*, in *Taiping
guangji*, p. 2137.
"Many thanks for sending" (p. 165): ibid.
"Jade fingers on red strings" (p. 165): ibid.
"Lady Sun of Lechang" (p. 165): *Taiping guangji*, p. 2137; *Beimeng suoyan*, in Zhou
Xunchu, comp., *Tangren yishi huibian*. Shanghai: Shanghai guji chubanshe,
1995, p. 2215.

Multiple Personalities

"Wang Fazhi, a girl from Tonglu" (p. 166): Dai Fu, "Wang Fazhi," *Guangyi ji*, in
Taiping guangji, p. 2414.

Conversations in Dreams

"Penumbra asked Shadow" (p. 169): *Zhuangzi jishi*. Peking: Zhonghua shuju, 1961, pp. 110–111.

"Niu Su's eldest daughter" (p. 169): Niu Su, "Niu Su nü," *Jiwen*, in *Taiping guangji*, pp. 2135–2136.

"Du Gao's wife, lady Liu" (p. 173): *Nanbu xinshu*, in *Tangren yishi huibian*, p. 1034.

Public Women

"When young, a man should not hesitate" (p. 174): Lu Qinli, pp. 1041–1043.

"Her smart intelligence" (p. 175): Gao Yanxiu, *Queshi*, "Wei jinshi jian wangji," in Li Shiren, ed., *Quan Tang Wudai xiaoshuo*. Xi'an: Shaanxi renmin chubanshe, 1998, p. 2085.

Poet and Traitor: Li Ye

"Cease your useless craving" (p. 176): *QTS*, p. 9058; Chen Wenhua, ed., *Tang nüshiren ji sanzhong* (hereafter "*TNSR*"). Shanghai: Shanghai guji chubanshe, 1984, pp. 6–8.

"A square of silk" (p. 176): *QTS*, p. 9059; *TNSR*, pp. 16–17.

"So filled with love, before the mirror" (p. 177): *QTS*, p. 9059; *TNSR*, p. 16.

"The one departing" (p. 177): *QTS*, p. 9059; *TNSR*, pp. 17–18.

"Most near and most far" (p. 177): *QTS*, p. 9059; *TNSR*, p. 14.

"I love most your slender form" (p. 177): *QTS*, p. 10039; *TNSR*, pp. 19–20.

"Nothing, they say, is deeper" (p. 177): *QTS*, p. 9058; *TNSR*, pp. 11–12.

"I climbed the hill to gaze upon the streams" (p. 178): *QTS*, p. 9057; *TNSR*, pp. 4–5.

"On the old riverbank" (p. 178): *QTS*, p. 3542; *TNSR*, p. 21.

"Originally I lived among the clouds" (p. 179): *QTS*, p. 9058; *TNSR*, pp. 8–11.

"In the form of morning clouds" (p. 180): *QTS*, p. 9058; *TNSR*, p. 12.

"Li Jilan was famed" (p. 179): Wang Renyu, "Li Xiulan," *Yutang xianhua*, in *Taiping guangji*, p. 2150; also in *Tangren yishi huibian*, p. 841.

"For a gentleman" (p. 180): Gao Zhongwu, *Zhongxing xianqi ji*, quoted in *TNSR*, p. 21.

"A heavenly aspara" (p. 181): *QTS*, p. 9268; *TNSR*, p. 21.

"At that time there was a woman" (p. 181): Zhao Yuanyi, *Fengtian lu*, quoted in *TNSR*, pp. 21–22.

"We must not belittle her" (p. 182): *Siku quanshu zongmu* 186: 25a.

Courtesan and Collator: Xue Tao

"One day, her father pointed" (p. 182): *Gaojian zhuibi*, in *Tangren yishi huibian*, p. 1128.

"Xue Tao's style name was Hongdu" (p. 183): *Xiaozhuan*, in *TNSR*, p. 90.

"I had heard about" (p. 184): *QTS*, p. 9036; *TNSR*, pp. 30–31.

"The fireflies above the overgrown fields" (p. 184): *QTS*, p. 9045; *TNSR*, pp. 81–82.

"The woman Xue Tao" (p. 184): *Xuanhe shupu*, quoted in *TNSR*, p. 89.

"During the reign period Primal Harmony" (p. 185): *Mushu xiantan*, in *Tangren yishi huibian*, pp. 1129–1130.

"The blossoms open" (p. 185): *QTS*, p. 9035; *TNSR*, pp. 26–27.

"The Second Month" (p. 186): *QTS*, p. 9043; *TNSR*, pp. 68–69.

"The most docile" (p. 186): *QTS*, p. 9043; *TNSR*, p. 74.

"Only when made of bamboo" (p. 186): *QTS*, pp. 9043–9044; *TNSR*, p. 74.

"Snow-white ears" (p. 186): *QTS*, p. 9044; *TNSR*, p. 74.

"As a solitary and lonely" (p. 186): *QTS*, p. 9044; *TNSR*, pp. 74–75.

"In and out" (p. 187): *QTS*, p. 9044; *TNSR*, p. 75.

"Brilliant and pure" (p. 187): *QTS*, p. 9044; *TNSR*, p. 75.

"It frolicked" (p. 187): *QTS*, p. 9044; *TNSR*, p. 75.

"Its talons" (p. 187): *QTS*, p. 9044; *TNSR*, p. 75.

"Thick and lush" (p. 187): *QTS*, p. 9044; *TNSR*, p. 76.

"When, forged from gold" (p. 187): *QTS*, pp. 9044–9045; *TNSR*, p. 76.

"As soon as Minister Yuan . . . heard" (p. 188): Fan Shu, *Yunxi youyi*, quoted in *TNSR*, pp. 86–87.

Concubine, Daoist Nun, and Murderer: Yu Xuanji

"The Yangzi encircles Wuchang" (p. 189): *QTS*, p. 9051; *TNSR*, pp. 113–114.

"Where has she gone" (p. 190): *QTS*, p. 9052; *TNSR*, p. 121.

"By the stones of the stairs" (p. 190): *QTS*, p. 9053; *TNSR*, pp. 122–123.

"The style name of Yu Xuanji" (p. 191): Huangfu Mei, "Yu Xuanji," *Sanshui xiaodu*, in *TNSR*, pp. 139–140.

"The chatter of orioles" (p. 194): *QTS*, p. 9049; *TNSR*, p. 107.

"Their verdant color" (p. 194): *QTS*, p. 9047; *TNSR*, pp. 95–96.

"Tender chrysanthemums" (p. 194): *QTS*, p. 9052; *TNSR*, pp. 118–119.

"Facing the wind" (p. 194): *QTS*, p. 9048; *TNSR*, pp. 101–102.

"Cloudy peaks fill" (p. 195): QTS, p. 9050; TNSR, pp. 111–112.

Part Two: *Between New Possibilities and New Limitations*

"From the age of five" (p. 201): Sima Guang, *Sima shi shuyi*, in *Tushu jicheng*, vol. 1040, p. 45; also quoted in Chen Dongyuan, *Zhongguo funü shenghuo shi*, reprint. Shanghai: Shanghai shudian, 1984, p. 133.

"From her earliest youth" (p. 202): Lu You, *Lu You ji*. Beijing: Zhonghua shuju, 1976, pp. 2328–2329.

"When it comes to women" (p. 202): Yang Weizhen, "*Cao shi Xuezhai xuange ji xu*" (*Dongweizi ji*, j. 7), quoted in Wang Xuechu, ed., *Li Qingzhao ji jiaozhu* (hereafter "*Li*"). Beijing: Renmin wenxue chubanshe, 1979, p. 319.

Chapter 4: *Li Qingzhao*
Li Qingzhao's Life

"On the tenth day of the Eighth Month" (p. 205): *Li*, pp. 131–133.
"What is this Inscriptions on Bronze and Stone" (p. 207): ibid., pp. 176–189.
"Since youth I have been versed in the norms of righteousness" (p. 215): ibid., pp. 167–176.

Li Qingzhao's Poetry

The Rise of the Ci

"After completing my toilette" (p. 218): Zhang Zhang and Huang Yu, eds., *Quan Tang wudai ci*. Shanghai: Shanghai guji chubanshe, 1986, p. 235.
"I often recall that night" (p. 219): *Li*, pp. 7–8.
"Once darkness falls" (p. 219): *Quan Tang wudai ci*, pp. 203–204.
"A tender breeze" (p. 219): *Li*, pp. 13–14.

Lady Wei's Lyrics

"Beyond the tower" (p. 221): Tang Guizhang, comp., *Quan Song ci*. Beijing: Zhonghua shuju, 1965, p. 268.
"The hills in the river appear" (p. 222): ibid., pp. 268–269.
"The east wind has already" (p. 222): ibid. p. 269.
"The red tower slanting" (p. 222): ibid.
"A full moon" (p. 223): ibid., p. 268.
"The light of the lamp" (p. 223): ibid., pp. 269–270.
"Over the waves a clear breeze" (p. 223): ibid., p. 269.
"How easy it was" (p. 224): ibid.
"The little courtyard" (p. 224): ibid.

Li Qingzhao's Lyrics

"The silent and lonely inner chamber" (p. 225): *Li*, pp. 70–71.
"The incense chilled in golden lions" (p. 225): ibid., pp. 20–23.
"Seeking, seeking, searching, searching" (p. 227): ibid., pp. 64–70.
"The red lotus has lost its fragrance" (p. 227): ibid., pp. 23–27.
"Last night the rain was scattered" (p. 228): ibid., pp. 8–11.
"The breeze has dispelled the dust" (p. 228): ibid., pp. 61–64.
"The courtyard desolate" (p. 229): ibid., pp. 49–53.

"In the Capital spring" (p. 230): ibid., pp. 80–81.

"The endless night stretches on and on" (p. 230): ibid., pp. 60–61.

"Light mist and heavy clouds" (p. 231): ibid., pp. 34–39.

"Yi'an [Li Qingzhao] sent her lyric on Double Nine" (p. 231): Yi Shizhen, *Langhuanji*, quoted in *Li*, pp. 35–36.

"The setting sun melts into gold" (p. 232): *Li*, pp. 53–57.

"Despite the snow I know that news of spring has arrived" (p. 233): ibid., pp. 46–47.

"Last night I was too tipsy to remove my headdress" (p. 233): ibid., p. 40.

"Whenever people of the present" (p. 234): ibid., pp. 42–43.

Li Qingzhao's Ci–criticism

"Ballads and song-poems" (p. 235): *Li*, pp. 194–201

"Cloudy waves to the horizon" (p. 237): ibid., pp. 6–7.

Li Qingzhao and Her Critics

"After exerting herself on the swing" (p. 239): *Li*, pp. 83–85.

"Out of the basket of the flower-seller" (p. 239): ibid., pp. 71–72.

"Yi'an jushi [Li Qingzhao] is the daughter" (p. 240): Wang Zhuo, *Biji manzhi*, in *Zhongguo gudian xiqu lunzhu jicheng*, vol. 1, p. 118; also quoted in *Li*, p. 319.

Li Qingzhao's Poems

"Why do I suffer" (p. 241): *Li*, pp. 130–131.

"The *shi* poems of Qingzhao are not very beautiful" (p. 241): Lu Chang, *Lichao minyuan shici*, j. 7, quoted in *Li*, p. 131.

"In life one should be a hero amongst men" (p. 241): *Li*, pp. 127–128.

"My dawn dream follows" (p. 242): ibid., pp. 129–130.

Chapter 5: *Talent and Fate*

An Unhappy Marriage: Zhu Shuzhen

"Combining phrases and linking sentences" (p. 245): Wei Duanli, "Xu," in Zhang Zhang and Huang Yu, eds., *Zhu Shuzhen ji* (hereafter, "*Zhu*"). Shanghai: Shanghai guji chubanshe, 1986, pp. 303–334.

"I get up but take no pleasure" (p. 249): ibid., pp. 141–142.

"On official business" (p. 249): ibid., pp. 168–169.

"Weary of facing the drifting blossoms," (p. 249): ibid., p. 76.

"The blossoms fall" (p. 249): ibid., p. 124.

"Dozing under the gauze netting" (p. 250): ibid., p. 178.

"The steamy heat" (p. 250): ibid., p. 179.

"Laying down my needle" (p. 250): ibid., pp. 82–83.

"Outside the window crickets chirp" (p. 250): ibid., pp. 86–87.

"Whose flute could that be" (p. 250): ibid., pp. 98–99.

"Although women's eyes may not be strong" (p. 250): ibid., p. 103.

"Freezing sparrows silently huddle" (p. 251): ibid., p. 115.

"Stop lamenting the passing of time" (p. 251): ibid., pp. 209–210.

"The sun-wheel pushes its fiery way" (p. 251): ibid., pp. 70–71.

"The fiery red sun" (p. 252): ibid., pp. 78–79.

"Alone I walk, alone I sit" (p. 253): ibid., pp. 275–276.

"How quickly the season hurries by" (p. 253): ibid., p. 278.

"Outside the tower millions of threads" (p. 254): ibid., pp. 281–282.

"Annoyed by the mist" (p. 254): ibid., pp. 278–279.

"Ingenious clouds adorn the evening" (p. 254): ibid., p. 285.

"A mountain pavilion" (p. 255): ibid., p. 283.

"The wind so fierce, the clouds so thick" (p. 255): ibid., pp. 280–281.

"The virility to dominate the world" (p. 256): ibid., p. 224.

"[Zhu Shuzhen's] poems" (p. 256): *Siku quanshu zongmu* 174: 54b.

"A woman who dabbles in writing" (p. 256): *Zhu*, pp. 154–155.

Doomed Love: Zhang Yuniang

"On the ridge the pines" (p. 257): Zhang Yuniang, *Lanxue ji*, in *Tuobachan congke* 1:4a; Du Xun, ed., *Zhongguo lidai funü wenxue zuopin jingxuan* (hereafter "Du"). Beijing: Zhongguo heping chubanshe, 2000, p. 179.

"In mid-journey" (p. 258): *Lanxue ji* 1: 6b; Du, pp. 181–182.

"Zhang Yuniang's style name was Ruoqing" (p. 258): Zhi Hengchun, comp., *Songyang xianzhi* (1875), in *Zhonghua fangzhi congshu, Huazhong difang*, vol. 170, 9: 67a–68a.

"In recent years" (p. 260): Ye Ziqi, *Caomuzi*. Beijing: Zhonghua shuju, 1959, p. 76.

"Wang Zhao's sobriquet was Longxi" (p. 261): *Songyang xianzhi* 9: 23b–24a.

"Zhang Yuniang's style name was Ruoqiong" (p. 262): Wang Zhao, "Zhang Yuniang zhuan," in *Lanxue ji*, "Fulu": 1a–2b.

"Lady Zhang was an outstandingly fine girl" (p. 264): ibid., 2b.

"From ancient times there have been women" (p. 266): Meng Chengshun, "Zhenwenji xu," in *Zhang Yuniang guifang sanqing yingwumu Zhenwen ji*, in *Guben xiqu congkan erji*, p. 1.

"Alone I sit, a flower without a branch" (p. 267): *Lanxue ji* 1: 6b.

"The autumn wind" (p. 267): ibid., 1: 6b–7a.

"Outside the door" (p. 267): ibid., 1: 7b.

"The autumn stream and autumn sky" (p. 267): ibid., 1: 11a.

"Outside the gate" (p. 268): ibid., 2: 10a.

"Gazing at the distant trees" (p. 268): *Lanxue ji* 2: 8a–b; Su, p. 270.

A Wifely Poetics: Zheng Yunduan

"I, lady Zheng, was born to a noble family" (p. 269): Zheng Yunduan, *Suyong ji* (hereafter *SYJ*), in Wang Yunwu, comp., *Hanfenlou miji (san)*. Taibei: Taiwan shangwu yinshuguan, 1967, "Tici," 1a–b.

"The beauty removes" (p. 270): ibid., 13a.

"My younger sister followed her husband" (p. 270): ibid., 4b–5a.

"I am the owner" (p. 271): ibid., 1a.

"I really love" (p. 272): IBID, 13a; Su, p. 264.

"How lovely was that Lady Jiang of Lu" (p. 273): *SYJ* 5a.

"Liu Ling's style name was Bolun" (p. 273): *Mingshi zhuan*, in Liu Yiqing, comp., Liu Xiaobiao, ann., *Shishuo xinyu huijiao jizhu*. Shanghai: Shanghai guji chuban she, 2002, p. 225.

"A hundred years flashes by" (p. 273): *SYJ* 17b.

"The Ban family for generations" (p. 274): ibid., 7b.

"Heaven granted me talent" (p. 274): ibid., 22b.

"The blossoms of the flowering peach" (p. 274): ibid., 14b–15a.

"The bones of a poet" (p. 275): ibid., 16a.

"I used to be an immortal" (p. 275): ibid., 6a.

"Hemp Maiden, that immortal of ancient times" (p. 275): ibid., 4b.

"I have observed that commoner families" (p. 276): *SYJ* 1b; Su, pp. 257–258.

"Her husband went off" (p. 277): *SYJ* 3b; Su, pp. 258–259.

"At fifty, one may use a staff" (p. 277): *SYJ* 3b.

"Bright and shiny" (p. 278): ibid., 4a.

"Where there is birth, there must be death" (p. 279): ibid., 22b–23a.

"Shallow and weak" (p. 280): *Siku quanshu zongmu* 174: 73b.

"Zheng Yunduan was the wife of Shi Boren" (p. 280): Zhong Xing, *Mingyuan shigui*, in *Siku quanshu cunmu congshu*. Jinan: Qi Lu shushe, 1997, vol. 339, p. 259 (23: 3a).

Guan Daosheng and Huang E

Artist and Artist's Wife: Guan Daosheng

"The personal name of the Lady was Daosheng" (p. 281): Zhao Mengfu, *Songxuezhai shiwen wai ji*, quoted in Chen Gaohua, comp., *Yuandai huajia shiliao*. Shanghai: Shanghai renmin meishu chubanshe, 1980, pp. 43–45.

"The day you left" (p. 284): Chen Yan, comp., *Yuanshi jishi*. Shanghai: Shanghai guji chubanshe, 1987, p. 815.

"After the snow" (p. 284): *Mingyuan shigui*, p. 265 (23: 16b); Su, pp. 249–250; Du, p. 185.

"From afar, I think of my mountain cottage" (p. 285): *Yuanshi jishi*, pp. 814–815; Su, p. 250; Du, pp. 184–185.

"Once, when Zhao Mengfu wanted to buy some concubines" (p. 286): Jiang Yikui, comp., *Yaoshantang waiji*, in *Xuxiu Siku quanshu*, vol. 1194, pp. 644–645 (70: 6b–7a).

An Exile's Wife: Huang E

"Even the geese on their return south" (p. 288): Huang E, *Yang furen shi ji*, in *Yang Shen ciqu ji*. Chengdu: Sichuan renmin chubanshe, 1984, p. 430; Su, pp. 296–297; Du, p. 228.

"Too listless to send this letter" (p. 289): ibid., p. 433; Du, p. 228.

"My pearly tears fall in profusion" (p. 289): ibid., p. 432.

"With my golden needle" (p. 290): ibid., p. 434.

"The ceaseless rain" (p. 290): Yang Shen, *Sheng'an Taoqing yuefu*, in *Yang Shen ciqu ji*, pp. 169–170; Du, p. 229.

"One is picking a rose" (p. 290): *Yang furen ciqu ji*, in *Yang Shen ciqu ji*, pp. 423–424.

Chapter 6: *Empresses, Nuns and Actresses*
Empresses and Palace Ladies

Lady Huarui and Her Palace Songs

"Inside the phoenix walls" (p. 294): *QTS*, pp. 8971–8981; Xu Shiwen, ann., *Huarui gongci jianzhu*. Chengdu: Ba Shu shushe, 1992, pp. 22–176.

"Lady Fei was a native of Qingcheng in Shu" (p. 295): Wei Qingshi, *Shiren yuxie*, quoting *Houshan shihua*, as quoted in *Huarui gongci jianzhu*, pp. 217–218.

"When Our Dynasty had subjugated" (p. 296): Cai Tao, *Tieweishan congtan*. Beijing: Zhonghua shuju, 1983, p. 109; also quoted in *Huarui gongci jianzhu*, pp. 203–204.

"Meng Chang, the illegitimate ruler of Shu" (p. 296): Wu Zeng, *Nenggaizhai manlu*. Beijing: Zhonghua shuju, 1960, p. 478; also quoted in Pu Jiangqing, "Huarui furen gongci kaozheng," in his *Pu Jiangqing wenlu*. Beijing: Renmin wenxue chubanshe, 1958, p. 51.

Empress Yang and More Palace Songs

"Willow branches snatch" (p. 298): Shen Lidong, comp., *Lidai houfei shici jizhu*. Beijing: Zhongguo funü chubanshe, 1990, pp. 337–361.

"All of a sudden our lord" (p. 299): ibid.

Xiao Guanyin and Her Sorry Fate

"Lady Xiao, the Xuanyi Empress" (p. 300): *Liaoshi.* Beijing: Zhonghua shuju, 1974, p. 1205.

"I sweep the hidden hall" (p. 301): Wang Ding, *Fenjiao lu,* in *Zhongguo guyan xipin congkan,* vol. 1 (*Ruyijun zhuan deng shizhong*), pp. 116–117.

"Despite a meager fortune I was greatly blessed" (p. 300): ibid., p. 126.

Empress Xu and the Bodhisattva Guanyin

"The Humane and Filial [Renxiao] Empress" (p. 305): *Mingshi.* Beijing: Zhonghua shuju, 1974, pp. 3509–3511.

"From my earliest years" (p. 308): *Neixun,* in Zhang Fuqing, comp., *Nüjie,* pp. 22–23.

"Guanyin was born in the western regions" (p. 312): Guan Daosheng (Lady Guan of the Yuan), "Guanyin dashi zhuan," in *Lüchuang nüshi,* quoted in Du Deqiao (Glen Dudbridge), *Miaoshan chuanshuo: Guanyin pusa yuanqi kao.* Taibei: Juliu tushu gongsi, 1990, pp. 44–48.

"In the spring of the thirty-first year" (p. 315): *Da Ming renxiao huanghou menggan Fo shuo diyi xiyou da gongde jing,* in *Xuzangjing* (hereafter "*XZJ*"), Yinyin Xuzangjing weiyuanhui. Hong Kong: Longmen shudian, 1967, vol. 1, pp. 342–343.

Nuns

Chan Buddhism and Women

"For the first time [Zhixian] bowed" (p. 322): *Jingde chuandeng lu,* in *Taishō shinshū daizōkyō,* vol. 51, pp. 288b–289a.

Miaodao, Miaozong, and Other Female Disciples of Chan Master Dahui Zonggao

"At that time it was as hot as a furnace" (p. 324): *Dahui Pujue chanshi pushuo, Dai nihon zokuzōkyō.* Kyoto: Zōkyō Shoin, 1902–1905, vol. 31, 5: 441c–443c. The translation is based on that of Miriam Levering, "Miao-tao and her Teacher Ta-hui," in Peter N. Gregory and Daniel A. Getz, Jr., eds., *Buddhism in the Sung.* Honolulu: University of Hawaii Press, 1999, p. 203.

"elegant, polished and literary" (p. 325): Miriam Levering, "Miao-tao and her Teacher Ta-hui," in *Buddhism in the Sung,* p. 209.

"Chan is not a matter of concepts and thoughts" (p. 325): *Wudeng huiyan,* in *XZJ,* vol. 138, pp. 347d–348a.

"When Yantou was in Shatai, he was a ferryman at Ezhu Lake" (p. 326): ibid., pp. 401b–402a.

"A leaf of a boat drifts across a vast stretch of water" (p. 327): ibid.

"Don't you know that afflictions are nothing more than wisdom" (p. 328): ibid., p. 412.

"Suddenly I find myself upside-down on level ground" (p. 329): Zhenhua, *Xu biqiuni zhuan*, in *Biqiuni zhuan quanji*. Taibei: Fojiao shuju, 1989, p. 31.

Other Writing Nuns

"Master Sixin, knowing of Kongshi's accomplishments" (p. 329): ibid., p. 30.

"Since there is nothing that exists" (p. 331): ibid.

"A spring morning on the lake: wind and rain" (p. 333): ibid., p. 36.

Courtesans and Actresses

"You swore an oath, proclaimed a vow" (p. 333): Xu Zhenbang, ed., *Gudai nüzi aiqing shixuan*. Beijing: Dazhong wenyi chubanshe, 1998, pp. 196–197.

Courtesan, Poet, and Philosopher: Wen Wan

"Around this time the prime minister Sima Guang" (p. 334): Qingxuzi, "Wen Wan," in Liu Fu, comp., *Qingsuo gaoyi*. Shanghai: Shanghai guji chubanshe, 1983, p. 169.

"As in the silent little flower courtyard" (p. 335): Cai Zichun, "Gantang yishi houxu," in Liu Fu, comp., *Qingsuo gaoyi*. Shanghai: Shanghai guji chubanshe, 1983, pp. 175–176.

"Those who by nature are rich" (p. 336): ibid., p. 176.

"Everyone loves the white moon" (p. 336): ibid., p. 178.

Smartass Wang and the Romance of Su Xiaoqing

"The river scene is desolate and bare" (p. 338): Sui Shusen, comp., *Quan Yuan sanqu*. Beijing: Zhonghua shuju, 1964, pp. 1274–1278.

"She was surnamed Wang" (p. 344): Xia Tingzhi, *Qinglou ji*, in *Zhongguo gudian xiqu lunzhu jicheng*, vol. 2, p. 37.

"She enjoyed quite a reputation" (p. 344): ibid., pp. 26–27.

Part Three: *The First High Tide of Women's Literature*

"Poems are sounds that arise naturally" (p. 350): Zhong Xing, *Mingyuan shigui*, "Zhong Xing xu," quoted in Hu Wenkai, pp. 883–884.

"The Way of Poetry may have many beginnings" (p. 351): ibid.

"In the transmission of prose and poetry" (p. 352): Zhou Lianggong, *Shu ying*. Shanghai: Gudian wenxue chubanshe, 1957, p. 24.

"One will not find in this book" (p. 352): Ma Rong, ed., *Nü caizi shu*. Shengyang: Chunfeng wenyi chubanshe, 1983, p. 6.

"It is more difficult for those" (p. 354): Liang Mengzhao, "Ji di shu," quoted in Hua Wei, "Wusheng zhi sheng: Ming Qing funü xiqu zhong zhi qing yu shuxie," in her *Ming Qing funü zhi xiqu chuangzuo yu piping*. Taibei: Zhongyang yanjiu yuan, Zhongguo wenzhe yanjiusuo, 2003, p. 42.

"Of course it is a good thing for women to be literate" (p. 357): Jin Fu, *Tingxun*, in Xu Zi, ed., *Jiaxun*. Beijing: Zhongyang minzu daxue chubanshe, 1996, p. 333.

Chapter 7: *Courtesans*

Liang Xiaoyu and the Tale of Huang Chonggu

"Liang Xiaoyu was a native of Hangzhou" (p. 359): Qian Qianyi, *Liechao shiji xiaozhuan* (hereafter "*LCSJ*"). Shanghai: Gudian wenxue chubanshe, 1957, pp. 771–772.

"Once the leather sack sank" (p. 361): Du, pp. 241–242.

"The rustling pine trees play" (p. 362): ibid., p. 241.

"Once when Zhou Xiang" (p. 362): *Taiping guangji*, pp. 2924–2925 (j. 367).

Jing Pianpian and Ma Xiaolan

"Jing Pianpian, who had the style name Sanwei" (p. 364): *LCSJ*, p. 764.

"Of all the famous courtesans of the Ming dynasty" (p. 365): *Yujing yangqiu*, quoted in Su, p. 326.

"How can you say the road is long" (p. 365): ibid., p. 327.

"The ninety days of springtime" (p. 365): ibid.

"The personal name of courtesan Ma was Shouzhen" (p. 366): *LCSJ*, pp. 765–766.

"All through the day I watch the parrot" (p. 367): Su, p. 310.

Wang Wei and Yang Wan

"Wei's style name was Xiuwei" (p. 368): *LCSJ*, p. 760.

"Her *shi* poems are like those of Xue Tao" (p. 369): Chen Jiru, "Ti *Xiuwei cao*," quoted in Su, p. 346.

"Sharing spring, we talked and talked" (p. 369): ibid.

"When my friend said goodbye" (p. 370): ibid., 347–348.

"The courtyard tree looks" (p. 370): ibid., p. 348.

"Yang Wan's style name was Wanshu" (p. 370): *LCSJ*, pp. 773–774.

"When Wan married me, she was barely sixteen" (p. 371): Mao Yuanyi, "Xu," quoted in Hu Wenkai, p. 184.

"Together we watch the jade-white arms" (p. 372): Su, pp. 349–350.

"Solitary, I rest my chin on my hand" (p. 373): Du, p. 284.

"Flying on and on" (p. 373): Su, pp. 350–351.

"The long-expected rendezvous" (p. 373): Du, p. 285.

Liu Shi

"She was his most favorite concubine" (p. 374): Qian Zhao'ao, *Zhizhi tan'er*, in Liu Yanyuan, ann., *Liu Rushi shici pingzhu* (hereafter "*LRSSC*"). Beijing: Beijing guji chubanshe, 2000, p. 280.

"In the Sixth Month of the *xinsi* year" (p. 375): Shen Qiu, "Hedongjun zhuan," in Liu Yanyuan, comp., *Liu Rushi shiwen ji*. Beijing: Zhonghua quanguo tushuguan wenxian suoweifuzhi zhongxin, 1996, p. 227.

"The time of spring completes" (p. 377): Zhou Shutian, ed., *Liu Rushi ji* (hereafter "*LRSJ*"). Shenyang: Liaoning jiaoyu chubanshe, 2001, p. 18; *LRSSC*, pp. 70–72.

"Willow floss returns from dreams" (p. 377): *LRSJ*, p. 34; *LRSSC*, pp. 194–195.

"Flower-patterned, moon-shaped" (p. 378): *LRSJ*, p. 35; *LRSSC*, pp. 204–206.

"Hidden birds multiply" (p. 378): *LRSJ*, p. 50; *LRSSC*, pp. 259–261.

"Qiantang was once upon a time the capital" (p. 380): *LRSJ*, pp. 48–49; *LRSSC*, pp. 249–251.

"The Junior Guardian was a hero without equal" (p. 380): *LRSJ*, p. 76; *LRSSC*, pp. 254–258.

"Why is it that foxes and birds" (p. 381): *LRSJ*, pp. 21–22; *LRSSC*, pp. 96–100.

"In her early years" (p. 382): *Shenshitang shihua*, quoted in *LRSSC*, pp. 99–100.

"It refuses to show off" (p. 382): *LRSJ*, p. 113; *LRSSC*, pp. 270–271.

Chapter 8: *Matrons and Maidens*
Shen Yixiu and Her Daughters

Shen Yixiu

"Shen Yixiu's style name was Wanjun" (p. 384): *LCSJ*, pp. 753–754

"Sad and distressed" (p. 385): Ye Shaoyuan, ed., *Wumengtang ji* (hereafter "*WMTJ*"). Beijing: Zhonghua shuju, 1998, pp. 34–35.

"The eastern breeze tonight" (p. 386): ibid., pp. 40–41.

"The endless night drags on and on" (p. 386): ibid., p. 82.

"To heaven's farthest reaches" (p. 387): ibid., pp. 145–146.

"The west wind is piercing" (p. 387): ibid., p. 165.

"The plum bud startled by the storm" (p. 388): ibid., p. 178.

"Busily we float up and sink down" (p. 388): ibid., p. 82.

"In Suzhou there was a deity" (p. 389): *LCSJ*, pp. 755–756.

Ye Xiaoluan

"Qianqian was the wife of Shen Zizheng" (p. 390): *LCSJ*, p. 757.

"I have no way to repay" (p. 391): *WMTJ*, p. 312

"I hold up my mirror" (p. 391): ibid., p. 311.

"The Master of the Cooking Dream hides herself away" (p. 392): ibid., pp. 352–353.

"The Lake Fen Stones are so called because" (p. 394): ibid., pp. 354–355.

"There was a girl" (p. 396): ibid., p. 348.

"Whenever I try to call out to Heaven" (p. 397): ibid., p. 330.

"One scroll of the *Lankavatara Sutra*" (p. 397): ibid., pp. 339–340.

"Several notes of clear chimes" (p. 400): ibid., p. 324.

"My daughter's name was Xiaoluan" (p. 400): ibid., pp. 201–204.

Ye Wanwan

"Wanwan's style name was Zhaoqi. Her appearance was beautiful" (p. 406): *LCSJ*, pp. 754–755.

"Alas, how can one bear to speak of poems" (p. 406): *WMTJ*, pp. 237–238.

"How many people grieve" (p. 407): ibid., p. 239.

"The shadows of red candles" (p. 408): ibid., pp. 241–242

Huichou

"Wounded by partings" (p. 409): *WMTJ*, p. 757.

"The light chill, cutting out leaves and petals" (p. 410): ibid., p. 749.

"[*The male lead enters*] I am Hui Baifang" (p. 412): ibid., pp. 398–399.

Gu Ruopu and Liang Mengzhao

Gu Ruopu

"Gu Ruopu had the style name Hezhi" (p. 414): Gu Ruopu, *Woyuexuan gao*, in *Wulin wangzhe yizhu qianbian* 1a.

"When I read the *Odes*" (p. 415): ibid., "Zixu," 2a–2b.

"As soon as yin and yang were separated" (p. 418): ibid., 2: 1b–2a.

"At the end of spring" (p. 419): ibid., 2: 2a–2b.

"Quietly I turn the sutra pages" (p. 419): ibid., 2: 1b.

"In my dream I was idly reciting" (p. 420): ibid., 2: 6a.

"What has become" (p. 420): ibid., 3: 1a.

Liang Mengzhao

"She is naturally gifted" (p. 420): Ge Zhengqi, "Xu," quoted in Hu Wenkai, p. 163.

"In her *shi* poems she strives for startling strangeness" (p. 421): *Gonggui shiji yiwen kaoliie*, quoted in Hu Wenkai, p. 164.

"From afar, the boatman calls" (p. 421): Wang Duanshu, comp., *Mingyuan shiwei chubian* (hereafter "*MYSW*"), woodblock ed. N.p.: Qingyintang, 1667, 12: 1b.

"In my yearning for nature's scenes" (p. 421): ibid.

"The boundless expanse" (p. 422): ibid., 12: 2b–3a.

"One would think that the mermaids had come out" (p. 423): ibid., 12: 3a.

"I stand alone in the little courtyard" (p. 423): ibid., 12: 3b.

"From all sides the sounds of the border" (p. 423): ibid., 12: 4b.

"Dimly discernable hangings and banners" (p. 423): ibid., 18: 15b–16a.

Chapter 9: *Women Writers of the Conquest Period*
Shang Jinglan and Xu Can

A Loyalist's Widow: Shang Jinglan

"You have achieved the reputation" (p. 426): Shang Jinglan, "Shang Furen Jinnang ji," in *Qi Biaojia ji*. Beijing: Zhonghua shuju, 1960, p. 260.

"The plum and willow" (p. 427): ibid., p. 268.

"The old garden has now grown wild" (p. 427): ibid., p. 268.

"A boat passing through mist" (p. 427): ibid., p. 269.

"Music is played" (p. 427): ibid., pp. 272–273.

"The Tenth Month of the year *jiawu*" (p. 428): ibid., p. 272.

"I am a seventy-two-year-old widow" (p. 430): ibid., p. 289.

Exiled to Manchuria: Xu Can

"The lady's personal name was Can" (p. 431): Xu Can, *Zhuozhengyuan shi ji*, in *Baijinglou congshu* (hereafter "*ZZYSJ*"). Shanghai: Boguzhai, 1922, 1a–2a.

"Before the Junior Guardian" (p. 433): Shi Shuyi, comp., *Qingdai guige shiren zhengliie*. Taipei: Dingwen shuju, 1971, p. 81 (2: 1a).

"Gone in a flash the splendors of spring" (p. 433): *Zhuozhengyuan shi yu* 3: 5a–5b.

"To grow old" (p. 434): *ZZYSJ* 1: 15a–b.

"The single moon above the inner quarters" (p. 434): ibid., 1: 16a–b.

"From far away I gaze on the high walls" (p. 435): ibid., 1: 32a.

"The entire family has taken refuge" (p. 435): ibid.

"Since our times in the Capital" (p. 435): ibid., 1: 43b–44a.

"I had heard played on strings songs" (p. 436): ibid., 1:34a–34b.

"The loom for weaving brocade grows cold" (p. 437): ibid., 1: 36a.

Wang Duanshu and Huang Yuanjie

Ming Loyalist: Wang Duanshu

"She was lovely in face and figure" (p. 437): Wang Youding, "Wang Duanshu zhuan," quoted in Zhong Huiling, *Qingdai nüshiren yanjiu.* Taibei: Liren shuju, 2000, p. 360.

"I wrote the six biographies" (p. 440): Wang Duanshu, *Yinhong ji* (hereafter "*YHJ*"), woodblock ed. N.p., ca. 1670, 20: 9a–b.

"Huang Duanbo had the style name of Yuangong" (p. 441): ibid., 20: 2a–4a.

"Lady Jin was a native of Guiji" (p. 443): ibid., 23: 1a–2b.

"The peaks of Yue, the hills of You" (p. 444): ibid., 5: 3b–4a.

"Lush and overgrown the riverbank grasses" (p. 445): ibid., 7: 1a–b.

"Cold and dilapidated the house of Han" (p. 445): ibid., 3: 1a–b.

"Who says that New Year's Eve is full of activity" (p. 446): ibid., 4: 9a–b.

"In the desolate and dusty bare wastes" (p. 447): ibid., 5: 4a–b.

"So unexpectedly the prime of my life has passed" (p. 447): *Qingdai nüshiren yanjiu*, pp. 364–365.

"The leaves were falling" (p. 448): *YHJ* 8:6b–7a.

"Climbing to a high place" (p. 449): ibid., 5:10b–11a.

"Between heaven and earth" (p. 449): ibid., 18: 3a–b.

"The water loves the flowers' reflection" (p. 450): ibid., 16: 1a.

"Tunes and songs line the path" (p. 450): ibid., 16: 1b.

"The butterflies coldly chase smiles" (p. 451): ibid., 16: 1b.

"Slapping the face the bitter cold wind" (p. 451): ibid., 16: 2a.

"Wine I love to drink when melancholy" (p. 451): ibid., 11: 4b–5a.

Painter, Calligrapher, and Poet: Huang Yuanjie

"We stir the flowers on winding paths" (p. 453): *MYSW* 9: 20b.

"Clutching fly whisks like immortal companions" (p. 453): ibid., 9: 21b–22a.

"The stream can print the moon" (p. 454): ibid., 9: 20a.

"Inside the house one feels" (p. 454): Huan Yuanjie, *Huang Jieling shi*, in *Shiyuan ba mingjia ji*, 1655 edition, 14b.

"Each and every one" (p. 454): ibid., 15a.

"Entering the mountains" (p. 455): *MYSW* 9: 23a–b.

"Who, traveling far from home" (p. 455): ibid., 9: 21b.

Writing Nuns

"In these degenerate days" (p. 456): Qian Qianyi, "Li Xiaozhen zhuan xu," in *Muzhai youxueji* 15: 27b, in *Xuxiu Siku quanshu*, vol. 1391.

Teacher and Convent-Builder: Yikui Chaochen

"My secular surname was Sun" (p. 458): Cantong Yikui, *Cantong Yikui chanshi yulu*, in *Mingban Jiaxing Dazangjing*, reprint. Taibei: Xinwenfeng chuban gongsi, 1987, vol. 37, p. 18.

"The master said: 'The ancients would cook 'a white ox of the open field'"" (p. 460): ibid., pp. 8–9.

"She who spent years humbling, shaping, and polishing us" (p. 461): ibid., p. 9.

"The ancestral hall is tall and lofty" (p. 462): ibid.

"Waking from my dream" (p. 462): ibid.

"My whole body burns with fever" (p. 462):ibid., p. 12.

"Once the layered gates" (p. 463): ibid., p. 10.

"You've forgotten the dusty world" (p. 464): ibid., p. 11.

"The ancient hall stands tall and proud" (p. 464): ibid., p. 10.

Pilgrimage and Poetry: Jizong Xingche

"I come from Hengzhou" (p. 464): *Jizong Che chanshi yulu*, in *Mingban Jiaxing dazangjing*, vol. 28, p. 453.

"The several decades since I left home" (p. 466): ibid., p. 469.

"The masters of old said" (p. 466): ibid., p. 452.

"From the mountain torrent" (p. 468): ibid., p. 462.

Chapter 10: *The Banana Garden Poetry Club*

"At that time, talented poets of the inner chambers" (p. 472): *Zhongxiangci*, "Yüe ji," Shanghai: Dadong shuju, 1933, 50b.

"At that time, the fashions in Wulin" (p. 472): *Hangjun shiji*, quoted in *Qingdai nüshiren yanjiu*, p. 178.

"Each month we would meet a number of times" (p. 472): Lin Yining, *Jiefang ji*, j. 27, "Feng Xian," quoted in *Qingdai nüshiren yanjiu*, p. 175.

Gu Zhiqiong

"The stars glow and glimmer" (p. 473): *Zhongxiangci*, "Li ji," 38a.

"Willow floss drifts about on the wind" (p. 473): ibid., 39a.

"The late night so still" (p. 474): ibid., 38a.

"My body, skinny and wasted" (p. 474): ibid.

Chai Jingyi

"From jade-white face and cloud-like hairdo" (p. 475): Du, p. 330.

"Don't you see / In the houses of nobles" (p. 475): Wanyan Yun Zhu, *Guochao guixiu zhengshi ji*, woodblock ed. N.p.: Hongxiangguan, 1831–1836 (4: 5a–b); Du, p. 330; Su, p. 381.

"The storm-tossed waves" (p. 476): *Guochao guixiu zhengshi ji* 4: 6a; Du, p. 330.

"Why do young men" (p. 476): *Zhongxiangci*, "Yüe ji," 51b; Du, p. 330.

"The wide expanse" (p. 477): Su, pp. 381–382.

Feng Xian

"Li Guang was also not yet enfeoffed" (p. 477): Du, p. 369.

Qian Fenglun

"My grandson's wife Qian Fenglun" (p. 478): Gu Ruopu, "Xu," quoted in Hu Wenkai, pp. 757–758.

"When many years ago" (p. 479): *Guochao guixiu zhengshi ji* 4: 6b–7a; Du, p. 508.

"All around one hears songs of Chu" (p. 479): *Zhongxiangci*, "Li ji," 41a.

"They've heard the crab apple tree" (p. 480): ibid., 41b.

"The lotus-flowers are ablaze" (p. 480): Du, p. 508.

"A secluded courtyard, a spring day of leisure" (p. 481): Su, pp. 423–424.

"Idly we leaned on the red railings" (p. 481): *Zhongxiangci*, "Li ji," 43a.

"The sun is warm and the spring is glorious" (p. 482): ibid., 42b–43a.

"One of the five people" (p. 482): Du, pp. 509–510.

"The path is blocked" (p. 483): ibid., p. 509.

"Leaning on the balustrade" (p. 483): *Zhongxiangci*, "Li ji," 39b.

"Tossed about by the waves" (p. 484): ibid., 42a–b.

"Where in the world" (p. 484): Du, pp. 510–511.

"A hundred years last but a moment" (p. 485): ibid., p. 510.

Lin Yining

"Crossing the most perilous mountains and rivers" (p. 486): *Guochao guixiu zhengshi ji* 4: 2b–3a; Du, p. 468.

"A full year filled by the feelings of parting" (p. 486): Du, p. 468.

"In eerie silence, the spring wood" (p. 487): ibid., pp. 468–469.

"A lifetime's failure and success" (p. 487): ibid., p. 469.

Gu Si

"Plum blossoms and bamboo leaves" (p. 487): Du, p. 381.

"Passing over the red towers, piercing through the green window silk" (p. 487): *Zhongxiangci*, "Yüe ji," 38b–39a; Du, p. 381.

"A slender boat, no bigger than a leaf" (p. 488): *Zhongxiangci*, "Yüe ji," 40a; Du, pp. 380–381.

Zhu Rouze

"Living at home you didn't have a worry" (p. 489): Xu Zhenbang, ed., *Gudai nüzi aiqing shixuan*. Beijing: Dazhong wenyi chubanshe, 1998, pp. 394–397.

"Outside the city, masses of people" (p. 491): Du, pp. 745–746.

"Let's meet to view the spring sights" (p. 491): Su, p. 393.

"[Zhu Rouze's husband] Fangzhou had a concubine" (p. 492): *Hangjun shiji*, quoted in Shi Shuyi, *Qingdai guige shiren zhenglüe*. Taibei: Dingwen shuju, 1971, p. 182 (3: 18b).

Zhang Hao

"Hao's style name was Chayun" (p. 492): Deng Hanyi, *Tianxia mingjia shiguan* 12: 31b–32b.

"The wind is fierce" (p. 493): *Tianxia mingjia shiguan* 12: 32b; Du, p. 703.

Mao Ti

"Rising at dawn I comb my hair" (p. 493): *Zhongxiangci*, "She ji," 34b.

"In the mountains, hungry crows clamor on a thousand trees" (p. 494): Du, p. 492.

"I love poetry" (p. 494): *Zhongxiangci*, "She ji," 33b–34a.

Interlude: *Ideal and Reality*

Chapter 11: *Ideal*

Du Liniang and Her Female Commentators

"a morbid fascination" (p. 499): Dorothy Ko, *Teachers of the Inner Chambers: Women and Culture in Seventeenth-Century China*. Stanford: Stanford University Press, 1994, p. 99.

"In the last month of the winter" (p. 502): Zhang Chao, comp., *Yuchu xinzhi*, in *Yuchu zhi heji*, reprint. Shanghai: Shanghai shudian, 1986, vol. 2, pp. 223–224.

Long-Suffering Concubines

Xiaoqing

"Xiaoqing was the concubine" (p. 505): Zhanzhan waishi, comp., *Qingshi*. Shenyang: Chunfeng wenyi chubanshe, 1986, pp. 422–427.

"The threat of snow stops the clouds" (p. 509): ibid., p. 424.

"I bow my head and pray" (p. 509): ibid.

"My spring blouse: tears of blood" (p. 509): ibid.

"If I, newly made-up, would've been compared with paintings" (p. 510): ibid.

"Cold rain outside the dark window" (p. 510): ibid., p. 425.

"A couple of birds, from who knows where" (p. 510): ibid.

"Cai Yan became a bride far away" (p. 510): ibid.

"When at some future date" (p. 511): ibid., p. 426.

"Twisted innards in a hundred knots" (p. 511): ibid.

"When I read the compositions of Xiaoqing" (p. 511): ibid.

"There was a girl from Yangzhou" (p. 513): Wang Duanshu, *Yinhong ji* 5: 3a–3b.

"Sulan's [White Orchid] personal name was Ru" (p. 513): *LCSJ*, p. 773.

Skinny Mares

"On the night of the sixth of the Sixth Month" (p. 515): Miao Lianbao, ed., *Guochao Zhengshi xuji* 2: 18b–20b.

"Zhao Juntai from Hangzhou" (p. 518): Yuan Mei, *Suiyuan shihua*. Nanjing: Jiangsu guji chubanshe, 2000, p. 87 (4: 37).

Poems on Walls

"It is unknown from where she hailed" (p. 518): *Qingshi*, p. 427.

Lyrics on Flower Petals: Shuangqing

"Shuangqing was a girl from Xiaoshan" (p. 521): Shi Zhenlin, *Xiqing sanji*, in *Zhongguo wenxue zhenben congshu*. Shanghai: Shanghai zazhi gongsi, 1935, vol. 9, pp. 66–67.

"Brows half in a frown" (p. 521): ibid., p. 70.

"At the beginning of the Ninth Month" (p. 525): ibid., p. 91.

"By the end of the Ninth Month" (p. 525): ibid., p. 92.

"Shuangqing was working one night" (p. 526): ibid., pp. 92–93.

"On the twentieth day of the Tenth Month" (p. 529): ibid., pp. 102–103.

"A neighbor woman said" (p. 531): ibid., p. 103.

"On the twenty-sixth day" (p. 532): ibid., pp. 103–104.

"Once when Shuangqing admonished" (p. 533): ibid., pp. 105–106.

"I left Xiaoshan" (p. 534): ibid., pp. 127–128.

"I had planned to return" (p. 536): ibid., pp. 128–129.

"I left Xiaoshan in the year *kuichou*" (p. 538): ibid., pp. 175–176.

"The lyrics of Shuangqing resemble" (p. 541): Huang Xieqing, *Guochao cizong xubian*, quoted in Zhang Gongliang, "*Xiqing sanji* cankao ziliao," p. 8, appendix to *Xiqing sanji*.

"Her lyrics represent the acme" (p. 541): Miao Quansun's preface, quoted in "*Xiqing sanji* cankao ziliao," p. 8.

Chapter 12: *Reality*

In a Script of Their Own

Formalized Friendship

"New Year's Day of the First Month" (p. 545): Zhao Liming, ed., *Zhongguo nüshu jicheng*. Beijing: Qinghua daxue chubanshe, 1992, pp. 437–438.

"I went to the garden" (p. 545): ibid., pp. 421–422.
"We had finished our meal" (p. 547): ibid., p. 605.

Getting Married

"I take in my hand a brush" (p. 548): *Zhongguo nüshu jicheng*, pp. 154–156.
"With a writing brush I write these words" (p. 549): ibid., pp. 201–202.
"I take up my brush and write a letter" (p. 550): ibid., pp. 125–126.
"In the Sixth Month it's burning hot" (p. 552): ibid., pp. 597–599.

Autobiographical Ballads

"I write this letter myself" (p. 553): *Zhongguo nüshu jicheng*, pp. 373–374.
"As I sit here in my empty room" (p. 555): ibid., pp. 378–381.

The Sorrows of Pregnancy and Motherhood

"Let me say to you a few simple words" (p. 558): *Zhongguo nüshu jicheng*,
   pp. 718–723.

How to Escape the Female Condition

"Yingtai was the daughter of the Zhu family" (p. 562): Zeng Yongyi, "Liang
   Zhu gushi de yuanyuan yu fazhan," in his *Shuo suwenxue*. Taibei: Lianjing
   chuban shiye gongsi, 1980, p. 122. (This summary is said to derive from
   Zhang Du's *Xuanshi zhi*, but modern editions of the text do not contain
   this story; the earliest text to quote this summary as deriving from *Xuan-
   shizhi* would appear to be eighteenth-century *Tongsupian*.)

Part Four: *The Second High Tide of Women's Literature*

"Because it really would be terrible" (p. 569): Cao Xueqin and Gao E,
   Honglou meng. Beijing: Renmin wenxue chubanshe, 1964, p. 826
   (chap. 64).
"Whenever they were sitting together" (p. 569): Wu Jingzi, *Rulin waishi huijiao
   huiping ben*, ed. by Li Hanqiu. Shanghai: Shanghai guji chubanshe, 1984,
   pp. 155–156 (chap. 11).
"Wen Pu's style name was Chuheng" (p. 570): *Guochao guixiu zhengshi ji*. 7:
   12b–13a.
"Nowadays there is a shameless fool" (p. 571): Zhang Xuecheng, *Bingchen
   zhaji*, in *Zhang Xuecheng yishu*. Beijing: Wenwu chubanshe, 1985, p. 399
   (a–b).
"Tomorrow morning We will visit the Park" (p. 572): Li Ruzhen, *Jinghua yuan*.
   Hong Kong: Zhonghua shuju, 1965, p. 18 (chap. 4).

Chapter 13: *Poetry*
Poetry and Piety

Tao Shan

"A cold wind whistles through the myriad ravines" (p. 579): *Qionglou yingao,* in
    XZJ, vol. 110, p. 359b.
"The small courtyard is filled with a perfect stillness" (p. 579): ibid., 360a.
"On Su terrace frost is cold" (p. 579): ibid.
"It is early winter" (p. 580): ibid., 360b.
"On the empty mountain" (p. 580): ibid.
"Deep in seclusion we share the spring chill" (p. 581): ibid.
"During the long summers of leisure" (p. 582): ibid., 361a.
"I am ashamed for not having cultivated" (p. 583): ibid.
"Mahaprajapati Gotami made a vast and limitless vow" (p. 583): ibid., 362a.
"Last year, my poetic inspiration evaporated" (p. 583): *Guochao guixiu zhengshi ji*
    13: 11a–b.
"How do these trees differ" (p. 584): *Qionglou yingao,* p. 361b.
"Madame Tao's given name was Shan" (p. 585): ibid., 362b–363a.
"In the year *gengzi*" (p. 587): ibid., 359b.
"In the interval between rains" (p. 588): Peng Jiqing, *Xifang gongju,* in *XZJ,*
    vol.109, p. 369a.

Jiang Zhu

"After I read the poetry drafts" (p. 589): Zhang Yunzi, comp., Ren Zhaolin, ed.,
    Wuzhong nüshi shichao, 68b.
"The night rain sad and sorrowful" (p. 590): ibid., 69a–69b.
"The green fat, the red skinny" (p. 590): ibid., 69a.
"On the first day of the Fourth Month" (p. 591): ibid., 61b–62a.
"I had recovered from my [previous] illness" (p. 592): ibid. 67b.
"The wine flows, the flowers gleam white" (p. 593): ibid., 64a.
"With a cup of wine in my hand" (p. 593): ibid., 65a.

Disciples of Yuan Mei

Xi Peilan

"At fifteen I had never been separated from you" (p. 594): Xi Peilan,
    Changzhenge ji (1891) 1: 2b.
"In the courtyard the lamps are aglow" (p. 594): ibid., 1: 4a–b.
"Lonely and quiet has become our mother's life" (p. 595): ibid.
"My love is like the moon" (p. 596): ibid., 1: 4b.

"I want to sew winter clothes for you" (p. 596): ibid., 1: 4b–5a.

"Since you left: months and years" (p. 596): ibid., 1: 5a.

"I am suddenly startled" (p. 596): ibid.

"I remember how long ago" (p. 596): ibid., 1: 6a–b.

"All of a sudden this boat" (p. 598): ibid., 1: 7a.

"At dawn we travel" (p. 598): ibid., 1: 8a–b.

"In the First Month of last year" (p. 599): ibid., 1: 12a–b.

"Don't you see" (p. 601): ibid., 1: 10a–b.

"I still recall that the day" (p. 603): ibid., 3: 7a–8b.

"Each and every word issues" (p. 607): Yuan Mei, "Xu," *Changzhenge ji* 1a.

"When one dragon raises its head" (p. 607): *Changzhenge ji* 3: 6a.

"A full moon from the time of the Qin" (p. 608): ibid., 3: 6b.

"The night is late, your clothes are thin" (p. 608): ibid., 2: 12b.

"From outside the gate" (p. 609): ibid., 3: 11a.

"Don't say that love" (p. 610): ibid., 3: 13a–b.

"At midnight the little serving girl" (p. 611): ibid., 3: 12a.

"The light of the moon" (p. 611): Wang Qi, ann., *Li Taibai quanji*. Beijing:
Zhonghua shuju, 1977, p. 346.

Luo Qilan

"For a woman it is harder" (p. 612): Luo Qilan, "*Guizhong tongren jishi* xu," reproduced in Robyn Hamilton, "The Pursuit of Fame: Luo Qilan (1755–
1813?) and the Debates about Women and Talent in Eighteenth-century
Jiangnan," *Late Imperial China* 18 (1997): 62–66.

"I had heard that the three peaks" (p. 615): Luo Qilan, *Tingqiuxuan shiji*. Jinling:
Gong shi, 1795, 3: 1a–b.

"When you are in the clouds" (p. 616): ibid., 1: 5a.

"When I was young" (p. 616): ibid., 1: 11b–12a.

"When I was very young" (p. 616): ibid., 2: 1a–2a.

"The windows open all around" (p. 617): ibid., 1: 7b.

"South of the Yangzi" (p. 617): ibid., 1: 13a–b.

"For over twelve years" (p. 618): ibid., 2: 10b–11a.

"I moor the boat and return again" (p. 618): ibid., 3: 6b–7a.

"In the women's quarters" (p. 618): ibid., 1: 12b.

"The mirror is eight feet long" (p. 619): ibid., 3: 7b–8a.

Poetry, Scholarship, and Vernacular Prose Fiction

Wang Duan

"*Thirty Poets of the Ming* was compiled by my niece" (p. 621): Liang Desheng,
Guchunxuan wenchao 2: 2a–3a.

"After I had finished compiling" (p. 624): Wang Duan, *Ming sanshijia shixuan*, "Jimeng" (1a–2b).

"Cruel and vindictive" (p. 628): Du, p. 560.

"The painting of Cockcrow Hill's scenery" (p. 629): *Qingdai nüshiren yanjiu*. p. 488.

"The heavens' blue" (p. 629): Du, p. 559.

Gu Chun (Taiqing)

"On summer's longest day" (p. 631): Gu Taiqing and Yihui, *Gu Taiqing Yihui shici heji* (hereafter "*Gu Taiqing*"). Shanghai: Shanghai guji chubanshe, 1998, p. 76.

"The many mountains" (p. 631): ibid., p. 196.

"My son Tong had not yet lived" (p. 632): ibid., p. 43.

"Forty-two years" (p. 632): ibid., p. 112.

"The immortal has already become a crane" (p. 633): ibid., p. 104.

"I had not written any poems" (p. 633): ibid., p. 103.

"The Heavenly Wandering" (p. 634): ibid., p. 280.

"The beauty of Taiqing's song lyrics" (p. 635): Long Muxun, quoted in *Gu Taiqing*, p. 712.

"Beautiful flowers" (p. 636): *Gu Taiqing*, p. 187.

"Long separated: our feelings" (p. 637): ibid., p. 257.

"What a fine easterly wind" (p. 637): ibid., p. 209.

"How beautiful the weather" (p. 637): ibid., p. 247.

"Flowers bloom and flowers fall" (p. 638): ibid., p. 251.

"Tired of embroidery" (p. 638): ibid., p. 274.

"Yesterday I sent spring back home" (p. 639): ibid., p. 231.

"Clear, clear dew" (p. 639): ibid., p. 218.

"Lonely in the empty courtyard" (p. 640): ibid., p. 279.

"A cold mist envelops the trees" (p. 641): ibid., pp. 261–262.

"Here and there the cocks" (p. 641): ibid., p. 291.

"Staying up late, discussing the sutras" (p. 642): ibid., pp. 203–204.

"My friend has sent me a letter" (p. 643): ibid., p. 238.

"Each and every affair" (p. 644): ibid., p. 194.

"Mist locks in the cold stream" (p. 644): ibid., p. 207.

"When the marionettes take the stage" (p. 645): ibid., p. 210.

"Spring is almost here" (p. 645): ibid., p. 223.

"Warmly resting on my chest" (p. 646): ibid., p. 220.

"Happiness and wisdom cultivated" (p. 646): ibid., p. 296.

"[Jia Lian] had no sooner fallen asleep" (p. 648): Yuncha waishi, *Hongloumeng ying*. Beijing: Beijing daxue chubanshe, 1988, pp. 65–67 (chap. 9).

"After a friendship of thirty years" (p. 651): *Gu Taiqing*, pp. 169–170.

Women and Warfare

Zhang Chaixin

"He let those bandits devour" (p. 653): Guang Tiefu, comp., *Anhui mingyuan shici zhenglüe*. Hefei: Huangshan shushe, 1986, p. 317.

"Lord Shen had a daughter" (p. 654): Chen Xiang, comp., *Qingdai nüshiren xuanji*. Taipei: Taiwan Shangwu yinshuguan, 1977, pp. 193–195.

Zhang Yin

"In her youth, Zhang Yin" (p. 656): Xu Shichang, comp., *Qingshihui*. Beijing: Beijing chubanshe, 1996, p. 3183 (188: 62a).

"When long ago I applied myself" (p. 657): ibid., p. 3183 (188: 62b).

"The ancient sages left us" (p. 658): ibid., pp. 3185–3186 (188: 66a–67a).

"By nature I love working" (p. 662): ibid., p. 3184 (188: 64a).

"I'd always heard" (p. 663): ibid., pp. 3186–3187 (188: 68a–69a).

"Even though the bandits had fled" (p. 666): ibid., p. 3187 (188: 69b).

"That year so long ago" (p. 666): ibid., p. 3188 (188: 71a–b).

"In last night's dream I saw" (p. 667): ibid., p. 3190 (188: 75a).

"When long ago my mother-in-law" (p. 668): ibid., p. 3190 (188: 75a–b).

Li Chengxia

"My carriage stops" (p. 669): *Qingshihui*, p. 3192 (189: 1a–b).

"We are going to stop for the night" (p. 669): ibid., p. 3193 (189: 2a).

"As the dew settles" (p. 669): ibid.

"On the empty steps" (p. 670): ibid., p. 3193 (189: 3a).

"A guest arrived from a faraway place" (p. 670): ibid., p. 3194 (189: 5a).

"Bereft of assistance" (p. 670): ibid., p. 3194 (189: 5b).

"Yesterday we departed" (p. 671): ibid., p. 3195 (189: 7b).

"Oh fierce, so fierce" (p. 672): ibid., pp. 3195–3196 (189: 7b–8a).

"The endless expanse of blue ocean" (p. 672): ibid., pp. 3198–3199 (189: 13b–14a).

"For three years this was our house" (p. 672): ibid., p. 3200 (189: 16b).

"The sporadic willows hide" (p. 673): ibid., p. 3193 (189: 2b).

"The shelves with five thousand books" (p. 674): Du, p. 457.

"To Fujian's mountains" (p. 675): *Qingshihui*, p. 3194 (189: 5a).

"A rainfall has dispelled" (p. 675): ibid., p. 3196 (189: 8b).

"Fighting to the south of the city" (p. 675): ibid., p. 3197 (189: 10b).

"I had a younger brother" (p. 676): ibid., p. 3202 (189: 20b).

Chapter 14: *Drama*
Wang Yun and He Peizhu

"Intelligent and talented" (p. 678): Zhang Lingyi, "Ziti," quoted in Hu Wenkai, p. 509.

"Lou Cheng, a woman from Dongyang" (p. 678): *Nanshi*, Beijing: Zhonghua shuju, 1975, p. 1143.

"Submerged and buried in" (p. 681): Wang Yun, *Fanhuameng*, in Hua Wei, ed., *Ming Qing funü xiqu ji*. Taibei: Zhongyang yanjiuyuan Zhongguo wenzhe yanjiusuo, 2003, p. 33.

"If I were a man" (p. 681): ibid., pp. 34–35.

"While melodic music is played offstage" (p. 682): ibid., p. 36.

"All of a sudden I wake up" (p. 683): ibid., p. 137.

"I am Du Lanxian" (p. 684): He Peizhu, *Lihuameng*, in *Ming Qing funü xiqu ji*, pp. 269–270.

Wu Zao

"In the autumn of the year *yiyou*" (p. 686): Wu Zao, *Qiaoying*, in Zheng Zhenduo, comp., *Qingren zaju erji*. N.p., 1934 (rep. in Zheng Zhenduo, *Qingren zaju chu er ji hedingben*. Hong Kong: Longmen shudian, 1969), p. 301; *Ming Qing funü xiqu ji*, pp. 264–265.

"[*The* xiaosheng *enters in a long gown, hair in a scarf*]" (p. 687): Wang Yongkuan, Yang Haizhong, and Yao Shuyi, eds., *Qingdai zaju xuan*. Zhengzhou: Zhongzhou guji chubanshe, 1991, pp. 336–341.

"With your jingling and jangling" (p. 693): Wu Zao, *Hualianci*, in Xu Naichang, ed., *Xiaotanluanshi huike guixiuci, di wu ji* 15a.

"Her jade feelings" (p. 694): Chen Wenshu, *Xileng guiyong* 16b.

"When I think back on the South" (p. 694): *Hualianci* 35a.

"There is no year that lacks falling blossoms" (p. 695): Zhao Qingxi, "Xu," quoted in Zhong Huiling, *Qingdai nüzuojia zhuanti: Wu Zao ji qi xiangguan wenxue huodong yanjiu*. Taibei: Lexue shuju, 2001, p. 134.

"The long nights drag on" (p. 695): *Hualianci* 1b.

"The bamboo mat" (p. 696): ibid., 6b–7a.

"The covered walkway" (p. 696): ibid., 12a–b.

"Depressed I demand a statement" (p. 697): ibid., 4b–5a.

"On one side 'Encountering Sorrow'" (p. 698): ibid., 37a.

"In the darkening dusk" (p. 698): ibid., 19a.

"From the time Zhu Shuzhen" (p. 699): Shen Xiong, *Gujin cihua*, quoted in *Zhu*, p. 318.

"I do not fear the blossoming" (p. 699): *Hualianci* 9a.

"Last night a gentle rain fell" (p. 699): ibid., 8b.

"The swallows have not yet left" (p. 700): ibid., 5a.

"The low balustrade" (p. 700): ibid., 5b–6a.

"A heart and mind of snow and ice" (p. 701): Wu Zao, *Xiangnan xuebei ci,* in Xu Naichang, comp., *Xiaotanluanshi guixiu huike ci, di wu ji* 24a–b.

Liu Qingyun

"In the spring of the year *dingyou*" (p. 702): Yu Yue, "*Xiaopenglaige chuanqi* xu," in Guan Dedong and Che Xilun, eds., *Liaozhai zhiyi xiqu ji*. Shanghai: Shanghai guji chubanshe, 1983, pp. 709–710.

"[*The* chou *enters, gaudily dressed*]" (p. 704): Liu Qingyun, *Danqingfu,* in *Liaozhai zhiyi xiqu ji,* pp. 686–687.

"[*The bit player enters, dressed as a woodcutter*]" (p. 706): Liu Qingyun, *Feihongxia,* in *Liaozhai zhiyi xiqu ji,* pp. 775–776.

"[*The* laodan *enters*]" (p. 710): Liu Qingyun, *Tianfengyin,* in *Liaozhai zhiyi xiqu ji,* pp. 742–743.

"[*The* xiaosheng *enters, his hair tied up*]" (p. 712): Liu Qingyun, *Tianfengyin,* pp. 735–736.

"[*The* sheng *(i.e. Ma Longmei) speaks*]" (p. 714): *Tianfengyin,* p. 739.

"[*They halt their horses, uncertain of what to do*]" (p. 714): ibid., p. 740.

"Four large Heavenly Kings" (p. 715): *Hongloumeng ying,* pp. 37–38.

Chapter 15: *Plucking Rhymes*

A Rain of Heavenly Flowers

"I was born in a time of warfare" (p. 719): Tao Zhenhuai, *Tianyuhua,* ed. by Li Ping. Zhengzhou: Zhongzhou guji chubanshe, 1984, "Yuanxu" (unnumbered page).

"During the reign of" (p. 721): Tan Zhengbi and Tan Xun, comp., *Tanci xulu*. Shanghai: Shanghai guji chubanshe, 1981, pp. 106–107.

"Why was *A Rain of Heavenly Flowers*" (p. 724): *Tianyuhua,* "Yuanxu" (unnumbered page).

"'Now when it comes to our daughter'" (p. 725): ibid., pp. 268–269.

"I cannot deny responsibility" (p. 726): ibid., p. 889.

"When Yizhen returned" (p. 727): ibid., pp. 1192–1193.

"'Ah, father, I will carry no grudge'" (p. 728): ibid., pp. 1197–1198.

Text and Performance: Zhu Suxian

"Lady Zhu from Yunjian" (p. 730): Yuting zhuren, "*Yulianhuan* xu," quoted in Tan Zhengbi, *Zhongguo nüxing wenxue shihua*. Tianjin: Baihua wenyi chuban she, 1984, p. 431.

"A certain Liang Qi" (p. 731): *Tanci xulu*, pp. 131–132.

"This book is not a performance text" (p. 733): *Huizhenji*, "Fanli," quoted in Bao Zhenpei, *Qingdai nüzuojia tanci xiaoshuo lungao*. Tianjin: Tianjin shehui kexueyuan chubanshe, 2002, p. 71.

"Lord Zuo said with a scornful smile" (p. 733): *Tianyuhua*, p. 1017.

Karmic Bonds of Reincarnation: Chen Duansheng and Hou Zhi

"Plays for the most part" (p. 734): Zheng Danruo, *Mengyingyuan*, quoted in Bao Zhenpei, *Qingdai nüzuojia tanci xiaoshuo lungao*, p. 103.

"During the reign of Emperor Ningzong" (p. 735): *Tanci xulu*, pp. 132–134.

"During the reign of Emperor Chengzong" (p. 737): *Tanci xulu*, pp. 154–155.

"Our story goes that" (p. 740): Chen Duansheng, *Zaishengyuan*, ed. by Du Zhijun. Beijing: Huaxia chubanshe, 2000, pp. 256–257.

"Just as the prime minister" (p. 743): ibid., pp. 658–659.

"'My parents, just think about'" (p. 746): ibid., pp. 663–664.

"People say that Mrs. Duansheng" (p. 749): *Guiyuan congkan*, quoted in *Zhongguo nüxing wenxue shihua*, p. 388.

"I scratch my head" (p. 750): *Zaishengyuan*, pp. 1006–1007.

"As a female ruler" (p. 753): Hou Zhi, *Zaizaotian*, quoted in *Zhongguo nüxing wenxue shihua*, p. 403.

Other Plucking Rhymes

More Cross-Dressing Heroines

"*Karmic Bonds of Reincarnation*, just recently" (p. 755): Qiu Xinru, *Bishenghua*, quoted in *Zhongguo nüxing wenxue shihua*, pp. 409–410.

"She wanted to draft" (p. 755): ibid., p. 410.

"Since ancient times" (p. 757): Niu Ruyuan, "Xu," in Tan Zhengbi and Tan Xun, comps., *Pingtan tongkao*. Beijing: Zhongguo quyi chubanshe, 1985, pp. 265–266.

"She said: 'Master, do not say'" (p. 760): Zheng Huiying, *Fengshuangfei*, quoted in *Zhongguo nüxing wenxue shihua*, pp. 424–425.

"Cheng Huiying [style name Chenchou]" (p. 761): *Queming biji*, cited in *Xiaoshuo kaozheng*, j.7, quoted in *Zhongguo nüxing wenxue shihua*, p. 421.

Loyalty and Patriotism

"The colored clouds scattered" (p. 762): Zhou Yingfang, *Jingzhongzhuan*, quoted in *Zhongguo nüxing wenxue shihua*, p. 456.

Epilogue: *Nationalism and Feminism: Qiu Jin*

Chapter 16: *The Beheaded Feminist: Qiu Jin*

Poet and Nationalist

"The Day of Flowers" (p. 771): *Qiu Jin ji.* Shanghai: Shanghai guji chubanshe, 1979, p. 102; Liu Yulai, *Qiu Jin shici zhushi.* Yinchuan: Ningxia renmin chuban she, 1983, pp. 277–278.

"Since leaving the river city" (p. 771): *Qiu Jin ji,* p. 56; *Qiu Jin shici zhushi,* pp. 12–13.

"A woman neighbor sent me" (p. 771): *Qiu Jin ji,* p. 58; *Qiu Jin shici zhushi,* pp. 28–31.

"Last year I came here" (p. 772): *Qiu Jin ji,* p. 65; *Qiu Jin shici zhushi,* pp. 81–82.

"Singing of willow floss" (p. 773): *Qiu Jin ji,* p. 74; *Qiu Jin shici zhushi,* pp. 142–144.

"The palaces of the house of Han" (p. 774): *Qiu Jin ji,* p. 82; *Qiu Jin shici zhushi,* pp. 197–201.

"Recently I've come to the capital" (p. 776): *Qiu Jin ji,* p. 101; *Qiu Jin shici zhushi,* pp. 269–271.

"Facing the mirror I mumble" (p. 777): *Qiu Jin ji,* p. 110; *Qiu Jin shici zhushi,* pp. 323–324.

"By boat I crossed the sea" (p. 778): *Qiu Jin ji,* p. 77; *Qiu Jin shici zhushi,* pp. 162–164.

"Looking around me" (p. 778): *Qiu Jin ji,* p. 70; *Qiu Jin shici zhushi,* pp. 114–116.

Student and Feminist

"Alas, the most unfair treatment" (p. 780): *Qiu Jin ji,* pp. 4–6.

"Sun and moon have grown dim" (p. 783): *Qiu Jin ji,* p. 87; *Qiu Jin shici zhushi,* pp. 229–231.

"A single expanse of autumn water" (p. 783): *Qiu Jin ji,* p. 79; *Qiu Jin shici zhushi,* pp. 175–178.

"In this ugly and dirty world" (p. 784): *Qiu Jin ji,* p. 110; *Qiu Jin shici zhushi,* pp. 325–326.

"Beset with emotion" (p. 785): *Qiu Jin ji,* p. 111; *Qiu Jin shici zhushi,* pp. 330–332.

"In her lonely study" (p. 785): *Qiu Jin ji,* p. 111; *Qiu Jin shici zhushi,* pp. 332–334.

"To my regret" (p. 786): *Qiu Jin ji,* pp. 125–129.

Teacher and Revolutionary

"Riding the wind for a myriad miles" (p. 794): *Qiu Jin ji,* p. 79; *Qiu Jin shici zhushi,* pp. 178–180.

"Who could this person be" (p. 795): *Qiu Jin ji,* p. 78; *Qiu Jin shici zhushi,* pp. 168–169.

"The lady scholar had a great capacity" (p. 795): Guo Yanli, ed., *Qiu Jin yanjiu ziliao.* Jinan: Shandong jiaoyu chubanshe, 1987, pp. 63–64.

"Later, when she returned" (p. 795): ibid., pp. 71–72.

"My dearly beloved elders" (p. 796): *Qiu Jin ji*, pp. 13–16.

"We women love our freedom" (p. 799): ibid., p. 117.

"Our neighbors encircle us" (p. 800): ibid., p. 116.

"Alas, our country cannot compete" (p. 800): ibid.

"They have liberty" (p. 800): ibid., pp. 116–117.

"Overcome with emotion" (p. 801): *Qiu Jin ji*, p. 112; *Qiu Jin shici zhushi*, pp. 334–335.

"Alas! As I wrote the account" (p. 802): *Qiu Jin yanjiu ziliao*, pp. 73–76.

"The lady scholar Qiu Jin" (p. 806): ibid., pp. 68–69.

Glossary

An Lushan 安祿山
Anle, Princess 安樂

Bai Juyi 白居易
Baitou yin 白頭吟
ban 班 [or 斑] (striped)
Ban, Concubine 班婕妤
Ban Biao 班彪
Ban Chao 班超
Ban Gu 班固
Ban Hui 班回
Ban Kuang 班況
Ban Yong 班勇
Ban You 班斿
Ban Zhao 班昭
Bao Linghui 鮑令暉
Bao Zhao 鮑照
Baochang 寶唱
Bao'en 報恩
baojuan 寶卷
Baopuzi 抱朴子
Baosi 褒姒
Beichuang yingao 北窗吟稿

Beilizhi 北里志
Beimeng suoyan 北夢瑣言
Brush Records, Biji 筆記
Biqiuni zhuan 比丘尼傳
Bishenghua 筆生花
Biyan lu 碧岩录
Bo Yi 伯夷
Bomingnü 薄命女
Bubujiao 步步嬌

cai 才 (talent)
cai 材 (timber)
Cai Tao 蔡條
Cai Yan 蔡琰
Cai Yong 蔡邕
Caicha ge 採茶歌
Caizi jiaren xiaoshuo 才子佳人小說
Cankui yin 慚愧吟
Cao Cao 曹操
Cao Cheng 曹成
Cao Dagu 曹大家
Cao E 曹娥
Cao Fengsheng 曹豐生

Cao Pi 曹丕

Cao Shishu 曹世叔

Cao Xueqin 曹雪芹

Cao Yanniang 曹燕娘

Cao Ye 曹鄴

Cao Yin 曹寅

Cao Zhi 曹植

Caomuzi 草木子

Chai Jingyi 柴靜儀

Chai Shiyao 柴世堯

Chai Zhenyi 柴貞儀

Chaitou huang 釵頭鳳

Chang'an 長安

Chang E 嫦娥

Changhen ge 長恨歌

Changmenfu 長門賦

Changning, Princess 長寧

Chao Cuo 晁錯

Chen, Empress 陳

Chen, Lady 陳氏

Chen Bo 陳柏

Chen Duansheng 陳端生

Chen Jiru 陳繼儒

Chen Peizhi 陳裴之

Chen Shou 陳壽

Chen Tong 陳同

Chen Wenshu 陳文述

Chen Yuanlong 陳元龍

Chen Yunqiao 陳云嶠

Chen Zhaolun 陳兆崙

Chen Zilong 陳子龍

Cheng, Emperor 成帝

Cheng'an Shou 程安壽

Cheng Huiying 程蕙英

Cheng Zheng 程鄭

Chisongzi 赤松子

Chongjun 重俊

chou 丑

Chou yilan ling 愁倚欄令

Chouyan 愁言

Chu 楚

chuanqi 傳奇

Chuci 楚辭

Chun cong tianshang lai 春從天上來

Chunguanghao 春光好

ci 詞

Cilun 詞論

Cixi, Empress Dowager 慈禧

Cixin baojian 慈心寶鑑

Cui Shi 崔湜

Cuishi furen xunnüwen 崔氏夫人訓
    女文

*Da Ming renxiao huanghou menggan
    Foshuo diyi xiyou dagongde jing* 大
    明仁孝皇后夢感佛說第一稀
    有大功德經

Dahui Zonggao 大慧宗杲

Daling tie 大令帖

dan 旦

Danqingfu 丹青副

Daozi 道子

Daque fu 大雀賦

Daxue 大學

Dayan ta 大雁塔

Dazhao 大召

Deng, Empress 鄧皇后

Deng Hanyi 鄧漢儀

Deng Sui 鄧綏

Deng Xun 鄧訓

Deng Yu 鄧禹

Deng Zhi 鄧騭

dengcaixi 燈彩戲

Dezong, Emperor 德宗

Dianjiang chun 點絳唇

Dielian hua 蝶戀花

Ding, lady 丁氏

Dingfeng bo 定風波

Dong Si 董祀
Dong Zhuo 董卓
Dong'a, Prince of 東阿
Dongxiang, Princess 東鄉
Dongxiange 洞仙哥
Dongzheng fu 東征賦
Dou anchun 鬥鵪鶉
Dou Lang 竇朗
Dou Tao 竇滔
Dou Xian 竇憲
Dou Zizhen 竇子真
Du Fu 杜甫
Du Gao 杜羔
Du Guangting 杜光庭
Du Lanxian 杜蘭仙
Du Liniang 杜麗娘
Du Yu 杜預
Duji 妒記

Faguo nü yingxiong tanci 法國女英雄
彈詞
Fan, lady 樊姬
Fan Tan 範菼
Fan Ye 范曄
Fan Zhen 范鎮
Fan Zuyu 范祖禹
Fanhuameng 繁華夢
Fansheng xiang 返生香
Fanxiang ling 翻香令
Feihong xiao 飛虹嘯
Fendie'er 粉蝶兒
Feng Menglong 馮夢龍
Feng shuang fei 鳳雙飛
Feng xi wu 鳳息梧
Feng Xian 馮嫻
Fengguang hao 風光好
Fengliu zi 風流子
Fenjiao lu 焚椒錄
fu 賦 (rhapsody)

Fu'ou fu 涪漚賦
Fu Jian 符堅
Fu Sheng 伏勝
fudao 婦道
fugu 復古
Fuxue 婦學

Gan huang'en 感皇恩
Gantang yishi houxu 甘棠遺事
後序
Gao Chang 高昌
Gao Lishi 高力士
Gao Qi 高啓
Gao Yanxiu 高彥休
Gao Yinxian 高銀仙
Gao Zhongwu 高仲武
Gaoshan liushui 高山流水
Gaozong, Emperor 高宗
Ge Hong 葛洪
Genglouzi 更漏子
Gong Chuo 公綽
gongci 宮詞
Gu, Lady 顧
Gu Ceyun 顧策雲
Gu Ruopu 顧若璞
Gu Si 顧姒
Gu Taiqing 顧太清
Gu Zhiqiong (Yurui) 顧之瓊
(玉蕊)
Guan Daosheng 管道昇
Guan Panpan 關盼盼
Guan Zhong 管仲
Guangyi ji 廣異記
Guanxi zhixian 灌溪
志閑
Guanyin 觀音
guci 鼓詞
guibin 貴嬪
Guiji, Prince of 會稽王

guiyuan 閨冤
Gujin lienüzhuan 古今列
　女傳
Gujin nüshi 古今女史
Guluan 孤鸞
Gumeijiu 沽美酒
Guo, Empress 郭后
Guo Maoqian 郭茂倩
Guo Sanyi 郭三益
Guochao guixiu zhengshi ji 國朝閨秀
　正始集
Gushi shijiushou 古詩十九首
Guwutu 穀於檡
Guxianglou ji 古香樓集
Guyan'er 孤雁兒
Guzhu 孤竹

Haifu 海賦
Han Boyu 韓伯瑜
Han Lanying 韓蘭英
Han Shizhong 韓世忠
Han Yu 韓愈
Hanshan 寒山
Hanshan Deqing 憨山德清
Hanshu 漢書
He, Emperor 和帝
He Guizhi 何桂枝
He Peizhu 何佩珠
He xinliang 賀新涼
He yuan ji 合元記
Hehuoling 喝火令
Helin yulu 鶴林玉露
Hongjia 鴻嘉
Honglou meng 紅樓夢
Hongloumeng ying 紅楼夢影
Hongxiuxie 紅繡鞋
Hou, Lady 侯夫人
Hou Hanshu 後漢書
Hou Zhi 侯芝

Houmochen Chao 侯莫陳邈
Hu Daying 胡大瀠
Hu Yinglin 胡應麟
Hua Wei 華瑋
huaigu 懷古
Huainanzi 淮南子
Hualianci 花簾詞
Huan, Duke of Qi 齊桓公
Huan, Emperor 桓帝
Huanchao luanfeng 換巢鸞鳳
Huang 皇
Huang Chonggu 黃崇嘏
Huang E 黃峨
Huang Ke 黃珂
Huang ying'er 黃鶯兒
Huang Yuanjie 黃媛介
Huangfu Mei 皇甫枚
Huangfu Shaohua 皇甫少華
Huangshi baojuan 黃氏寶卷
Huantiandang 黃天蕩
Huanxisha 浣溪沙
Huarui, Lady 花蕊
Huhanye 呼韓邪
Hui, Emperor 惠帝
Hui Baifang 蕙百芳
Huiban 惠班
Huichou 蕙綢
Huizhen ji 繪真記
Huizong, Emperor 徽宗

Ji (another name of Ban Zhao) 姬
Ji Zha 季札
Jia Baoyu 賈寶玉
Jia Sidao 賈似道
Jia Yi 賈誼
Jiang, lady 姜氏
Jiang Dehua 姜德華
Jiang Zhu 江珠
Jiangcheng meihua yin 江城梅花引

Jiangchengzi 江城子

Jiangdu, Prince of 江都王

Jiangershui 江兒水

Jiangnan chun 江南春

Jiangxi 江西

Jianjingsi 簡靜寺

Jianping, Marquis of 建平侯

Jianwen Emperor 建文

Jianzi mulanhua 減字木蘭花

Jiaojiaoling 僥僥令

Jiaoran 皎然

Jiaxing Xuzang jing 嘉興續藏經

Jiemin, Crown Prince 節愍太子

Jin Fu 靳輔

Jin shu 晉書

Jinfeng yulu xiangfeng qu 金風玉露相
逢曲

Jing Pianpian 景翩翩

Jingang 金剛

Jingde chuandenglu 景德傳燈錄

Jingdi, Emperor 景帝

Jinghua yuan 鏡花緣

Jingwei shi 精衛石

Jingzhi dashi 淨智大師

Jingzhong zhuan 精忠傳

Jingzong, Emperor 敬宗

Jinlüqu 金縷曲

Jinpingmei 金瓶梅

Jinshanghua 錦上花

Jinshi lu 金石錄

Jinyuyuan 金魚緣

Jiu Tang shu 舊唐書

Jiwen 紀聞

Jizong Xingche 季總醒徹

juan 卷

jueju 絕句

Juling 巨靈

Jushi zhuan 居士傳

Kaiyuansi 開元寺

Kang Aide (Cheng) 康愛德 (成)

Kang Tongwei 康同微

Kang Youwei 康有為

Ke Shaomin 柯劭忞

Kongshi daoren 空室道人

Kunmo 昆莫

Langhuan ji 嫏嬛集

Lanxue ji 蘭雪集

Laozi 老子

leng 冷 (cold)

Lengyan Sutra 楞嚴經

Li 禮

Li Bai 李白

Li Baozhen 李抱真

Li Changxia 李長霞

Li Guang 李廣

Li Guiyu 李桂玉

Li Hanzhang 李含章

Li Jilan 李季蘭

Li Lin 李璘

Li Longji 李隆基

Li Ping 李平

Li Qingzhao 李清照

Li Ruzhen 李汝珍

Li Shangyin 李商隐

Li Si 李斯

Li Xun 李訓

Li Ye 李冶

Li Yu (Last Ruler of Southern Tang)
李煜

Li Yu (seventeenth-century dramatist)
李漁

Li Zongmin 李宗閔

lian 蓮 (lotus)

lian 憐 (love)

Lianbo 連波

Liandeng huiyao 聯燈會要
Liang, Prince of 梁王
Liang Hong 梁鴻
Liang Hongyu 梁紅玉
Liang Mengzhao 梁孟昭
Liang Qichao 梁启超
Liang Shanbo 梁山伯
Liang Xiaoyu 梁小玉
Liangdu fu 兩都賦
Liang shu 梁書
Lianlizhi 連理枝
Liaoshi 遼史
Liaozhai zhiyi 聊齋志異
Lichui 鸝吹
Liechao shiji 列朝詩集
Lienü zhuan 列女傳
Liexian zhuan 列仙傳
Lihuameng 梨花夢
Liji 禮記
Lin Bu 林逋
Lin Daiyu 林黛玉
Lin Yaqing 林亞清
Lin Yining 林以寧
Lin Zhiyang 林之洋
Lingbao jing 靈寶經
Lingfei jing 靈飛經
Lisao 離騷
Lishu 吏書
Liu, Lady (wife of Xie An) 劉夫人
Liu, lady (wife of Yuan Shao) 劉夫人
Liu An 劉安
Liu Bang 劉邦
Liu Caichun 劉採春
Liu Changqing 劉長卿
Liu Ji 劉基
Liu Jian 劉建
Liu Jie 劉捷

Liu Jun 劉峻
Liu Kuibi 劉奎璧
Liu Lingxian 劉令嫻
Liu Liu 劉柳
Liu Pu 劉璞
Liu Qingyun 劉清韻
Liu (Ru) Shi 柳(如)是
Liu Shang 劉商
Liu Shuying 劉淑姝
Liu Tao 劉濤
Liu Tiemo 劉鐵磨
Liu Wen 劉文
(Liu) Xia (劉)瑕
Liu Xiang 劉向
Liu Xiaochuo 劉孝綽
Liu Xie 劉勰
Liu Xijun 劉細君
Liu Xiu 劉秀
Liu Yiqing 劉義慶
Liu Yong 柳永
Liu Yuxi 劉禹錫
Liu Zhen 劉臻
Liu Zongyuan 柳宗元
Liuhuameng 榴花夢
Lizong, Emperor 理宗
Loudong fu 樓東賦
Lu Hu 盧壺
Lu Ji 陸機
Lu You 陸游
Lunyu 論語
Luo Qilan 駱绮蘭
Luocha haishi 羅刹海市
Luoshen fu 洛神賦
Lü, Empress 呂后
Lü Bu 呂布
Lü Dongbin 呂洞賓
Lü Qu 呂姁
lüshi 律詩

Ma Rong 馬融
Ma Xianglan 馬湘蘭
Ma Xu 馬續
Manjiang hong 滿江紅
Mantingfang 滿庭芳
Manyuan hua 滿園花
Mao Kun 茅坤
Mao Ti 毛媞
Mao Xianshu 毛先舒
Mao Yanshou 毛延壽
Mao Yuanyi 茅元儀
Mei Chong 梅沖
Mei Zengliang 梅曾亮
Meifei zhuan 梅妃傳
Meifeng bi 眉峰碧
Meng Chang 孟昶
Meng Chengshun 孟稱舜
Meng Guang 孟光
Meng Jiangnan 夢江南
Meng Lijun 孟麗君
Meng Zhixiang 孟知祥
Mengying yuan 夢影緣
Mengzi jieyi 孟子解義
Mi Fei 米芾
Miaodao 妙道
Miaoshan 妙善
Miaoyin 妙音
Miaozong 妙總
Milou ji 迷樓記
Ming sanshijia shi xuan 明三十家詩選
Ming Taizu 明太祖
Mingdi, Emperor 明帝
Mingshi 明史
Mingshi biecai 明詩別裁
Mingshi daoren 明室道人
Mingshi zong 明詩綜
Mingxin lu 明心錄
Mingyuan shigui 名媛詩歸
Mingyuan shihua 名媛詩話

Mingyuan shiwei 名媛詩緯
Mituo 彌陀
Miyun Yuanwu 密雲圓悟
Moling ji 秣陵集
Moshan Liaoran 末山了然
Mudanting 牡丹亭
Muzong, Emperor 穆宗

Nangezi 南歌子
Nanshi 南史
Nanyue Chan denglu 南越禪燈錄
Neixun 內訓
Niannujiao 念奴嬌
Ningzong, Emperor 寧宗
Niu Su 牛肅
Niu Yingzhen 牛應貞
Niu Yingzhen zhuan 牛應貞傳
Nü caizi shu 女才子書
Nü jie 女誡
Nü kaike zhuan 女開科傳
Nü lunyu 女論語
nü shu 女書
Nü sishu 女四書
Nü xian 女憲
Nü xiaojing 女孝經
Nü xun 女訓
Nü ze 女則
Nüwa 女媧

Ouyang Xiu 毆陽修
Ouyang Xuan 歐陽玄

Pan Yue 潘岳
Pang Yun 龐蘊
Pei, Lady of 沛國夫人
Pei Songzhi 裴松之
Peng Shaosheng 彭紹升
Peng Xiluo 彭希洛
Pinhua baojian 品花寶鑑

Pu Songling 蒲松齡
Pusaman 菩薩蠻
Putianle 普天樂

Qi, Lady 戚姬
Qi Biaojia 祁彪佳
Qi Chongli 綦崇禮
Qi Xiangjun 祁湘君
Qi Xiuyan 祁修嫣
Qian Fenglun 錢鳳綸
Qian Meipo 錢梅坡
Qian Qianyi 錢謙益
Qian Tingmei 錢廷枚
Qian Yi 錢宜
Qian Zhaoxiu 錢肇修
Qiang (name of proto-Tibetan tribes) 羌
Qiang (Wang Zhaojun's personal name) 嬙
Qiaoying 喬影
Qin, Emperor 欽宗
Qin Guan 秦觀
Qin Jia 秦嘉
Qin Liangyu 秦良玉
qing 情 (feelings)
Qing Xilun 慶錫綸
Qingjiangyin 清江引
Qinglou ji 青樓集
Qingpingle 清平樂
Qingshi 情史
Qinshi huangdi 秦始皇帝
Qingshihui 清詩匯
Qingxi 清溪
Qinlou yigao 琴樓遺稿
Qiong Longdiao 瓊龍雕
Qionglou yingao 瓊樓吟稿
Qiu Jin 秋瑾
Qiu Xinru 邱心如
Qiugan 秋感

Qiuxing bashou 秋興八首
Qu Yuan (poet from Chu) 屈原
Qu Yuan (sage from Wei) 蘧瑗
Quan Song shi 全宋詩
Quan Tang shi 全唐詩
Quan Yuan sanqu 全元散曲
Quanshan shu 勸善書
Queqiaoxian 鵲橋仙
Quting yong 趨庭詠
quzi ci 曲子詞

Ran You 冉有
Ren 任
Ren Zhaolin 任兆麟
Renxiao, Empress 仁孝
Ruan Ji 阮籍
Ruan Xian 阮咸
Ruan Yuan 阮元
Ruanlanggui 阮郎歸
Ruci jiangshan 如此江山
Ruizong, Emperor 睿宗
Rulin waishi 儒林外史
Rumengling 如夢令
Ruolan 若蘭
Rusai 入塞
Ruyi 如意

sangjian Pushang 桑間濮上
Sanguo yanyi 三國演義
Sanhua yin 三花吟
sanqu 散曲
Sansheng zhuan yucanji 三生傳玉簪記
Sanshui xiaodu 三水小牘
Shang 商 (constellation)
Shang Jinglan 商景蘭
Shang xiaolou 上小樓
Shangguan Tingzhi 上官庭芝
Shangguan Wan'er 上官婉兒

Shangguan Yi 上官儀
Shanglin chun 上林春
Shangqing 上清
Shanhai qunguo zhi 山海羣國志
Shannü zhuan 善女傳
Shanyang, Duke of 山陽公
Shen Chong 沈琉
Shen Quanqi 沈佺期
Shen Shanbao 沈善寶
Shen Yi 沈 蘁
Shen Yixiu 沈宜修
Shen Yongji 沈用濟
Shen Yongzhen 沈永禎
Shen Yue 沈約
Shen Yunying 沈雲英
Shen Zhixu 沈至緒
Shengruhua 盛如花
Shengshengman 聲聲慢
Shennü fu 神女賦
shewen 設問
shi 詩
Shi Chong 石崇
Shi Zhenlin 史震林
Shi'eryue 十二月
Shigui shu 石匱書
Shihui 士會
Shiji 史記
Shijing 詩經
Shijun zhi 十郡志
Shiliuhua 石榴花
Shipin 詩品
Shishuo xinyu 世說新語
Shizu, Emperor 世祖
Shou Jiangnan 收江南
Shu jing 書經
Shu Qi 叔齊
Shuahai'er 耍孩兒
Shuang Jian 雙漸
Shuangqing 雙卿

Shuilongyin 水龍吟
Shulian danyue 疏簾淡月
Shun 舜
shuochang wenxue 說唱文學
Shuyi 書儀
Shuying 書影
Si (mother of King Wu of Zhou)
     姒
si 思 (longing)
si 絲 (thread)
Siku quanshu zongmu tiyao 四庫全書總
     目提要
Sima Guang 司馬光
Sima Qian 司馬遷
Sima Rangju 司馬穰苴
Sima Xiangru 司馬相如
Sixin 死心
song 頌
Song, lady 宋
Song bo fu 松柏賦
Songgu hexiangji 頌古合響集
Song Lian 宋濂
Song Ruohua 宋若華
Song Ruolun 宋若倫
Song Ruoxian 宋若憲
Song Ruoxin 宋若莘
Song Ruoxun 宋若荀
Song Ruozhao 宋若昭
Song Tingfen 宋廷芬
Song Yu 宋玉
Song Yuan 宋遠
Song Zhiwen 宋之問
Songshu 宋書
Su Daozhi 蘇道質
Su Hui 蘇蕙
Su Shi 蘇軾
Su Song 蘇頌
Su Wu 蘇武
Su Xiaoqing 蘇小卿

Su Xiaoxiao 蘇小小
Suiyuan shihua 隨園詩話
Suiyuan shihua buyi 隨園詩話補遺
Sun Deying 孫德英
Sun En 孫恩
Sun Guangxian 孙光憲
Sun Qi 孫棨
Suochuanghan 瑣窗寒
Suojizi 蓑鷄子
Suyong ji 肅雝集
Suzhongqing 訴中情
Suzong, Emperor 肅宗

Taibo 太伯
Taiping, Princess 太平
Taiping guangji 太平廣記
Taiping tianguo 太平天國
Taiping yulan 太平御覽
Taishang dongshen Tiangong xiaomo huguo jing 太上洞神天公消魔護國經
Taiyuan 太元
Taizong, Emperor 太宗
Tan Ze 談則
Tan Zhengbi 譚正璧
Tan Xun 譚尋
tanci 彈詞
tanci changben 彈詞唱本
Tang caizi zhuan 唐才子傳
Tang Guichen 唐閨臣
Tang jian 唐鑒
Tang Xianzu 湯顯祖
Tanpo Huanxisha 攤破浣溪沙
Tao Qian 陶潛
Tao Shan 陶善
Tao Zhenhuai 陶貞懷
Taoye 桃葉
Tasuoxing 踏莎行
Teng Chuanyin 滕傳胤

Tian Qilang 田七郎
Tianfeng yin 天風引
Tianwen 天問
Tianxia mingjia shiguan 天下名家詩觀
Tianxianzi 天仙子
Tianyuhua 天雨花
Tingqiuxuan gao 聽秋軒稿
Tingxun 庭訓
Tongqiu shixuan 同秋詩選
Tu Long 屠隆

Wang, Empress 王皇后
Wang Anguo 王安國
Wang Anshi 王安石
Wang Ao 王鏊
Wang Bogu 王伯穀
Wang Ding 王鼎
Wang Duan 汪端
Wang Duanshu 王端淑
Wang Fajin 王法進
Wang Fazhi 王法智
Wang Fuchen 王黻臣
Wang Gang 汪綱
Wang haichao 望海潮
Wang Ji (father of King Wen) 王季
Wang Ji (magistrate of Linqiong) 王吉
Wang Jian 王建
Wang Mang 王莽
Wang Ningzhi 王凝之
Wang Shuying 王叔英
Wang Siren 王思任
Wang Tingjun 王廷鈞
Wang Wei (late Ming courtesan) 王微
Wang Wei (Tang dynasty poet) 王維
Wang Wenzhi 王文治

Wang Xianzhi 王顯芝

Wang Xizhi 王羲之

Wang Yangming 王陽明

Wang Youding 王猷定

Wang Yun 王筠

Wang Zhao 王詔

Wang Zhaojun 王昭君

Wang Zhaoyuan 王照圓

Wang Zhiheng 王穉登

Wang Zhuo 王灼

Wang Ziqiao 王子喬

Wangliang wen ying fu 魍魎問影賦

Wanyan Yun Zhu 完顏惲珠

Wei, Concubine 衛

Wei, Empress (Han dynasty) 衛皇后

Wei, Empress (Tang dynasty) 韋后

Wei, Lady 衛夫人

Wei Cheng 韋逞

Wei Duanli 魏端禮

Wei Hong 衛宏

Wei Huacun 魏華存

Wei Jie 衛玠

Wei Qing 衛青

Wei Shu 魏舒

Wei Wan 魏玩

Wei Wen 韋溫

Wei Zhonggong 魏仲恭

Wei Zhuang 韋莊

Wei Zifu 衛子夫

Weifang 偉方

Wen, Emperor 文帝

Wen, King 文王

Wen Tingyun 溫庭筠

Wen Wan 溫琬

Wenhui 文惠

Wenxin diaolong 文心雕龍

Wenxuan 文宣

Wenxuan 文選

Wenyi 文漪

Wenzong, Emperor 文宗

Woyuexuan gao 臥月軒稿

Wu, Emperor 武帝

Wu, Empress 武后

Wu, King 武王

Wu Gang 吳剛

Wu Jingzi 吳敬梓

Wu Ren 吳人

Wu Sansi 武三思

Wu Weiye 吳偉業

Wu Zao 吳藻

Wu Zetian 武則天

Wu Zhao 武曌

Wu Zhiying 吳芝瑛

Wubeizhi 武備志

Wudi, Emperor 武帝

Wuliang shou jing lun 無量受經論

Wulingchun 武陵春

Wumengtang ji 午夢堂集

Wushan 巫山

wusheng laomu 無生老母

Wusun 烏孫

Wuxin 無心

wuyue 五嶽

Xi huanghua manci 惜黃花慢詞

Xi Kang 嵇康

Xi Peilan 席佩蘭

xiang 香

Xiang Sheng 項昇

Xiang Yu 項羽

Xiangnan Xuebei ci 香南雪北詞

Xiangshan baojuan 香山寶卷

Xiangsi yan chuanqi 相思硯傳奇

Xianzong, Emperor 憲宗

Xiao, Concubine 蕭

Xiao Guanyin 蕭觀音

Xiao He 蕭何

Xiaojing 孝經

xiaopin 小品

Xiaoqing 小青

xiaosheng 小生

Xiaowu, Emperor 孝武

Xiaozhao 小召

Xie An 謝安

Xie Daoyun 謝道韞

Xie He 謝遏

Xie Lingyun 謝靈運

Xie Wuyi 謝無奕

Xie Yuhui 謝玉輝

Xifenchai 惜分釵

Xijing zaji 西京雜記

Xiling guiyong ji 西泠閨詠集

Xin Tang shu 新唐書

Xin Wenfang 辛文房

Xin Yuanshi 新元史

Xingxiangzi 行香子

Xiongnu 匈奴

Xiqianying 喜遷鶯

Xiqing sanji 西青散記

Xiqunyao 繫裙腰

Xiuyi 修儀

Xu 徐

Xu, Empress 許皇后

Xu Can 徐燦

Xu Fei 徐悱

Xu Jinpingmei 續金瓶梅

Xu Mian 徐勉

Xu Shichang 徐世昌

Xu Shu 徐淑

Xu Tingfu 許廷輔

Xu Wei 徐渭

Xu Xilin 徐錫麟

Xu Zihua 徐自華

Xuan Huazi 玄華子

Xuanwen jun 宣文君

Xuanzong, Emperor 玄宗

Xue Baozhai 薛寶釵

Xue Meng 薛蒙

Xue Tao 薛濤

ya 雅

Yan, Lady 顏氏

Yan Hui 顏回

Yan Jin 嚴謹

Yan Juchuan 嚴巨川

Yan Kejun 嚴可均

Yan Shu 晏殊

Yan Ying 晏嬰

Yan Yu 嚴羽

Yang, Emperor 煬帝

Yang, Empress 楊太后

Yang Guifei 楊貴妃

Yang Guozhong 楊國忠

Yang Ji 楊基

Yang Qidan 楊契丹

Yang Shen 楊慎

Yang Wan 楊宛

Yang Weizhen 楊維楨

Yang Xi 楊羲

Yang Xiong 揚雄

Yang Yuhuan 楊玉環

Yantou Quanhuo 巖頭全奯

Yao 堯

Yao Nai 姚鼐

Yaomin ge 堯民歌

Ye Shaokui 葉紹奎

Ye Shaoyuan 葉紹袁

Ye Wanwan 葉紈紈

Ye Xiaoluan 葉小鸞

Ye Xiaowan 葉小紈

Ye Xie 葉燮

Ye Ziqi 葉子奇

Yesou puyan 野叟曝言

Yi Jiangnan 憶江南

Yi Nianhua 義年華

Yi Qin'e 憶秦娥

Yi wangsun 憶王孫
Yide, Empress 懿德
Yigong Chaoke 一恭超珂
Yijianmei 一剪梅
Yijing 易經
Yikui Chaochen 一揆超琛
Yin, lady 陰
Yin Hao 殷浩
Yin Xi 尹喜
Yinanwang 憶難忘
Ying 英
Ying xianke 迎仙客
Ying Zheng 贏政
Yingying zhuan 鶯鶯傳
Yinhong ji 吟紅集
Yong, Prince of 永王
Yongcheng jixianlu 墉城集仙錄
Yongyule 永遇樂
You, King 幽王
youxianshi 遊仙詩
Youxuan ji 又玄集
Yu Ji 虞集
Yu meiren 虞美人
Yu Qian 于謙
Yu Qiu 虞丘
Yu Tongzhi 虞通之
Yu Xuanji 魚玄機
Yuan Mei 袁枚
Yuan Ming yishi 元明佚史
Yuan Shao 袁紹
Yuan Xi 袁熙
Yuan Zhen 元稹
Yuandi, Emperor 元帝
Yuanfang 元方
Yuanlin hao 園林好
Yuanwangsun 怨王孫
Yuanwu Keqin 園悟克勤
Yuanyang meng 鴛鴦夢
Yuchuanyuan 玉釧緣

Yue Fei 岳飛
yuefu 樂府
Yuefu shiji 樂府詩集
Yueguan shi 樾館詩
Yuezhang ji 樂章集
Yufu 漁父
Yujia'ao 漁家傲
Yujingqiu 玉京秋
Yulianhuan 玉連環
Yulin, Prince of 鬱林王
Yulouchun 玉樓春
yulu 語錄
Yuquanzi 玉泉子
Yutai xinyong 玉臺新詠
Yuzhen, Princess 玉真公主
Yuzhonghua 雨中花

zabian 雜編
Zaishengyuan 再生緣
Zaizaotian 再造天
zaju 雜劇
Zeng Bu 曾布
Zeng Gong 曾鞏
Zeng Guofan 曾國藩
Zeng Yu 曾燠
Zengzi 曾子
Zhang Chaixin 張苈馨
Zhang Chayun 張槎雲
Zhang Chuxiang 張楚纕
Zhang Dai 張岱
Zhang Hao 張昊
Zhang Lei 張耒
Zhang Liang 張良
Zhang Lingyi 張令儀
Zhang Qiongru 張瓊如
Zhang Sheng 張嵊
Zhang Shicheng 張士誠
Zhang Xianzhong 張獻忠
Zhang Xuan 張玄

Zhang Xuecheng 章學誠
Zhang Yin 張印
Zhang Yue 張說
Zhang Yuniang 張玉孃
Zhang Yunzi 張允滋
Zhao, Prince of 趙王
Zhao Feiyan 趙飛燕
Zhao Kuo 趙括
Zhao Mengfu 趙孟頫
Zhao Mingcheng 趙明誠
Zhao Qicheng 昭綦成
Zhao She 趙奢
Zhao Tingzhi 趙挺之
Zhao Yangtai 趙陽臺
Zhao Yuanyi 趙元一
Zhaoming, Crown Prince 昭明
Zhaorong 昭容
Zheguiling 折桂令
Zhegutian 鷓鴣天
zhen 鍼 (needle)
Zhen, Empress 甄皇后
Zhen Han 甄邯
Zhen Yi 甄逸
Zheng, lady 鄭氏
Zheng Danruo 鄭澹若
Zheng Ruzhao 鄭如昭
Zheng Yunduan 鄭允端
Zheng Zhu 鄭注
Zhisheng 智勝
Zhitong Weijiu 智通惟久
Zhiyi 智顗
Zhiyuan Xinggan 祇院行剛
Zhong Rong 鍾嶸
Zhong Jun 終軍
Zhong Xing 鍾惺
Zhongzong, Emperor 中宗
Zhongguo nübao 中國女報
Zhongqing zhuan 鍾情傳
Zhongxing fu 中興賦

Zhongxing jianqi ji 中興間氣集
Zhongxun 仲遜
Zhou Chang 周昌
Zhou Lianggong 周亮工
Zhou Shuoyi 周碩沂
Zhou Yingfang 周穎芳
Zhouguan 周官
Zhouli 周禮
Zhu Ci 朱泚
Zhu Rouze 朱柔則
Zhu Xiyan 朱睎顏
Zhu Xi 朱熹
Zhu Shuzhen 朱淑真
Zhu Yingtai 祝英台
Zhu Yuanzhang 朱元璋
Zhu Zhaobi 朱照璧
Zhu Zundu 朱遵度
Zhuang, King of Chu 楚莊王
Zhuang, Marquis of Wei 衛莊侯
Zhuang Zhou 莊周
zhuangyuan 狀元
Zhuangzi 莊子
zhugongdiao 諸宮調
Zhuo Wangsun 卓王孫
Zhuo Wenjun 卓文君
Zhuozhengyuan 拙政園
Zhuozhengyuan shiyu chukan 拙政園
    詩餘初刊
Zhuying yaohong 燭影搖紅
Zi Lu 子路
Ziye 子夜
Ziyege 子夜歌
Zui chunfeng 醉春風
Zuihuayin 醉花蔭
Zuo Fen 左芬
Zuo Si 左思
Zuo zhuan 左傳
Zutang ji 祖堂集

Index

abandoned children, 116, 117, 118, 125, 126

abandoned women, 130, 197, 554; and absent husbands, 473–74, 486, 489–90; Huang E as, 287–90; lament of, 110–13; as lyric theme, 220–21, 225

"Aboard a Ship on the Yellow Sea . . ." (Qiu), 794

"About the Weaving Maid One Day after Double Seven" (Yang), 373–74

Addenda to the Sui Garden Poetry Talks (Yuan), 607

Address to My Two Hundred Million Women Compatriots in China, An (Qiu), 780–82

"Admiring the Blossoms at Heavenly Peace Monastery . . ." (Gu), 637

"Admonishing My Younger Brothers" (Xi), 594–95

"Admonition on Love, An" (Xi), 610–11

"After Completing My Toilette" (Hou), 98–99

"After Returning at Night I Remember the Girl on the Neighboring Boat" (Wang), 369

Amitabha Buddha, 314, 582, 584, 585

An Lushan rebellion, 67, 101, 106, 436, 669

Analects (Confucius), 13, 26, 35, 55, 57, 201; on Master Zeng, 60, 152n

Analects for Women (Song), 55, 57, 58, 310

Ancient Fragrance Tower Collection (Qian), 478

"Ancient Mirror, The" (Xi), 608

Anecdotal History of the Yuan and Ming (Duan), 627

Anecdotes from Gantang, 334

Anle, Princess, 65, 66–67, 72
Annals of Spring and Autumn, 169
anthologies of women's writing,
349, 350, 576. *See also specific
anthology*
"Apricot Flowers by Xu Xi"
(Zheng), 272
arias *(qu),* 336, 396, 412–13, 683; of
Huang E, 287, 290–91; "Sent to
My Loved One," 337–43
aristocratic society, 15, 132, 137–38,
200; and Daoism, 142–43, 161.
See also elite families
"As in a Dream" (melody), 218–19,
228, 268, 639, 700
"Ascending the Small Tower"
(tune), 340–41
"Ascending to the Heavenly
Wandering Pavilion…" (Gu),
637
"A Night on a Boat" (Haiyin), 158
authorship, 3, 77, 238, 501, 718
autobiography, 4, 238, 553–57; of
Yikui Chaochen, 457–59; of
Jizong Xingche, 464–67
"Autumn Crab Apple" (Gu), 639–40
"Autumn Emotions, Eight Poems"
(Du), 436
"Autumn Feelings" (Xu), 436
"Autumn Feelings" (Yang), 373
"Autumn Lament" (Wang), 451
"Autumn Night is Long, The"
(Zhang), 267
"Autumn Nights" (Zhu), 250
autumn poems, 226–28, 250–51
"Autumn Window, Describing My
Emotions" (Zheng), 275
Avalokiteshvara, 311. *See also*
Guanyin, Bodhisattva of Com-
passion

"Azure-Tipped Arrows" (melody),
481

"Bad Dream, A" (Gu), 644
Bai Juyi, 405n, 426n, 614n
"Ballad of a Soldier's Life"
(Zhang), 663–65
"Ballad of General Shen, The"
(Zhang), 654–56
"Ballad of Golden Threads" (mel-
ody), 646–47, 697
"Ballad of Resentment" (Wang),
446
"Ballad on the Way in Which the
People of Wu Marry Off Their
Daughters" (Zheng), 276–77
ballads, 8; autobiographical, 553–
57; in women's script, 544. *See
also* plucking rhymes
"Bamboo Separated from the Pa-
vilion, The" (Xue), 187
Ban, Imperial Concubine, 18, 22,
49, 75, 77–82, 181, 259; as abandoned woman, 197; and *Books of
the Han,* 77, 78–80; and Emperor Cheng, 19, 77, 78–79, 82;
Liu Xiaochuo's poem on, 148–
49; *shi* poetry of, 77–78
Ban Biao, 19, 20, 22
Ban Chao, 22, 27, 28–29, 681n
Ban family, 18–20, 22, 26, 77
Ban Gu, 21, 77, 84–85
Ban Zhao (Madam Cao), 17, 18–43,
52, 57–58, 60, 202, 586; and Ban
family, 77; and *Books of the Han,*
18–19, 21, 26–27, 34; and Empress Deng, 19, 31–33, 34–35;
memorial to the throne by, 28–
30, 35–36; as model, 570; "Nee-

dle and Thread," 30–31; poem in praise of, 657–58; *Rhapsody on a Journey to the East*, 22, 23–26; *Rhapsody on the Ostriches*, 27–28; Ye Xiaoluan compared to, 394, 400; Zhang Yuniang compared to, 262, 263. *See also Precepts for My Daughters*; Cao Dagu

Banana Garden Poetry Club, 383, 414, 471–95; Chai Jingyi, 475–77; Feng Xian, 477–78; Gu Si, 487–88; Gu Zhiqiong, 473–74; Lin Yining, 486–87; Mao Ti, 493–95; Qian Fenglun, 478–86; Zhang Chayun, 429, 430–31; Zhang Hao, 492–93; Zhu Rouze, 489–92

Bao Hongtai, 414–15

Bao Linghui, 49, 50

Bao Zhao, 49, 180, 773

Baochang, 153–56, 158, 319–20

Baochi Jizong, 326

Baopuzi (Ge). See *Master Who Embraces Simplicity, The*

Baosi, Imperial Concubine, 80, 82n

barbarians, 566, 722, 783n; customs of, 119, 680, 803; marriages to, 9, 91, 94, 120–21, 247–48

Basic Facts on All the Titles in the Complete Books of the Four Treasuries, 130

"Beautiful Weather" (melody), 637–38

"Because of the Long Rains I Was Concerned about the Peasants . . ." (Zhang), 666

behavior, rules of, 11. *See also* moral behavior

Beichuang yingao (Cheng). See *Songs of Lament by the Northern Window*

Beilizhi (Sun). See *Records of the Northern Ward*

Beimeng suoyan (Sun). See *Trifling Words from the Northern Marshlands*

Big Goose Pagoda, 68

biographical accounts, 3–4. *See also* autobiography

Biographical Sketches of Women of Chastity from Ancient Times to the Present, 304

Biographies of Bhiksunis (Baochang), 153–56, 158, 319–20, 900

Biographies of Exemplary Women (Liu), 12, 42, 136n, 201, 265, 273, 627

Biographies of Pious Women (Peng), 581

Biography of Concubine Plum, 101, 107

"Biography of My Youngest Daughter Qiongzhang, A" (Shen), 400–406

Biography of Niu Yingzhen, 168, 169

"Biography of the Loyal and Virtuous Huang Duanbo," 441–42

Biography of the Mahasattva Guanyin (Guan), 312–14

Biqiuni zhuan (Baochang). See *Biographies of Bhiksunis*

Birrell, Anne, 149

Bishenghua (Qiu). See *Flowers from a Brush*

Biyan lu. See *Blue Cliff Record*

black magic, 74, 77

Blue Cliff Record, 326, 332n

Bo Yi, 35

"Bodhisattva Barbarian" (melody), 219–20, 222, 255, 450

Bodhisattvas, 321, 329, 588. *See also* Guanyin, Bodhisattva of Compassion

book burning, 52, 209n, 214n

book collections, 209–11, 212, 214

Book of Changes, 41, 210

Book of Documents, 52–53

Book of Odes, 28, 29, 42, 152, 271, 288, 541; commentaries on, 627; on evergreens, 47, 48; "Grass-Insects," 259; "The Green Coat," 75–76, 82n; jealousy in, 140; on neglected women, 75–76; "The Ospreys," 37, 40; on sexual assault, 273; women writers of, 613

Book of Rites. See Rites

Books of the Han, 18–19, 21, 26–27, 34, 84, 91

Books of the Jin, 43, 46, 53, 127–28, 627; "Exemplary Women" in, 139, 143–44

Books of the Later Han (Fan), 13, 92, 113, 119, 308; Ban Zhao's biography in, 28–30, 31, 33, 34

Books of the Liang, 151

Books of the Song, 110, 111, 627

Boxer movement, 773

Broken Heart, A (Zhu), 244–53; *shi* poems in, 248–53, 256; Wei Duanli's preface to, 245–48, 257

brothers- and sisters-in-law, 40–41

Buddha, 590; Amitabha, 314, 582, 584, 585; as Ancient Master, 176

Buddhahood, 313, 317, 592, 605. *See also* enlightenment

Buddhism, 376, 406, 431, 432, 441, 580; and dualism, 321, 331, 694; lotus symbol in, 167, 532n; Mahayana, 304, 314, 319, 331; Pure Land, 314, 578, 581–85, 586, 588. *See also* Chan (Zen) Buddhism

Buddhism, poets inspired by, 588. *See also* Jiang Zhu; Tao Shan

Buddhist chants *(dharanis),* 318, 319, 586

Buddhist monasteries, 68, 160, 198–99

Buddhist nuns, 5, 15, 153–59, 201, 312, 319–33; Baochang's biographies of, 153–56, 158, 319–20; Chitong Weijiu, 329–32; enlightenment of, 158–59, 320–21, 324; Guiyuan, 718; Kongshi Daoren, 329–31; Mingshi Daoren, 327–28; poetry of, 321, 328, 329, 333; sutras by, 156–58.

Buddhist sutras, 156–58, 293, 321, 718; *Diamond Sutra,* 283, 564; of Empress Xu, 304, 310–11, 314–19; *Heart Sutra,* 505; *Lankavatara Sutra,* 397; *Surangama Sutra,* 538; Tao Shan's study of, 582, 584, 586

Buddhist verses *(gatha),* 399–400

bureaucracy/officials, 11, 18, 53, 204, 786, 787–88. *See also* examinations

Burnt Pepper (Wang), 301

"Butterfly Loves Flowers, The" (melody), 230–31, 254

"Buying Fine Wine" (tune), 692

Cai Jing, 204

Cai Tao, 296

Cai Yan, 3, 108, 112, 113–19, 138,
    185n, 445; on abandonment of
    children, 116, 117, 118, 125, 126;
    accounts of warfare by, 114–15,
    118; "Eighteen Stanzas for the
    Barbarian Reed Pipe," 121–27;
    marriage of, 122, 510; ransom by
    Cao Cao, 113–14; Ye Xiaoluan
    compared to, 394, 400
Cai Yong, 112, 113, 138, 185n
Cai Zichun, 334, 335
Caizi Mudanting. See *Talented
    Scholar's Peony Pavilion, The*
calligraphy, 138, 184–85, 283–84,
    371
"Calls of the Flower-Seller"
    (Zheng), 270
"Candle Shadows Swaying Red"
    (melody), 484, 590
Cankui yin (Tao). See *Chants of
    Shame and Remorse*
Cantong Chan Cloister, 458–59,
    461
Cao Cao, 85, 87, 88, 89–90; poetry
    of, 86; ransom of Cai Yan by,
    113–14
Cao Dagu (Venerable Madam
    Cao), 22, 32, 55, 308. *See also* Ban
    Zhao
Cao E, 343, 493, 720
Cao Fengsheng, 42
Cao Pi, 86, 87–88, 89, 90; as Em-
    peror Wen, 85, 87, 95, 135
Cao Xueqin, 571; *Dream of the Red
    Chamber,* 499, 567–69, 642, 647,
    648
Cao Ye, 101
Cao Zhi, 350, 351n, 406–7, 656;
    poetry of, 86, 90

Caomuzi (Ye). See *Master Grass and
    Tree*
"Cave of the Immortals" (melody),
    693
"Celebrating the Fresh Coolness"
    (melody), 641–42
censorship, 164–65, 354–55, 567,
    571, 721
Chai Jingyi, 471, 472, 475–77, 486,
    489
Chan (Zen) Buddhism, 332, 397n,
    576, 578, 592; and courtesan po-
    ets, 368; *gong'an (koan)* collec-
    tions, 323, 325–26, 327; Pure
    Land Buddhism compared to,
    581–82; Qian Qianyi on, 456–57
Chan (Zen) Buddhist nuns, 7, 320–
    31, 356, 455–70; enlightenment
    of, 320–21, 324, 327, 466–67;
    Jizong Xingche, 464–70; Miao-
    dao, 323–25; Miaozong, 325–27,
    456; Yikui Chaochen, 457–64
Changhen ge (Bai). See *Song of Lasting
    Regret*
Changmenfu (Sima). See *Rhapsody of
    the Long Gate [Palace]*
Changning, Princess, 65, 69, 72
Chantings of Red Collection (Wang),
    439
*Chants of Rushing through the Court-
    yard* (Zhang), 493
Chants of Shame and Remorse (Tao),
    582–83, 586
Chao Cuo, 52, 53
character, judgment of, 58–59
Charter for Women, 33, 39, 307,
    308–9
chastity, 130, 265, 273, 364; model
    of, 257; and neo-Confucianism,

113; symbols of, 96–97, 278; of widows, 201. *See also* purity
"Checking on the Plum" (Wang), 370
Chen, Empress, 76, 79n
Chen, Lady, 144–46
Chen Bo (Chen Yunqiao), 344–45
Chen Duanlin *(The Jade Bracelet),* 735
Chen Duansheng: family life of, 748–49; *Karmic Bonds of Reincarnation,* 734, 737–52
Chen Huiying, 759–61
Chen Jiru, 357, 369
Chen Peizhi, 620, 622, 628
Chen Sen, 759
Chen Shou, 86
Chen Tong, 501
Chen Wenshu, 571, 620–21, 622, 694
Chen Yuanlong, 431–33
Chen Yunqiao, 344–45
Chen Zilim (Su'an), 431, 432, 433
Cheng Qiong, 504
Cheng Yi, 803, 804, 805
Cheng, Emperor, 19, 77, 78–79, 82
"Cherishing the Chrysanthemums, Long Version of" (melody), 528–29
children, abandoned, 116, 117, 118, 125, 126. *See also* abandoned children; daughters; sons
China Women's Journal, 796, 798–99, 800, 807
Chitong Weijiu (nun), 329–32
Chongjun, Jiemin crown prince, 66–67, 71
Chongzhen emperor, 724, 775
Chouyan (Ye). See *Words of Sorrow*

"Chrysanthemum Party" (song), 344
chrysanthemums, as symbol, 227, 231
Chu Sanzang jiji (Sengyou). See *Collected Notes on Texts from the Tripitaka*
Chuci (Qu). See *Songs of the South*
Chunqiu. See *Annals of Spring and Autumn*
ci lyrics. *See* lyrics *(ci)*
Cilun (Li). See *On Lyrics*
Cixi, Empress Dowager, 17, 769–70, 773
Classic of Filiality for Women (Zheng), 13, 58–60, 201, 258, 310
Classic of Numinous Treasure (Lu), 352
Classic of Soaring and Flying Spirits (Yuzhen), 161
Classic of the Grotto-God . . . (anonymous), 163
Classic Poetry of Famous Women (Wang, ed.), 439, 454
Classics, 11, 31, 32, 52, 202; and neo-Confucianism, 200. *See also Book of Changes; Book of Odes; Rites*
"Clear and Level" (melody), 253, 254
Clear Brook Poetry Club, 589
"Clear River Intro" (tune), 683, 692
"Climbing the Highest Peak of Maoshan" (Luo), 615–16
clouds and rain, symbolism of, 179, 180
"Coda" (tune), 343
"Cold Carved Window, The" (tune), 708
Cold Food Festival, 229, 230, 771

Collected Notes on Texts from the Tripi-
taka (Sengyou), 156–58

Collected Poems of the Successive Reigns
(Qian and Liu), 287, 355, 359,
376, 622, 625; on Liang Xiaoyu,
359–64; on Jing Pianpian, 364–
66; on Ma Xiaolan, 366–67; on
Wang Wei, 368–69; on Yang
Wei, 370–71; on Xiaoqing, 513–
14; on Yu Sulan, 514

Collection from the Halls of the Foun-
ders, 323

Collection of Music Bureau Poems, 121

Collection of Texts for Music, A (Liu),
236

"Comforting My Husband on Our
Boat Tied Down for the Night on
the Huai" (Gu), 488

Commentary of Mr. Zuo, 168, 169

Comments on Poems by Famous Ladies
(Shen, ed.), 626

Compendium of Ming Poetry (Zhu),
622, 625

Compendium of Qing Poetry (Xu), 656

Complete Arias of the Yuan Dynasty,
337

Complete Poems of the Song Dynasty,
334

Complete Poems of the Tang Dynasty,
158, 295

"Composing Poems to the Same
Rhyme in Yu Garden . . ."
(Huang), 453

Comprehensive Records of the Reign Pe-
riod Great Peace, 161

"Concubine Ban's Resentment"
(Liu), 149

concubine poets, 286, 295, 515–20;
anonymous, 518–20; He Guizhi,

515–18. *See also* imperial concubines; Gu Chun (Taiqing);
Shuangqing; Xiaoqing

Confucian scholars, 623, 624,
674n, 781

Confucianism, 1, 146, 269, 327,
357, 578; canon of, 200; and loyalty, 261, 264. *See also* neo-
Confucianism

Confucius, 23, 31, 41, 43, 209n, 536;
Analects of, 26, 35, 55, 57, 60,
428n; and education, 11; on
sense of shame, 582; and Zeng,
60, 614

"Congratulating My Husband . . ."
(Xi), 609

"The Conquest of the South"
(tune), 691

"Consulting the Oracle" (tune),
707

Correct Beginnings: Women's Poetry of
Our August Dynasty (Wanyan,
ed.), 570, 626

coup d'états, 61, 65, 67, 72

courtesan poets, 6, 174–76, 198,
333, 359–82; *ci* lyrics of, 199, 220;
Daoist nuns as, 164, 175–76; and
elite women writers compared,
355; in Jiangnan area, 7; Jing
Pianpian, 364–66; Liang Xiaoyu,
359–62; literary exams for, 574;
Liu Shi, 374–82; Li Ye, 16, 164,
175, 176–82, 178, 180; Ma
Xiaolan, 366–68; in Ming society, 383; Su Xiaoqing, 337–43,
345, 366; Wang Wei, 69, 70,
226n, 368–70; Wen Wan, 334–
36; Yang Wan, 370–74. *See also*
Xue Tao; Yu Xuanji

"Courtyard Filled with Fragrance, A" (melody), 638–39

Cowherd and the Weaving Maiden, 254–55, 608n. *See also* Double Seven festival

cremation, 246, 247

cross-dressing heroines, 570, 677–94, 776; of He Peizhu, 677, 683–85; Huan Chonggu, 677–78, 680; Jiang Dehua/Jiang Junbi, 754–56; Meng Lijun, 737, 738–43, 746–48, 749, 752; Mulan, 656, 679, 720, 779; in plucking rhymes, 7, 577, 719, 735–36; Qian Shurong, 756–57; of Wang Yun, 677, 680–83; in Wu's *The Fake Image,* 685–94; in Zhu's *Linked Rings of Jade,* 731, 732, 734; Zhu Yingtai, 562–64, 565. *See also* Lou Cheng; Qiu Jin

"Crossing the Confluence of the Yi and the Luo" (Lin), 486–87

"Crossing the Yangzi" (Xi), 598

Crouching Lion Chan Cloister, 457, 458, 459, 461

"Cursing the Lover" (tune), 290

Da Ming Renxiao huanghou menggan Foshuo diyi xiyou dagongde jing. See *Rarest Sutra of Great Merit Spoken by the Buddha . . .*

Dahui Zonggao, 323, 324, 326, 327, 329

Dai Fu, 166, 167

Dang, General, 507

Danqingfu (Liu). See *Kept Promises*

Daoism, 142–43, 168, 282, 327, 578, 582; Highest Clarity, 143, 159; holy places of, 615–16; immor-tals in, 141–42, 143, 159–60, 162, 455; Orthodox Unity, 142, 143, 160, 161

Daoist mystics, 159–63

Daoist nuns, 5–6, 158, 164, 184, 197–98; Yu Xuanji, 175–76, 189–90, 191

Daque fu (Ban). See *Rhapsody on the Ostriches*

daughters, 760; and fathers in *A Rain of Heavenly Flowers,* 720, 725–29; poems addressed to, 550–52, 658–62. *See also Precepts for My Daughters*

"Dawn Dream" (Li), 242

"Delighting in the Rain" (Zhu), 252–53

Deng Hanyi, 492, 520

Deng Shengzhao, 439

Deng Sui, Empress, 19, 31–33, 34–35

Deng Zhi, 33, 34

"Describing My Emotions" (Wen), 336

"Describing My Feelings on an Autumn Day" (Zhu), 250–51

"Describing My Puppy, Double-Topknot" (Gu), 646

Description of the Ten Commanderies (Yu), 351

"Despair" (He), 515–17

Dezong, Emperor, 55–56, 181–82

Dharma, 154, 157, 460–61, 586, 587

Ding, Commander, 344

Ding, Prince of Changsa, 772

Ding Yaokang, 574

"Dirge for Myself, A" (Zheng), 279–80

discourse records (*yulu*), 356

"Diversion" (Hou), 97, 99

Divine Land Women's Magazine, 802

"Dog Barked Out Front, The . . ." (Yi), 547

"Dog Separated from Its Master, The" (Xue), 186

"Doll, The" (tune), 342

Dong Si, 113, 114

Dong Zhuo, 112–13, 114

Dongzheng fu (Ban). See *Rhapsody on a Journey to the East*

"Dotting Red Lips" (melody), 223–24, 225, 239, 255

Dou Tao, 128–29, 130

Double Nine festival, 68, 229, 231, 449

Double Seven festival, 254n. *See also* Cowherd and the Weaving Maiden

Double Three festival, 229, 230–31

Draft Chants of the Lovely Tower (Tao), 587

Drafts from the Reclining in the Moonlight Studio (Gu), 414, 415, 417

"Dragon Well" (Zhang), 423–24

drama, 7, 130, 677–716; cross-dressing heroines in, 677–85; of He Peizhu, 677, 683–85; immortals in, 684, 716; lamp-and-props shows, 715–16; of Liu Qingyun, 701–16; *Mandarin Ducks' Dream* (Ye), 411–14; monologues in, 119, 686, 688, 704; *Peony Pavilion* (Tang), 349, 591, 686; suite of arias in, 337–43; of Wang Yun, 677, 680–83; of Wu Zao, 621, 677, 685–701; *zaju,* 364, 390, 411, 687. *See also* playwrights

Dream Affinities (Zheng), 734–35, 761

Dream of Splendor (Wang), 680–83, 693

Dream of the Red Chamber (Cao), 500, 567–69, 576, 627, 647, 648

"Dreaming of Junyong" (Shen), 385

"Dreaming of My Deceased Daughter, Qiongzhang" (Shen), 386

"Dreaming of South of the River" (melody), 218

dreams: conversations in, 168–73; poems of, 385–86; records of, 275–76, 616–17, 643–44, 667–68

"Drinking in Come-Again Pavilion" (Jiang), 593

"Drunken Spring Breezes" (tune), 338–39, 413

Du Fu, 71, 175, 214n11, 354, 436, 467; as model for Li Changxia, 669, 675; in Xi Peilan's poems, 601, 602, 609

Du Gao, 173–74

Du Guanting, 163

Du Lanxian *(Pear Blossom Dream),* 684–85

Du Liniang *(Peony Pavilion),* 500–504, 510

Du Yu, 134

dualism, Buddhism and, 321, 331, 694

Duan Yuhan (Lover of Flowers), 521, 522–23, 524, 536, 537

Duanchang ji. See *Broken Heart, A*

Duji (Yu). See *On Jealousy*

"During a Visit to the Southern Tower . . ." (Yu), 195

"During the Time When I Was Ill, I Put My Scattered Drafts in Order . . ." (Ye), 409–10

dutiful daughters, 756

dynastic histories, 13, 21. *See also specific dynasty*

"Each Step Lovely" (tune), 688

"Early Autumn" (Yu), 194

"Early Spring" (Tao), 583–84

"Early Summer: Visiting the River Isle..." (Qian), 483

economic growth, 203, 348

education of women, 12, 201–3, 564, 726; Gu Ruopu on, 416–19; of palace ladies, 18; private girls' academics, 199; and Qiu Jin, 767, 782, 794, 797–98, 800, 808; in Tang dynasty, 15–16; writing of poetry, 201–2. *See also* literacy, female

"Eight Extremes" (Li), 177

"Eighteen Stanzas for the Barbarian Reed Pipe" (Cai), 121–27

elite families, 132, 348, 568; Buddhist nuns from, 201, 456; and Daoism, 142–43; lifestyle of, late Ming dynasty, 357; literacy in, 199; marriage alliances of, 91, 138; nuns from, 153, 154

elite women writers, 6, 203, 356, 358; and cult of *qing*, 353; examinations for, 574–75; and feminine poetic style, 200; and footbinding, 201; freedom of, 15; in Jiangnan area, 575–76; literacy rate of, 567; lyric poetry of, 220;

on military heroines, 566; networks of, 383; plays of, 7; plucking rhymes of, 718–19, 729; private sphere of, 4–5, 12; public roles of, 15–16; self-censoring, 164–65, 354–55; spontaneous expression of, 351, 354. *See also* palace ladies

emancipation of women, 770, 782–83. *See also* feminism

emotion, 134; and cult of *qing*, 349–50, 352, 353; in lyric poems, 225, 237, 238, 240; of neglected women, 75; in *shi* poetry, 51, 275, 397. *See also* feelings; *shi* poems

"Emotions" (Hou), 98

"Emotions" (Li), 205

emperor: devotion to, 77; and palace ladies, 74–75; poems in praise of, 252–53. *See also specific emperor*

empress dowagers, 17–18; as regent, 32, 34–35. *See also specific empress dowager*

"Encountering Sorrow" (Qu), 686, 687, 697, 698

"End of Spring Feelings" (Zhu), 249

"End of Spring, The" (Li), 241

"End of Spring, The" (Zhang), 267

"Enjoying the Cool on a Summer Night" (Luo), 617

"Enjoying the Moon at South Tower" (Jiang), 593

enlightenment, 314, 319, 327, 368, 587, 642; as Buddhahood, 313, 317, 592, 605; of Buddhist nuns, 158–59, 320–231, 324, 466–67; Ye sisters on, 399–400, 413, 414

"Entering the Pass" (melody), 636

erotic poems, 167–68, 175.

estate poetry, 69–70

Eternal Mother cult, 718

"Eternal Pleasure" (melody), 232–33

"Evening Entertainments on the Qinhuai River" (Liang), 423

evergreens, symbolism of, 47–48

Examination for Women, 574

examinations, 11, 15, 247, 622; failure to pass, 585, 601–2; and neo-Confucianism, 200–201, 349; passing of, 173–74, 339n, 608, 609, 611, 680, 722, 732; and social status, 198, 200; and women, 195, 569–70, 573–75

"Exhortation for My Younger Sisters on My Departure, An" (Xi), 595

Exhortations (Xu), 304, 307

"Expressing My Emotions" (Ye), 397

"Expressing My Emotions" (Zheng), 275

Extensive Collection of Miracles (Dai), 166

Faguo nü yingxiong tanci. See *Female Hero from France*

Fake Image, The (Wu), 677, 685–94

"Falling Flowers" (Gu), 638

"Falling Petals" (Lin), 487

Family Rituals (Sima), 201–2

famine, 161–62

Fan, Concubine, 58–59

Fan, lady, 79

Fan Lihua, 566

Fan Ye, 308

Fan Zhen, 333

Fan Zuyu, 332

Fang Congzhe, 723, 725

Fanhuameng (Wang). See *Dream of Splendor*

Fansheng xiang (Ye). See *Fragrance of a Returned Life*

feelings *(qing),* 245; cult of, 203, 349, 350. *See also* emotion; *shi* poems

"Feelings in the Last Month of Spring; Sent to a Friend" (Yu), 194

"Feelings of Separation" (Zhang), 268–69

"Feelings on a Rainy Night" (Jiang), 590

"Feelings on a Spring Day" (Zhu), 249

"Feelings on the Double Ninth" (Wang), 449

"Feelings While Watching Flowers on a Spring Day" (Ye), 407–8

Feihongxiao (Liu). See *Sword of Vengeance*

Feilong *(Recreated Heaven),* 753

female friendship, "sworn sisters," 544–47

Female Hero from France, The, 779

female impersonation, 759; by male writers, 2, 6, 76–77.

Female Poets (Xu), 352–53

female virtue, 101, 357, 679, 725, 753; wifely, 100, 273, 283. *See also* chastity

feminine poetic style, 2, 199–200, 256, 280, 767; of Li Qingzhao, 235, 238, 269; of Zheng Yunduan, 269, 270 feminism, 8, 574, 767, 773, 780, 808. *See also* Qiu Jin

Feng *(Shadow Dream of the Red Chamber)*, 648, 649–50

Feng Kui ("Sent to My Loved One"), 337–38, 339, 342

Feng Menglong, 504, 518–19

Feng shuang fei (Cheng). See *Phoenixes Flying Together*

Feng Xian, 471, 472, 477–78

Fenggan, 624, 626

Fenjiao lu (Wang). See *Burnt Pepper*

festival performances, 544

festival poems, 229–33. *See also specific festival*

"Fifth Daughter of Wang," 564–65

"Fighting Quails" (tune), 340

"Fighting Song for Women's Rights, A" (Qiu), 795

"Fighting South of the City" (Li), 675–76

filiality, 35, 264, 354–55, 750; and cross-dressing, 679; and loyalty, 35, 264, 720; of Shuangqing, 538; as theme in poetry, 560–61. *See also Classic of Filiality for Women*

"Filled with Emotion" (Qiu), 783

"Filled with Emotions" (Liang), 421–22

"Fine Gardens" (tune), 691

"Finer Than Flowers" (tune), 710, 711

First Night poems, 232–33

"First" (tune), 342–43

"Fish Separated from Its Pond, The" (Xue), 187

"Fisherman's Boat, The" (Zhang), 267

"Fisherman's Song" (tune), 284

"Fishes Knotted of White Silk; Presented to a Friend" (Li), 176–77

"Fleeing from the Bandits by Taking to the Sea" (Li), 672

flirtation and teasing, 38

Flower Screen Lyrics (Wu), 694–95

"Flowers Fill the Garden" (melody), 589–90

Flowers from a Brush (Qiu), 754–56

Flowers in the Mirror (Li), 572–75, 627

Flower-Scattering Chants (Jing), 364

"Following the Original Rhyme Words . . ." (Gu), 639

"Following the Rhymes of My Husband's 'Expressing My Emotions'" (Feng), 477

Fonu (pseudonym), 802–6

footbinding, 201, 518, 680, 770; Qiu Jin's critique of, 780, 781, 782, 789–91

"For My Daughter Quan" (Zhang), 658–62

"For the Dancer Zhang Yunrong" (Yang), 100–101

Forbidden City, 73. *See also* Inner Palace

foreign rulers, marriage to, 91, 94

Fragrance of a Returned Life (Ye), 385

Frankel, Hans H., 119

Fu'ou fu (Zuo). See *Rhapsody on a Water Bubble*

Fu Jian, 54, 129, 138

Fu Sheng, 674; daughter of, 52, 53

Fuchai, King of Wu, 361

"Full River Red" (melody), 433–34, 488, 493–94, 776, 784–85

funeral laments, 542. *See also* mourning/grieving poems

Furth, Charlotte, 353

Fuxue (Zhang). See *Women's Learning*

Gantang yishi houxu (Cai). See *Postface to Anecdotes from Gantang*

Gantang yishi. See *Anecdotes from Gantang*

Gao Lishi, 102, 104

Gao Qi, 621, 622, 624

Gao Yanxiu, 175

Gao Yinxian, 544, 545–46

Gao Zhongwu, 180, 360

Gaozong, Emperor, 62–63, 64, 206

"Gazing on Shenyang" (Xu), 435

"Gazing to Jiangnan" (melody), 522

Ge Hong, 13–15

"Geese" (Yang), 373

gender, limitations of, 195, 256, 616, 693

gender-switching, 70–71, 687, 734; in drama, 677, 687. *See also* cross-dressing heroines; Lou Cheng; Qiu Jin

Gengniang *(Sword of Vengeance),* 706–9

"Getting Up, Two Poems" (Zhu), 249

"God Erlang, The" (melody), 527

Goddess of Compassion. *See* Guanyin

Goddess of Shamanka Mountain, 178–79, 180, 250n, 502

Goddess of the Xiang, 502

"Going to My Mother's Place in the Burning Heat of the Sixth Month" (Yi), 552–53

"Going to Visit Refining Master Zhao but Not Finding Her at Home" (Yu), 189–90

Golden Fish Affinity, The (Sun), 756–59

gong'an (koan) collections, 323, 325–26, 327

Gong Chuo, 26

Gong Zichen, 633

"Goose Falls, The" (tune), 690

"Grand Canal," 95

"Grass-Insects" (poem), 259

"Grateful for the Emperor's Favor" (melody), 290–91

"Grave Inscription for Lady Guan . . ." (Zhao), 281–84

"Great Peace Tune," 692

"Green Coat, The" (anonymous), 75–76, 82n

"Greeting the Immortal Guest" (tune), 339, 413

grieving/mourning poems, 65, 632–34, 676. *See also* sorrow, in poetry

"Groping for Fish" (melody), 534–35

Gu Chun (Taiqing), 630–52; *Shadow Dream of the Red Chamber,* 647–52, 715–16; song lyrics of, 631–32, 634–47

Gu family, 141

Gu Lanzhou, 686

Gu Ruopu, 414–20, 471, 478; on children's education, 416–19; poetry of, 418–20

Gu Si (Qiji), 477, 482, 487–88, 504

Gu Sili, 626

Gu Taiqing. *See* Gu Chun (Taiqing)

Gu Zhiqiong, 471, 473–74

Guan Daosheng, 280, 281–87, 312; poetry of, 284–85, 286; Zhao Mengfu's biography of, 281–84

Guan Panpan, 360, 362

Guangxu emperor, 769–70, 773

Guangyi ji (Dai). *See Extensive Collection of Miracles*

Guanqi Zhixian, 322

Guanyin dashi zhuan (Guan). *See Biography of the Mahasattva Guanyin, The*

Guanyin, Bodhisattva of Compassion, 311–18, 509, 605, 716, 792; and Empress Xu's sutra, 304, 314–18; as Mahasattva, 505; as Princess Miaoshan, 311–14, 718; and Eternal Mother cult, 718

Guided by Heaven's Storm (Liu), 709–14; "A Mother's Offering," 710–12

Guifu, 802, 803, 805

Guiji, girl of, 518, 520

Guiyuan (Buddhist nun), 718

Gujin lienüzhuan. See Biographical Sketches of Women of Chastity from Ancient Times to the Present

Gulik, Robert Hans van, 193

Guo, Empress, 90

Guo Maoqian, 121

Guochao guixiu zhengshi ji (Wanyan, ed.). *See Correct Beginnings: Women's Poetry of Our August Dynasty*

Gushi shijiushou (anonymous). *See Nineteen Old Poems*

Guwutu, 19

Guxianglou ji (Qian). *See Ancient Fragrance Tower Collection.*

Haiyin (nun), 158

Han Boyu, 45

Han dynasty, 17; Western, 20, 21, 93, 110

Han Fei, 216

Han Lanying, 49–52, 181

Han Shizhong, 475

Han shu. See Books of the Han

Han Xi, 488, 534

Han Yu, 394

Hangzhou Bore, 490–91, 493

Hangzhou poets, 414–23, 571; Gu Ruopu, 414–20, 471, 478; Liang Mengzhao, 420–23. *See also* Banana Garden Poetry Club

Hanshan, 470

Hao Yixing, 627

"Hard to Forget" (melody), 473–74

Harmonious Echoes Collection of Poems about Ancient [Cases], 326

Harvard-Yenching Library, 623

"Hawk Separated from the Gauntlet, The" (Xue), 187

He, Emperor, 26, 32, 34

He Guizhi, 515–18

He Peizhu, 683–85

He Wanqing *(Kept Promises)*, 704

"Hearing a Flute at Mid-Autumn" (Zhu), 250

"Heavenly Immortal" (melody), 510

Heavenly Kingdom of Great Peace (sect), 575

Helin yulu (Luo). *See Jade Dew from Crane Forest*

"Her Own Story by He Huanshu from Baishui," 553–54

heroism, 440–44, 687; in warfare, 257, 379, 381–82

Heyuan ji (Liang). See *United Primes*

"High Hills and Flowing Rivers" (melody), 631

History of the Liao, 300–301

History of the South, 678

History of the Three Kingdoms (Chen), 86, 87–88

"Hometown Landscape" (Zhu), 490

homoerotic desire, 683, 685, 693, 759

Hong Xiuquan, 575

Honglou meng (Cao). See *Dream of the Red Chamber*

Hongloumeng ying (Gu). See *Shadow Dream of the Red Chamber*

Hongwu emperor, 305, 306

"Horse Separated from Its Stable, The" (Xue), 186

Hou Han shu. See *Books of the Later Han*

Hou, lady, 95, 96–100

Hou Zhi, 734, 753–54

Household Instructions (Xu), 304, 307, 308, 309–10

Houses of Pleasure (Xia), 337, 343–44

"How Mournful" (Li), 676

Hu Weiyong, 623

Hu Yinglin, 134–35

Hua Wei, 677, 683–84

Hualianci (Wu). *Flower Screen Lyrics*

Huang and Ying (Xiang goddesses), 165

Huang Chonggu, 362–64, 570, 677–78

Huang Duanbo, 441–42

Huang E, 280, 281, 287–91

Huang Maowu (Dongsheng), 414–15

Huang Ruheng (Yuyong), 414, 415

Huang Shang, 324

Huang Yuanjie, 426, 452–55

Huangfu Changhua, Empress Dowager, 753

Huangfu Mei, 190–93

Huangfu Shaohua *(Karmic Bonds of Reincarnation),* 737–39, 743, 747, 748, 752, 755

Huangshi baojuan. See *Precious Scroll on Lady Huang*

"Huangtiandang: On Lady Liang" (Chai), 475

Huarui, Lady, 245, 293–97, 299

Huhanye, khan of Southern Xiongnu, 91, 92

Hui, Emperor, 84, 85

Hui Baifang *(Mandarin Ducks' Dream),* 411–14

Huiguang (Jingzhi dashi), 332

Huizhen ji. See *Painted Portrait, The*

Huizong, Emperor, 184, 206, 292

husbands: absent, 473–74, 486, 489–90; mourning for, 426, 632–34; poems to, 150, 284, 419, 488, 596, 608, 609–10; return of, 289–90; Xi Peilan's poems to, 596, 601–2, 608, 611

"Husband-Watching Rock, The" (Zheng), 277

husband-wife relations, 37–40, 58, 111, 791. *See also* marriage; wifely duties; wifely virtues

"Hymn on the Pepper Blossom" (Chen), 145

"I Attended Xiao Shuzi While He Was Listening to Someone Playing the Zither . . ." (Li), 179

"I Have Been a Widow Since the Age of Twenty-Eight . . ." (Yi), 555–57

"Imitations of Old Poems" (Bao), 50–52

immortality, poems on, 47–48

"Immortals at the Bridge of Magpies" (melody), 254–55

immortals, 141–42, 313–14; Daoist, 141–42, 143, 159–60, 162; in drama, 411–12, 413–14, 684, 716; in poetry, 275–76

"Impending Snow" (Zhu), 251

imperial concubines, 568; Baosi, 80, 82n; Concubine Plum, 101–7; poetry of, 18, 74, 76, 80, 294; Zuo Fen as, 46. *See also* Ban, Imperial Concubine; palace ladies

imperial harem, 5, 18

Imperial Reading Matter of the Great Peace Reign Period (anthology), 135–36

"Impromptu Verses" (Wang), 452

"In Front of My Study Window" (Zhu), 249

"In Imitation of 'A Traveler Came from a Distant Land'" (Bao), 51

"In Imitation of 'Border Lyrics'" (Chai), 476

"In Reply to a Poem by Jilan" (Jiaoran), 181

"In the Mountains" (Huang), 455

"In the Old Style; Sent to a Contemporary Man" (Bao), 51

"In the Old Style" (Liu), 147

"In the Old Style" (Xi), 596

"In the Rain . . . the Rhymes of Jian Zhushan" (Gu), 641–42

"Incense Offering" (melody), 695

independence of women, 793, 797–98. *See also* emancipation of women

"Inkstones of Mutual Love, The" (Liang), 421

"Inn at Nanliu, The" (Li), 672

Inner Palace, 5, 15, 18, 42, 50; central role of, 6; daily life in, 46; disbanding of, 212; and elite families, 132; Forbidden City, 73; literate women of, 197, 292; nuns in, 155. *See also* palace ladies; palace songs

inner sphere, of women, 4–5, 12

"Inscription for a Portrait of Myself, An" (Qiu), 795

"Inscription for Lady Scholar Yu Caizhuang's *Wisdom and Happiness Tower Poetry Collection*" (Luo), 646–47

"Inscription for My Painting . . ., An" (Luo), 617

"Inscription on a Painting by Lin Yaqing" (Gu), 487

"Inscription on a Wall in Shanghai, An" (Qiu), 778

Inscriptions on Bronze and Stone (Li), 207–14

"Instruction in the Womb" (Zheng), 59–60

Instructions for My Sons (Zhuo), 357

Instructions for Women, 258

intellectuals, 356, 357, 374, 571, 769

"Intertwined Branches" (melody), 699

Jade Bracelet, The (Chen), 734, 735–37
"Jade Butterflies" (melody), 268–69
Jade Dew from Crane Forest (Luo), 158
"Jade Metropolis Autumn" (melody), 524
Japan: Chinese nationalists in, 773, 779; feminism in, 777, 808; war with (1894–1895), 769, 777; war with Russia (1904–1905), 794
jealousy, 74, 289, 566
Ji (nun), 141
Jia Baoyu *(Dream of the Red Chamber)*, 499, 568–69
Jia Lian *(Shadow Dream of the Red Chamber)*, 648, 649–50, 653, 655
Jia Sidao, 506
Jia Yi, 151, 216, 772
Jiadai pudenglu. See *Jiadai Universal Record of the Lamps, The*
Jiadai Universal Record of the Lamps, 323, 324
Jian Zhushan, 641–42
Jiang, Lady, 75–76
Jiang Dehua/Jiang Junbi *(Flowers from a Branch)*, 754–56
Jiang Zhu, 588–93; lyric poems of, 589–91; spirit-writing of, 591–92
Jiangnan region, 7, 347–48, 353, 357, 452, 571; literary courtesan culture in, 575–76; plucking rhymes of, 719
"Jiangnan Spring" (melody), 473
Jiao Hong zhuan (Song). See *Wang Jiaoniang and Feihong*

Jiaoran, 181, 365, 467
Jiaxing Extended Tripitika (Buddhist canon), 457
Jiaxing Xuzang jing. See *Jiaxing Extended Tripitika*
Jin, lady, 443–45
Jin Dayong *(Sword of Vengeance)*, 706, 707
Jin dynasty (265–419), 127–28, 137–38; conquest of, 48–49. *See also Books of the Jin*
Jin dynasty (1115–1234), 205, 211, 213, 379, 475; plucking rhyme set in, 736–37, 761. *See also* Jürchen
Jin Fu, 357
Jin shu. See *Books of the Jin*
Jing Ke, 774, 775
Jing Pianpian, 364–66
Jingde chuandeng lu (Moshan). See *Jingde Period Record of the Transmission of the Lamp, The*
Jingde Period Record of the Transmission of the Lamp, The (Moshan), 322, 323
Jingdi, Emperor, 108
Jinghua yuan (Li). See *Flowers in the Mirror*
Jingwei shi (Qiu). See *Stones of the Jingwei Bird*
Jingzhong zhuan (Zhou). See *Utter Loyalty*
Jinpingmei. See *Plum in the Golden Vase, The*
Jinshi lu (Li). See *Inscriptions on Bronze and Stone*
Jintuo, 552–53
Jinyuyuan (Sun). See *The Golden Fish Affinity*

Jiu Tang shu. See *Old Books of the Tang*

Jiwen (Niu). See *Records of Rumors*

Jizong Xingzhe, 464–70; autobiographical account, 464–67; poetry of, 467–70

"Journeying to Weiyang" (Li), 671

"Joy of the World, The" (tune), 340

judgment of character, 58–59

Jürchen, 205, 247, 379, 475, 574, 762. *See also* Jin dynasty (1115–1234)

Kang Aide, 770

Kang Tongwei, 808

Kang Youwei, 769–70

Karmic Bonds of Reincarnation (Chen), 734, 737–52, 755, 759; author's introduction to, 749–52; cross-dressing heroine in, 737, 738–43, 746–48, 749, 752

karmic debt, 531, 564

Kept Promises (Liu), 703–5

Khitan, 206

kite-flying poems, 372–73, 377–78

Ko, Dorothy, 499

Kongshi Daoren, 329–31

Labyrinth, The, 96, 97–100

"Lady Cui's Instructions to Her Daughter," 61

"Lady Yan" (Han), 50

"Lady Yu" (melody), 479–80

"Lament at the Qiantang Battlefield" (Wang), 445

"Lament for China" (Qiu), 800

"Lamenting My Elder Dharma Sister Yigong" (Yikui), 462

"Lamenting My Fate" (Hou), 99

"Lamenting My Teacher, the Venerable Nun Zhiyuan" (Yikui), 461

"lamenting the past" poems, 628–29

laments, of abandoned women, 110–13

Lang Ying, 298, 299, 300

Langhuan Collection (Liang), 359

Langhuan ji (Liang). See *Langhuan Collection*

Lankavatara Sutra, 397

Lanxue ji (Zhang). See *Orchid and Snow*

Laozi, 146, 153, 163, 216. *See also* Daoism

"Late Autumn Afternoon" (Tao), 579–80

"Late Spring Impromptu Verse, A" (Jiang), 590–91

Later (Eastern) Han dynasty, 20

Later Shu dynasty, 293, 295

"Leaving through the Passes" (Zhang), 666–67

leisure reading, 348–49, 357

lesbianism, 685, 693. *See also* homoerotic desire

"Letter to Lin Yaqing, A" (Qian), 482–83

"Letter to My Younger Brother, Youkun, A" (Qian), 484–85

Lezi, Great Master, 388–89, 399

Li, Empress Dowager, 310

Li, Master, 235

Li. See *Rites*

Li Bai, 71, 164n, 288, 354, 467, 675; quoted by Wu Zao, 686, 689; in

Xi Peilan's poems, 601, 602,
604n, 609, 611
Li Changxia, 668–76; traveling poems of, 669, 671–74
Li Gefei, 204
Li Guiyu, 719
Li Jilan, 180
Li Jinglong, 305–6
Li Junyu. *See* Meng Lijun/Li Junyu
(Karmic Bonds of Reincarnation)
Li Mingtang *(Karmic Bonds of Reincarnation)*, 744, 745–46,
752
Li Qingzhao, 202, 204–17, 268,
272, 611; book collection of,
209–11, 212, 214; emotional expression of, 225, 237, 238, 240;
feminine tradition of, 235, 238,
256, 269; festival poems of, 229–
33; *Inscriptions on Bronze and Stone*,
207–14; lost works of, 6, 244;
lyric poems of, 219–20, 221, 225–
40, 243, 635; *On Lyrics*, 234–37;
patriotic poems of, 241–42, 256;
renown of, 201, 245, 808; remarriage of, 214–17, 240; *shi* poems
of, 205, 217, 240, 241–42; and
Wang Wei, 369; and Zhao
Mingcheng, 204–5, 206, 208–12,
231–32
Li Ruzhen, 572–75
Li Shangyin, 350, 351n
Li Si, 628
Li Xun, 56
Li Ye, 175, 176–82, 362; as courtesan, 16, 164, 178, 180, 182, 361
Li Yi, 189
Li Yu, 439, 452
Li Yu, Emperor, 220, 781n

Li Zhongyue, 804, 805
Liandeng huiyao. See *Outline of Linked
Lamps*
Liang, Prince of, 108, 453n
Liang Desheng, 620, 621–23,
752
Liang Hong, 136
Liang Hongyu, 475
Liang Jun *(Linked Rings of Jade)*,
732–33
Liang Mengzhao, 354, 414, 420–23
Liang Qi *(Linked Rings of Jade)*, 731–
32
Liang Qichao, 769–70, 773
Liang Shanbo, 199, 562–64, 565, 679
Liang shu. See *Books of the Liang*
Liang Xiaoyu, 359–62, 364, 365,
677
Liangdu fu (Ban). See *Rhapsody on the
Two Capitals*
Liangdu fu (Liang). See *Rhapsody on
the Two Capitals*
Liao dynasty, 206, 300, 301
Liaoshi. See *History of the Liao*
Liaozhai zhiyi (Pu). See *Stories of the
Strange from Make-do Studio*
Lichui (Shen). See *Oriole Pipings*
Liechao shiji (Qian and Liu). See
*Collected Poems of the Successive
Reigns*
Lienü zhuan (Liu). See *Biographies of
Exemplary Women*
Liji. See *Notes on the Rites*
Lin Daiyu *(Dream of the Red Cham-
ber)*, 499, 500, 568–69
Lin Shoutu, 656, 657
Lin Yining, 471, 472–73, 486–87
Lin Zhiyang *(Flowers in the Mirror)*,
573

Lin'er *(Kept Promises)*, 704

Lingbao jing (Lu). See *Classic of Numinous Treasure*

"Lingering Fragrance" (Liu), 173

Lingfei jing (Yuzhen). See *Classic of Soaring and Flying Spirits*

Lingzhao, 583

Linked Rings of Jade (Zhu), 730–33, 740, 743

"Listening to the Blackbirds" (Liu), 148

literacy, female, 5, 154, 292, 542, 575, 770; of elite women, 199, 567; and leisure reading, 348–49, 357. *See also* education of women

literary criticism, 9, 238, 242, 243, 349–50

Literary Mind and the Carving of Dragons, The (Liu), 128

literary societies, 589. *See also* Banana Garden Poetry Club; poetry clubs

"Little Town on the River" (melody), 224, 638, 644

Liu, Lady, 139–40

Liu An, 507

Liu Bang, 17, 82–83, 241, 380n, 479, 776–77

Liu Caichun, 189

Liu Changqing, 180–81

Liu family *(Karmic Bonds of Reincarnation)*, 737–39

Liu Ji, 622, 623, 624, 625

Liu Jian, 91

Liu Jun, 137

Liu Lingxian, 146, 148–53

Liu Liu, 144

Liu Mengmei *(Peony Pavilion)*, 501

Liu Qingyun, 701–15, 716; *Guided by Heaven's Storm*, 709–14; *Kept Promises*, 703–5; *Sword of Vengeance*, 706–9; Yu Yue on, 702–3

Liu Shang, 121, 405

Liu Shi, 374–82, 406, 454, 513; and Chen Zilong, 374–75, 377; on courtesan poets, 368, 370; on Liang Xiaoyu, 359–61; poetry of, 376–82; and Qian Qianyi, 375–76, 513–14; on Ye Xiaoluan, 390–91. *See also Collected Poems of the Successive Reigns*

Liu Shuying, 654, 721

Liu Tao, 143

Liu Xiachuo, 146–48, 149

Liu Xiang, 18, 19; *Biographies of Exemplary Women*, 12, 42, 136n, 201, 265, 273, 627

Liu Xie, 128

Liu Xijun, 91, 94

Liu Xiu, 20

Liu Yiqing, 137

Liu Yong, 234, 236

Liu Yuxi, 690

Liu Zhen, 350

Liu Zongyuan, 394

Liuhuameng (Li). See *Pomegranate Blossom Dream*

"Living in a Village" (Li), 675

"Living in Seclusion on Southern Peak" (Jizong), 467–70

"Lonely Phoenix" (melody), 527–28

"Longing for My Mother" (Xi), 594

"Looking at the Plum Tree" (Hou), 98

lotus, symbolism of, 167–68, 532

Lotus Sutra, 321, 328n

"Lotus-Gathering Songs" (Qian), 480

Lou Cheng, 678–79; and cross-dressing, 678–79

Loudong fu (Plum). See *Rhapsody on the East of My Residence*

love, symbols of, 111, 167–68

"Love-Longing" (Li), 177–78

"Love for the Way; Sent to Vice-Minister Cui" (Li), 176

love poems, 134, 220, 287

love stories, 101, 261, 262, 627, 719; Liang Shanbo and Zhu Yingtai, 562–64, 565. *See also* plucking rhymes

loyalty, 35, 296, 379, 720; to fiancé, 258, 264–65, 266, 581; in marriage, 136n, 277, 561–63; patriotic, 475, 761–63; poems on, 47–48; to the ruler, 257, 258

Lu, Mademoiselle *(The Scholars)*, 569–70

Lu Hu, 54

Lu Ji, 151, 170

Lu Meiniang, 352

Lu You, 202, 332

"Lunar New Year's Eve (1649)" (Wang), 446–47

Lunyu, (Confucius). See *Analects*

Luo Dagang, 158

Luo Guanzhong, 86

Luo Qilan, 612–20; poems of, 615–20; on women poets, 612–15; and Yuan Mei, 612, 613, 614, 618–20

Lü Dongbin *(Mandarin Ducks' Dream)*, 411–12, 413–14

Lü, Empress Dowager, 17, 83–84, 85

Lüqiao, 191–93

lyrics *(ci)*, 201, 217–41, 369, 576; and abandoned women, 220–21, 225; autumn theme, 226–28; of courtesans, 199, 220, 333–36, 377–78; criticism of, 234–37; and feminine mode, 6; festival days in, 229–33; of Guan Daosheng, 284–85; of Gu Chun (Taiqing), 631–32, 634–47; of Jian Zhu, 589–90; of Lady Wei, 221–25; of Li Qingzhao, 219–20, 221, 225–40, 243, 635; love theme in, 220; of Qian Fenglun, 479–83, 484–86; of Shen Yixiu, 387–88; of Shuangqing, 522–24, 526–29, 533–36, 538–40; structure of, 9; of Xu Can, 431, 432, 433–34; of Ye Xiaoluan, 396–99; of Zhu Shuzhen, 253–56

Lyrics from South of Incense Mountain and North of Snowy Mountains (Wu), 701

Ma, Empress, 305, 308, 309, 623, 625, 657

Ma Longmei *(Guided by Heaven's Storm)*, 709–10, 712, 714

Ma Rong, 26, 27, 34, 42

Ma Xiaolan, 366–68

"Magnolia Flower Abbreviated" (melody), 223, 239, 253

"Magpie Bridge Immortals," 333–34

Mahaprajapati Gotami, 583

Mahayana Buddhism, 304, 314, 319, 331

"Making an Appointment with Gu Chunshan for Enjoying the Plum Blossoms . . ." (Zhu), 491–92

male dress, women in. *See also* cross-dressing heroines; gender-switching; Lou Cheng; Qiu Jin

male homosexuality, 759

male poets, impersonating women, 2, 6, 8, 76–77

male relatives, 354. *See also* husbands; sons

Manchurian exile poems, 431, 432, 435–37

Manchus, 630, 769, 775, 805; censorship by, 571; conquest of, 7, 355, 425, 576, 721; court of, 773; customs of, 647; dress code of, 679–80; protest against, 779, 807; threat to China, 381, 420; Yue Fei cult in, 762–63. *See also* Qing dynasty

Mandarin Ducks' Dream (Ye), 411–14

Manuscripts from the Listening to Autumn Study, 613

Mao Kun, 371, 421

Mao Ti, 471, 493–95

Mao Xianshu, 493, 494–95

Mao Yanshou, 93, 99

Mao Yuanyi, 371, 373

Mao Zhisheng, 370, 371

"Marionettes" (Gu), 645

marriage, 53, 276–77, 612; arranged, 433, 564; to barbarians, 9, 91, 94, 120–21, 247–48; delayed-transferral, 552; elite alliances in, 91, 138; forced, 337–38, 339; frustration in, 245–46, 247–48, 280, 751; loyalty in, 277, 561–63; Qiu Jin's critique of, 770, 780–81, 793; wedding laments, 542–43. *See also* husband-wife relations; widows, remarriage of

marriage poems, 547–53

Master Grass and Tree (Ye), 260–61

Master Jade Source (anonymous), 173

"Master of the Cooking Dream," 392–93, 394

"Master Ruan Returns" (melody), 221

Master Who Embraces Simplicity, The (Ge), 13–15

Master Zhuang, 168–69, 170, 171, 173. *See also* Zhuang Zhou

May Fourth Movement (1919), 808

"Maze Pattern, The" (Su), 129–31

McLaren, Anne, 543

Meaning of Mencius Explained, The (Wen), 334, 335

Meifei zhuan. See Biography of Concubine Plum

memorial to the throne (Ban), 28–30, 35–36

"Memories after the Destruction of Our Library" (Li), 674–75

Mencius, 334, 335, 536–37

Meng Chang, 293, 295, 296, 297

Meng Chengshun, 265–67

Meng Jiangnü, 562

Meng Lijun/Li Junyu (*Karmic Bonds of Reincarnation*), 737, 738–43, 746–48, 749, 752; and Jiang Dehua compared, 755, 756

Mengying yuan (Zheng). *See Dream Affinities*

Mengzhan, 523, 524, 530

Mengzi jieyi. See Meaning of Mencius Explained, The

Miaodao (nun), 323–25

Miaoshan, Princess, 311–14, 718

Miaoyin (nun), 154–55

Miaozong (nun), 325–27, 456

"Midnight Song" (melody), 771

Milou ji. See *Labyrinth, The*

Ming dynasty, 18, 347, 349, 629;
    Chan Buddhism in, 356; collapse
    of, 7, 425; courtesan culture of,
    355, 383; drama of, 190, 337; es-
    tablishment of, 622–24, 623,
    624, 625; female chastity in, 265;
    moral decay of, 725; moral tracts
    for women in, 348; palace songs
    (gongci) in, 293, 295; plucking
    rhymes of, 720, 724

Ming History, 305–7, 310

Ming loyalists, 721; suicide of, 426;
    writings of Wang Duanshu on,
    438, 440–45

Ming sanshijia shi xuan (Wang, ed.).
    See *Selections of Thirty Poets of the
    Ming*

Ming shi zong (Zhu). See *Compendium
    of Ming Poetry*

Mingdi, Emperor, 86, 89, 91

Mingshi. See *Ming History*

Mingshi biecai (Shen). See *New Selec-
    tion of Ming Poetry*

Mingshi Daoren, 327–28

Mingxin lu. See *Record of Mind
    Illumination*

Mingyuan shigui (Zhong, ed.). See *Se-
    lections of Poems by Famous Ladies*

Mingyuan shihua (Shen, ed.). See
    *Comments on Poems by Famous
    Ladies*

Mingyuan shiwei (Wang, ed.). See
    Classic Poetry of Famous Women

Minor Writings from Shanshui
    (Huangfu), 190–93

miracle tales, 161–62, 168

"Mirror Separated from Its Stand,
    The" (Xue), 187–88

"Mocking Myself" (Luo), 616

Moling ji. See *Nanjing Collection*

"Moon on Border Mountain"
    (Xu), 434–35

"Moonlight Shadows" (Gu), 487–
    88

moral behavior, 349, 623, 648, 679;
    and degeneracy, 261; education
    in, 12, 32; and integrity, 47–48;
    in plucking rhymes, 725, 729,
    730, 755, 759

moral tracts for women, 12, 43, 61,
    308–10, 348; *Analects for Women*
    (Song), 13, 55, 57, 58; *Classic of
    Filiality for Women,* 13, 58–60, 201,
    258, 310; *Household Instructions*
    (Empress Xu), 304, 307, 308,
    309, 310. *See also Precepts for My
    Daughters*

moralistic poems, 270–74, 276,
    277–78

"Morning Toilette on a Spring
    Day" (Ye), 391

Moshan Liaoran (nun), 322

"Mother's Offering, A," 710–12

motherhood, 59–60, 557–61

mothers: admonition to sons by,
    23, 25–26, 357, 475–76, 485–86;
    mourning for, 65

mothers-in-law, 526, 528, 529

Mount Lu, 272

"Mountain Climbing" (Xie), 142

"Mourning at the Tomb of Prince
    Yue" (Zhang), 653

"Mourning My Husband" (Shang), 426

mourning/grieving poems, 65, 632–34, 676. *See also* sorrow, in poetry

"Moved by Events" (Xu), 433–34

"Moved by Separation" (Zuo), 43–44

"Moved by What I Hear the Farmers Say during a Heat Wave" (Zhu), 251–52

Mu Guiying, 566

Mudanting (Tang). See *Peony Pavilion*

Mulan, 656, 679, 720, 779

multiple personalities, 165–68

murder, 192–93. *See also* suicide

musical traditions, 179, 217. *See also* arias; lyrics *(ci)*

Muzong, Emperor, 56

"My Feelings on My Fiftieth Birthday" (Shang), 427–28

"My Mirror" (Zheng), 278–79

"My Servant Girl Wenqin Married a Certain . . ." (Luo), 617–18

"My Woman Friend Zheng Er Mingzhan Stopped to See Me . . ." (Wang), 448–49

Mystery upon Mystery (Wei, ed.), 189

mystical literature, 159–63

Nanchuan Puyuan, 320

Nanjing Collection, 625

Nanshi. See *History of the South*

Narrow-Minded, Master (pseudonym), 504, 511–12

nationalism, 763, 770, 773, 775, 783; and feminism, 767

"Needle and Thread" (Ban), 30–31

Neixun (Xu). See *Household Instructions*

neo-Confucianism, 280, 357, 567, 578; and examinations, 200–201, 349; morality of, 216, 623; on remarriage of widows, 113, 201. *See also* Confucianism

New Account of Tales of the World, A (Liu, ed.), 137, 138, 140–41, 273

New Books of the Tang, 55–56, 57, 61

New Selection of Ming Poetry (Shen), 622

New Songs from a Jade Terrace (Zhen), 89, 110, 112, 132, 148

"New Water Tune," 687–88

"New Year's Eve of the Year *Yihai*" (Xu), 435

"New Year's Eve" (Zhu), 251

Nian rebellion, 669

"Niannu's Charms" (melody), 229

"Night of Double Seven, The" (Zhu), 254–55

"Night of Full Moon, A; For Someone Seeing Me Off" (Li), 177

Nineteen Old Poems (anonymous), 52

nirvana, 319. *See also* enlightenment

Niu Ruyuan, 757–59

Niu Su, 168, 169

Niu Yingzhen zhuan. See *Biography of Niu Yingzhen*

Niu Yingzhen, 168–73; and Zhuang Zhou, 168–69, 170, 171, 173

Nizi (nun), 156–58, 310

Noon Dream Hall Collection (Ye), 390, 392, 406, 410, 411

Notes on Poetry from the Sui Garden (Yuan), 518

Notes on the Rites (Li), 204

Nü caizi shu (Xu). See *Female Poets*

Nü kaike zhuan. See *Examination for Women*

Nü Lunyu (Song). See *Analects for Women*

Nü shishuo (Yan). See *Tales of the World about Women*

Nü xian. See *Charter for Women*

Nü Xiaojing (Zheng). See *Classic of Filiality for Women*

Nü ze. See *Regulations for Women*

Nüjie (Ban). See *Precepts for My Daughters*

Nüxun. See *Instructions for Women*

"Offered to the Great Master Lezi" (Shen), 388

Offices of the Zhou, 11, 20, 52, 53–54

Old Books of the Tang, 57–58, 62–63, 71–72

"On a Cold and Sleepless Night, Remembering My Deceased Daughter" (Shen), 387–88

"On a Moonlit Night Drinking Alone" (Gu), 640

"On a Rainy Day Receiving a Letter from Yingjiang" (Gu), 643

"On a Sleepless Summer Night Thinking of My Deceased Son" (Shen), 386–87

"On a Spring Day in Yu Garden Gazing at the Plum Blossoms" (Shang), 427

"On a Spring Day Longing for Home" (Li), 670

"On a Spring Night in the Year *renshen,* I Wrote the Following . . ." (Ye), 397–98

"On a Winter Night I Was Listening to My Husband Expounding the Way . . ." (Gu), 642–43

"On Chan Master Dongyun's Fiftieth Birthday" (Yikui), 464

"On Double Three I Invited My Relatives to a Banquet" (Li), 230–31

"On Flying Kites" (Liu), 377–78

"On Hearing a Zither" (Sun), 165

"On His Birthday in the Year *gengzi,* Mourning My Departed Husband" (Gu), 632–33

On Jealousy (Yu), 140

On Lyrics (Li), 234–37

"On My Shadow" (Wu), 701

"On Myself" (Liang), 359–60

"On Receiving a Letter from My Husband" (Lin), 486

"On Receiving a Letter from Yan Bojun" (Li), 177

"On the Assigned Topic of Willows by the River" (Yu), 194

"On the Day Following the Mid-Autumn Festival . . ." (Gu), 641

"On the First Prime of the Year *yiwei* Lady Wu Zixia Invited the Club Sisters . . ." (Huang), 453–54

"On the Night of the Fifteenth of the Eighth Month, I Think of My Father" (Li), 669–70

"On the Ninth Day of the Ninth Month His Imperial Majesty Visited . . ." (Shangguan), 68

"On the Original Topic" (Qian), 479–80

"On the Picture of Liu Lang and the Man with a Spade . . ." (Zheng), 273–74

"On the Road between Jiaozhou and Laizhou" (Li), 669

"On the Road through Nine Pines" (Huang), 454

"On the Seventh Day of the Seventh Month My Husband Departed . . ." (Gu), 633

"On the Sixteenth of the Fifth Month . . ." (Liang), 423

"On the Twenty-first of the Seventh Month of the Year . . . Where We Used to Stay" (Gu), 635

"On the Twenty-second Day . . . Weeping for Ninth Son, Zaitong" (Gu), 632

"One Cut-out Plum" (melody), 640

"One Day . . . Thereupon I Composed This Lyric by the Light of the Lamp" (Gu), 637

oppression of women, 33, 788–89, 791–92, 793, 808. *See also* footbinding; subordination of women

oral tradition, 8, 248, 542

Orchid and Snow (Zhang), 257–58, 259

Oriole Pipings (Shen), 385

"Orphaned Goose" (melody), 234

Orthodox Unity Daoist church, 142, 143, 160, 161

"Ospreys, The," 37, 140

"Our Mutual Love Will Not Be Broken" (Gao), 545–46

"Our Youngest Son A'an Suffered from . . ." (Xi), 599–601

Outline of Linked Lamps, 323

Ouyang Xuan, 259–60

Owen, Stephen, 69, 70–71

"Painted Plum Trees" (Guan), 284

Painted Portrait (plucking rhyme), 733

"Painting of Palace Ladies, A" (Huang), 290–91

paintings, 209, 214; poems inspired by, 271–72

palace ladies, 18, 97–98; and literate women, 197, 292; neglect of, 73–76; poetry about, 147–48. *See also* imperial concubines; Inner Palace

palace songs *(gongci)*, 292–304; by Empress Yang, 293, 298–300; of Lady Huarui, 293–97, 299

palindromes, 127, 128, 450–51; brocade palindromes, 129–31

"Pallid Moon behind the Curtain" (melody), 698–99

Pang E, 478–79

parents-in-law, 40, 58. *See also* mothers-in-law

"Parrot Separated from Its Cage, The" (Xue), 186–87

parting songs, 226, 227

"Partridge Sky" (melody), 373–74, 397, 403, 642–43, 645, 681, 801–2

"Passing By My Old House in Yangzhou" (Luo), 618

"Passing Mood, A" (Zheng), 274

patriotism, 241–42, 256, 475, 653; in Zhou's *Utter Loyalty*, 761–63. *See also* Yue Fei

Pear Blossom Dream (He), 683–85

"Pearl Separated from the Palm of the Hand, The" (Xue), 187

peasant ballads, 8

peasant life, 524–26

Pei Songzhi, 86–87

Peng Shaosheng, 581–82, 586, 587–88, 591

Peng Xiluo, 581, 584, 585, 587

Peony Pavilion (Tang), 349, 500–504, 569, 591, 686, 704; Xiaoqing's reference to, 501, 510, 512, 694, 717

People's Republic of China, 242, 251

performative literature, 542. *See also* drama; playwrights

Perovskaia, Sofia, 779

"Phoenix on Her Hairpin" (melody), 639–40

"Phoenix Roosting on the Acacia, A" (melody), 480

"Phoenixes Exchanging Their Nest" (melody), 482

Phoenixes Flying Together (Cheng), 759–60

"Pine Tree" (Tao), 579

Ping'er *(Shadow Dream of the Red Chamber)*, 648, 649–50

Pinhua baojian (Chen). See *Precious Mirror of Ranked Flowers*

"Planting Vegetables" (Zhang), 662

"Playing a Game of Go with Yaqing" (Qian), 481

playwrights, 7, 364, 367, 576, 677; Tang Xianzu, 349, 591. *See also* drama

plucking rhymes *(tanci)*, 7, 9, 577, 717–63; *Dream Affinities*, 734–35; and elite women, 718–19, 729; *The Female Hero from France*, 779; *Linked Rings of Jade*, 730–33, 734; moral behavior in, 725, 729, 730, 755, 759; *Phoenixes Flying Together*, 759–60, 761; *A Rain of Heavenly Flowers*, 719–29, 733; *Recreated Heaven*, 734, 753–54; *Stones of the Jingwei Bird* (Qiu), 786–94; on Yue Fei, 761–63. *See also Karmic Bonds of Reincarnation*

Plum, Concubine, 100–107; poetry of, 102, 104–5, 106; rivalry with Lady Yang, 103–4, 106, 107

Plum in the Golden Vase, The, 574, 718

plum tree poems, 284, 370, 427, 509, 635–36; of Concubine Plum, 101–2; of Lady Hou, 96–98; of Li Qingzhao, 233–34; of Shuangqing, 538–40; of Zhu Rouze, 491–92

"Poem on a Parrot" (Ma), 367

"Poem Utilizing the Same Rhyme as the One Used in Concubine Ban's 'Resentment,'" 149

"Poems in the Ancient Style from the Year *gengshen*" (Li), 670

Poems of Foliage Hall (Wang), 369

"Poems Written in Response to the Spirit of the Planchette" (Jiang), 591–92

poems written on walls, 518–20

poetic genres: and Buddhist nuns, 321, 328, 329, 333; imitation in, 351; "lamenting the past" (*huaigu*), 628–29. *See also* lyrics (*ci*); feminine poetic style; *shi* poems

poetry clubs, 453, 568, 571, 589. *See also* Banana Garden Poetry Club

Poets and Murder (Gulik), 193

Polo, Marco, 343

Pomegranate Blossom Dream (Li), 719

"Pomegranate Flower" (tune), 340

"Poorly-Fated Girl" (melody), 474

Postface to Anecdotes from Gantang (Cai), 334

"Postscript to a Letter; Sent to a Traveling Man" (Bao), 50

"Potted Plum Trees" (Gu), 636

"Powdered Butterflies" (tune), 338, 412

Precepts for My Daughters (Ban), 19, 26, 33–34, 36–42, 201; Ma Rong's praise for, 27, 42; and other moral tracts, 13, 57, 307, 308, 309, 310; Zheng Yunduan's poem on, 274

Precious Mirror of Ranked Flowers (Chen), 759

Precious Scroll of Incense Mountain, 718

Precious Scroll on Lady Huang, 718

precious scrolls (*baojuan*), 718

pregnancy, 59–60, 557–61

"Pride of the Fisherman" (melody), 233, 237

printing, 5, 6, 198, 201, 292, 348–49

prosimetrical ballads, 7, 577, 717–18. *See also* plucking rhymes

Pu Songling, 703, 706, 709

public women, 15–16, 174, 572. *See also* courtesan poets

publishers and publishing, 7, 203, 349

Pure Land Buddhism, 314, 578, 581–85, 586, 588

purity, 97, 167, 364, 580; of women writers, 351, 352, 354

"Purposely Written as a 'Rebuttal of Ridicule' After Having Been Criticized for Hiring a Teacher to Instruct My Daughters" (Gu), 418–19

Qi, Lady, 82–85

Qi, state of, 380

Qi Biaojia, 426

Qi Chongli, 215–16

Qian Fenglun, 471, 472, 478–86, 486; letters of, 482–83, 484–86; lyrics of, 479–82, 483–84

Qian Meibo, 701–2

Qian Qianyi, 390–91, 406, 452, 513, 576; on Chan Buddhism, 456–57; and Liu Shi, 375–76, 513–14; on Shen Yixiu, 384, 389. *See also Collected Poems of the Successive Reigns*

Qian Shurong (*The Golden Fish Affinity*), 756–57

Qian Yi, 501–4

Qian Youkun, 484

Qiannü, 511

Qiantang River (Hangzhou) Bore, 490–91, 493

Qiao, Concubine, 329

Qiaoying (Wu). See *Fake Image, The*

Qin, kingdom of, 628, 686, 775

Qin Guan, 237, 570n

Qin Jia, 132–33, 135, 720

Qin Kui, 379, 653

Qin Liangyu, 653, 783

qing, cult of, 349–50, 352, 353

Qing dynasty, 18, 238, 699, 767,
    807; anti-Manchu sentiment in,
    762–63; censorship in, 567;
    Manchu dress code in, 679–80;
    poetry revolution of, 783;
    women writers in, 8, 347, 425,
    626

Qinglou ji (Xia). See *Houses of Pleas-
    ure*

Qingshi (Feng). See *History of Passion*

Qingshihui (Xu). See *Compendium of
    Qing Poetry*

Qionglou yingao (Tao). See *Draft
    Chants of the Lovely Tower*

Qiu Jin, 770–808; arrest and be-
    heading of, 767, 802–7; biogra-
    phy of, 806–7; early poems of,
    770–73; on footbinding, 780,
    781, 782, 789–91; on marriage,
    770, 780–81, 793; nationalist
    martyr, 8; "Song of the Precious
    Sword," 773–75, 783; songs and
    poems of, 776–77, 778, 783–86,
    799–802; and cross-dressing,
    776, 780, 795; *Stones of the Jingwei
    Bird,* 786–94; as student and
    feminist in Japan, 779–94, 806;
    as teacher and revolutionary,
    794–802; "To My Sisters," 796–
    99

Qiu Xinru, 754–55

Qu Yuan (poet), 45, 502, 777; in
    drama of Wu Zao, 686–87, 691,
    692; "Encountering Sorrow,"
    686, 687, 697, 698

Qu Yuan (sage), 23, 25, 214, 428n,
    661

Quan Song shi. See *Complete Poems of
    the Song Dynasty*

Quan Tang shi. See *Complete Poems of
    the Tang Dynasty*

Quan Yuan sanqu. See *Complete Arias
    of the Yuan Dynasty*

Quanshan shu (Xu). See *Exhortations*

"Queen Mother of the West," 393,
    414, 573

"Questions to Heaven" (Qu), 686–
    87

"Quiet Night Thoughts" (Xi), 611–
    12

Qinlou yigao (Zhang). See *Remaining
    Drafts of Zither Tower*

Quting yong (Zhang). See *Chants of
    Rushing through the Courtyard*

"rags to riches" myth, 198

Rain of Heavenly Flowers, A (Tao),
    719–29; father-daughter relation-
    ship in, 720, 725–29; historical
    villains in, 723, 724, 725; preface
    to, 719–20, 724; summary of,
    721–24

"Rain on the First Day of the
    Fourth Month" (Jing), 365

Rankin, Mary Backus, 780

Ranking of Poets (Zhong), 49, 134

*Rarest Sutra of Great Merit Spoken by
    the Buddha . . .,* 314–19

"Reading" (Tao), 580

rebirth, 564, 565

"Record of a Dream" (Gu), 644

"Record of a Dream" (Wang), 623

"Record of a Dream" (Zhang),
    667–68

"Record of a Dream" (Zheng), 275–76

"Record of a Night at the Banana Window" (Ye), 392–94

"Record of a Visit to a Garden in Bloom, Four Poems" (Qiu), 771–72

Record of Mind Illumination, 332

"Record of the Lake Fen Stones, A" (Ye), 394–96

"Records of Dreams . . ." (Luo), 616–17

Records of Rumors (Niu), 168

Records of the Assembled Immortals of Yongcheng (Du), 163

Records of the Historian (Sima), 20–21, 83, 84, 108, 112

Records of the Northern Ward (Sun), 175

Recreated Heaven (Hou), 734, 753–54

"Red Embroidered Slippers" (tune), 339, 413

"Red Pine, Master," 47, 48

"Reduplications, Extended" (melody), 227

"Regret over the Parted Hairclasp" (melody), 645–46

Regulations for Women, 308

"Rejoicing That My Husband Has Finally Returned" (Xi), 596

religious life, 320, 564. *See also* Buddhist nuns; Chan (Zen) Buddhist nuns; Daoist nuns

religious literature, 323. *See also* Buddhist sutras

Remaining Drafts of Zither Tower (Zhang), 430–31

"Remembering an Absent Husband" (Gu), 473

"Remembering My Husband" (Gu), 419

"Remembering the Beauty of Qin" (melody), 387–88

"Remembering the Flute-Player on Phoenix Terrace" (melody), 225–26, 535–36

"Remembering the Prince" (melody), 387

"Remembering the South" (melody), 694

Ren Zhaolin, 571, 589

"Rendezvous, The" (Zhang), 337

Renzong, Emperor, 307

"Resentment against My Prince" (melody), 230

"Resentment against the Plum" (Wang), 370

resentment, 77–78, 114, 124

"Resentment" (Wang), 93–94

"Resting at White Cloud Cloister after Climbing. . ." (Luo), 616

Restoration Collection (Gao, ed.), 180

"Returning to Our Old House in West Village" (Li), 672–73

Reverential Harmony (Zheng), 269–74

revolutionaries, 780, 796, 801. *See also specific rebellion*

rhapsodies *(fu),* 9, 22, 43. *See also specific rhapsody*

Rhapsody of the Long Gate [Palace] (Sima), 76, 104

Rhapsody of the Questioning of Shadow by Penumbra (Niu), 168–73

Rhapsody on a Journey to the East (Ban), 22, 23–26

Rhapsody on a Water Bubble (Zuo), 48

Rhapsody on Feelings of Separation (Zuo), 44–46

Rhapsody on Pine and Cypress (Zuo), 47–48

Rhapsody on the Apparition of Empress Zhen (Cao), 91

Rhapsody on the Goddess of the Luo (Cao), 90, 91

Rhapsody on the Ostriches (Ban), 27–28

Rhapsody on the Two Capitals (Ban), 22–23

Rhapsody on the Two Capitals (Liang), 359

Rhapsody on the East of My Residence (Plum), 104–5

"Rising at Dawn" (Mao), 493–94

"Rising Early, an Impromptu Poem" (Gu), 420

"Rising Early One Morning . . . An Experience of Enlightenment" (Ye), 400

Rites, 11, 37, 38, 39, 114, 174; commentary on, 204; on separation of sexes, 14

ritual behavior, 201

"River Town Plum Blossoms Intro" (melody), 643, 699–700

"River's Water" (tune), 689

"Rivers and Mountains Like This" (Qiu), 785–86

Rolland, Madame (Jeanne-Manon Philipon), 779

Romance of the Three Kingdoms, The (Luo), 86

"Romantic Lover" (melody), 696–97

romantic tales, 265, 348–49. *See also* love stories

Ruan Ji, 179

Ruizong, Emperor, 64, 67, 161

Rulin waishi (Wu). See *Scholars, The*

Russo-Japanese War (1904–1905), 794

Rustic Greybeard's Idle Words, A, 721

sadness in poems, 114, 228. *See also* sorrow, in poetry

"Sands of Washing Brook Expanded" (melody), 487

"Sands of Washing Brook" (melody), 397, 474, 522, 646, 698, 701

Sanguo yanyi (Luo). See *Romance of the Three Kingdoms, The*

Sanguo zhi. See *History of the Three Kingdoms*

Sanhua yin (Jing). See *Flower-Scattering Chants*

Sansheng zhuan yucanji (Ma). See *Tale of Three Lives, A*

"Saying Goodbye to Li Jilan" (Zhu), 178

Scattered Records of Xi and Qing (Shi), 520–21, 522, 529, 536, 538, 540, 542

"Scenes from a Journey by Boat, Two Poems" (Liang), 421

Schipper, Kristofer, 163

Scholars, The (Wu), 567, 569–70

"Scroll-Painting of Qiu Hu Trying to Seduce His Own Wife" (Zheng), 272–73

"Second" (tune), 342

"secret games" poems, 362

"Seeing Off Gu Qiji (and Her Husband) on Her Journey to Peking" (Qian), 482

"Seeing Off Lady Fang on Her Return to the West" (Xu), 435–36

"Seeing Off My Younger Brother Youkun on His Journey to Peking" (Qian), 484

"Seeing Off Spring" (Zhu), 254

"Seeing Off the Two Sisters . . ." (Qiu), 785

Selections of Poems by Famous Ladies (Zhong, ed.), 350, 354

Selections of Refined Literature (anthology), 23, 90

Selections of Thirty Poets of the Ming (Wang, ed.), 621, 622, 623, 624, 626

self-censorship, 164–65, 354–55

"Self-Description at Fifty" (Shang), 428–29

"Self-Reproach, Two Poems" (Zhu), 256

"Selling Wilted Peonies" (Yu), 194–95

"Sending a Letter" (Liu), 378

"Sending Off My Younger Sister Qiongzhang upon Her Departure from Home to be Married" (Ye), 408–9

"Sending off Spring" (Gu), 639

Sengyou (monk), 156–58

sensuality, 176, 179

"Sent to a Traveling Man" (Bao), 51

"Sent to My Elder Dharma Sister Yigong" (Yikui), 462

"Sent to My Husband: Painted Bamboo" (Guan), 284

"Sent to My Husband" (Gu), 473–74

"Sent to My Husband" (Huang), 289

"Sent to My Loved One" (suite of arias), 337–43; authorship of, 344; forced marriage in, 337–38, 339

"Sent to Someone Far Away" (Wen), 335

"Sent to Younger Lady Yao" (Li), 675

"Sent to Zhu Fang" (Li), 178

"Setting Sail at Dawn on the Yangzi" (Liang), 422

"Settling Stormy Waves" (melody), 644

Seven Sages of the Bamboo Grove, 141, 179, 382n

sexual assault, 273

sexual identity, 678, 756. *See also* cross-dressing heroines; gender-switching; homoerotic desire; Lou Cheng; Qiu Jin

sexual relations, 362, 648

sexual symbolism, 167–68, 175, 179, 180

Shadow and Penumbra dialogues, 168–73

Shadow Dream of the Red Chamber (Gu), 647–52, 715–16; poetry in, 650–52

Shadows of Books (Zhou), 352

Shamanka Mountain, goddess of, 178–79, 180, 250n, 502

shame, 273, 582, 630

Shang Jinglan, 425, 426–31, 493; children of, 426, 429; and Huang Yuanjie, 453, 454; poetry of, 426–29

Shangguan Wan'er, 60, 61, 63–72; biography of, 71–72; and Empress Wu, 60, 63, 64–65; as judge in poetry competition, 65–66; poetry of, 68–70

Shannü zhuan (Peng). See *Biographies of Pious Women*

Shanshui xiaodu (Huangfu). See *Minor Writings from Shanshui*

Shen Deqian, 475, 622

Shen Hui, 259, 263

Shen Quan, 262, 263

Shen Junyong, 390–91

Shen Quanqi, 66

Shen Shanbao, 626, 650, 701

Shen Yixiu, 383–89, 391; "A Biography of My Youngest Daughter Qiongzhang," 400–406; poems of, 385–89

Shen Yixiu, daughters of. *See* Ye Wanwan; Ye Xiaoluan; Ye Xiaowan

Shen Yue, 110, 146

Shen Yunying, 653–56, 783

Shen Zhixu, 653, 654

Shen Zizheng, 411

Shenzhou nübao. See *Divine Land Women's Magazine*

Shi Boren, 269, 280

Shi Chong, 119–20

shi poems, 6, 43, 61, 134, 369, 576; of Concubine Ban, 77–78; emotion in, 51, 275, 397; of Gu Chun (Taiqing), 630–31; of Han Lanying, 49, 50–52; of Huang E, 288, 290; of Li Qingzhao, 205, 217, 240, 241–42; and lyrics compared, 199, 234–35, 236; of Xiaoqing, 509; of Xu Can,

434–36; of Ye Xiaoluan, 391–92; of Zhu Shuzhen, 244–45, 248–53, 256

Shi Zhenlin, 520–21, 537–38, 540

Shigui shu (Zhang, ed.). See *Stone Chest Writings*

Shiji (Sima). See *Records of the Historian*

Shijing. See *Book of Odes*

Shijun zhi (Yu). See *Description of the Ten Commanderies*

Shipin (Zhong). See *Ranking of Poets*

Shishuo xinyu (Liu, ed.). See *New Account of Tales of the World, A*

"Shouting Fire" (melody), 636–37, 696

"Shrine of the Loyal and Dignified Prince Yu" (Liu), 380–81

"Shrine of the Martial and Revered Prince Yue" (Liu), 380

Shuang Jian ("Sent to My Loved One"), 337, 338, 339, 341, 345

Shuangqing, 500, 502, 520–41, 569; lyrics of, 522–24, 526–29, 533–36, 538–40; malaria of, 525–26, 529, 534, 537; nine quatrains of, 529–31

Shujing. See *Book of Documents*

Shusun Tong, 674

Shuyi (Sima). See *Family Rituals*

Shuying (Zhou). See *Shadows of Books*

Siku quanshu zongmu tiyao. See *Basic Facts on All the Titles in the Complete Books of the Four Treasuries*

Sima Guang, 334–35, 336; *Family Rituals*, 201–2

Sima Qian: *Records of the Historian,* 20–21, 83, 84, 108–10, 112

Sima Xiangu, 76, 108–10, 135, 488

"Since We Are Going to . . ." (Xi), 597–98

Sino-Japanese War (1894–1895), 769, 777

"Sitting Alone, Two Poems" (Liu), 377

"Sitting Idly; An Impromptu Song" (Zhang), 267

"Sitting in Meditation during the Daytime" (Zhang), 668

Six Inscriptions on Paintings (Zhang), 267

Sixin Wuxin, 329–31

"Sleeping Alone during the Hottest Month" (Zhu), 250

"Sleepless Due to a Cold" (Yikui), 462–63

"Snapping Off a Sprig of Cassia" (tune), 689

"Snow" (Mao), 495

"Soaked Gauze Gown" (melody), 523

social consciousness, 251

social criticism, 276, 629

social Darwinism, 769

social satire, 704

social status, 198, 200, 276–77. *See also* elite families

Song, lady, 43, 52, 53–55, 60, 128

Song dynasty (420–478), 49; political chaos at end of, 155;

Song dynasty (960–1278), 94, 101, 185, 253, 293, 379; conquest of, 205–6; defeat of Shu by, 295–96; examinations in, 198; footbinding in, 201; imperial family in, 281; remarriage in, 217; Southern, 242, 247, 761–62; women's poetry in, 199; writing nuns of, 320, 323, 329, 456. *See also* Southern Song dynasty

Song Lian, 623, 624–25

Song Lyrics of the Inept Administrator's Garden, First Collection (Xu), 431, 432

"Song of a Landscape Painting on a Folding Screen" (Zheng), 271–72

"Song of a Merchant's Wife" (Xi), 596

"Song of China Expelling Its Demons" (Qiu), 800

Song of Lasting Regret (Bai), 389, 405, 406

"Song of Meeting of Metal Wind and Jade Dew" (melody), 641

"Song of Mulan," 679

"Song of People of Yao" (tune), 341

"Song of Sending Winter Clothes, A" (Xi), 596

"Song of the Large Mirror" (Luo), 619–20

"Song of the Old Tree . . ." (Xi), 607–8

"Song of the Precious Sword" (Qiu), 773–75, 783

"Song of the Red-Haired Barbarian's Sword" (Qiu), 783–84

"Song of Wang Mingjun, The" (Shi), 120–21

"Song of Watching the Bore on Hangzhou's Qiantang River, A," 491

Song Ruoxin, 55, 56, 57

Song Ruozhao, 55, 56–57, 168

Song sisters, 43, 55–57, 60, 182

Song Tingfen (father), 55, 56

Song Yu, 502, 687

Song Yuan, 265

Song Zhiwen, 66

Songgu hexiang ji. See *Harmonious Echoes Collection of Poems about Ancient [Cases], The*

"Songs for the Zither" (Guo), 121

"Songs of a Broken Heart" (Xi), 603–7

Songs of Lament by the Northern Window (Cheng), 760

"Songs of Resentment" (Jing), 365

Songs of the South (Qu), 391, 404, 417, 502n, 686, 697, 698n

"Songs Sent to an Absent Husband" (Zhu), 489–90

Songshu. See *Books of the Song*

sons: mother's admonition to, 23, 25–26, 357, 475–76, 485–86; of palace ladies, 73, 74; poems on illness and death of, 599–601, 603–7, 632

sorrow, in poetry, 44–46, 76, 123–24, 125, 239–40; Cao Zhi on, 406–7; mourning/grieving, 65, 632–34, 676; Wu Zao on, 695–99

"Sorrowfully Leaning on the Balustrade" (melody), 483–84

"Sound Reduplications" (melody), 377

"Southern Song" (melody), 483

Southern Song dynasty (1127–1278), 242, 247, 761–62

spirit messages, 388–89, 400, 588, 591–92

spirit possession, 166–68

"Spring Day" (Gu), 637–38

"Spring Day, A: Living in Seclusion" (Tao), 579

"Spring Day, A" (Huang), 290

"Spring Descends from Heaven" (melody), 538–40

"Spring in the Imperial Park" (tune), 705

"Spring Lament (In Imitation of the Style of Zhu Huiweng)" (Wang), 450

"Spring Night Moon" (Xi), 611

"Spring of the Year *yisi* (1629): Weeping at the Grave of My Aunt . . ." (Ye), 391

"Spring Outing" (Gu), 474

"Spring Outing" (Qian), 480

"Spring Prospects, Four Songs" (Xue), 185–86

"Springtime in Wuling" (melody), 224, 228, 240

"Springtime Window" (Huang), 455

Stone Chest Writings (Zhang, ed.), 441

Stones of the Jingwei Bird (Qiu), 786–94; critique of footbinding in, 789–91; critique of officials in, 786, 787–88; on oppression of women, 788–89, 791–92, 793

"Stopping for the Night at a Mountain Inn and Listening to the Rain" (Li), 669

Stories of the Strange from Make-do Studio (Pu), 703, 706, 709

Su Hui, 127–31

Su Shi, 127, 199, 204, 234, 286n, 570

Su Xiaoqing ("Sent to My Loved One"), 336, 337–43, 345

Su Xiaoxiao, 360, 362

Su Yingxue/Liang Suhua, 740–43

Su Zhecong, 239, 334

subordination of women, 13, 38, 131

suffering: and Buddhist thought, 326–27; in

"Suffering from the Rain" (Huang), 455

suffering young poets, 566, 569; anonymous poems of, 518–20; Du Liniang, 500–504; He Guizhi, 515–18. *See also* Shuangqing; Xiaoqing

Sui dynasty, 55, 95

suicide, 33, 56, 67, 79, 94, 208n, 273, 368, 680, 727–29, 779; of Lady Hou, 95, 96, 98; of Lady Yang, 406n; of Liu Shi, 355, 376; of Ming loyalists, 426; of Wu Zixu, 361; of Xiao Guanyin, 300, 303

Suiyuan shihua (Yuan). See *Notes on Poetry from the Sui Garden*

Suiyuan shihua buyi (Yuan). See *Addenda to the Sui Garden Poetry Talks*

Summary of the Poems of the Most Famous Masters of the Whole World (Deng), 492

"Summer Lament" (Wang), 450–51

"Summer Night, For My Husband" (Xi), 608

Sun, lady, of Lechang, 164–65, 202

Sun Deying, 756–59

Sun En rebellion (399), 143

Sun Hao *(Linked Rings of Jade),* 731, 732–33

Sun Qi, 175

Sun Yuanxiang, 594, 607, 608, 610, 611

sutras. *See* Buddhist sutras

Suyong ji (Zheng). See *Reverential Harmony*

"Swallows Separated from Their Nest" (Xue), 187

"Sweeping the Graves on a Spring Day" (Shang), 427

Sword of Vengeance (Liu), 706–9

"Swordsmanship" (Liu), 381–82

"Sworn Sisters Song of the Twelve Months of the Year" (Wu), 545

Taiching Emperor, 723

Taiping, Princess, 67

Taiping guangji. See *Comprehensive Records of the Reign Period Great Peace*

Taiping rebellion (1843–1863), 575, 650, 652, 758, 768–69

Taiping yulan. See *Imperial Reading Matter of the Great Peace Reign Period*

Taishang dongshen Taingong xiaomo huguo jing (anonymous). See *Classic of the Grotto-God*

Taizong, Emperor, 61–62, 296, 297

Taizu, Emperor, 295, 296–97

Tale of Three Lives, A (Ma), 367

Tale of Yingying (Yuan), 188

Talented Scholar's Peony Pavilion, The, 504

Tales of the World about Women (Yan), 627

Tan Xun, 721–25, 730–33, 735–39

Tan Zhengbi, 721–25, 730–33, 735–39

Tang Ao *(Flowers in the Mirror),* 573

Tang dynasty, 42, 55–58, 61, 332; Buddhist nuns in, 153, 158; Chan Buddhism in, 320–21, 322; concubine/courtesan poets of, 100, 101, 174–76, 198, 365; Daoist convents in, 160–61; elite women of, 15–16, 163–65; music in, 179, 235; poetry of, 23, 158, 189, 199, 217, 295

Tang Xianzu, 349, 414, 500–504, 591

Tao Qian, 226n, 579

Tao Shan, 578–88, 591; biography of, 585–87; *Chants of Shame and Remorse*, 582–83, 586; and Peng Xiluo, 581, 584, 585; and Pure Land Buddhism, 578, 581–83, 584–85, 586, 588; and sister Ren, 578, 580–81

Tao Zhenhuai: as pseudonym, 720–21; *A Rain of Heavenly Flowers*, 719–29

"Tea-Picking Song" (melody), 290–91

"Telling My Story" (Wang), 447–48

"Ten Months of Pregnancy, The" (Zhou, ed.), 558–61

"Ten Pecks of Pearls" (Plum), 106

Teng Chuanyin, 166–67

"Thanks for a Gift of Wine" (Sun), 165

"Thinking Fondly of My Sister-in-Law Chai Jixian . . ." (Qian), 481–82

"Thinking of My Son in Jiangxi Province" (Chai), 476

"Thinking of My Younger Sister" (Zheng), 270–71

"Third Daughter Wang," 561

"Third Day Letter to Her Daughter, A . . ." (Yi), 550

"Third Day Letters," 548

"Third Precoda, The" (tune), 342

"Thoughts on Reading the 'Biography of Ban Zhao'" (Zhang), 657–58

Tian Qilang *(Kept Promises),* 703

Tianfeng yin (Liu). See *Guided by Heaven's Storm*

Tianxia mingjia shiguan (Deng). See *Summary of the Poems of the Most Famous Masters of the Whole World*

Tianyuhua (Tao). See *Rain of Heavenly Flowers, A*

Tingqiuxuan gao. See *Manuscripts from the Listening to Autumn Study*

Tingxun (Zhuo). See *Instructions for my Sons*

"Tipsy in the Shade of Flowers" (melody), 231

"To My Chan Companion Dongyun" (Yikui), 464

"To My Sisters" (Qiu), 796–99

"To My Son Zhao" (Qian), 485–86

Together with Autumn Poetry (Xuan), 449–50

"Tomb of General Wang, The" (Zhang), 257

Tong Zilin, 526, 529

Tongqiu shixuan (Xuan). See *Together with Autumn Poetry*

"Tossing over Fragrance" (melody), 590–91

"Traveler Came from a Distant Land, A," 51

"Traveling at Dawn and Watching the Sunrise" (Xi), 598–99

"Traveling on the River" (Yu), 189

"Traveling, Three Poems" (Li), 673–74

"Treasuring Autumn Flowers" (melody), 634

Treatise on Military Preparedness (Mao), 371

Trifling Words from the Northern Marshlands (Sun), 164

"Trip by Steamboat, Two Poems, A" (Qiu), 778–79

"Trying Out My Walking Staff after Recovering from an Illness" (Zheng), 277–78

"Twelfth Month, The" (tune), 341

"Two Poems Written in Reply to My Husband" (Liu), 150

"Tying Up My Skirt" (melody), 223

United Primes (Liang), 362

"Untitled" (Gu), 419

"Upright and Loyal Lady Jin, The" (Wang), 443–44

Utter Loyalty (Zhou), 761–63

Various Notes on the Western Capital, 93, 110, 112

"Venting My Innermost Feelings" (melody), 233

"Victory Tune," 690

Vimalakirti, 588

virago (jealous wife), 566. *See also* jealousy

"Visit to the Lake on a Summer Day, A" (Zhu), 254

"Visiting Again a Spot I Had Visited Before . . ." (Qiu), 772–73

"Visiting Master Yuan Mei in His Garden" (Luo), 618–19

"Visiting the New Cloister at Dragon Well" (Liu), 378–79

"Voicing My Ambition" (Lin), 487

"Walking through the Sedge-Grass" (melody), 378, 388, 777

Waltner, Ann, 131

Wang, Empress, 62–63

Wang, General, 257

Wang, lady: aria suite of, 337–43

Wang, Smartass, 336, 344–45

Wang, "Ten-Percent," 344

Wang Anguo, 293, 295, 297

Wang Anshi, 199, 293

Wang Bogu (Zhiheng), 364–65, 366–67

Wang Ding, 301, 303

Wang Duan, 620–29, 694, 701; and Liang Desheng, 620, 621–23; marriage to Chen Peizhi, 620, 622, 628; poems of, 628–29; *Selections of Thirty Poets of the Ming*, 621, 623, 624, 626

Wang Duanshu, 425, 437–52, 453, 512–13; childhood of, 437–38; *Classic Poetry of Famous Women*, 439, 454; heroic biographies of, 440–44; lyrics of, 450–51; as Ming loyalist, 438, 440–45; poetry of, 444–52

Wang Fajin, 161–63

Wang family, 138

Wang Fazhi, 166–67

Wang Ganbo, 621–22

Wang Ji, 35n8, 108

Wang Jian, 292, 293, 295, 297, 299

Wang Jiaoniang and Feihong (Song), 265

Wang Kui, 367–68

Wang Mang, 20

Wang Menglin *(Dream of Splendor)*, 680–83

Wang Ningzhi, 138–39, 143

Wang Tangzuo, 246, 248

Wang Wei, 69, 71, 226n, 368–70, 371, 588

Wang Wencai *(Linked Rings of Jade)*, 731

Wang Wenzhi, 612, 613, 614

Wang Xianding, 437–38

Wang Xianzhi, 139, 550

Wang Xizhi, 138, 185, 186, 363n

Wang Yan, 170, 297

Wang Yangming, 349

Wang Yuanchang, 680

Wang Yun, 677, 680–83, 693

Wang Zhao, 258, 261–65

Wang Zhaojun, 91–95, 97, 510, 714; barbarian marriage of, 9, 94, 120, 247; impersonation of, 119–20; poems about, 149, 420, 423

Wang Zhaoyuan, 627

Wang Zhuo, 240–41

Wang Ziqiao, 141, 690

Wangliang wen ying fu (Niu). See *Rhapsody on the Questioning of Shadow by Penumbra*

Wanru Tongwei, 466

Wanyan Yun Zhu, 570, 626

Wanzhen *(A Rain of Heavenly Flowers)*, 727, 728–29, 733

warfare: women's poetry in, 114–15, 118; heroes of, 257, 379, 381–82; Li Changxia, 668–76; Ming loyalists, 440–45; Shen Yunying,

653–56; *Utter Loyalty,* 761–63; Zhang Chaixin, 652–56; Zhang Yin, 656–68. *See also* Taiping rebellion

"Watching Beauties Flying Kites" (Yang), 372–73

"Watching Children Play with a Noisemaker" (Gu), 645–46

"Watching the Bore" (Zhang), 493

"Watching the Clouds on a Summer Day" (Huang), 455

"Watching the Tide" (melody), 785

"Water Dragon's Chant, The" (melody), 481

Way, the, 537, 720. *See* Buddhism

Way of Five Pecks of Rice, 142, 143. *See also* Orthodox Unity Daoist church

"We Envy the People of Europe and America" (Qiu), 800–801

wedding laments, 542–43. *See also* marriage

"Weeping for My Brothers" (Qian), 479

"Weeping for My Daughters" (Shen), 388

"Weeping for My Sister Roujia" (Qian), 483–84

"Weeping for the Death of the Loyalist Wife Jin and Her Husband" (Wang), 444–45

"Weeping for Third Younger Sworn-Sister Xianpei" (Gu), 651–52

"Weeping over Student Shen" (Zhang), 258

Wei, Empress (ca. 100), 79

Wei, Empress (ca. 700), 15, 61, 65, 66, 67, 71, 72; coup d'etat by, 67,

72; and Emperor Xuanzong, 67,
107
Wei, Lady, 138, 185, 221–25, 244
Wei Cheng, 54, 128
Wei Duanli, 245–48, 257
Wei dynasty, 85–86
Wei Gao, 183, 184
Wei Hong, 53
Wei Huacun, 159–60, 161, 163
Wei Zhongxian, 724
Wei Zhuang, 189, 604n
Wen, Emperor, 85, 87, 95, 135. *See
also* Cao Pi
Wen Pu, 570
Wen Tingyun, 190, 199, 200, 218,
219, 350
Wen Wan, 334–36
Wenhui, crown prince, 155, 156
Wenxin diaolong. See *Literary
Mind and the Carving of Dragons,
The*
Wenxuan. See *Selections of Refined Lit-
erature*
*West Lake Collection of Poems about
Women* (Chen, ed.), 621
Western Han dynasty, 20, 21, 93,
110
"When My Woman Friend . . .
Came for a Visit, There Was
No Cooked Food" (Wang),
447
"White Blossom, The," 82n
"White Hair Lament" (Zhuo), 110–
13
"White Wax Candle" (Sun), 164–65
Widmer, Ellen, 514, 754
widows, 144; empress dowagers,
17–18, 32, 34–35; Gu Ruopu,
414–20, 471, 478

widows, remarriage of, 39, 113, 135–
36, 201, 562; Li Qingzhao, 214–
17, 240; and loyalty, 136n, 581
wife, lament of, 110–13. *See also*
abandoned women
wifely duties, 131, 306–10, 531, 572.
See also husband-wife relations;
marriage
wifely virtues, 101, 273, 283. *See also*
female virtue; loyalty
"Willow Floss" (Xue), 186
Willow of Zhangtai (courtesan),
506
"Willow, The" (Li), 177
"Wind Entering Pines" (melody),
476
"Winter Day: An Impromptu
Verse" (Tao), 580
"Winter Lament" (Wang), 451
"With a Brush Made of Goat's
Hair, I Write a Letter to You in
Your Noble Mansion" (Yi),
548–49
"With a Writing Brush, I Write
These Words on a Paper
Fan . . ." (Zhou), 549–50
women poets: hardships of, 612–13;
patrons of, 620–21; talent of, 614
women warriors, 565–66. *See also*
Mulan
Women's Learning (Zhang), 572
women's networks, 643, 734
women's rights song, 799
women's script: themes in, 543–65;
autobiography, 553–57; escaping
the female condition, 562–66;
female friendship, 544–47; loyal
wives, 561–63; marriage poems,
547–53; origins of, 543–44;

pregnancy and motherhood, 557–61; unfilial son, 560–61

"Woodpecker" (Zuo), 46–47

Words of Sorrow (Ye), 385, 406–9

Woyuexuan gao (Gu). See *Drafts from the Reclining in the Moonlight Studio*

"Writing Brush Separated from the Hand, The" (Xue), 186

"Written at Imperial Command . . . in the Unicorn Virtue Hall" (Song), 56–57

"Written at the End of *Phoenixes Flying Together,* for Yang Xiang-wan" (Chen), 761

"Written by Moonlight" (Wen), 336

"Written in a Besieged City" (Li), 670–71

"Written on a Summer Night" (Zhu), 250

"Written on the Occasion of My Departure . . ." (Qiu), 771

"Written to Comfort My Eldest Son Yongji . . ." (Chai), 475–76

"Written to the Rhymes of 'Sitting in Meditation Gathas': Five Poems" (Yikui), 463

"Written to the Rhymes of a Lyric . . . at the Clear Breeze Pavilion" (Gu), 631–32

Wu, Emperor, 20, 35, 76, 110, 146, 157

Wu Chengxiu *(Kept Promises),* 703, 704

Wu Dongyu, 545

Wu Jingzi, 567, 569–70, 571

Wu Lai *(Kept Promises),* 703

Wu Ren, 501

Wu Sansi, 66, 67, 71

Wu Weiye, 452, 629

Wu Yuanheng, 183, 184, 189

Wu Zaigong, 686

Wu Zao, 621, 677, 685–701; and Buddhism, 694; *The Fake Image,* 685–94; *Flower Screen Lyrics,* 694–95; and Qu Yuan, 686–87, 691; sorrow-filled lyrics of, 695–99

Wu Zetian, Empress Dowager (Wu Zhao), 15, 18, 71, 74, 753; in *Flowers in the Mirror,* 572–73, 575; and Su Hui's palindrome, 128, 130, 131. *See also* Wu Zhao, Empress

Wu Zhao, Empress (Wu Zetian), 60, 61–65. *See also* Wu Zetian, Empress Dowager

Wu Zhensheng, 504

Wu Zhiying, 795–96, 806–7

Wu Zixu, 361, 493

Wubeizhi (Mao). See *Treatise on Military Preparedness*

Wudi, Emperor, 48, 49

Wumengtang ji (Ye). See *Noon Dream Hall Collection*

Xi Kang, 141, 190, 382n, 430

Xi Peilan, 593–612, 618; "Admonishing My Younger Brothers," 594–95; poems to her husband, 596, 601–2, 608–11; poems to her son, 599–601, 603–7; "Songs of a Broken Heart," 603–7; traveling poems of, 596–99

Xi Shi, 361

Xia dynasty, 171

Xia Tingzhi, 337, 343–44

Xiang goddesses, 165

Xiang Jin, 729, 730

Xiang Sheng, 97

Xiang Yu, 83, 241–42, 256, 479, 776–77

Xiang'e *(The Jade Bracelet)*, 735, 736

Xiangnan Xuebei ci (Wu). See *Lyrics from South of Incense Mountain and North of Snowy Mountains*

Xiangshan baojuan. See *Precious Scroll of Incense Mountain*

Xiao, Concubine, 62–63

Xiao Guanyin, 300–304

Xiaoqing, 3, 499–500, 504–14, 621; illness and death of, 507–8; on *Peony Pavilion*, 501, 502, 510, 512, 694, 717; poetry of, 508–11; as suffering young poet, 566, 569

"Xiaoqing" (Wang), 512–13

Xiaowu, Emperor, 75

Xie An, 137, 138, 139–40, 563

Xie Daoyun, 137–44, 138, 145, 402, 478, 773; and Daoism, 142–43; and Lady Liu, 139–40; poetry of, 141–42, 144

Xie family, 138–41

Xie He, 140–41

Xie Huixin *(Linked Rings of Jade)*, 731–32

Xie Xucai *(The Fake Image)*, 686, 687

Xie Yuhui *(The Jade Bracelet)*, 735–37

Xijing zaji. See *Various Notes on the Western Capital*

Xiling guiyong ji (Chen, ed.). See *West Lake Collection of Poems about Women*

Ximen Qing *(Plum in the Golden Vase)*, 718

Xin Tang shu. See *New Books of the Tang*

Xionghu, 91–93, 113, 119, 120, 123

Xiqing sanji (Shi). See *Scattered Records of Xi and Qing*

Xu, Empress, 79, 293, 304–11; biography of, 305–7; Buddhist sutra of, 304, 310–11, 314–19; moral tracts by, 304, 307, 308–10

Xu Can, 425, 431–37, 471; biography of, 431–33; Manchurian exile of, 432, 435–37

Xu Fei, 150, 151

Xu Mian, 151

Xu Shichang, 656–57

Xu Shipu, 352–53

Xu Shu, 132–36, 137

Xu Wei, 364

Xu Xi, 209, 272

Xu Xilin, 801, 802, 807

Xu Yuqing, 368–69

Xu Zihua, 795

Xuan Huazi, 449–50

"Xuanwu Lake" (Wang), 629

Xuanzong, Emperor, 60, 67–68, 69, 72, 164n, 405n; concubines of, 100–104, 106, 107

Xue Baochai *(Dream of the Red Chamber)*, 499, 569

Xue Meiying *(The Jade Bracelet)*, 735, 736

Xue Tao, 16, 164, 175–76, 182–89, 360, 369; biography of, 183–84; calligraphy of, 184–85; poems of, 182, 184, 185–89; and Yuan Zhen, 188–89

Xuedou Chongxian, 326

Yama, King, 564–65

Yan Heng, 626

Yan Juchuan, 181–82

Yan Kejun, 135

Yang, Emperor, 95–96, 97, 100, 214

Yang, Empress, 46, 293, 298–300

Yang Guifei (Concubine Yang), 67, 100, 405n; rivalry with Concubine Plum, 103–4, 106, 107

"Yang Pass" songs, 226

Yang Shen, 281, 287, 288, 289

Yang Wan, 370–74

Yang Weizhen, 202, 280

Yang Xi, 143, 159, 160

Yang Yuhuan, 100–101. *See also* Yang Guifei

Yantou Quanho, 326, 327

Yao, Emperor, 35, 306, 343

Yao Lingze (Roujia), 483–84

Ye, lady (Zhengjue), 333

Ye Qiongzhang. *See* Ye Xiaoluan

Ye Shaoyuan (Zongshao), 383–84, 385, 390, 400, 406–7; on daughter Xiaoluan, 391, 392, 394

Ye Wanwan, 383, 384, 385, 389, 406–9

Ye Xiaoluan (Qiongzhang), 383, 384, 389–406, 408–9, 499; death of, 385, 404, 405–6; enlightenment of, 399–400; lyrics and arias of, 396–99; on *Peony Pavilion,* 501; poetry of, 391–94, 403; precocious childhood of, 389–90, 401; "A Record of the Lake Fen Stones," 394–96; Shen Yixiu's biography of, 400–406

Ye Xiaowan (Huichou), 383, 384, 389, 409–14; plays of, 390, 411–14, 678

Ye Xie, 390, 410

Ye Ziqi, 260–61, 265

"Yellow Oriole" (tune), 290, 396

Yesou puyan. See Rustic Greybeard's Idle Words, A

Yi Nianhua, 544, 547, 548–49, 550–57

Yigong Chaoke (nun), 461–62, 466

Yihui, 630, 632, 633

Yijing. See Book of Changes

Yikui Chaochen (nun), 457–64, 466; autobiographical account, 457–59; dharma talk (sermon) of, 460–61; poems of, 461–64

Yin Xi, 163

Yingying zhuan (Yuan). *See Tale of Yingying*

Yinhong ji (Wang). *See Chantings of Red Collection*

Yizhen *(A Rain of Heavenly Flowers),* 723, 725–29

Yongcheng jixianlu (Du). *See Records of the Assembled Immortals of Yongcheng*

Yongle emperor, 305, 306, 307, 622, 623

You, King of Zhou dynasty, 80n, 82n

You *(Shadow Dream of the Red Chamber),* 648, 649–50

Youxuan ji (Wei, ed.). *See Mystery upon Mystery*

Yu, lady, 479–80

"Yu Garden" (Shang), 427

Yu Ji, 259–60

Yu Qian, 379

Yu Qiu, 58–59

Yu Shiji, 351–52

Yu Sulan, 513–14

Yu Tongzhi, 140

Yu Xuanji, 16, 189–95, 361, 362; as
    Daoist nun, 164, 175–76, 189–90,
    191; as murderess, 192–93; poems
    of, 191, 193–95
Yu Yue, 702–3
Yuan, Emperor, 120, 214
Yuan dynasty, 94, 300, 326, 625;
    chaos at end of, 270; classical
    tales of, 265; drama in, 337; po-
    etry of, 626
Yuan Mei, 576, 589, 618–20, 620;
    disciples of, 571–72, 749. *See also*
    Luo Qilan; Xi Peilan
Yuan Ming yishi (Duan). See *Anecdo-
    tal History of the Yuan and Ming*
Yuan Xi, 87–88
Yuan Zhen, 188–89
Yuandi, Emperor, 91, 92, 93, 94–95
Yuanwu Keqin, 326
Yuanyang meng (Ye). See *Mandarin
    Ducks' Dream*
Yuchuanyuan (Chen). See *Jade Brace-
    let, The*
Yue Fei, 379, 380–81, 653, 761–63
Yuefu shiji. See *Collection of Music Bu-
    reau Poems*
Yueguan shi (Wang). See *Poems of Fo-
    liage Hall*
Yuezhang ji (Liu). See *A Collection of
    Texts for Music*
Yulianhuan (Zhu). See *Linked Rings
    of Jade*
Yulin, Prince of Qi dynasty, 49, 50
Yunlin Zhuren, 638–39
Yuquanzi (anonymous). See *Master
    Jade Source*
Yutai xinyong (Zhen). See *New Songs
    from a Jade Terrace*
Yuzhen, Princess, 161

Zaishengyuan (Chen). See *Karmic
    Bonds of Reincarnation*
zaju drama, 364, 390, 411, 687
Zang Qinchen, 443
Zaozaotian (Hou). See *Recreated
    Heaven*
Zen. *See* Chan (Zen) Buddhism
Zeng Guofan, 768
Zeng Yu (Master Zeng), 60, 152n,
    612, 613, 614
Zhang, lady, 337
Zhang Chaixin, 652–56
Zhang Chayun, 429, 430–31
Zhang Dai, 438, 440–41
Zhang Hao, 471, 492–93, 627
Zhang Lingyi, 678
Zhang Mao, 262
Zhang Qian, 604
Zhang Qianqian, 390–91, 400
Zhang Qiongru, 423–24
Zhang Ruzhou, 215–16
Zhang Shicheng, 270, 621
Zhang Shifang, 565
Zhang Songyuan, 619
Zhang Xiang, 694
Zhang Xuan, 141
Zhang Xuecheng, 571–72
Zhang Yin, 656–68; "Ballad of a
    Soldier's Life," 663–65; "For My
    Daughter Quan," 658–62;
    "Leaving through the Passes,"
    666–67; life of, 656–57; "Record
    of a Dream," 667–68
Zhang Yue, 72
Zhang Yuniang, 244, 257–69; biog-
    raphy of, 258, 261–65; critics of,
    259–61; fiancé of (student Shen),
    258, 259, 260, 262, 263–64, 266;
    and Meng Chengsun, 265–67;

poetry of, 267–69

Zhang Zhao, 680

Zhao, Prince of, 83–84, 85

Zhao Chang, 84

Zhao Feiyan, 77, 79, 148

Zhao Juntai, 518

Zhao Mengfu, 281–84, 285–87

Zhao Mingcheng, 204–5, 206, 208–12, 231–32

Zhao Qingxi, 694–95

Zhao sisters, 79–80

Zhao Tingzhi, 204

Zhao Weiyi, 300

Zhao Yangtai, 129, 131

Zhao Yuanyi, 181

"Zhaojun's Resentment" (Xu), 434

Zhaoming crown prince, 146

Zhaozhou, 320–21, 328n

Zhen, Empress, 85, 86–91, 135; biography of, 86–87; legend of, 90–91

Zheng, lady, 58–60

Zheng Danruo, 734–35, 761

Zheng Feng, 166, 167

Zheng Guotai, 723, 725, 726

Zheng Yunduan, 244, 269–80; moralistic poetry of, 270–74, 276, 277–78; poem on marriage, 276–77; poems on immortals, 275–76; poems on paintings, 271–72; *shi* poems of, 270–80

Zhengjue (lady Ye), 333

Zhenru (nun), 329

Zhisheng (nun), 155–56

Zhiyuan Xinggang, 457, 461

Zhong Rong, 49, 50, 51, 134

Zhong Xing, 350–52

Zhongguo nübao. See *China Women's Journal*

Zhonglü mode, 338, 412

Zhongxing jianqi ji (Gao, ed.). See *Restoration Collection*

Zhongzong, Emperor, 64, 67, 72; and Shangguang Wan'er, 61, 65, 66, 71

Zhou, Duke of, 53

Zhou dynasty, 20, 35, 52, 64, 80

Zhou Lianggong, 352

Zhou Shuoyi, 549–50

Zhou Xiang, 362–63, 364

Zhou Yingfang, 761–63

Zhouguan. See *Offices of the Zhou*

Zhu, Master of Hui'an, 308

Zhu Ci rebellion (783), 181

Zhu Fang, 178

Zhu Fengrui, 756–57

Zhu Rouze, 489–92

Zhu Shuzhen, 201, 202, 244–56, 269; *A Broken Heart*, 244–51; lyrics of, 253–56; marriage of, 245–46, 247–48, 699; *shi* poems of, 244–45, 248–53; and Zheng Yunduan compared, 274, 280

Zhu Suxian, 729–33, 734

Zhu Xi, 200, 221, 349, 537

Zhu Yingtai, 199, 562–64, 565, 679

"Zhu Yingtai" (melody), 700–701

Zhu Yizun, 622

Zhu Yuanzhang, 621, 622, 623

Zhuang, King of Chu, 58, 59

Zhuang Zhou, 168–69, 170, 171, 173, 692n. *See also Master Zhuang*

Zhuangzi. See *Master Zhuang*

Zhuo Wangsun, 109–10

Zhuo Wenjun, 108, 109–12, 135

Zhuozhengyuan shiyu chukan (Xu). See
  *Song Lyrics of the Inept Administra-
  tor's Garden, First Collection*
Zi Lu, 23, 26
Zongshao. *See* Ye Shaoyuan
Zukui Jifu (nun), 326
Zuo Fen, 43–48, 49, 384

Zuo Weiming *(Rain of Heavenly
  Flowers)*, 721, 722–24, 725, 733
Zuo Yi, 721–22
Zuo zhuan. See *Commentary of Mr.
  Zuo*
Zutang ji. See *Collection from the Halls
  of the Founders*

Harvard East Asian Monographs
(* out-of-print)

*1. Liang Fang-chung, *The Single-Whip Method of Taxation in China*

*2. Harold C. Hinton, *The Grain Tribute System of China, 1845-1911*

3. Ellsworth C. Carlson, *The Kaiping Mines, 1877-1912*

*4. Chao Kuo-chün, *Agrarian Policies of Mainland China: A Documentary Study, 1949-1956*

*5. Edgar Snow, *Random Notes on Red China, 1936-1945*

*6. Edwin George Beal, Jr., *The Origin of Likin, 1835-1864*

7. Chao Kuo-chün, *Economic Planning and Organization in Mainland China: A Documentary Study, 1949-1957*

*8. John K. Fairbank, *Ching Documents: An Introductory Syllabus*

*9. Helen Yin and Yi-chang Yin, *Economic Statistics of Mainland China, 1949-1957*

*10. Wolfgang Franke, *The Reform and Abolition of the Traditional Chinese Examination System*

11. Albert Feuerwerker and S. Cheng, *Chinese Communist Studies of Modern Chinese History*

12. C. John Stanley, *Late Ching Finance: Hu Kuang-yung as an Innovator*

13. S. M. Meng, *The Tsungli Yamen: Its Organization and Functions*

*14. Ssu-yü Teng, *Historiography of the Taiping Rebellion*

15. Chun-Jo Liu, *Controversies in Modern Chinese Intellectual History: An Analytic Bibliography of Periodical Articles, Mainly of the May Fourth and Post-May Fourth Era*

*16. Edward J. M. Rhoads, *The Chinese Red Army, 1927-1963: An Annotated Bibliography*

17. Andrew J. Nathan, *A History of the China International Famine Relief Commission*

*18. Frank H. H. King (ed.) and Prescott Clarke, *A Research Guide to China-Coast Newspapers, 1822-1911*

19. Ellis Joffe, *Party and Army: Professionalism and Political Control in the Chinese Officer Corps, 1949-1964*

*20. Toshio G. Tsukahira, *Feudal Control in Tokugawa Japan: The Sankin Kōtai System*

21. Kwang-Ching Liu, ed., *American Missionaries in China: Papers from Harvard Seminars*

22. George Moseley, *A Sino-Soviet Cultural Frontier: The Ili Kazakh Autonomous Chou*

23. Carl F. Nathan, *Plague Prevention and Politics in Manchuria, 1910-1931*

*24. Adrian Arthur Bennett, *John Fryer: The Introduction of Western Science and Technology into Nineteenth-Century China*

25. Donald J. Friedman, *The Road from Isolation: The Campaign of the American Committee for Non-Participation in Japanese Aggression, 1938-1941*

*26. Edward LeFevour, *Western Enterprise in Late Ching China: A Selective Survey of Jardine, Matheson and Company's Operations, 1842-1895*

27. Charles Neuhauser, *Third World Politics: China and the Afro-Asian People's Solidarity Organization, 1957-1967*

28. Kungtu C. Sun, assisted by Ralph W. Huenemann, *The Economic Development of Manchuria in the First Half of the Twentieth Century*

*29. Shahid Javed Burki, *A Study of Chinese Communes, 1965*

30. John Carter Vincent, *The Extraterritorial System in China: Final Phase*

31. Madeleine Chi, *China Diplomacy, 1914-1918*

*32. Clifton Jackson Phillips, *Protestant America and the Pagan World: The First Half Century of the American Board of Commissioners for Foreign Missions, 1810-1860*

33. James Pusey, *Wu Han: Attacking the Present Through the Past*

34. Ying-wan Cheng, *Postal Communication in China and Its Modernization, 1860-1896*

35. Tuvia Blumenthal, *Saving in Postwar Japan*

36. Peter Frost, *The Bakumatsu Currency Crisis*

37. Stephen C. Lockwood, *Augustine Heard and Company, 1858-1862*

38. Robert R. Campbell, *James Duncan Campbell: A Memoir by His Son*

39. Jerome Alan Cohen, ed., *The Dynamics of China's Foreign Relations*

40. V. V. Vishnyakova-Akimova, *Two Years in Revolutionary China, 1925-1927*, tr. Steven L. Levine

*41. Meron Medzini, *French Policy in Japan During the Closing Years of the Tokugawa Regime*

42. Ezra Vogel, Margie Sargent, Vivienne B. Shue, Thomas Jay Mathews, and Deborah S. Davis, *The Cultural Revolution in the Provinces*

*43. Sidney A. Forsythe, *An American Missionary Community in China, 1895-1905*

*44. Benjamin I. Schwartz, ed., *Reflections on the May Fourth Movement.: A Symposium*

*45. Ching Young Choe, *The Rule of the Taewŏngun, 1864-1873: Restoration in Yi Korea*

46. W. P. J. Hall, *A Bibliographical Guide to Japanese Research on the Chinese Economy, 1958-1970*

47. Jack J. Gerson, *Horatio Nelson Lay and Sino-British Relations, 1854-1864*

48. Paul Richard Bohr, *Famine and the Missionary: Timothy Richard as Relief Administrator and Advocate of National Reform*

49. Endymion Wilkinson, *The History of Imperial China: A Research Guide*

50. Britten Dean, *China and Great Britain: The Diplomacy of Commercial Relations, 1860-1864*

51. Ellsworth C. Carlson, *The Foochow Missionaries, 1847-1880*

52. Yeh-chien Wang, *An Estimate of the Land-Tax Collection in China, 1753 and 1908*

53. Richard M. Pfeffer, *Understanding Business Contracts in China, 1949-1963*

54. Han-sheng Chuan and Richard Kraus, *Mid-Ching Rice Markets and Trade: An Essay in Price History*

55. Ranbir Vohra, *Lao She and the Chinese Revolution*

56. Liang-lin Hsiao, *China's Foreign Trade Statistics, 1864-1949*

*57. Lee-hsia Hsu Ting, *Government Control of the Press in Modern China, 1900-1949*

58. Edward W. Wagner, *The Literati Purges: Political Conflict in Early Yi Korea*

*59. Joungwon A. Kim, *Divided Korea: The Politics of Development, 1945-1972*

*60. Noriko Kamachi, John K. Fairbank, and Chūzō Ichiko, *Japanese Studies of Modern China Since 1953: A Bibliographical Guide to Historical and Social-Science Research on the Nineteenth and Twentieth Centuries, Supplementary Volume for 1953-1969*

61. Donald A. Gibbs and Yun-chen Li, *A Bibliography of Studies and Translations of Modern Chinese Literature, 1918-1942*

62. Robert H. Silin, *Leadership and Values: The Organization of Large-Scale Taiwanese Enterprises*

63. David Pong, *A Critical Guide to the Kwangtung Provincial Archives Deposited at the Public Record Office of London*

*64. Fred W. Drake, *China Charts the World: Hsu Chi-yü and His Geography of 1848*

*65. William A. Brown and Urgrunge Onon, translators and annotators, *History of the Mongolian People's Republic*

66. Edward L. Farmer, *Early Ming Government: The Evolution of Dual Capitals*

*67. Ralph C. Croizier, *Koxinga and Chinese Nationalism: History, Myth, and the Hero*

*68. William J. Tyler, tr., *The Psychological World of Natsume Sōseki,* by Doi Takeo

69. Eric Widmer, *The Russian Ecclesiastical Mission in Peking During the Eighteenth Century*

*70. Charlton M. Lewis, *Prologue to the Chinese Revolution: The Transformation of Ideas and Institutions in Hunan Province, 1891-1907*

71. Preston Torbert, *The Ching Imperial Household Department: A Study of Its Organization and Principal Functions, 1662-1796*

72. Paul A. Cohen and John E. Schrecker, eds., *Reform in Nineteenth-Century China*

73. Jon Sigurdson, *Rural Industrialism in China*

74. Kang Chao, *The Development of Cotton Textile Production in China*

75. Valentin Rabe, *The Home Base of American China Missions, 1880-1920*

*76. Sarasin Viraphol, *Tribute and Profit: Sino-Siamese Trade, 1652-1853*

77. Ch'i-ch'ing Hsiao, *The Military Establishment of the Yuan Dynasty*

78. Meishi Tsai, *Contemporary Chinese Novels and Short Stories, 1949-1974: An Annotated Bibliography*

*79. Wellington K. K. Chan, *Merchants, Mandarins and Modern Enterprise in Late Ching China*

80. Endymion Wilkinson, *Landlord and Labor in Late Imperial China: Case Studies from Shandong by Jing Su and Luo Lun*

*81. Barry Keenan, *The Dewey Experiment in China: Educational Reform and Political Power in the Early Republic*

*82. George A. Hayden, *Crime and Punishment in Medieval Chinese Drama: Three Judge Pao Plays*

*83. Sang-Chul Suh, *Growth and Structural Changes in the Korean Economy, 1910-1940*

84. J. W. Dower, *Empire and Aftermath: Yoshida Shigeru and the Japanese Experience, 1878-1954*

85. Martin Collcutt, *Five Mountains: The Rinzai Zen Monastic Institution in Medieval Japan*

86. Kwang Suk Kim and Michael Roemer, *Growth and Structural Transformation*

87. Anne O. Krueger, *The Developmental Role of the Foreign Sector and Aid*

*88. Edwin S. Mills and Byung-Nak Song, *Urbanization and Urban Problems*

89. Sung Hwan Ban, Pal Yong Moon, and Dwight H. Perkins, *Rural Development*

*90. Noel F. McGinn, Donald R. Snodgrass, Yung Bong Kim, Shin-Bok Kim, and Quee-Young Kim, *Education and Development in Korea*

91. Leroy P. Jones and II SaKong, *Government, Business, and Entrepreneurship in Economic Development: The Korean Case*

92. Edward S. Mason, Dwight H. Perkins, Kwang Suk Kim, David C. Cole, Mahn Je Kim et al., *The Economic and Social Modernization of the Republic of Korea*

93. Robert Repetto, Tai Hwan Kwon, Son-Ung Kim, Dae Young Kim, John E. Sloboda, and Peter J. Donaldson, *Economic Development, Population Policy, and Demographic Transition in the Republic of Korea*

94. Parks M. Coble, Jr., *The Shanghai Capitalists and the Nationalist Government, 1927-1937*

95. Noriko Kamachi, *Reform in China: Huang Tsun-hsien and the Japanese Model*

96. Richard Wich, *Sino-Soviet Crisis Politics: A Study of Political Change and Communication*

97. Lillian M. Li, *China's Silk Trade: Traditional Industry in the Modern World, 1842-1937*

98. R. David Arkush, *Fei Xiaotong and Sociology in Revolutionary China*

*99. Kenneth Alan Grossberg, *Japan's Renaissance: The Politics of the Muromachi Bakufu*

100. James Reeve Pusey, *China and Charles Darwin*

101. Hoyt Cleveland Tillman, *Utilitarian Confucianism: Chen Liang's Challenge to Chu Hsi*

102. Thomas A. Stanley, *Ōsugi Sakae, Anarchist in Taishō Japan: The Creativity of the Ego*

103. Jonathan K. Ocko, *Bureaucratic Reform in Provincial China: Ting Jih-ch'ang in Restoration Kiangsu, 1867-1870*

104. James Reed, *The Missionary Mind and American East Asia Policy, 1911-1915*

105. Neil L. Waters, *Japan's Local Pragmatists: The Transition from Bakumatsu to Meiji in the Kawasaki Region*

106. David C. Cole and Yung Chul Park, *Financial Development in Korea, 1945-1978*

107. Roy Bahl, Chuk Kyo Kim, and Chong Kee Park, *Public Finances During the Korean Modernization Process*

108. William D. Wray, *Mitsubishi and the N.Y.K, 1870-1914: Business Strategy in the Japanese Shipping Industry*

109. Ralph William Huenemann, *The Dragon and the Iron Horse: The Economics of Railroads in China, 1876-1937*

110. Benjamin A. Elman, *From Philosophy to Philology: Intellectual and Social Aspects of Change in Late Imperial China*

111. Jane Kate Leonard, *Wei Yüan and China's Rediscovery of the Maritime World*

112. Luke S. K. Kwong, *A Mosaic of the Hundred Days:. Personalities, Politics, and Ideas of 1898*

113. John E. Wills, Jr., *Embassies and Illusions: Dutch and Portuguese Envoys to K'ang-hsi, 1666-1687*

114. Joshua A. Fogel, *Politics and Sinology: The Case of Naitō Konan (1866-1934)*

*115. Jeffrey C. Kinkley, ed., *After Mao: Chinese Literature and Society, 1978-1981*

116. C. Andrew Gerstle, *Circles of Fantasy: Convention in the Plays of Chikamatsu*

117. Andrew Gordon, *The Evolution of Labor Relations in Japan: Heavy Industry, 1853-1955*

*118. Daniel K. Gardner, *Chu Hsi and the "Ta Hsueh": Neo-Confucian Reflection on the Confucian Canon*

119. Christine Guth Kanda, *Shinzō: Hachiman Imagery and Its Development*

*120. Robert Borgen, *Sugawara no Michizane and the Early Heian Court*

121. Chang-tai Hung, *Going to the People: Chinese Intellectual and Folk Literature, 1918-1937*

*122. Michael A. Cusumano, *The Japanese Automobile Industry: Technology and Management at Nissan and Toyota*

123. Richard von Glahn, *The Country of Streams and Grottoes: Expansion, Settlement, and the Civilizing of the Sichuan Frontier in Song Times*

124. Steven D. Carter, *The Road to Komatsubara: A Classical Reading of the Renga Hyakuin*

125. Katherine F. Bruner, John K. Fairbank, and Richard T. Smith, *Entering China's Service: Robert Hart's Journals, 1854-1863*

126. Bob Tadashi Wakabayashi, *Anti-Foreignism and Western Learning in Early-Modern Japan: The "New Theses" of 1825*

127. Atsuko Hirai, *Individualism and Socialism: The Life and Thought of Kawai Eijirō (1891-1944)*

128. Ellen Widmer, *The Margins of Utopia: "Shui-hu hou-chuan" and the Literature of Ming Loyalism*

129. R. Kent Guy, *The Emperor's Four Treasuries: Scholars and the State in the Late Chien-lung Era*

130. Peter C. Perdue, *Exhausting the Earth: State and Peasant in Hunan, 1500-1850*

131. Susan Chan Egan, *A Latterday Confucian: Reminiscences of William Hung (1893-1980)*

132. James T. C. Liu, *China Turning Inward: Intellectual-Political Changes in the Early Twelfth Century*

133. Paul A. Cohen, *Between Tradition and Modernity: Wang T'ao and Reform in Late Ching China*

134. Kate Wildman Nakai, *Shogunal Politics: Arai Hakuseki and the Premises of Tokugawa Rule*

135. Parks M. Coble, *Facing Japan: Chinese Politics and Japanese Imperialism, 1931-1937*

136. Jon L. Saari, *Legacies of Childhood: Growing Up Chinese in a Time of Crisis, 1890-1920*

137. Susan Downing Videen, *Tales of Heichū*

138. Heinz Morioka and Miyoko Sasaki, *Rakugo: The Popular Narrative Art of Japan*

139. Joshua A. Fogel, *Nakae Ushikichi in China: The Mourning of Spirit*

140. Alexander Barton Woodside, *Vietnam and the Chinese Model.: A Comparative Study of Vietnamese and Chinese Government in the First Half of the Nineteenth Century*

141. George Elision, *Deus Destroyed: The Image of Christianity in Early Modern Japan*

142. William D. Wray, ed., *Managing Industrial Enterprise: Cases from Japan's Prewar Experience*

143. T'ung-tsu Ch'ü, *Local Government in China Under the Ching*

144. Marie Anchordoguy, *Computers, Inc.: Japan's Challenge to IBM*

145. Barbara Molony, *Technology and Investment: The Prewar Japanese Chemical Industry*

146. Mary Elizabeth Berry, *Hideyoshi*

147. Laura E. Hein, *Fueling Growth: The Energy Revolution and Economic Policy in Postwar Japan*

148. Wen-hsin Yeh, *The Alienated Academy: Culture and Politics in Republican China, 1919-1937*

149. Dru C. Gladney, *Muslim Chinese: Ethnic Nationalism in the People's Republic*

150. Merle Goldman and Paul A. Cohen, eds., *Ideas Across Cultures: Essays on Chinese Thought in Honor of Benjamin L Schwartz*

151. James M. Polachek, *The Inner Opium War*

152. Gail Lee Bernstein, *Japanese Marxist: A Portrait of Kawakami Hajime, 1879-1946*

153. Lloyd E. Eastman, *The Abortive Revolution: China Under Nationalist Rule, 1927-1937*

154. Mark Mason, *American Multinationals and Japan: The Political Economy of Japanese Capital Controls, 1899-1980*

155. Richard J. Smith, John K. Fairbank, and Katherine F. Bruner, *Robert Hart and China's Early Modernization: His Journals, 1863-1866*

156. George J. Tanabe, Jr., *Myōe the Dreamkeeper: Fantasy and Knowledge in Kamakura Buddhism*

157. William Wayne Farris, *Heavenly Warriors: The Evolution of Japan's Military, 500-1300*

158. Yu-ming Shaw, *An American Missionary in China: John Leighton Stuart and Chinese-American Relations*

159. James B. Palais, *Politics and Policy in Traditional Korea*

160. Douglas Reynolds, *China, 1898-1912: The Xinzheng Revolution and Japan*

161. Roger R. Thompson, *China's Local Councils in the Age of Constitutional Reform, 1898-1911*

162. William Johnston, *The Modern Epidemic: History of Tuberculosis in Japan*

163. Constantine Nomikos Vaporis, *Breaking Barriers: Travel and the State in Early Modern Japan*

164. Irmela Hijiya-Kirschnereit, *Rituals of Self-Revelation: Shishōsetsu as Literary Genre and Socio-Cultural Phenomenon*

165. James C. Baxter, *The Meiji Unification Through the Lens of Ishikawa Prefecture*

166. Thomas R. H. Havens, *Architects of Affluence: The Tsutsumi Family and the Seibu-Saison Enterprises in Twentieth-Century Japan*

167. Anthony Hood Chambers, *The Secret Window: Ideal Worlds in Tanizaki's Fiction*

168. Steven J. Ericson, *The Sound of the Whistle: Railroads and the State in Meiji Japan*

169. Andrew Edmund Goble, *Kenmu: Go-Daigo's Revolution*

170. Denise Potrzeba Lett, *In Pursuit of Status: The Making of South Korea's "New" Urban Middle Class*

171. Mimi Hall Yiengpruksawan, *Hiraizumi: Buddhist Art and Regional Politics in Twelfth-Century Japan*

172. Charles Shirō Inouye, *The Similitude of Blossoms: A Critical Biography of Izumi Kyōka (1873-1939), Japanese Novelist and Playwright*

173. Aviad E. Raz, *Riding the Black Ship: Japan and Tokyo Disneyland*

174. Deborah J. Milly, *Poverty, Equality, and Growth: The Politics of Economic Need in Postwar Japan*

175. See Heng Teow, *Japan's Cultural Policy Toward China, 1918-1931: A Comparative Perspective*

176. Michael A. Fuller, *An Introduction to Literary Chinese*

177. Frederick R. Dickinson, *War and National Reinvention: Japan in the Great War, 1914-1919*

178. John Solt, *Shredding the Tapestry of Meaning: The Poetry and Poetics of Kitasono Katue (1902-1978)*

179. Edward Pratt, *Japan's Protoindustrial Elite: The Economic Foundations of the Gōnō*

180. Atsuko Sakaki, *Recontextualizing Texts: Narrative Performance in Modern Japanese Fiction*

181. Soon-Won Park, *Colonial Industrialization and Labor in Korea: The Onoda Cement Factory*

182. JaHyun Kim Haboush and Martina Deuchler, *Culture and the State in Late Chosŏn Korea*

183. John W. Chaffee, *Branches of Heaven: A History of the Imperial Clan of Sung China*

184. Gi-Wook Shin and Michael Robinson, eds., *Colonial Modernity in Korea*

185. Nam-lin Hur, *Prayer and Play in Late Tokugawa Japan: Asakusa Sensōji and Edo Society*

186. Kristin Stapleton, *Civilizing Chengdu: Chinese Urban Reform, 1895-1937*

187. Hyung Il Pai, *Constructing "Korean" Origins: A Critical Review of Archaeology, Historiography, and Racial Myth in Korean State-Formation Theories*

188. Brian D. Ruppert, *Jewel in the Ashes: Buddha Relics and Power in Early Medieval Japan*

189. Susan Daruvala, *Zhou Zuoren and an Alternative Chinese Response to Modernity*

190. James Z. Lee, *The Political Economy of a Frontier: Southwest China, 1250-1850*

191. Kerry Smith, *A Time of Crisis: Japan, the Great Depression, and Rural Revitalization*

192. Michael Lewis, *Becoming Apart: National Power and Local Politics in Toyama, 1868-1945*

193. William C. Kirby, Man-houng Lin, James Chin Shih, and David A. Pietz, eds., *State and Economy in Republican China: A Handbook for Scholars*

194. Timothy S. George, *Minamata: Pollution and the Struggle for Democracy in Postwar Japan*

195. Billy K. L. So, *Prosperity, Region, and Institutions in Maritime China: The South Fukien Pattern, 946-1368*

196. Yoshihisa Tak Matsusaka, *The Making of Japanese Manchuria, 1904-1932*

197. Maram Epstein, *Competing Discourses: Orthodoxy, Authenticity, and Engendered Meanings in Late Imperial Chinese Fiction*

198. Curtis J. Milhaupt, J. Mark Ramseyer, and Michael K. Young, eds. and comps., *Japanese Law in Context: Readings in Society, the Economy, and Politics*

199. Haruo Iguchi, *Unfinished Business: Ayukawa Yoshisuke and U.S.-Japan Relations, 1937-1952*

200. Scott Pearce, Audrey Spiro, and Patricia Ebrey, *Culture and Power in the Reconstitution of the Chinese Realm, 200-600*

201. Terry Kawashima, *Writing Margins: The Textual Construction of Gender in Heian and Kamakura Japan*

202. Martin W. Huang, *Desire and Fictional Narrative in Late Imperial China*

203. Robert S. Ross and Jiang Changbin, eds., *Re-examining the Cold War: U.S.-China Diplomacy, 1954-1973*

204. Guanhua Wang, *In Search of Justice: The 1905-1906 Chinese Anti-American Boycott*

205. David Schaberg, *A Patterned Past: Form and Thought in Early Chinese Historiography*

206. Christine Yano, *Tears of Longing: Nostalgia and the Nation in Japanese Popular Song*

207. Milena Doleželová-Velingerová and Oldřich Král, with Graham Sanders, eds., *The Appropriation of Cultural Capital: China's May Fourth Project*

208. Robert N. Huey, *The Making of 'Shinkokinshū'*

209. Lee Butler, *Emperor and Aristocracy in Japan, 1467-1680: Resilience and Renewal*

210. Suzanne Ogden, *Inklings of Democracy in China*

211. Kenneth J. Ruoff, *The People's Emperor: Democracy and the Japanese Monarchy, 1945-1995*

212. Haun Saussy, *Great Walls of Discourse and Other Adventures in Cultural China*

213. Aviad E. Raz, *Emotions at Work: Normative Control, Organizations, and Culture in Japan and America*

214. Rebecca E. Karl and Peter Zarrow, eds., *Rethinking the 1898 Reform Period: Political and Cultural Change in Late Qing China*

215. Kevin O'Rourke, *The Book of Korean Shijo*

216. Ezra F. Vogel, ed., *The Golden Age of the U.S.-China-Japan Triangle, 1972-1989*

217. Thomas A Wilson, ed., *On Sacred Grounds: Culture, Society, Politics, and the Formation of the Cult of Confucius*

218. Donald S. Sutton, *Steps of Perfection: Exorcistic Performers and Chinese Religion in Twentieth-Century Taiwan*

219. Daqing Yang, *Technology of Empire: Telecommunications and Japanese Imperialism, 1930-1945*

220. Qianshen Bai, *Fu Shan's World: The Transformation of Chinese Calligraphy in the Seventeenth Century*

221. Paul Jakov Smith and Richard von Glahn, eds., *The Song-Yuan-Ming Transition in Chinese History*

222. Rania Huntington, *Alien Kind: Foxes and Late Imperial Chinese Narrative*

223. Jordan Sand, *House and Home in Modern Japan: Architecture, Domestic Space, and Bourgeois Culture, 1880-1930*

224. Karl Gerth, *China Made: Consumer Culture and the Creation of the Nation*

225. Xiaoshan Yang, *Metamorphosis of the Private Sphere: Gardens and Objects in Tang-Song Poetry*

226. Barbara Mittler, *A Newspaper for China? Power, Identity, and Change in Shanghai's News Media, 1872-1912*

227. Joyce A. Madancy, *The Troublesome Legacy of Commissioner Lin: The Opium Trade and Opium Suppression in Fujian Province, 1820s to 1920s*

228. John Makeham, *Transmitters and Creators: Chinese Commentators and Commentaries on the Analects*

229. Elisabeth Köll, *From Cotton Mill to Business Empire: The Emergence of Regional Enterprises in Modern China*

230. Emma Teng, *Taiwan's Imagined Geography: Chinese Colonial Travel Writing and Pictures, 1683–1895*

231. Wilt Idema and Beata Grant, *The Red Brush: Writing Women of Imperial China*